International Management

**Managing in a Diverse
and Dynamic Global Environment**

Second Edition

Arvind V. Phatak
Temple University

Rabi S. Bhagat
University of Memphis

Roger J. Kashlak
Loyola College in Maryland

**McGraw-Hill
Irwin**

Boston   Burr Ridge, IL   Dubuque, IA   New York   San Francisco   St. Louis
Bangkok   Bogotá   Caracas   Kuala Lumpur   Lisbon   London   Madrid   Mexico City
Milan   Montreal   New Delhi   Santiago   Seoul   Singapore   Sydney   Taipei   Toronto

McGraw-Hill Irwin

INTERNATIONAL MANAGEMENT:
MANAGING IN A DIVERSE AND DYNAMIC GLOBAL ENVIRONMENT

Published by McGraw-Hill/Irwin, a business unit of The McGraw-Hill Companies, Inc., 1221 Avenue of the Americas, New York, NY, 10020. Copyright © 2009, 2005 by The McGraw-Hill Companies, Inc. All rights reserved. No part of this publication may be reproduced or distributed in any form or by any means, or stored in a database or retrieval system, without the prior written consent of The McGraw-Hill Companies, Inc., including, but not limited to, in any network or other electronic storage or transmission, or broadcast for distance learning.

Some ancillaries, including electronic and print components, may not be available to customers outside the United States.

This book is printed on acid-free paper.

1 2 3 4 5 6 7 8 9 0 QPD/QPD 0 9 8

ISBN 978-0-07-321057-5
MHID 0-07-321057-9

Vice president and editor-in-chief: *Brent Gordon*
Publisher: *Paul Ducham*
Managing developmental editor: *Laura Hurst Spell*
Editorial assistant: *Jane Beck*
Executive marketing manager: *Rhonda Seelinger*
Senior project manager: *Harvey Yep*
Full service project manager: *Erika Jordan, Pine Tree Composition, Inc.*
Production supervisor: *Gina Hangos*
Designer: *Matt Diamond*
Senior photo research coordinator: *Jeremy Cheshareck*
Media project manager: *Suresh Babu, Hurix Systems Pvt. Ltd.*
Cover design: *Matt Diamond*
Cover image: *© Getty Images*
Typeface: *10.5/12 Times New Roman*
Compositor: *Laserwords Private Limited*
Printer: *Quebecor World Dubuque Inc.*

Library of Congress Control Number: 2008940396

www.mhhe.com

Arvind V. Phatak:
- To all my students from the past and in the future
- To Temple University for giving me the opportunity to be in a profession that is spiritually uplifting and emotionally rewarding
- To Dr. Meena Phatak, my sister and best friend
- To Rhoda, Vikram, Raj, Viveca, and Anniina

Rabi S. Bhagat:

To my family, Ebha, Monika, and Priyanka, and three significant individuals who urged me to undertake a project of this magnitude and encouraged me throughout the process:
- Hashmukh Shah, thoracic surgeon at Baylor University and Medical Center, Dallas, Texas
- S. P. Krishnamurthy, global entrepreneur, Dallas, Texas
- Jyoti P. Bhatia, information technology consultant, Dallas, Texas

Roger J. Kashlak:

To the next generation of scholars, including:
- My sons, Adam and Jake
- Their cousins Stephanie, Brian, and Rebecca Newman; Samuel and Maggie Blair; and Josh and Sarah Brunermer
- And my past and current students

Brief Contents

Preface xii

SECTION ONE
The International Environment 1

1. An Introduction to International Management 2
2. The Global Macroeconomic Environment 25
3. The Political and Legal Environments 55
4. The Cultural Environment 108

Case I: Hong Kong Disneyland 148

SECTION TWO
Managing International Strategic Planning and Implementation 161

5. Strategies for International Competition 162
6. Analyzing and Managing Foreign Modes of Entry 202
7. Organizing and Controlling International Operations 249
8. Managing Technology and Knowledge 289

Case II: Nora-Sakari: A Proposed JV in Malaysia 317

SECTION THREE
Managing People and Processes across Borders and Cultures 329

9. Communicating across Borders and Cultures 330
10. Negotiation and Decision Making across Borders and Cultures 360
11. Motivating and Leading across Borders and Cultures 392
12. International Human Resources Management 436

Case III: Christina Gold Leading Change at Western Union 459

SECTION FOUR
Social Initiatives 469

13. Global Social Enterprise 470
14. Ethics and Social Responsibility for International Firms 485

Case IV: The Tata Way: Evolving and Executing Sustainable Business Strategies 516

Name Index 523
Subject Index 529

Contents

Preface xii

About the Authors xvi

SECTION ONE
THE INTERNATIONAL ENVIRONMENT 1

Chapter 1
An Introduction to International Management 2

Chapter Learning Objectives 2
Opening Case: Trained Manpower and Low Cost Attract Global Giants 2
The International Management Setting 3
What Is International Business? 5
What Is International Management? 6
International Companies and Entry Modes 7
   International Companies 7
   Foreign Market Entry Modes 9
Why Firms Seek to Engage in International Business 9
   Market-Seeking Motives 9
   Cost-Reduction Motives 11
   Strategic Motives 13
Strategic Objectives and Sources of Competitive Advantage 16
   Achieving Efficiency 17
   Managing Risks 17
   Practical Insight 1.1: Dell Computer's Supply Chain Extends into China 18
   Innovation and Learning 18
The Environment of International Management 19
Summary 20
Key Terms and Concepts 22
Discussion Questions 22
Minicase: Want to Be More Efficient, Spread Risk, and Learn and Innovate at the Same Time? Try Building a "World Car" 22

Chapter 2
The Global Macroeconomic Environment 25

Chapter Learning Objectives 25
Opening Case: High-tech Transnationals Take "Stateless" to the Next Level 25
A New Global Economy 27
The General Agreement on Tariffs and Trade and the World Trade Organization 28
   What GATT Left Undone 28
   The World Trade Organization 29
   Settlement of Disputes by the WTO 29
Country-Level Economic Integration 30
The Effects of Economic Integration 32
   Static Effects of Economic Integration 32
   Dynamic Effects of Economic Integration 33
   Supply-Side Economics Effects 33
Major Regional Economic Agreement Initiatives 34
   The North American Free Trade Agreement 34
   Practical Insight 2.1: Is This NAFTA's Fault? 36
   Association of Southeast Asian Nations 37
   MERCOSUR 38
   The European Union 39
Will Regional Trade Blocs Promote Global Free Trade? 42
Globalization 44
   Specific Drivers of Globalization 44
   Practical Insight 2.2: Back-Room Operations in India 47
   The Two Sides of Globalization 47
Country-Specific Economic Environments and Country Competitiveness 50
Summary 52
Key Terms and Concepts 52
Discussion Questions 53
Minicase: A Global European Consumer? 53

Chapter 3
The Political and Legal Environments 55

Chapter Learning Objectives 55
Opening Case: A Love-Hate Relationship with Chavez 55
Macro-Level Environments and Uncertainties 57
   Practical Insight 3.1: Changing Political Risk Forecast in Kenya in 2008 59
The Political System 59
   The Players in the Political System 59
   The Concepts of Legitimacy and Consensus 61
   The Political Process 61
The Global Political System 62
The Interaction between International Politics and International Economics 62
   The Influence of the International Political System on the International Economic System 65
   Political Concerns and Economic Policy 66
   International Economic and Political Relations 67
Political Risk and the International Firm 67
   The Nature of Political Risk 68
   Types of Political Risk 69
   The Scope of Political Risk 70
   Assessing Host-Country Political Risk 71
   Changes in Government 73
   Changes in Party Leaders 73
   Religious Influences on Government 73
   Civil Strife in the Host Country 73
   The Risk of Kidnapping 75
A Global Framework for Assessing Political Risk 76
Managing International Political Risk 77
   Proactive Hedges 77
   Reactive Hedges 79
   Practical Insight 3.2: OPIC Hedges against Politically Imposed Risk to Multinational Corporations 80
Understanding Laws in the International Context 80
   The Concept of Law 81
   The Requirements of an Effective Legal System 81
   Functions of Law 82
International Law 82
   The Nature of International Law 82
   The Role of the World Court and the WTO 83
International Law and the Risk of Intellectual Property Theft 84
   International Law Creation 84
   International Custom 84
   International Treaties and Conventions 85
   Examples of Commercial Treaties 85
   Practical Insight 3.3: Did Spark Spark a Copycat? 90
Laws of Regional Trade Blocs 90
Laws of Nation-States 92
   Common Law and Civil Law 92
   Islamic Law 93
   Practical Insight 3.4: Profit and the Prophet: Indonesian Bank Offers No-Interest Services 95
Host-Country-Specific Laws 95
The Foreign Corrupt Practices Act and Antibribery Provisions 96
   Background 97
   Basic Provisions Prohibiting Foreign Corrupt Payments 97
   Payment by Intermediaries 97
   Enforcement 97
   Practical Insight 3.5: Siemens Braces for a Slap from Uncle Sam; China's New Posture on Commercial Bribery 98
   Antibribery Provisions—Elements of an Offense 98
   Third-Party Payments 99
   Permissible Payments and Affirmative Defenses 100
   Sanctions against Bribery 100
The OECD Convention on Combating Bribery 101
   Practical Insight 3.6: Asia-Pacific Countries Strengthen Co-operation in the Fight against Corruption 102
Summary 102
Key Terms and Concepts 104
Discussion Questions 104
Minicase: Leadership Changes in China and Russia 104

Chapter 4
The Cultural Environment 108

Chapter Learning Objectives 108
Opening Case: Cross Culture in Business and Everyday Life 108
What Is Culture? 111
   Practical Insight 4.1: Yankee, We Want You. Yankee, Go Home 112
   Difference between Learning a New Language and Learning a New Culture 114
   Culture and Its Effects on Organizations 114
The Dimensions of Culture 117
   Kluckhohn and Strodtbeck's Framework 117
   Practical Insight 4.2: Coping with Culture Shock 118
   Hofstede's Framework 120

Trompenaars's Framework 127
Ronen and Shenkar's Framework 129
Schwartz's Framework 130
Hall's Framework 131
Triandis's Framework 132
Cultural Dimensions from the GLOBE Studies 133
Practical Insight 4.3: How to Do Business in Islamic Countries 134
Hooker's Framework for Cultural Differences 136
Language Barriers 137
Religious Differences 137
Organizational Cultures 137
Practical Insight 4.4: Signs in English All Over the World 138
Culture and Management Styles in Selected Countries 139
Cultural Patterns of Japan 139
Cultural Patterns of Germany 140
Cultural Patterns of China 140
Cultural Patterns of Mexico 141
Summary 141
Key Terms and Concepts 142
Discussion Questions 142
Minicase: The Controversy over the Islamic Head Scarf: Women's Rights and Cultural Sensibilities 142
Case I: Hong Kong Disneyland 148

SECTION TWO
MANAGING INTERNATIONAL STRATEGIC PLANNING AND IMPLEMENTATION 161

Chapter 5
Strategies for International Competition 162

Chapter Learning Objectives 162
Opening Case: Maytag—Three Countries, One Dishwasher 162
The Roots of International Strategy 164
Strategically Expanding Overseas 165
Facilitators of International Expansion 165
Practical Insight 5.1: Global Internet Initiatives 166
Where to Expand Internationally 167
Strategic Planning for Foreign Market Entry 168
Managing a Portfolio of Country Subsidiaries 171
Host-Country Attractiveness versus Competitive-Strength Matrix 171
The International Risk versus Return Portfolio 173
Modern International Strategic Orientations 174
Global versus Multidomestic Strategic Orientations 174
The Transnational Orientation Imperative 176
The Value Chain Configuration and Strategic Orientations of Firms 176
Worldwide Dispersal and Reintegration of Value Chain Activities 178
The Functional Scope of Value Chain Dispersal and Integration Strategies 178
Stand-Alone Strategies 179
Simple Integration 180
Practical Insight 5.2: Dispersal of the Value Chain across Continents: India as a Center for Backroom Operations 181
Complex Integration 181
Merging Strategic Orientations and Functional Integration Strategies 183
Firm-Level Strategies for International Competitiveness 183
Core Competency Leveraging 183
Counterattack 185
Glocalization 187
Practical Insight 5.3: Cheese Katsu Burger Anyone? 190
Strategies That Fit the Emerging Market Environments 191
The Mammoth Middle-Class Market 191
How Can MNCs Capitalize on the Middle-Class Market Segment? 193
Practical Insight 5.4: Tata Unveils the World's Cheapest Car 194
Summary 195
Key Terms and Concepts 196
Discussion Questions 196
Minicase: CIENA's Globalization Decision (2000–2007) 196

Chapter 6
Analyzing and Managing Foreign Modes of Entry 202

Chapter Learning Objectives 202
Opening Case: Tata Cummins Limited (1993–2008)—an IJV Success Story! 202
Environmental Influences on the Foreign Entry Mode Decision 204

Exporting   206
   Indirect Exporting   206
   Direct Exporting   207
Countertrade   208
   Pure Barter   208
   Switch Trading   209
   Counterpurchase   209
   Buyback   209
   Practical Insight 6.1: The Arab World Wants Its MTV   210
Contract Manufacturing   210
Licensing   211
Franchising   215
   The Franchise Agreement   216
   Advantages and Disadvantages of Franchising   217
Equity-Based Ventures through Foreign Direct Investment   217
The International Collaboration Imperative   218
Equity International Joint Ventures   219
   Conditions Influencing the IJV Choice   221
   Motives for Equity International Joint Ventures   222
   Practical Insight 6.2: The Great Indian Beer Rush   223
   Advantages of Equity International Joint Ventures   224
   Disadvantages of Equity International Joint Ventures   225
   The Importance of Having the Right IJV Partner   227
   Negotiating the International Joint Venture   227
International Strategic Alliances   228
   Rationale for International Strategic Alliances   229
   Risks of International Strategic Alliances   229
   Practical Insight 6.3: Successful Alliance between Renault and Nissan   230
Making International Collaborative Initiatives Work   232
Mode of Foreign Entry and Control Implications   234
Factors Influencing the Entry Mode Choice by International Firms   235
   Determinants of Foreign Mode of Entry   236
Theory of Multinational Investment   238
   The O-L-I Framework and Internationalization   239
   An Alternative View on the Evolution of an International Company   242
Summary   243
Key Terms and Concepts   244
Discussion Questions   244
Minicase: Tommy Hilfiger in India, 2007   244

Chapter 7
Organizing and Controlling International Operations   249

Chapter Learning Objectives   249
Opening Case: The Americanization of a Japanese Icon   249
The Strategy–Structure Linkage for the International Firm   252
Pre–International Division Phase   255
International Division Structure   256
Global Hierarchical Structures   258
   The Global Product Structure   259
   The Global Area Structure   260
   Practical Insight 7.1: Rogue Wave Software Announces New International Structure and Strategy   262
Multidimensional Global Structures   263
   The International Matrix Structure   264
   Heterarchical Structures and Transnational Mind-Sets   266
   Practical Insight 7.2: AIS Goes "Matrix": New Structure Hailed for Its Efficiency   267
   Practical Insight 7.3: No-Cubicle Culture: Hearing Aid Maker Oticon Removed All Office Boundaries   270
Global Strategy, Structure, and Organizational Control   271
The Managerial Control Process   271
   Types of Control Systems   272
   Problems of Control in a Global Firm   274
International Environments and Control Systems   275
   Cultural Distance   276
   Political Risk and Host-Country Restrictions   276
   Host-Country Economic Factors   277
   A Comprehensive Framework of International Control   278
Designing an Effective International Control System   279
   Parent–Subsidiary Relationships and Strategic Control Mechanisms   280
Summary   282
Key Terms and Concepts   284
Discussion Questions   284
Minicase: A Guide for Multinationals   284

Chapter 8
Managing Technology and Knowledge   289

Chapter Learning Objectives   289
Opening Case: Transferring Knowledge in Global Corporations   289

Understanding Technology   291
   Practical Insight 8.1: At China's Gates: Microsoft Boss Conquers a Key Asian Market   292
Technology and Technology Transfer   294
The Role of Strategy and Cultural Issues   296
Knowledge in Organizations   298
The Process of Knowledge Management   300
Managing the Knowledge Life Cycle   303
   Practical Insight 8.2: Acer's Shih on Taiwan's Future: "Knowledge Is Our Business"   305
Integration of Strategic Processes with Knowledge Management   306
The Learning Organization   309
Summary   309
Key Terms and Concepts   310
Discussion Questions   310
Minicase: He Loves to Win. At I.B.M., He Did   311
Case II: Nora-Sakari: A Proposed JV in Malaysia   317

SECTION THREE
MANAGING PEOPLE AND PROCESSES ACROSS BORDERS AND CULTURES   329

Chapter 9
Communicating across Borders and Cultures   330

Chapter Learning Objectives   330
Opening Case: Understanding Others   330
What Is Communication?   332
The Cross-Cultural Communication Process   332
The Medium of Communication   334
   Verbal Communication   334
   Practical Insight 9.1: The Great English Divide   335
   Computer-Mediated Communication   337
   Nonverbal Communication   338
Environmental Context of Communication   340
   Practical Insight 9.2: The Relative Importance of Encoding Messages in Words   341
Barriers to Effective Communication   341
   Practical Insight 9.3: Culture Clashes Harm Offshoring   342
   Selective Perceptions and Stereotypes   345
   Practical Insight 9.4: Crossing the Cultural Chasm   346
   Importance of Self-Disclosure   346
   Etiquette in Communication   347
   Humor in Communication   349
   Truthfulness in Communication   349
   Elaborate versus Succinct Communication   349
   Practical Insight 9.5: Ad Citing Kashmir Stirs Fury in India   350
   Silence   350
The Role of Information Technology in Communication across Borders and Cultures   350
   Practical Insight 9.6: Potential Hot Spots in Cross-Cultural Communication   351
   Practical Insight 9.7: The Way to Reach an Italian? Not E-Mail   352
Guidelines for Managing across Borders and Cultures   353
Summary   354
Key Terms and Concepts   354
Discussion Questions   354
Minicase: Johannes van den Bosch Sends an Email   355

Chapter 10
Negotiation and Decision Making across Borders and Cultures   360

Chapter Learning Objectives   360
Opening Case: Political Impact on Global Negotiation   360
What Is Negotiation?   361
   Practical Insight 10.1: Culture Shock: If You Don't Learn to Bridge the Gap, You May Risk Alienating Potential Business Partners   363
The Negotiation Process   363
   Preparation   364
   Relationship Building   365
   Information Exchange   365
   Persuasion   365
   Making Concessions and Reaching Agreement   365
   Practical Insight 10.2: Building Trust with the Japanese   366
Environmental Context of International Negotiations   368
   Cultural Variables   368
   National Variables   369
   Organizational Variables   371
   Practical Insight 10.3: How to Avoid Being the "Ugly American" When Doing Business Abroad   372
   Negotiating with the Chinese   374
   Using the Internet to Manage Negotiations   376
Managing Negotiation and Conflict   376
Ethics in International Negotiations   378
What Is Decision Making?   379

The Decision-Making Process 379
   Practical Insight 10.4: A Whole World of Ethical Differences 380
   Practical Insight 10.5: Culture Quiz 383
Internal and External Factors 383
Sources of Errors in Decision Making across Borders and Cultures 384
   Different Approaches to Heuristics and Biases 384
   Escalation of Commitment 385
Implications for Managers 385
   Practical Insight 10.6: A Cultural Dilemma 386
Summary 387
Key Terms and Concepts 387
Discussion Questions 387
Minicase: Conflict Resolution for Contrasting Cultures 387

Chapter 11
Motivating and Leading across Borders and Cultures 392

Chapter Learning Objectives 392
Opening Case: My Way or the Highway at Hyundai and Kia 392
What Is Motivation? 395
Theories of Work Motivation 396
   Needs Theories 397
   Practical Insight 11.1: Employee Motivation the Ritz-Carlton Way 398
   Process Theories 402
The Meaning of Working across Nations and Cultures 405
Applying Cultural Frameworks 407
   The Role of Cultural Variations in Work Motivation and Job Satisfaction 408
   Practical Insight 11.2: Treat Employees Right in Tough Times 411
Motivation in International and Global Corporations 412
What Is Leadership? 413
Perspectives on Leadership 414
   Trait-Based Perspectives 414
   Behavioral Perspectives 415
   Contingency Perspectives 416
   Implicit Perspectives 416
   Transformational Perspectives 417
Leadership across Cultures and Borders 417
   Functions of Leadership across Borders and Cultures 418

   Leadership in Guilt versus Shame Cultures 418
   The GLOBE Project on Leadership 419
Non-Western Styles of Leadership 423
   Leadership in Japan 423
   Leadership in India 423
   Leadership in the Arab World 423
Leading in an Increasingly Interconnected World 424
Implications for the Practice of Global Leadership 424
   Practical Insight 11.3: Remote Leadership 425
   Practical Insight 11.4: A Leader's Real Job Description 426
   Practical Insight 11.5: India's Got a Job for You 427
Summary 428
Key Terms and Concepts 428
Discussion Questions 429
Minicase: All Eyes on the Corner Office 429

Chapter 12
International Human Resources Management 436

Chapter Learning Objectives 436
Opening Case: How to Avoid Culture Shock 436
What Is International Human Resources Management? 438
   Managing and Staffing Subsidiaries 439
Major IHRM Functions 441
   Recruitment and Selection 441
   Classifying Employees 442
   Performance Evaluation 443
   Compensation and Benefits 444
   Training and Development 444
   Labor Relations 445
   Practical Insight 12.1: The Right Perks 446
Selecting Expatriates 448
   Culture Shock 449
Managing Expatriates 450
   Cost of Failure 450
   Compensation Issues 450
   Practical Insight 12.2: Staying Safe on Foreign Assignments 451
   Managing Dual-Career Expatriates 453
   Repatriation 453
International Human Resources Management and Competitive Advantage 454
   Practical Insight 12.3: Culture Shock in America? 455

Summary   456
Key Terms and Concepts   456
Discussion Questions   456
Minicase: Cracks in a Particularly Thick Glass Ceiling   456
Case III: Christina Gold Leading Change at Western Union   459

SECTION FOUR
SOCIAL INITIATIVES   469

Chapter 13
Global Social Enterprise   470

Chapter Learning Objectives   470
Opening Case: Beyond the Green Corporation   470
The Foundation of Global Social Enterprise   474
Global Development and Emerging-Nation Objectives   475
Micro-Enterprise Collaboration and Global Development   475
   Practical Insight 13.1: Taking Tiny Loans to the Next Level   476
Innovation and Knowledge from Global Enterprise Initiatives   479
   Practical Insight 13.2: Minetti of Argentina   480
Global Enterprise Networks and Sustainability   480
Summary   482
Key Terms and Concepts   482
Discussion Questions   482
Minicase: Rise of the Asian D-School: More Students Are Opting for Programs—and Jobs—at Home   482

Chapter 14
Ethics and Social Responsibility for International Firms   485

Chapter Learning Objectives   485
Opening Case: Scandals and Corruption—A Historical Perspective   485
Business Ethics and Corporate Social Responsibility Defined   487
Moral Philosophies of Relevance to Business Ethics   489
   Teleology   489
   Deontology: The Theory of Rights   491
   The Theory of Justice   491
   Cultural Relativism   492
The Basic Moral Norms   494
Incorporating Corporate Social Responsibility and Ethics into International Business Decisions   495
Integrating Corporate Social Responsibility with Business Operations   496
   Responsive CSR   497
   Strategic CSR   497
International Ethical Codes of Conduct for International Companies   501
The Issues of Bribery and Corruption   501
   Practical Insight 14.1: Unlawful Payments to Foreign Officials   502
   Why Payoffs?   503
   Types of Payoffs   503
   The Social Costs of Bribery and Corruption   503
   Practical Insight 14.2: Halliburton Discloses Bribes in Nigeria   504
   Child Labor and Sweatshops   504
What Companies Can Do to Integrate Ethics and Business Conduct   507
   Practical Insight 14.3: U.S. Companies Back Out of Burma, Citing Human-Rights Concerns, Graft   509
Summary   510
Key Terms and Concepts   511
Discussion Questions   511
Minicase: Hondurans in Sweatshops See Opportunity   511
Case IV: The Tata Way: Evolving and Executing Sustainable Business Strategies   516

Name Index   523

Subject Index   529

Preface

The world of international management not only is dramatically different than it was in the early 1990s but has changed significantly since the first edition of this textbook was published in 2005. Macro-level developments in information technology, political landscapes, energy costs, and subsequent economic implications have grown exponentially. The U.S. trade deficit has approached $700 billion even as the dollar has continued to weaken. The economies of China and India are exploding as companies not only seek cost efficiencies and comparative advantage benefits but also seek pieces of the new markets that these countries represent for all products and services. More than half of the approximate 400 million households in China now have color televisions, and the rise of the driving class's demand on automobiles in China, India, and many other emerging nations has combined with random and, in many cases, unnecessary wars to send energy prices skyrocketing since our first edition of this text. Significant political change has occurred in Canada and Mexico, while greater levels of political risk have arisen in countries from Venezuela to Zimbabwe. These influences, along with the rise of the creative class in all parts of the globe, have had tremendous impact on the management of multinational and global corporations. There is a current mandate for these corporations to market their products and services on a global scale unimaginable just a few years ago in order to quickly and simultaneously gain the cost and market benefits of their respective innovations before new technologies make those innovations obsolete. At the same time, an imperative for businesses is to continue to learn from internal initiatives as well as external linkages such as international alliances and joint ventures in order to always be innovating at all levels—product, process, and managerial.

Countries that differ in their business practices and paradigms are becoming interconnected through the rapid transfer of technology, knowledge, products, processes, and ideas regarding desirable life styles. Trillions of U.S. dollars in currencies are traded every day in response to fluctuations in currency exchange rates, changes in interest rates, and the ups and downs of securities markets worldwide. Interest rates, stock markets, and currency values in the major markets in the United States, Europe, and Japan are dynamically interdependent. The 2008 housing and banking crisis in the United States has affected global borrowing to a level that rivals the Asian currency crisis of the late 1990s.

Even as the drive toward free trade is in full swing, U.S. presidential candidates are rethinking where the United States should be on the protectionist–free trade continuum. Still, the European Union has expanded and continues to accept new members. The falling trade barriers have opened up new markets that were once closed, for products and services in countries of eastern Europe, south Asia, the Pacific Basin, and many other parts of the world. International trade has been growing at a skyrocketing pace. Subsequently, world exports of merchandise and services have exploded to trillions of U.S. dollars.

Innovations in information technology and the Internet have enabled people in different countries to collaborate on projects without leaving home. Global teams comprising members from two or more countries can develop new products and processes via videoconferencing without leaving home. Now one can communicate with friends and business associates at the other end of the world through instant messaging simply by clicking the "send" button. Distance is measured not in miles or kilometers but in the time it takes to communicate from one end of the world to another.

People do not have to go where the jobs are. Jobs come to where the people are. Indian engineers and scientists who serve the needs of companies in Europe and America staff the software industry in India. Countries such as China, India, and Mexico, with comparatively low manufacturing costs and cheap labor, are becoming leaders in the manufacturing and information services sectors. Companies continue to shift jobs globally as long as the worldwide supply of skilled and unskilled workers is greater than the demand.

These developments lead to new opportunities, new threats, and new risks for industries and firms. This book is about the unique opportunities and concerns that confront international managers as they navigate their respective companies through the extremely complex and ever-changing global economic, political, legal, technological, and cultural environments. Choices made by international managers—such as plant location, strategies for marketing of products and services, the entry mode to penetrate foreign markets, the hiring of personnel to manage foreign operations, and the leadership and motivational techniques adopted in different foreign operations—must take into account limits imposed by the external environment, as well as the imperative to simultaneously adapt to local conditions while functioning efficiently on a global scale.

International Management is designed to help students gain insights into the complexities of managing across borders and cultures. Our goal is to provide a robust, yet lively, discussion of the various issues involved in managing operations of international, multinational, transnational, and global firms. This book describes theories of international management in the context of current and emerging realities in the global marketplace. For example, we learn that communication in the global economy, while it might appear simple, is complicated by the fact that there might not be an adequate level of trust between employees of a global corporation.

As a team, we have decades of collective experience in teaching undergraduate, MBA, and executive MBA international and comparative management courses. In addition, we have witnessed the challenges and opportunities that managers from advanced countries encounter in their attempts to globalize areas of the world that are distinctly different from their own countries. We have presented seminars and workshops for academics and practicing managers in numerous countries, collectively, from Europe to East Asia to Latin America, Africa, Australia, and New Zealand. We have been teaching students from many countries in our respective universities and have become familiar with their distinctive preferences in dealing with events and situations. We have also served on faculties and lectured at various universities in Asia, Europe, South America, and New Zealand as well as worked with governments and corporations from over 80 countries.

This book starts with a section dealing with macro-level perspectives in international management. In order to fully comprehend the various challenges that international managers face, it is imperative that they understand the various facets of the environment where they will function. We discuss the characteristics of the economic, legal, political, and cultural environments that impact on the operations of international companies and on the choices they make in their international business transactions.

The second section of the book focuses on strategic issues of managing corporations in the global context. Chapters 5 through 8 deal with the various anchors that international managers must wrestle with before they can successfully launch their operations abroad. In Chapter 5, we discuss the forces that drive the internationalization of firms and the strategic planning process for international expansion. We also discuss in this chapter the global, multidomestic, and transnational orientations of international companies. Chapter 6 focuses on the different modes of entry for expansion of operations abroad, such as licensing, franchising, and management service contracts. Equity joint ventures and nonequity collaborative ventures, also known as strategic alliances, have become increasingly popular among international companies. Chapter 7 explores the role of strategy on the choice of organization structure by international companies. Various models of organizing international operations are covered in this chapter. Furthermore, we investigate the main elements in the managerial control process, such as output control, behavior control, and input control, concluding with a discussion of the problems of control that are characteristic of international companies. The concepts of technology and technology transfer, and the relevance of appropriate technology transfer for international management, are discussed in Chapter 8.

In Section Three, we discuss the organizational behavior issues of managing employees within the context of global corporations and their subsidiaries and in the various networks of global corporations. Gone are the days when traditional concepts of management discussed in textbooks can be applied in today's interrelated world. A clash of civilizations and cultures is eminent, and global corporations face challenges in adapting to the habits and preferences of global customers. In this section, we discuss the challenges of communicating across borders, managing negotiation and decision-making processes, instilling work motivation, and instituting leadership processes. We end this section with a chapter on international human resource management and focus on the expatriate experience, which has always connected with our students, both graduate and undergraduate, who desire careers that take them overseas. In an era where knowledge-based resources inherent in various segments of the global workforce are the primary key for sustaining competitiveness in the global economy, it is crucial that we teach our students various strategies and methods associated with managing human resources in global corporations.

In Section Four, we have added a new chapter on global social enterprise that melds international management, profits, community building, and knowledge attainment and suggests that a new strategic imperative for global corporations is to serve the underserved markets of many emerging and undeveloped countries. This leads directly into our final chapter, on ethical and social responsibilities that global corporations face today. These challenges are critical to sustaining the health and vitality of global corporations. These issues confront the pivotal balance between the abstract concepts of fair play and equity, on one hand, and practical concepts of growth and return on capital, on the other. We believe that such an intricate topic is presented best after the students have grasped some of the major issues underlying the fundamentals of international management rather than during the initial stages of learning.

Examples from the business press are embedded throughout the text. Also included are practical insights captured from the business press that illustrate the application of theoretical concepts in the functioning of global companies and in today's business environment.

As instructors often look for small cases to end a classroom session, we have inserted one minicase after each chapter. The minicases are aimed at fostering discussion and bring to life concepts covered in the chapter. As this book is organized into four distinct sections, a comprehensive case is included after each section. Each case has been widely used in classrooms throughout the world and has been proved as an effective vehicle to capture the broad concepts covered in the section chapters.

This second edition of *International Management* is the beneficiary of many new insights from our own research and corporate activities. More important, it is the beneficiary of comments from the many students and professors who have used this book in more than 20 countries.

Teaching and Learning Supplements

A comprehensive teaching supplement package is available to adopters of this text. An Instructor's Manual, a Test Bank, and PowerPoint slides are included at the Instructor's Resource Center of the book's Web site, **www.mhhe.com/phatak2e.** Self-grading quizzes and additional study aids for students are available at the Student Resource Center.

In addition, a collection of videos featuring original business documentaries as well as PBS and NBC news footage is also available on the International Business Video DVD Vol. 4 (ISBN 0073272922). Featured titles include "Will Rallies Help Immigrants?" "Is China Cheating When It Comes to Trade?" "Cirque du Soleil: A Truly Global Workforce," and "J&J: Creating a Global Learning Organization."

Additional current videos are available for student purchase via iGlobe, www.mhhe.com/iGlobe, an online video Web site providing instructors and students with on-demand videos from the PBS TV show *The News Hour with Jim Lehrer*. Updated with two new clips monthly, these videos cover breaking stories surrounding international business issues.

Acknowledgments

We would like to sincerely thank the people who reviewed our text in the early stages of this revision, including Bonita Barger, of Tennessee Technical University, Fred Ware, Jr, of Valdosta State University, Sonia Ketner of Towson University, Dilek Yunlu, of Northeastern Illinois University, Bonnie McNeely of Murray State University and Mindy West of Northern Arizona University.

Arvind: I would like to thank my co-author Roger Kashlak for taking the lead in designing the chapter contents and for carrying the very heavy work load that was desperately needed in completing this edition of the book on schedule. Many thanks also to my students for their constructive criticisms of the book's first edition.

Rabi: My family in Memphis made significant sacrifices of time in order to let me focus on revising the second edition of this book. They deserve my thanks. Therefore, I dedicate this book to them along with three other individuals from Dallas, Texas, who have encouraged me to write books that are friendly to students and at the same time convey complexities of the process of management in the world. Karen South Moustafa, an assistant of management at Indiana University–Purdue University in Fort Wayne, Indiana, provided some interesting insights into practical issues as well as cases that I have used in the second edition. I have also been guided by Dr. Annette McDevitt, who is on the faculty at the University of Memphis. She provided helpful suggestions in improving the chapter on negotiation and decision making across cultures. I am also thankful to Charlotte Davis and Julie Hancock Barker for their help during the revision process. Finally I must thank many of my students in both undergraduate and gradute classes at the University of Memphis and at the University of Hawaii for their feedback on the various chapters. I hope that the second edition has incorporated some of the interesting developments in the world of multinational and global management since 2005.

Roger: I express my sincere thanks to my colleagues at Loyola College in Maryland, in particular, Professor Ray Jones, who passed away in June 2008 and was my friend, cheerleader, and voice of reason. The Sellinger School of Business at Loyola College has supported my many global initiatives that have helped to give me both the theoretical and practical backgrounds needed to co-author this text. Also, Hugh Sherman, Dean of the College of Business at Ohio University, has been a valuable friend and confidant since we both came from the corporate world to begin our PhD program 20 years ago. I also thank my lifelong friends Michael Kitsis, Richard McMonigle, John Bevilacqua, and Sam Jacob for their continued support and encouragement in all aspects of my life, including this text. My sincere thanks must also go to my family for the support they have given to me, including my sons Adam and Jake, to whom this edition is dedicated; my mother, Rose; my father, Walter, who passed away in August 2007 and whose love for education was a catalyst for my own academic initiatives; and my sisters Jane and Rosemary and their families.

About the Authors

Arvind V. Phatak

Arvind V. Phatak is Laura H. Carnell Professor of Management and International Business at Temple University's School of Business and Management. Currently he is the executive director, Institute of Global Management Studies, and the Temple University CIBER at the Fox School of Business. Dr. Phatak was the founding director of the international business program at Temple University. He has served as chairman of the General and Strategic Management Department from 1978 to 1981 and from 1987 to 1990.

Dr. Phatak has taught international management, strategic management, and general management courses at Temple University and at several colleges and universities abroad. He is the recipient of several awards, including the Great Teacher Award of Temple University (Pioneer Recipient), the Distinguished Faculty Award, the MBA Professor of the Year Award (Pioneer Recipient), and the Musser Award for Excellence in Service.

He is the author of four books and coauthor of two others in the field of strategic and international management. Currently he is the consulting editor of the *Journal of International Management*. He has also published several articles in reputable management journals. Dr. Phatak was the recipient of the Fulbright Senior Research Fellowship in 1986 for research on joint ventures in India.

Dr. Phatak has lectured on various international management topics for the U.S. State Department throughout Asia, as well as at numerous professional groups. He has presented several seminars on international and corporate business strategy in corporate settings in the United States and abroad. His corporate clients include the U.S. State Department, John Hancock Company, Dominion Textile (Canada), Federal Reserve Bank of Philadelphia, Hiro Honda (India), CIGNA, and New York Life. Dr. Phatak has an MSW from M.S. University, Baroda India; MBA from Temple University; and PhD in management from U.C.L.A.

Rabi S. Bhagat

Rabi S. Bhagat is professor of organizational behavior and international management at the Fogelman College of Business and Economics of the University of Memphis. He was awarded the Suzanne Downs Professorship for Research (2003–2004) by the University of Memphis.

Dr. Bhagat was professor at the University of Texas at Dallas (1976–1990). He was visiting professor at the University of Illinois at Urbana–Champaign, the University of Hawaii at Manoa, and Louisiana State University. He received his PhD and MA from the University of Illinois at Urbana–Champaign and his BS from the Indian Institute of Technology in Kharagpur, India.

His teaching and research interests are in organizational behavior and international management. His research focus is in the area of megatrends in world cultures and their implications for organizational behavior and international management. He is directing a major international study on the significance of time orientation and organizational stress. He is also a collaborator in the GLOBE Project on Leadership Effectiveness, directed by Professor Robert J. House of the Wharton School at the University of Pennsylvania.

Dr. Bhagat has published more than 50 articles and chapters in leading academic journals and research volumes. He is currently serving or has been on the editorial boards of nine journals, including *Journal of International Business Studies, Journal of International Management, Journal of Cross-Cultural Management, Applied Psychology: An International Review, Academy of Management Review, Journal of Cross-Cultural Psychology, Journal of Management, Global Focus,* and *Journal of Occupational Health Psychology.* In addition, he serves as a reviewer or as an editorial consultant for many leading journals.

Previous books include the *Handbook of Intercultural Training* (with D. Landis, Sage Publications, 1996), *Human Stress and Cognition in Work Organizations: An Integrated Perspective* (with T. A. Beehr, Wiley-Interscience, 1985), and *Work Stress: Health Care Systems in the Work Place* (with J. C. Quick, J. D. Quick, and J. Dalton, Praeger, 1987). His interest in the development of the global mind-set is reflected in two books, *On Becoming a Global Manager* (with B. L. Kedia and K. S. Moustafa, Sage Publications, 2004) and *Work Stress and Coping in an Era of Globalization* (LEA Publications, 2005).

Dr. Bhagat is a member of seven international, regional, and professional associations and has presented over 60 papers in their annual meetings in the United States and other countries. He is a fellow of the American Psychological Association, the American Psychological Society, the Society for Industrial and Organizational Psychologists, and the International Academy for Intercultural Research. He was awarded the James McKeen Cattell Award from the Society for Industrial and Organizational Psychologists, a division of the American Psychological Association. He was also awarded the University of Memphis Alumni Distinguished Research Award in Social Sciences and Business for 2004, and he was awarded the Suzanne Downs Palmer Professorship for Research for 2003–2004.

He has been a consultant for Bell Laboratories (AT&T Corporation), General Electric, Hilton Corporation, the U.S. Army, Franklin University (Ohio), and other organizations. National Public Radio, the *Commercial Appeal* (Memphis, TN), the *Dallas Morning News,* the *Richardson Morning News,* and NBC and ABC news affiliates, as well as *Psychology Today* and *APA Monitor* (American Psychological Association), have reported results of his research.

Roger J. Kashlak

Roger J. Kashlak is professor of international business and senior associate dean at the Sellinger School of Business and Management at Loyola College in Maryland. He has been with Loyola College since 1993. He received a BS in economics from the Wharton School of the University of Pennsylvania, an MBA in international business from Temple University, and a PhD in international business and strategy from Temple University.

Dr. Kashlak has been a member of the International Business Department at the University of Auckland and has also served as visiting professor of international business there. He has been a research fellow at the Voinovich Center for Leadership and Public Affairs at Ohio University. He has been an invited lecturer and developed courses and seminars at institutions including Thunderbird (the American Graduate School of International Management), Temple University–Japan, Manipal University (India), Katholiek University Leuven (Belgium), Institut Technologi Mara (Malaysia), and Universidad Jesuita Alberto Hurtado (Chile).

Dr. Kashlak's research has focused on topics such as international reciprocity; international alliances; global expansion in telecom, health care and other industries; global control and corporate governance issues; executive education pedagogies; and comparative analyses of leadership and work attitudes. His research has been published in journals such as *Journal of International Business Studies, Strategic Management Journal, Management International Review, Journal of Business Research, Group & Organization Management, Long Range Planning, Journal of International Management,* and *Women in Management Review* and presented at over 60 national and international conferences. He serves on various editorial boards and as a reviewer for journals in the international business and strategic management disciplines.

Dr. Kashlak's teaching focuses on international management and global strategy at undergraduate, MBA, and executive MBA levels. He has developed and conducted executive MBA courses throughout the world, including China, Vietnam, Malaysia, Thailand, South Africa, Chile, Argentina, the Netherlands, and the Czech Republic. He is the recipient of Loyola's 27th Annual Distinguished Teacher Award (1997) and other teaching honors from Beta Gamma Sigma, Loyola's Sellinger School, and Alpha Sigma Nu (the Jesuit Honor Society).

Prior to entering academia, Dr. Kashlak worked for AT&T-Communications International, where he developed the initial international rate negotiation strategy and was responsible for financial negotiations with host governments and telecom entities throughout the world. Subsequent to that job, he established AT&T-Communication's Italian subsidiary. Dr. Kashlak has continued to be involved in the corporate world through executive education with firms such as AEGON (N.V.), AT&T, Northrop-Grumman, Ericsson, Motorola, and Lucent Technologies. He currently serves on various corporate and nonprofit boards of directors in the Baltimore area.

SECTION ONE

The International Environment

CHAPTER ONE

An Introduction to International Management

Chapter Learning Objectives

After completing this chapter, you should be able to:

- Define the concepts of international business and international management.
- Examine the dramatic growth and global impacts of international companies.
- Define and understand the strategic, marketing, and economic motives of firms seeking to expand internationally.
- Explain the strategic objectives and sources of competitive advantage for an international firm.

Opening Case: Trained Manpower and Low Cost Attract Global Giants

NEW DELHI: It has all the ingredients of a corporate blockbuster: a growing middle class, rising income levels and low production costs. That's the Indian market as seen by the global biggies from the world of car-making.

No wonder then that an increasing number of car manufacturers from across the world are making India—the second fastest growing car market in Asia after China—a hub for most of their manufacturing activities.

To name a few: Suzuki has decided to make India the only hub for making cost-effective small cars outside Japan. It is also Suzuki's R&D hub for developing new small cars.

The country is also the production and export base for Hyundai's Santro. Toyota is building a utility vehicle for the world market and India features in the small list of destinations where it will be produced. India has also been named the hub for Fiat's R&D activities.

Low production costs and a high number of trained manpower are the reasons behind this newfound fascination among global car makers. Also, the local laws in some European nations, like Italy and Greece, favor shipping cars from India over other Asian nations, with tax breaks.

This has helped South Korea's Hyundai Motor Corp. establish its Indian arm as the export hub for the compact car Santro. The made-in-India hatchback is today being sold in Greece, Germany and Italy, besides being sourced by DaimlerChrysler to be sold under its Dodge badge in Mexico.

"We have proved that India can become a cost-competitive base for producing technologically superior cars," said Hyundai Motor India (HMI) president BVR Subbu. Riding on this growing acceptance among global buyers, HMI drove home export earnings to the tune of Rs 1,000 crore (1,000 crore = 10 billion rupees) in the first eight months of 2004. That's not all. The firm is now gearing up to become the largest exporter of manufactured goods this calendar year in non-metallurgy and non-refinery sectors in India with an export earning of around Rs 1,500 crore (15 billion rupees).

Independent surveys by leading consultants also pointed out that India is fast emerging as the most-preferred sourcing base for global auto majors. U.S. auto executives have even picked India over China as the most popular business process outsourcing (BPO) destination as far as automotive activities are concerned. Even Nissan has last week procured the government nod to set up a subsidiary in India that will explore opportunities for sourcing low-cost components besides locally building cars. Above all, there's a burgeoning local population of professionals that can be targeted with soft loans. The industry is hopeful of selling 1 million units in the domestic market this fiscal. It's this captive industry that's working as an added bait for the global players.

As Maruti Udyog Managing Director Jagdish Khattar said: "There are about 40 million Indians who ride two-wheelers. I want them to upgrade to cars and that's what we are trying to achieve with our finance and exchange schemes." A recent ICRA study had also pointed out that the overall car segment in India is poised to grow at a compounded annual growth rate of 8 percent from 2004–2008, with compact and mid-range cars leading the growth. With an eye on this potential market, Suzuki has announced plans to invest Rs 6,000 crore in India over the next few years for setting up a new car-making venture.

With the Indian car market maturing, manufacturers are also experimenting with new vehicle types and segments that appeal to the new-age buyer. If 2003 was the year when manufacturers rolled out one SUV after the other, 2004 became the year of premium hatchbacks with Hyundai Getz, Ford Fusion and Indigo Marina vying for buyer attention. "We want to play in the heart of volume segment and that's why we are looking at locally making a volume car here," said Aditya Vij, president, GM India.

They are also playing the 24x7 service card to pull customers to win over working couples. Car makers led by Maruti, Hyundai, GM and Fiat are also driving into the call centre market to offer a slew of support services like round-the-clock assistance in case of breakdowns and even for vehicle servicing. Hyundai has also announced an extended four-year warranty program on its big cars

Source: Anand Byas, *Times of India*, November 21, 2004 (http://timesofindia.indiatimes.com/articleshow/930106.cms).

Discussion Questions

1. Why are foreign car companies making India a premium car market for car manufacturing?
2. Under what conditions will India serve as an export base for foreign cars made in India?
3. What are the competitive advantages of India in car manufacturing?

The International Management Setting

The world is becoming a smaller place. Look around you. The clothes you wear, the gadgets in the kitchen, the car you drive—all may be made in China, India, or Japan. Perhaps in your refrigerator you have Mexican tacos or Indian chicken curry. Now people can communicate with friends and business associates across the world through instant messaging simply by clicking the "send" button. Distance is measured not in miles or kilometers but in the time it takes to reach from one end of the world to another. Who is responsible for "shrinking" the world in which we live? This responsibility has been shouldered by the numerous small and large international companies, from different countries, that produce and market their wares worldwide.

Even though the world is becoming "smaller," significant political, legal, economic, and technological differences still distance us from our fellow inhabitants of Earth. In their quest to reach markets and customers in foreign countries, international companies have to navigate across the often turbulent international environment.

Consider an American company with, among other business units, sales offices in Buenos Aires, Toronto, and New York City, wholly owned manufacturing subsidiaries in Jakarta and Taipei, an equity joint venture in Shanghai, a research and development facility in Tel Aviv, and call service centers in Bangalore and Manila. In recent times, the economic collapse of Argentina, the political implosion of Indonesia, and the severe acute respiratory syndrome (SARS) scares in China, Taiwan, and Canada have exerted increased pressures, risks, and costs for that firm. Furthermore, the ongoing conflicts in the Middle East and southern Asia as well as the threat of terrorism aimed at Western targets worldwide have further increased risk and the cost of managing that risk for this company.

The excitement and opportunities of the new millennium have been accompanied by many new risks and associated costs of doing business internationally. This book is about the challenge of managing these risks of such international activities of international companies within the various international environments. Also, this book is about understanding and managing the tremendous amount of new opportunities internationally. Thus it is about the unique opportunities and problems that confront managers in international companies as they navigate through the extremely complex and ever-changing economic, political, legal, technological, and cultural environments of a world of increasingly interdependent nation-states. The choices that international managers make—plant location, products and services marketed in different countries or regions of the world, the mode used to penetrate foreign markets, the hiring of personnel to manage foreign operations, and so on—must take into account the limits imposed on such choices by the external environment, as well as the imperative to simultaneously adapt to local conditions and function efficiently on a global scale.

The need for international management arises with a firm's initial involvement in international operations by way of exports of its products, technology, or services to foreign markets. This need becomes even more critical when a company becomes involved in foreign direct investment. **Foreign direct investment (FDI)** is a long-term equity investment in a foreign affiliate or subsidiary; it gives the parent company (the investor) varying degrees of managerial control over the foreign operation, depending on the percentage of ownership by the parent company.[1] The more FDI that a company makes in a foreign affiliate, the greater the managerial control that it has over that foreign affiliate. FDI involves the establishment of facilities, buildings, plants, and equipment for the production of goods and/or services in a foreign country. And FDI is accompanied by the need to manage, market, and finance the foreign production. People manage enterprise functions like marketing, production, and finance. Managing the various enterprise functions abroad requires that managers in the parent company, as well as in every foreign affiliate, have the necessary skills and experience to manage the affairs of affiliates in countries whose political, cultural, economic, and financial environments may be very different from one another. It therefore follows that the greater a company's FDI, the greater will be its need for skilled international managers.

Figure 1.1 represents the multilevel focus of this text. We discuss international management from a variety of perspectives. In Section 1, we paint a picture of the various macro-level environments where managers must effectively manage. Section 2 elaborates on strategic management issues. That is, what are the firm-level strategic considerations necessary to consider when expanding overseas? In Section 3, we focus on the manager level and the need to effectively communicate, motivate, lead, and

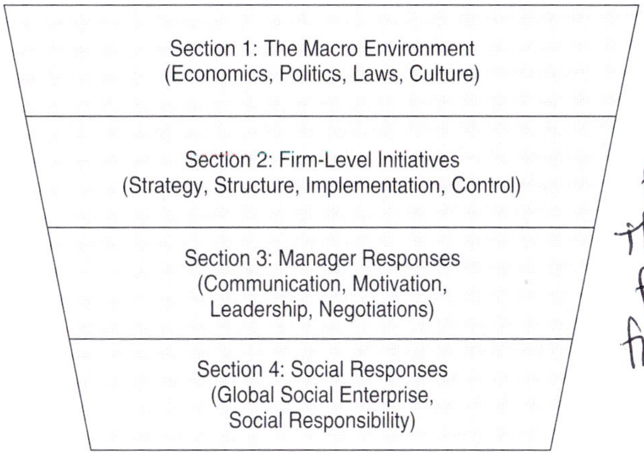

FIGURE 1.1
Managing in the International Environment

Section 1: The Macro Environment
(Economics, Politics, Laws, Culture)

Section 2: Firm-Level Initiatives
(Strategy, Structure, Implementation, Control)

Section 3: Manager Responses
(Communication, Motivation, Leadership, Negotiations)

Section 4: Social Responses
(Global Social Enterprise, Social Responsibility)

negotiate in order to manage internationally. Finally, Section 4 integrates serving the world's poor profitably and corporate social responsibility initiatives.

International management activities in a firm begin either when the firm's managers initiate the establishment of a foreign affiliate from the ground up, which is called a greenfield investment, or when it acquires an existing host-country firm. Furthermore, they continue as long as the parent company owns one or more functioning foreign affiliates.

What Is International Business?

Besides their involvement in foreign acquisition and greenfield investments, international companies may be simultaneously involved in several other international business activities such as export, import, countertrade, licensing, and strategic alliances. Before delving into the distinctions of these various forms of international involvement, we should first understand what international business is. Several definitions of international business have been advanced through the years. The most basic definition is "all business transactions that involve two or more countries."[2] These business transactions or relationships may be conducted by private, nonprofit, or government organizations, as well as through a combination of the various organizations. In the case of private firms the transactions are for profit. Government-sponsored activities in international business may or may not have a profit orientation, and a nonprofit firm may be competing in an industry that has firms with profit motives.

Other definitions suggest that an international business is "a business whose activities involve the crossing of national boundaries"[3] or is "any commercial, industrial or professional endeavor involving two or more nations."[4] To Charles W. L. Hill, "an international business is any firm that engages in international trade and investment . . . all the firm has to do is export or import products from other countries."[5] Kolde and Hill say that "one cannot ignore the contrasts between domestic and international business, or in a more general phrase between uninational and multinational business. The primary distinction between the two lies in the environmental framework and the organizational and behavioral responses that flow from that framework."[6]

Taking the foregoing definitions of international business into account, we define **international business** as those business activities of private or public enterprises that involve the movement of resources across national boundaries. The resources that may be involved in the cross-national transfers include raw materials, semifinished and finished goods, services, capital, people, and technology. Specific services transferred may include functions such as accounting, consulting, legal counsel, and banking activities. Technology transferred may range from simple managerial and marketing know-how to higher level managerial and technical skills to ultimately high-end technological advancements.

What Is International Management?

The noted international management theorist and scholar Jean J. Boddewyn argues that a definition of international management must include an interpretation and "elaboration of the key terms *international* and *management* as well as of their *interaction*."[7] We also agree with him that the term international means "crossing borders and [applies] to processes intersected by national borders."[8] In very general terms, international management is the management of a firm's activities on an international scale. But before we define international management in specific terms, let us define management.

Management is defined in numerous ways. We would define management as the process aimed at accomplishing organizational objectives by (1) effectively coordinating the procurement, allocation, and utilization of the human, financial, intellectual, and physical resources of the organization and (2) maintaining the organization in a state of satisfactory, dynamic equilibrium within the environment—that is, the firm's strategies and operational plans are responsive to the demands and constraints embedded in the economic, political, legal, cultural, political, and competitive environment.

This definition of management has two basic premises. First, management is needed to coordinate the human, financial, intellectual, and physical resources and to integrate them into a unified whole. Without such coordination the resources would remain unrelated and disorganized and therefore inefficiently used. The second premise in the definition is that an organization lives in a dynamic environment that constantly affects its operations. To further complicate the manager's job, the various environments have different degrees of dynamism. "The multinational setting is more dynamic than the uninational (domestic) setting. This is due partly to the different rates of speed at which the various environmental parameters are changing in the different countries and in part to the nature of the parameters themselves."[9] For instance, some of the environmental factors, such as the distinct national cultures, evolve and converge over time. Others, like the political environments, have the ability to be radically changed through elections and revolutions. Furthermore, the financial environment, especially when one considers foreign exchange rates, is continually in a state of change. Note that "for domestic businesses, the external factors are relatively constant and homogeneous. Any changes that occur are gradual and generally do not lead to any sudden differentiation among the opportunities and constraints among different industries or types of enterprises."[10] However, with expansion abroad of a firm's operation, the environmental setting can no longer be called constant. Thus one managerial task is to effectively forecast the varying environmental forces that are likely to have a significant impact on the firm in the immediate and distant future and to determine the probable impact. Also, managers must respond to the environmental forecasts by designing appropriate strategies to ensure the survival and growth of the organization as it interacts with its dynamic environment.

On the basis of the preceding meaning of the term *international* and definition of *management,* we can now define **international management** as a process of accomplishing the global objectives of a firm by (1) effectively coordinating across national boundaries the procurement, allocation, and utilization of the human, financial, intellectual, and physical resources of the firm and (2) effectively charting the path toward the desired organizational goals by navigating the firm through a global environment that is not only dynamic but often very hostile to the firm's very survival. Note that our definition is focused on the *business firm* as the primary level and unit of analysis of international management, and it excludes the management of all international organizations such as the World Trade Organization, the International Labor Organization, and the United Nations. Focusing on the international business firm as an organization allows us to define the international management domain in terms of two central themes:

1. Why, when, and how does a business firm (as an organization) decide to "go international," including the expansion and reduction of such internalization?
2. Why, when, and how is its organizational behavior—a broad term covering mission, objectives, strategies, structures, staff, and processes [particularly decision making], internal and external transactions and relations, performance, impact, etc.—altered by internationalization?[11]

International Companies and Entry Modes

International Companies

All firms, regardless of size, are affected by international competition. Specifically, any firm that has one or more foreign affiliates is involved in international management; it does not have to be a billion-dollar corporation. Even small and medium-sized firms can and do have international operations in several countries. Many international companies do not qualify for the exclusive list of the Fortune 500 or the BusinessWeek Global 1000 list of the largest international corporations. Even though they do not come close to Microsoft, Toyota, Wal-Mart, or Deutsche Bank in terms of total sales, gross profits, total assets, and similar measures of company size, they are still multinational companies. Many firms in Europe and Japan have also developed a multinational structure; and in the last 10 years or so, we have seen many government-owned enterprises that have become privatized and subsequently multinational. The 1960s laid the foundations for the massive growth of international companies. The growth of that decade far exceeded any achieved earlier by the United States or the other industrialized countries of the world. Since then, the growth in international business activities has been exponential, culminating during the last 10 years with the significant increase in privatization and deregulation in many industries and countries.

Although international enterprises are dissimilar in many respects—size of sales and profits, markets served, and location of affiliates abroad—they all have some common features. To begin, an **international company** is an enterprise that has operations in two or more countries. If it has operations in several countries, then it may have a network of wholly or partially (jointly with one or more foreign partners) owned producing and marketing foreign affiliates or subsidiaries. The foreign affiliates may be linked with the parent company and with each other by ties of common ownership and by a common global strategy to which each affiliate is responsive and committed. The parent company may control the foreign affiliates via resources that it allocates to each affiliate—capital, technology, trademarks, patents, and workforce—and through the right to approve each affiliate's long- and short-range plans and budgets.[12]

As pointed out earlier, there are many small- and medium-sized multinational companies. However, generally we are talking about a large corporation whose revenues, profits, and assets typically run into hundreds of millions of dollars. For example, the most profitable international company in 2007 was ExxonMobil with profits of $39.51 billion. In 2007, Wal-Mart Stores ranked number one in the world on the basis of sales, which approached $351 billion. In the same year, 30 companies accrued global revenues in excess of $100 billion. Table 1.1 lists the 15 largest international companies in terms of 2007 sales.

The top 100 international companies hold almost $5 trillion of assets outside their home countries. The economic power of these companies is evident in the fact that they are estimated to account for more than one-third of the combined outward FDI of their home countries. Because the largest international companies control such a large pool of assets, they exercise considerable influence over the home and host countries' output, economic policies, trade and technology flows, employment, and labor practices.

In 2005, the world's largest global (the terms *global* and *transnational* are used interchangeably) companies held 54.5 percent of their total assets in foreign countries and generated 56.5 percent of total sales from foreign countries. The foreign affiliates of these companies employed 8 million personnel, which amounted to 53.1 percent of their total employment. Global foreign direct investment in 2006 reached $1,306 billion, of which $857 billion flowed into the developed countries, as opposed to $379 billion to developing countries. This goes to show that the rich countries are getting the infusion of capital, technology, and knowledge that usually accompanies foreign direct investment, whereas the poorer countries do not enjoy such benefits from foreign direct investment. The world's gross domestic product (GDP) in 2006 amounted to almost $48.29 trillion, of which almost $4.8 trillion, or 11.5 percent, was accounted for by the production of foreign affiliates. The total world exports in 2006 amounted to $13.9 trillion, of which $4.7 trillion, or almost 34 percent, was generated by exports of foreign affiliates. In that same year, the total sales of foreign affiliates amounted to $25.2 trillion. Therefore, sales of goods and services produced by foreign affiliates are five times greater than their own exports and, not counting affiliates' exports, almost twice as large as total world exports. One could interpret this data to mean that local production by foreign affiliates to serve local markets has replaced exports to those markets.[13]

International companies have been growing in size at rates exceeding those of the economies of many countries. The size of the large international companies is often compared with that of countries' economies as an indicator of the power and influence

TABLE 1.1
Largest International Companies, by Sales

Source: Fortune Global 500, July 23, 2007.

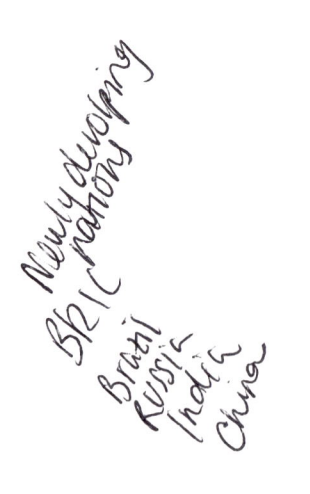

Global Rank	Company	2007 Revenues ($ millions)
1	Wal-Mart Stores	$361,139.0
2	ExxonMobil	347,250.0
3	Royal Dutch Shell	318,845.0
4	BP	274,316.0
5	General Motors	207,349.0
6	Toyota Motor	204,746.4
7	Chevron	200,567.0
8	DaimlerChrysler	190,191.4
9	Conoco Phillips	172,451.0
10	Total	168,356.7
11	General Electric	168,307.0
12	Ford Motor	160,126.0
13	ING Group	158,274.3
14	Citigroup	146,777.0
15	AXA	139,738.1

of international companies in the world economy. Table 1.2 shows a comparison of the 100 largest country economies and global companies ranked by their GDP and total revenue respectively. This is a crude comparison as the domestic sales of foreign affiliates get included in the computation of a nation's GDP. Nevertheless, it is quite interesting to notice that Wal-Mart Stores (number 24), ExxonMobil (number 25), and Royal Dutch Shell (number 26) are "bigger" than 29 countries in the list. And of the 100 countries and companies in Table 1.2, there are 48 global companies.

Foreign Market Entry Modes

A company can achieve its international business aims through different forms of foreign market entry modes, such as:

- Exporting.
- Countertrade.
- Contract manufacturing.
- Licensing.
- Franchising.
- Turnkey projects.
- Nonequity strategic alliances.
- Equity-based ventures such as wholly owned subsidiaries and equity joint ventures.

We examine these entry modes in detail in later chapters

Why Firms Seek to Engage in International Business

An international company may have several motivations for establishing various types of foreign operations. Let us examine some of the motivations for foreign operations that are illustrated in Figure 1.2 and grouped into three categories: market-seeking motives, cost-reduction motives, and strategic motives.

Market-Seeking Motives

Historically, companies have initially looked to overseas markets when their home market became saturated. In his landmark *product life cycle theory,* Vernon theorizes that firms will search foreign markets for product that has been standardized and has reached the maturity stage in its life cycle.[14] Because of social and regulatory pressures

FIGURE 1.2
Motives to Go International

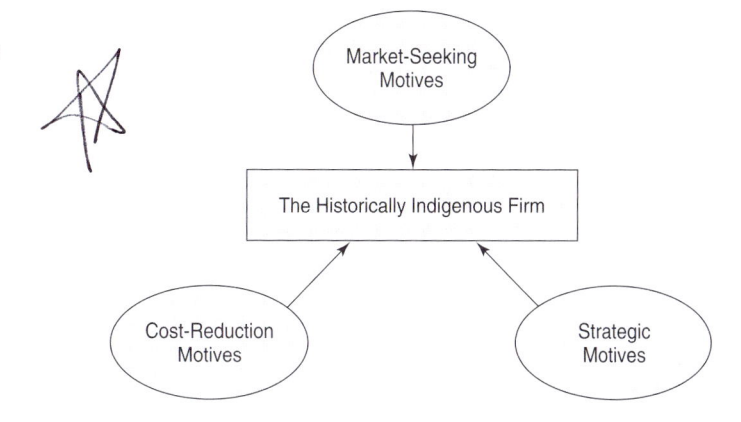

TABLE 1.2 How Large Are Global Companies in Comparison with Countries of the World?

Source: Fortune Global 500, *Fortune*, July 23, 2007, and 2007 CIA *World Factbook*.

Rank	Country/Company	GDP/Revenue ($ millions)	Rank	Country/Company	GDP/Revenue ($ millions)	Rank	Country/Company	GDP/Revenue ($ millions)
1	World	46,660,000	34	Greece	222,500	67	American International Group	113,194
2	European Union	13,620,000	35	Argentina	210,000	68	Hungary	113,100
3	United States	13,220,000	36	General Motors	207,349	69	United Arab Emirates	110,600
4	Japan	4,911,000	37	Toyota Motor	204,746	70	China National Petroleum	110,520
5	Germany	2,858,000	38	Ireland	202,900	71	BNP Paribas	109,214
6	China	2,512,000	39	Chevron	200,567	72	ENI	109,014
7	United Kingdom	2,341,000	40	South Africa	200,500	73	UBS	107,835
8	France	2,154,000	41	Thailand	196,600	74	Siemens	107,342
9	Italy	1,780,000	42	Finland	196,200	75	State Grid	107,186
10	Canada	1,089,000	43	Iran	194,800	76	Colombia	105,500
11	Spain	1,081,000	44	DaimlerChrysler	190,191	77	Assicurazioni Generali	101,811
12	India	796,100	45	Hong Kong	187,100	78	Chile	100,300
13	Korea, South	768,500	46	Portugal	176,600	79	J.P. Morgan Chase & Co.	99,973
14	Mexico	741,500	47	ConocoPhillips	172,451	80	Carrefour	99,015
15	Russia	733,000	48	Total	168,357	81	New Zealand	98,770
16	Australia	645,300	49	General Electric	168,307	82	Berkshire Hathaway	98,539
17	Brazil	620,700	50	Ford Motor	160,126	83	Philippines	98,480
18	Netherlands	612,700	51	ING Group	158,274	84	Pemex	97,469
19	Switzerland	386,800	52	Venezuela	147,900	85	Deutsche Bank	96,152
20	Sweden	371,500	53	Citigroup	146,777	86	Dexia Group	95,847
21	Belgium	367,800	54	AXA	139,738	87	Honda Motor	94,791
22	Turkey	358,200	55	Volkswagen	132,323	88	McKesson	93,574
23	Taiwan	353,900	56	Malaysia	131,800	89	Verizon Communications	93,221
24	Wal-Mart Stores	351,139	57	Sinopec	131,636	90	Algeria	92,220
25	ExxonMobil	347,254	58	Crédit Agricole	128,481	91	Nippon Telegraph Telephone	91,998
26	Royal Dutch Shell	318,845	59	Allianz	125,346	92	Hewlett-Packard	91,658
27	Austria	309,300	60	Pakistan	124,000	93	International Business Machines	91,424
28	Saudi Arabia	286,200	61	Israel	121,600	94	Valero Energy	91,051
29	BP	274,316	62	Singapore	121,500	95	Home Depot	90,837
30	Poland	265,400	63	Fortis	121,202	96	Nissan Motor	89,502
31	Indonesia	264,400	64	Czech Republic	118,900	97	Samsung Electronics	89,476
32	Norway	261,700	65	Bank of America Corp.	117,017	98	Credit Suisse	89,354
33	Denmark	256,300	66	HSBC Holdings	115,361	99	Hitachi	87,615
						100	Egypt	84,510

in the United States that leveled off a once-growing market, the U.S. cigarette industry firms had to look to the foreign markets of eastern Europe and Asia to maintain sales volumes. Similarly, as revenue growth declined and the fast-food industry edged toward maturity in the United States, various fast-food firms like McDonald's and Pizza Hut expanded overseas to countries such as Russia, Japan, China, and India. Today, product life cycles in many industries have become very short because of next-generation technologies, so firms are seeking to penetrate overseas markets simultaneously with their respective home markets in order to recoup costs and make a profit before the next generation of technology comes to market.

Once firms have internationally expanded, many try to protect and maintain a market position abroad by establishing production facilities in foreign markets that had been served through exports. In this way companies bypass the threat of trade barriers such as the imposition of high tariffs or quotas. For instance, the so-called voluntary restrictions in 1980 on the export of Japanese automobiles to the United States was one factor that prompted Japanese auto companies like Toyota and Nissan to build car manufacturing plants in the United States. Toyota, Honda, and Nissan have established significant shares in the U.S. automobile market. Similarly, many U.S. and Japanese companies established plants in the 15-country European Union (EU) to circumvent potential trade barriers raised by the member countries against imports from non-EU countries. Over the years, through the efforts of the World Trade Organization (WTO), tariffs and quotas have been reduced dramatically. We elaborate on the practical and strategic implications of the EU, other trade blocs, and the WTO in Chapter 2.

The expectation of immense business opportunities in an integrated and unified market of the 27-nation European Union has brought an upsurge of both Japanese and American direct investment in Europe. As an example, for the past decade, Japanese banks and companies in the manufacturing sector have been continually investing, buying European companies, setting up manufacturing subsidiaries, and boosting sales forces throughout Europe. Japan's business activities in Europe intensified in 1990 when Japanese companies decided Europe was serious about market unification after 1992. The Japanese companies wanted a foothold in Europe before protectionism possibly kept them out. Japanese companies have responded by building new manufacturing plants and buying existing manufacturing capacity inside what could become a European fortress.

Historically, U.S. firms in many industries have been able to gain cost efficiencies and needed experience in their home market before venturing overseas. However, when a company's home market is not large enough to gain necessary cost efficiencies, that firm must look to international markets. The small size of the domestic market is the reason given by European companies that have developed international presences. Pharmaceuticals companies Hoffman–La Roche and Novartis (in 1996, in one of the largest corporate mergers in history, Ciba-Geigy and Sandoz merged to form Novartis), based in Switzerland—a nation whose population is less than 8 million—could not have survived in their industry had they limited their business horizons to the Swiss market. These companies, and others like them in other European countries with small populations like Holland and Belgium, were forced to seek markets abroad, which eventually led to the creation of foreign manufacturing facilities in their major markets.

Cost-Reduction Motives

Companies venture overseas to lower factor costs. Intense competitive pressures and the resulting fall in profit margins serve as a powerful inducement for affected companies to seek cost-reduction measures. Firms therefore seek countries with low wages to shift manufacturing operations.[15]

Comparitively Cheap Labor

Comparatively cheap labor is often the strongest incentive for companies to establish foreign operations.[16] For example, over the past two decades more than 2,000 maquiladoras have sprung up near the United States–Mexico border. These plants take advantage of cheap labor to assemble American-made components for reexport to the United States. Further inside Mexico, Japanese, German, and American automotive firms all have assembly facilities that ship final products to the United States and global markets. The economics of assembly in Mexico are favorable because jobs that are higher priced in the United States and fully "burdened" with benefits, Social Security, and so on, can be had in Mexico for a fraction of the cost.

In the 1950s and 1960s, many American companies had established not just assembly plants but fully integrated manufacturing plants in newly industrializing countries such as Taiwan and Singapore and the crown colony of Hong Kong. Even more foreign investment in manufacturing operations has flowed into Asia since then. Research indicates that "the high-wage differential between West Europe and Asia has been the most significant contribution to the restructuring of U.S. foreign direct investment (FDI) during 1981–2000."[17] As wages in Taiwan, Singapore, and Hong Kong rose in comparison to lesser developed Southeast Asian countries, the companies shifted their investment sights and moved to Malaysia, Thailand, and Indonesia. Most recently, even lower cost labor has been found in locales like southern China and Vietnam. During the 1990s and into the twenty-first century, Black & Decker, the U.S. power tools manufacturer, aggressively expanded production facilities for power drills throughout China, not to serve the Chinese market but rather to export to Europe. Automobile companies have engaged in several contracts with Indian suppliers for the supply of parts and components.

transportation costs

Another reason companies set up foreign plants is to eliminate or reduce high transportation costs, particularly if the ratio of the per-unit transportation expenditures to the per-unit selling price of the product is very high. For instance, if the product costs $10 to ship but it can be marketed for no more than $25 in the foreign market, all other things being nearly equal, the company may decide to produce it in the market to improve its competitiveness and profit margin. The trade-off for the company is giving up the economy-of-scale efficiencies of long production runs in one country in order to reduce transportation costs.

govt incentives

Costs can also be reduced for a firm through favorable host-government incentives and inducements. Local production often allows the company to take advantage of incentives that the host government may be offering to foreign companies that make direct investments in the country.[18] These incentives include reduced taxes for several years, free land, low-interest loans, and a guarantee of no labor strife. This was a principal motive for Intel to establish manufacturing operations in Costa Rica and for Mercedes, the German luxury car company, to build a manufacturing plant in Alabama.

Firms in industries with relatively high allocation of funds to research also look to overseas markets. Companies in pharmaceutical and high-technology industries that must spend large sums of money on research and development for new products and processes are compelled to look for ways to improve their sales volume in order to support their laboratories. If the domestic sales volume and exports do not raise the necessary cash flow, then strategically located manufacturing and sales affiliates are established abroad with the objective of attaining higher levels of sales volume and cash flow to support future research endeavors.

exchange rates wages

A factor that companies take into account in locating production plants is the comparative production costs in their major country markets. For example, a company that has major market positions in Japan, Germany, and the United States would be concerned about how costs are affected by the cross-exchange rates between the Japanese yen, the euro, and the U.S. dollar. If the yen were to rise significantly in value against the U.S. dollar and the euro, then exports to the United States and Germany of the company's Japanese-produced products could become relatively noncompetitive because of the rise of the yen-denominated Japanese wage rates and exports, especially if labor costs added significantly to the total product value. In such an event, the economics of production and distribution permitting, the company would gain if it could shift its production to either the United States or Germany. In fact, during the 1990s, when the yen appreciated against the U.S. dollar, Japanese auto companies used their U.S. plants to ship cars to Europe and even back to Japan! BMW and Mercedes, two of the major luxury carmakers of Germany, decided to commence manufacture of some models in the United States because of the highly noncompetitive labor rates in Germany largely due to the high value of the German mark. Global companies invest in favor of operational flexibility and in the ability to shift the sourcing of products and components from country to country. Global companies are therefore motivated to make major investments in operations and supply sites in their major country markets.

Firms have been known to move their operations to ecologically and environmentally friendly countries in order to reduce costs of adherence, both from the operations perspective and from the political perspective. Companies have been alleged to have moved their environmentally harmful operations to countries in Africa, Asia, and Latin America whose laws for environmental protection are less strict than those in the United States and therefore are considered ecologically and environmentally friendly to businesses. But companies do not have to migrate to developing countries to avoid environmental risks. A case in point is Germany's BASF, which moved its biotechnology research laboratory focusing on cancer and immune-system research from Germany—where it faced legal and political challenges from the environmentally conscious Green movement—to Cambridge, Massachusetts, which, according to BASF's director of biotechnology research, had more or less settled any controversies involving safety, animal rights, and the environment.[19] These and other types of social responsibility issues that confront the international company are expanded upon in Chapter 14.

Strategic Motives

Firms venture overseas for many long-term strategic reasons. Strategic decisions are those that are made to maintain or enhance the competitive position of a company in an industry or market. According to Hymer, who was the first to offer an explanation of why firms start production abroad, firms use foreign production as a means of transferring and taking advantage of the host country's specialized assets, knowledge, and capabilities, both tangible and intangible.[20] Firms also engage in foreign operations in several countries to diversify their strategic risk.[21] Both Caves and Dunning explain foreign production by firms as a means of taking advantage of their assets, knowledge, and capabilities that are superior to firms in the foreign markets.[22] A firm can accrue many distinct strategic advantages by producing a product in a foreign market. These include the ability to meet the demand for the product quickly, good public relations with customers and the host government, and improved service.

A firm may simply follow its major customers abroad. When the Japanese automakers Honda, Toyota, Nissan, Mazda, Subaru, and Isuzu established car manufacturing plants in the United States, their Japanese suppliers followed and set up their own plants in the United States. There are today more than 300 Japanese-owned parts suppliers in the United States, representing an investment in excess of $7 billion and employing more than 30,000 workers. Most of these supplier firms provide glass, brake systems, seats, air conditioners, heaters, filters, fuel pumps, and other components directly to the production plants. This pattern has been seen in the service industries as well. As major American corporations were expanding worldwide, they demanded better and more reliable services, including telecommunications services. Consequently, AT&T began the international expansion initiative of its communications line of business in the latter half of the 1980s, setting up overseas operations in five countries. AT&T now has major subsidiary locations in more than 50 countries.

The hardware line of business of AT&T, which was eventually spun off into a separate entity named Lucent, also made a big push overseas, mainly to satisfy the telecommunications needs of its large global customers, which had made their own push into overseas markets. Fearing that its major customers—the global companies—would turn to rival companies such as France's Alcatel, Italy's Italtel, IBM, and Japan's NEC if it did not operate advanced voice and data networks around the world, the company formed several joint ventures and strategic alliances around the globe.[23] Combined employment abroad for AT&T and Lucent jumped from a mere 50 people in 1983 to more than 50,000 today. Like AT&T, Federal Express followed the lead of its customers who increasingly wanted packages sent to Asia and Europe. Accordingly, with the aim of "keeping it purple"—the color of FedEx's planes and vans—the company set out to duplicate its business abroad.

Besides following their important customers, firms exhibit a *bandwagon effect,* venturing abroad to follow their major competitors.[24] This is especially true in an industry that is characterized by an oligopolistic rivalry. A competitor's inroads in certain foreign markets may translate to losing business in other markets. Years ago, fearing that they would eventually lose some of their U.S. business with Ford and General Motors if European tire manufacturers were able to sell to those auto manufacturers in Europe, U.S. tire manufacturers followed each and established plants in Europe to better service their major accounts. Similarly, Japanese tire manufacturers like Bridgestone have established manufacturing plants in the United States to serve Japanese carmakers. More recently, from the telecommunications service perspective, MCI followed AT&T to many overseas markets.

The competitive perspective is another strategically based motive for international expansion. If a company's competitor can make unencumbered profits in a specific host country, that competitor can use a portion of those profits to attack the firm in the firm's major markets. This is called *cross-subsidization,* that is, using profits generated in one market to compete in another market. Firms strategically look overseas to gain cross-subsidization possibilities as well as to block competitors from that advantage.[25]

Rapid expansion of a foreign market for the company's product and the desire to obtain a large market share in it before a major competitor can get in are other strong driving forces for companies to engage in foreign production. By being first into a new market, a firm may be able to obtain favorable deals with customers and suppliers. Furthermore, the firm may be able to secure the most efficient distribution channels and set both the strategic and technological agendas for the industry in that host country. This is an important reason for American and European companies wanting to enter the market in China.

The need for vertical integration is another strategic reason often responsible for the international expansion of operations. Companies are pushed into making direct investment abroad so that they can capture a source of supply or new markets for their products. For example, a company in the oil exploration and drilling business may integrate "downstream" by acquiring or building an oil refinery in a foreign country that has a market for its refined products. Conversely, a company that has strong distribution channels (e.g., gas stations) in a country but needs a steady source of supply of gasoline at predictable prices may integrate "upstream" and acquire an oil producer and refiner in another country.

Numerous companies have established operations abroad to exploit the strong brand name of their products. Realizing that they could not fully exploit their advantage by way of exports, they have set up plants in their major foreign markets. Examples of companies that have used this strategy are Coca-Cola, Pepsi-Cola, Budweiser, and Heineken. Scotch whiskey is now produced in India, replacing exports from abroad.

A global company may decide to locate its manufacturing plant in a country that is of strategic importance for the company's exports to a third country. For instance, Japanese companies have strictly observed the Arab boycott of Israel and therefore cannot export to Israel directly from Japan. However, Japanese plants in the United States can export their U.S.-made products to Israel, and this is exactly what Honda is doing. It is exporting Honda Civic sedans to Israel from its plant in Ohio. In the same vein, Northern Telecom Ltd. (Nortel), the Canadian telecommunications giant, has moved many of its manufacturing operations to the United States to gain the competitive edge that an American company can obtain in securing Japanese contracts. Nortel made this strategic move to the United States knowing that the Japanese would favor U.S. companies because of Japan's huge trade surplus with the United States.

As organizational knowledge is becoming a key competitive weapon, firms have recognized that scientific talent and brainpower are not the monopoly of any one country or group of countries. Thus international companies are establishing technological research and development centers around the world. Companies like IBM and Microsoft have established such centers in Japan and India respectively to tap into the "innovation culture" of those countries. Several global companies in a variety of knowledge-based industries such as biotechnology, pharmaceuticals, and electronics have set up such centers in the countries of the so-called Triad of Europe, the Pacific Basin (including Japan), and the United States. This strategy has paid rich dividends for Xerox, which has introduced 80 different office copier models in the United States that were engineered and built by its Japanese joint venture, Fuji-Xerox Company. Another example is Bangalore, India, which has become the global center for software development for major computer and software companies. The number-one global carmaker, General Motors, plans to invest $60 million in a technology center in Bangalore, India's technology hub. General Motors plans to hire 260 engineers, who will collaborate with the company's American and European research center through high-speed communication links. Most planes flying between Mumbai (Bombay), the major international gateway to India, and Bangalore are filled with U.S. technology executives looking to source business in this emerging Silicon Valley.[26] Similarly, firms in Malaysia have proactively marketed themselves to North American and European companies as the appropriate places to outsource their technology needs.

Paralleling financial planning thinking, firms have strategically ventured overseas to diversify their operations and, in effect, to hedge against the many environmental risks of doing business in one country. This strategy ranges from simply distribution and sales in multiple countries to rationalization of production across key countries. Regarding distribution and sales, firms relying solely on the Japanese market have been hurt due to the long-lasting recession in Japan. Firms with a portfolio of country businesses have somewhat hedged against such a recession. Likewise, firms try to balance the efficiencies of long production runs with the flexibility of being able to switch production should trouble arise in a certain country. For instance, auto parts are produced in many countries, including the United States, Japan, Argentina, Mexico, India, and Indonesia. Although the comparative costs in Argentina, Mexico, India, and Indonesia are lower than in the United States and Japan, the former countries are less stable than the latter. Mexico had a financial problem in the mid-1990s. From the late 1990s until today, Indonesia saw a combination of financial and political upheaval that put many foreign investments at risk. And most recently, Argentina's financial problems have bubbled over into increased instability of the market and workforce. Thus producing all of a firm's components in any one of these countries would have proved catastrophic to a firm.

In this section, we have introduced some of the many reasons why a firm may choose to "go international." However, it is important to remember that each company's decision should be based on a careful assessment of its own distinctive strengths (and weaknesses) and the potential for it to strengthen its overall competitive position by making the international move. In the next section, we look at one proposed framework for assessing such potential benefits.

Strategic Objectives and Sources of Competitive Advantage

Sumantra Ghoshal, in his seminal article "Global Strategy: An Organizing Framework,"[27] offered an excellent framework that explains the broad categories of objectives of a global firm and the sources for developing an international/global firm's competitive advantage. The framework is presented in Exhibit 1.1.

As seen in Exhibit 1.1, in its **global strategy,** a global firm pursues three categories of objectives: (1) achieving efficiency, (2) managing risks, and (3) innovating, learning, and adapting. The key is to create a firm's competitive advantage by developing and implementing strategies that optimize the firm's achievement of these three categories of objectives. This may require trade-offs to be made between the objectives because on occasion they may conflict. For example, the objective of achieving efficiency through economies of scale in production may conflict with the objective of minimizing risks emanating from economic or political conditions in a country where the plant is located.

Ghoshal identifies three sources through which a global firm may derive its competitive advantage: (1) national differences, (2) scale economies, and (3) scope economies. According to Ghoshal, the strategic task of managing globally is to use all three sources of competitive advantage to optimize efficiency, risk, and learning simultaneously in a

EXHIBIT 1.1 Global Strategy: An Organizing Framework

Source: From Sumantra Ghoshal, "Global Strategy: An Organizing Framework," *Strategic Management Journal,* Vol. 8. Copyright © 1987 John Wiley & Sons Limited. Reproduced with permission.

Strategic Objectives	Sources of Competitive Advantage		
	National Differences	**Scale Economies**	**Scope Economies**
Achieving efficiency in current operations	Benefiting from differences in factor costs (wages and cost of capital)	Expanding and exploiting potential scale economies in each activity	Sharing investments and costs across products, markets, and businesses
Managing risks	Managing different kinds of risks arising from market- or policy-induced changes in comparative advantage of different countries	Balancing scale with strategic and operational flexibility	Portfolio diversification of risks and creation of options and side-bets
Innovation, learning, and adapting	Learning from societal differences in organizational and managerial processes and systems	Benefiting from experience, cost reduction, and innovation	Sharing learning across organizational components in different products, markets, or businesses

worldwide business. The key to a successful global strategy is to manage the interactions between these different goals and means.[28]

Achieving Efficiency

If a firm is viewed as an input–output system, its overall efficiency is defined as a ratio of the value of all its outputs to the costs of all its inputs. A firm obtains the surplus resources needed to grow and prosper by maximizing this ratio. It may enhance the value of its products or services (outputs) by making them of higher quality than those of its competitors, and at the same time it may lower the costs of inputs by obtaining low-cost factors of production such as labor and raw materials.[29] Different business functions—production, research and development, marketing, and so on—have different factor intensities. A firm could exploit *national differences* by locating a function in a country that has a comparative advantage in providing the factors required to perform it. Thus it could locate labor-intensive production in low-wage countries like Malaysia or Mexico and locate R & D activities in countries that have capable scientists who can do the work but who do not have to be paid high salaries. As an example, many American companies—Microsoft, Oracle, Hewlett-Packard, Novell, Motorola, and Texas Instruments—established centers for software development work in India, where personnel qualified to write innovative software are plentiful and can be employed for as little as $300 a month. Similarly, many U.S.-based companies have established service centers outside America in order to gain added cost efficiencies. For instance, when talking with a Compaq computer service representative, a customer is actually talking with a technical adviser in Ottawa, Canada. Service centers for various firms have been established in countries like Ireland, India, and the Philippines as well during the first part of the twenty-first century.

A firm could enjoy the benefits of *scale economies* like lower costs and higher quality resulting from specialization by designating one plant to serve as the sole producer of a component for use in the final assembly of a product. For example, a plant in the Philippines may make transmissions, another in Malaysia the steering mechanisms, and one in Thailand the engines. Each country would then do the final assembly of the complete automobile. Toyota Motor Company is rapidly moving in this direction. Practical Insight 1.1 illustrates steps taken by Dell Computer to take advantage of scale economies and proximity to key markets to reduce transportation costs.

The concept of *scope economies* is based on the notion that savings and cost reductions will accrue when two or more products can share the same asset, such as a production plant, distribution channel, brand name, or staff services (legal, public relations, etc.). A global company like Coca-Cola enjoys a competitive advantage because it is in a position to produce two or more products in one plant rather than two separate plants, market its products through common distribution channels, and share its world-famous brand name across a wide range of products.

Managing Risks

A global company faces a number of different types of risk including economic, political, cultural, legal, and competitive. The nature and severity of such risks are not the same for all countries. A global company is in a position to manage such risks effectively by planning and implementing effective strategies aimed at diffusing risk.[30] For example, in a country that has high levels of unemployment, a global company could deflect restrictive and unfriendly governmental policies by sourcing products for world markets in that country, thus increasing much-needed employment opportunities for the local populace. An example of such a strategy is the transfer of significant amounts of car production to the United States by Japanese automakers like Toyota, Honda,

> **PRACTICAL INSIGHT 1.1**

DELL COMPUTER'S SUPPLY CHAIN EXTENDS INTO CHINA

Dell Computer's competitive advantage lies in its manufacturing acumen, an upstream activity in the value chain. Dell has dispersed its manufacturing operations to large manufacturing plants strategically located in various parts of the globe primarily to take advantage of scale economies and proximity to key markets to reduce transportation costs. Now Dell is making a big push to lower costs and prices across the board—especially in the two largest markets, Japan and China. In the past, most of the Dell computers that ended up in Japan were built at the company's giant facility in Malaysia.

Now Dell is making PCs for the Japanese market at a factory in the southeastern Chinese city of Xiamen. The switch means Dell saves a third off its manufacturing and shipping costs—savings Dell can pass on to customers. Dell's market share in Japan jumped from 3.8% in 2000 to 5.8% in 2001, according to Gartner Group Inc. consultants, a surge that Dell execs attribute to better management and lower prices.

Source: Reprinted from Bruce Einhorn, Andrew Park, and Irene M. Kunii, "Will Dell Click in Asia? The PC Maker Is Going All Out to Win a Bigger Piece of the Pie," April 22, 2002 issue of *BusinessWeek* by special permission. Copyright © 2002 by The McGraw-Hill Companies, Inc.

and Nissan. One of the principal motivations behind this strategy was to minimize the growing anti-Japanese sentiment in the United States due to the alleged job losses caused by Japanese imports.

The benefits of scale economies must be weighed against their risks. A plant located in a country because of its low wages could lose its locational advantage if the wage rates in the country rise significantly because of economic development or appreciation of the country's currency. Global companies manage such risks by distributing production in more than one country even at the expense of benefits derived from lower scale economies. Japanese car companies have managed currency and wage-rate risks caused by rising wage rates in Japan and the much stronger Japanese yen compared to the U.S. dollar by exporting cars made in U.S.-based plants back to Japan. The flexibility afforded to Japanese car companies by having plants in both the United States and Japan was responsible for their effective management of risk. Chapters 3 and 4 further delineate the various political, legal, economic, and cultural environments and associated risks.

Innovation and Learning

A global company has a distinct advantage over its purely domestic competitor because of the multiple environments in which the global company operates. A company that has operations in many countries is exposed to a diversity of experiences and stimuli. Being in many countries allows it to develop a variety of capabilities.[31] A global company has opportunities to learn skills and acquire knowledge of a country, which can be transferred and applied in many other countries where it has operations.[32] For example, a company that has operations in Japan can learn about the very best aspects of the Japanese management system and adapt and use those that are most useful in its American or European operations. General Electric is marketing in India an ultrasound unit designed by Indian engineers, using technology developed in GE's Japanese operations.

Hewlett-Packard has continued pouring resources into the Asian region, opening a laboratory in Japan and new manufacturing facilities in Japan and Malaysia, while simultaneously beefing up its engineering, project management, and design capacity in Singapore. Such investments provide not only increased sales in the region but also skills and expertise in how to improve the production process, something that it lacks in the United States. Hewlett-Packard has learned process improvement techniques from its Asian operations and transferred the knowledge not only to its U.S. operations but also to operations worldwide.

Eli Lilly & Company, a global pharmaceutical corporation, and Ranbaxy Laboratories Limited, India's largest pharmaceutical company, have formed a path-breaking alliance to set up joint ventures in India and the United States. In the first phase, a state-of-the art research, development, and manufacturing facility is being set up in India to develop products for the U.S. market by undertaking chemical, pharmaceutical, and analytical research. Lilly's strategy apparently is to tap into the research capabilities of Indian scientists, and thereby to learn and develop innovative new products and processes. Moreover, the development of a new patented pharmaceutical product costs $800 million or more in the United States, but it may cost as little as $200 million in India.[33]

The framework we have discussed in this chapter is very useful in identifying possible sources of competitive advantage for an international company. However, the suggested strategies must be translated into operating decisions that can realize the broader goals. We explore this topic in depth in Chapter 6 and illustrate how an international firm establishes the optimum mix of functional and geographic integration to achieve its strategic objectives. But before we take up the issue of strategy, we turn in the next section to a discussion of the environmental context within which the international firm must operate. In the next chapter, we set the stage with an overview of the current global economic environment, highlighting some trends that are important for international managers.

The Environment of International Management

A manager in an international company performs her or his managerial functions in an environment that is far more complex than that of her or his counterpart in a domestic company (see Figure 1.3). The international environment is the total world environment. However, it is also the sum total of the environments of every nation in which the company has its foreign affiliates. The environment within each nation consists

FIGURE 1.3
The International Environment

- Political: Governments, Ideology, Stability, Civil Strife
- Economic: Trade Agreements, Trading Blocs, GDP/Wages, Inflation
- Cultural: Customs, Values, Language, Religion
- Legal: International Law, Host-Country Laws, Home Laws, International Piracy
- Infrastructure: Communications, Internet, Transportation, Technology
- The International Company

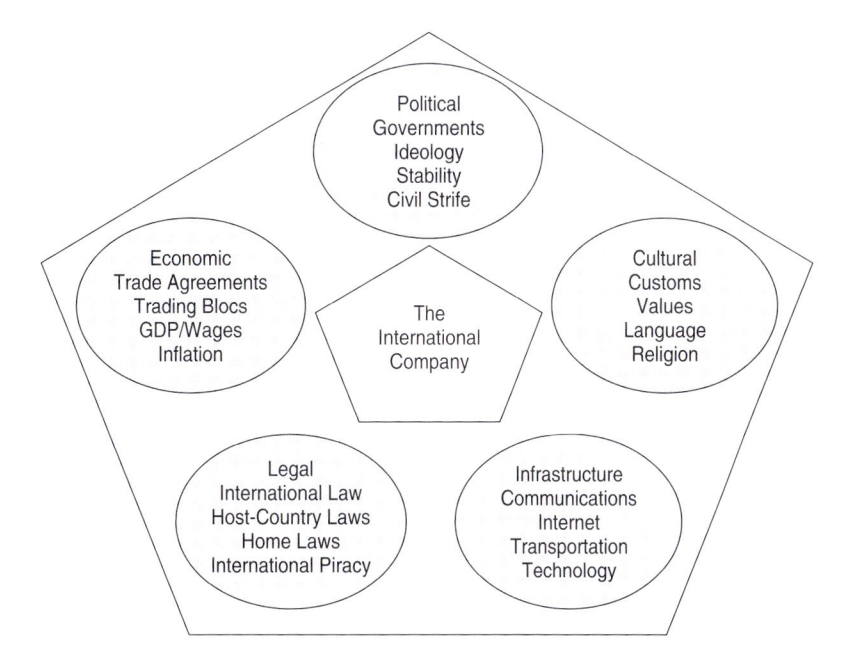

EXHIBIT 1.2
The International Environment

Economic Environment	Legal Environment
Economic system	Legal tradition
Level of economic development	Effectiveness of legal system
Population	Treaties with foreign nations
Gross national product	Patent trademark laws
Per capita income	Laws affecting business firms
Literacy level	**Cultural Environment**
Social infrastructure	Customs, norms, values, beliefs
Natural resources	Language
Climate	Attitudes
Membership in regional economic blocs (EU, NAFTA, LAFTA)	Motivations
Monetary and fiscal policies	Social institutions
Wage and salary levels	Status symbols
Nature of competition	Religious beliefs
Foreign exchange rates	**Technological Environment**
Currency convertibility	Inventions
Inflation	New-product development
Taxation system	New-process innovations
Interest rates	Internet capabilities
Political Environment	
Form of government	
Political ideology	
Stability of government	
Strength of opposition parties and groups	
Social unrest	
Political strife and insurgency	
Governmental attitude toward foreign firms	
Foreign policy	

of five dimensions: economic, political, legal, cultural, and technological. Exhibit 1.2 lists the factors typically found in each of these environments. We examine the new economic infrastructure that includes trade agreements and regional economic integration initiatives in Chapter 2, the political and legal dimensions in Chapter 3, and the cultural dimension in Chapter 4.

Summary

This chapter provides an introduction to international management and to the world of the so-called international company. The nature of international business was explained first, and we saw that the need for international management and managers arises for many strategic and market reasons.

Although there are scores of small international companies, generally when one speaks about them, the reference is to the large multinationals. Increasingly, people are referring to these giant companies with operations throughout the world as international, multinational, and global companies. Because the other connotations are used more specifically in later chapters, we use the term *international companies* to define the entities with overseas sales and/or operations. International management and international companies are more or less like conjoined twins or the two sides of a coin. The growth of international companies has resulted from the astute management of these enterprises by international managers. And the management of these corporations epitomizes what international management is all about.

We saw something of the dimensions and drastic growth of multinational companies since the 1960s. We also examined the market-based, cost-based, and strategic motives a firm has to expand internationally. After this, we studied how global companies exploit economies of scale, economies of scope, and national differences to achieve their three generic objectives: (1) efficiency in current operations, (2) managing risks, and (3) innovation, learning, and adaptation. We concluded by introducing the nature and complexity of the international environment of international companies. Figure 1.4 illustrates the roadmap for the remainder of the book.

FIGURE 1.4 International Management: A Model of International Management

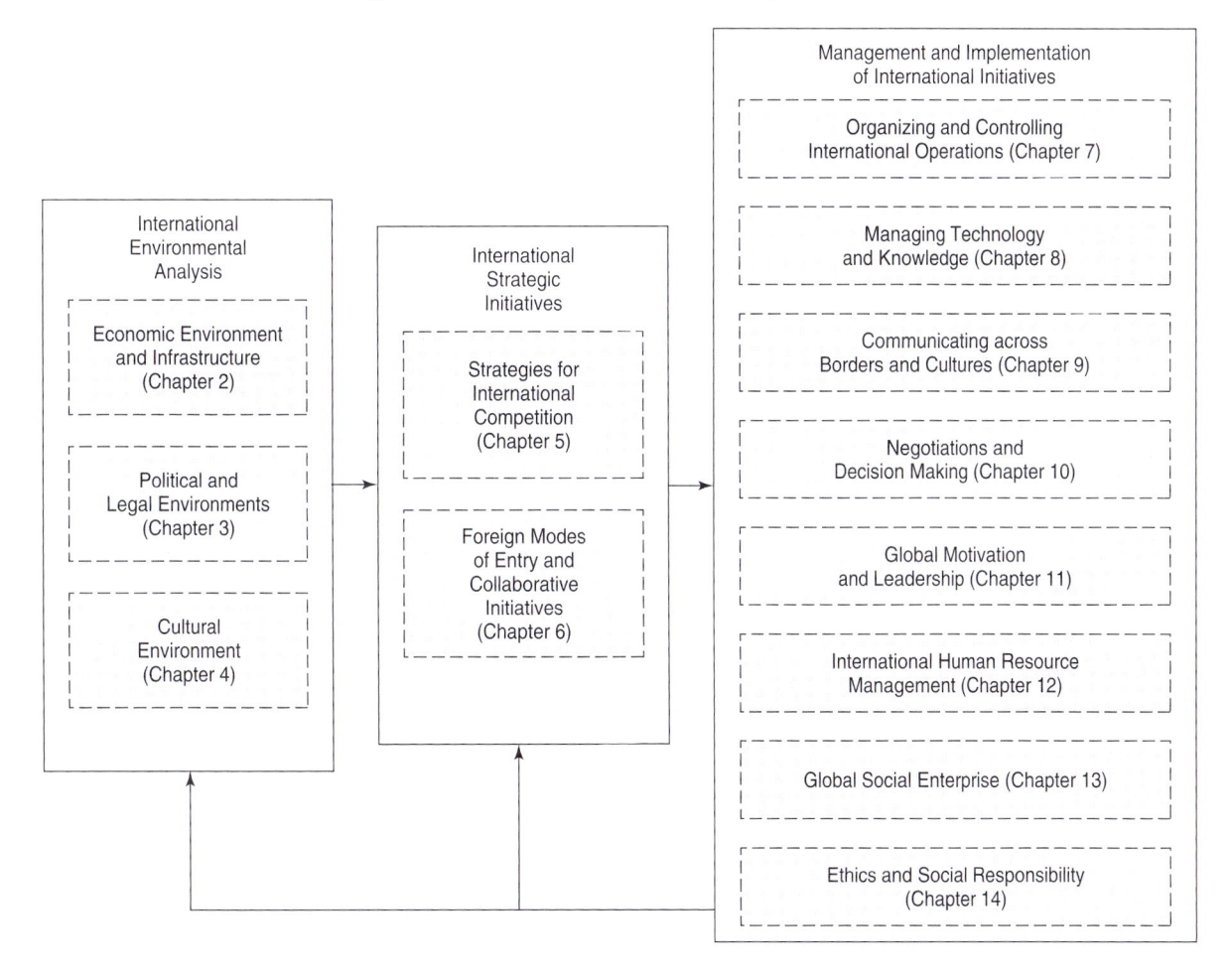

```
International                                    Management and Implementation
Environmental                                    of International Initiatives
Analysis
                                                 ┌─────────────────────────────┐
┌─────────────────────────┐                      │ Organizing and Controlling   │
│ Economic Environment    │                      │ International Operations     │
│ and Infrastructure      │                      │ (Chapter 7)                  │
│ (Chapter 2)             │                      └─────────────────────────────┘
└─────────────────────────┘   International
                              Strategic          ┌─────────────────────────────┐
┌─────────────────────────┐   Initiatives        │ Managing Technology          │
│ Political and           │                      │ and Knowledge (Chapter 8)    │
│ Legal Environments      │   ┌──────────────┐   └─────────────────────────────┘
│ (Chapter 3)             │   │ Strategies   │
└─────────────────────────┘   │ for          │   ┌─────────────────────────────┐
                              │ International│   │ Communicating across         │
┌─────────────────────────┐   │ Competition  │   │ Borders and Cultures         │
│ Cultural                │   │ (Chapter 5)  │   │ (Chapter 9)                  │
│ Environment             │   └──────────────┘   └─────────────────────────────┘
│ (Chapter 4)             │
└─────────────────────────┘   ┌──────────────┐   ┌─────────────────────────────┐
                              │ Foreign Modes│   │ Negotiations and             │
                              │ of Entry and │   │ Decision Making (Chapter 10) │
                              │ Collaborative│   └─────────────────────────────┘
                              │ Initiatives  │
                              │ (Chapter 6)  │   ┌─────────────────────────────┐
                              └──────────────┘   │ Global Motivation            │
                                                 │ and Leadership (Chapter 11)  │
                                                 └─────────────────────────────┘

                                                 ┌─────────────────────────────┐
                                                 │ International Human Resource │
                                                 │ Management (Chapter 12)      │
                                                 └─────────────────────────────┘

                                                 ┌─────────────────────────────┐
                                                 │ Global Social Enterprise     │
                                                 │ (Chapter 13)                 │
                                                 └─────────────────────────────┘

                                                 ┌─────────────────────────────┐
                                                 │ Ethics and Social            │
                                                 │ Responsibility (Chapter 14)  │
                                                 └─────────────────────────────┘
```

Key Terms and Concepts

cost-reduction motives for international expansion, *11*
foreign direct investment (FDI), *4*
global strategy, *16*
international business, *5*
international company, *7*
international management, *6*
market-seeking motives for international expansion, *9*
strategic motives for international expansion, *13*

Discussion Questions

1. What is international business? How does it differ from international management?
2. Discuss the characteristics of multinational companies. What forces have contributed to their development and growth?
3. What are strategic, cost-based, and marketing-based company motives for expanding overseas?
4. Identify and explain the three categories of broad objectives of global companies. What strategic actions can a global company take in order to develop competitive advantage against its competitors?
5. Discuss the key differences between economies of scale and economies of scope.
6. Discuss how national differences can serve as a source of competitive advantage for a global company.

Minicase

Want to Be More Efficient, Spread Risk, and Learn and Innovate at the Same Time? Try Building a "World Car"

Japanese car companies like Toyota and the Honda Motor Company are pioneering the auto industry's truly global manufacturing system. The companies' aim is to perfect a car's design and production in one place and then churn out thousands of "world" cars each year that can be made in one place and sold worldwide. In an industry where the cost of tailoring car models to different markets can run into billions of dollars, the "world car" approach of Toyota and Honda—and which Ford is hoping to emulate—is targeted at sharply curtailing development costs, maximizing the use of assembly plants, and preserving the assembly line efficiencies that are a hallmark of the Japanese "lean" production system.

As for Honda, the goal is to create a "global base of complementary supply," says Roger Lambert, Honda's manager of corporate communications. "Japan can supply North America and Europe, North America can supply Japan and Europe, and Europe can supply Japan and the United States. So far, the first two are true. This means that you can more profitably utilize your production bases and talents."

The strategy of shipping components and fully assembled products from the U.S. to Europe and Japan couldn't have come at a more opportune time for the Japanese car companies, especially when political pressures are intense to reduce the Japanese trade surplus with the United States. The task was made easier due to the strength of the Japanese yen, which has risen about 50 percent against the U.S. dollar. That has made production of cars in the United States cheaper, by some estimates, by $2,500 to $3,000 per car. That saving more than compensates for the transportation costs for a car overseas. For the first time, Toyota is creating a system that will give it the capability to manage the car production levels in Japan and the United States. It is moving toward a global manufacturing system that will enable it to enhance manufacturing efficiency by fine-tuning global production levels on a quarterly basis in response to economic conditions in different markets.

Source: Adapted from Paul Ingrassia, "Ford to Export Parts to Europe for a New Car," *The Wall Street Journal*, September 29, 1992, p. A5; Jane Perlez, "Toyota and Honda Create Global Production System," *The New York Times*, March 26, 1993, pp. A1, D2.

DISCUSSION QUESTIONS

1. Discuss the strategies implemented by Toyota and Honda to achieve greater efficiency in car production.
2. How do the automobile companies plan to simultaneously manage risk and gain efficiencies?
3. Discuss how the car companies use national differences to gain a strategic advantage in the global car industry.

Notes

1. Richard E. Caves, "International Corporations: The Industrial Economics of Foreign Direct Investment," *Economica* 38, no. 141 (1971), pp. 1–27.
2. John D. Daniels and Lee H. Radebaugh, *International Business: Environment and Operations,* 6th ed. (Reading, MA: Addison-Wesley, 1992), p. 8.
3. Donald A. Ball and Wendell H. McCulloch Jr., *International Business: Introduction and Essentials,* 4th ed. (Homewood, IL: BPI/Irwin, 1990), p. 17.
4. Betty Jane Punett and David A. Ricks, *International Business* (Boston: PWS/Kent, 1992), p. 7.
5. Charles W. L. Hill, *International Business,* 4th ed. (New York: McGraw-Hill /Irwin, 2003), p. 29.
6. Endel J. Kolde and Richard E. Hill, "Conceptual and Normative Aspects of International Management," *Academy of Management Journal,* June 2001, p. 120.
7. Jean J. Boddewyn, "The Domain of International Management," *Journal of International Management* 5, no. 1 (Spring 1999), p. 5.
8. Ibid.
9. Ibid., p. 121.
10. Kolde and Hill, "Conceptual and Normative Aspects of International Management."
11. Boddewyn, "The Domain of International Management," p. 9.
12. Arvind V. Phatak, *International Management: Concepts and Cases* (Cincinnati: South-Western College Publishing, 1997), p. 3.
13. All statistics in this paragraph are from United Nations Conference on Trade and Development, *World Investment Report 2007* (Geneva: UNCTAD, 2007), chap. 1.
14. R. Vernon, "International Investment and International Trade in the Product Life Cycle," *Quarterly Journal of Economics* 80 (1965), pp. 190–207.
15. D. Sethi, S. E. Guisinger, S. E. Phelan, and D. M. Berg, "Trends in Foreign Direct Investment Flows: A Theoretical and Empirical Analysis," *Journal of International Business Studies* 34, no. 4 (2003), pp. 315–326.
16. Peter J. Buckley and Mark Casson, *The Economic Theory of the Multinational Enterprise* (London: St. Martin's Press, 1985).
17. Sethi, Guisinger, Phelan, and Berg, "Trends in Foreign Direct Investment Flows," p. 325.
18. Ibid., p. 319.
19. Ibid., p. 100.
20. S. H. Hymer, *The International Operations of National Firms: A Study of Direct Investment* (Cambridge, MA: MIT Press, 1960).
21. A. M. Rugman, *International Diversification and the Multinational Enterprise* (Lexington, MA: Lexington Books, 1979).
22. R. E. Caves, "Industrial Corporations: The Industrial Economics of Foreign Direct Investment," *Economica* 38 (1971), pp. 1–27; J. H. Dunning, "Toward an Eclectic Theory of International Production: Some Empirical Tests," *Journal of International Business Studies* 11, no. 1 (1980), pp. 9–31.
23. Roger Kashlak, former director for Italy for AT&T International, personal communication.

24. F. T. Knickerbocker, *Oligopolistic Reaction and the Multinational Enterprise* (Cambridge, MA: Harvard University Press, 1973).
25. Gary Hamel and C. K. Prahalad, "Do You Really Have a Global Strategy?" *Harvard Business Review* 63, no. 4 (1985), pp. 139–149.
26. Saritha Rai, "World Business Briefing, Asia: India: G. M. to Invest in Technology Center," *New York Times,* June 26, 2003, p. W1.
27. Sumantra Ghoshal, "Global Strategy: An Organizing Framework," *Strategic Management Journal* 8 (1987), pp. 425–440.
28. Ibid., p. 427.
29. Alan M. Rugman, *Inside the Multinationals: The Economics of International Markets* (New York: Columbia University Press, 1981).
30. Kent D. Miller, "A Framework for Integrated Risk Management in International Business," *Journal of International Business Studies* 23, no. 2 (1992), pp. 311–334.
31. Bruce Kogut and Sea-Jin Chang, "Technological Capabilities and Japanese Foreign Direct Investment in the United States," *Review of Economics and Statistics* 73 (1991), pp. 401–413.
32. John J. Dunning, "Multinational Enterprises and the Globalization of Innovative Capacity," *Research Policy* 23 (1994), pp. 67–68.
33. Comments made by G. P. Garnier to Arvind V. Phatak at the Greater Philadelphia Global Award of which Mr. Garnier was the awardee, June 12, 2003.

Economies of scale = the cost advantage that arises w/ increased output of a product
- arises because of the inverse relationship between the quantity produced and per-unit fixed costs
  i.e. the greater the quantity of a good produced, the lower the per-unit fixed cost because these costs are shared over a large number of goods

Economies of scope = an economic theory stating that the average total cost of production decreases as a result of increasing the number of different goods produced.
  i.e. McDonalds can produce both hamburgers and french fries at a lower average cost than what it would cost two seperate firms to produce the same goods

CHAPTER TWO

The Global Macroeconomic Environment

Chapter Learning Objectives

After completing this chapter, you should be able to:

- Discuss potential effects of the growth of regional trade blocs on global free trade.
- Explain the differences between and similarities of a free trade area, a customs union, a common market, an economic union, and a political union.
- Describe the static and dynamic benefits of regional economic integration as well as the supply-side-led benefits that will accrue to member countries.
- Describe the key features of the Uruguay Round of the General Agreement on Tariffs and Trade and the World Trade Organization and their implications for the conduct of business between member countries.
- Discuss the significance of the World Trade Organization to international trade.
- Describe the important characteristics of the North American Free Trade Agreement and the European Union.
- Discuss the ways in which the major regional economic agreements can be expected to improve business opportunities and problems associated with their implementation.
- Examine the phenomenon of globalization and its meaning.
- Evaluate the significance of country-specific economic features and competitiveness rankings to international companies.

Opening Case: High-Tech Transnationals Take "Stateless" to the Next Level

When the first reports surfaced at 12:17 p.m. Pacific Time on Aug. 11, 2003, that the Blaster computer virus was on the loose, researchers at antivirus-software company Trend Micro Inc. scrambled to come up with a fix. Meanwhile, the company's five global alert commanders began sizing up Blaster via cell-phone calls and e-mails. At 1:55 p.m., Hammud Saway, the commander based in Japan, declared a global alert, signaling that this virus was nasty enough to require all the company's resources. Just 51 minutes later, a cure was ready. The company routinely is among the first responders to viruses, often delivering 30 minutes before market leader Symantec Corp., according to GEGA IT-Solutions in Germany, a response tester.

Trend Micro is able to respond so quickly partly because it's not organized like most companies. It has spread its top executives, engineers, and support staff around the world to improve its response to new virus threats—which can start anywhere and spread like wildfire. The main virus response center is in the Philippines, where 250 engineers are willing to work the evening and midnight shifts necessary to keep ever-vigilant. Then there are six other labs scattered from Munich to Tokyo. "With the Internet, viruses became global. To fight them, we had to become a global company," says Chairman Steve Chang, a Taiwanese who started the company in 1988.

Trend Micro is among a new breed of high-tech companies that defy conventional wisdom about how corporations ought to operate. While most large companies have extensive worldwide operations, these companies go much further—aiming to transcend nationality altogether. C. K. Prahalad, a professor at the University of Michigan Business School, calls this the fourth stage of globalization. In the first stage, companies operate in one country and sell into others. Second-stage multinationals set up foreign subsidiaries to handle one country's sales. And the third stage involves operating an entire line of business in another country.

What's different about these outfits—call them transnationals—is that even the executive suite is virtual. They place their top executives and core corporate functions in different countries to gain a competitive edge through the availability of talent or capital, low costs, or proximity to their most important customers. Trend Micro's financial headquarters is in Tokyo, where it went public; product development is in PhD-rich Taiwan; and sales is in Silicon Valley—inside the giant American market. When companies fragment this way, they are no longer limited to the strengths, or hobbled by the weaknesses, of their native lands. "This is very new, and it's important," says Prahalad. "There's a fundamental rethinking about what is a multinational company," he says. "Does it have a home country? What does headquarters mean? Can you fragment your corporate functions globally?"

There has long been talk of the stateless corporation—*BusinessWeek* even ran a cover story on it in 1990. Yet the dispersal of key corporate functions takes the idea one step further, and it's made possible by advances in technology, especially the Internet. Harvard Business School Professor Christopher A. Bartlett says improved communication is allowing an evolution toward "an integrated global network of operations." To deal with the gaps between time zones and cultures, these tech transnationals operate like virtual computer networks. Thanks to the Internet, they can communicate in real time via e-mail, instant messenger, or Web videoconferencing. Over time, these scattered experiments could coalesce into a powerful new model for business. Bartlett and other management experts say the strategy of truly globalizing core corporate functions is applicable for all kinds and sizes of companies.

Tech's transnationals are popping up all around the world. They range from business-intelligence-software maker Business Objects (BOBJ) with headquarters in France and San Jose, Calif., to Wipro (WIT), a tech-services supplier with headquarters in India and Santa Clara, Calif., to computer-peripherals maker Logitech International (LOGI) with headquarters in Switzerland and Fremont, Calif. While no one tracks the numbers, *BusinessWeek* interviewed executives at a dozen such companies, and new ones keep popping up. For instance, 24/7 Customer, a business-services provider with headquarters in Los Gatos, Calif., and Bangalore, India, just raised $22 million from Silicon Valley venture capitalists.

Running a transnational company is a tough management challenge, though. Executives are separated by oceans and time zones, making it difficult to maintain basic communications and routines that old-style companies take for granted. Then there are the cultural chasms. "The curse is that national cultures can be very different," says Trend Micro's Chang. "We have to figure out how to convert everybody to one business culture—no matter where they're from." That's why Chang is visiting the company's 20-plus sites and laying out a set of common values. Chang, who learned to do magic tricks when he performed at his parents' bowling alley in Taiwan during his youth, breaks the ice by performing sleight-of-hand with cards or coins.

In spite of the complexities of spanning the globe and a sluggish economic environment, most of these tech transnationals have been delivering outstanding financial results. Of the dozen companies

BusinessWeek studied, the average revenue increase last year was 25.4%, vs. a 4% decline for the overall tech industry, says market researcher IDC.

These companies use geo-diversity to great advantage. Logitech, for instance, has placed its manufacturing headquarters in Taiwan to capitalize on low-cost Asian manufacturing. Meanwhile, its business-development headquarters in Europe has lined up strategic partnerships that have kept the company at the cutting edge of peripherals design, particularly for optical pens and mice. That has helped Logitech hold its own against mighty Microsoft in worldwide markets for peripherals.

For Wipro Ltd., there are clear pluses to locating sales in the U.S. and engineering in India. Wipro's vice-chairman, Vivek Paul, is based in Silicon Valley to be close to the mammoth U.S. market. At the same time, the company can underprice Western rivals because 17,000 of its 20,000 software engineers and consultants are in India, where the annual cost per employee is less than one-fifth that of Silicon Valley. There are even some unintended benefits from operating transnationally. To collaborate smoothly in spite of the geographic barriers, all of the Wipro managers file electronic activity reports with their superiors on Monday, who in turn pass them along, via e-mail, until summaries reach Paul, who travels nearly constantly. Not only does Paul stay plugged in wherever he is, but the report process "steps up the pace of the organization," he says.

This next big step in globalization won't be steady—or fast. Expect startups to experiment with new ways of operating, and a few innovative established companies to tinker with their geographic organizations. But being transnational requires fundamental and difficult shifts for the giants that might not be worth the trouble. Often, the transformation requires a unique leader—and extremely flexible business unit managers. Still, given the necessity to exploit new markets and to operate ever more efficiently, the pressure won't let up to create something approaching a corporation without a country.

Source: Reprinted from Steve Hamm, "Borders Are So 20th Century: High-Tech Transnationals Take 'Stateless' to the Next Level," September 22, 2003 issue of *BusinessWeek* by special permission. Copyright © 2003 by The McGraw-Hill Companies, Inc.

Discussion Questions

1. Explain the effects of technology on globalization.
2. What are the effects of globalization on firms like Trend Micro and Wipro?
3. In your opinion, why has globalization occurred? What are your concerns regarding globalization?

A New Global Economy

During the past 15 years, many of the world's nations have increasingly tried to erase barriers to free trade that had been erected over time. Efforts to bring about freer trade among nations were begun with the General Agreement on Tariffs and Trade (GATT) negotiations as early as 1948 and with the Treaty of Rome in 1957, which created the European Economic Community. The real impetus to freer trade, however, was given by the recognition by nation-states that, in the long run, the economic benefits of free trade would spread to the peoples of all countries. The success of the original European Economic Community and its evolution into the modern-day European Union (EU) promoted freer trade and investment flows among its member countries and raised the living standards of people in the union, demonstrating the power of the free market. Moreover, the fall of the Soviet Union in 1991 has demonstrated the economic power of the free market over state regulation of economic activity. These developments played a major role in the global push favoring freer world trade.

Major developments favoring free trade include (1) the emergence of the World Trade Organization (WTO) and (2) the emergence of regional trade blocs, such as the North American Free Trade Agreement (NAFTA), the expanded EU, and other regional trade arrangements like MERCOSUR in South America. In this chapter we review the movement toward global free trade, starting with the General Agreement on Tariffs and Trade and its successor, the World Trade Organization.

The General Agreement on Tariffs and Trade and the World Trade Organization

The **General Agreement on Tariffs and Trade (GATT)** was created in 1947, with 23 industrialized countries as the founding members, to set fair and common rules for the way each country must conduct its trade with others.[1] GATT was created after World War II for the principal purpose of reducing tariffs and removing nontariff barriers to international trade.* The single most important principle at the heart of GATT was that discrimination poisons trade. In keeping with this principle, GATT strove to ensure that every country in GATT open its markets equally to every other. And GATT upheld the principle of "national treatment," which requires countries to treat foreign businesspeople and foreign companies as they do locals.

Eight rounds of GATT-sponsored multilateral trade negotiations spawned significant reductions in tariff and nontariff barriers. From the 23 countries that took part in the first round in Geneva in 1947, the number of member countries in the eighth Uruguay Round had grown to 117. (Each round is identified by the name of the place where it took place.) The Uruguay Round was concluded in Geneva on December 15, 1993, after seven years of strenuous negotiations, and the biggest-ever world trade treaty was signed in Marrakesh, Morocco, on April 15, 1994, amid hopes of a more equitable and cooperative world economic order.

What GATT Left Undone

The intent of GATT was to remove nontariff barriers altogether, and its new rules were designed to discourage their proliferation. However, countries inevitably continued to impose nontariff barriers against foreign competitors. These barriers included government procurement procedures that favor domestic suppliers; weak enforcement of antitrust laws designed to foster competition; restrictions on inward direct foreign investment; and arbitrary application of food safety regulations to block imports.

The issue of a uniform code for cross-border investments was not addressed by the Uruguay Round. Thus countries were left with no restrictions on under-the-table subsidies to attract foreign investments. Although the U.S. movie industry won eventual copyright protection worldwide for its movies, U.S. negotiators failed to break a European quota system that limited foreign programming and other domestic film subsidies. Also, much was left undone in the area of free trade and investment in services. U.S. negotiators were unable to secure agreement from Asian and developing countries to permit broader entry of U.S. financial services firms into their markets.

GATT has contributed significantly to a more harmonious world trade regime. However, new issues like trade and the environment, competition and antitrust policies,

---

* A tariff (or customs duty) is a tax imposed by a government on physical goods as they move in and out of a country. Examples of nontariff barriers are import and export quotas; subsidies to domestic producers or exporters; dumping of products (selling a product in one national market at a cheaper price than in another market); regulations to imports with respect to safety, health, marketing, labeling, packaging, and technical standards; and local content requirements.

and regionalism in trade (e.g., NAFTA, which is discussed later in this chapter) are coming to the fore as the world economy evolves.

The World Trade Organization

The Uruguay Round of GATT created the **World Trade Organization (WTO)** to enforce the GATT agreement.[2] In 1995 the WTO replaced GATT. GATT had always been considered a partial agreement among member nations, which allowed them to effectively ignore any GATT rulings they did not like. The WTO, by contrast, is an institution, not an agreement, which has the authority to set and enforce rules governing trade between more than 151 member countries. Thus GATT, which was set up in 1947 as a temporary entity, was transformed into a permanent trade body.

The WTO, with an elaborate institutional mechanism of councils and committees, oversees the implementation of the GATT agreement by member countries. All members of the WTO, large and small alike, have equal representation in the WTO's Ministerial Conference. The conference meets at least once every two years to vote for a director general, who appoints other officials.

Settlement of Disputes by the WTO

The **WTO dispute settlement procedure** calls for the establishment of a panel of trade experts who would be called upon to resolve disputes. The WTO selects the panel from a list of trade experts provided by member countries. If the two countries involved in the dispute are unable to agree on the members of the panel, the WTO director general selects the panel. The WTO must rule on member complaints within one year, which is quite an improvement over the five or more years it took under the GATT procedures. The panel hears from both sides and makes its decision in secret.

Decisions by the trade panels are binding unless overturned by consensus of the WTO membership. As was mentioned earlier, this is quite a departure from the GATT procedures that, absurdly, allowed countries found in violation of fair-trade rules to unilaterally block unfavorable panel decisions by merely ignoring them. Under the WTO process, countries that win a case they filed before the WTO receive an automatic green light to undertake retaliatory measures against the offending country if that country does not change its practices. The country that is found guilty of violating fair-trade rules has two choices: (1) change its law or (2) face sanctions, most likely in the form of tariffs slapped on its exports by the complaining country.

Critics, especially in the United States, have expressed fears that the WTO could become a foreign-dominated Supreme Court that would result in a loss of national sovereignty of member countries. These critics are afraid that the WTO could make rulings that would put the U.S. environmental, health, and safety laws at risk by labeling them nontariff barriers, thus requiring the United States to repeal them. In reality, the WTO does not have the legal power to change U.S. laws—only the U.S. Congress can do that. This is equally true for every country in the WTO. No outside body can force a country to do anything it does not want to. However, the fears of the critics are valid to the extent that in choosing not to abide by the WTO rulings, the United States, or any other country, is subjecting itself to sanctions imposed by the complaining country or countries. International business experts believe that because of its economic strength and market size, the United States has little to fear from retaliation. Experts reason that even countries that win cases before the WTO would hesitate before retaliating and are more likely to negotiate with each other to arrive at a reasonable compromise.

Country-Level Economic Integration

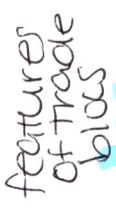

Continental trade blocs are emerging in many parts of the world almost in tandem. This current wave of regionalism has three important features. First, almost every country belongs to at least one trade bloc. Second, most trade blocs have been formed among neighboring countries, many along continental lines. Third, regional arrangements are put forward or accelerated in various parts of the world. For example, in the Western Hemisphere, efforts are under way to expand NAFTA to include most countries of the Americas. In South America, countries have joined together to create the Free Trade Area of the Americas (FTAA). Also, in western Europe, the European Union is continuing to add more countries that once belonged to the now-defunct Soviet bloc. In Asia and the Pacific, the ASEAN bloc is expanding to include more countries in East Asia.[3] NAFTA, FTAA, the European Union, and ASEAN will be covered later in this chapter.

Regional economic integration through trade blocs, such as the North American Free Trade Agreement (NAFTA), which includes Canada, the United States, and Mexico, and the European Union have served as primary catalysts in promoting the elimination of trade barriers and trade liberalization among bloc members. One or more of the following reasons may explain why regional groupings of countries in trade blocs are formed:

- Geographic proximity and often the sharing of common borders, as in the European Union and NAFTA.
- Common economic and political interests, as in the European Union and the ASEAN.
- Similar ethnic and cultural backgrounds, as in the Free Trade Area of the Americas.
- Similar levels of economic development, as in the European Union.
- Similar views on the mutual benefits of free trade, as in NAFTA.
- Regional political needs and considerations, as in the ASEAN.

Figure 2.1 illustrates the various levels at which countries may economically integrate. There are five major types of trade blocs:

1. **Free trade area (FTA).** The loosest form of economic integration is the free trade area. Many of today's stronger agreements began as simple free trade areas. In a free trade area, bloc member countries eliminate trade barriers on trade among member countries but retain the right to impose their own separate trade barriers on trade with countries outside the trade bloc. According to this definition, NAFTA is a free trade area.

2. **Customs union.** This agreement among member countries eliminates the duties and also establishes common external positions regarding trade with non–bloc members. For instance, a tariff on bicycles being imported from China would be the same for all countries participating in a customs union.

3. **Common market.** A common market is a customs union that also allows factor mobility, that is, the free movement of resources such as labor and capital. The European Union from the 1970s through the early 1990s is an example of a common market. Citizens of its member countries could move freely throughout the other countries.

4. **Economic union.** An economic union is a common market wherein the national economic policies of member countries are also harmonized. That is, the member

FIGURE 2.1
A Hierarchy of Regional Economic Integration Initiatives

- Free Trade Area → Elimination of Trade Barriers
- Customs Union → + Common External Trade Positions
- Common Market → + Labor/Capital Mobility
- Economic Union → + Coordinated Economic and Fiscal Policy
- Political Union → + Coordinated Political and Social Policy

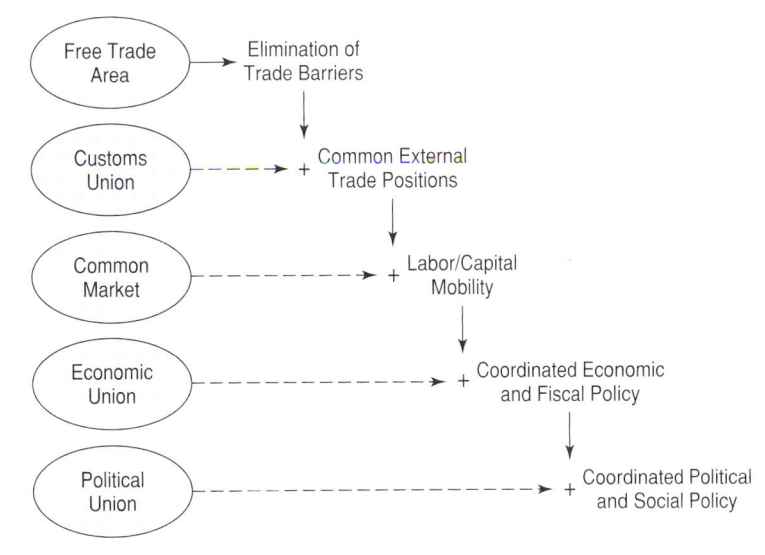

TABLE 2.1 Types of Trade Blocs
Source: Adapted from Franklin R. Root, *International Trade and Investment* (Cincinnati, OH: South-Western Publishing Company, 1992), p. 254.

Level of Integration	No Tariffs and Quotas	Common Tariffs and Quotas	No Restrictions on Factor Movements	Harmonized and Unified Economic Policies and Institutions	Unified Economic and Political Policies and Institutions
Free trade area	Yes	No	No	No	No
Customs union	Yes	Yes	No	No	No
Common market	Yes	Yes	Yes	No	No
Economic union	Yes	Yes	Yes	Yes	No
Political union	Yes	Yes	Yes	Yes	Yes

countries harmonize monetary and fiscal policies, environmental regulations, health and safety measures, agricultural policy, and technical standards. As opposed to a free trade area, a customs union, and a common market, which are created mainly by the removal of trade restrictions, an economic union demands the transfer of considerable economic sovereignty to supranational institutions. The European Union has moved to this status and has now implemented a common currency, called the *euro,* as ultimate evidence of economic integration.

5. **Political union.** A political union is the ultimate step in regional integration. Beyond the ties delineated as part of an economic union, the member countries of a political union will coordinate government and social policy as well. The former Soviet Union is an example of a political union, one that was forced upon its members. The Civil War in the United States between the North and the South was fought by the northern states to restore a political union called the Unites States of America after the South had seceded.

The essential features of each type of trade bloc are illustrated in Table 2.1.

The Effects of Economic Integration

Two main categories of effects result from **economic integration**: *static* and *dynamic*. We next examine how these effects emerge in a **common market** that provides common external tariffs and quotas against third countries and free movement of people, capital, and goods and services among member countries. Except for an economic union, a common market is the most advanced form of economic integration among countries.

Static Effects of Economic Integration

Common external trade barriers and free trade among member countries have both positive and negative effects on trade patterns. In his study of economic integration, particularly that of a customs union, Jacob Viner[4] formalized their economic benefits and costs, which may be called trade creation and trade diversion, respectively. The positive trade effect occurs when free trade among member countries leads to the substitution of inefficient domestic production in a common market country for efficient production in another country also in the common market. As an example, in the European Union, German consumers would be better off, after the lowering of tariffs, by importing products produced by a lower-cost producer in Spain rather than a high-cost producer inside Germany. Trade is created between Germany and Spain, which did not exist before because tariffs on imports made the Spanish products noncompetitive against the German-made products. This is good, as it manifests comparative advantage at work. When such new trade is created among member countries without displacing third-country imports, the process is called *trade creation*.

Trade creation is a positive effect of free trade. However, lowering intraregional barriers leaves relatively high barriers on nonmembers. If this leads to a substitution of efficient third-country production by inefficient production in a common market country, *trade diversion* may result. Trade diversion occurs when consumers within a common market find that goods produced inefficiently in a member country are cheaper than efficiently produced goods in a country outside the common market, primarily because of the high tariffs imposed on imports from non–common market countries. As an example, suppose that the unit production cost of a car is $6,000 in Germany and $4,500 in South Korea. If the European Union imposes a 50 percent import tariff on imports of South Korean automobiles, the cost of Korean cars in Germany and in other European countries would be pushed above $6,000. Consumers in the European Union would therefore be more inclined to buy German cars, as opposed to Korean cars, resulting in a diversion of trade. This is bad: Comparative advantage is denied. Why? Because before the free trade was established, exporters of German and Korean cars faced the same tariff, so the importing country chose its suppliers on price and quality alone. With free trade within the common market, the importer switched to the less efficient supplier in Germany.

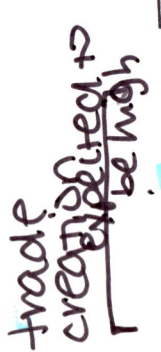

Under what circumstances would a common market lead to trade creation as opposed to trade diversion? Trade creation can generally be high when the economies of the member countries are very competitive and not specialized in the production of certain industries or products—that is, production is overlapping and diffused among member countries. Such conditions provide opportunities for specialization and intra–common market trade. On the other hand, if the economies of the countries prior to the formation of the common market were complementary, then opportunities for *new* trade are limited, because the economies are already specialized with respect to each other. Trade creation is expected to be high also when (1) the member countries in the common market are at similar levels of economic development; (2) the preunion tariffs of member countries were high, inducing trade creation in products that were once protected from imports; (3) transport costs are low; and (4) the size of the common market is large, because the larger the size, the greater the probability that producers would be able to lower costs through the scale effect. Trade diversion is more likely to occur in a common market of small economic size, because member countries would be inclined to protect their own relatively less efficient companies (due to higher unit costs because of the absence of the scale effect) against more efficient outsiders by raising the tariff barriers against imports.

The net effect of a common market depends on the size of trade creation relative to trade diversion. Trade creation improves the world's economic efficiency, and thus its potential welfare, by substituting lower-cost production for higher-cost production. Potential world welfare is lowered when trade diversion causes the substitution of higher-cost production within the common market for lower-cost production outside the union.

The best solution to ensure trade creation in a free trade area is to insist that "(a) members of a free-trade area set a common external tariff (and thus form a customs union) and (b) that the common tariff for any item should be set equal to the lowest tariff applied to that good by any member of the free-trade area before the union was formed."[5]

The ultimate solution to avoid trade diversion would be to eliminate all import tariffs. However, given the internal political realities of member countries, this solution may not be possible. The next best alternative would be to keep external tariffs at a bare minimum that would allow exporters in nonmember countries to compete against member country producers on factors such as quality, service, and design, but not necessarily on price.

Dynamic Effects of Economic Integration

Free trade arrangements can also have significant dynamic effects on economic growth. *Market extension* is one benefit of a common market. Producers have free access to the national markets of all member countries, unhindered by import restrictions. Similarly, consumers have access to products produced in all countries of the union. The enlarged market serves as a catalyst for many forces. It promotes *economies of scale,* not only in production but also in marketing, research and development, and purchasing, as the large market size is able to support larger scale in these functions. Higher capital investment also boosts the returns to skilled labor by improving *productivity,* which in turn increases the accumulation of human capital, thus raising growth further. In common markets, labor mobility also increases productivity and growth as firms are able to hire skilled workers and professionals who are able to move freely in search of jobs where their abilities are most in demand. A larger market size also promotes entry of new competitors and intensifies *competition,* forcing producers to improve product and service quality and to search for ways to lower costs by improving efficiency in all business functions. Intensified competition fosters the growth of efficient firms and the demise of inefficient ones. Growth of firms, either by internal growth, acquisition of smaller firms, or merger, results in increases in *firm size*. And large firms generally have much greater capacity to fund research and development and to compete by marketing innovative products.

Supply-Side Economics Effects

Figure 2.2 illustrates two streams of benefits of regional economic integration agreements. The first stream is derived from the lowering of per-unit costs as demand increases—assuming normal price elasticities—due to the initial lowering of price

FIGURE 2.2
Regional Economic Integration Benefits

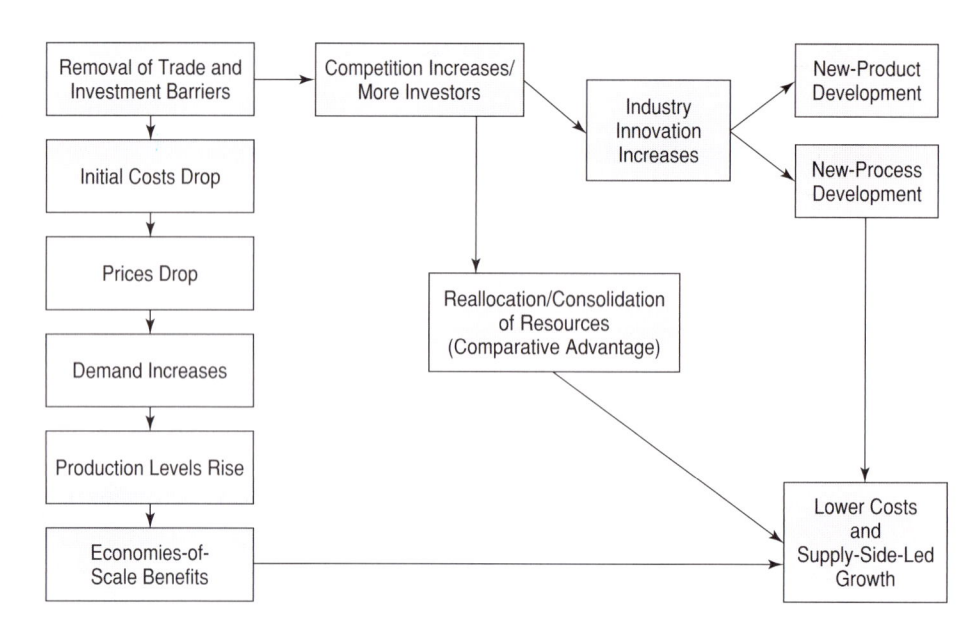

```
Removal of Trade and    →    Competition Increases/         →    Industry        →    New-Product
Investment Barriers          More Investors                      Innovation           Development
       ↓                            ↓                             Increases      →    New-Process
Initial Costs Drop                  ↓                                                 Development
       ↓                     Reallocation/Consolidation
Prices Drop                  of Resources
       ↓                     (Comparative Advantage)
Demand Increases                    ↓
       ↓                     Lower Costs and
Production Levels Rise    →  Supply-Side-Led Growth
       ↓
Economies-of-Scale Benefits
```

based on the removal of trade and investment restrictions. The second stream of benefits is based on the increase of competition due to the emergence of a new mass market. The risk of investing is lowered and the purchasing power of the cooperative increases, thereby stimulating more investment. Increased competition will lead to new technological breakthroughs in systems and processes, which in turn lower cost. Furthermore, because of the dropoff of trade restrictions, companies can now consolidate operations in countries that have the comparative advantage within the integration agreement.

Regional economic agreements thus are supply-side-led initiatives. The producers are given the initial cost break, which is passed on to primary consumers and eventually trickles down to the entire economy.

Major Regional Economic Agreement Initiatives

The two most prominent regional trade blocs formed to promote regional economic integration are the North American Free Trade Agreement and the European Union. After we discuss these two agreements, we consider other significant trade blocs throughout the world.

The North American Free Trade Agreement

The **North American Free Trade Agreement (NAFTA)** is a *free trade agreement*. It was ratified by the Congress of the United States in November 1993, and the agreement went into effect on January 1, 1994. NAFTA links the United States, Canada, and Mexico in a free trade area of 450 million consumers and over $15.4 trillion of annual output. NAFTA unites the United States with its largest (Canada) and third-largest (Mexico) trading partners. (See Figure 2.3.)

Building on the earlier United States–Canada Free Trade Agreement, NAFTA is expected to contribute to productive efficiency, enhance the ability of North American producers to compete globally, and raise the standard of living of all three countries. By improving the investment climate in North America, and by providing innovative

FIGURE 2.3
Map of NAFTA

companies with a larger market, NAFTA is expected to also increase economic growth. Mexico should benefit from more open and secure access to its largest market, the United States, increased confidence on the part of foreign firms to invest in Mexico, a more stable economic environment, and the return from abroad of Mexican-owned capital into the Mexican economy. The clearest proof of NAFTA's success is that total trade among the three members more than tripled from 1993 (the year before NAFTA's implementation) to 2001, from $297 billion to $930 billion.[6]

Notwithstanding the long-term benefits of NAFTA to all three member countries, there has been grumbling from those industries that are affected by NAFTA's free trade initiatives. Loud complaints can be heard of job exports to Mexico by American companies to take advantage of Mexico's cheap labor. Similarly complaints have been voiced by industries in Mexico that have suffered lost markets to industries located north of the border. Practical Insight 2.1 illustrates one such complaint lodged by Mexican farmers.

In addition to dismantling trade barriers in industrial goods, NAFTA includes agreements on services, investment, intellectual property rights, agriculture, and strengthening of trade rules. There are also side agreements on labor adjustment provisions, protection of the environment, and import surges. The side agreement on labor adjustment was in response to American workers' concerns that jobs in the United States would be exported to Mexico because of the latter's lower labor wages and weak child labor laws and other conditions that afford Mexican labor an economic advantage over its American counterpart. The side agreement is an attempt to manage the terms of the potential change in labor markets brought about by the NAFTA accord. The agreement involves such issues as restrictions on child labor, health and safety standards, and minimum wages. In addition to signing the labor side agreement, the Mexican government has pledged to link increases in the Mexican minimum wage to productivity increases.

The side agreement on environmental cooperation explicitly ensures the rights of the United States to safeguard the environment. NAFTA maintains all existing U.S. health, safety, and environmental standards. It allows states and cities to enact even

PRACTICAL INSIGHT 2.1

IS THIS NAFTA'S FAULT?

On January 1, 2003, as the North American Free-Trade Agreement (NAFTA) enters its tenth year, a new phase of tariff reductions on farm produce will take place. The United States will eliminate tariffs completely on several Mexican items, including limes and winter vegetables. Mexico will eliminate them on a range of produce, including wheat, barley, rice, apples, potatoes and pork. This moves the two countries a step closer to the point, in 2008, when the last few tariffs on agricultural produce are due to be scrapped.

The Americans may be cheering, but Mexicans are not. These tariff reductions have occasioned the gloomiest predictions about the decline and fall of the entire agriculture sector, the end of the Mexican countryside, even the demise of the tortilla, the staff of Mexican life. In 2001, Mexico ratcheted up a deficit of more than $2 billion in farm trade with America. Once tariffs go, the country will surely be flooded by cheap American imports. Opposition politicians have been calling for the tariff reductions to be postponed, and even for NAFTA to be renegotiated.

Slim chance of that. But any Mexican government has to listen seriously to farmers, who make up a huge political constituency. About 8m people—22% of Mexico's active labor force—work in the countryside, although they generate only 4.4% of GDP. Yet rather than taking any difficult, strategic decisions, the government of President Vicente Fox has spent the past few months producing a tranche of subsidies, price supports and anti-dumping measures (such as a tariff of 46.5% on Yanqui Golden Delicious apples) to appease the farming lobby.

On November 18th, the government announced a $10-billion programme to "armour-plate" farmers against the supposed effects of the January tariff reductions, including higher price supports for certain grains.

Unfortunately, these measures have appeased nobody in Mexico, while escalating what is, in effect, a trade war with the United States. Farmers' groups in Mexico are unimpressed with the armour-plating, arguing that the $10 billion is in fact a re-formulation of existing funds. On the other hand, the only items that now seem to be freely traded between Mexico and the United States are recriminations over each country's subsidies. This week the under-secretary at the Department of Agriculture in Washington, J. B. Penn, argued that Mexico's subsidies "question the efficacy of agreements like NAFTA."

Sheer hypocrisy, the Mexicans reply. They are merely responding to President George Bush's farm bill, which will lavish about $180 billion on American farmers over the next ten years. Farmers north of the Rio Bravo are much more heavily subsidised than Mexicans; but they argue, in turn, that their subsidies are piffling compared with those enjoyed by farmers in Europe and Japan.

A subsidy war with America is one the Mexican government can never win in terms of hard cash. Neither will it help Mexico's farmers in anything but the shortest term, since subsidies merely entrench the manifest inefficiencies in the system. One government official in the rural state of Sinaloa, in the north-west, estimates that about 15% of subsidies, siphoned off by corrupt bureaucrats, never reach the farmers and producers in any case. More thoughtful Mexican farmers,

---

tougher standards, while providing mechanisms to encourage all parties to harmonize their standards upward.

The side agreement on import surges creates an early warning mechanism to identify those sectors where explosive trade growth may do significant harm to domestic industry. It also establishes that, in the future, a working group can provide for revisions in the treaty text based on the experience with the existing safeguard mechanisms. During the transition period, safeguard relief is available in the form of a temporary snapback to pre-NAFTA duties if an import surge threatens serious injury to a domestic industry. These three side agreements were obviously negotiated to alleviate the fears of U.S. labor and industry groups that felt threatened by the immediate adverse impact on their members. NAFTA is supposed to be the first step in the creation of the so-called Free Trade Area of the Americas (FTAA), a unified megamarket stretching from Alaska to Argentina in South America. This concept is supported by many Latin American countries, which are moving away from their protectionist economic policies toward privatization of state-owned enterprises and free enterprise. Still, because of political and economic concerns among countries in the region, NAFTA has been slower to expand than anticipated.

such as Eduardo Palau in Sinaloa, would rather see steadily liberalising trade than subsidies.

The 2003 tariff eliminations will, in fact, make almost no material difference. These tariffs have been gradually reduced since 1994; most of them will come down from only 1.5% or 2% to zero on January 1st. The real problem is not NAFTA and American subsidies, but Mexico's failure to adapt to trade liberalisation in general since the mid-1980s, when it first acceded to the General Agreement on Tariffs and Trade (GATT). Since gaining access to all those shiny new markets in America and the European Union, Mexican agricultural production has either declined, collapsed or grown only slightly. For all types of beans, for instance, production fell on average by 0.7% a year between 1980 and 2001. Wheat production has fallen by 57% since 1980, and soyabean production by about one-sixth. NAFTA merely accelerated all this. Mexicans, and world markets, have preferred cheaper alternatives.

It is the high cost of Mexican farming that makes it so uncompetitive. Mexican governments failed to take advantage of the ten-year transition period, while the tariffs were being phased out, to invest in infrastructure improvements such as irrigation. It is the high cost of Mexican farming that makes it so uncompetitive. Mr. Palau argues that farming in the state of Sinaloa has become almost as efficient as in the United States, with yields per hectare increasing from 2.9 tons in 1981 to 8.5 tons in 2001. But local farmers are still going out of business because their costs—from diesel to electricity to credit—are about a third higher than those north of the border. Poor transport makes a crucial difference: it costs about three times as much to deliver corn by rail from Sinaloa to Mexico City as it does to ship it there from New Orleans to Veracruz.

These are what the Americans this week politely, and correctly, called Mexico's "structural" challenges. While the country's farmers are being exposed to the full force of world competition, they are saddled with artificially high costs because much of the rest of the economy consists of public or private monopolies sheltering behind legal and constitutional barriers to competition.

The worst moment will come in 2008, when tariffs are eliminated on American corn. Because corn is so central to Mexican agriculture—using about 55% of cultivated land—it was afforded special protection under NAFTA in 1994, with a tariff of 206% on imports over 2.6m tons a year and a 15-year phase-out to zero. But so feebly have Mexican farmers risen to the challenge of feeding their own protected market that, since 1994, Mexican governments have regularly imported much more than the import quotas. Furthermore, they have not collected the revenue from the tariffs, arguing that they need cheap corn to keep the poor supplied with tortillas.

There are about 3m corn-growers in Mexico, with an average of five dependants each. Mexico's government has squandered the first ten years of NAFTA's transition period. It now has five years left to make its farms competitive. Don't hold your breath.

Source: From "Is This NAFTA's Fault?" *The Economist Newspaper.* Copyright © 2003 The Economist Newspaper Ltd. All rights reserved. Reprinted with permission. Further reproduction prohibited. www.economist.com.

Association of Southeast Asian Nations

The **Association of Southeast Asian Nations (ASEAN)** was established on August 8, 1967, in Bangkok by the five original member countries, Indonesia, Malaysia, Philippines, Singapore, and Thailand.[7] Member nations include Brunei Darussalam, Cambodia, Indonesia, Lao PDR, Malaysia, Myanmar, Philippines, Singapore, Thailand, and Vietnam. (See Figure 2.4.) The ASEAN region has a population of about 565 million, a total area of 4.6 million square kilometers, a combined gross domestic product of almost $1,100 billion, and a total trade of $1,400 billion.

The objectives of ASEAN are no different from those of any other trade bloc: (1) to accelerate the economic growth, social progress, and cultural development in the region, (2) to strengthen the foundation for a prosperous and peaceful community of Southeast Asian nations, and (3) to promote regional peace and stability.

In 1997, the ASEAN leaders adopted the ASEAN Vision 2020, aimed at forging closer economic integration within the region. The vision statement also resolved to create a stable, prosperous, and highly competitive ASEAN Economic Region, in which there is a free flow of goods, services, investments, capital, and equitable economic

FIGURE 2.4
Map of ASEAN Members, 2000

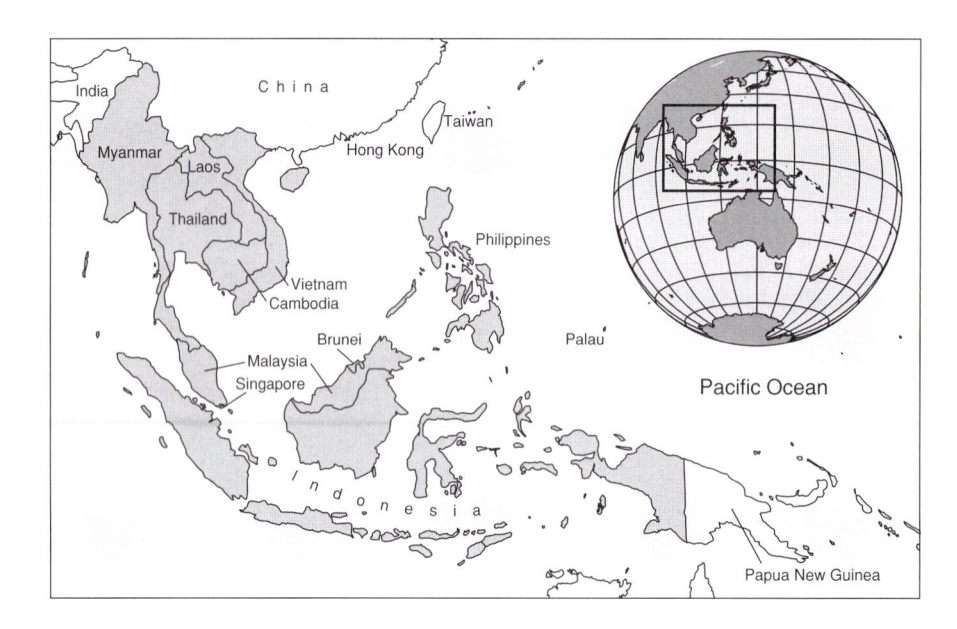

development and reduced poverty and socioeconomic disparities. The Hanoi Plan of Action, adopted in 1998, serves as the first in a series of plans of action leading up to the realization of the ASEAN vision.

ASEAN cooperation has resulted in greater regional integration. The share of intraregional trade from ASEAN's total trade rose from $81,929 million in 1999 to $352,771 million in 2006, an increase of 23 percent.

The expansion of ASEAN into a formidable trade bloc is quite possible given that cooperation with other East Asian countries has accelerated with the holding of an annual dialogue among the leaders of ASEAN, China, India, Japan, and the Republic of Korea.

MERCOSUR

By far the most promising free trade agreement, the MERCOSUR (Mercado Común del Sur, the Common Market of the South), comprising Argentina, Brazil, Paraguay, and Uruguay, was set up under the Treaty of Asuncion in 1991. Venezuela, a leading oil producer, became the fifth member in July 2006. (See Figure 2.5.) The MERCOSUR treaty committed the member nations to cut tariffs every six months, aiming to eliminate tariff barriers altogether and to create a full customs union behind a common external tariff by December 31, 1994. To meet the demands of the treaty, governments must continue to deregulate their economies. The aim is to link the five member countries in a market of nearly 266.6 million people covering an area of about 4.9 million square miles with a combined gross regional product in excess of $1.1 trillion, and $2.8 trillion in purchasing power parity, creating Latin America's largest industrial base.[8] Other aims include increasing the negotiating power of the member nations in world trade negotiations, and competing more efficiently in international markets.

In August 1994, the presidents of the four original member countries formally agreed to form a customs union on January 1, 1995. This deadline was met, and both a free trade zone and a customs union have been in operation from that date. The customs union has common external tariffs in the modest range of zero to 20 percent on 85 percent of the products, with a common tariff for all MERCOSUR countries

FIGURE 2.5
Map of MERCOSUR

instituted in 2006. Tariffs between the member countries were eliminated, although a few products still remain protected by each member nation. The MERCOSUR nations reached their agreement only after agreeing to disagree on areas where a lot of trade takes place. Capital goods, advanced electronics, and petrochemicals, which together comprise 15 percent of the trade, are treated differently from the rest.

MERCOSUR's founders envisioned not only free trade in goods but also free movement of capital, labor, and services. Thus far, free trade in goods is almost in place, and steps have been taken to promote free movement of capital. However, no agreement for free trade in services or free mobility of labor appears likely in the near future. Nevertheless, experts in the area suggest that MERCOSUR is on the right track. The reason for such optimism is that technocrats in charge of all five countries are committed to free trade. Chile, the continent's most liberal economy, Colombia, Ecuador, Bolivia, and Peru are associate members of MERCOSUR, with the expectation of eventually gaining full membership.

The European Union

The **European Union (EU)**—historically known as the Common Market—is an institutional framework for the construction of a unified Europe.[9] It was created after World War II to unite the nations of Europe through peaceful means and to create conditions for the economic recovery and growth of Europe after the devastation caused by the war. Twenty-seven countries are now members of the EU, and more than 1 billion people share the common institutions and policies that have brought an unprecedented era of peace and prosperity to western Europe. (See Figure 2.6.)

There are many similarities between the European Union and the United States. EU member countries have agreed to pool some of their sovereign powers for the sake of unity, just as the American states did to create a federal republic. In fields where such delegation of national sovereignty has occurred—for example, in trade and agriculture—the EU acts as a full-fledged country, and it negotiates directly with the United States and other countries. EU member states retain their full sovereign powers in such fields as security and defense. The search for political unity is inspired by the U.S. federative model; however, Europeans realize that Europe will have to

FIGURE 2.6
Map of the EU

Source: *The Economist*, October 23, 1999. Copyright © 1999 The Economist Newspaper Ltd. All rights reserved. Reprinted with permission. Further reproduction prohibited. www.economist.com.

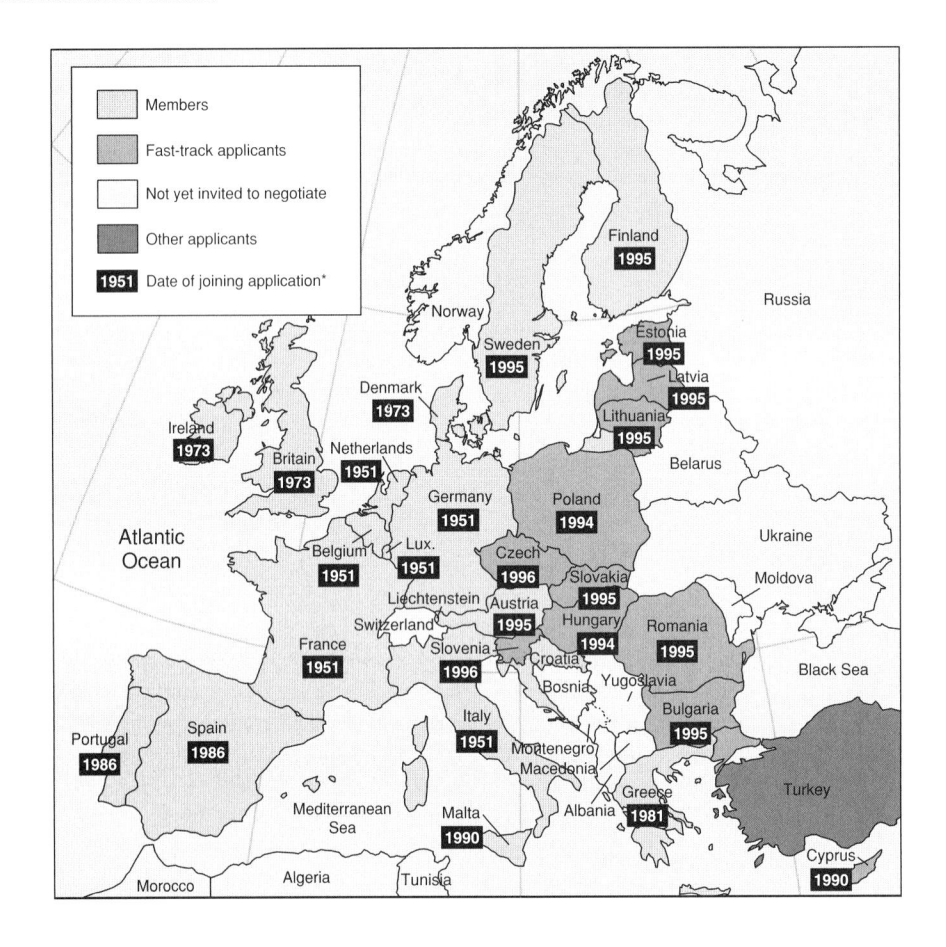

construct its own model for unification, one that takes full account of the rich historical, cultural, and linguistic diversity of the European nations.

The European Community Origins On May 9, 1950, Robert Schuman, the French foreign minister, presented the so-called Schuman Declaration, a bold plan for lifting Europe out of the rubble of World War II. He proposed the pooling of European coal and steel industries as a first step toward a united Europe. Schuman's proposal called for the placement of coal and steel production of France and Germany under a common authority within an organization open to other European countries. The long-term objective of the Schuman Declaration was to lay the foundation for the economic integration of Europe, starting with coal and steel. Belgium, the Federal Republic of Germany, Italy, Luxemburg, and the Netherlands (Holland) accepted the French proposal. The six countries signed the European Coal and Steel Community (ECSC) Treaty in Paris on April 18, 1951. The six countries created the ECSC High Authority, to which each country transferred some of its sovereign power.

The Treaty of Rome On March 25, 1957, in Rome, the six nations signed two treaties, creating the European Economic Community (EEC) and the European Atomic Energy Community (EAEC). Both treaties were ratified by the parliaments of the six member countries before the end of the year. The EEC was created to merge the separate national markets of the six into a large single market, within which there would be free movement of goods, people, capital, and services. Common economic policies were also a goal of the EEC. The EAEC, or Euratom, was created to promote the use of nuclear energy for peaceful purposes.

The European Community (EC) is in fact three separate entities governed by separate treaties: the European Coal and Steel Community, the European Atomic Energy Community, and the European Economic Community. However, the name "European Community" has been in common use to refer to the three communities, since together they form a single political whole.

EC in 1992: Moving from a Common Market to an Economic Union Squabbles over the common agricultural policy coupled with the persistence of some old barriers and the creation of new ones during the 1970s—a period of "stagflation" (high inflation together with low economic growth) for most developed countries—compelled the EC to admit in the mid-1980s that its goal of a real common market was still far from reach. The main source of the EC's poor performance was attributed to the absence of an integrated Europe-wide market, which prevented European businesses from launching and implementing competitively efficient strategies. The answer was the 1985 White Paper by the EC Commission, which put forth a road map for the completion of an integrated internal market by the end of 1992. The 1985 White Paper listed almost 300 legislative measures needed to eliminate all physical, technical, and financial barriers to trade and commerce among the member countries. Specifically it called for a wide variety of reforms, including:

- An end to intra-EC customs checks and border controls.
- An EC-wide market for services, such as banking, insurance, securities, and other financial transactions.
- The mutual recognition of professional diplomas.
- The harmonization or mutual recognition of technical standards.
- The approximation of national rates and assessment criteria for EC's indirect taxes.

The EC member states signed the Single European Act (SEA) in February 1986. It became effective on July 1, 1987, after ratification by the 12 national parliaments (including the 6 original members and 6 additional countries that had joined the union). The SEA contains amendments to the EC treaties necessary to ensure the timely achievement of the 1992 program. The SEA not only aims at the completion of the integrated internal EC market, but it also calls for significant developments in economic and monetary policy, social policy, industrial relations, research and technology, and the environment. It also formalized procedures for cooperation in the sphere of foreign policy. Finally, the SEA renewed the commitment to transform relations among the member states into a European union.

At the end of 1992, the internal market became a reality. All frontiers between member countries were removed, as far as goods, services, and capital were concerned. There are no longer any customs controls on the EC's internal borders (between member states). Citizens of non-EC countries must show their passports and entry visas only at the first point of entry into any EC country, after which they can freely move anywhere within the EC member countries. Travelers may buy as many goods as they wish in any EC country for their own or their family's use, provided that they pay the appropriate tax on the goods in the country of purchase. Community citizens may take up residence in a member state other than their own as long as they wish. Professional qualifications are mutually recognized in all member states.

The EU and the Maastricht Treaty The success of the Europe 1992 program and the changed political framework prompted the EC members to take a new step along the path of integration, creating the European Union. In Maastricht, the Netherlands, in December 1991, the heads of states of the EC member countries agreed on the Treaty on European Union. It was signed in February 1992, and after ratification by the parliaments of the EC member countries it came into force in November 1993. The Maastricht Treaty on European Union was just one more step on the road to a European constitution. Built on the structures that have been handed down, it forms an overall framework for various stages of integration.

Since Maastricht, economic integration has progressed rapidly in Europe. Trade statistics show that most of the trade of the European Union countries is with each other. With the introduction of the common currency, the euro, in 2001, the union of 27 member countries has matured into a unified market like the unified market of the United States.

Achievements to Date

1. All border controls within the EU on goods have been abolished, together with customs controls on people. Random spot checks by police (part of the fight against crime and drugs) still take place when necessary.
2. The *Schengen Agreement,* which was signed by a first group of EU countries in 1985 and later extended to others (although Ireland and the United Kingdom do not participate), governs police cooperation and a common asylum and immigration policy, so as to make it possible to completely abolish checks on persons at the EU's internal borders.
3. For the majority of products, EU countries have adopted the principle of mutual recognition of national rules. Any product legally manufactured and sold in one member state must be allowed to be placed on the market in all others.
4. An EC-wide market for services, such as banking, insurance, securities, and other financial transactions, has been established.
5. Mutual recognition or coordination of national rules concerning professional diplomas and access to or practice of certain professions (law, medicine, tourism, banking, insurance, etc.) has been adopted. Action has been taken to improve worker mobility, and particularly to ensure that educational diplomas and job qualifications (for plumbers, carpenters, etc.) obtained in one EU country are recognized in all the others.
6. The opening of national services markets has brought down the price of national telephone calls to a fraction of what they were 10 years ago. Helped by new technology, the Internet is being increasingly used for telephone calls. Competitive pressure has led to significant falls in the price of budget airfares in Europe.

Will Regional Trade Blocs Promote Global Free Trade?

Will the existing trade blocs serve as catalysts for worldwide free trade? Trade among members of regional trade agreements has shown dramatic increases from 1990 to 2006. Intra-bloc exports in NAFTA, MERCOSUR, and ASEAN have grown dramatically. Within NAFTA, trade grew from $127.5 billion in 1990 to $528.9 billion in 2006. Within MERCOSUR, exports grew from $4.1 billion in 1990 to $25.7 billion in 2006. And within ASEAN, exports grew from $29 billion in 1990 to $193 billion in 2006.[10]

Will the trade blocs be able to achieve the vision of global free trade enshrined in the GATT and WTO charters discussed earlier? On one side, those who believe that trade blocs will not lead to global free trade base their opinion on events in the EU and NAFTA. In the EU, quotas were imposed on imports of Japanese automobiles to protect the European carmakers. In NAFTA, quotas restrict imports of some types of steel and textile products. The fear is that companies protected by common external tariff walls against competing imports will become complacent and inefficient, and they will ultimately demand ever-increasing protectionist measures for their own survival against foreign competition. Jagdish Bhagwati, one of the world's top trade theorists and adviser to the director-general of GATT (the precursor to the WTO), believes that "it is all too likely that regional trade blocs will advance the frontiers of liberal trade more slowly than the GATT, because governments will find it harder to resist the argument, put by protectionist lobbies, that 'our market is already large enough.' "[11]

On the other side are those who believe that trade blocs will expand their membership and add more countries. For instance, NAFTA has already made overtures to Chile, and there is speculation that NAFTA may eventually evolve into a large trade bloc—FTAA—that will include 34 countries in the Western Hemisphere. Similarly, the European Union, with 27 current members, is expected to expand to include all countries of western and eastern Europe during the first decade of this century.

Finding that they are being discriminated against by the trade bloc countries, those countries that are left out of the trade blocs may seek to form their own trade blocs or, alternatively, seek special free trade agreements with existing trade blocs. Bhagwati offers such advice to countries like India. He believes that, in response to NAFTA and the EU, an Asian bloc may be formed, possibly centered on Japan, and countries like India that are marginalized on the outside should seek special free trade agreements with it. He believes that the Asian bloc, if it does materialize, would be inclined to seriously consider India's request because of its huge internal market and its potential as a sourcing country for foreign firms. Thus, hypothetically, the number of trade blocs will multiply because each new trade bloc will serve as a stimulant for countries left on the periphery to form their own trade blocs.

Proponents of the theory that trade blocs will eventually lead to global free trade also suggest that free trade negotiations between and among trade blocs may lead to their becoming merged with one another. For instance, NAFTA and the EU may initially negotiate free trade in automobiles, which may be extended to other industries, and which in turn may eventually lead to a merger of the two blocs to form one mega–trade bloc that comprises all of the Americas and Europe. However distant the realization of this scenario may be, the thrust of the argument that free trade blocs would lead to global free trade seems valid.

Regardless of their ultimate effect on global free trade, the increasing importance of regional trade blocs will be a major consideration for international managers in the years to come, shaping the environment in which the international company does business. A significant phenomenon that was partly an outcome of the drive toward free trade is what is commonly known as *globalization,* a process that has resulted in increasing interconnectedness and interdependence among the nations of the world. Globalization has changed the landscape on which competitive battles are fought among companies in global industries. Globalization has opened up new markets that were once closed to foreign companies. Globalization has also brought into the forefront new opportunities and new challenges for international companies. The economic, political, legal, and cultural landscape has been altered by the forces that are driving the globalization engine faster and faster. We look at this phenomenon in the following pages.

Globalization

A dominant context that has had the greatest influence on the strategies and operations of international companies is the phenomenon of globalization. Much has been written about how the forces of globalization—the unremitting expansion of market forces, the breakneck speed with which capital moves around the globe, and the constant search for greater economic efficiencies—influence everything from indigenous cultures and environmental regulations to labor standards and patterns of productivity. The general catalysts of globalization were reviewed in Chapter 1. Now, we add to those general trends.

Globalization is a phenomenon that has remade the economy of virtually every nation, reshaped almost every industry, and touched billions of lives, often in surprising and ambiguous ways. Definitions of globalization abound. For example,

> "Globalization is a process fueled by, and resulting in, increasing cross-border flows of goods, services, money, people, information and culture."[12]

> "The increasing interdependence of national economies in trade, finance, and macroeconomic policy."[13]

We define **globalization** as the growing economic interdependence of countries worldwide and the increasing integration of economic life across political boundaries, through the increasing volume and variety of cross-border transactions in goods, services, capital flows, and rapid and widespread diffusion of technology. Globalization is meant to signify integration and unity—yet it has proved, in its way, to be no less polarizing than the cold war divisions it has supplanted. The lines between globalization's supporters and its critics run not only between countries but also through them, as people struggle to come to terms with the defining economic force shaping the planet today. The debate over globalization's true nature has divided people in third-world countries since the phenomenon arose. It is now an issue in the United States as well, and many Americans—those who neither make the deals inside World Trade Organization meetings nor man the barricades outside—are perplexed.

The two sides in the discussion describe what seem to be two completely different forces. The issues debated by the proponents and opponents of globalization revolve around the role of international companies in the world economies. Questions such as the following are subjects of intense debate:

> Is the world embedded in a global network of companies like Citicorp, CNN, Unilever, Microsoft, and IBM that will lead to the betterment of the quality of life of all mankind? Or is the welfare of mankind subservient to the domination and whims of greedy and corrupt global companies?

In all probability, this debate will not end in the foreseeable future. Managers in global companies would be challenged to implement corporate strategies that would induce the opponents to lower their criticism of the globalization phenomenon. To manage effectively in a globalized world, students of international management should understand the globalization phenomenon. So at the onset, let us review the forces that have served as the principal drivers of globalization.

Specific Drivers of Globalization

Tremendous Growth in International Trade and Commerce If shop windows everywhere seem to be filled with imports, there is a reason. International trade has been growing at a skyrocketing pace. In 2006 the global economy (GDP) grew at the rate of 3.5 percent, whereas the volume of world merchandise trade grew by 8 percent. World merchandise trade has been growing at twice the rate of world GDP since 2000.[14]

Foreign products play a more important role in almost every country in the world. Just look at what you and I purchase and consume: To go to work, we drive cars made by Honda, Toyota, and Volkswagen in countries such as Brazil and Mexico in addition to the United States and Japan. To listen to music, we use a Korean-made CD player by Sanyo or Samsung or one made by Sony from Japan. We wear Levi jeans made in Bangladesh. We drink Colombian-made coffee and Heineken beer from Holland. Parts of our Dell, Sony, and Compaq computers are sourced from dozens of countries. Similar consumption patterns exist in almost every country in the world. What is behind this dramatic growth in world trade? Some reasons follow.

Innovations in Information Technology and Transportation The world has shrunk because of new developments in information technology, geopolitical changes, rapid growth in the speed at which people can travel around the world, and the push toward free and open trade. The countries in this world are connected by the rapid flows of knowledge and information carried by people, satellites, computers, and television.

A telephone call from the United States to India cost $5 per minute in 1960, and it took several hours to book the call through an international operator.[15] The transmission was very poor, and calls were disconnected without notice. Today it costs as little as 35 cents a minute for the same call, and all it takes to make the call is to dial the numbers on a land-line or cellular telephone. In most countries cellular telephones have become as ubiquitous as toasters. One can now successfully place international telephone calls from anywhere to anywhere in the world.

Years ago, mail sent from India took two weeks to reach the United States. Now we can communicate via e-mail and chat on the Internet via Yahoo.com, Rediff.com, and AOL.com. Travel from India to the United States used to take four days by plane. Now, we can take off from Philadelphia and reach New Delhi 18 hours later.

Two decades ago there was no television in most of the developing countries in Asia, Africa, and Latin America. Now CNN, BBC, and Star TV blanket the television screens worldwide from transmissions originating in the United States, England, and Hong Kong, respectively. Satellite dishes on rooftops almost everywhere in the world allow villagers in the remotest parts of a country to see TV broadcasts emanating from all over the world.

Innovations in technology and transportation have promoted the interconnectedness of nations through the rapid dispersal and transfer of knowledge of products, processes, and lifestyles worldwide. Companies can now market their products worldwide via television commercials and banners on commercial Web sites. People can travel from one nation to another for in-person meetings and return home within days. Global teams comprising members from two or more countries can develop new products and processes via videoconferencing without leaving home.

Porous Borders between Countries Before the 1970s, most countries placed strict limitations on the immigration of foreigners. Western European countries, the United States, and Australia have now opened the door to immigrants from other parts of the world. The Indian and Chinese diaspora has footprints worldwide, creating links between the adopted and mother countries of these two ethnic groups. Chinese and Indian expatriates have been transferring billions of U.S. dollars to their home countries. A similar phenomenon is being played out in the case of Turkish immigrants to

Europe and Koreans and Filipinos to the United States and East Asia. Furthermore, citizens of countries that belong to the European Union can travel freely, without passports or visas, throughout western Europe. They can work in any country in the EU without work permits.

Globalization and interconnectedness of countries have been enhanced by the lowering of barriers to immigration. We have witnessed an increase in the transfer of wealth, often accompanied by knowledge and technology from country to country, thereby contributing to the economic links between the adopted and mother countries. Multinational companies have been the beneficiaries of this trend as well. People with skills and expertise, from any country, can now be employed where they are most needed, anywhere in the world.

The Globalization of Financial Markets What happens in the United States has an impact on Europe and the rest of the world. Interest rates, stock markets, currency values are all interconnected. Globally $3.2 trillion in currencies are traded every day.[16] The currency and stock markets never sleep. Portfolio managers "hand off" portfolios from one market to another.

Today, the ability of a country to compete in world markets is often dictated by events in distant parts of the world. When coffee prices drop in Brazil because of a bumper crop in that country, prices of coffee drop in other parts of the world because coffee prices are set by the world commodity market. This would not have happened had there not been free trade among countries.

A recent implication of the global financial markets is the Asian crisis of the late 1990s. Chinese devaluation and a prolonged Japanese recession put downward pressures on the yuan and yen, respectively, as compared to currencies from Southeast Asia. The financial meltdown was helped as well as perpetuated because the Thai baht was linked with the U.S. dollar. As the U.S. dollar became stronger, the baht's value rose as well. Thai products and foreign investment opportunities became noncompetitive compared to those of countries like China.

The Creation of a Global Labor Force People do not have to go where the jobs are. Jobs come to where the people are. The software industry in India is manned by Indian engineers and scientists who serve the needs of companies in Europe and America. Countries like China that can produce the cheapest products are dictating the world prices of consumer products. Yet, during 2007 and 2008, there has been a variance regarding product quality, especially regarding safety of consumer goods. India is dictating the global prices of software development. We are fast approaching a global wage rate for skilled and unskilled workers. The global workforce determines the global prices of goods and services. This phenomenon is illustrated in Practical Insight 2.2.

Rapidly Falling Freight Costs One force that has gone unnoticed in promoting international trade is rapidly falling freight costs, that is, the costs of getting goods to market. High freight costs as a percentage of the sales price, or delays in shipments because of slow shipment of goods, can make trade impractical or impossible. Freight costs can have a huge impact both on the overall volume of trade and on individual countries' trade patterns. Trade costs today are less formidable than they used to be. This reflects three notable economic trends:

1. The world economy has become far less transport-intensive than it once was. At the turn of the twentieth century, international commerce was dominated by raw materials, such as wheat, wood, and iron, or processed commodities, such as meat

PRACTICAL INSIGHT 2.2

BACK-ROOM OPERATIONS IN INDIA

Thanks to the Internet and satellites, India has been able to connect its millions of educated, English-speaking, low-wage, tech-savvy young people to the world's largest corporations. They live in India, but they design and run the software and systems that now support the world's biggest companies, earning India an unprecedented $60 billion in foreign reserves—which doubled in just the last three years. But this has made the world more dependent on India, and India on the world, than ever before.

If you lose your luggage on British Airways, the techies who track it down are here in India. If your Dell computer has a problem, the techie who walks you through it is in Bangalore, India's Silicon Valley. Ernst & Young may be doing your company's tax returns here with Indian accountants. Indian software giants in Bangalore, like Wipro, Infosys and MindTree, now manage back-room operations—accounting, inventory management, billing, accounts receivable, payrolls, credit card approvals—for global firms like Nortel Networks, Reebok, Sony, American Express, HSBC and GE Capital.

You go to the Bangalore campuses of these Indian companies and they point out: "That's G.E.'s back room over here. That's American Express's back office over there." G.E.'s biggest research center outside the U.S. is in Bangalore, with 1,700 Indian engineers and scientists. The brain chip for every Nokia cellphone is designed in Bangalore. Renting a car from Avis online? It's managed here.

Source: Reprinted from Thomas Friedman, "India, Pakistan and GE," August 11, 2002, issue of *BusinessWeek* by special permission. Copyright © 2002 by The McGraw-Hill Companies, Inc.

---

and steel. These products are heavy and bulky. The cost of transporting them is relatively high compared to the value of the goods themselves, so transport costs had much to do with the volume of international trade, and countries tended to trade with their geographic neighbors. Today, finished manufactured goods, not raw commodities, dominate the flow of trade. And these are high-value goods such as computers, disk drives, and laser printers. The relative cost of transportation as a percentage of the value of goods shipped even for heavy goods like cars and refrigerators has fallen precipitously because lightweight composites have replaced steel and light microprocessors do the job of huge control panels. And computer software can be "exported" without ever loading it on a cargo plane simply by transmitting it over telephone lines or satellites from one country to another.

2. The transportation industry has changed in remarkable ways, making it far cheaper and easier to ship goods around the world. "Containerization" and "intermodal transportation" have led to steep drops in the cost of cargo handling—and in the process, have lowered one of the biggest obstacles to trade.

3. The deregulation of the airlines and telecommunications has brought about a huge drop in the cost of air transport and data transfer. The cost of a three-minute telephone call has fallen from $300 (in 1996 dollars) in 1930 to $1 today.

The protests against globalization at the World Trade Organization's meetings in the United States, Europe, and the Middle East have brought to the forefront arguments both for and against the trend toward the increasing interdependence of nations. We now examine these differing views regarding globalization.

The Two Sides of Globalization

The growth of globalization has triggered a heated debate between constituencies supporting this phenomenon and those dramatically opposing it. We now present the arguments offered by scholars and practitioners who are in favor of globalization, followed by those of its opponents.

Arguments That Favor Globalization

The architects of globalization argue that international economic integration not only is good for the poor but is essential. To embrace self-sufficiency or to deride growth, as some protesters do, is to glamorize poverty. The London-based Center for Economic Policy Research (CEPR) recently released a study on the positive aspects of globalization. The authors of the study noted that economic growth benefits the poor and trade is good for growth. Closer economic ties between countries, lower tariff rates, and greater investment flows have had a large impact in reducing the poverty levels of low-income countries. Poverty levels can be further reduced as well if a low-income country accepts globalization policies and increases foreign investment opportunities. No nation has ever developed over the long term without trade. East Asia is the most recent example. Since the mid-1970s, Japan, South Korea, Taiwan, China, and their neighbors have lifted 300 million people out of poverty, chiefly through trade.

Proponents of globalization claim that it has improved the lot of hundreds of millions of poor people around the world. Poverty can be reduced even when inequality increases. And in some cases inequality can even decrease. The economic gap between South Korea and industrialized countries, for example, has diminished in part because of global markets. No poor country, meanwhile, has ever become rich by isolating itself from global markets; indeed, North Korea and Myanmar have impoverished themselves by doing so. Economic globalization, in short, may be a necessary, though not sufficient, condition for combating poverty. Markets have unequal effects, and the inequality they produce can have powerful political consequences. But the cliché that markets always make the rich richer and the poor poorer is simply not true.

As Hernando de Soto wrote in his book, *The Mystery of Capital,* "Globalization is occurring because developing and former communist nations are opening up their once protected economies, stabilizing their currencies and drafting regulatory frameworks to enhance international trade and private investment."[17] De Soto says that globalization will allow low-income countries to sell more exports, increase the wages of workers, entice new foreign capital, and become successful participants in the global marketplace. A salary of $5 a day is regarded as "shockingly poor" to antiglobalization protesters living in wealthy countries. Yet this salary level of a worker in a low-income country is five times higher than what a worker would have earned by remaining in an agricultural society. In other words, the switch to globalization policies has gradually improved workers' salaries in low-income countries. It is therefore up to wealthy countries to help integrate low-income countries in the free market economy by reducing tariffs and subsidies on agricultural products and textiles.

Globalization critics claim that corporations find the cheapest places to do business, which forces wealthy countries to purge their social safety nets and environmental standards. If this were true, say the proponents of globalization, then more investment would have flowed to the poorest countries in Africa, rather than predominantly to a small number of middle-income countries in Asia and Latin America. All things being equal, corporations shift production to those countries where labor is most productive, not cheapest. Cheap labor is not always the most productive. This critique is further discounted when figures show that 65 percent of employment of U.S. multinational corporations (MNCs) was in relatively high-wage countries, like those in western Europe, and the balance in relatively low-wage countries.[18] The notion that U.S. MNCs establish foreign operations in low-wage countries to produce for the U.S. market is also unfounded, as only 17 percent of sales of foreign subsidiaries were to U.S. customers.[19] Moreover, MNCs establish foreign operations not just to take advantage of cheap labor but also for strategic reasons, such as exploiting a potentially large market, tapping into technology and knowledge, taking advantage of competitive forces, following major customers abroad, using locational advantage (e.g., advantage derived from being in the EU or in Hong Kong for entry into the Chinese market).

Lately, technology has been the main driver of globalization. The advances achieved in computing and telecommunications in the West offer enormous, indeed unprecedented, scope for raising living standards in the third world. New technologies promise not just big improvements in local efficiency but also the further and potentially bigger gains that flow from an infinitely denser network of connections, electronic and otherwise, with the developed world.

What has growth through integration meant for all the developing countries that have achieved it so far? Proponents of globalization claim that in terms of improving living standards of the common citizen, globalization is the difference between South Korea and North Korea, between Malaysia and Myanmar, between Europe and Africa.

If there is a showcase for globalization in Latin America, it lies on the outskirts of Puebla, Mexico, at Volkswagen Mexico. Every new VW Beetle in the world is made here, 440 a day, in a sparkling clean factory with the most sophisticated technology. The Volkswagen factory is the biggest single industrial plant in Mexico, employing 11,000 people in assembly-line jobs, 4,000 more in the rest of the factory—with 11,000 more jobs in the industrial park of VW suppliers across the street making parts, seats, dashboards, and other components. The average monthly wage in the plant is $760, among the highest in the country's industrial sector. The factory is the equal of any in Germany, the product of a billion-dollar investment in 1995, when VW chose Puebla as the exclusive site for the new Beetle. It is estimated that more than 50,000 people work in other companies around Mexico that supply VW.[20]

Arguments against Globalization

Having discussed the arguments in favor of globalization, let us not ignore contrary points of view. In the 1980s, the so-called Washington Consensus—highly influenced by the Reagan and Thatcher administrations in the United States and United Kingdom, respectively—held that government was in the way. The administrations pushed for privatization, deregulation, fiscal austerity, and financial liberalization in countries' economies.

Opponents of globalization argue that globalization and deregulation of the economy do not work if the institutions required to make them work are absent. A case in point is Russia, where open markets and globalization have not worked as well as anticipated due to the absence of institutions such as a reliable banking system, an effective legal system, and a culture that understands the market economy and how it should function.

To revisit the VW Mexico "showcase" example above, the value Mexico adds to the Beetles it exports is mainly labor. Technology transfer is limited in part because most foreign trade today is intracompany trade, which is particularly impenetrable to outsiders. Although Volkswagen buys 60 percent of its parts in Mexico, the "local" suppliers are virtually all foreign-owned and import most of the materials they use. Although the country has gone from assembling clothing to assembling high-tech goods, nearly 40 years later 97 percent of the components used in Mexican "maquiladoras" are still imported, and the value that Mexico adds to its exports has actually declined sharply since the mid-1970s.[21] Without technology transfer, work in maquiladoras is marked for extinction. As transport costs become less important, Mexico is increasingly competing with China and Bangladesh—where labor goes for as little as 9 cents an hour. This is one reason that real wages for the lowest-paid workers in Mexico dropped by 50 percent from 1985 to 2000. Businesses, in fact, are already leaving to go to China.

Joseph Stiglitz suggests that "the gap between the poor and the rich has been growing, and even the number in absolute poverty—living on less than one dollar a day—has increased." He also suggests that "the developed world needs to do its part to reform the international institutions that govern globalization."[22]

Arguments that favor or oppose globalization can affect the operations of multinational companies. There have been instances of firebombing of the offices of multinational companies in various parts of the world. Hostility toward globalization could inhibit the flow of capital, technology, and people to parts of the world that are inhospitable and dangerous to the safety of human life and property. The same forces that have contributed to globalization of companies have done the same for Osama bin Laden. His terror network could not exist without the infrastructure that is now available to him to carry out his terrorist activities. The significance of hitting the World Trade Center's twin towers in Manhattan cannot be ignored. It was a direct hit at the global financial system of the world led by the United States and the Western world.

Many of the things that have left sophisticated Western societies vulnerable to terrorist attacks are the very efficiencies that have come as a consequence of persons', companies', and countries' relentless search for efficiency and maximum productivity. Curbside check-in, e-tickets, streamlined procedures for border crossings, freer immigration policies in industrialized societies, and just-in-time delivery of international packages and shipping were all introduced to help improve productivity and advance competitiveness.

Several of these efficiencies have been either temporarily discontinued or curtailed in the name of improving security. The fundamental question is whether all, or just some, of these globalization-era improvements will be among the early casualties of the war on terrorism, sacrificed in order to reduce societal vulnerabilities and to restore domestic tranquility. This remains to be seen.

Country-Specific Economic Environments and Country Competitiveness

The macroeconomic environment has been the focus of the chapter thus far. The macroeconomic environment is the global canopy under which international business is conducted. As they create the global strategies for their companies, managers must also examine the country-specific economic environments to look for particular opportunities or challenges that each country environment has to offer.

India and China have very large populations. More than a third of the populations in all five countries are 65 years and older, and more than 400 million people in India and China are in this age group. Which industries would stand to gain from marketing their products in these two countries? Probably those industries that serve the older citizens with services and products such as nursing homes, geriatric pharmaceuticals, and wheelchairs.

How products are marketed depends on the literacy rate. Printed advertisements and product-user manuals would not be effective in countries like India, with a large incidence (48 percent) of illiteracy. Companies in India have resorted to use of pictures and symbols to convey marketing messages. For example, to promote the benefits of a small family, billboards in India show a picture of a couple with two healthy children, and another picture next to it depicting a couple with five skinny children. The message on this billboard is "two are better than five."

Although the average gross domestic product per capita is low in India and China, various sources have estimated that almost 100 million to 200 million Indians have purchasing power equal to that of the middle class in the United States, which has a total population of approximately 280 million. This means that the market in India for products that the typical middle-class population can afford to buy is at least one-third the total population of the United States and more than three times larger than the total population of Canada. Companies should not therefore merely look at the very low per capita income in India and conclude that the Indian market is negligible at best. Rather, companies would be prudent to look more deeply at the total number of people in the country who have the purchasing power to buy the products sold by the company.

The United States, Japan, and Germany have a much larger density of telephone and cellular phone use than India and China. People in the United States and Europe take for granted the ease of use of telephones and cell phones for domestic and long-distance calls. Communications within a company and with customers and suppliers is not that easy in India and China, although in large metropolitan areas in these countries the availability and use of telephones and cell phones are extensive. It is next to impossible to conduct telephone surveys for market research in India and China. In contrast, citizens in the United States are constantly bombarded by telemarketers.

The density per square mile of radio and television stations is far lower in India and China than in the United States, Japan, or Germany. Similarly, there is a very low density per capita of ownership of radios and televisions in India and China. Only 6 and 31 percent of the Indian and Chinese populations own a television set, whereas 78 percent of Americans have at least one set. The use of radio and television for advertisements is pervasive in developed countries like the United States, Japan, Germany, and most wealthy countries in Europe. Millions of U.S. dollars are spent on 30-second advertisements on the major television networks. Companies spend such huge sums because of the high density per capita of television set ownership. This is not the case in India and China. Although both countries now can get several domestic television stations and all major international networks, the penetration of the marketing message is quite shallow because of the low television set ownership in these countries.

International companies are obliged to use other methods, in addition to radio and television, to advertise their products in India and China. Advertising on billboards, buses, trains, and taxis is the preferred method of communicating with customers. Multinational companies must therefore do the following before deciding on the foreign entry mode:

1. Determine the key success factors for the business, that is, the conditions that must be present in the foreign market in order to succeed in achieving the objectives of the market entry.
2. Study whether these conditions exist in the target market.
3. Determine changes in implementation strategies that would be required in order to succeed in the target market.

In general, the international firm must understand the economic environments, infrastructure development relative to other nations, and effects of membership in a regional economic integration agreement for various countries. This understanding will subsequently lead to a deeper understanding of relative country competitiveness. As has been implied throughout this chapter, countries compete in global trade markets as well as for foreign direct investment inflows. Thus international firms must be aware of each country's relative competitiveness before deciding where to expand.

In the next few chapters, we turn to an examination of additional macro-level dimensions of the environment seen in Figure 1.3 in Chapter 1: the political, legal, and cultural dimensions of international business. Our discussion generally assumes the standpoint of individual country differences. However, to the extent that countries are united into trade blocs, the blocs themselves may also be a useful focus for addressing these environmental dimensions.

Summary

A major environmental context within which international companies conduct their global business is the WTO and its push toward global free trade, taking into account the progress toward integration of member countries of regional trade blocs such as NAFTA and the European Union. Not all trade blocs are alike; some are more developed in integrating the economies of the member countries than others. The European Union and its 27 member countries represent the most developed of the trade blocs.

Economic trade blocs can cause trade creation when new trade among member countries does not displace third-country imports. Trade creation is a positive effect of free trade. However, lowering intraregional barriers leaves relatively high barriers on nonmembers. If this leads to a substitution of efficient third-country production by inefficient production in a common market country, it may result in trade diversion. Trade blocs should create economic conditions that would not require policies leading to trade diversion.

Free trade arrangements can also have significant dynamic effects on economic growth. Market extension is one benefit of a common market. Producers have free access to the national markets of all member countries, unhindered by import restrictions. Similarly, consumers have access to products produced in all countries of the union.

GATT and its successor, the WTO, have been the driving forces to promote free trade. International companies stand to gain from the push in favor of free trade because free trade opens new markets around the world. Through its dispute settlement mechanism, the WTO provides global companies and member nations with a mechanism for resolving trade disputes.

The phenomenon called globalization is the driving force that is pushing the depth and breadth of international business and international companies in the world economy. Globalization is the cause of, as well as the result of, the growing interdependence of nation-states throughout the world. Several forces are the drivers of globalization. These drivers will, in all probability, intensify the speed of globalization in the years ahead. Globalization has ardent supporters as well as vehement opponents. Only time will tell which viewpoint prevails.

Key Terms and Concepts

Association of Southeast Asian Nations (ASEAN), *37*
common market, *30*
customs union, *30*
economic integration, *32*
economic union, *30*
European Union (EU), *39*
free trade area (FTA), *30*
General Agreement on Tariffs and Trade (GATT), *28*
globalization, *44*
North American Free Trade Agreement (NAFTA), *34*
political union, *31*
World Trade Organization (WTO), *29*
WTO dispute settlement procedure, *29*

Discussion Questions

1. Will NAFTA evolve into an economic union like the European Union in the future?
2. Are you in favor of free trade, even if it causes unemployment in some domestic industries?
3. Does the WTO impinge on the sovereignty of nation-states?
4. Is globalization inevitable in the world today? Can the drivers of globalization be controlled by nation-states?

Minicase

A Global European Consumer?

In 1983 Leif Johansson was a manager at Electrolux, a Swedish appliance maker. Electrolux was ready for expansion beyond the small Swedish market. Johansson was swayed by studies that showed Europe was becoming more homogeneous. In particular the study showed that unexpected parts of Europe had increased pasta consumption. It was assumed that all types of European markets would begin to show the same type of homogeneity. Johansson envisioned being able to sell the same appliance models across all of Europe, as is done in America. He persuaded his superiors to purchase Zanussi, an Italian appliance manufacturer, to increase Electrolux's European market share.

A decade later, Johansson, now Electrolux's president, has found that lifestyles in Europe are not quite as homogeneous in the appliance market as they are in the pasta market. The different parts of Europe show drastic differences in preferences when it comes to refrigerators. These preferences are mostly derived from cultural differences. In northern Europe, customers prefer larger refrigerators because they shop weekly in supermarkets. They also prefer to have the freezer on the bottom. In southern Europe, customers prefer smaller refrigerators because they shop almost daily at outdoor markets. They prefer the freezer on top. In Britain customers prefer mostly freezer, about 60 percent, as they eat lots of frozen foods. Because of such strong preferences, Johansson found that he was unable to pursue his corporate vision of selling the same models of appliances to all of Europe.

To compete in Europe, Electrolux has found that it must have 120 basic designs with 1,500 variants. The company has come to realize that its strategic vision for Electrolux in Europe was wrong. The idea of only a few brands did not work due to the cultural differences. Johansson had to review his strategic vision and alter it to fit the European market. He found he had to alter his products for each country. His new goal is "to be a good Frenchman in France and a good Italian in Italy. My strategy is to go global only when I can and stay local when I must."

Johansson is still trying to expand the market of Electrolux. He still feels a global strategy is important for Electrolux, only he has learned that culture must be taken into account in each new market. Electrolux is growing. The company has entered the American market and is looking to enter the former Soviet Union and Asia.

Source: Adapted from William Echikson, "Electrolux: The Trick to Selling in Europe," *Fortune*, September 20, 1993, p. 82.

DISCUSSION QUESTIONS

1. How is the European environment different from that of the United States? What factors are responsible for the fragmentation of the European home appliance market?
2. Are there any circumstances under which there will be a single homogeneous market for home appliances in Europe?
3. Can you identify products for which there is, or could be, a homogeneous market in all of Europe?
4. Identify and explain the functional strategies (e.g., distribution channels, advertising, purchasing) that a company like Electrolux could use to take advantage of the European Union's common market.

Notes

1. For information on the WTO, refer to www.ciesin.org/TG/PI/TRADE/gatt.html.
2. For information on GATT, refer to www.wto.org.
3. Jeffrey Frankel and Shan-Jin Wei, "Open Regionalism in a World of Continental Trade Blocs," IMF Working Paper (Washington, DC: International Monetary Fund, 1998).
4. Jacob Viner, *The Customs Union Issue* (New York: Carnegie Endowment for International Peace, 1950).
5. "The Trouble with Regionalism," *The Economist,* June 27, 1992, p. 79.
6. NAFTA Facts, Office of the U.S. Trade Representative, March 2008, www.ustr.gov/assets/Trade_Agreements/Regional/NAFTA/Fact_Sheets/asset_upload_file202_14592.pdf.
7. Information on the ASEAN was obtained from the official site of Association of South-East Asian Nations, www.aseansec.org.
8. UNESCO, www.unesco.org/most/p80.htm.
9. Information on the European Union was obtained from various public sources and from "Europa: The European Union On-Line," http://europa.eu.int/index_en.htm.
10. World Trade Organization, "World Trade Developments in 2006," *International Trade Statistics 2007* (Geneva: WTO, 2007), www.wto.org/english/res_e/statis_e/its2007_e/its07_world_trade_dev_e.htm.
11. Jagdish Bhagwati, "Negotiating Trade Blocs," *India Today,* July 15, 1993, p. 65.
12. D. Held, A. McGrew, D. Goldblatt, and J. Perraton, *Global Transformations* (Stanford, CA: Stanford University Press, 1999), p. 16.
13. R. Gilpin, *The Political Economy of International Relations* (Princeton, NJ: Princeton University Press, 1987), p. 389.
14. WTO, "World Trade Developments," *International Trade Statistics 2007,* www.wto.org/english/res_e/statis_e/its2007_e/section1_e/its07_highlights1_e.pdf.
15. Experience of Arvind V. Phatak, who immigrated to the United States in 1960.
16. Bank of International Settlements, Quarterly Review, December 2007, www.bis.org/publ/qtrpdf/r_qt0712g.pdf?noframes=1.
17. Hernando DeSoto, *The Mystery of Capital* (New York: Basic Books, 2000).
18. Raymond J. Matoloni Jr., "U.S. Multinational Companies' Operations in 1998," *Survey of Current Business,* July 2000, table 12.1, p. 40.
19. Ibid., table 2, p. 4.
20. Tina Rosenberg, "Globalization," *New York Times,* August 18, 2002, sec. 6, p. 28.
21. Ibid.
22. Joseph E. Stiglitz, *Globalization and Its Discontents* (New York: Norton, 2003).

CHAPTER THREE

The Political and Legal Environments

Chapter Learning Objectives

After completing this chapter, you should be able to:

- Describe the components, relationships, and interactions involved in the political systems model, and explain how the one-nation model can be extended into a global business context.
- Define and differentiate among the various types of political risk, and discuss their implications for the multinational firm.
- Discuss comprehensive frameworks for assessing political risk, from a global as well as a single-country perspective.
- Understand alternative methods used to hedge against risk from political and politically imposed economic changes in a host country.
- Understand practical implications of political risk for the manager working overseas.
- Identify the distinct levels of the international legal system that businesses must understand.
- Describe the implications of various international treaties concerning intellectual property rights.
- Understand the Foreign Corrupt Practices Act and its implications for a firm's global operations.

Opening Case: A Love-Hate Relationship with Chavez

Just how hard is it to do business in Venezuela? As President Hugo Chavez leads his country toward "21st century socialism," hardly a day passes without another change in the rules restricting companies. Want to export? First get government certification that there's no domestic shortage of your product. Want to import? Prove that the goods aren't available locally. Chavez has already forced global oil giants, phone carriers, and power companies to hand over control of key assets. Now he says he might nationalize banks, hospitals, and steel companies. No wonder foreign direct investment, which averaged $3.2 billion annually during Chavez's first three years in office, plunged to a net outflow of $2.6 billion last year. "It's a bit like the . . . French Revolution," says Edmond J. Saade, president of the Venezuelan American Chamber of Commerce (VenAmCham). "Power to the people, death to the nobility."

No doubt, Venezuela is a pretty scary place to invest these days. But in some respects business is better than ever. Thanks to soaring oil revenues, Chavez is spending heavily—some $13.3 billion last year alone—to win support for his "Bolivarian Revolution." For the past three years the economy has grown at an 11%-to-12% clip, while consumption has expanded by 18% annually. The poor, 58% of all

Venezuelans, have seen their meager household incomes more than double since 2004 thanks to cash stipends, subsidized food, and scholarships from the government's social-development programs. The result: Sales of everything from basics such as Coca-Cola and Crest toothpaste to big-ticket items like Ford SUVs and Mercedes-Benz sedans have taken off.

You might call it business' love-hate relationship with Chavez. Local and foreign companies alike are raking in more money than ever in Venezuela. Two-way trade between the U.S. and Venezuela has never been higher. Venezuela exported more than $42 billion to the U.S. last year, including 1 million barrels of oil daily, and imported $9 billion worth of American goods, up 41% from 2005. But since Chavez declared President George W. Bush Public Enemy No. 1, Americans prefer to keep a low profile, even though VenAmCham's 1,100 member companies account for more than 650,000 jobs. "Consumption has been going through the roof, and commercial relations between the U.S. and Venezuela are still workable, but on the political front there is confrontation," says Saade. "American business is caught in the middle."

Even global oil companies—Chavez's chief targets so far—are likely to stay put. Although they have been forced to turn over control of their projects to the state-owned Petroleos de Venzuela (PDVSA), Chavez can't afford to alienate them. Ventures involving foreign companies account for 40% of Venezuela's output of 2.4 million barrels a day. For the multinational oil giants, the country is too important to ignore, even if it means they no longer call the shots. "Venezuela's oil potential is so great," says a foreign oil executive who declined to be identified. "We're not making huge returns, but it's not a financial black hole, either."

Other industries are not only putting up with Chavez but also benefiting directly from his programs. Take Intel Corp.: Sales of its microprocessors in Venezuela jumped by 15% in 2006 and look set to grow at the same pace this year as the government equips schools and public offices with new computers. In December, Caracas started a joint venture with China's Lanchao Group to manufacture low-cost machines called "Bolivarian PCs." The venture, 60% owned by Lanchao, will produce 80,000 computers in Venezuela the first year and 150,000 in 2008, including a stripped-down desktop model that will cost $450. Intel says the government alone could buy as many as 300,000 computers. "There's a lot of money in the Venezuelan market now, and it's important to take advantage of that," says Guillermo Deffit, Intel's's business-development manager in Venezuela.

Sales of cars and cola are booming, too. Ford and General Motors Corp. have manufactured cars in Venezuela for nearly a half-century, but with the strength of the bolivar, imports of pricier models such as the Ford Expedition sport-utility vehicle and GM's Silverado pickup are on the rise. Last year, Ford's sales increased 52%, to nearly 62,000 cars and trucks, as its imports more than tripled, to 28,000. GM's sales jumped 21% last year, to 71,000 vehicles, and so far this year are on track to climb by 50%. And sales of Coke and other beverages made by bottler Coca-Cola Femsa in Venezuela jumped 25% in the first quarter of 2007, in spite of a two-day shutdown of the company's distribution center in March for a surprise audit by tax authorities.

For local companies that have managed to survive Chavez's ever-changing business rules, the fast-growing economy offers some small solace—but few guarantees for the future. "We have fewer competitors every year because people throw in the towel," says the owner of a family company that provides raw materials for a variety of industries. He declined to give his name, fearing government retaliation, but he says his profit margins are getting fatter as he faces less competition. Still, his company has shrunk to just 100 employees from 300 since Chavez came to power in 1999, and sales have fallen by half. Dozens of his friends have left the country in recent years, and one of his top managers is decamping soon for Florida, where many middle-class Venezuelans have made their homes. But he's determined to stick it out.

As Chavez continues his socialist crusade, there are signs of rising discontent: A recent decision to revoke a popular TV network's license sparked outrage among university students, who took to the streets in early June. And the consumption boom is fueling inflation, now running at 18% annually. In any event, the fiery President can hardly do without business. Private companies account for half the government's non-oil tax receipts and 83% of jobs, says Ruth de Krivoy, a former Central Bank president who runs Sintesis Financiera, a Caracas think tank. "The government believes that state-run companies . . . will take the place of the exploiting business class," she notes. "But if you erase the private sector from the map, what do you have left? Not much."

Source: Geri Smith, *BusinessWeek,* June 25, 2007, p. 42.

Discussion Questions

1. What are the sources of risk for multinational firms operating in Venezuela?
2. Discuss risks for specific industries that may originate from President Chavez's policies.
3. How may the risks of doing business in Venezuela affect investment and trade with other South American countries?

Macro-Level Environments and Uncertainties

In the previous chapter, we discussed in detail several important dimensions of the global business environment—elements that shape the context within which international business must be conducted. We continue this macro-environmental discussion in the next two chapters by considering the governance infrastructure of host countries, which includes the political and legal institutions of those countries.[1] Many of the cross-nation differences referred to in Chapter 2 regarding economic environment and associated growth and productivity levels have been related to differences in the political and legal environments of countries.[2]

In this chapter, we start the discussion of host-country governance infrastructure by considering the political environment facing the international business manager and the problems it can pose for international operations in the form of politically imposed risk. Furthermore, we link other general environmental factors and uncertainties to a host nation's political environment. Table 3.1 illustrates various uncertainties that may arise in a host country for a manager of an international firm and that are all linked to a nation's political environment.[3]

TABLE 3.1 Macro-Environmental Uncertainties

Political Uncertainties	Macroeconomic Uncertainties
War	Inflation
Revolution	Changes in relative prices
Coup d'état	Foreign exchange rates
Democratic changes in government	Interest rates
Government Policy Uncertainties	Terms of trade
Fiscal and monetary reforms	**Social Uncertainties**
Price controls	Changing social concerns
Trade restrictions	Social unrest
Nationalization	Riots
Government regulation	Demonstrations
Barriers to earnings repatriation	Small-scale terrorist movements
Inadequate provision to public service	

International business has consistently emphasized the need to both understand the political dimension regarding the management of overseas activities and include inter-country differences and changes in political environments[4] when researching strategic initiatives and expansion activities of international firms.[5]

Politics and political interests are powerful forces in every country throughout the world, and their ability to support or disrupt business operations is of major interest to the global manager. For instance, the chapter's opening case illustrates how a powerful leader in Venezuela can cause certain disruptions to business operations there. Similarly, although China represents both a major production center and a significant market for many industries, the international manager can never forget that the current government of China may interfere with business plans in that country. During this decade, direct-marketing companies like Mary Kay Cosmetics and Avon Products were suddenly forbidden to use this business model in China. Furthermore, this policy was reversed by the Chinese government only after negotiations and diplomatic pressure by the U.S. government. Likewise, even in the United States, where there was business-friendly Republican-controlled government until 2006, the shift in Congress and possibly the executive office to the Democratic Party could exert new pressures on businesses operating there. In contrast, the conservative Harper government that came to power in Canada in 2007 has relaxed some restrictions for businesses operating in that country. Thus, international managers must think not only about political risks in the turbulent Middle East and southern Asia and the effects of the sustained conflicts in Iraq and Afghanistan; they must also think about the effect on their respective firms of the changes in government in relatively stable environments both home and abroad.

Only through an understanding of the fundamental elements and dynamics of political systems can one adequately appreciate their effect on the multiple operating environments facing the global firm and properly assess the degree of politically imposed risk involved in commencing or continuing operations in each. Policymakers and managers must have the tools to assess the extent of political and regulatory risk faced by a given investment project in a given country.[6]

Because of the dynamic changes taking place in various parts of the world, political forecasting is now big business. Why would international companies pay huge sums of money, sometimes amounting to thousands of U.S. dollars, to obtain such forecasts? Because firms prefer that there not be any uncertainty in the external environment that would affect the preferred outcomes of their strategies. The greater is the uncertainty, the greater is the perceived risk of operating in a particular country. Ignorance and misperceptions of facts often cause uncertainty. Therefore, firms attempt to minimize uncertainty and risk in a country through forecasts about the country's future business environment and prospects.

A firm understanding of political risk allows companies to decide how attractive a country is for exports, licensing, or direct investment in a manufacturing operation. Each of these modes of entry requires varying amounts of financial investments. The greater is the investment required to penetrate a foreign market, the greater is the risk involved in doing so. Companies therefore engage in assessing the amount of investment that they would be willing to make in the country, based on their assessment of the risks involved with each entry mode and the corresponding financial and other tangible and intangible benefits. As delineated in Practical Insight 3.1, the country of Kenya represents an example of how a seemingly stable country for business operations can quickly present a significant risk for international firms.

PRACTICAL INSIGHT 3.1

CHANGING POLITICAL RISK FORECAST IN KENYA IN 2008

During 2007, Kenya enjoyed a 5% economic growth. It was perceived as one of the more stable countries in Africa in which to invest and thus as an emerging-market leader for the future. However, contrary to this perception by Western firms especially, in its 2007 rankings, Transparency International ranked Kenya as the 150th most corrupt country in the world. Elections at the end of 2007 confirmed Transparency International's ranking and changed world perceptions of this East African country regarding politically imposed risk.

In December of 2007, President Mwai Kibaki, who succeeded the 24-year rule of Daniel Moi, won a bitterly disputed election in Kenya. The opposition party, the Orange Democratic Movement, felt that the election had been stolen. Widespread violence based on ethnic lines—much aimed at Kibaki's Kikiyu tribe—followed Kibaki's claim that he was re-elected. Neutral observers verified that the election was seriously flawed, adding more fuel to the burning that Kenya experienced into 2008.

In hopes of ending the violence, the president and the Orange Democratic Movement leader, Raila Odinga, attempted to promote bipartisanship by signing a power-sharing deal in February, 2008. Still, a bitter dispute over the role of Mr. Odinga, the new prime minister, emerged as a major obstacle to a coalition government in the country as Mr. Odinga would be actually ranked below the sitting Vice-President in Kenya. During the first quarter of 2008, the country seemed to vacillate between complete turmoil and further tribal-based violence and a peaceful coalition government. Messrs. Kibaki and Odinga were actually seen golfing with each other in March, 2008.

Western nations, led by the United States, the United Kingdom, and France, urged a peaceful coalition government founded upon power-sharing. Kenya represents a long-term business and political oasis for the West in an already unstable part of the world that includes East Africa and the Persian Gulf countries. Indeed multinational firms already in Kenya or looking to invest in the country were confused and needed to perform a risk assessment and subsequently reevaluate both current business plans and expansion strategies regarding Kenya. The country is heavily dependent on the tourism industry and firms in this industry sector began to bypass Kenya for other exotic locales such as South Africa and Botswana that were perceived as less risky.

However, other firms are predicting longer-term peace and economic stability. For instance, Kenya's mobile phone market underwent a change during the January, 2008, violence as France Telecom took a 51% stake (approximately 400 million USD) in Kenya's state-owned telecom company, Telkom Kenya, which was drowning due to high debt. Interestingly, the mobile phone brand will be known as Orange.

The Political System

When a firm crosses international boundaries, new and different political environments force that firm into various modes of adaptation.[7] Thus, because a firm must first understand the nature of the international political system and how it works, it should initially understand just what a political system is as well as its specific characteristics. Furthermore, we need to first separate the political and economic systems before integrating them into a more comprehensive framework. In this section, we examine a generic model of political and economic systems. The generic model of a political system is presented in Figure 3.1.

The Players in the Political System

The **political system** consists of a set of "players," each with its own unique set of aspirations and goals, which are often in conflict with those of the other "players" in the system. The *government* is only one of many players in this system, although a key one, as it alone has the legitimacy to make authoritative decisions and to enforce those decisions by force. The other key players in the system are the various significant *groups* that exist in a society. Examples of societal groups are labor unions, environmental

FIGURE 3.1
The Political System

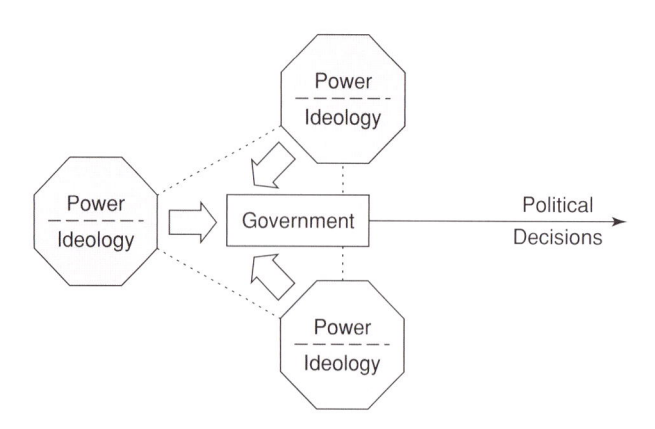

activist organizations, special-interest groups, and religious organizations. Some of these groups, such as political parties, armed forces, labor unions, and religious organizations, are significant institutions of society; others, such as the National Rifle Association and Amnesty International, are primarily lobby groups. Finally, groups, including various terrorist organizations, exist that conduct illegal activities.

Each of these groups has a certain amount of power it can exert to control and influence the behavior of other groups and of various host governments. The amount of power in the hands of each group is not equally distributed. Some groups may be more powerful than others. The power of each group is derived from the total number of people who are firmly committed to the group's ideals and goals and from the group's stockpile of key financial, technical, and human resources.

Each societal group also has its unique political ideology. *Ideology* has been defined as "a set of closely related beliefs, or ideas, or even attitudes, characteristic of a group or community."[8] Similarly, a "political ideology is a set of ideas or beliefs that people hold about their political regime and its institutions and about their position and role in it."[9] The ideology of a group is the set of values and beliefs pertaining to the way in which society should be organized—politically, economically, morally—that are shared by its members. For example, in the United States the ideology of the National Rifle Association is grounded in the belief that every person has the right to bear arms, whereas on the opposite side is Hand Gun Control, Inc., which is committed to restricting the possession of handguns by lay members of the society. The labor unions have as their primary objective the protection of workers from unfair treatment by the employer. The Democratic Party in the United States and the Labour Party in the United Kingdom have been historically committed to worker welfare, whereas the Republican Party in the United States and the Tory party in the United Kingdom have been generally committed to the development and growth of business firms with little or no interference by the government.

Various groups within a society

> at given times and under given conditions, challenge the prevailing ideology. Interests, classes, and various political and religious associations may develop a "counter ideology" that questions the status quo and attempts to modify it. They advocate change rather than order; they criticize or reject the political regime and the existing social and economic arrangements; they advance schemes for the restructuring and reordering of the society; and they spawn political movements in order to gain enough power to bring about the changes they advocate. In this sense, a political ideology moves people into action. It motivates them to demand changes in their way of life and to modify the existing political, economic, and social relations, or it mobilizes them on how to preserve what they value.[10]

Thus, the two important features that characterize all ideologies include a given ideology that rationalizes the status quo and competing ideologies that challenge it.

One must make note of the fact that institutions and groups that appear to be alike may perform different functions in different countries. For example, in the United Kingdom, labor unions have a leftist ideology and are politically affiliated with the Labour Party, whereas in the United States the labor unions are basically "business unions" with an ideological bias in favor of private enterprise and a capitalist society. In the United States, Republican Party members believe that the Democratic Party is politically left of center, whereas in some countries outside the United States, the Democratic Party is seen as a right-of-center party. It should be noted that the United States never had politically viable socialist or communist parties. Such is not the case in many countries, like Italy, India, Sweden, and Greece. The role played by the church also varies from country to country. For instance, the Catholic Church played a crucial role in the "liberation" of Poland from Soviet domination and in the overthrow of the Marcos dictatorship in the Philippines, whereas the Catholic Church in India is politically neutral.

The Concepts of Legitimacy and Consensus[11]

Every group in the political system has its own objectives and aspirations, and all the groups attempt to influence the government and thereby translate their particular interests into authoritative political decisions. A key prerequisite for the efficient functioning of any political system is the presence of a high level of "consensus." *Consensus* is the widespread acceptance of the decision-making process in the political system by the individuals and groups in the system. Consensus is the instrument by which a government itself becomes legitimized. *Legitimacy* is the use of the power of the state by officials in accordance with prearranged and agreed-on rules. A legitimate act is legal, but a lawful command is not always legitimate. For example, the commands issued by the Nazi government in Germany were legal; however, they were not legitimate because they violated a code of civilized behavior and morality that brought into question their legitimacy. Legitimacy and consensus are key indicators of the effectiveness and performance of the political system. Conversely the absence of legitimacy and consensus can cause an undermining instability of the system. A government that has no legitimacy does not have the right to issue authoritative directives and thus is likely to lead to political instability, unless it is backed up by massive coercive force to keep it in power. Examples have included the now-deposed brutal Taliban regime in Afghanistan, which was in power through coercive means until recently, and the ongoing dictatorship in North Korea.

The Political Process

The political process constitutes a political bargaining process in which different groups representing different interests conflict over different preferred outcomes. The outcomes of the political process include a myriad of political decisions made by the government in response to the pressures applied by the different interest groups. Group conflict is common in an effective political system, and the strength of the political system is its ability, through the agency of the government, to resolve the intergroup conflicts peacefully. Group conflict occurs, for example, between groups that favor free trade and lower tariff barriers and those that advocate protectionism. The role of the government is to engage in the constructive management of conflict among the various interest groups.

The Global Political System

The international political system, like the political system of a nation, also consists of numerous players, each of whom have their own particular interests, goals, and aspirations. The various countries of the world, the various regional trade blocs discussed in the previous chapter, and the different international organizations, including the United Nations, the World Bank, the International Monetary Fund (IMF), and the World Trade Organization (WTO), are the major participants in the international political system.

> In domestic politics, goal-seeking behavior is regulated by government which has the authority to make decisions for a society and the power to enforce those decisions. The characteristic that distinguishes international politics from internal politics is the absence of government. In the international system, no legitimate body has the authority to manage conflict or achieve common goals by making and enforcing decisions for the system; instead, decision-making authority is dispersed among many governmental, intergovernmental, and non-governmental groups.[12]

As seen in the previous chapter, the WTO is approaching a world-type government for international trade. In 1994 the WTO was empowered by an international treaty signed by over 100 countries to regulate world trade and investments in accordance with the rules of the treaty provisions. The WTO has the power to adjudicate in trade disputes between countries and to impose punitive measures against those that are found to be guilty of violating the treaty provisions. Similarly, international law, characterized by treaties such as the treaty for the protection of intellectual property, is designed to manage conflict and cooperation in the area of intellectual property rights.

Because of the absence of a legitimate "world government" with the capability for making and enforcing authoritative decisions, it has been up to the various nations and international groups to create the appropriate rules, institutions, and procedures that manage international conflict and cooperation. Within this framework, conflict occurs within agreed-on limits, and cooperation among nations is enhanced. However, when there are no effective rules, procedures, and institutions to manage conflict and cooperation, international conflict may rise to undesirable levels and may even escalate into war.

The Interaction between International Politics and International Economics

In today's world the international economic system and the international political system do not function independently of each other. The international economic relations between nation-states are determined to a large extent by their political and diplomatic relations, while the reverse holds true as well. Figure 3.2 illustrates the extreme political and economic systems. As depicted on the vertical axis, politically, a country may range from far-right totalitarianism, or fascism, to far-left totalitarianism, or communism. At both extremes, there is government oppression. In the former, it is in the name of a select group in the population such as the military. In the latter, the government represents the entire people. In the depiction seen in Figure 3.2, democracy as it is seen in the United States lies in the middle. From the managerial perspective, it is interesting to realize that the United States lies within a small band relative to the world. For example, the most liberal politicians in Washington, D.C., are still seen as

FIGURE 3.2
Political and Economic Systems

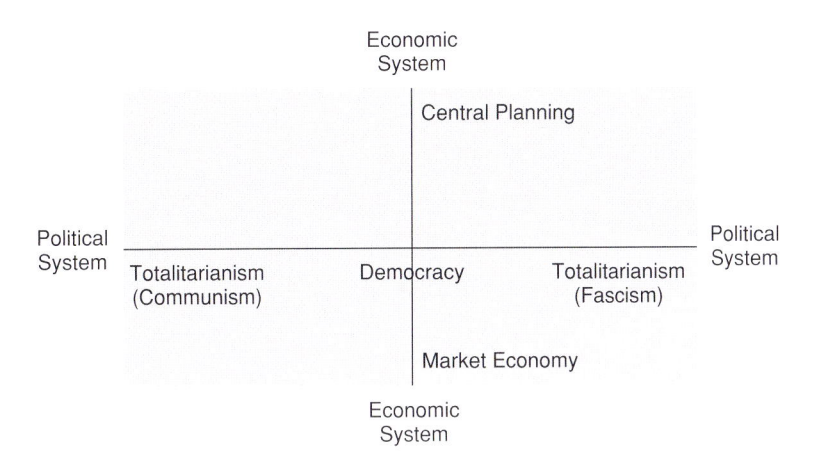

```
                          Economic
                           System
                             |
                      Central Planning
                             |
 Political                   |                    Political
 System  ─────────────────────────────────────── System
         Totalitarianism   Democracy  Totalitarianism
         (Communism)                  (Fascism)
                             |
                      Market Economy
                             |
                          Economic
                           System
```

very moderate by the extreme left throughout the world. Likewise, the most conservative Washington politicians are seen as moderates by extreme right-wingers throughout the world.

Extreme economic systems are depicted on the horizontal axis in Figure 3.2. At one extreme, there exists a market economy. In this economic environment, market forces without government intervention set price and quantity levels in all industries. Supply and demand principles rule, and the private sector owns the factors of production. At the other extreme, a centrally planned economy, the government owns the factors of production and establishes the price and quantity levels. Subsequently, the government tries to harmonize economic plans across all industry sectors. Both extreme economic systems are theoretical, with most countries falling along the continuum where the government has some role. In these mixed economies, the government can interfere in the economic process in distinct ways. For instance, it can actually own industries or pieces of industries. Also, governments that do not have equity stakes in industries may provide financial incentives as well as strategic direction for the firms and industries in their countries.

A manager cannot assume that a country that has tendencies toward a market economy is democratic. For instance, the government of Singapore has historically promoted capitalism while being less than a fully functioning democracy. Likewise, South Korea and various South American countries during the 1980s had military-based governments that promoted capitalism. From another perspective, many governments that have historically been democratically driven have had both government ownership and influence of industries. India provides a good example here. Also, Japan has historically choreographed the strategic initiatives of industries deemed to be critical to the country's economic future. There are even many versions of democracies throughout the world. For instance, both Malaysia and Mexico have claimed the "democracy" label. In both countries, however, the same party held national office for decades. In fact, the elections in Mexico in July 2000 marked the first time since the 1910 Mexican Revolution that the opposition defeated the party in government, the Institutional Revolutionary Party (PRI). Vicente Fox of the National Action Party (PAN) was sworn in on December 1, 2000, as the first chief executive elected in free and fair elections.

To begin the political analysis of a country, it is important to realize where the country falls economically and politically relative to other countries. Beyond that, the international manager must understand political and economic changes that have occurred

FIGURE 3.3
25 Years of Political and Economic Change, 1983–2008

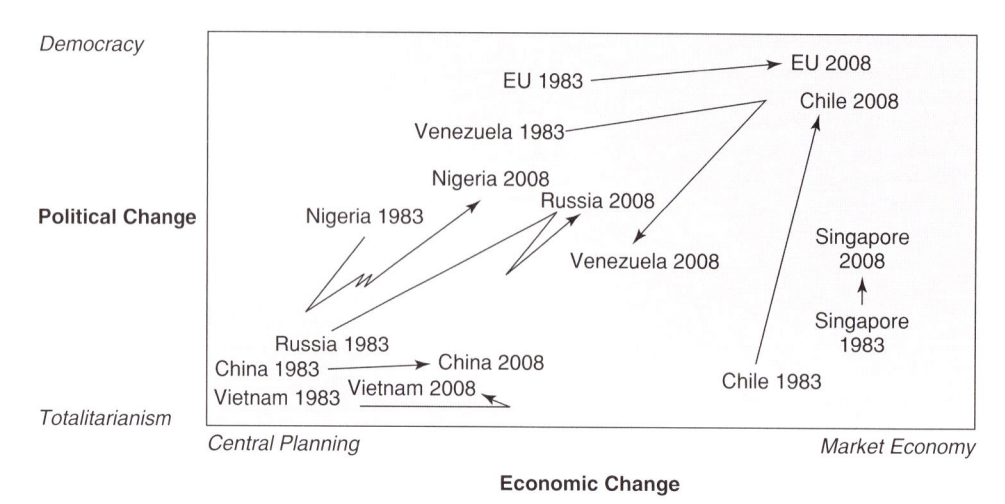

Democracy / Political Change / Totalitarianism (vertical axis)
Central Planning — Economic Change — Market Economy (horizontal axis)

Points plotted: EU 1983 → EU 2008; Venezuela 1983 → Venezuela 2008; Chile 1983 → Chile 2008; Nigeria 1983 → Nigeria 2008; Russia 1983 → Russia 2008; China 1983 → China 2008; Vietnam 1983 → Vietnam 2008; Singapore 1983 → Singapore 2008.

in the recent past as well as changes expected to occur in the future. Figure 3.3 presents a tool for managers to use in analyzing political and economic shifts of countries deemed important to their respective firms and industries.

During the past 25 years, there has been a significant shift toward democracy and market economies. In some countries like China, even though the political tone has remained totalitarian, more and more pockets of capitalism have been introduced into the historically planned economy. From another perspective, Chile represents a country that has always tended toward capitalism and, since the removal of General Pinochet as leader during the mid-1990s, has recently moved strongly toward democracy. Other countries have been more volatile in their respective political and economic movements. Nigeria has seen various military rulers as well as attempts at free elections and subsequent political corruption scandals during the past 25 years. Vietnam, although politically unwavering, has economically experimented after the general embargo was lifted by the United States in the mid-1990s. In that country, pockets of capitalism were introduced, then pulled back, and then a slower movement toward free market postures began. As illustrated in the chapter's opening case, Venezuela has begun to drift to socialism under the heavy-handedness of President Chavez. Still, in general, there has been a worldwide trend toward democracy during the past 25 years. Government privatization and deregulation activities, as well as the fall of major planned economies around the world, have led to a shift toward market economies.

There are three ways in which political factors affect economic outcomes:

1. The political system shapes the economic system, because the structure and operation of the economic system is, to a great extent, determined by the structure and operation of the international political system.

2. Political concerns often shape economic policy, because economic policies are frequently dictated by overriding political interests.

3. International economic relations themselves are political relations, because international economic interaction, like international political interaction, is a process by which state and nonstate actors manage, or fail to manage, their conflicts and by which they cooperate, or fail to cooperate, to achieve common goals.[13]

What follows is a look in some detail at these three political dimensions of international economics.

The Influence of the International Political System on the International Economic System

The influence of the international political system on the international economic system is apparent when we review the political developments during three distinct periods in history. The first is the period of nineteenth-century imperialism, the second is the post–World War II era of cold war between the Soviet Union and the Western free world, led by the United States, and the third is the post-Berlin Wall demolition and the demise of the Soviet Empire era.

Nineteenth Century Imperialism and the International Economic System

Nineteenth-century imperialism and mercantilism were driven by two major political factors: (1) powerful nation-states in Europe—the United Kingdom, France, Germany, and Holland—of nearly equal military power and (2) rampant nationalism practiced by these powerful nation-states, which drove each nation to engage in practices designed to enhance national pride, national identity, self-sufficiency, wealth, and economic power. National independence, rather than collective or cooperative relations among nation-states, was in vogue. These two conditions led to the pursuit of "empire building," characterized by the policy of colonialism under which each European power engaged in colonizing countries in Asia, Africa, and Latin America. The objective of the colonial powers was to obtain raw materials and minerals from the colonies, to process them into finished products at home, and to market the products in the captive markets of the colonies. The overriding objectives of the colonial powers were to accumulate wealth and power and to provide full employment to their citizens, at the expense of the colonized countries whose markets and production capabilities were totally controlled by the imperial powers.

The European colonial powers divided the world into parts that each controlled. Thus the British controlled most of West and South Asia and parts of Africa. The French controlled Southeast Asia and northwest Africa. The Dutch controlled Indonesia and parts of Central and South America, and the Germans took control of parts of West Africa. Wars erupted between the colonial powers as each attempted to increase its respective power by colonizing more countries. The British and the French fought for the control of India, and the British and the Dutch fought for parts of Africa. European imperialism determined the patterns of trade and investments—each colonial power concentrated on trade and investments within its colonial empire.

The Cold War Era and the International Economic System

The imperialist system and the residual domination of the United Kingdom in the West ended following the end of World War II. Two major superpowers emerged in the post–World War II period, namely, the United States and the Soviet Union. A new political and economic system emerged based on the rivalry between these two superpowers for world political and economic domination. Politically, the new system was bipolar and hierarchical. The United States was the leader of the West and a weakened Japan, as well as the dominant military power; in the East, the Soviet Union was the dominant military power and leader of the so-called Soviet bloc, which comprised countries behind the "iron curtain." The developing countries of the third world, most of which had gained their freedom from the old imperial powers, remained politically subordinate to their once colonial "mother" countries. On the global arena, the United States and its allies confronted the Soviet Union and its allies in the cold war. Such was the political system that determined the post–World War II international economic system.

For political reasons, the West and East were isolated in two disparate economic systems. The United States and its allies in the West adhered to the capitalist system, which championed the free enterprise and free market economic system. In the East, the Soviet Union and its allies in the Communist bloc adhered to the so-called Socialist/Marxist economic model, which called for the centralized control of the economy by the government and the absence of private property. In the West, the United States was the dominant economic power, and its free market vision shaped the economic order; trade, commerce, and capital flows occurred predominantly among the free market economies. In the East, the Soviet Union forced the Eastern bloc countries to adhere to the socialist model for their economies, and for political reasons it made them economically dependent on the Soviet Union and economically isolated from the West. Thus politics shaped economics in the post–World War II period.

The Demise of the Soviet Union and Its Impact on the International Economic System

As before, the changing political scene in the late 1980s and the 1990s caused the breakdown of the post–World War II international economic system. The birth of democracy in Poland and Hungary, the demolition of the Berlin Wall, which resulted in the union of East and West Germany into one nation, and the subsequent breakup of the Soviet Union caused a sea change in the international economic system. Countries that once loathed capitalism and a free enterprise economy acknowledged its superiority over the socialist model and gradually adopted its salient features. Russia became a democracy, and China, Vietnam, and India opened their respective markets to foreign investments and trade.

Political Concerns and Economic Policy

In addition to influencing the international economic system, political concerns influence a nation's economic policies as well. Internal political processes play a role in determining a national economic policy. Economic policy is the outcome of the political bargaining process that is responsible for resolving the conflict over the outcomes preferred by different groups, each representing distinct and often conflicting interests. The outcome of the political conflict is determined by the relative power of each group vis-à-vis other groups. For instance, conflict occurs between labor unions that want to protect domestic employment, and are therefore opposed to free trade, and business organizations that favor free trade, with the group that has more power exerting stronger influence on determining the international economic policy.

The overriding political and strategic interests of a nation very often determine its international economic policy. In effect, international economic policy becomes a tool for fulfilling a nation's strategic and foreign policy objectives. For example, the embargo has been used as a tool of political warfare throughout history, such as when the United States placed an embargo on trade with Cuba after Fidel Castro came to power in that country. Similarly, the United Nations placed an embargo on all trade and investments in South Africa in the 1980s as a means of dismantling the apartheid system in that country.

International economic policy, driven by political considerations, can be beneficial to international companies. For example, because of larger political and strategic interests such as maintaining a correct political balance of power among countries, nations have often overlooked the human rights violations committed by repressive governments, and continued to promote trade, commerce, and investments with the repressive nations. An example of this strategy is the huge investments by Western nations and Japan in communist China, which by all accounts has an overtly repressive regime.

International Economic and Political Relations

Earlier in this chapter, we discussed the nature of the international political system as being characterized by the absence of a legitimate body like a "world government" to manage conflict or achieve cooperation among and between the various members in the system (e.g., the nation-states, global companies, and various financial and nonfinancial institutions such as the World Bank, the OPEC oil cartel, and Amnesty International). In the absence of a world government with the requisite authority and legitimacy to make and enforce decisions for the political system, decision-making authority to manage conflict and cooperation among the various members of the political system is dispersed among the members themselves.

International economic relations may be viewed as the outcome of the political process involving the management of conflict and cooperation over the acquisition of scarce resources among the various members of the political system in the absence of a centralized world government. As with all international political interaction, economic interaction ranges from pure conflict to pure cooperation. The conflict among the members of the political system is often rooted in a struggle for greater power and national sovereignty. National sovereignty is associated with national wealth. A country that is not independently wealthy becomes dependent on others and hence loses some of its national sovereignty. Therefore, the pursuit of wealth is the goal of most members in the political system, and the pursuit of this goal in the presence of scarce resources frequently leads to conflict among the system members.

The debate over whether the international political system influences the international economic system or whether the international economic system influences the international political system will continue unabated. However, when one accepts the notion that nations interacting with each other are the dominant players in both economic and political systems, then unquestionably the political interests embodied in national power and national sovereignty will be the primary determinants of their political as well as economic relations with other nations in the world community of nations.

Political Risk and the International Firm

Since Kobrin's work on political risk,[14] this important macro-level topic has received much attention by business research scholars. Political risk has been linked to all aspects of international business and international management behavior. Some linkages include foreign investment flows,[15] foreign entry mode,[16] reciprocity among international alliance partners,[17] and international control systems.[18] As suggested earlier in this chapter, it is the change in political and economic positions that causes risk for the international firm. Much of the risk stems from a change in the national laws discussed in the preceding section. Political risk in this sense has been operationalized in two distinct ways. The first is grassroots instability arising from demonstrations, riots, strikes, and political assassinations. The second is government instability arising from irregular power transfers and the imposition of political restrictions.[19]

Political risk is the likelihood that political forces will cause unexpected and drastic changes in a country's environment that significantly affect the opportunities and operations of a business enterprise. This definition of political risk puts emphasis on political forces as being the primary determinants of political risk in a country's environment. *Political forces* are the different participant groups in the political system. Earlier in this chapter we examined the characteristics of a political system and the role played by the major political groups in a society in influencing the authoritative decisions of the government in power. Political risk is the degree of uncertainty associated with the pattern of decisions made by the government. There is no political risk when there is certainty about the future decisions made by the government. The higher the degree of uncertainty regarding the policy decisions made by the government, the higher is the political risk perceived by those most affected by government decisions.

The likelihood of political change is referred to as *political hazard*.[20] When the political institutions in a host country constrain the freedom to change policy, there is less uncertainty. When there are few constraints, there is greater uncertainty and political hazard is said to be high. International business researchers have developed measures of political hazards from the perspective of industry-level foreign investment[21] and country-level foreign investment.[22]

Countries in which the governments do not show consistency in the pattern of their decision making are more likely to be perceived as having higher political hazard and therefore being riskier than those in which the government's decisions show a pattern of consistency. Two major emerging economies—India and China—are cases in point. Since 1990, the Indian government has embarked on a slow but steady program of opening the huge Indian market to foreign competition and investments. Billions of dollars of foreign investments, mostly from the United States, have entered the Indian market. Although, in the opinion of many observers, the rate at which the Indian government is opening up the market is rather slow, the (adverse) political risk that is perceived by firms doing business in India is moderate to low. In contrast, China, which also has a huge market potential for many business firms, has made much bigger strides in opening the market to foreign firms. However, the perception of the degree of political risk is much higher in China than is the case with India. This is because China as yet does not have an effective legal system, a reliable commercial code that establishes the rules of commercial interactions and obligations does not exist, and decisions made by one agency of the government are often negated by decisions of some other agency.

The Nature of Political Risk

Political risk can have positive consequences also. Political risk is positive in nature when the unexpected changes in government policies result in favorable conditions for business. An example of positive political risk is the Indian government's policy change that now allows foreign investments in almost all industries in India. The Indian government is allowing equity participation in industries that were forbidden to foreign companies, such as banking, insurance, airports, oil and gas, pharmaceuticals, fast foods, and some defense-related industries. Not many years ago, few observers would have predicted such an opening of the Indian economy to foreign trade and investments. This newly opened Indian market has provided companies worldwide with new business opportunities, and it illustrates the potentially favorable impact of political risk. The same can be said about the changes that have occurred in Russia, which has embraced capitalism and the free enterprise system following the demise of what once was the Soviet Union. Hence political risk can be positive as well as negative, depending on how it affects company operations.

There is no established relationship between the political ideology of the government and the nature of risk incurred. Regardless of the government's ideology, it is the behavior of the government that determines the degree of risk prevalent in a country. A government with a capitalist ideology may pose more risk to businesses if it abruptly changes its policies than a socialist government, which has a record of maintaining consistent policies over extended periods of time.

The form of government is also not necessarily associated with the amount of risk generated in a country. Dictatorships may pose the same amount of risk as democracies. Once again, it is the behavior of the government that determines the amount of risk present in a particular country.

Political risk can be country-, company-, or project-specific. *Country-specific* political risk is manifested in the mutual hostility between Israel and Syria. One would expect that Israeli companies would find little support in Syria, and the same would apply for Syrian companies in Israel. *Company-specific* risk invokes either a favorable or an unfavorable response aimed at a particular company. For example, companies that are known for their technological superiority, such as Motorola and Hewlett-Packard, may receive favorable treatment in some countries through special incentives such as inducements to form joint ventures or to establish wholly owned subsidiaries. On the other hand, large companies may not be welcomed in a country that is afraid that they may destroy local firms. *Project-specific* risk involves special treatment bestowed on a certain type of project. For example, countries like Libya and Iran, which are very unfriendly to foreign investments from the United States, are nonetheless eager to collaborate with American oil companies in oil exploration and drilling even though they reject business with companies in other industries.

Types of Political Risk

The impact of political decisions can be felt in three different ways: transfer risk, operational risk, and ownership risk.

Transfer risk is the change in the degree of ease or difficulty experienced in making transfers of capital, goods, technology, and people into and out of a country. Capital controls include restrictions placed on the remittance of money to or from a country through foreign exchange controls. Similarly, governments may impose controls over the flow of goods into a country through quotas and high tariffs. The tariffs imposed on imported steel by President Bush in 2003 are examples of transfer risk incurred by steel-importing companies like the automobile makers. Technology transfer may be constrained by government policy. For instance, the U.S. government has forbidden exports of technology to China and India that could be used to develop products with military applications such as missiles and nuclear weapons. Similarly, most countries require work visas for foreigners, while some place limits on the number of foreign nationals who can be employed in a company, thereby limiting the free flow of human resources among the subsidiaries of international companies. American high-tech and software companies are hurting from the severe restrictions on visas granted to foreign engineers and scientists after the tragic bombing of the World Trade Center.

Operational risk is the impact on the operations of a firm caused by changes in the government's policies. For example, the enforcement of strict new environmental protection legislation may cause a firm to shift its production site from one location to another within a country or to another country altogether. Similarly, a change in minimum-wage laws may induce a company to farm out some production work to contractors in countries with more competitive wage rates.

Ownership risk involves a change in the proportion of equity owned by a company in a foreign subsidiary. Until the late 1960s and early 1970s, the nature of the ownership risk experienced by international companies was predominantly negative. The nationalistic ideology of most developing countries—countries that had become independent from the bondage of colonialism—called for economic independence and self-sufficiency. This ideology fomented a wave of nationalization, expropriation, or forced divestment of equity of foreign companies in such countries as India, Egypt, Zimbabwe, Zambia, and Indonesia. Since the 1980s and 1990s, however, there has been a rise in the wave of sentiment in favor of foreign enterprise. The thirst for foreign technology and access to foreign markets, both of which international companies are in a good position to provide, has motivated governments in countries that once abhorred foreign companies to now throw them a welcome mat. Foreign companies that were once asked to divest their share of the equity in foreign subsidiaries are now being asked to increase their share to a majority or wholly owned status. Such is the case in India and China, where the governments are actively seeking foreign investments in industries that were once government-owned, such as banking and insurance. In these cases, ownership risk has now shifted from negative to positive. For all practical purposes, ownership risk has disappeared globally, except in countries like Zaire, where President Mugabe has embarked on a policy of expropriating property owned by the country's white citizenry. However, as shown in the following quote, expropriation by a foreign government does occur:

> A U.S. investor established a fishing venture in Somalia. After a military coup occurred, the new government began a series of repeated and continuous acts of harassment and interference against the U.S. investor's personnel and operations. For example, the U.S. investor's personnel were repeatedly threatened by military and police officials, arrested and, in one instance, deported from the country. In addition, the Government interfered with the company's operation of its aircraft, which was used to transport the fish, and ordered the company to permit a military observer to accompany all flights. This extra passenger displaced several hundred pounds of seafood products and added substantially to the cost of the company's operations. Viewing these and other government actions together, OPIC* found that the Somalian Government had expropriated the investor's project and compensated the investor.[23]

The Scope of Political Risk

The scope of transfer, operational, and ownership risk may range from macro to micro.[24] Macro risk and micro risk can be looked at as two ends of a continuum. There are degrees of macro and micro risk. **Macro risks** affect the full spectrum of firms and businesses operating in a host country.[25] One can conceive of macro risk as risk in which all private enterprise is confiscated or nationalized, as was the case when Cuba became a communist country. In a macro risk of lesser scope, only foreign companies or only certain industries are nationalized, as was the case when Saudi Arabia nationalized the oil industry in that country, removing American, British, and French oil companies' operations. Likewise, in current-day Venezuela, the same oil industry nationalization is occurring.

At the other extreme are **micro risks,** which may entail a specific action against a specific company by a group or government. Micro risks may also affect specific business activities exclusively.[26] The targeting of El Al Airlines by various terrorist organizations, the bombing of the World Trade Center by al-Qaeda terrorists, or the pressure put on Coca-Cola by the Indian government to reveal its secret syrup formula (which forced Coke to abandon the Indian market for some time) are examples of micro risk.

---

*The Overseas Private Insurance Corporation (OPIC) is a U.S. government agency that provides insurance to protect the foreign operations of U.S. companies against currency inconvertibility, expropriation, and political violence. The functions of OPIC are discussed later in the chapter.

FIGURE 3.4
Classification of Types of Risk for Company A in Country XYZ

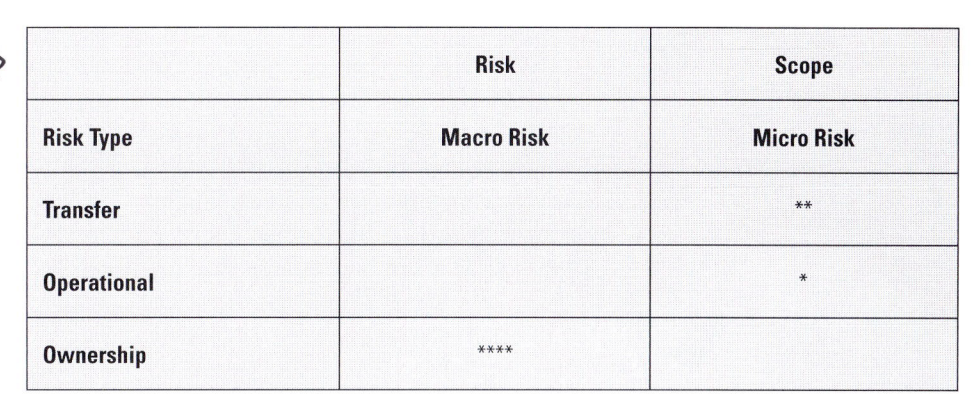

	Risk	Scope
Risk Type	**Macro Risk**	**Micro Risk**
Transfer		**
Operational		*
Ownership	****	

Note: ***** = high, * = low.

The table in Figure 3.4 shows the relationships among the three types of risk—transfer, operational, ownership—and the scope of such risks—micro and macro. The table shows that for Country XYZ, there are three different categories of political risk: transfer, operational, and ownership, with each type falling anywhere along the macro–micro risk continuum. As the table shows, company A in country XYZ is experiencing a medium level of micro transfer risk, a low level of micro operational risk, and a high level of macro ownership risk.

Assessing Host-Country Political Risk

Doing business internationally requires that the business risks caused by the political climate be assessed in every host country in which the international firm conducts business. A valid and reliable evaluation of host-country political risk provides managers with a realistic view of the probability of being able to achieve the proposed venture's objectives. Armed with this information, managers are in a position to determine the minimum levels of expectations from the venture in areas such as the rate of return (discounted for the level of risk), market share, and profits and to employ this knowledge in the ensuing negotiations with either the foreign government's officials or potential business associates.

Assessing the political risk in a host country begins with an exhaustive study of the political system and the corresponding political process in the country. As stated earlier, the political process constitutes a political bargaining process in which different groups in the political system, representing different interests, conflict over different preferred outcomes. Assuming that the government in power has the legitimacy to govern, the outcomes of the political process are the various political decisions made by the government. The government's decisions are in response to the lobbying efforts by the various interest groups in favor of their respective viewpoints. An exhaustive study of the political process would involve the following steps.[27]

1. **Study the relative power of the dominant groups in the society, and become familiar with their ideologies.** Groups that are more powerful are more likely to have their way with the politicians in the government than are those with less power. Look for any dominant coalitions among one or more groups whose political aspirations may be overlapping. Coalitions among groups may help less powerful groups gain more influence in the political process than would be possible if each of the relatively less powerful groups were to operate on its own.

2. **Study the decision-making process in the government.** Which political parties are represented in the legislative branch of the government? For example, the British Parliament includes members whose party affiliations include Tory, Labour, Liberal, and Communist. The U.S. Senate and House of Representatives includes members who are either Democrat or Republican. Understand the ideologies of the political parties in the legislative branch and the dominant groups in society that they represent. For instance, the British Tory Party and the Republican Party in the United States both represent the interests of the various business associations within their respective business communities.

3. **Evaluate the relative strength and bargaining power of the political parties in the legislative branch.** Assess the relative bargaining power of the various dominant coalitions in the legislative branch. The political party(s) and dominant coalitions that have greater bargaining power are more likely to have their ideologies implemented through legislation that is enacted by the legislative body. In a parliamentary democracy there is no separation between the legislative branch and the executive branch of government as the prime minister (the chief executive) is chosen by the majority party in the parliament. However, in the presidential system the legislative branch is separate from the executive, and therefore, as has often been the case in the United States, the party in power in the legislature may not be the same as the party to which the president belongs. Therefore, in a presidential system, one must evaluate the relative power between the president, who represents the executive branch of government, and the dominant political party in the legislative branch, because the political decisions made by the government are outcomes of the bargaining and negotiations between the legislative and the executive branches of government.

4. **Identify the key decision makers in both the legislative and executive branches of government.** The key decision makers are those who have the most influence on the policy choices of the government. The key person may be the chairperson of a subcommittee of the parliament or congress or a senior civil servant in a government agency. Occasionally the most influential person may not be in the government at all. For example, Senior Minister Lee (the former prime minister) is supposedly the person who is most influential in developing the policies of the Singapore government, although he is not officially in the government itself. Identifying the key decision makers may provide valuable clues on the future policy initiatives of the government.

5. **Study the path traveled by the government in power over the past several years in terms of its economic, social, and foreign policies.** This information, in conjunction with the information accumulated in the previous three steps, may be used to make informed judgments as to the future policy initiatives of the government.

6. **Evaluate the impacts on the industry and your company of the anticipated political decisions of the government.** The political risk facing the industry and company in the host country is a critical factor. Assess the nature of the political risk—transfer, operational, ownership? Will the risk be macro or micro? What is the probability of the political risk, and what is the time frame within which it is likely to materialize?

Diligently following the steps outlined above should provide international managers with a fairly good picture of the probability, intensity, and nature of the political risk that their companies are likely to face in the target country. Furthermore, assessing major changes and influences within a host country's political structure will supplement the above analysis.

Changes in Governments

When a host-country government changes, political uncertainty will heighten. For example, the election in February 1999 in Venezuela of President Hugo Chavez brought a government with leftist leanings. The chapter's opening case illustrates the significant risk to foreign companies—especially U.S. foreign direct investment—almost a decade after the election. Furthermore, there continues to be uncertainty in Venezuela caused by ongoing civil strife and drug-related conflicts along the Colombian border. The implications of the current Venezuela political situation parallel past changes in governments such as what happened in the Philippines during the late 1980s and 1990s when President Marcos was deposed and President Aquino's government took control. Subsequently, U.S. business and military interests were put at risk and eventually collapsed under the new regime.

Though not as dramatic, political risk can arise in countries like the United States, Canada, and Australia when governments change. As Stephen Harper's Conservative government recently took power in Canada, as Australian Prime Minister John Howard lost his seat in Parliament in 2007 to a more liberal member of his own party, and as President George Bush leaves office in 2008, all three countries will see various changes in tax, trade, and environmental policies with their new respective governments.

Changes in Party Leaders

Even if a government remains in power in a host country, a change in leadership can trigger political and economic change and subsequent risk to businesses in that country. When Vladimir Putin of Russia took office, there were concerns that Russia could move backward in terms of both economics and political openness. The closing minicase of this chapter discusses planned leadership changes and their possible implications in China and Russia. India has had considerable political stability since its independence from the British in 1947. Still, the economic policies of the government have varied widely and frequently under different leaders, creating considerable political risk for businesses over the years. Current Prime Minister Manmohan Singh has regained some stability for foreign firms investing in India, but there is always the risk that the next leader may revert to less friendly postures toward foreign investors.

Religious Influences on Government

The more a host country does not separate political matters from religious influences, the higher the political risk. Countries such as Pakistan, Iran, and Afghanistan are examples of countries in which strong religious overtures in society not only have influenced government actions but have controlled the political process. The more fundamentalist a country's religion, and the more that religion becomes intertwined in political matters, the more political risk will increase for a firm doing business in that country. Islamic law (as we shall see later in this chapter) prohibits business practices that are taken for granted in most countries of a different persuasion. Banks may not be allowed to charge interest on money loaned to borrowers.

Civil Strife in the Host Country

Civil strife of any kind must have as a precondition relative deprivation, which is the citizens' perceptions of discrepancy between the goods and conditions of the life to which they believe they are justifiably entitled and the amounts of those goods and conditions that they think they are able to get and keep.[28] The citizens' response to perceived deprivation is discontent and anger, which may ultimately find an outlet through aggressive acts. The more intense and widespread deprivation is among the people of a

FIGURE 3.5
Framework for Assessing Civil Strife

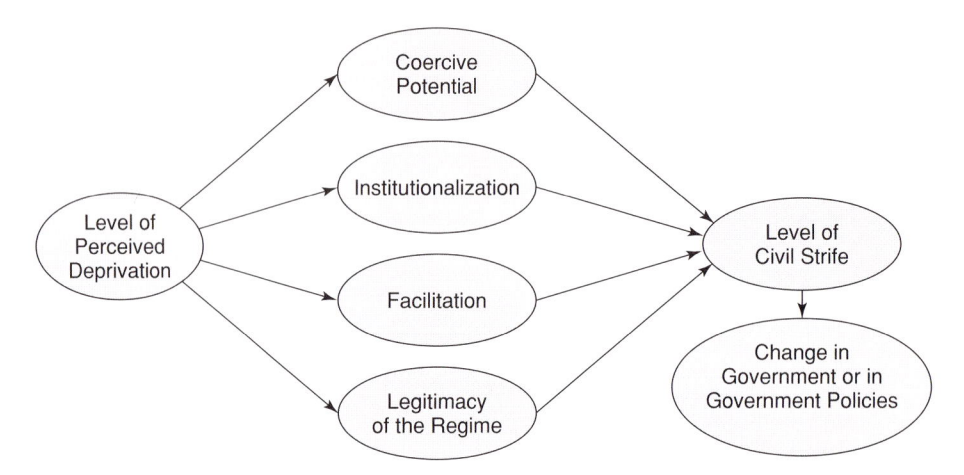

country, the greater is the potential for civil strife. The greater is the level of civil strife, the higher is the probability that there will be a change in the government or significant changes in the government's policies. The political risk inherent in either of these two possible outcomes is that a change could lead to the enactment of policies that are detrimental to a company's operations. Discontent and anger do not necessarily result in civil strife because of the mediating effects of four variables (see Figure 3.5):[29]

1. **Coercive potential.** The government could apply high levels of coercion, which could limit the extent of strife. Also, the more loyal the coercive forces are to the government, the more effective they are in deterring strife. The brutal regime of Saddam Hussein in Iraq is an example of this dimension.

2. **Institutionalization.** This is "the extent to which societal structures beyond the primary level are broad in scope, command substantial resources and/or personnel, and are stable and persisting." Societal structures such as labor unions and political parties serve two purposes. First, they provide alternative means by which the citizens can attain satisfaction. Second, they provide citizens with outlets to channel their dissatisfactions and anger in a nonviolent manner. Therefore, the greater the institutionalization, the lower the magnitude of strife is likely to be. The post–Saddam Hussein chaotic conditions in Iraq exemplify the outcomes caused by the destruction of societal institutions.

3. **Facilitation.** Social and structural conditions in a country might promote the outbreak and persistence of strife. Examples of such conditions are (a) the belief held by the population, partly based on the historical experience of chronic civil strife, that violence is justified as a means of overcoming deprivation; (b) the transportation network and terrain of a country; (c) the presence of organized groups that facilitate social strife; and (d) the extent of foreign assistance to the initiators of strife. The greater the levels of past strife, and of social and structural facilitation, the greater is the magnitude of strife. Vietnam is often cited as a country that personified all of these characteristics, which led to the civil strife and the eventual unification of North and South Vietnam into a single country.

4. **Legitimacy of the regime.** This variable refers to the popularity of the regime. The greater is regime legitimacy at a given level of deprivation, the less the magnitude of consequent strife. There are divergent opinions on whether Fidel Castro was in power for so long because he had earned legitimacy in the eyes of the Cuban people or because of his coercive tactics.

Thus, in assessing the magnitude of civil strife, it is necessary not only to establish the level of perceived deprivation but also to evaluate the *cumulative* impact of the above four mediating variables. Staff groups in multinational companies specializing in political risk forecasting could devise ways of composing indexes to measure the level of deprivation, coercive potential, institutionalization, facilitation, and legitimacy of the regime in a country. These indexes could then be used together to obtain the magnitude of civil strife in the country. Indexes based on uniform parameters could be constructed for various countries and, in turn, facilitate the comparison of potential political risk in two or more countries.

The country of Iran is a good example of how civil strife led to a change of the regime in power—the shah of Iran was replaced by the Ayatollah Khomeini—which eventually resulted in unacceptable risks and the withdrawal of American firms from that country. Other countries in which civil strife has resulted in a change of government include the former republics of the Soviet Union, which have now emerged as independent countries, and South Africa. Civil strife was also one of the factors that led to the breakup of Yugoslavia into several smaller countries.

The Risk of Kidnapping

A new type of risk has emerged and is increasing, particularly in developing countries and countries of the former eastern European Communist bloc, especially Russia. There are examples galore of kidnappings for ransom of senior executives of foreign multinationals. For example, on September 13, 2002, a top executive of Russia's largest oil company, Lukoil, was abducted on his way to the office. The executive, Sergei P. Kukura, 48, first vice president for finance at Lukoil, was riding in a Mercedes from his country home in Vnukova, southwest of Moscow, when masked men carrying Kalashnikov submachine guns stopped the car at a railroad crossing at about 8 A.M., a Lukoil spokesman said. The gunmen handcuffed the driver of the car and Mr. Kukura's bodyguard, and both men were then "injected with a sleep-inducing substance," Lukoil said. The driver and bodyguard awoke in a wooded area outside Moscow late in the afternoon.[30]

It is routine for multinational company executives to ride in bulletproof cars with armed guards, take different routes to work and back, have armed guards protecting homes and family members, and have huge insurance policies purchased by their companies to cover the risk of millions of dollars in ransom payments. Unquestionably, the risk of kidnappings is a risk that companies must manage. As evidenced by the above insight on kidnapping, the individual manager must understand personal risks that arise because of politics, political opinion, and political change. During this first decade of the new millennium, with increased terrorism aimed at Western and industrialized-nation targets throughout the world, the managers of these entities in various countries are advised to rethink their behaviors in the host country. Exhibit 3.1 lists some of these behaviors for U.S. and British workers abroad, especially in the Middle East, south Asia, and Africa.

EXHIBIT 3.1
Staying Safe While Working Overseas

Source: Adapted from "Post 9-11: The View from Abroad," *Computerworld*, April 29, 2002.

- Always remain aware of your surroundings and avoid unusual circumstances.
- Walk with authority and purpose when in public areas.
- Call ahead to notify others of your travel plans or appointments.
- Alternate your routes to work on a regular basis.
- Alternate your timing to and from your work location.
- Avoid wearing American or British flag pins or other insignia in public.
- Speak in the native language where you're working.

A Global Framework for Assessing Political Risk

Up to this point we have focused on the process for evaluating political risk in a particular country. The proposed frameworks for making such an evaluation have assumed that the host country was insulated from forces and events outside the country's political boundaries. However, in the real world of interdependent nation-states such is really not the case, since the political risk faced by a company is caused not only by the events and environmental changes occurring in the host country but also by those occurring in the home country and in the international political system. Figure 3.6 depicts a framework with four basic environments: host country, home country, international environment, and international events. The framework can help the international manager identify the key actors and developments affecting an analysis of political risk.[31]

As has been the case in this chapter, one always first considers the *host country*. Analysis of political risk in the host country may follow the frameworks offered earlier in this chapter, and forecasts of the anticipated probability, degree, and nature of risk faced by the enterprise in the target country can be made by international managers.

However, political risk can originate in environments beyond the host country. For instance, there are many ways in which the *home country* can be the source of political risk to a company's operations in the host country. Policy decisions by the home-country government directed at a particular foreign country can have a serious impact on companies that have business dealings and operations in that country. As an example, the home-country government can place restrictions on technology transfers to the target country, or it may impose economic sanctions on goods exported to and imported from the target country. Companies that do business in the targeted country would be affected by such home-country actions. Thus, the political risk can be sourced not just in the host country; in certain cases, the home country can also become a major source of political risk for an international company. In recent years, the U.S. government has pressured various countries, such as China before its accession to the WTO, because of alleged human rights violations. If the U.S. government imposes trade restrictions on these countries, then U.S. firms that went to those countries to produce at low cost and export products back to America would be penalized.

Another environmental dimension in which political risk can arise is the impact of *international organizations and groups*. This environment consists of third parties beyond the host and home countries: International organizations and groups can also cause repercussions. These groups include Amnesty International, the various Islamic fundamentalist groups that have branches in numerous countries, the WTO,

FIGURE 3.6
The Environments of Political Risk

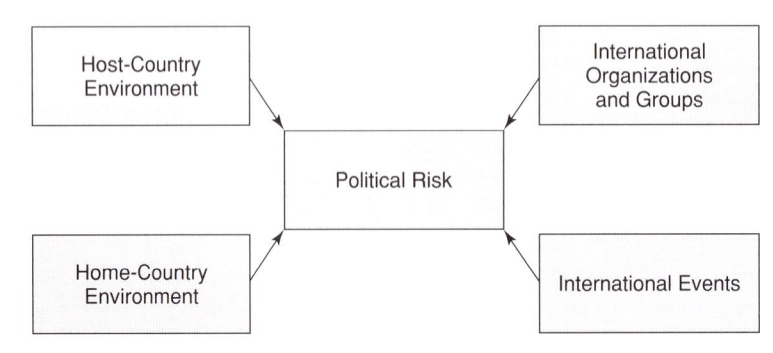

the International Monetary Fund, and the United Nations and its various agencies. International organizations and groups can create political risk for an international company through the influence that they can exert on the political decisions of nation-states. For instance, the United Nations sanctions on trade and investments in South Africa, aimed at bringing down the minority white government in that country, forced countries to pass laws that prohibited trade and investments in that country. Companies such as Polaroid, IBM, and many other large and small companies worldwide had to withdraw from South Africa.

Political risk may originate in major *international events* as well. In this environment, the effects of political risk can transcend the political boundaries of any one country or region. Political risk implications will therefore affect a firm wherever it is in the world. American interests in Kuwait were put at risk in the early 1990s when Iraq invaded Kuwait. Both this conflict and the current conflict in Iraq caused major disruptions in global economic conditions. The price of oil and energy skyrocketed. As a result, manufacturing operations worldwide were hurt by higher fuel costs. The global airline industry suffered from higher operating costs. The threat of global terrorist groups like al-Qaeda, Hamas, and others based in the Philippines, Pakistan, and elsewhere is another example of a third entity that can cause political risk for a home country's investment in a particular host country. American companies and properties have been attacked in Kenya, Somalia, Pakistan, and Saudi Arabia. Financial crises such as the financial and currency-related crisis that hit countries in Southeast Asia, Russia, and Brazil in the late 1990s had repercussions felt not only in the United States but also throughout the world. Similarly, the Argentine financial crisis of 2002 affected debt and borrowing of firms worldwide. Most recently, the subprime crisis in the United States has led to a global borrowing crisis, one that has affected many multinational firms.

Managing International Political Risk

International firms cannot avoid politically risky regions because investments in these markets may provide returns that outweigh the risks.[32] An international manager cannot completely eliminate the risk that arises from changes in the political, economic, and legal environments. However, there are various hedges that the manager and firm can employ to help mitigate this type of risk. Figure 3.7 illustrates a framework that helps understand different postures international managers can take. On one hand, the international firm and manager can proactively hedge against the implications of politically imposed risk through various collaborative and strategic initiatives. The firm can also take a more defensive posture by seeking to protect itself from an expected loss. In each of these postures, the international firm can be directly or indirectly involved, as illustrated in Figure 3.7.

Proactive Hedges

A basic way that international firms shield themselves from politically imposed risks is through the appropriate mode of entry. Equity joint ventures with a host-country firm will help spread risks because the firm will not be responsible for 100 percent of the investment in a given host country. Additionally, a local partner may have closer connections to the key political players, and thus the venture may be politically shielded. Also, when partnering with a host-country organization, an international firm may be further shielded from government interference because the government would, in effect, be also interfering with its own firm or entity. Still, downsides for

FIGURE 3.7
Managing Political, Legal, and Economic Risk

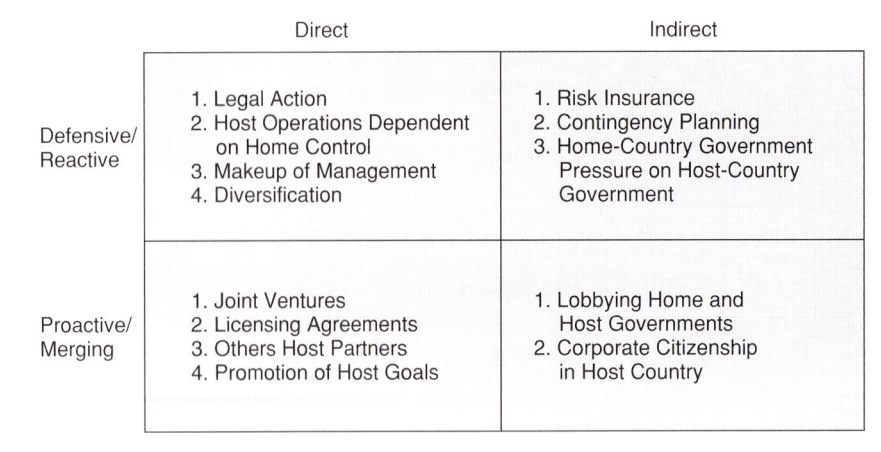

	Direct	Indirect
Defensive/ Reactive	1. Legal Action 2. Host Operations Dependent on Home Control 3. Makeup of Management 4. Diversification	1. Risk Insurance 2. Contingency Planning 3. Home-Country Government Pressure on Host-Country Government
Proactive/ Merging	1. Joint Ventures 2. Licensing Agreements 3. Others Host Partners 4. Promotion of Host Goals	1. Lobbying Home and Host Governments 2. Corporate Citizenship in Host Country

the firm include some loss of control as well as the sharing of potential economic returns. Licensing activities, where the international firm contracts a local firm (rather than investing with it), also help hedge against political risk. However, the firm loses much more control with this entry mode. Joint ventures, licensing activities, and other modes of entry will be reviewed in detail in Chapter 7.

The international firm can form other collaborative relationships in the host country. For instance, linking with a local bank has proved to help protect against political risks. Also, the international firm can proactively promote a host country's goals, including employment, technology transfer, managerial and management skill development, and the establishment of exports and export channels. Bringing both new technology and export channels to the host country will increase the likelihood of technology exports and, subsequently, increase hard currency. During the 1990s, the Malaysia government looked favorably on Nokia's investment there because the Finnish firm brought new technology and the "export promise" to the joint venture.

Indirect proactive actions by the international firm include lobbying activities. In recent years, firms have understood that effective lobbying of both the home and host governments will help to deflect political risk. This can even be done at local levels, as has been seen in the United States. Toyota, Nissan, and Honda have all located in midwest states and have effectively used those states as lobbying springboards to the U.S. government in Washington. Lobbying in international service industries has also been helpful in avoiding political risk. Since 1982, firms from the U.S. telecom industry have continually lobbied both the U.S. and host governments to gain better completion rates for international calling in order to shield themselves from radical political changes in the host countries while also lowering the cost to customers. Thus, even in countries that have undergone political upheaval, including the Philippines, Indonesia, and many African nations, the business of international calling has not been disrupted.

International firms have also realized that being a good citizen of the country helps to deflect political interference. This goes beyond the proactive reinforcement of the country's economic goals and includes the integration of the firm into the local communities. For example, McDonald's (India) has transferred its entire supply chain for lettuce, potatoes, hamburger buns, cheese, and tomatoes to India. It has also transferred knowledge and technology for food processing and horticulture to its Indian suppliers. A strong public relations campaign usually reinforces the social and socially responsible role of the firm as it applies in each host country. Each country will have a different perspective of what indeed is social responsibility and socially responsible behavior at both the organization and individual-manager levels.[1]

Reactive Hedges

From a defensive position, firms hedge against political risk through diversification. That is, they establish operations and sales expectations in many countries rather than relying on one country or region. International business scholars have suggested that diversification among politically risky countries reduces overall political risk.[33] For example, if there is a political/economic problem in one country, operations can be shifted to another country. Also, if the political/economic problem is expected to affect future revenues, the appropriately diversified international firm has other markets to which it can shift its focus. International firms also try to control the makeup of management teams by hiring more locals who understand and have connections with key political players. An extreme defensive political hedge is the use of the host-country, home-country and international legal systems to protect its interests.

Indirectly, a firm can hedge against political risk through insurance. State agencies like the **Overseas Private Investment Corporation (OPIC)** and the Multilateral Investment Guarantee Agency (MIGA) of the World Bank offer U.S. firms low–interest rate funding as well as insurance for operations in many emerging and less developed countries. OPIC has the power of the United States behind it, while MIGA's strength is derived from the World Bank. Both OPIC and MIGA provide up to a few hundred million dollars of political risk insurance for equity protection shields that protect the foreign operations of U.S. companies against currency inconvertibility, expropriation, and political violence for investments and returns with tailored insurance policies. This includes various forms of investments, such as capital, in-kind contributions, and loan guarantees. MIGA provides additional insurance against breach of contract should a corporation's profits be hurt due to changes in the contract that are imposed unilaterally by the host government. OPIC suggests:

> The risks investors face in today's world are not always the same. OPIC recognizes this and is committed to customizing its Political Risk Insurance coverage to meet every client's unique project-specific risks. From large corporate investments valued in millions to those of the U.S. small business entrepreneur and everything in-between, OPIC political risk insurance can be tailored to each individual investor, providing maximum security on their investments.[34]

OPIC premiums vary for different industries and are higher for the industries and initiatives most vulnerable to political risk. As an example, the oil and gas industry function of exploration has higher premiums regarding loss from political violence than those for loss from expropriation, inconvertibility, or interference with operations. However, the industry function of development/production has the highest premiums relating to expropriation. Thus, *political risk is not just country-specific. It is also industry-specific within a country as well as function-specific within an industry.* Practical Insight 3.2 gives various examples of political risks that were protected by OPIC's insurance.

Complementing the insurance against politically imposed risk illustrated in Practical Insight 3.2, international firms have increasingly put into action strategic contingency plans to exit countries that become too politically and economically unstable and set up similar operations in other countries. Many U.S and European oil and gas companies had these plans in place during the late 1990s before Indonesia experienced the political upheaval that it did. Their operations and expatriates were relocated to other Asian nations and Latin America and even consolidated back in their respective home countries. Contingency plans are not seen as being as proactive as a strategy of diversification. Nevertheless, these plans have the diversification mentality that is ready to spring to action.

PRACTICAL INSIGHT 3.2

OPIC HEDGES AGAINST POLITICALLY IMPOSED RISK TO MULTINATIONAL CORPORATIONS

Political Violence

A U.S. company made an investment in a Liberian subsidiary in order to operate a rubber plantation. Due to the Liberian civil war, the subsidiary's property was seized by rebels and then damaged and destroyed by the general military activities. OPIC found the claim to be valid and compensated the investor.

Expropriation

A U.S. investor established a fishing venture in Somalia. After a military coup occurred, the new government began a series of repeated and continuous acts of harassment and interference against the U.S. investor's personnel and operations. For example, the U.S. investor's personnel were repeatedly threatened by military and police officials, arrested and, in one instance, deported from the country. In addition, the Government interfered with the company's operation of its aircraft, which was used to transport the fish, and ordered the company to permit a military observer to accompany all flights. This extra passenger displaced several hundred pounds of seafood products and added substantially to the cost of the company's operations. Viewing these and other government actions together, OPIC found that the Somalian Government had expropriated the investor's project and compensated the investor.

Currency Inconvertibility

A U.S. company made an equity investment in a subsidiary in the Philippines in order to process coconuts. Sixteen years later, the subsidiary declared a dividend of over 9 million Philippine pesos payable to the U.S. parent company. The Central Bank of the Philippines had adopted restrictions on foreign currency so that the subsidiary was unable to pay the dividend in dollars. The U.S. parent company filed an inconvertibility claim with OPIC and was compensated, since the Central Bank restrictions were not in effect when the U.S. parent company originally obtained its insurance.

Source: OPIC Insurance Department, www.opic.gov/Insurance.

Finally, from a defensive position, the international firm can use its home-country government to put pressure on a host government in a country where there is potential political risk. For instance, it was reported that the U.S. government pressured the Indian government to refrain from attacking Pakistan in 2002. This action was initiated by the U.S. government in response to lobbying by companies like IBM, HP, and Microsoft, which have significant operations in India.

Understanding Laws in the International Context

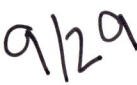

The legal environment is intricately tied to the various political environments discussed earlier in this chapter. As already suggested, a host country's legal environment and associated legal institutions are a critical part of the governance infrastructure that an international firm must confront when expanding overseas.[35] Whereas stable legal environments may lead to greater economic growth within a country,[36] the instability of the same environment will put increased pressure on a manager of an international firm and affect firm-level strategic choices and performance.[37]

An international company is obligated to operate within the boundaries of the international legal environment and, specifically, within the legal precepts that pertain to international business activities. One could conceptualize the legal environment of international business as consisting of three concentric circles, as shown in Figure 3.8. The outer circle includes international *treaties, conventions,* and *custom,* which have been and continue to be the most important sources of international legal rules.[38] The middle circle represents the legal constraints and requirements imposed and incorporated in the laws of nation-states by the overarching *laws of the regional trade blocs* such as the European Union, North American Free Trade Agreement, and

FIGURE 3.8
The Legal Environment of International Business

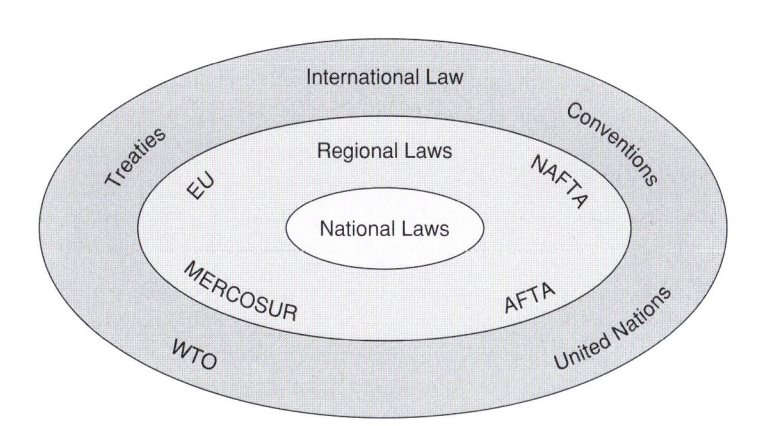

Diagram: Concentric ovals showing International Law (outer, with Treaties, Conventions, NAFTA, AFTA, United Nations, WTO, MERCOSUR), Regional Laws (middle, with EU), and National Laws (inner).

MERCOSUR. The inner circle depicts the laws of nation-states designed to govern the behavior of the nations' citizens and business firms.

To understand the degree to which international law meets the requirements of an effective legal system, we shall examine, first, the concept of law; second, the requirements of an effective legal system; third, the functions of law; and, fourth, the degree to which international law meets the requirements of an effective legal system.

The Concept of Law

Law has three basic characteristics in a civilized society. First, law is a norm that prescribes what is assumed to be a proper mode of behavior. It attempts to regulate the behavior of the subjects according to certain standards set by the society or by those who control the society. Second, law not only prescribes a certain pattern of behavior but also requires that the prescribed mode be followed. We are bound to obey the law because it is the official desire of the society in which we live. Third, law includes a process approved by society for applying coercive sanctions against those who do not obey and therefore perform illegal acts.

The Requirements of an Effective Legal System

Several factors determine the effectiveness of a legal system. First, the people in the society must clearly understand and have knowledge of what the society prescribes as legal behavior. Without this knowledge one could not expect the law to be obeyed. Second, the members of society, the subjects of the legal system, must have agreed that the laws deserve to be obeyed; that is, they must regard the laws as being fair and just. And third, an effective system for punishing illegal behavior must be in place. A number of writers have taken the position that an effective system of sanctions is all that is needed to make a legal system effective and, thus, whether the members of society believe that the law is worthy of obedience is immaterial. The position taken in this book is that both prerequisites must be met before a legal system is deemed effective: the belief and sentiment that the law ought to be obeyed as well as a system for sanctioning illegal behavior.

In a democratic society, the government, which is duly elected by the people, provides the machinery for an effective legal system. The legislative branch of the government makes the laws; and the judicial and executive branches together perform the tasks of identifying illegal behavior and applying sanctions on the lawbreaker. A legal system functions effectively when there is a centralized process, like the government, to make and enforce the laws. The more effective that law enforcement is through the government,

Functions of Law

The principal function of law in a democratic society is to promote law and order with justice. Four functions of law promote this principal function:

1. Law communicates to individuals in a society their rights and duties in their daily interactions with other people in the society. The definition of rights and duties of individuals helps prevent frequent conflicts among members of the society and also provides a basis for the settlement of disputes among them as they occur.
2. Law helps in controlling and preventing behavior that the society considers undesirable.
3. Governments use law to promote the social and economic welfare of society. Examples of such laws are those concerned with child labor, social security, workers' compensation, minimum wage, health care, and food and drugs. Such laws promote law and order indirectly and in the long run, in so far as they help lay a solid foundation for [...]
4. Laws of [...] general beliefs of a society. To [...] the motivation of the members [...]

International Law

Figure 3.8 [...] international firm must be aware. Th[...] the seventeenth century, observers [...] this question: Is international law [...] meet the requirements of an effective [...] international law, if it exists, exists [...] national law is true law if (1) there is [...] world (and, by implication, among the [...] of behaviors by nations and their [...] (2) nations feel obliged to obey the laws, and (3) there is a mechanism for applying sanctions against nations and their citizens if they behave in a manner deemed to be unacceptable according to generally recognized international standards.

The real underlying issue is whether an effective legal system—national or international—can exist without a centralized system, such as a government, that has the legitimacy and power, conferred on it by the subjects, to enact and enforce laws that conform with the values and beliefs of the members of the society who are the subjects of the law.

The Nature of International Law

It is generally accepted that there exists in international law what is known as *illegal conduct*. One is able to establish that illegal conduct has occurred because international law consists of a set of norms prescribing patterns of behavior, although those patterns are often vaguely defined. For example, expropriating the property of a foreign company without just and fair compensation for the property seized is generally considered to be unacceptable by the world community. Similarly, invasion by one

---

Handwritten margin notes:

4 functions

International Law

International Law:
1) General agreement among nations of the world regarding the natures & types of behaviors by nations and their citizens that are acceptable & those that are not
2) nations feel obliged to obey laws
3) There is a mechanism for applying sanctions against nations and their citizens if they behave in a manner deemed to be unacceptable according to generally recognized international standards.

country of another country merely to expand the latter's national boundaries is viewed as illegal aggression under international law.

Moreover, in the past, as well as today, certain norms and reasons have obliged states to obey the law. The reasons are usually generated internally rather than from a central source, but they nonetheless exist in a subtle and often unarticulated form.

Finally, a system of sanctions in international law contributes to the coercive enforcement of the law. For instance, Iraq's invasion of Kuwait led to the Gulf War in which a U.N. multinational force was involved in ousting the Iraqis from Kuwaiti soil. The United Nations enforced the international law enshrined in the principle that it is illegal for a nation to invade and seize the land and property of another sovereign nation. However, the United Nations is far from being a world government. The United Nations is in a position to take positive action against "lawbreaker" states only if all countries that are the permanent members of the Security Council agree to not cast a veto against it. Since there is no world government in the true sense of the term, the system of sanctions in international law is not controlled by a centralized force but is primarily administered according to the principle of self-help.

Therefore, at least in terms of the criteria employed in discussing law in democratic societies, international law can be defined as law. However, due to the absence of a single formal supranational institution with the authority delegated to it by the various countries to enact laws, and to force compliance by the countries and their citizens to the laws through enforceable sanctions, international law remains a decentralized or unsophisticated system of law.

The Role of the World Court and the WTO

The International Court of Justice (the World Court) in the Hague, Holland, is the principal judicial organ of the United Nations. It is often mistakenly presumed to have the authority to adjudicate commercial disputes between companies and citizens of different countries and to have the power to enforce its decrees. There are three scenarios under which disputes could arise: (1) between two countries; (2) between a country and a company; and (3) between two companies. The International Court of Justice can adjudicate disputes between two countries only when *both* governments involved agree to submit to its authority. This limits the scope of this world judicial body. Disputes between a country and a company, or between two companies, can be settled in the courts of one of the parties to the dispute or through arbitration.

The WTO has a dispute settlement system. When there is a dispute between two countries or trade blocs, the director general of the WTO appoints a panel of experts to examine the dispute and then make its decision, which is binding unless overturned by consensus of the WTO membership. Under the WTO process, the country or trade bloc that wins a case before the WTO receives an automatic approval to undertake retaliatory measures against the offending country if that country does not change its practices. The country that is found guilty of violating fair-trade rules has two choices: It can change its law or face sanctions, most likely in the form of tariffs slapped on its exports by the complaining country. Thus, even in this case, the winner of the case must take punitive actions by itself against the offending country or trade bloc. If the offending country is an economically powerful country like the United States or Japan, and hence could absorb the punitive actions imposed on it without much harm to its economy, then there is not much that the aggrieved party can do about it. Thus, international managers must realize that no centralized judicial body exists to resolve commercial disputes between citizens and companies of different countries.

We shall next examine how international law is created and the role that custom and treaties play in this process.

International Law and the Risk of Intellectual Property Theft

International Law Creation

International law derives from four acknowledged sources that are recognized in the statutes of the International Court of Justice and taught in every international law course.[40] These sources, depicted in Figure 3.9, include:

- International treaties and conventions, whether general or particular, establishing rules expressly recognized by the contesting states.
- International customs, as evidence of a general practice accepted as law.
- General principles of law recognized by civilized nations.
- Judicial decisions and the teachings of the most highly qualified publicists of the various nations.

Today, these four main sources—treaties, customs, general principles of law, and judicial decisions/teachings of publicists—do not stand in isolation.[41] While the two preeminent sources, treaty and custom, certainly are the clearest and most frequently used, often all four work as an interrelated system to develop international law.[42]

International Custom

Historically, when international interactions were sporadic and less complex, custom was the primary source of international law. Under such conditions, habitual patterns of behavior that had evolved over a number of years often reached the level of obligatory rules, that is, international law, which governed how nations and their subjects interacted with one another. Customary international law must meet two requirements: habituality and a feeling of legal obligation. A rule of customary international law comes into existence when almost all states behave almost exactly the same way for a long time and feel a legal obligation to do so. Thus, the essential elements of international custom include:

1. Concordant practice by a number of states regarding the type of situation falling within the domain of international relations.
2. Continuation and repetition of the practice over a considerable period of time.
3. Conception that the practice is consistent with prevailing international law.
4. General acquiescence in the practice by other states.[43]

Even though it is important to understand that individual countries control the creation and legitimization of international customary law, custom in the form of unwritten but clearly understood norms has diminished as a source of international law

FIGURE 3.9
Sources of International Law

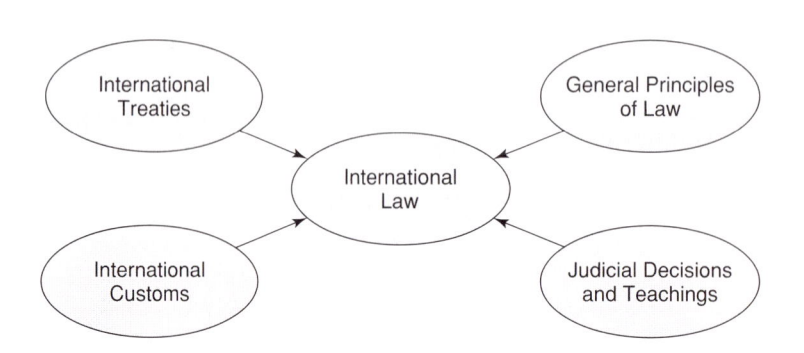

because of the increasing interdependence and complexity of the modern world and the expansion of the international legal system beyond the confines of the "Western world." Thus, we focus next on international treaties and conventions.

International Treaties and Conventions

The working definition of an international treaty was provided in the 1969 Vienna Convention on the Law of Treaties. It defined the **international treaty** as an international agreement concluded between states in written form and governed by international law.[44] A treaty is an agreement entered into by two or more states under general international law. If only two states are the contracting parties, it is called a *bilateral* treaty. A *multilateral* treaty is one in which more than two states are contracting parties. Sometimes a treaty is called an international *convention,* an *agreement,* a *protocol,* or a *declaration.* In most cases the title is not important. However, in the United States a distinction is made between a "treaty" and an "agreement." The U.S. Constitution stipulates that treaties are international agreements made by the president of the United States "by and with the advice of the Senate." The so-called executive agreements are treaties entered into by the president, or with his authorization by someone else, without consultation with the Senate.

A treaty, like a contract, is a legal transaction by which the contracting parties intend to establish mutual obligations and rights. Countries that have signed the treaty are legally obliged and correspondingly entitled to behave as they have declared that they will behave. Therefore, if they do not behave in conformity with the contract or treaty, they are exposed to sanctions and punishment. A treaty becomes incorporated into the laws of a nation when the nation's legislative body ratifies it. For example, in the United States, a two-thirds majority in the Senate must ratify a treaty.

Even though treaties are considered the major source of international law, one must be careful in taking such a statement too literally. The thousands of treaties concluded among nations do not create one single general rule of international law. For instance, a commercial treaty between the United States and China, or a treaty to prevent double taxation between France and Morocco, does not create any rule of conduct for the family of nations. However, so-called *lawmaking treaties,* which are concluded among a number of countries in their joint interest, are intended to create a new rule. When a treaty is ratified by many nations, it creates general norms that regulate the mutual conduct among the signatory countries. A lawmaking treaty, then, is a means by which a substantial number of countries reach an agreement about a particular rule of law. It may promote new general rules for the future conduct of the member countries. A lawmaking treaty may also cause an existing customary or conventional rule of law to be modified, abolished, or codified. It may, as well, lead to the creation of a new international agency. The International Labor Organization is an example of an international agency that was created by a multilateral treaty signed by almost all nations to protect the health, safety, and working hours of workers and to prevent the abuse of child labor. It is through this kind of treaty that conventional international law is created.

Examples of Commercial Treaties

Treaties of Friendship, Commerce, and Navigation

Many different types of treaties are in force that govern the behavior of nations and, in turn, their citizens, such as the Law of the Sea, military alliances like NATO, and treaties that govern global aviation and navigation. Certain treaties are of particular significance to business enterprises. For instance, the various treaties regarding friendship, commerce, and navigation (FCN) apply to an international company doing business in another country. This is seen not as a right but as a privilege. Subsequently, this privilege and its conditions are negotiated between the host-country government and the home-country government. The United States has treaties with several dozen nations that formulate the conditions of the privilege under which American firms may do business in these nations, and vice versa. They usually include, among other things, reciprocal pledges by each of the signatory countries to honor the property of the other country's companies located within their respective national borders and to give the other country's companies *national treatment,* meaning treatment that is no less favorable than that which is given to business firms that are its own citizens. Also included are guarantees that property will not be seized illegally and without proper compensation. Most treaties include in them the *most-favored-nation (MFN)* treatment clause. The MFN clause obligates the country to give to the imports of goods from the other country, with which it has signed a treaty, tariff treatment that is no less favorable than that given to imports from third countries.

FCN laws continue to be a current international business issue. For example, as Japanese firms have increasingly expanded into the United States during the past two decades, problems have developed between U.S. employees and Japanese employees in the United States. Because many Japanese companies limited senior management positions to Japanese expatriates, many discrimination claims were filed. Under the FCN laws between the United States and Japan (JFCN), Article VIII provides that U.S. companies in Japan and Japanese companies in the United States can fill certain positions without restriction. In effect, Article VIII appears to exempt certain companies from complying with antidiscrimination laws in certain employment circumstances. Thus, a central issue of conflict lies between the JFCN treaty and antidiscrimination laws of the United States.[45] Furthermore, the foreign companies' placing of expatriates of choice in host countries has been found to have national security implications for the hosts.[46]

Treaties for the Protection of Intellectual Property Rights

Of particular significance today for an international company is the protection of its proprietary property or intellectual capital. While many countries have officially signed the various treaties governing the protection of intellectual property, there is still the serious problem of enforcing the treaties' provisions. A very serious problem facing American industry and therefore America itself is the theft of intellectual property—ideas and innovations protected by copyright, patents, and trademarks—due to the absence of effective domestic legislation in other countries for the protection of intellectual property.

When blockbuster movies such as the three movies comprising the *Spiderman* trilogy were released from 2002 to 2007 in theaters in the United States, they had already been available on DVD in Shanghai, Beijing, and Bangkok at the price of U.S. $1. Likewise, a new Tom Clancy novel or Tom Friedman book may be obtained in paperback in Bombay, Hong Kong, and even Singapore before its U.S. hardback release. Many "entrepreneurs" throughout the world illegally copy or even create music CDs for sale. There have been ongoing but unsuccessful attempts to protect authors' and performers' international rights, as seen in the passage below:

> In December 2000, efforts to sign a global treaty for the protection of performers' rights in audiovisual works failed because of a disagreement between the United States and the European Union over the issue of transferring rights from performers to producers. Now, WIPO is trying again. WIPO hopes to restart negotiations and has announced that it will schedule an informal conference for early 2003.

In 2000, WIPO members reached an agreement on 19 of the draft treaty's 20 articles, recognizing for the first time audiovisual performers' moral rights against any distribution and/or modification of their work that would somehow prejudice their reputations. The EU has long advocated for language that would require the permission of the authors or performers themselves before allowing a transfer of rights to producers. This is already the law in several EU nations.

The United States, however, takes a different view. U.S. officials insisted on the recognition of existing contractual arrangements that allow for the automatic transfer of rights from performers to producers. As a result, they wanted a performer's "entitlement" to exclusive rights based on consent to be governed by the law of the country most closely related to the parties or the agreement. Thus, if U.S. law applied, consent would not be necessary. The European Union refused, claiming that such a provision would effectively impose U.S. law on other countries. How this issue will be resolved remains to be seen.[47]

Beyond the obvious concerns for the music, cinema, and publishing industries, the concern of protecting intellectual property has reached new heights regarding software and high technology. It has become increasingly important for international companies with new technologies to develop (1) mechanisms that protect against illegal pirating of their intellectual property and (2) patent programs that protect their inventions throughout the international market. In fact, companies that remain ignorant of foreign patent procedures and apply for patents in the traditional, one-nation manner can inadvertently destroy their opportunities to obtain foreign patents.

U.S. patents give rights only within the United States. The same rule applies to patents granted in foreign countries. In order to protect its foreign patent rights, a company's patent strategy and business practices must accommodate foreign rules and deadlines, making sophisticated use of complex national, regional, and global patent application strategies. To obtain patent protection in a foreign country or region, companies must ultimately obtain a patent from the appropriate foreign patent office, and the patent must be enforced in that country's or region's courts. By following proper procedures, international companies can achieve these goals.

In the United States, utility patents (patents for "any new and useful process, machine, manufacture, or composition of matter") are distinguished from design patents. Within different industries, these patents have different practical lives depending on the ease with which the patent can be extended. As an example, in 2002, extending patents in the U.S. pharmaceutical industry was made more difficult, thus allowing generic drugs easier entry into the market. A further complicating factor is that the life of various types of patents can be very different from country to country. Also, there is the distinction between a patent system based on a *first-to-invent* standard and one based on a *first-to-file* standard. When two or more independent inventors file overlapping patent applications, a rule must be applied to determine which one will be granted the patent. Under the *first-to-invent* rule, an inventor who can prove that she was the first to invent a device and diligently pursue its development will obtain the patent rights. In countries using the *first-to-file* rule, the first party to file a patent application in a given jurisdiction is awarded the patent.

International patent protection has steadily increased for international firms. There have been ongoing efforts to secure a new global patent system for firms operating internationally.[48] Major changes finally occurred in 2002 as exemplified in the passage below:

WIPO members agreed to procedural changes to the Patent Cooperation Treaty (PCT) at the annual meeting of the WIPO General Assemblies held September 23 to October 21, 2002. The changes are intended to streamline and simplify the system for filing patents under the PCT. Included among the changes is a single flat fee for applications. Additionally, WIPO adopted changes relating to the language in which applications must be filed, the restatement of rights after failing to comply with filing requirements, and the availability of priority documents from digital libraries. These additional changes were made in order to bring the PCT into compliance with the Patent Law Treaty that was finalized in 2002.

Another change decreased the filing fees for electronic filings under the PCT by 200 Swiss francs (approximately $135). Filing fees are reduced by 75 percent for applications that originate from developing countries. The new discount took effect on October 17, 2002, and reflected the sixth consecutive year that fees have decreased. The General Assemblies also instituted changes in regard to preliminary reports used by applicants to determine whether to proceed in seeking patent protection. Under current rules, the international phase begins with Chapter I proceedings, in which a report is prepared by an International Searching Authority (ISA) as to the patentability of the claimed invention. Then, in a separate procedure, an applicant may choose a preliminary examination report under Chapter II of the process, which involves a more extensive preliminary and non-binding opinion as to the patentability of the invention. These reports are used by the applicant to determine whether to continue to seek patent protection at the national level.

Under new procedures promulgated by WIPO, the ISA will now be responsible for drafting a report on whether an invention appears to be novel, involves an inventive step, and appears to be industrially applicable. According to WIPO, this change allows for the combination of "the international search and international preliminary examination procedures to a much greater extent than is the case at present." These changes were instituted because many applicants are forced to proceed without the benefit of a Chapter II report because of the 30-month time limit to begin the national phase.[49]

Other types of intellectual property include trademarks, copyrights, and processes. Combined company losses resulting from the piracy of these proprietary properties have skyrocketed to billions of U.S. dollars. The potential piracy of a trademark, copyright, or manufacturing process represents a significant risk for the international company as well as a potential loss of worldwide competitive positioning. Historically, many treaties have attempted to limit piracy of proprietary property. For instance, under the Trademark Law Revision Act of 1988, federal registrations of trademarks and service marks in the United States have a renewable term of 10 years (formerly 20 years), provided that the mark is in use in interstate commerce and a specimen proving use is provided to the Patent and Trademark Office. Also, the Paris Convention for the Protection of Industrial Property was established as an international convention to protect trademarks. The Berne Convention for the Protection of Literary and Artistic Works was multilaterally instituted to protect copyright infringement around the world. Still, the piracy of a company's intellectual property continues to grow exponentially.

One of the newest intellectual property treaties is the **Madrid Protocol.** Signed into law by U.S. President Bush in November 2002, this treaty provides an international system for registering trademarks. It is administered by the World Intellectual Property Organization (WIPO). It is important for firms to realize that the Madrid Protocol does not replace any one country's trademark registration system. Instead, it allows a trademark owner to file a single application, called a *basic registration,* in his home country and then designate extension of the application or registration to some or all of the member countries at a reduced fee.[50] As a result of the United States joining this treaty, its businesses will have the means to accomplish the closest thing to international trademark registration. This is a key element to success in today's evolving global marketplace. That is, businesses must be able to protect their

TABLE 3.2
The 2002 Madrid Protocol: Implications for U.S. Firms Registering International Trademarks

Advantages to U.S. Firms	Disadvantages to U.S. Firms
Less expensive	Fewer international rights
Simpler	Linked to valid U.S. registration
Less need for foreign counsel	Trademark must be used in U.S.
Quicker	Broader foreign definitions

identities throughout the world in order to maintain sustainable competitive advantages.[51] International firms obtain some distinct benefits from the Madrid Protocol. Still, there are a few drawbacks, as depicted in Table 3.2, which highlights the implications for U.S. firms.

The Madrid Protocol is a simple and inexpensive option for securing international trademark protection. The trademark applicant may forgo the hiring of foreign attorneys in each country where trademark protection is sought. Furthermore, international firms are not required to file national applications, to deal with translations from and into foreign languages, and to administer a trademark portfolio on a country-by-country basis. Also, because international applications must be acted on within 12 to 18 months, the application process is now quicker than it had been in countries where examination used to take three or four years (e.g., India). Still, there are potential drawbacks. The Madrid Protocol may offer fewer rights to U.S. companies. For instance, because the international registration depends on the original U.S. application, international protection will be canceled if the mark is not registered in the United States, even if it is able to be registered overseas. The entire application will fail if the U.S. firm has not used the mark at home within three years of allowance. Another potential drawback involves U.S. and foreign-based definitions. U.S. law requires a narrowly defined specification of goods and services, whereas many foreign laws allow much broader definitions. Under the Madrid Protocol, a U.S. applicant's international registration would be limited to the narrow U.S. description. While the Madrid Protocol will make it easier for U.S. applicants to achieve registrations abroad, it also will make it easier for foreign applicants to obtain rights in the United States, making the U.S. register even more crowded and increasing the risk that a U.S. firm will be forced to contend with conflicting trademarks owned by foreign entities.[52]

From counterfeit Rolex watches on Canal Street in Manhattan to modern software factories in Asia to the automotive industry in China (described in Practical Insight 3.3), international companies stand to lose from piracy of intellectual property in a number of ways. These include:

1. The international company loses sales in the copycat country itself as it is forced to compete against pirated products.
2. It loses sales in third countries where it has to compete against exported pirated products.
3. Its reputation as a producer of quality products and service suffers because pirated products of inferior quality are quite often sold under the company's brand name (e.g., Polo, Ralph Lauren, Rolex, Gucci, Microsoft, Zantac).
4. It may be prevented entry into a foreign market because a company in the foreign market may have established a dominant market share using the international company's pirated technology or trademark.

PRACTICAL INSIGHT 3.3

DID SPARK SPARK A COPYCAT?

It's close to noon on a sunny January day, and the Chery dealership at the Asian Games Village car market in north Beijing is bustling. That's because the price of the popular Chery QQ minicar was just slashed by as much as $725, to a highly affordable $3,600. "The best thing is the low price," says one customer preparing to buy a gray QQ, which he says has "a fashionable shape." General Motors Corp. execs would agree with that—which is why they're apoplectic. GM Daewoo Auto & Technology Corp., the Korean subsidiary of GM, says the QQ is a knockoff of its own Matiz minicar, sold in China as the Chevrolet Spark since 2003. "The cars are more than similar," says Rob Leggat, vice-president for corporate affairs at GM Daewoo. "It really approaches being an exact copy." Same cute, snubby nose. Same bug-eyed headlights. Same rounded, high back. And most components in the QQ, Leggat says, can easily be interchanged with parts on the Spark. So on Dec. 16, GM Daewoo filed suit in a Shanghai court alleging that Chery Automotive stole its trade secrets to make the QQ. Chery declined to comment.

This is not the first time a foreign auto maker has felt ripped off in China. In 2003, Toyota Motor Corp. sued Hangzhou-based Geely Group Co. for copying the Japanese company's logo and slapping it on Geely models. Toyota lost the case. Yet Honda Motor Co. in December won a ruling that bars Chongqing Lifan Industrial from selling motorcycles under the "Hongda" brand. Honda is also suing Shuanghuan Automobile Co., saying the Chinese company's Laibao SRV is a copy of the Honda CR-V sport-utility vehicle. "Chinese car companies still have limited [design] capabilities," says Jia Xinguang, an analyst at China National Automotive Industry Consulting & Developing Corp., a consultancy. "That is why so many [of them] copy bigger car companies' models."

Some, though, believe China will need to clean up its act on intellectual property if Chery and other auto makers hope to be successful overseas. "Intellectual-property rights violations will be a major impediment to the aspirations" of Chinese car companies looking to export, says Charlene Barshefsky, former U.S. Trade Representative and now a Washington attorney.

Chery already has global ambitions. Last year the company exported 8,000 vehicles to Cuba, Malaysia, and elsewhere and started assembling cars in Iran. In January, Chery announced plans to export five models, ranging from a compact sedan to an SUV, to the U.S. by 2007—though the QQ isn't part of the mix.

At home, the QQ is Chery's mainstay. The model made up 57% of the 87,000 cars it sold in China last year—outselling the Chevy Spark nearly five to one, according to researcher CSM Asia. And sales show no sign of slowing. In the first three weeks of January, the Asian Games dealership sold 118 QQs, says manager Zhang Ying, noting that the model costs about $1,000 less than the Spark after the recent discount. With such a price gap, it's unlikely that the Spark will outsell the QQ anytime soon. So GM had better hope it outmaneuvers Chery in court.

Source: Dexter Roberts, *BusinessWeek,* February 7, 2005, p. 64.

Laws of Regional Trade Blocs

As alluded to in Chapter 2, the various regional economic agreements have laws that pertain to doing business in each of those pacts, regardless of whether the firm originates from one of the countries in the cooperative or does not. For instance, new standards for different industries now apply to all locations within the European Union. There are many categories of these laws. Some of the more prominent include laws regarding:

- Agriculture
- Competition
- Consumer protection
- Education and training
- Environmental protection
- Food safety
- Fraud

- Internet marketing
- Public health
- Research and innovation
- Taxation

As an example, environmental laws within the EU apply to every firm operating in the member countries and state:

> Damage to the environment has been growing steadily worse in recent decades. Every year, some 2 billion tons of waste are produced in the Member States and this figure is rising by 10% annually, while CO_2 emissions from our homes and vehicles are increasing, as is our consumption of "dirty" energy. The quality of life for people living in Europe, especially in urban areas, has declined considerably because of pollution, noise and vandalism.
>
> Protection of the environment is therefore one of the major challenges facing Europe. The European Community has been strongly criticized for putting trade and economic development before environmental considerations. It is now recognized that the European model of development cannot be based on the depletion of natural resources and the deterioration of our environment.
>
> Environmental action by the Community began in 1972 with four successive action programs, based on a vertical and sectoral approach to ecological problems. During this period, the Community adopted some 200 pieces of legislation, chiefly concerned with limiting pollution by introducing minimum standards, notably for waste management, water pollution and air pollution. The introduction of this legislative framework, however, could not of itself prevent deterioration of the environment, and with the growth in public awareness of the risks posed by global environmental problems it has become clear that concerted action at European and international levels is absolutely essential.
>
> Community action developed over the years until the Treaty on European Union conferred on it the status of a policy. A further step was taken with the *Treaty of Amsterdam*, which enshrines the principle of sustainable development as one of the European Community's aims and makes a high degree of environmental protection one of its absolute priorities.
>
> To set about achieving this as effectively as possible, the *Fifth Community Action Programme on the Environment* "Towards Sustainability" established the principles of a European strategy of voluntary action for the period 1992–2000 and marked the beginning of a "horizontal" Community approach which would take account of all the causes of pollution (industry, energy, tourism, transport, agriculture, etc.).
>
> This across-the-board approach to environmental policy was confirmed by the Commission in the wake of its 1998 Communication on *integrating the environment into European Union policies* and by the Vienna European Council (11 and 12 December 1998). The Community institutions are now obliged to take account of environmental considerations in all their other policies. Since then, this obligation has been taken into account in various Community acts, particularly in the fields of employment, energy, agriculture, development cooperation, single market, industry, fisheries, economic policy and transport.
>
> A communication on the *European strategy for sustainable development* was approved in May 2001. It sets out the long-term objectives for sustainable development and essentially concerns climate change, transport, health and natural resources. The need for Community action on liability for damage caused to the environment and on making good such damage has been gaining ground since the adoption of the White Paper on *environmental liability* in February 2000.
>
> The *sixth action program for the environment,* which is currently being adopted, sets out the priorities for the European Community up to 2010. Four areas are highlighted: climate change, nature and biodiversity, environment and health and the management of

natural resources and waste. Measures to achieve these priorities are outlined: improving the application of environmental legislation, working together with the market and citizens and ensuring that other Community policies take greater account of environmental considerations. An innovation which is worth mentioning is the integrated product policy. This aims to develop a more ecological product market by making products more environmentally sustainable throughout their life cycle.[53]

Laws of Nation-States

Now we move to the inner concentric circle in Figure 3.8—the laws of nation-states, or country laws. In conjunction with international law (created through treaties and conventions) and regional trade bloc laws, country laws shape the legal environment of international business with which international firms must comply. We live in a world of sovereign states. Scholars have historically classified numerous countries according to the origin of their commercial or corporate legal codes. These classifications include:

- English common law.
- Civil law of French, German, or Scandinavian origin.
- Socialist law, based on Communist principles.[54]

A disadvantage of this system is that it classifies all formerly Communist countries in the last category and so possibly combines the role of legal systems with other factors. Still, these classifications may be initially used to clarify that there are distinctions in the legal systems of various host countries.[55] The system also fails to explicitly recognize Islamic law. We explore the implications of Islamic law below.

Sovereignty grants each independent nation the supreme authority to legislate laws meant to govern those within its jurisdiction. Although a country is obligated to obey the provisions and code of conduct of any international treaty or agreement to which it is party, it still retains the right to make its own laws. The international legal framework as it exists today consists of an umbrella of international law embracing various treaties and regional trade bloc law, under which are the separate national laws of independent nations.

An international company has to live within this global legal framework. It must comprehend international law, as well as national laws of countries in which it has subsidiaries; and it must understand how international law and national laws affect the different subsidiaries individually as well as collectively. This can be quite a problem because not only are the legal systems of countries continuously evolving and changing but quite often the laws of two or more countries might be in conflict. Additionally, international companies must be knowledgeable of not only the treaties that the home country has with other countries but also the treaties that the host country has with third countries. This is because the foreign subsidiaries must obey the national laws and treaty obligations of both the home and host countries.

Common Law and Civil Law

The legal systems of different countries can be grouped into two main categories—common law and civil law. **Common law** is a set of legal principles that has emerged from the feudal law of medieval England. **Civil law,** often referred to as *code law* or *Roman law,* has its roots in the legal system of the Roman Empire. Civil law was compiled initially by Napoleon Bonaparte. The legal systems of English-speaking countries, such as England, Canada, the United States, and Australia, and of the former British colonies, such as India, Pakistan, Nigeria, Kenya, and Jamaica, are based on common law. Nations of continental Europe, such as France, Spain, and Italy, and their former colonies base their legal systems on civil law.

What are the major differences between common law and civil law? Common law is based on tradition and legal precedents formulated by past court rulings, statutes, and government decrees. Included in common law, therefore, are sets of legal precepts that have gradually evolved over a number of years. The bases for common law, then, are past practices and precedents. Under civil law, one finds a comprehensive set of written codes or rules of law, which have been stated in general terms. These codes are then applied to specific cases as they arise because civil law recognizes that business problems are often unique and consequently need special status under the law. Therefore, civil law provides a separate code to handle commercial problems. There is no such commercial code specially designed for business under common law, although there is one set of codes that is applied to either civil or commercial disputes. International companies must understand the differences in the natures of these two systems because the due process of law may differ considerably between civil law and common law countries.

Islamic Law

As major Islamic countries such as Indonesia, Saudi Arabia, and Malaysia have become more prominent regarding international business activity, legal issues unique to the Islamic world arise. The *Koran,* the holiest of all holy books in Islam, is the basis for the legal system and the nature of laws in most countries that have a majority of the population belonging to the Islamic faith. **Islamic law** *(Shari'ah)* is the interpretation of the Koran. The word *Islam* means "submission" (i.e., to the will of God), and the word *Muslim* means "one who submits."[56] There are differences in the extent to which Islamic precepts govern the laws of the various predominantly Muslim countries in the world. For example, by far the strictest Islamic country in the world is Saudi Arabia, which has the holy Koran as its constitution. This means that all laws in Saudi Arabia, whether civil or criminal, must reflect the principles enunciated in the Koran. Pakistan is another country that has declared itself an Islamic republic and therefore professes to legislate according to Islamic precepts.

At the core of Islamic thinking is the right of every man or woman, Muslim or non-Muslim, to own property. Similarly, the importance of business and trade is recognized. The prophet Muhammad was himself a businessman.[57] Islam forbids "excessive" profit, which is considered to be a form of exploitation. Islam preaches moderation and a sharing of wealth with others less fortunate, so individuals are held accountable for the well-being of the community. The concept of sharing of wealth is manifested in the *zakat,* which is an annual individual tax used for the benefit of the community. Islam also forbids usury or interest. The Islamic law of contracts requires that any transaction must be free of *riba,* defined as the unlawful advantage by way of excess of deferment (i.e., usury or interest). To Western economists an interest rate should reflect, among other things, "pure time preference"—that is, the notion that consumption today is worth more than consumption tomorrow. The interest that is charged by the lender is meant to be a reward for forgone consumption. However, Islamic scholars argue that this justification for charging interest implies that mere hoarding of cash in a safe deposit box at home also deserves an economic reward because it too reflects forgone consumption. Moreover, an economic reward becomes available for distribution only if consumption forgone is translated into investment that yields a real economic return, that is, creates wealth. While Islamic scholars would agree with Western economists that lenders are entitled to have their fair share (in the form of interest) of any such return, they argue that this should be only to the extent that the lenders help to create wealth. This means that lenders must accept a share of the risk. Islamic contract law is very strict in its application of the concept that risks should be shared. It insists that wherever there is uncertainty, contracts that assure one party of a fixed return (interest), even though no wealth was created, are not permitted.[58]

Banks in fundamentalist Islamic nations have banking systems that follow, at least in part, Islamic principles. Some circumvent the prohibition against making interest-bearing loans by buying some of the borrower's stock and selling it back to the company at a higher price. The size of the markup is determined by the riskiness of the venture and the amount and maturity period of the loan. This loan-granting tactic is no different from the traditional criteria used in determining interest rates.[59] This practice is not approved of by strict fundamentalists. Alternatively, banks may buy equity in the venture being financed and share profits as well as losses in the joint ventures.

A variety of partnership agreements allow lending without interest. Schemes such as *mudarabha* and *musharaka* have been designed to allow banks to receive a contractual share of the profits generated by the borrowing firms. Under the mudarabha arrangement, the bank supplies capital to a client and in return the bank gets a percentage of the client's net profits every year until the loan is repaid. The bank's share of the profits serves to repay the principal and provide a profit for the bank that is passed on to its depositors. If the client does not make a profit, the bank, its depositors, and the borrower jointly absorb the loss, thereby putting into practice the Islamic principle that both lenders and borrowers should share in the risks and rewards of an investment. A musharaka contract is similar to the Western concept of a limited partnership. The bank and the client both share the equity capital, and sometimes even the managerial and technical expertise, of the investment project. Both the bank and the client share the profits or losses of the project according to a previously negotiated ratio. Such practices for making loans in the face of the Islamic prohibition of interest-bearing loans are examples of how the strict principles of Islamic law can be harmonized with the laws of non-Islamic legal systems.[60] Practical Insight 3.4 explores Islamic law.

The acceptance of Islamic banking has been mixed. People have the choice of opting for Islamic or traditional banking. Because international companies mostly conduct business with international banks that do not follow practices based on Islamic banking precepts, banks in Islamic countries have two options on introduction of Islamic banking. They can establish a full-fledged subsidiary for Islamic banking or open special windows for Islamic banking at their branches. Nowhere in the Islamic world is the Islamic banking system enforced in totality. Partial Islamic banking is in vogue in 75 countries, including Pakistan, Saudi Arabia, Iran, Kuwait, Malaysia, and Indonesia, but the total volume of deposits governed by the system is not more than $200 billion, which is far less than the amount in conventional banking. International companies generally do not conduct business with customers in Islamic countries with Islamic banks. However, international banks could take the opportunity afforded by Islamic banking though subsidiaries or divisions that function on Islamic banking principles. HSBC, Chase Manhattan, Citicorp, ABN Amro, Grindlays, Kilienwont Benson, Union Bank, and Australian Girozentale Bank have introduced Islamic banking alongside their extant, much larger, traditional banking systems.[61]

PRACTICAL INSIGHT 3.4

PROFIT AND THE PROPHET: INDONESIAN BANK OFFERS NO-INTEREST SERVICES

Bank Muamalat Indonesia (BMI), Indonesia's first Islamic bank, met with a mixed reaction when it opened its doors for business on 1 May. While many Islamic groups welcomed the new institution, saying it would draw new funds into the banking system, bankers criticized it as being too risky, and political analysts labeled it a thinly veiled attempt by the government to woo Muslim support. The financial sector in Indonesia, home to the world's largest Muslim community, has risen sharply in the past five years, with funds in the system increasing by more than 200% in 1987–91. Supporters believe BMI will attract business from those Muslims who object to placing their money in banks that violate the Islamic proscription on charging interest on loans.

The principle of Islamic banking is founded on a verse in the Koran in which the Prophet Mohammad forbids the practice of usury. "Usury and interest are synonymous in Islamic terminology," Seyed Ali Asghar Hedayati, a faculty member at the Iran Institute of Banking, said at a Jakarta symposium in October. While a more moderate interpretation defines usury as excessively high rates of interest, BMI subscribes to the stricter view. The issue is sensitive in Indonesia because the existence of one Islamic bank suggests that conventional banks are violating Muslim teachings. "BMI is an alternative for Muslims," says the bank's managing director, Maman Natapermadi. "If they switch to us, then Allah will forgive them (for banking at conventional banks). If they don't switch, they run the risk of (Allah's) punishment."

An Islamic bank works on a profit-sharing principle. Depositors, treated as investors, are allocated a return based on how profitably the bank invests their money. On the asset side, an Islamic bank acts like a venture-capital investor, injecting funds into companies instead of loans. Islamic banks also participate in a kind of trade financing in which they buy goods and sell them, at a mark-up, to customers.

BMI divides its assets into three kinds: trade finance, venture-capital-type investments and "benevolent lending," in which the bank lends to customers who must repay the principal, but with no interest or additional charges. Trade finance is the simplest to compute. Instead of lending money to customers for purchases of raw materials or capital goods, BMI acquires the items on its own behalf and re-sells to the customer at a higher price. The mark-up usually will be equivalent to the rate customers would pay elsewhere for conventional financing. For its venture-capital investments, BMI will provide start-up capital, and the client will manage the business. "Together, we share the risks and rewards," says Natapermadi. To depositors, BMI offers products that are similar to demand and savings deposits. In an Islamic bank, the latter are called profit-sharing deposits and are distinguished by the absence of a pre-determined reward.

Theoretically, the return that depositors receive depends on how well the bank "invests" its available funds. The bank and the depositor agree to a "revenue-sharing ratio" which stipulates how much of the bank's profits are kept and how much are to be paid out to the depositor. In practice, BMI's depositors will receive a return close to that offered by conventional banks. "We don't want our depositors to make less than they would make elsewhere," says Natapermadi. Periodically, BMI will adjust the revenue-sharing ratio so that the portion of profits allocated to depositors will be close to the rate of interest offered by other banks.

Source: Adam Schwarz, "Profit and the Prophet: Indonesian Bank Offers No-Interest Services," *Far Eastern Economic Review,* May 21, 1992, pp. 44–46.

Host-Country-Specific Laws

Different nations have their own peculiar laws, which in one way or another affect the international operations of multinational companies. In the following paragraphs we shall take a brief look at a few such laws. The examples given in this section are by no means all-inclusive. There are certainly many more interesting differences in the legal requirements of various countries, but our purpose here is merely to acquaint the reader with situations that may be legal in one country but not in another. Multinational companies need to give particular attention to the impact of national laws on such crucial areas as advertising, patent protection, ownership of subsidiaries, finance, and personnel.

Many countries place various restrictions on the use of premiums in the promotional efforts of companies. Specific restrictions are placed on what can be advertised in some countries. For instance, regarding tobacco and alcohol advertising, country restrictions range from highly lenient to highly stringent. The United States is comparatively stringent relative to many other countries in this regard. Various countries place restrictions on how a firm can advertise. In the United States, direct comparisons (e.g., Burger King vs. McDonald's; Avis vs. Hertz; Verizon Wireless vs. AT&T) are allowed. In other countries, the firms must change their approach as direct comparisons are prohibited.

Beyond understanding laws that apply to marketing, the international company must understand other host-country-specific laws. For instance, some countries have very unique employment laws. This is seen in severe restrictions placed on the employment of foreigners. It is also seen in the employment of locals, whose salary, benefits, and dismissel may be dictated by host-government rules.

Vacation days vary among countries. A sampling of vacation and leave policies and practices from around the world provides an interesting base of comparison. Recently, a U.S. manager setting up a new subsidiary in Italy was surprised to find that the first person he hired as his secretary was entitled to—and took—six weeks' vacation during her first six months on the job, leaving him to perform many of the office tasks during the start-up.

There are other laws that are host-country specific as well. The problem of environmental pollution is worldwide. Subsidiaries operating in industrialized countries where air pollution has become a major problem must comply with the local air pollution standards or face stiff penalties. It is debatable whether air pollution curbs in the United States are any stricter than those in many European countries. Still, the laws of emerging and developing countries are often more lax than similar industrialized country standards. One major problem concerning environmental laws is the various definitions and meanings in different host countries. It is therefore difficult to extend and enforce laws in specific host countries.[62]

Many emerging countries do not allow private ownership of certain industries. It is said that the purpose of this law is to prevent industries vital to the economic welfare and safety of the country from falling into foreign hands. As seen previously, there is a worldwide trend toward greater privatization of many industries, thus mitigating the control that many countries once had over vital industries.

Another locally sensitive law deals with manufacturing. A company could have serious problems with a subsidiary located in a country that requires that a certain percentage of the components and subassemblies used in the production of a product must be sourced from local suppliers. Such laws are in effect in India, the United States, Chile, Spain, and several other countries. Problems also arise when local suppliers are not in a position to meet the quality standards of the subsidiary and/or supply the inputs at competitive world prices.

The Foreign Corrupt Practices Act and Antibribery Provisions

A U.S. law that applies to U.S. firms and their respective subsidiaries throughout the world is the **Foreign Corrupt Practices Act (FCPA)**, which was established in 1977. The FCPA specifically permits certain types of payments, called *facilitating payments*, whereas it prohibits other types of payments that could be categorized as bribes. At this point in our discussion of law, it is important to examine the antibribery provisions of the FCPA in some detail since an understanding of this legislation is crucial for international companies in order to stay clear of making illegal payments.[63] In general, the FCPA prohibits American companies from making corrupt payments to foreign officials for the purpose of obtaining or keeping business. The Department of Justice is the chief enforcement agency, with a coordinating role played by the Securities and Exchange Commission (SEC).

Background

Investigations by the SEC in the mid-1970s revealed that over 400 U.S. companies admitted making questionable or illegal payments in excess of $300 million to foreign government officials, politicians, and political parties. The abuses ran the gamut from bribery of high foreign officials in order to secure some type of favorable action by a foreign government to so-called facilitating payments that allegedly were made to ensure that government functionaries discharged certain ministerial or clerical duties. Congress enacted the FCPA to bring a halt to the bribery of foreign officials and to restore public confidence in the integrity of the American business system. The antibribery provisions of the FCPA make it unlawful for a U.S. person to make a corrupt payment to a foreign official for the purpose of obtaining or retaining business for or with, or directing business to, any person.

The FCPA also requires that issuers of securities meet its accounting standards. These accounting standards, which were designed to operate in tandem with the antibribery provisions of the FCPA, require that corporations covered by the provisions maintain books and records that accurately and fairly reflect the transactions of the corporation and that they design an adequate system of internal accounting controls.

Basic Provisions Prohibiting Foreign Corrupt Payments

The FCPA makes it unlawful to bribe foreign government officials to obtain or retain business. The antibribery provisions apply both to certain issuers of registered securities and issuers required to file periodic reports with the SEC (referred to as *issuers*) and to others (referred to as *domestic concerns*). A "domestic concern" is defined as any individual who is a citizen, national, or resident of the United States or any corporation, partnership, association, joint-stock company, business trust, unincorporated organization, or sole proprietorship that has its principal place of business in the United States or is organized under the laws of a state of the United States or of a territory, possession, or commonwealth of the United States.

The FCPA's antibribery provisions extend to two types of behavior. The basic prohibition is against making bribes directly; a second prohibition covers the responsibility of a domestic concern and its officials for bribes paid by intermediaries. The FCPA's basic antibribery prohibition makes it unlawful for a firm (as well as any officer, director, employee, or agent of a firm or any stockholder acting on behalf of the firm) to offer, pay, promise to pay (or even authorize the payment of or promise of) money, or anything of value, to any foreign official for the purpose of obtaining or retaining business for or with, or directing business to, any person.

Payment by Intermediaries

It is also unlawful to make a payment to any person while knowing that all or a portion of the payment will be offered, given, or promised, directly or indirectly, to any foreign official (or foreign political party, candidate, or official) for the purposes of assisting the firm in obtaining or retaining business. "Knowing" includes the concepts of conscious disregard or willful blindness.

Enforcement

The Department of Justice is responsible for all criminal enforcement and for civil enforcement of the antibribery provisions with respect to domestic concerns. The SEC is responsible for civil enforcement of the antibribery provisions with respect to issuers. Enforcement also stretches to non-U.S. firms, as depicted in Practical Insight 3.5.

PRACTICAL INSIGHT 3.5

SIEMENS BRACES FOR A SLAP FROM UNCLE SAM

Peter Loscher, the new CEO of German electronics and engineering giant Siemens, is desperately trying to dig his company out of the biggest bribery scandal in German corporate history. On Nov. 8, Siemens disclosed that its own internal investigation had uncovered $1.9 billion in questionable payments made to outsiders by the company from 2000 to 2006. That staggering sum deeply interests U.S. authorities in Washington who want to make an example of Siemens.

How did the long arm of the U.S. law reach into the offices of Germany's most important company? Because its shares are listed on the New York Stock Exchange and it has extensive operations in the U.S., Siemens is subject to the provisions of the U.S. Foreign Corrupt Practices Act. The act has given the Justice Dept. and Securities & Exchange Commission the authority to launch investigations, with which Siemens is cooperating. Munich prosecutors, who uncovered evidence that Siemens used bribes to land contracts around the globe, have already extracted $290 million in fines. But Siemens is bracing for an even nastier bite from the Americans. "The potential fines are much bigger than what companies have been used to in Germany," says Peter von Blomberg, deputy chair of the German chapter of Transparency International.

Washington wants to hold foreign companies to the same standards as their U.S. competitors. To make their point, U.S. regulators have been known to deliberately upstage foreign governments in the penalties they hand out. Dissatisfied with a $3 million penalty Norway imposed on energy producer Statoil for paying bribes in Iran, U.S. authorities last year hit the company with an additional $18 million in penalties. (The company did not admit guilt in the case.)

The financial penalty may not be the worst of it. As part of a settlement with U.S. authorities, Siemens will likely have to install a team of monitors to make sure the company banishes palm-greasing permanently. The monitors, who could number in the hundreds, will have carte blanche to snoop anywhere in the company they want, never mind the cost. They will report directly to U.S. authorities, but Siemens will have to pay the bill. Siemens has already spent $500 million on its own internal investigation, which was overseen by New York–based law firm Debevoise & Plimpton.

Given the looming presence of U.S. investigators, it's no surprise that Siemens is showing contrition. "We will go wherever the evidence takes us," says Peter Y. Solmssen, a U.S. lawyer and Siemens board member responsible for compliance.

But before they devise a fitting penalty, Justice and SEC lawyers want to determine how much profit Siemens earned from its bribes—an inquiry that could take months, even years. Says Solmssen: "We still have a long way to go."

CHINA'S NEW POSTURE ON COMMERCIAL BRIBERY

Enforcement of anticorruption statutes is on the rise in China, says the November, 2007, issue of legal newspaper *The Metropolitan Corporate Counsel.* China was required to pass anticorruption laws as a condition of joining the World Trade Organization in 2001 and has turned into one of the world's most aggressive prosecutors of bribery, writes Jeffrey Harfenist, managing director of UHY Advisors, an international tax consultancy. Since 2005, Beijing has prosecuted more than 21,000 cases of commercial bribery, creating huge headaches and potential liabilities for U.S. companies that rely on local agents to get deals done. The U.S. Justice Dept. is interested in following up on Chinese investigations involving the local representatives of U.S. companies.

Source: Jack Ewing and Eamon Javers, *BusinessWeek,* November 26, 2007, p. 78.

Antibribery Provisions—Elements of an Offense

With respect to the basic prohibition of the FCPA, there are five elements that must be met to constitute a violation of the act. These are identified below.

1. **Who.** The FCPA applies to any individual firm, any officer, director, employee, or agent of the firm, and any stockholder acting on behalf of the firm. Individuals and firms may also be penalized if they order, authorize, or assist someone else to violate the antibribery provisions or if they conspire to violate those provisions. A foreign-incorporated subsidiary of a U.S. firm is not subject to the FCPA, but its U.S. parent may be liable if it authorizes, directs, or participates in the activity in question. Individuals employed by or acting on behalf of such

foreign-incorporated subsidiaries may, however, be subject to the antibribery provisions if they are persons within the definition of "domestic concern." In addition, U.S. nationals employed by foreign-incorporated subsidiaries are subject to the antibribery provisions of the FCPA.

2. **Corrupt intent.** The person making or authorizing the payment must have a corrupt intent, and the payment must be intended to induce the recipient to misuse his or her official position in order wrongfully to direct business to the payer. You should note that the FCPA does not require that a corrupt act succeed in its purpose. The offer or promise of a corrupt payment can constitute a violation of the statute. The FCPA prohibits the corrupt use of the mails or of interstate commerce in furtherance of a payment to influence any act or decision of a foreign official in his or her official capacity, to induce the official to do or omit to do any act in violation of his or her lawful duty, or to induce a foreign official to use his or her influence improperly to affect or influence any act or decision.

3. **Payment.** The FCPA prohibits paying, offering, promising to pay (or authorizing to pay or offer) money or anything of value.

4. **Recipient.** The prohibition extends only to corrupt payments to a foreign official, a foreign political party or party official, or any candidate for foreign political office. "Foreign official" means any officer or employee of a foreign government, department, or agency or any person acting in an official capacity. You should consider utilizing the Department of Justice's Foreign Corrupt Practices Act Opinion Procedure for particular questions as to the definition of a *foreign official,* such as whether a member of a royal family, a member of a legislative body, or an official of a state-owned business enterprise would be considered a foreign official. Prior to the amendment of the FCPA in l988, the term *foreign official* did not include any employee of a foreign government or agency whose duties were essentially ministerial or clerical. Determining whether a given employee's duties were "essentially ministerial or clerical" was a source of ambiguity, and it was not clear whether the act prohibited certain "grease" payments, such as those for expediting shipments through customs or placing a transatlantic telephone call, securing required permits, or obtaining adequate police protection. Accordingly, recent changes in the FCPA focus on the purpose of the payment, instead of the particular duties of the official receiving the payment, offer, or promise of payment, and there are exceptions to the antibribery provision for "facilitating payments for routine governmental action" (see below).

5. **Business purpose test.** The FCPA prohibits payment made in order to assist the firm in obtaining or retaining business for or with, or directing business to, any person. It should be noted that the business to be obtained or retained does not need to be with a foreign government or foreign government instrumentality.

Third-Party Payments

Generally, the FCPA prohibits corrupt payments through intermediaries. It is unlawful to make corrupt use of the mails or of interstate commerce in furtherance of a payment to a third party while knowing that all or a portion of the payment will go directly or indirectly to a foreign official. "Knowing" includes conscious disregard and deliberate ignorance. The elements of an offense are essentially the same as those described above, except that in this case the recipient is the intermediary who is making the payment to the requisite foreign official.

Permissible Payments and Affirmative Defenses

As amended in 1988, the FCPA now provides an explicit exception to the bribery prohibition for "facilitating payments" for "routine governmental action" and provides affirmative defenses that can be used to defend against alleged violations of the FCPA.

Exception for Facilitating Payments for Routine Government Actions

There is an exception to the antibribery prohibition for facilitating or expediting performance of "routine governmental action." The statute lists the following examples: obtaining permits, licenses, or other official documents; processing government papers, such as visas and work orders; providing police protection and mail pick-up and delivery; providing phone service, power, and water supply; loading and unloading cargo; protecting perishable products; and scheduling inspections associated with contract performance or transit of goods across country. "Routine governmental action" does not include any decision by a foreign official to award new business or to continue business with a particular party.

Affirmative Defenses

A person charged with a violation of the FCPA's antibribery provisions may assert as a defense that the payment was lawful under the written laws of a foreign country or that the money was spent as part of demonstrating a product or performing a contractual obligation. Whether a payment was lawful under the written laws of a foreign country may be difficult to determine. Moreover, because such defenses are "affirmative defenses," the defendant would be required to show in the first instance that the payment met these requirements. The prosecution would not bear the burden of demonstrating in the first instance that the payments did not constitute this type of payment.

Sanctions against Bribery

The following criminal penalties may be imposed for violations of the FCPA's antibribery provisions: Firms are subject to a fine of up to $2 million; officers, directors, and stockholders are subject to a fine of up to $100,000 and imprisonment for up to five years; employees and agents are subject to a fine of up to $100,000 and imprisonment for up to five years. You should also be aware that fines imposed on individuals may not be paid by the firm.

There can be civil penalties as well. The attorney general or the SEC, as appropriate, may bring a civil action for a fine of up to $10,000 against any firm, as well as any officer, director, employee, or agent of a firm or any stockholder acting on behalf of the firm, that violates the antibribery provisions. In addition, in an SEC enforcement action, the court may impose an additional fine. The specified dollar amount may vary depending on the egregiousness of the violation, ranging from $5,000 to $50,000 for a person and from $100,000 to $500,000 for a firm.

Critics of the FCPA argue that the law exports the values of the culture of one country—namely, the United States—to countries that do not share similar values. They claim that bribery is a perfectly acceptable practice in most countries and that "while in Rome, do as the Romans do." However, the fact remains that probably every country has laws that prohibit domestic bribery. Hence, companies that bribe local officials in foreign countries would be breaking local laws against giving bribes to corrupt officials and bureaucrats. But local laws against giving or accepting bribes are not strictly enforced, which leaves open the opportunities for companies to engage in behavior that corrupts local officials in host countries.

The OECD Convention on Combating Bribery

The U.S. government began to receive numerous complaints from U.S. companies that the FCPA had placed them at a competitive disadvantage in obtaining foreign contracts against their competitors from other nations that did not have any prohibitions against the bribing of foreign officials. For instance, Germany permitted resident corporations to deduct foreign bribes, known as *sonderspesen,* or "special expenses," from corporate taxes. After considerable pressure from the government of the United States, the Convention on Combating Bribery of Foreign Public Officials in International Business Transactions was adopted by the Organization for Economic Cooperation and Development (OECD) on November 21, 1997. With South Africa's ratification in June 2007, there are currently 37 countries that have ratified the **OECD Antibribery Convention** (see Table 3.3). Complying with the convention requires unwavering support from the OECD and its Working Group on Bribery. Country monitoring and extensive follow-up ensure that all 37 countries win the fight against bribery.[64]

This is the first legally binding international instrument that aims to curb the behavior of corrupt multinational corporations operating overseas. The convention is a historic achievement in the fight against bribery. Countries that have signed the convention were required to put in place legislation that criminalizes the act of bribing a foreign public official. All member countries have now ratified this convention, thereby incorporating the treaty's provisions into their respective legal systems. Although its text does not specifically cover political parties, the negotiators agreed that the convention would cover business-related bribes to foreign public officials made through political parties and party officials.

Also, OECD anticorruption regional actions focus on countries not party to the OECD Antibribery Convention. The regional actions promote international anticorruption instruments in order to strengthen regional capacity to fight corruption. Practical Insight 3.6 discusses the Asia-Pacific initiatives against corruption.

TABLE 3.3
Signatories to the OECD Convention

Argentina	Australia	Austria	Belgium	Brazil
Bulgaria	Canada	Chile	Czech Rep	Denmark
Estonia	Finland	France	Germany	Greece
Hungary	Iceland	Ireland	Italy	Japan
Korea	Luxembourg	Mexico	Netherlands	New Zealand
Norway	Poland	Portugal	Slovak Rep	Slovenia
South Africa	Spain	Sweden	Switzerland	Turkey
U.K.	U.S.A.			

PRACTICAL INSIGHT 3.6

ASIA-PACIFIC COUNTRIES STRENGTHEN CO-OPERATION IN THE FIGHT AGAINST CORRUPTION

Government representatives and experts from some thirty countries and jurisdictions gathered in Bali, Indonesia, from 5–7 September 2007, for a two-day international seminar on Asset Recovery and Mutual Legal Assistance. The seminar provided a forum for exchanging knowledge and discussing formal and informal measures to obtain international legal assistance across jurisdictions, particularly as this assistance relates to the confiscation and recovery, from foreign jurisdictions, of assets obtained through corrupt practice.

"Corruption is a financial crime, with no boundary of states, considering that the crime proceeds are often laundered and hidden in foreign countries," said the Chairman of the Commission for Eradication of Corruption in Indonesia (KPK), Mr. Taufiqurrahman Ruki, as he welcomed the 170 experts to the seminar.

The tracking and recovery of assets is an important issue on the international anticorruption agenda. The fight against corruption involves prevention, detection and effective prosecution. The ability of prosecutors and courts to access evidence and recover the proceeds of corruption is critical to this process. The issue entered the international arena with the OECD Convention on Combating Bribery of Foreign Public Officials in International Business Transactions (1997) and the discussion has gained momentum as a result of the United Nations Convention Against Corruption (2003). Both instruments include provisions for international cooperation in the area of mutual legal assistance and asset recovery.

The seminar is hosted by the Government of Indonesia and organized by the Asian Development Bank and the Organisation for Economic Co-operation and Development (OECD) Anti-Corruption Initiative for Asia and the Pacific, the Basel Institute on Governance, and the United Nations Office on Drugs and Crime in collaboration with KPK. It follows the 10th Steering Group meeting of the Initiative during which members reviewed their policies for mutual legal assistance, extradition, and asset recovery. Members also discussed their priorities, strategies and ongoing reforms to fight corruption in the Asian and Pacific Region. The Initiative welcomed Bhutan as its 28th member.

The ADB/OECD Anti-Corruption Initiative was launched in 1999 and the 2001 Anti-Corruption Action Plan for Asia and the Pacific has been endorsed by 28 member countries and jurisdictions.

Source: www.oecd.org/corruption/asiapacific, 2008.

Summary

A political system comprises a set of players, each of which has a unique ideology and some degree of power, which it uses to control and influence the behavior of other groups. One group, government, has an additional attribute—legitimacy—which it uses along with its generally greater influence to make and enforce authoritarian decisions. It does so by means of the political process, the bargaining process by which the conflicting interests and relative power of different groups are constructively managed in attaining political decisions. Today's international economic and political systems and processes are highly interdependent. Economic relations between countries are shaped to a large extent by their political relations, and vice versa. As a result of this complex interaction, political considerations can generate actions by nation-states in the economic sphere that may be detrimental to the interests of private enterprise.

The likelihood that such political forces will unexpectedly and drastically affect a firm's operations is embodied in the concept of political risk. High levels of political risk are generally associated with low levels of stability and consistency in the political system of a nation-state. Political risk may be felt in three ways: transfer risk, operational risk, and ownership risk. Each of these three types of risk can be further classified as macro or micro in nature, depending on the particular circumstances. Key determinants of political risk in many countries include a change in a country's government, a change in a country's leadership within the same party, religious influences on government, and the likelihood of civil strife leading to a mass uprising that would result in destabilizing the incumbent political system. Although political risk is generally discussed in the context of one particular country at a time, today's global firms are exposed to such risk on a much broader front. The complex nature of the dynamics between political and economic relations requires that the modern firm extend its risk assessment framework to include not only the forces within the host- and home-country environments but also the role played by international groups and international events. International firms must take appropriate precautions regarding the risks that arise from international politics, economics, and law. Firms can proactively hedge these risks through vehicles such as joint ventures, promotion of a host country's goals, and lobbying efforts. Firms can also defensively deflect risk through diversification initiatives and the purchase of insurance.

The international legal environment can be viewed as comprising three concentric levels around the company: the laws of the nation-states within which the firm operates, laws of the regional trade blocs to which those nation-states belong, and international law. International law is set apart from national legal systems as it is implemented by the mutual agreement of nation-states, not through the power of a central enforcement authority.

International law, the outer level of the legal environment, may be based on custom—the historical practice of generally accepted patterns of behavior—or on treaties and conventions—signed agreements governing activity between sovereign states. Treaties may be bilateral or multilateral, depending on the number of signatory countries. We discussed two types of treaties of particular importance to international companies: treaties of friendship, commerce, and navigation (FCN) and treaties for the protection of intellectual property rights. Protection of intellectual property—patents, trademarks, and copyrights—is a primary concern of international companies. Laws governing what can and cannot be protected and for how long vary widely among nations. While many countries are party to the Paris Convention, which standardizes and simplifies intellectual property protection, practical problems of enforcement are still widespread. Historically, GATT and, more recently, the WTO have attempted to improve intellectual property protection. The Madrid Protocol, signed in 2002, offers international filers of trademarks simplicity, ease, and cost efficiency while promoting protection of trademarks globally.

The second level of the international legal environment of business is the regional laws that have developed along with the various regional trade blocs in recent years. These laws, particularly well developed in the European Union, standardize activity and requirements among the member nations and are designed to facilitate intraregional trade. The third level of the international legal environment is represented by the specific laws of nation-states. National legal systems are generally based on common law, civil law, or Islamic law and reflect the social, cultural, and religious norms of the people. Accordingly, there are many significant differences and peculiarities among the laws of different nations. Activity or behavior that is perfectly acceptable in one country may be patently illegal in others. Managers in international companies must research and be aware of these differences as they affect foreign investment and operations.

The international manager of a U.S. firm must understand the basic provisions of the Foreign Corrupt Practices Act (FCPA) as well as what constitutes an offense under the law. Furthermore, the FCPA applies to foreign subsidiaries of U.S corporations, including majority and minority ownership in foreign companies and participation in strategic alliances. The OECD Convention has 37 signatory countries and increasing regional initiatives from non-member-country consortia. It monitors and imposes sanctions on commercial corruption.

The legal climate for multinational operations varies widely from country to country. Even for a given country, laws affecting investment policies and operating decisions can change markedly and quickly as different political regimes and changing economic circumstances alter a nation's goals and priorities. Supranational influences, such as the WTO worldwide, NAFTA for Mexico, Canada, and the United States, or the EU in Europe, also may result in significant changes in trade-related laws. Failure to keep abreast of changes in the various legal environments in which the multinational firm operates can subject the firm and its assets—financial, plant, and intellectual property—to unnecessary risk or even to loss.

Key Terms and Concepts

civil law, *92*
civil strife, *73*
coercive potential and civil strife, *74*
common law, *92*
facilitation and civil strife, *74*
Foreign Corrupt Practices Act (FCPA), *96*
intellectual property rights, *86*
Islamic law, *93*
institutionalization and civil strife, *74*
international law, *82*
international treaties and conventions, *85*
macro risk, *70*
Madrid Protocol, *88*
micro risk, *70*
OECD Antibribery Convention, *101*
operational risk, *69*
Overseas Private Investment Corporation (OPIC), *79*
ownership risk, *69*
political system, *59*
proactive hedge, *77*
reactive hedge, *79*
regime legitimacy and civil strife, *74*
transfer risk, *69*

Discussion Questions

1. What are the components of the political system model? Apply the political system model to your country of choice.
2. Discuss how the global political system impacts the global economic system. To what extent does the global economic system influence the global political system?
3. Discuss the concept of political risk. When can political risk be favorable for international firms? Give examples of countries where such risk has been favorable to international business.
4. Apply the comprehensive framework for assessing political risk to companies doing business in the Middle East or to a country or region of your choosing.
5. Select a target country for establishing a foreign subsidiary.
   a. Develop a political risk index for the target country.
   b. Choose an industry in your home country and develop a political risk index for this industry in the target country.
6. Does international law measure up to the requirements of an effective legal system? Will there ever be an effective international legal system?
7. Discuss the different ways in which Islamic law can impact the operations of international companies in Islamic countries.
8. Discuss the risks an international firm incurs overseas regarding intellectual property rights and subsequent control of its proprietary technology and knowledge.

Minicase

Leadership Changes in China and Russia

During the first week of March 2008, both China and Russia were braced for new political leadership. In China, Xi Jinping was being positioned to succeed Hu Jintao as the general secretary of China's Communist Party. Mr. Xi will assume this role in 2012 and is also expected to assume the role of Chinese president in 2013. Both Mr. Xi and his opponent, Li Kequiang, were appointed to the powerful Inner Committee of China's Communist Politburo in fall 2007. These appointments signaled that one of the two men was to be Mr. Hu's chosen successor. Once the party agreed on Mr. Xi as China's next general secretary, the leaders gave him many titles, some real and others honorary. For instance, Mr. Xi was placed in charge of the 2008 Olympics in Beijing. He was also chosen to lead the Central Party School, the most important Communist Party education and training institute. Mr. Xi represents an economic reformer, one who has developed excellent relations with foreign investors.

During the same time period, in Russia, Dmitry Medvedev was elected to succeed Vladimir Putin as Russia's next president. Mr. Medvedev has been seen as a protégé and anointed successor to President Putin. Mr. Putin assumed the office of Russia's prime minister, and as a result, the two men vowed to rule as a team even though the presidency is the highly visible position while the prime minister has been a historically subservient position, one with economic responsibility but without direct control over Russia's military. Unlike Mr. Xi in China, Mr. Medvedev does not have the reputation as an economic reformer or one who has made deep inroads with foreign investors, especially from the West.

Source: Roger Kashlak, Loyola College, Maryland, 2008.

DISCUSSION QUESTIONS

1. Contrast the processes of becoming the political leader in China and Russia. How does each differ from your own country's process?
2. Apply the global risk assessment framework to demonstrate how both home- and host-country environments can create political risks for international companies doing business in either China or Russia.

Notes

1. Stephen Globerman and Daniel Shapiro, "Governance Infrastructure and U.S. Foreign Investment," *Journal of International Business Studies* 33, no. 1 (2003), pp. 61–74.
2. R. Hall and C. I. Jones, "Why Do Some Countries Produce So Much More Output per Worker Than Others?" *Quarterly Journal of Economics* 114, no. 1 (1999), pp. 83–86; D. Kaufmann, A. Kraay, and P. Zoido-Lobaton, *Governance Matters,* World Bank working paper no. 2196, 1999.
3. Kent Miller, "A Framework for Integrated Risk Management in International Business," *Journal of International Business Studies* 23, no. 2 (1992), pp. 311–331.
4. G. V. Stevens, "Politics, Economics and Investment: Explaining Plants and Equipment Spending by U.S. Direct Investors in Argentina, Brazil and Mexico," *Journal of International Money Finance* 19, no. 2 (2000), pp. 115–135.
5. C. Altomonte, "Economic Determinants and Institutional Frameworks: FDI in Economies in Transition," *Transnational Corporations* 9, no. 2 (2000), pp. 75–106.
6. Witold Henisz, *Politics and International Investment* (Cheltenham, England: Elgar Publishing, 2002).
7. J. Boddewyn and T. Brewer, "International Business Political Behavior: New Theoretical Directions," *Academy of Management Review,* January 1994, pp. 119–143.
8. John Plamenatz, *Ideology* (New York: Praeger, 1970), p. 15.
9. Roy C. Macridis, *Contemporary Political Ideologies,* 5th ed (New York: HarperCollins, 1992), p. 2
10. Plamenatz, *Ideology,* p. 2
11. For more on the concepts of consensus and legitimacy, please read Roy C. Macridis and Bernard E. Brown, eds., *Comparative Politics: Notes and Readings,* 3rd ed. (Homewood, IL: Dorsey Press, 1968), pp. 107–114.
12. Joan Edelman Spero, *The Politics of International Economic Relations,* 4th ed. (New York: St. Martin's Press, 1990), p. 9.
13. Ibid., p. 4.
14. S. Kobrin, "Political Risk: A Review and Reconsideration," *Journal of International Business Studies* 10, no. 1 (1979), pp. 67–80.
15. D. Sethi, S. Guisinger, S. Phelan, and D. Berg, "Trends in Foreign Direct Investment Flows: A Theoretical and Empirical Analysis," *Journal of International Business Studies* 34, no. 2 (2003), pp. 315–326.
16. K. Brouthers, "Institutional, Cultural and Transaction Cost Influences on Entry Mode Choice and Performance," *Journal of International Business Studies* 33, no. 2 (2002), pp. 203–221.
17. R. Kashlak, R. Chandran, and A. DiBenedetto, "Reciprocity in International Business: A Study of Telecommunications Contracts and Alliances," *Journal of International Business Studies* 29, no. 2 (1998), pp. 281–304.

18. R. Hamilton and R. Kashlak, "National Influences on Multinational Control System Selection," *Management International Review* 39, no. 2 (1999), pp. 167–189.
19. K. Fatehi, "Capital Flight from Latin America as a Barometer of Political Instability," *Journal of Business Research* 30 (1994), pp. 165–173.
20. W. Henisz, "The Institutional Environment for Multinational Investment," *Journal of Law, Economics and Organization* 16 (2000), pp. 334–364.
21. W. Henisz and B. Zellner, "The Institutional Environment for Telecommunications Investment," *Journal of Economics and Management Strategy* 10 (2001), pp. 123–147.
22. W. Henisz and A. Delios, "Uncertainty, Imitation and Plant Location: Japanese MNCs, 1990–1996," *Administrative Science Quarterly* 46 (2001), pp. 443–475; A. Delios and W. Henisz, "Policy Uncertainty and the Sequence of Entry by Japanese Firms, 1980–1998," *Journal of International Business Studies* 34, no. 2, (2003), pp. 227–241.
23. OPIC Insurance Department, www.opic.gov/Insurance.
24. Stefan A. Robock, "Political Risk: Identification and Assessment," *Columbia Journal of World Business,* pp. 9–10.
25. S. Kobrin, *Managing Political Risk Assessment* (Berkeley: University of California Press, 1982).
26. K. Miller, "Industry and Country Effects on Managers' Perceptions of Environmental Influences," *Journal of International Business Studies* 24, no. 4 (1993), pp. 693–713.
27. Based on Robock, "Political Risk: Identification and Assessment," p. 16.
28. Ted Gurr, "A Causal Model of Civil Strife: A Comparative Model Using New Analysis," *American Political Science Review* 62, no. 4 (December 1968), p. 1104.
29. Ibid., pp. 1105–1106.
30. *New York Times,* September 13, 2002, p. w1.
31. J. Simon, "A Theoretical Perspective on Political Risk," *Journal of International Business Studies,* Winter 1984, pp. 123–142.
32. V. Errunza and E. Losq, "How Risky Are Emerging Markets?" *Journal of Portfolio Management,* Fall/Winter 1987, pp. 83–99.
33. J. Cosset and J. Suret, "Political Risk and the Benefits of International Portfolio Diversification," *Journal of International Business Studies* 27, no. 3 (1996), pp. 301–318.
34. OPIC Insurance Department, www.opic.gov/Insurance.
35. Globerman and Shapiro, "Governance Infrastructure and U.S. Foreign Investment."
36. O. Havrylyshyn and R. van Rooden, "Institutions Matter in Transition, but So Do Policies," *Comparative Economic Studies* 45 (2003), pp. 2–24.
37. Brouthers, "Institutional, Cultural and Transaction Cost Influences on Entry Mode Choice and Performance."
38. W. Coplin, *The Functions of International Law* (Chicago: Rand McNally, 1966), pp. 8–9
39. Ibid., pp. 3–4.
40. J. Gamble and C. Lu, "International Law—New Actors and New Technologies: Center Stage for NGOs?" *Law and Policy in International Business* 31, no. 2 (2000), pp. 221–263.
41. Statute of the International Court of Justice, Article 38(I).
42. O. Schachter and C. Joyner, eds., *United Nations Legal Order 31* (New York: United Nations, 1995).
43. Gamble and Lu, "International Law—New Actors and New Technologies."
44. Vienna Convention on the Law of Treaties, May 23, 1969, Article 2.1 (a).
45. Y. Hamabe, "The JFCN Treaty Preemption of U.S. Anti-discrimination Laws in Executive Positions: Analysis in International Contexts," *Law and Policy in International Business* 27, no. 1 1995, pp. 67–136.
46. C. Saban and E. Fealy, "Making the Most of the 'FCN Treaty' and Related National Origin Defenses," *Employee Relations Law Journal* 21, no. 3 (1996), pp. 149–161.

47. K. Josephberg, J. Pollack, J. Victoriano, and, O. Gitig, "WIPO Conference on Performers' Rights to Be Held in 2003," *Intellectual Property & Technology Law Journal* 15, no. 1 (2003), pp. 22.
48. R. Fishman, K. Josephberg, J. J. Linn, and J. Pollack, "US to Work toward Global Patent Treaty," *Intellectual Property & Technology Law Journal* 14, no. 7 (2002), pp. 30–32; J. Boyarski, R. Fishman, K. Josephberg, and J. Linn, "WIPO Members Extend Patent Cooperation Treaty Time Limit," *Intellectual Property & Technology Law Journal* 14, no. 1 (2003), pp. 26–28.
49. K. Josephberg, J. Pollack, J. Victoriano, and O. Gitig, "WIPO Agrees to Changes in Patent Application Process," *Intellectual Property & Technology Law Journal* 15, no. 1 (2003), p. 23.
50. M. Retsky, "New Law Protects Marks Worldwide," *Marketing News* 37, no. 8 (2003), p. 10.
51. L. Perez, "Protecting Brand Names Overseas," *World Trade* 16, no. 3 (2003) p. 50.
52. I. Haleen and A. Scoville, "United States Ratifies the Madrid Protocol: Pros and Cons for Trademark Owners," *Intellectual Property & Technology Law Journal* 15, no. 4 (2003), pp. 1–4.
53. *Activities of the European Union,* November 12, 2001.
54. R. La Porta, F. Lopez-de-Silanes, A. Shleifer, and R. Vishny, *The Quality of Government* (Cambridge, MA: National Bureau of Economic Research, 1998).
55. S. Kalemli-Ozcan, B. Sorensen, and O. Yosha, "Risk Sharing and Industrial Specialization: Regional and International Evidence," *American Economic Review* 93, no. 3 (2003), pp. 903–930.
56. Jessica M. Bailey and James Sood, "The Effect of Religious Affiliation on Consumer Behavior: A Preliminary Investigation," *Journal of Managerial Issues* 5, no. 3 (Fall 1993), p. 333.
57. Mushtaq Luqmani, Zahir A. Quaraeshi, and Linda Delene, "Marketing in Islamic Countries: A Viewpoint," *MSU Business Topics,* Summer 1980.
58. "Banking Behind the Veil," *The Economist,* April 4, 1992, p. 76.
59. Luiz Moutinho and M. Hisham Jabr, "Perspective on the Role of Marketing in Islamic Banking," *Journal of International Consumer Marketing* 2, no. 3 (1990), pp. 29–47; Geraldine Brooks, "Riddle of Riyadj: Islamic Law Thrives amid Modernity," *Wall Street Journal,* November 9, 1989, p. A1.
60. "Islamic Banking Rules Spell More Paperwork but the Same Result," *Business Asia,* March 11, 1991, p. 81.
61. Pakistan Newswire, March 25, 2003.
62. D. French, "Environmental Damage in International and Comparative Law: Problems of Definition and Valuation," *Journal of Environmental Law* 15, no. 2 (2003), p. 266.
63. The material in this section was obtained from the government document "Foreign Corrupt Practices Act Antibribery Provisions" (Washington, DC: U.S. Department of Commerce, Office of the Chief Counsel for International Commerce). It is presented in its entirety except for minor deletions and changes.
64. OECD Convention, 2008.

CHAPTER FOUR

The Cultural Environment

Chapter Learning Objectives

After completing this chapter, you should be able to:

- Understand the concepts of culture and cultural variations in international management.
- Explain the influence of environmental factors on societal culture.
- Understand the concept of organizational culture and its relationship with societal culture.
- Discuss the significance of various frameworks for understanding cultural differences around the world.
- Identify distinctive management styles that exist in different countries.

Opening Case: Cross Culture in Business and Everyday Life

The phone rings at 3:00 a.m. and it is not a prank call. It is your son. "Hi Dad, I'm sorry I forgot what time it is for you in California. I just left the Bangkok airport . . . sorry to wake you. Bye."

After an interrupted night's sleep, Mr. Vice President of Technology Inc. heads into the office, "Tall Latte" in hand, to prepare for the conference call with the international sales team in Milan, Italy. Figures are reported and the outline for the next quarter is set.

"It would be great if you could send me the report by the end of the week," said Mr. VP. By Friday the report has not arrived. Mr.VP is disappointed and the Italian staff has no idea why. "We were extremely busy and sending one report did not seem to be priority! You said 'it would be great'—meaning good if you get the report and not a problem if you don't. Right?"

Wrong. Any North American reading this at the moment is sure what Mr. VP meant. The report is priority number one! Simply receiving the language without grasping the cultural background can lead to miscommunication. How well do we really know each other?

Trust in Business (TiB), an international relocation company based in Munich, Germany, works together with business partners from the Americas, Asia and Europe, to ensure that these types of culture bumps are smoothed out. Here are several tips from TiB to help you integrate cross culturally into business and everyday life. Begin to untangle the mysteries in the life of the expatriate.

Understanding the Expatriate

If you have family living in other countries; are an expatriate yourself; work in a global company; have a neighbor who is from another country or ethnicity; have friends, business partners, or classmates of cultures different than your own, then you are automatically trying to understand the vibrant display of cultural backgrounds around you.

Here are some simple tips to bring you cross-culture success. Take your difficult yet glamorous, adventurous yet tiring expatriate life and transform it into a rewarding experience.

Even if you are not the one living in another country but have frequent contact with someone who does, our hints will enable you to help the expatriates you know integrate into the culture, while teaching you a bit about their culture as well. It is a win-win philosophy that is moving up the ranks in global business and will move you up the ladder of success.

"There has never been a more important time for the world to reach out to each other and be more than just tolerant but willing to learn," said Anne Koark from Britain who is President and founder of Munich-based Trust in Business.

What Makes it Tricky?

We often take it for granted that our sense of being *polite, normal, rude, friendly, etc.* must be understood by the people we deal with. But this is not the case.

Christian Steuer, German, 26, attending a Texas university, replied, "I wondered why a woman from Japan did not reply to a question from a professor in my class right away. She was looking down on her desk and it took her at least one minute, of what I felt was extreme awkward silence, until she looked up again and responded to the professor. In the beginning of my cross culture class I thought her behavior was rude. But I learned that my behavior in the same situation (answering as soon as possible) would have been very rude and impolite in her culture. The difference in our cultures is that in Japan people expect you to think deeply about what you reply to an authority or person of respect." Western European culture tries to answer a person's question quickly—otherwise it is assumed that there is insecurity or doubt about his/her response.

Europeans living in America experience confrontation difficulties. At an American restaurant, diners automatically receive the check without asking for it. For most Europeans unfamiliar to the American style of dining, it is rude. The dining atmosphere can turn from cozy and enjoyable to uncomfortable and rushed for Europeans eating in typical North American restaurants.

Cultures' Basic Similarities and their Expressions

It's true that we all share the same basic human emotions in our lives, such as love, hate, anger and passion. However, each culture has a distinct way of expressing those emotions and has different attitudes behind this expression—also in business matters. We have to learn to overcome *culture bumps* beyond the simple belief of tolerance.

Living as an Expatriate

Everybody who decides to live in another culture goes through a *cultural adjustment* cycle before he/she adapts to the new environment. People go through the cycle at their own pace—some take longer to go through the cycle and others pass through it quickly.

There are five different stages of the adjustment cycle, taking the expatriate from the first day of residence in the new culture to a settled life in the new environment.

Expatriate Amy Hart, North Carolina native now living and working for 11 months in Munich, Germany, helps us differentiate between the five different stages of the adjustment cycle.

1. Honeymoon Stage

The first stage Hart went through was the honeymoon stage. Everything in her new surroundings was new to her and exciting and interesting. She had the feeling of a dream finally coming true and being right in the middle of a great adventure. It was interesting to organize a German bank account and find the perfect German apartment to live in. Overall, Hart was in a light-hearted mood. Just like a honeymoon, the bliss of beginning a new life can be rose-colored, and happy and hopeful for most expatriates.

2. Culture Shock

After approximately six to eight weeks, Hart moved into the *culture shock* stage. "Overall, I hated the feeling of not being able to be independent. It is as if you are a child again. Your personal freedom is suddenly taken away from you," said Hart.

Typical for this stage of the cycle you can physically feel that something is not right. Hart complained about frequent headaches, and her stomach was upset at random times. She felt a little tired and not able to concentrate and focus on her work perfectly. Her sleeping patterns changed as well. She started thinking of her friends and family back home and felt homesick.

The fear of not being able to succeed cast shadows on her initial honeymoon stage dreams. Hart felt she was living with one foot in her American culture—and at the same time having the other foot in the German culture. This stage lasted for about another eight weeks.

3. Initial Adjustment Stage

After the culture shock period, Hart went into what we call *initial adjustment stage* and started connecting with people from Germany in social and business situations. Though she was still missing her home country, she gained self-reliance in Germany. Being needed in her company helped her make a bigger step into finding her place in German culture.

It was hard for her to realize that she then had to go through another stage of negative feelings. And for many expatriates this stage feels like it should be the end of the cycle. It is not.

Pennsylvania expatriate Kelly Payne lived and worked in Germany and Japan. She found it easier to enter this stage of *initial adjustment* when she learned to relax and flow with the lifestyle of her new host country as it differed from her own.

Typically, North Americans are constantly active. Overall, trying to crowd as many activities into an hour as possible is considered productive. Wasting time is seen as wasting money. In cultures where there is less emphasis on competition, people are able to let time "fill itself," or place more emphasis on quality of actions rather than quantity of actions. North Americans, in contrast, need to do something useful every second.

Many North Americans will use time while they are driving a car to learn a new language or dictate letters, rather than just meditating or enjoying the landscape.

During the initial 40-minute subway rides to work in Germany, Payne felt the urge to not waste time but rather to be "doing something."

"When I forgot to take my book at home or my Walkman with me, I felt so useless just sitting in the subway without any task to do. It took a while until I learned not to feel guilty when I just enjoyed watching people or letting my mind wander around," said Payne.

4. Mental Isolation

Mental isolation follows what seems to be the end for expatriates adjusting into their new culture. Step 3—the "Initial Adjustment" stage—is a beginning adjustment but is temporary, to be followed by another wave of integration ups and downs.

During this stage, Hart really needed support and help from her friends and co-workers. Hart felt anger against the host culture and had self-doubt, wondering if she did the right thing in her decision to live in Europe. "Maybe the people back home are forgetting about me," said Hart.

She complained about the fact that everything is "verboten" (forbidden) in Germany and the food was different. People were staring at her in a way she was not used to. "I sometimes felt as if I had an imaginary American flag on my forehead. People just knew even before I spoke. I got the 'you're different' type of look," said Hart. She lost her motivation for learning German and you could see a difference in her personality. She was not the girl straight off the plane from America. The sparkles in her eyes were dimming but the knowledge in her mind was blossoming as she transitioned.

I understand completely what Amy went through. My *mental isolation* stage was identical when I left my native Germany to study at a university in Texas. One incident remains vivid in my mind. I wrote a letter to a company and received a "short and sweet" answer in return. I found it rude and way too short for my experience in German business matters. I complained about the "rude and impolite way to deal with clients," because I did not know at that point that this style of "coming to the point quickly" is just a way of responding fast and saving time. Time is money in American culture.

5. Acceptance and Integration

Finally, Hart entered the last stage of the culture adaptation cycle. This stage we call *acceptance and integration*. She stopped trying to change the host culture and stopped making constant comparison to her own American way. She developed strategies for everyday life here in Germany. She was willing to take German classes again, tried to speak German to everyone in the office and seemed to be more content and less moody.

"My sense of time was mixed up in the first months here in Germany. When I went to a restaurant with my German friends, I always felt strange when my European peers kept sitting at the table for another hour after finishing dinner. I felt the urge to pay for the meal and leave. I was ready to go to another bar or café.

"I learned to not be in such a rush and to have dinner for two and a half hours compared to 45 minutes. I began to let go of the feeling that having a tight schedule was important and productive."

Source: Reprinted with permission from Daniela Montabaur, Leadervalues.com.

Discussion Questions

1. What are some of the cultural differences that are going to be of relevance to managers working in dissimilar cultures?
2. Why do members of different cultures express their ideas differently?
3. What are some of the lessons that are worth remembering from the various episodes discussed in this case?

What Is Culture?

Culture is a concept that has been used in several social science disciplines to explain variations in human thought processes in different parts of the world. Culture is to a society what memory is to an individual.[1] Anthropologists believe that cultures provide solutions to problems of human adaptation to the environment. Humans have evolved over the past 4 million years from apes to highly sophisticated beings and control most of the ecological environment of the world. In the course of this development, their adaptation has been enhanced by the development of culture.

Culture is the human-made part of environment.[2] It has both subjective and objective components. **Objective culture** components are such things as infrastructure of roads, architecture, patterns of music, food, and dress habits. **Subjective culture** components include the ways that people categorize experience, associations, beliefs, attitudes, self-definitions, role definitions, norms, and values. Subjective culture helps people survive the various demands that are present in an ecological setting since they do not have to reinvent adaptive behaviors but can imitate them or learn from previous generations. Triandis[3] suggested these two components of culture, and these distinctions provide a helpful way of understanding cultural differences. Subjective culture–related differences and the way they influence attitudes and values of people in different parts of the world are the focus of this chapter.

When you come across a man wearing an Arabic headdress or a woman in burka, you immediately think that these people have a different culture from your own. Countries also have distinctive architectural preferences—buildings in Cairo often look different from those in New York or Frankfurt, Germany. When you go to Moscow, the golden domes on the churches tell you that you are in a country whose culture is different from your own. Similarly, when you listen to the distinctive rhythms of Japanese music, you realize that it is a different culture. All of these are examples

PRACTICAL INSIGHT 4.1

YANKEE, WE WANT YOU. YANKEE, GO HOME
When Henri Poole took the helm at a French software outfit, he became the latest American to learn just how easy it is to ruffle Old World feathers

It seemed like a fantastic opportunity for the entrepreneurial Henri Poole. He had co-founded and run Vivid Studios, a San Francisco-based Web consulting shop, before selling it in 1998 to Platinum Technology for $13 million. Then, after taking an 18-month break to travel and spend time with his newborn, Poole was approached by a group of European venture capitalists about becoming CEO of a French software company. In May, 2000, after a quick mating dance, Poole signed on to lead Paris-based MandrakeSoft, a two-year-old seller of Linux software.

Though Poole, then 36, was primed for a challenge, the Mandrake experience was tougher than he anticipated. Less than a year after joining MandrakeSoft, he departed after a split with the company's French founders over strategy. Poole had been hired to transform the company from a small Linux publisher into "a major software player," says Edward Walsh, former vice-president of communications, who resigned in July. In the end, the founders got cold feet about Poole's plan to turn the startup into a technology services provider.

Tougher Rules
"My vision was more aggressive than some of the founders and investors were comfortable with," Poole says. "They wanted the benefits at the end of the rainbow, but didn't like my plan for getting there." (MandrakeSoft executives wouldn't comment, saying the company is in the midst of a $3.7 million stock offering on the Paris Euronext Marché Libre, scheduled to close July 27.)

Poole's story highlights the difficulties many U.S. executives face when they take on the job of managing technology companies under Europe's more confining business rules. During the Internet boom, says James Hand, manager of the Global Technology Fund at London's Investec Asset Management, experienced American execs were in hot demand across Europe. But when the bubble burst and the Old Economy reasserted itself, old habits returned. As Hand puts it: "People are content to stay with the less dynamic European way, taking longer to do things."

Case in point: former Hewlett-Packard exec Antonio Perez, who was hired in the fall of 2000 to head French smart-card giant Gemplus. Perez is now under fire from unions for plans to lay off workers and close factories. His travails illustrate Europeans' limited tolerance for the tougher management style many American executives practice.

Outsider's Perspective
Then there's former Microsoft exec James Kinsella, hired last year to salvage Dutch Internet service provider World Online after its founder left amid a stock scandal. In January, Kinsella sold the company to Italian ISP Tiscali and was named its provisional CEO. Less than a month later, Kinsella was on the street, thanks to strategy and culture clashes with Tiscali Chairman Renato Soru.

The divergence between New Economy management and Old World thinking helped bring down Poole. At first, he was unconcerned about the differences in business culture and philosophy he found at MandrakeSoft. After all, he'd been recruited precisely because he was an outsider. "I had a more democratic management style," Poole says. "I also understood how to put together an agenda and stick to it." MandrakeSoft co-founder Jacques Le Marois, who has now stepped into the CEO slot, had sought out Poole—not just for his skills, but also because he was an American. Having an American CEO would lend the company a certain cachet, the thinking went.

Also, Poole believed technology transcends borders. Linux is at the heart of a global movement called Open Source, whose proponents believe software should be free and available in its original form to anybody who wants to improve it. Millions of people around the world now use Linux, and hundreds of thousands tinker with it, sharing their improvements with the rest of the community. When MandrakeSoft's investors, who have invested $18 million in the company, approached Poole about the CEO job, he was intrigued by the idea of collaborative software development and developing

---

of objective culture, and they are easily seen and experienced. However, the man wearing an Arabic headdress may be fluent in English and educated in the West, and he may understand how Westerners think and behave. He can therefore be said to have a very good grasp of the subjective culture found in the West. Subjective culture differences are not easily visible to the eye, and they must be interpreted in terms of differences in rituals, customs, and other practices.

In this chapter and throughout this book we are concerned with subjective culture, and we use the concept of culture to reflect the subjective culture of groups of people in a given geographic location. Two countries may show differences in objective parts of their culture but be quite similar in terms of their underlying subjective cultures,

intellectual property across borders. He also knew that some of MandrakeSoft's U.S. rivals, such as Red Hat and VA Linux, had been among the hottest stock offerings of 1999.

Language Barrier
Despite his enthusiasm, Poole faced some immediate hurdles. The first was language. He speaks little French, and even though MandrakeSoft's managers and investors had agreed to conduct the company's business in English, the CEO couldn't communicate fluently with every employee. To win them over and inject a note of fun, he sang to the staff in French at a company meeting. Even so, says Walsh, who spoke to *BusinessWeek* Online before the start of MandrakeSoft's share offering: "To get along with a bunch of people who program all day, you have to speak their language." Before long, Walsh adds, "There began to be discontentment and it bubbled up to the founders."

Poole also had to get used to the Continent's different business rules: Employee stock options are harder to hand out. It's much tougher to fire people in France than in rough-and-tumble Silicon Valley. French bureaucracy and regulations are truly daunting. Another factor: The government taxes net worth, including illiquid stock holdings, unless a shareholder is on the management team—something that often sees inexperienced entrepreneurs remain in executive positions for which they might not be suited.

There were also surprising cultural differences: Poole discovered that French employees cared deeply about titles and perks—more than the Americans with whom he was accustomed to working—yet he thought many lacked "the same results-oriented work ethic."

A Gulf Grows Wider
Poole set out to professionalize MandrakeSoft and sharpen its operations. To whip the company's finances into shape, he brought in an old friend, Jon Zimman, as acting CFO. Zimman was shocked to discover the startup had no budget and few controls. Mandrake's top-ranked financial manager was more of an accountant than a strategist. Writing a three-year business plan took months of effort and required placing big, risky bets.

That's when visions began to diverge. MandrakeSoft, with expected 2001 revenues of $3.7 million, was already a big seller of Linux. In fact, it sold more units through U.S. retail channels in 2000 than any other company, according to researcher PC Data.

Trouble was, those boxes didn't carry big margins, and Poole felt the company needed to find a more profitable niche for the long haul. His plan: Offer a suite of technical support services to MandrakeSoft's customers, including offering non-Linux products. For the founders, who had a strong emotional attachment to Linux, that was too much. "His business plan was really aggressive," says Walsh. "People here are just more conservative."

Bon Voyage!
Poole concedes the point but argues that his plan was necessary to produce the return on investment that MandrakeSoft's backers were seeking. He was thus surprised when Le Marois approached him one day in April to say he was concerned about Poole's strategy—especially since Le Marois had helped develop it. "It turned out that we weren't on the same page, but I hadn't seen it coming," Poole says. He speculates that the miscommunication may have derived from cultural factors. And he admits that he may have pushed people harder than they expected. "We were a young company with a lot of work to do, and we were really turning up the heat," he says. "Unfortunately, when you do that, some people can feel really threatened."

Like several other American imports, Poole left the company. He remains intrigued by Open Source and is looking for another gig in that area. For its part, MandrakeSoft says it hopes to continue working with Poole on a consulting basis. "He brought in a lot of vision and dynamism," says Walsh. Now, with its IPO in process, MandrakeSoft will likely have greater resources available to invest in its own growth.

Unfortunately for Poole, who gave up his stock options when he left, that windfall comes too late. But he now understands better than ever before how high the barriers of global business really are.

Source: Reprinted from "Yankee, We Want You. Yankee, Go Home," *BusinessWeek*, July 26, 2001, by special permission. Copyright © 2001 by The McGraw-Hill Companies, Inc.

such as the United Kingdom and the United States. Although the castles and royal palaces found in the United Kingdom are strikingly different from most of the houses of the rich and famous in the United States, the underlying subjective cultures are very similar. However, two countries may have similar objective cultures and considerably different subjective cultures, such as Sweden and the United Kingdom. Although both countries have similar patterns of buildings and roads and dress habits (objective culture), their subjective cultures are very different; the societal norms and values of the English differ considerably from those of the Swedes.

Practical Insight 4.1 shows the importance of cultural awareness and some of the difficulties in bridging the culture gap.

Difference between Learning a New Language and Learning a New Culture

In many ways, the language of a country influences the evolution of cultural patterns. Leading researchers find sharp similarities and contrasts in learning a new language and learning a new culture.[4] Table 4.1 presents the parallel principles of learning a new language and a new culture. Just as the first language greatly influences the way we learn both content and verbal intonation patterns of the second language, values of one's native culture continue to influence and sometimes even distort the learning of a new culture. When an individual is in a new cultural setting, whether in the role of a manager of a subsidiary or in a joint venture, people treat him or her differently and expect conformity to the norms and mores of the host culture. These expectations make it necessary for the manager to quickly learn new patterns of thinking, valuing, and behaving. The longer it takes to learn the values of the new culture, the more difficult it becomes for the manager to function successfully.

Culture and Its Effects on Organizations

As stated previously, culture is to a society what memory is to an individual. It consists of standard operating procedures and unstated assumptions—ways of perceiving, evaluating, and acting—for a group of people who live in the same historical period in the same geographic region of the world. The shared outlook results in common codes of conduct and expectations that influence and control a large majority of beliefs, norms, and values. Individuals are born into a given culture, and they gradually experience the subtle internalizing effects of their culture through various social institutions, such as family, school systems, and work organizations.

Over time, cultures evolve as societies adapt to transitions in their internal and external environments. Internal environments consist of the political system, customs,

TABLE 4.1
Similarities and Contrasts in Learning a New Language and a New Culture

Source: Adapted from G. M. Guthrie, "A Behavioral Analysis of Culture Learning," in R. W. Brislin, S. Bochner, and W. J. Lonner, eds., *Cross-Cultural Perspectives on Learning* (New York: Sage, 1975), pp. 95–116.

Learning Language	Learning Culture
• Learned in early childhood, generally by age 5.	• Learned in early childhood, generally by age 5.
• New languages can be learned somewhat easily by children.	• New culture can be learned somewhat more easily by children than by adults.
• One's native language largely determines one's style of thinking.	• One's native culture largely determines one's values.
• One's native language largely influences the mistakes made in learning a second language.	• One's native culture introduces errors of judgment in interpreting the new culture.
• One must learn a new set of pitch levels and intonation patterns in learning a second language.	• One's native culture has some unique gestures and body language that are always correctly interpreted by members of that culture.
• An accent remains, which reveals the nature of the native language.	• Values of the native culture often introduce "noise" when learning the values of the second culture.
• In dealing with significant difficulties and stressful experiences, one is usually more comfortable thinking in the native language.	• In dealing with significant difficulties and stressful experiences, one is usually more comfortable with coping styles learned in childhood.
• One's most affectionate feelings are best expressed in one's native language.	• One's behavior is best understood in terms of one's long-standing, deeply rooted values. It is easier for us to learn to appreciate a different cuisine than to learn a new way of expressing affection or love.
• One tends to think in one's native language when reflecting on personal values or problems.	• One's native culture determines how one views and values an event, either favorably or unfavorably. Profound emotions are generally determined by one's native culture.

and traditions that are found in a given locale, whereas external environments consist of the ecological setting where the members of a society reside and other events (such as war with another nation) that are not controlled directly by the group. Cultures of traditional societies, such as Greece, India, China, Japan, and Egypt, have gone through changes due to internal and external adaptations through their experiences during the colonial era, independence movement, and globalization in the later part of the last century. As depicted in Exhibit 4.1, several layers of environmental variables affect the functions of the international manager, and the cultural layer is very important. Cultural variables determine basic attitudes toward time, work, materialism, and norms concerning how relationships are maintained and sustained over time.

It is clear that cultural variables—shared beliefs, values, and attitudes—affect how managers in global corporations develop their policies and execute various tasks. One example of how culture affects organizational processes is reflected in the frequent resistance in some countries to technological improvements that might otherwise lead to improvements in quality of life. Clashes between culture and technology can often be unpleasant, and we (from a Western point of view) might wonder why certain nations are not willing to absorb technology in the way we do. Some have argued that the effects of culture are much clearer at the individual level than at the organizational level.[5]

Convergence of cultures around the world is taking place continuously, but at a relatively slow pace. A group of scholars in the 1960s published a study, called *Industrialism and the Industrial Man*,[6] in which they argued that as colonial influences

EXHIBIT 4.1
Environmental Influences on International Management Functions

```
┌─────────────────────────────┐        ┌─────────────────────────────┐
│  Country-Specific Influences│        │   Customs and Traditions    │
│       Economic System       │        │        of the Country       │
│       Political System      │        │          Religion           │
│      Technological Level    │        │    Dialects and Languages   │
│  Important Historical Events│        │          Education          │
└─────────────────────────────┘        └─────────────────────────────┘

              ┌─────────────────────────────┐
              │  Cultural Orientation and   │
              │       Value Patterns        │
              └─────────────────────────────┘
                         │ Influences
                         ▼
              ┌─────────────────────────────┐
              │      Attitudes Toward       │
              │                             │
              │   Work        Authority     │
              │   Money       Change        │
              │   Time        Risk          │
              │   Family      Equality      │
              └─────────────────────────────┘
                         │ Influences
                         ▼
              ┌─────────────────────────────────┐
              │ International Management Functions │
              │     Organizing and Controlling    │
              │   Managing Technological Change   │
              │            Motivating             │
              │           Communicating           │
              │          Decision Making          │
              │            Negotiating            │
              │  Ethical and Social Responsibility│
              └─────────────────────────────────┘
```

decline around the world, the governing elites of many of these countries would like to see their cultures **converge**, that is, come together, with those of the developed countries. While this has taken place, **divergence**, that is, the refusal to accept foreign cultural values, has also been persistent. Many parts of the world, such as the Middle East, Africa, and Latin America, do not necessarily like to change their dominant value orientations. It is important to realize that convergence and divergence are parallel processes and are taking place all the time.

The effect of culture on a specific management activity becomes evident when the manager of a global corporation attempts to impose his or her values and systems on the workers of another society that is culturally dissimilar from the manager's.

A first step toward increasing adaptation of a subsidiary of a global corporation in a new country is to encourage expatriate managers to develop cultural sensitivity. **Cultural sensitivity** may be defined as a state of heightened awareness for the values and frames of reference of the host culture.[7] Managers with higher levels of cultural sensitivity tend to be less parochial in their thinking and are often willing to examine the way management practices might be implemented in dissimilar cultures.

- **Parochialism** is the belief that there is no way of doing things other than that found within one's own culture, that is, that there is no better alternative. This notion is very common, and this tendency is found in all cultures of the world. An American manager who assumes that people in non-U.S. cultures will take a very short time for bereavement leave and fails to consider the custom in other countries is being parochial.
- **Ethnocentrism** is similar to parochialism and tends to reflect a sense of superiority. Ethnocentric individuals believe that their ways of doing things are the best, no matter which cultures are involved.
- **Geocentrism** is very different from both parochialism and ethnocentrism. It reflects a belief that being responsive to local cultures and markets is necessary. Companies exhibiting geocentrism usually use both local and international managers. Executives in the headquarters can come from any region of the world.

Improvements in cultural sensitivity will occur only after managers examine the deep-seated values of their own culture. Examples of the organizational problems that result from being insensitive are numerous. A few examples are striking:[8]

> Procter and Gamble blundered in Japan when trying to sell Camay soap. It seems that it aired a popular European television advertisement showing a woman bathing. In the ad, her husband enters the bathroom and touches her approvingly. The Japanese, however, considered this behavior to be inappropriate and in poor taste for television.
>
> Saudi Arabia nearly restricted an airline from initiating flights when the company authorized "normal" newspaper advertisements. The ads featured attractive hostesses serving champagne to the happy airline passengers. Because in Saudi Arabia alcohol is illegal and unveiled women are not permitted to mix with men, the photo was viewed as an attempt to alter religious customs.
>
> Green, for instance, is often associated with disease in countries that have dense, green jungles, but is associated with cosmetics by the French, Dutch, and Swedes. Various colors represent death. Black signifies death to Americans and many Europeans, while in Japan and many other Asian countries white represents death. Latin Americans generally associate purple with death, but dark red is the appropriate mourning color along the Ivory Coast. And even though white is the color representing death to some; it expresses joy to those living in Ghana.

Managers of international and global corporations should be aware of the flux of cultural variables that they might be submerged in and realize their effects on workplace

EXHIBIT 4.2
Cultural Emphases on Important Dimensions

Source: Adapted from F. Kluckhohn and F.L. Strodtbeck, *Variations in Value Orientations* (Evanston, IL: Row, Peterson, 1961).

Dimensions	Emphasis in Culture		
Relation to nature	Subjugation	Harmony	Mastery
Basic human nature	Evil	Mixed	Good
Time orientation	Past	Present	Future
Space orientation	Private	Mixed	Public
Activity orientation	Being	Thinking	Doing
Relationships among people	Hierarchical	Group-based	Individualistic

behaviors. Appreciation of cultural diversity and the ability to develop effective relationships across cultures should be important goals of managers in this increasingly global marketplace.

The Dimensions of Culture

Countries differ in terms of their underlying cultures. Just to say that the culture of Japan is different from that of the United States is not enough. It is correct, but it does not give us enough insight in terms of how the Japanese workers might react to certain managerial practices, compared to American workers. It would be more useful to say further that the Japanese worker places a great deal of emphasis on the hierarchical arrangements within the company. This attitude prevails because in a Japanese company, a superior has more access to certain important resources than an American or Australian in the same position. Cultural differences result from the variation given to different values. Conflicts and misunderstandings occur when members of a group take the view that their values are correct and best. Practical Insight 4.2 illustrates these cross-cultural misconnections.

Cultural dimensions are basic concepts that help us understand how two or more cultures might be different or similar along each dimension. Various frameworks have been developed, and we will discuss a few of these frameworks as a guide to understanding the various cultures of the world. These frameworks have been developed at different times using different approaches. However, they have resulted in very similar descriptions of the various issues or dimensions that different countries and cultures of the world emphasize. We will describe the very first framework developed by Kluckhohn and Strodtbeck and end with the framework described by Triandis, dealing with the notions of vertical and horizontal types of cultures.

These frameworks represent average tendencies or norms of the major value systems that define a culture. They are meant neither to describe exactly how a culture evolves and functions nor to stereotype how a particular person may behave. Not everyone in a particular culture or country behaves in the same way. By defining the United States in terms of its ranking on different dimensions of a framework, we are not saying that all Americans behave the same way. These cultural dimensions represent general tendencies found in a particular region of the world.

Kluckhohn and Strodtbeck's Framework

Kluckhohn and Strodtbeck developed a framework to describe the emphasis a culture places on various dimensions.[9] These are called *dimensions of value orientation,* and they are described in Exhibit 4.2.

PRACTICAL INSIGHT 4.2

COPING WITH CULTURE SHOCK

From business cards to handshakes and working hours—working in a different country is littered with hidden traps. One faux pas could scupper the deal—and your credibility.

Living in a new culture gives you time to observe, learn and adapt. The business traveler does not have that luxury.

Japanese woman Hisako Imura spent ten years in New York after graduating in her hometown of Tokyo.

"For me as a Japanese woman, a foreign country gave me a much better opportunity than maybe I would have had in Japan. Now it's changing but it's still a very much male-dominated society," Imura said.

She moved to Sydney this year, but found the change hard.

"I noticed the Japanese way of doing business, also the relationship with other people, was quite different from in New York or in Sydney."

"In Japan as a business person your life revolves around your business. Your colleagues are like part of your family."

"In Australia they maybe work shorter hours, but work very hard, then they leave the office and spend as much time with their family as possible."

Chris Brewster, a professor of human resources at London's South Bank University, says Imura has begun to understand some of the cultural differences between Japan and Australia.

"These differences are much more than the handing out of business cards. These are about deep-seated cultural values, ideas of what's good and bad, right and wrong, and these spill over into business.

"It's the way that you have to deal with those when you're in business that creates the problem because often you have very little time to learn."

One option when entering a different culture is to explain that it is a new experience for you, Brewster advises.

"You can say to people: 'I respect your culture, but I don't understand it. I'm going to make mistakes, it's bound to happen but I'm really trying to do the best I can.'"

He also advises being modest when it comes to selling a product. "There's a lot of process involved in reaching deals, in coming to agreement. And if people don't understand that, however good their product or their service is, they're not going to be successful in the deal. They've got to be modest, they've got to realise that it's not just about their product, it's also about the process."

From her own experience, Imura suggests learning about the culture before you visit, and talk to friends and colleagues who have been where you are going.

"Then when you arrive you should really abandon your preconception about other people. You just open up yourself first. And don't be afraid of rejection."

Source: From "Coping with Culture Shock," November 27, 2002. Copyright © 2002 Cable News Network LP, LLLP.

The dimension of *relation to nature* is concerned with the extent to which a culture copes with its relation to nature most of the time by subjugating to it, being in harmony with it, or attempting to master it. Polynesians from islands in the South Pacific have a *subjugation orientation.* They believe that what happens to them is their luck or destiny, and they are not able to change it by their behavior. A culture that emphasizes *harmony,* like the Japanese, emphasizes the value of coexisting with nature, rather than changing it. For example, Japanese planned areas of parks within cities before this became a popular aspect of city planning in the United States. Cultures with a *mastery orientation,* like the United States and most of the Western world, believe that some of nature's forces can be controlled. Continuous emphasis of technology, such as air-conditioning systems and flood control, reflects this tendency to seek mastery over nature to the greatest extent possible.

The dimension of *basic human nature* reflects how cultures socialize individuals to develop beliefs about the inherent character of human beings: as evil, good, or mixed. Cultural values greatly determine whether people believe that the fundamental nature of humans is changeable. In Japan, for example, executives have historically trusted each other enough so that verbal agreements are used for major business deals. In a culture that believes that people are basically evil, there is a lack of trust in business deals and explicit contracts are needed. The *Wall Street Journal* reported that American workers are among the most carefully watched workers in the world, due to electronic monitoring devices.[10] The primary reason for careful monitoring initially was to check on the rate of production and theft and industrial espionage. We might speculate that the tendency to monitor people increased a great deal in the United States after suicide bombers struck the Pentagon and demolished the World Trade Center's twin towers on September 11, 2001. The notion that human beings can be easily trusted has been completely discarded in favor of tight monitoring at the airports and in many office buildings. A society with a mixed orientation views people as basically good and trustworthy but recognizes that they are capable of committing serious acts, violating society norms, in some situations. Norway reflects this orientation in that there is a general atmosphere of goodwill and trust among its citizens but very strict laws governing the use of alcohol.

The dimension of *time orientation* reflects a society's emphasis on the past, present, or future. A *past orientation* emphasizes customary, tradition-bound, and time-honored approaches. Asian Indians, Middle Easterners, and those from Mediterranean countries such as Greece, Italy, and Turkey have a profound tendency to emphasize past precedents in resolving important issues. The relevance of past approaches is not the point. Rather, the way a similar issue was resolved in the past and the extent to which deviating from the past pattern might be considered inappropriate in that culture are the overriding factors. A *present-oriented* culture generally focuses on short-term approaches. Americans are particularly present-oriented in terms of time, and managers are socialized to look at quarterly financial reports and daily returns on stock market performance. A *future-oriented* society emphasizes long-term approaches. Many Japanese and Korean global companies have plans for improving their performance in the long term, which may range from 5 to 10 years. East Asians often engage in activities that are designed to benefit future generations rather than providing immediate gratification for themselves.

The dimension of *space orientation* indicates how people define the concept of space in relation to other people: Is it public, private, or mixed? In a society that emphasizes a *public orientation,* space belongs not just to one person but to everyone. It is not uncommon in Japanese companies to arrange office space in the form of an open layout. In societies that value *privacy,* such as Germany, the United Kingdom, and the United States, employees consider it important to have their own space. Senior managers and other high-status employees are often provided large private office spaces. In societies reflecting a *mixed orientation,* the tendency is to combine both public and private emphases on space. In India, for example, whereas lower-level employees may share a common area of work, senior managers have private offices that are not easily accessible.

The *activity orientation* of a culture focuses on doing, being, or thinking. In a culture emphasizing *doing,* such as the United States, people are always moving from one activity to another, and their days are heavily scheduled or organized to accomplish a series of things from morning to evening. Continuous focus on getting tasks done is the primary orientation of these cultures, and it contrasts with those cultures where a *being orientation* is emphasized. Rural areas of Mexico, India, and Latin America are examples of being-oriented cultures, where spontaneous reactions to feelings are expected, decisions and rewards are based on emotions, and performance criteria are broad and variable. A *thinking orientation* is also known as a controlling and containing orientation. Individuals are socialized to take time off from work, enjoy each other's company, exchange greetings, and achieve a balance in their work and nonwork lives. The French, the Spanish, and those from Mediterranean countries adopt this mode of functioning.

The dimension of *relationships among people* reflects the extent to which a culture emphasizes individualistic, group-oriented, or hierarchy-focused ways of relating to one another. Cultures emphasizing *individualistic orientation* tend to focus on people relating to each other in terms of their personal characteristics and achievements. In the United States, Canada, and most parts of the Western world, employees receive rewards for their own achievements, work on their own personal agendas, and relate to each other one on one. In a *group-oriented society,* people relate to each other in terms of focusing on the needs of the group to which they belong. Emphasis is on harmony, equality, unity, and loyalty to group objectives. The Japanese make decisions by referring to group consensus and working from lower levels and moving upward. *Hierarchical societies,* while valuing group relationships, emphasize awareness of the status of the individual that one is talking to or relating with. Venezuela, Colombia, Mexico, the Philippines, and India reflect this orientation.

Hofstede's Framework

Geert Hofstede, a Dutch researcher, used five dimensions of culture to explain differences in behaviors from one culture to another.[11] His work is based on questionnaires completed by IBM employees from 70 countries, one of the largest studies in international management ever conducted. Although Hofstede's work has been criticized because his data reflect a single company, he believed that using employees from the same company would clearly show national cultural differences because the IBM employees were matched in other respects, such as their type of work and educational levels for similar occupations. Hofstede's five dimensions are (1) individualism and collectivism, (2) power distance, (3) uncertainty avoidance, (4) masculinity and femininity, and (5) time orientation.

Individualism and Collectivism   Hofstede identified **individualism versus collectivism**[12] as an important dimension of culture. A number of other scholars have argued that this dimension of cultural variation is the major distinguishing characteristic in the way that people in various societies of the world analyze social behavior and process information.[13] Individualism and collectivism are social patterns that define cultural syndromes.[14] *Cultural syndromes* are shared patterns of beliefs, attitudes, norms, values, and so on, organized as one theme. Some countries are more individualistic than others. *Individualism* may be defined as a social pattern that consists of loosely linked individuals who view themselves as independent of groups and who are motivated by their own preferences, needs, rights, and contracts. *Collectivism,* on the other hand, may be defined as a social pattern that consists of closely linked individuals who see themselves as belonging to one or more groups (e.g., family, co-workers, in-groups, organizations, tribes) and who are motivated by norms, duties, and obligations identified by these groups. People give priority to the goals of these groups over their own personal goals. People of a given culture emphasize and sample different segments of information from a given body of knowledge, but they believe that their ways of thinking about themselves and their groups are obviously correct, and they do not question their validity. Exhibit 4.3 summarizes key differences between individualistic and collectivist societies.

Included in Hofstede's work is the idea that countries with higher per capita gross national product (GNP) exhibit more individualism. In other words, countries that are more individualistic are also wealthier, more urbanized, and more industrialized.[15] Hofstede also found that countries with moderate and cold climates tend to show more individualistic tendencies, and he speculated that this finding was a result of the personal initiative required for survival in these climates.[16] Exhibit 4.4 compares individualism with GNP per capita in selected countries.

EXHIBIT 4.3
Key Differences between Individualistic and Collectivist Societies

Source: From Geert Hofstede, *Culture's Consequences: International Differences in Work-Related Values*, 2nd ed. (Sage Publications, 2001). Reprinted with permission of the author.

Collectivist	Individualist
People are born into extended families or other in-groups which continue to protect them in exchange for loyalty.	Everyone grows up to look after himself or herself and his or her immediate (nuclear) family only.
Identity is based in the social network to which one belongs.	Identity is based in the individual.
Children learn to think in terms of "we."	Children learn to think in terms of "I."
Harmony should always be maintained and direct confrontations avoided.	Speaking one's mind is a characteristic of an honest person.
The purpose of education is learning how to *do*.	The purpose of education is learning how to *learn*.
The employer–employee relationship is perceived in moral terms, like a family link.	The employer–employee relationship is a contract based on mutual advantage.
Hiring and promotion decisions take into account the employee's in-group.	Hiring and promotion decisions are based on skills and rules only.
Management is management of groups.	Management is management of individuals.
Relationship prevails over task.	Task prevails over relationship.

Power Distance Another cultural dimension to consider is **power distance**, "the extent to which the less powerful members of institutions and organizations within a country expect and accept that power is distributed unequally."[17] Power distance scores inform us about dependence relationships in a country. In small power distance countries there is limited dependence of subordinates on bosses, and a preference for consultation, that is, interdependence between bosses and subordinate. In large power distance countries there is considerable dependence of subordinates on bosses.[18]

In high power distance societies, a centralized authority generally designates the procedures for employees to follow, and inequalities in rewards are easily accepted.

EXHIBIT 4.4 1970 Individualism Scores versus 1990 GNP per Capita for 50 Countries

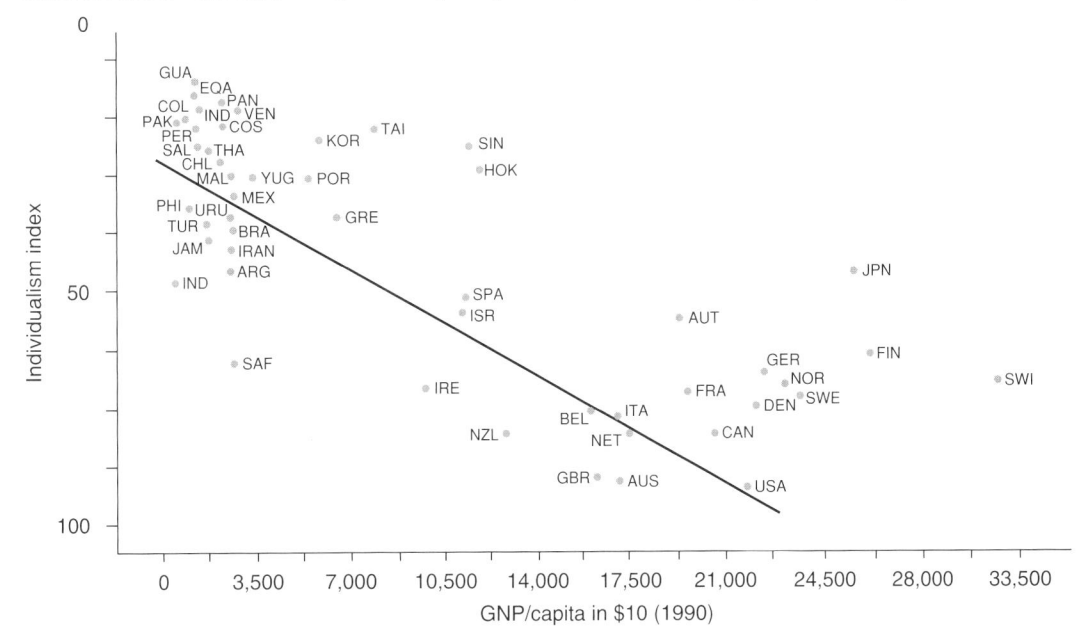

Source: From Geert Hofstede, *Cultures and Organizations: Software of the Mind* (McGraw-Hill/UK, 1991), p. 75. Reprinted with permission of the author.

EXHIBIT 4.5
Key Differences between Low and High Power Distance Societies

Source: Geert Hofstede, *Cultures and Organizations: Software of the Mind* (McGraw-Hill/UK, 1991), p. 37. Reprinted with permission of the author.

Low Power Distance	High Power Distance
Inequalities among people should be minimized.	Inequalities among people are both expected and desired.
Teachers are experts who transfer impersonal truths.	Teachers are gurus who transfer personal wisdom.
Hierarchy in organization means an inequality of roles, established for convenience.	Hierarchy in organization means there are inequalities between superiors and subordinates.
Decentralization is popular.	Centralization is popular.
The salary range between the top and bottom of the organization is narrow.	The salary range between the top and bottom of the organization is wide.
Subordinates expect to be consulted.	Subordinates expect to be told what to do.
The ideal boss is a resourceful democrat.	The ideal boss is a benevolent autocrat, or good father.
Privileges and status symbols are frowned upon.	Privileges and status symbols for managers are both expected and popular.

On the other hand, centralized authority and severe inequalities in rewards are difficult to maintain in low power distance societies.

Lower-level employees in low power distance societies follow procedures outlined by their superiors unless they disagree or feel that the directions are wrong. In high power distance countries, strict obedience to superiors is expected even when their judgments are considered to be wrong. Power distance is reflected in the way that companies are organized. In high power distance societies, centralized organizations are the norm, whereas decentralized decision making is more common in low power distance societies. Exhibit 4.5 summarizes differences between low and high power distance societies.

Individualism and Collectivism versus Power Distance Hofstede compared the scores of societies that ranked high on individualism or collectivism with their scores on power distance. The result is the graph in Exhibit 4.6.

Cultures that are relatively individualistic generally have lower power distance, whereas those that are relatively collectivistic generally have higher power distance. There are exceptions. Costa Rica is a strongly collectivistic country with small power distance. Other countries rank toward the middle on both dimensions, such as Spain and India.

Uncertainty Avoidance The degree to which individuals avoid uncertainty in their environments and the resulting anxiety varies from society to society. Hofstede found this dimension as a derivative of power distance and coined the term **uncertainty avoidance** to define the "extent to which the members of a culture feel threatened by uncertain or unknown situations"[19] or by ambiguity in a situation. Cultures that are high in uncertainty avoidance tend to be more expressive; that is, they use body language to release their anxiety and to ensure their message is conveyed. Weak and strong uncertainty avoidance societies are contrasted in Exhibit 4.7.

Masculinity and Femininity The use of **masculinity versus femininity** as a measure has been controversial, but Hofstede indicates that he developed these dimensions from male and female stereotypical gender roles:

> *Masculinity* pertains to societies in which social gender roles are clearly distinct (i.e., men are supposed to be assertive, tough, and focused on material success whereas women are supposed to be more modest, tender, and concerned with the quality of life); *femininity* pertains to societies in which social gender roles overlap, i.e., both men and women are supposed to be modest, tender, and concerned with the quality of life.[20]

EXHIBIT 4.6
The Position of 50 Countries and Three Regions on the Power Distance and Individualism–Collectivism Dimensions

Source: Geert Hofstede, *Cultures and Organizations: Software of the Mind* (McGraw-Hill/UK, 1991), p. 54. Reprinted with permission of the author.

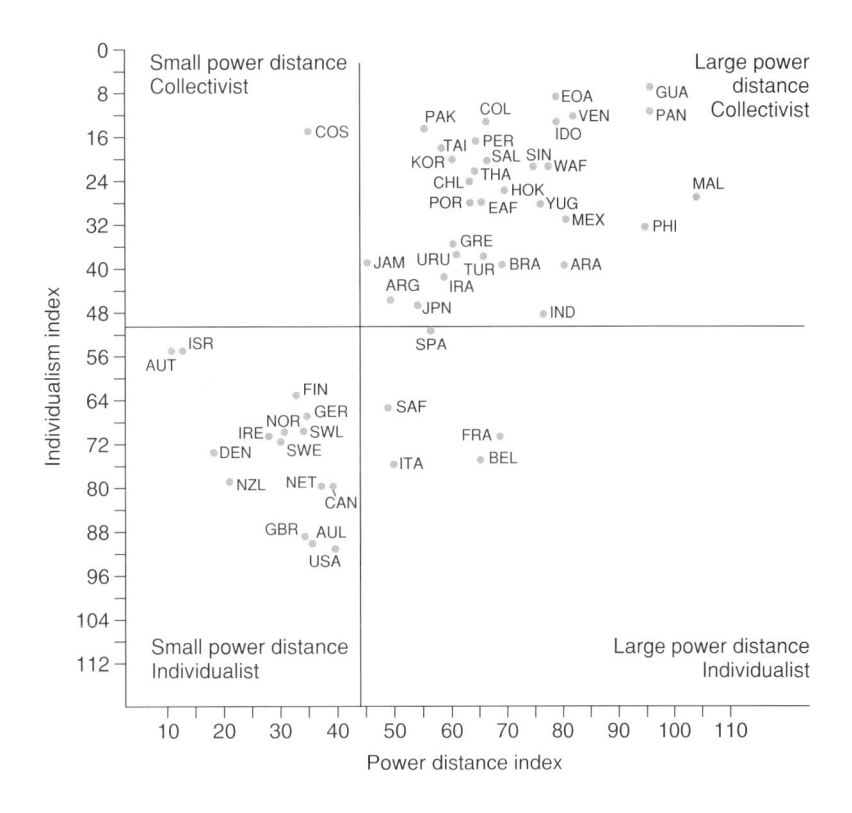

EXHIBIT 4.7
Key Differences between Weak and Strong Uncertainty Avoidance Societies

Source: From Geert Hofstede, *Cultures and Organizations: Software of the Mind* (McGraw-Hill/UK, 1991), p. 125. Reprinted with permission of the author.

Weak Uncertainty Avoidance	**Strong Uncertainty Avoidance**
• Uncertainty is a normal feature of life and each day is accepted as it comes.	• The uncertainty inherent in life is felt as a continuous threat that must be fought.
• Low stress; subjective feeling of well-being.	• High stress; subjective feeling of anxiety.
• Aggression and emotions should not be shown.	• Aggression and emotions may be ventilated at appropriate times and places.
• Ambiguous situations and unfamiliar risks cause no discomfort.	• Familiar risks are accepted; ambiguous situations and unfamiliar risks raise fears.
• What is different is curious.	• What is different is dangerous.
• Rules should be limited to those that are strictly necessary.	• There is an emotional need for rules, even if they will never work.
• Comfortable feeling when lazy; hard work only when needed.	• Emotional need to be busy; inner urge to work hard.
• Tolerance of deviant and innovative ideas and behavior.	• Suppression of deviant ideas and behavior; resistance to innovation.
• Motivation by achievement and esteem or belongingness.	• Motivation by security and esteem or belongingness.

In masculine societies, success and money are dominant values; in feminine societies, the quality of life is the dominant value. For example, in masculine societies such as Japan, the workplace is generally high in job stress and supervisor oversight. However, in more feminine societies such as Scandinavia, cooperation and security are emphasized. Female managers are more common in organizations in feminine societies than in masculine societies. Exhibits 4.8 and 4.9 summarize this dimension.

EXHIBIT 4.8 Masculinity Index Values for 50 Countries and 3 Regions

Source: From Geert Hofstede, *Cultures and Organizations: Software of the Mind* (McGraw-Hill/UK, 1991), p. 84. Reprinted with permission of the author.

Score Rank	Country or Region	MAS Score	Score Rank	Country or Region	MAS Score
1	Japan	95	28	Singapore	48
2	Austria	79	29	Israel	47
3	Venezuela	73	30/31	Indonesia	46
4/5	Italy	70	30/31	West Africa	46
4/5	Switzerland	70	32/33	Turkey	45
6	Mexico	69	32/33	Taiwan	45
7/8	Ireland (Republic of)	68	34	Panama	44
7/8	Jamaica	68	35/36	Iran	43
9/10	Great Britain	66	35/36	France	43
9/10	Germany FR	66	37/38	Spain	42
11/12	Philippines	64	37/38	Peru	42
11/12	Colombia	64	39	East Africa	41
13/14	South Africa	63	40	Salvador	40
13/14	Equador	63	41	South Korea	39
15	USA	62	42	Uruguay	38
16	Australia	61	43	Guatemala	37
17	New Zealand	58	44	Thailand	34
18/19	Greece	57	45	Portugal	31
18/19	Hong Kong	57	46	Chile	28
20/21	Argentina	56	47	Finland	26
20/21	India	56	48/49	Yugoslavia	21
22	Belgium	54	48/49	Costa Rica	21
23	Arab countries	53	50	Denmark	16
24	Canada	52	51	Netherlands	14
25/26	Malaysia	50	52	Norway	8
25/26	Pakistan	50	53	Sweden	5
27	Brazil	49			

EXHIBIT 4.9
Key Differences between Feminine and Masculine Societies

Source: From Geert Hofstede, *Cultures and Organizations: Software of the Mind* (McGraw-Hill/UK, 1991), p. 96. Reprinted with permission of the author.

Feminine	Masculine
• Dominant values in society are caring for others and quality of life.	• Dominant values in society are material success and progress.
• People and warm relationships are important.	• Money and things are important.
• Everyone is supposed to be modest.	• Men are supposed to be assertive, ambitious, and tough.
• Both men and women are allowed to be tender and concerned with relationships.	• Women are supposed to be tender and take care of relationships.
• Sympathy for the weak.	• Sympathy for the strong.
• Work in order to live.	• Live in order to work.
• Managers use intuition and strive for consensus.	• Managers should be decisive and assertive.
• Stress on equality, solidarity, and quality of work life.	• Stress on equity, competition, and performance.
• Conflicts are resolved through compromise and negotiation.	• Conflicts are resolved by fighting them out.

Power Distance versus Masculinity and Femininity This comparison is not as distinct as the comparison between individualism and collectivism versus power distance. Exhibit 4.10 displays the position of 50 countries and 3 regions on the masculinity–femininity and uncertainty avoidance dimensions.[21] Exhibit 4.11 shows country scores on all dimensions.

Time Orientation Societies place different emphasis on time. In some cultures, efficient use of time is emphasized. In the United States, the common phrase "time is money" denotes the fact that time has value. Western Europeans and Canadians are also very time-conscious. However, in other countries, time is considered to be not limited and valuable but an inexhaustible resource. This attitude makes individuals in these cultures very casual about such things as keeping appointments and deadlines. The differences in **time orientation** can cause anxiety and frustration on the part of individuals from both types of culture.

In the United States, the time spent waiting for a person beyond the appointed time is a measure of the importance of the person kept waiting. The longer the waiting time, the less important the person kept waiting is deemed to be. This is why Americans consider having to wait to be an affront. In other areas, such as the Middle East, there is no such interpretation of waiting time. A visitor may wait for a long time, but once the visitor is seen, the interview will last as long as necessary to complete the business between the individuals. However, the next visitor may be kept waiting a long time as a result of this practice. This happens at all levels of society.

EXHIBIT 4.10
The Position of 50 Countries and 3 Regions on the Masculinity–Femininity and Uncertainty Avoidance Dimensions

Source: From Geert Hofstede, *Cultures and Organizations: Software of the Mind* (McGraw-Hill/UK, 1991), p. 87. Reprinted with permission of the author.

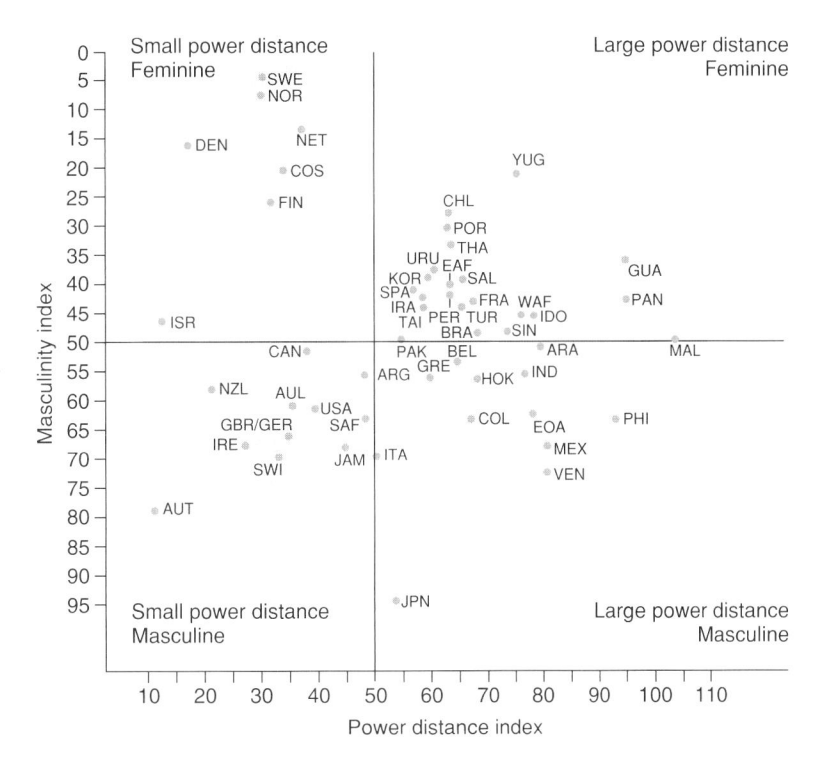

EXHIBIT 4.11
Scores for Countries Using Hofstede's Dimensions and Data

Source: From Geert Hofstede, *Cultures and Organizations: Software of the Mind* (McGraw-Hill/UK, 1991). Reprinted with permission of the author.

Country	Power Distance	Individualism	Masculinity	Uncertainty Avoidance
Argentina	49	46	56	86
Australia	36	90	61	51
Austria	11	55	79	70
Belgium	65	75	54	94
Brazil	69	38	49	76
Canada	39	80	52	48
Chile	63	23	28	86
Colombia	67	13	64	80
Costa Rica	35	15	21	86
Denmark	18	74	16	23
Equador	78	8	63	67
Finland	33	63	26	59
France	68	71	43	86
German FR	35	67	66	65
Great Britain	35	89	66	35
Greece	60	35	57	112
Guatemala	95	6	37	101
Hong Kong	68	25	57	29
India	77	48	56	40
Indonesia	76	14	46	48
Iran	58	41	43	59
Ireland	28	70	68	35
Israel	13	54	47	81
Italy	50	76	70	75
Jamaica	45	39	68	13
Japan	54	46	95	92
Malaysia	104	26	50	36
Mexico	81	30	69	82
Netherlands	38	80	14	53
New Zealand	22	79	58	49
Norway	31	69	8	50
Pakistan	55	14	50	70
Panama	95	11	44	86
Peru	64	16	42	87
Philippines	94	32	64	44
Portugal	63	27	31	104
Salvador	66	19	40	94
Singapore	74	20	48	8
South Africa	49	65	63	49
South Korea	60	187	39	85
Spain	57	51	42	86
Sweden	31	71	5	29
Switzerland	34	68	70	58
Taiwan	58	17	45	69
Thailand	64	20	34	64
Turkey	66	37	45	85
United States	40	91	62	46
Uruguay	61	36	38	100
Venezuela	81	12	73	76
Yugoslavia	76	27	21	88
Regions				
East Africa	64	27	41	52
West Africa	77	20	46	54
Arab countries	80	38	53	68

The following incident during Secretary of State Warren Christopher's visit to Saudi Arabia illustrates this point:

> Secretary of State Warren Christopher was on a visit to Saudi Arabia to discuss critical Middle East issues with King Fahd. The King kept his guest waiting for more than six hours beyond the expected meeting time and met him shortly before 10 p.m. Mr. Christopher used the free time to tour the old section of Jedda, rest, and have dinner. The King apologized for the delay but offered no explanation. The whole incident was written off by the U.S. State Department saying that it was nothing personal and that such things happen all the time in that part of the world.[22]

If the individuals involved had both been from countries where "time is money," the incident would have caused a furor.

When two individuals engaged in a business transaction have different time orientations, problems are likely to develop. For example, in most Middle Eastern cultures, deadlines are considered an affront in the same way that Americans would be offended if someone backed them into a corner in a threatening manner. Americans set deadlines to get things done. Middle Easterners use a different method, which Americans consider rude: needling. An Arab businessman explained how he gets his car repaired in a timely manner:

> First, I go to the garage and tell the mechanic what is wrong with my car. I wouldn't want to give him the idea that I didn't know. After that, I leave the car and walk around the block. When I come back to the garage, I ask him if he has started to work yet. On my way home for lunch, I stop in and ask him how things are going. When I go back to the office, I stop by again. In the evening, I return and peer over his shoulder for a while. If I didn't keep this up, he'd be off working on someone else's car.[23]

FedEx first entered the European market with a final pickup time set for 5 p.m., although the Spanish, for example, work as late as 8 p.m. FedEx had assumed that work schedules and times were the same in Europe as in the United States.[24]

A second aspect of time orientation concerns a society's view of the future. Most Eastern countries (e.g., Japan, Hong Kong, Taiwan, and China) have a long-term future orientation. Individuals from these societies learn self-restraint and learn to delay gratification from an early age. These individuals are concerned with saving money, working toward long-term future goals, and respecting the elderly. In these societies, family and work are not separated, status is respected, and persistance is valued. In contrast, individuals from countries with a short-term orientation (e.g., United States, United Kingdom, Canada, and Pakistan) are more concerned with leisure time, short-term investments, and obsession with youth. Businesses in these societies are concerned with the bottom line and control systems, where managers are rewarded for immediate financial outcomes.

Trompenaars's Framework

Another European researcher, Fons Trompenaars, conducted research with 15,000 managers from 28 countries, representing 47 national cultures.[25] He describes cultural differences using seven dimensions. Five dimensions are concerned with how people relate to each other: (1) universalism versus particularism, (2) individualism versus collectivism, (3) neutral versus affective relationships, (4) specific versus diffuse relationships, and (5) achievement versus ascription. The sixth dimension deals with time—whether the culture emphasizes the past, present, or future and whether the time is sequential or synchronic. The seventh and final dimension is the relation to nature, focusing on internal or external orientation.

Universalism versus Particularism In cultures emphasizing a *universalistic orientation,* people believe in the definition of goodness or truth as being applicable to all situations. Judgments are likely to be made without regard to situational considerations. On the other hand, people in *particularistic societies* take the notion of situational forces more seriously, and judgments take into account contingencies that affect most circumstances. In universalistic cultures, such as the United States, the United Kingdom, and Germany, there is a tendency to rely on legal contracts defining a business relationship. These legal contracts are considered to reflect what the parties should do and are referred to in times of disputes and conflicts. In particularistic cultures, such as China and parts of Latin America, legal contracts do not carry much significance. The contract may reflect an initial agreement, but how the parties relate to each other depends on many factors in the situation.

Individualism versus Collectivism This dimension is almost identical to Hofstede's dimension. In *individualistic societies,* an individual pursues his or her own personal goals, and the focus tends to be on continuous improvement of one's self-worth. Laws and regulations make the rights of individuals of paramount importance. Most Western cultures share this value orientation. *Collectivistic societies* emphasize group well-being, and an individual learns to subordinate his or her personal goals in favor of group goals. Cultures in most parts of east and south Asia, as well as Latin America, the Middle East, and Africa, are collectivistic in their orientation. About 70 percent of the world's cultures are collectivistic.[26]

Neutral versus Affective Relationships In this dimension, Trompenaars focuses on the appropriateness of expressing emotions in different cultures. In *neutral cultures,* the tendency is to control one's emotion so that it does not interfere with judgment. In contrast, *affective cultures* encourage expression of emotions as one relates to others. In a business situation, members of affective cultures, such as Brazil, Mexico, and Italy, may express emotions such as anger, joy, or frustration more freely compared to members of neutral cultures, such as the United Kingdom, Singapore, and Japan.

Specific versus Diffuse Relationships This dimension of culture focuses on how a culture emphasizes notions of privacy and access to privacy. In *specific cultures,* individuals have large public spaces and relatively small private spaces. The distinction between public and private spaces is clear, and the private space retains its private character with limited access to people except those in one's inner circle. The United States is a good example of a specific culture, but the United Kingdom is even more specific. One often must go through several levels of receptionist, secretary, and personal assistant to reach the manager, even for a specified appointment. On the other hand, members of *diffuse cultures,* such as those found in parts of Latin America and southern Europe, draw no clear distinction between public and private spaces. In diffuse cultures, a business executive's office and home are not divided as clearly as they are in specific cultures, and work relationships often extend into personal relationships.

Achievement versus Ascription This dimension describes the methods used to achieve power and status. Achievement cultures, such as the United States and the United Kingdom, are those emphasizing competence (special skills, knowledge, and talent) in attaining position status and power. Ascription cultures, such as Saudi Arabia and China, are those where position status and power come from membership in groups—those in power have been born into influence.

Relationship to Time The first aspect of Trompenaars's time dimension is similar to Hofstede's: There are different emphases on the past, present, and future. The second, sequential versus synchronic, is quite different. In *sequential cultures,* time is viewed as being linear and divided into segments that can then be divided and scheduled. In sequential cultures, such as the United States and the United Kingdom, schedules rule the business and private lives of individuals and are generally more important than relationships. On the other hand, in *synchronic cultures,* time is viewed as circular and indivisible, and relationships are more important than schedules. In synchronic cultures such as Portugal and Egypt, activities are not scheduled with definite starting or ending times, and individuals move from event to event, rather than from deadline to deadline.

Relationship to Nature This dimension is similar to Kluckhohn and Strodtbeck's dimension. In *internal-oriented cultures,* individuals control situations. In the United States, for example, if one is late to an appointment, it is his or her fault. In *external-oriented cultures,* individuals do not control situations. In Argentina, for example, if one is late for an appointment, the fault is not considered to be his or hers but is seen as the fault of the situation that prevented a prompt arrival.

Ronen and Shenkar's Framework

In this framework, shown in Exhibit 4.12, countries of the world are clustered on the basis of attitudinal dimensions that Ronen and Shenkar found by conducting a smallest-space analysis of their data.[27] This framework provides another interesting way of clustering countries and naming them in a fashion that is somewhat consistent with the regions of the world in which they are located. Nine clusters were found based on employee attitudes toward importance of work roles, need fulfillment, job satisfaction, managerial and organizational variables, and interpersonal orientation. In addition to the country clusters resulting from smallest-space analysis, per capita gross national

EXHIBIT 4.12
Ronen and Shenkar's Framework

Source: S. Ronen and O. Shenkar, *Academy of Management Review,* September 1985. Copyright © 1985 by Academy of Management. Reproduced with permission of Academy of Management via Copyright Clearance Center.

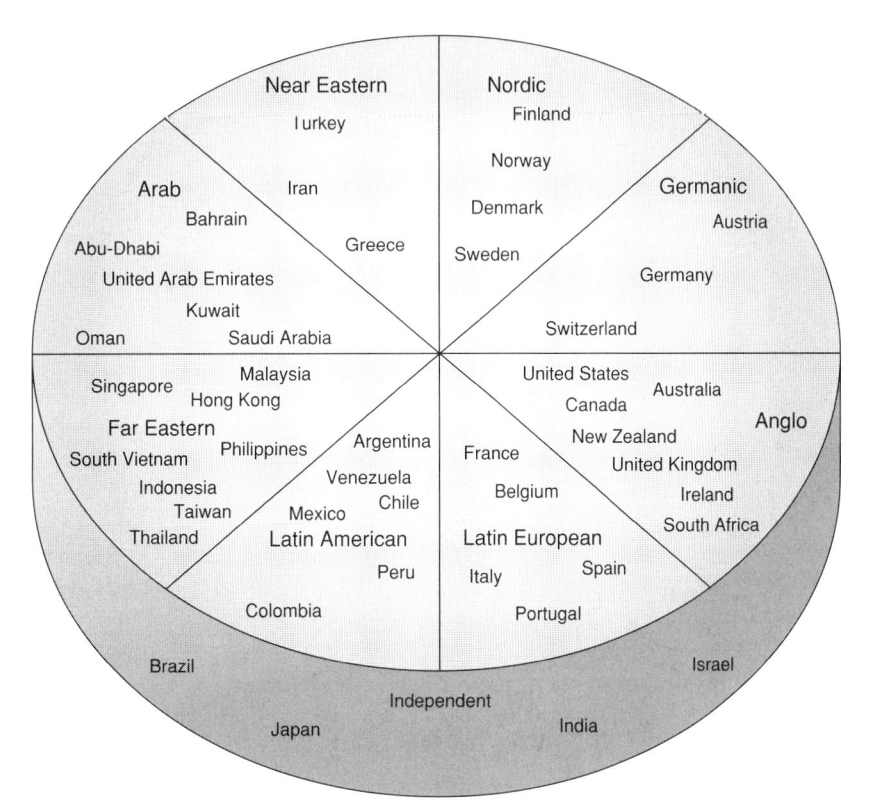

Near Eastern: Turkey, Iran, Greece

Arab: Bahrain, Abu-Dhabi, United Arab Emirates, Kuwait, Oman, Saudi Arabia

Nordic: Finland, Norway, Denmark, Sweden

Germanic: Austria, Germany, Switzerland

Far Eastern: Singapore, Malaysia, Hong Kong, Philippines, South Vietnam, Indonesia, Taiwan, Thailand

Latin American: Argentina, Venezuela, Chile, Mexico, Peru, Colombia

Anglo: United States, Canada, Australia, New Zealand, United Kingdom, Ireland, South Africa

Latin European: France, Belgium, Italy, Spain, Portugal

Independent: Brazil, Israel, Japan, India

product was used to determine the relative placements in the circle. It seems as though most highly developed countries are on the right side of the circle. While this may indicate some consistency between a country's level of economic development and generally endorsed patterns of values and work attitudes, no firm conclusions can be drawn.

Schwartz's Framework

Another important framework is based on the work of Shalom Schwartz, an Israeli cross-cultural researcher, and his collaborators from different parts of the world.[28] They were interested in identifying the content and organization of human values based on their similarities and differences. Schwartz proposed that fundamental issues facing mankind need to be identified before one can meaningfully sample all of the important value differences. Three fundamental needs were regarded as the basis for this value study: social coordination needs, biological needs, and survival and welfare needs. Working from this foundation, Schwartz identified 56 values and constructed a method in which respondents from more than 50 countries in all regions of the world indicated the extent to which each value was a guiding principle in his or her life. The human values were grouped into three dimensions, based on the fundamental needs Schwartz identified. Schwartz's dimensions are significant because they show that the values have the same meanings and are important concepts in all cultures. The value dimensions are shown in Exhibit 4.13.

EXHIBIT 4.13
Schwartz's Value Dimensions

Source: S. H. Schwartz, "Beyond Individualism/Collectivism: New Dimensions of Values," in U. Kim et al., *Individualism and Collectivism: Theory, Application, and Methods.* Copyright © 1994 by Sage Publications, Inc. Reprinted by permission of Sage Publications, Inc.

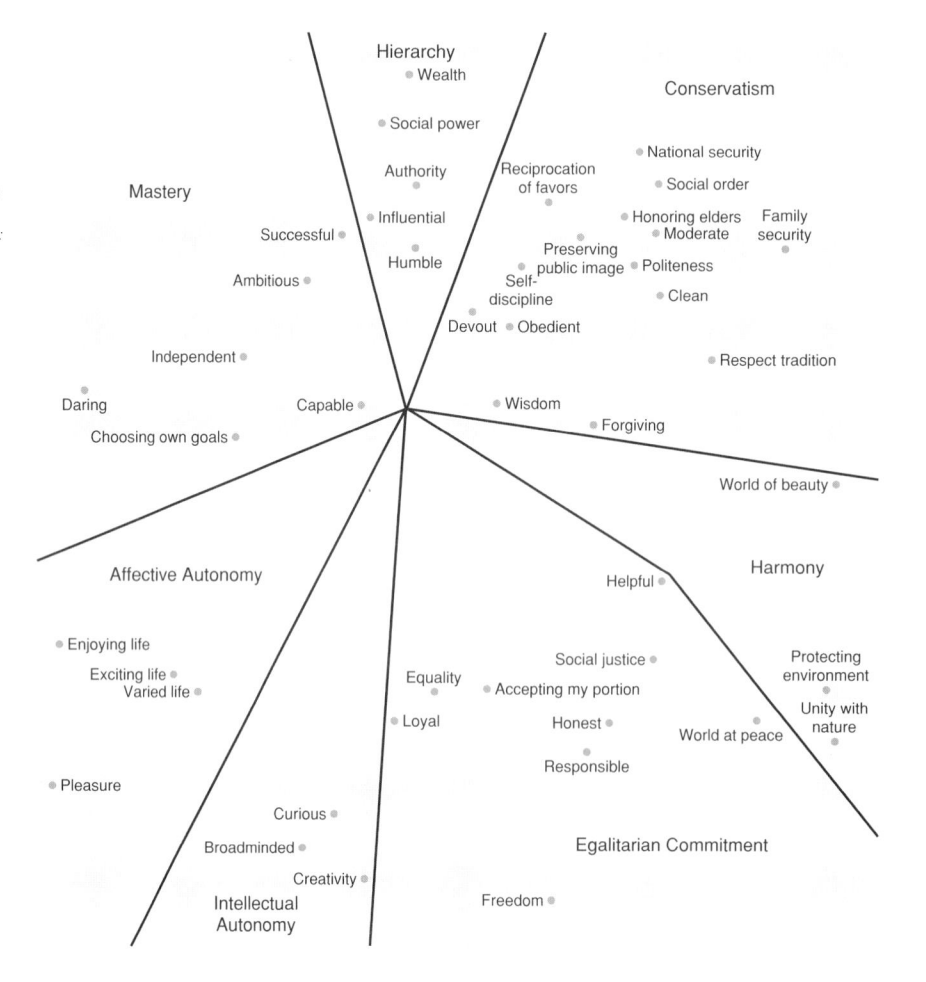

Conservatism versus Autonomy In countries where *conservatism* is emphasized, maintenance of the status quo and restraint of personal actions that disrupt solidarity, cohesiveness, and traditional order are valued. Examples of such values include obedience, respect of tradition, family security, social order, and reciprocation of favors. *Intellectual autonomy,* in contrast, emphasizes independence of ideas and the rights of an individual to pursue his or her own intellectual goals. Examples include values of curiosity, broad-mindedness, and creativity. *Affective autonomy,* which is also opposite to conservatism, focuses on individuals' right to have pleasurable experiences, such as enjoying life, having an exciting life, having a varied life, and pursuing pleasure. Countries that emphasize conservatism include China, India, and Greece as well as the Middle East. Emphasis on intellectual autonomy is found in countries that are also high on Hofstede's dimension of individualism, such as the United States, United Kingdom, Australia, and Germany. Affective autonomy is especially emphasized in the United States and other individualist countries, such as Australia and the United Kingdom.

Hierarchy versus Egalitarianism In countries that emphasize the value of *hierarchy,* individuals are socialized to respect the obligations and rules attached to social roles. Sanctions are imposed if they deviate from these expectations. This value type accepts the unequal distribution of power, wealth, authority, and influence. On the other hand, countries emphasizing the value of *egalitarianism* reinforce the need for individuals to cooperate voluntarily and feel a sense of genuine concern for everyone's welfare. This value type deemphasizes personal interests in favor of equality, responsibility, and freedom. Hierarchy is particularly found in countries that are also high in Hofstede's dimension of power distance, such as Latin American countries, Middle Eastern countries, and some eastern and southern Asian countries. Egalitarianism is found in countries that are low in power distance and high in femininity, such as the Scandinavian countries of Denmark, Sweden, and Norway.

Mastery versus Harmony In countries that emphasize *mastery,* people are socialized to control and change the natural and social world, to exert some degree of control, and to exploit it. This value type stresses the importance of getting ahead through assertiveness. Ambition, success, independence, and individual capability are highly valued in these countries. *Harmony,* on the other hand, advances the preservation of the ecological and social worlds as they are. This value type emphasizes protection of the environment and unity of nature. The value of mastery is found in the United States and some western European countries, whereas the value of harmony is found in east Asian countries, particularly in Japan. However, the ecological movement is becoming very strong in the United States and western European countries, and time will show whether the values of mastery retain their hold on these countries.

Hall's Framework

Edward T. Hall, an American anthropologist, used the concept of context to explain cultural differences between countries.[29] *Context* refers to cues and other information present in a given situation. In *high-context cultures,* such as Japan, Spain, and the Middle Eastern countries, information is embedded in the social situation and is implicitly understood by those involved in the situation. Use of body language and tone of voice in conveying sentiments and messages is common. In *low-context cultures,* such as Switzerland, Germany, and the United States, information tends to be explicitly stated. Use of words to convey meaning is emphasized, and little information is left that is not explicitly stated. For example, Swiss and Germans are relatively direct in their style of communication, whereas Japanese and Chinese expect that implicit messages that are in the context will be easily understood.

Triandis's Framework

Harry C. Triandis, a prominent cross-cultural researcher, developed a framework around the concept of subjective culture.[30] He advanced the notion that to analyze culture systematically, one needs to understand the significance of the *cultural syndrome,* which is composed of (1) cultural complexity, (2) tightness versus looseness, and (3) two aspects of individualism versus collectivism.

Cultural complexity is largely determined by the ecology and history of the society. Societies in which people are hunters and gatherers of food tend to be simple. Agricultural societies are a little more complex, and industrial societies tend to be still more complex. Societies in which large volumes of information are continuously being exchanged tend to be the most complex. According to this scheme, the culture of the Eskimos is relatively simple, whereas the culture of cities like metropolitan New York is one of the most complex. Most international business occurs in more complex societies that have established infrastructure.

The second aspect of the syndrome, *tightness versus looseness,* is concerned with the degree of enforcement of social norms in the society. In the United States, where culture is loose, deviation from social norms is tolerated more easily than in tight cultures, such as those found in most east Asian (e.g., Japan and China), Mediterranean (Greece), and Middle Eastern (e.g., Egypt and Jordan) countries. Impulsive behaviors and those that lead to self-gratification appear more frequently in U.S. and Western television programs than in those of countries that are tighter in the enforcement of norms. Tight cultures do not tolerate deviation from norms and expected role behaviors, and severe sanctions are imposed on those who violate expectations. Triandis noted that self-control and control of impulsive behavior are learned more easily in cultures that are tight.[31] The significance of this aspect of the cultural syndrome is discussed in the chapter on leadership (Chapter 11) as well as the chapter on negotiation and decision making (Chapter 10).

The third aspect of this syndrome is concerned with cultural patterns of individualism versus collectivism coupled with the notion of *verticalness versus horizontalness.* Triandis and his colleagues suggest that there are two kinds of collectivism and two kinds of individualism.[32]

The first kind of collectivism, *horizontal collectivism,* emphasizes interdependence of action and equality with others. The second type of collectivism, *vertical collectivism,* emphasizes interdependence of action but the concept of being different from others. Horizontal collectivism is found in Israeli *kibbutim.* This particular cultural pattern is not widely observed. Vertical collectivism cultures are traditional China, India, most of Latin America, and many of the Mediterranean and African countries.

The first kind of individualism, *horizontal individualism,* emphasizes independence of action and equality with others. Australia, Sweden, and Denmark are good examples of countries that are high on horizontal individualism. The second type of individualism, *vertical individualism,* emphasizes independence of action and the need to stand out from others. This is a characteristic of most wealthy Western countries and is particularly prevalent in the United States, United Kingdom, and France.

Triandis's framework is important because the preference for management style differs in part due to these cultural syndromes. The significance of the framework will also be seen in the chapter on managing technology and knowledge (Chapter 8).

TABLE 4.2
A Synthesis of the Basic Cultural Dimensions

Areas	Dimensions	Authors
Relation to nature	Mastery, harmony, subjugation	Kluckhohn and Strodtbeck
	Internal versus external	Trompenaars
	Mastery versus harmony	Schwartz
Basic human nature	Good, mixed, evil	Kluckhohn and Strodtbeck
Time orientation	Past, present, future	Kluckhohn and Strodtbeck
	Long-term versus short-term	Hofstede
	Sequential versus synchronic	Trompenaars
Space orientation	Public, mixed, private	Kluckhohn and Strodtbeck
	Specific versus diffuse	Trompenaars
Activity orientation	Doing, being, thinking	Kluckhohn and Strodtbeck
Relationship orientation	Individualistic versus group	Kluckhohn and Strodtbeck
	Individualism versus collectivism	Hofstede
	Power distance	Hofstede
	Uncertainty avoidance	Hofstede
	Masculinity versus femininity	Hofstede
	Universalism versus particularism	Trompenaars
	Individualism versus collectivism	Trompenaars
	Neutral versus affective	Trompenaars
	Conservatism versus intellectual autonomy	Schwartz
	Hierarchy versus egalitarianism	Schwartz
	High versus low context	Hall
	Cultural complexity	Triandis
	Tightness versus looseness	Triandis
	Verticalness versus horizontalness	Triandis

Table 4.2 outlines the basic cultural dimensions. Practical Insight 4.3 illustrates some of the intricate details that international managers must know about the cultures they want to do business with.

Cultural Dimensions from the GLOBE Studies

A recent large-scale study on global leadership and organizational behavior effectiveness (GLOBE) led by Robert House of the Wharton School has identified cultural dimensions that are relevant for distinguishing one society from another. These dimensions are individualism, in-group collectivism, institutional collectivism, power distance, uncertainty avoidance, gender egalitarianism, human orientation, performance orientation, future orientation, and assertiveness. Since these dimensions are the latest findings on cultural variations, it is important that we understand their significance in terms of their practical implications. The dimensions of individualism, power distance, future orientation, and uncertainty avoidance were discussed earlier in the section on Hofstede's framework of culture; therefore, we discuss only the remaining dimensions here.

In-group and Institutional Collectivism In-group collectivism concerns the readiness of individuals to subordinate personal goals in favor of goals of the in-group. In east Asian societies, individuals learn to put primary emphasis on the goals of the collectives to which they belong; they do not feel particularly concerned about giving up their personal goals in order to uphold or sustain the goals of their families, close friends, and other groups that are important in the immediate social context. Such tendencies are not found in the affluent societies of the West. In countries such as the

PRACTICAL INSIGHT 4.3

HOW TO DO BUSINESS IN ISLAMIC COUNTRIES

The business scene in the Islamic world may be as complex as its 1.3 billion people, but one rule is nevertheless quite straightforward for Westerners who want to do deals.

"One thing you do not bring up is the Palestinian–Israeli situation," advised Samuel L. Hayes III,[*] an expert on Islamic finance and an emeritus professor of investment banking at Harvard Business School.

Hayes, who continues to travel regularly to Islamic countries for research and consulting, offered advice to HBS students on January 23 as part of the school's post–September 11 speaker series, "Rising to the Challenge." He was joined by a specialist in Islamic law, Harvard Law School professor Frank E. Vogel,[†] for the series' discussion on doing business in the Islamic world. Vogel and Hayes are also co-authors of the book *Islamic Law and Finance: Religion, Risk and Return* (Kluwer Law International, 1998).

According to Hayes and Vogel, businesspeople, particularly Westerners who work in the Persian Gulf and other Islamic regions such as Asia and North Africa, need to appreciate the extent to which religion and Islamic law are intertwined and permeate all levels of society, including commerce, to greater and lesser degrees depending on the country. "This law is seen as deriving from direct, divine command," said Vogel. "This is important to grasp."

Executives who understand the basic tenets of the Islamic religion as it relates to commerce will have an easier time abroad, they said. According to Hayes, the following principles of comportment are expected among businesspeople:

- Contracts should be fair to all parties. Partnership is preferred over hierarchical claims.
- Speculation is prohibited. "They don't like gambling," said Hayes. "For instance, if you invested in an Islamic mutual fund, among those industries which would be barred from representation as funds would be the gambling industry. But gambling also relates to futures; it relates to currency hedging; so it's a major situation that you have to be aware of."
- Interest is prohibited. "This is probably the thing that is most often identified with Islamic finance. Back in the time of the prophet Mohammed, some of the most rapacious individuals were the moneylenders; and so as a response to the things that these moneylenders did which were so reprehensible, part of the religious belief is that you do not charge interest or accept interest. Now, of course, that isn't always practiced, but it is the theory."
- Compassion is required when a business is in trouble. "In any country that has Islamic influences in its legal structure, if somebody is in bankruptcy or if somebody is experiencing financial reversals, you can't put pressure on them, because that is not an appropriate thing to do when somebody is down. You don't kick them when they're down," said Hayes.

Like religious people everywhere, Vogel said, not all Muslims follow the faith in every respect. Some do deal in futures, for instance. "What Frank and I found after working with religious mullahs for most of the 1990s—and Frank a lot longer than that—is that it's a process of education," Hayes told the group. "When they get to understand what's involved in an international transaction, they are more willing to interpret an option, for instance, as not being speculative.

"There are very few who are doing that yet," he added. "As a result, truly few Muslims who are international businesspeople are exposed to the vagaries of currency exchanges." There are religiously acceptable options for commodities, but they're very cumbersome, he said.

United States, United Kingdom, France, and Australia individuals put more emphasis on their personal goals and objectives and are not typically willing to subordinate their personal goals in favor of the goals that might be important for the various groups to which they belong.

Institutional collectivism is concerned with the degree of identity that individuals have in regard to various institutions, particularly their own work organization. In Japan, South Korea, China, and India individuals are proud to identify themselves with their employing organization. "I work for Toyota" (in the context of Japan) or "I work for the Tata Consulting Services" (in the context of India) are proud utterances of individuals working for these organizations. In the West, the tendency is to identify oneself with the values and goals of one's occupation. It is not deemed necessary or even appropriate to take pride in being identified with one's employing organization.

More Tips

On a practical basis, names are very important for doing deals in Islamic countries, as in most of the world, the professors said. Who you know is key. Similarly, relationships and family connections are vital in business. "Relationships that have gone on over time inspire confidence, and of course that's no different than in [the U.S.]," said Hayes.

Personal staff can be very influential and should not be underestimated, he continued. The man who meets you at the airport or who chats you up in a company's waiting room may turn out to be a relative or confidant of the person you're there to do business with.

While it's good for Westerners to be able to speak Arabic socially in the Gulf region, Hayes said, many people would be insulted if you try to speak Arabic about something as important as a deal: "That would be like suggesting that they don't speak English well enough." Those at the business level have usually gone to college in the U.S., Britain, or Australia. Speaking English is a status symbol.

Perhaps surprisingly, Western women sometimes have an advantage doing business in some Islamic countries, Hayes pointed out. They're seen as special and different, almost a "third sex," since most companies send men on the assumption that men will be more acceptable. "Women seem to be able to get to people quicker than the men can," he observed.

Forward and Back

Membership in the World Trade Organization should loosen up the Middle East and particularly the Gulf economically, said Vogel, yet only countries around the periphery of the Arabian peninsula have joined so far. "The big elephant," he said, is Saudi Arabia. It is nowhere near being able to join the WTO, according to Vogel, in part because it is unwilling to enforce foreign arbitration awards.

"It's very important to watch how fast Saudi Arabia moves toward WTO membership. It will have a great deal to do with the political stability of the country, its dealing with the challenges of the future—very serious ones like a demographic bubble that is terribly frightening, affecting, particularly, young males otherwise prone to all sorts of radical beliefs—and a lot of other things, such as the status of women.

"Adaptation and liberalization can happen quickly if the government is in the mood," said Vogel. "It hasn't got there. So far there's too much freight Saudi Arabia is holding back."

Asked if they see a lessening of dependence on Gulf oil since the September 11 terrorist attacks, Vogel said Central Asia should be tapped to counterbalance dependence on Gulf countries and OPEC, while Hayes offered a realist perspective. The U.S. political system is very short sighted, Hayes said. American politicians, who only look two years down the road to the next election, try to "placate the electorate" with short-term benefits at the expense of long-term solutions.

"I think President Carter was right when he tried to initiate a number of long-term energy projects which would have given us greater independence from the Gulf area," said Hayes. "But of course they were completely chucked as soon as he left office.

"So I'm not optimistic about this, and I therefore think we will find ourselves continuing to be vulnerable to that part of the world."

[*] Samuel L. Hayes III holds the Jacob H. Schiff Chair in Investment Banking at the Harvard Business School, Emeritus.

[†] Frank E. Vogel is the Custodian of the Two Holy Mosques Adjunct Professor of Islamic Legal Studies and director of the Islamic Legal Studies Program at Harvard Law School.

Source: Martha Lagace, "How to Do Business in Islamic Countries," *HBS Working Knowledge,* February 4, 2002. Reprinted with permission of HBS Working Knowledge.

Gender Egalitarianism This dimension reflects the beliefs and values of a society regarding whether sex differences should have any importances in determining the roles that members of the society play in their work settings, communities, and homes. In societies that emphasize high gender egalitarianism, biological sex differences have much less importance in determining the allocation of different types of roles between males and females. Females and males are encouraged to play any kind of role that they might deem important in their various life stages. It is not unlikely for females to occupy roles that have been viewed as traditionally masculine in nature, such as firefighter, factory foreman, police officer, and senior manager in a large corporation.

The primary differentiating factor in occupying different roles is the ability of the individual to perform the role despite sex differences. Countries such as Sweden, Denmark, Norway, Finland, and other Scandinavian countries do not make much distinction as to which sexes would occupy which types of roles. However, in much of the Middle East, Africa, Latin America, and Asia, men and women are encouraged to play different types of roles that are traditionally either masculine or feminine. You will hardly find a female police officer in Saudi Arabia, United Arab Emirates, Iran, and the like. In addition, in societies that do not put much emphasis on gender egalitarianism, women are not supposed to be assertive in making their viewpoints known. They are socialized to follow the various rules developed by men and religious doctrines. Education of women in these societies is not encouraged, leading to a workforce at all levels that is predominantly composed of male members.

Human Orientation   The **human orientation** dimension is concerned with the extent to which a society encourages members to be fair, altruistic, generous, kind, and caring for their fellow members. GLOBE studies find that Ireland, Malaysia, Egypt, and the Philippines are high on this dimension. In other words, in these societies there is a strong tendency to foster paternalism and benevolent autocratic regimes. People are usually friendly with each other, are tolerant of each other's ways of behaving in societies, and value harmony. Societies with low human orientation give more importance to power and material possessions as well as self-enhancement. Germany, France, and Spain scored low on the dimension of human orientation in the GLOBE project. Research on this dimension is likely to be helpful for managers in establishing successful cross-cultural interactions. Individuals from countries emphasizing high human orientation might get offended by strong acts or tendencies toward sustaining competition in the workplace that are common among members of societies whose human orientation is low.

Performance Orientation   This dimension of culture indicates the importance of ongoing concern with improving various types of performance in the workplace. Most individuals are engaged in striving for excellence. Societies such as Singapore, Hong Kong, and the United States are high on performance orientation, whereas Russia and Italy scored low on this dimension. Other important aspects of life such as tradition, loyalty, and respect for family integrity are viewed as being more important in societies where performance orientation is not valued highly.

Assertiveness   In societies that value assertiveness, individuals are supposed to be tough, willing to confront important adversaries, and competitive in obtaining valued outcomes in the workplace. Modesty and tenderness are not as valued as assertiveness. According to the GLOBE data, the United States, Austria, and Germany are highly assertive societies and value competition, in contrast to the societies of Sweden and Japan, which were found to be less assertive in the GLOBE studies. These less assertive societies value warm interpersonal and social relations, and maintaining harmony in the workplace is desired more than obtaining valued outcomes by employing confrontative methods. These societies also have sympathy for the weak and value loyalty and solidarity in the workplace and in other social contexts.

The dimensions of the GLOBE studies are important in predicting various outcomes in work organizations, and it is important to be familiar with the issues that are associated with these dimensions.[33]

Hooker's Framework for Cultural Differences

Another framework for understanding cultural differences across societies has been proposed by Hooker. The major dimension of this framework that is useful for understanding international differences in cultural orientation of societies is concerned with relative emphasis on *rules versus relationships.* **Rule-oriented societies** are interested in designing work organizations according to certain guiding principles that have been found useful in the past. There is a strong emphasis on formal organizational procedures and contractual arrangements. Employees do not necessarily receive special consideration of any kind (e.g., a longer maternity leave or a larger bonus) for being warm individuals in the workplace. Human resource policies and practices are strongly followed in distributing rewards and other benefits. On the other hand, in **relationship-oriented societies,** there is a strong concern for maintaining harmonious relationships. In work organizations in these societies, productivity may be temporarily sacrificed at the expense of maintaining peaceful relationships among various segments or groups in the organization. Research using this framework is beginning to emerge,[34] and it is likely that this framework will highlight some issues that are not easily understood by applying the Hofstede or Triandis frameworks of cultural differences.

Language Barriers

Language is another problem for international managers. In English-speaking countries alone, the variety can cause difficulties. In England, India, New Zealand, and Australia, the word *trousers* is used to connote a two-legged garment worn by both men and women; the word *pants* denotes undergarments worn under the trousers. Many Americans have made this error in polite conversation. In the same way, the U.S. auto body shop becomes a panelbeater's shop, the wrench becomes a spanner, the trunk of a car becomes its boot, and granulated sugar becomes caster sugar. And this is just in English. Imagine the difficulties in other, less familiar languages.

American brand names can take on unexpected meanings when they are translated. Companies have become more careful recently, but there are some interesting examples. The famous Pepsi-Cola slogan "Come alive with Pepsi" became "Come out of the grave" in Germany and "Bring your ancestors back from the dead" in Taiwan. More examples are shown in Practical Insight 4.4.

Religious Differences

In the past decade religion-based differences among societies are beginning to emerge as important determinants of how international business functions in various parts of the world. The spiritual beliefs held by members of different societies are so powerful that they are likely to overwhelm cultural values in many parts of the world. It has been noticed in many reports that religious practices are integrated with business practices in the Middle East. For example, the new shopping mall at the airport in Riyad, Saudi Arabia, has a very large mosque that can hold over 4,000 individuals with space for another 3,000 in the attached courtyard. It is unlikely that such influences of religion would be present in the West or in the eastern societies of the world. Long-standing traditions based on the Koran and sayings of Muhammad provide important guidelines for many business transactions. In India, McDonald's and other Western fast-food restaurants do not serve beef or pork out of respect for Hindu and Muslim customers. It is unlikely that these patterns of food consumption based on religious preferences are going to change soon.

Organizational Cultures

Just as societies vary according to cultural values, organizations also vary in the way they emphasize a set of shared values, beliefs, norms, customs, and practices. *Organizational culture* reflects a pattern of shared basic assumptions that an organization learns in the process of solving problems of external adaptation and internal integration. These patterns are regarded as valid, taught to new members as the correct way of thinking about various practices in the organization.[35] Organizational culture controls the way employees perceive their work environment and how they process information to make decisions.

PRACTICAL INSIGHT 4.4

SIGNS IN ENGLISH ALL OVER THE WORLD
Here are some signs and notices written in English that were discovered throughout the world.

- **In a Tokyo hotel:** Is forbidden to steal hotel towels please. If you are not a person to do such a thing is please not to read notis.
- **In a Bucharest hotel lobby:** The lift is being fixed for the next day. During that time we regret that you will be unbearable.
- **In a Leipzig elevator:** Do not enter lift backwards, and only when lit up.
- **In a Belgrade hotel elevator:** To move the cabin, push button wishing floor. If the cabin should enter more persons, each one should press a number of wishing floor. Driving is then going alphabetically by national order.
- **In a Paris hotel elevator:** Please leave your values at the front desk.
- **In a hotel in Athens:** Visitors are expected to complain at the office between the hours of 9 and 11 a.m. daily.
- **In a Japanese hotel:** You are invited to take advantage of the chambermaid.
- **In the lobby of a Moscow hotel across from a Russian Orthodox monastery:** You are welcome to visit the cemetery where famous Russian and Soviet composers, artists and writers are buried daily except Thursday.
- **In an Austrian ski lodge:** Not to perambulate the corridors during the hours of repose in the boots of ascension.
- **On the menu of a Swiss restaurant:** Our wines leave you nothing to hope for.
- **On the menu of a Polish hotel:** Salad a firms' own make; limpid red beet soup with cheesy dumplings in the form of a finger; roasted duck let loose; beef rashers beaten up in the country people's fashion.
- **Outside a Hong Kong tailor shop:** Ladies may have a fit upstairs.
- **In a Bangkok dry cleaners:** Drop your trousers here for best results.
- **Outside a Paris dress shop:** Dresses for street walking.
- **In a Rhodes tailor shop:** Order your summer suit. Because is big rush we will execute customers in strict rotation.
- **From the *Soviet Weekly*:** There will be a Moscow Exhibition of Arts by 150,000 Soviet Republic painters and sculptors. These were executed over the past two years.
- **A sign posted in Germany's Black Forest:** It is strictly forbidden on our black forest camping site that people of different sex, for instance, men and women, live together in one tent unless they are married with each other for that purpose.
- **In a Zurich hotel:** Because of the impropriety of entertaining guests of the opposite sex in the bedroom, it is suggested that the lobby be used for this purpose.
- **In an advertisement by a Hong Kong dentist:** Teeth extracted by the latest Methodists.
- **In a Rome laundry:** Ladies, leave your clothes here and spend the afternoon having a good time.
- **In a Czech tourist agency:** Take one of our horse-driven city tours—we guarantee no miscarriages.
- **Advertisement for donkey rides in Thailand:** Would you like to ride on your own ass?
- **In a Swiss mountain inn:** Special today—no ice cream.
- **In a Bangkok temple:** It is forbidden to enter a woman even a foreigner if dressed as a man.
- **In a Tokyo bar:** Special cocktails for the ladies with nuts.
- **In a Copenhagen airline ticket office:** We take your bags and send them in all directions.
- **On the door of a Moscow hotel room:** If this is your first visit to the USSR, you are welcome to it.
- **In a Norwegian cocktail lounge:** Ladies are requested not have children in the bar.
- **In the Budapest zoo:** Please do not feed the animals. If you have any suitable food, give it to the guard on duty.
- **In the office of a Roman doctor:** Specialist in women and other diseases.
- **In an Acapulco hotel:** The manager has personally passed away all the water served here.
- **In a Tokyo shop:** Our nylons cost more than common, but you'll find they are best in the long run.
- **From a Japanese information booklet about using a hotel air conditioner:** Cooles and Heates: If you want just condition of warm in your room, please control yourself.
- **From a brochure of a car rental firm in Tokyo:** When passenger of foot heave in sight, tootle the horn. Trumpet him melodiously at first, but if he still obstacles your passage then tootle him with vigor.
- **Two signs from a Majorcan shop entrance:** English well speaking . . . and . . . Here speeching American.

Source: *Air France Bulletin,* December 1, 1989.

Organizational cultures of the same corporation differ across national boundaries. For example, subsidiaries of Microsoft located in the United Kingdom, Australia, Germany, Ireland, and India exhibit considerable differences in the way they organize work activities and value various outcomes. It is important for managers of multinational and global corporations to understand the nature of the organizational cultures of the subsidiaries in which they are going to work in their overseas employment. Many reports published in business periodicals reveal that organizational cultures of subsidiaries can and do exert greater influences on work behavior than do the cultures of the societies in which they are located.

Culture and Management Styles in Selected Countries

Management practices based on cultural differences vary. For example, in high power distance cultures such as those found in Asia, an effective leader is one who is a benevolent autocrat. In low power distance countries such as the United States, the effective leader is the one who is people-oriented and practices participative decision making. In collectivistic societies such as those in Latin America, the most appropriate reward to individuals is based on the performance of their group. However, in individualistic countries such as those in western Europe, the most appropriate reward system is to reward individuals for their own performance, as opposed to group performance.

In countries with masculine cultures, such as Japan, women are expected to play certain roles, such as staying home and taking care of the children or working as nurses or secretaries. In Japan, women may be fired when they get married, and they are not expected to assume managerial positions at any time. In cultures with a more feminine perspective, such as the Scandinavian countries, women have equal status with men, reflected in the societal expectation that women should work. Businesses are required to make this easier by providing both paternity and maternity leave so that parents can take care of newborn children. In high uncertainty avoidance cultures, such as Japan and Italy, organizations generally have rules and procedures for reducing uncertainty about behaviors in particular circumstances. This creates stability and certainty, and individuals are less likely to change jobs readily. Low uncertainty avoidance countries, such as the United States and Great Britain, favor organizations that provide managers with freedom to take prudent risks. These countries are also known for very high rates of job mobility.

Now we examine the cultural patterns of four countries. These countries were chosen because of their importance in international trade with the largest economic power of the world, the United States.

Cultural Patterns of Japan

About 140 million Japanese live on four main islands in the Pacific that are shaped like a crescent. These islands are largely mountainous, and the population is crowded in a small part of the total surface of the land, near coastal areas. Japan's industrial growth over the past 50 years has been astounding, especially in light of its defeat in World War II. There are huge urban areas about 300 miles long running northeast from the enormous industrial city of Tokyo through Osaka and Kobe. It is the second-largest economic power in the world, after the United States, with a gross GDP of more than $3 trillion.

The Japanese are a homogeneous people, and they have lived relatively independently for thousands of years. The royal family claims ancestry back over 2,000 years. The people practice a unique combination of Shintoism and Buddhism. The Japanese were known to reject foreign influences, often feeling that they had little to learn from the *gaijins* (foreigners), until their self-imposed isolation ended in the 1700s.

Japanese culture is based on the principle of *wa* (peace and harmony). Wa is connected to the value of *amae* (spiritual harmony). Amae, in its turn, leads to *shinyo* (mutual interdependence, faith, and honor), which is necessary to execute business relationships. Although Japan is a country that is high in pragmatism, as well as masculinity, power distance, and uncertainty avoidance (three of Hofstede's value dimensions), much significance is given to the values of loyalty, interpersonal empathy, and continuous guidance and development of subordinates. This results in a curious mix of authoritarianism and humanistic values, and the company is often seen as a reflection of one's family.

In competing with Japan, one often encounters the phrase "competing with Japan, Inc." In several visits to Japan, the authors of this book noted the remarkable sense of affinity that the Japanese have with their community, company, and country. They take great pride in their country's achievement.

Cultural Patterns of Germany

Germany is the largest country located in central Europe, with more than 90 million people. Despite its current status as the third-largest economic power in the world, it has had one of the most turbulent political histories of any western European country in the last two centuries. After World War II, Germany was completely devastated, and the United States developed the Marshall Plan for the economic recovery of Europe, which led to the reconstruction of West Germany. West Germany's economic performance after 1945 was no less than remarkable. It reflected the tremendous resilience of Germans to rebuild the country's economic backbone, which was one of the strongest in western Europe throughout the last two centuries. The reunification of Germany after 1990 led to considerable economic difficulties, particularly because the economic infrastructure of East Germany had been much weaker than that of West Germany. Despite the economic difficulties that accompanied unification, Germany has emerged as the economic leader of the European Union (see Chapter 2).

One of the most important aspects of German culture is the continuous emphasis on planning and orderliness for managing uncertainty. The German emphasis on low power distance is expressed in the formal structures of corporations—a practice somewhat uncommon in the United Kingdom and the United States. This approach to managing business leads to a structural rather than liberal view of management.[36] Long-term thinking in all aspects of organizational planning is valued, and high product quality is important. Management qualifications focus more on highly technical knowledge than on work experience, in contrast to other countries. Adherence to procedures is strongly encouraged, and the decision-making style tends to be based on appropriate risk calculations and tends to be slow.

Cultural Patterns of China

About 1.1 billion people live in the world's largest communist state, the People's Republic of China. The population density of mainland China tends to be high in coastal regions and in the fertile plains along the Yangtze River. Even though Mandarin is spoken by all of the Chinese, different dialects are found throughout China. In 1979, Deng Xiaoping opened the economy to foreign investment. The annual increases in foreign direct investment averaged more than 40 percent during the 1990s, reaching a high point in 1993 at 175 percent. In the world's economic history, increases of this magnitude over such a short time have not been seen. After the political integration of Hong Kong with mainland China in 1997, the interest of international and global companies to invest in China increased again.

How people in society should relate to each other and behave is strongly influenced by Confucian thought and has been for many centuries. To understand the cultural pattern of China and its emergence as a leading economic power in the twenty-first century, we must understand the role of Confucian Dynamism, which values thrift and persistence, as well as concern for future generations. In the Chinese culture, the influence of current actions on future generations is a significant concern. Investments in work organizations, both in human and monetary terms, are regarded as long term. Michael Bond's research shows the importance of four cultural characteristics: persistence (or perseverance), respect for relationships according to status and family connections, thrift, and a sense of shame.[37] The Chinese Culture Connection Study of 1987 showed that Asian nations do not all hold the same exact values,[38] but they do generally hold these four basic cultural values in common.

Cultural Patterns of Mexico

Mexico borders the United States on the south. It has a population of 103 million, living in an area slightly less than three times the area of Texas. The population is mixed with mestizo (Amerindian-Spanish) at 60 percent, Amerindian (Native American) at 30 percent, and white at 9 percent. Spanish is the predominant language. Mexico's economy is a free market economy mixing old and new industry and agriculture, with the private sector becoming increasingly dominant. Income is not consistently distributed, and 40 percent of households fall below the poverty level. Currently, Hispanics, and especially people of Mexican origin, are the largest ethnic minority in the United States.[39] Since NAFTA was implemented in 1994, trade with the United States and Canada has tripled. Because of the importance of Mexico for the NAFTA community, an understanding of some of the dominant cultural patterns of Mexico is necessary.

The cultural pattern of Mexico is highly collectivistic, high in power distance, and high in uncertainty avoidance. Using Triandis's framework, discussed earlier, Mexico is a good example of a vertical collectivistic country. Mexicans do not value time and the concept of punctuality in the same way they are valued in the United States and would not find a half hour to an hour wait for a business meeting unusual. Mexicans value formality and should be addressed by their title and family name. Triandis noted that the concept of *sympatia* (understanding another's feelings as one's own) is crucial to understanding the way that Mexicans expect colleagues to behave.[40] The importance of family should never be underestimated in doing business with Mexico. The cultural significance of work and business is not the same in Mexico as in the United States and Canada. The negotiation process can be long and filled with interruptions, and one must exercise patience.

Summary

The cultural environment of international business is the focus of this chapter. Culture is to a society what memory is to an individual. Many problems facing managers who live abroad arise from conflicts between the value orientations of different cultures.

Many frameworks can be used to analyze cultural differences. Hofstede's framework, for example, includes (1) individualism and collectivism, (2) power distance, (3) uncertainty avoidance, (4) masculinity and femininity, and (5) time orientation. These frameworks help us understand the differences in cultures. Hall's work on context of cultures helps managers understand such things as communication and use of space in cultures. Language difficulties, along with cultural differences, make it difficult for subsidiaries around the world to function effectively, even as they are brought closer together by the Internet.

In this chapter, we discuss management styles around the world. International managers must learn the intricacies of cultural differences that are present and should develop cultural sensitivity as they expand global operations.

Key Terms and Concepts

convergence of cultures, *116*
cultural sensitivity, *116*
culture, *111*
divergence of cultures, *116*
ethnocentrism, *116*
geocentrism, *116*
human orientation, *136*
in-group collectivism, *133*

individualism versus collectivism, *120*
institutional collectivism, *134*
masculinity versus femininity, *122*
objective culture, *111*
parochialism, *116*
power distance, *121*

relationship-oriented societies, *137*
rule-oriented societies, *136*
subjective culture, *111*
time orientation, *125*
uncertainty avoidance, *122*

Discussion Questions

1. Define the concept of culture, and explain some of its consequences for international management. Why should managers of multinational and global corporations be concerned with cultural issues in different countries?
2. Discuss the differences between learning a new language and learning a new culture.
3. What is cultural sensitivity? What steps should international companies take to improve the cultural sensitivity of managers?
4. Discuss the significance of Kluckhohn and Strodtbeck's values framework.
5. Describe Hofstede's framework for understanding cultural differences. Explain the significance of each of the dimensions.
6. What are the differences between Trompenaars's framework and Hofstede's framework? Provide a few examples along the dimensions in which there are differences.
7. What is a cultural syndrome as proposed in Triandis's framework? Distinguish between the concepts of vertical individualism and horizontal collectivism. Give examples.
8. What are the nine cultural dimensions of the GLOBE study? Distinguish between performance orientation and human orientation and their implications for international management.
9. Discuss the differences between rule-oriented and relationship-oriented societies according to Hooker's framework. What are some of the implications of rule- versus relationship-oriented societies for international management?

Minicase

The Controversy over the Islamic Head Scarf: Women's Rights and Cultural Sensibilities

Taraneh Assadipour walked briskly through the international arrival terminal of the Orly Airport in Paris. Her flight from Tehran had landed a few minutes earlier and Taraneh, accompanied by her 13-year-old daughter Shireen, was back in the city she had known as an undergraduate student, more than 20 years ago. She felt exhausted: it had been only a six-hour flight from Tehran, but a long and arduous journey for the 44-year-old woman. Taraneh was leaving behind the constraints and rigors of life under the strict Islamic code enforced in her homeland, to start a new life abroad.

She had not left Iran for 15 years, and the sight of bare-headed, smartly dressed Parisian women was startling. Taraneh loosened her scarf and let her neatly combed black hair free. Her daughter looked on disapprovingly; the slightly built teenager, her round face enveloped by a tightly knotted white scarf, had been reluctant to leave the only country that she had ever known. In contrast to her mother, she wholeheartedly embraced the Islamic code of behavior and vehemently rejected any suggestion that they restricted women's basic rights.

Shireen had been raised in an environment where gender segregation had become the norm. Women were separated from men in all public places, in schools as well as on city buses, at cultural and sporting events, even on the beaches. Shireen maintained, with all the conviction of her 13 years, that the constraints imposed on women, such as the mandatory use of head scarves and loose fitting garments in public, actually enhanced the status of women. Toeing the arguments put forth by the fundamentalist rulers of Iran, the young girl denounced Western attire as demeaning to women: fashionable clothing made them physically attractive to men, she said, thus reducing them to mere objects of desire. Modesty, on the other hand, underscored the Muslim woman's dignity.

Taraneh, a professional woman who had fought to preserve women's rights in her country, and had suffered subsequently the consequences of their loss, had resigned herself to her daughter's intransigence. She felt confident that once Shireen was exposed to a different environment, her views would moderate. One day, maybe, they could understand each other better. For now, however, mother and daughter were walking silently side by side.

A sensation of freedom seized Taraneh: she felt eager to rush forward and embrace a new life full of promise as well as uncertainties. Memories, however, kept racing through her mind. She remembered the heady days of 1979, when like so many other young Iranians, she had left a lucrative job abroad to come home and help build the new postrevolutionary Iran.

"How enthusiastic and naive we were!" she thought to herself. Like many other members of the secular middle class, she had been slow to acknowledge the ominous signs of a new dictatorship taking shape: anticlerical publications were shut down, peaceful demonstrations were repeatedly and violently disrupted by young toughs—the self-described members of a shadowy and nebulous "Party of God"— and increasingly stringent demands were raised for the so-called Islamization of public life. As the noose of the newly established theocracy tightened, fear fast replaced the enthusiasm of yore. Taraneh vividly recalled how the newly consolidated regime required all women to wear the "hijab," either a full-length cloth covering from head to toe, or, at the very minimum, a head scarf concealing the hair.

To protest these new restrictions on clothing, a group of educated urban women, braving the rising tide of intimidation, had called for a demonstration on the International Woman's Day, March 8, 1980. Taraneh could never forget that day: as demonstrators gathered to march, they were quickly surrounded by young toughs, some carrying clubs or chains, who mercilessly threatened and taunted them, before actually assaulting many. Taraneh remembered the fear that gripped her as the bearded young men lunged at her, chanting "Yah roossaree, yah toossaree!" ("either scarf on the head or blows to the head!"), and the stream of insults, especially the cries of "Prostitute! Prostitute!" leveled at female demonstrators. Soon, panic set in, and the demonstrators, some wounded or badly beaten, dispersed. That night, Taraneh watched in dismay as the state television news broadcast reported, "The outraged citizens of our Islamic country spontaneously stopped a group of provocateurs, remnants of the ousted imperial regime and other counterrevolutionaries, from defiling the dignity of the Muslim woman."

The short-lived transition period between the fall of the imperial tyranny and the consolidation of the new dictatorship, which had witnessed the blossoming of freedoms and the rise of great expectations, had drawn to an end.

Most people withdrew from the public sphere and took refuge in their private lives. Many women were forced to resign from their jobs in public and private institutions as the expropriations and policy uncertainties contributed to deepen an economic downturn. Then came the Iraqi attack and a protracted and bloody war that was to last eight years. It was a time of extreme hardship with scant hope for better days. It was also then that Taraneh met Behrooz.

Like Taraneh, Behrooz had pursued graduate studies in the United States. It was difficult and risky to meet and virtually impossible to go out together, given the extraordinary circumstances of war and the newly enacted rules banning intermingling and socialization between the sexes as being tantamount to debauchery and perversity. As a result, the two married before they could get to know each other well. It was an unhappy marriage. The only fleeting moment of joy came when Shireen was born. After several years of strained relations, Taraneh sought a divorce. She then discovered, much to her dismay, that profound changes had taken place in the country's judicial system: the civil laws had been replaced by an Islamic code in various legal areas, from business practices to laws governing family matters. The rights of women, in particular, had been severely curtailed. Taraneh could not get a divorce unless her estranged husband consented to it. Further, the courts gave custody of children to fathers, in most cases.

For four long years, Taraneh tried to obtain a divorce and leave the country to join her brother Khosrow in France or her sister Afsaneh, a resident of the United States. Finally, shortly after Behrooz met and married another woman, he consented to the divorce and gave his first wife the custody of their daughter. It took Taraneh another year to sell off her belongings and secure the necessary documents to travel. She had eagerly awaited the day when she could start a new life abroad and that day had finally arrived.

Taraneh quickened her pace, tugging Shireen along. After undergoing extensive questioning by stern and suspicious immigration officials, the mother and daughter emerged into the crowded arrival hall. Khosrow was waiting there, beaming. The brother and sister embraced. Khosrow then turned to the niece he had never met. Shireen gingerly stepped back and extended her arm. They shook hands.

It took several months for Taraneh to adjust to the new environment. France had much changed from the days when Taraneh haunted the hallways of its venerable universities. The number of immigrants from Third World countries had risen and so had resentment against them. This hostility extended to the French-born children of immigrants, especially those of North African origin. Known as "Beurs," these young French citizens of Arab origin were mostly the offspring of unskilled workers who had settled in France during the 1960s and 1970s to work in the factories or to take menial jobs that the French-born increasingly shunned. They grew in the sprawling housing developments that ringed the major cities. As economic conditions deteriorated in the 1980s and 1990s, unskilled immigrants were the first to lose their jobs and many became dependent on public assistance. The younger generation of people of North African ancestry was also besieged by a high incidence of unemployment. Some of its members had turned to petty larceny or other illegal activities. Most felt alienated from their parents' culture and, at the same time, rejected by French society.

Indeed, populist and outright xenophobic political parties were successfully exploiting the resentment and fears of the populace. The National Front, in particular, had grown from a marginal and insignificant organization of the extreme right in the 1970s into a major political party of the 1990s, capturing 15 percent of the popular vote in the 1995 presidential elections. Its leader, the charismatic Jean-Marie Le Pen, repeatedly demanded that France be for the French, denouncing the loss of national character, rising crime rates, unemployment and empty public coffers, all allegedly resulting from the presence of immigrants and their offspring.

A National Front mayoral candidate darkly warned of a future where a mayor could be named Mohammed, while others raised questions about the influence of Islamic fundamentalists among the several million Muslims living in France. The specter of a rising Islamic tide lapping at the borders of the secular French republic and threatening its very foundations had become a popular and entrenched image. Muslim residents, especially observant or pious individuals, were facing deep suspicion. Although many among them rejected religious intolerance, they were widely viewed as the Trojan horses of fundamentalism.

Taraneh was anxious. She was especially concerned about her daughter Shireen, who steadfastly refused to take off her head scarf in public. Shireen had made great strides in learning French and had started to attend the local public school. Her attire, however, had given rise to strong objections from the school administrators.

The principal and her associates were well prepared to manage the situation. As early as 1989, indeed, in the Paris suburb of Creil, a schoolgirl's insistence on covering her hair with a scarf had caused a nationally publicized confrontation. School authorities considered that wearing the scarf was tantamount to religious proselytism, and thus incompatible with the secular nature of the French republic and its institutions. The public school system was always considered a pillar of secularism and a conduit through which children of immigrants could be inculcated with ideas and beliefs that would facilitate their insertion in the French society. Thus the defiance of Muslim schoolgirls, first in Creil and later in a number of other localities, was considered a serious threat that had to be thwarted. The tug-of-war between school administrators and a majority of instructors, on the one hand, and devout Muslim girls and their parents on the other resulted in several expulsions of students and a call for national guidelines. In the fall of 1994, Francois Bayrou, then minister of education, issued a decree, formally prohibiting the use of any "ostentatious religious signs" in public schools and mandating punishments, starting from initial warnings to eventual expulsions, for those who did not obey the new regulations. As a result, scores of Muslim high school students were forced to stop attending the public school system.

Taraneh had tried to coax her daughter into removing her scarf during school hours, but to no avail. The school had already issued several warnings to Shireen, and Taraneh knew that ultimately, she may have to leave for a country where her daughter's beliefs, as well as her own, could be accommodated. In fact, Taraneh had decided to move to the United States, should the pressure on her daughter become unbearable. She had already contacted the Houston, Texas, company where she had worked in the late 1970s, and knew that she could be rehired.

One day Shireen came home in tears. "I am not allowed to go to school anymore," she announced. Taraneh took her daughter into her arms, and while consoling her, tried one last time to persuade her to submit to the school regulations. "Never!" cried out the adolescent girl. "It is not my head scarf that they hate, it is me!"

Three months later, Taraneh was sitting in the personnel manager's office of the Houston company, listening intently. "Things have changed a lot since you were last here, Terry—I can call you Terry, right?" The lanky Texan continued without waiting for an answer. "Our company has grown tremendously, but we have maintained our employee-friendly orientation: indeed, we are very much aware of the diverse backgrounds of our staff and try to be very responsive to their special needs. In particular, we are committed to create an environment where cultural diversity can thrive. As you have noticed, you will be working with people of many different ethnic backgrounds. Our company has been a leader in promoting multiculturalism in the workplace."

Source: Written by Farid Sadrieh, PhD student in international business, Temple University. Copyright © 1997 by Arvind V. Phatak.

DISCUSSION QUESTIONS

1. It is said that a person's freedom ends where it encroaches on another person's rights. Give your interpretation of this idea using examples. Do freedom and individual rights have a universal meaning, or should they be defined differently in different countries?
2. Consider the head scarf controversy as a symbol of the broader debate on the status of women. Develop a cultural relativist approach, and take sides in the events depicted in the case accordingly. What can you say about the mandatory use of head scarves in Iran? About their mandatory removal in French public schools?
3. In the controversy over head scarves in French schools, many liberals and intellectuals have found themselves siding with extreme rightists and nationalist groups denouncing the use of head scarves. What are the likely motivations of the first group, and what probably incites the nationalist groups to oppose head scarves?
4. What may explain American society's greater tolerance for publicly expressed differences in religious or cultural behavior? Does the emphasis on multiculturalism reduce the possibility for minority groups to fully participate in mainstream society? How could it strengthen or weaken the national unity and sense of purpose of a country?
5. What factors, besides the cultural tradition, affect the status of women in a society? How are attitudes toward women in conservative Muslim countries reminiscent of those prevailing in America at an earlier time?
6. Imagine that you are the manager of a French subsidiary of an American multinational company. How would you handle the problem of several of your French managers objecting to the Islamic dress code observed by immigrant women secretaries?

Notes

1. H. C. Triandis, "Greek Identity: Implications for Individual Development in English Speaking Countries," paper presented at the Fifth International Conference on Greeks in English Speaking Countries, Speros Basil Vryonis Center for the Study of Hellenism, Sacramento, California, 2000; H. C. Triandis, *Individualism and Collectivism* (Boulder, CO: Westview Press, 1995); H. C. Triandis, *Culture and Social Behavior* (New York: McGraw-Hill, 1994).
2. M. J. Herskovits, *Cultural Anthropology* (New York: Knopf, 1955).
3. H. C. Triandis, *The Analysis of Subjective Culture* (New York: Wiley, 1972).
4. G. M. Guthrie, "A Behavioral Analysis of Culture Learning," in R. W. Brislin, S. Bochner, and W. J. Lonner, eds., *Industrialism and the Industrial Man* (New York: Oxford University Press, 1964).
5. J. Child, "Culture, Contingency, and Capitalism in the Cross-National Study of Organizations," in B. Staw and L. L. Cummings, eds., *Research in Organizational Behavior* (Greenwich, CT: JAI Press, 1981); J. Veiga, M. Lubatkin, R. Calori, and P. Very, "Measuring Organizational Culture

Clashes: A Two-Nation Post-hoc Analysis of a Cultural Compatibility Index," *Human Relations* 53, no. 4 (2000), pp. 539–557.

6. C. Kerr, J. L. Dunlop, M. Harbison, and J. Meyer, *Industrialism and the Industrial Man* (New York: Oxford University Press, 1964).

7. K. Cushner and D. Landis, "The Intercultural Sensitizer," in D. Landis and R. S. Bhagat, eds., *Handbook of Intercultural Training,* 2nd ed. (Thousand Oaks, CA: Sage, 1996), pp. 185–202.

8. D. A. Ricks, *Blunders in International Business,* 3rd ed. (Malden, MA: Blackwell, 1999). Examples from pp. 50, 67, and 32, respectively.

9. F. Kluckhohn and F. L. Strodtbeck, *Variations in Value Orientations* (Evanston, IL: Row, Peterson, 1961).

10. A. Q. Nomani, "Labor Letter: A Special News Report on People and Their Jobs in Offices, Fields, and Factories," *Wall Street Journal,* August 2, 1994, p. A1.

11. G. Hofstede. *Culture's Consequences: International Differences in Work-Related Values,* 2nd ed. (Thousand Oaks, CA: Sage, 2001); G. Hofstede, *Cultures and Organizations: Software of the Mind* (New York: McGraw-Hill, 1991); G. Hofstede, *Culture's Consequences: International Differences in Work-Related Values* (Beverly Hills, CA: Sage, 1980).

12. Ibid.

13. P. C. Earley and C. B. Gibson, "Taking Stock in Our Progress on Individualism–Collectivism: 100 Years of Solidarity and Community," *Journal of Management* 24 (1998), pp. 265–304; M. Erez. and P. C. Earley, *Culture, Self-Identity, and Work* (New York: Oxford University Press, 1993); H. C. Triandis, "Vertical and Horizontal Individualism and Collectivism: Theory and Research Implications for International Comparative Management," in J. L. Cheng and R. B. Peterson, eds., *Advances in International Comparative Management,* vol. 12 (Greenwich, CT: JAI Press, 1998), pp. 7–35; Triandis, *Individualism and Collectivism;* Triandis, *Culture and Social Behavior;* H. C. Triandis, "Cross-Cultural Studies of Individualism and Collectivism," in J. J. Berman, ed., *Nebraska Symposium on Motivation,* Vol. 37 (Lincoln: University of Nebraska Press, 1990), pp. 41–133; H. C. Triandis, "The Self and Social Behavior in Differing Cultural Contexts," *Psychological Review* 96 (1989), pp. 269–289.

14. Earley and Gibson, "Taking Stock in Our Progress on Individualism–Collectivism"; Hofstede, *Culture's Consequences,* 2nd ed.; Hofstede, *Cultures and Organizations;* Triandis, "Vertical and Horizontal Individualism and Collectivism"; Triandis, *Individualism and Collectivism;* Triandis, *Culture and Social Behavior.*

15. Hofstede, *Cultures and Organizations,* p. 75.

16. Ibid., p. 76.

17. Ibid., p. 28.

18. Ibid., p. 25.

19. Ibid., p. 113.

20. Ibid., pp. 82–83.

21. Ibid., p. 87.

22. Adapted from E. Sciolino, "Christopher Confers with Saudi King on Aid and Arms," *New York Times,* March 13, 1995, p. A7.

23. E. T. Hall and W. F. Whyte, "Intercultural Communication: A Guide to Men of Action," *Human Organization* 19, no. 1 (1960), p. 9.

24. D. Pearl, "Federal Express Finds Its Pioneering Formula Falls Flat Overseas," *Wall Street Journal,* April 15, 1991, p. A1.

25. F. Trompenaars, *Riding the Waves of Culture: Understanding Diversity in Global Business* (London: Economist Books, 1993).

26. Triandis, *Culture and Social Behavior.*

27. S. Ronen and O. Shenkar, "Clustering Cultures on Attitudinal Dimensions: A Review and Synthesis," *Academy of Management Review* 10, no. 3 (1985), pp. 435–454.

28. L. Sagiv and S. H. Schwartz, "Value Priorities and Readiness for Outgroup Social Contact," *Journal of Personality and Social Psychology* 69 (1995), pp. 245–272; S. H. Schwartz, "Universals in the Content and Structure of Values: Theoretical Advances and Empirical Tests in 20 Countries," in M. P. Zanna, ed., *Advances in Experimental Social Psychology* (San Diego: Academic Press, 1992), pp. 1–65; S. H. Schwartz, "Beyond Individualism/Collectivism: New Dimensions of Values," in U. Kim, H. C. Triandis, C. Kagitcibasi, S. C. Choi, and G. Yoon, eds., *Individualism and Collectivism: Theory, Application, and Methods* (Newbury Park, CA: Sage, 1994); S. H. Schwartz and W. Bilsky, "Toward a Universal Psychological Structure of Human Values," *Journal of Personality and Social Psychology* 53 (1990), pp. 550–562.

29. E. T. Hall, *Beyond Culture* (New York: Anchor/Doubleday, 1976).

30. Triandis, *Culture and Social Behavior.*

31. Ibid., p. 160.

32. H. C. Triandis, D-K. Chan, D. P. S. Bhawuk, S. Iwao, and J. B. P. Sinha, "Multimethod Probes of Allocentrism and Ideocentrism," *International Journal of Psychology* 30 (1995), pp. 461–480; H. C. Triandis and M. Gelfand, "Converging Measurement of Horizontal and Vertical Individualism and Collectivism," *Journal of Personality and Social Psychology* 74 (1998), pp. 118–128.

33. R. J. House, P. J. Hanges, M. Javidan, P. W. Dorfman, and V. Gupta, *Culture, Leadership, and Organizations: The GLOBE Study of 62 Societies* (Thousand Oaks, CA: Sage, 2004).

34. J. Hooker, *Working across Cultures,* (Stanford, CA: Stanford University Press, 2003).

35. E. H. Schein, "Organizational Culture," *American Psychologist,* February 1990, pp. 109–119.

36. D. J. Hickson and D. S. Pugh, *Management Worldwide: The Impact of Societal Culture on Organizations around the Globe* (London: Penguin, 1995).

37. M. H. Bond, ed., *The Handbook of Chinese Psychology* (Hong Kong: Oxford University Press, 1996).

38. Chinese Culture Connection, "Chinese Values and the Search for Culture-Free Dimensions of Culture," *Journal of Cross-Cultural Psychology* 18 (1987), pp. 143–16

39. *USA Today,* June 19, 2003.

40. Triandis, *Culture and Social Behavior.*

Case 1
Hong Kong Disneyland

Michael N. Young and Donald Liu

September 12, 2006, marked the one-year anniversary of the opening of Hong Kong Disneyland (HKD). Amid the hoopla and celebrations, media experts were reflecting on the high points and low points of HKD's first year of operations, including several controversies that had generated some negative publicity.

At a press conference and interview to discuss the first year of operations, Bill Ernest, HKD's executive vice-president, acknowledged that the park had learnt a lot from its experiences and that the problems had made it stronger. Ernest also announced that HKD attendance for the year had been "well over" five million visitors. Still, this figure was short of the 5.6 million visitors that had earlier been projected by park officials. Ernest stated that the park was on sound financial footing but would not release the details.[1] He also announced the appointment of two non-executive directors; Payson Cha Mou-sing, managing director of HKR International, and Philip Chen Nan-lok of Cathay Pacific would be joining the board of directors in a move calculated to counter charges of a lack of transparency. The criticisms were, in part, coming from members of the Hong Kong Legislative Council as HKD was 57 percent owned by the Hong Kong Government, which had invested HK$23 billion.[2]

Since plans for the high-profile HKD project were first announced, there had been criticisms of a lack of transparency from Hong Kong government officials, the Consumer Council and members of the public. The dissatisfaction was reflected in a survey conducted by Hong Kong Polytechnic University in March 2006.[3] Although 56 percent of the 524 respondents believed the government's HK$13.6 billion (about US$1.74 billion) investment to be of a "fair" value, 70 percent of respondents had a negative impression of the public investment in HKD. This response was a considerably more pessimistic result than previous surveys. It was in the interests of HKD to turn this situation around.

HKD was the third park that Disney had opened outside of the United States, following the Tokyo Disney Resort and Disneyland Resort Paris. The Tokyo Disney Resort was the most successful of all of the Disney parks worldwide, and indeed one of the most successful theme parks in the world; the Disneyland Paris Resort was much less successful.[4] Pundits had begun to wonder whether the outcome of HKD would more closely resemble that of its successful Far Eastern Japanese cousin or whether it would more closely resemble that of the French park. That outcome depended in part on how well Disney would be able to translate its strategic assets, such as its products, practices and ideologies, to the Chinese context.

COMPANY BACKGROUND

The Walt Disney Company (Disney) was founded in 1923, and was committed to delivering quality entertainment experiences for people of all ages. As a global entertainment empire, the company

Michael N. Young and Donald Liu wrote this case solely to provide material for class discussion. The authors do not intend to illustrate either effective or ineffective handling of a managerial situation. The authors may have disguised certain names and other identifying information to protect confidentiality. Ivey Management Services prohibits any form of reproduction, storage or transmittal without its written permission. Reproduction of this material is not covered under authorization by any reproduction rights organization. To order copies or request permission to reproduce materials, contact Ivey Publishing, Ivey Management Services, c/o Richard Ivey School of Business, The University of Western Ontario, London, Ontario, Canada, N6A 3K7; phone (519) 661-3208; fax (519) 661-3882; e-mail cases@ivey.uwo.ca. Copyright © 2007, Ivey Management Services. Version: (A) 2007-08-27. Reprinted with permission of Ivey Management Services on August 5, 2008.

[1] Linda Choy and Dennis Eng, "5 Million Visit Disney Park, Short of Target," *South China Morning Post*, electronic edition, September 5, 2006, available at http://scmp.com, accessed December 3, 2006.

[2] In 2006, the Hong Kong dollar was pegged to the U.S. dollar at approximately US$1 = HK$7.80.

[3] May Chan, "Disneyland's Image Has Soured Since Its Opening," *South China Morning Post*, p. CITY3.

[4] Mary Yoko Brannen, "When Mickey Loses Face: Recontextualization, Semantic Fit, and the Semiotics of Foreignness," *Academy of Management Review*, October 2004, pp. 593–616.

EXHIBIT 1
Current Holdings of the Walt Disney Company

Source: *Annual Report 2005*, The Walt Disney Company.

Business Segments	Performance (2005)
Studio Entertainment	This segment had the greatest decrease, of 69%, which the company attributed to the overall decline in unit sales in worldwide home entertainment and at Miramax.
Consumer Products	This division reported decrease in operating income of 3% due to lower revenue generated from the sales of Disney goods and merchandise.
Media Networks	The higher rates paid by cable operators for ESPN and the Disney Channels and higher advertising revenue at ESPN and ABC were the primary factors driving the 27% growth in revenue at the Media Network unit.
Parks & Resorts	The Parks and Resorts division also enjoyed a 5% increase in revenue, largely due to the higher occupancy at the resorts, theme park attendance, and guest expenditure.

leveraged its amazing heritage of creativity, fantasy and imagination established by its founder, Walt Disney. By 2006, Disney's business portfolio consisted of four major segments: Studio Entertainment, Parks and Resorts, Consumer Products and Media Networks. Exhibit 1 summarizes the details of the company's holdings and their respective financial performance in 2005.

OTHER DISNEY PARKS AND RESORTS

Disney opened the first Disneyland, Disneyland Resort, at Anaheim, California, in July 1955. The company's second theme park, Walt Disney World Resort, was opened at Lake Buena Vista, Florida, in 1971. After the establishment of these two large theme parks in the United States, Disney sought to expand internationally. Disney's international expansion strategy was straightforward, consisting of "bringing the original Disneyland model to a new territory, and then, if feasible, adding a specialty theme park."[5] Tokyo Disney Resort was Disney's first attempt at executing this strategy.

Tokyo Disney Resort

Disney opened its first non-U.S. park in Tokyo, Japan, in 1983. The scope and thematic foundation of the Tokyo park was modeled after the Disney parks in California and Florida. The US$1.4 billion cost to develop Tokyo Disney Resort was financed solely by Oriental Land Co., a land-reclamation company formed under a joint-venture agreement between Mitsui Real Estate Development Co. and Keisei Electric Railway Co.[6] Disney did not assume any ownership of Tokyo Disney Resort to minimize risks. The contract signed in 1979 spelled out Oriental Land as the owner and licensee, whereas Disney was designated as the designer and licensor. Although Disney received a US$100 million royalty every year, this amount was less than would have been the case if Disney were the sole owner or even a co-owner of Tokyo Disney Resort. By 2006, the 23-year-old Tokyo Disney Resort, along with the addition of Tokyo DisneySea, at an additional cost of US$3 billion in 2000,[7] was a huge success, with a combined annual attendance of more than 25 million visitors and an operating income of ¥28,957 million (about US$245.47 million) generated in 2005 alone.[8]

Tokyo Disney Resort was well received by the Japanese, owing in part to the Japanese interest in Western cultures and the Asian love of fantasy and costume. The secret underlying this success was to provide the visitors with "a slice of unadulterated Disney-style Americana," proclaimed Toshio Kagami, president of Oriental Land Co. Tokyo Disney Resort had attracted wide support from the local Japanese, who accounted for more than 95 percent of the annual attendance. Moreover, around 15 percent of the total visitors had visited the park 30 times or more, making Tokyo Disney Resort

[5] Sara Bakhshian, "The Offspring," *Amusement Business*, May 2005, pp. 20–21.

[6] Eva Liu and Elyssa Wong, "Information Note: Tokyo Disneyland: Some Basic Facts," Research and Library Services Division of the Legislative Council Secretariat, Hong Kong, 1999, retrieved March 10, 2006, from www.legco.gov.hk/yr99-0/english/sec/library/990in02.pdf.

[7] Ibid.

[8] Oriental Land Co., *2005 Annual Report*, retrieved March 10, 2006, from http://olc.netir-wsp.com/medias/1656486483_OLCAR2005final.pdf.

one of the world's most popular theme parks in terms of annual attendance.[9] The Tokyo Disney Resort also had the highest sales of souvenirs of all the Disney land resorts, in part because it was the only Disney property to give special admission just for the purpose of purchasing souvenirs.

Disneyland Resort Paris

France was the largest consumer of Disney products outside the United States, particularly in the area of publications, such as comic books.[10] However, this status did not provide much help to Disneyland Resort Paris (formerly named Euro Disney), Disney's second attempt at international expansion. Disneyland Resort Paris came into operation in 1992, after two-and-a-half years of negotiations with the French Government. Disney was determined to avoid the mistake of forgoing majority ownership and profits, as had been the case with Tokyo Disney Resort. Thus, Disney became one of the partners in this project. Under the initial financial arrangement, Disney had a 49 percent stake in the project. The French Government provided cash and loans of US$770 million at interest rates below the market rates, and financed the majority of the US$400 million infrastructure.

However, cost overruns pushed overall construction costs to US$5 billion—five times the previous estimate of US$1 billion. This increase was due to alterations in design and construction plans. This higher cost, coupled with the theme park's mediocre performance during its initial years of operation and other factors, caused the park severe difficulties between 1992 and 1994. The park did not report a profit until 1995, which was largely due to a reduction of interest costs from US$265 million to US$93 million and the rigorous financial re-engineering efforts in late 1994.[11]

Despite poor results between 1995 and 2001, Disney added a new park, Walt Disney Studios, which brought Hollywood-themed attractions to the French park. At its opening in 2004, the second park attracted only 2.2 million visitors, 5.8 million short of its original projections. At the end of the fiscal year on September 30, 2004, Disneyland Resort Paris announced a loss of €145.2 million (about US$190 million).[12]

Part of the problem with the Paris resort was the resistance by the French to what they considered American cultural imperialism. French cultural critics claimed that Disney would be a "cultural Chernobyl," and some stated publicly a desire for the park's failure. For example, critic Stephen Bayley wrote:

> The Old World is presented with all the confident big ticket flimflam of painstaking fakery that this bizarre campaign of reverse-engineered cultural imperialism represents. I like to think that by the turn of the century Euro Disney will have become a deserted city, similar to Angkor Wat [in Cambodia].[13]

Disney had to assure the French government that French would be the primary language spoken within the park. Even the French president, Francois Mitterand, joined in the fray, declining to attend the opening-day ceremony, dismissing the expensive new investment with Gallic indifference as "pas ma tasse de thé" ("just not my cup of tea").[14]

Robert Fitzpatrick, the first chairman of the Disneyland Resort Paris, was a French-speaking American who knew Europe quite well, in part because of his French wife. Fitzpatrick did not, however, realize that Disney could not approach France in the same way as it had approached Florida when setting up its second theme park. For example, the recruitment process and training programs for its staff were initially not well-adapted to the French business culture. The 13-page manual specifying the dress code within the theme park was apparently unacceptable to the French; the court had even ruled that imposing such a dress code was against the labour laws.

The miscalculations of cultural differences were found in other operational aspects as well. For instance, Disney's policy of banning the serving of alcoholic beverages in its parks, including in California, Florida and Tokyo, was unsurprisingly extended to France. This restriction outraged the

---

[9] James Zoltak, "Lots of Walks in the Parks the Past Year," *Amusement Business,* December 2004, pp. 6–7.

[10] Mary Yoko Brannen, "When Mickey Loses Face: Recontextualization, Semantic Fit, and the Semiotics of Foreignness," *Academy of Management Review,* October 2004, pp. 593–616.

[11] James B. Stewart , *Disney War,* Simon & Schuster, New York, 2005.

[12] Jo Wrighton and Bruce Orwall, "Mutual Attractions: Despite Losses and Bailouts, France Stays Devoted to Disney," Wall *Street Journal,* January 26, 2005, p. A1.

[13] James B. Stewart, *Disney War,* Simon & Schuster, New York, 2006, p. 128.

[14] Ibid.

EXHIBIT 2 How Disney's Assets and Practices Recontextualize to Japan and France

Source: Mary Yoko Brannen, "When Mickey Loses Face: Recontextualization, Semantic Fit and the Semiotics of Foreignness," *Academy of Management Review*, October 2004, p. 593.

	United States	**Japan**	**France**
Products			
Mickey Mouse	Squeaky-clean, all-American boy representing wholesome American values	Safe and reliable (used to sell money market accounts)	Cunning, street-smart detective epitomized in *Le Journal Mickey*—squeaky-clean version is boring
Cowboy	Rugged, self-reliant individualist	Quintessential team player	Carefree, somewhat dim-witted anti-establishment individual
Souvenirs	Fun, part of the experience	Legitimating mementos that fit into the formalized system of gift giving, known as *sembetsu*	Tacky, waste of money
Practices			
Service Orientation	Hypernormal	Cultural norm	Abnormal
Personnel Management	Hypernormal	Cultural norm	Invasive/illegal
Training	Hypernormal	Cultural norm	Totalitarian
Ideologies			
Disneyland	Modernist theme—fun, clean, wholesome entertainment	Translated modernist theme—fun, clean, safe foreign vacation	Postmodernist theme—resistance to Disney's meta narrative
Foreignness	• Fantasized European roots • Marginalized native and minority others	• Keeping the U.S. exotic • Marginalizing the Asian other	• Politicized repatriation • Schizophrenic relationship with the U.S.

French, for whom enjoying wine during lunch and dinner was part of their daily custom. In May 1993, Disney yielded to the external pressure, and altered its policy to permit the serving of wines and beers in the theme park. With the renaming and the retooling of the entire theme park complex to better appeal to European taste, Disneyland Resort Paris finally began to profit in 1995.

WHY SUCH DIFFERENT OUTCOMES FOR TOKYO AND PARIS?

Why was Disney so successful in Tokyo but largely a failure in Paris? Professor Mary Yoko Brannen maintains that it may in part have been due to the way that Disney's strategic assets—such as products, practices and ideologies—were translated to and interpreted in the Japanese and French contexts.[15] According to Brannen, the "Americana" represented by Disney was an asset in Japan, where a trip to Disney was seen as an exotic, foreign-like experience. However, this association with the pure form of all things American was a liability in France, where it was seen as a form of reverse cultural imperialism. The result was a "lost-in-translation" effect for many of Disney's most valued icons and established business practices. For example, Mickey Mouse was seen as a squeaky-clean all-American boy in the United States, and he was viewed as conservative and reliable enough to sell money market accounts in Japan. However, in France, he was seen as a street-smart detective because of the popularity of a comic book series *Le Journal Mickey*.

Likewise, Disney's service training, human resource management (HRM) practices and training required to achieve the "happiest place on earth" were quite easy to implement in Japan, where such practices represented the cultural norm. In France, however, the same training practices were perceived as invasive and totalitarian. Exhibit 2 summarizes how other strategic assets of Disney were recontextualized to the Japanese and French environments.

In 2006, it remained to be seen how Disney's strategic assets would translate to, and be interpreted in, the Chinese culture of Hong Kong, the topic to which we turn next.

---

[15] Mary Yoko Brannen, "When Mickey Loses Face: Recontextualization, Semantic Fit and the Semiotics of Foreignness," *Academy of Management Review*, October 2004, pp. 593–616.

MICKEY MOUSE GOES TO CHINA

> We know we have an addressable market just crying out for Disney products.
> —Andy Bird, Walt Disney International president, discussing China's potential[16]

The Chinese "have heard so much about the parks around the world, and they want to experience the same thing," said Don Robinson, the former managing director of HKD. Chinese consumers wanted to connect with the global popular culture and distance themselves from their previous collective poverty and communist dictate. Kevin Wong, a tourism economist at the Hong Kong Polytechnic University, remarked that the Chinese "want to come to Disney because it is American. The foreignness is part of the appeal." The Chinese needed Disney, and Disney needed China. For example, Ted Parrish, co-manager of the Henssler Equity Fund, an investment fund house, said, "If Disney wants to maintain earnings growth in the high teens going forward, China will be a big source of that."[17]

Because the Chinese economy was booming, Disney thought it would be a good time to set up a new theme park there. China's infrastructure was still substandard by world standards. In addition, the Chinese currency, the renminbi, was not fully convertible. These and other factors increased the attractiveness of Hong Kong—a Special Administrative Region of China since the handover of sovereignty from the United Kingdom in 1997. Hong Kong had world-class infrastructure and a reputation as an international financial center. Most importantly, Hong Kong had always been a gateway to China. These factors gave Hong Kong an edge as a location for Disney's third international theme park.

THE HONG KONG TOURISM INDUSTRY

> Hong Kong, with its unusual blend of East and West, of Chinese roots and British colonial heritage, of ultramodern sophistication and ancient traditions, is one of the most diverse and exciting cities in the world. It is an international city brimming with energy and dynamism, yet also a place where peace and tranquility are easily found.[18]

Tourism was one of the major pillars of the Hong Kong economy. In 2005, the total number of visitors was more than 23 million, a new record and approximately a 7.1 percent increase over 2004 (see Exhibit 3). Visitors came from all over the world, including Taiwan, America, Africa, the Middle East and Macao (see Exhibit 4). Mainland China was the biggest source of visitors, accounting for 53.7 percent of the total in 2005.[19] The dominance of this group was, in part, supported by the Individual Travel Scheme[20] introduced in 2003.

LOCAL ATTRACTIONS

Popular tourist attractions in Hong Kong included, but were not limited to, Victoria Peak, Repulse Bay, open-air markets and Ocean Park. Hong Kong's colonial heritage provided several attractions, such as Cenotaph, Statue Square and the Government House. Traditional Chinese festivals, such as Tin Hau Festival, Cheung Chau Bun Festival and Temple Fair, added local flavor. Visitors often took part in the celebration of these annual festive events during their stay. The Hong Kong Tourism Board had designated 2006 as "Discover Hong Kong Year" to attract more travelers and encourage them to extend their stay. Furthermore, the AsiaWorld-Expo opened in early 2006, and it was expected to attract more business travelers. Other initiatives included a sky rail to the world's largest sitting Buddha statue and Hong Kong Wetland Park. In addition, the Dr. Sun Yat-sen Museum was being renovated and was scheduled to reopen in early 2007.

---

[16] Jeffrey Ressner and Michael Schuman, "Disney's Great Leap into China," *Time*, July 11, 2005, pp. 52–54.

[17] Paul R. La Monica, "For Disney, It's a Small World after All," CNNmoney.com, September 12, 2005, retrieved March 10, 2006, from http://money.cnn.com/2005/09/12/news/fortune500/hongkongdisney/.

[18] Hong Kong Tourism Board, www.discoverhongkong.com, accessed August 17, 2007.

[19] Hong Kong Census & Statistics Department, "Hong Kong Monthly Digest of Statistics," Hong Kong Census & Statistics Department, Hong Kong, March 2006.

[20] The Individual Travel Scheme was a policy that permitted urban residents from selected cities in Mainland China to apply for visas from the Public Security Department to visit Hong Kong. In 2006, the Scheme covered 38 mainland cities. Until the implementation of this policy, mainlanders could only visit Hong Kong through business or travel groups.

EXHIBIT 3
Annual Visitor Arrivals in Hong Kong

Source: Hong Kong Tourism Board (2006).

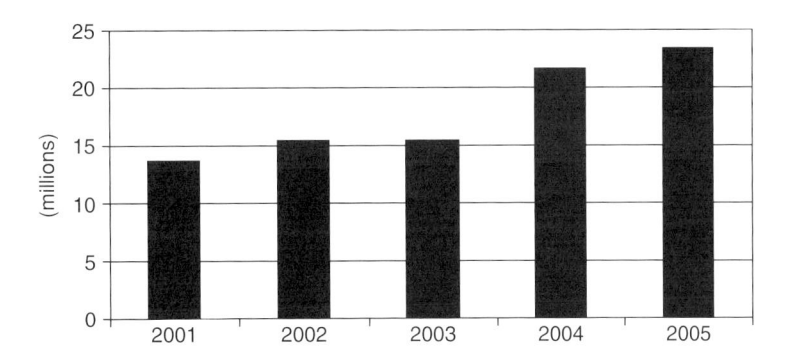

EXHIBIT 4
Visitor Arrivals by Country/Territory of Residence

Source: *Hong Kong Monthly Digest of Statistics* (March 2000).

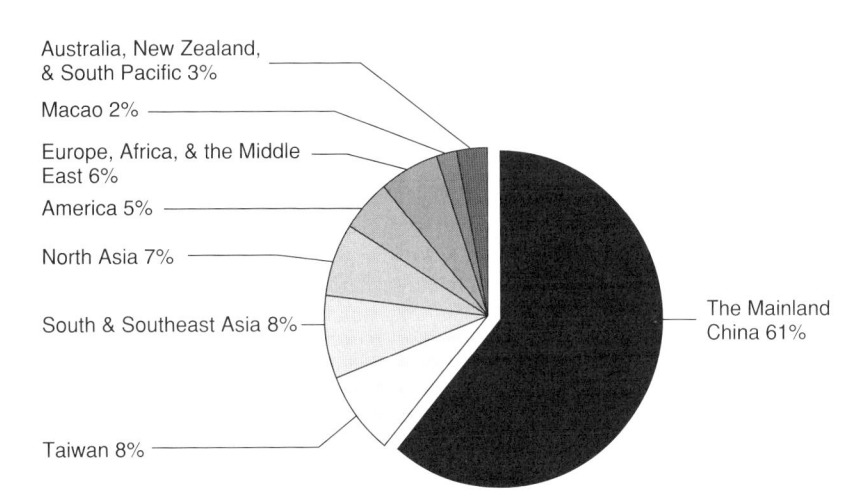

- Australia, New Zealand, & South Pacific 3%
- Macao 2%
- Europe, Africa, & the Middle East 6%
- America 5%
- North Asia 7%
- South & Southeast Asia 8%
- Taiwan 8%
- The Mainland China 61%

OCEAN PARK

Ocean Park was another prime attraction in Hong Kong and was well-recognized worldwide. Prior to Disney's entry, Ocean Park occupied a quasi-monopoly position as the only local theme park. Founded in 1977, Ocean Park was located near Hong Kong's Central district, the heart of the bustling city. Ocean Park had an annual attendance of more than four million visitors and had been ranked recently as one of the top 10 amusement parks in the world by Forbes magazine.[21] Ocean Park sought to blend entertainment with educational elements, thus offering the dual experience for its guests termed as "edutainment."

For the 2004/05 fiscal year, Ocean Park's gross revenue was HK$684 million (US$87.8 million), which represented a 12 percent increase over the previous year. The surplus of HK$119.5 million (US$15.3 million) was the best performance ever achieved at the Park.[22] In 2006, Ocean Park received necessary financing for a HK$5.55 billion (about US$0.71 billion) makeover, including a government-guaranteed portion of HK$1.39 billion (about US$0.18 billion).[23] Ocean Park's redevelopment was expected to bring HK$23 billion (about US$2.95 billion) to HK$28 billion (about US$3.59 billion) over the first 20 years of operation, with visitors projected to increase to more than five million annually by 2011.

---

[21] Norma Connolly, "Top 10 Accolade a Boost to Ocean Park," *South China Morning Post*, electronic edition, June 3, 2006, http://www.scmp.com, accessed December 3, 2006.

[22] The Walt Disney Company, *Annual Report*, 2005, retrieved March 10, 2006 from http://corporate.disney.go.com/investors/annual_reports/2005/index.html.

[23] Charis Yau, "Ocean Park Eyes $4.1B Loan to Finance Makeover," *South China Morning Post*, April 13, 2006, p. BIZ1, retrieved May 3, 2006, from WiseNews Database.

HONG KONG'S VERY OWN DISNEYLAND

> Hong Kong Disneyland will be the flagship for the Disney brand in this huge and growing country and play a pivotal role in helping to bring entertainment to this . . . part of the world. . . . It is our first destination opening in a market where [there] isn't a very deep knowledge of Disney culture and stories.
>
> —Jay Rasulo, chairman of Walt Disney Parks and Resorts[24]

Disney initiated a conversation with the Hong Kong Special Administrative Region (SAR) government in August 1998 about the possibility of setting up a Disney theme park. To avoid a situation like the one encountered by Disneyland Resort Paris, Disney initially planned to simply run the park on a management fee and licensing contract basis. After extended talks and negotiations, however, Disney agreed to take an ownership stake as well.

HKD was expected to bring a number of economic benefits to Hong Kong. First, approximately 18,400 jobs would be created directly or indirectly at HKD's opening, and this number was expected to increase to 35,800 in 20 years. Plus, 3.4 million visitors, mainly from Hong Kong and Mainland China, would be attracted to the park, and attendance was projected to increase to 7.3 million after 15 years. The additional spending by tourists would amount to HK$8.3 billion (about US$1.1 million) in Year 1, rising to HK$16.8 billion (about US$2.2 billion) annually by Year 20 and beyond. There would be "soft" benefits as well, such as with the acquisition of first-class technological innovations and facilities and gaining hands-on experience with quality service training. Over a period of 40 years, it was forecast that HKD would generate an economic benefit equivalent to HK$148 billion (about US$19 billion). This forecast sounded promising during the 1998/99 period when negotiations were taking place, when Hong Kong was still feeling the effects of the 1997 Asian financial crisis.

THE CONCLUDED DEAL

> This is a happy marriage between a world-class tourism attraction and a world-class tourist destination. We hope that Hong Kong Disneyland will not just bring us more tourists, but also wholesome quality entertainment for local families as well.[25]

After a year of negotiations, the final contract was signed in December of 1999. The theme park and hotels would cost US$1.8 billion to construct over six years. In addition, US$1.7 billion would be spent for land reclamation as no other suitable location was available in the densely populated territory. The park would be situated on Penny's Bay of Lantau Island, the largest of Hong Kong's outlying islands. The Hong Kong Government and Disney would invest US$416 million and US$314 million, respectively. In return, Disney held a 43 percent stake in HKD, and the government held the remaining 57 percent, which could later be increased to 73 percent by converting subordinate shares. A further US$1.1 billion was put up in the form of government and commercial loans.

Hong Kong International Theme Park Limited (HKITP), the joint venture formed between Disney and the Hong Kong Government in December 1999, oversaw the construction and running of HKD. While the government developed the infrastructure, Disney provided master planning, real estate development, attraction and show design, engineering support, production support, project management and other development services. Disney also set up a wholly owned subsidiary, Hong Kong Disneyland Management Limited, to manage HKD on behalf of HKITP.

A ROCKY START

> There was a palpable excitement when the new Disneyland theme opened, but the skeptics and critics were not so easily impressed. Press reports described the first few months as a "rocky start." Some locals called the park's management policies "absurd."[26]

Four weeks prior to the official opening, HKD invited 30,000 selected individuals per day to visit the park to test the rides and other attractions. During the trial period, a thick haze hovered over

---

[24] Greg Hernandez, "Mickey Gains Recognition in Hong Kong," *Knight Ridder/Tribune Business News,* September 8, 2005, p. 1, retrieved March 10, 2006, from Lexis-Nexis Academic Universe Database.

[25] Stephen Ip, Hong Kong secretary for Economic Services, press release from Hong Kong government, "Hong Kong Disneyland Final Agreement Signed," www.info.gov.hk/gia/general/99912/10/1210286.htm, accessed August 17, 2007.

[26] "Mousekeeping," *South China Morning Post,* December 28, 2005, features section, p. 12.

the whole park, a result of the air pollutants passing down from Mainland China. This problem was well-recognized by Hong Kong authorities and was particularly acute during low wind periods, which trapped all of Hong Kong in smog.[27] Smog virtually engulfed Sleeping Beauty's Castle.

The first problem noticed was that the capacity limit of 30,000 visitors may have been too high. For example, on September 4, 2005, approximately 29,000 local visitors went to the park. The average queuing time was 45 minutes at the restaurants and more than two hours for the rides. The park faced pressure to lower the daily capacity limit. Instead, the park proposed other measures, such as extending the opening time by an hour and encouraging visits during weekdays by offering discounts, as opposed to reducing the actual limit.[28]

The park faced another problem when inspectors from the Hygiene Department were asked to remove their badges and caps prior to carrying out an official investigation of a food-poisoning case. Park officials later apologized and pledged to operate in compliance with all local regulations and customs. But problems continued. The police could not get into the park—even when deemed necessary—unless pre-arranged with the park's security unit.[29]

OPERATIONS

PRODUCT OFFERINGS

HKD, like its counterparts in the United States, Japan and France, symbolized happiness, fantasy and dreams, and sought to offer an unparalleled experience to its visitors. The admission price was initially set at HK$295 (US$38) during the weekdays and HK$350 (US$45) on weekends and peak days, the lowest pricing among the five Disney theme parks. A day pass for a child was HK$250 (US$32), while it was HK$200 (US$27) for seniors aged 65 and above. Tickets were sold primarily via the company's website (http://www.hongkongdisneyland.com), which allowed three-month advance bookings. Tickets were sold through travel agencies. These two measures aimed to control the daily number of visitors and avoid long queues at the entrance. Only a small portion of tickets were available for walk-in customers.

HKD, like other Disney theme parks, was divided into four parts, including Main Street, U.S.A.; Fantasyland; Adventureland and Tomorrowland. Disney's classic attractions, such as Space Mountain, Mad Hatter Tea Cups and Dumbo, were included in the park. In Main Street, U.S.A., guests could ride a steam train to tour the park. A large part of Fantasyland was the Sleeping Beauty Castle, which included Dumbo and Winnie the Pooh. Guests could find Mickey, Minnie and other popular Disney characters available for photos in the Fantasy Garden, which was unique to HKD. Adventureland was home to Tarzan's tree house, the jungle river cruise and the Festival of the Lion King show. Tomorrowland featured science fiction and space adventures.

To cater to the time-pressed Hong Kong residents, HKD offered a Fastpass ticketing system, which provided a one-hour window to bypass queues for favored rides. Guests preferring an extended stay could check in to one of the two hotels, HKD Hotel and Disney's Hollywood Hotel, which offered on-site lodging services.

MARKETING

HKD collaborated with the Hong Kong Government to jointly promote the theme park. It was estimated that one-third of the visitors would come from Hong Kong, one-third would come from Mainland China and the remaining third would come from Southeast Asian countries.[30] The free-to-air TV program, *The Magical World of Disneyland*, was broadcast in Hong Kong, and could be received in various regions across Southern China. In each episode, famous pop stars from the region (for example, Jacky Cheung, who was also the official ambassador of HKD) would introduce some behind-the-scene

---

[27] Bruce Einhorn, "Disney's Not-So-Magic New Kingdom," *Business Week Online*, September 13, 2005, retrieved March 10, 2006, from http://www.businessweek.com/bwdaily/dnflash/sep2005/nf2005/nf20050913_9145_db046.htm?chan=search.

[28] "HK Disneyland Considers Longer Opening Hours to Beat Long Lines," *The Associated Press*, retrieved March 10, 2006, from http://english.sina.com/taiwan_hk/p/1/2005/0906/44951.html.

[29] Jonathan Hill and Richard Welford, "A Case Study of Disney in Hong Kong," *Corporate Social Responsibility Asia Weekly*, November 16, 2005, retrieved March 10, 2006, from http://www.csr-asia.com/index.php?p=5318.

[30] Suchat Sritama, "HK Disneyland to Boost Thai Visitor Numbers," *The Nation*, September 13, 2005, retrieved March 10, 2006, from http://www.nationmultimedia.com/2005/09/13/business/index.php?news=business_18587589.html.

stories about HKD, such as interviews with rides designers. Disney believed that the widespread popularity of Jacky Cheung would connect well with the audience in Asia. HKD also launched a special TV channel on local cable TV. This channel included background stories on founder Walt Disney, information about The Walt Disney Company and its evolution, interesting facts about the company's state-of-the-art animated films, and regular updates on the construction progress of the park.

The theme park also introduced a line of Disney-themed apparel at Giordano, a Hong Kong–based clothing retailer with more than 1,500 outlets in Asia, Australia and the Middle East.[31] Giordano featured low-price fashionable clothes similar to The Gap in the United States. The Disney line featured adult and children's T-shirts and sweatshirts with popular Disney cartoon characters, such as Mickey Mouse and Nemo. The T-shirts were about HK$80 (US$10) at Giordano, much less expensive than comparable items at HKD for HK$380 (US$49).

HKD outsourced part of its marketing effort to *Colour Life*, a Guangzhou-based magazine. In September 2005, 100,000 extra copies were printed, featuring the grand opening of HKD that month. It was hoped the extra publicity would increase awareness of the theme park among the residents of Guangzhou, the major metropolitan area of southern China, just north of Hong Kong. The company also donated 200 HKD umbrellas to key newsstands in Guangzhou to provide even more publicity. In addition, HKD partnered with the Communist Youth League of China to run special events for children, such as Mickey Mouse drawing contests.

HUMAN RESOURCE MANAGEMENT

The magical experience of an HKD visit depended upon the quality of service. HKD treated human resource management (HRM) as one of the cornerstones of its competitive advantage. To fill the remaining positions at the park, in April 2005, HKD launched one of the city's largest recruitment events ever. The park screened job candidates according to qualities such as service orientation, language capabilities, passion for excellence and friendliness. Employees were referred to as cast members because "they are always on stage when interacting with guests, and therefore represent a very important element of the show," said Greg Wann, vice-president for HRM at HKD.[32]

In January 2005, HKD sent the first cohort of 500 cultural representatives to Walt Disney World in Orlando for a six-month training program. The cast members would learn about the magical Disney culture and would have a platform to share their Chinese cultural experience with other cast members at Walt Disney World. During their stay at Orlando, the Hong Kong crew was trained according to standards set by The Walt Disney Company worldwide. They also had the opportunity to work in other divisions, including merchandising, food and beverage operations, park operations, custodial services and hotel operations. In addition to training, HKD provided handbooks to each cast member, which literally detailed the regulations from head to toe. For example, male cast members could not have goatees or beards, and female cast members were not allowed to have fingernails longer than six centimeters.

LOCAL CULTURAL RESPONSIVENESS

Given the cultural faux pas that occurred with Disneyland Resort Paris, Disney paid special attention to cultural issues pertaining to HKD. Because the prime target customer segment was the growing group of affluent Mainland Chinese tourists, feng shui[33] masters were consulted for advice on the park layout and design. New constructions often began with a traditional good-luck ceremony featuring a carved suckling pig.[34] One of the main ballrooms was constructed to be 888 square meters since eight was an auspicious number in Chinese culture, signifying good fortune. The hotels

---

[31] "Hong Kong Disneyland Rolls Out Fashions: Hong Kong Disneyland Takes Publicity Blitz to Masses with Fashion Line," *The Associated Press*, retrieved March 10, 2006, from http://abcnews.go.com/Business/wireStory?id=963083&CMP=OTC-RSS-Feeds0312, archived at http://news.ewoss.com/articles/D8BFNL1O0.aspx.

[32] Based on: Steven Knipp, "The Magic Kingdom Comes to the Middle Kingdom: What It Took for Hong Kong Disneyland to Finally Open in 2005," *Fun World*, February 2005, retrieved March 10, 2006, from http://www.funworldmagazine.com/2005/february05/features/magic_kingdom/magickingdom.html.

[33] Feng shui is the Chinese art and practice of positioning objects in accordance to the patterns of yin and yang, and in flow with chi, the energy source that resides in all matter.

[34] Jeffrey Ressner and Michael Schuman, "Disney's Great Leap into China," *Time*, July 11, 2005, pp. 52–54.

deliberately skipped the fourth floor because the Chinese associated four with bad luck. Other finer details were incorporated throughout the park to better fit the local culture. For example, the theme park sold mooncakes during the Chinese Mid-Autumn Festival. Phyllis Wong, the merchandising director, stated that green hats were not sold at the park because they were a symbol of a wife's infidelity in Chinese culture.[35]

Cast members at HKD were expected to converse proficiently in English, Cantonese and Mandarin, and signs in the park were written in both Chinese and English. Another local adaptation was the squat toilets, which were popular throughout China. "These toilets benefit those Mainland Chinese who prefer squatting and those who don't want to see muddy footprints on toilet seats," commented a Hong Kong visitor.[36]

Restaurants offered a wide variety of food, ranging from American-style burgers and French fries to Chinese dim sum and sweet and sour pork. Although some animal activists groups initially protested, shark fin soup was on the menu as "it is what the locals see as appropriate," said Esther Wong, a spokeswoman of HKD.[37]

NEGATIVE PUBLICITY

THE LUNAR NEW YEAR HOLIDAY FIASCO

The park faced several public relations problems during its first year of operations, none bigger than that which occurred during the popular Chinese Lunar New Year holiday period. HKD had introduced a new, discounted, one-day ticket that could be used at any time during a given six-month period. These tickets could not be used on "special days" when the park anticipated an influx of visitors. The first period of special days was the Lunar New Year holidays.[38] In Hong Kong, the 2006 Lunar New Year period started on January 28 (Saturday) and ended on January 31 (Tuesday). However, HKD failed to take into account that the following two days (i.e., February 1 and 2) were still public holidays in Mainland China. Mainland tour agencies had purchased large batches of the discounted tickets and escorted large groups of Mainland tourists to HKD during those two days.

This influx created a major problem for HKD as thousands of mainland tourists clinching their tickets swarmed the front gates of the park. The park could not accommodate the additional guests, and the steel gates were locked shut. Many of these Mainland Chinese tourists had saved all year for this trip and had accompanied their extended families to Hong Kong to experience the Disney magic. Needless to say, they were understandably upset. The crowd turned into an angry mob, and, brandishing their tickets, started shouting profanities and hurling objects at the police and security guards. Some tourists even tried to climb over the gates, which were topped with sharp spikes. The front page of the local paper next morning showed a Mainland tourist throwing a young child over the closed gates to his parents who had managed to get inside the park. As one disgruntled customer commented from that fateful day, "I won't come again, even if I am paid to."[39]

To China observers, the behavior was not entirely surprising, given that Mainland Chinese consumers can be very vocal when they are dissatisfied with a product or service. For example, in 2001, the dissatisfied owner of a Mercedes Benz SLK230 had his car towed to the center of town by a pair of oxen, where workers with sledgehammers demolished the car in front of media crews, creating a publicity nightmare for DaimlerChrysler.[40]

---

[35] "Disney Uses Feng Shui to Build Mickey's New Kingdom in Hong Kong," *The Associated Press*, retrieved March 10, 2006, from http://english.sina.com/taiwan_hk/1/2005/0907/45097.html.

[36] "Disneyland with Chinese Characteristics," *Letters from China: China and Independent Travel*, July 22, 2005, retrieved March 10, 2006, from http://voyage.typepad.com/china/2005/07/disneyland_with.html.

[37] "HK Disneyland Draws Fire over Soup," *Chinadaily.com.cn*, May 24, 2005, retrieved March 10, 2006, from http://www.chinadaily.com.cn/english/doc/2005-05/24/content_445139.htm.

[38] The Lunar New Year Holiday, or Chinese New Year, was one of the most important traditional Chinese festivals. A series of celebrations usually took place during the period, starting from the first day of the first month on the Chinese calendar.

[39] Helen Wu, "Queues Take the Magic out of a Crowded Kingdom," *South China Morning Post*, February 4, 2006, p. CITY1.

[40] "Luxury Car Under Hammer," *Herald Sun*, December 28, 2001, retrieved May 3, 2006, from Lexis-Nexis Academic Universe Database.

There was plenty of finger-pointing for the fiasco. Fengtan Peiling, the commissioner of the Hong Kong Consumer Council, claimed that Disney had failed to learn about the cultural traditions and consumption habits of Chinese people. Wang Shuxin, from the Shenzhen Tourism Tour Group Centre, blamed HKD of falsely accusing the travel agents for the predicament. His center, which oversaw Mainland tourists traveling to Hong Kong, had more than 300 claims for compensation through travel agencies. Some agencies wanted to sue HKD for a possible breach of contractual terms.[41] Soon afterwards, the Hong Kong Government released a statement requesting the park to improve its ticketing and guest-entry procedures. Bill Ernest, HKD's executive vice-president, later apologized, stating "every market has unique dynamics that must be taken into consideration and must be learned over time," and that Disney was still learning.[42]

CUSTOMER COMPLAINTS

Customers also complained that the park was too small and that it had too few Hong Kong–themed attractions. HKD had only 22 attractions, 18 fewer than the other Disney theme parks. Other guests claimed that they were mistreated during their stay at the park. Some guests even planned to take legal action against HKD. For example, a park visitor from Singapore alleged negligence and discrimination of Disney's staff because they refused to call an ambulance for her mother who later died of heart failure at an HKD hotel. A spokesperson for HKD denied the allegations, saying that the staff handled the case in the "most appropriate" manner.[43] In another case, a guest and his daughter were in a bakery shop on Main Street, U.S.A., when they were hit by falling debris. The guest stated "the park does not seem to regard customers' safety as its priority" and threatened to take legal action against HKD, adding that they tried to placate him with a Winnie the Pooh for his daughter.[44]

WORKING CONDITIONS

The character performers at HKD complained that they were overworked and underpaid. The spokesperson of the staff union stated that workdays of more than 12 hours and inadequate rest breaks had overwhelmed many workers, causing work-related injuries, such as joint and muscle strain. In response, Lauren Jordan, the theme park's vice-president of entertainment, claimed that "there are a few cast members who have found this work to be less rewarding than others and perhaps more physically challenging than they anticipated."

In addition the character performers, who performed in the daily parade and met visitors, were petitioning for the same salaries as stage performers. The entry salaries for parade performers averaged about HK$9,000 per month (US$1,153) per month compared to about HK$11,000 (US$1,409) for stage performers.[45] In response to the staff's concerns, management announced extended breaks of 40 minutes for every 20-minute session with guests during the hot and humid summer season. Cooling vests, designed for the character performers, were also being tested.

Complaints were not limited to the line staff; there was also turnover among the executive staff. As one disgruntled executive complained:

> The Americans make all the key decisions and often the wrong ones. Finance is also king here, and when things go wrong, they look for local scapegoats. The mood and morale is very low here. I know a lot of us are actively looking for jobs [and many of us] are totally disillusioned.[46]

---

[41] Meng Chu, "Disneyland Suffers Crowd Problems in Hong Kong," *Voice,* February 10, 2006, retrieved March 10, 2006, from http://bjtoday.ynet.com/article.jsp?oid=7653476.

[42] "HK Disneyland Underestimates Lunar New Year Holiday Potential," *Asia Pulse,* February 6, 2006, retrieved March 10, 2006, from Lexis-Nexis Academic Universe Database.

[43] Patsy Moy and Ravina Shamdasani, "Call for Inquest into Disney Visitor's Death," *South China Morning Post,* February 20, 2006, p. CITY1.

[44] May Chan, "Disney's Pooh Unable to Mollify Irate Father," *South China Morning Post,* December 8, 2005, p. CITY4.

[45] Dennis Eng, "Mickey and Friends Call for a Better Work Environment," *South China Morning Post,* April 10, 2006, p. CITY3.

[46] Dennis Eng, "Two More Executives Quit Disney Park," *South China Morning Post,* p. CITY1.

HKD'S RESPONSE

To combat problems highlighted through the media, such as low park attendance, limited attractions, long queues, disgruntled employees and guests' accounts of rude treatment, HKD implemented several recovery strategies.

NEW PROMOTION

To boost attendance, HKD adjusted its pricing strategy. In November 2005, the park offered ticket discounts in which the price for local residents was reduced by HK$50 (US$6.41). Moreover, HKD promoted a ticket express package: guests could purchase a one-day rail pass for an extra HK$6.4 over the admission price. This pass gave unlimited rides to and from the park plus a souvenir showcase of the popular Disney characters. Many believed that these new policies were intended to boost attendance but park spokespersons dismissed such a claim.

In mid-2006, 50,000 taxi drivers were invited to HKD free of charge. Every taxi driver who took up the offer was given free admission to the park between May 15 and June 11, 2006. In addition, a 50 percent discount was provided to up to three family members or friends who accompanied each driver. The aim of this promotion was to give taxi drivers a personal experience of the park that they could share with others. The Urban Taxi Drivers Association Joint Committee welcomed this scheme but it was not clear whether it was successful.

HKD also introduced a "one-day trip guide" in Chinese during November of 2005.[47] This initiative was intended to explain HKD to local travel guides. Furthermore, special VIP treatment was extended to local celebrities in the form of a Dining with Disney program. Local TV commercials also featured testimonials of previous guests and enticing scenes from inside HKD.

EXTERNAL LIAISON WITH MAINLAND TRAVEL AGENTS

Since Mainland visitors were a primary target of HKD, more proactive and collaborative moves were made with Chinese travel agencies, some of which were reluctant to sell HKD tickets in view of their slim profitability and extensive hassles: "when there are problems, [travel agencies] have to eat the cost and other troubles." To overcome this resistance, HKD offered Chinese travel agents a 50 percent discount on visits to the park and hotels. Incentives of approximately US$2.50 per adult ticket were also given to tour operators who incorporated an HKD visit into their package tours. HKD also changed the sales packages to open-ended tickets, from just fixed-date tickets, which offered greater flexibility for visitors and minimized the number of returned tickets.[48]

SETTING THE COURSE FOR EVENTUAL SUCCESS

The performance of HKD during its first year of operation had not turned out as good as had been hoped, with some potentially devastating mistakes. Tour operators further complained that HKD was not big enough to keep the guests occupied for a whole day. Worse still, HKD had faced much negative publicity: from overcrowding, to customer lawsuits, to chaotic incidents during the Chinese Lunar New Year that were front page news in Hong Kong. Further, a survey of current visitors to HKD revealed that 30 percent of guests opted not to revisit the park, which did not bode well for HKD's future.[49]

Disney had experience in operating parks internationally in both good and bad conditions. Inevitably comparisons had begun being made between HKD and Disneyland Resort Paris in France, which attracted a mere 1.5 million visitors by the end of its second month of operation and nowhere could it match Disney management's original projection of 15 million in the first year. However,

---

[47] Geoffrey A. Fowler and Merissa Marr, "Hong Kong Disneyland Gets Lost in Translation," *The Wall Street Journal Asia*, February 9, 2006, p. 26.

[48] Ibid.

[49] "Feature: Concerns Growing over HK Disneyland's Future," *Knight Ridder/Tribune Business News*, October 20, 2005, p. 1, retrieved March 10, 2006, from Lexis-Nexis Academic Universe Database.

some academics believed that it might take another five years to determine whether HKD could be judged as an economic success or failure.

Although maintaining an optimistic public face, the management team at HKD was facing pressures to turn things around. How could HKD steer through the cultural minefield to ensure Hong Kong Disneyland's success? How well had Disney achieved its goal of translating its strategic assets to the Chinese cultural context? What could HKD do to ensure a successful outcome along the lines of Tokyo Disney and avoid the type of embarrassment experienced with Disneyland Paris? What could the company do to rescue the park from the onslaught of continuing negative publicity? The park's management certainly had its challenges cut out for it.

The initial research and a first draft of this case were completed by Edwina H. S. Chan, Lutricia S. M. Kwok, John C. M. Lee, Jacky W. Y. Shing and Sally P. M. Tsui as an assignment under the direction of Professor Michael Young.

SECTION TWO

Managing International Strategic Planning and Implementation

CHAPTER FIVE

Strategies for International Competition

Chapter Learning Objectives

After completing this chapter, you should be able to:

- Discuss the roots of international strategy, including ethnocentric, polycentric, and geocentric organizations.
- Explain the facilitators of international expansion for firms.
- Employ various types of analytical and portfolio thinking to understand how firms decide which countries to expand to.
- Distinguish among the global, multidomestic, and transnational mind-sets of firms and industries.
- Describe the fit of various value chain activities into a firm's total international strategy.
- Explain the levels of strategic integration, including stand-alone, simple integration, and complex integration.
- Integrate the specific firm-level initiatives of core competency leveraging, counterattack, and glocalization to a firm's international strategy.
- Explain how companies can take advantage of opportunities in the huge middle class in emerging markets.

Opening Case: Maytag—Three Countries, One Dishwasher

Maytag dishwashers have Chinese motors, Mexican wiring, and are put together in a sprawling American factory in Tennessee. Some refer to this three-tiered approach to manufacturing as a triad strategy. Maytag calls it trying to keep ahead of imports. For a long time, bulky appliances like washing machines and refrigerators largely were insulated from competition with cheap imports because of their cavernous size. "Big boxes of air are expensive to ship across the ocean," says Maytag Corp.'s Jim Starkweather.

Over time, though, sharply lower labor and production costs in Asia have offset high freight costs, enabling some imported appliances to be sold in the U.S. at lower prices. China's Haier and South Korea's LG Electronics started out small with microwaves and minirefrigerators, but are moving to bigger appliances. At the same time, Maytag's U.S. competitors, General Electric and Whirlpool, have already turned Mexico into a prime location for making appliances for the U.S. market. GE owns 48% of Mexico's largest appliance maker and Whirlpool recently acquired full control of the second largest. Both are exporting Mexican-made appliances to the U.S. by the truckload, which means Maytag's biggest import threat is, ironically, its domestic rivals. Now Asian appliance makers, including LG, are opening plants in Mexico to save on shipping.

With the arrival of low-priced imports, Maytag had to radically rethink how and where it builds refrigerators, washing machines and dishwashers; it found the triad strategy works best for now. "It's a logical progression for us," says Art Learmonth, senior vice president of supply chain, noting that Maytag wants to avoid a wholesale shift of production out of the U.S. The company says it wants to stay as close as possible to its end market and avoid shedding American jobs whenever possible. In the case of dishwashers, Maytag buys motors in China, from a plant owned by GE, because the design is standardized and stable and China offers the lowest price. Maytag makes wire harnesses for dishwashers in Mexico because those harnesses tend to be different in each dishwasher model, so sudden shifts in demand could make it difficult to supply from farther away.

European companies are also using a version of the triad approach, increasingly buying components in the Far East and setting up production in Eastern Europe to augment what they do at home, says Anand Sharma, president of TBM Consulting Group Inc., which specializes in "lean manufacturing" techniques.

For Maytag, the strategy involves dissecting appliances to determine the cost of every component. Whenever a competitor introduces a new dishwasher, for example, Maytag buys one and brings it here to Jackson to dismantle it. In a makeshift workshop known as "the aquarium" because blue plastic sheeting conceals work on new models, engineers examine rival appliances' every O-ring and steel tube and estimate what it costs to make the appliance in the United States and compare that to what it would cost to make it in Mexico. Competitors aren't making dishwashers in Mexico yet, but Maytag thinks it's only a matter of time. "Everything we do is aimed at staying competitive once product starts coming from Mexico," says Mr. Learmonth.

Maytag's new approach to production began three years ago, when other companies had already established footholds in Mexico. Rather than build a plant there, Mr. Learmonth leased a small factory in the Mexican border town of Reynosa and ordered every division to determine what portions of their subassembly work could be sent there. Subassembly work tends to be labor intensive, but not very skill intensive. The moves lowered Maytag's costs because Mexican workers are paid less than U.S. workers. Since then, the company has bought another factory in Reynosa for subassembly work. Sometimes, work that leaves the U.S. returns. Subassembly work for dishwashers, essentially putting pumps and motors together in one piece with cables and connectors, was done in Reynosa, and shipped to Tennessee. But eventually it grew more cost-effective to do the work in Tennessee: A simpler design was introduced, reducing labor, and it used less-expensive motors from China rather than Mexico.

Still, Maytag says it wouldn't build certain items in China. Maytag teamed with a German supplier to develop a "turbidity sensor" that scans water coming out of a dishwasher to determine how clean the dishes are. As long as it detects the tiniest bits of macaroni or mashed potatoes, the dishes are deemed dirty and the machine keeps churning. Mr. Learmonth says the company wouldn't try to have the sensors built in China, because the Chinese "aren't as protective of new technology" and so such proprietary technology is at greater risk of being stolen.

Maytag does the same cost analysis with its other appliances. It took apart one of GE's Mexican-made side-by-side refrigerators and decided it couldn't match GE prices without building its side-by-sides in Mexico, too. So Maytag is building a plant in Reynosa dedicated to making those models. It is set to open next year.

In some cases, after a careful review, Maytag decides it simply can't compete with imports. Profit margins on refrigerators with the freezer on top, rather than alongside or on the bottom, were so measly due to cheap imports that Maytag decided to quit making them. Instead, next year it will pay Daewoo Electronics Corp. in Korea to produce those models and ship them to the U.S. to be sold under the Maytag name. That decision was linked to the anticipated closing of a sprawling two-million-square-foot refrigerator factory in Galesburg, Ill., where those models are made. That plant, shutting down in stages, is expected to close its doors for good late next year.

Source: T. Aeppel, *The Wall Street Journal, Online,* October 6, 2003. Copyright © 2003 by Dow Jones & Co. Inc. Reproduced with permission of Dow Jones & Co. Inc. via Copyright Clearance Center.

Discussion Questions

1. How does international diversification of operations fit into Maytag's strategy?
2. In your opinion, what factors should Maytag consider when deciding where to produce its appliances? Where to sell them?
3. What are the overall pressures for firms competing in the global appliance industry?

The Roots of International Strategy

A pioneer in the field of international business, Howard V. Perlmutter, identified three states of mind or attitudes that can be inferred from examining the managerial practices of international firms.[1] He called them "ethnocentric," "polycentric," and "geocentric." It is from these foundations that a discussion on international strategies may be approached.

As depicted in Figure 5.1, **ethnocentrism** represents an extreme orientation. An ethnocentric attitude looks upon everything that originates from an organization's home country as the best in the world. Thus the international firm's headquarters controls all that goes on in the world for that firm, including managerial personnel, management techniques and practices, products, marketing techniques, and overall strategy. The approach of ethnocentric companies is one of centralization. The firm's primary purpose is to extend to foreign subsidiaries that which has proved to be effective for it in its home country. Standardization of both products and processes is emphasized.

Polycentrism represents the opposite extreme. A polycentric attitude is an orientation that assumes that countries have vast differences in their economic, political, and legal systems deriving from culture, language, and race. Because of the great differences in these aspects, home-country nationals would be unable to really understand the foreign environments. Hence management in the parent company should give foreign subsidiaries as much freedom as is possible to manage their own affairs. This creates a highly decentralized organization where headquarters control is not emphasized. The subsidiaries may therefore have different operations and human resource processes. Furthermore, the product offered throughout the world may be adapted to each individual country.

Geocentrism is a world-oriented attitude, with no predisposition regarding degree of control or centralization. Rather, interdependence among headquarters and all foreign subsidiaries is emphasized. Communications and shared perspectives are key. Subsequently, managers at the parent company and in the foreign subsidiaries are in

FIGURE 5.1 International Orientations

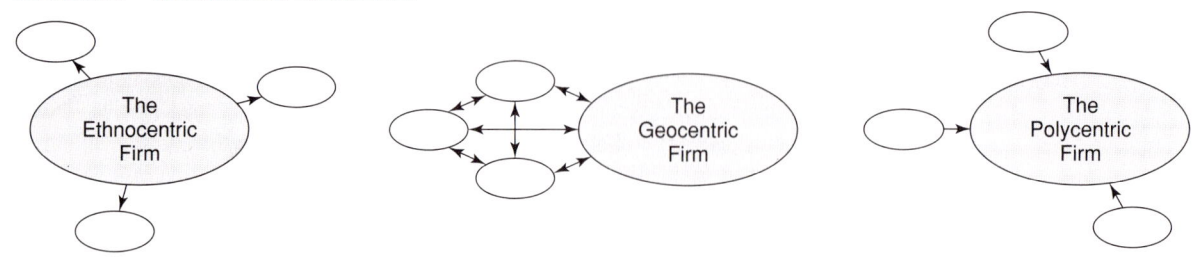

close communication with one another and are aware of the objectives of the entire enterprise. Decisions are made at the parent-company level as well as in subsidiaries only after a thorough analysis of worldwide opportunities and threats. The geocentric attitude is characterized by an absence of parochial thinking within the parent and subsidiaries. This does not mean that the host country's needs are ignored. On the contrary, a geocentric firm wants to be a good citizen of the host country and makes its global plans after taking into account the aspirations of host countries. The incentive system is designed to motivate each subsidiary manager to attain not only the objectives of the subsidiary but also those of the entire international company. Unlike those in a polycentric firm, managers of foreign subsidiaries in a geocentric firm have the opportunity to move into parent-company management. This is in response to the philosophy of a geocentric firm to place in each job the person who can do it best, regardless of nationality or other considerations like race or religion—provided that mobility across national borders is permitted by immigration laws of sovereign states.

Strategically Expanding Overseas

Facilitators of International Expansion

During the past decade, international business researchers have suggested various rationales for firms to expand overseas. Chapter 1 presented factors specifically oriented to the firm's strategy. Macro-environmental forces, discussed in Chapter 2, are higher-level facilitators of internationalization. Combining these factors, we find that global strategy is initially determined by the external industry globalization drivers related to market, cost, government, and competitive factors[2] and, most recently, the emergence of technological factors. The cost, market, and competitive factors were evidenced in this chapter's opening case regarding Maytag.

Internationalization has been facilitated through various factors as seen in Figure 5.2. From the mid-1980s through today, *government and political forces* have gone through dramatic upheavals worldwide. These changes have been key catalysts in internationalization. A significant example is the shift of many countries from communism and planned economies toward democracy and markets unencumbered by significant government intervention. Many industries worldwide have been privatized. In 1998, for instance, 69 countries agreed to a schedule of privatization of their respective telecom industries. This opened the door for many foreign firms in that industry to expand internationally. Complementing the privatization initiatives, many governments of the world have proactively instigated increasing deregulation to many of their respective industries.

A second facilitator of internationalization has been *technological forces*. Initially, technology gave the firm the simple ability to communicate more efficiently with

FIGURE 5.2
Macro-Environmental Facilitators of Internationalization

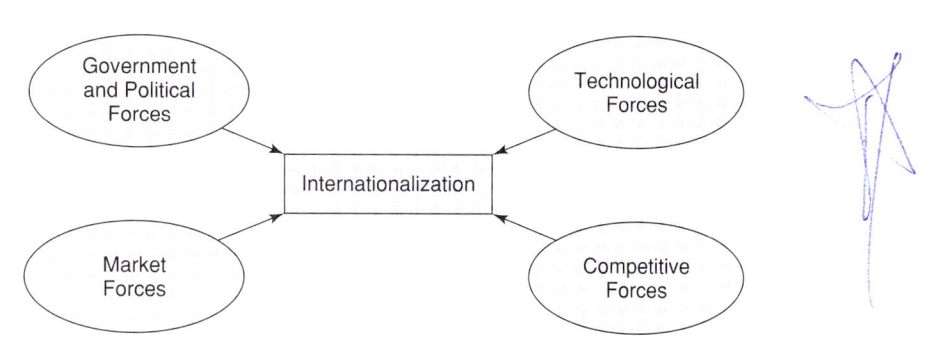

PRACTICAL INSIGHT 5.1

GLOBAL INTERNET INITIATIVES

New Zealand Baby and Child Products Are Now Global

Historically, New Zealand has had a well-developed baby and child products industry nationally. Since 2000, many firms in the industry have begun to leverage their competitive advantages in design and relative costs through exports to other Anglo nations. For instance, approximately 20 brands of New Zealand baby and child products were exported and sold in the United Kingdom in 2001. Many of the industry firms, small in size relative to firms from other Western countries, have banded together to promote the industry through the Internet. An example of these firms is Baby Shade Limited, a designer and supplier of woolen liners and shades for baby carriages, strollers, and car seats. Women from a coffee circle, who simply wanted to have fun and make extra money, formed the company in the late 1990s. The products that the firm sells have a distinct New Zealand design and are manufactured to be able to fit any baby apparatus worldwide. Thus there is a global standardized approach in this industry, as exhibited by Baby Shade's worldwide consistent marketing message and production of goods. From 2000 to 2003, Baby Shade began a proactive promotion of its products to Australia and the United Kingdom through the Internet. Today, the Internet reach has expanded to the United States and is poised to market to most of continental Europe.

Surat Diamond Jewelry's International Expansion

In 1997, a small mail-order jewelry manufacturer in India, Surat Diamond Jewelry (SDJ), began to target overseas customers exclusively through the Internet. During the first year that SDJ began to market on the Internet, the company received more orders from Americans who had no family or cultural connections to India as compared to Indians residing in the United States. There was a similar pattern in the other regions. Eventually, SDJ began offering products adapted to the cultural tastes of each region, while keeping the traditional product line for the Indians living both in India and worldwide. Because of the ease and efficiency of using the Internet, SDJ was able to better investigate specific customer needs in different countries. The company found that, in the jewelry industry, the tastes and preferences across cultures were differentiated. Furthermore, the Internet allowed the company to efficiently yet selectively serve targeted customer needs, while keeping the assets centralized in Mumbai, India. Today, SDJ has regular clients in 15 different countries and is investigating further country expansion. Thus the Internet provided the pathway for a small, indigenous firm to compete internationally in a locally responsive, multidomestic fashion, without the capital resources historically deemed necessary.

Source: Written by Mahesh Joshi, Hugh Sherman, and Roger Kashlak, 2003.

---

overseas subsidiaries and partners, including agents and export intermediaries. This ability led to a higher level of control not previously afforded the firm. Technology also leads to increased efficiencies in transportation. For instance, because of improvements in transportation technology for wine, many nations, including Chile, Argentina, and Slovenia, now have the ability to compete in lower and middle-end wine markets in the United States. Most important, technological advances dealing with the Internet have opened up international markets to many smaller and medium-size firms that do not possess the cost efficiencies or global resources to expand internationally. Today, a small firm in Bombay, Beijing, or Barcelona may market its goods worldwide without the costs and resources once associated with this initiative. For example, a small start-up in Ambler, Pennsylvania, Lucidsecurity, has a Web page for its Internet intrusion prevention product called *ip*Angel that has elicited inquiries and brought in customers from countries such as Brazil, Taiwan, India, and Hungary. Practical Insight 5.1 depicts global Internet initiatives of firms and industries in New Zealand and India.

A third facilitator of internationalization has been *market forces*. Because of increased travel, 24-hour global news, and ease of communication and associated knowledge transfer, once-distinct cultures now are overlapping. Demand for American fast food and soft drinks cuts across all cultures. Similarly, demand for new Japanese electronics technology developed by Sony is not bound by national borders. The

French hotel firm Accor offers its Sofitel and Novatel hotels from New Zealand to the Ivory Coast. That same Paris-based firm has a discount hotel strategy as well, including Red Roof Inn and Motel 6 in the United States. Complementing the overlap of cultures is the increase of disposable income in many countries. Thus a higher percentage of people can now afford the luxury of goods imported from another country or a differentiated good made in their own country.

Beyond these forces, *competitive forces* within industries have facilitated internationalization. As we will discuss in Chapter 7, international joint ventures and international strategic alliances have proliferated during the past 15 years. Firms that wanted to internationalize have increased options besides going at it alone. Also, many industries have had tremendous cost pressures. Subsequently, we have seen a significant rise in international mergers and acquisitions. For example, in the global pharmaceutical industry, the cost of research and development—even for a blockbuster drug—has become prohibitive for many companies. Thus, besides various joint venture initiatives, full mergers and buyouts have increased in the past 15 years. Likewise, in technology-based industries, where the life cycle of a generation of technology is sometimes too short to recoup costs of investment in traditional ways, cross-national mergers have allowed companies to pool resources in order to compete. Consumer nondurables are affected as well. For example, the Chinese beer industry has seen activity during 2003 where South African Breweries (SAB), the world's second-largest brewer, purchased a 29.6 percent stake of China's fourth-biggest brewer, Harbin Brewery Company, at a cost of $86.6 million. This gives SAB stakes in 31 Chinese brewers and makes it the biggest foreign brewer in China.

Where to Expand Internationally

How do firms decide where to expand overseas? This question was posed in the opening case of this chapter. Maytag needed to examine various alternatives before deciding on the triad approach to manufacturing its dishwashers.

In general, a number of tools are available to each firm. For instance, country attractiveness ratings will rate countries on a variety of aspects, including the following dimensions:

- Political risk
- Cultural distance
- Geographic distance
- Economic environment
- Foreign exchange volatility
- Market size
- Market growth
- Regulatory environment

These various ratings will then be combined to yield an overall attractiveness rating relative to other countries. Firms may then derive (1) a measure of *country risk* from these ratings and (2) a measure of *expected return*. Subsequently, each country may be comparatively viewed from this risk–return perspective.

Firms also use the *analytical hierarchy process*[3] for making internationalization decisions. In this approach, the firm develops a list of important variables to consider (e.g., political instability, market growth). Then the firm uses these variables to rate each country under consideration for expansion. Complementing this rating is the firm's determination of relative weights given to each variable. For instance, if

EXHIBIT 5.1
An Analytical Hierarchy Approach in International Expansion

Factor	Weighting	Chile	Brazil	Ecuador	Venezuela
Political stability	.1	10	6	3	2
Market size	.4	2	10	3	5
Cultural nearness	.1	8	6	5	9
Regulatory leniency	.2	10	6	5	6
Repatriation of profits	.2	9	8	4	6
Total score		39	36	20	28
Total weighted score		6.4	8.0	3.8	5.5

market size as determined by level of disposable income is deemed most critical, the weighting given to that factor would be higher than that of other factors. Using this approach, firms will develop the type of grid illustrated in Exhibit 5.1, which depicts an international expansion analysis for BellSouth, the American telecom firm, into Latin America. As seen in this exhibit, five factors enter into the decision: political stability, market size, cultural nearness, regulatory leniency, and the ability to repatriate profits. Each of the four countries in Latin America has relative strengths when compared to the others. Before the effect of weighting the variables, Chile appears to be the best candidate for expansion. However, when market size is weighted as the most critical factor for the firm, Brazil emerges as the best opportunity for expansion.

Strategic Planning for Foreign Market Entry

In today's global environment, many businesses have a set of strategic goals in addition to the traditional financial goals.[4] Any company that wants to assume global leadership in its industry must be adept at discovering new market opportunities, establishing a presence in those markets, and subsequently securing a sustainable competitive advantage.[5] There are more than 200 countries in the world, and obviously not all would be of interest to an international company. Many countries are eager to get foreign direct investments for a variety of reasons, including the importation of new technology and products that the foreign companies would bring, the creation of new jobs, and the building of much-needed infrastructure. The process of planning for foreign market entry consists of seven discrete steps that are explained in the following paragraphs. Note that the entire process is iterative.

1. Identify the Company's Objective in Its Foreign Market Entry

At the outset, management must clearly identify the reasons for its foreign market entry. In Chapter 1 we discussed the different motives for entering foreign markets. They include, but are not limited to, motives such as exploiting a large and virgin market, obtaining a competitive advantage over a competitor, securing essential raw materials, or cutting costs by employing a relatively inexpensive skilled and unskilled labor force in the production of components or product assembly. There may be many more, and different, foreign market entry objectives driving a company's foray into foreign markets.

Establishing the objectives for foreign market entry is important because those countries that, at first glance, meet the foreign market entry objectives are included in the group of countries subjected to further analysis, and those that do not are dropped from further consideration.

2. Preliminary Country Screening

As a start, a comparative analysis of different countries may yield a select few that meet the needs of the "investment screen." The investment screen is based on the company's predetermined market entry objectives. It allows countries to go through the preliminary approval process only if they meet certain minimum predetermined criteria. As one would expect, the nature of the investment screen and the embedded criteria would be different for different industries and companies. For example, the investment screen of a large pharmaceuticals company with innovative products may include criteria such as guaranteed patent protection and a big-enough pool of host-country chemists and scientists. On the other hand, countries like Germany, France, and the United States would not seep through the investment screen of an automobile parts company that is searching for countries with low labor costs; however, India, China, and Sri Lanka would pass this screening test.

A country with a small population of 25 million would be eliminated in favor of one with a population of 900 million by a breakfast cereal company like Kellogg or General Mills, provided that the population in the latter country has the purchasing power to afford its products. However, lack of patent protection would be of no concern. Large insurance companies like the U.S.-based AIG search for countries with large populations, in which a significant percentage is uninsured. This criterion has induced AIG to enter the huge markets of China and India because both countries pass the test of this investment screen.

The country screening process generates a select group of countries in which a market entry is contemplated. The countries in this group are subjected to an intensive, detailed investigation from which emerges a selected few that are the most attractive investment opportunities. For instance, the preliminary investment screen might produce 10 countries that meet the investment criteria. From this small group of companies a smaller number of countries—probably only two or three—are chosen for market entry by the company.

3. What Are the Opportunities and Constraints in the Target Market?

In Chapters 2, 3, and 4 we examined the characteristics of the global, regional, and country-specific economic, legal, political, and cultural environments. Each of these environmental sets would influence the types of opportunities and constraints imposed on a foreign company. For instance, opportunities may exist for a product that has a huge potential market. However, the country may be a developing economy and therefore have poor infrastructure such as roads and a transportation network. The legal system of the target country may be extremely sophisticated in its protection of a company's patents and trademarks. Such countries offer opportunities for companies that market patented products and those that leverage their trademarks and brand names like Coca-Cola, Mercedes, and Sony. However, the lack of such protections has been the principal constraint for companies selling patented pharmaceutical products and branded men's and women's clothing.

4. What Capabilities, Resources, and Skills Are Needed to Succeed in the Foreign Market?

The analysis and determination of the various opportunities and constraints leads to a set of factors, called *key success factors,* in which the company must excel in order to succeed in the targeted foreign market. For example, a franchiser like McDonald's, which is required to maintain a consistent image worldwide, must excel in the following key success factors in every country in which it operates its restaurants: (1) consistent product quality, (2) consistency in taste, (3) standardized production process (e.g., how long its french fries must be fried), (4) cleanliness in the seating areas and in the toilet areas, (5) identical service standards and procedures, and (6) standardized menu in all restaurants worldwide. One of the authors of this book visited the chief executive officer (CEO) of McDonald's India, who related his experiences in opening a McDonald's restaurant in Mumbai (Bombay):

- Potatoes did not contain the required moisture. The CEO had to teach local suppliers how to grow potatoes that met the required moisture standard.
- Tomato farmers were taught to grow tomatoes that met the quality standards.
- The staff was not used to serving customers with the courtesy and speed that signified McDonald's standards.
- The restaurant was vandalized because of the rumor that its french fries were fried in animal fat.
- McDonald's India was the only franchisee that sold lamburgers because religious beliefs prohibited the consumption of beef. The restaurant subsequently temporarily dropped meat from its hamburgers because customers suspected that beef was added to the ingredients.

This example illustrates the key success factors for all McDonald's restaurants worldwide and the resources and capabilities that the CEO of McDonald's India had to deploy to make the franchise succeed in India.

It is well known that the success of Wal-Mart stores is based on superior logistical capabilities. The company is able to maintain a very small inventory of goods in stores and warehouses because of its effective and efficient system of transporting goods by trucks from the supplier to the stores. Wal-Mart also has a system to detect the sales volume and stock of each product sold in every store, so that it knows which store needs which product and when. This information is used to replenish the inventory needed in every store. This system has allowed Wal-Mart to obtain goods at the lowest prices from suppliers and pass the low prices to its customers. Wal-Mart has scored high on the key success factors of speed of delivery, reliability of service, and low prices. Other companies like Kmart have tried to emulate Wal-Mart's business practices, but they have not succeeded. Wal-Mart has now opened stores in several countries. The success of Wal-Mart in foreign markets will depend on its ability to score high on the aforementioned key success factors.

Other industries may include key success factors such as channels of distribution, a constant stream of innovative products, and product design. The U.S.-based company Procter & Gamble has had considerable trouble in gaining market share for its soap and laundry products in the huge market of 1 billion people in India. The constraint facing Procter & Gamble was the country's poor infrastructure, which prevented the products from reaching markets in distant small towns and villages. On the other hand, its main competitor, Lever Brothers, has been extremely successful. Over several decades, ever since it entered the country when it was a colony of Great Britain, Lever has developed a distribution network that extends deep into the hundreds and thousands of villages by means of trucks, rickshaws and bicycles, and by foot. In this example, the size and quality of the distribution network in India was quite different from that which Procter & Gamble had in its home market—the United States—or in advanced countries in Europe. In these countries a huge network of supermarkets and chain stores was there to be exploited.

Other key success factors include the ability to withstand substantial financial loss in the market development stage, the ability to develop good relationships with governmental bureaucrats, and high tolerance by expatriate staff of cultural differences.

5. Does the Company Have the Core Capabilities and Resources to Score High on the Key Success Factors? What Are Our Strengths and Weakness on the Key Success Factors?

This is the extension of the previous step. Comparing the country market's key success factors to the core capabilities and resources of the company leads to the evaluation and determination of the company's strengths and limitations for success.

6. Should the Company Enter the Target Market, and How?

Now the management is ready to decide whether to enter the target market. If the answer is in the affirmative, then a further examination of the areas in which the company has strengths and weaknesses leads to an evaluation and decision on the most appropriate mode of entry. Should it enter the foreign market via exports or through contractual agreements like licensing, franchising, contract manufacturing, or management contracts. Or is the best mode of entry through a foreign direct investment in a joint venture or in a wholly owned subsidiary?

7. Compare and Rank the Targeted Countries

The process discussed in Steps 1 to 7 is carried out in each target foreign market under consideration. A ranking of the attractiveness of each foreign market is made based on the company's assessment of its own propensity to take risk and the expected level of achievement of the objectives (Step 1) for seeking the particular market entry. An executive decision is then made on which foreign markets to enter and in which sequence, as well as the most desirable mode of entry in each market.

Managing a Portfolio of Country Subsidiaries

Beyond the decision on where to expand next, most firms also need to understand the various strategies and linkages that may be associated with each of their respective overseas subsidiaries. In this section, two portfolio approaches are presented. The first approach is based on the intersection of host-country attractiveness and the firm's competitive strength within that host country. The second approach enhances the portfolio analysis perspective by integrating the risk–expected-return perspective borrowed from financial management thinking.

Host-Country Attractiveness versus Competitive-Strength Matrix

As illustrated in Figure 5.3, the firm may have a portfolio of international subsidiaries. These overseas positions may be in a variety of host countries. The relative attractiveness of these countries may be determined through the political, economic, cultural, and market factors delineated above. The firm's competitive strength in a given host country may be measured through many different factors. These factors, which are compared to the firm's competition in each host country, include:

- Relative market share
- Relative market support
- Technology fit with the host country
- Relative contribution margin
- Brand recognition

In Figure 5.3, one can see that when a host country has high attractiveness and the firm has relatively strong competitive strength in that country, the firm should leverage

FIGURE 5.3
Managing a Portfolio of International Subsidiaries

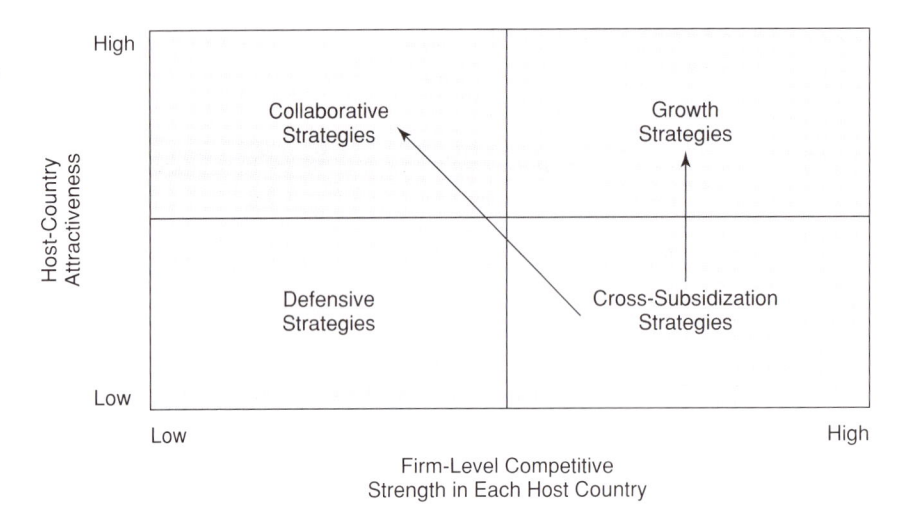

	Low Firm-Level Competitive Strength	High Firm-Level Competitive Strength
High Host-Country Attractiveness	Collaborative Strategies	Growth Strategies
Low Host-Country Attractiveness	Defensive Strategies	Cross-Subsidization Strategies

its competitive advantages and pursue *growth strategies*. This strategic initiative will correlate to a strong capital commitment by the firm. Depending on the industry, this commitment may be geared toward increased production, increased research and development, or increased marketing and promotion efforts. From 1995 to 2007, U.S firms like Black & Decker and Wal-Mart aggressively expanded into Latin America and Asia, attractive regions in which each firm showed competitive strength.

When the host country is attractive but the firm does not possess relative competitive strength in that country, the firm faces a difficult decision. Because of its attractiveness, the country will demand more investment. However, because of its competitive weakness in that country, the firm will not be able to fully fund the necessary strategic initiatives. Because the country represents a long-term opportunity, the firm cannot look to divest away from it. Subsequently, the firm should consider a *collaborative strategy* such as an international joint venture or strategic alliance. Here the firm will give up some control and future profits to a partner, but in return it will receive the ability to maintain a presence in this attractive country. Various types of collaborative efforts and the specific implications of these strategic endeavors are developed in Chapter 6.

When the host country is not attractive and the firm has relatively little competitive strength in that country, a *defensive* (or *reactive*) *strategy* must be undertaken. The firm can divest its holdings in that country. By doing this, the firm acknowledges the unattractiveness of doing business in that country, although it still may have strategic reasons to maintain a presence there. The country could be a source of low-cost inputs into other country subsidiaries. The country may also be a piece of an international marketing message. For instance, the ability to use a service or buy a product "anywhere in the world" may be an important part of a company's international brand positioning. Thus many firms may consider nonequity arrangements to stay in the country.

When the country is unattractive and the company has little strength there, a significant number of licensing initiatives may keep a firm interested. Types of licensing arrangements are further elaborated on in the next chapter. During the 1990s through the early part of the twenty-first century, U.S. health care providers divested many of their overseas holdings because of a combination of strict host-country regulations and lack of competitive advantage compared to host-country health care providers.

Finally, when the host country is unattractive but the firm has substantial competitive strength in that country, a recommended strategy is one of *cross-subsidization*.

Because the country is unattractive, it does not demand the investment and associated resources necessary for future growth. Still, because the firm has some strength, it is accumulating more profits relative to its competitors. These profits may subsequently be sent to fight other strategic battles in more highly attractive countries. Another way to effect cross-subsidization would be to share resources (marketing, manufacturing, etc.) from the subsidiary in this country with those countries that are looking for future growth. During the past decade, many U.S. and Japanese firms have seen their respective home markets mature and thus become less attractive for added investment. They then use home-country-generated profits to help facilitate international expansion. An example of this is the U.S. cigarette industry, where firms like Philip Morris have fueled expansion into eastern Europe and Asia through a highly competitive position in the United States, which represents a declining market for cigarettes due to social and legal environmental changes.

The International Risk versus Return Portfolio

In the host-country attractiveness versus competitive-strength matrix, the underlying perspective is one of profitability. It implicitly suggests where profits are going (the high-attractive countries) and where profits are coming from (the high-strength countries). By collapsing this matrix into one dimension, we begin to form a basis for the next portfolio matrix to consider. The horizontal axis of Figure 5.4 illustrates this perspective: expected future profits in a specific host country. It is the intersection of a country's attractiveness and the firm's competitive position in that country. The vertical axis represents risk, or uncertainty. From a statistical perspective, risk represents variance about an expectation. Thus this axis measures how uncertain an outcome is in a particular host country. A high level of uncertainty will have different strategic implications for the firm than a country with relatively low risk.

The underlying premise in this matrix is that a firm, to manage risk or uncertainty, must expend more resources. Thus when a relatively high level of risk (usually associated with developing or emerging countries) is combined with minimal or negative expected return, a firm usually looks to exit that country. However, if there is a strategic imperative to stay there, the various licensing options will deflect much of the associated risk. With the same level of expected return coupled with a low level of risk (as seen in many developed countries), a firm may truly understand the future and opt to stay in that country to pursue a cross-subsidization initiative as described above. In countries where there is a medium level of expected profits, a firm will look to pursue

FIGURE 5.4
International Risk–Return Portfolio

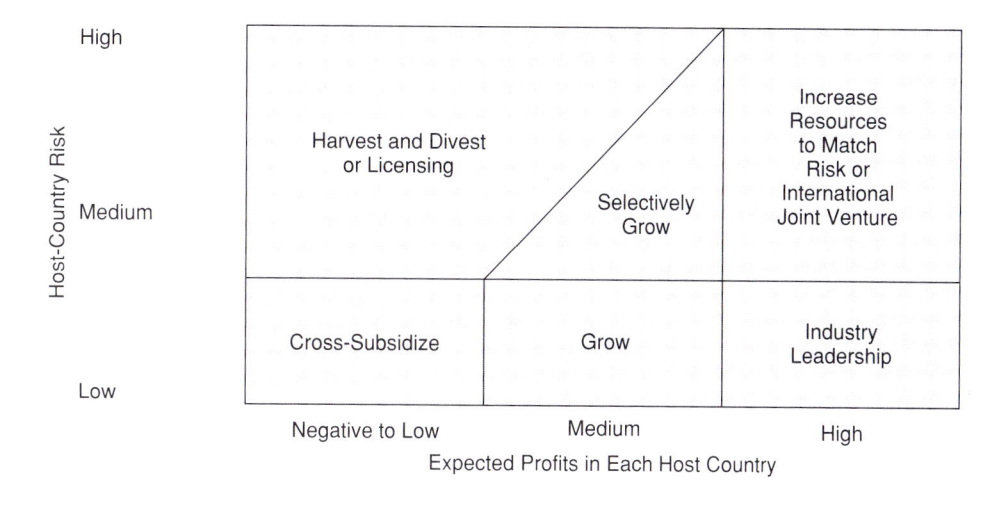

Host-Country Risk	Negative to Low	Medium	High
High / Medium	Harvest and Divest or Licensing	Selectively Grow	Increase Resources to Match Risk or International Joint Venture
Low	Cross-Subsidize	Grow	Industry Leadership

Expected Profits in Each Host Country

growth. This growth will be more aggressive as risk drops and more selective as risk increases. Finally, when the expected profits from the host country are high, the firm must take advantage of its strongly competitive position in a highly attractive country. If risk is low, it may look beyond growth and pursue industry leadership in that country. This initiative may include setting both the strategic and technological standards for the industry in that host country. As risk increases, the firm must dedicate more and more resources to manage and deflect that uncertainty. If the resource commitment becomes too great, the firm will consider an equity-based joint venture, where it will cede some control in return for assets and resources that complement its current position.

Modern International Strategic Orientations

At the beginning of this chapter, the roots of international strategic thinking were introduced. That thinking has evolved into broader international orientations and mind-sets. These mind-sets, although grounded from a strategic perspective, will also be used as we discuss various organizational behavior and human resource issues in later chapters. Many scholars and observers have chosen to classify companies with international operations into four categories: international, multinational, global, and transnational. These orientations and the associated pressures leading to each are illustrated in Figure 5.5. Both global integration pressures and local responsiveness pressures will affect competition in industries and firms crossing national boundaries.[6] When an industry or firm has no overriding pressures to be globally integrated, cost-efficient, or locally responsive, an **international orientation** is observed. An international company is defined by some as one in which top management focuses on domestic operations, and the international operations are treated as accessories whose main purpose is to support the domestic operations by providing critical raw materials or components or incremental sales of the domestic product lines. Besides the international orientation, three orientations—global, multidomestic, and transnational—form a basis for much of international management behavior. We discuss these orientations next.

Global versus Multidomestic Strategic Orientations

Roth, Schweiger, and Morrison linked organizational design by international firms to two strategies: (1) a global orientation that relies on coordination of worldwide

FIGURE 5.5
Strategic Orientations of International Firms and Industries

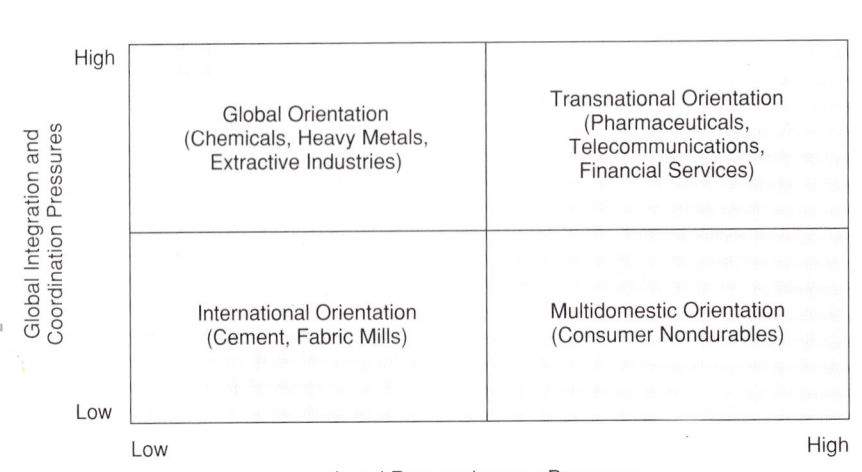

	Local Responsiveness Pressures Low	Local Responsiveness Pressures High
Global Integration and Coordination Pressures High	Global Orientation (Chemicals, Heavy Metals, Extractive Industries)	Transnational Orientation (Pharmaceuticals, Telecommunications, Financial Services)
Global Integration and Coordination Pressures Low	International Orientation (Cement, Fabric Mills)	Multidomestic Orientation (Consumer Nondurables)

activities to maximize the collective organization, and (2) a multidomestic orientation that responds to individual country opportunities and constraints.[7]

Global Orientations In some industries, the former strategy dominates, so a firm's position in one competitive market is significantly affected by its competitive position in other markets.[8] These firms follow a **global orientation,** deriving the cost benefits of scale or scope economies. This strategic orientation matches the integration approach, where the international firm seeks to increase efficiency through the optimum allocation of global resources.[9] Of primary importance to the international firm is the strategic need to maximize its collective organization through an efficient configuration of all of its global activities. Simply put, the international firm will have an orientation toward cost and efficiency.[10] Subsequently, there will be a relatively high level of centralization and control, similar to the ethnocentric perspective. Thus a company with a global orientation is described as one that searches for commonality among countries in aspects such as consumer tastes and preferences, market segments, and lifestyles. As such, global companies attempt to standardize products and marketing approaches that are sold globally, and they also find ways to squeeze efficiency from the production function by manufacturing the products on a global scale in a few very efficient plants strategically located in different parts of the world. Such companies require a considerable degree of coordination among the various worldwide operations, and generally it is provided by various product or business managers with worldwide responsibility. Strategic decisions are made at the parent-company level and foreign subsidiary managers are expected to play the role mainly of implementers of centrally designed strategies. Some aspects of the simple and complex integration strategies that are discussed later in this chapter are present in the functioning of a global company.

Companies with global strategies aim to have standardized products with strong brand names that have global recognition. Adaptations to local or regional conditions and tastes are kept to a minimum. Marketing strategies are designed to be implemented uniformly worldwide, except for minor modifications to suit local and regional differences in cultural attributes and legal requirements. Competitive moves in any particular country market are undertaken only after forethought of their impacts on other country markets.

An integrated network of interdependent value chain activities supports the global strategy. The value chain illustrated previously is broken up, and activities are strategically placed in different parts of the world to take advantage simultaneously of locational advantages, risk reduction, and counterattack capability against a competitor. These issues are elaborated upon later in this chapter.

Multidomestic Orientations Not all industries and firms that compete internationally exhibit the market interdependencies fitting the global orientation profile. Doz and Prahalad suggested that certain factors will contribute to an industry's need to be more responsive to local environments. These factors include different local tastes, different cultures, different regulatory requirements, and different laws. Thus the international firm will forgo an attempt at maximizing the global organization.[11] For example, product or service requirements may substantially differ from one geographical region to another, making standardization impossible. Furthermore, the benefits from scale or scope economies derived from the sharing of costs across markets may be constrained by governments imposing protectionist policies limiting international trade opportunities.

Roth and Morrison found that these local responsiveness pressures are industry forces necessitating local context-sensitive strategic decisions. The resulting multidomestic strategy is an approach that attacks each market individually rather than attempting to gain cost advantages from a global integration effort.[12] To exploit potential sources of competitive advantage, firms must be able to identify and manage risk in individual foreign markets.[13] Sources of systematic risk of particular importance to multidomestic firms include a host government's regulatory, monetary, and fiscal policies as well as market risk derived from various levels of cultural differences between the home and host countries.[14]

A company with a **multidomestic orientation** is defined as a company whose top management appreciates the importance of foreign operations to its overall profitability and competitive strength. Companies in this category adopt products, strategies, and management practices country by country. Their worldwide strategy is an amalgam of the multiple, country-based approaches of its foreign subsidiaries. A multidomestic strategy requires that each foreign affiliate serve primarily the host-country market. Products and services are customized to the needs of each country market. Marketing strategies are fully tailored for each country. All or most of the value chain is reproduced in every country. Few efforts are made by the parent company to integrate the operations in host countries with parent-company operations or with operations in other host countries, although some functions in the value chain may be integrated across countries. Competitive moves are made without consideration of their impact on other countries. Multidomestic strategies allow for differentiated strategic approaches across country locations. The strategy of each affiliate is driven by local conditions. Affiliates have considerable autonomy to respond effectively to local conditions. Stand-alone and simple integration strategies, which are discussed below, are most commonly found in multidomestic strategies.[15]

The Transnational Orientation Imperative

Companies with a **transnational orientation** attempt to balance the need to be responsive to host-country markets through adaptation of the product, marketing strategies, and management practices to suit local conditions with the need to obtain global efficiencies by linking and coordinating the dispersed operations. The resources and activities are distributed to specialized foreign operations, and they are integrated into an interdependent network of worldwide operations.[16] Complex integration strategies discussed below are representative of the functioning of a transnational company. Firms in industries like pharmaceuticals and telecommunications are examples of companies that must strive toward global efficiency. Because of the high cost of research and development, pharmaceutical firms must closely integrate and coordinate worldwide efforts. Similarly, as international calling and peripheral services have tended toward commoditylike status, telecom firms must have highly efficient global networks and close coordination of all activities. Firms in these industries must also strive to respond to local markets. In pharmaceuticals, both government regulation and social norms dictate the demand for specific drugs. In telecom, patterns of phone usage as well as various technological protocols are locally determined.[17]

The Value Chain Configuration and Strategic Orientations of Firms

One approach to understanding global versus multidomestic industries is to examine the concept of a firm's "value chain." The famous management scholar Michael Porter introduced the **value chain** concept: "The value chain groups a firm's activities into several categories, distinguishing between those directly involved in producing, marketing, delivering, and supporting a product or service; those that create, source, and improve inputs and technology; and those performing overarching functions such as raising capital, or overall decision making."[18]

FIGURE 5.6 Upstream, Support, and Downstream Activities and Competitive Advantage

Source: Michael E. Porter, *On Competition* (Boston; 1998), p. 314. Copyright © 1998 by Michael E. Porter; all rights reserved. Reprinted by permission of Harvard Business School Press.

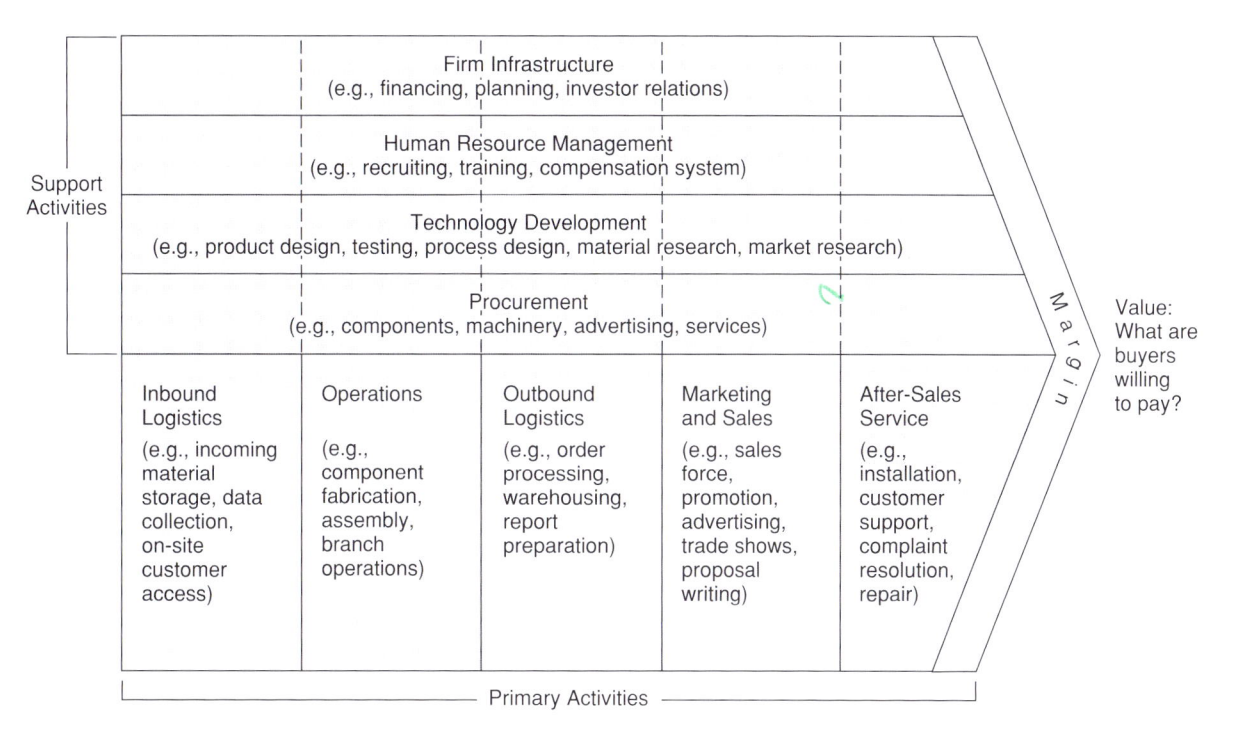

Support Activities	Firm Infrastructure (e.g., financing, planning, investor relations)				
	Human Resource Management (e.g., recruiting, training, compensation system)				
	Technology Development (e.g., product design, testing, process design, material research, market research)				
	Procurement (e.g., components, machinery, advertising, services)				
	Inbound Logistics (e.g., incoming material storage, data collection, on-site customer access)	Operations (e.g., component fabrication, assembly, branch operations)	Outbound Logistics (e.g., order processing, warehousing, report preparation)	Marketing and Sales (e.g., sales force, promotion, advertising, trade shows, proposal writing)	After-Sales Service (e.g., installation, customer support, complaint resolution, repair)
	⎯⎯⎯⎯⎯⎯⎯⎯⎯⎯⎯⎯⎯ Primary Activities ⎯⎯⎯⎯⎯⎯⎯⎯⎯⎯⎯⎯⎯				

Margin → Value: What are buyers willing to pay?

Figure 5.6 illustrates a typical value chain of a firm. The value chain consists of two distinct types of activities. *Primary activities* are those activities that are directly involved in producing and marketing goods or services of a firm. *Support activities* are those that facilitate and enhance the effectiveness and efficiency of the various links in the primary-activities chain. Furthermore, the primary value chain activities could be labeled as either *upstream* (inbound logistics, operations) or *downstream* activities (outbound logistics, marketing and sales, after-sales service).

Downstream activities are generally closely associated with the customer, and therefore are performed in close proximity to the customer. For instance, the sales force, advertising in newspapers, channels of distribution like stores, shops, and supermarkets, and service centers are situated where the customer lives and works. On the other hand, *upstream* and support functions, like purchasing and shipping raw materials to the production plants, manufacturing operations, and plant maintenance can at least conceptually be uncoupled from where the buyer is located.

The distinction between upstream and downstream activities has strategic implications for how companies compete in an industry. Competitive advantage in upstream and support activities often grows more out of the *entire system of countries* in which a firm competes than from its position in any one country. Downstream activities create competitive advantages that are largely *country-specific,* such as product or service brand name and distribution network in a country.[19]

In industries where upstream and support activities are vital to competitive advantage, companies tend to have global strategic orientations. Companies in such industries emphasize the gaining of efficiencies in current operations through economies of scale and scope in upstream activities in the value chain—for example, operating large manufacturing plants in a few countries rather than many small plants in many countries; bulk purchases of raw materials to be used in strategically located plants worldwide as opposed to buying locally; centralized research and development of new products and processes to be used globally; sharing of huge warehouse spaces; and sharing of advertisements in many countries. Companies in industries where downstream activities connected to buyer satisfaction are key to competitive advantage—such as a superior brand image, service satisfaction, adaptation of products and services to suit local tastes and culture—are more multidomestic in orientation.[20]

Gupta and Govindarajan argue that in the twenty-first century, international firms need to redesign their value chains because of the turbulent environment that exists in many global industries. Three principles should guide the firm's redesign of its value chain: (1) redesigning the set of activities as well as the interfaces across activities, such as supplier and customer linkages; (2) redesigning in order to accrue significant gains in the firm's cost structure, asset investment, and/or speed of responsiveness to external environmental changes; and (3) redesigning to ensure rapid growth in market share and economies of scope from expansion into other related products and services.[21]

Worldwide Dispersal and Reintegration of Value Chain Activities

Complementing its direction of international expansion and overall international orientation, the international firm must integrate its various functions into the larger worldwide mosaic. Thus international firms have rapidly moved to put in place integrated systems of international production and distribution capable of most effectively achieving the three objectives discussed in Chapter 1: efficiency in current operations, risk management, and global learning and innovation. Such a system incorporates (1) the dispersal of the company's various activities and functions in the value chain, and their location in different parts of the world to take advantage of national differences, and (2) a reintegration of the dispersed activities and functions to benefit from scale and scope economies. In this section we examine the characteristics of this system.

First we study the functional scope of the value chain dispersal and reintegration strategies, and then we describe the geographic scope of such strategies.

The Functional Scope of Value Chain Dispersal and Integration Strategies

In the initial stages of internationalization, products are exported by the company to foreign markets from the home country. As the company expands its markets abroad to include several countries, it may choose to perform one or more activities in the value chain in foreign locations with the principal purpose of taking advantage of national differences, scale economies, and scope economies. The foreign location of a particular activity may, or may not, be in a country where the company's products or services are currently marketed. Factors such as the following induce companies to disperse the different activities in the value chain to various locations throughout the world:

- Comparative advantage of the country (competitive input costs, low levels of political risk, market size, proximity to major markets or supply sources, availability of knowledge and skills in the population, etc.).
- Efficiency gains from economies of scale and scope derived from an increased internal functional specialization and international division of labor.
- Competitive pressures from domestic and foreign-based companies and the necessity to compete in competitors' home and third-country markets.

- The benefits of flexibility and risk reduction derived from multiple sourcing points and destination points for components, products, and capital.
- The opportunities to innovate and learn from diverse cultures and economic systems.
- The dispersal of human, capital, material, and knowledge-based resources throughout the world, not in any one country or region; and tariff and nontariff barriers that prevent market penetration via exports.

Having dispersed the value chain activities in different parts of the world, international companies implement plans to reintegrate those activities in response to a global strategy designed to enable the company to achieve its objectives most efficiently and effectively, under an umbrella of an acceptable level of risk.

The level of integration, which varies from company to company, can be categorized as (1) stand-alone, (2) simple integration, and (3) complex integration. The value chain of a firm describes how it organizes and performs the many discrete activities that add value to the goods and services the firm produces and markets. Some of these activities are vertically and sequentially linked, and others are linked horizontally and cut across the various vertical links in the value chain. The vertically linked activities are inbound logistics, components production, assembly, distribution, marketing, and after-sales service. The horizontally linked activities include research and development, human resource management, procurement, finance, accounting, and other management functions like planning, organizing, and controlling. The horizontally linked activities are performed in all links of the value chain; for example, human resource management—which includes salary administration and staffing—is carried out in each and every operation in the horizontally linked value chain. The same can be said of the other horizontally linked activities. How effective and efficient a firm is in managing the most critical links in the value chain is what ultimately determines how competitive it will be in the industry.

Stand-Alone Strategies

Highly differentiated national tastes and habits or trade barriers such as high tariffs, import quotas, and local content requirements are some factors that have motivated companies to establish stand-alone affiliates in some countries. Under a **stand-alone strategy,** each foreign affiliate is responsible for the performance of almost all of the required activities in the value chain in the host country. The output produced by an affiliate is marketed primarily in the host country, although some of the output may be "exported" to other affiliates and to the parent company. The foreign affiliate may also "import" the output produced by other affiliates for sale in the host-country market. For instance, an affiliate in France may produce camcorders, another in Germany may produce VCRs, and the parent company may produce television sets. Each unit may export its respective outputs to the other two and each would then have three products to sell in each country market.

Except possibly for the export and import of outputs, there is no integration of value chain activities among the affiliates themselves or between the parent and affiliates. The principal linkage between the parent and an affiliate is through ownership, supply of long-term capital, and transfer of technology. The parent does not interfere in the activities of an affiliate as long as the affiliate is profitable and does not deviate from the company's mission and business portfolio.

Factors such as trade barriers (tariffs and quotas), high transportation costs, and communications barriers may cause a company to establish a stand-alone affiliate abroad. Stand-alone strategies are particularly prevalent in service industries. Services like fast-food restaurants, advertising agencies, computer services, management consulting, banking, insurance, and engineering and construction are not tradable, and hence affiliates in these industries are established as self-contained units, mirroring the "production" organization of their parents.

Simple Integration

A **simple integration strategy** calls for the integration of a few activities in the value chain among some or all affiliates of an international company. The integration might be unidirectional or multidirectional. In unidirectional, or one-way, integration, an affiliate might be responsible for producing components for use in another affiliate. For instance, an affiliate in China may have the sole responsibility for the efficient production of an engine, which is then used in a tractor assembled in Taiwan, Australia, and Brazil. Or an affiliate in Switzerland or Singapore might be responsible for raising funds from local banks and financial institutions for use in other affiliates. These affiliates may also serve as a cash cow for investments in other functions such as research and development or advertising expenditures to gain a bigger market share in a key country market.

In multidirectional integration, there is *interdependence* among the affiliates and between the affiliates and the parent. For example, an English affiliate may manufacture and export an engine to an Italian affiliate, and in return it may import a transmission manufactured by the Italian affiliate. Or the parent might import and assemble different components produced in different affiliates and subsequently export the assembled products to the affiliates for marketing through their respective distribution channels.

The practice of *outsourcing* by some international companies represents simple integration in its most popular form. Outsourcing is performing some activities in the value chain in foreign countries and linking them to work done elsewhere, mainly in the home country. International outsourcing is the farming out of some value chain activities to countries other than the home country and the major market countries of the product or service. The unit producing the outsourced product may be controlled by the international parent either through equity control or through nonequity contractual arrangements with nonaffiliated foreign contractors. Outsourcing enables an international company to focus on certain activities in the value chain and to delegate other activities in the chain to subcontractors who specialize in those activities. Contractors who have associated with an international company for many years, in effect, become part of the value chain of the international company. In such cases, contractors not only produce a component but also design it for the international company. Nike and Adidas (basketball shoes), Levi Strauss & Company (jeans), and Wal-Mart and Marks and Spencer (clothing) have significant outsourcing operations in countries like Bangladesh, Turkey, and China. Many software developers use foreign affiliates or subcontractors in India and Ireland to process data or write software. Advances in telecommunications have made possible the transfer of computer programs by communications satellites. India, for example, has the second-largest information technology base in Asia after Japan, and it has emerged as the primary development center for sophisticated software and hardware for international companies like IBM, Motorola, and Hewlett-Packard.

Practical Insight 5.2 illustrates the dominant role that India now plays in performing so-called backroom operations. Companies like General Electric, Dell, British Airways, Nortel Networks, Reebok, Sony, American Express, HSBC, and GE Capital have established operations in India to perform various skilled functions like

PRACTICAL INSIGHT 5.2

DISPERSAL OF THE VALUE CHAIN ACROSS CONTINENTS: INDIA AS A CENTER FOR BACKROOM OPERATIONS

Thanks to the Internet and satellites, India has been able to connect its millions of educated, English-speaking, low-wage, tech-savvy young people to the world's largest corporations. They live in India, but they design and run the software and systems that now support the world's biggest companies, earning India an unprecedented $60 billion in foreign reserves—which doubled in just the last three years. But this has made the world more dependent on India, and India on the world, than ever before.

If you lose your luggage on British Airways, the techies who track it down are here in India. If your Dell computer has a problem, the techie who walks you through it is in Bangalore, India's Silicon Valley. Ernst & Young may be doing your company's tax returns here with Indian accountants. Indian software giants in Bangalore, like Wipro, Infosys and Mind-Tree, now manage back-room operations—accounting, inventory management, billing, accounts receivable, payrolls, credit card approvals—for global firms like Nortel Networks, Reebok, Sony, American Express, HSBC and GE Capital.

You go to the Bangalore campuses of these Indian companies and they point out: "That's G.E.'s back room over here. That's American Express's back office over there." G.E.'s biggest research center outside the U.S. is in Bangalore, with 1,600 Indian engineers and scientists. The brain chip for every Nokia cellphone is designed in Bangalore. Renting a car from Avis online? It's managed here.

Source: Thomas L. Friedman, "India, Pakistan and GE," August 11, 2002. Copyright © 2002 The New York Times Co. Reprinted with permission.

---

accounting, inventory management, billing, accounts receivable, payroll, credit card approval, technical support, and the answering of service calls.

To a large extent, outsourcing is cost-driven as companies search for locales that offer cheap production inputs like labor, raw materials, and energy. However, companies also source abroad in more than one locale, through affiliates or subcontractors, as a hedge against economic, political, and currency risks. Having more than one source country allows an international company to reduce the risk of overdependence on only one source of supply. Thus, all other things being equal, a company that has operations in Japan as well as in Italy could easily shift its supply source from Japan to Italy in response to an exorbitant rise in the value of the Japanese yen or in the Japanese wage rates that makes imports from Japan expensive and economically nonviable. Also, firms that play the role of subcontractors need to be functionally integrated into the parent company's value chain through the establishment of functional linkages. For instance, a subcontractor in Taiwan that manufactures desktop computers for an American company would have its research and development, manufacturing, and purchasing functions integrated with those of the American company. Thus integration of some functions of the parent company with those of the subcontractor may be necessary. In a similar vein, affiliates in various parts of the world that serve as suppliers of parts or subassembly modules, or perform some other value chain activities, also must be functionally integrated with the parent.

Complex Integration

The ability of international companies to transfer goods, services, components, capital, technology, and information among the parent and affiliate companies has been facilitated by major changes in the world economy including diminishing market barriers in developed and developing countries; the liberalization of international trade; the emergence of trade blocs like the European Union, NAFTA, and MERCOSUR; advances in global telecommunications and computer networks; and the spread of information technology. This business-friendly environment has precipitated the entry of new firms from developed and developing countries, which has led to intensified global competition in most industries.

Convergence of consumer tastes for some products (refrigerators, automobiles, television sets, personal computers, VCRs, camcorders, etc.) has reinforced the standardization of products across national boundaries. Standardization of products provides companies with the opportunity to reduce unit production costs through economies of scale. There is still the simultaneous need to engage in product adaptation to make some products suitable to local and regional tastes. For example, refrigerators in Europe are half the size of those in the United States; and washing machines in Europe are side-loaded with a horizontal rotating drum, whereas those in the United States are top-loaded with an agitator action. Shortened product life cycles and the corresponding imperative to develop new and innovative products have propelled companies to search for new ideas and human capital throughout the world.

This process has led international companies to redesign the pattern by which they manage and organize their physical, financial, technological, and human assets worldwide. Through **complex integration strategies,** international companies are transforming their geographically dispersed affiliates and fragmented production, financial, and marketing systems into functionally integrated regional or global networks of affiliates.

Complex integration strategies are characterized by a dispersal of the value chain into discrete functions—component production, assembly, finance, research and development, distribution, and so on—and their location in the place where they can be best carried out in response to the overall goals and strategy of the firm as a whole. A foreign affiliate may be selected by the parent to perform functions for the international company as a whole (either by itself or in close interaction with other affiliates or the parent company) on the basis of a sophisticated intrafirm division of labor. For example, an affiliate in England may be responsible for research and development for the whole company, an affiliate in Switzerland for finance, and those in the United States and Belgium for marketing of products in North America and Europe respectively. Similarly, the production chain for the manufacture of an electric fan might be dispersed as follows: purchasing done by a central purchasing office in France; manufacturing of components in Mexico (frame), Germany (motor), and India (blades) for final assembly in Singapore (electric fan); and marketing in North America and Europe by affiliates in the United States and Belgium respectively.

Complex integration strategies create a network of linkages among the various affiliates including the parent. The linkages among the various units represent substantial unidirectional and multidirectional flows of technology, people, products, services, components, capital, and information. The distinction between the parent and affiliates becomes blurred in the corporate network as an increasing number of affiliates assume primary responsibilities for functions that are supposed to serve as inputs to other functions performed elsewhere in the network.

Complex integration represents the most advanced level of globalization of a company. Firms that have a complex integration strategy in place are not just a collection of discrete affiliates at home and abroad but, rather, a system of interdependent affiliates in which each affiliate's functions are designed and carried out in response to a unified strategy for the company as a whole.

EXHIBIT 5.2 Integration Strategies and Antecedent Factors

Integration Strategy	Type of Intrafirm Linkage	Degree of Integration	Environment

Stand-alone strategy
   Multidomestic orientation
   Polycentric firm
	Ownership, technology, intracompany trade in goods and services	Weak, self-contained affiliates	Host-country barriers; market entry allowed via direct investment

Simple integration strategy
   Early global orientation
   Ethnocentric firm
	Financial, technology, components, uni- or multidirectional	Strong at some links in the value chain, frequent outsourcing to independent contractors	Moderate financial, political, currency risks; significant differences in comparative advantages of countries; free trade

Complex integration strategy
   Later global and transnational orientations
   Geocentric firm
	All functions, multidirectional network	Strong linkages and interdependencies throughout value chain links	Free trade, trade blocs, convergence of consumer tastes, intense competition from global competitor

Merging Strategic Orientations and Functional Integration Strategies

Our discussion of (1) the global-multidomestic-transnational orientations and (2) the functional integration strategies discloses a clear overlap. To conclude our brief look at the different types of global strategies that a firm may employ in its international activities, Exhibit 5.2 summarizes international orientations and integration strategies. It also integrates the roots of international strategy discussed at the beginning of this chapter. Finally, it illustrates the intrafirm linkages, degree of integration, and environmental characteristics most associated with each functional integration strategy.

Firm-Level Strategies for International Competitiveness

The global-multidomestic-transnational distinction is indeed at the heart of international strategic thinking. Thus these orientations connect throughout the remainder of this book. We have also identified the overlap and consistency with various integration strategies. A final piece of the international strategic discussion now focuses on three specific firm-level initiatives that must be identified: core competency leveraging, counterattack, and glocalization.

Core Competency Leveraging

Core competency leveraging is a strategy being used by companies that are gaining prominence in a variety of businesses. It is a strategy that is not readily apparent to their less perceptive competitors. The thrust here is to gain superiority by building on one or more core competencies. Fundamental to the concept of core competence is the recognition of the distinction among core competence, core product, and end products.

Core competence may be defined as the distinctive ability to excel in a key area, upon which a company can build a variety of businesses and develop new generations of products, some of which customers may need but have not yet imagined.[22] *Core products* are the intermediate linkages between core competencies and end products. They are the subassemblies or components that actually make significant additions to the value of the end products. To be in a position of world leadership, a company must be in a position of strength at all three levels: core competencies, core products, and end products. For example, Honda has developed core competence in engines and power-train technology that was physically embodied in its core product (the engine), which it skillfully incorporated in a variety of end products such as lawn mowers, generators, marine engines, motorcycles, and cars. At the core competence level, the goal is to attain state-of-the-art, world-class leadership in a key field. For example, Sony developed the capacity to miniaturize, and Canon's competencies are in 3-D technologies, optics, imaging, and microprocessor controls, which are used in computers, digital cameras, document scanners, and video camcorders.

At the core products level, the goal is to maximize world manufacturing share. This goal is achieved by manufacturing a core product for sale to both internal and external customers. For example, Briggs and Stratton focuses on the manufacture of engines that are used in lawn mowers, power washers, chainsaws, and generators by many other companies. Korean companies such as Goldstar and Samsung began by manufacturing VCRs for American and European consumer electronics companies. The objective of such supply relationships was to build core product leadership in key components such as diverse displays and semiconductors. Another strategic objective of these Korean companies is to prevent their potential American and European customer competitors from making manufacturing investments in the Korean companies' core products and thus displacing them from value-creating activities.

Serving as a manufacturing base for other companies gives core product manufacturers an opportunity to build manufacturing share without the risk and expense of building downstream brand share. Product feedback received from buyer companies provides free and invaluable market research data on customer preferences and market needs. Such information is used by a core product manufacturer to improve the core product. Furthermore, this kind of information serves as a lever to develop the end product by itself and to enter the end product market independently. This strategy was used quite effectively by Japanese television makers such as Sony and Hitachi in their quest to enter the U.S. market. They first served as original equipment manufacturers (OEMs) of private-label, black-and-white television sets for American department stores. Subsequently, they used the experience and knowledge gained in the process to upgrade their presence in the United States from OEMs to independent marketers of color TV sets under their own brand names. More important, in doing so the Japanese companies managed to displace American TV manufacturers like RCA, GE, and Sylvania.

A dominant world manufacturing share in a core product may not necessarily mean an equally strong position in the market for end products. For example, Canon supposedly has a dominating world manufacturing share in desktop laser printer engines; however, its brand share in the laser printer business is actually quite small. Similarly, Matsushita has a huge market share worldwide in compressors, its core product. Its brand share in the air conditioner and refrigerator businesses, however, is negligible. Clearly, the strategic objective for obtaining the maximum possible manufacturing market share for core products is to generate revenue and customer feedback, which in turn can be used to improve and extend core competencies. The focus is on enhancing and replenishing a company's core competencies and leveraging them to later develop and market a variety of end products, with core products serving as their backbone.

Examples of companies that have effectively leveraged their core competencies are Casio, 3M, and Canon. Casio drew on its expertise in semiconductors and digital displays by producing calculators, small-screen television sets, musical instruments, and watches. The 3M Company combined competencies in substrates, coatings, and adhesives to produce Post-it Notes, magnetic tape, photographic film, pressure-sensitive tapes, and coated abrasives—quite a diversified product portfolio driven by only a few shared core competencies. Canon has leveraged its competencies in optics, imaging, and microprocessor controls to produce copiers, laser printers, cameras, and image scanners. Core competence is important because, in the short run, the quality of a company's product and its performance determine its competitiveness. In the long run, however, the global competitiveness of a company depends more on its ability to grow through internal development, licensing deals, or strategic alliances. Its core competencies, however, are what give birth to new generations of products, and at a rate faster than the competition.

Thus far, we have focused on technological core competence. However, companies can develop core competencies in a variety of functional areas. For example, the Maine-based catalogue sales retailer L.L. Bean's core competence is in logistics and distribution, and Philip Morris (Altria Group) is unbeatable in its ability to identify emerging market segments for consumer products, which it has leveraged in businesses other than cigarettes, like soft drinks, beer, and fast foods. Core competency may also be developed in other functions like purchasing, service after sales, product design, and advertising. For instance, the Italian company Benneton, retailer of sportswear and casual clothing, has a celebrated expertise in developing extremely successful and relatively inexpensive, albeit often controversial, advertising campaigns.

Counterattack

The typical response of U.S. companies to foreign competition in the home market was to assume that foreign companies, especially those from Japan and the Pacific Basin countries, were able to effectively compete in the U.S. market because of lower costs derived from cheap labor rates in their own countries. In response, U.S. companies **counterattacked** by establishing offshore assembly and manufacturing sites in Asia to lower their own production costs.[23] American companies also observed that the Japanese were taking advantage of lower costs from scale economies derived from production in large world-scale plants. In response, American companies followed suit and also established world-scale plants. However, such strategies did not prevent a market share decline in the U.S. market of American companies as Japanese companies continued to take over the market share. What the American companies did not recognize was that a strategy based on low labor costs was vulnerable to fluctuating exchange rates and rising labor costs. This phenomenon is exactly what has taken place in Japan. Wage rates there have risen significantly in the last three decades and are now high enough to be noncompetitive in comparison to wage rates in other Asian countries such as China, Malaysia, Thailand, and Sri Lanka. Moreover, the strategy of lowering production costs through scale advantages derived from large-scale plants also proved to be vulnerable to technological improvements in the production process brought about by such factors as robotics and computer-aided, flexible manufacturing.

With the increasing globalization of industries, international companies have come to realize that a competitive attack against a home market can be launched by foreign companies that, at the time of the attack, may have a relatively small presence in it. Today, global competition is characterized by a series of competitive attacks and counterattacks by global companies in each other's home and third-country markets. Companies that cannot engage in such battles are doomed to lose market share, both at home and abroad. For example, an American company that is attacked by a Japanese company cannot spend all its resources only on defending its home market, while the Japanese company faces no such threat in its own home market. The American company must be capable of attacking the Japanese company in the Japanese market or in a third-country market where the Japanese company is vulnerable. The Japanese aggressor, when attacked by the American defender on its (Japanese) home ground, is forced to divert resources to defend its home market and is thus averted from attacking the foreign American market. In actual military combat, a defender must be able to attack the enemy in the enemy's home territory in order to repel the enemy's attack. The same holds true in business warfare. To launch a counterattack, however, one must have the required "firepower," which, in business terms, is the cash flow to launch an attack.

Cash flows are needed to develop the various capabilities required to make an effective attack or counterattack. The types of capabilities needed are (1) channels of distribution through which to direct an attack, (2) investment in key core competencies, and (3) a wide range of products that can benefit from the same distribution channels. With these capabilities in place in major world markets, companies can engage in cross-subsidizing across countries and markets.

Cross-subsidization, identified in the matrices illustrated earlier in this chapter, involves the deployment of resources generated in one area or country for use in another location. For instance, using cash flows generated in Japan or elsewhere, a Japanese company can launch an attack on an American company in the U.S. market or in a third-country market in which the American company is weak. Such an attack might involve lowering the Japanese company's prices in the U.S. market just enough to squeeze the profit margins of the U.S. company. The objective here is to reduce the cash flows of the American company and drain them away from activities such as marketing and research and development. Without channels of distribution in the foreign company's home market, the American company is in no position to cross-subsidize and counterattack. The American company is thus weakened and unable to make necessary improvements in its products or to launch expensive advertising and marketing campaigns. Consequently, the American company loses market share, and the Japanese company then proceeds to raise its prices and increase its margins, which are, in turn, used to continue such attacks in other countries and markets.

Cash flows are also required to develop effective channels of distribution in major markets of the world. To be a global player in a global industry, a company must have an effective presence in three areas of the world—the United States, Europe, and Asia. Developing channels of distribution is an expensive endeavor for which enormous amounts of cash are needed. Cash flows are also vitally needed to develop core technologies and core competencies, which, as just discussed, are key requisites of a global company's competitive advantage. Companies that can generate such competencies can leverage them in the ways that were discussed earlier. Cash flows are also needed to develop a large-enough portfolio of contiguous products that can be funneled through the existing distribution channels to utilize the channels to their maximum capacity. Examples of contiguous products are cereals, soups, and frozen foods, which can be marketed through a company-owned distribution channel in a region.

Each of the above activities, carried out on a global scale, requires cash flows. These activities, in turn, generate necessary cash flows, and the cycle of cross-subsidization, attack, and counterattack continues on a global scale. Companies that do not perceive the strategic intent of global companies playing the game of cross-subsidization are paving the path to their own extinction. The strategic intent of global competitors is to wage battles worldwide. They want not only to capture world volume but also to generate the cash flow necessary to support the creation of new core technologies; enhance core competencies; establish strong distribution channels; acquire or build world-class, efficient plants; and achieve global brand recognition through massive advertising and marketing campaigns. A historical example of an effective counterattack strategy is the invasion by Eastman Kodak of the home market of Japan's Fuji Photo Film.[24] Kodak launched the attack against Fuji in response to Fuji's attack on Kodak's lucrative markets in America and Europe, where for decades Kodak had maintained a dominant market share in the color film business. Fuji's attack shrank Kodak's margins and forced it to cut prices. Realizing that it faced a global challenge from Fuji that would only grow stronger, Kodak struck back and invaded its rival's home market. The results were dramatically favorable for Kodak, whose sales jumped sixfold within a few years. It put Fuji on the defensive; Fuji's domestic margins were squeezed, and some of Fuji's best executives were recalled to Tokyo. In Kodak's estimation, its invasion of the Japanese market forced Fuji to divert its resources from overseas in order to defend its home market, where it had enjoyed a commanding 60 percent share of the market in color film.

The implementation of a counterattack strategy has several critical implications for the management of a global company. For instance, to assist a parent company in a global counterattack, the foreign affiliates in the company have to relinquish much of their autonomy to the parent company or to divisional management. The relationship between and among the affiliates and the parent company has to be one of resource interdependence rather than independence. The strategies and implementation plans of each affiliate have to be coordinated with those of the parent company and the other affiliates. This coordination is necessary so that resources required for launching offensive or preemptive cross-subsidization strikes against competitors can be marshaled from the most appropriate sources within the global network of the company. The managerial philosophy underlying a counterattack strategy is that in a global industry, competition in an affiliate country does not always emanate from other local companies; rather, it can come from affiliates of foreign companies that are members of powerful networks of global companies having worldwide access to resources. Therefore, a foreign affiliate left to fend for itself with only its own country-based resources would be no match for an aggressive global company's attack without help from sister affiliates or the parent company. Collaboration among the affiliates and the parent company in the sharing of resources through cross-subsidization is the only way to deflect an attack by a global company against a weak affiliate.

At the parent-company level, divisional management and strategic business units (SBUs) have to abandon a "my division" or "my business unit" attitude and think more in terms of interdivisional and cross-SBU relationships. Like foreign affiliates, they, too, have to collaborate and share resources among themselves and seek to agree on, and implement, strategies that add value and strength to the company as a global whole.

Investments abroad in manufacturing, research and development, marketing, and other functional areas have to be made for strategic reasons, such as establishing a beachhead in major markets of the world or in the home market of a foreign competitor. Such investments are based primarily on their strategic importance to any future offensive or defensive counterattack strategies, and not necessarily on financial considerations, such as return on investment or profitability.

Glocalization

In core competency leveraging and counterattack, the parent company clearly plays a central role in coordinating its network of globally dispersed affiliates. The parent company makes the network operate as one integrated, collective global unit. Global companies, however, must be careful that, in their zealous pursuit of an effective global strategy, they do not neglect managerial initiative at lower levels in the organizational hierarchy, especially at the regional and subsidiary levels. Phatak coined the word **glocalization** to represent a firm-level strategic response that parallels the industry-level, total-firm transnational orientation. Glocalization is simply thinking globally but acting locally. It includes an optimal mix of parental control where it counts and local initiative at regional and subsidiary levels. This structural balance has proved to be most fruitful for well-managed global companies.[25] More recently, the following thoughts have been offered to further delineate Phatak's glocalization:

> The introduction of the terms "glocal strategy" and "glocalization" may be a compromise to improve the present usage of the term global strategy. The glocal strategy approach reflects the aspirations of a global strategy approach, while the necessity for local adaptations and tailoring of business activities is simultaneously acknowledged. The "glocal strategy" concept comprises local, international, multinational, and global strategy approaches.[26]

A successful strategy incorporates the glocalization of the following interrelated elements: management, foreign affiliates, exports, products, and production.[27]

Glocalization of Management Adopting a global strategy that does not stifle local initiative requires a delicate balancing act. It often means giving regional and subsidiary managers the freedom to develop their own implementation plans for products, marketing, financing, and production that are consistent with local political, economic, legal, and cultural demands. For example, Levi Strauss & Company, the jeans maker, maintains tight headquarters control where it matters most. As a company that cherishes brand identity and quality, Levi's has organized several foreign manufacturing subsidiaries rather than relying on a patchwork of licensees that are hard to control. It has also exported its pioneering use of computers to track sales and manufacturing and, in so doing, keep a step ahead of fashion trends. Levi's also allows local managers to make decisions about adapting products to suit local tastes. In Brazil, Levi's local managers make decisions regarding distribution. For example, local initiative and knowledge of the market enabled Levi's to establish a chain of over 400 *Levi's Only* stores, some of them in tiny, rural towns in Brazil's fragmented market. Levi's approach represents a slogan that is symbolic of what glocalization stands for: "Be global, act local."

In the Sony Corporation, apart from the long-term strategy handed down from Tokyo, regional managers make all their own investment and product decisions on the spot. Top managers from Sony's subsidiaries around the world meet twice a year to hammer out the basic details of the company's operations.[28] Insiders say that this international-top-meeting arrangement is the main reason for Sony's ability to respond to market changes and launch new products so swiftly.

A glocalization of management philosophy is also evident in Toshiba and Matsushita Electric Industrial Company, which have delegated decision-making authority to regional headquarters. Toshiba has a tripolar regional management structure for Asia, Europe, and the United States. Each area manager has decision-making authority for manufacturing, sales, and some research and development. At Matsushita Electric, which has regional headquarters for Asia, Europe, and the United States based in Singapore, London, and New Jersey, respectively, most local decisions are now made locally, and the three top regional heads are all members of Matsushita Electric's board of directors. Again, each region has manufacturing, marketing, and product-related research and development capability, and Matsushita plans to develop some regional basic research facilities as well.[29]

Glocalization of Foreign Affiliates Strong presence in a foreign market requires the physical presence of manufacturing facilities in the market itself. Governments are making market entry easier for companies, provided that company management agrees to base production of the product in the foreign country as soon as possible. Companies are also realizing that, as good corporate citizens, they ought to make a significant contribution to the economic development and social welfare of their host countries. Transferring production technology to the host country and increasing the ratio of locally produced items in the production process or the final product are two ways to contribute to a host country's economic well-being. Training and developing local suppliers of components and subassemblies enhances the technological base of a nation. Such a transfer of technology could be brought about by entering into technical collaboration agreements with local partners, forming joint ventures with local capital, or establishing a wholly owned subsidiary that is owned by the parent company.

The economic and political conditions in a country or region, as well as market size and the capabilities of the local partner, often dictate the mode of collaboration. For example, Japanese manufacturers have chosen to enter European markets mainly through joint ventures because of a preference, in Europe, for such collaborations and the hostility toward wholly owned Japanese plants exhibited by European governments. In the United States, Japanese companies have shown a preference for wholly owned plants, although they have also established several joint ventures with American companies.

Glocalization of Exports Using foreign production plants as export bases to third-country markets is yet another way to become a "local" company in a foreign country. The Japanese have been exporting U.S.-made Japanese automobiles back to Japan and to European markets. Similar strategies have been adopted by global companies that export from developing countries in Asia and other parts of the world. Glocalization of exports is the outcome of a deliberate strategy of helping host countries earn foreign exchange from exports of products and becoming a good citizen of the host country. The benefits accrued from goodwill may far outweigh the added costs of exports from a country that may not be the most suitable from a purely economic measure.

Glocalization of Products Should a company standardize its product or service throughout the world by selling the same product without making variations to suit differences in local taste and use? Or should the product or service be tailored and customized to comply with local taste and use? This issue has been debated ad infinitum, and the answer to the question is that, to the extent that standardization is possible, a company should attempt it. Some products and services can be standardized globally, such as fax machines and telephones. On the other side of the scale, however, are products such as coffee and soups, which must be modified to make them more palatable to the tastes of people in various countries and cultures.

Companies are resolving this dilemma by realizing that some products have certain core technologies, subassemblies, or components that can be standardized on a worldwide basis, while other parts or configurations of the same product require adaptation to local conditions. For example, Whirlpool Corporation saw a growing market in India for washing machine sales to the growing number of middle-class, two-income families in that country. The washing machines sold in Europe and America, however, were not suited to wash the traditional, five-yard-long saris worn by Indian women. Whirlpool formed a joint venture with an Indian partner to produce and market a Western-style automatic washing machine that is compact enough to fit into Indian homes and that incorporates specially designed agitators that will not tangle saris. Variations of the same machine, internally dubbed the "World Washer," are also built and sold in Brazil and Mexico. In the aftermath of the glocalization-of-exports strategy discussed above, Whirlpool exports these machines from factories in those countries to other

PRACTICAL INSIGHT 5.3

CHEESE KATSU BURGER ANYONE?

For Toshihiro Imagawa, a recent breakfast under the Golden Arches consisted of two rice balls and a cup of what you might call McMiso soup.

"So finally, it's come this far," says the 23-year-old fast-food fan, sampling items from McDonald's newest breakfast offerings here. Squirting concentrated miso paste into a cup of hot water, he wonders: "Do Americans know about this stuff?"

Perhaps not, but rising competition on Japan's fast-food front is forcing McDonald's Corp. to stretch its imagination beyond the Egg McMuffin. Local rivals are bombarding the market with increasingly exotic menus, such as rice burgers (which sandwich shredded beef between grilled rice in the shape of a bun) and seaweed soup. In particular, the Mos Burger chain is putting McDonald's—Japan's biggest fast-food company—on the defensive.

"Consumers are now looking for the homemade touch, the Japanese taste," says Toshio Hayashi, a McDonald's spokesman. So the company is fighting back by launching more new items than any other chain, including such localized fare as steamed Chinese dumplings, curry with rice and roast pork-cutlet burgers oozing with melted cheese.

Last year, McDonald's added fried rice to its menu, four years after Mos Burger introduced its Rice Burgers in 1986.

Also last year, McDonald's came up with a Cheese Katsu Burger, which encloses cheese in the traditional Japanese roast pork cutlet, drenched in the traditional katsu sauce and topped with shredded cabbage. But that was patterned after Mos Burger's Mos Roast Katsu Burger, which hit the menu in 1988. KFC, meanwhile, deep-fried the chicken cutlet, topped it with cabbage and splashed it with teriyaki sauce.

In the meantime, fast-food chains are trying new ways to increase profits. KFC, which bought Pizza Hut's Japanese operation, will soon start delivery of Japanese-style box lunches as well. McDonald's hopes to set the scene for big outlets—seating 250, compared with 100 in most standard outlets—by building them next to Toys 'R' Us and Blockbuster video-rental stores, both of which the company or an affiliate has a stake in.

Japan's fast-food chains say they are also continuing their experiments in the kitchen. But they will take a while longer to win over the likes of 22-year-old Kento Yamada, who would rather stick to the good old Big Mac.

Source: Yumiko Ono, *The Wall Street Journal, Online,* May 29, 1992. Copyright © 1992 by Dow Jones & Co Inc. Reproduced with permission of Dow Jones & Co. Inc. via Copyright Clearance Center.

Asian and Latin American markets. Except for minor variations in controls, the three bare-bones washers are nearly identical; They all handle only 11 pounds of wash, which is about half the capacity of the typical U.S. model.[30] Whirlpool illustrates the slogan of product glocalization: Standardize worldwide what you can, and adapt what you cannot.

Fast-food chains have given up on the strict code of offering the same menu globally. In response to local cultural demands, McDonald's has vastly modified its menu in its restaurants in India. It does not offer its traditional beef hamburger because the majority Hindu population will not eat beef. For some time, McDonald's India offered instead the lamburger, which was made from lamb meat, but that item was temporarily dropped because of the customers' suspicion that it could contain beef. The company now offers such offbeat menu items as the Chicken Maharaja Mac; Paneer Salsa Wrap made from ricotta cheese; McVeggie, a vegetable burrito; and the McAllo, a potato patty burger. McDonald's has made similar glocalization moves in other countries, including Japan, described in Practical Insight 5.3.

Glocalization of Production   Companies are splitting the production process and farming out parts of it to different countries. They are doing so in order to exploit the advantages of lower costs derived from scale economies, international specialization (where some countries are better at doing certain things than others), and locational advantages such as proximity to markets, cheap labor, freedom from significant political risk, and local incentives such as tax holidays and government subsidies. Japanese automobile companies have targeted Asian countries for the expansion of their production activities because of the long-term growth potential of markets there. For example, one result of the Japanese expansion is the beginning of a parts-supply network that spans Southeast Asia. To achieve economies of scale, Japan's carmakers produce different parts in different countries. Nissan, for example, wants to concentrate on production of diesel engines in Thailand, mechanical parts in Indonesia, wire harnesses in the Philippines, and clutches and electrical parts in Malaysia. Toyota has also invested in facilities to support a similar parts production program.

The farming out of production to different countries also extends to finished products. For instance, a company that produces a variety of models of the same product might assign a subsidiary in one country to specialize in the production of one model and a subsidiary in yet another country to specialize in a second model. The two subsidiaries then export to each other the models they produce. In this way, both subsidiaries have two models to market in their respective regions, but each is responsible for the production of only one of them. This strategy is common in the global automobile industry, and General Motors and Ford already practice it in Europe.[31]

With the emergence of the so-called emerging markets, companies are examining market penetration opportunities offered by the increasing number of middle-class consumers in such countries. We study this in the discussion below.

Strategies That Fit the Emerging Market Environments

MNCs are now very eager to tap into the potentially profitable opportunities in the so-called emerging markets. Countries like Brazil, Russia, India, and China, to name a few, have been growing at rates in excess of 7 percent per annum and, unlike the case in the past, have become a lot more welcoming toward investments by foreign companies. However, MNCs have been unable to take full advantage of the opportunities presented by the emerging markets because of the tendency to look upon emerging markets as a place to transplant existing products that have sold well in the home and developed-country markets. The failure to perceive the necessity of tailoring the pricing, promotion, packaging, distribution, and design strategies to suit the conditions in the emerging markets has led to disappointing outcomes for many MNCs in those markets. Quite often, little effort is devoted to tailoring the marketing mix to the emerging markets' conditions because senior managers in MNCs think that a very small segment of the local population could afford to buy their products. Such thinking could prove to be a costly mistake, as we shall see in the following paragraphs.

The Mammoth Middle-Class Market

Some companies fail to realize that even though the average living standards of the majority of the population in emerging markets may not be equal to those of the populations in the economically advanced countries of Western Europe and North America, there exists in emerging markets a very large population belonging to the middle class with incomes that approximate the purchasing power of their middle-class counterparts in the richer countries of the world. To illustrate this concept, let us look at the Indian market characteristics. Similar characteristic also exist in the demographic profile of other emerging markets.

In their *BusinessWeek* article, "Next Big Spenders: India's Middle Class," Diana Farrell and Eric Beinhocker classified the Indian population into the following five tiers (see Figure 5.7):[32]

FIGURE 5.7
The Indian Income Pyramid

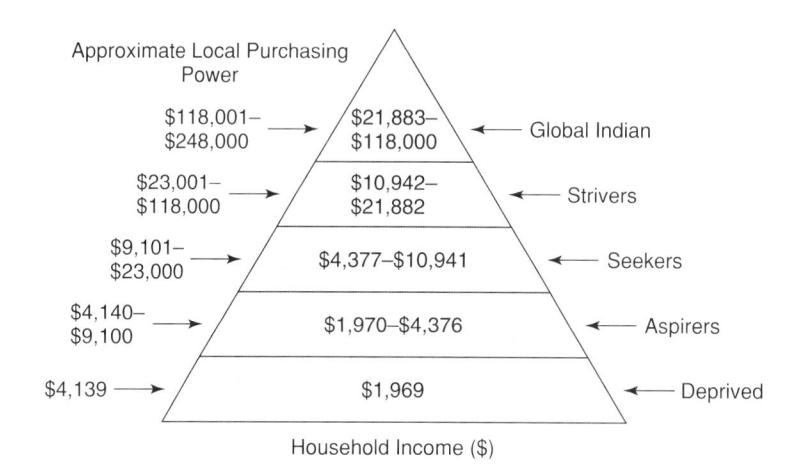

```
                    Approximate Local Purchasing
                              Power

       $118,001–            $21,883–
       $248,000    ──→      $118,000      ←── Global Indian

       $23,001–             $10,942–
       $118,000    ──→      $21,882       ←── Strivers

       $9,101–
       $23,000     ──→      $4,377–$10,941  ←── Seekers

       $4,140–
       $9,100      ──→      $1,970–$4,376   ←── Aspirers

       $4,139      ──→      $1,969          ←── Deprived

                        Household Income ($)
```

- **Tier 1: Global Indians.** Indians in this tier earn more than 1 million rupees ($21,882, or $118,000, taking into account the cost of living). By 2025, there will be 9.5 million Indians in this class, and their spending power will hit 14.1 trillion rupees—20 percent of total Indian consumption. Today there are about 1 million people in this grouping. By 2025, there will be 9.5 million Indians in this class, and their spending power will hit 14.1 trillion rupees—20 percent of total Indian consumption. Their consumer tastes are similar to those of the affluent class in advanced countries, with a penchant for designer clothes, French perfume, and luxury cars.

- **Tiers 2 and 3: The middle class.** The middle class segment in India is currently estimated at between 50 and 250 million people, and it is expected to grow to 583 million people by 2025, about 41 percent of the total population of India. Their incomes balloon to 51.5 trillion rupees ($1.1 billion)—11 times the level of today and 58 percent of total Indian income. While their incomes would place them below the poverty line in the United States, things are much cheaper in India. When the local cost of living is taken into account, the income of the seekers and strivers looks more like $23,000 to $118,000, which is middle class by most developed-country standards. This segment consists of two subgroupings: (1) strivers and (2) seekers.

  Tier 2: Strivers. With incomes of between 500,000 and 1 million rupees ($10,941–$21,882), this group comprises the upper end of the middle class. Included in this grouping are senior government officials, managers of large businesses, professionals, and rich farmers. Strivers are successful and upwardly mobile. They are very brand-conscious and tend to buy the latest fashion apparel and electronic gadgets. Their homes are likely to be air-conditioned, and they can afford to indulge in yearly vacations somewhere in India.

  Tier 3: Seekers. With incomes of between 200,000 and 500,000 rupees ($4,376–$10,941), people in this group are young college graduates, midlevel government officials, traders, and businesspeople. Their lifestyle is similar to that of the middle class in most advanced countries. Typically they own a television, a refrigerator, a mobile phone, and perhaps even a scooter or a car. They stretch their earnings for their children's education and for their own modest retirement.

- **Tier 4: Aspirers.** Over the next 20 years, this group will shrink from 41 percent of the population to 36 percent, as many of its members move up into the middle class. With incomes of between 90,000 and 200,000 rupees ($1,969–$4,376) per year, members of this group are typically small shopkeepers, farmers, or semiskilled industrial and service workers. They have enough food and might own items such as a small television, a propane stove, and an electric rod for heating water. They spend about half of their income on basic necessities, and many of their other purchases are bought secondhand or in what Indians call the "informal economy."

- **Tier 5: The deprived.** The deprived earn less than 90,000 Indian rupees a year ($1,969 per household, or about a dollar per person per day). If growth in the Indian economy continues at its recent pace, a further 291 million people are expected to move out of poverty over the next two decades.

How Can MNCs Capitalize on the Middle-Class Market Segment?

With a middle-class population in India as large as the total population of many European countries, and projected to grow to more than one half billion by the year 2025, it would be a folly for MNCs to ignore the potential for making volume sales to consumers in this segment.

While luxury-goods makers may be able to sell to India's global consumers with little modification to their products, those selling to India's new middle class will need to be innovative to square the difference between the rising aspirations of consumers and their still-modest pocketbooks. The same holds true for the middle-class market segment in other emerging markets. Companies that fail to understand the unique desires and tastes of the new Indian consumer will miss out on huge volume sales to a half-billion-strong market that, along with China, ranks as one of the most important growth opportunities of the next two decades.

Pricing MNCs should sell their products at a price that a middle-class consumer can afford to pay. This may take some innovative thinking by MNCs. For example, instead of selling a box of chocolates or cough lozenges, which may be beyond the purchasing power of a middle-class consumer, one could package the chocolates or cough lozenges in single-serve packets. Products as varied as shampoos, detergents, pickles, and cooking oil are sold in single-serve packets in India, and they make up 20 to 30 percent of the sales in their categories.[33] Single-serve packets are becoming popular in China as well. Single-serve packets allow consumers to conserve cash and to buy only what they need.

Packaging In emerging markets, the highways and roads, especially those away from the main cities, may be quite poor. Therefore, distribution by trucks to markets serving the middle class may require packaging that can prevent breakage and damage from the shocks and bumps on bad roads leading to the various distribution points.

Distribution Consumers in emerging markets generally live in the outskirts of major cities or in hamlets and villages scattered throughout the country. The distribution of products, especially to the hamlets and villages, may require a transportation network consisting of trains, trucks, rickshaws, and bicycles for the final phase of delivery to the millions of kiosks scattered throughout the country.

Promotion The literacy rates in emerging countries could be as low as 10 percent, as is the case in countries in sub-Saharan Africa. In India the literacy rate is estimated to be 60 percent. Advertising must account for the fact that vast numbers of people cannot read or write. Therefore, although written messages in advertisements may reach those who can read, they would be of no use in targeting the illiterate population. In such cases, it would be prudent to resort to pictures and images to convey the promotional message in an advertisement. For example, to promote birth control in India,

PRACTICAL INSIGHT 5.4

TATA UNVEILS THE WORLD'S CHEAPEST CAR
The $2,500 Nano, met with extreme enthusiasm, will have lighter steel and innovative distribution. It also could further snarl India's roads.

It's called the Nano, for its high technology and small size. It's cute, compact, and contemporary. It's a complete four-door car with a 623-cc gas engine, gets 50 miles to the gallon, and seats up to five. It meets domestic emissions norms and will soon comply with European standards. It's 8% smaller in outer length than its closest rival, Suzuki's Maruti 800, but has 21% more volume inside. And at $2,500 before taxes (value-added taxes increase the price by about $300), it is the most inexpensive car in the world. Starting this fall, the Nano will roll off the assembly lines at a Tata Motors (TTM) plant in Singur, Bengal, and navigate India's potholed roads.

The Nano, also known as the People's Car, is Ratan Tata's dream come true, and is India's contribution to changing the global auto industry. "The car has put India on the global map," says Fionna Prims, head of business development for Segment Y, a Goa-based automotive consultant for emerging markets. "Tata has done in four years what the Japanese took 30 years to do. It will change the whole industry." Even rivals are gushing. "It's a red letter day for Indian industry, a day India should be proud of," says Venu Srinivasan, chairman of motorcycle maker TVS Motors. "Ratan Tata has the vision to create a new business model and all the naysayers are looking at it with concern. The Nano is a path breaker."

Judging by the extreme enthusiasm that greeted the launch of the car Jan. 10 at the biennial Auto Expo 2008 in New Delhi, the Nano has exceeded industry expectations. For the four years that the car has been in the making, Tata Motors, which makes trucks, sport-utility vehicles, and the Indica, India's second most popular car, has endured skepticism and disbelief (BusinessWeek.com, 1/3/08) from rivals both domestic and international.

Ratan Tata Never Lost Faith
In the past week alone, domestic rival Bajaj Auto unveiled a hastily configured concept car with a price tag of $2,700, and Osamu Suzuki, chairman of Japan's Suzuki Motor, said the $2,500 price point was not where the market is (BusinessWeek.com, 12/5/07) in India. International carmakers and media doubted Tata's ability to meet international environment and safety standards, and wondered aloud what the appearance of an affordable car would do to India's already congested roads.

Throughout, Ratan Tata remained unfazed, despite his own doubts of meeting his timeline and price goal at a time when the costs of raw materials, from steel to rubber, were rising. But Tata promised a $2,500 car, and "a promise is a promise," he said to an audience spilling out into the streets and packed with government officials, industry chiefs, international carmakers, and reporters. "I hope it will be seen as the car . . . which changes the manner in which people in rural and semi-urban India will travel," said Tata. And, he added, "it will be a profitable venture for the company."

---

companies have used billboards with two pictures, one showing a family with two healthy children and the other showing a family with five emaciated children.

Design How the product will be used influences its design. For example, in middle-class homes in India, Videocon, the Indian consumer electronics company, launched a washing machine that is responsive to the frequent power outages that still occur all over India. The richer families have their own diesel electricity generators to ensure a continuous power supply during power outages, but the middle class cannot afford them. Videocon's washing machine not only is cheap but also completes the wash during a power outage, and it does not have the standard drying feature, which is costly to operate.

Managers in MNCs must answer the following questions:

1. Who is the middle class in the emerging market?
2. What are the needs of people in this class?
3. How big is their discretionary income; that is, how much money is available for spending after meeting the basic needs for food, housing, and clothing?
4. Can our product be downsized to make it affordable to the consumer?
5. Can our product be redesigned to make it economical to use?

The Nano has broken ground on many different levels—in price, in size, in distribution, and technology. By using lighter steel, a smaller engine, and having longer-term sourcing agreements with parts suppliers, Tata was able to keep the price of the Nano down. Its length of 3.1 meters, width of 1.5 meters, and height of 1.6 meters, with wheels at the outer corners and engine, gears, and transmission in the rear, creates space inside the car.

A Diesel Nano Will Come Next Year

Tata has filed 34 new patents on the Nano, says Girish Wagh, chief engineer and leader of the 500-man engineer and design team that created and developed the car. Most are in the engine; the Nano will have a two-cylinder, 30-hp engine with a four-speed manual transmission. Analysts say the true engine innovation will come next year, when Tata introduces the diesel version of the Nano.

Finally, the distribution of the car will also be an innovation. Just like a bicycle, it will be sold in kits that are distributed and serviced by the entrepreneurs who will assemble it for the consumer. Tata won't elaborate, and will only say "the distribution system will be a variant from the norm. It will remove some of the layers in distribution and service."

The Nano basic will sell for $2,500, but there will be many versions of it, including an air-conditioned one, and prices could go up to $4,000, still less than the Maruti 800, until now the world's cheapest car at $4,810. And it will be customized for overseas markets and exported. Ratan Tata intends to export the car to emerging markets in Africa, Latin America, and Asia, where it'll be a natural fit, says Paul Blokland, director of Segment Y, who has been following the auto sector in emerging markets, particularly China, for a decade. The Chinese, he adds, have been only making copies of cars all these years, and have a lot to learn from Tata Motors' innovative vehicle.

Dealers' Phones Ringing Off the Hook

The Nano, having created a new market segment, has already begun to spawn an industry around it. India's Apollo Tyres has said it will start to make tires for small cars like the Nano, and the industry could clearly grow if the Nano proves to be popular.

Will Ratan Tata shift to a lower gear now that his dream has been fulfilled? He'd like nothing better, he says, but it's unlikely. "We have to now deliver a reliable product, and the Indian consumer has still to ratify it," he said. "We have only just put a stake in the ground." Does he worry about rivals? "We were driven by a desire to achieve what we set out to do, and it can be achieved by anyone who tries to achieve their dream. Someone else may be able to do it better than us," he said.

Certainly there's interest from consumers. At Bafna Motors in Mumbai, the phones were ringing all day, according to S.M. Bafna, managing director of the auto dealer. He had to keep his phone off the hook to ward off prospective buyers. Bafna wouldn't hazard a guess of how many Nanos he might sell, for "I might underestimate the demand," he said. "People are desperately waiting for the car."

Source: Manjeet Kripalani and Nandini Lakshman, *BusinessWeek*, January 10, 2008.

6. How can we distribute the product to the consumer? What sorts of distribution patterns and networks exist in the country?

A good example of how companies can innovate their business models to market to the middle class is Tata Motors' production of the Nano, discussed in Practical Insight 5.4.

Summary

This chapter begins Section 2 of the book, our discussion of the strategic initiatives international firms use in response to the changing environments we discussed in Section 1. We presented Perlmutter's ethnocentric, polycentric, and geocentric attitudes, which the international firm may exhibit, and offered a three-dimensional framework for classifying international firms on the basis of those three attitudinal orientations and the functional and geographic orientations to integration strategies described in the chapter.

We identified various decision processes, including the analytical hierarchy process, that firms may use when they look to overseas markets and international locations for production. We then introduced the portfolio-analysis framework to help the firm manage its various international subsidiaries. Subsequently, the implications of global, multidomestic, and transnational mind-sets were linked into the discussion.

We also used the concept of the value chain to illustrate the functional and geographic scope of integration strategies available to the international firm in responding to different environmental contexts. Stand-alone strategies, based on a high degree of autonomy for operating units, require the least amount of centralized coordination. Simple and complex integration strategies offer more opportunity to capitalize on global economies of scale and scope, but they require greater degrees of coordination and control among the different subunits.

The chapter concluded with specific strategic initiatives that international firms must undertake to sustain their respective competitive advantages. These include core competency leveraging, counterattack, glocalization, and a discussion of how companies can take advantage of the huge middle-class market in emerging markets like China, India, Brazil, and Russia.

Key Terms and Concepts

complex integration strategy, *182*
core competency leveraging, *183*
counterattack, *185*
ethnocentrism, *164*
geocentrism, *164*
global orientation, *175*
glocalization, *188*
international orientation, *174*
internationalization, *165*
multidomestic orientation, *176*
polycentrism, *164*
simple integration strategy, *180*
stand-alone strategy, *179*
transnational orientation, *176*
value chain, *176*

Discussion Questions

1. Pick an industry and develop a list of factors that you believe are critical to consider when deciding to expand overseas.
2. Why will implementation of the transnational approach require more of a firm's resources?
3. Why is the value chain important to understand in relation to a firm's international strategic approach?
4. Link the levels of integration strategies to (a) ethnocentrism, polycentrism, and geocentrism and (b) the global, multidomestic, and transnational approaches.
5. Give examples of the various ways a firm can glocalize.

Minicase

CIENA's Globalization Decision (2000–2007)

CIENA'S CORE COMPETENCY AND GROWTH

In the early nineties, CIENA began to capitalize on the changes in U.S. rules relating to telecom carriers. The firm introduced equipment using disruptive technology of dense wave division multiplexing (DWDM) for long-range transmission of digital data. In very simple terms, DWDM is multiplexing signals using different colors of light over a single fiber pair.

This technology increased the data transmission capacity of telecom carriers beyond imagination. It enabled transmission of 196 channels over a fiber pair with each channel carrying 10 gigabytes per second (GB/sec) (OC-192) of digital data; this is many times more than the size of a computer's hard drive and can provide millions of phone calls all on the same fiber pair. This paved the way for development of CIENA's Optical Switch. This switch has been very well received by the telecom carrier industry. It saves both millions of dollars and floor space for the carriers. Until now, due to technological limitations, carriers had been using older telecom equipment like the add drop multiplexers (ADMs).

CIENA continues to innovate not only by offering new hardware but also by offering complete solutions for telecom carriers to enable them to upgrade their networks and offer cost-efficient solutions to their customers. In doing so, software plays a major role by efficiently utilizing the hardware and automating manual tasks.

CIENA was recently added to the Standard & Poor's 500; yet that is only a part of the story. It is the change in the size of its hardware and software R&D teams that is worth noting. As of April 2003, the senior vice president responsible for hardware had 269 engineers and managers, while the senior vice president responsible for software had 480 direct reports. The reason for this increase in software team numbers is that software improves the efficiency and reliability of the deployed hardware. Software also allows the carrier to manage (monitor and control) hundreds of network elements deployed across the continental United States and Europe from a single location.

Using this ability to control from a single location, carriers can now provision and monitor circuits for their customers in a few seconds, rather than the hours and even days required in the past. These circuits can originate from a building in one city and terminate at a building in the same city or in a different state or country. The carriers love this ability; it enables them to save huge amounts of money on training and personnel expenses. Consequently, they can now pass on some of the savings to their customer, which increases revenue and allows the carriers to competitively price their offerings.

In 2002, British Telecom (BT) signed CIENA to supply equipment and solutions for its next-generation network. Before signing, they approached AT&T to observe firsthand CIENA's capabilities. AT&T uses CIENA's switches and metro transmission equipment. An AT&T executive demonstrated to his BT counterpart the efficiency and cost savings achieved because of CIENA's innovations. He took the BT executive to a nearly deserted operations center and told him that the reason for the empty chairs is that they have been replaced by CIENA's software.

DRIVERS FOR GLOBALIZATION: REVENUE AND PROFIT GROWTH

The dot-com boom of the late 1990s brought into play the need for increased data transmission. That in turn brought about the birth of many new telecom carriers, and since they were starting from scratch they bought a lot of equipment from CIENA. The traditional carrier already had networks in place and hence orders from them were limited. Also, these carriers wanted to continue to use their traditional suppliers.

The dot-com boom is history and those new carriers have either gone under or are struggling. But the traditional carriers have realized the benefits of CIENA's solutions and now buy more from CIENA. A few of CIENA's traditional telecom carrier customers are AT&T, BT, Sprint, Qwest, and Verizon. But the traditional carriers are not spending as much compared to a few years ago and the revenue from the new carriers has all dried up.

Experiences in Europe have shown that the carriers there are more resistant to change and continue to buy from traditional suppliers like Alcatel, Marconi, Ericsson, Nokia, and Nortel. Currently, there is an ongoing initiative with French Telecom and Telia but orders from them and other European carriers are expected to be limited. Additionally now there are price threats from companies like Huawei, which have started to offer products in the transmission segment. In comparison to CIENA, Huawei is based in China and has very low R&D and manufacturing costs. CIENA continues to enjoy a great lead in the switching segment. But this competitive threat pressures CIENA to look for ways to cut its cost and increase its market share.

To reduce costs and to increase its market, CIENA is considering the following:

1. Reduce costs by moving some of its software development operations to India.
2. Aggressively expand into China for revenue enhancement and also to further prevent the expansion of companies such as Huawei into the U.S. and European markets by competing with them on their home turf (similar to the Kodak and Fuji situation in Japan). And once substantial sales are realized in China, establish a manufacturing base in China.

In the following sections, India's emergence as a location of choice for software development and the benefits offered to companies by regional (state) and central governments to establish and operate from India will be analyzed. In addition to outsourcing issues, CIENA must also address how it wants to enter China and, specifically, how to ensure that its mode of entry protects its proprietary product technology. There is the specific need to explore the area of legal risk in China and discuss why creating a wholly owned subsidiary makes the most sense for CIENA.

INDIA'S EMERGENCE AS A PREFERRED LOCATION FOR SOFTWARE DEVELOPMENT

Due to the economic liberalization in the early nineties, India has continued to see an increase in multinational companies setting up software development centers within its borders. Initially this growth was presumed to be dot-com driven; however, other factors also explain the rise of software development in India. Listed below are a few internationally renowned technical companies that have expanded into India in the post-dot-com era for advanced/innovative research and development:

EDS opened a new offshore facility in 2003.

Siemens located its global applications development function in 2003.

Oracle chose India as a key overseas hub in 2002.

Ford opened an IT hub in 2001.

Since 2000, Microsoft, IBM, and Lucent all have expanded their existing Indian facilities.

The Indian laws are continuing to improve providing protection against illegal copying of intellectual property; this makes India more lucrative for businesses thinking of outsourcing work to India. Also, the policies of the U.S. government continue to favor software development in India, having few restrictions regarding movement of U.S. software initiatives into India. The Indian education system puts a lot of stress on science and technology. A 2002/2003 report on CBS's *60 Minutes* talked about the Indian Institute of Technology. It demonstrates the quality and capabilities of technical graduates from India. In the late 1990s, a great number of IT workers were needed in the United States and a large number of them came from India. Since the bust of the dot-com era, many of these workers have returned to India. Being trained in U.S. methods of operation, they are valuable assets for U.S. companies in India.

Another attraction for U.S. companies is the salary in India. For the same qualifications, Indian salaries were nearly 10 times less than U.S. salaries in 2003. Given the huge population and education system that stresses math and science in India, every year there are a significant number of technical graduates to choose from for companies setting up in India. Last, English is widely spoken and accepted in India. Not only is English the medium of instruction in technical colleges and universities, but it is the accepted language for interbusiness and business-to-government interactions. It is also used widely within subsidiaries in India and for those subsidiaries' interactions with headquarters in the United States. In general, when considering expansion to India, the pros and cons may be summarized as follows. The pros are:

1. Lower labor cost for same levels of qualifications.
2. English as a prevalent language.
3. A large pool of qualified high-tech labor.
4. Government subsidies and tax breaks.
    a. Software Technology Parks of India (STPI) certification to provide a 10-year tax holiday on revenues if the product is marked 100 percent export from India.
    b. No import tax on factors of production such as computers and network equipment.
    c. Subsidies on floor space.
    d. Subsidies and promise of continued power.
    e. Subsidies on telephone charges.

The cons are:

1. Weak antipiracy laws.
2. Changes in government policies.
    a. In its 2002–2003 budget, the government imposed a 10 percent tax on STPI exempt exports.
    b. The costs of various factors of production (floor space, telecom charges, power charges) can increase if the government subsidies are reduced or eliminated.

3. Cost of facilities.
    a. Telecom and electricity, if not subsidized, can become very expensive.
    b. Good office locations with air-conditioned floors are expensive.
4. Hidden labor costs.
    a. 13 months' salary. It is customary to pay one month's salary as bonus, which is not tied to the performance of the company.
    b. Overhead of 20 to 25 percent relating to benefits.

The Indian government is going ahead with its economic liberalization programs. It is expected that with the privatization of telecom and power companies the costs for both will become comparable to or lower than those in the United States and subsidies will not be required. The tax breaks will continue to be available to global companies, to attract them to continue to invest in India. The reason is that these investments create employment that in return creates a tax base for the government. The exports of software helps the Indian government balance the imports it needs to improve the infrastructure of the country to support the overall economic development of the country. Additionally, the benefit for business because of this is the improvement in quality of labor and factors of production. But with overall economic improvements the costs of labor will go up too. As the income levels increase, the purchasing power of people in India will increase, which will in turn make India a lucrative market for the products of these foreign firms. Increased revenue from sales will be much more than increased labor costs.

CIENA'S PROPOSED ENTRY INTO CHINA AND INTELLECTUAL PROPERTY ISSUES

A second issue is how CIENA should proceed into China. What is China's legal environment like? How are intellectual property rights (IPRs) enforced? Clearly, competitive threats exist. The aforementioned Chinese rival Huawei Technologies Company has produced products "similar" to CIENA's product line. CIENA cites patent infringements by Huawei. In January 2003, Cisco, another high-tech firm, sued Huawei, charging that the company had copied and misappropriated Cisco software, copied copyrighted Cisco manuals, and infringed Cisco patents. A U.S. federal judge temporarily blocked Huawei from distributing software and user manuals related to Cisco software or having employees familiar with that software develop similar products. Will the same thing happen when CIENA begins selling its products in China? What are the business risks?

Intellectual property refers to products of the mind, ideas (e.g., books, music, software, designs, technological know-how). Patents, copyrights, and trademarks can protect intellectual property. The patent protects the owner for a limited period, generally 20 years in this industry. The owner of a U.S. patent can stop anyone from making, selling, or offering for sale the invention in the United States. In addition, a U.S. patent owner can stop anyone from importing unauthorized copies of the invention into the United States. However, U.S. patent rights stop at the American border. An inventor cannot use a U.S. patent to stop someone from making, selling, or using the invention in another country. To do that, American inventors must acquire patent rights in that country and rely on rules of reciprocity in international treaties. Reciprocity means that when an inventor from Country A applies for a patent in Country B, the inventor will be treated in the same manner as inventors living in Country B. This reciprocal treatment extends only to inventors who live in nations that have signed the treaty.

Trade Related Aspects of Intellectual Property Rights (TRIPS) is an agreement among members of the World Trade Organization (WTO) to enforce stricter intellectual property regulations, including granting and enforcing patents lasting at least 20 years and copyrights lasting 50 years. China committed to full compliance with the TRIPS agreement upon its year 2001 admission to the WTO. Chinese leaders have acknowledged that protection of patents, copyrights, and trademarks is needed to promote a knowledge-based economy. China has completed a revised patent law and is now reviewing and revising its trademark and copyright laws to ensure consistency with the TRIPS requirements. In spite of steady, significant progress in improving its intellectual property legal and regulatory regime, IPR protection in China remains weak. Trademark and copyright violations are blatant and widespread. While Chinese officials are increasing enforcement efforts, IPR violations, including growing exports of counterfeit products, continue to outpace enforcement. Enforcement of existing IPR laws is uneven and is sometimes impeded by local interests. The Business Software Alliance estimates that more than 90 percent of business software used in China is pirated. China's criminal sanctions against IPR violations are seldom used, in part because of restrictions on types of admissible evidence and cumbersome procedures.

Combating IPR violations in China is a long-term, multifaceted undertaking. China has established special IPR courts in all provinces and major cities. Judges in Chinese courts are charged with fact-finding and have greater discretion in the adjudication of cases than those in the United States. However, the lack of legal training of many trial court judges undermines the effectiveness of these courts. Laws and regulations in China tend to be far more general than in other countries. This vagueness allows Chinese courts and officials to apply them flexibly, which results in inconsistencies.

CIENA'S ENTRY INTO INDIA

In September 2005, CIENA Corporation announced the expansion of its global presence with the launch of a research and development (R&D) center located in Gurgaon, India. The 95,000-square-foot facility is CIENA's first core research and development center outside North America and is expected to employ as many as 300 product development engineers within the next three years. CIENA's Gurgaon center will supplement and work collaboratively with CIENA's existing research and development organization in North America. CIENA India will be led by Neeraj Gulati as vice president and managing director and Dimple Amin as vice president of engineering. "The India centre will be an addition to the five CIENA establishments in the world equipped with advanced design, development and testing laboratories," said Dimple Amin. "CIENA is regarded as a pioneer in networking technology worldwide, with a number of industry and technology firsts to its name, proof of CIENA's commitment to research and development. We are confident that the Gurgaon centre will serve as a strong addition to CIENA's R&D capabilities." Ciena's Gurgaon R&D center will focus on technologies such as storage extension and optical transport, including ultra-long-haul, long-haul, regional, and metropolitan applications, as well as multiservice switching, broadband access, and network management.

In November 2007, CIENA India announced the appointment of Kanwal Jawanda, a veteran telecom engineering professional, as its vice president, engineering. With more than 20 years of rich experience in the telecommunication industry, Kanwal will serve as a significant leader to CIENA India's research and development (R&D) team. In this capacity, he will drive the evolution of CIENA's world-class R&D center in Gurgaon. Also as part of his role, Kanwal will lead the end-to-end product development for several CIENA solution sets, which are utilized worldwide by leading telecom carriers, cable operators, enterprises, research institutions and government agencies.

Source: Sanjay Kumar, Dena Lorenzi, and Roger Kashlak, 2003; Roger Kashlak, 2008; www.ciena.com.

DISCUSSION QUESTIONS

1. Why did CIENA eventually move software development operations into India? What were potential concerns?
2. Should CIENA pursue the Chinese market, establish production facilities there for export purposes, or do both?
3. How should CIENA protect its intellectual property in each country?

Notes

1. Howard W. Perlmutter, "The Tortuous Evolution of the Multinational Corporation," *Columbia Journal of World Business* 3, no.1 (1969), pp. 9–18.
2. J. Johansson, *Global Marketing: Foreign Entry, Local Marketing and Global Management* (New York: Irwin/McGraw-Hill, 2000); G. S. Yip, "Global Strategy . . . in a World of Nations?" *Sloan Management Review,* Autumn 1989, pp. 29–41.
3. T. Saaty, *The Analytical Hierarchy Process* (New York: McGraw-Hill, 1980).
4. S. T. Cavusgil and S. Zou, "Marketing Strategy–Performance Relationship: An Investigation of the Empirical Link in Export Market Ventures," *Journal of Marketing* 58, no. 1 (1994), pp. 1–21.
5. A. Gupta and V. Govindarajan, *Global Strategy and Organization* (New York: John Wiley & Sons, 2004).

6. C. Prahalad and Y. Doz, *The Multinational Mission: Balancing Local Demands and Global Vision* (New York: Free Press, 1987).
7. K. Roth, D. Schweiger, and A. Morrison, "Global Strategy Implementation at the Business Unit Level: Operational Capabilities and Administrative Mechanisms," *Journal of International Business Studies* 22, no. 3 (1991), pp. 369–402.
8. T. Hout, M. Porter, and E. Rudden, "How Global Companies Win Out," *Harvard Business Review,* September/October 1982, pp. 98–108.
9. Y. Doz and C. Prahalad, "Patterns of Strategic Control within Multinational Corporations," *Journal of International Business Studies* 15, no. 3 (1984), pp. 55–72.
10. Michael E. Porter, *Competitive Strategy: Techniques to Analyzing Industries and Competitors* (New York: Free Press, 1980).
11. Doz and Prahalad, "Patterns of Strategic Control."
12. K. Roth and A. Morrison, "An Empirical Analysis of the Integration–Responsiveness Framework in Global Industries," *Journal of International Business Studies* 21, no. 4 (1990), pp. 541–564.
13. S. Ghoshal, "Global Strategy: An Organizing Framework," *Strategic Management Journal* 8 (1987), pp. 428–448.
14. S. Chatterjee and M. Lubatkin, "Corporate Mergers, Stockholder Diversification and Changes in Systematic Risk," *Strategic Management Journal* 11 (1990), pp. 256–280.
15. C. Bartlett and S. Ghoshal, *Managing across Borders: The Transnational Solution* (Boston: Harvard Business School Press, 1989).
16. C. Bartlett and S. Ghoshal, "Organizing for Worldwide Effectiveness: The Transnational Solution," *California Management Review,* Autumn 1988, pp. 54–74.
17. R. Kashlak, "Establishing Financial Targets for Joint Ventures in Emerging Countries: A Conceptual Model," *Journal of International Management* 4, no. 4 (1998), pp. 241–258.
18. M. Porter, *Competitive Advantage* (New York: Free Press, 1985), p. 11.
19. M. Porter, *On Competition* (Boston: Harvard Business School Press, 1998), p. 6.
20. Michael E. Porter, "Changing Patterns of International Competition," *California Management Review* 28, no. 2 (1986), pp. 9ff.
21. Gupta and Govindarajan, *Global Strategy and Organization.*
22. C. K. Prahalad and G. Hamel, "The Core Competence of the Corporation," *Harvard Business Review,* May/June 1990, pp. 79–91.
23. G. Hamel and C. K. Prahalad, "Do You Really Have a Global Strategy," *Harvard Business Review,* July/August 1985, pp. 139–148.
24. "The Revenge of Big Yellow," *The Economist,* November 10, 1990, pp. 66–68.
25. A. Phatak, *International Management: Concept and Cases* (Cincinnati: Southwestern Publishing, 1997).
26. G. Svensson, "Glocalization of Business Activities: A Glocal Strategy Approach," *Management Decision* 39, no. 1 (2001), pp. 6–22.
27. Phatak, *International Management: Concept and Cases.*
28. Nicholas Valery, "Consumer Electronics Survey," *The Economist,* April 13, 1991, p. 16.
29. "The Goal Is Genuine Internationalism," *BusinessWeek,* July 16, 1990, p. 81.
30. David Woodruff, "A Little Machine That Won't Shred a Sari," *BusinessWeek,* June 3, 1991, p. 100.
31. Phatak, *International Management: Concept and Cases.*
32. Diana Farrell and Eric Beinhocker, "Next Big Spenders: India's Middle Classs," *BusinessWeek,* May 19, 2007.
33. C. K. Prahalad and Kenneth Lieberthal, "The End of Corporate Imperialism," *Harvard Business Review,* August 2003, p. 5.

CHAPTER SIX

Analyzing and Managing Foreign Modes of Entry

Chapter Learning Objectives

After completing this chapter, you should be able to:

- Understand the different modes of entry into foreign markets.
- List the advantages, disadvantages, and risks in various entry modes.
- Understand the nonequity entry modes such as licensing, franchising, and nonequity strategic alliances.
- Explain the factors that influence the choice of entry modes.
- Explain the equity-based and nonequity-based control mechanisms.
- Understand various types of international collaborative agreements.
- Discuss the various motivations firms have for entering into international joint ventures.
- Delineate the many advantages as well as potential pitfalls associated with international joint ventures.
- Gain the ability to pick the right international alliance partner.

Opening Case: Tata Cummins Limited (1993–2008)—an IJV Success Story!

The Tata Cummins Limited (TCL) international joint venture (IJV) was incorporated in October 1993, with commercial production commencing on January 1, 1996. Located in India, in Jamshedpur, the IJV began as a 50-50 joint venture between Tata Engineering, India's largest automobile manufacturer, and Cummins Engine Company Inc. (USA), a world leader in the manufacturing and design of diesel engines, to manufacture fuel-efficient, low-emission, environment-friendly diesel engines. Tata Engineering was the largest manufacturer of commercial vehicles in India, while Cummins Engine Company is the largest 200+ HP diesel engine manufacturer in the world.

The IJV was set up at Jamshedpur for the manufacture of diesel engines to power Tata Motors Limited's commercial vehicles. The decision to locate at Jamshedpur was based on the desire to be near the customer. These engines were used in Tata Engineering's new-generation medium and heavy commercial vehicles that conform to Euro-I standards. The primary market was the Indian commercial vehicle business. Cummins brought new technology, including both manufacturing and distribution, and capital to the partnership. Tata had the India market knowledge and embedded base of customers. Commercial production of engines from kits commenced in January 1996, and the machining lines for in-house manufacture of components started in March 1997.

Through the new millennium, the mission of TCL continued to be widely acknowledged, and TCL was benchmarked as one of the best companies in the world. Its core values were to care for its customers, have an obsession for quality, care deeply about people, do what's right and not what's convenient, guarantee leadership, practice responsible citizenship, and strive for relentless improvement. End users of TCL's engines continually perceived the products to be more powerful and more efficient; have higher reliability, lower life cycle cost, and lower emissions; be easier to recondition; have lower maintenance costs, and use up to 40 percent fewer parts in comparison to competitive designs.

TCL's goal of bringing delight to customers through excellent customer support, and making them "Customers for Life," was highly successful. The engines reached the end users quickly through TCL's delivery partners, Tata Engineering and Cummins India. Technical training was provided to various dealers as well as roadside mechanics. Expert service engineers were able to be reached 24 hours a day through a help line at TCL. A TCL distinct competency was its very strong systems and IT infrastructure, which controlled and facilitated its operations. In June 2000, a Web-based supply chain management system was implemented to further increase efficiency. TCL was awarded excellence awards by the Eastern Region and was a QS 9000 company.

While mainly poor, India is very labor-intensive and boasts top-notch intellectual capital. Its human talent makes an excellent target for industrial development. Both Cummins Engine Company and Tata Engineering Company were looking for continual learning, innovation, and efficiency. Cummins' option to pursue this joint venture was fueled by highly attractive future profitability prospects in a high-risk country. It was a place where Cummins wanted to expand its core technologies, but it didn't want to risk going into the country alone. Tata's existing infrastructure and cultural knowledge made it an excellent prospective partner. Also, Cummins low competitive strength in the highly attractive country further suggested joint venturing.

The transfer of technology and knowledge between Cummins and Tata benefited both companies and their markets. Teaming up and sharing technology put the joint venture at a competitive advantage. The two companies were well ahead of their competition, and this partnership would ensure keeping them the biggest and best in the business. There was a good strategic fit between the companies, as they were in the same industry, excelled in the same expertise, and targeted the same markets. Strong parent companies help make the transition into a joint venture a little bit easier. Strong financial backgrounds for both companies indicate a history of success and determination, which are favorable in looking for a joint venture partner.

By 2006, Tata Cummins employed about 850 people and had a capacity of 72,000 engines per annum, and it had plans to increase its capacity up to 120,000. The IJV developed world-class manufacturing systems that were benchmarked against the best international manufacturing operations. Assembly of engines was performed on a state-of-the-art automated electrified monorail system, which was roof-mounted for clean floor assembly. The system was linked to a computerized assembly management system. It incorporated "fail-safing" at each station and in-process-verification systems at critical points for defect-free assembly. Laser pulse tools, pneumatic manipulators, and ergonomically designed workstations and facilities were provided to reduce operator fatigue.

Into the year 2007, the company's efforts in achieving manufacturing excellence were guided by the principles and practices of the Cummins operating system (COS) and the customer-led quality objectives. The company had a flat organization structure. The level of first-line supervisors had been eliminated, with the operatives (known as associates) organized in teams. The formally structured team-based work system constituted an integral part of the COS and was a key initiative to involve and empower shop-level employees to work toward continuous improvement and customer delight. Total quality systems, or TQS, had been adopted from the early stages in the company, in line with Cummins' quality systems. The latest communications and computing systems were installed for connectivity internally and with Cummins systems in the United States to provide real-time online information integrating the manufacturing and management information/control systems.

Significant milestones of the successful Cummins-Tata partnership that resulted in TCL included:[*]

July 1993	Foundation stone laid
March 1995	First engine manufactured
July 1995	Official plant inauguration
January 1996	Commercial production begins
November 1997	10,000th engine manufactured
February 1998	ISO-9002 certification granted
January 1999	Launch of TATA vehicles with TCL engines
May 1999	QS-9000 certification granted
June 2000	Launch of supply chain management business applications
May 2001	Export of first consignment to Cummins, China
August 2001	100,000th engine manufactured
November 2001	Rajiv Gandhi Quality Award
July 2003	ISO 14001 (EMS) certification
April 2005	300,000th engine built
September 2005	ISO 14001-2004 version award
December 2005	TS 16949 certification

In 2007, Cummins Inc., which had entered other strategic initiatives with the Tata Group including Tata Holstet Ltd., a manufacturer of turbochargers, announced that it had acquired Tata's 50 percent stake in that IJV and renamed the organization Cummins Turbo Technologies (CTT), consistent with Cummins' worldwide branding strategy. Cummins' partnership with Tata Motors was deemed a success story, and the 100 percent–owned subsidiary of Cummins Inc. continues to boast both Tata Motors and Tata Cummins as key strategic customers.

[*] From TCL Supply Chain Management System, www.tatacummins.com, 2008.

Source: Written by Melissa deWitt and Roger Kashlak, Loyola College in Maryland, 2003; Roger Kashlak, Loyola College in Maryland, 2008.

Discussion Questions

1. Why did Cummins choose an international joint venture to expand to India?
2. Why was TCL initially successful? Why was the international joint venture able to sustain its success over 15 years?

Environmental Influences on the Foreign Entry Mode Decision

The choice of foreign entry mode has been identified for over two decades as one of the most critical decisions associated with a firm's international strategy. The mode of foreign entry has been an important conceptual subject[1] as well as the subject of many empirical studies, especially in manufacturing industries, including Andersen's 1997 study[2] and Agarwal and Ramaswami's 1992 work. From a service industry perspective, there has been an increase in research initiatives regarding both internationalization and foreign entry mode, beginning with Erramilli and Rao in 1993[3] and continuing with Roberts in 1999[4] and Domke-Damonte in 2000.[5]

The external environmental factors that were studied in the first section of this book, including the cultural, political, legal, and economic environments, have been identified as contingency variables that affect foreign market entry choice. Ekeledo and Sivakumar generally proved this in their 1998 study. More specifically, Kogut and Singh in 1988,[6] as well as Barkema, Bell, and Pennings in 1996,[7] linked cultural distance to the mode of foreign entry. Host-country market size and market potential have also been found to affect the mode of foreign entry.[8] Furthermore, firms have entered highly competitive foreign markets differently than they have oligopolistic ones,[9] and a host country's geographic proximity to the home country would affect the firm's choice of entry mode into new countries.[10]

Besides the external environmental factors, the strategic decision on choice of mode of entry into foreign markets has also been related to various internal factors of the firm. These factors include the firm's size, the firm's marketing strategy,[11] its cumulative international experience, its degree of control and resource commitments, and its overall profitability relative to its competition.[12] An international company can avail itself of several different modes of entry into foreign markets. These include:

- Exporting
- Countertrade
- Contract manufacturing
- Licensing
- Franchising
- Nonequity strategic alliances
- Equity-based joint ventures
- Wholly owned subsidiaries

Typically, an international company may engage in each of the above foreign market entry modes in different world markets. And in any one country market, a subsidiary may be engaged in one or more of the above entry modes. The parent company of the international enterprise decides which foreign affiliate will be responsible for which of the above international business activities. Pan and Tse illustrated the entry mode choices through a hierarchical framework.[13] They separated entry modes into equity and nonequity categories. They further delineated equity modes as equity joint ventures and wholly owned subsidiaries. Similarly, they separated nonequity modes into exports and contractual agreements. As Figure 6.1 illustrates, mode of foreign entry can also be viewed from a cooperative perspective as well as from a wholly owned perspective. As internationalization has exponentially grown during the past two decades, increasing emphasis, as depicted in Figure 6.1, has been on equity

FIGURE 6.1 Foreign Mode-of-Entry Choices

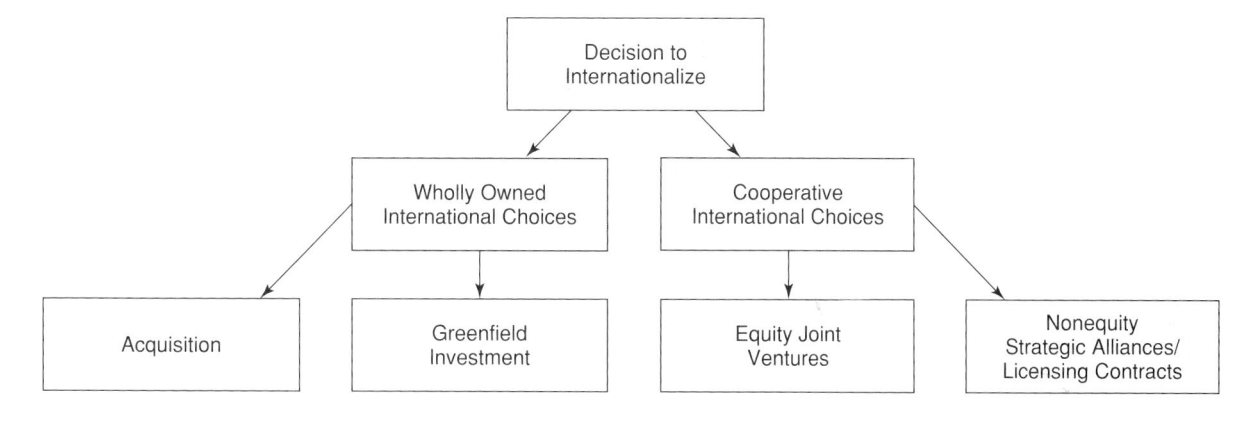

choices. For instance, firms that once exported to culturally and politically distant countries like China, and eventually invested in those countries, are now seeking to "go it alone."

In this chapter, we first examine various entry modes. Some, like exporting, countertrade, and licensing, will be reviewed first because of their historical and current importance in international business. Furthermore, because of the increasing importance of equity choices for the firm during the past 10 years, and because of the organizational complexity that comes with foreign investment and a network of subsidiaries, the entry modes that include collaborative alliances will be reviewed in this chapter.

Exporting

The process of *exporting* is sending a firm's products or services to international destinations. A company seeking international markets has various choices regarding how it will export its products. In some instances, the company itself does nothing more than supply the products for export. For example, the company may deal with a home-based export firm that buys on its own account, sells abroad through its own affiliates or branches, and often maintains its own logistical support systems including warehouses, shipping docks, and transportation facilities. A company could also sell through an export commission house or through an export buyer, who acts as a purchasing agent for various foreign buyers. For the company these processes are exporting in name only, since the sales transactions take place in the home country itself; the actual export activity is accomplished by the buyer of the company's products. There are two basic methods of export management, the indirect approach and the direct approach.

Indirect Exporting

In indirect exporting, a firm's products are eventually sent overseas without the firm's ultimate involvement. Many small and medium-size firms do not have the cost efficiencies, scale economies, or foreign market knowledge to export directly. In contrast, a large international company would not generally resort to this method of exporting as it has the efficiencies to internalize the export function. Thus, small and medium-size firms, particularly those just getting started in export, may prefer to begin with the indirect approach by entering into a contract with a combination export manager or with a manufacturer's export agent, both of which would be based in the company's home market.

A *combination export manager (CEM)* is an independent firm that acts as the export department of the company. The CEM sells the company's products together with allied, but noncompetitive, lines of other companies through its own network of foreign distributors, who conduct business in the name of the company they represent. To potential buyers abroad, the CEM is the export department of the product manufacturing firm. Contracts with buyers are negotiated in the manufacturer's name. Correspondence may be on the manufacturer's letterhead, thus affording it an opportunity to establish its brand name abroad. All quotations and orders are subject to approval by the manufacturer. Most CEMs operate mainly on a commission basis. A CEM often takes over all risks and problems associated with exporting.

The CEM provides a manufacturer with one of the fastest routes of entering foreign markets, as well as with the CEM's ready-made experience—a very important factor in international marketing because of the differences between the markets in various countries in areas such as culture, channels of distribution, product liability laws, and so on. The CEM is actually a ready-made export department for the manufacturer, considering that the CEM not only researches foreign markets but also chooses the type of distribution channel to be used and does its own advertising and sales promotion. The CEM may also give credit assistance to the manufacturer when buy-and-sell arrangements are involved. It is essential, therefore, for the manufacturer to maintain close liaison with the CEM on policies concerning advertising, sales promotion, pricing, financing, and credit extension.

An alternative to hiring a CEM is engaging a manufacturer's export agent. A *manufacturer's export agent,* unlike the CEM, does not make sales in the name of each manufacturer it represents but retains its own identity by operating in its own name. This firm works on a straight-commission basis. Unlike a CEM, a manufacturer's agent does not assume responsibility for advertising and financing.

Direct Exporting

Direct exporting happens when a company internalizes the export function and takes responsibility for selling its products, without an intermediary, to an importer or buyer located in a market abroad. The direct approach involves more expense and detail than the indirect method. However, over the long haul, the results can be far superior in comparison to the indirect approach.

A separate *export department* may be created by the company to enable its own staff to concentrate on developing new markets abroad. An export department is a distinct, self-contained department that handles most of the export activities. The export department may be organized by territory, product, customer, or any combination of these. A separate export department enables exporting to be handled by specialists in the area who are committed to its success.

Companies that want to separate international marketing from its domestic counterpart may form a separate export sales subsidiary. An *export sales subsidiary* is a semi-independent corporation, that is, a separate corporation wholly owned by the parent company. Very often the export sales subsidiary is made a profit center to enable the parent company to better monitor how successful its foreign marketing efforts have been. A major advantage of an export sales subsidiary is that it can be organized as a domestic international sales corporation (DISC), a Western Hemisphere trade corporation (WHTC), or an export trade corporation—any of which, if properly utilized, could accrue substantial tax benefits to the parent company.

Companies that feel the need for closer supervision over the sales of their products in a certain market may choose to establish their own selling offices abroad that function as *foreign sales branches* of the home company. Foreign sales branches are usually located only in large markets because the sales volume must justify the cost involved in establishing and operating a branch office. The sales branch handles all sales and promotional activities in a specified market and generally sells to wholesalers, dealers, and, at times, to industrial users. Usually, a foreign sales branch is established only after representatives and distributors have developed a market for the company's products.

In time, the foreign sales branch may be incorporated by the company as a *foreign sales subsidiary,* the foreign counterpart of the home-based export sales subsidiary. A foreign sales subsidiary is far more independent than a foreign sales branch because of its foreign incorporation and domicile. The staff of the subsidiary can evaluate the market, suggest product changes, and analyze the effectiveness of advertising, public relations, and promotional efforts from the foreign consumer's point of view.

Countertrade

As liquidity pressures have increased in emerging, economically transitioning, and lesser developed nations during the past two decades, pressure to fund global trade and investment without using capital has increased. Subsequently, various and unique forms of countertrade have emerged. In regular business transactions, goods or services flow in one direction while the money being paid for them flows back in the other. **Countertrade** refers to arrangements whereby the flow of goods or services in both directions is an integral element of the specific terms of the business transaction.

In recent years, a large number of U.S. corporations have found it increasingly difficult to conduct business with many countries without relying on countertrade. They include IBM, Heinz, PepsiCo, General Motors, and Boeing. Many U.S. commercial banks have decided to set up their own countertrade departments. Conversely, for American executives who face, more than ever before, worldwide economic and competitive pressures, countertrade offers previously untapped opportunities, particularly since it is "more attractive than having no sales in a given market."[14] Indeed, it has been described as "a rational response . . . to environmental constraints and market imperfections,"[15] particularly for those nations lacking either hard currency or the ability to borrow. Thus countertrade operations add another dimension of particular benefit to developing countries seeking to circumvent structural trade imbalances.

Countertrade initiatives, similar to general strategy motivations, correlate to various industry and environmental opportunities and threats. For instance, through countertrade activities, firms may gain access to emerging markets that otherwise would be closed. Countertrade also is used to enter growth markets with technologies already on the decline in home and similar markets. Overriding the strategic rationale for countertrade is the hard-currency issue: Many emerging countries do not have the adequate capital to purchase necessary technology on world markets. Defense and aerospace giant Northrop Grumman frequently relies on countertrade activities to offset the lack of hard currency from its various emerging-country customers. Countertrade relates to foreign exchange hedging strategies for multinational firms by eliminating exchange valuations and risks, especially in countries with volatile exchange rates.

Countertrade, however, has potential strategic downsides and risks. It is a complicated mode of entry, usually requiring a third party or agent as an intermediary. Subsequently, costs rise. In many cases, countertrade may also take a firm into industries and functions where it does not possess relative competencies, leading to incremental inefficiencies and, once again, an associated rise in costs. These activities are also more complex than traditional foreign entry modes, especially regarding price setting. They tend not to have long-term strategic viability and have the potential to help develop the countertrade partner as a longer-term global competitor. Of the many varieties of countertrade, we discuss four principal ones: pure barter, switch trading, counterpurchase, and buyback.

Pure Barter

In *pure barter,* both sides in the business arrangement agree to accept each other's goods as payment for the transaction. The most famous historically is PepsiCo's agreement with Russia nearly 40 years ago to trade its syrup for cases of Stolichnaya vodka. Russia marketed Pepsi domestically under a franchising arrangement with PepsiCo, which received an equivalent value of Stolichnaya vodka in return for the franchise rights and syrup that it sold to the Soviets. PepsiCo in turn marketed the Russian vodka in the United States.

Another countertrade example was Chrysler's (before its integration into Daimler-Benz) agreement with South Africa to exchange autos for platinum. The platinum was then used in Chrysler's manufacturing operations, especially for catalytic converters. In another interesting deal involving PepsiCo, the company agreed to sell Ukrainian-built commercial ships in the world market in exchange for the opportunity to market Pepsi and open several Pizza Hut restaurants (which PepsiCo owned at the time) in the Ukraine. This arrangement between PepsiCo and the Ukrainian government and another between McDonnell Douglas and the Ugandan government represent barter agreements. In the latter case, Uganda wanted to buy 18 helicopters to help eradicate elephant and rhino poaching but did not have the $25 million in hard currency that was the cost. McDonnell Douglas Helicopter set up several projects in Uganda to generate the hard currency required. One of these initiatives was a plant to catch and process Nile perch. Another was the construction of a factory that produced both pineapple and passion fruit concentrate. McDonnell Douglas subsequently found buyers in Europe. Uganda received the helicopters and McDonnell Douglas got paid in a convertible currency.[16]

Switch Trading

Switch trading is trade involving three or more countries. For instance, England agrees to trade computers worth $500,000 to Brazil in exchange for coffee that has an equivalent market value of $500,000. The English may not want the coffee, and so, with the help of a switch specialist, they sell the coffee to an Italian company for $450,000. England gets the cash for the sale minus the 5 to 10 percent that may be paid to the switch trader. Because the English side knows in advance that the coffee will be sold elsewhere at a discount, it will have hiked the price of the computers upward to compensate for the discount and the commission paid to the switch trader.

Counterpurchase

In a *counterpurchase* deal, Country A exports to Country B and, in return, promises to spend some or all of the receipts on imports from B. The details of those imports need not be specified, but they must be bought within a particular period, usually two to three years. When Peru was undergoing liquidity problems under President Alain Garcia's first term in office, he insisted that firms exporting to Peru accept most of their expected revenues in Peruvian goods. Since then, many countries have employed this type of countertrade. When the good being exported is more valued by the importing country, the counterpurchase demands become less stringent. This is especially the case with high-technology goods. For example, Northrop Grumman has received more lenient agreements with countries like Algeria, who are in need of the aerospace technology being supplied.

Buyback

Buyback involves licensing of patents or trademarks, selling production know-how, lending capital, or building a plant in another country and agreeing to buy part or all of its output as payment. In one case of buyback, the General Electric Company provided Poland with the technology and equipment to manufacture electrocardiogram meters, which, in turn, Poland shipped back to General Electric. In another famous deal, Fiat built an automobile factory in Russia, and the Russians paid Fiat for the

PRACTICAL INSIGHT 6.1

THE ARAB WORLD WANTS ITS MTV

Matthew Noujaim lives and breathes hip-hop. But the 19-year-old Beirut university student, who raps about "anything and everything, including the Arab cause" in English and Arabic, has struggled to get his music noticed. Although rap is hugely popular among Middle Eastern youth, it's still underground and largely ignored by the region's record labels, radio stations, and music television channels. "There's lots of good hip-hop made here that never gets played," Noujaim says. "No one's willing to promote local talent."

That's about to change. MTV Arabia, a new 24-hour free satellite channel, will begin broadcasting in Arabic across the Middle East on Nov. 16. The Viacom-owned network's flagship show, *Hip HopNa* ("my hip-hop"), will be co-hosted by Saudi rapper Qusai Khidr and Palestinian-American producer Farid Nassar, aka Fredwreck, who has worked with Snoop Dogg, 50 Cent, and other marquee names. The show will visit 10 cities across the Middle East in search of talent, giving would-be Arab rap stars an international platform. Noujaim won the show's first competition, and Fredwreck has produced one of his tracks. "This is a music genre that is bubbling underneath the surface here, and we want to claim it as our own," says Bhavneet Singh, head of emerging markets for MTV Networks International.

How will the likes of Justin Timberlake and Rihanna go down in a region that's not exactly brimming with goodwill toward Americans? Better than you might think. Middle Eastern youth may not agree with U.S. politics, but they can't get enough of Western music and fashion. "The myth about the Arab world is that people go to bed at night hating the U.S. and wake up hating Israel," says James Zogby, president of the Arab American Institute, a think tank in Washington. "But go to any mall in Saudi Arabia, and you'll see kids in jeans and baseball caps hanging out at Starbucks and McDonald's. Globalization is real."

For Viacom, MTV Arabia is just the beginning. The region is attractive because it's awash in petrodollars and two-thirds of the population is under 25. Viacom has signed a 10-year licensing deal between MTV Networks and Tecom Investments, controlled by Dubai's ruler. On Oct. 12, 2007, Viacom planned to announce another decade-long licensing deal with Tecom for children's channel Nickelodeon Arabia. That's set for the second half of 2008, and the company reckons an Arabic version of *Comedy Central* won't be far behind. Also under discussion: Paramount Pictures productions in the region and licensing of Nick's characters for clothing, toys, and games. "The Middle East may be the world's most underappreciated growth story," says Viacom Chairman Sumner M. Redstone.

No wonder U.S. media giants are pouring in. NBC Universal in May struck a licensing deal for a $2.2 billion amusement park in Dubai. Days later, Viacom announced plans to create a Nickelodeon section in Dubailand, a $2.5 billion development in the emirate that aims to be the world's largest theme park when it opens in 2011. And in September, Warner Brothers Entertainment announced a multibillion-dollar deal in Abu Dhabi that includes film production, a Warner Brothers theme park and hotel, and a chain of cinemas.

The Westerners will face plenty of homegrown competition. More than 50 music TV channels broadcast in the

---

factory partly in Russian-made Fiats. Likewise, Levi-Strauss was compensated for building a blue-jeans manufacturing facility in Hungary with guaranteed output from the plant. In another example of buyback, Occidental Petroleum was paid in output from the ammonium plant the firm built in Russia.

Contract Manufacturing

A contractual agreement between a company and a foreign producer under which the foreign producer manufactures the company's product is called **contract manufacturing**. Under this agreement the company retains responsibility for the promotion and distribution of its product. For example, an American pharmaceutical company may contract a company in India to manufacture its cough syrup. The Indian company manufactures it and does all the packaging of the product as required by the American company. Then the American company takes the packaged product and markets it in India or even globally. Nike, the athletic gear company, uses contract manufacturers throughout Asia to manufacture its footwear and sportswear. In this sense, the company limits its politically imposed and economically imposed financial risk.

region. The dominant player, Rotana, owned by Saudi Prince Al Waleed bin Talal, is also the Middle East's largest record label and has exclusive contracts with most top-selling pop and folk artists. But MTV is betting it will win viewers by offering an alternative. "No one in this market is going out and asking the viewers what they want," says Abdullatif Al Sayegh, CEO of Arab Media Group, the Tecom unit that runs the channel. "We're spending our time in malls and cafes talking to young people; we're not getting our ideas from watching TV."

MTV Arabia is the biggest test to date of the network's two-decade-old localization strategy. MTV's flagship music channel has seen its American TV ratings slip and has struggled online. Management believes the biggest growth will come overseas, and the network now pumps out a blend of international and local tunes from Russia to Indonesia to Pakistan. That has helped MTV and sister operations, such as VH1 and Nickelodeon, reach 508 million households in 161 countries. "This isn't going to be MTV U.S.," Bill Roedy, vice-chairman of MTV Networks, says of the latest offering. "It is Arabic MTV made by Arabs for Arabs."

That means it'll be pretty tame by American standards. At noon every Friday, Islam's holiest day, the channel will air an animated call to prayer. During peak family viewing hours from 8 to 11 p.m., shows will introduce audiences to acts from the West and from other emerging markets such as India and Pakistan. And there will be Arabic versions of popular MTV shows such as *Made,* which gives young people coaching in fields like cooking and film.

Later in the evening things will loosen up a bit. *Al Hara* ("the neighborhood") is an Arabic version of *Barrio 19,* a program that shows what young people do for fun. In the Middle East, that apparently includes dune-bashing (driving all-terrain vehicles over, and into, steep sand dunes) and water soccer, played in what looks like a vast inflatable kiddie pool. Says Rasha Al Emam, the 30-year-old Saudi woman who heads MTV Arabia's programming production: "The idea is to encourage kids to go out and do something edgy and fun instead of sitting around smoking a shisha," or waterpipe.

While plenty of U.S. and European videos will never make it into the line-up, others will be sanitized for the Arab audience. At MTV Arabia's offices, a vast warehouse in Dubai, editors from across the region pore over clips frame by frame to remove offensive content. Bad language? Bleep it out. Shots of kissing, revealing outfits a la Britney Spears, or people on a bed? Blur them, or insert some less racy bit of the video.

That'll be fine with Maram Alhabib. The 23-year-old Saudi studying special education at Jeddah's Dar Al Hekma University loves metal group Seether and American alternative band Three Doors Down, but she finds many music videos to be too provocative. "The Arab channels are boring, they all play the same music and a lot of the videos ... are all about seduction," she says. "If MTV focuses on music and issues Arabs care about, people will watch."

Source: Kerry Capell, *BusinessWeek,* October 22, 2007, p. 79.

Licensing

An alternative route to markets abroad, one that falls somewhere between exporting and manufacturing abroad, is licensing. In a foreign **licensing** agreement the international company, or licensor, agrees to make available to another company abroad, the licensee, use of its patents and trademarks, its manufacturing processes and know-how, its trade secrets, and its managerial and technical services. In exchange, the foreign company agrees to pay the licensor a royalty or some other form of payment according to a schedule agreed on by the two parties. The licensing agreement could be between the parent company of the international enterprise and one or more of its foreign affiliates, or it could be between the international enterprise and an independent foreign, private, or government enterprise. For example, beer manufacturers have used the licensing of their brand names and trade secrets to foreign companies as an alternative to exporting. Movies and television programs have been licensed to foreign distributors and television networks mainly after they have run their course in the home market. First-run programming is a growing international licensing business for Western media firms. Practical Insight 6.1 explores Viacom's 10-year licensing agreement in Saudi Arabia.

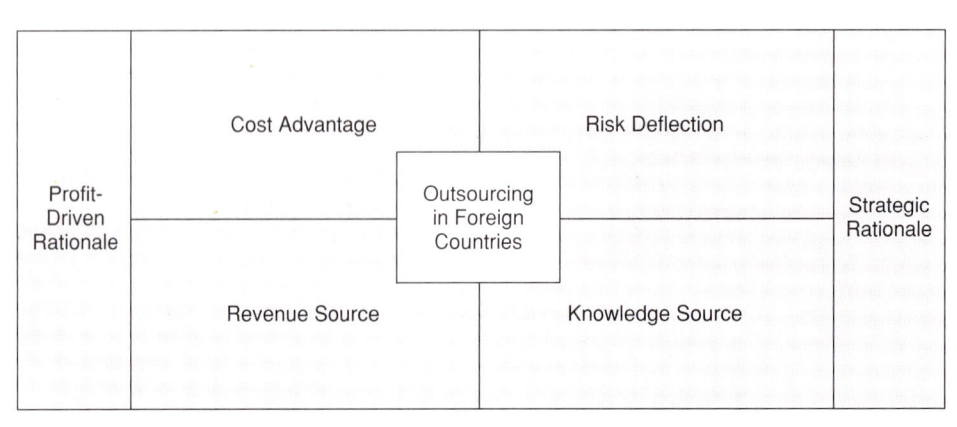

Foreign licensing involves more risk than straight exporting from the home country, but it does not have in it the risks that go with the start-up of foreign manufacturing facilities abroad. The licensor is in fact exporting its know-how instead of products. There are many reasons that a company might decide to use licensing as a means of tapping foreign markets. Figure 6.2 illustrates some of these reasons. In general, overseas licensing activities may be a source of additional immediate profit for the firm through lowering costs and/or increasing revenues. Licensing is a way to capitalize on revenues in foreign markets when the capital expenditures of foreign investment into those markets are beyond a firm's internal capabilities. Licensing is also a way to accrue additional revenues when trade barriers are blocking or raising the cost of potential export activities. Licensing gives the firm the ability to quickly, at a lower cost, enter a new market as well. Furthermore, licensing may help a firm gain the potential low-cost advantages of particular host countries without committing the resources abroad. This may come from comparative low-cost labor or efficient access to necessary components or raw materials.

Overseas licensing activities may have a strategic rationale as well. For instance, when an international firm allows another firm to incur the cost of sales in a foreign country, that licensee incurs the bulk of the various economic risks, whether politically or culturally imposed. Licensing is also a way for a firm to scope out and then develop a potential market for long-term investment activity. It adds to the firm's knowledge of the nuances of the overseas markets without incurring the potential associated risks. Strategically, licensing may help a firm diversify not only its scope of country operations but also its mode of entry. Thus, the international firm may have a portfolio of both countries and types of operations within those countries. As knowledge creation and accumulation have become important pieces of international competitive advantage, licensing offers the international firm the ability to acquire reciprocal benefits from foreign know-how, research, and technical services.

License agreements are defined by the nature and content of the rights granted by the licensor to the licensee. A simple licensing agreement is limited to a patent or trademark. But more complex licensing agreements include the delivery by the licensor to the licensee of one or more of the following:

- A patented product or process.
- A trademark or trade name.
- Manufacturing techniques.
- Proprietary rights generally referred to as *company* or *industry know-how*.

FIGURE 6.2
Licensing as a Foreign Entry Choice

	Cost Advantage	Risk Deflection	
Profit-Driven Rationale		Outsourcing in Foreign Countries	Strategic Rationale
	Revenue Source	Knowledge Source	

FIGURE 6.3
Concerns of Foreign Licensing

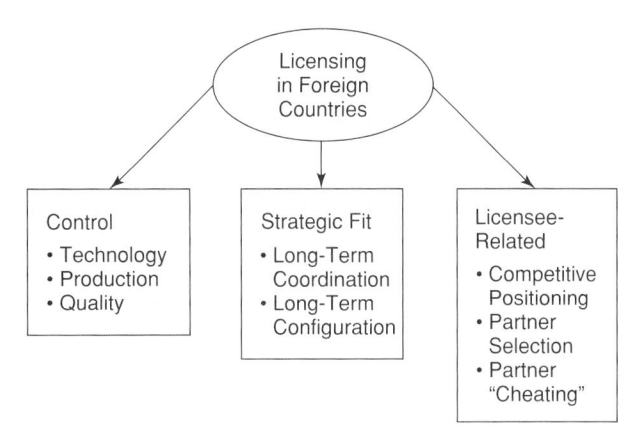

```
                    Licensing
                    in Foreign
                    Countries
           ┌────────────┼────────────┐
           ▼            ▼            ▼
    ┌──────────┐  ┌──────────┐  ┌──────────┐
    │ Control  │  │Strategic │  │Licensee- │
    │•Technology│ │   Fit    │  │ Related  │
    │•Production│ │•Long-Term│  │•Competitive│
    │•Quality  │  │Coordination│ │ Positioning│
    │          │  │•Long-Term│  │•Partner  │
    │          │  │Configuration│ │ Selection│
    │          │  │          │  │•Partner  │
    │          │  │          │  │ "Cheating"│
    └──────────┘  └──────────┘  └──────────┘
```

- Supply of components or equipment.
- Technical advice and services of various sorts.
- Marketing advice and assistance of various sorts.
- Capital and/or managerial personnel.

As illustrated in Figure 6.2, licensing has several advantages. It opens the way to getting a foothold in a foreign market without a large capital investment. Thus it can be less risky than starting a manufacturing operation. Licensing is most attractive to firms that are new to the international business arena. Most countries require that patents and trademarks be used within a certain number of years of their grant and registration, respectively, or they are canceled; this makes licensing a viable option for protecting the company's patents and trademarks.

Import restrictions and tariffs that are suddenly imposed after a company has established a market for its products in the country through exports pose a difficult problem for the company: Should it abandon the proven market for its products? Should it establish a manufacturing facility in the country? Is licensing the best alternative, given the global strategic interests of the company? It may resort to licensing if it decides not to jump over the trade barriers by establishing its own manufacturing plant in the country. Licensing of the products to a local company enables the firm to retain a foothold in such markets, which would otherwise be completely lost. Some licensors consider the acquisition of patents from foreign patent holders to be one of the major benefits of foreign licensing operations. Reciprocal license grants are frequently made by the licensee as partial compensation for the rights and know-how made available by the licensor.

As illustrated in Figure 6.3, licensing also has disadvantages. The disadvantages regarding licensing as a technique for penetrating foreign markets should be recognized and clearly understood by multinational companies. Every licensee is a potential competitor of the licensor. If the original licensing agreement does not stipulate the region within which the licensee may market the licensed product, the licensee could create problems for the licensor by insisting on marketing the product in third-country markets in competition with products already served in the market by the licensor.

The licensee may develop a formidable market with the use of licensed patents, trademarks, technology, or processes, and thus reap huge profits, much to the chagrin of the licensor, who did not foresee the huge markets developing and therefore is receiving a comparatively negligible royalty under the license agreement in effect at the time. The experience of many firms indicates that it is very difficult for the licensor to have completely satisfactory control over the licensee's manufacturing and marketing operations. This situation could result in damage to the licensor's trademark and reputation.

Also, several companies have had difficulties with licensees who refuse to pay royalties, claiming that the original product or process was altered and no longer in use. Moreover, if the licensing agreement calls for a payment of royalties in local currency, devaluation of the local currency would result in a decline of the value of royalty payments in the home-country currency.

It is extremely important for a company to consider how its licensing program fits into its overall long-range strategic objectives and policies. If a company can establish its own manufacturing and sales facilities, it should do so, because it is to its advantage to develop and run its own business abroad and reap maximum benefits from the global markets for its products. Possible repercussions on domestic, export, and other foreign operations, as well as prospective return in terms of resources and risks involved, must be carefully determined prior to signing any license agreement with a foreign firm. If a company does decide to enter into a licensing agreement, it should consider the following steps: Before entering into a licensing agreement, the licensor must know the market's potential and the cost of developing it. The company must do its own research and gather its own information and not rely solely on data provided by the licensee. It is important that the company does not underestimate or overestimate the market potential. If it does the former, it might sell itself short; if it does the latter, it may make unrealistic demands of the licensee in terms of royalties and market development expectations. One company made just such arrangements in a foreign country. It oversold its franchise, demanded unrealistic results, and then expected the licensee to expend unreasonable sums of money to develop the market without hope of commensurately adequate compensation. The result was disastrous. Legal proceedings ensued, with the licensor demanding compensation for loss of profits and the licensee counterclaiming on the grounds that it had been deliberately misled on the value of the franchise.

The company must clearly state in the licensing agreement what it expects in terms of income from royalties and the effort to be expended, in terms of financial and managerial resources, by the licensee to develop the market. Unrealistic demands should not be made of the licensee, which should be fairly compensated for the time, effort, and money it spends on the task. A successful licensing arrangement should result if both parties to the agreement feel that they are getting a fair bargain for their efforts.

The quality of the partner must be thoroughly investigated by the licensor company. The licensee need not be a big firm; however, it must have the managerial and financial strength to carry out its side of the agreement. It is also important that the licensee have a good image in the host country.

Serious problems could occur if a multinational company does not retain control over the production and marketing of its products by the licensee. A company can retain control over production by providing for quality control in the agreement. Agreement could be reached with the licensee that provides for the permanent stationing of a technical representative in the licensee's plant to check on the quality of the products produced or the process being used. Or the licensee could be required to submit samples of production runs to the multinational company for approval. Periodic visits to the production site by the multinational company's production and quality control personnel could also help prevent the marketing of inferior-quality products.

Most troublesome of all for potential licensors is accurately gauging the size of the market, obtaining meaningful clues as to the nature of the market and probable competition, and verifying such information by effective test marketing or market research. Some companies reported their failure to realize that their "new" products would not be sufficiently "new" or different enough to capture the overseas public's fancy. One food company executive said he discontinued one of his products because consumers would not use it properly. Housewives insisted on adding milk rather than water, making it uneconomical to use.

Regarding the actual licensing contract, the following specific questions should be considered by a company:

- How may patents, processes, or trademarks will be used?
- How will technical assistance be rendered?
- Which products are included in the agreement, and to what extent?
- What territory is to be covered by the license?
- How should the licensee be compensated?
- In which currency will payments be made to the licensor?
- What happens if compensation cannot be paid by the licensee?
- If sublicensing is permitted, how should it be carried out?
- Are there any geographic limitations on the marketing of the licensed product or service?
- What are the provisions regarding duration of the agreement and its cancellation?
- What rights does the licensor have in developments by the licensee?
- What visitation and inspection privileges are held by the licensor?
- Can the parent company inspect accounts?
- What provisions are there for satisfactory promotional/sales performance and adequate quality control?
- What home- and host-government approvals are required?
- What tax factors are involved?
- How will disputes be settled?

Franchising

Franchising, a very common form of licensing, is defined as a transfer of technology, business system, brand name, trademark, and other property rights by a franchisor to an independent company or person who is the franchisee. There has been an explosion of franchising throughout the world in recent years. Estimates indicate that almost 50 percent of all major retail businesses are franchises.[17] Franchising involves two businesspeople or entities: the franchisor, which has developed the business or product and lends its name or trademark to it, and the franchisee, which buys the right to operate the business under the franchisor's brand name or trademark. Usually a company initially establishes a brand name for its products, service, quality, and so on, in the home market, as well as a standardized business system to operate the business. It then franchises the entire business system, including the trademark and brand name, to the franchisee in a foreign country. The franchisee depends on the franchisor for the business system, and the franchisor depends on the franchisee for royalties or fees. Most developed and developing countries have drafted specific legislation to attract foreign franchisors.

The franchisee operates the business under the franchisor's trademark or brand name and is contractually obligated to adhere to the procedures and methods of operation prescribed in the business system. The franchisor generally maintains the right to control the quality of the franchisee through quality control of products and service so that the franchisor cannot harm the company's image. In exchange, the franchisor receives a fee based on the volume of sales. Sometimes the franchisor mandates that the franchisee must buy from it the equipment and some key ingredients used in the products. For example, Burger King and McDonald's require that the franchisee buy from the company cooking equipment and other products that bear the company name. Or the franchisor requires that the franchisee obtain the ingredients from local sources, provided they retain the franchisor's quality requirements. For example, McDonald's has helped its franchisee in India to set up a domestic supplier network for items such as potatoes and buns. It even helped the Indian franchisee to grow potatoes that contained the right amount of moisture. Coca-Cola and PepsiCo send the syrup, which is the key ingredient in the soda, to their franchisees, which bottle and market the drink. Marriott, Holiday Inn, Hilton, McDonald's, Burger King, Hertz, and Coca-Cola are examples that have become household names throughout the world using the franchising entry mode.

The Franchise Agreement

Franchise agreements vary from franchise to franchise. It would be impossible to identify every term and issue that should be considered in every situation. However, the checklist below should be a valuable tool if you're interested in buying a franchise. A franchise agreement includes four major areas:[18]

1. **A detailed list of issues to consider regarding the cost of the franchise.** What does the initial franchise fee purchase? What are the payment terms: amount, time of payment, lump sum or installment, financing arrangements, and so on? Are there periodic royalties? If so, how much are they and how are they determined? How and when are sales and royalties reported, and how are royalties paid? How are advertising and promotion costs divided? Must premises be purchased or rented?

2. **A detailed list of issues to consider regarding the location of the franchise.** Does the franchise apply to a specific geographic area? If so, are the boundaries clearly defined? Who has the right to select the site? Will other franchisees be permitted to compete in the same area, now or later? Is the territory an exclusive one, and is it permanent or subject to reduction or modification under certain conditions? Does the franchisee have a first-refusal option as to any additional franchises in the original territory if it is not exclusive? Does the franchisee have a contractual right to the franchisor's latest products or innovations? Will the franchisee have the right to use its own property and buildings?

3. **A detailed list of issues pertaining to the buildings, equipment, and supplies.** Must equipment or supplies be purchased from the franchisor or approved supplier, or is the franchisee free to make its own purchases? What controls are spelled out concerning facility appearance, equipment, fixture and furnishings, and maintenance or replacement of the same? Is there any limitation on expenditures involved in any of these? When the franchisee must buy from the franchisor, are sales considered on consignment?

4. **A detailed list of issues pertaining to the operating practices.** Must the franchisee participate personally in conducting the business? If so, to what extent and under what specific conditions? What degree of control does the franchisor have over franchise operations, particularly in maintaining franchise identity and product quality? What continuing management aid, training, and assistance will be provided by the

franchisor, and are these covered by the service or royalty fee? Will advertising be local or national, and what will be the cost-sharing arrangement, if any, in either case? If local advertising is left to the franchisee, does the franchisor exercise any control over such campaigns or share any costs? Are operating hours and days set forth in the franchise contract?

5. **A detailed list of issues pertaining to termination and renewal.** Under what conditions (illness, etc.) can the franchisee terminate the franchise? In such cases, do termination obligations differ? Is the franchisee restricted from engaging in a similar business after termination? If so, for how many years? If there is a lease, does it coincide with the franchise term? Has the franchisor, as required, provided for return of trademarks, trade names, and other identification symbols and for the removal of all signs bearing the franchisor's name and trademarks?

Advantages and Disadvantages of Franchising

The advantages and disadvantages of franchising are similar to those of licensing. The main advantages are the following: Franchising is an inexpensive way of exploiting a foreign market. Little or no political risk is involved. The risks of failure and its associated costs are borne by the franchisee. And it is a fast and relatively easy avenue for leveraging globally a company's assets such as a brand name and standardized business system. Because the franchisees have made a significant financial investment in the business, they are more likely to be better motivated to maximize sales and minimize costs than are hired managers. Franchisees can be significant providers of innovative ideas. For instance, the KFC's franchisee in Japan was responsible for the concept of the KFC kiosk restaurants. This idea has been implemented by KFC worldwide.

Franchising has disadvantages as well, however. The franchisee may spoil the franchisor's image by not upholding the standards for quality established by the franchisor. Sometimes it may be very difficult to exercise control over the franchisee because of the absence of a traditional management–employee relationship. At times, franchisees may attempt to deviate from the policies and standards established by the franchisor. Franchisees may fight attempts by the franchisor to implement changes, such as introducing a new product line or eliminating one already in place. Even if the franchisor is able to terminate the agreement, the franchisee may still stay in business by slightly altering the company's brand name or trademark. For example, the former franchisee of TGI Friday's in Mexico City merely changed its name to TGI Freeday and continued to do business. A citywide noodle shop in Shanghai uses an almost identical logo to KFC. Thus a franchisee may actually help to establish a competitor.

Equity-Based Ventures through Foreign Direct Investment

As opposed to the modes of entry discussed above, in equity-based foreign market entry an international company has equity ownership and control of a foreign venture through foreign direct investment (FDI). The foreign venture may serve several purposes. It may be established to obtain raw materials for use by the company in production in other countries or for sale on world markets. Companies in the petroleum, aluminum, steel, and copper industries have established numerous foreign ventures for these purposes. An equity-based venture may also be established to produce components or products that are mainly exported to the home country or to third countries. A company may establish such an enterprise in a foreign country to take advantage of the availability of labor, energy, or other inputs at competitive prices. International companies, especially in the electronics industry, have established subsidiaries to source components and products in Mexico, China, and many countries in the Pacific Basin. In fact, the governments of Malaysia, India, and several other countries have established high-tech centers to facilitate foreign investment in high-technology ventures.

An equity-based foreign venture need not necessarily involve production. A company may establish one that is involved in the distribution of the company's products or in the marketing of a service such as advertising, accounting, engineering, legal services, or management consulting. An international company may decide to establish an equity-based venture in a foreign country to produce and/or market a product or service mainly to serve the foreign market itself. It may export some of the production to the home market or to third-country markets; however, the host-country market is the principal target market for the products produced by the venture. For example, several Japanese multinational automobile companies such as Nissan, Honda, Toyota, Subaru, and Mazda have set up manufacturing plants in the United States that have the latest manufacturing technology and management techniques. Their purpose is to give the Japanese companies not only the greatest competitive edge in serving the domestic U.S. market but also a base for sales to Europe, which tightly limits imports from Japan but not from the United States.

An equity-based venture abroad could be a *greenfield* investment—which involves establishing the venture from the ground up—or it may involve the *acquisition* of an existing firm. A company may finance the new venture abroad from its own funds, or it may borrow the necessary funds from financial institutions and equity markets in the home-, host-, or third-country markets.

An equity-based venture could be *wholly owned* by the parent international company, or it could be a *joint venture* in which the international company shares its ownership with another company. Managing a wholly owned foreign subsidiary is a relatively less complex endeavor than managing a joint venture. Sharing of the management of the enterprise with a foreign partner is the reason for the greater complexity of managing a joint venture. The joint venture route is a popular mode for foreign market entry among international companies.

The International Collaboration Imperative

Globalization has both prompted and been prompted by interfirm collaboration across borders to control against the various macro-level environmental risks that were discussed in the first section of this book. Managing a collaborative relationship is a relatively more complex endeavor than managing a wholly owned subsidiary. For our purposes, even though many of the benefits and risks overlap, we distinguish between the equity international joint venture and the international strategic alliance.

The complexity of managing an equity joint venture or a strategic alliance is caused by the sharing of the management of the enterprise with a foreign partner. The collaborative route is a popular mode for foreign market entry among international companies. These strategic initiatives have many characteristics.[19] For instance, they may be:

- Explorative or exploitative.[20]
- Cross-border or home-country based.
- Equity- or contractual-based.
- Two or multiple partners.
- Short-term project-based or long-term.[21]

Furthermore, the collaborative initiatives can be focused on various stages of the respective firms' value chains. Link alliances connect different stages of the partners' value chains and subsequently bring together different knowledge levels and skills. Scale alliances focus on similar stages of partner firms to gain increased economies of scale and cost efficiencies.[22]

Although many companies shun international joint ventures and strategic alliances, insisting upon wholly owned subsidiaries as a mode of foreign market entry, an increasing number of companies often conclude that under certain circumstances a joint venture mode of market entry can be mutually beneficial to all parties involved in its formation. As discussed throughout this text so far, the current environment of international business is an environment in which globalization is being affected by various initiatives. These include governments moving more toward market economies and subsequently initiating increased privatization and deregulation activities. Also, regional economic integration, like NAFTA and the EU, are catalysts to increasing globalization. In Chapter 5, we saw that firms are continually balancing global efficiency with national responsiveness. Overall, because of the increased pressures of globalization, an international firm must do many activities simultaneously and quickly. The international firm must also accumulate more and more knowledge, as well as enhance its capacity to learn, in order to keep current competitive advantages and develop new ones. The international joint venture has become a strategic means for firms to penetrate markets without exhausting respective capital, to deflect some of the risks associated with going overseas, and to increase their respective knowledge bases.

Equity International Joint Ventures

As exemplified by Tata Cummins Ltd., depicted in the chapter opening case, an equity international joint venture (EIJV) is a business collaboration between companies that are based in two or more countries and that share ownership in an enterprise established jointly for the production and/or distribution of goods or services. More narrowly defined, it is an arrangement in which two or more firms from different nations pool a portion of their respective resources within a common, legal organization.[23] The separate entity can be a partnership or a closely held corporation and can issue corporate securities in its own right.[24] In this text, we adopt the following definition:

> An **equity international joint venture** is a separate legal organizational entity representing the partial holdings of two or more parent firms, in which headquarters of at least one is located outside of the country of operations of the joint venture. The entity is subject to joint control of its parent firms, each of which is economically and legally independent of the other(s).[25]

As illustrated in Figure 6.4, equity international joint ventures are a form of international cooperation in which the level of interdependence between partners is the highest. As will be seen later in this chapter, the level of control is the highest as well, although the international firm does give up some control and profits, in contrast to going it alone. In the following sections, we examine the nature of joint ventures, their advantages and disadvantages, and how they can be best utilized by international companies.

Equity international joint ventures are often established to jointly develop a new technology or to obtain resources that require huge amounts of capital, as in jointly exploring for oil and natural gas. Pure trade agreements are excluded from our concept

FIGURE 6.4
Cooperative Strategies

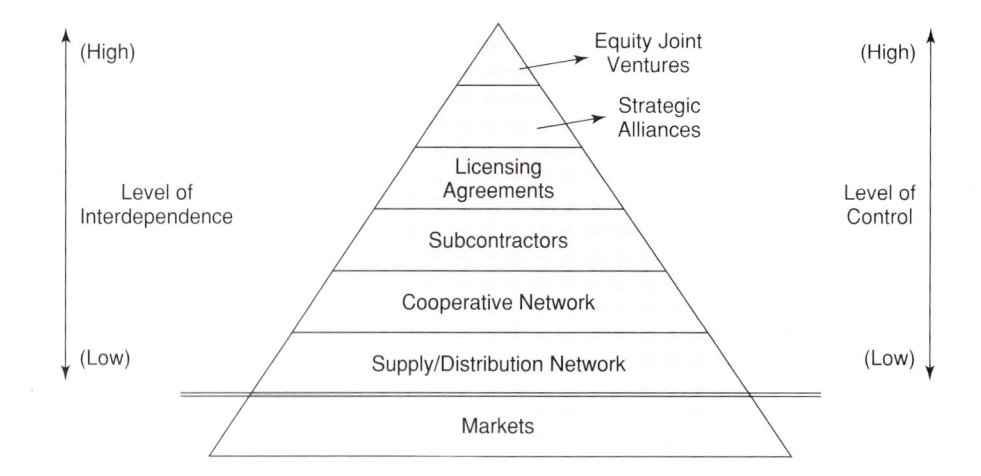

(High) — Level of Interdependence — (Low)

- Equity Joint Ventures
- Strategic Alliances
- Licensing Agreements
- Subcontractors
- Cooperative Network
- Supply/Distribution Network
- Markets

(High) — Level of Control — (Low)

of a joint venture. Of particular interest to us are joint ventures in which one of the partners is an international company and the other is a national of the host country. Figure 6.5 illustrates a typical EIJV in which partnering firms form a new, autonomous company. International joint ventures can take many forms depending on the needs and circumstances of the partners and the conditions under which the collaboration agreement is consummated.

International entry, where the firm maintains wholly owned control, has been identified as highly risky, especially in terms of expected profits and risk. Researchers have suggested that the total costs of international acquisitions, including the costs of procuring additional resources and the costs of control, are higher relative to cooperative international entry modes and that EIJVs outperform international acquisitions.[26] Specifically regarding international joint ventures, this entry mode mitigates the political, cultural, and financial risks associated with foreign direct investments. Furthermore, this risk-sharing function is more critical in research-intensive industries, where high costs of technology and short product life cycles leave little time to amortize development costs.[27]

EIJVs can vary depending on such factors as the percentage of the total equity in the joint venture held by each partner, the number of partners involved in the joint venture, and the characteristics of the partners. An international company could have

FIGURE 6.5
The Equity International Joint Venture

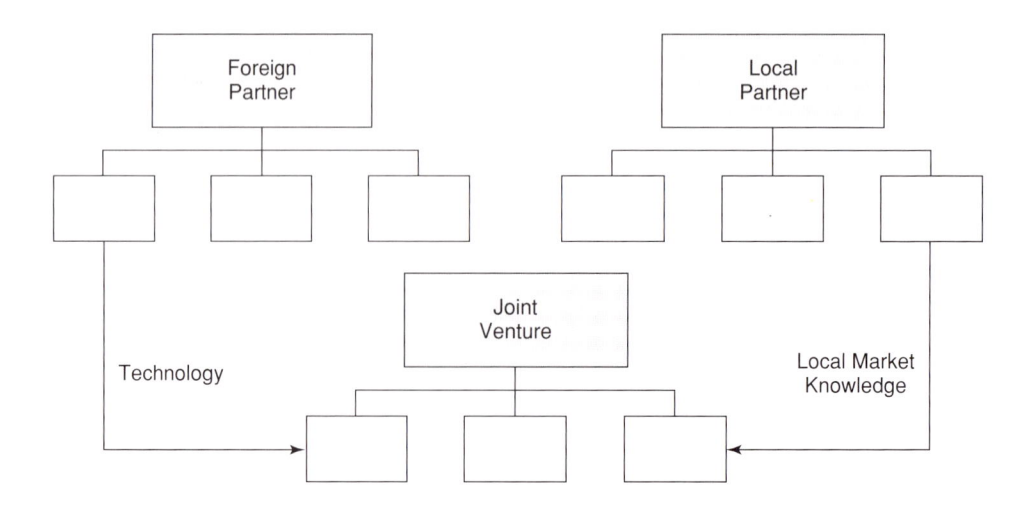

a variety of partners, including a local company, another international company, or the host-country government. Also, an international company's ownership of a joint venture may vary from majority to equal or minority participation in the total equity capital of the joint venture.

Conditions Influencing the IJV Choice

The affinity of companies for joint ventures abroad is influenced by several factors. The following are some of the most influential.

Legislation The laws in some countries mandate that foreign firms must form joint ventures with local partners (as opposed to wholly foreign-owned subsidiaries) in order to conduct business within their borders. Often this rule is applied for certain industries only. At times no such legal requirement may exist, but nevertheless the attitude of the host government may be so heavily biased in favor of joint ventures that it almost becomes the only practical entry mode available to a foreign company. Historically, China represented this type of environment. However, international firms are increasingly going it alone in China. In contrast, Vietnam represents a turbulent environment today where EIJVs are a primary way of gaining a foothold in the country.

Protecting a Profitable Market Tariffs or import barriers imposed by a host-, home-, or third-party government may threaten a profitable export market developed in a country by an international company. If the local government has policies that discourage or disallow wholly owned subsidiaries, the multinational company can choose to effect a licensing agreement with a local company. However, if the international company decides that neither licensing nor contract manufacturing are attractive alternatives to pursue, it is left with two alternatives: (1) Form a joint venture with a local partner, or (2) abandon the market altogether. Only if an international company has a firm policy of its own of not forming joint ventures under any circumstances will it decide to abandon the market despite its already established position.

Intellectual Property Considerations Companies whose value is based on a unique production process, trademark, brand name, or trade secret are quite hesitant to form joint ventures because of the danger that the production process or trade secret may be leaked to third parties. Such companies hesitate to form joint ventures also because of the risk of eroding the value and prestige associated with the quality of their product, brand name, or trademark, which could happen if the joint venture is unable to maintain the original quality standards.

Integrated Network of Subsidiaries Companies that have several subsidiaries abroad that are integrated globally or regionally in a network of production-assembly-distribution systems are likely to oppose joint ventures. The reason for this is that joint ventures with local partners decrease their flexibility, as well as increase the control required to optimally integrate the different subsidiaries involved in this network. For example, local partners are more likely to be interested in the profitability of the joint venture and would therefore be inclined to oppose any plans to curtail production in the joint venture and shift it to another subsidiary or to supply third markets from another subsidiary, even though the multinational company considered such plans to be in the interests of its global operations. Therefore, a joint venture that has been established primarily to produce products for the national market only may be more suitable for an international company than one that may have to be integrated in a global or regional network of subsidiaries.

Acquisition of Knowledge and Expertise Companies seek joint ventures when they need expertise that can be best provided by a local company, such as a well-developed marketing and service organization, well-established and proven contacts with important officials in the host government, an established name and place in the host country's industrial sector, and a competent management team and labor force.

Motives for Equity International Joint Ventures

Figure 6.6 illustrates a matrix that suggests four distinct reasons a firm will form an international joint venture.[28] The first rationale is seen in quadrant 1. There, a firm desires to further penetrate its current market with its existing products and technologies. Thus, the firm relies on its existing products and existing market knowledge. In many cases, it is the small or medium-size firms that basically need more cost efficiencies to compete against the larger firms in the industry. Often, the cooperating companies, large or small, limit the joint venture to a platform technology or product to gain cost efficiencies, as evidenced by the GM-Fiat IJV that develops automotive engines and strategically reaps platform synergies and related cost efficiencies. Subsequently, the cooperating firms each take responsibility for integrating that jointly developed platform into their respective autonomous downstream activities.

These types of quadrant 1 ventures are often seen in the pharmaceutical industry, where small, limited-product firms collaborate to develop research and development to an intermediate level. For example, the two American companies Merck and ProMetic BioSciences formed a comarketing and technological cooperation alliance for monoclonal antibody purification. By pooling their respective resources and technologies, Merck and ProMetic can now offer clients an integrated solution to problems. The value of this comarketing agreement is substantial for both companies because the combined product offerings complement each one's core competencies. The partners hope that the alliance will bolster sales of their respective products and strengthen the respective market position of each.

In quadrant 2, the firm is looking to extend and leverage its product offerings or core competencies to a new country. That is, it has a core technology or knowledge that is giving it a competitive advantage in its home country and now desires to extend that advantage overseas. The new country may be a market that has high future attractiveness but be one in which the firm has little competitive strength. Or it can be a higher-risk market where the firm wishes to hedge against that risk. Furthermore, the firm may not have the necessary capital or knowledge to expand in that market on its own; thus, it requires a local partner. During the 1990s and into the twenty-first century, various Japanese auto parts firms have sought to follow their customers (Toyota, Honda, Nissan, and Mitsubishi) to the United States in order to continue to provide the low-cost, innovative technology that they did in Japan. Because of capital costs and perceived new-market risks, the Japanese firms decided to expand through joint ventures. In the Nora-Sakari case at the end of this section, Sakari, a Finnish firm, has the imperative to expand to and compete in Asian telecom markets; however, lacking the critical knowledge of Asia, it needs a local Asian partner to facilitate its entry.

Quadrant 3 is actually the reverse of quadrant 2. Here, the firm is the foreign partner that wishes to collaborate with a home international firm. As was seen in the U.S. auto parts industry, U.S. firms were anxious to collaborate with Japanese partners in order to learn newer, low-cost industry technologies. As seen above, the Japanese firms were actually examples of firms in quadrant 2. They were seeking local market knowledge and contacts in the United States as well as deflecting some financial

PRACTICAL INSIGHT 6.2

THE GREAT INDIAN BEER RUSH

Locals disdain suds, but foreign brewers are betting they'll switch to the stuff. Indians love their booze, but beer, it seems, leaves them cold. The country ranks tops globally in consumption of whisky, but it's somewhere near the bottom in beer drinking. So why is just about everyone in the brewing industry scrambling to get a piece of the market?

Despite the obvious preference Indians have for distilled spirits, beermakers worldwide think there's great potential for selling their brews in the country. A hot climate, an even hotter economy, and an enormous youth population look like an unbeatable combination in the eyes of Britain's SABMiller and Scottish & Newcastle, Heineken of the Netherlands, and Denmark's Carlsberg. Facing flat sales in many Western markets, all have set up India operations in recent years, either on their own or in tieups (IJVs).

The latest to join the fray is Anheuser-Busch Cos. The No. 1 American beermaker has just inked a 50-50 joint venture with local player Crown Beers. In May, the two plan to start churning out Budweiser and other brands at a new brewery in the southern Indian city of Hyderabad. "India is still pretty small," says Stephen J. Burrows, CEO of Anheuser-Busch International. "But it has great potential."

Pretty small is putting it mildly. Although India boasts the world's second most populous nation, when it comes to beer it barely figures on the map—leaving plenty of upside for brewers who can get in early. Annual per capita consumption stands at just 0.6 liters, or about a pint, compared with 23 liters in China, an average of 73 across Europe, and 78 in the U.S. "Why should I waste money on beer when whisky does the trick much faster?" says Sudnya Bordoloi, a 21-year-old saleswoman at a Mumbai department store.

Getting Indians to switch from liquor to beer won't be easy. Brewers must contend with a dizzying list of bureaucratic restrictions that make it tough and expensive to win customers and to build a national footprint. Steep tariffs render imports uncompetitive. And state excise taxes of as much as 150% can push the price of a pint of domestic brew up to more than $3, or about triple what a shot of local whisky might cost. "The market has huge complexities," says Jean-Marc Delphon de Vaux, managing director of SABMiller India. "You have to work it bottom-up, state by state."

Ads for beer are banned. As a result, brewers have to be creative in building their brands on a national scale. SABMiller, for instance, sells a mineral water called Royal Challenge—not coincidentally the name of one of its lagers. TV spots for the water are indistinguishable from traditional beer ads, down to the label on the bottle. The only difference: The actors guzzle a clear liquid rather than amber-colored suds. "It looks like a beer ad, but we sell water," says Delphon de Vaux. The boldest ploy, though, comes from Bangalore-based United Breweries. Its chairman, Vijay Mallya, launched Kingfisher Airlines—named after United's flagship brew, India's top seller—and emblazoned the planes with its logo.

In short, international brewers will be charged with crafting a beer culture in India largely from scratch. In that, at least, they have demographics in their favor. Roughly 60% of the population is under 30. What's more, incomes are rising, powered by an economy that's growing at 9%-plus. These trends are expected to fuel growth in beer consumption of up to 15% a year through the end of the decade.

To date, the biggest beneficiary of the surge has been Kingfisher. The brand rules the market, with a 45% share. But closing in is SABMiller, which over the past six years has spent an estimated $600 million in India to buy 11 local breweries. Today, the company's five brands command 37% of the market. And Heineken, though it's small today, is hoping to boost its profile following its $18 million purchase last year of a controlling stake in India's Aurangabad Breweries Ltd. "India," says Vivek Chhabra, Heineken's country chief, "is the place to be."

Source: Nandini Lakshman and Adrienne Carter, *BusinessWeek*, April 23, 2007, p. 50.

---

risks. Likewise, in the Nora-Sakari case, Nora, a Malaysian firm, is in need of a new infusion of state-of-the-art telecom technology. Practical Insight 6.2 focuses on the beer industry in India during 2007 and illustrates market complexities requiring that foreign firms interested in investing in India pursue the IJV option.

Finally, firms located in quadrant 4 of Figure 6.6 are those that are looking to diversify away from current products, technologies, and markets and enter both different industries and newer markets. As seen in Chapter 5, firms attempt to enter new industries and new markets simultaneously for distinct reasons, including home-market saturation, as illustrated by the U.S. cigarette industry during the past 15 years. In 2008, the results of a specific IJV formed years earlier for strategic diversification reasons further elaborate on this IJV rationale. As Mitsubishi led a consortium of Japanese firms in

FIGURE 6.6
Motives for International Joint Ventures

Source: Adapted from P. Beamish, A. Morrison, A. Inkpen, and P. Rosenzweig, *International Management: Text and Cases,* 5th ed. (New York: McGraw-Hill/Irwin, 2003), p. 123.

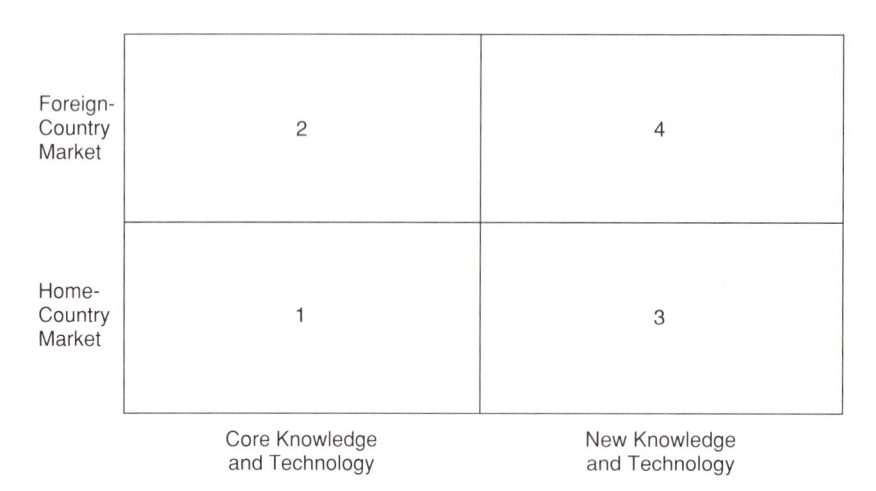

	Core Knowledge and Technology	New Knowledge and Technology
Foreign-Country Market	2	4
Home-Country Market	1	3

exploring entry into regional jet manufacturing, the partners needed the expertise and technology of a major airline manufacturer. With Boeing as a partner, the Japanese group sought to enter the crowded market for regional jets and compete with established industry giants like Bombardier of Canada and Embraer of Brazil. In March 2008, All Nippon Airways of Japan announced its plans to purchase 15 regional jets from the joint venture and, furthermore, took the option to purchase 10 additional jets during the next five years.

Advantages of Equity International Joint Ventures

A joint venture may be the only possible way to set up a business in a country. This may be particularly true in the case of certain industries that are regarded as politically sensitive such as the petroleum industry, aircraft manufacture, or transportation or utility companies. A firm with limited resources is able to enter a greater number of markets through the joint venture route than would be possible with a policy of establishing only wholly owned subsidiaries abroad. In some developing countries in particular, where large local firms have capital but are short on technical and managerial know-how, a multinational company can form a joint venture with a local firm without making any capital outlays, by receiving equity in the joint venture in exchange for its patents and know-how.

In countries where the fervor of nationalism is high, a joint venture with a local firm or government agency could help in substantially lowering the governmental and societal hostility against a foreign firm. In many instances, the local partner is able to circumvent red tape and bureaucratic harassment, which afflict multinational companies in many countries. Through well-established contacts with the right people, the local partner is often able to obtain important permits and licenses for imports, foreign exchange, plant expansion, water and electricity supply, and so on.

First-class managerial talent is difficult to find everywhere, but this is particularly evident in developing countries. The best way of obtaining high-quality managerial talent that is knowledgeable about local conditions is often through a joint venture with a successful local firm. Another advantage of an intangible nature is the effect on the local employees of a joint venture. It was reported that in India the sale of 10 percent of the stock of a once wholly owned subsidiary to the Indian public had a significantly positive impact on the morale of the Indian staff.

Government contracts are sometimes given only to domestic firms. International firms in certain industries are therefore obliged to form joint ventures with local companies in order to qualify for government contracts. Developing countries have been insisting that joint ventures include the government because of a historical distrust of foreign countries, arising from their experience with colonialism. This distrust is transferred to foreign companies, which, it is feared, might exert undue political and social influence. A minority participation of the government in a joint venture would allow its representatives to sit on the board of directors, thus permitting direct scrutiny of the workings of the joint venture. However ill-founded such anxiety may be, allaying it may be a valid motive for a multinational company to form a joint venture with the government. Civil servants on the board of directors can be helpful in obtaining favorable rulings from the government on vital matters such as price increases and import permits. As a partner in the joint venture, the host government is in a position to examine the problems and needs of the joint venture, as well as its contributions to the country's economy, from the inside.

International companies are often confronted with a peculiar problem that forces them to form joint ventures. For example, foreign companies planning to establish manufacturing facilities in a country may find that certain prominent local business firms have managed to corner permits that are no longer granted by the government but are required for producing the products that the international companies want to produce. Hence they are compelled to form joint ventures with local firms that own the required permits to produce the products.

Many companies form joint ventures with local firms that have the ability to provide the foreign partner with a steady stream of quality raw materials and/or components. A joint venture with a local firm is especially useful when imports of the required materials have been cut off by the government and when a license for their production has been given to the local firm.

Disadvantages of Equity International Joint Ventures

Joint ventures can have several disadvantages as well, and therefore international companies should carefully weigh the advantages against the disadvantages before deciding for or against joint ventures. Consider a company with a planning system that attempts to mobilize and deploy its worldwide resources with the aim of achieving its global objectives effectively and efficiently. This requires that actions be taken based on decisions that are in the interests of the company as a whole, even though the interests of one or more of its subsidiaries may have to be sacrificed in the process. A multinational company can take such actions only if each subsidiary's objectives are derived from, and dovetail with, the global company objectives. Problems with achieving global objectives could arise if a foreign joint venture partner refuses to go along with decisions of the international company that may be in the best interests of its global objectives but may not be in the best interests of the joint venture partner. For example, the local partner may resist efforts by the international company to have one of its wholly owned subsidiaries in another country, rather than the joint venture, serve third-country markets. A multinational company may favor such an arrangement if it is more efficient and cheaper than serving a third-country market from the joint venture. For example, it may be more efficient to serve the Australian market from a newly established subsidiary in Indonesia, rather than from a joint venture in Mauritius or Sri Lanka. The local partner is likely to resist such a shift because it may mean a loss in sales revenue, particularly when exports are essential to keeping the joint venture operating at full capacity.

Sourcing of components and raw materials could also cause problems in a joint venture. For example, it might be cheaper to manufacture certain components in a third county and have them imported for final assembly in the joint venture. The local partner is not likely to look favorably on this idea, especially if, as is very often the case, the joint venture partner is capable of making the components, and importing them would mean an increase in costs and a decrease in the joint venture's profits.

Problems could arise if the local partner—in the absence of any prior agreement precluding any such action—insists on exporting the products of the joint venture into world markets. A multinational company may find itself in a very grave predicament if the products of the joint venture were to compete in third markets with similar products produced by its other subsidiaries. Worse still would be for the joint venture products to find their way into the home market of the multinational company itself.

The above examples illustrate how a joint venture could disrupt a multinational company's plans for a regional or worldwide integration of its production-assembly-marketing operations in view of its total company objectives. There are also other areas in which problems could arise. The long-term success of a joint venture depends not only on how and to what extent the capabilities and contributions of both partners reinforce each other but also on the combination of their respective risk–gain and time–return attitudes. Let us see how the risk–gain and time–return attitudes of the partners could affect a joint venture's prospects.

The desire for growth and the propensity to assume corresponding risks to achieve it may differ between the partners. For example, a multinational company, because of its bigger size and stronger financial position, might be willing to assume financial risks on projects that have prospects of high returns. Such high-risk–high-return projects might seem like reckless behavior to the local partner, which might be relatively more conservative because of its smaller size and weaker financial position. Because of the differences in the willingness to assume risks, friction could arise between the joint venture partners on issues such as the extent to which the joint venture company is an aggressive price leader, the debt-to-equity ratio assumed, whether some budget items are capitalized or expensed, the handling of employee pension funds, the amount of resources committed to marketing capabilities to exploit new markets, and the aggressiveness of marketing policies.

The time–return attitudes of the two partners might also vary and cause problems. This is not to be confused with the conservative–liberal attitude toward risks, which has to do with a company's propensity to take risks. The time–return attitude of a company is concerned with its tendency to wait in anticipation of a future return. For example, the local partner might be unwilling to commit the company's resources to research and marketing programs that may promise high long-term returns but sacrifice the joint venture's short-term competitive edge and immediate profits.

Conflicts could also occur due to the different tax laws and foreign exchange considerations affecting the two partners. A U.S. international company, for example, may wish to forgo dividends in order to defer U.S. taxes on dividends repatriated to the United States. But this may conflict with the desire of the local partner for dividends and immediate cash.

An international company that has a joint venture in a country with a history of currency devaluations would prefer to keep the joint venture's current assets to a minimum to limit its losses from local currency depreciation. It would also prefer to borrow from the local capital markets to meet the joint venture's working capital needs. This again may not be acceptable to the local partner, which has no such losses to worry about and may therefore object to the idea of incurring heavy interest payments by borrowing for working capital requirements. Joint ventures could, in this way, reduce an international company's flexibility to respond strategically and exploit profit opportunities arising from differences in tax laws and currency fluctuations.

Disagreements also could arise over staffing practices in the joint venture. In some countries it is a common practice for top management personnel to be recruited from a certain social class. It is also common in some countries, like India, for owners of firms to give good jobs to family members or members of the same community. An international company, which desires to employ competent managerial personnel in the joint venture, might have a conflict over such a policy.

The Importance of Having the Right IJV Partner

New organizational structures, such as joint ventures, have a greater chance of releasing conflicts that past old structures were able to contain within their hierarchies and regulations.[29] Thus, conflicts that arise in front-end negotiations of IJVs may threaten the sustainability of these agreements. Lyles studied various mistakes of international joint ventures, grouping these errors into technological, human resources, negotiations, partner, and strategic goal categories. The truth is that many international joint ventures fail. That is, either they are dissolved before they were expected to be or they do not meet the objectives that were laid out at the beginning of the collaboration. For instance, due to a poor partner selection, British drugstore chain Boots Co. had to close its retail outlets in Japan. Many other retailers, such as U.S. clothing and outdoor goods retailer L.L. Bean, closed many stores and revamped marketing strategies in response to stagnating sales. Among other reasons, these withdrawals directly correlated to the poor selection of joint venture partners.

In general, some of the reasons that EIJVs fail include:

- Lack of trust between partners.
- Different partner objectives.
- Hidden partner objectives.
- Changing partner objectives.
- Clashing partner national cultures.
- Clashing partner organizational cultures.
- No real strategic fit between partners.
- Opportunistic behavior by a partner.
- Lack of knowledge reciprocity between partners.[30]

Negotiating the International Joint Venture

In international joint ventures, as in the case of negotiations in general, the power of each prospective partner relative to the other will influence the front-end negotiations process.[31] If this, in turn, leads to contentious communications, the ultimate success of the venture may be jeopardized.[32] Thus, the partner with the most relative power will have the ability to influence front-end discussions and ultimately the joint venture structure.

Weiss proposed a framework for analyzing the negotiations leading to international joint ventures. Studying a proposed alliance in the international telecommunications industry, he suggested a complex web of interrelationships that must be addressed during the negotiation. External environmental conditions as well as internal conditions such as EIJV partner objectives were proposed to influence the negotiations, strategy, implementation, and eventual partner benefits of the EIJV.[33] Past international business researchers suggested that three distinct entities—the international firm, the local firm, and the host government—will each have their objectives directly influenced by external environmental forces that include the various cultural, economic, and political systems. Each entity will bring its desired goals to the EIJV table. In turn, these objectives, diverse in nature, will lead to varying degrees of negotiating conflicts and cooperation.[34] Comparing U.S. problem-solving negotiation methods with the cultures of the Japanese, South Koreans, and Taiwanese, researchers found that the perceived satisfaction with negotiation outcomes was based primarily on partner attractiveness and compatibility.[35]

Incorporating a political dimension into negotiations, the international firm must realize that in many countries the host government is a key stakeholder in the venture and thus will exert power during the negotiations.[36] Doz argued that negotiations between an international firm and a host government will center on the division of profits. Consistent with the strategic thinking identified in Chapter 5, he identified three strategies that the international firm may adopt when dealing with host governments:

- **Integration.** The firm seeks to increase efficiency through the optimum allocation of global resources.
- **Multifocal.** The firm permits a degree of influence over its strategies in exchange for host-government support.
- **National responsiveness.** The international company positions itself as a partner to the local government.[37]

Incorporating lessons learned from previous chapters that explored the external environment in which international firms must exist, Table 6.1 illustrates the effect of environmental factors on the front-end negotiations of international joint ventures.[38] A perceived riskier environment will clearly influence the firm to seek higher financial guarantees during negotiations.

During international joint venture negotiations, the financial targets alluded to in Table 6.1 may include (1) cost-based criteria such as share of global research and development, share of central overheads, and technology transfer costs and (2) market-based criteria pertaining to the net incremental revenues from the new market.[39] International negotiations, with applications formation and partner decisions, will be explored further in Chapter 10.

International Strategic Alliances

Not a week goes by without an announcement in the business press of a strategic alliance between two or more companies. Almost every internationally minded company trying to become global will consider forging a strategic alliance with another company as a fast track to that goal. A strategic alliance is a collaborative arrangement that a company makes with competitors, suppliers, customers, distributors, or firms in the same or different industries in order to develop, produce, distribute, or market a product or service. Strategic alliances are also formed to obtain technology, minimize

TABLE 6.1
Host-Country Effects on EIJV Negotiations' Financial Targets

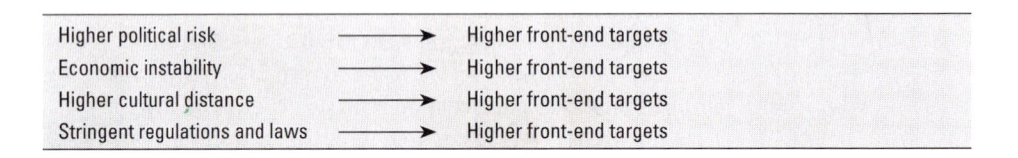

Higher political risk	→	Higher front-end targets
Economic instability	→	Higher front-end targets
Higher cultural distance	→	Higher front-end targets
Stringent regulations and laws	→	Higher front-end targets

environmental risks, or acquire key human and material resources. The joint venture discussed to this point in this chapter is actually an equity-based strategic alliance that establishes a new company. In this section, we focus on strategic alliances as collaborative initiatives directly between or among companies, with or without equity.

Thus, compared to the equity-based joint venture, the **international strategic alliance** is an association between the companies without an offshoot company being formed. An example is the alliance begun between the Japanese company Mitsubishi and the German company Daimler-Benz before it merged with Chrysler from the United States. The two companies worked on 11 joint projects involving cars, aerospace, and integrated circuits. Likewise, Sony, the dominant Japanese and world firm in the electronics and entertainment industries, has forged such alliances with many small, high-technology companies in the United States and Europe during the past 15 years. The company shares its research staff, production facilities, and even business plans for specific products with small companies. Sony has worked with Panavision Inc. to develop a lens for high-definition television cameras now in use, with Compression Labs Inc. on a videoconferencing machine, and with Alphatronix Inc. to develop rewritable, optical-disk storage systems for computers.[40] Practical Insight 6.3 depicts the successful alliance between Renault and Nissan, especially in emerging countries—markets critical in the automotive industry.

A specific type of nonequity strategic alliance is the noncash partnership, in which each company has a stake in the other and the companies trade assets. It is believed that such cash-neutral transactions may become a trend in a credit-sensitive international environment. Examples of such alliances abound in the international airline industry, where clusters of firms have forged marketing and operations alliances. Star Alliance, a consortium that includes United Airlines, Lufthansa, and Air New Zealand, among other carriers, is an alliance in which each member carrier markets, operationally supports, and logistically offers ease of connection with the other member routes. Delta and Air France have a similar arrangement, as do British Air and Qantas.

Rationale for International Strategic Alliances

Beyond the apparent marketing and operations synergies suggested in the above discussion, there are, of course, other reasons for strategic alliances. Many of these rationales are similar to the reasons identified earlier in this chapter regarding international joint ventures. They include:

- Penetrating new foreign markets.
- Sharing marketing costs.
- Sharing research and development costs and risks.
- Launching a counterattack against competitors.
- Pooling global resources.
- Learning from partners.

Risks of International Strategic Alliances

Potential concerns of international strategic alliances are similar to those regarding international joint ventures. It is assumed, incorrectly of course, that all strategic alliances are successful. In fact, many alliances are terminated for a variety of reasons. Many risks affect the international strategic alliance. One is deemed *relational risk*. This risk is concerned with the probability and potential consequences of a partner firm's not fully committing itself to the alliance. This lack of commitment may affect the attainment of front-end alliance strategic objectives, based on the premise that

PRACTICAL INSIGHT 6.3

SUCCESSFUL ALLIANCE BETWEEN RENAULT AND NISSAN
Putting Ford in the Rearview Mirror
Ghosn's Repair Job Could Make Renault-Nissan the World's No. 3 Carmaker

Just about everyone in the auto industry knows that Toyota Motor Corp is on pace to pull ahead of General Motors as the world's largest carmaker this year or next. But less noticed has been a race just down the ranking tables, where another storied U.S. giant is facing similar pressure: Ford Motor Co. is on the verge of being edged out by Renault-Nissan for the No. 3 spot globally. As Ford shrinks to projected sales of 6.3 million vehicles for 2007, the French-Japanese alliance is likely to grow to 6.4 million, according to data from Morgan Stanley and UBS.

Ford's catastrophic $12.7 billion loss in 2006, and impending production cuts this year, have shifted it into reverse, letting Renault-Nissan catch up fast. (Ford owns 33% of Mazda, which sold 1.3 million cars last year, but doesn't include those sales in its total.) Carlos Ghosn, chief executive at both Renault and Nissan, has pushed the two companies to collaborate on engineering and research and development. It's a formula that seems to be working. As Detroit has struggled, Ghosn has quietly boosted design and quality, cut costs, and attacked high-growth Asian markets.

It hasn't always been easy for Ghosn, who saved Nissan from near-bankruptcy in 1999. Last year was filled with setbacks and troublesome distractions, such as failed talks on expanding the Renault-Nissan alliance to include GM. Ghosn ordered improvements in new models, causing costly delays. But getting it right was essential, especially in the wake of earlier quality problems. All told, 2006 sales for the Renault-Nissan alliance fell 3.6% worldwide.

Now the repair work seems largely done, and both companies are poised to rebound. Nissan's U.S. third-quarter sales rose 1%, reversing a first-half slide. For the next fiscal year, Nissan's global sales will rise 7%, Standard & Poor's forecasts. That's largely thanks to the launch of nine new models, including revamped versions of high-volume cars such as the Altima, Sentra, and Infiniti G35 sedan. Renault's global sales are also expected to jump 7% this year, Morgan Stanley estimates, as the Twingo subcompact, a revamped Laguna sedan, and a minivan version of the low-cost Logan all hit the market. That should help Ghosn start delivering on his promise of 6% margins at Renault in 2009.

The Logan is key to Ghosn's push in emerging markets. Competitors had dismissed the $7,500 compact, built in Romania, as an underpowered, low-margin ugly duckling. Yet it went on to be a hit following its 2004 launch. Last year sales jumped to 247,000, and Ghosn aims to sell 1 million Logans worldwide by 2010, many of them in India and China. Renault also aims to produce a low-cost pickup based on the Logan for South Africa, the Middle East, and Southeast Asia. As the new models roll off the assembly line, many expect Ghosn's restructuring to start kicking in. Says David Weinstein, a professor at the French business school INSEAD: "The real dimensions of the Renault-Nissan iceberg are not yet visible."

Renault-Nissan's strategy of designing many models from one platform gives the alliance an edge. In 2008, Renault will introduce a new generation of its Megane compact family based on Nissan's Rogue and Qashai crossover SUVs. With the Megane family accounting for about half of Renault's sales and 75% of its profit, the shared platform will especially help the bottom line.

The complementary reach of Renault and Nissan lets Ghosn carry out a surprisingly powerful global strategy. Nissan is

---

both (or all) partners forgo opportunistic behavior.[41] As an illustration of this risk, partners that are direct competitors have been found to incur more relational risk in their alliance, and thus such alliances are not predicted to be as successful as alliances between noncompetitors.[42]

A second risk posed is *performance risk*. This refers to external environmental factors, in the home country, the host country, or globally, that jeopardize the attainment of the alliance's strategic objectives. These factors include political changes, economic changes, and shifts in law. Whereas performance risk deals with many strategic initiatives of an international firm, relational risk focuses on the internal dynamics of international alliances in particular. Figure 6.7 illustrates the linkages between these external and internal risks and international alliance type.[43]

strong in Japan, China, and the U.S., while Renault is a market leader in Europe and spearheading the push into India. "As a result, they can play bigger than they are," says Morgan Stanley analyst Adam Jonas. "Their ultimate competitor is Toyota."

RENAULT-NISSAN ALLIANCE

The Renault-Nissan alliance, established in March 1999, was the first industrial and commercial partnership involving a French and a Japanese company. The two global companies are linked by cross-shareholdings and at year-end 2007 had an estimated global market share of 9% (by volume). The alliance has a significant presence in major world markets both developed and emerging (United States, Europe, Japan, China, India, Russia). The alliance develops and implements a strategy of profitable growth. The objective is to establish a powerful automotive group and develop synergies while conserving the corporate culture and identity of each brand. The alliance is built on values of trust and mutual respect and relies on its partners combined expertise and technology sharing. For instance, Nissan pilots the development of new gasoline engines while Renault focuses on diesel engines. Furthermore, Nissan has actively participated in the development of the Renault group's first cross-over, which was conceived and designed by Renault, and is manufactured by Renault Samsung Motors in South Korea. Currently, a focus is on international development in emerging markets including (1) a project to build a joint factory in Chennai (India), (2) an agreement for the installation of a shared production site in Tangiers (Morocco), (3) a partnership announced with Bajaj, an Indian manufacturer, to develop an ultra-low-cost vehicle by 2010, and (4) an alliance with the Russian automaker AvtoVAZ.

Renault holds a 44.3% stake in Nissan, while Nissan holds 15% of Renault shares. Each company has a direct interest in the results of its partner. A strategic management company, Renault-Nissan b.v., was founded to define a common strategy and manage synergies. It was created under Dutch law and is jointly and equally owned by the two partners.

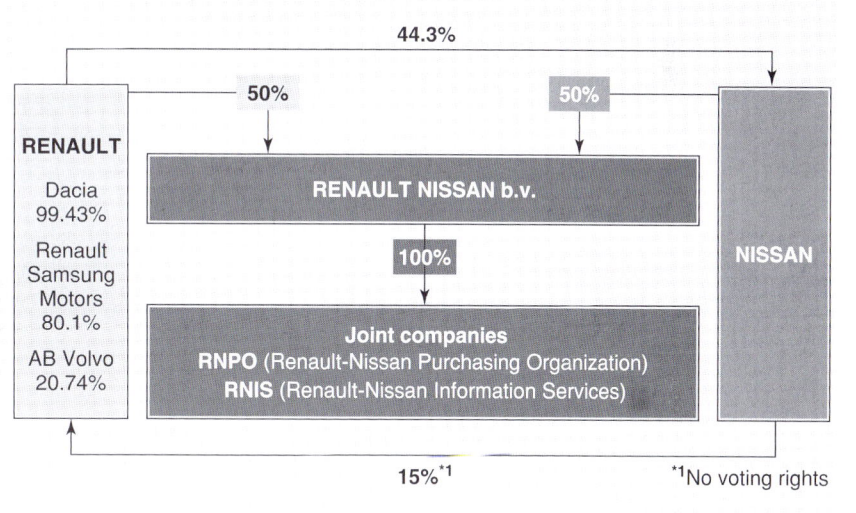

RENAULT
Dacia 99.43%
Renault Samsung Motors 80.1%
AB Volvo 20.74%

Renault → 44.3% → NISSAN
Renault → 50% → RENAULT NISSAN b.v. ← 50% ← NISSAN
RENAULT NISSAN b.v. → 100% → Joint companies
RNPO (Renault-Nissan Purchasing Organization)
RNIS (Renault-Nissan Information Services)
NISSAN → 15%*1 → Renault
*1 No voting rights

Source: Gail Edmondson and Ian Rowley, "Putting Ford in the Rearview Mirror," *BusinessWeek,* February 12, 2007, p. 44; "Renault-Nissan Alliance," www.renault.com, 2008.

Thus, in terms of the relational or internal risks specific to international alliances, among the most common reasons for the failure of these partnerships are the following:

- **Clash of cultures.** Communication and decision-making differences because of cultural differences (discussed in Chapter 4) could lead to serious problems between the alliance partners.
- **Unrealized partner expectations.** One or both partners might conclude that the alliance is not realizing the objectives that were the predominant reasons for forming the alliance.
- **Surrender of sovereignty.** A smaller partner in an alliance may lose its independence if it becomes overly dependent on the larger partner for things like money, newer technology, or market access in a key country.

FIGURE 6.7
Risks in International Collaborative Initiatives

Source: T. Das and B. Teng, "A Risk Perception Model of Alliance Structuring," *Journal of Management*, 2001. Copyright © 2001 *Journal of Management*. Reprinted with permission.

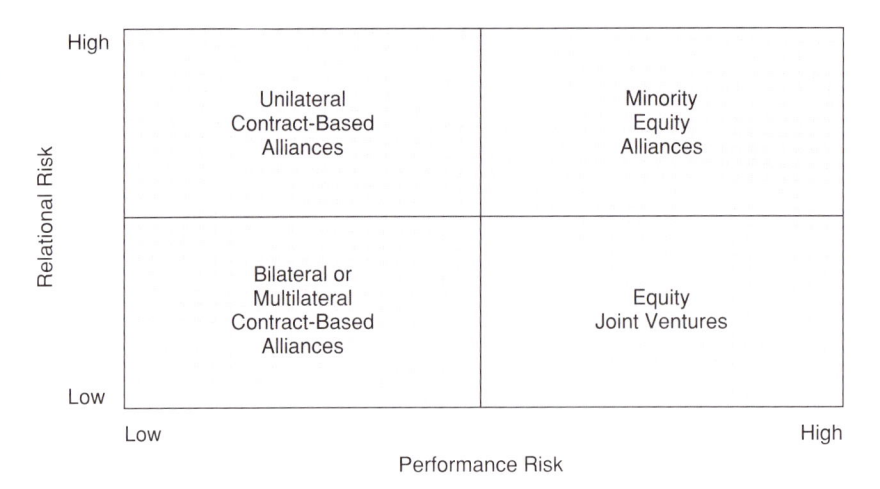

	Low Performance Risk	High Performance Risk
High Relational Risk	Unilateral Contract-Based Alliances	Minority Equity Alliances
Low Relational Risk	Bilateral or Multilateral Contract-Based Alliances	Equity Joint Ventures

- **Risk of losing core competence to a partner.** When an alliance is formed, there is generally a transfer of knowledge among the partners. For example, Company X may learn how to market a product in Company Y's home market, and Company Y may learn from Company X a secret process for manufacturing a patented product. Later, Company Y may enter a foreign market and compete with Company X with products made by using the secret process. The original alliance may fail because of this strategy implemented by Company Y.

Making International Collaborative Initiatives Work

Whether the international cooperative arrangement is equity-based or nonequity-based, a joint venture or a strategic alliance, there are certain aspects to consider in order to help ensure the success of the initiative. Parkhe suggested that reciprocity, trust, and lack of opportunistic behavior between and among partner firms were critical components for the success of the international partnership.[44] Steensma and Lyles studied EIJVs in economically transitioning nations and suggested that an imbalance in the management control structure of the partnership may lead to conflict and ultimate failure.[45]

Although there are no magical prescriptions to ensure the success of joint ventures and strategic alliances there are some guidelines that can enhance the chances of their survival.

Trust Is Built in Small Steps

Trust among partners is critical to the success of any joint venture or strategic alliance. But trust cannot be written into a legal document in the form of a contract. It is each participant's observed behavior that builds trust in any relationship, and this fact is true in a strategic alliance as well. Partners must keep trust in mind and behave in an open manner that enhances the bonds of that trust between them. Each of the partners must attempt to find ways of working together without either one feeling that the other is trying to steal technology or take advantage in any way. Such trust takes time to develop, and relationships based on trust need to be developed in a deliberate fashion.[46]

Pick a Compatible Partner

To begin with, the alliance must be important enough to make a strategic impact on the future well-being of both partners. If one of the partners considers the alliance of

FIGURE 6.8
International Collaborative Initiative: Partner Success Factors

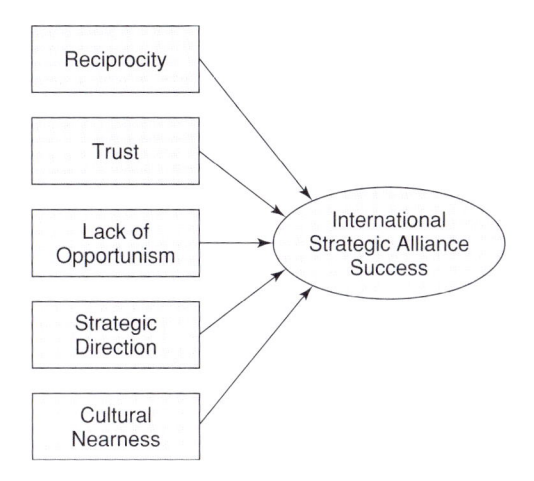

merely peripheral importance, the seeds of dissolution are sown. Cultural compatibility is an absolute prerequisite for the success of any partnership. Therefore, if the partners in an alliance have greatly divergent cultures, it would be advisable to have one of the partners play a dominant role in the day-to-day management of the venture once the strategic intent of the alliance has been mutually agreed on. This arrangement is the one under which the NUMMI partnership between General Motors and Toyota was administered, with Toyota managing the venture on a daily basis. Figure 6.8 illustrates partner factors that correlate with eventual alliance success. They include:

- **Reciprocity.** Both partners have equal give and take regarding knowledge (market knowledge, technology, etc.). Equal, as opposed to unequal, reciprocity among alliance partners has been linked to long-term alliance profitability.[47]
- **Trust.** Both partners honor the commitments and duties of the final strategic alliance agreement. Interorganizational trust has been linked to improved market performance of international alliances.[48] Trust between partners helps to deter opportunistic behavior, which is discussed next.[49]
- **Lack of opportunism.** In the case of a changing environment and new opportunities, neither partner uses the joint venture or strategic alliance exclusively to its own benefit and to the detriment of the other partner.[50]
- **Strategic direction convergence.** Both partners have similar strategic goals for the international alliance.
- **Cultural nearness.** Both from an organizational perspective and from a national context, the organizations understand each other's motives and actions.

Create and Maintain an Alliance with Equal Power

An alliance in which one of the partners is more powerful than the other is in danger of collapsing unless the more powerful partner treats the weaker partner as an equal. Power derives from one's ability to deliver something (technology, capital, information, or resources) to another, something that the other party cannot obtain in the marketplace or develop by itself at an acceptable cost. The power that a company can muster in an alliance is not necessarily associated with its relative size vis-à-vis its partner. For example, a company that has the proprietary knowledge and expertise to develop a breakthrough drug for the treatment of a fatal disease, or one that can develop a better and faster computer chip, will have the power to deal on equal terms with a much larger company. The power balance in an alliance is what matters. A small company may have the technology, but a large firm could provide the required capital to develop and commercialize it. As long as the relationship maintains a power balance, the partnership should not expect trouble. However, when a power imbalance develops in an alliance, the company emerging as the more powerful should be careful not to act as such in order for the alliance to survive.

Understand the Control Structure of the Partnership

Overlapping with the power balance is the control structure of the partnership. Two types of control exist for an EIJV. The first, *ownership control,* is the legitimate authority each partner has over specific assets.[51] This is based on the relative equity each firm has in the partnership. The second, *management control,* is the decision-making power that each partner has. It may be linked to ownership control, but it may also be an offshoot of various informal practices, implementation techniques, and political processes.[52] As seen in the Renault-Nissan alliance, the overall structure and control process is clearly communicated to both partners.

Be Patient

An infinite amount of patience is needed on both sides during the various stages of an alliance. During the initial negotiation phase, patience is necessary to ensure that the alliance is properly structured in terms of who is responsible for what types of decisions, and so forth. Spending extra time and effort on ironing out such issues early in the alliance helps prevent future problems. Patience is also needed when the alliance begins to function. Expecting immediate results can prove fatal. Managers on both sides must recognize that delays and unexpected technical- and people-related problems will emerge in any organization and that the chances of such problems arising increase greatly when two companies are engaged in a collaborative effort.

Mode of Foreign Entry and Control Implications

Each foreign entry mode includes varying degrees of control through different control mechanisms. Contractor and Kundu have classified these into four types: (1) daily operational and quality control in each foreign entry; (2) control over the physical assets or the real estate and its attendant risks; (3) control over tacit expertise embedded in the routines of the firm; and (4) control over the codified assets such as a global reservation system or the firm's internationally recognized brand name.[53] The degree of control for each type of mechanism in each entry mode is depicted in Table 6.2.

TABLE 6.2
Type and Degree of Parent Company Control over Foreign Operations

Source: Adapted from Farok J. Contractor and Sumit Kundu, "Modal Choice in a World of Alliances," *Journal of International Business Studies* 29, no. 2 (Second Quarter, 1998), p. 330.

Mode of Entry	Strong Control	Weak Control	Nonexistent Control
Contract manufacturing		A	B, C, D
Licensing	D	C	A, B,
Franchising	D	C	A, B
Management service contract	D	A, C	B
Joint venture	D	A, B, C	
Wholly owned subsidiary	A, B, C, D		

Key:
A = daily management and quality control.
B = control over physical assets.
C = control over tacit expertise and knowledge.
D = control over codified assets.

Table 6.2 shows that a multinational company can exert control over its foreign operations through various means and that it does not necessarily need a significant equity in the foreign operation to obtain control. For example, a hotel chain like Marriott can impose considerable influence over a franchisee hotel abroad because it controls the global reservation system. The franchisee hotel depends on filling its hotel rooms through customers that the global reservation system provides.

Factors Influencing the Entry Mode Choice by International Firms

The choice of the mode of entry in a foreign country by a firm is perhaps one of the most widely researched areas in the international business arena. It ranks with the most significant decisions that a firm will make as it embarks on a global strategy to penetrate foreign markets. The choice of an entry mode is critical in a firm's globalization strategy. As shown in Table 6.2, each entry mode discussed earlier in this chapter differs in the degree of control, the degree of systemic risk experienced, the degree of dissemination risk experienced, and the amount of the firm's resources committed. *Degree of control* is the authority over operational and strategic decision making that a company has over its foreign operations.[54] **Systemic risk** is the level of political, economic, and financial risks faced by the particular entry mode. **Dissemination risk** is the risk that firm-specific advantages in know-how will be expropriated by a partner in a foreign venture.[55] *Resource commitment* refers to the amount of resources invested in revenue-generating assets in a foreign venture, such as plant and equipment, training imparted to personnel, and the costs of penetrating a foreign market, all of which cannot be redeployed to alternative uses without incurring substantial sunk costs.[56]

The degree of control of a foreign operation ranges from low for exporting, countertrade, and licensing to high for wholly owned subsidiaries. Systemic risk varies from low for exporting, countertrade, licensing, franchising, management service contracts, and turnkey projects to high for the wholly owned entry mode. Dissemination risk is highest for licensing, and resource commitments are highest for wholly owned ventures. Table 6.3 is a suggested representation of these concepts as they are compared across the various modes of entry.

Several theoretical perspectives, such as transaction cost economics, industrial organization, and strategic behavior, have been advanced to explain the choice of entry mode by global companies. Over the past two decades, researchers have empirically tested several existing explanations for this phenomenon, and new explanations have been offered.

TABLE 6.3 Characteristics of Entry Modes

Type of Entry Mode	Degree of Control	Systemic Risk	Dissemination Risk	Resource Commitment
Export	Low	Low	Low	Low
Countertrade	Low	Low	Low	Low
Contract manufacturing	Medium	Medium	Low to medium	Low
Licensing	Low	Low	High	Low
Franchising	Low to medium	Low	Medium	Low
Management service contract	Medium	Low	Medium	Low
Turnkey	Low	Low	Low	Low
Equity-based entry: joint venture	Medium-high	Medium-high	Medium to high	Medium to high
Equity-based entry: wholly owned subsidiary	High	High	Low	High

Determinants of Foreign Mode of Entry

Research on entry mode strategies has yielded 25 different factors as determinants in the entry mode choice. However, the research findings do not agree on the significance of some of these factors. Some studies identify certain factors as being significant in their impact on the entry mode decision, and others negate such conclusions. We have therefore selected 17 variables that were tested and found to be statistically significant in eight empirical studies conducted between 1987 and 1992. The eight studies were built on the accumulated knowledge and findings of previous research and therefore reflect the key findings of earlier studies as well as new developments in the area. In the following list, we present a brief review of each of these 17 variables.

1. **Firm size.** Firm size is one of the measures of managerial capabilities and resources of a firm, and as such it could influence the choice of entry mode. Empirical evidence shows that firm size has a positive impact on foreign direct investment; that is, firm size would generally have a positive correlation with foreign market entry and, in particular, with entry through wholly owned or joint venture modes.[57]

2. **Multinational experience.** Multinational experience reduces the uncertainty associated with assessing the true economic worth of entry into a foreign market. It follows, therefore, that firms with little or no experience with international business or multinational operations would seek to limit their risk exposure. Such firms would prefer low-control–low-resource, noninvestment-type entry modes like exporting or licensing.[58] In contrast firms with significant multinational experience would prefer high-control–high-resource, investment-type modes like joint ventures or wholly owned affiliates.

3. **Industry growth.** Industry growth in the target country is an indicator of the degree of competition and profitability that a firm would experience in that country. Industry growth is therefore expected to influence the entry mode choice. Kogut and Singh found that the entry mode preference of a firm is dependent on competitive assumptions.[59] They also found evidence (albeit weak) for the proposition that the joint venture entry mode is encouraged when the industry is growing.

4. **Global industry concentration.** Hamel and Prahalad have argued that in a global industry characterized by global competition, firms that function under a global strategy umbrella respond to their competitor's competitive moves not only in their home market but also in the competitor's home market or in third-country markets.[60] It is imperative that such firms have control of their foreign affiliates, without which it would be impossible to implement a global response to a competitor's onslaught.[61] Assuming that high global industry concentration would be associated with a high degree of global competition, firms operating in such industry conditions would prefer high-control entry modes like wholly owned subsidiaries.

5. **Technical intensity.** According to most studies, failure of markets to mediate the exchange of technology and tacit knowledge is the reason that firms in technically intense industries prefer the wholly owned affiliate entry mode.[62] However, an entering firm that is seeking technology and tacit knowledge is more likely to enter the foreign market through a joint venture with a firm that has the needed technology.

6. **Advertising intensity.** When a firm is in an industry that is characterized by high advertising intensity, it is inclined to shy away from joint ventures and to seek entry modes that provide full control over the foreign venture.[63]

7. **Country risk.** Firms prefer to avoid countries with high political risk, like expropriation or nationalization, or economic risk, like restrictions on remittances of

assets and limitations on operational and managerial choice. But if they do choose to make an entry into such countries, they would do so utilizing noninvestment (low-control) entry modes.[64]

8. **Cultural distance.** Firms entering culturally distant countries will prefer licensing agreements or joint ventures over wholly owned affiliates.[65]

9. **Market potential.** In high-market-potential countries, firms are inclined to pursue joint ventures or wholly owned entry modes since such modes provide higher profitability and market presence.[66]

10. **Market knowledge.** Firms can be expected to pursue the wholly owned entry mode rather than a joint venture as firms gain experience and learn more about the local environment.[67] Firms are likely to use high-control entry modes when following a client into a country market.[68] For example, firms that are suppliers of components to major automobile companies have followed them in their foreign market entries by establishing manufacturing plants that are either wholly owned or joint ventures with local partners. Therefore, having prior experience with a country market and/or following a buyer is expected to be associated positively with high-control entry modes.

11. **Value of firm-specific assets.** If the firm-specific assets, such as specific technologies that give the firm a sustainable competitive advantage, are highly valued in the venture, firms are likely to prefer entry modes that allow full control of the venture and to avoid joint ventures with local partners for fear of self-serving actions by the latter.* Researchers have used different variables to capture the value of firm-specific assets. Agarwal and Ramaswami used the firm's "ability to develop differentiated products."[69] Gatignon and Anderson used the "value of firm-specific know-how" to represent the value of firm specific assets involved in a venture.[70]

12. **Contractual risk.** If the cost of making and enforcing contracts to prevent opportunism by local partners is high, the firm will prefer entry modes that offer high control over their assets and skills.[71] Therefore, when the contractual risk is high, firms are likely to pursue high-control entry modes.

13. **Tacit nature of know-how.** If the nature of the firm-specific know-how is tacit (i.e., not able to be efficiently transferred to a partner), wholly owned operations increase the firm's ability to efficiently utilize the accumulated tacit knowledge.[72] Therefore, tacit know-how is expected to be positively associated with degree of control.

14. **Venture size.** Gatignon and Anderson have argued that the size of the operation will have an impact on the extent of control sought by the entrant.[73] Empirical evidence supports the proposition that firms shy away from wholly owned entry modes in favor of joint ventures when the size of the venture is big.[74]

15. **Intent to conduct joint R&D.** Modes of entry that do not involve an equity stake may not provide the requisite control to manage the complex judgmental tasks involved in conducting R&D.[75] Therefore, if the intent of a firm entering a foreign market is to conduct research and development work in conjunction with a partner, the firm will be inclined to favor a joint venture as opposed to other low-control governance structures.

16. **Global strategic motivation.** It has been argued by researchers that foreign market entries are motivated by strategic factors that go beyond immediate efficiency considerations.[76] Strategic goals like establishing a strategic outpost and developing

---

*For examples, the joint venture partner might take the technology, upgrade it, and refuse to give royalties to the international company.

a global sourcing site, or moving into a market to deny a profit sanctuary for competitors, motivate firms to prefer wholly owned or joint venture entry modes as opposed to low-control licensing agreements.[77]

17. **Global synergies.** Firms seek hierarchical control over affiliates when there is a high degree of interaction between and among the foreign affiliates and the parent company in pursuit of an integrated global strategy.[78] Therefore, when the potential synergies from global integration of companywide strategies are high, firms are likely to pursue high-control entry modes like wholly or majority-owned affiliates.

Theory of Multinational Investment

Thus for, we have discussed the various types of entry modes. However, one should also explore the various theories proposed by scholars to explain the reasons for foreign involvement by international companies and the circumstances underlying the entry mode choices.

One can postulate that two main reasons motivate a firm to engage in international investment: (1) to serve a local market better and (2) to get lower-cost inputs.[79] Foreign direct investment (FDI) to serve local markets better is known as *horizontal FDI (HFDI)* since it generally involves the duplication of the production process as additional plants are established to supply different locations. HFDI replaces exports with local production and thus substitutes for trade. The motive for HFDI is either to improve the firm's competitive position in the market or to reduce the costs associated with supplying the foreign market (such as transportation costs or tariffs).

Foreign direct investment made to obtain low-cost inputs is often referred to as *vertical FDI (VFDI)*. VFDI involves splitting the vertical chain of production (the value chain) and locating parts of this chain in a low-cost location; for example, computers may be assembled in Taiwan even though the components are manufactured in, and the computers are marketed in, the United States. The low-cost inputs might be unskilled labor, a cheap energy source, highly educated scientists or engineers, or even access to the knowledge embedded in an industrial cluster (such as the electronic industry clusters in the Silicon Valley, Boston, or Austin). Vertical FDI usually creates trade because different links in the value chain may be dispersed to different locations and also shipped between different locations. The economic rationale for this phenomenon rests on the idea that different parts of the production process have different input requirements. Furthermore, because input prices vary across countries, it may be profitable to split the value chain and distribute the performance of the various links and activities to the countries in which they could be performed most efficiently and effectively.

Although fundamental differences exist between horizontal and vertical integration, very often the distinction can become fuzzy as the strategic intent to establish a plant abroad might be based on the low costs as well as the demand for the final product in the local market.

A number of factors that influence the choice of an entry mode in a specific market have been identified by earlier studies in the fields of international trade, international organization, and market imperfections. Normally a firm is likely to choose a foreign entry mode that offers the best *return* after discounting for the level of *risk* that is associated with it. However, researchers in the field have found that the choice of an entry mode is also influenced by two other factors: (1) the *resources* available to the firm in the form of the financial and managerial capacity needed to serve a specific foreign market, and (2) the firm's felt need for *control* over the strategies and operations in the foreign market in order to improve its position and maximize the returns on the assets and skills it dedicated to the foreign venture.[80]

A higher level of ownership of the foreign venture results in greater operational control over it. However, it is also accompanied by a greater level of risk due to the higher commitment of resources required to sustain the firm's presence in the market.

Experience shows that the level of risk-adjusted return on investment, resource commitments, and degree of control increase as the firm's involvement in foreign operations increases from exporting to licensing/franchising to a joint venture and finally to a wholly owned subsidiary. The wholly owned subsidiary has the greatest level of risk-adjusted return on investment, high resource commitment, and a high level of control, whereas the exporting mode has the smallest of each of these attributes. The choice of an entry mode is a compromise involving a trade-off between the risk, return, resource commitment, and control associated with each entry mode.

There are two fundamental questions that one could ask: Under what circumstances would a firm export products abroad or choose to produce locally in the foreign market? Furthermore, if a firm chooses to produce the product locally, how would it do so? Would it choose to adopt nonequity entry modes such as licensing, franchising, or management service contracts, or would it choose equity modes like joint ventures or wholly owned subsidiaries?

The O-L-I Framework and Internationalization

Dunning proposed a comprehensive framework that includes the impact of firm-specific and location-specific factors that influence a firm's choice of entry mode after taking into account the risk, return, control, and resource commitments associated with each mode.[81] Specifically, Dunning's framework proposed that an entry mode for a target market is influenced by three determining factors: **ownership advantages**, **location advantages** (or *disadvantages*) of the target market, and **internalization** (by which he meant the advantages that would accrue to the firm from retaining specific transactions within the firm). As Dunning puts it:

> The propensity of an enterprise to engage in international production—that financed by foreign direct investment—rests on three main determinants; first the extent to which it possesses (or can acquire, on more favorable terms) assets which its competitors (or potential competitors) do not possess; second whether it is in its interest to sell or lease these assets to other firms, or make use of—internalize—them itself; and third, how far it is profitable to exploit these assets in conjunction with the indigenous resources of foreign countries rather than of the home country. The more the *ownership-specific advantages* possessed by an enterprise, the greater the inducement to *internalize* them; and the wider *the attractions of a foreign rather than a home country production base,* the greater the likelihood that an enterprise, given the incentive to do so, will engage in international production.[82]

We discuss the principal elements of Dunning's ownership, location, and internalization framework in the following paragraphs.

Ownership Advantages

Over the past four decades, international business literature has identified several reasons that international companies enter foreign markets financed by foreign direct investment. One of the most frequently mentioned reasons focuses on so-called ownership advantages. A firm's assets and skills include proprietary rights such as patents, trademarks, brand names, brand reputation, customer base, technological and marketing capability, particular raw materials essential to the production of the product, economies of large-scale production, and exclusive control over particular market outlets.[83] Firms enter foreign markets to exploit ownership advantages developed in their home or third-country markets. In doing so, they endeavor to choose an entry mode that offers a high degree of control. Ownership advantages also include tacit assets such as complex learning capabilities and organizational and operational routines that cannot be taught or learned through written or spoken words.[84] The net ownership advantages give international firms absolute advantage over firms in almost all locations. To compete with host-country firms in their own markets, firms must possess superior and additional ownership advantages sufficient to outweigh the costs of servicing an unfamiliar or distant environment.[85] This competitive advantage of firms is explained by imperfections in markets for goods or factors of production. In a theoretical world of perfect competition, firms produce homogeneous products and have equal access to all productive factors. In the real world of imperfect competition, as explained by industrial organization theory, firms acquire competitive advantages through product differentiation, brand names, marketing expertise, and technological superiority. A foreign firm that enjoys such a competitive advantage can extract a high-enough rent because of the inability to gain, or lack of access to, the knowledge, and skills owned by the foreign competitor.

Internalization

An international company can choose among a variety of entry mode choices, each of which affords the company varying degrees of control. The international operations of firms can be organized *internally,* within wholly owned subsidiaries, or *externally,* under arm's-length contracts with independent local producers. Internalization involves keeping activities and ownership of assets used in foreign operations within the firm. For example, a pharmaceutical company organizing internally would establish a wholly owned subsidiary abroad, rather than enter into a contractual agreement with a foreign company to manufacture its patented product in the latter's plant in the foreign country.

The main arguments for internalization extend the market imperfections approach by focusing on imperfections in intermediate-product markets, such as the knowledge and expertise embodied in patents, rather than on final-product markets, such as the knowledge underlying production, marketing, or other activities. As claimed by Johnson,[86] McManus,[87] and Magee,[88] knowledge is a public good,* and as such it can be transferred at zero or marginal cost from one party to another. Consequently, the firm that is responsible for its creation faces the difficulty of reaping the appropriate financial and nonfinancial benefits by itself. The optimal pricing of intermediate-product markets, particularly for types of knowledge and expertise embodied in patents and human capital, is extremely difficult under arm's-length transactions.[89] Property rights on the knowledge embodied in R&D-intensive products cannot be easily defined and enforced through contracts. It is difficult to write complete contracts between the international firm and third parties for the production of innovative products embodying breakthrough knowledge and technology. According to Kogut and Zander, the less codifiable, less teachable, and more complex the knowledge is, the more difficult it is to replicate and transfer across firms.[90] When production is carried out abroad, there is

---

*Bruce Kogut and Udo Zander explain the concept of a public good as follows: "By public good, it is meant that one party may enjoy the use of a common good (such as the rose bush planted on the property of the other party) without diminishing its availability to the other. The issue of market failure arises out of a problem whether the owner of the rose can "appropriate" a pecuniary payment from the neighbor." In "Knowledge of the Firm and Evolutionary Theory of the Multinational Corporation," *Journal of International Business Studies* 24, no. 4 (1993), p. 643.

always the danger that proprietary knowledge can easily be dissipated to third parties in production because of knowledge spillover or because of their opportunistic behavior. Moreover, the characteristics of such products cannot be specified a priori without disclosing proprietary information. Such market failures lead to a preference for internalizing transactions; that is, the system of hierarchical intrafirm relations replaces market-based transactions.[91]

The fact that the public good character of knowledge makes it easily transferable and hard to protect lies at the core of the theory of internalization. Buckley and Casson bring this idea to the fore:

> There is a special reason for believing that internalization of the knowledge market will generate a high degree of multinationality among firms. Because knowledge is a public good which is easily transmitted across national boundaries, its exploitation is logically an international operation; thus unless comparative advantage or other factors restrict production to a single country, internalization of knowledge will require each firm to operate a network of plants on a worldwide basis.[92]

Market failures of the type discussed in the above paragraph can occur also in a purely national firm and for transactions taking place in one country alone. However, the likelihood of market failures is greater when transactions occur between parties across national boundaries (e.g., an American international company conducting business transactions with a company based in India). Market failures occur more frequently in foreign operations because of the higher uncertainty involved (e.g., exchange rate fluctuations, political instability), insufficient information on the foreign market, problems with legal protection of property rights, and looser enforcement of contracts.

Location Advantages

It is assumed that an international company will invest in the most advantageous and attractive location. The attractiveness of a location is determined by its market potential and investment risk; investment incentives offered by the host-country government; location within, or in proximity to, a trade bloc (e.g., European Union, NAFTA); resource endowments; inexpensive unskilled or highly educated labor force (e.g., high-tech telecommunications and computer-related U.S. firms in India and China); and so on.

Several authors, including Buckley,[93] Casson,[94] and Dunning,[95] have emphasized that an international company's ownership or firm-specific advantages should be evaluated in relation to its competitors or in light of the competitive environment in host countries. This is because a specific advantage is valued in relation to the capabilities of competitors and peculiar characteristics of host countries.[96] For instance, a technologically intensive company like the U.S. company Hewlett-Packard may conceivably enjoy a greater competitive advantage over firms in a less developed country like Indonesia than over those in western Europe. Table 6.4 is a representation of the O-L-I theory of FDI.

TABLE 6.4
The O-L-I Theory of FDI

	Ownership	Location Advantage	Internalization
Export	X		X
Contractual/licensing, etc.	X	X	
Wholly owned	X	X	X

The O-L-I framework proposed by Dunning has been updated and revised and so remains the standard theoretical model for explaining the development of the multinational enterprise. This is not to say that there have not been challenges and variations proposed by other scholars.

An Alternative View on the Evolution of an International Company

The notion that *all* knowledge is a public good has been challenged by Kogut and Zander. They argue against the notion that all types of knowledge can be transferred at a cost to a third party. They argue that knowledge, especially that which is tacit and learned over a period of time within an organization (which they refer to as a *social community*) cannot be transferred (sold) to a third party at a price.

> The decision to transfer technology within the firm or in the market can be explained by the attributes of knowledge that constitute the ownership advantage of firms. A firm is a repository of knowledge that consists of how information is coded and action coordinated. The mode by which technology is transferred, e.g., within the firm or by licensing to other parties, is influenced by the characteristics of the advantage that motivates the growth of the firm across borders.[97]

They also challenge the notion that market failure (i.e., the hazard or cost of relying on the market) for intermediate goods leads their internalization within the firm, which leads to the creation of international companies when such a transaction occurs across national boundaries. They write:

> The multinational corporation arises not out of failure of markets for the buying and selling of knowledge, but out of its superior efficiency as an organizational vehicle by which to transfer this knowledge across borders. . . . The view we develop is that firms are social communities that serve as efficient mechanisms for the creation and transformation of knowledge into economically rewarded products and services. The relevant benchmark for whether a firm will transfer a technology internally is its efficiency in this respect relative to other firms. Market considerations are not required.[98]

Another view on the theory of FDI is the notable behavioral-based international network theory. This theory describes a multinational company as an internally differentiated and heterogeneous organizational system.[99] The MNC is viewed as a company that approaches global production, sales, and competition through a network of differentiated and interdependent subsidiaries that fulfill different objectives for the MNC. In addition, the MNC is not viewed as a static entity in the global marketplace but as one that is constantly changing. There are three central elements in this description of the MNC:

1. Strategic diversity in its organizational structure.
2. Internal relations and coordination mechanisms.
3. Internal flexibility and dynamism.

International network theory claims that the overseas subsidiaries of a multinational company can play different roles and have different responsibilities in the MNC global strategy that reflect differences in external environments and internal capabilities. Therefore, although O-L-I rationale would argue that a firm engage in direct investment in a certain country, the international network theory may conclude that from a global strategic viewpoint, it may make sense to engage in licensing in that country regardless of the resources and capabilities of the firm. The organizational structure and entry mode choices of the MNC are a function of its overall strategic goals.

Summary

We looked in this chapter at the factors affecting an international company's choice of mode for entering a foreign market. Generally, markets are entered to improve a company's competitive position, as an outgrowth of the corporate strategic process that we discussed in Chapter 5. A company desiring to enter foreign markets can choose from among several different modes of entry: exporting, countertrade, contract manufacturing, licensing, franchising, and equity-based ventures. Each mode involves different levels of control over foreign operations, capital investment, risk, and potential returns.

Exporting, the selling of one's goods or services in another country, is the simplest means of entering foreign markets, and it is usually the first step for a company going international. Exporting can be accomplished either indirectly, via an agent or forwarder, or directly, by an organizational subunit or subsidiary of the exporting company.

Countertrade refers to transactions involving a flow of goods or services in two or more directions. This is an important aspect of world trade, especially with developing and controlled economies. Countertrade can ease problems with inconvertible and fluctuating currencies, but it requires the ability to profitably dispose of the goods acquired through the countertrade agreement.

Licensing agreements allow a foreign company to use, in exchange for fees or royalties, another's patents and trademarks, manufacturing processes and know-how, trade secrets, or managerial and technical services. Foreign licensing involves more risk than straight exporting or countertrade, but it is less risky than direct investment in foreign production. Essentially, the firm is exporting its know-how instead of its products.

Franchising is a special type of licensing agreement. It involves a transfer of technology, business system, brand name, trademark, and other property rights by a franchisor to an independent company or person who is the franchisee. The franchisee is expected to duplicate the business model of the franchisor. The fast-food chain of McDonald's has franchise restaurants all over the world.

Equity-based ventures—both wholly owned and joint ventures—involve some degree of ownership and control of a foreign venture by the international company. The choice of joint venture will be influenced by company, industry, market, and country conditions. Maintaining the necessary control over a joint venture is crucial for the international company. However, control can be imposed by equity as well as nonequity mechanisms. In this chapter, we emphasized the importance as well as the risks of collaborating with international partners. The equity-based joint venture was discussed initially from the perspective of environmental conditions that influence this choice of entry mode. Then we looked at firm-specific motives for international joint ventures and illustrated a matrix that delineates product and geographic diversification rationale. Advantages and disadvantages of this entry mode were delineated, and we emphasized the importance of the right partner because with the wrong partner many international joint ventures do not meet stated objectives and dissolve prematurely. Also, issues dealing with control over and negotiation of the international joint venture were covered.

The chapter then identified another form of international collaboration, the international strategic alliance. We paralleled the motives, advantages, and risks with those already discussed for international joint ventures. Furthermore, we discussed tactics for actually making both equity and nonequity alliances work, including partner selection, trust established continually yet incrementally, a balanced power structure between alliance partners, and patience by the alliance partners. We also discussed the framework for partner selection, which includes reciprocity, trust, lack of opportunism, strategic direction convergence, and cultural nearness.

The chapter concluded with a discussion of the theories that try to explain different entry mode choices by a multinational company. Specifically we discussed Dunning's O-L-I theory and some dissenting viewpoints on this theory. The choice of entry mode by an international firm is among the most significant decisions that a firm will make, and it is influenced by firm capability, industry factors, location-specific factors, venture-specific factors, and strategic factors. Risk and resource requirements must be balanced in a manner appropriate to each entry mode decision.

Key Terms and Concepts

contract manufacturing, *210*
countertrade, *208*
dissemination risk, *235*
equity international joint venture, *219*
franchising, *215*
internalization, *239*
international reciprocity, *233*
international strategic alliance, *229*
licensing, *210*
location advantage, *239*
ownership advantage, *239*
partner trust, *232*
systemic risk, *235*

Discussion Questions

1. What factors do international firms consider when choosing how to enter a foreign market?
2. What are the pros and cons of international licensing agreements as compared to exporting and foreign direct investment?
3. Why do firms pursue international joint ventures? (*Hint:* Think of the "four-quadrant" framework.)
4. What are the various advantages and disadvantages of international joint ventures for the international firm?
5. Create a profile of a foreign partner for your international joint venture. What characteristics are desirable? What characteristics would you wish to avoid?
6. What is the O-L-I framework? Give examples of each dimension of this framework.

Minicase

Tommy Hilfiger in India, 2007

Mohan Murjani, the Hong Kong–based nonresident Indian who owns the rights for Tommy Hilfiger in India, was instrumental in bringing about a strategic licensing agreement between the $6 billion Tommy Hilfiger Corporation and the Arvind Group of Ahmedabad. Under the licensing agreement, Arvind Brands, a wholly owned subsidiary of Arvind Mills of the Lalbhai Group, will sell Tommy Hilfiger apparel in India. Arvind Murjani Brands is a joint venture between the Murjani Group and Arvind brands. Plans to market the products through exclusive Tommy Hilfiger stores and departmental chains were developed in 2002. The approvals from the Reserve Bank of India and Foreign Investment Promotion Board were granted in 2003.

During 2006, the retailer launched four new outlets in India, in Ahmedabad, Bangalore, Delhi, and Lucknow. These sites are in addition to stores already located in Bangalore, Chandigarh, Gurgaon, Hyderabad, and Kolkata. As of 2007, all nine Hilfiger outlets in India were franchised.

DISCUSSION QUESTIONS

1. Evaluate the long-term implications of the decision of Tommy Hilfiger to sell the rights to Mr. Murjani for Tommy Hilfiger products in India.
2. What should Tommy Hilfiger consider in the licensing agreement with the Arvind Group?
3. How can Tommy Hilfiger ensure its brand reputation in India?
4. Can Tommy Hilfiger control the operations of Arvind Brands?
5. Given the expansion in 2006 and 2007, should Tommy Hilfiger consider the equity international joint venture option?

Notes

1. Y. Wind and H. Perlmutter, "On the Identification of Frontier Issues in International Marketing," *Columbia Journal of World Business* 12 (1977), pp. 131–139; I. Ekeledo and K. Sivakumar, "Foreign Market Entry Mode Choice of Service Firms," *Academy of Marketing Science Journal* 26, no. 4 (1998), pp. 274–292.
2. O. Andersen, "Internationalization and Market Entry: A Review of Theories and Conceptual Frameworks," *Management International Review* 37, no. 2 (1997), pp. 27–42.
3. M. Erramilli and C. Rao, "Service Firms' International Entry Mode: A Modified Transaction-Cost Analysis Approach," *Journal of Marketing* 57, no. 3 (1993), pp. 19–38.
4. J. Roberts, "The Internationalisation of Business Service Firms: A Stages Approach," *The Service Industry Journal* 19, no. 4 (1999), pp. 68–88.
5. D. Domke-Damonte, "Interactive Effects on International Strategy and Throughput Technology on Entry Mode for Service Firms," *Management International Review* 40, no. 1 (2000) pp. 41–59.
6. B. Kogut and H. Singh, "The Effect of National Culture on the Choice of Entry Mode," *Journal of International Business Studies* 19, no. 4 (1988), pp. 411–432.
7. H. Barkema, J. Bell, and J. Pennings, "Foreign Entry, Cultural Barriers and Learning," *Strategic Management Journal* 17 (1996), pp. 151–166.
8. S. Agarwal, "Socio-cultural Distance and the Choice of Joint Venture: A Contingency Perspective," *Journal of International Marketing* 2, no. 2 (1994), pp. 63–80.
9. F. Root, *Entry Strategies for International Markets* (Lexington, MA: Lexington Books, 1994).
10. V. Terpstra and C. Yu, "Determinants of Foreign Investment in U.S. Advertising Agencies," *Journal of International Business Studies* 19, no. 1 (1988) pp. 33–46.
11. K. Banerji and R. Sambharya, "Vertical Keiretsu and International Market Entry: The Case of the Japanese Automobile Ancillary Industry," *Journal of International Business Studies* 27, no. 1 (1996), pp. 89–113.
12. Y. Pan, S. Li, and D. Tse, "The Impact of Order and Mode of Entry on Profitability and Market Share," *Journal of International Business Studies* 30, no. 1 (1999), pp. 81–103.
13. Y. Pan, and D. Tse, "The Hierarchical Model of Market Entry Modes," *Journal of International Business Studies* 31, no. 4 (2000), pp. 535–554.
14. J. W. Dizard, "The Explosion of International Barter," *Fortune,* February 1983, pp. 88–95.
15. "Economic Incentives for Countertrade," with Rolf Mirus, *Journal of International Business Studies,* Autumn 1986, pp. 27–39.
16. M. J. McCarthy, "Why Countertrade Is Getting Hot," *Fortune,* June 29, 1992, p. 25.
17. A. S. Konigsberg, "Around the World with Franchise Legislation," *Franchising World,* May–June 1999, pp. 18–22.
18. "CCH Business Owners Toolkit: Checklist of Basic Franchise Agreements," www.toolkit.cch.com/tools/franch_m.asp.
19. A. Arino, "Measures of Strategic Alliance Performance: An Analysis of Construct Validity," *Journal of International Business Studies* 34 (2003), pp. 66–79.
20. M. Koza and A. Lewin, "The Co-evolution of Strategic Alliances," *Organization Science* 9, no. 3 (1998), pp. 255–264.
21. A. Arino, "Measures of Strategic Alliance Performance: An Analysis of Construct Validity," *Journal of International Business Studies* 34 (2003), pp. 66–79.
22. P. Dussuage, B. Garrette, and W. Mitchell, "Learning from Competing Partners: Outcomes and Durations of Scale and Link Alliances in Europe, North America and Asia," *Strategic Management Journal* 21, no. 2 (2000), pp. 99–126.
23. B. Kogut, "Joint Ventures: Theoretical and Empirical Perspectives," *Strategic Management Journal* 9 (1988), pp. 319–332.
24. K. Harrigan, "Joint Ventures and Competitive Strategy," *Strategic Management Journal* 9 (1988), pp. 141–158.
25. W. Newberry and Y. Zeira, "Generic Differences between Equity International Joint Ventures, International Acquisitions and International Greenfield Investments: Implications for Parent Companies," *Journal of World Business* 32, no. 2 (1997), pp. 87–102.

26. C. Woodcock, P. Beamish, and S. Makino, "Ownership-Based Entry Mode Strategies and International Performance," *Journal of International Business Studies* 25, no. 2 (1994), pp. 253–273.
27. F. Contractor and P. Lorange, "Why Should Firms Cooperate? The Strategy and Economics Basis for Cooperative Ventures," *International Marketing Review* (Spring 1986), pp. 74–85.
28. Adapted from P. Beamish, A. Morrisom, A. Inkpen, and P. Rosenzweig, *International Management* (New York: McGraw-Hill/Irwin, 2003), p. 123.
29. J. Brett, D. Shapiro, and A. Lytle, "Breaking the Bonds of Reciprocity in Negotiations," *Academy of Management Journal* 41, no. 4 (1998), pp. 410–424.
30. M. Lyles, "Common Mistakes of Joint Venture Experienced Firms," *Columbia Journal of World Business,* Summer 1987, pp. 79–85.
31. A. Inkpen and P. Beamish, "Knowledge, Bargaining Power and the Instability of International Joint Ventures," *Academy of Management Review* 22, no. 1 (1997), pp. 177–202.
32. J. Brett, D. Shapiro, and A. Lytle, "Breaking the Bonds of Reciprocity in Negotiations," *Academy of Management Journal* 41, no. 4 (1998), pp. 410–424.
33. S. Weiss, "Analysis of Complex Negotiations in International Business: The RBC Perspective," *Organization Science,* May 1993, pp. 269–283.
34. D. Datta, "International Joint Ventures: A Framework for Analysis," *Journal of General Management,* Winter 1988, pp. 78–91.
35. J. Graham, "The Influence of Culture on the Process of Business Negotiations," *Journal of International Business Studies,* Spring 1988, pp. 81–96.
36. K. Brouthers and G. Bamossy, "The Role of Key Stakeholders in International Joint Ventures: Case Studies from Eastern Europe," *Journal of International Business Studies* 28, no. 2 (1997), pp. 359–373.
37. Y. Doz, "Government Policies and Global Industries," in M. E. Porter, ed., *Competition in Global Industries* (Boston: Harvard Business School Press, 1986), pp. 225–266.
38. R. Kashlak, "Establishing Financial Targets for Joint Ventures in Emerging Countries: A Conceptual Model," *Journal of Management* 4 (1998), pp. 241–258.
39. F. Contractor, "Strategies for Structuring Joint Ventures: A Negotiations Planning Paradigm," *Columbia Journal of World Business,* Summer 1984, pp. 30–39.
40. U. Gupta, "Sony Adopts Strategy to Broaden Ties with Small Firms," *Wall Street Journal,* February 28, 1991, p. B2.
41. T. Das and B. Teng, "A Risk Perception Model of Alliance Structuring," *Journal of Management* 7(2001), pp. 1–29.
42. S. Park and M. Russo, "When Competition Eclipses Cooperation: An Event History Analysis of Joint Venture Failure," *Management Science* 42 (1996), pp. 875–890.
43. T. Das and B. Teng, "A Risk Perception Model of Alliance Structuring," *Journal of Management* 7(2001), pp. 1–29.
44. A. Parkhe, "Messy Research, Methodological Predispositions and Theory Development in International Joint Ventures," *Academy of Management Review* 18 (1993), pp. 794–829.
45. H. Steensma and M. Lyles, "Explaining IJV Survival in a Transitional Economy through Social Exchange and Knowledge-Based Perspectives, *Strategic Management Journal* 21 (2000), pp. 831–851.
46. Anoop Madhok, "Revisiting Multinational Firms' Tolerance for Joint Ventures: A Trust-Based Approach," *Journal of International Business Studies,* First Quarter, 1995, pp. 117–137; Paul W. Bemish and John C. Banks, "Equity Joint Ventures and the Theory of the Multinational Enterprise," *Journal of International Business Studies* 18, no. 2 (1987), pp. 1–16; Arvind Parkhe, "Interfirm Diversity, Organizational Learning, and Longevity in Global Strategic Alliances," *Journal of International Business Studies* 20 (1991), pp. 579–601.
47. R. Kashlak, R. Chandran, and A. DiBenedetto, "Reciprocity in International Business: A Study of Telecommunications Contracts and Alliances," *Journal of International Business Studies* 29 (1998), pp. 281–304.

48. P. Aulakh, M. Kotabe, and A. Shay, "Trust and Performance in Cross-Border Marketing Partnerships: A Behavioral Approach," *Journal of International Business Studies* 27, no. 5 (1996), pp. 1005–1032.
49. J. Bradach, and R. Eccles, "Price, Authority and Trust: From Ideal Types to Plural Forms," *American Review of Sociology,* 15 (1989), pp. 97–118; A. Parkhe, "Strategic Alliance Restructuring: A Game Theoretic and Transaction Cost Examination Of Interfirm Cooperation," *Academy of Management Journal* 36, no. 4 (1993), pp. 794–829.
50. Parkhe, "Strategic Alliance Restructuring."
51. A. Yan, "Structural Stability and Reconfiguration of International Joint Ventures," *Journal of International Business Studies* 29 (1998), pp. 773–796.
52. H. Mjoen and S. Tallman, "Control and Performance in International Joint Ventures," *Organization Science* 8 (1997), pp. 508–527.
53. Contractor and Kundu, "Model Choices in a World of Alliances," p. 329.
54. Charles W. Hill, Peter Hwang, and Chan W. Kim, "An Eclectic Theory of the Choice of International Entry Mode," *Strategic Management Journal* 11 (1990), pp. 117–128.
55. Ibid.
56. Ibid.
57. Sanjeev Agarwal and Sridhar Ramaswami, "Choice of Foreign Market Entry Made," *Journal of International Business Studies* 23, no. 1 (1992), pp. 1–28.
58. Krishna M. Erramilli, "The Experience Factor in Foreign Market Entry Behavior of Service Firms," *Journal of International Business Studies* 22, no. 3 (1991), pp. 479–501.
59. Bruce Kogut and Harbir Singh, "Entering United States by Joint Venture: Competitive Rivalry and Industry Structure," in Farok Contractor and Peter Lorange, eds., *Cooperative Strategies in International Business* (Lexington, MA: Lexington Books, 1988).
60. Gary Hamel and C. K Prahalad, "Do You Really Have a Global Strategy," *Harvard Business Review,* July–August 1985.
61. Hill, Hwang, and Chan, "An Eclectic Theory of the Choice of International Entry Mode."
62. Oliver E. Williamson, *Markets and Hierarchies: An Analysis of Antitrust Implications* (New York: Free Press, 1975); David J. Teece, "The Multinational Enterprise: Market Failure and Market Power Considerations," *Sloan Management Review,* September 1981.
63. Kogut and Singh, "Entering United States by Joint Venture."
64. Agarwal and Ramaswami, "Choice of Foreign Market Entry Mode."
65. Chan W. Kim and Peter Hwang, "Global Strategy and Multinationals' Entry Mode Choice," *Journal of International Business Studies* 23, no. 11 (1992), pp. 29–53.
66. Agarwal and Ramaswami, "Choice of Foreign Market Entry Mode."
67. Bruce Kogut and Harbir Singh, "The Effect of National Culture on the Choice of Entry Mode," *Journal of International Business Studies,* Fall 1988.
68. Krishna M. Erramilli and C. P. Rao, "Choice of Market Entry Modes by Service Firms: Role of Market Knowledge," *Management International Review* 30, no. 22 (1990).
69. Ibid.
70. Hubert Gatignon and Erin Anderson, "The Multinational Corporation's Degree of Control over Foreign Subsidiaries: An Empirical Test of a Transaction Cost Explanation," *Journal of Law Economics and Organization* 4, no. 22 (1988).
71. Agarwal and Ramaswami, "Choice of Foreign Market Entry Mode."
72. Kim and Hwang, "Global Strategy and Multinationals' Entry Mode Choice."
73. Ibid.
74. Gatignon and Anderson, "The Multinational Corporation's Degree of Control"; Kogut and Singh, "The Effect of National Culture on the Choice of Entry Mode."
75. Richard N. Osborn and Christopher C. Baughn, "Forms of Inter-organizational Alliances," *Academy of Management Journal* 33, no. 33 (1990), pp. 503–519.

76. Hamel and Prahalad, "Do You Really Have a Global Strategy?"
77. Kim and Hwang, "Global Strategy and Multinationals' Entry Mode Choice."
78. Ibid.
79. Georgio Barba Navaretti, Jan I. Haaland, and Anthony Venables, "Multinational Corporations and Global Production Networks: The Implications for Trade Policy," report prepared for the European Commission Directorate General for Trade (London: Centre for Economic Policy Research, 2002).
80. Frank V. Cespedes, "Control vs. Resources in Channel Design: Distribution Differences in One Industry," *Industrial Marketing Management* 17 (1988), pp. 215–227; John M. Stopford and Louis T. Wells, *Managing the Multinational Enterprise: Organization of the Firm and Ownership of the Subsidiaries* (New York: Basic Books, 1972); Erin Anderson and Hubert Gatignon, "Modes of Foreign Entry: A Transaction Cost Analysis and Propositions," *Journal of International Business Studies* 17 (Fall 1986), pp. 1–26.
81. John H. Dunning, "Toward an Eclectic Paradigm of International Production: A Restatement and Some Possible Extensions," *Journal of International Business Studies* 19 (Spring 1988), pp. 1–31.
82. John H. Dunning, "Toward an Eclectic Theory of International Production: Some Empirical Tests," *Journal of International Business Studies* 11, no. 1 (Spring–Summer 1980), p. 9.
83. Ibid., p. 10.
84. Alan M. Rugman and Alain Verbeke, "Extending the Theory of the Multinational Enterprise: Internalization and Strategic Management Perspectives," *Journal of International Business Studies* 34, no. 2 (2003), p. 127.
85. Dunning, "Toward an Eclectic Theory of International Production," p. 9; Agarwal and Ramaswami, "Choice of Foreign Market Entry Mode," p. 4.
86. J. Johnson, "The Efficiency and Welfare Implications of the Multinational Corporation," in Charles Kindelberger, ed., *The International Corporation* (Cambridge, MA: MIT Press, 1970).
87. J. McManus, "The Theory of the International Firm," in G. Paquet, ed., *The Multinational Firm and the Nation State* (Ontario: Collier Macmillan Canada, 1972).
88. Stephen Magee, "Information and the Multinational Corporation: An Appropriability Theory of Foreign Direct Investment," in Jagdish N. Bhagwati, ed., *The New International Economic Order* (Cambridge, MA: MIT Press, 1977).
89. Peter J. Buckley and Mark Casson, *The Future of the Multinational Enterprise* (New York: Holmes and Meier, 1976), p. 33.
90. Bruce Kogut and Udo Zander, "Knowledge of the Firm and the Evolutionary Theory of the Multinational Corporation," *Journal of International Business Studies* 24, no. 4 (1993), pp. 625–646.
91. Navaretti, Haaland, and Venables, "Multinational Corporations and Global Production Networks."
92. Buckley and Casson, *The Future of the Multinational Enterprise*, p. 45
93. Peter J. Buckley, "Problems and Developments in the Core Theory of International Business," *Journal of International Business Studies* 21, no. 4 (1990), pp. 657–666.
94. Mark C. Casson, *The Firm and the Market* (Oxford, England: Basil Blackwell, 1987).
95. Dunning, "Toward an Eclectic Theory of International Production," pp. 9–31.
96. Sanjay Lall and S. Siddharthan, "The Monopolistic Advantages of Multinationals: Lessons from Foreign Investment in the U.S.," *Economic Journal* 92 (September 1982), p. 679.
97. Kogut and Zander, "Knowledge of the Firm and the Evolutionary Theory of the Multinational Corporation," p. 626.
98. Ibid., p. 627.
99. Christopher A. Bartlett and Sumantra Ghoshal, *Managing across Borders: The Transnational Solution* (Boston: Harvard Business School Press, 1989); Nitin Nohria and Sumantra Ghoshal, *The Differentiated Network: Organizing Multinational Corporations for Value Creation* (San Francisco: Jossey-Bass, 1997).

CHAPTER SEVEN

Organizing and Controlling International Operations

Chapter Learning Objectives

After completing this chapter, the student will be able to:

- Understand the relationship between organizations' international strategies and their respective organizational structures and control systems.
- Understand the factors that affect an organization's choice of structure.
- Distinguish among various types of global structures, including product structure, geographic structure, global matrix structure, and transnational and heterarchical structures.
- Discuss the benefits and potential problems of each distinct global-oriented structure.
- Compare and contrast output control, behavior control, and input control.
- Discuss problems of control that are particular to international companies.
- Discuss the different categories of parent–subsidiary relationships and the strategic control mechanisms appropriate to each.
- Identify the effects of various host-country environments on a firm's international control system.

Opening Case: The Americanization of a Japanese Icon

Since moving to the U.S. 15 years ago, Nicaragua-born Roberto Castillo has had a series of jobs at car dealerships—first Ford, then Pontiac, and eventually Hyundai. But two years ago, he landed the job he really wanted: selling Toyotas. "Toyotas are easier to sell than any other car," he says. "Everyone knows the reputation, so you never have to sell [people] on the benefits." Nowadays, Castillo works at Longo Toyota in the Los Angeles suburb of El Monte. Castillo isn't Longo's top salesman, but last year he piled up commissions worth more than $80,000. As he says: "You can make good money with Toyota."

Tell that to Tetsuo Kawano. He runs a Toyota dealership in a beachfront Yokohama suburb in Japan. Recently Kawano held a promotion featuring FM deejay Haruhisa Kurihara. The event drew about 75 young Japanese with bleached hair, baggy pants, and goatees. The idea was to move a few Toyota Vitz subcompacts; the crowd enjoyed the music and free doughnuts, but there wasn't much interest in the product. "I'm here because I like the deejay," said Kidokoro Katsumi, 21. And the cars? "I just bought a Honda." Says a rueful Kawano: "We're selling into a shrinking market."

Booming in the U.S., but running out of gas in Japan? That was never Toyota's global strategy. Ten years ago, Japan's foremost auto maker had a multipronged attack plan: grow steadily at home, make modest gains in the U.S., make money in Europe, and take over Southeast Asia. Well, things have changed. Japan has become the incredible shrinking market. The European conquest, though still possible, is a dream deferred. And Southeast Asia has stalled out. That leaves the U.S., the one market where sales remain robust. Toyota's American strategy, in short, has become Toyota's lifeline.

The importance of the U.S. raises questions about what kind of company Toyota will become. How far will the Japanese leadership let the Americanization of Toyota go? How will the importance of the North American market affect Toyota's international thrust? And most important, with future profits so dependent on the U.S., how easy will it be for Toyota to drive its current 10% share of the U.S. market to 15%—or even 20%?

Toyota, the world's third-largest auto maker—2001 sales hit $108 billion and operating profits $4.2 billion—will struggle with these and other questions over the next few years. Still, despite trepidation about the company's increasingly American tilt back at headquarters in Toyota City, about 100 km east of Nagoya, the way forward seems clear. Says Toyota Chief Executive Fujio Cho: "We must Americanize." The process is already well under way. Consider the following facts, including some statistics that scare the wits out of Toyota's rivals in Detroit:

- Last year, Toyota sold more vehicles in the U.S. (1.74 million) than in Japan (1.71 million). Although Toyota doesn't break out foreign-derived earnings, analysts figure that almost two-thirds of the company's operating profit comes from the United States.
- Toyota's U.S. factories and dealerships currently employ 123,000 Americans—that's more than Coca-Cola (KO), Microsoft (MSFT), and Oracle (ORCL) combined.
- Toyota's top U.S. execs are, increasingly, local hires. The recently appointed manager of the key Georgetown (Ky.) plant, which makes the Camry, is Ford Motor Co. veteran Gary Convis. "Thirty years ago, we were more dependent on Japan," says James Press, chief operating officer of Toyota Motor Sales USA Inc. in Torrance, Calif. Now, "there's not much Japanese influence on a day-to-day basis."
- Toyota's biggest hits in the U.S.—the Camry sedan, Tundra pickup, and Sequoia SUV—were all designed with the American consumer in mind with significant input from U.S. design teams. Now, Toyota is launching a much-anticipated third brand: Scion, aimed at America's youth.
- With its 10% U.S. market share, Toyota is within striking distance of DaimlerChrysler's 14.5%. Some auto executives think it's only a matter of time before Toyota steals DaimlerChrysler's place in the Big Three.

It's easy to see why Toyota has become so focused on the U.S. market. While the company has never forfeited its dominant position in Japan, its market share is slipping steadily, while profit margins per vehicle are now an estimated 5%, vs. 13% in the U.S. In recessionary Japan, Toyota failed to shift production quickly enough into minivans and cheaper subcompacts, sticking instead with pricier sedans. Its rivals, by contrast, have adapted to changing demand, putting unaccustomed pressure on Toyota. "The Japanese market has gotten much more competitive, with Nissan back on track and Honda on a roll," says Chris Richter, an analyst at HSBC Securities Inc. in Tokyo. And Toyota's move into Europe has been slower than expected. While Toyota is doing better than Honda and Nissan, it still loses money on nearly every car it sells there.

Which brings us back to the U.S. Toyota's top brass won't discuss market-share goals: The last thing the company wants to do is ruffle feathers in Washington by publicly targeting DaimlerChrysler. But top Toyota officials are emphatic about where Toyota will direct its energies. "The American market is our top priority, bar none," says Cho, who in February became the first foreign exec to be inducted into the U.S. Automotive Hall of Fame. "We'll do whatever it takes to succeed there." The company is already planning to ramp up production capacity in the U.S. to more than 1.45 million units by 2005, from 1.25 million now. And in the next two to three years, it hopes to be selling a total of 2 million vehicles a year, including imports, in the U.S. market.

Of course, deep inside Toyota, ambivalence lingers about the growing clout of the American division. Toyota traditionalists are reluctant to stray even an inch from the Toyota Way, a philosophy set forth by the company's legendary founder, Kiichiro Toyoda, a zealot for consensus-style decision-making, merciless cost-cutting, and fanatical devotion to quality and customer satisfaction. Toyoda's focus on such basics has guided Toyota's growth over the past 65 years. In fact, it has been U.S. auto makers who learned from the Japanese, not the other way around.

To ensure that Toyota doesn't lose the essence of what makes it great, the company in February opened the Toyota Institute, an internal, MBA-style program near Toyota City whose faculty will comprise Toyota execs and visiting professors from the University of Pennsylvania's Wharton School. "We don't have the bench strength to rely solely on Japanese managers anymore," says Takashi Hata, Toyota's global human-resources guru. "But we must remain faithful to the fundamentals that got us where we are today as a company."

The fact is Toyota and its U.S. subsidiaries don't always see eye to eye, especially when it comes to making design choices for the American market. Sometimes the conflicts are over small issues; one Toyota official in Japan, for example, says interior color schemes are a constant source of friction. At other times, there are clashes over crucial product-strategy decisions. "They have to be dragged kicking and screaming into bigger products," says Jim Olson, a senior vice-president at Toyota Motor North America Inc. in New York City.

In the late 1990s, Japanese product planners resisted their U.S. colleagues' idea that the company should produce a V8 pickup truck for the American market. To change their minds, U.S. execs took their Japanese counterparts to a Dallas Cowboys football game—with a pit stop in the Texas Stadium parking lot. There, the Japanese saw row upon row of full-size pickups. Finally, it dawned on them that Americans see the pickup as more than a commercial vehicle, considering it primary transportation. Result: the red-hot Tundra, which sells for about $25,000.

Now, it's harder than ever for executives in Japan to second-guess their American colleagues. "Once we started building products [in the U.S.] and we were responsible for keeping those factories running," says Donald V. Esmond, senior vice-president of the Torrance sales arm, "then the chief engineers started listening a lot closer in terms of what products we need in the market." The proof that American marketers know their business is in the numbers. March sales of the $20,000 Camry, a sedan revamped for the U.S., surged 24.1% over the same month last year. Sales of the Highlander SUV were up 28.4%.

However successfully Toyota blends the essence of the Toyota Way with a dash of American salesmanship, increasing market share in the U.S. from now on will be a bigger challenge. "Toyota [has] very complete product coverage," says George Peterson, president of AutoPacific Group Inc., a market-research company in Tustin, Calif. "There are very few holes in its lineup." More ominously, Toyota could face in the U.S. the same problem it does in Japan: smaller rivals taking daring design steps that attract new customers. Already, Nissan Motor Co.'s redesigned Altima and Infiniti G35, with their head-turning styling, are luring Americans from the Camry and Lexus line. And South Korea's traditionally no-frills Hyundai is moving inexorably upscale with such cars as the XG350, a family sedan that is thousands of dollars cheaper than the Camry.

Still, given Toyota's U.S. momentum, even stiffer competition from Honda and Nissan won't have a dramatic impact in the short term. Indeed, to increase market share, all Toyota need do is crank up U.S. production. Right now there is more demand for such models as the Lexus RX 300 and Highlander SUVs than Toyota can fill. "They could get a full share point just by bringing Highlander production to the U.S.," says a well-placed analyst. The company already plans to make the RX 300 in Canada. As a result, Toyota should have no trouble "dialing up their U.S. sales through the remainder of the decade," says one analyst.

But Toyota does have an Achilles' heel: its aging customer base. The average age of a Toyota buyer in the U.S. is 45, the highest among Japanese carmakers. Press says Toyota has already halted the aging process by revamping the Celica coupe and MR2 Spyder roadster. Yet neither sold well last year. Nor did the Echo, the first Toyota subcompact aimed at Generation Y and younger. A moderate hit in Japan, it is a flop with young drivers in the U.S., who prefer the Ford Focus or any Volkswagen.

Toyota Chairman Hiroshi Okuda jokingly said last year that his company should move its headquarters to the U.S. That is extremely unlikely. Nonetheless, this most Japanese of Japanese auto makers knows its U.S. strategy is crucial to future prosperity. The company that Kiichiro Toyoda founded still has its roots in Japan, but its destiny is all-American.

Source: C. Dawson, L. Armstrong, J. Muller, and K. Kerwin, "The Americanization of a Japanese Icon; Toyota's Quandary: Should It Concentrate on Its U.S. Success or Shift Focus to Markets Sorely in Need of Help?" *BusinessWeek*, April 15, 2002.

Discussion Questions

1. What type of strategic mind-set (global, multidomestic, transnational) does Toyota exhibit?
2. How might the emerging importance of the U.S. market and the subsequent "Americanization of Toyota" affect the way the firm is organized internationally?
3. Is communication and knowledge flow important for Toyota? What international organization structure would you recommend for Toyota to implement?

The Strategy–Structure Linkage for the International Firm

As evidenced with Toyota in the opening case, the issue of designing an international firm's organization structure must be thought of as a continual process[1] that answers this question: How should an international business design its organization to achieve both effectiveness and efficiency of globally integrating its business functions? Toyota is facing this challenge as the American market has grown in strategic importance. Furthermore, this is a tremendous challenge for international firms as they disperse business activities worldwide to cope with increased global pressures.[2] The strategy–structure linkage is an international business topic that is both highly discussed and highly researched.[3] Organizations may have a variety of hierarchical and nonhierarchical structures[4] that are designed to effectively implement given strategic initiatives. In general, organizations are structured to link the behavior of individuals; to collect and pool information, skills, or capital; to engage in related actions toward the achievement of a set of goals; and to monitor performance, initiate corrections, and define new goals.

In a strictly domestic enterprise, these aims can be achieved with a two-dimensional organization, that is, an organization that concerns itself with resolving the potentially conflicting demands of functional (production, finance, marketing, etc.) and product-line requirements. As exemplified in the previous chapters, the organization has various strategic choices regarding expansion. Figure 7.1 illustrates these choices as:

- **Vertical expansion,** which takes the firm into new activities either forward or backward along the value chain of its existing product line.
- **Product expansion,** which takes the firm into new product markets, whether related or unrelated to its current core businesses.
- **Geographic expansion,** which takes the firm into new overseas markets, thus creating the multinational enterprise.

A two-dimensional organization is not the appropriate structure for a multinational enterprise because it must be able not only to resolve functional and product-line

FIGURE 7.1
Firm Expansion and Organization of Activities

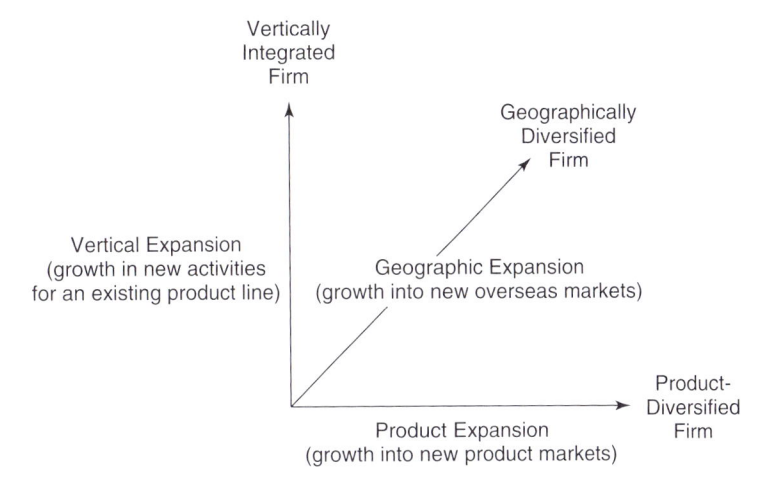

demands but also to deal effectively with the external environmental concerns outlined in Section 1 of this book. Thus, a more appropriate organizational form for a multinational enterprise may combine four dimensions:

1. **Functional expertise** of the value chain activities in which the firm is involved.
2. **Product and technical know-how** of the various lines of business in which the firm is involved.
3. **Knowledge of the countries and regions** where the firm has business interests.
4. **Customer expertise** regarding similar market segments and major accounts that cut across various regions and countries.

The manner in which these dimensions are combined should and does differ from one international company to another. There is no one best way for organizing an international company, and each company will combine these four dimensions in an organizational structure that it tries to make consistent with its own particular strategy.

As Figure 7.2 illustrates, to effectively implement its desired strategies, an international firm must effectively link its structure, culture, systems, and people with its stated strategy. In this chapter, we focus on the various structures that international firms use to effectively implement their respective strategies. We discuss the

FIGURE 7.2
Linking International Strategy Formulation and Implementation

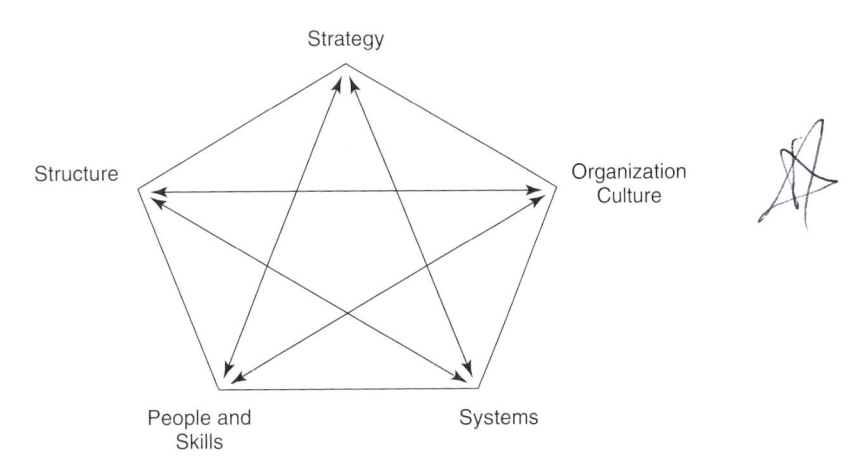

traditional structures as well as newer ways to organize in light of the tremendous changes occurring in the various industry and country environments.

In the early stages of international business as a discipline, the firm's international organization was identified as a response to three major strategic concerns: (1) how to encourage a predominantly domestic organization to take full advantage of growth opportunities abroad; (2) how to blend product knowledge and geographic area knowledge most efficiently in coordinating worldwide business; and (3) how to coordinate the activities of foreign units in many countries while permitting each to retain its own identity. Responses to each of these concerns will differ, depending on the firm's situation and the overall philosophy of top management. In this chapter we focus on the organizational design and ongoing control of international enterprises, that is, on the formal arrangement of relationships between the various domestic and foreign organizational units in the multinational network and the mechanisms provided for their coordination into a unified whole.

The organizational structures of international firms that are covered in this chapter include the following basic hierarchical structures: the pre–international division phase, the international division, the global product structure, and the global area structure. The benefits and concerns of these structures are identified. Furthermore, we identify newer structures that must be considered by firms operating in certain international industries. These structures include the matrix organization, the transnational structure, and the heterarchical structure. Figure 7.3 illustrates these structures and provides a framework for understanding how a firm may evolve its international structure. This framework is based on two critical dimensions for the international firm. The first is *foreign product diversity,* which is an indicator of the number of different products and services a firm sells internationally. It represents the breadth of the firm's international activities. The second dimension is *foreign sales as a percentage of total sales,* which is an indicator of the importance to the firm of the aggregate overseas markets. As will be seen in the discussions below, this framework will help provide a basis for the strategy–structure linkage as well as for changes in a firm's organizational structure.

In most cases, a multinational firm's organizational structure is neither predetermined nor permanently fixed; rather, it evolves continuously to correspond with changes in the firm's strategy. As a firm's operations grow and spread to new foreign markets, its organizational structure typically becomes overburdened. As the pressures intensify and threaten the current organizational structure, the firm is normally

FIGURE 7.3
International Strategy versus International Structure

Source: Adapted from W. Egelhoff, "Strategy and Structure in Multinational Corporations: A Revision of the Stopford and Wells Model," *Strategic Management Journal* 9 (1988), pp. 1–14.

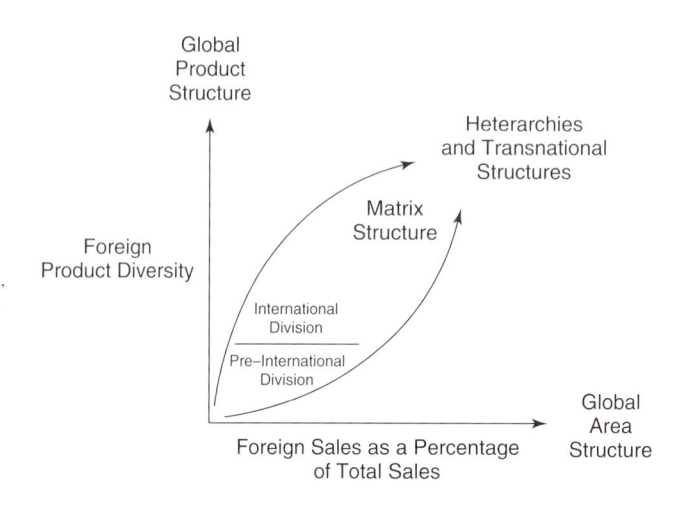

compelled to experiment with and evolve to alternate organizational forms. Furthermore, the structure must fit with the firm's international environment.[5]

Eventually the firm chooses a structure that is consistent with its new international expansion strategy and is capable of handling its expanding operations. The replacement structure chosen is typically influenced by the structure that preceded it because the experience of the company with one structure provides a building block for future structures.

Although we stated earlier that there is no one best organizational structure for multinational enterprises, this does not mean that every firm's organizational structure is unique or that there is no rationale for a firm's structural development. On the contrary, there are certain regular organizational patterns that firms of like strategy develop and through which multinational firms with changing strategies evolve.

Pre–International Division Phase

A firm with a technologically advanced product in the new-product stage is well positioned to exploit foreign markets. Generally, initial exploitation occurs through exports—the first stage in the evolution of a multinational company. At this stage, the firm is relatively small by multinational enterprise standards, and its activities are generally confined to a few products and markets. Thus, it has neither diversity in the breadth of its overseas offerings nor a critical mass of overseas sales as compared to its domestic sales. Therefore, the firm has to deal with a comparatively limited number of strategic dimensions, most of which are related to the domestic market and can be addressed directly by the president with input from managers who report directly to him or her. Since the firm's technologically advanced product stands on its own, there is little need to develop expertise in the foreign markets in which the firm sells. Assistance in exporting is usually provided initially by an independent export management company and later by an in-house export manager. In most cases, an in-house export manager is thought of as an adjunct to marketing, whose principal communication needs are with the marketing vice president and others in the marketing group. The organizational arrangements for a firm in this stage of multinational development are rather simple: In an organization with a narrow product line, an export manager reports to the chief marketing officer; in an organization with a broad product line, the export manager reports directly to the chief executive officer.

As the firm's exports increase and its product matures, certain pressures develop that tend to threaten the firm's foreign market share. Such threats can originate from one of two sources. First, competitors at home and abroad begin to share the firm's special knowledge and special skills. Thus, the threat of competition becomes more tangible. Second, as local demand and sales volume increase in a country, an importing country begins to encourage local production by imposing restrictions such as "buy-local" policies on its government agencies and other public buyers and enacting import restrictions such as tariffs and quotas.

Faced with increased competition from other producers and higher comparative costs resulting from freight and tariff costs, the exporting firm feels pressed to defend its foreign market position by establishing a production facility inside the foreign market. Once established, the foreign production unit supplies the foreign market as the former technologically advanced product matures or makes its way through the maturity stage and into the standardized-product stage of the product cycle. The same cycle may be repeated by the firm in the markets of other nations as the firm tries to protect its market share by establishing local production units to supply local markets. At first the management of the newly formed foreign subsidiaries remains quite polycentric and decentralized. The foreign subsidiaries report directly to company presidents or other designated company officers, who carry out their respective responsibilities without assistance from a headquarters staff group. As the firm increases its investment in foreign operating units, however, and as these units become more important to the firm's overall financial performance, greater emphasis is placed on international product coordination and operations control. This creates pressure to assemble a headquarters staff group to assist the officer in charge and to develop a specialized international expertise. The group essentially takes control of all international activities of the firm and evolves into a separate international division in a new and comparatively more complex organizational structure.

International Division Structure

As international activity increases, pressure mounts for the firm to evolve away from the simple structure described above. Still, the relative product diversity and overseas sales are not yet at a critical stage that would require that the firm have a more global structure. Thus, in the **international division** form of organization, all international activities are grouped into one separate division and assigned to a senior executive at corporate headquarters. The senior executive is often given the title of vice president of the international division or director of international operations and is at the same level in the organizational hierarchy as the other divisional and functional heads of the company.

The head of the international division is generally given line authority over the subsidiaries abroad, and the international division is made into a profit center. The formation of the international division in effect segregates the company's overall operations into two differentiated parts—domestic and international. As far as the top management at headquarters is concerned, the international division is expected to manage the nondomestic operations and therefore to be the locus of whatever international expertise there is or should be in the company. There is not much contact or interaction between the domestic and international sides, and coordination between the two segments of the company occurs at the company's top management level.

In general, companies that are still at the developmental stages of international business involvement are likely to adopt the international division structure. Other factors favoring the adoption of this structure are limited product diversity, comparatively small sales generated by foreign subsidiaries (compared to domestic and export sales), limited geographic diversity, and few executives with international expertise. Because the international division represents a structure in which domestic sales overshadow international sales, we see this structure as an intermediate one in countries with large domestic markets, where firms can attain cost efficiencies without leaving home. Thus, firms from the United States and Japan have been more likely to adopt this structure than are firms from relatively smaller market countries. The latter firms need to expand internationally more quickly in order to capture the economy-of-scale benefits of longer production runs and experience.

In this structure, executives are providing the concentration of managerial expertise necessary for the effective promotion of the company's international efforts. During the period in which the company is establishing itself in international markets, international operations tend to remain, in the minds of the corporate executives of domestic operations, a sideline of minor importance. There are several advantages to the use of an international division structure. The concentration of international executives within the division ensures that the special needs of emerging foreign operations are met. The presence of the head of international operations as a member of the top management planning team serves as a constant reminder to top management of the global implications of all decisions. The international group provides a unified position regarding the company's activities in different countries and regions as it makes an effort to coordinate the operations of foreign subsidiaries with respect to the various functional areas of finance, marketing, purchasing, and production. For example, central coordination of international activities enables the company to make more secure and more economic decisions about where to purchase raw materials, where to locate new manufacturing, and from where to supply world customers with products. Also, when the financial function of the international division is coordinated, investment decisions can be made on a global basis and overseas development can turn to international capital markets, instead of just local ones, for funds. The international division also will not strain the capabilities of product or functional managers within the domestic divisions because these persons are not required to work with unfamiliar environments.

Because of several drawbacks to the international division structure, a company will use this structure only if the benefits from its adoption as a coordination mechanism clearly outweigh the costs. One principal disadvantage of the international division structure is the separation and isolation of domestic managers from their international counterparts, which may prove to be a severe handicap as the company continues to expand abroad. If foreign operations should approach a level of equality with domestic ones in terms of size, sales, and profits, the ability of domestic managers to think and act strategically on a global scale could be critical to the success of the company. Also, an independent international division may put constraints on top management's effort to mobilize and allocate the resources of the company globally to achieve overall corporate objectives. Even with superb coordination at the corporate level, global planning for individual products or product lines is carried out at best awkwardly by two "semiautonomous" organizations—the domestic portions of the company and the international division. Additionally, there exists the potential of conflict between the domestic and international groups. Where the domestic business represents the current success of the firm and generates the majority of the revenues, the international business represents the future of the firm and has a seemingly disproportionate budget. Anecdotally, there have been many "sour-grape" stories from domestic managers who fly coach class to unglamorous meeting locations and regular hotels in the United States only to learn of their international counterparts flying business or first-class to Paris or Beijing and staying at five-star hotels.

Also, conflicts occasionally occur between the domestic product divisions and the international division, particularly when the international division asks for help from the domestic divisions and gets what it considers to be inadequate technical support and second-rate staff members for special assignments abroad. Still another problem with the international division is that the firm's research and development remains domestically oriented. Consequently, new ideas originating abroad for new products or processes are not easily transmitted to and enthusiastically tackled by the predominantly domestically oriented research and development personnel, who remain, after all, in the domestic setting of the organization.

A rule of thumb that many firms use is as follows: When the sales of the international division exceed those of the largest domestic division, the international division structure is disaggregated and a structure more in tune with the firm's evolving global posture is established. Thus, an alternative is to take the profit responsibility from the international division and reorganize the entire company on either a product or area division basis, keeping the international division in an advisory capacity.

Studies have shown that the following factors play a major role as indicators that the international division is no longer an appropriate structure for an international company: (1) The international market is as important as the domestic market. (2) Senior officials of the corporation have both foreign and domestic experience. (3) International sales represent 25 to 35 percent of total sales. (4) The technology used in domestic divisions has far outstripped that of the international.

Other studies have shown that the pressures to reorganize on an integrated, worldwide basis by dismantling the international division mount when the division has grown large enough to be equal in size to the largest product division.[6] This is to a large extent due to the struggles that take place between the international and domestic divisions over capital budgeting and transfer pricing issues. But, most importantly, it is the structural conflict between the geographic (foreign) orientation of the international division and the product orientation of the domestic divisions that motivates top management to reorganize the company in a fashion that merges the domestic and international sides of the business into one integrated global structure.

Global Hierarchical Structures

Up to this point we have been concentrating on the typical stages in the evolution of the organizational structure of a company as it becomes increasingly involved in international business activities. As the firm gains experience in operating internationally, the initially limited involvement in foreign direct investment gradually turns into a full-fledged commitment. Top management begins to perceive the company as a truly multinational enterprise, the company enters a new phase in its evolution, and the domestic–foreign bifurcation is abandoned in favor of an integrated, worldwide orientation. Hierarchical structures are the most common organization designs used by international firms. They involve the presence of experts who can be ranked according to the difficulty of the problems they can solve, resulting in a pyramidical structure.[7] These structures are based on authority over the implementation and control of a firm's assets[8] and information.[9]

Strategic decisions that previously were made separately for the domestic and international parts of the company are henceforth made at the corporate headquarters for the total enterprise, without any distinctions of domestic versus foreign. Top management considers the home market to be only one of many, and operational and staff groups are given global responsibility. Under such an attitudinal setup at corporate headquarters, corporate decisions are made with a total company perspective and for the purpose of achieving the company's overall mission and objectives. These decisions include where to establish a new production facility, where to raise capital, what businesses and products to be in, where to obtain resources, what methods to use for tapping foreign markets, what subsidiary ownership policies to adopt, and so on.

The shift to a global orientation in company management must be accompanied by the acquisition and allocation of company resources on the basis of global opportunities and threats. These changes require an organizational structure that is consistent with, and supportive of, this new managerial posture. The new organizational structure includes, as all structures do to varying degrees, three types of informational inputs: product, geography, and function. Although the structures adopted by various companies differ, the structure an international company adopts is certain to be based on one of these basic orientations: a worldwide area or a worldwide product (or, occasionally, a worldwide function).

FIGURE 7.4
The Global Product Division Structure

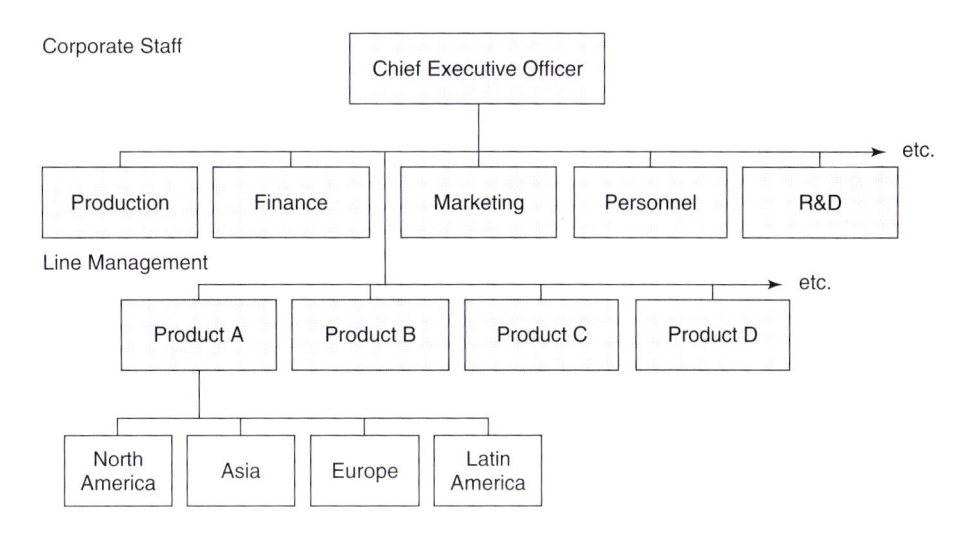

The Global Product Structure

When the international division is discarded in favor of a **global product structure,** the domestic divisions are given worldwide responsibility for product groups. The manager in charge of a product division is given line authority and responsibility for the worldwide management of all functional activities, such as finance, marketing, and production, that are related to a product or product group.[10] Within each product division, there may exist an international unit or even a more refined subdivisionalization on an area basis (see Figure 7.4).

Each product division functions as a semiautonomous profit center. Divisional management has considerable decentralized authority to run the division because of the unique multinational environmental pressures under which it must operate. However, corporate headquarters provides an umbrella of companywide plans and corporate strategy. This umbrella provides both the protection and the constraints under which product divisions are expected to formulate divisional plans and strategy. A product division receives general functional support from staff groups at the corporate level, but at the divisional level it may also have its own functional staff, specialized to provide services tailored to the division's unique market situation. The product division head is given worldwide responsibility for developing and promoting his or her product line.

Conditions favoring the global product structure include the following:

1. A high level of product diversity, with the firm manufacturing products that require different technologies and have dissimilar end users.
2. Little use of common marketing tools and channels of distribution among the various product divisions.
3. A significant need to globally integrate production, marketing, and research related to the product.
4. Little need for local product knowledge and product adaptation as the firm expands into new countries.
5. A product-related need for continuous technical service and inputs and for a high level of technological capability, requiring close coordination between divisional staff groups and production centers abroad.

Industries such as chemicals, pharmaceuticals, and computer manufacturing would be inclined to use this structure.

Some products require close, product-oriented technological and marketing coordination between the home-market affiliates and foreign affiliates. This interdependence between the home and foreign affiliates—the latter needing help from the former in matters pertaining to the production and promotion of the growth product in a foreign market—calls for products, and not markets, as the primary organizing dimension.

To maximize the benefits of divisionalization based on a global product structure, a firm must be able to produce a standardized product that requires only minor modifications for individual markets and for which world markets can be developed. Division managers are expected to take advantage of the structure to generate global economies of scale in production, resource acquisition, and market supply. This makes the structure particularly suited to firms that use capital-intensive technology.

Benefits of the Global Product Structure The major advantages of this form of organization are the ease and directness of the flow of technology and product knowledge from the divisional level to the foreign subsidiaries and back; this tends to put all facilities, regardless of location, on a comparable technological level. Additionally, the global product form preserves product emphasis and promotes product planning on a global basis; it provides a direct line of communication from the customer to those in the organization who have product knowledge and expertise, thus enabling research and development to work on the development of products that serve the needs of the world customer; and it permits line and staff managers within the division to gain expertise in the technical and marketing aspects of products assigned to them.[11]

In addition, the global product division structure facilitates the coordination of domestic and foreign production facilities according to natural resource availability, local labor cost and skill level, tariff and tax regulations, shipping costs, and even climate, in order to produce the highest-quality product possible at the lowest cost.

Drawbacks of a Global Product Structure Several critical problems are associated with a global product structure. One is the duplication of facilities and staff groups that takes place as each division develops its own infrastructure to support its operations in various regions and countries of the world. Another is that division managers may pursue geographic areas that offer immediate growth prospects for their products and may neglect other areas where the current prospects are not as bright but the long-run potential is significant. A far more serious problem is that of motivating product division managers to pursue the international market when the preponderance of their current profits comes from domestic business and most of their experience has been domestic.

Beyond these concerns lies an important inherent characteristic and subsequent concern of this structure. The global product structure represents a hierarchical organization structure, one that potentially limits communication, information flow, knowledge crossover, and, ultimately, organizational learning across divisions. It is a biased structure, in which every manager is concerned with his or her specific niche. Thus, there is no motivation to share knowledge across product boundaries. International companies have tried to alleviate these difficulties by adopting a multidimensional structure, which we discuss later in this chapter.

The Global Area Structure

Firms abandoning the international division as a structure may choose to coordinate their global operations by using geography as the dominant organizational dimension. Looking back at Figure 7.3, we see that firms favoring the **global area structure** more than likely will have a relatively large percentage of their total sales derived from the overseas markets.

In the international division structure, the company's worldwide operations are grouped into two regions—domestic and international. Thus, in a way, the international division structure is also an area-based structure. But in a truly area-based global structure, the company's worldwide operations are grouped into several coequal geographic areas, and the head of an area division is given line authority and responsibility over all affiliates in the area.[12] There is no one fixed pattern for carving up the geographic areas. Obviously, each enterprise has its own circumstances and needs that determine how countries get grouped into regions. Factors such as locations of affiliates, customers, and sources of raw materials influence the grouping of countries into manageable geographic units.

An area structure reflects a very significant change in the attitudes of top management toward international operations and the allocation of the company's resources. In the international division structure, the domestic–nondomestic bifurcation of the company's global operations reflects top management's view that the domestic side of the business is as important as all the international operations together. The area structure embodies the attitude that the domestic market is just one of many markets in the world (see Figure 7.5).

The manager in charge of an area is responsible for the development of business in his or her region. However, the firm's area plans and strategies have to be consistent with those of the company as a whole. Area managers and their counterparts participate in the formulation of companywide plans and strategies. Such participation in total company planning gives each area manager an appreciation of how his or her area operations and results fit with total company plans and performance. Practical Insight 7.1 illustrates a software firm's reorganization to a global area structure to better develop regional markets and business linkages.

Advantages of the Global Area Structure A global area structure is most suited to companies having these characteristics: They are businesses with narrow product lines; they have high levels of regional product differentiation; and they have the opportunity to attain high levels of economies of scale in production, marketing, and integrated resource procurement on a regional basis. Industries with these characteristics include cosmetics, food, beverage, and other consumer goods companies.

FIGURE 7.5
The Global Area Division Structure

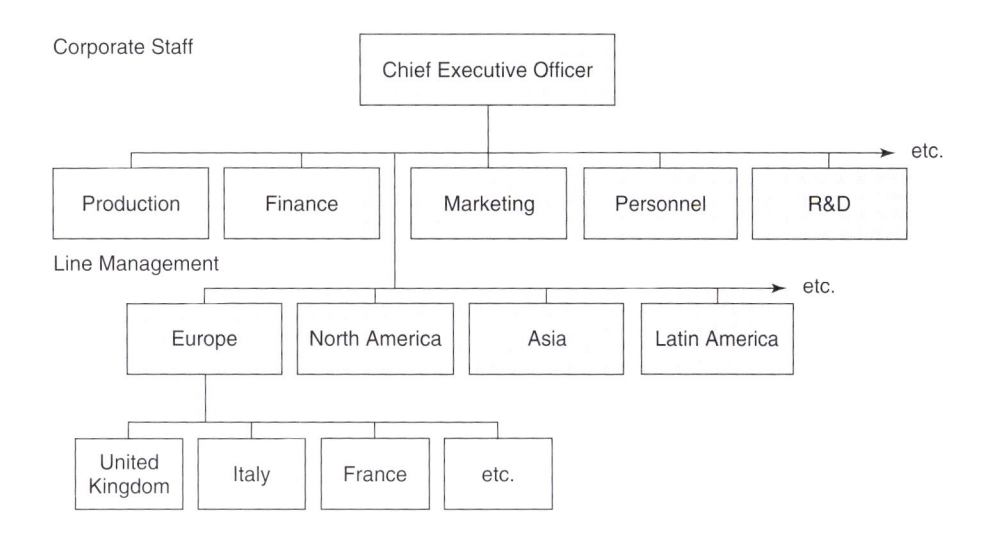

PRACTICAL INSIGHT 7.1

ROGUE WAVE SOFTWARE ANNOUNCES NEW INTERNATIONAL STRUCTURE AND STRATEGY
New General Managers to Help Company Focus on International Market Expansion and Development of Strategic Partnerships

Rogue Wave Software, Inc., of Boulder, Colorado, a leading global software and consulting services company, today announced an updated strategic direction for the future that positions the company as a global infrastructure supplier rather than a tools developer for the programming community. These initiatives are the first in a series of strategic moves planned by new CEO John Floisand, following his internal review of the company's operations. In support of its expanded international strategy, Rogue Wave announces the development of three new divisions and the appointment of three regional general managers to oversee operations in the Americas, Europe and Asia Pacific. All three general managers share a common background in previously helping the Borland Software Corporation transition its focus to that of an infrastructure player, as did Floisand. Their past experience is essential in assisting Rogue Wave to create both reseller and technology development partnerships.

Each manager is tasked with bringing greater sales and marketing discipline to their respective regions, as they work to develop a new customer base and reinvigorate existing relationships. While the Americas are Rogue Wave Software's largest and most stable geographic line of business, Europe and Asia Pacific represent significant growth opportunities.

In particular, the Asia Pacific region has three of the largest global markets for C++ products: Japan, China and India. As the regional general managers build operations in each market, they lay the groundwork for the future sale of the company's infrastructure technologies. The named regional heads include:

- John Racioppi, Vice President & General Manager of Americas
- Gidi Schmidt, Managing Director of Europe
- Raymond Bradbery, General Manager of Asia Pacific

"We are truly fortunate and excited to add leaders of this caliber and with their depth of experience to the Rogue Wave family," stated Floisand. "Their impact will be felt immediately. First in exploiting our core business opportunities internationally, and then longer-term, in our transformation up the value chain to become an infrastructure supplier to our customers. There is a large international market for leveraging both our core business, and future technologies and partnerships. It was crucial to commit to these three markets and reorganize our business structure to capitalize on revenue opportunities in each region. In addition, we need to ensure our customers, domestically as well as internationally, are serviced correctly. My direct experience in working with these individuals gives me great confidence we are headed in the right direction. Our initiatives will provide the framework to allow our core C++ business to grow."

Source: PR Newswire Association, Inc., March 25, 2002.

The principal advantage of an area structure is that the authority to make decisions is pushed down to the regional headquarters. This means that decisions on matters such as product adaptation, price, channels of distribution, and promotion can be made near the scene of action. For example, a company that makes soups, coffee, and prepared frozen foods must take into account regional and even country differences. The Italians and Turks like dark, bitter coffee, whereas Americans like the lighter and less bitter variety. The English like bland soups, whereas the French prefer those with a blend of mild spices. Different countries have different taste preferences. By and large the peoples of the Middle East and Asia like their foods spiced, whereas those in Europe and America like theirs bland. Information on such differences among regions and country markets can be considered at lower levels in the organizational hierarchy, and this helps in the making of plans and strategies consistent with the existing regional and country conditions.

The other advantage of the area structure is that it promotes the finding of regional solutions to problems. Ideas and techniques that have worked in one country are easier to transfer to other countries in the region. And the area manager can resolve conflicts between subsidiaries by finding solutions that optimize the operations in the region as a whole. For example, when a new country market opens up, which subsidiary in the region is in the best position to serve it through exports? Conflicts could occur if more than one subsidiary attempts to export to the new market, but with the area structure the area manager is in a position to resolve such problems.

Drawbacks of a Global Area Structure The main disadvantage of the area structure is the difficulty encountered in reconciling product emphasis with a geographically oriented management approach. Since a certain amount of product expertise has to be developed by the area unit, a duplication of product development and technical knowledge is often required. At the same time, functional staff responsibilities overlap with those of the worldwide headquarters. All of this adds to overhead costs and creates an additional tier of communications.

Other difficulties reported by executives are that research and development programs are hard to coordinate, that global product planning is difficult, that there is no consistent effort to apply newly developed domestic products to international markets, and that introduction to the domestic market of products developed overseas is too slow, or simply that product knowledge is weak. In many respects, the advantages of a global area structure are the disadvantages of a global product division structure, and vice versa. The answer to the product-versus-area dilemma may be an organizational structure that incorporates into its authority, responsibility, and communications lines a blend of these two dimensions.

As was the case with the global product structure, the hierarchical area structure leads to relative inefficiencies of communication (both formal and informal), information flow, knowledge crossover, and long-term organizational learning and the subsequent competitive benefits that come with this learning. Like the product structure, it is a biased structure, in which every manager is concerned with her or his specific niche. For instance, the salesperson in Palermo is concerned only with that city. His boss is concerned only with Sicily. Her boss's focus is strictly Italy. As you move up the European hierarchy, concerns rest in southern Europe and finally the vice president of Europe is focused on Europe. Just as there is no incentive for the Italian country manager to share information with the German or Dutch manager, so too is there no real incentive for the VP-Europe to share information and knowledge with regional vice presidents in other areas of the world, such as Latin America or Asia. Thus, there is no motivation to share knowledge across geographic boundaries.

Multidimensional Global Structures

In deciding whether to organize on a product or area basis, managers of international companies must weigh the benefits of each against the costs. The particular dimension that is chosen as the primary basis for organizing a company's operations should be that which offers the best benefits-costs ratio. When one of these structures is chosen as the primary organizational form, management still tries to utilize the advantages of the remaining dimension, along with a functional perspective, at lower levels in the structure. For example, a company that is organized on a product division basis may have its own functional staff at the divisional level, and each of the product divisions may be further subdivided on a geographic basis. However, many international companies have found that none of the global structures discussed above is a totally satisfactory means of organizing because some problems remain untouchable, and therefore unsolved.

The international firm needs to change the biased nature of the hierarchical structures. It needs to influence multidimensional perspectives. Some companies have attempted to do this by establishing product committees in area-based structures and area committees in product-based structures. Membership of such committees consists of divisional managers and staff specialists who are assigned the collective responsibility for coordinating transactions that cut across divisional lines.

Another alternative is to create staff positions for advisers and counselors. For instance, a product division structure might have area specialists for each of the major regions served by the company. These persons are given the task of exploring new opportunities and developing new markets for the company's products in their respective regions, thus maintaining the distinct advantages of the product structure without losing sight of the unique characteristics of each regional market. Similarly, in an area-based structure, the position of product manager would have responsibility for the coordination of the production and development of his or her product line across geographic areas.

Other tactics used by firms include cross-functional–cross-area task forces, management rotation, and liaison assignments. In each of these instances, the firm has its managers actually coming together with other parts of the organization to influence informal communication and longer-term knowledge transfer. Still, in each of the preceding structural arrangements, the implicit assumption is that an organizational structure can have only one dominant dimension. Because the advantages of the other dimensions are lost when only one is chosen, an attempt is sometimes made to correct the situation by overlaying the dominant dimension with some aspects of the others.

The International Matrix Structure

Some international companies are rejecting the notion that there must be a clear line of authority flowing from the top to the bottom in an organizational hierarchy, with a manager at a given level reporting to only one superior at the next-highest level in the hierarchy. Companies that have adopted what is known as the **matrix structure** have cast aside this so-called principle of the unity of command. In a matrix, the organization avoids choosing one dimension over another as the basis for grouping its operations; instead, it chooses two or more: "The foreign subsidiaries report simultaneously to more than one divisional headquarters; worldwide product divisions share with area divisions responsibility for the profits of the foreign subsidiaries."[13] Thus, the matrix, by its nature, involves dual-authority relations.[14]

For instance, a subsidiary manager may report to an area manager as well as a product manager. In a pure product division or area structure, only the manager in charge of the dominant dimension has line authority over a foreign subsidiary in her or his unit. In a matrix structure, both product and area managers have some measure of line authority over the subsidiary. Thus the unity-of-command principle is abrogated in favor of a coordinating mechanism that considers differences in products and areas to be of equal importance. Firms using the matrix structure are attempting to integrate their operations across more than one dimension simultaneously (see Figure 7.6). Firms should consider adopting the matrix structure if conditions such as the following exist:

1. Substantial product and area diversification.
2. Need to be responsive simultaneously to product and area demands.
3. Constraints on resources requiring that they be shared by two or more product, area, or functional divisions.
4. Significant problems created and opportunities lost due to emphasis on only the product or area dimension.
5. Formulation of corporate strategy requiring the simultaneous consideration of functional, product, and area concerns.

FIGURE 7.6
The International Matrix Structure

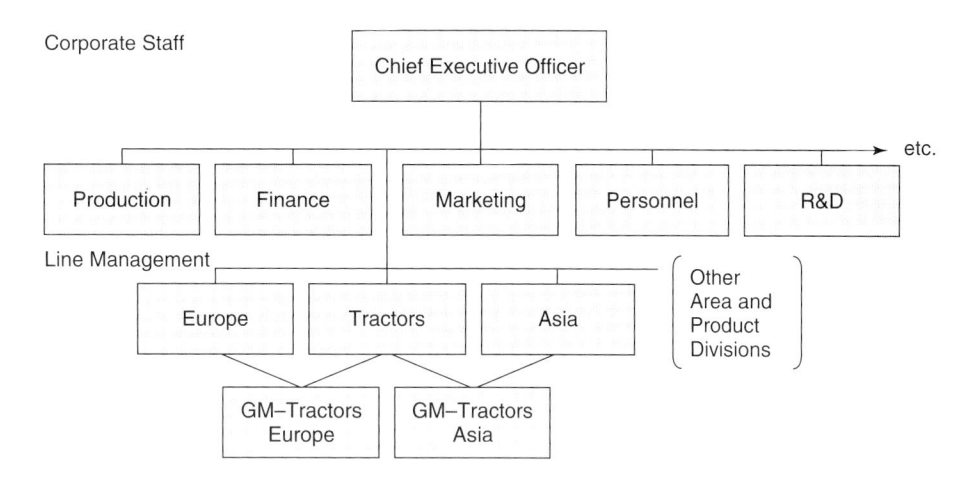

```
Corporate Staff
                    ┌─────────────────────────┐
                    │ Chief Executive Officer │
                    └─────────────────────────┘
                                │
    ┌───────────┬───────────┬───┴───────┬───────────┬──────────→ etc.
┌───────────┐┌─────────┐┌───────────┐┌───────────┐┌──────┐
│Production ││ Finance ││ Marketing ││ Personnel ││ R&D  │
└───────────┘└─────────┘└───────────┘└───────────┘└──────┘

Line Management                            ┌─────────────┐
    ┌────────┬──────────┬────────┐         │ Other       │
┌────────┐┌──────────┐┌──────┐             │ Area and    │
│ Europe ││ Tractors ││ Asia │             │ Product     │
└────────┘└──────────┘└──────┘             │ Divisions   │
              │                            └─────────────┘
      ┌───────┴────────┐
┌────────────┐ ┌────────────┐
│ GM–Tractors│ │ GM–Tractors│
│   Europe   │ │    Asia    │
└────────────┘ └────────────┘
```

Adoption of a matrix structure requires a commitment on the part of top management not only to the structure itself but also to the essential preparation required for it to be successful. Executive groundwork must be laid; executives must understand how the system works, and those who report to two or more superior managers, such as the subsidiary managers, must be prepared to work through the initial confusion created by dual reporting relationships. The structure must be reinforced by systems such as dual-control and -evaluation systems, by leaders who operate comfortably with lateral decision making, and by a culture that can negotiate open conflict and a balance of power. Thus, the mere adoption of a matrix structure does not create a matrix organization.

Adoption must be followed by some fundamental changes in technical systems and management behavior. Managers must recognize the need to resolve issues and choices at the lowest possible level, without referring them to a higher authority. A delicate balance of power must be maintained among managers face to face. A tilt in favor of one organizational dimension or another would cause the organization to fall back to the old single-dimensional, vertical hierarchy, with a resulting loss of the benefits of a matrix structure. Absence of cooperation between facing managers, even when a perfect power balance exists, could cause so many unresolved problems and disputes to be referred up the hierarchy that top management would become overloaded with interdivisional matters.[15]

The benefits of a matrix structure flow directly from the conditions that induce enterprises to adopt it. A matrix organization can respond simultaneously to all environmental factors that are critical to its success. Decision-making authority can be decentralized to an appropriate level. Policy decisions are made in concert with people who have relevant information, and the design also facilitates a flow of information that promotes better planning and the implementation of plans.

The matrix structure does take time, effort, and commitment by executives to make it work. Although Peter Drucker says that it "will never be a preferred form of organization; it is fiendishly difficult,"[16] he nevertheless concludes that "any manager in a multinational business will have to learn to understand it if he wants to function effectively himself."[17] Percy Barnevik, the former CEO of Asea Brown Boveri (ABB), suggested that any manager operating in the global environment must have, at the minimum, a matrix mind-set. In many industries, managers can no longer be focused on only a unitary, biased hierarchical perspective. ABB, the Swedish-Swiss diversified company that was created following the merger of Sweden's Asea and Switzerland's Brown Boveri, was one of the first examples of a global matrix structure, as evidenced in the following passage:

The Barnevik strategy for ABB is based on three internal contradictions. "We want to be global and local, big and small, radically decentralized with centralized reporting and control," he says. Barnevik manages this many-tentacled operation by way of a matrix system. A 12-member executive committee, which he heads, sets strategy and reviews the performance of the whole. Each committee member manages one of eight business segments—power plants, power transmission, power distribution, transportation, industry, environmental control, financial services and a miscellaneous segment, called "various activities," which embraces robotics and telecommunications—and/or a country or region. Each reports to the group at meetings held every three weeks in a different country. At the same time a centralized reporting system, named Abacus, collects performance data on the company's 5,000 profit centers, compares them with budgets and forecasts, converts them into dollars to enable cross-border analyses, and consolidates or breaks them down by segment, country and local company. The group is then divided vertically by business area and horizontally by country. Business area leaders set the rules on a global level, determining strategy, organization, manufacturing and product development. They also allocate export markets to specific factories. Country managers run line operations, establishing balance sheets and income statements and administering their own career ladders, while fulfilling their obligation to respect ABB's worldwide objectives—not always an easy task, Barnevik admits. "Thirty of the companies we have bought had been around for more than 100 years," he says. "We have to convince country managers that they gain more than they lose when they give up some autonomy." Answering to both business area managers and country managers are the bosses of the myriad local companies. "The only way to structure a complex, global organization is to make it as simple and local as possible," Barnevik says. "ABB is complicated from where I sit, but on the ground, where the real work gets done, all our operations must function as closely as possible to stand-alone operations."[18]

Practical Insight 7.2 studies AIS, the cell phone firm from Thailand, and its restructuring into the matrix mind-set to help become more efficient and better compete in the turbulent Asian telecom market.

The matrix structure provides better communications, movement of information, and creation of knowledge for the international firm; moreover, it promises to open up multiple channels of formal and informal communications, to nurture more perspectives, and to give the organization more flexibility. Nevertheless, the matrix is not an easy structure to implement on a global basis and has been a difficult structure to manage. The dual reporting structure leads to more conflicts and confusion. The proliferation of channels of reporting leads to corporate logjams. Overlapping responsibilities lead to power struggles and loss of accountability. More things slip through the cracks than is the case with a hierarchy. Furthermore, even though there are ultimately better decisions due to the multiple perspectives generated, the decisions many times take much longer to reach. When conflicts arise, the decisions are pushed up the corporate ladder, making inefficient use of executive time. If one adds in the complicating factors of distance, culture, time, and language that arise with international operations, an international matrix does not adequately serve many international firms. It is simply too cumbersome to manage effectively.

Still, firms need to be more efficient in communication, information flow, and knowledge creation across the various lines of business. This is especially true for firms in industries that are undergoing turbulence, where speed is of the essence and where the product life cycles have significantly shortened. Firms in these industries need malleable, flexible structures. Thus, the next section addresses these ever-evolving structures.

Heterarchical Structures and Transnational Mind-Sets

In Chapter 5, we distinguished among the multidomestic, global, and transnational orientations. Extending that thinking leads us to see the cost and efficiency benefits of

PRACTICAL INSIGHT 7.2

AIS GOES "MATRIX": NEW STRUCTURE HAILED FOR ITS EFFICIENCY

In 2002, Thailand's No. 1 cell-phone firm Advanced Info Service (AIS) decentralized its organizational structure as part of a major new change intended to enable it to move faster in capturing a larger market share. Termed the Matrix Organization, the new structure transformed AIS from a hierarchical firm to a network-oriented organization and will enable it to serve its customers four times faster, said Somprasong Boonyachai, AIS chairman and president.

[In 2002], AIS—the mobile-phone flagship of Shin Corp, founded by Prime Minister Thaksin Shinawatra—targeted 6 million new subscribers to add to its existing 7 million. Therefore, it must make the change first to be ahead of its rivals. "Now AIS signs up as many as 500,000 subscribers monthly and also plans to massively expand its subscription base, so the old structure is not responsive enough to support this mission," Somprasong said.

Under the new scheme, AIS created four new positions—chief of commercial and customer service, chief network officer, wireless corporate planning chief, and future business opportunities chief—which all are empowered with presidential authority. This allowed them to manage and make crucial decisions rapidly and more flexibly without reporting to Somprasong at all times, as was the case previously. For example, if the chief of network thinks it is time for AIS to quickly invest further in networks to respond to faster growth, he can make the decision without waiting for approval from the president. Somprasong claimed that AIS is the first cell-phone operator adopting the Matrix structure. "We're the first to embrace this kind of management, which we've adapted from the models of several global giant companies like IBM or Nokia," he said.

Decentralization would allow Somprasong to take time off from day-to-day management to concentrate on working on AIS' future plans and maximizing benefits for shareholders. "The restructuring also reflects our policy of giving priority to training executives, to allow them to shine in their capacity," Somprasong said.

AIS has also set up three regional headquarters in the North, East and Northeast as part of its plan to aggressively penetrate the provincial market. Provincial consumers account for 60 per cent of AIS' total subscribers. "AIS will open another headquarters in the South soon to help it increase the number of provincial customers," he added.

Source: Usanee Mongkolporn, "Cell Phone Sector: AIS Goes Matrix," *The Nation* (Thailand), May 10, 2002.

---

the global orientation matched to the global product structure. Likewise, the marketing and differentiation benefits associated with the multidomestic orientation overlap similar benefits discussed for the global area structure. As firms in many dynamic and turbulent industries are confronted with the dual mandate of global efficiency and national responsiveness, there must be newer organizational structures to complement these newer strategic initiatives.

Given the complexity and volatility of many industries within the global environment, a single, biased hierarchical structure will no longer fit for many firms in the future. These firms need to build strategic and operational flexibility. Thus, we need to explore some of the more subtle, as well as sophisticated, ways of thinking about the organizational challenges facing managers in international firms. This points to the necessity of understanding the transnational mentality and associated heterarchical[19] structures.

A **heterarchy** is distinguished from a hierarchical structure in various aspects. For instance, decision making is dispersed throughout the organization and not concentrated at the top levels. Also, lateral managerial relationships exist as complements to the usual vertical relationships, and firm-level activities are coordinated across multiple dimensions including, product, function and geography.[20] Scholars have suggested that emerging organizations are more likely to be characterized by decentralization of decision making and that, in order to facilitate this, they are likely to be designed as distributed organizations, such as heterarchies and transnationals.[21]

Specifically, these structures, as compared to the more traditional product and area structures, have the following characteristics:

1. Less systematic
2. More flexibly coordinated
3. Nimbler
4. Less hierarchical

Furthermore, these structures have:

1. Higher levels of interdependency among the subsidiaries.
2. Greater exchange of knowledge, especially informal knowledge.
3. Informal coordination processes.
4. Potentially shifting positions and relationships.
5. Lateral as well as vertical sharing of knowledge.
6. Consensual decision making.

When a firm moves to a **transnational structure,** it does so through a number of processes. For example, ABB used an internal entrepreneurial process in which even middle-level managers were given the autonomy to be entrepreneurs. Also, consistent with the autonomy given to managers is the underlying radical decentralization, in which business units and in-country offices are left alone from a control aspect. Still, the price that these units and managers pay is one of high-level accountability. Thus, the in-country managers have certain goals and the flexibility to reach those goals the way they see most beneficial.[22]

The horizontal integration process that is associated with transnational structures includes intensive informal communications implemented primarily by middle-level managers. Additionally, continual learning and renewal processes that shape the organizational purpose are led by the top management teams.[23]

Bartlett proposes a management structure that balances the local, regional, and global demands placed on companies operating across the world's many borders. In the volatile world of transnational corporations and heterarchical mind-sets, he sees various groups of specialists including business managers, country managers, and functional managers. Furthermore, the top executives of the international firm must not only manage the complex interactions between these three manager roles but also identify, develop, and socialize the talented personnel that the transnational requires.[24]

Another overriding feature of transnational structures is the emphasis on creativity at all levels of management. Complementing this emphasis is the critical role of socialization of the organization's managers to build a strong corporate culture and shared vision of just "who" the organization is and where it is headed. It is this last point, regarding the managers or people of the international firm, that leads to its success. Not all managers are able to handle the ambiguity of this structure and the systems associated with it. Not all managers are able to not only effectively move knowledge but also actually create knowledge. Thus, the front-end hiring process becomes critical.

As suggested above, the heterarchical structure and transnational orientation are ambiguous to say the least. What tangible form may these self-organizing structures take? One may start with a traditional hierarchy and relax its constraints. For instance, think of an organization built around multiple hierarchies, where a manager's position in one of the organization's hierarchies does not necessarily prevent or suggest a distinctly different position in another of the hierarchies. Suppose a firm has the following critical activities:

- Penetrating the Chinese market during the next three years.
- Building on its research and development capabilities.

Chapter 7 *Organizing and Controlling International Operations* **269**

- Successfully launching a newly developed standardized product in world markets during the upcoming quarter.
- Investigating various acquisitions and mergers with European firms.
- Effectively managing the 10 existing joint ventures and strategic alliances throughout the world.
- Managing major customer accounts consistently throughout the world.

Of course, these critical activities will overlap. That is, the international joint venture initiatives will affect the Chinese market as well as potential European acquisitions and marketing and R&D efforts. Thus, a structure that consists of multiple hierarchies might be appropriate. In this structure, the skills and knowledge necessary are brought to the forefront of each hierarchy. Thus, the manager who leads the Chinese initiative may actually be in the middle of a few of the hierarchies supporting other critical initiatives. To illustrate the effect of this orientation and shifting relationships, we have kept this example simple, using only six critical activities. Figure 7.7 illustrates the orientation and dynamic capabilities of this type of structure.

As seen, when the individual hierarchies are combined in Figure 7.7*b,* and when the individual managers' roles in each hierarchy are connected, we begin to form a spider's web. The ultimate effect is a networklike web structure, one that we all know will facilitate communication while efficiently and rapidly moving knowledge

FIGURE 7.7
(a) Multiple Hierarchies Structure and (b) Network Effect

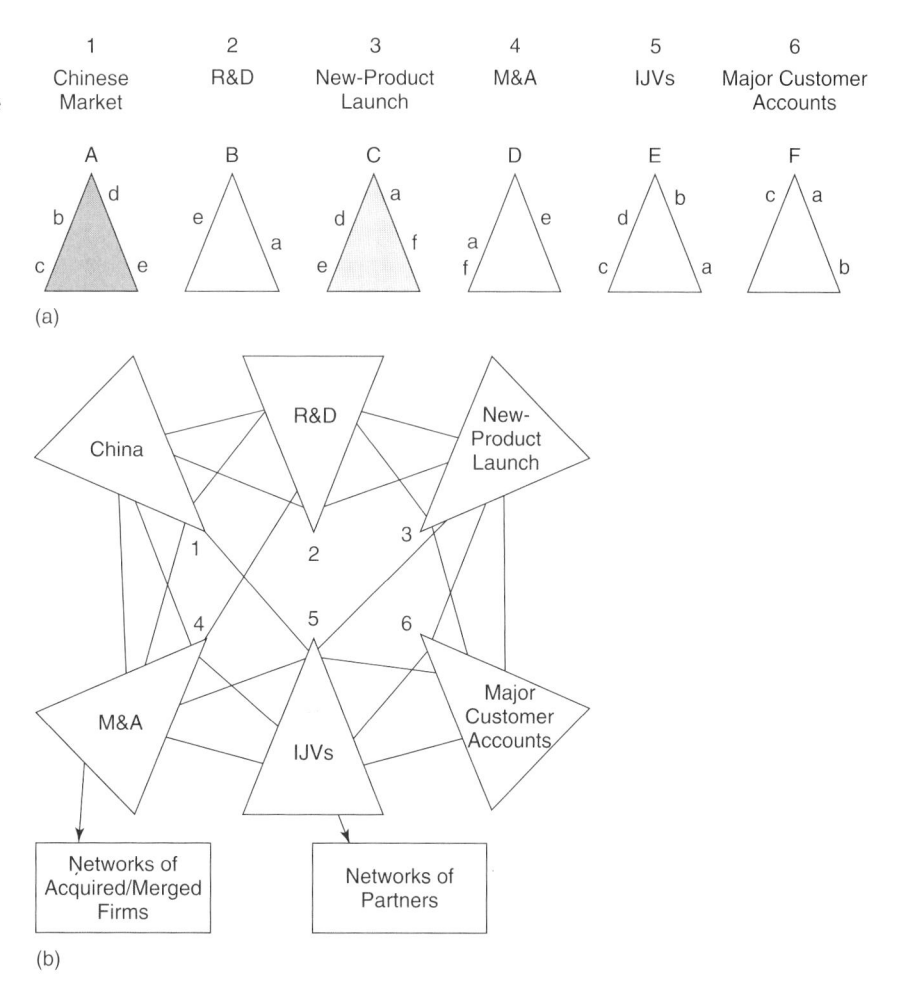

PRACTICAL INSIGHT 7.3

NO-CUBICLE CULTURE: HEARING-AID MAKER OTICON REMOVED ALL OFFICE BOUNDARIES

It sounds like the corporate paradise of the future. Workers organize themselves, coalescing around natural leaders and gravitating to the most exciting projects. There are no middle managers, no hierarchies, no fixed assignments.

At Oticon, a midsize Danish maker of hearing aids, the future started back in 1991. That's when its chief executive, Lars Kolind, turned traditional notions of the workplace upside down. Kolind, a corporate renegade trained as a mathematician, swept away old structures. Workers were suddenly free to concentrate on any project and join any team.

Kolind's radical idea was to transform the company's once-stodgy culture into a free marketplace of ideas. He moved headquarters to a new location where none of the 150 employees had a permanent desk or office, only filing cabinets on wheels that they pushed from project to project. Meeting areas had no tables or chairs. He called it the spaghetti organization, because the place had no fixed structure yet somehow held together. Ideas bubbled up and turned into hits such as a new hearing aid that required less adjustment. Sales and profits soared. The company became a model for management creativity. Even CNN showed up to tape a segment. Yet as the company grew and went public, many of the old structures crept back.

Kolind eventually left, and these days there's not much talk about his spaghetti revolution. Still, its spirit survives. None of the 500 head-office employees at Oticon has even a cubicle. The latest headquarters features few interior walls. Workers sit around the perimeter of the building at simple desks. They attend meetings on sofas in the middle of each floor.

The relaxed atmosphere helps retain top engineers, keeping Oticon at the forefront of innovation. Its unobtrusive Delta hearing aid has been a success. Sales of parent William Demant Holding Group, of which Oticon is the largest business, have grown 36% since 2002, to $927 million, while operating profit has risen 57%, to $232 million.

But some things have clearly changed. Everyone has a boss to whom they report and they no longer have total freedom to choose projects. That seems to suit people fine. A degree of freedom sparks creativity, but workers also crave leadership. The trick is striking the right balance. Says Mads Kamp, Oticon's director of human resources: "People want to be led."

Source: Jack Ewing, *BusinessWeek*, August 20, 2007, p. 60.

---

throughout the organization. Furthermore, when this weblike structure is connected to the skills, knowledge, and resources of joint venture and strategic alliance partners and acquisition firms, the communication and knowledge benefits can potentially grow exponentially. Network structures may be appropriate designs to cope with the complex and dynamic forces of globalization facing organizations,[25] and thus these structures may help international firms thrive in an era of turbulence due to new technologies, uncertain competition, and host-government involvement.[26]

The network structure illustrated in Figure 7.7b is one example of a malleable, flexible structure that can quickly bring the correct perspectives to critical decisions.[27] Still, it must be understood that such structures are much less defined than the traditional product and area orientations. As organizations shift toward the transnational orientation, a significant amount of knowledge that was based on industry and firm traditions may be lost. These new models are discontinuous with the old ones and give the firm a competitive advantage of developing new knowledge and technology rather than exploiting old knowledge and technology. These new structures support radical change rather than incremental change. Many firms in stable industries may be destabilized if they try to force this type of structure into their organizations. Indeed, a traditional consumer goods or industrial goods firm may be better off with an area or product structure, respectively.

However, firms in the truly transnational industries like pharmaceuticals and telecom may need to explore these new structures. Both of those industries, as we previously discussed, face intense pressures to be globally and efficiently coordinated while also responding to individual market needs. These industries are also good examples of industries whose conventional boundaries have been shattered during the past 20 years. Telecom is now a part of the larger infocom industry, which includes media, cable television, Internet, and entertainment. The global pharmaceuticals industry has seen the once-typical focused drug firms turn into full-line global companies while also venturing into the chemical and biotech businesses. Furthermore, linkages may be made to the automobile industry, as evidenced by Toyota's new critical contingencies in the United States (depicted in the opening case of this chapter).

Still, transnational models ignore some of the traditional social institutions on which the organization was based and from which it drew support and strength. These social institutions include the community, the family, specific ethnic groups, and a nationality. In contrast, the transnational firm is one whose boundaries venture beyond any one country or industry. Subsequently, the firm must have a structure that ventures beyond tradition as well. Practical Insight 7.3 depicts the benefits and implications of initiatives by the Danish firm Oticon to promote creativity through matching a radical change in structure to its strategy.

Global Strategy, Structure, and Organizational Control

An international company derives its strength from its ability to recognize and capitalize on opportunities anywhere in the world and from its capacity to respond to global threats to its business operations in a timely fashion. On the basis of an evaluation of global opportunities and threats and of a company's strengths and weaknesses, top management executives of a multinational at the parent-company level formulate corporate strategy for the whole company. The objectives of a multinational company serve as the umbrella under which the objectives of divisions and subsidiaries are developed. There is a considerable amount of give-and-take between the parent company, divisions, and subsidiaries before the divisional and subsidiary objectives are finally agreed to by executives at all three levels. As discussed earlier in the chapter, an international firm must link its global strategic initiatives to an appropriate organization structure in order to efficiently implement those initiatives. Similarly, controlling the network of domestic and overseas subsidiaries must be consistent with the strategies and structure of the firm.

The objective of managerial control is to ensure that strategic, operational, and tactical plans are implemented correctly. Thus, control can be defined as any process that helps align the actions of individuals with the interests of their employing firm.[28] In the remainder of this chapter, the focus is on the parent company's managerial control over its foreign subsidiaries. We examine first the salient features of the managerial control process. Then, because multinational companies experience problems controlling their far-flung operations, we look at those problems and their causes. Next, we review the typical characteristics of control systems used by international companies. We conclude by revisiting the external environments discussed in Section 1 of this book, focusing on their integration with and effects on control processes.

The Managerial Control Process

Managerial control is a process directed toward ensuring that operations and personnel adhere to parent-company plans. A control system is essential because the future, especially when dealing with the dynamic international environment, is uncertain.

Assumptions about the internal and external environment that were at one time the basis of a forecast may prove invalid. Furthermore, strategies may not be applicable, and current budgets and programs may not be effective in the longer term. Managerial control is a process that evaluates performance and takes corrective action when performance differs significantly from the company's plans. With managerial control, any deviations from forecasts, objectives, or plans can be detected early and corrected with minimum difficulty.

Managerial control involves several management skills: planning, coordinating, communicating, processing and evaluating information, and influencing people. The four main elements in the managerial control process are:

1. The setting of standards.
2. The development of methods to monitor the performance of an individual or an organizational system.
3. The comparison of actual performance measures to planned performance in order to determine whether current performance is sufficiently close to what was planned.
4. The employment of effectuating or action devices that can be used to correct significant deviations in performance.

There is a close relationship between managerial control and planning. Managerial control depends on the objectives set forth in tactical plans, which in turn are derived from the strategic plans of the organization. Tactical plans encompass the short-term contributions of each functional area to the strategic plans, goals, and objectives.

Types of Control Systems

The control process has two distinct parts: (1) the antecedent conditions and (2) the various forms of control. The antecedent conditions include the availability of output measures and the knowledge of the transformation process, that is, an organizational understanding of how inputs are converted into outputs.[29]

When both **output measure availability** and **knowledge of the transformation process** are high, an organization has the flexibility to use either output or behavior performance measurement systems. As output measures become less available, a firm must adopt more behavioral measures. Conversely, as the knowledge of the transformation process declines, an output measurement orientation is preferred. Finally, as both parameters simultaneously tend toward the negative extremes, a firm will tend to adopt ritual or clan control. This control form achieves efficiency under conditions of high performance and low opportunism and takes place when goal incongruence is high and performance ambiguity is low. Under conditions of low outcome observability, even when information about an agent's behavior is incomplete, a behavior control system is possible under the assumption that information and information systems play a proactive role.[30]

The discussion of output and behavior control has excluded two other organizational mechanisms to help align the interests of the employee and the firm. These are the recruitment and selection of new employees and the training of individuals after they have joined the organization. Both of these mechanisms fall under another type of control system, input control. Input control complements the output–behavior choice and incorporates organizational socialization, staffing procedures, and ongoing training and development programs. Furthermore, input control involves the formal bureaucratic human resource management systems, such as selection and training, rather than the less observable influences, such as socialization or clan control. Input controls regulate the antecedent conditions of performance including the knowledge, skills, abilities, values, and motives of employees. In contrast, behavior control regulates the transformation process, and output control regulates the results. The U.S. foreign service corps represents an example of input control where cause-and-effect relationships for the personnel are incomplete and results are difficult to measure. Subsequently, a difficult selection process and rigorous training process are both used to improve the organizational control.[31]

A firm's strategic context, including the extent of its product-market variation, its work flow integration, and its size, will affect the firm's ability to develop well-delineated, measurable performance standards as well as its knowledge of the cause–effect relationships. The strategic context influences administrative information, which, in turn, influences control. The various strategic control options for the international firm are delineated as follows:

- **Input control** is a control system that emphasizes employee selection and training,[32] as well as socialization of employees to the organization and its values, vision, and objectives.[33] This type of control can be assessed by the degree to which an employee of an international firm is provided substantial training before assuming responsibility. Also, within this system, the firm establishes the best staffing procedures available, becomes involved in the training and skill development of an employee, performs multiple evaluations before hiring an individual, provides opportunities for broadening a skill set of an employee, and takes pride in hiring the best employees possible. In turn, the employees are socialized within the organization and subsequently share the firm's overriding values and vision. Consistent with input controls are informal systems for continually integrating the managers into the organization.[34]

- **Behavior control** is a control system that emphasizes top-down control in the form of articulated operating processes and procedures.[35] This form of control can be assessed by analyzing the following organizational attributes:
  — The degree to which a firm weighs evaluations based on behavior.
  — Whether an employee is held accountable regardless of the outcome.
  — The degree to which there is concern for procedures or methods.
  — The degree to which performance programs are imposed from the top down.
  — The frequency at which employees receive feedback or performance information.

- **Output control** is a control system that sets and measures actual targets, such as financial results[36] and productivity. This system may be implemented by an international firm along the following dimensions:
  — The degree to which a firm uses evaluations with significant weightings on results.
  — Pay based on performance.
  — Preestablished targets used for evaluating personnel.
  — Numerical records as indices of effectiveness.
  — Performance linked to concrete results.
  — Appraisals based on goal achievement.

Ideally, control systems should regulate both motivation and ability. Whereas the use of behavior control ensures motivation through close supervision and, to a lesser extent, facilitates the ability of subordinates to perform well by articulating operating procedures, output control focuses on motivation through the use of incentives, providing virtually no direction about how results should be accomplished. Finally, input control ensures that employees have the requisite ability to perform well. These issues will be further elaborated on in Section 3, when we discuss motivation of the international workforce. Because there are overlapping effects of the three types of control, it is not surprising that firms tend to use elements of input behavior and output control simultaneously. Figure 7.8 shows that these control system options depend on various host-country environmental factors. We now begin to discuss those factors and the problems and concerns that arise with them.

Problems of Control in a Global Firm

An international firm's control system not only must support the firm's strategy but also must produce the behavior and flexibility needed by subsidiary managers to manage within various host-country environments.[37] Thus, control systems and the problems associated with them are far more complex in a multinational company than in one that is purely domestic because the multinational operates in more than one cultural, economic, political, and legal environment. Let us examine a few of the most important international variables having a major negative impact on the flow of information between headquarters and subsidiaries. These variables, in turn, influence the effectiveness of the international company's control system.

Despite the sophistication and speed of contemporary communication systems, the geographic distance between a parent company and a foreign affiliate continues to cause communication distortion. Differences in language between the parent company and its foreign affiliates are also responsible for distortions in communication. Language barriers caused by language differences involve both the content and the meaning of messages. Many ideas and concepts are not easily translatable from one language to another. Because of geographic distances, there is little face-to-face communication, so the messages of nonverbal communication are lost.

Problems are also caused by misunderstanding the communication habits of people in other cultures. Managers of different cultures may interact and yet block out important messages because the manner in which the message is presented may mean different things in the sending and receiving cultures. For example, a manager may make a wrong judgment about a subordinate's performance because he or she is unaware of culturally different communications habits. As an illustration, the aborigines in Australia exhibit attention by listening intently with their faces and bodies turned away from the speaker and with no eye contact.[38] Looking directly at the eyes of another is considered rude in Arab cultures, whereas in Western cultures it is interpreted as a sign of strength. Such behavior could easily be misread by a member of a different

FIGURE 7.8
A Model of MNC Control Selection

Source: From Hamilton and Kashlak, "National Influences on MNC Control System Selection," *Management International Review* 39, no. 2 (1999). Reprinted with permission.

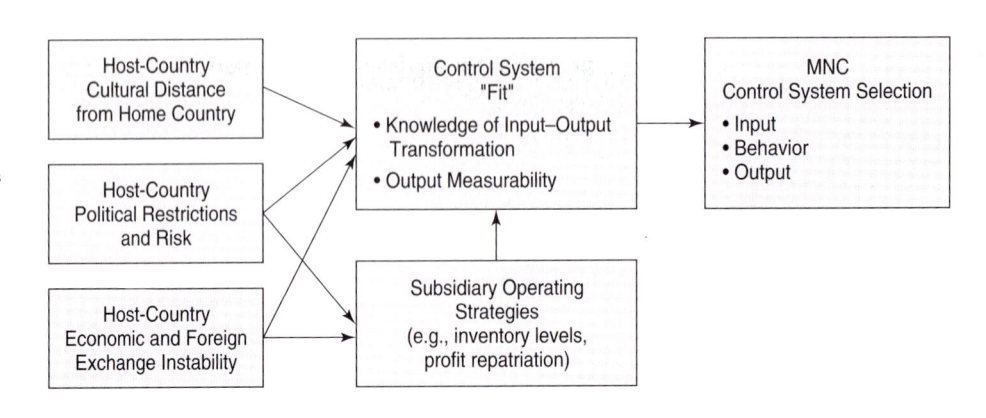

culture—one who is accustomed to associate body posture and eye contact with attention. Cultural distance is as significant as geographic distance in creating communication distortions. Lack of understanding and acceptance of the cultural values of a group may impair a manager's ability to evaluate information accurately, to judge performance fairly, and to make valid decisions about performance. This failure could create problems in an international company in the area of employee performance appraisal.

In some cultures one does not make criticism bluntly but, rather, discusses critical areas in an oblique fashion. In contrast, the American managerial style is direct in identifying responsibilities for achieving certain organizational goals with specific members in the organization. Other control mechanisms are also affected by cultural differences. For example, the detailed reporting required by some "tight" managerial control systems is not acceptable to some cultures. Also, the degree of harmony valued in a culture may make the accurate reporting of problems difficult.[39]

In the Japanese culture, maintaining group cohesiveness is considered to be far more important than reporting a problem to a superior who would place blame on the group or on an individual in the group. It is therefore not unusual for Japanese supervisors not to report a problem to upper management, in the hope that it can be resolved at the group level.

Communication distortion between the parent company and a foreign affiliate may occur because of the differing frames of reference of these two organizational units. The parent company may perceive each foreign affiliate as just one of many, and therefore it may have a tendency to view each affiliate's problems in light of the company's entire global network of operations. However, foreign affiliate heads may view the problems of their own operations as being very important to them and their affiliates. Both the parent company and the affiliate heads may try to communicate their feelings and views to each other without much success because each could be communicating from a different frame of reference.

International Environments and Control Systems

Differences and changes in the various host-country environments will affect a firm's ability to use the different forms of control described above. Specifically, the alterations along three external environmental dimensions—cultural differences, political risk, and economic factors—will affect the knowledge of cause-and-effect relationships as well as the degree of crystallization of standards and, subsequently, the choice of an international firm's control systems. As an organization increases its overseas presence, the process of coordination and communication with its overseas subsidiaries becomes strained,[40] requiring increased integration and interdependence among the affiliates as well as between the affiliates and headquarters. Thus, within the larger global structure, specific control systems must be adapted to host-country environmental influences.

Specific **host-country environmental factors** could increase market variation and must be considered when developing performance measurement and control systems. These factors include:

1. The cultural distance between the headquarters' home country and the country hosting the international firm's subsidiary.
2. The degree of host-country political risk as reflected in host-government restrictions on the international firm's operations.
3. Economic factors such as the volatility of a host country's foreign exchange rates and host-country inflationary pressures that are linked to foreign exchange movements.[41]

The effects of these three factors on an international firm's control system is discussed in the following sections. In general, as the host country moves further away from the origin in terms of cultural distance, political risk, and economic instability, the control system will tend more toward input control.

Cultural Distance

Both national culture and the distance among national cultures are significant influences on decision making and strategies. A firm will initially expand overseas to countries most similar in culture and business culture to the home country in order to more easily implement and control its strategies. Specifically, cultural distance affects many behaviors and managerial decisions, including work values, patterns of negotiations, international joint venture establishment and operations, overseas entry mode, and degree of partner reciprocity.

The greater the extent to which an organization's headquarters and subsidiaries are culturally distant, the more difficult it becomes to effectively supervise the various units. If the headquarters–subsidiary relationship is viewed from a transaction cost perspective, costs will increase relative to cultural distance. Thus, a decreasing level of cultural distance will reduce the expenses of adapting a firm's control system to a host-country subsidiary.[42] More explicitly, the degree of cultural distance between home and host countries will influence the parent–subsidiary performance ambiguity and task definition. As a result, knowledge of input–output transformation and output measurability will decline. Therefore, when cultural distance between the home and host countries is low, performance measurement in the host country will be determined by outcome measurability and knowledge of input–output transformation. As cultural distance increases, overseas subsidiary performance evaluation through output or behavior systems becomes increasingly difficult. As a result, an input control system becomes more attractive as a control mechanism.

Political Risk and Host-Country Restrictions

Differences in home- and host-country political systems and the resulting risk and restrictions arising in the host country may affect an international firm's control system. Politically imposed country-level restrictions may be seen as opportunistic behavior by the foreign government partners seeking to redistribute MNE gains within the host country.

In Chapter 3 of this text, the political environment was related to international business activities through the concept of political risk. Political differences and political risk have been identified as factors that influence strategic and tactical behavior. The political environment of a host country is a critical dimension in distinguishing among respective opportunities in foreign markets, and firms today view both the assessment and the management of changes in the various sociopolitical environments as critical components of strategic decision making. In general, when a firm crosses international boundaries, new and different political environments force that firm into various modes of adaptation. The implementation of control systems represents one critical mode of adaptation for the international firm.

Political risk may consist of government or societal actions, may originate either within or outside the host country, and will cause restrictions that limit an international firm's strategic flexibility in a host country. Specifically, various linkages, when politically strained, engender restrictions that affect both long-term and day-to-day flexibility of an MNC's in-country manager. These linkages include (1) host government–firm,

(2) host society–host business community–host government–firm, and, (3) home government–host government–firm.

One operationalization of political risk that helps with the discussion of control systems is government instability arising from irregular power transfers and the imposition of political restrictions. These politically based restrictions include profit repatriation limits, price controls, protectionistic trade policies, host-government tax policy, monetary policy, and legal restrictions. All of these factors are indicators of political uncertainty and will affect the international business sector. Some international firms cannot avoid politically unstable regions because investments in these markets may provide returns that outweigh the risks. Other firms pursue diversification initiatives among politically risky countries to reduce the overall political risk. Thus, there is an imperative for many international firms to continue expansion into countries where political risk and associated host-government restrictions limit the subsidiary managers' strategic flexibility. Subsequently, as it expands, a firm must meet these varied restrictions with more flexible control systems.

As political uncertainty rises and the potential for a host government to interfere with the operations of a firm also increases, the firm must be ready to adapt its control systems. Consistent with the cultural distance discussion above, host-country politically imposed restrictions will affect a firm's knowledge of input–output transformation and output measurability. Under conditions of low or nonexistent host-government restrictions, the organization can use either output control or behavior control. We make the assumption that output control, with less observation costs, will be the preferred choice. As political risk and corresponding restrictions in a host country increase, the input form of control system is increasingly employed because of the levels of complexity and uncertainty the firm faces.[43]

Host-Country Economic Factors

The third environmental factor suggested as an influence on an international firm's control system is the level of host-country economic stability. In many countries, foreign exchange rate fluctuations arbitrarily penalize or reward subsidiary managers after a global consolidation of financial statements. International firms have historically attempted to discount this uncontrollable element when accounting for and measuring performance. For instance:

> Losses or gains from foreign-exchange variations affect the units of a multinational enterprise just as they do any national enterprise. At times, however, in measuring the performance of a manager of the unit of an MNE (multinational enterprise), it may be necessary to consider whether the policies that generate gains or losses of this sort should be counted as part of a manager's responsibilities.[44]

Reliable financial control systems for international firms must include the complicating factors of exchange rate fluctuations, relative inflation rates, and government-imposed exchange controls. In fact, an international firm's accounting-related performance measurement process correlates directly to the host country's economic environment.[45] As a host country's economic climate becomes increasingly turbulent due to high inflation and volatile foreign exchange, a firm must move away from strict reporting measures. Thus, an international firm may need to consider alternative strategic control systems. Also, as a host country's financial and monetary environment becomes increasingly unstable, performance ambiguity increases for the MNC due to the negative effects on output measurability. The ability to have accurate performance

278 Section Two *Managing International Strategic Planning and Implementation*

measures declines. As a result, an MNC will increasingly tend to employ an input control system as its primary control system.

A Comprehensive Framework of International Control

Hamilton and Kashlak developed a framework linking the various external environmental variables to a firm's international control system selection. Each of the identified host-country environmental factors is individually an important variable for selecting an international firm's control system. A host country may, however, be on different positions along each of these dimensions simultaneously. All three of the host-country factors may be combined into a general framework to offer additional explanatory insights in situations that have two or three different environmental variables. Figure 7.9 illustrates the synthesis of the three host-country environmental variables and allows the manager to select control systems for host counties that vary along the three different dimensions. Each of the key intersections along these three dimensions has been numbered to identify the various intersections of cultural distance, host-government restrictions, and host-country economic environment.[46]

Maximum parental subsidiary control is represented by position 1. This situation occurs when comparatively stable foreign exchange and inflation rates are combined with low host-government restrictions and close cultural proximity. A Canadian MNC with a subsidiary in the United Kingdom would exemplify this situation. In the more stable country, the parent can accurately interpret outcomes and has limited performance ambiguity associated with behavior control. In short, the clarity of the situation allows for either market outcomes or behavior measures to be used, and no adjustment of the budgeted and actual rate of foreign exchange is required. Specifically, when host-country restrictions and cultural distance are low, the host-country manager may positively impact an overseas location's performance due to the knowledge of expected fluctuations and strategies to counter the potential effects of those

FIGURE 7.9 Host-Country External Environments and International Control Systems

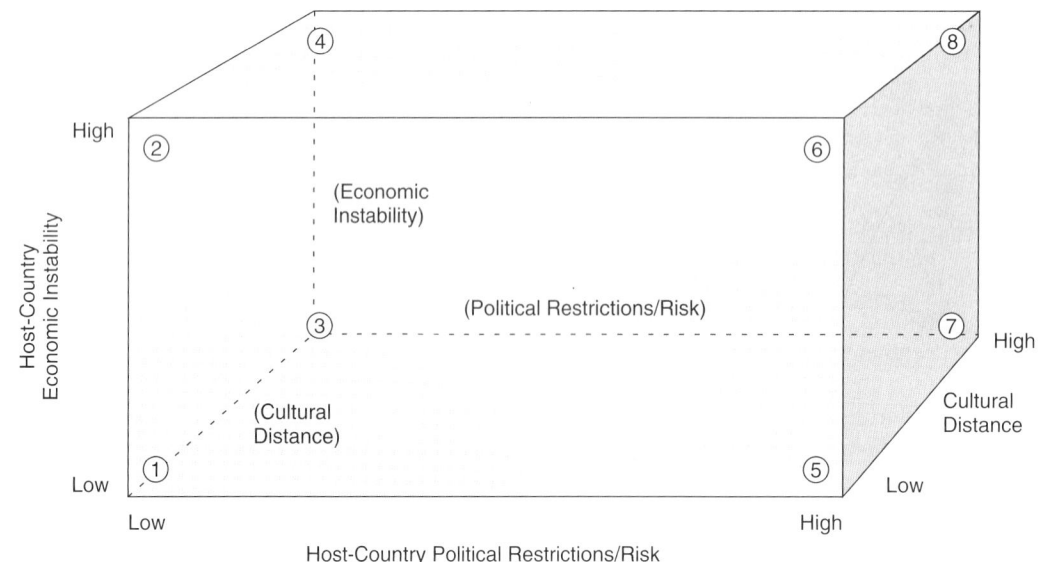

Source: R. Hamilton and R. Kashlak, "National Influences on MNC Control System Selection," *Management International Review* 39, no. 2 (1999). Reprinted with permission.

TABLE 7.1 Relationship of Host-Country Environment to Control System

Position	Cultural Distance	Political Risk	Economic Instability	Control System
1	Low	Low	Low	Output or behavior
2	Low	Low	High	Behavior
3	High	Low	Low	Output
4	High	Low	High	Input
5	Low	High	Low	Output
6	Low	High	High	Behavior and input
7	High	High	Low	Output and input
8	High	High	High	Input

movements derived from the planning process. Potential operating-level strategies include repatriating profits, maintaining inventory levels at a minimum, borrowing in host-country capital markets, and matching assets and liabilities. Furthermore, when the financial environment is relatively stable, the importance of these tactics is minimized. The overall situation allows the MNC headquarters a full range of options for monitoring overseas managers.[47]

Conversely, a host-country environment may be characterized by severe political constraints imposed by the host country coupled with a high degree of cultural distance and significant economic instability. This combination of conditions is identified in Figure 7.9 as position 8. As exemplified by Japanese subsidiaries in modern-day Russia, the instability and uncertainty in the environment make assessment of subsidiary performance exceptionally difficult even after using a transformational process on a subsidiary's results. In this example, the linkage of an inadequate outcome measurement combined with a lack of knowledge of the input–output transformation provides the managers with the highest degree of performance ambiguity. As a result of the headquarters' extreme difficulty in understanding the relationship between host-manager activity and performance, an input control system has the highest probability of being employed.

The remaining positions on the matrix (2 through 7) are characterized by at least one of the host-country variables constraining knowledge of the input–output transformation or output measurability. As a result, an international firm's ability to employ behavior and output control systems is correspondingly reduced. The firm must identify the form of control that maximizes the fit with the country characteristics. Table 7.1 further delineates Figure 7.9.

Designing an Effective International Control System

An effective control system cannot rely on reported profits and ROI as the dominant measures of performance of a foreign subsidiary, because the corporate headquarters of the company, rather than the subsidiary manager, makes most of the major decisions affecting the profitability of the subsidiary. To obtain a more accurate picture of a subsidiary's performance, one must be certain to eliminate extraneous factors—results, positive or negative, caused by decisions made above the subsidiary level; results due to environmental variables, such as unprecedented fluctuations in the price of raw materials (e.g., the dramatic increase in the price of petroleum from 2006 to 2008); or results due to government actions over which subsidiary management could not exercise any control. Thus, a subsidiary manager should be held accountable only for results that were caused by actions that he or she could initiate, without external interference, and by decisions that he or she could make unilaterally. The profit-and-loss statement or the ROI of a subsidiary may be adjusted to reflect its actual performance, taking into account the above-mentioned factors. It is conceivable, under such a system, for subsidiary managers to be rated quite favorably in spite of their having a poor profit-and-loss statement. The opposite is also possible: A manager who shows huge profits may still be judged a poor manager if his or her performance warrants such a judgment.

In addition to using financial measures, an assessment should also use nonfinancial measures of performance, such as market share, productivity, relations with the host-country government, public image, employee morale, union relations, and community involvement. Most companies do take into account some nonfinancial factors. However, it might be advisable to formalize the process, assigning scorecard ratings for all subsidiaries based on the same broad range of variables. Finally, the level of performance expected from a foreign subsidiary in the following year should consider the characteristics of its environment and any likely changes from the current year. Thus, an environment that was generally favorable one year might be expected to change for the worse the following year, and the level of performance expected should be appropriately lowered as well. Not doing so could lead to unhealthy pressure on the subsidiary manager, perhaps inducing him or her to make decisions about maintenance expenditures, service to customers, or the funding of process improvements that are detrimental in the long run to both the subsidiary and the company as a whole.

Parent–Subsidiary Relationships and Strategic Control Mechanisms

Two issues regarding the foreign subsidiaries of an international firm are the role that the subsidiaries play for the organization and the relationships between the subsidiaries and the organization's headquarters. Regarding the **foreign subsidiary roles**, Figure 7.10 depicts four separate roles for subsidiaries based on the competence of the subsidiary and the strategic importance of the host country.

In quadrant 1, when both the core competence of the subsidiary is high and the strategic importance of the host country is high, the foreign subsidiary takes on the role of *strategic leader*. Consistent with the geocentric orientation of a firm, the subsidiary partners with headquarters in strategy formulation and implementation on a global basis. Overall, the entities in this quadrant have a subsidiary mandate, that is, strategic responsibilities beyond their national market.[48]

FIGURE 7.10
Foreign Subsidiary Roles

Source: Adapted and reprinted by permission of *Harvard Business Review*. Exhibit from "Tap Your Subsidiaries for Global Reach," by Christopher Bartlett and Sumantra Ghoshal, November/December 1986. Copyright © 1986 by the Harvard Business School Publishing Corporation; all rights reserved.

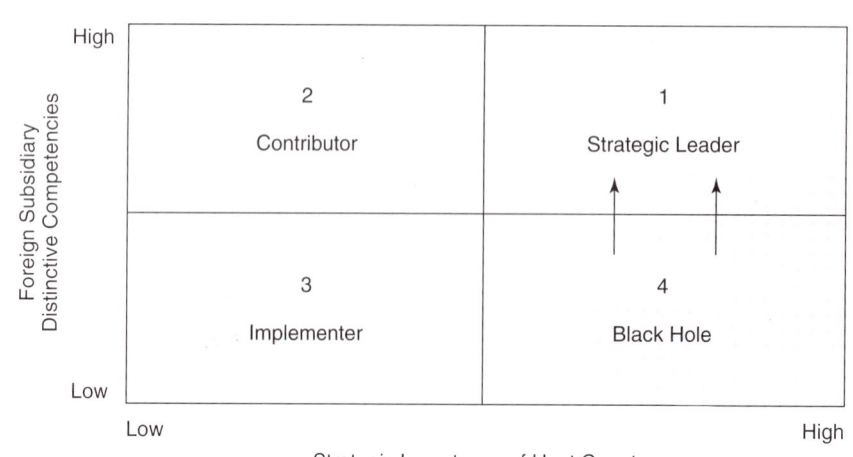

Foreign Subsidiary Distinctive Competencies	Low Strategic Importance of Host Country	High Strategic Importance of Host Country
High	2 Contributor	1 Strategic Leader
Low	3 Implementer	4 Black Hole

In quadrant 2, where the foreign subsidiary remains highly competent but the host country becomes an environment that is not strategically important, the role of the subsidiary becomes that of a *contributor.* That is, the firm must recognize and employ the distinctive competencies of the subsidiary to help the rest of the organization gain new knowledge and learning for future strategic initiatives.

Quadrant 3 represents an environment in which the host country is not strategically important and the foreign subsidiary lacks distinctive competencies. The resulting role for that subsidiary is *implementer.* Here, the local market potential is limited. Subsequently, consistent with an ethnocentric orientation of the firm, the foreign subsidiary reacts to headquarters' demands.

Finally, when the distinctive competency of the foreign subsidiary is low but the strategic importance of the host market is high, a problem exists for the international firm. Whereas in the other three segments of Figure 7.10, the challenge is to manage the situation with the appropriate role given to the foreign subsidiary, in quadrant 4 the *black hole* role represents an unacceptable position for the firm. The host country is a critical link within the greater international strategy of the firm. Thus, the firm must find a way to enhance the capabilities of the subsidiary in order for it to be strategically positioned within the host country.[49]

Regarding the headquarters–subsidiary relationship, the network of subsidiaries in an international company is characterized by three types of relationships between each subsidiary and the parent company: dependent, independent, and interdependent. A *dependent* subsidiary is one that is unable to generate strategic resources—such as technology, capital, management, and access to markets—independently of the parent company and must therefore obtain such resources from the parent company or from other subsidiaries after prior approval by the parent company. At the other extreme is the *independent* subsidiary, which can generate all the required strategic resources on its own. Between the two extreme positions is the *interdependent* subsidiary–parent relationship, in which the parent and the subsidiary are able to generate some, but not all, of the required strategic resources. In the interdependent relationship each side is dependent on the other for some strategic resources that it cannot generate by itself.

- **Example of a dependent subsidiary:** A subsidiary whose only role is to operate in the home market of a competitor and to launch strategic counterattacks locally against the competitor. The subsidiary is dependent on the parent company for the financial resources needed to stay in business. The strategic intent of the parent company in establishing the subsidiary was mainly to keep an eye on the competitor and to gather information on the competitor's strategic moves. The dependent subsidiary cannot survive for long without the strategic resources provided by the parent.

- **Example of an independent subsidiary:** A subsidiary in a country that has substantial restrictions on international trade that prevent the subsidiary from establishing production, marketing, financial, product, or service linkages with the parent and its other subsidiaries. The subsidiary is self-sufficient in the strategic resources required to implement its mission in the host country.

- **Example of subsidiary–parent interdependence:** A subsidiary that serves as a cash-cow to the parent company, and a parent that provides the subsidiary with state-of-the art technology to maintain the subsidiary's competitive advantage in the host country. Neither the parent nor the subsidiary can do without the strategic resource that each provides to the other.

Prahalad and Doz identified two principal methods by which a parent company could exercise *strategic control,* which they define as "the extent of influence that

FIGURE 7.11
Parent–Subsidiary Relationship and Strategic Control Mechanisms

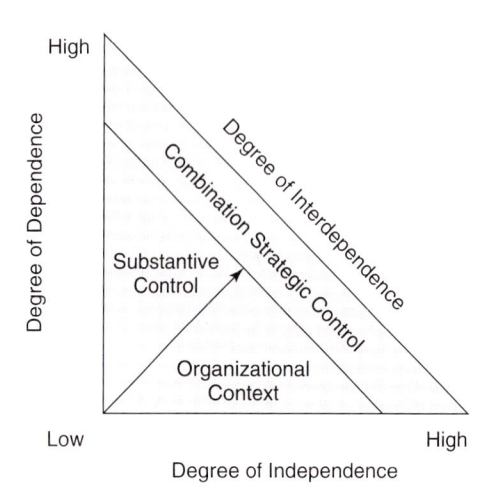

a head office has over a subsidiary concerning decisions that affect subsidiary strategy."[50] The two methods they identify are:

- **Substantive control,** restricting the flow of strategic resources.
- **Organizational context,** a blending of organizational structure, measurement and reward systems, career planning, and a common organizational culture, which would create the type of relationship between the parent and the subsidiary that would facilitate the continued influence of the former over the latter.[51]

Two examples of organizational contexts that would strengthen the parent's ability to exercise strategic control are (1) rewarding subsidiary managers for implementing strategies that support the global strategies of the international company and (2) making the position of subsidiary manager a "stop" on the way to higher-level positions in the company.

Substantive controls can be effective in influencing the strategy of dependent subsidiaries. Subsidiaries that are independent cannot be controlled with substantive controls alone because of their self-sufficiency from the parent company. In this case, the organizational context is most effective in compensating for the erosion of the parent's capacity to exercise strategic control. As the ability to use substantive control diminishes, the dependence of the parent company on organizational context to influence strategy of subsidiaries increases.[52]

The parent company will need to balance substantive control with effective use of organizational context to control the strategies of subsidiaries with which it is in an interdependent relationship. We shall call the joint use of both methods *combination strategic control*. Reliance solely on either substantive control or organizational context would cause loss of strategic control (see Figure 7.11).

Summary

This chapter was concerned with the typical stages in the evolution of the basic structures of international companies. Specific traditional organizational structures were discussed. They included the pre–international division phase, the international division structure, the global product structure, and the global area structure. Furthermore, the key current issues that face organizations today were discussed, including efficient communication, information sharing, and the creation and movement of knowledge throughout the entire organization.

Finding the organizational structure best suited to a company's global corporate strategy is a challenge that an international company's top management executives must meet effectively and efficiently. The imperative to coordinate functions, products, and areas has created problems and tensions in the internal transactions and management of international companies. Companies have usually modified the structures and made trade-offs among the various approaches while attempting to integrate their geographically far-flung operations. This has led to the exploration of multidimensional structures as well as ways that firms can enhance the traditional hierarchies. The international matrix structure was investigated and shown to offer a variety of advantages over the traditional structures as well as many distinct comparative disadvantages.

Another challenge facing international company managers is that, after finding a suitable structure for a particular global corporate strategy at a certain point in time, they must keep modifying the structure to suit evolving company strategy. This requirement for change is ever present in international enterprises. Thus, we illustrated the self-organizing structures that are becoming associated with transnational firms.

The managerial control process was then integrated into the international context. The focus was on the problems and characteristics of control systems adopted by multinational companies in order to manage their foreign subsidiaries, with emphasis on ways to improve the process. The purpose of control is to facilitate the implementation of plans by continuously monitoring the performance of the people responsible for carrying them out. There are four principal elements in the control process: (1) establishing standards against which performance is to be measured, (2) developing devices or techniques for monitoring individual or organizational performance, (3) comparing actual performance with planned performance, and (4) taking corrective action to eliminate significant deviations of performance from plans.

There are three separate types of control processes. Output control is based on specific measures of performance. Behavior control measures processes and the means–ends relationships within an organization. Input control is grounded in rigorous attention to hiring the right people and subsequently socializing them in order to "buy in" to the shared values and mission of the firm.

The process of control and the problems associated with it are far more complex in an international company than in its purely domestic counterpart because of the multiple cultural, economic, political, and legal environments in which its subsidiaries operate. Several divisive factors, such as geographic distance, language barriers, cultural distance, and differing frames of reference between the parent company and foreign subsidiary managers, are responsible for distortion in the information that is required for control purposes.

Different host-country environmental factors limit the ability of the international firm to globally standardize its control systems. As host-country cultural distance, political risk, and economic instability increase, the firm has less and less ability to accurately hold its subsidiary managers to specific, tangible outputs or behaviors.

The choice of strategic controls on a subsidiary also depends on the role that the subsidiary plays in the host country as well as globally and on whether the subsidiary is highly dependent on the parent, is highly independent from the parent, or has a high degree of interdependence with the parent. Substantive controls and control by means of organizational context can be balanced as appropriate to each relationship.

Key Terms and Concepts

behavior control, *273*
foreign subsidiary roles, *280*
global area structure, *260*
global product structure, *259*
heterarchy, *267*
host-country environmental factors, *275*
input control, *273*
international division, *256*
knowledge of the transformation process, *272*
matrix structure, *264*
organizational control, *282*
output control, *273*
output measure availability, *272*
substantive control, *282*
transnational structure, *268*

Discussion Questions

1. Compare and contrast the international product division structure and the international area division structure. What are the major benefits and drawbacks of each?
2. Why is the international matrix structure used by some firms? What are the problems in trying to implement this structure globally?
3. The heterarchy is a new form of organization structure. Why has it evolved? In your opinion, within which industries does this structure fit best? Why?
4. Why is the control process more difficult to implement in a multinational company than in a purely domestic company? Discuss factors that influence the effectiveness of a multinational company's control system.
5. What are output, behavior, and input controls? Give examples.
6. Explain why the reported profits of a foreign affiliate may not be a good measure of its true performance.
7. Explain how a host country's cultural distance, economic instability, and political risk can affect a company's control system for its subsidiaries in that country.

Minicase

A Guide for Multinationals

One of the great challenges for a multinational is learning how to build a productive global team.

Willy Chiu was parked outside a Palo Alto (Calif.) convenience store early one evening in January with his notebook PC switched on. Suddenly he heard the ping of an instant message arriving. It was the Tokyo-based head of IBM's Asia operations with urgent news: A major competitor was homing in on a pivotal project IBM had been chasing. The job, to develop a new IT system for a Korean bank, could be worth up to $100 million. Chiu, who runs IBM's worldwide network of elite labs, was needed to help develop a pilot product.

That plea ignited a flurry of online, BlackBerry, and cell-phone conversations across four continents. Within minutes, Chiu had 18 chat windows open simultaneously on his laptop. "How do we mobilize resources worldwide?" he typed in one message to the head of worldwide operations in San Jose. "I'll take the lead," responded IBM's country manager in Seoul. Chiu dashed off a note asking a team in Beijing to free up staff and quickly received confirmation that they were on the case. Then a banking specialist from England chimed in: "Our team can provide reference cases from Spain." Chiu to his administrative assistant: "Stella, please change my flight to a later time tonight. Also, looks like I may go to Korea again in a few weeks." Chiu to his wife: "Will be working late."

For global corporations, the borderless world of Willy Chiu offers a glimpse of what's to come. International success once meant having bodies and factories on the ground from Sao Paulo to Silicon Valley to Shanghai. Coordinating their activities was a deliberately planned effort handled by headquarters.

The challenge now is to weld these vast, globally dispersed workforces into superfast, efficient organizations. Given the conflicting needs of multinational staff and the swiftly shifting nature of competition brought about by the Internet, that's an almost impossible task. And getting workers to collaborate instantly—not tomorrow or next week, but now—requires nothing less than a management revolution.

Complicating matters is the fact that the very idea of a company is shifting away from a single outfit with full-time employees and a recognizable hierarchy. It is something much more fluid, with a classic corporation at the center of an ever-shifting network of suppliers and outsourcers, some of whom only join the team for the duration of a single project.

To adapt, multinationals are hiring sociologists to unlock the secrets of teamwork among colleagues who have never met. They're arming staff with an arsenal of new tech tools to keep them perpetually connected. They include software that helps engineers co-develop 3D prototypes in virtual worlds and services that promote social networking and that track employees and outsiders who have the skills needed to nail a job. Corporations are investing lavishly in posh campuses, crafting leadership training centers, and offering thousands of online courses to develop pipelines of talent.

To function in this Age of Diffusion, businesses are rethinking traditional practices. In human resources, the era of standardized benefits and work requirements is vanishing. Instead, to keep prized talent, companies need to accommodate a wide range of cultural and generational idiosyncrasies. In China, where personal relationships are paramount, employers have to tread carefully with hard-edged practices such as management reshuffles and 360-degree performance reviews. To keep valued Indian workers from jumping ship, companies are offering one-on-one career planning and reaching out to parents and spouses. Multinationals that viewed Eastern Europe as a terrific low-cost engineering shop are finding that if they don't give the local scientists a crack at real innovation, they soon are coping with a brain drain.

Dow Chemical is trying to navigate this complex new territory. Dow expects 30% of its 20,000 workers to retire in the next five years. Meanwhile, enrollment in U.S. chemical engineering schools is declining, forcing Dow to fight against deep-pocketed oil and gas companies for scarce talent. To persuade veterans to stay as long as possible, Dow is offering flexible hours, three-day workweeks, and reminders that the door is always open should they want to come back after retirement. But when recruiting college grads, says Dow human resources manager Deborah Berg, the company stresses its efforts to develop green technologies and improve living standards in developing nations.

The hard part for multinationals is getting people to work well together, especially given that day-and-night collaboration across the globe is growing. Over the past decade many companies rushed to spread key functions, such as product development, to the far corners of the earth. The idea was to save time and money. But corporations are finding that running these new operations requires much more effort than connecting staff by phone and e-mail. "One problem with distributing work is that you lose the intimacy of talking things through at a local cafe," says Forrester Research network innovation expert Navi Radjou. London Business School management professor Lynda Gratton, who led a study of 52 global teams in 15 leading multinationals, spotted the same problem. "Complex teams really struggle to be productive," says Gratton.

Such pressures put a premium on recruiting staff who are globally minded from the outset rather than being mere technicians. Gratton found that global marketing and product development teams at Nokia were especially effective, even though they involve scores of people working in several countries. She says Nokia is careful to select people who have a "collaborative mindset" and carefully includes in task forces a range of nationalities, ages, and education levels. Teams also are made up of people who have worked together in the past and others who have never met, Gratton adds. Members are encouraged to network online and share their photographs and personal biographies.

Training is essential to making staffers globally minded. Accenture, which spent $700 million on education last year, says its 38,000 consultants and most of its services workers take courses on collaborating with offshore colleagues. And each year, Accenture puts up to 400 of its most promising managers through a special leadership development program. They are assigned to groups that can include Irish, Chinese, Belgians, and Filipinos, and specialists in fields such as finance, marketing, and technology. Over 10 months, teams meet in different international locations. As part of the program, they pick a project—developing a new Web page, say—and learn how to tap the company's worldwide talent pool to complete it.

IBM aims to set itself apart with a spate of Web-based services that make it easier for its 360,000-member staff to "work as one virtual team," says Lab chief Chiu. Big Blue has launched what it calls an innovation portal, where any employee with a product idea can use online chat boxes to organize a team, line up resources, and gain access to market research. Developers in IBM labs around the world then can collaborate on prototypes and testing. This way, enterprising staff can build a global team in as little as half an hour and cut the time to start a business from at least six months to around

30 days. An example: For a major U.S. telecom client that needed a Web-based tool to launch new services such as video streaming for cell phones, IBM organized a 20-member group including staff from Japan, Brazil, and Britain. These IBMers built a working prototype in two weeks and delivered a finished product in two months. Since IBM introduced the portal, in early 2006, 93,000 workers have logged on, leading to 70 businesses and 10 new products. Creating a seamless global workforce is hard. But certain multinationals are slowly figuring out how to do it.

Source: Pete Engardio. *BusinessWeek,* August 20, 2007, p. 48.

DISCUSSION QUESTIONS

1. Using the companies mentioned in this case, discuss the factors that must be considered to effectively implement a strategy for a multinational firm.
2. In your opinion, what are the linkages of the strategic orientations (global, multidomestic, and transnational) discussed in Chapter 5 with the initiatives seen by the firms analyzed in this case.
3. What control issues must be addressed by each of these firms?

Notes

1. R. Engdahl, R. Keating, and K. Aupperle, "Strategy of Structure: Chicken or Egg?" *Organization Development* 18, no. 4 (2000), pp. 21–34.
2. K. Kim, J. Park, and J. Prescott, "The Global Integration of Business Functions: A Study of Multinational Businesses in Integrated Global Industries," *Journal of International Business Studies* 34, no. 4 (2003), pp. 327–344.
3. A. Harzing, "An Empirical Analysis and Extension of the Bartlett-Ghoshal Typology of Multinational Corporations," *Journal of International Business Studies* 31, no. 1 (2000), pp. 101–120.
4. M. Harris and A. Raviv, "Organization Design," *Management Science* 48, no. 7 (2002), pp. 852–866.
5. S. Ghoshal and N. Nohria, "Horses for Courses: Organizational Forms for Multinational Corporations," *Sloan Management Review* 34, no. 2 (1993), pp. 23–36.
6. J. Stopford and L. Wells Jr., *Managing the Multinational Enterprise* (New York: Basic Books, 1972), p. 51.
7. L. Garicano, "Hierarchies and the Organization of Knowledge in Production," *Journal of Political Economy* 108 (2000), pp. 874–904.
8. O. Hart and J. Moore, "On the Design of Hierarchies: Coordination versus Specialization," working paper, Department of Economics, Harvard University, Cambridge, MA, 1999.
9. D. Vayanos, "The Decentralization of Information Processing in the Presence of Interactions," working paper, MIT, Cambridge, MA, 2002.
10. J. Daniels, D. Pitts, and R. Tretter, "Strategy and Structure of U.S. Multinationals: An Exploratory Study," *Academy of Management Journal* 27, no. 2 (1984), pp. 292–308.
11. A. Phatak, *Managing Multinational Corporations* (New York: Praeger, 1974), p. 183.
12. Daniels, Pitts, and Tretter, "Strategy and Structure of U.S. Multinationals."
13. Stopford and Wells, *Managing the Multinational Enterprise,* p. 87.
14. P. Jennergren, "Decentralization in Organizations," in Paul C. Nystrom and William H. Starbuck, eds., *Handbook of Organizational Design* (New York: Oxford University Press, 1981).
15. C. Bartlett and S. Ghoshal, "Matrix Management: Not a Structure, a Frame of Mind," *Harvard Business Review,* July–August 1990, pp. 138–145.
16. P. Drucker, *Management: Tasks, Responsibilities, Practices* (New York: Harper & Row, 1974), p. 598.
17. Ibid.
18. R. Joyce, "Global Hero," *International Management,* September 1992, pp. 82 and 85.
19. G. Hedlund, "A Model of Knowledge Management and the N-Form Corporation," *Strategic Management Journal* 15 (1994), pp. 73–90.

20. J. Birkinshaw and A. Morrison, "Configurations of Strategy and Structure in Subsidiaries of Multinational Structure," *Journal of International Business Studies* 26, no. 4 (1995), pp. 729–753.
21. J. Galbraith and E. Lawler, "Effective Organizations: Using the New Logic for Organizing," in Galbraith et al., eds., *Organizing for the Future* (San Francisco: Jossey-Bass, 1993).
22. Hedlund, "A Model of Knowledge Management."
23. G. Hedlund, "The Hypermodern MNC—a Heterarchy," *Human Resource Management* 25, no. 1 (1986), pp. 9–25.
24. C. Bartlett, "What is a Global Manager?" *Harvard Business Review* 81, no. 8 (2003), p. 101.
25. C. Bartlett and S. Ghoshal, *Managing across Borders: The Transnational Solution* (Boston: Harvard Business School Press, 1989); M. S. Gerstein and R. B. Shaw, "Organizational Architecture for the Twenty-First Century," in D. A. Nadler, M. E. Gerstein, R. B. Shaw, and Associates, eds., *Organizational Architecture: Designs for Changing Organizations* (San Francisco: Jossey-Bass, 1992), pp. 263–273.
26. M. Gerstein and R. B. Shaw, "Organizational Architecture for the Twenty-First Century."
27. A. Mukherti, "The Evolution of Information Systems: Their Impact on Organizations and Structures," *Management Decision* 40, no. 5/6 (2002), pp. 497–508.
28. S. Snell, "Control Theory in Strategic Human Resource Management: The Mediating Effect of Administrative Information," *Academy of Management Journal* 35, no. 2 (1992), pp. 292–318.
29. W. Ouchi, "The Relationship between Organizational Structure and Organizational Control," *Administrative Science Quarterly,* March 1977, pp. 95–113.
30. V. Govindarajan and F. Fisher, "Strategy, Control Systems and Resource Sharing: Effects on Business-Unit Performance," *Academy of Management Journal* 33 (1990), pp. 259–285.
31. Snell, "Control Theory in Strategic Human Resource Management."
32. A. Jaeger and B. Baliga, "Control Systems and Strategic Adaptation: Lessons from the Japanese Experience," *Strategic Management Journal* 6 (1985), pp. 115–134.
33. V. Govindarajan and F. Fisher, "Strategy, Control Systems and Resource Sharing."
34. B. Chakravarthy and Y. Doz, "Strategy Process Research: Focusing on Corporate Self-Renewal," *Strategic Management Journal* 13 (1992), pp. 5–14; Bartlett and Ghoshal, *Managing across Borders.*
35. M. Hitt, R. Hoskisson, and R. Ireland, "Mergers and Acquisitions and Managerial Commitment to Innovation in M-Form Firms," *Strategic Management Journal* 11 (1990), pp. 29–47.
36. C. Hill and R. Hoskisson, "Strategy and Structure in Multiproduct Firms" *Academy of Management Review* 12 (1987), pp. 331–341.
37. W. Chan and R. Mauborge, "Effectively Conceiving and Executing Multinationals' Worldwide Strategies," *Journal of International Business Studies* 24, no. 3 (1993), pp. 419–448.
38. David Clutterbuck, "Breaking Through the Cultural Barriers," *International Management,* December 1980, p. 41.
39. Phatak, *Managing Multinational Corporations,* p. 225.
40. R. Vernon, L. Wells, and S. Rangan, *The Manager in the International Economy,* 7th ed. (Upper Saddle River, NJ: Prentice Hall), 1996.
41. R. Hamilton, V. Taylor, and R. Kashlak, "Designing a Control System for a Multinational Subsidiary," *Long Range Planning* 29, no. 6 (1996), pp. 857–868.
42. L. Gomez-Meija and L. Palich, "Cultural Diversity and the Performance of Multinational Firms," *Journal of International Business Studies* 28, no. 2 (1997), pp. 309–335; K. Roth and S. O'Donnell, "Foreign Subsidiary Compensation: An Agency Theory Perspective," *Academy of Management Journal* 39, no. 3 (1996), pp. 678–703.
43. R. Hamilton and R. Kashlak, "National Influences on MNC Control System Selection, Management," *International Review* 39, no. 2 (1999), pp. 167–189.
44. Vernon, Wells, and Rangan, *The Manager in the International Economy.*
45. D. Lessard and P. Lorange, "Currency Changes and Management Control: Resolving the Centralization–Decentralization Dilemma," *Accounting Review,* July 1977, pp. 628–637.

46. Hamilton and Kashlak, "National Influences on MNC Control System Selection."
47. Ibid.
48. J. Birkinshaw, "How Multinational Subsidiary Mandates Are Gained and Lost," *Journal of International Business Studies* 27, no. 3 (1996), pp. 467–496.
49. C. Bartlett and S. Ghoshal, "Tap Your Subsidiaries for Global Reach," *Harvard Business Review,* November–December 1986, pp. 1–11.
50. C. K. Prahalad and Yves I. Doz, "An Approach to Strategic Control in MNCs," *Sloan Management Review,* Summer 1981, pp. 5–13.
51. Ibid., p. 8.
52. Ibid.

CHAPTER EIGHT

Managing Technology and Knowledge

Chapter Learning Objectives

After completing this chapter, you should be able to:

- Understand the concept of technology and the process of technology transfer.
- Explain the relevance of appropriate technology transfer for international management.
- Define and distinguish among the concepts of data, information, and knowledge.
- Understand the relevance of these three commodities for international management.
- Explain the process of creation, transformation, and transfer of knowledge.
- Identify the processes that integrate management of technology and knowledge with strategic processes of international and global corporations.
- Understand the roles of strategic factors, administrative heritage, and technical systems in the process of knowledge transfer.
- Understand the concept of learning organizations.

Opening Case: Transferring Knowledge in Global Corporations

Ford: Europe Has a Better Idea
Can Detroit Replicate the European Turnaround at Home?

In the annals of Ford Motor Co., 2001 will go down as its *annus horribilis*. The world's No. 2 auto maker was hit by a second Firestone tire recall, recalls of key vehicles like the Explorer, other quality glitches, and launch delays. Not to mention angry dealers, demoralized employees, and the autumn ouster of its CEO—all culminating in a $5.4 billion annual loss. Amid all this gloom and doom, though, there was one bright spot. Ford of Europe Inc., a subsidiary with almost $30 billion in sales, battled its way to breakeven after a $1.1 billion loss in 2000. This year a modest profit is likely, thanks to aggressive cost-cutting and a refreshed lineup.

Nice work. But Europe isn't just a bright spot for Ford—it's the model for the entire turnaround effort for Ford in North America. Nicholas V. Scheele, Ford president and chief operating officer, and Chairman William C. Ford Jr.'s right-hand man, engineered the rescue of Ford of Europe. Bill Ford is gambling that Scheele can replicate his lifesaving strategies in Detroit: "Ford of Europe was the biggest turnaround of any unit in Ford's history," he says. "In many ways, it's the template for what to do here." But this strategy is not without risks. If the rebound at Ford of Europe stalls, then doubts about Ford's overall strategy will quickly multiply.

For clues, investors will be watching Scheele, the 58-year-old Briton who led the turnaround of Ford of Europe after having overhauled the Ford-owned Jaguar marque. The European unit racked up $2.5 billion in losses through the 1990s. "It was a broken business," says David W. Thursfield,

Scheele's former No. 2 and current Ford of Europe Chairman. Development time for new models was laughably slow: The Fiesta compact bumped along for 12 years without a major remake. And Europeans had concluded that Fords were duds to drive and embarrassing to own. From 1994 to 2000, the Ford brand's share of the European car market shrank by one-fourth, to 8.2%. Nearly one-third of Ford's European production network sat idle. Capacity utilization—a key gauge—sank to 71% in 2000, well below the break-even level.

Scheele and Thursfield embarked on an overhaul. In just two years, they shuttered three plants and slashed more than 2,000 jobs—or nearly 2% of the unit's total workforce. The pair whittled away a fourth of the Ford brand's production capacity—600,000 units. One painful move was the decision to stop assembling cars at the Dagenham (Britain) factory after 69 years.

Just as important, Scheele and Thursfield overhauled Ford's four big car-assembly plants in Europe so they could produce more than one model on the same line. Such "flex factories" can save the company hundreds of millions of dollars it otherwise would have to spend on separate assembly lines. "Ford did it right in Europe," says J. P. Morgan Securities analyst Himanshu Patel.

The duo also attacked the lackluster lineup. Luckily, Ford already had one hit on its hands, the stylish $12,200 Focus compact, launched in 1998, and another in the pipeline, the $17,500 Mondeo, which debuted two years ago. *Auto Motor und Sport* magazine rated the Mondeo best in its class in 2001, ahead of VW's popular Passat. And this year's edition of the annual TUV quality survey showed the Focus had fewer defects than any other car sold in Germany since 1999. Bolstered by the success of these two models, Ford's market share in Europe has climbed to 8.8%, ahead of Fiat Auto. "The Focus is selling very well. It's a good value for the price," says Hans-Joachim Kremer, owner of the Ford Autohaus Kremer dealership in Frankfurt.

Ford of Europe is now rolling out more new cars—and faster. A new $10,200 Fiesta was launched last year nine months ahead of schedule, and the Fusion, a compact minivan, is due out in October. The Fusion is targeted at the growing number of Europeans who want something small and fuel-efficient but more versatile than a sedan.

These are the broad outlines of the Ford turnaround. But the little moments count, too. Thursfield convened weekly meetings in a "war room" at Ford's Merkenich design studio near Cologne (no sitting allowed). At one of those encounters, executives discovered they were paying one gas-tank supplier twice as much as another for the same-quality product. By picking up on those discrepancies, Scheele saved $900 million over the past two years. Thursfield wants to wring out a further $400 million this year. Says one Ford official: "The trick is to look at everything."

That's what Scheele plans to do in Michigan, where staff already has adopted some of the European methods. Dearborn headquarters now boasts its own war room, though officials prefer to call it the "energy room." Ford is also looking across the Atlantic for lessons on how to make better use of its plants. Ford's revamped Cologne factory is capable of assembling any model in the European lineup, from the Ka minicar to the Galaxy van. Bill Ford wants that kind of versatility in North America, where the company has no flex factories. "You don't need all your plants to be flexible, but you need a portion, probably about a third," he says.

To stanch the red ink at domestic operations, Bill Ford is adopting many of the measures the company implemented in Europe even before it's clear whether they are working there. Ford models are doing well now in Europe, but it's an unusual moment in the Continent's car cycle. Market heavies Renault and Volkswagen are both in the midst of major makeovers of their lineup. That's giving Ford some needed breathing room—but it won't last forever. PSA Peugeot Citroen is on a product roll, and GM's Opel is about to embark on a restructuring. Meanwhile, luxury marques such as Mercedes-Benz and BMW are putting the squeeze on middle-market players by producing smaller, more affordable models.

And the trade-offs Ford of Europe made between savings and quality may still come back to haunt the company. The new Fiesta has gotten knocks for its plasticky, cheap-looking dashboard. And the Focus comes less richly equipped than rivals. Antilock brakes are standard on the Fiat Stilo and the Peugeot 307. On most of the Focus range, they're an option. Small details, but they add up—and sometimes they turn potential customers off. Bill Ford can learn some lessons from Europe. He just has to make sure they're the right ones.

Source: Reprinted from Christine Tierney and Kathleen Kerwin, "Ford: Europe Has a Better Idea: Can Detroit Replicate the European Turnaround at Home?" *BusinessWeek*, April 15, 2002, by special permission. Copyright © 2002 by The McGraw-Hill Companies, Inc.

Discussion Questions

1. How will Ford replicate European practices, that is, technological know-how, in its Detroit location?
2. What are the potential effects of ineffective transfers on global companies such as Ford?
3. What are some of the difficulties of transfers of technology and scientific know-how across borders and cultures?

Understanding Technology

Consider an international company that, among other business units, has a sales office in Argentina, a manufacturing subsidiary in China, and a research and development office at corporate headquarters in the United States. As we discussed in Chapter 1, international management is about the challenge of managing the international activities of such companies. Among the many activities of international companies, the management of technology and knowledge is crucial. An international company must answer questions such as: How does the company create new forms of technology that are needed in the manufacturing subsidiary in China? How does it successfully transfer knowledge created in Argentina about the emerging market trends to its headquarters in the United States?

Technology and knowledge transfer are not new. They have existed in the field of international business for more than a century. The complexities surrounding the process of transfer of technology and new forms of knowledge created in important subsidiaries around the world are important to understand, especially in today's highly competitive international environment. Consider the experience of the Ford Motor Company. In the past, the Ford Motor Company created new forms of innovation in the design of cars solely in the corporate headquarters located in the United States. In 1994, the company moved its design office, where new technology and knowledge are created, to one of its European subsidiaries in Germany. The company decided that moving the design office from Detroit would strengthen the technology and knowledge transfer process from the German subsidiary, which was relatively more effective in developing new designs for cars.[1]

The People's Republic of China is becoming one of the fastest-growing markets for software products from companies such as Microsoft and Intel. However, vast linguistic, cultural, and legal differences characterize China and the United States, where the headquarters of some of the largest software companies in the world are located. Microsoft's and other software companies' success in China depends heavily on their effectiveness in customizing the user interface of their products, something more easily planned than accomplished. Thus, given the large market, Microsoft decided to locate one of the biggest research programs in language recognition and speech input in China. Technological advances and knowledge emerging from these activities in China will assist Microsoft to increase its market share, not only in China and East Asia, but also in other parts of the world.[2] Details are discussed in Practical Insight 8.1.

PRACTICAL INSIGHT 8.1

AT CHINA'S GATES: MICROSOFT BOSS CONQUERS A KEY ASIAN MARKET

On the expressway running north from Hong Kong to the Chinese city of Guangzhou, a small convoy is creating quite a commotion. A white Mercedes-Benz, escorted by a police car with blaring sirens and flashing lights, speeds past construction ditches, shacks and bicycles, dodging container lorries on the way. The scene startles other road users—and small wonder. In a little liberty taken to avoid a detour caused by road works, the cars are racing up a southbound lane, forcing oncoming vehicles to move out of the way.

Stopping at a city pier, the Mercedes' occupant boards a boat for a river crossing to the back entrance of a hotel. Inside, more than a thousand admirers and local dignitaries, squeezed into not one but two auditoriums, eagerly await his entrance.

Who is this great man? Some icon from the communist pantheon in Beijing, a Western pop superstar?

No, this is Bill Gates: chairman of Microsoft, supplier of computer programs to the world.

There is some irony in the reception that awaited Gates's December visit. Less than two years ago, the Microsoft boss travelled practically unnoticed in China. Even to those who recognized the name, he was the American who lost a fight with President Jiang Zemin over a Chinese version of Windows (Microsoft's flagship operating system) that had been developed partly in Taiwan.

The transformation in Microsoft's profile in China since then, coupled with its increasing inroads in other parts of Asia, underlie the software giant's jump into top spot among multinationals in the REVIEW 200 survey. And it's a development that has enormous implications not only for Microsoft but also for the future of computing throughout the region.

In an interview, Gates acknowledges the importance of the huge Chinese market and the rest of Asia for his company. "It's the highest-growth region" in the world, he says, and Microsoft can expect "a lot of growth" itself. China, he adds "has a low level of sales right now, but that's okay. We're taking the long-term view."

The first step was to resolve Microsoft's problems with the Chinese government, which has now approved Windows 95 as one of several standard platforms for software development. That means program writers will have government approval to produce software that works with the Windows operating system. In turn, this will help Microsoft increase its market share. The company reckons that over half of all PCs in China already use authentic or pirated versions of Windows.

China, though, isn't the only Asian country Microsoft has mastered since it set up its first Asian office—in Japan— about a decade ago. It is now No. 1 in sales of software for desktop PCs in Japan, South Korea and Hong Kong, counting both operating systems and applications, says Charles Stevens, Microsoft's vice-president for the Far East.

Microsoft's success is putting other software developers —American and Asian alike—on edge, not to mention government officials trying to jumpstart indigenous software industries. "We don't want anyone to dominate," says Chen Chong, deputy director of the computer department at China's Ministry of Electronics. "China wants to create a fair and competitive environment."

Gates plays down the fears that Asia will become swamped with American computer software—a worry exacerbated by the increasing popularity of the Internet, the worldwide computer network, which will help American programs to reach Asia faster than ever before. "If people have such a pessimistic view, they need to be in a different business," he quips. As for the Internet, he notes, it provides a channel for a two-way flow of information, removing geographical constraints on selling all sorts of goods and services. "You have an opportunity to be in markets that you could not participate in before."

In any case, it's not that easy for even mighty Microsoft to dominate Asia. "We don't have indigenous competition in other places," Gates says, acknowledging the rise of Asian software developers, particularly in Japan. And as strong as Microsoft is in the region, he notes, "our market share in Asia is lower than anywhere else in the world."

Asian software developers, moreover, can sometimes play rough. South Korean on-line service providers, for example, recently misinformed the press that Seoul had banned Microsoft Service Network, an adjunct of Windows 95 that helps users connect to the Internet. Once it became clear

---

Before we can understand the process and the complexities that accompany the transfer of technology across various subsidiaries of a global corporation, such as in the case of Microsoft (Practical Insight 8.1), we need a better grasp of the concept of technology. When the clock radio comes on in the morning, waking you with the news, it is also sharing $73 billion in annual advertising spending by various international corporations. Your toothpaste is a product of millions of dollars of research investment and much more in building technological facilities to create the product. On a purely cost basis, 50 percent of the price represents the cost of technological knowledge. The car you drive

that wasn't the case, they threatened to follow the American Justice Department's lead and file an antitrust suit. "But they won't do anything unless the United States does," Stevens, the Microsoft vice-president, predicts.

The fiercest competition comes from copycats. Pirated versions of Windows 95, the latest version of the operating system, were available in Hong Kong as soon as the authentic version was officially released. "There are a lot of strong local competitors," says Stevens. "But the biggest competition by far is piracy."

Piracy, however, has helped Asia's PC markets grow rapidly—and with them Microsoft's market share. The easy availability of copied Microsoft software has thwarted potential local competitors by making it tougher for them to enter the business. The downside for Microsoft is that although it has a high market share, its Asian revenues are low. The region accounts for only about 10% of its worldwide sales, according to industry sources. (Microsoft declines to confirm the number.) Describing his company's prospects in the Chinese market, where piracy is rampant, Gates wryly told a Hong Kong audience: "Hopefully, as it grows, people will actually pay for the software as well."

Whatever the misgivings about Microsoft's dominance, more Asian software developers are switching to its Windows platform. Microsoft boasts of conferences attended by thousands of Chinese developers anxious to learn more about the program. Wee Liang Toon, a software analyst at International Data Corp., which watches the computer industry, concurs: "Developers are beginning to see the advantage of developing on a Windows platform."

Despite rampant piracy, Microsoft's Asian sales are doing well. IDC forecasts that as many as one million copies of Windows 95 will be sold in Japan this year—out of more than 10 million that Gates says are now in use worldwide.

Microsoft's Japanese office employs around 1,000 people and is its largest subsidiary in terms of revenues outside the United States, exceeding the company's operations in France, Britain or Germany. Microsoft has also invested in software development in Japan—as it has in China, South Korea and Taiwan.

These local labs, the only ones of their kind in Microsoft's empire outside the U.S., customize the company's products for Asian markets, enabling it to deliver local versions faster than if it was developing them in the U.S. When the company introduced Windows 3.0 in Hong Kong in 1990, it took two more years to come out with a Chinese version. This year, it released a local version of Windows 95 in Hong Kong only three months after the English one. A version based on the simplified Chinese script used in the mainland is due out in the first quarter of 1996.

In addition to customizing Microsoft's products for local users, the company's developers in Asia are also researching leading-edge programs for the future. Among other things, these may eventually enable users to speak instructions to their PCs rather than use a keyboard. Microsoft's biggest research program in language recognition and speech input is in China.

The company has also built up a sizable support network for Asian developers and customers. It claims to have more than 30 engineers in Hong Kong manning phone lines to answer questions from customers. The company has also begun to offer consultancy services. In Hong Kong, it has helped set up a telephone betting system for the Jockey Club and a database for Hongkong Telecom.

As for Microsoft's future in Asia, its executives talk of expanding its presence in software businesses ranging from traditional spreadsheet and database-management systems to consumer applications and interactive television. The one thing Microsoft says it doesn't want to do in Asia is design company-specific programs that have to conform with local accounting, inventory and tax requirements. "If we had a million people we couldn't develop that expertise," says Stevens.

In Guangzhou, Gates tells his Chinese audience he wants local help in turning his vision of an information age into reality. As for worries that Asian developers might be squelched in the process by the Microsoft juggernaut, he says: "Somebody's confused. Software is a huge industry."

Source: Emily Thornton, "At China's Gates: Microsoft Boss Conquers a Key Asian Market," *Far Eastern Economic Review*, December–January 1996. Copyright © 1996 by Dow Jones & Co., Inc. Reproduced with permission of Dow Jones & Co., Inc., via Copyright Clearance Center.

to work in probably has more computing power than was available for Apollo 11 scientists to put two men on the moon. Today's automobiles "know" how much fuel you have and when your tires are low, and they can give you directions and even maps. The information-infused car, with voice-activated Internet access, real-time traffic information, and the ability to diagnose problems, is a phenomenon that 1960s automobile engineers could not imagine. Information, technology, and knowledge are embedded in almost all the products that we use in today's world, and more and more products, even those sold in developing parts of the world, contain these three commodities.

Technology and Technology Transfer

Technology comprises a systemically developed set of information, skills, and processes that are needed to create, develop, and innovate products and services. This definition suggests that new forms of technology are developed in organizations that would like to launch new products or services in order to increase their market share. **Technology transfer** is the movement of technology from one person to another, one unit to another, or one company to another.

Technological competence is important, not only for sustaining international competitiveness but also for emerging economies, such as India and China, and less developed countries, such as the African states. Sophisticated technologies are transferred to these countries when prevailing economic conditions are appropriate. For example, computer use is very difficult in countries where the electric infrastructure is inconsistent—that is, where the electricity supply can go on and off without warning—and baby-food processing plants have difficulty operating in countries that do not have clean water. In addition, the transfer of technologies has to meet local objectives and priorities, such as government regulations, export requirements, and licensing agreements. One of the key factors that influences technology transfer is the extent of capital participation and payments for technology as agreed on by the two countries. Technology transfers are relatively quicker and more efficient among subsidiaries of global corporations, because policies and programs pertaining to implementation are relatively uniform.[3]

Organizational cultures also play a role. Global corporations that emphasize technology transfer among subsidiaries routinely are generally successful. International and global companies compete fiercely to launch new technologies today. They concentrate on three types of technology: product-embodied technology, process-embodied technology, and person-embodied technology.[4]

Global companies transfer *product-embodied technologies* by transferring the physical product itself. When the Caterpillar Company, headquartered in Peoria, Illinois, or Komatsu Incorporated of Japan transfers heavy earth-tilling machinery and related products, such as bulldozers, to a country such as Kuwait or Argentina, it is engaging in the process of transferring product-embodied technology. Transferring product-embodied technologies is routine. Global corporations from the major industrialized countries, as well as those in emerging economies such as India, Brazil, and China, transfer technologies to countries that are less developed and are able to pay for such technologies.

Developers transfer *process-embodied technology* by transferring blueprint or patent rights of the actual scientific processes and engineering details. Examples include transfer of chemical technology for the manufacture of synthetic fabrics and offshore oil exploration technology. When ExxonMobil or Texaco transfers oil-drilling technology to its subsidiaries in Saudi Arabia or Nigeria, it is transferring process-embodied technology. Blueprints and working know-how of these technologies can be transferred relatively easily by means of the Internet or by trained technical personnel who physically carry the manuals and procedures with them.

By contrast, *person-embodied technology* is transferred through continuous dialogue between the supplier and the recipient organizations pertaining to the intrinsic nature, diffusion, and utilization of scientific details that are hard to articulate in the form of either process or product. The intrinsic nature of person-embodied technology makes transfer as a one-shot or quick process difficult. A series of exchanges may be needed for a global company, such as Bechtel, headquartered in San Francisco, to transfer its technology for creating nuclear power plants to a company located in

Bombay, India, or Seoul, South Korea. Person-embodied technology is the most difficult of the three types to transfer. An advanced technological infrastructure and a trained workforce at the receiving end are required before such exchanges can be successfully initiated. In addition, strong regulations govern transfers of nuclear fuel, rocket, satellite, and other advanced technology.

In recent years, almost all types of technology that have been created involve some form of product-, process-, and person-embodied technologies. Competition for creating new forms of process- and person-embodied technologies is increasingly fierce among various companies within a particular industrial sector.

Success in creating a certain highly marketable technology does not imply that a company will be successful in transferring this technology to its various subsidiaries. In international management, the common expression used is "technology transfer," not "technology sale."[5] A global company, such as Procter & Gamble, may license a producer in a different country to manufacture its popular forms of toothpaste or health care products, but it does not engage in *selling* its technology. Licensing, which was discussed in Chapter 7, is the most common method of gaining royalties from technologies. Technology is typically considered a public good or common resource that should be used for improving the quality of life for all. Dangerous military technologies, such as nuclear missiles and biological and chemical weapons, are an exception. Problems in transfer can result from differences in the legal and economic systems of countries in which the subsidiaries of the global organizations are located, or problems can arise when two diverse corporations are involved. Among the factors influencing technology transfer are:[6]

- **Similar language.** Transfer of technology from an English-speaking country, such as the United States, to another English-speaking country, such as the United Kingdom, is relatively easy.
- **Common ancestry and shared history.** Common elements in ancestry and historical background facilitate technology transfer. For example, the Japanese are traditionally successful in transferring technology they create in their cultural context to countries such as South Korea, Taiwan, and Singapore.
- **Physical proximity.** The physical proximity between the United States and Latin America, as well as between Germany and east European countries, facilitates technology transfers. U.S. companies have typically succeeded in transferring technology from the U.S. headquarters to Canadian subsidiaries, such as Ford Motor Company's transfer from Detroit headquarters to its manufacturing subsidiary in Ontario, Canada.
- **Technical competence of the workforce.** This is particularly germane to new, high-tech industries. For example, Microsoft is able to transfer its advanced software technology to various high-tech ventures in India because of the technical competence of Indian software engineers and developers.
- **Complexity of the technology at the time of transfer.** Transfer of complex technology is not likely to be successful when companies have very different levels of expertise. For example, transfer of nuclear power plant technology from the United States to Peru would be difficult because Peru lacks a trained workforce to understand and implement the complex technology. It would be easier to transfer such technologies to France or Japan, which already have basic nuclear technology.
- **Number of successful prior transfers.** Two companies succeed more easily if attempts to transfer similar forms of technology have been successful in the past. Microsoft and General Motors have been successful in transferring technology and establishing research centers of strategic importance in India because past attempts have been successful.[7]

The Role of Strategy and Cultural Issues

When we examine the history of technology transfer, one factor stands out immediately: In the past, such transfers took place primarily among Western nations. However, in today's globalized world, transfers from the United States to various countries in Southeast Asia, Africa, South America, and central and southern Europe are becoming as frequent as transfers between the United States and western Europe.

Technology transfers among developed nations rely on the strategic orientations of the transacting organizations. However, transfers to developing countries in parts of the world that are culturally dissimilar are likely to be difficult. Transferring technology from the headquarters to various subsidiaries of a multinational company can be a mixed blessing. Some subsidiaries are eager to absorb the technology and realize the need for such technologies for improving market share, efficiency, and innovativeness. Other subsidiaries might resist the absorption because of differences in strategic orientation or because of repeated failures in past transfers. However, such difficulties seem to be relatively minor in global companies because of the centralized method that these companies use for innovation and technology diffusion.

Difficulties in technology transfer across various subsidiaries of a multinational or global corporation or between two organizations located in dissimilar economies and cultures often arise from the following concerns:

1. **Differences in strategic thinking.** When senior managers in the companies involved have differing views on the strategic significance of the technology involved in the transfer, the transfer of technology is rarely smooth. Microsoft, as the leading creator of software technology, might not feel inclined to share such technologies with Fujitsu of Japan because both of these companies are competing for global market share.

2. **Characteristics of the technology involved.** We have seen that some technologies are easier to transfer than others. Product-embodied technologies are easier to transfer than process- and person-embodied technologies. In transferring product-embodied technology, the supplying organization or the creator of the technology in the multinational network is simply physically transporting the technology to its needed location. The sophistication of the technical personnel at the recipient organization or other factors that might inhibit the technology's effective absorption and diffusion offer little cause for concern. However, in the case of process- and person-embodied technologies, transferring and diffusing the technology may entail major problems. If the recipient organization does not have well-trained technical personnel who understand the complexities of the technology, or if the infrastructure for diffusing the technology is poor, then product- and person-embodied technologies cannot be transferred easily.

3. **Differences in organizational and corporate cultures.** An organization's receptivity to absorbing new technology often reflects the dominant values of the organizational and corporate cultures. Some organizations value what has been termed "process orientation" in their cultures.[8] As a rule, process orientations facilitate absorption of new technology that comes from another organization. In addition, organizations that are more professional than parochial are better able to absorb technology that is imported from dissimilar national or cultural settings.[9] In professional organizations, the identity of the individuals working for the company comes more from the job than from the organization. In parochial organizations, the social and family backgrounds are more important in defining individuals' identity.

Professional organizations are generally better prepared to understand the complexity of technologies that are being imported for diffusion in the organization.

4. **Differences in societal cultures.** As with organizational cultures, the nature of the societal culture in which the organizations are located greatly influences the success of technology transfer. Consider two organizations that are located in two societies, say, the United States and Greece. One of the hallmarks of Greek culture is its high uncertainty avoidance, as discussed in Chapter 4. On the one hand, managers of Greek work organizations are less likely to be willing to import technologies from other countries because of their need to avoid uncertainty. On the other hand, managers in the United States would be more willing to import technologies from other countries, because their need to avoid uncertainty is not as high as that of Greek managers. The difference between individualist tendencies that managers in different countries exhibit is also important. Managers who are highly individualistic are more effective in their willingness to create, absorb, and diffuse new forms of technology. Naturally, companies located in such cultures are more creative in the way they come up with new technologies and in the way they absorb imported technologies.

Exhibit 8.1 shows that the rate of creation of new technologies is very high in the United States, the United Kingdom, and Germany—countries that rank significantly higher than other countries in terms of the value they put on individualism. With the exception of Japan, which is a collectivistic country, the rate at which technology is created and transferred is higher in western European nations and in the United States. Along with an emphasis on individualism, the per capita expenditure on research and development in Germany and Japan was higher than that in the United States during the 1990s.[10] While the level of education and professional orientation of managers make significant differences, the value put on individualism is clearly much more important. Moreover, the number of R&D scientists in Japan alone is higher than the combined number of R&D scientists in Spain, the United Kingdom, and France.

Exhibit 8.2 presents a framework developed by Kedia and Bhagat that summarizes the various differences.[11] This figure shows the relevance of some of the major factors that influence or inhibit the process: differences in technology, company cultures, societal cultures, and capacities of organizations to absorb the technology. The major factors that directly influence the effectiveness of technology transfer between companies in different countries are the nature of technology—whether it is product-, process-, or person-embodied—and the differences between cultures of the transacting

EXHIBIT 8.1
Rate of Innovation and New Technology Creation

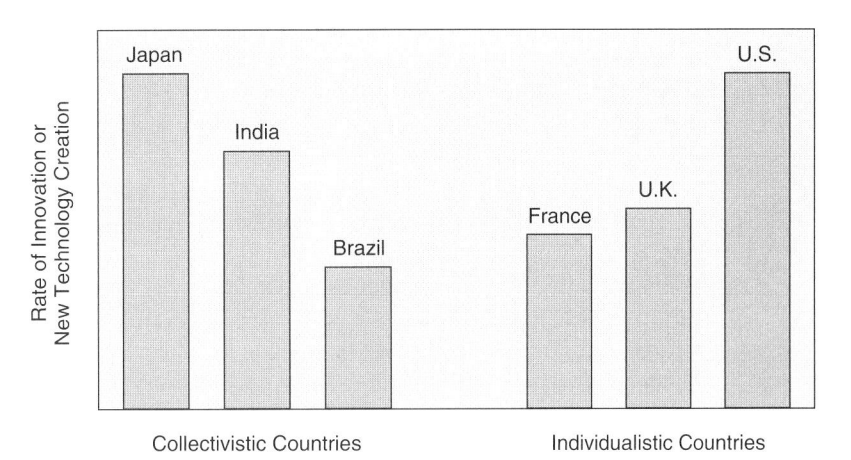

EXHIBIT 8.2
A Conceptual Model for Understanding Cultural Constraints on Technology Transfer

Source: B. Kedia and R. S. Bhagat, "Cultural Constraints of Transfer of Technology across Nations: Implications for Research in International and Comparative Management," *Academy of Management Review* 13, no. 4 (1988), p. 561.

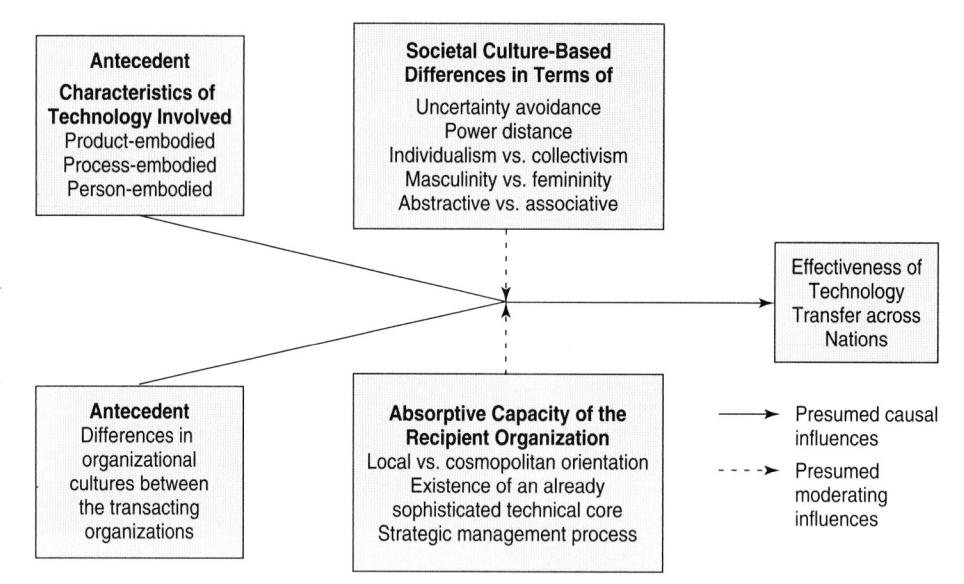

Antecedent Characteristics of Technology Involved
Product-embodied
Process-embodied
Person-embodied

Societal Culture-Based Differences in Terms of
Uncertainty avoidance
Power distance
Individualism vs. collectivism
Masculinity vs. femininity
Abstractive vs. associative

Effectiveness of Technology Transfer across Nations

Antecedent
Differences in organizational cultures between the transacting organizations

Absorptive Capacity of the Recipient Organization
Local vs. cosmopolitan orientation
Existence of an already sophisticated technical core
Strategic management process

⟶ Presumed causal influences
- - -▸ Presumed moderating influences

companies. Product-embodied technologies are relatively easy to transfer. Transfer of process-embodied technologies is slightly more difficult and may involve barriers of language or culture. Person-embodied technologies are the most difficult to transfer when the societal or organizational cultures of transacting companies are substantially different and when the senior managers have conflicting strategic objectives. These technologies are easier to transfer among subsidiaries of a vertically integrated firm (see Chapter 7).

As discussed in Chapter 7 and shown in Figure 7.2, the five points of the figure (strategy, structure, people and skills, systems, and organizational culture) are important considerations in transferring technology in subsidiaries of a global corporation, but they are more significant for two unrelated companies located in dissimilar cultural contexts that have not successfully transferred technology previously.

Knowledge in Organizations

Like technology, knowledge is an important commodity for multinational and global organizations. In fact, it has become so important that organizations competing globally cannot be effective without understanding the significance of knowledge and processes surrounding the management of knowledge.[12] In this section, we discuss the **strategic significance of knowledge** created by organizations for making their processes effective and their products or services competitive in the global marketplace. Knowledge is embedded in the context of the organization, and managers must make every effort to harness its creation and diffusion for accomplishing the kinds of activities that they need to improve.

Knowledge has been defined in many different ways, and most people have an intuitive sense that knowledge is broader, deeper, and richer than either data or information.[13] Davenport and Prusak have done extensive work on the topic of knowledge management in a large number of global corporations and define knowledge as a "fluid mix of experience, values, contextual information, and expert insight that provides a framework for evaluating and incorporating new experiences and information."[14] Knowledge is typically generated in the minds of "knowers" and is made sense of by others in the organization through a process of continuous interactions with the knowers. This interaction results in the creation of working documents or repositories and archives that organizations use for guiding them in the present and in the future. In addition, interaction with knowers creates organizational routines, processes, practices, and norms that are important for enhancing organizational productivity and performance. Knowledge has certain features, summarized by Nonaka and Takeuchi:

> First, knowledge, unlike information, is about *beliefs* and *commitment.* Knowledge is a function of a particular stance, perspective, or intention. Second, knowledge, unlike information, is about *action.* It is always knowledge "to some end." And third, knowledge, like information, is about *meaning.* It is context-specific and relational.[15]

The *intellectual capital* of a global corporation is the sum total of its stock of knowledge, which is described in procedures and manuals as well as systematically embedded in the organization's unique culture and its individuals. For example, knowledge held in the mental and organizational processes of American Express, a U.S.-based global corporation, would be referred to as its intellectual capital.

Data, which are related to the concept of knowledge, reflect discrete, objective facts about events.[16] Think of a gas station keeping count of how many customers fill up their tanks. Without any other details, these transactions, by themselves, constitute what we might call "raw data." When we know how many are filling up with regular gasoline versus premium gasoline, we have **information.** Information is meant to change a receiver because she perceives something; that is, it typically makes an impact on the judgment and behavior of the decision maker. In the example we just gave, if the gas station owner would like to have more of his customers buy premium gasoline, then he must provide some incentives to the customers to convince more of them to buy premium gasoline. The word *inform* means "to give shape to," and important information created in organizational contexts makes some difference in the outlook or insight of the receiver. Strictly speaking, then, it is not the sender but the receiver who typically decides whether the message he or she receives is information or not. Global organizations keep numerical and quantitative measures of information, such as the degree of connectivity with customers in different parts of the world and the kinds of transactions customers are engaging in. However, having a great deal of information technology does not necessarily enhance the state of information in an organization.

Information can lead to knowledge, the next important concept that we alluded to earlier. Knowledge is typically composed of information that has been transformed through the following processes:

- **Comparison.** How does a given piece of information about an organizational event, such as a sales transaction in a global subsidiary, differ from other information that the company might have had before? If the senior managers feel that the new piece of information is more indicative of a trend that is taking place in the global marketplace, then this new information becomes knowledge of some significance. Consider the case of cell phone use. The number of cell phones sold in the United States is estimated to be increasing exponentially every day. Comparison of sales data of various companies, such as AT&T Wireless, Cingular, and Verizon Communications, on an ongoing basis can inform managers of these companies about how successful they are or will be in capturing an increased market share.
- **Consequences.** If a piece of information spells out a significant course of action that managers must undertake, then that information is clearly knowledge. Reliable information about a possible tornado hitting an important manufacturing facility

of a global corporation quickly becomes knowledge because it tells the plant managers what they should do in the event the tornado does strike the facility.
- **Connections.** When a piece of information is related to other bits of information that the company already has, it becomes knowledge. Information that sales figures for a product are low and, moreover, that sales figures for other products are high can be combined to allow managers to decide which products should make up their bundle of offerings. Such information is typically used as reliable knowledge by global companies such as Procter & Gamble of Cincinnati in tracing the growth of their overall offerings in the area of consumer products, health care products, and pharmaceutical products.
- **Conversation.** Related and unrelated pieces of information have the potential to become knowledge when managers begin to talk about such information and to make sense of it to arrive at meaningful and clear decisions. FBI professionals in the United States use this process in detecting criminals. Seemingly unrelated pieces of information eventually may lead to significant amounts of knowledge about the motives of a criminal and his or her whereabouts. In the case of global corporations, various unrelated acts taking place in a developing country when a new product is introduced may, on reflection by a group of senior marketing managers, yield significant knowledge about what the company should do to enhance the quality of the product or change the product to suit the market.

The Process of Knowledge Management

Increasingly, knowledge work is replacing manual labor.[17] In many places, automation is taking the place of assembly line work, and documents are often delivered by e-mail instead of by messengers. In areas where physical labor is still employed, computers are used to enhance workers' efficiency. To understand how knowledge is managed in the global corporation, we must first understand how knowledge is created in organizations. Then we must focus on the art and science of transmission and diffusion of knowledge.

Knowledge is an intangible asset in an organization, composed of the skills and knowledge of key individuals within the organization, patents, databases, and networks, as well as information regarding relationships with customers, suppliers, and regulatory agencies such as the government. General Electric has been successful in converting knowledge assets by creating a department of learning, and many companies have chief knowledge officers (CKOs).[18]

Knowledge in organizations is accumulated and held collectively in the working memories of individuals in the context of their work roles, and unique experience in their specialized positions is developed over time.[19] To convert the personal knowledge and expertise of these individuals, organizations, whether they are global or not, must find appropriate ways of managing (i.e., creating and transferring) knowledge for new-product and process development.[20] Such processes cannot always be spelled out ahead of time.

Two distinct types of knowledge—tacit and explicit—are important to an understanding of knowledge transfer across cultures. **Tacit knowledge** is knowledge that is highly personal, difficult to communicate, and highly specialized. Processing and transferring it is difficult because it is a part of the historical and cultural context in which the organization exists.[21] Tacit knowledge is a process of continual knowing. It consists of specific information and know-how that is obtained through the experience of having "lived" in the environment or having performed a particular task many times over—like walking. Tacit knowledge is transferred, for example, when teaching a child how to walk—although we know how to walk, the knowledge cannot be transferred except by showing the child how to walk and letting the child try to follow. On the other hand, **explicit knowledge** is knowledge that can be written and transmitted.[22] It is discrete or digital, stored in repositories such as libraries and databases. Generally, explicit knowledge can be accessed quickly with little distortion. Blueprints of a building that are printed in a book allow the transfer of explicit knowledge from the author to the reader.

Tacit knowledge is becoming increasingly recognized as an essential part of organizational knowledge.[23] Sometimes managers have to use their own experience in learning to convert knowledge that is held in a tacit form into more explicit knowledge. For example, professional skills and know-how, a significant part of tacit knowledge, are often so deeply ingrained that they are taken for granted.

Transferring tacit knowledge is much more difficult than transferring explicit knowledge. One cannot say in advance that tacit knowledge is either more or less significant than explicit knowledge in enhancing the quality of products or services that the global organization might offer in the marketplace. It all depends on the nature of the task or technology to be improved.

Tacit knowledge was not recognized as a valued form of knowledge in organizations before the publication of Nonaka and Takeuchi's *The Knowledge-Creating Company* in 1995.[24] They explained how Matsushita Electric Company (parent company of Panasonic brand products) was able to develop bread-making machines by encouraging its software engineers to watch the process used by the master baker of the Osaka International Hotel in Osaka, Japan. The process of making bread is something that cannot be taught by spelling out in writing all the steps that are involved in kneading a loaf of bread. The software engineers observed the minute details that the master baker used in the process of kneading dough, which was a major problem in bread-making machine technology up to that time. The computer simulation they created, by converting the tacit knowledge that the head baker processed into various steps that a machine must go through in order to knead a lump of dough, is a good example of how global companies create explicit knowledge from tacit knowledge.

The four modes of knowledge creation, as described by Nonaka and Takeuchi, are depicted in Exhibit 8.3. It is important that managers be aware of all of the four modes that multinational and global companies use in the process of managing explicit and tacit knowledge.

EXHIBIT 8.3
Four Modes of Knowledge Creation

Source: Based on Nonaka and Takeuchi's scheme; I. Nonaka and H. Takeuchi, *The Knowledge-Creating Company: How Japanese Companies Create the Dynamics of Innovation* (New York: Oxford University Press, 1995), p. 58.

Mode 1: Combination	Mode 2: Internationalization
Explicit ⟶ Explicit	Explicit ⟶ Tacit
Is much easier to codify and convey to significant parties and recipients in the transnational and global organizations	Cannot be easily codified, cannot be easily conveyed and transmitted to significant parties and recipients
Mode 3: Externalization	**Mode 4: Socialization**
Tacit ⟶ Explicit	Tacit ⟶ Tacit
Cannot be easily codified and conveyed to those who might need this kind of knowledge	Most difficult to codify; the process of such knowledge creation is essentially focused on developing shared mental models among the important members and others who need this kind of knowledge

Creation of new knowledge always begins with an individual. A brilliant R&D researcher may have an insight that can lead to the development of a significant patent for a successful product. An experienced marketing manager's sense of market trends, even without a lot of data, may become an inspiration for a product concept. Sony's chairman, Akio Morita, proposed the idea of the Walkman in the 1980s, when most of his senior managers thought it was not a good product idea for the Western market. Morita, however, knew that most Western consumers tend to be individualistic and might like the idea of a stereo system designed for individual listeners.[25]

Nonaka and Takeuchi explain the process of the creation of new knowledge and its transmission, in other words, how knowledge moves from tacit to explicit.[26] They visualize the process of transferring tacit to explicit knowledge, as well as explicit to tacit knowledge, as a spiral. When explicit knowledge is converted into usable explicit knowledge, the process is called *combination*. The process of converting explicit knowledge into tacit knowledge is *internalization*. Becoming an effective leader after going through a series of seminars on leadership is an example of internalization. The process of converting tacit knowledge into explicit knowledge is called *externalization*. The development of the bread machine, discussed previously, is an excellent example of externalization. The process of converting tacit knowledge into tacit knowledge is *socialization*. Learning about product development from an effective mentor is an example of socialization. Such processes cannot be explicitly described.

Countries that are collectivistic are better in their ability to convert tacit knowledge into explicit knowledge.[27] Tacit knowledge tends to be a favored mode of knowledge creation and retention on the part of individuals in collectivistic societies. In their extensive analysis of knowledge transfer across national boundaries, Bhagat and his colleagues found that explicit knowledge tends to be favored more in individualistic societies—societies where individuals are encouraged to think independently from their childhood and socialization processes are geared toward developing an abstractive mode of thinking.

Transfer of knowledge from a collectivistic culture to another collectivistic culture is likely to be easier when the knowledge transferred is of the tacit variety.[28] Tacit knowledge is better absorbed in cultures where there is a focus on "give-and-take" and consensual decision making. Consensual decision making is facilitated when individuals in a society consider themselves to be very similar to others. In general, members of a collectivistic society have similar thought patterns because of the trust they have in each other and the continual communication they have with the same individuals over time.[29]

Transferring tacit knowledge from a company located in a collectivistic society to a company located in an individualistic society is generally difficult.[30] Individualists are predisposed to use their own perspectives in understanding knowledge and are more accustomed to doing things by absorbing explicit knowledge from company manuals, policy and procedure manuals, and similar material. The transfer becomes even more difficult if the countries involved are horizontal (collectivists) and vertical (individualists) in their orientation. The vertical–horizontal dimension increases the difficulty of transferring knowledge because in vertical societies individuals in organizations like to stand out from each other whereas the opposite pattern is found in horizontal societies.[31]

Companies in the individualistic countries are more inclined to use certain types of knowledge transfer than are companies located in collectivistic contexts. Emphasis on explicit types of knowledge is more common in individualistic contexts, whether the transfers take place within a given multinational or global organization or between two or more multinationals or global organizations. (See Exhibit 8.4, which depicts the role of cultural differences within and across transnational and global organizations.[32]

EXHIBIT 8.4 Cultural Differences Affecting the Transfer of Knowledge within and across Transnational and Global Organizations

Source: R. Bhagat, P. Englis, and B. Kedia, "Creation, Diffusion and Transfer of Organizational Knowledge in Transnational and Global Organizations," in Linda L. Neider and Chester A. Schriesheim, eds., *Research in Management: International Perspectives* (Charlotte NC: Information Age, 2007), p. 118.

Cultural Differences	Within	Across
Individualism–Collectivism	Transferring implicit knowledge from a collectivistic context to an individualistic context, even though difficult, could still be accomplished with relative ease due to similarities in strategic considerations, administrative heritage, and technical systems.	Transferring implicit knowledge from a collectivistic context to an individualistic context will be more difficult due to differences in strategic considerations, administrative heritage, and technical systems.
	Transferring explicit knowledge from a collectivistic context to an individualistic context, even though difficult, could still be accomplished with relative ease due to similarities in strategic considerations, administrative heritage, and technical systems.	Transferring explicit knowledge from a collectivistic context to an individualistic context will be more difficult due to differences in strategic considerations, administrative heritage, and technical systems.
Power Distance	Transferring implicit knowledge from a high power distance context to a low power distance context and vice versa, while difficult, could still be accomplished with relative ease due to above-mentioned similarities.	Transferring implicit knowledge from a high power distance context to a low power distance context and vice versa will be more difficult due to differences in strategic considerations, administrative heritage, and technical systems.
	Transferring explicit knowledge from a high power distance context to a low power distance context and vice versa, while difficult, could still be accomplished with relative ease due to above-mentioned similarities.	Transferring explicit knowledge from a high power distance context to a low power distance context and vice versa will be more difficult due to differences in strategic considerations, administrative heritage, and technical systems.

This exhibit also incorporates the role of power distance in the process of transferring knowledge.)

Managing the Knowledge Life Cycle

Most executives today realize that knowledge is strategically significant and their companies must be able to manage it effectively. Just how one goes about developing that ability is a challenge. As in other areas of international management, there is no shortage of useful frameworks, models, and checklists that one can choose from. However, some of these solutions are only Band-Aids, conceived as being applicable in any and all situations. Many international managers are left to make their own mistakes as they choose one failing framework after another. A knowledge management model that has potential for significant gain in one context, such as electronic groupware or communities of practice, may have limited use in others.

It seems useful for us to think about knowledge management as a process of evolution through the **knowledge life cycle,** shown in Exhibit 8.5. In the *creation* stage, very few managers understand the idea of the emerging body of knowledge, including those who are creating it. The process of creation is messy, and it does not always respond to rigid timelines. An effective method for working with early stage knowledge is to

EXHIBIT 8.5
The Knowledge Life Cycle

Source: Reprinted from J. Birkinshaw and I. Sheehan, "Managing the Knowledge Life Cycle," *MIT Sloan Management Review,* Fall 2002, pp.75–83, by permission of publisher. Copyright © 2002 by Massachusetts Institute of Technology. All rights reserved.

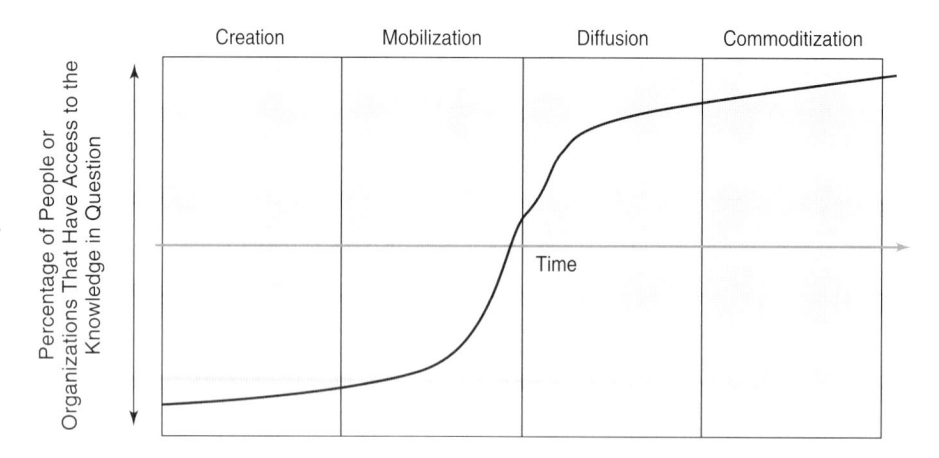

solidify an idea to the point where its commercial viability can be tested. To encourage knowledge creation at this stage, companies need to create an environment allowing ongoing experimentation and creativity within some structure and discipline. Individuals need to be allowed to make mistakes, as discussed in Practical Insight 8.2.

In the *mobilization* stage, knowledge in organizations continues to be defined and redefined as its use becomes more apparent. Companies that have developed the idea tend to extract value from it. Mobilization is the process of circulating the significance of newly emergent knowledge in the internal organization. It also includes hiding the knowledge from outsiders and keeping it proprietary. Acquisition of patent protection is a good example of this stage.

In *diffusing* the knowledge, the company no longer tries to keep the knowledge or new technology under its continuous vigil. In fact, senior managers accept the idea that leakage and imitation are bound to occur. They also invite other companies to join the bandwagon, actively selling the knowledge to a broad base of customers and marketing the concept through various media. Many knowledge-based service companies, such as McKinsey and Company and Booz, Allen, and Hamilton, appear to gain significantly by moving their ideas rapidly into the diffusion stage. In the case of computer software, diffusing the product has the effect of building a client base, creating a network of users, and preempting competitors.

The last stage, *commoditization,* is about how to manage knowledge that has gone through the three previous stages and is already well known. Some companies take the view that once knowledge is widely understood, nothing more can be done with it. They tend to move on to other interesting ideas. However, we should remember that international managers have a lot to gain from exploiting opportunities and extracting value from knowledge that has reached the status of a commodity. A good example is baking soda. For many years, it was a product used only in baking. It has since been rejuvenated as a toothpaste additive, a refrigerator freshener, a sink cleaner, and now a trash can deodorizer. Commoditized knowledge will not last forever. Consider an engineering firm that specializes in the construction of skyscrapers. While the knowledge required to build the skyscrapers has been known for a long time, the events of September 11, 2001, may mean that the old principles of structural engineering, which have been considered to be a commodity, will have to be revised.

Managing the knowledge life cycle is important for companies that function in the domestic context of any country. However, it becomes more important for multinational and global companies because the centers of knowledge creation are not necessarily located in a single geographic place. Continuous interchange is necessary among

PRACTICAL INSIGHT 8.2

ACER'S SHIH ON TAIWAN'S FUTURE: "KNOWLEDGE IS OUR BUSINESS"
The computer maker's chairman talks about his nation's need to plan now for a postindustrial tomorrow.

As more and more Taiwanese electronics companies shift their manufacturing to mainland China, policymakers, business leaders, and ordinary citizens are debating the future direction of the island's economy. For many Taiwanese, the answer lies in developing new industries like financial services, software, and biotechnology while further expanding capital-intensive ones such as semiconductors and liquid-crystal displays.

Taiwanese technocrats believe these businesses are the foundation of the island's postindustrial future, one in which Taiwan lets workers in mainland China do most of the manufacturing that Taiwanese used to do. Taiwan's workers would then work mainly in industries in which human capital plays a greater role—the so-called knowledge economy.

One of the leading proponents of this knowledge-economy vision is Acer Group chairman Stan Shih. I recently spoke to Shih at his Spartan corporate headquarters in suburban Taipei and asked him about the role he sees for Taiwan and Acer in this new kind of economy (for more on this topic, see BW, 11/27/00, "Taiwan: Minds over Matter").

Q: You and many other Taiwanese speak these days about the island developing more of a "knowledge-based" economy. What's causing this transformation?

A: The overall global economy is moving toward more of a knowledge base. You have to find a way to play a role in the future economy. Taiwan doesn't have any choice: We have to move all of our efforts to new, knowledge-based business lines like software or to segments of [manufacturing] that have more knowledge such as research and development, services, or global logistics.

Q: Why?

A: Today in Asia, wealth is created through the competence of manufacturing. That is our advantage. The strategy is not to neglect that advantage, but to develop it. Ten years from now, if we don't have knowledge capability, all of our manufacturing may become a burden. We can't afford to invest in manufacturing in Taiwan, so it's obvious that we need to leverage our resources outside of Taiwan.

Q: Does that mean that there is nothing left to manufacture in Taiwan?

A: Taiwan is still good for capital-intensive businesses like semiconductors and TFT-LCDs. To move those operations to China would be too risky. Capital-intensive industries should be in Taiwan, labor-intensive in mainland China.

Q: How do you respond to critics who say that Taiwan without its manufacturing base will be a "hollowed-out" economy?

A: Hollowing out is not an issue. Hollow of what? Hollow of low-value-added portion, of wasted resources. If Taiwan is talking about having to keep [old labor-intensive] industries in Taiwan, that's not only a waste of resources but also a lost opportunity to develop new industries.

Q: But Taiwan's 3.1% unemployment rate—while low by American standards—is steadily rising. That's leading to fears about social dislocation caused by the loss of manufacturing jobs. How do you respond to such worries?

A: It's much easier to take care of those people through social programs than to keep those industries in Taiwan. Taiwan has very limited resources. The only way to enhance our strength is to leverage those resources. Japan [in the 1990s] was so concerned about hollowing out, so the Japanese developed automation [to keep manufacturing from moving outside Japan]. And they ended up less competitive.

Q: You've launched a Web site called www.stantalk.com. How does that fit into your new model?

A: To us, knowledge is our business. But to create knowledge is really high-cost. So how to reuse that knowledge becomes a key issue. I'm trying to develop the model. All the experience I have is put into the Web site, so students and customers can hook into the site for questions, tests, and workshops. The subject is international management. All the experience of my 24 years [at Acer] is relevant to them.

Q: How do you see that kind of electronic classroom evolving?

A: Taiwan has a lot of knowledge that is useful, especially to mainland China. But how to put that into software and marketing it is the key question. Later on, I can duplicate this model. I can have Morris Chang [chief of Taiwan Semiconductor Manufacturing Corp.] give a talk. We can deal with 10,000 students.

Source: Reprinted from Bruce Einhorn, "Fear of Mistakes Stifles IT Innovation in Government," *BusinessWeek,* November 20, 2000, by special permission. Copyright © 1999 by The McGraw-Hill Companies, Inc.

country managers to determine how knowledge is to be created, diffused, transferred, and commoditized.

Integration of Strategic Processes with Knowledge Management

Consider the case of Buckman Laboratories, located in Memphis, Tennessee. When Bob Buckman inherited Buckman Labs, a specialty chemical producer, in the 1960s, it was a top-heavy company with management layers and bureaucratic regulations and it was slow to respond to environmental changes. Knowledge management was not an issue in those days.

Today, Buckman Labs is a model of the knowledge-era company. Its 1,600 staff members are not just "grunt" workers; they are knowledge workers. Buckman, in his efforts to create a knowledge-managed and knowledge management company, asked himself, "How do I close the gap between my workforce and my customers?" He perceived the importance of his workers and created mechanisms for reinventing, not necessarily reengineering, Buckman Labs around people who can create knowledge.[33]

Many other companies link knowledge management with strategic intent. Canon, Ricoh, Matsushita (parent company of Panasonic), and Microsoft are a few of the leading high-technology-based companies that routinely engage in knowledge management. Senior managers in charge of knowledge management operations must recognize that effective management of knowledge is a product of three systems:

- **Strategic considerations.** The strategic intent of management emphasizes knowledge creation through innovation and tangible administrative support for innovation.
- **Technical systems.** Management stresses research and development systems, the sophistication of management information systems, quality, and competence of technical and administrative staff.
- **Administrative heritage.** The firm has a historical emphasis on knowledge creation, the values and practices of founders and senior managers (leadership legacy and organizational culture), the nature of organizational communication, and the quality of professional interactions.

A comprehensive view of these three systems indicates that they are influenced by the distinctive cultural context of the society in which the organization is located. When the organization is viewed as a *knowledge-production system* that directly impacts the effectiveness of management systems, the sophistication of electronic data interchanges (EDIs) and related computer-mediated communication is important, but so is the interaction among the various technical systems, strategic management processes, and administrative heritage of the organization, as illustrated in Exhibit 8.6.

Creators of organizational knowledge do not necessarily use knowledge in an instrumental fashion. Often, they draw from their personal sources as well as collective sources of knowledge.[34] In other words, managers in global and multinational organizations should have the capability to create new knowledge at least within the constraints and demands of the foregoing three systems. Exhibit 8.6 depicts the strategic considerations, administrative heritage, and technical systems of an organization as influenced by the immediate cultural context. The effectiveness of management knowledge and systems is also dependent on the dominant values of the cultural context in which the organization operates. In the case of global organizations, the process of managing knowledge is dependent on these three systems in the particular cultural contexts of the various subsidiaries.

EXHIBIT 8.6
Knowledge Management Effectiveness as a Product of Strategic Considerations, Technical Systems, and Administrative Heritage

Source: Reprinted from R. S. Bhagat, D. L. Ford, Jr., C. A. Jones, and R. R. Taylor, "Knowledge Management in Global Organizations: Implications for International Human Resource Management," *Research in Personnel and Human Resources Management*, Vol. 21, pp. 243–274. Copyright © 2002, with permission from Elsevier.

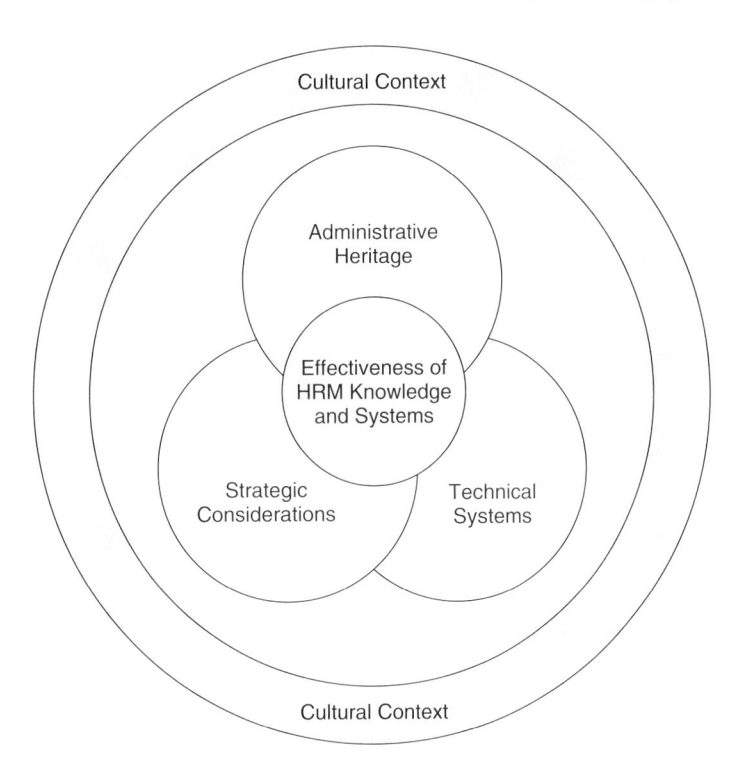

Denning notes that a company must engage in the following seven steps in order to continuously link strategic management processes with the process of managing technological innovation and knowledge creation:[35]

1. **Assembling a large knowledge base.** A company may have a knowledge management system composed of high-quality staff with appropriate knowledge, but the knowledge within the company needs continuous upgrading and monitoring.

2. **Going beyond the "Help Desk."** Having dedicated staff that can answer questions is not enough. A company must also think of going beyond the Help Desk, developing a mechanism for linking the operational activities of the organization with various features of the environment. In Chapter 1, we discussed the various features that the global organization must monitor.

3. **Establishing a directory of experts.** A director of "who knows what" is useful to have. Another tricky but essential tool to establish is a directory of experts who are developing useful knowledge.

4. **Maintaining developmental data.** Developmental data comprise information about current knowledge development. Each figure in development data is a judgment about the situation in the country. This differs from pure data, in the sense of stock market data, for example.

5. **Encouraging information.** When organizationally created knowledge has made a major impact, it must be acknowledged. In addition, the parties responsible for its development should be acknowledged by the company's reward system and other mechanisms.

6. **Creating a dialogue space.** The ability to ask questions around the organization and get the answers through dialogue is tremendously important. This concept is still in the development stage, but it has the potential to be the most powerful aspect of knowledge management systems.

EXHIBIT 8.7 Factors Affecting the Transfer of Knowledge within and across Transnational and Global Organizations

Source: R. Bhagat, P. Englis, and B. Kedia, "Creation, Diffusion and Transfer of Organizational Knowledge in Transnational and Global Organizations," in Linda L. Neider and Chester A. Schriesheim, eds., *Research in Management: International Perspectives* (Charlotte, NC: Information Age, 2007), pp. 112–113.

Similar	Within	Across
Strategic Considerations		
Strategic intent for knowledge creation	• Transferring knowledge in subsidiaries located in distinctive cultural contexts such as GM in U.S. and Glaxco-Wellcome of U.K. Strategic intent generally facilitates such processes.	• Transferring knowledge between two global organizations (e.g., IBM in the U.S. with Fujitsu in Japan), differences in strategic intent generally prevent effective transfer in subsidiaries located in distinctive cultural contexts.
Emphasis on innovation	• Transfer of knowledge generally emphasizes creation of new knowledge at the point of absorption.	• Transfer of knowledge to fulfill licensing requirements and enhance functioning of recipient organization.
Tangible and administrative support for innovation	• Making resources available throughout network to facilitate knowledge transfer is easier to accomplish when there is significant top management support.	• Differences in available resources to facilitate knowledge transfer processes may lead to selective absorption, retention, and diffusion.
Administrative Heritage		
Historical emphasis on knowledge creation	• Knowledge transfer is more effective if emphasis is on continuous innovation throughout network.	• Differences in historical emphasis on knowledge management may lead to ineffective knowledge transfer.
Values and practices of founders and senior managers	• Likely consistency in managerial practices throughout network might aid knowledge transfers across subsidiaries.	• Differences in managerial values and practices infused throughout distinct organizations are likely to inhibit successful knowledge transfer.
Nature of organizational communication and quality of professional interactions	• Processes, systems, and support infrastructure to facilitate creation of knowledge.	• Processes, systems, and support infrastructure to facilitate creation of knowledge.
Technical Systems		
Research and development (R&D) systems	• Likely compatibility of R&D systems throughout the world facilitates knowledge transfer.	• Differences in compatibility and sophistication of R&D systems throughout the world inhibit effective knowledge transfer.
Sophistication of management information system	• Continuous investments in MIS systems facilitate knowledge transfer.	• Differences in MIS systems inhibit effective transfer of knowledge.
Quality and competence of technical and administrative staff	• Competent technical and administrative staff facilitate knowledge transfer.	• Differences in skill levels of technical and administrative staff inhibit knowledge transfer.

7. **Offering external access.** This is the process of making organizationally created knowledge available in immediately usable form by clients of the organization. McKinsey and Company has been very successful in its management consulting practice by engaging in this technique.

Along with considering cultural differences that influence the effectiveness of knowledge transfer, we should also consider the roles of strategic considerations, administrative heritage, and technical systems. These three factors work in conjunction with cultural differences and influence the quality of flow of knowledge within the same multinational or global organization or between two or more multinational or global organizations (see Exhibit 8.7).[36]

The Learning Organization

The concept of the **learning organization** is very important for senior managers. A learning organization is one that is capable and skilled at creating, acquiring, transferring, and defusing knowledge and, at the same time, modifying the behavior and expectations of its participants to reflect new knowledge.[37] An organization must be effective in:

- Gathering and creating relevant knowledge.
- Storing it for future use.
- Diffusing it throughout the entire organization.
- Engaging everyone in unlearning ineffective knowledge.
- Evaluating the significance and timeliness of accumulated knowledge.
- Implementing and encouraging appropriate changes based on the knowledge.

Learning organizations are more than organizations with a desire to learn. They reflect an organizational culture that values the desire to learn. Some of the techniques for continually creating and using knowledge are listed in Exhibit 8.8.

EXHIBIT 8.8

Techniques for Enhancing the Creation and Use of Organizational Knowledge

Source: From P. R. Ferguson and G. J. Ferguson, *Organisations: A Strategic Perspective.* Copyright © 2002 P. R. Ferguson and G. J. Ferguson. Reprinted with permission of Palgrave Macmillan.

- Incorporate learning on an individual and team basis as an important part of corporate culture.
- Encourage systematic collection and recording of knowledge in blueprints and manuals.
- Evaluate the contribution of existing knowledge to the value chain.
- Appoint "knowledge brokers" to foster and disseminate knowledge in various subsidiaries.
- Nominate senior managers who can act as "boundary spanners" to sense and monitor the development of new knowledge from the external environment.
- Encourage the formation of multifunctional project groups and quality circles.
- Create networks of professionals who can share information within the organization as well as with relevant parties outside.
- Develop appropriate organizational structures and information systems.
- Encourage professional competence and team development.
- Provide rewards for creating and sharing knowledge.
- Develop routines and rules for sharing knowledge continuously.
- Encourage experimentation with knowledge creation and accept occasional failures as part of the process.
- Provide valued resources, including uninterrupted time, for learning.
- Encourage job rotation leading to a breadth and depth of knowledge and experience.
- Provide opportunities for learning by doing.
- Follow examples of leading organizations in the global marketplace.
- Encourage learning as a primary objective during joint ventures and strategic alliances.
- Make effective use of consultants.

Summary

Management of technology and knowledge has become the most important source of competitive advantage in multinational and global corporations. The Internet has revolutionized the way that international business is conducted. As a tool for managing knowledge, its implications for international management are significant. One must understand the difference between data, information, and knowledge. This chapter presented the concepts of technology and knowledge and discussed their crucial role in enhancing the competitiveness of multinational and global organizations.

Management of knowledge is rapidly becoming the most important topic in the field of international management, and global managers are being entrusted with the responsibility of creating learning organizations that facilitate the process of creating, diffusing, transferring, and commoditizing important types of organizational knowledge. Two types of knowledge—tacit and explicit—present different difficulties for firms transferring them within and across national and cultural boundaries, as do the various methods of knowledge creation. Some cultures are better able to create and diffuse tacit forms of knowledge than others. International managers should recognize strategic and cultural differences before undertaking technology and knowledge transfer. The roles of strategic considerations, administrative heritage, and technical systems should be understood.

The knowledge management cycle is essential in understanding the utility of knowledge within the organization over time. The importance of this topic will continue to grow, particularly in countries where knowledge management is the key to international competitiveness. The quest for global dominance will be realized for companies that are able to manage and master this process.[38]

Key Terms and Concepts

administrative heritage, *306*
data, *299*
explicit knowledge, *301*
information, *299*
knowledge, *298*
knowledge life cycle, *303*
learning organization, *309*
strategic significance of knowledge, *298*
tacit knowledge, *300*
technical systems, *306*
technology, *294*
technology transfer, *294*

Discussion Questions

1. Define *technology*. What are the three different types of technology that are considered for cross-border transfers? Define each, and give examples. Why is person-embodied technology the most difficult to transfer across cultural boundaries?
2. List the various factors that influence the success of technology transfer, and give examples of each.
3. Define *knowledge*. Distinguish it from the concepts of data and information. Give examples of each from your personal experience and from other sources.
4. Explain the difference between tacit and explicit knowledge. Discuss why explicit knowledge is easier to transfer between individualist countries. Explain why tacit knowledge is difficult to transfer from collectivistic countries to individualistic countries.
5. How do strategic management and administrative heritage influence the process of knowledge management in global organizations? Give some examples.
6. How do cultural differences influence transfer of knowledge within and between multinational and global organizations?
7. What are the various factors that affect transfer of knowledge within and between multinational and global organizations? Give examples.

Minicase

He Loves to Win. At I.B.M., He Did

The revival of I.B.M. over the last nine years is most tellingly measured not in numbers but by its return to pre-eminence as the industry leader. Once again, I.B.M. is the model others follow.

Consider the strategic debate behind the fevered proxy fight at Hewlett-Packard. Its planned purchase of Compaq Computer makes sense, Hewlett-Packard says, because the merger will make it more like I.B.M. A dangerous delusion, reply the deal's opponents. Who, they ask, could possibly compete broadly with I.B.M.?

Even the main question these days about I.B.M.'s future lends perspective. Sure, the skeptics say, I.B.M. is back with a vengeance, a powerhouse in the marketplace with strong profits. But, they ask, how much growth can be expected from a corporate giant with sales last year of $86 billion?

In 1993, when Louis V. Gerstner Jr. became chairman and chief executive, the question asked about I.B.M. was whether it would survive. And in choosing him, the I.B.M. board had taken a historic gamble on a professional manager with no experience in the computer industry.

Last Monday was Mr. Gerstner's first day at I.B.M. bearing just one title—chairman. He will keep it until year-end, then depart. On March 1, he was succeeded as chief executive by Samuel J. Palmisano, a 29-year I.B.M. veteran who built up the vital services business, which now represents about half of I.B.M.'s revenue and profits.

The rearview mirror holds little interest for Mr. Gerstner, who is 60. Yet in a lengthy interview last Monday at the company's headquarters in Armonk, N.Y., he reflected on his worries in taking the job, the challenges he faced and the reasoning behind his crucial strategic, organizational and technical decisions there. He spoke of where he thought I.B.M. had been smart and when luck had helped a lot.

He spoke of matters beyond I.B.M. as well. He explained why he believes there is no new economy, a statement that prompted boos from the dot-com world when he first made it in 1998. He answered the criticism he received in the industry in 1993, when he said, "The last thing I.B.M. needs now is a vision," and explained why he was right. And, ever the outsider in the computer business, he discussed what he thought was special about the industry, what was ordinary and what still irritates, even amuses, him about it.

Mr. Gerstner also offered a bit of personal reflection. After leading three large corporations and achieving vast personal wealth, he said that the enduring thrill of being a chief executive—and the part he would miss—was really quite simple. "I love winning," he said, pausing briefly before answering the question emphatically, "I love the process of leading an institution and being part of an institution that succeeds, that wins. I get excited by our success. I get very frustrated by our failures, too, but I enjoy the game."

At I.B.M., the Gerstner record is mainly a success story. "Lou Gerstner re-established the company's belief in itself," observed Andrew S. Grove, the chairman of Intel, who has known I.B.M. as a partner and competitor for more than two decades. "It's hard to describe how beaten down that company was."

When he took the job, Mr. Gerstner, a former McKinsey consultant who went on to become president of American Express and then chief executive of RJR Nabisco Holdings, was far from the obvious choice for guiding Big Blue, the fallen icon of American technology, back from the brink. Among I.B.M. directors, there had been a sharp debate over whether to hire a technologist or a professional manager. In the end, the board bet that I.B.M. needed a leader, a strategist and a manager—Mr. Gerstner's portfolio of skills—not an executive with a deep understanding of computer technology.

He also had qualms. "If the board had been wrong, and that was my big concern—that underlying it all there was a technical problem in I.B.M.—then it would have been a very short tenure for me," he said, smiling and shrugging.

Those misgivings are a distant memory. Even last week, it was clear that he does not plan to slow down until he leaves. Monday was his first day at the headquarters in two weeks. He had been on the road, going to Philadelphia, Boca Raton and Salt Lake City, and abroad in Stuttgart, Munich, London and Edinburgh, mostly meeting with I.B.M. customers.

The day was the equivalent of a corporate pit stop; he was headed out again on Tuesday, adding to the more than 1.1 million air miles he has logged since 1993. His travel regimen reflects his management philosophy: getting out of the office to deal with customers and dwell in the marketplace is an antidote to the corporate insularity that was nearly I.B.M.'s downfall.

He began traveling to meet customers and to visit I.B.M. outposts as soon as he took over, and what he heard guided his action. He also read. As a former McKinsey consultant, he asked first for the I.B.M. strategic plans, current and recent. There were plans aplenty, he found strategic blueprints for each division, even down to the product level. By the end of his first month, Mr. Gerstner, who always carries two briefcases of reading material when he travels, had read thousands of pages of strategic documents.

The reading left him enlightened—and appalled. I.B.M., he said, was filled with smart people who had recognized the industry's major technological and economic shifts. Yet I.B.M. had repeatedly failed to respond. "Part of the culture was a tendency to debate and argue and raise every issue to the highest level of abstraction," Mr. Gerstner said. "The process almost became one of the elegance of the definition of the problem rather than the actual execution of an action plan."

So, a few months after arriving at I.B.M., when he said the last thing it needed was a vision, he was declaring a break with the old culture of introspection and foot-dragging. Had he spoken of vision at I.B.M., he said, he knew it would have started "a yearlong debate."

"And we didn't need the vision," he added. "We needed to save the company economically."

Instead, he gave marching orders to the I.B.M. troops. "We were going to build this company from the customer back, not the from the company out," he said. "That was the big message from my first six months in the company, that the company was going to be driven from the marketplace."

As one symbolic step, he abolished the ritual of the I.B.M. organization chart. These fold-out charts were minor masterpieces of draftsmanship and printing, an intricate latticework of lines, color-coded boxes and asterisks. Lovely to behold, they recalled the engineering drawings of Leonardo da Vinci, according to one executive. Producing them was a cottage industry within I.B.M., and thousands of them were pinned on the office walls of its workers.

When asked about how to revise the organization chart under his management, Mr. Gerstner declared there would be no more organization charts, that anyone asking for one was focusing on the wrong thing.

Early on, he also changed incentives to put I.B.M. and its people more in step with the marketplace. When he came to the company, only 300 employees received stock options. Today, more than 60,000 do. He told his top 100 executives soon after he arrived that he expected them to own I.B.M. stock equal to one to four times their yearly compensation.

Mr. Gerstner argues that strategy and corporate culture are intimately linked. "You can't talk a culture into changing," he said. "You can't just exhort people to be different. You've got to point to fundamental strategic changes you're going to implement in a company and then drive the execution of that strategy. And it is in the execution of the strategy that the culture begins to change."

The first major decision Mr. Gerstner made was to decide to keep the company together, not split it up into 13 loosely linked "Baby Blues." Under that plan, put forward by his predecessor, John F. Akers, in December 1992, some would be spun off as separate companies with their own names, like AdStar, for the disk storage unit.

This so-called federation plan was moving ahead briskly when Mr. Gerstner arrived. "It was an extraordinary Balkanization of the company under way when I walked in," he said. "There were investment bankers sticking their flag on every piece of I.B.M. they could."

Auditors had been hired, costing millions of dollars, to create stand-alone financial statements for the spinoff candidates. "Every unit had run for the hills," Mr. Gerstner recalled, "creating their own human resources policies, their own communications policies."

In theory, the federation plan addressed I.B.M.'s fundamental trouble—that as an integrated company it was not quick and nimble. It would be better off aping the personal computer industry, where fast-moving technology specialists like Microsoft and Intel prevailed.

"That was the industry model that I.B.M. was responding to," Mr. Gerstner said. "And I looked at that and I said, 'Wait a minute, as a customer of I.B.M.'s, I'm not terribly drawn to that as a model for I.B.M.'"

Mr. Gerstner, an I.B.M. customer at American Express and RJR, liked the concept of "integrated solutions"—that I.B.M. could distill the complexity of computing to solve business problems for companies. In his early travels for I.B.M., he heard similar sentiments from customers.

Aside from its breadth, in Mr. Gerstner's view, I.B.M. had another unique feature: its research prowess. "Now, I walk in and they're atomizing the company," he said. "I see both of I.B.M.'s distinctive competencies being destroyed."

Within 90 days of his arrival, Mr. Gerstner irrevocably decided to keep the company together. "I knew it was a big risk, but I never doubted that it was the right thing to do at I.B.M.," he said.

"What scared me," he added, was the need to do three things at once: change I.B.M.'s economic model, its strategy and its culture.

First, though, Mr. Gerstner had to cut costs. Work force cutbacks and plant closings were already under way, but he went deeper. In July 1993, he announced the company would eliminate an additional 35,000 jobs, bringing the declared total for the year to 50,000 and bringing the charge against earnings to $8.9 billion. As a result, I.B.M. reported a record loss of $8.1 billion in 1993, and the next year, its worldwide employment fell to a low point of 220,000, from 302,000 in December 1992.

Looking back, Mr. Gerstner pointed to three strategic decisions that were "the fundamental underpinnings of building an integrated company." First, he created a broad computer services unit that sold bundles of hardware, software, consulting and maintenance to manage business processes like manufacturing, purchasing or marketing.

I.B.M. had a services arm before, but it merely kept the company's machines up and running for customers. To be a real computer services company, Mr. Gerstner noted, "I had to be product agnostic."

"The customer would not accept a services company if all it did was flog I.B.M. products," he said.

His decision to move into services set off "an incredible bomb in the company," Mr. Gerstner recalled, adding, "Here was a part of I.B.M. that was going to work closely with Oracle, Sun Microsystems and, God forbid, Microsoft." Yet IBM Global Services became the company's biggest business, the corporate vehicle that would, as Mr. Gerstner observed, "look at technology through the eyes of the customer."

His second crucial decision struck at another I.B.M. heritage, that of relying almost exclusively on its own homegrown technology. Before, when the company had gone outside—when it plunged into the personal computer business in 1981 using Intel's microprocessor and Microsoft's operating system—the move had been regarded as a grave mistake.

But by early 1994, Mr. Gerstner had decided that I.B.M. would move to "open systems." In other words, Mr. Gerstner said, "All of I.B.M.'s software would run on major competitive hardware, and all of I.B.M.'s hardware would support competitive software." To do that, the company would have to adopt standard software protocols that allowed different hardware and software products to talk to each other.

To Mr. Gerstner, the move toward openness was a technical manifestation of his broader strategy. "There's no way that you can get a company built around proprietary control to accept the open model unless they start with the customer and realize this is what the customer wants," he explained.

His third decision, made in 1995, was to fully embrace the Internet and what I.B.M. calls the "networked world" model of computing. Moving to open systems made it easier for the company to adapt to the Internet early. But the networked model of computing suited I.B.M.'s strengths—big data-serving computers are the equivalent of power plants on the network, and the Internet shift moved the center of computing away from the personal computer.

As the Internet moved into the mainstream in the mid-1990's, it brought an explosion of computing complexity, as all kinds of hardware and software had to be able to connect to the global network. I.B.M.'s breadth and its services group were big advantages in this new environment.

"Here was a chance for I.B.M. to lead again," Mr. Gerstner declared. "We were able to articulate a role for I.B.M. in the networked world that spoke of the value of all we did."

I.B.M. welcomed the sudden spread of Internet-style computing as a gift, Mr. Gerstner admitted. "The company was extraordinarily lucky that the networked model of computing arrived in the mid-90's," he said. "And let me tell you, having worked in industries where the cycle of change is measured in decades, if not centuries, one of the things that is extraordinary about this industry is that if you miss a turn of the wheel you have a chance to get back in the game" every 10 years or so.

Still, it was his earlier decisions that put I.B.M. in a position to ride the Internet wave. Given the company's size, that strategy evolved quite rapidly. In late 1995, it formed an Internet division, which was not a product group, but more a corporate SWAT team to make sure the entire company was marching toward the Internet. Then, it carved out its niche, trumpeted in a massive advertising and marketing campaign, beginning in 1997, to push "e-business."

Competitors scoffed and advertising experts scratched their heads, but the message resonated with corporate customers.

The message—helping companies do "e-business," documented in ads by examples—remained consistent, as did the strategy. Amid the dot-com mania in 1999, Mr. Gerstner told Wall Street analysts that he regarded the hot Internet start-ups as "fireflies before the storm," suggesting that the big impact of e-business would be in the old economy. At the time, that was hardly conventional wisdom.

At the conclusion of Mr. Gerstner's tenure, his three strategic pillars have come together in what could be mistaken for the very word he avoided, a vision. And that strategy shift actually executed, insured a real change in the corporate culture.

The company's sheer number of recent hires is a clear sign of that—and the buildup of the services business is a big reason IBM Global Services employs 150,000 people, up from 7,600 in 1992. All told more than half of I.B.M.'s employees have worked for the company for five years or less. In 1992, the figure was 14 percent.

Having succeeded in an industry skeptical of outsiders, Mr. Gerstner feels free to assess it. The computer industry tends to go astray, he said, when it "tends to reach to promise value in utopian schemes"—the paperless office, the cashless society, the notion that shopping Web sites would bring the demise of bricks-and-mortar stores.

"The payoff from information technology is going to be in making transactions and processes more effective and efficient," he asserted. "So it's not about creating a new economy, it's not about creating new models of behavior or new models of industry. It's about taking a tool, a powerful tool, and saying. 'How can I make my supply chain more effective and efficient, how can I make any purchasing process more efficient, how can I make my internal employee communications more effective and efficient, how can I as a government deliver services to constituents more efficiently and more effectively?'"

"So the computer," he continued, "is in a sense like the electric motor 120 years earlier. It's an invention that in and of itself is kind of interesting, but doesn't have a lot of value unless you like hitting the alt, control, and delete keys, and all the other things you can do on a keyboard. Its value is in the application to other processes."

His reference to alt, control, delete—the keys users strike to try to reanimate a personal computer, running Windows, that has crashed—was a slap at Microsoft. Like many people, Mr. Gerstner, who travels everywhere with an I.B.M. Thinkpad notebook computer, finds PC's too hard to use. He believes the problem reflects the technical parochialism of the industry.

"There's an absence of concern about ease of use and almost a pride in technical complexity," he said. "What other industry would give you a product that, to turn it off, you first have to press a button labeled start? And you tell me one other industry where somebody could sell a product that you have to reboot on average five or six times a day to get it to work?"

Yet, unlike so many in the software business, Mr. Gerstner did not let his critique of Microsoft drive his business decisions.

In 1996, he decided that I.B.M.'s OS/2 operating system could not compete with Microsoft's Windows. "Most of the big technical decisions we made were half as much business as they were technical," Mr. Gerstner explained. "I mean, the decision to basically stop fighting Microsoft with OS/2 was hardly a technical decision. It was a decision on my part that it looked like we had lost, so why don't we get on with doing something else?"

That kind of unsentimental pragmatism has served I.B.M. pretty well for the last nine years.

Source: From S. Lohr, "He Loves to Win. At I.B.M. He Did," *New York Times,* March 10, 2002. Copyright © 2002 The New York Times Co. Reprinted with permission.

DISCUSSION QUESTIONS

1. How did IBM, under the leadership of Louis Gerstner, improve its technological leadership in the global marketplace?
2. What role did the Internet play in improving the strategic competitiveness of IBM?
3. How did Mr. Gerstner combine the various processes of structure, technology, and people to make IBM a more competitive global company?
4. What lessons have you learned from this case that are useful for analyzing the situation of a similar company, like Apple Computers?

Notes

1. Christine Tierney and Kathleen Kerwin, "Ford: Europe Has a Better Idea: Can Detroit Replicate the European Turnaround at Home? *BusinessWeek,* April 15, 2002.
2. Emily Thornton, "At China's Gates: Microsoft Boss Conquers a Key Asian Market," *Far Eastern Economic Review* 159, no. 1 (1996), pp. 54–55.
3. K. Marton, *Multinational, Technology, and Industrialization* (Lexington, MA: Heath, 1986); K. Marton and R. K. Singh, "Technology Transfer," in I. Walter and T. Murray, eds., *Handbook of International Management* (New York: Wiley, 1988), pp. 17.3–17.26.
4. G. Hall and R. Johnson, "Transfer of United States Aerospace Technology to Japan," in R. Vernon, ed., *The Technology Factor in International Trade* (New York: Columbia University Press, 1970), pp. 305–358.
5. Marton, *Multinational, Technology, and Industrialization.*
6. B. Kedia and R. S. Bhagat, "Cultural Constraints on Transfer of Technology across Nations: Implications for Research in International and Comparative Management," *Academy of Management Review* 13, no. 4 (1988), pp. 559–571.
7. V. Govindarajan and A. K. Gupta, *The Quest for Global Dominance: Transforming Global Presence into Global Competitive Advantage* (San Francisco: Jossey-Bass, 2001).
8. G. Hofstede, B. Neuijen, D. D. Ohayv, and G. Sanders, "Measuring Organizational Cultures: A Qualitative and Quantitative Study across Twenty Cases," *Administrative Science Quarterly* 35 (1990), pp. 286–316.
9. Ibid.
10. P. W. Beamish, A. J. Morrison, P. M. Rosenzweig, and A. C. Inkpen, *International Management: Text and Cases,* 5th ed. (Boston: McGraw-Hill/Irwin 2002).
11. Kedia and Bhagat, "Cultural Constraints on Transfer of Technology across Nations."
12. Govindarajan and Gupta, *The Quest for Global Dominance;* T. H. Davenport and L. Prusak, *Working Knowledge: How Organizations Manage What They Know* (Boston: Harvard Business School Press, 1998); T. A. Stewart, *The Wealth of Knowledge: Intellectual Capital and the Twenty-First Century Organization* (New York: Doubleday, 2001).
13. Davenport and Prusak, *Working Knowledge.*
14. Ibid., p. 5.
15. I. Nonaka and H. Takeuchi, *The Knowledge-Creating Company: How Japanese Companies Create the Dynamics of Innovation* (New York: Oxford University Press, 1995), p. 58.
16. Davenport and Prusak, *Working Knowledge.*
17. M. H. Best, *The New Competitive Advantage: The Renewal of American Industry* (New York: Oxford University Press, 2001).
18. Ibid.
19. S. F. Matusik and C. W. L. Hill, "The Utilization of Contingent Work, Knowledge Creation, and Competitive Advantage," *Academy of Management Review* 23, no. 4 (1998), pp. 680–697; U. Zander and B. Kogut, "Knowledge and Speed of the Transfer and Imitation of Organizational Capabilities: An Empirical Test," *Organization Science* 6, no. 1 (1995), pp. 76–92.
20. D. Leonard-Barton, *Wellsprings of Knowledge: Building and Sustaining the Source of Innovation* (Boston: Harvard Business School Press, 1995); I. Nonaka, "The Knowledge-Creating

Company," *Harvard Business Review* 69, no. 6 (1991), pp. 96–104; Nonaka and Takeuchi, *The Knowledge-Creating Company.*

21. R. Reed and R. DeFillippi, "Casual Ambiguity, Barriers to Imitation, and Sustainable Competitive Advantage," *Academy of Management Review* 15 (1990), pp. 80–102.
22. Nonaka and Takeuchi, *The Knowledge-Creating Company.*
23. D. Lei, M. Hitt, and J. Goldhar, "Advanced Manufacturing Technology: Organizational Design and Strategic Flexibility," *Organization Studies* 17, no. 3 (1996), pp. 501–523.
24. Nonaka and Takeuchi, *The Knowledge-Creating Company.*
25. G. Nathan, *Sony* (New York: Norton, 1998).
26. Nonaka and Takeuchi, *The Knowledge-Creating Company.*
27. R. S. Bhagat, B. L. Kedia, P. Harveston, and H. C. Triandis, "Cultural Variations in the Cross-Border Transfer of Organizational Knowledge: An Integrative Framework," *Academy of Management Review* 27, no. 2 (2002), pp. 204–221.
28. Ibid.
29. I. Nonaka, "A Dynamic Theory of Organizational Knowledge Creation," *Organization Science* 5, no. 1 (1994), pp. 14–37.
30. Bhagat, Kedia, Harveston, and Triandis, "Cultural Variations in the Cross-Border Transfer of Organizational Knowledge."
31. Ibid.
32. R. Bhagat, B. Englis, and B. Kedia, "Creation, Diffusion and Transfer of Organizational Knowledge in Transnational and Global Organizations," in Linda L. Neider and Chester A. Schriesheim, eds., *Research in Management: International Perspectives* (Charlotte, NC: Information Age, 2007), p. 118.
33. R. Ruggles and D. Holtshouse, *The Knowledge Advantage* (Dover, NH: Capstone, 1999), p. 46.
34. J. C. Spender, "Making Knowledge the Basis of a Dynamic Theory of the Firm," *Strategic Management Journal* 17 (1996), pp. 45–62.
35. S. Denning, "The Knowledge Perspective: A New Strategic Vision," in Ruggles and Holtshouse, eds., *The Knowledge Advantage,* pp. 143–162.
36. Bhagat, Englis, and Kedia, "Creation, Diffusion and Transfer of Organizational Knowledge in Transnational and Global Organizations," pp. 112–113.
37. D. A. Garvin, "Building a Learning Organization," in *Harvard Business Review, On Knowledge Management* (Boston: Harvard Business School Press, 1998), p. 422.
38. Govindarajan and Gupta, *The Quest for Global Dominance.*

Case II

Nora-Sakari: A Proposed JV in Malaysia (Revised)

Paul Beamish and R. Azimah Ainuddin

On Monday, July 15, 2003, Zainal Hashim, vice-chairman of Nora Holdings Sdn Bhd[1] (Nora), arrived at his office about an hour earlier than usual. As he looked out the window at the city spreading below, he thought about the Friday evening reception which he had hosted at his home in Kuala Lumpur (KL), Malaysia, for a team of negotiators from Sakari Oy[2] (Sakari) of Finland. Nora was a leading supplier of telecommunications (telecom) equipment in Malaysia while Sakari, a Finnish conglomerate, was a leader in the manufacture of cellular phone sets and switching systems. The seven-member team from Sakari was in KL to negotiate with Nora the formation of a joint-venture (JV) between the two telecom companies.

This was the final negotiation which would determine whether a JV agreement would materialize. The negotiation had ended late Friday afternoon, having lasted for five consecutive days. The JV Company, if established, would be set up in Malaysia to manufacture and commission digital switching exchanges to meet the needs of the telecom industry in Malaysia and in neighbouring countries, particularly Indonesia and Thailand. While Nora would benefit from the JV in terms of technology transfer, the venture would pave the way for Sakari to acquire knowledge and gain access to the markets of South-east Asia.

The Nora management was impressed by the Finnish capability in using high technology to enable Finland, a small country of only five million people, to have a fast-growing economy. Most successful Finnish companies were in the high-tech industries. For example, Kone was one of the world's three largest manufacturers of lifts, Vaisala was the world's major supplier of meteorological equipment, and Sakari was one of the leading telecom companies in Europe. It would be an invaluable opportunity for Nora to learn from the Finnish experience and emulate their success for Malaysia.

The opportunity emerged two and half years earlier when Peter Mattsson, president of Sakari's Asian regional office in Singapore, approached Zainal[3] to explore the possibility of forming a cooperative venture between Nora and Sakari. Mattsson said:

> While growth in the mobile telecommunications network is expected to be about 40 per cent a year in Asia in the next five years, growth in fixed networks would not be as fast, but the projects are much larger. A typical mobile network project amounts to a maximum of 50 million, but fixed network projects can be estimated in hundreds of millions. In Malaysia and Thailand, such latter projects are currently approaching contract stage. Thus it is imperative that Sakari establish its presence in this region to capture a share in the fixed network market.

The large potential for telecom facilities was also evidenced in the low telephone penetration rates for most South-east Asian countries. For example, in 1999, telephone penetration rates (measured by the number of telephone lines per 100 people) for Indonesia, Thailand, Malaysia and the Philippines ranged from three to 20 lines per 100 people compared to the rates in developed countries such as Canada, Finland, Germany, United States and Sweden, where the rates exceeded 55 telephone lines per 100 people.

R. Azimah Ainuddin prepared this case under the supervision of Professor Paul Beamish solely to provide material for class discussion. The authors do not intend to illustrate either effective or ineffective handling of a managerial situation. The authors may have disguised certain names and other identifying information to protect confidentiality. Ivey Management Services prohibits any form of reproduction, storage or transmittal without its written permission. This material is not covered under authorization from CanCopy or any reproduction rights organization. To order copies or request permission to reproduce materials, contact Ivey Publishing, Ivey Management Services, c/o Richard Ivey School of Business, The University of Western Ontario, London, Ontario, Canada, N6A 3K7; phone (519) 661-3208; fax (519) 661-3882; e-mail cases@ivey.uwo.ca. Copyright © 2006, Ivey Management Services. Version: (A) 2006-09-07. Reprinted with permission of Ivey Management Services on August 5, 2008.

[1] *Sdn Bhd* is an abbreviation for Sendirian Berhad, which means private limited company in Malaysia.

[2] *Oy* is an abbreviation for Osakeyhtiot, which means private limited company in Finland.

[3] The first name is used because the Malay name does not carry a family name. The first and/or middle names belong to the individual and the last name is his/her father's name.

THE TELECOM INDUSTRY IN MALAYSIA

Telekom Malaysia Bhd (TMB), the national telecom company, was given the authority by the Malaysian government to develop the country's telecom infrastructure. With a paid-up capital of RM2.4 billion,[4] it was also given the mandate to provide telecom services that were on par with those available in developed countries.

TMB announced that it would be investing in the digitalization of its networks to pave the way for offering services based on the ISDN (integrated services digitalized network) standard, and investing in international fiber optic cable networks to meet the needs of increased telecom traffic between Malaysia and the rest of the world. TMB would also facilitate the installation of more cellular telephone networks in view of the increased demand for the use of mobile phones among the business community in KL and in major towns.

As the nation's largest telecom company, TMB's operations were regulated through a 20-year license issued by the Ministry of Energy, Telecommunications and Posts. In line with the government's Vision 2020 program which targeted Malaysia to become a developed nation by the year 2020, there was a strong need for the upgrading of the telecom infrastructure in the rural areas. TMB estimated that it would spend more than RM1 billion each year on the installation of fixed networks, of which 25 percent would be allocated for the expansion of rural telecom. The objective was to increase the telephone penetration rate to over 50 percent by the year 2005.

Although TMB had become a large national telecom company, it lacked the expertise and technology to undertake massive infrastructure projects. In most cases, the local telecom companies would be invited to submit their bids for a particular contract. It was also common for these local companies to form partnerships with large multinational corporations (MNCs), mainly for technological support. For example, Pernas-NEC, a JV company between Pernas Holdings and NEC, was one of the companies that had been successful in securing large telecom contracts from the Malaysian authorities.

NORA'S SEARCH FOR A JV PARTNER

In October 2002, TMB called for tenders to bid on a five-year project worth RM2 billion for installing digital switching exchanges in various parts of the country. The project also involved replacing analog circuit switches with digital switches. Digital switches enhanced transmission capabilities of telephone lines, increasing capacity to approximately two million bits per second compared to the 9,600 bits per second on analog circuits.

Nora was interested in securing a share of the RM2 billion contract from TMB and, more importantly, in acquiring the knowledge in switching technology from its partnership with a telecom MNC. During the initial stages, when Nora first began to consider potential partners in the bid for this contract, telecom MNCs such as Siemens, Alcatel, and Fujitsu seemed appropriate candidates. Nora had previously entered into a five-year technical assistance agreement with Siemens to manufacture telephone handsets.

Nora also had the experience of a long-term working relationship with Japanese partners which would prove valuable should a JV be formed with Fujitsu. Alcatel was another potential partner, but the main concern at Nora was that the technical standards used in the French technology were not compatible with the British standards already adopted in Malaysia. NEC and Ericsson were not considered, as they were already involved with other local competitors and were the current suppliers of digital switching exchanges to TMB. Their five-year contracts were due to expire soon.

Subsequent to Zainal's meeting with Mattsson, he decided to consider Sakari as a serious potential partner. He was briefed about Sakari's SK33, a digital switching system that was based on an open architecture, which enabled the use of standard components, standard software development tools, and standard software languages. Unlike the switching exchanges developed by NEC and Ericsson which required the purchase of components developed by the parent companies, the SK33 used components that were freely available in the open market. The system was also modular, and its software could be upgraded to provide new services and could interface easily with new equipment

---

[4] RM is Ringgit Malaysia, the Malaysian currency. As at December 31, 2002, US$1 = RM3.80.

in the network. This was the most attractive feature of the SK33 as it would lead to the development of new switching systems.

Mattsson had also convinced Zainal and other Nora managers that although Sakari was a relatively small player in fixed networks, these networks were easily adaptable, and could cater to large exchanges in the urban areas as well as small ones for rural needs. Apparently Sakari's smaller size, compared to that of some of the other MNCs, was an added strength because Sakari was prepared to work out customized products according to Nora's needs. Large telecom companies were alleged to be less willing to provide custom-made products. Instead, they tended to offer standard products that, in some aspects, were not consistent with the needs of the customer.

Prior to the July meeting, at least 20 meetings had been held either in KL or in Helsinki to establish relationships between the two companies. It was estimated that each side had invested not less than RM3 million in promoting the relationship. Mattsson and Ilkka Junttila, Sakari's representative in KL, were the key people in bringing the two companies together. (See Exhibits 1 and 2 for brief background information on Malaysia and Finland respectively.)

NORA HOLDINGS SDN BHD

THE COMPANY

Nora was one of the leading companies in the telecom industry in Malaysia. It was established in 1975 with a paid-up capital of RM2 million. Last year, the company recorded a turnover of RM320 million. Nora Holdings consisted of 30 subsidiaries, including two public-listed companies: Multiphone Bhd, and Nora Telecommunications Bhd. Nora had 3,081 employees, of which 513 were categorized as managerial (including 244 engineers) and 2,568 as non-managerial (including 269 engineers and technicians).

The Cable Business

Since the inception of the company, Nora had secured two cable-laying projects. For the latter project worth RM500 million, Nora formed a JV with two Japanese companies, Sumitomo Electric Industries Ltd. (held 10 percent equity share) and Marubeni Corporation (held five percent equity share). Japanese partners were chosen in view of the availability of a financial package that came together with the technological assistance needed by Nora. Nora also acquired a 63 percent stake in a local cable-laying company, Selangor Cables Sdn Bhd.

The Telephone Business

Nora had become a household name in Malaysia as a telephone manufacturer. It started in 1980 when the company obtained a contract to supply telephone sets to the government-owned Telecom authority, TMB, which would distribute the sets to telephone subscribers on a rental basis. The contract, estimated at RM130 million, lasted for 15 years. In 1985 Nora secured licenses from Siemens and Nortel to manufacture telephone handsets and had subsequently developed Nora's own telephone sets—the N300S (single line), N300M (micro-computer controlled), and N300V (hands-free, voice-activated) models.

Upon expiry of the 15-year contract as a supplier of telephone sets to the TMB, Nora suffered a major setback when it lost a RM32 million contract to supply 600,000 N300S single line telephones. The contract was instead given to a Taiwanese manufacturer, Formula Electronics, which quoted a lower price of RM37 per handset compared to Nora's RM54. Subsequently, Nora was motivated to move towards the high end feature phone domestic market. The company sold about 3,000 sets of feature phones per month, capturing the high-end segment of the Malaysian market.

Nora had ventured into the export market with its feature phones, but industry observers predicted that Nora still had a long way to go as an exporter. The foreign markets were very competitive and many manufacturers already had well-established brands.

The Payphone Business

Nora's start-up in the payphone business had turned out to be one of the company's most profitable lines of business. Other than the cable-laying contract secured in 1980, Nora had a 15-year contract to install, operate and maintain payphones in the cities and major towns in Malaysia. In 1997, Nora started to manufacture card payphones under a license from GEC Plessey Telecommunications (GPT) of the United Kingdom. The agreement had also permitted Nora to sell the products to the neighboring countries in South-east Asia as well as to eight other markets approved by GPT.

While the payphone revenues were estimated to be as high as RM60 million a year, a long-term and stable income stream for Nora, profit margins were only about 10 percent because of the high investment and maintenance costs.

Other Businesses

Nora was also the sole Malaysian distributor for Nortel's private automatic branch exchange (PABX) and NEC's mobile telephone sets. It was also an Apple computer distributor in Malaysia and Singapore. In addition, Nora was involved in: distributing radio-related equipment; supplying equipment to the broadcasting, meteorological, civil aviation, postal and power authorities; and manufacturing automotive parts (such as the suspension coil, springs, and piston) for the local automobile companies.

THE MANAGEMENT

When Nora was established, Osman Jaafar, founder and chairman of Nora Holdings, managed the company with his wife, Nora Asyikin Yusof, and seven employees. Osman was known as a conservative businessman who did not like to dabble in acquisitions and mergers to make quick capital gains. He was formerly an electrical engineer who was trained in the United Kingdom and had held several senior positions at the national Telecom Department in Malaysia.

Osman subsequently recruited Zainal Hashim to fill in the position of deputy managing director at Nora. Zainal held a master's degree in microwave communications from a British university and had several years of working experience as a production engineer at Pernas-NEC Sdn Bhd, a manufacturer of transmission equipment. Zainal was later promoted to the position of managing director and, six years later, the vice-chairman.

Industry analysts observed that Nora's success was attributed to the complementary roles, trust, and mutual understanding between Osman and Zainal. While Osman "likes to fight for new business opportunities," Zainal preferred a low profile and concentrated on managing Nora's operations.

Industry observers also speculated that Osman, a former civil servant and an entrepreneur, was close to Malaysian politicians, notably the Prime Minister, while Zainal had been a close friend of the Finance Minister. Zainal disagreed with allegations that Nora had succeeded due to its close relationships with Malaysian politicians. However, he acknowledged that such perceptions in the industry had been beneficial to the company.

Osman and Zainal had an obsession for high-tech and made the development of research and development (R&D) skills and resources a priority in the company. About one percent of Nora's earnings was ploughed back into R&D activities. Although this amount was considered small by international standards, Nora planned to increase it gradually to five to six percent over the next two to three years. Zainal said:

> We believe in making improvements in small steps, similar to the Japanese *kaizen* principle. Over time, each small improvement could lead to a major creation. To be able to make improvements, we must learn from others. Thus we would borrow a technology from others, but eventually, we must be able to develop our own to sustain our competitiveness in the industry. As a matter of fact, Sakari's SK33 system was developed based on a technology it obtained from Alcatel.

To further enhance R&D activities at Nora, Nora Research Sdn Bhd (NRSB), a wholly-owned subsidiary, was formed, and its R&D department was absorbed into this new company. NRSB operated as an independent research company undertaking R&D activities for Nora as well as private clients in related fields. The company facilitated R&D activities with other companies as well as government organizations, research institutions, and universities. NRSB, with its staff of 40 technicians/engineers, would charge a fixed fee for basic research and a royalty for its products sold by clients.

Zainal was also active in instilling and promoting Islamic values among the Malay employees at Nora. He explained:

> Islam is a way of life and there is no such thing as Islamic management. The Islamic values, which must be reflected in the daily life of Muslims, would influence their behaviours as employers and employees. Our Malay managers, however, were often influenced by their western counterparts, who tend to stress

knowledge and mental capability and often forget the effectiveness of the softer side of management which emphasizes relationships, sincerity and consistency. I believe that one must always be sincere to be able to develop good working relationships.

SAKARI OY

Sakari was established in 1865 as a pulp and paper mill located about 200 kilometers northwest of Helsinki, the capital city of Finland. In the 1960s, Sakari started to expand into the rubber and cable industries when it merged with the Finnish Rubber Works and Finnish Cable Works. In 1973 Sakari's performance was badly affected by the oil crisis, as its businesses were largely energy-intensive.

However, in 1975, the company recovered when Aatos Olkkola took over as Sakari's president. He led Sakari into competitive businesses such as computers, consumer electronics, and cellular phones via a series of acquisitions, mergers and alliances. Companies involved in the acquisitions included: the consumer electronics division of Standard Elektrik Lorenz AG; the data systems division of L.M. Ericsson; Vantala, a Finnish manufacturer of color televisions; and Luxury, a Swedish state-owned electronics and computer concern.

In 1979, a JV between Sakari and Vantala, Sakari-Vantala, was set up to develop and manufacture mobile telephones. Sakari-Vantala had captured about 14 percent of the world's market share for mobile phones and held a 20 percent market share in Europe for its mobile phone handsets. Outside Europe, a 50-50 JV was formed with Tandy Corporation which, to date, had made significant sales in the United States, Malaysia and Thailand.

Sakari first edged into the telecom market by selling switching systems licensed from France's Alcatel and by developing the software and systems to suit the needs of small Finnish phone companies. Sakari had avoided head-on competition with Siemens and Ericsson by not trying to enter the market for large telephone networks. Instead, Sakari had concentrated on developing dedicated telecom networks for large private users such as utility and railway companies. In Finland, Sakari held 40 percent of the market for digital exchanges. Other competitors included Ericsson (34 percent), Siemens (25 percent), and Alcatel (one percent).

Sakari was also a niche player in the global switching market. Its SK33 switches had sold well in countries such as Sri Lanka, United Arab Emirates, China and the Soviet Union. A derivative of the SK33 main exchange switch called the SK33XT was subsequently developed to be used in base stations for cellular networks and personal paging systems.

Sakari attributed its emphasis on R&D as its key success factor in the telecom industry. Strong in-house R&D in core competence areas enabled the company to develop technology platforms such as its SK33 system that were reliable, flexible, widely compatible and economical. About 17 percent of its annual sales revenue was invested into R&D and product development units in Finland, United Kingdom and France. Sakari's current strategy was to emphasize global operations in production and R&D. It planned to set up R&D centers in leading markets, including South-east Asia.

Sakari was still a small company by international standards (see Exhibit 3 for a list of the world's major telecom equipment suppliers). It lacked a strong marketing capability and had to rely on JVs such as the one with Tandy Corporation to enter the world market, particularly the United States. In its efforts to develop market position quickly, Sakari had to accept lower margins for its products, and often the Sakari name was not revealed on the product. In recent years, Sakari decided to emerge from its hiding place as a manufacturer's manufacturer and began marketing under the Sakari name.

In 1989 Mikko Koskinen took over as president of Sakari. Koskinen announced that telecommunications, computers, and consumer electronics would be maintained as Sakari's core business, and that he would continue Olkkola's efforts in expanding the company overseas. He believed that every European company needed global horizons to be able to meet global competition for future survival. To do so, he envisaged the setting up of alliances of varying duration, each designed for specific purposes. He said, "Sakari has become an interesting partner with which to cooperate on an equal footing in the areas of R&D, manufacturing and marketing."

The recession in Finland which began in 1990 led Sakari's group sales to decline substantially from FIM22 billion[5] in 1990 to FIM15 billion in 1991. The losses were attributed to two main factors:

---

[5] FIM is Finnish Markka, the Finnish currency until January 1, 1999. Markka coins and notes were not withdrawn from circulation until January 1, 2002, when Finland fully converted to the Euro. As at December 31, 2000, US$1 = FIM6.31, and €1 = FIM5.95.

weak demand for Sakari's consumer electronic products, and trade with the Soviet Union which had come to almost a complete standstill. Consequently Sakari began divesting its less profitable companies within the basic industries (metal, rubber, and paper), as well as leaving the troubled European computer market with the sale of its computer subsidiary, Sakari Macro. The company's new strategy was to focus on three main areas: telecom systems and mobile phones in a global framework, consumer electronic products in Europe, and deliveries of cables and related technology. The company's divestment strategy led to a reduction of Sakari's employees from about 41,000 in 1989 to 29,000 in 1991. This series of major strategic moves was accompanied by major leadership succession. In June 1992, Koskinen retired as Sakari's President and was replaced by Visa Ketonen, formerly the President of Sakari Mobile Phones. Ketonen appointed Ossi Kuusisto as Sakari's vice-president.

After Ketonen took over control, the Finnish economy went through a rapid revival in 1993, followed by a new period of intense growth. Since the mid 1990s the Finnish growth had been bolstered by intense growth in telecommunications equipment manufacturing as a result of an exploding global telecommunications market. Sakari capitalized on this opportunity and played a major role in the Finnish telecommunications equipment manufacturing sector.

In 2001, Sakari was Finland's largest publicly-traded industrial company and derived the majority of its total sales from exports and overseas operations. Traditionally, the company's export sales were confined to other Scandinavian countries, Western Europe and the former Soviet Union. However, in recent years, the company made efforts and succeeded in globalizing and diversifying its operations to make the most of its high-tech capabilities. As a result, Sakari emerged as a more influential player in the international market and had gained international brand recognition. One of Sakari's strategies was to form JVs to enter new foreign markets.

THE NORA-SAKARI NEGOTIATION

Nora and Sakari had discussed the potential of forming a JV company in Malaysia for more than two years. Nora engineers were sent to Helsinki to assess the SK33 technology in terms of its compatibility with the Malaysian requirements, while Sakari managers traveled to KL mainly to assess both Nora's capability in manufacturing switching exchanges and the feasibility of gaining access to the Malaysian market.

In January 2003, Nora submitted its bid for TMB's RM2 billion contract to supply digital switching exchanges supporting four million telephone lines. Assuming the Nora-Sakari JV would materialize, Nora based its bid on supplying Sakari's digital switching technology. Nora competed with seven other companies short listed by TMB, all offering their partners' technology—Alcatel, Lucent, Fujitsu, Siemens, Ericsson, NEC, and Samsung. In early May, TMB announced five successful companies in the bid. They were companies using technology from Alcatel, Fujitsu, Ericsson, NEC, and Sakari. Each company was awarded one-fifth share of the RM2 billion contract and would be responsible for delivering 800,000 telephone lines over a period of five years. Industry observers were critical of TMB's decision to select Sakari and Alcatel. Sakari was perceived to be the least capable of supplying the necessary lines to meet TMB's requirements, as it was alleged to be a small company with little international exposure. Alcatel was criticized for having the potential of supplying an obsolete technology.

THE MAY 21 MEETING

Following the successful bid and ignoring the criticisms against Sakari, Nora and Sakari held a major meeting in Helsinki on May 21 to finalize the formation of the JV. Zainal led Nora's five-member negotiation team which comprised Nora's general manager for corporate planning division, an accountant, two engineers, and Marina Mohamed, a lawyer. One of the engineers was Salleh Lindstrom who was of Swedish origin, a Muslim and had worked for Nora for almost 10 years.

Sakari's eight-member team was led by Kuusisto, Sakari's vice-president. His team comprised Junttila, Hussein Ghazi, Aziz Majid, three engineers, and Julia Ruola (a lawyer). Ghazi was Sakari's senior manager who was of Egyptian origin and also a Muslim who had worked for Sakari for more than 20 years, while Aziz, a Malay, had been Sakari's manager for more than 12 years.

The meeting went on for several days. The main issue raised at the meeting was Nora's capability in penetrating the South-east Asian market. Other issues included Sakari's concerns over the efficiency of Malaysian workers in the JV in manufacturing the product, maintaining product quality and ensuring prompt deliveries.

Commenting on the series of negotiations with Sakari, Zainal said that this was the most difficult negotiation he had ever experienced. Zainal was Nora's most experienced negotiator and had single-handedly represented Nora in several major negotiations for the past 10 years. In the negotiation with Sakari, Zainal admitted making the mistake of approaching the negotiation applying the approach he often used when negotiating with his counterparts from companies based in North America or the United Kingdom. He said:

> Negotiators from the United States tend to be very open and often state their positions early and definitively. They are highly verbal and usually prepare well-planned presentations. They also often engage in small talk and "joke around" with us at the end of a negotiation. In contrast, the Sakari negotiators tend to be very serious, reserved and "cold." They are also relatively less verbal and do not convey much through their facial expressions. As a result, it was difficult for us to determine whether they are really interested in the deal or not.

Zainal said that the negotiation on May 21 turned out to be particularly difficult when Sakari became interested in bidding a recently-announced tender for a major telecom contract in the United Kingdom. Internal politics within Sakari led to the formation of two opposing "camps." One "camp" held a strong belief that there would be very high growth in the Asia-Pacific region and that the JV company in Malaysia was seen as a hub to enter these markets. Although the Malaysian government had liberalized its equity ownership restrictions and allowed the formation of wholly-owned subsidiaries, JVs were still an efficient way to enter the Malaysian market for a company that lacked local knowledge. This group was represented mostly by Sakari's managers positioned in Asia and engineers who had made several trips to Malaysia, which usually included visits to Nora's facilities. They also had the support of Sakari's vice-president, Kuusisto, who was involved in most of the meetings with Nora, particularly when Zainal was present. Kuusisto had also made efforts to be present at meetings held in KL. This group also argued that Nora had already obtained the contract in Malaysia whereas the chance of getting the U.K. contract was quite low in view of the intense competition prevailing in that market.

The "camp" not in favor of the Nora-Sakari JV believed that Sakari should focus its resources on entering the United Kingdom, which could be used as a hub to penetrate the European Union (EU) market. There was also the belief that Europe was closer to home, making management easier, and that problems arising from cultural differences would be minimized. This group was also particularly concerned that Nora had the potential of copying Sakari's technology and eventually becoming a strong regional competitor. Also, because the U.K. market was relatively "familiar" and Sakari has local knowledge, Sakari could set up a wholly-owned subsidiary instead of a JV company and, consequently, avoid JV-related problems such as joint control, joint profits, and leakage of technology.

Zainal felt that the lack of full support from Sakari's management led to a difficult negotiation when new misgivings arose concerning Nora's capability to deliver its part of the deal. It was apparent that the group in favor of the Nora-Sakari JV was under pressure to further justify its proposal and provide counterarguments against the U.K. proposal. A Sakari manager explained, "We are tempted to pursue both proposals since each has its own strengths, but our current resources are very limited. Thus a choice has to made, and soon."

THE JULY 8 MEETING

Another meeting to negotiate the JV agreement was scheduled for July 8. Sakari's eight-member team arrived in KL on Sunday afternoon of July 7, and was met at the airport by the key Nora managers involved in the negotiation. Kuusisto did not accompany the Sakari team at this meeting.

The negotiation started early Monday morning at Nora's headquarters and continued for the next five days, with each day's meeting ending late in the evening. Members of the Nora team were the same members who had attended the May 21 meeting in Finland, except Zainal, who did not participate. The Sakari team was also represented by the same members in attendance at the previous meeting plus a new member, Solail Pekkarinen, Sakari's senior accountant. Unfortunately, on the third day of the negotiation, the Nora team requested that Sakari ask Pekkarinen to leave the negotiation. He was perceived as extremely arrogant and insensitive to the local culture, which tended to value modesty and diplomacy. Pekkarinen left for Helsinki the following morning.

Although Zainal had decided not to participate actively in the negotiations, he followed the process closely and was briefed by his negotiators regularly. Some of the issues which they complained were difficult to resolve had often led to heated arguments between the two negotiating teams. These included:

1. Equity Ownership

In previous meetings both companies agreed to form the JV company with a paid-up capital of RM5 million. However, they disagreed on the equity share proposed by each side. Sakari proposed an equity split in the JV company of 49 percent for Sakari and 51 percent for Nora. Nora, on the other hand, proposed a 30 percent Sakari and 70 percent Nora split. Nora's proposal was based on the common practice in Malaysia as a result of historical foreign equity regulations set by the Malaysian government that allowed a maximum of 30 percent foreign equity ownership unless the company would export a certain percentage of its products. Though these regulations were liberalized by the Malaysian government effective from July 1998 and new regulations had replaced the old ones, the 30-70 foreign-Malaysian ownership divide was still commonly observed.

Equity ownership became a major issue as it was associated with control over the JV company. Sakari was concerned about its ability to control the accessibility of its technology to Nora and about decisions concerning the activities of the JV as a whole. The lack of control was perceived by Sakari as an obstacle to protecting its interests. Nora also had similar concerns about its ability to exert control over the JV because it was intended as a key part of Nora's long-term strategy to develop its own digital switching exchanges and related high-tech products.

2. Technology Transfer

Sakari proposed to provide the JV company with the basic structure of the digital switch. The JV company would assemble the switching exchanges at the JV plant and subsequently install the exchanges in designated locations identified by TMB. By offering Nora only the basic structure of the switch, the core of Sakari's switching technology would still be well-protected.

On the other hand, Nora proposed that the basic structure of the switch be developed at the JV company in order to access the root of the switching technology. Based on Sakari's proposal, Nora felt that only the technical aspects in assembling and installing the exchanges would be obtained. This was perceived as another "screw-driver" form of technology transfer while the core of the technology associated with making the switches would still be unknown.

3. Royalty Payment

Closely related to the issue of technology transfer was the payment of a royalty for the technology used in building the switches. Sakari proposed a royalty payment of five percent of the JV gross sales while Nora proposed a payment of two percent of net sales.

Nora considered the royalty rate of five percent too high because it would affect Nora's financial situation as a whole. Financial simulations prepared by Nora's managers indicated that Nora's return on investment would be less than the desired 10 percent if royalty rates exceeded three percent of net sales. This was because Nora had already agreed to make large additional investments in support of the JV. Nora would invest in a building which would be rented to the JV company to accommodate an office and the switching plant. Nora would also invest in another plant which would supply the JV with surface mounted devices (SMD), one of the major components needed to build the switching exchanges.

An added argument raised by the Nora negotiators in support of a two percent royalty was that Sakari would receive side benefits from the JV's access to Japanese technology used in the manufacture of the SMD components. Apparently the Japanese technology was more advanced than Sakari's present technology.

4. Expatriates' Salaries and Perks

To allay Sakari's concerns over Nora's level of efficiency, Nora suggested that Sakari provide the necessary training for the JV technical employees. Subsequently, Sakari had agreed to provide eight engineering experts for the JV company on two types of contracts, short-term and long-term. Experts employed on a short-term basis would be paid a daily rate of US$1260 plus travel/accommodation. The permanent experts would be paid a monthly salary of US$20,000. Three permanent experts would be attached to the JV company once it was established and the number would gradually be reduced to only one, after two years. Five experts would be available on a short-term basis to provide specific training needs for durations of not more than three months each year.

The Nora negotiation team was appalled at the exorbitant amount proposed by the Sakari negotiators. They were surprised that the Sakari team had not surveyed the industry rates, as the Japanese and other western negotiators would normally have done. Apparently Sakari had not taken into consideration the relatively low cost of living in Malaysia compared to Finland. In 2000, though the average monthly rent for a comfortable, unfurnished three-bedroom apartment was about the same (660 US$) in Helsinki and Kuala Lumpur, the cost of living was considerably lower in KL. The cost of living index (New York = 100) of basket of goods in major cities, excluding housing, for Malaysia was only 83.75, compared to 109.84 for Finland.[6]

In response to Sakari's proposal, Nora negotiators adopted an unusual "take-it or leave-it" stance. They deemed the following proposal reasonable in view of the comparisons made with other JVs which Nora had entered into with other foreign parties:

Permanent experts' monthly salary ranges to be paid by the JV company were as follows:
(1) Senior expert (seven to 10 years experience)....RM24,300–RM27,900
(2) Expert (four to six years experience)............. RM22,500–RM25,200
(3) Junior expert (two to three years experience)... RM20,700–RM23,400
(4) Any Malaysian income taxes payable would be added to the salaries.
(5) A car for personal use.
(6) Annual paid vacation of five weeks.
(7) Return flight tickets to home country once a year for the whole family of married persons and twice a year for singles according to Sakari's general scheme.
(8) Any expenses incurred during official travelling.

Temporary experts are persons invited by the JV company for various technical assistance tasks and would not be granted residence status. They would be paid the following fees:

(1) Senior expert.. RM1,350 per working day
(2) Expert... RM1,170 per working day
(3) The JV company would not reimburse the following:
  - Flight tickets between Finland (or any other country) and Malaysia.
  - Hotel or any other form of accommodation.
  - Local transportation.

In defense of their proposed rates, Sakari's negotiators argued that the rates presented by Nora were too low. Sakari suggested that Nora's negotiators take into consideration the fact that Sakari would have to subsidize the difference between the experts' present salaries and the amount paid by the JV company. A large difference would require that large amounts of subsidy payments be made to the affected employees.

5. Arbitration

Another major issue discussed in the negotiation was related to arbitration. While both parties agreed to an arbitration process in the event of future disputes, they disagreed on the location for dispute resolution. Because Nora would be the majority stakeholder in the JV company, Nora insisted that any arbitration should take place in KL. Sakari, however, insisted on Helsinki, following the norm commonly practiced by the company.

At the end of the five-day negotiation, many issues could not be resolved. While Nora could agree on certain matters after consulting Zainal, the Sakari team, representing a large private company, had to refer contentious items to the company board before it could make any decision that went beyond the limits authorized by the board.

THE DECISION

Zainal sat down at his desk, read through the minutes of the negotiation thoroughly, and was disappointed that an agreement had not yet been reached. He was concerned about the commitment Nora had made to TMB when Nora was awarded the switching contract. Nora would be expected to fulfill the contract soon but had yet to find a partner to provide the switching technology. It was foreseeable that companies such as Siemens, Samsung and Lucent, which had failed in the bid, could still be potential partners. However, Zainal had also not rejected the possibility of a reconciliation with Sakari. He could start by contacting Kuusisto in Helsinki. But should he?

---

[6] IMD & World Economic Forum. 2001. "The World Competitiveness Report."

EXHIBIT 1
Malaysia: Background Information

Sources: Ernst & Young International. 1993. "Doing Business in Malaysia." Other online sources.

Malaysia is centrally located in South-east Asia. It consists of Peninsular Malaysia, bordered by Thailand in the north and Singapore in the south, and the states of Sabah and Sarawak on the island of Borneo. Malaysia has a total land area of about 330,000 square kilometers, of which 80 percent is covered with tropical rainforest. Malaysia has an equatorial climate with high humidity and high daily temperatures of about 26 degrees Celsius throughout the year.

In 2000, Malaysia's population was 22 million, of which approximately nine million made up the country's labor force. The population is relatively young, with 42 percent between the ages of 15 and 39 and only seven percent above the age of 55. A Malaysian family has an average of four children and extended families are common. Kuala Lumpur, the capital city of Malaysia, has approximately 1.5 million inhabitants.

The population is multiracial; the largest ethnic group is the Bumiputeras (the Malays and other indigenous groups such as the Ibans in Sarawak and Kadazans in Sabah), followed by the Chinese and Indians. Bahasa Malaysia is the national language but English is widely used in business circles. Other major languages spoken included various Chinese dialects and Tamil.

Islam is the official religion but other religions (mainly Christianity, Buddhism and Hinduism) are widely practiced. Official holidays are allocated for the celebration of Eid, Christmas, Chinese New Year and Deepavali. All Malays are Muslims, followers of the Islamic faith.

During the period of British rule, secularism was introduced to the country, which led to the separation of the Islamic religion from daily life. In the late 1970s and 1980s, realizing the negative impact of secularism on the life of the Muslims, several groups of devout Muslims undertook efforts to reverse the process, emphasizing a dynamic and progressive approach to Islam. As a result, changes were introduced to meet the daily needs of Muslims. Islamic banking and insurance facilities were introduced and prayer rooms were provided in government offices, private companies, factories, and even in shopping complexes.

Malaysia is a parliamentary democracy under a constitutional monarchy. The Yang DiPertuan Agung (the king) is the supreme head, and appoints the head of the ruling political party to be the prime minister. In 2000 the Barisan Nasional, a coalition of several political parties representing various ethnic groups, was the ruling political party in Malaysia. Its predominance had contributed not only to the political stability and economic progress of the country in the last two decades, but also to the fast recovery from the 1997 Asian economic crisis.

The recession of the mid 1980s led to structural changes in the Malaysian economy which had been too dependent on primary commodities (rubber, tin, palm oil and timber) and had a very narrow export base. To promote the establishment of export-oriented industries, the government directed resources to the manufacturing sector, introduced generous incentives and relaxed foreign equity restrictions. In the meantime, heavy investments were made to modernize the country's infrastructure. These moves led to rapid economic growth in the late 1980s and early 1990s. The growth had been mostly driven by exports, particularly of electronics.

The Malaysian economy was hard hit by the 1997 Asian economic crisis. However, Malaysia was the fastest country to recover from the crisis after declining IMF assistance. It achieved this by pegging its currency to the USD, restricting outflow of money from the country, banning illegal overseas derivative trading of Malaysian securities and setting up asset management companies to facilitate the orderly recovery of bad loans. The real GDP growth rates in 1999 and 2000 were 5.4% and 8.6%, respectively (Table 1).

Malaysia was heavily affected by the global economic downturn and the slump in the IT sector in 2001 and 2002 due to its export-based economy. GDP in 2001 grew only 0.4% due to an 11% decrease in exports. A US $1.9 billion fiscal stimulus package helped the country ward off the worst of the recession and the GDP growth rate rebounded to 4.2% in 2002 (Table 1). A relatively small foreign debt and adequate foreign exchange reserves make a crisis similar to the 1997 one unlikely. Nevertheless, the economy remains vulnerable to a more protracted slowdown in the U.S. and Japan, top export destinations and key sources of foreign investment.

In 2002, the manufacturing sector was the leading contributor to the economy, accounting for about 30 percent of gross national product (GDP). Malaysia's major trading partners are United States, Singapore, Japan, China, Taiwan, Hong Kong and Korea.

TABLE 1
Malaysian Economic Performance, 1999 to 2002

Source: IMD. Various years. "The World Competitiveness Report."

Economic Indicator	1999	2000	2001	2002
GDP per capita (US$)	3,596	3,680	3,678	3,814
Real GDP growth rate	5.4%	8.6%	0.4%	4.2%
Consumer price inflation	2.8%	1.6%	1.4%	1.8%
Unemployment rate	3.0%	3.0%	3.7%	3.5%

EXHIBIT 2
Finland: Background Information

Sources: Ernst & Young International. 1993. "Doing Business in Finland." Other online sources.

Finland is situated in the north-east of Europe, sharing borders with Sweden, Norway and the former Soviet Union. About 65 percent of its area of 338,000 square kilometers is covered with forest, about 15 percent lakes and about 10 percent arable land. Finland has a temperate climate with four distinct seasons. In Helsinki, the capital city, July is the warmest month with average mid-day temperature of 21 degrees Celsius and January is the coldest month with average mid-day temperature of –3 degrees Celsius.

Finland is one of the most sparsely populated countries in Europe with a 2002 population of 5.2 million, 60 percent of whom lived in the urban areas. Helsinki had a population of about 560,000 in 2002. Finland has a well-educated work force of about 2.3 million. About half of the work force are engaged in providing services, 30 percent in manufacturing and construction, and eight percent in agricultural production. The small size of the population has led to scarce and expensive labor. Thus Finland had to compete by exploiting its lead in high-tech industries.

Finland's official languages are Finnish and Swedish, although only six percent of the population speaks Swedish. English is the most widely spoken foreign language. About 87 percent of the Finns are Lutherans and about one percent Finnish Orthodox.

Finland has been an independent republic since 1917, having previously been ruled by Sweden and Russia. A President is elected to a six-year term, and a 200-member, single-chamber parliament is elected every four years.

In 1991, the country experienced a bad recession triggered by a sudden drop in exports due to the collapse of the Soviet Union. During 1991–1993, the total output suffered a 10% contraction and unemployment rate reached almost 20%. Finnish Markka experienced a steep devaluation in 1991–1992, which gave Finland cost competitiveness in international market.

With this cost competitiveness and the recovery of Western export markets the Finnish economy underwent a rapid revival in 1993, followed by a new period of healthy growth. Since the mid 1990s the Finnish growth has mainly been bolstered by intense growth in telecommunications equipment manufacturing. The Finnish economy peaked in the year 2000 with a real GDP growth rate of 5.6% (Table 2).

Finland was one of the 11 countries that joined the Economic and Monetary Union (EMU) on January 1, 1999. Finland has been experiencing a rapidly increasing integration with Western Europe. Membership in the EMU provide the Finnish economy with an array of benefits, such as lower and stable interest rates, elimination of foreign currency risk within the Euro area, reduction of transaction costs of business and travel, and so forth. This provided Finland with a credibility that it lacked before accession and the Finnish economy has become more predictable. This will have a long-term positive effect on many facets of the economy.

Finland's economic structure is based on private ownership and free enterprise. However, the production of alcoholic beverages and spirits is retained as a government monopoly. Finland's major trading partners are Sweden, Germany, the former Soviet Union and United Kingdom.

Finland's standard of living is among the highest in the world. The Finns have small families with one or two children per family. They have comfortable homes in the cities and one in every three families has countryside cottages near a lake where they retreat on weekends. Taxes are high, the social security system is efficient and poverty is virtually non-existent.

Until recently, the stable trading relationship with the former Soviet Union and other Scandinavian countries led to few interactions between the Finns and people in other parts of the world. The Finns are described as rather reserved, obstinate, and serious people. A Finn commented, "We do not engage easily in small talk with strangers. Furthermore, we have a strong love for nature and we have the tendency to be silent as we observe our surroundings. Unfortunately, others tend to view such behaviour as cold and serious." Visitors to Finland are often impressed by the efficient public transport system, the clean and beautiful city of Helsinki with orderly road networks, scenic parks and lakefronts, museums, cathedrals, and churches.

TABLE 2
Finnish Economic Performance, 1999 to 2002

Source: IMD. Various years. "The World Competitiveness Report."

Economic Indicator	1999	2000	2001	2002
GDP per capita (US$)	24,430	23,430	23,295	25,303
Real GDP growth rate	3.7%	5.6%	0.4%	1.6%
Consumer price inflation	1.2%	3.3%	2.6%	1.6%
Unemployment	10.3%	9.6%	9.1%	9.1%

EXHIBIT 3
Ten Major Telecommunication Equipment Vendors

Source: International Telecommunication Union. 1999. "Top 20 Telecommunication Equipment Vendors 1998." http://www.itu.int/ITU-D/ict/statistics/at_glance/Top2098.html.

Rank	Company	Country	1998 Telecom Equipment Sales (US$ billions)
1	Lucent	USA	26.8
2	Ericsson	Sweden	21.5
3	Alcatel	France	20.9
4	Motorola	USA	20.5
5	Nortel	Canada	17.3
6	Siemens	Germany	16.8
7	Nokia	Finland	14.7
8	NEC	Japan	12.6
9	Cisco	USA	8.4
10	Hughes	USA	5.7

SECTION THREE

Managing People and Processes across Borders and Cultures

CHAPTER NINE

Communicating across Borders and Cultures

Chapter Learning Objectives

After completing this chapter, you should be able to:

- Understand the meaning and significance of communication in international companies and the way that culture differences and cultural context influence the process of communication.
- Discuss the significance of various forms of communication, such as verbal and nonverbal.
- Identify the possible barriers to communication across borders and cultures.
- Understand the implications of computer-mediated communication in global companies.
- Discuss the convergence and divergence of communication patterns around the world.
- Apply concepts that improve communication processes across borders and cultures.

Opening Case: Understanding Others

Much of the debate surrounding the Washington–Beijing standoff over a downed U.S. spy plane involved parsing the linguistic differences of the words regret, sorrow, and apology.

But the incident provides a public illustration of the intricacies that often complicate cross-cultural communication—whether in words, body language, or manners. An unsuspecting person can send the wrong message by how close he stands to someone, how loudly he speaks or by patting someone on the back or even smiling. "I think there are probably more stunning (cultural) contrasts in Asia . . . but boy, you can also get in a lot of trouble in any other part of the world," said Gary P. Ferraro, a cultural anthropologist and author of *The Cultural Dimension of International Business*. Language is perhaps the biggest land mine. Even the best translations can fail when trying to interpret phrases and concepts that have no cultural equivalent.

Americans may be particularly at risk of making mistakes because "ours is a society where words don't mean very much," said Seymour Chatman, a linguist and professor emeritus of rhetoric at the University of California at Berkeley. For many Americans, getting to the point is more important than choosing words carefully.

In some cases, a cultural gaffe might be dismissed as the funny misstep of a foreigner; other times it can infuriate. In the business sector, companies must be careful in choosing the words for advertising and marketing campaigns for other countries—it can make the difference between success and failure.

"It's about making people comfortable . . . and if they find something offensive, they may not buy from the company," said Michele Scott, a senior account executive with Transperfect Translations in San Francisco. Scott said her company sends clients some particularly egregious examples of mistakes—such as the infamous Chevy Nova campaign that flopped in Latin America because "no va" means "it does not go" in Spanish.

In 1993, the wildly popular "Got Milk?" campaign was revamped for Spanish-speaking markets after advertisers learned that Latinos interpreted the query more intimately, as in: "Are you lactating?" That same year, confectioner Mars Inc. confused Russians with billboards advertising that M&M's "melt in your mouth, not in your hands." It backfired because the cold climate keeps pretty much anything from melting in anyone's hands.

Soda companies Coca-Cola and Pepsi both faced marketing challenges in China. Coca-Cola can mean "bite the wax tadpole" or "female horse stuffed with wax," depending on the dialect. Coke switched its name to a phonetic equivalent that translated to "happiness in the mouth." Pepsi had its own share of trouble with the advertising slogan it "brings you back to life," which when translated literally means "Pepsi brings your ancestors back from the grave."

The film industry frequently provokes laughs when adding subtitles or renaming movies for foreign distribution. The consensus among Hollywood marketing executives is that Asian distributors give more colorful and descriptive titles for their versions of movies than do their American counterparts. For example, *As Good As It Gets* was shown in Chinese theaters as *Mr. Cat Poop*.

Linguistic misunderstandings can be funny, expensive, even embarrassing for advertisers, tourists or business travelers. But when it comes to international incidents—such as an 11-day dispute over a spy plane—the stakes are great. And often such gaffes point up more profound communications problems between countries.

"This (standoff) was not really about the language per se . . . but the deeper cultural differences," said Kaiping Peng, who teaches classes in Chinese psychology at UC Berkeley. Many Chinese were baffled when American legislators decided to air their opinions publicly by speaking out on television. Elected officials in China are considered government mouthpieces, not independent politicians with individual opinions, said Peng, who comes from China and has published numerous studies on the differences between Asian and American perceptions. The rhetoric "really did not go over very well," he said.

Another culturally telling detail was the Chinese government's insistence that the United States make a statement in writing. "What is interesting is that to Americans, a letter is just a letter, but in Chinese culture, giving a letter symbolizes a show of respect that translates as a letter of apology, even if the words don't exactly say that," Peng said.

There are also major differences in the way Americans and Chinese perceive "group responsibility." Peng said his research has shown that Americans are far more individualistic and reject the notion that an entire country can or should be held responsible for a military action. "One of the good things that will come out of this (standoff) is that people will see that we need to understand people in different cultures better," he said. "Not just the Americans understanding the Chinese perspective, but the Chinese having a greater appreciation of Americans also. Here, we're a superpower, so we tend to take everything for granted and in other places they pay much more attention to the details," Peng said. "And we need to be aware of that."

Source: Anastasia Hendrix, "The Nuances of Language," *San Francisco Chronicle*, April 15, 2001. Copyright © 2001 by San Francisco Chronicle. Reproduced with permission of San Francisco Chronicle via Copyright Clearance Center.

Discussion Questions

1. In this case what are the effects of language use on effective communication?
2. What are the effects of ineffective communication on companies such as Coke and Pepsi?
3. In communicating with people from different cultures, did you have any difficulties? Refer to this case as you discuss the unique difficulties you had.

What Is Communication?

The social and cultural environment influences the process that managers use to accomplish tasks in various countries. The variation in beliefs, values, expectations, and the amount of information available influences the process of managing communication. Maintaining effective channels of communication is central in the functioning of multinational and global organizations. Organizations, whether domestic or global, are essentially communication systems, and without an adequate understanding of how communication processes work, managers cannot function effectively.

Communication is the process of conveying data, information, ideas, and thoughts from one person to another. Communicating in the form of writing, talking, or listening or over the Internet is essential to a manager's role and consumes a great deal of time. Previous studies on managerial behavior demonstrate the importance of face-to-face communication. Managers spend 50 to 90 percent of their time communicating orally.[1]

Interpersonal communication is the key to managing the process of motivation, leadership, group interaction, team building, negotiation, and decision making, not only in the home country but also in subsidiaries around the world. Whether intended or not, cultural values are both explicitly and subtly conveyed in the process of communicating, regardless of the type of communication used. As corporations become global, the success of international business transactions will depend on the ability of managers to communicate effectively across national and cultural boundaries. In culturally diverse countries, such as the United States, United Kingdom, and India, the process of managing heterogeneous work groups and building teams requires an understanding of the role of culture in the communication process.

The Cross-Cultural Communication Process

The person who initiates the communication process is called the *sender,* and the person receiving the communication is the *receiver.* A message is transmitted to the receiver through a *medium,* which can be a face-to-face meeting, a telephone call, an e-mail, or a videoconference, for example. The message is received and interpreted by the receiver and understood. Feedback uses the same processes, with the receiver changing roles with the sender. *Communication effectiveness* is the extent to which the receiver understands the sender's message. *Noise* is distortion or interruption of the message. It can be caused by changes in the message, due to technical problems like phone distortion, or by people talking nearby. It can also be caused by selective perception, filtering, language difficulties, information overload, and cultural differences. Exhibit 9.1 outlines the communication process.

Effective communication is accomplished through the use of appropriate language. For example, the variety of English leads to the question: Which English? English spoken in countries where English is the primary business language (such as Britain, Ireland, Scotland, the United States, Australia, New Zealand, India, Nigeria, and South Africa) sounds very different in each country. In some countries, a wrench is a spanner, granulated sugar is caster sugar, and an auto repair shop is a body shop or a panelbeater. In Singapore, Singlish is used, a combination of English, Malay, and a Chinese dialect.

> When I first went to New Zealand, I expected the language to be the same as in the US. After all, I spoke English. My rude awakening came with a television show, a favorite of my husband, who had lived in New Zealand for 30 years. The show was based in Manchester,

EXHIBIT 9.1
National and Cultural Influences on the Communication Process

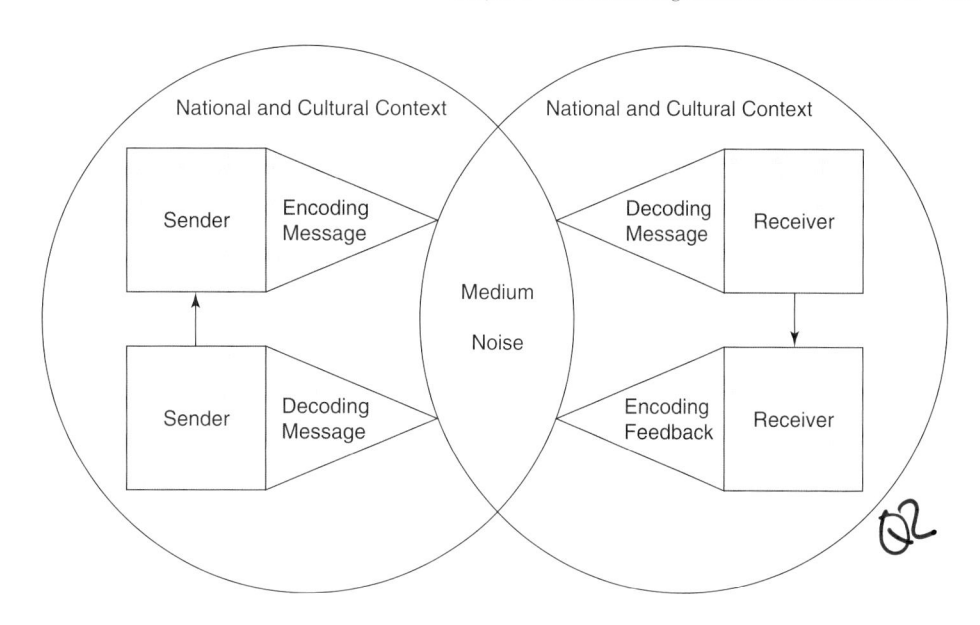

England, and I could not understand the heavy English dialect at all. In tears, I begged my husband to turn it off. Instead, he explained the words to me. At the beginning, he had to repeat almost every sentence, and luckily the program was rather slow moving. Before we returned to the US, I could "listen with an accent" and understood almost all of the programs on New Zealand television, most of which originated in England or Australia.[2]

Language is closely aligned with environment.[3] Alaskan natives have a myriad of words for different types of snow, depending on the shape, how much is falling, how wet it is, and so on. However, people living at the equator have only the word *snow* to describe the phenomenon. Those living in deserts at the equator have numerous words for different types of dust storms. Whether we are discussing the language use of Alaskan natives or of people living at the equator, different terms for snow and dust have evolved to help them adapt quickly to changing patterns in their environment.

Some cultures have terms for modern technology, but others do not. Maoris (native New Zealanders) have no word for automobile or car, so they use the English words. When the Navaho were enlisted as technicians in World War II, their language was used as code, because it is unique and spoken by only a small group of American natives. However, their language did not have all of the words necessary for military communication, so they created new ones.

People in some cultures object to the encroachments of other languages that might "dilute" their own. The French, for example, have resisted the use of English words for various expressions, and a group of people watch for the infiltration of English language into native French. This group is called the *Académie Française*. The use of words like *sandwich, weekend,* and *jogging,* for example, is common in French society, but their use is frowned on by the Académie Française.[4] In modern business, the frequent use of jargon is designed to provide explicit information using only a few words. *Jargon* is technical terminology used in business, science, or art that is specific to the environment in which it evolves. For example, in countries such as Alaska and Siberia, where the climate is generally cold and air-conditioning is not needed, jargon for the technology of air-conditioning has not developed.

Cultural values influence the development of vocabulary. The language of the Navaho, like many other native languages, has few words for the different uses of time.[5] This happens because, in these environments, the flow of time is regulated by seasonal activities and is not based on the movements of an objective clock, as is the case in modern cultures. Because of this, Navaho workers, in the past, might have been late for work because the concept of being in a particular place at a specific time was not part of their culture. The concept of "clock time" was not translatable.

Similarly, privacy is not a Chinese cultural value, so there is no word for this concept in the Chinese language.[6] Understanding these differences is important, because if the concept does not exist in the language, then substitutions must be made—but there is no guarantee that such substitutions will be understood correctly. In translations of the word *privacy* from English to Chinese, the Chinese word for "reclusiveness" is often used. In the U.S. context, a recluse is considered strange, but in China the word has a much more negative connotation. Therefore, discussing concepts such as "privacy" with Chinese people can lead to noise in communication.

Cultural influences on the use of language cannot be ignored.[7] The choice of words and the form of the messages that we send to each other is based on cultural preferences, norms, and values. For example, sending greetings of a personal nature by e-mail is not acceptable in many cultures, particularly in East Asia and Latin America. If the birth of a child or wedding announcement of a daughter were conveyed to a colleague or supervisor by e-mail, many in these countries would find this insulting.

An understanding of the importance of the underlying cultural values is essential when we communicate, particularly across national boundaries. For example, when we say "How are you?" in the United States, most of us do take it not as a question about health but as an alternative to saying "Hello." In other countries, the other person is likely to interpret the phrase literally and reply in terms of how he or she might be feeling. The importance of language as a critical component in international business is illustrated in Practical Insight 9.1. After the integration of European economies, the importance of English as the *lingua franca* of international business has increased tremendously, and this Practical Insight shows that while 41 percent of the people on the European continent can speak English, only 29 percent can speak it fluently. The result is a gap of language that increases cultural difficulties associated with the conduct of international business.

The Medium of Communication

A very important part of learning how to communicate in one's own culture, as well as across cultures, is learning how to use appropriate media to convey a message. There are two types of media: verbal and nonverbal. **Verbal communication** consists of any oral or written means of transmitting a message through words. **Nonverbal communication** is the art and science of communicating without using words, either in written or spoken form.

Verbal Communication

Different types of verbal communication are used in conducting different types of business transactions. Face-to-face interaction is the preferred method for transmitting emotions or subtle messages and for persuading the receiver to act in a certain way, because nonverbal cues, such as tone of voice, use of silence, and body language, are important. Furthermore, in face-to-face interactions, the sender receives immediate feedback that is rich with both informational and emotional content and has the opportunity to act appropriately.

Telephone communication is the next-richer form of communication. It has the potential to transmit some nonverbal cues, such as tone of voice and use of silence, but

PRACTICAL INSIGHT 9.1

THE GREAT ENGLISH DIVIDE

In Europe, speaking the lingua franca separates the haves from the have-nots. Antonio Sanz might as well have won the lottery. In 1965, when the small, curly-haired Spaniard was 10, an American professor asked his parents if she might take the boy to the U.S. and enroll him in public school. They agreed. America seemed to offer a brighter future than the dairy farms where his father worked in the foothills north of Madrid. Sanz left, but came back to Spain every summer with stories from Philadelphia and boxes of New World artifacts: Super Balls, baseball cards, and Bob Dylan records.

His real prize, though, was English. Sanz learned fast, and by senior year he outscored most of his honors English classmates in the verbal section of the Scholastic Aptitude Test. In those days, back in his hometown of Colmenar Viejo, English seemed so exotic that kids would stop him on the street and ask him to say a few sentences. By the time he graduated from Hamilton College in Clinton, N.Y., and moved back to Spain, American companies there were nearly as excited. He landed in Procter & Gamble Co.

Sanz, now 46 and a father of three, employs his Philadelphia English as an executive at Vodafone PLC in Madrid. But something funny has happened to his second language. These days, English is no longer special, or odd, or even foreign. In Paris, Düsseldorf, Madrid, and even in the streets of Colmenar Viejo, English has put down roots. "What else can we all speak?" Sanz asks.

Basic Tool

No surprise there. English is firmly entrenched nearly everywhere as the international language of business, finance, and technology. But in Europe, it's spreading far beyond the elites. Indeed, English is becoming the binding agent of a continent, linking Finns to French and Portuguese as they move toward political and economic unification. A common language is crucial, says Tito Boeri, a business professor at Bocconi University in Milan, "to take advantage of Europe's integrated labor market."

English, in short, is Europe's language. And while some adults are slow to embrace this, it's clear as day for European children. "If I want to speak to a French person, I have to speak in English," says Ivo Rowekamp, an 11-year-old in Heidelberg, Germany.

The implications for business are enormous. It's no longer just top execs who need to speak English. Everyone in the corporate food chain is feeling the pressure to learn a common tongue as companies globalize and democratize. These days in formerly national companies such as Renault and BMW, managers, engineers, even leading blue-collar workers are constantly calling and e-mailing colleagues and customers in Europe, the U.S., and Japan. The language usually is English, an industrial tool now as basic as the screwdriver.

But there's one fly in the ointment. While English is fast becoming a prereq for landing a good job in Europe, only 41% of the people on the Continent speak it—and only 29% speak it well enough to carry on a conversation, according to a European Commission report. The result is an English gap, one that divides Europe's haves from its have-nots. In the 19th and 20th centuries, Europeans brought peasants into the workforce by teaching them to read and write the national language. These days, the equivalent challenge is to master Europe's international language. Those that fail—countries, companies, and individuals alike—risk falling far behind.

How much is English worth? In jobs from offices to the factory floor, recruiters say that workers who speak English often command salaries 25% to 35% above those who don't. More important, they can aspire to a host of higher-level jobs that are off-limits to monolinguists. "English is an imperative," says Didier Vuchot, chairman of recruiter Korn/Ferry International in Europe.

A generation ago, this wasn't the case. Most European companies did the bulk of their business at home. They maintained only a small phalanx of English-speaking "international experts" to deal with bankers in London and machine shops in Chicago. Ambitious anglophones such as Antonio Sanz often landed at American multinationals. "I was with a bunch of aristocrats at Procter," Sanz recalls. "In Spain, they were the ones who spoke English."

That was when Europe boasted only a handful of multinational corporations. Now there are hundreds. When European governments freed up their economies during the 1980s and '90s, a host of newly private companies burst onto the scene. As they pushed for growth, giants such as Deutsche Telekom and France's Alcatel spread across borders in a frenzy of mergers and acquisitions. Suppliers followed them into foreign markets. In most of these companies, managers who didn't know English soon found themselves confined to sleepy domestic operations. Their English-chattering colleagues, by contrast, flew the globe and advanced.

The need for a lingua franca is most pressing for global technology players. "We need a common language," says Alcatel CEO Serge Tchuruk. "There aren't many choices." So in the early '90s, Alcatel and Finland's Nokia embraced English as the corporate language. In Europe, where the Germans and French have long battled for supremacy, English also makes political sense: It's the closest thing to linguistic neutral territory. When France's Rhone Poulenc and Germany's Hoechst joined forces to found Aventis two years ago, they set up headquarters in the border city of Strasbourg. And they further defused cultural tensions by adapting English as the company language.

continued

> **PRACTICAL INSIGHT 9.1** *continued*
>
> The other European languages are hardly dying, of course, and British and American managers working in Europe would do well to pick up bilingual skills. But new forces, including the Internet, are pushing Europe toward a common language. Take KPNQwest, the pan-European phone company based in the Netherlands. There, all e-mail must be written in English, even communiqués between German engineers. Why? CEO John A. McMaster sees e-mail as strings of communication that often spread through the corporate system. "If you shift the language from Spanish to German to Italian, you leave out lots of people," he says.
>
> As companies like KPNQwest cross one border after another, companies across the Continent are doubling as language schools. At Germany's gas and water utility, RWE, fully 30% of the employees are busy studying English—a necessity for advancement in a company that operates in more than 100 countries. At Ravensburger, a German game-maker, human-resources officials used to conduct interviews in German. Now, they need English to interview applicants in Poland or Britain, says Martin Hurtha, personnel chief. Europeans who don't know English, says Lorenzo Targetti, CEO of Targetti Sankey, an Italian lighting company, are "running a marathon in house shoes."
>
> More and more, even the rank and file must know English—or risk missing out on vital job opportunities. For example, 1½ years ago the Dutch cable company United Pan-European Communications was building a $20 million TV studio in Amsterdam. This job required scores of electricians, far more than UPC could find in the Netherlands. Only a two-hour train ride south of Amsterdam, however, in the rust belt of French-speaking Belgium and northern France, plenty of electricians were available. But the Dutch and American managers at UPC wanted everyone at the project to speak and understand the same language. So UPC flew in a platoon of electricians from Britain, put them up in hotels during the week, and sent them home every weekend.
>
> Across all sectors and ranks, non-English-speakers face a harder hunt for fewer and poorer jobs. Many of the leading employers in Europe, including Vivendi Universal and CAP Gemini rarely even consider job applicants without English. Secretaries who lack English can expect to make 30% less—if they're lucky enough to find a job, says temporary-work agency Manpower Inc. And for headhunters such as Sarah Mulhern of Spencer Stuart in Paris, English is not a option anymore: "It's a requirement." She recalls working with one French technical whiz who didn't know English. She landed him a job at Excite—but only after he had completed an intensive language course.
>
> True, line workers in many manufacturing plants can still get by in their native language. But workers who want to advance find themselves back at school—learning English. At DaimlerChrysler, workers seeking a promotion to team leader on the shop floor take English classes after hours. Even union representatives duck into English classrooms at the company's Unterturkheim plant. Says one union official at the plant: "We need it to speak to union officials in America."
>
> Europe's English divide closely mirrors its economy. The wealthy parts—Sweden, the Netherlands, western Germany, and cosmopolitan cities such as Paris and Milan—are also rich in English, and getting richer. English-poor regions, from the Mediterranean to Eastern Europe, lose out on foreign investment and jobs. Only 5% to 10% of the workforce at Italian banks speaks good English, estimates Michele Appendino, co-founder of European venture fund Net Partners. If those banks merge with German or French banks, as expected, the common language will likely be English. Those who don't speak it risk becoming foreigners in their own banks—if they're lucky enough to hold on to their jobs.
>
> For the flip side, look no further than Ireland. It has enjoyed job growth averaging 5% a year since the mid-'90s, with many of the new employment resulting from U.S. investments. Ireland's greatest advantage? Its young, English-speaking

it is not as effective as face-to-face communication in communicating the content of the total message.

Written communication conveys a great deal of data and information in explicit form and is used widely in all organizations in different parts of the world. Explicit knowledge useful for organizational innovation is best communicated in written form. However, the problem with written communication is that some of the subtleties are not likely to be conveyed effectively, because they can be communicated only by nonverbal means. For example, while the decision to move a manager to a different part of the world can be transmitted in writing, it would be more effectively conveyed face-to-face. We must remember that written communication is the primary method of communicating across subsidiaries of multinational and global communication, and its use is increasing.

workforce, says Aidan Brady, CEO of Citigroup in Dublin, is the main reason Citigroup put down roots there.

"Goners"
The pressure to be an anglophone has resulted in a bonanza for English-language schools. Barcelona's Wall Street Institute, for example, has opened 35 new language centers throughout Europe in the past 1½ years, making a total of roughly 300 schools across the Continent. Students pay an average of $1,400 for 120 hours of courses. "They've realized that they're goners if they don't take English classes," says Wall Street Institute Paris President Natanael Wright. European governments are also pitching in. In France, Italy, and Spain, political leaders are pushing to introduce their nations' children to English at earlier ages. Nearly 300,000 Spaniards are piling into state language schools this year.

But teaching English to the whole Continent is no easy task. Teachers are scarce: Their English often provides them with more lucrative opportunities than teaching in a public school. "All our English teachers are getting swallowed up by DaimlerChrysler," complains one school administrator near the company's Stuttgart headquarters. When they don't have the chance to learn English in the classroom, high school graduates from Europe's south and east flock to Britain and Ireland to wait tables and learn English on the cheap.

French Farce
A rearguard action is being fought against the English advance. When French Defense Minister Alain Richard approved English as the common language of a joint French-German army battalion, *Le Figaro* dubbed him "the gravedigger" of the French language. In Brussels, the European Commission is bending over backwards to avoid the impression that it favors English, even as English establishes itself as the de facto language of the EC. Its current effort, known as Europe's Year of Languages, pushes English as one of 11 languages, no more important than Greek or Finnish.

Europe's leaders, of course, know how vital English is: Just like CEOs and software engineers, they need it to talk to each other. Politicians such as Spanish Prime Minister José Maria Aznar and Italy's Silvio Berlusconi, who both require interpreters, miss out on English-language dinner chatter and one-to-one schmoozing at Euro-gatherings. One Italian language school, International House, offers English lessons by phone to politicians on the run.

The English divide is age-related, too. According to a European Union study, 67% of Europeans between 15 and 24 say they can speak English, compared with only 18% of those over 55. Thus Europe's relentless drive for English empowers kids around the Continent, wreaking havoc with hierarchies in companies and families alike. Take a look at the families of Spaniards and Italians visiting Paris: The English-speaking children appear to be in charge, ordering food in English for their parents, and arranging early-morning taxis to the airport.

But what's amusing in families is dead serious in the workplace. Thirty-nine-year-old Nadine Koulecheff, a high school graduate in Paris, saw in the late '90s that one answering machine could put an end to her career as a receptionist. She spent three months in a 40-hour-per-week English class associated with France's National Employment Office. At the end, she successfully interviewed in English for a secretarial job at a medical laboratory. "My English got me the job," she says. She uses it every day—mostly to talk to her Italian boss.

That's the Europe that's taking shape. For the ever-growing masses of English speakers, basic communication is now a breeze. The Babel of old hardly interferes, and instead adds richness and texture to life in Europe. But for those on the other side of the Great Divide, Europe's unification—its opportunities and pitfalls alike—is still shrouded in mystery. The operating instructions for Europe, it's now clear, are written in English.

Source: Stephen Baker, Inka Resch, Kate Carlisle, and Katharine A. Schmidt, "The Great English Divide," *BusinessWeek*, August 13, 2001.

Computer-Mediated Communication

Communication through the use of electronic mail (e-mail)—**computer-mediated communication**—has revolutionized communication processes in organizational settings. It is particularly prevalent in global organizations where effective management information systems are the key to maintaining and improving coordination of activities, as discussed in Section 2. In 1970, transmitting the *Encyclopedia Britannica* as an electronic data file from coast to coast within the United States would have cost $187. Today the entire Library of Congress could be transmitted across America for just $40.[8] As the technology of bandwidth expands, costs will fall further, causing even more dramatic improvements in the way managers of multinational and global organizations send and receive information and implement decisions.

E-mail messages are quickly formed, edited, and stored, and they can be transmitted to many people with a simple click of a mouse. There is no need to coordinate a communication session. E-mail allows random access to information, no matter which part of the globe a manager is located in. One can access any message in any order and then move on to others, depending on their usefulness for accomplishing a task or coordinating an activity across geographic boundaries.

E-mail has reduced the need for face-to-face and telephone communication, and it has altered the flow of organizational information. While reducing the need for other types of communication, it has increased the movement of communication across all parts of organizations. Organization- and culture-specific differences in power and status between the sender and receiver are less important in e-mail use than in face-to-face and telephone communication.

However, one problem with e-mail that often causes difficulties is the increased frequency of "flaming"—the act of sending emotional messages without considering the implications. In this respect, e-mails can cause more problems than traditional forms of written communication, which allow more time for reflection before transmission.

Instant messaging is the next step in computer-mediated communication. Instant messaging software connects two or more people located in different parts of the globe, enabling them to communicate with each other instantaneously. For example, if a manager in the United States sends an instant message to a colleague in another part of the world, such as Brazil, the message will instantly appear not only on the monitor of the Brazilian colleague but on other monitors connected in the network. Coordinating tasks of multinational and global organizations is becoming easier to accomplish through the technology of instant messaging and networking. Their use is predicted to increase dramatically—from 5.5 million in 2000 to more than 180 million in 2004 and beyond.[9]

Nonverbal Communication

E-mail and other types of computer-mediated communication are changing the way managers of global corporations communicate. But they cannot replace the role of nonverbal communication, which includes facial expressions, tone of voice, physical distance, and the use of silence. For example, Japanese negotiators allow long periods of silence in order to communicate their messages in a manner seldom understood by Western counterparts.[10]

Nonverbal communication is also important in tasks that involve a great deal of emotional labor—the effort, planning, and control needed to express organizationally valued emotions. Individuals in all countries make extensive use of nonverbal cues to transmit necessary feelings to co-workers, customers, and supervisors in the conduct of their duties.

Nonverbal communication differs from verbal communication in many ways. While verbal communication is typically a conscious process, nonverbal communication tends to be somewhat unconscious and culture-specific. For example, Australians tend to be less verbal than Americans in communicating their messages.[11] In many Scandinavian countries, listeners' silence is interpreted as encouragement for the communicator.[12]

The term **kinesic behavior** refers to body movements—physical posture, gestures, facial expressions, and eye contact. While such body movements are universal in nature, their meaning depends on the cultural context, and they cannot be generalized across cultures. People worldwide can recognize displays of basic emotions, such as joy, contempt, anger, disgust, fear, and sadness, but the interpretation of special facial expressions that are unique to a cultural context entails significant differences. International managers and visitors who are unaware of the meaning of different facial expressions in different cultures may react incorrectly because they do not have adequate knowledge of the meaning of such expressions. For example, most Westerners would not correctly understand many of the facial expressions of East Asian cultures—sticking out the tongue expresses surprise, scratching the ears and cheeks indicates happiness, and widening of the eyes displays anger.[13]

Gestures that individuals use in organizations to emphasize a point also vary widely across nations. A study done by a group of researchers showed that the frequency of the use of 20 different hand gestures and the meaning associated with each of them across 40 distinct locations in western Europe varied considerably.[14] There is substantially more gesturing in some nations than in others. Gesturing improved the effectiveness of communication in Italy more than in other locations. Low rates of gestures are typically found in countries where there is greater emphasis on formality and formal modes of transactions—whether in the business or in interpersonal or social situations. As a general rule, northern and Anglo-Saxon countries (e.g., United Kingdom, Ireland, Netherlands, Germany, and Scandinavia), use gestures much less than members of countries in southern Europe (e.g., Italy, Greece, or Spain). Use of bowing is largely found in hierarchical countries (i.e., countries that are characterized by high power distance, such as Japan).

Proxemics is the study of the role of physical distance between persons and the use of personal space and office layout in the process of communication. Private office space for each manager is common in U.S. organizations. As the manager achieves higher status, the office generally becomes larger and more private. In contrast, in much of Asia as well as in Latin America, an open office layout is more common. Whereas a corner office on the top floor of the building tends to communicate power in the United States and Germany, an office in the middle of the floor reflects power in the United Kingdom and India. The French, on the other hand, like to occupy an office in the middle of subordinates, signifying that they have a central role in the information network, since they like to be in control.[15]

Hall and Hall noted that cultural differences influence how close we allow another person when communicating face-to-face.[16] Americans generally feel uncomfortable when someone is too close. This is because they feel that the person is invading their "space." Proper use of physical distance in maintaining personal space is very important, and unfamiliar approaches that violate our sense of personal space are not appreciated. Some of these distances in the U.S. culture are illustrated in Exhibit 9.2.

Some cultures encourage people to use their senses—stay close to each other and touch each other in the process of communicating—as part of the communication process. These cultures are called **high-contact cultures,** and they are found among countries around the Mediterranean, the Middle East, Latin America, and southern and eastern Europe. In contrast, cultures of North America, East Asia, and western and

EXHIBIT 9.2
A Typology of Physical Distances

Source: E. T. Hall and M. R. Hall, *Understanding Cultural Differences* (Yarmouth, ME: Intercultural Press, 1990).

Intimate distance	Contact–18 inches—a distance reserved for comforting, protecting, and lovemaking
Personal distance	18 inches–4 feet—a bubble of personal space the size of which depends on the relationship to the other person
Social distance	4–12 feet—used by acquaintances and strangers in more formal settings
Public distance	12–25 feet—distance at which the recognition of others is not required

northern Europe encourage much less sensory involvement in the communication process. In these **low-contact cultures,** the preference is to stand apart and not touch each other while communicating. We find low-contact cultures in cooler climates of the world, whereas high-contact cultures are found mostly around the equator. For example, Americans stand roughly 18 inches apart when they communicate, and standing closer will result in a person backing away from the contact.

Environmental Context of Communication

Hall and Hall discuss the significance of context in determining the amount of communication that can be accomplished without a great deal of communication noise.[17] Communication takes place in a context, and the specific meaning and interpretation that are provided by individuals in the context are a part of the message.

Cultures of Asia, the Middle East, Latin America, the Mediterranean, and parts of Africa are called **high-context cultures.** In these cultures, members do not convey feeling and thoughts very explicitly and must develop an ability to detect subtle meanings and nonverbal messages that are present in the physical context of the communication. Information and knowledge of relationships are important, such as whether one is communicating with the members of the in-group or out-group, the nature of historical relationships that existed among the parties, and the various patterns of obligations and norms.

In **low-context cultures,** which are found in Canada and the United States, as well as countries of western and northern Europe, such attention to the context is not needed. Communication in these cultures does not need the detailed information demanded for communication in high-context cultures. Explicit forms of communication, especially written communication, are preferred. The Swiss culture is least concerned with context in communication, as depicted in Exhibit 9.3.[18]

When people from low-context cultures communicate with those in high-context cultures, the potential for distortion and misunderstanding is significant, as illustrated in Practical Insight 9.2. Those in high-context cultures would like individuals from low-context cultures to understand the importance of things that are not clearly stated. Proxemics, subtle gestures, and various cues that are present in the physical context are important in communicating with members of high-context cultures. Similarly, managers from low-context cultures get the impression that those in high-context cultures are not open in their communication of views and opinions. For example, East

EXHIBIT 9.3
Contrasting Patterns of Communication in Low- versus High-Context Cultures

Source: Based on information drawn from Edward T. Hall and M. R. Hall, *Understanding Cultural Differences* (Yarmouth, ME: Intercultural Press, 1990); and Martin Rosch, "Communications: Focal Point of Culture," *Management International Review* 27, no. 4 (1987), p. 60.

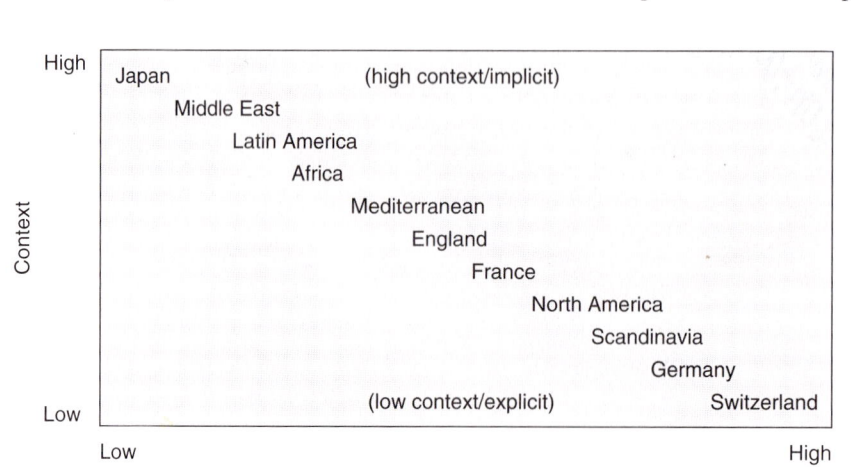

Context	Explicitness of Communication
High	Japan (high context/implicit)
	Middle East
	Latin America
	Africa
	Mediterranean
	England
	France
	North America
	Scandinavia
	Germany
Low	(low context/explicit) Switzerland
	Low High

PRACTICAL INSIGHT 9.2

THE RELATIVE IMPORTANCE OF ENCODING MESSAGES IN WORDS

In a training session to orient mainland Chinese to North American work practices, one of the authors delivered a half-day session about putting "messages into words." The theme was that in North American business environments, if you have a problem, you should articulate it to someone rather than struggle along trying to cope in silence.

At mid-day, the trainer and trainees sat together around their conference table to eat lunches they had brought. The room had a kettle along with a box of Chinese tea so the trainees could enjoy a cup of tea with their lunch and throughout the day. The trainees were not accustomed to having trainers eat lunch with them, but nevertheless they graciously asked her if she would like some tea. She said yes, thank you very much, she would like tea.

A few minutes later, she was politely presented with a cup of boiled water. Where was the tea? She asked. All gone, she was told. When? A few days ago. Why, she asked, didn't anyone say anything sooner?

After some exploratory discussion, several reasons emerged. One trainee volunteered that they weren't sure the trainer, a teacher who automatically had high status in their eyes, was the right person to ask about something like tea. They didn't want to insult her. Another trainee said they didn't want to mention the exhausted tea supply to the trainer in case that made her feel obliged to buy tea, paying out of her own pocket. They weren't certain the program had funds for additional tea for her to be reimbursed if she did buy them tea. They also felt perhaps they should have replaced the tea themselves, but hadn't worked out an equitable mechanism yet for doing so. In any case, that meant the risk of an expenditure that might turn out to be unnecessary.

No doubt the unannounced presence of a trainer at their lunch table raised another uneasy question in their minds: Were they supposed to have reserved some tea in case a trainer decided to have some? Finally, a young man daringly offered the opinion that in China, the person who identified a problem was then identified with the problem and in his words, "became the problem." It was better not to draw attention to a problem, he said, and the others agreed that this could be true.

This episode says a number of things about expectations by the trainer and different expectations by the trainees about communication. The Chinese were conscious of the social impact of their words, and therefore chose to communicate in actions rather than risk a consequence that was difficult for them to calculate accurately. The act of offering a cup of boiled water in a context where tea was expected was as eloquent as any specifically worded message.

Source: K. Beamer and I. Varner, *Intercultural Communication in the Global Workplace,* 2nd ed. (New York: McGraw-Hill, 2001), p. 144. Copyright © 2001 The McGraw-Hill Companies, Inc. Reprinted with permission.

Asians tend to like people who are not talkative, whereas Americans dislike silence and will talk to fill silent spaces.[19]

In Germany and the United States, dominance frequently is expressed through talking, but the manner of speaking of the one wishing to dominate the conversation differs between the two countries. Americans who dominate the conversation speak loudly with a greater use of expressive movements, whereas dominant Germans show a lesser range of expressive movements but a high degree of verbal fluency.

Barriers to Effective Communication

Communicating across cultures is more difficult than communicating in one's own culture, because people with different cultural backgrounds have less common information about how to communicate effectively. In Exhibit 9.1, "national and cultural context" refers to culturally based elements of a person's background, such as:

- Beliefs about what is correct to communicate.
- The status of the sender and the receiver.
- Attitude toward the content of the message.

PRACTICAL INSIGHT 9.3

CULTURE CLASHES HARM OFFSHORING

An Accenture study shows cultural differences, such as communications styles, are by far the biggest reason outsourcing deals fail.

Cultural differences are one of the biggest reasons why offshore outsourcing deals fail or run into problems, according to new research.

In an Accenture study, two-thirds of 200 U.S. business executives said that miscommunication arising from cultural differences has caused problems when outsourcing offshore.

Different communication styles was identified as the key factor causing problems between onshore and offshore workers by over three-quarters (76 per cent) of the managers questioned.

Different approaches to completing tasks, different attitudes toward conflict and different decision-making styles were cited as the other main cultural factors that frequently cause upsets when managing an offshore outsourcing relationship.

Kris Wadia, senior executive in Accenture's network of global delivery centres, said that the physical obstacles to offshore outsourcing such as telecoms and facilities have largely been resolved.

He said in a statement: "However, the soft issues, particularly cross-cultural communication, will continue to present the main challenges to realising global sourcing's full potential for the foreseeable future."

Over half of National Outsourcing Association (NOA) members surveyed recently also said cultural differences are still an issue in offshore outsourcing deals.

At a NOA event last week David Skinner, partner at law firm Morrison & Foerster, said this is particularly true in multi-sourcing where the client is often dealing with many managers from different suppliers in different countries.

He said: "It is one of the biggest multi-sourcing issues. You have got to manage the cultural differences."

Source: Andy McCue, "Culture Clashes Harm Offshoring," *BusinessWeek,* July 17, 2006.

- Stereotypes of the other culture.
- Cultural preferences regarding the medium used.
- Educational level and professional competence of the sender and the receiver.

Practical Insight 9.3 shows that cultural differences in communication styles are one of the major factors that negatively affect offshoring activities of multinational and global companies. Different communication styles between onshore and offshore employees were key factors causing problems in over 76 percent of the managers who participated in the study conducted by Accenture.

Other barriers that frequently contribute to ineffective communication across national borders and cultures are as follows:

1. Differences in Status between the Sender and the Receiver of Communication

As a general rule, members of countries that are strongly collectivistic in their orientations pay more attention to status differences than do people from countries that are more individualistic. A message from a high-status individual will be received and paid attention to more carefully in collectivistic cultures than is likely to be the case in individualistic cultures. In addition, in many of the collectivistic cultures of the world, words that one should use in communication depend a great deal on the relative status of the parties engaged in communication.

In India, for example, the manner (i.e., the style of addressing) in which a supervisor is approached by his or her subordinate is different from the way a co-worker would be addressed by the same subordinate. The word *you* in the English language has three different status connotations in India. In Japan, too, there are at least three levels of status differences when talking to another person, as well as three levels of polite self-reference.[20] It is important for employees of multinational corporations to be sensitive to status differences that are uniquely present in different cultural contexts. While there are some similarities in the way status differences play a role in the process of communication, differences do exist among collectivistic nations in East Asia, Latin America, and Africa. It is important to note that individualists from western Europe and North America are much more concerned with the exactness of the content of communication and are not very sensitive to the role of status differences in the process of receiving or sending messages in the context of organizational communication.

2. Content of Communication

Content of communication is valued differently in different countries. Exaggerating peripheral elements may be valued in some nations and cultures but not in others. Compared with individuals from Western cultures, individuals from Middle Eastern cultures (e.g., Saudi Arabia, UAE, Jordan) generally place more emphasis on some interpersonal and social aspects of communication that are not necessarily linked with the central message(s) that are to be conveyed in the process of communication. Individualists prefer to emphasize as well as receive specific aspects of the message that are immediately relevant for thought or action. They are interested in knowing the exact point of the message that is necessary for decision making or action. Peripheral elements are considered extraneous and are regarded as a waste of time. In fact, emphasis on peripheral, as opposed to central, issues is likely to annoy individualists. However, collectivists, particularly from some of the Middle Eastern cultures, tend to focus on some of the peripheral aspects before discussing the issues of central importance. Part of the reason this happens can be attributed to the fact that individuals from these cultures are interested in developing a sense of cordial relationships prior to engaging in business transactions.

The issue of developing and maintenance of **trust** is more important while communicating with collectivists. In contrast, managers from multinational and global corporations of individualistic countries are more inclined to get to the specifics of the message and don't necessarily see the relevance of developing trust in matters that are purely related to business transactions. Collectivists, on the other hand, need to feel a degree of comfort in communicating substantive aspects of a business proposal or idea with a person or a group of persons whom they feel they can trust. As global businesses extend their reaches in dissimilar nations and cultures of the world, we will get more insights into the role of trust in communication.

3. Differences in Goals and Face-Saving Tendencies

One of the important goals that individuals from collectivistic cultures emphasize is harmony and saving face for both the sender and the receiver of communication.[21] The concept of face is concerned with the issue of identity and respect in a given social context. **Saving face** is the process of preserving one's reputation and connectedness. In a sense, it is related to the concept of politeness, and it has both verbal and nonverbal connotations. Ting-Toomey suggested that people from all cultures like to save face,[22] but "saving face" is especially important in the collectivistic cultures of East Asia and the Middle East. In individualistic cultures, the concept of face is primarily focused on highlighting the person's positive qualities and deemphasizing the negative qualities. Since smooth maintenance of social connectedness is of secondary importance in individualistic cultures, there is less of an emphasis on saving face. Despite our best intentions, sometimes we might find ourselves in situations where we lose face. For example, when a manager is told in public that his or her analysis of the marketing strategy is wrong, he or she loses face. Criticizing someone in public, in the

East Asian context, is particularly forbidden. Managers wishing to achieve successful communication networks in East Asia and the Middle East should pay particular attention to the concept of saving face.

Collectivists tend to feel more comfortable in situations where **harmony** is maintained and face is preserved—that is, there is no loss of identity. Communications that adversely affect the process of maintaining face are detrimental. Collectivistic cultures are more concerned with the importance of maintaining relationships, not only within their in-groups but also with members of groups with which they conduct business on a routine basis. It is important to remember the strong importance of harmony and saving face as two important elements in communicating with collectivists. The process of communication, whether within the collectivistic context or across the individualism–collectivism divide, needs to be sensitive to the importance of developing and maintaining harmony.

4. The Role of Ideology versus Pragmatism

Some nations as well as cultures put a premium on the role of ideology in communication. The ideology can be political (such as Marxism), religious (Judeo-Christian, Islamic, Buddhist, etc), or world-view (i.e., strong emphasis on self-interest versus strong concerns for the less fortunate). The sender of the communication tends to assume that the other party is aware of the central values that are enshrined in the nation or in the culture. Pragmatic cultures concentrate on what works and are not necessarily concerned with framing messages to make them consistent with the dominant values of the nation or culture. Members of socialist and communist countries tend to emphasize the role of ideology (such as emphasis on central planning and state ownership of lands, factories, etc.) as a general rule in communicating with members of countries where market-driven processes are emphasized. Managers from countries where market-related transactions are important, and the primary factor driving the economic enterprise, tend to be more pragmatic and therefore expect communication to be direct, focused, and free from ideological jargon. These individuals do not want to waste time worrying about ideological concerns slowing the speed or efficacy of business transactions.[23]

5. Associative versus Abstractive Norms

Another important barrier is concerned with the difference between associative and abstractive modes of thinking and its effect on the process of communication. Countries that are primarily populated by people of one distinct culture are homogeneous, and those that are populated by people of different cultures are heterogeneous. In homogeneous cultures (such as Japan, South Korea), communication tends to be dependent on the nature of relationships between the parties. Long-term associations between people and groups who have lived together develop some rules of communication that are also context-dependent and are not necessarily logical by standards of individualistic cultures, which tend to be more heterogeneous. Individualistic cultures are more abstractive in nature and communication, largely governed by cause–effect relationships and Judeo-Christian modes of thinking. In collectivistic cultures, especially those that are homogeneous such as Japan, Korea, and China, associative modes of thinking are important. Sometimes, associations are emphasized among events that may not be logically related. The context of communication and the nature of relationships between the parties are clearly more important than they are in individualistic cultures, where logical connections among events and scientific rationale are more important in the process of communication.[24]

6. The Role of Symbols

The symbols that are used to express an idea can exert a powerful effect on the message content. Symbols are generally highly culture-specific and may introduce noise easily when used excessively. Just as symbols have to be appropriate and communicated with skill, both the sender and the receiver must be skilled in adopting appropriate media to convey the message. Some uniformities in the use of symbols are developing in many of the globalized and globalizing countries of the world, but we have not yet reached the stage where the importance of symbols and symbolic processes can be ignored in the process of communicating across nations and borders. Managers should learn as much as possible about the symbols of the dissimilar cultures in which they conduct international business in order to be more effective.

Other barriers that cause difficulties when communicating across borders and cultures include selective perception and stereotypes, self-disclosure, etiquette, humor, truthfulness, elaborate versus succinct discourse, and silence. Discussion of these barriers follows.

Selective Perception and Stereotypes

Perception is the process of receiving information from the external world around us. We decide what kind of information we should notice carefully, how to categorize the information, and how to incorporate it into our existing knowledge framework. **Stereotyping** is the process of attributing traits to people on the basis of their group membership. Stereotypes tend to define people by their demographic, ethnic, organizational, and national memberships. For example, some stereotypes about cultural groups are reflected in the beliefs that Germans are methodical, Italians are emotional, British are domineering, and Japanese are highly work-oriented.

In Chapter 4, we discussed the role of cultural differences in influencing the way people perceive and stereotype individuals from other countries and cultures. Because of the cultural context in which they function, individuals develop tendencies to pay more attention to certain informational cues from the environment and to ignore others. For example, if a German manager asks German subordinates for some ideas about improving work processes, the subordinates will likely understand that the questions are truly seeking their opinions and perceive them positively. However, these questions asked by a German manager to a group of Greek subordinates create the perception that the German manager is not knowledgeable about the work.

Another example of mistaken perceptions concerns the way colleagues and superiors are addressed in the workplace. Whereas informality is emphasized in the United States, surnames with the appropriate title are more frequently used in India. For example, someone named Rajen Singh would be called "Mr. Singh" as opposed to "Rajen" or "Raj." A U.S. manager who uses the American practice of calling a person by the first name might be introducing some barriers to communication.

Stereotyping acts as a major barrier to effective intercultural communication because it creates certain expectations that may not be true. For example, if an American manager has preconceived notions that Mexican employees do not work hard, then he or she might not be willing to emphasize the rewards associated with hard work. This can lead to potential misunderstandings in communication and conflict, especially because this stereotype is inaccurate when generalized to Mexican workers. Research has shown that managers who are most effective internationally are able to change their stereotypes quickly as they come into contact with people of different cultures. Managers who are least effective internationally are unable to change their

PRACTICAL INSIGHT 9.4

CROSSING THE CULTURAL CHASM
Keeping communication clear and consistent with team members from other countries isn't easy, says author Maya Hu-Chan. But the rewards are huge.

Long past the era of the "sleeping giant," China is the epicenter of an industrial and economic transformation whose effect is being felt everywhere—from the boardrooms of Boston to the banks of London. Global systems are shifting so dramatically in China and other emerging countries that we're all challenged to come up with new skills to work across cultures. What are the implications for management communication?

My friend and respected colleague Maya Hu-Chan and I reflected on this and other cross-cultural questions recently when we were the keynote speakers at the Global Leadership Conference in Shanghai. She's the co-author (with Cathy Greenberg, Alistair Robertson, and me) of *Global Leadership: The Next Generation*. Maya conducts workshops on cross-cultural communication (in both English and Chinese) around the world and has worked with more than 3,000 leaders in global corporations. You can contact her at mayahuchan@earthlink.net, or visit her Web site at mayahuchan.com. She and I recently spoke about the challenges of leading global teams. Edited excerpts of our conversation follow:

What do managers tell you about the challenges they're facing in this new global business environment?
It's sink or swim, and swimming the Pacific is only one of the cultural marathon events for a modern CEO. We're in an era of interwoven global cultures, each with its own character and subtleties. Over the past three years, I've surveyed over 1,200 global managers of multinational companies in telecommunications, financial services, manufacturing, and engineering/construction industries. I asked them, "What are your greatest challenges?" Ultimately, it boils down to a few areas: cultural gaps, lack of trust in each other, failure to value each other's skills, and the big one: We just don't communicate effectively.

Doesn't speaking English make it easier?
Global team members have a hard time understanding one another even when they're all speaking the same language. One global manager found it was hard for his team members in China and India to say no. He would think they were agreeing and move forward, only to find out later that they disagreed. Another manager was amazed at how many ways people found to say no, and yet it always sounded like yes to him!

To stay on course, you've got to be constantly asking yourself, "Am I reading this right?" Even if everyone speaks English, you have to test your assumptions. In a group situation, encourage everyone to slow down their speech, speak clearly, and periodically take a stop to recap what has been said or decided upon.

Communication styles come into play, right? For example, being up front is prized in the U.S. but may be considered rude in some other cultures.
There is the issue of "face." For example, Marshall, I have known you for over 20 years. I'm sure that most of your friends and clients would agree that your communication style is sometimes in their face!

But seriously, American culture rewards outspokenness. In this English-dominant world, an American may admit point blank

stereotypes, even after working with people who acted differently from the established cultural stereotypes.[25]

Importance of Self-Disclosure

Self-disclosure is the process of revealing personal information about oneself to others.[26] Self-disclosure is important in maintaining improved communication ties in Western (individualistic) cultures. But excessive self-disclosure regarding social and personal situations in collectivistic cultures may lead to difficulties unless the person communicates with members of an already established in-group. Barnlund's study of private and public self in Japan and the United States illustrates the importance of self-disclosure in the communication process.[27] Japanese prefer a communication style where relatively little about oneself is made available to others in everyday interaction. A majority of information that one knows about oneself is kept strictly private—the private self is relatively large. In contrast, the preferred style of communication in the United States is one in which an apparently large amount of information about oneself is given to others—the public self is relatively large—while little information about

that he/she doesn't speak another language—no big deal. People from other countries are proud to have studied English from grade school on, and are likely to fall silent rather than risk "losing face" when they realize that they aren't being understood, or if they don't completely understand what's being said.

To turn this dynamic around, cultivate an intellectual grace and kindness which will allow you to ensure that a point is understood without shaming your colleague. Get on the same playing field by being curious, with respect. Thank your listener for speaking in English, and allow silence for him to reflect on the content on the table.

Are there other solutions to the communication problem?
For starters, cut the slang. Using too many culturally narrow expressions, idioms, colloquialisms, and even too much humor can cause your message to be totally lost in translation. Your global associates may misinterpret what you said, or not understand you at all, but remain too polite to ask what has been said. For instance, one global manager from Malaysia was upset that his boss said "no-brainer" in a recent conversation. He thought his boss was insulting him by calling him stupid.

Can you talk about your work with global virtual teams, to help them build trust and improve productivity?
Research showed that building trust is one of the greatest challenges for global and virtual teams. There are some unfortunate behavioral trends common to all of us on this planet—like lack of communication and inclusion. Intentionally or not, remote team members can feel left "out of the loop," [because they're] unaware of changes or new developments in the project, [or due to] decisions made without getting their input or phone calls and e-mails not responded to in a timely manner.

The list goes on. All of our classic problems—blaming others, not keeping commitments, giving negative feedback in public, and lack of positive recognition—become magnified in importance when we deal with colleagues from other cultures.

How do things look when trust is part of a global business relationship?
There is honest, open, and consistent communication. You provide full disclosure. You are an active listener and provide feedback, especially praise and recognition, and you share information regularly. Consistency is key.

What other things are important to do?
Do what you say you're going to do—deliver what you promise. Don't overpromise—plan effectively. Beyond that, develop trustworthy habits of relaying information. Be clear about responsibilities, authority, delegation. Don't forget that your team members may have other responsibilities and other "virtual" bosses. Budget the time to "do it right the first time." Don't assume that understanding is automatic.

Effective cross-cultural communication isn't easy. But a small investment in clear communication and sensitivity at the beginning of the project can save millions of dollars and hurt feelings at the end of the project!

Goldsmith's new book, *What Got You Here Won't Get You There*, was recently listed as America's best-selling business book in *The Wall Street Journal*. He can be reached at Marshall@MarshallGoldsmith.com, and he provides his articles and videos online at www.MarshallGoldsmithLibrary.com.

Source: Marshall Goldsmith, "Crossing the Cultural Chasm," *BusinessWeek*, May 30, 2007.

---

oneself is hidden from public exposure—the private self is considered to be relatively small. This is shown in Exhibit 9.4. The French consider Americans easy to make friends with in the work context but difficult to develop deep and meaningful relationships with. The difficulty of getting to know an American manager at the personal level has been found by Greeks, Egyptians, Chinese, and other cultures as well.

Etiquette in Communication

Cultures differ in what they consider to be polite communication, and **etiquette** is concerned with the way requests can be conveyed, approved, or refused.[28] For example, social interactions in Filipino and Japanese cultures are based on smooth interpersonal relationships, and, as discussed earlier, saving face is important. Americans assigned to the Philippines as Peace Corps volunteers were instructed to be frank and direct in requesting information or supplies from the local community leaders. This turned out to be a big mistake—the American directness was considered impolite and inconsiderate, that is, lacking knowledge of the etiquette of the local culture.[29] Note these other examples:

EXHIBIT 9.4
Self-Disclosure and Intercultural Communication

Source: Reprinted with permission from *Business Horizons,* March–April 1989. Copyright © 1989 by the Trustees at Indiana University, Kelley School of Business.

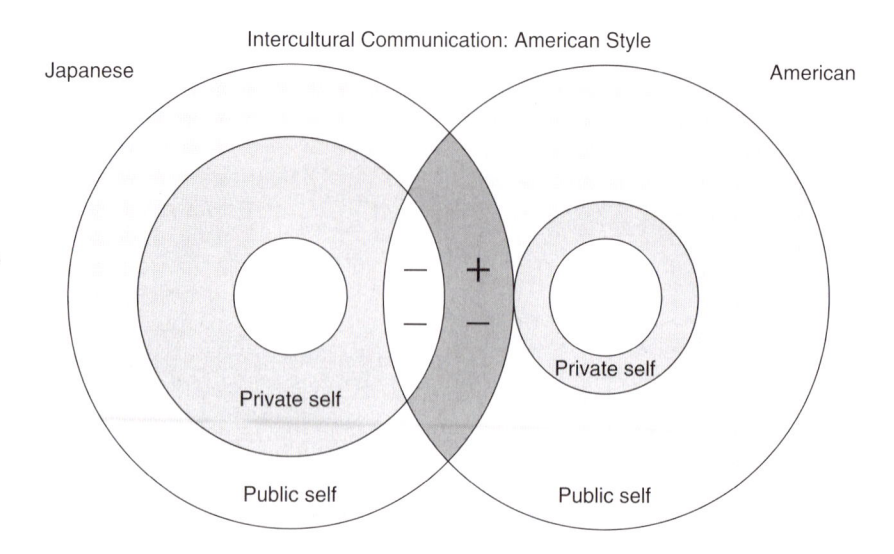

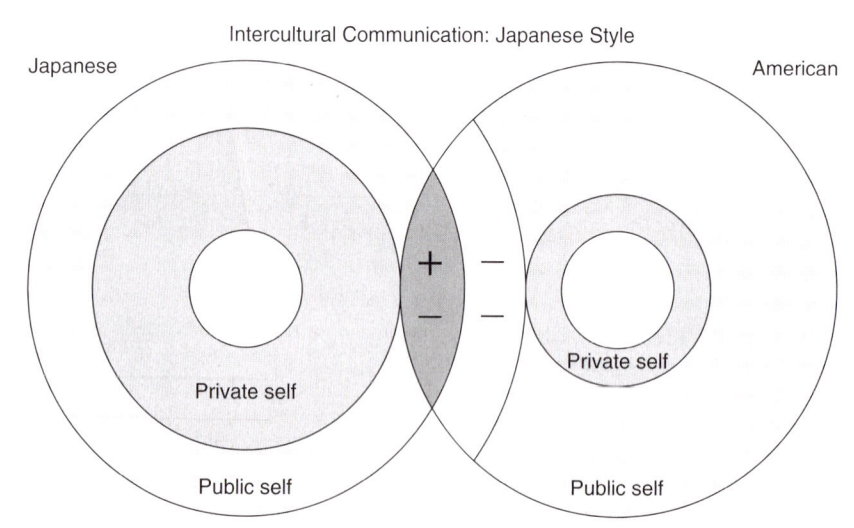

Intercultural Communication: American Style

Intercultural Communication: Japanese Style

- The Chinese are known to use ambiguous terms in communication, to a much greater extent than is the case in western Europe and the United States, mainly because of their greater emphasis on face saving.[30]
- In work group discussions, Japanese take shorter turns, and everyone is given equal time. Americans take longer turns, distributed unevenly, and the initiator of the topic is given more time to express his or her point of view.[31]
- The use of the word *no* is infrequent in many Asian countries, so that a "yes" can mean "no" or "maybe."

Rules about extending and accepting invitations are also related to the communication etiquette of the culture. A Westerner may invite an Asian and receive what would be considered an affirmative reply, only to be surprised when the visitor does not arrive. The Asian's response is not affirmative to *coming to the American's home* but simply indicates that he received the invitation and was pleased.[32] Triandis tells the story of an American visitor asking his Greek acquaintance what time he should arrive for dinner. The Greek villager replied "Anytime."[33] In the United States, the expression "anytime" is a noninvitation that people give to appear polite, and it is not necessarily a serious invitation. The Greek, however, meant that the American would be welcome anytime at all, because in his culture it would be rude to give a guest a definite time of arrival. In some cultures, "thank you" is expressed in written form, but in other cultures "thank you" can be conveyed by appropriate polite gestures.[34]

The intensity of speaking also varies around the world. Arabs and those from countries around the Mediterranean tend to speak loudly, and northern Europeans interpret this as shouting or disagreement. Americans and French speak louder than the English, who sometimes find this overly assertive.

Japanese differ from Americans with respect to situations that might require an apology and the manner that an acceptable apology is phrased and communicated.[35] In Japan, a remark that might cause a co-worker to lose face in public would be considered a situation requiring immediate remedy and verbal apology. In the United States, the remedy and apology may come later and may be in writing.

Humor in Communication

Not all cultures appreciate the significance of **humor.** Although smiling is associated with happiness in all cultures, a smiling face may not be appreciated as communicating direct and honest information in all cultures.[36] The Chinese associate smiling with a lack of self-control and tranquillity—two culturally significant and valued outcomes in Chinese societies. Research has also shown that Americans tend to associate smiling with intelligence, but Japanese do not make such associations. Individuals from Thailand are known to laugh when they find themselves in embarassing situations. Such expression is often misconstrued by members of dissimilar cultures who are not familiar with the unique significance of laughter for Thais. Americans are offended if they are told that they lack a sense of humor in communication, but this is not the case in East Asia and other collectivistic cultures, where such associations are rare. An instance where humor backfired is illustrated in Practical Insight 9.5.

Truthfulness in Communication

An important aspect of communicating across cultures that can be tricky is the concept of what is considered **truthfulness.** In cultures that emphasize universalistic values (see Chapter 4), truth is thought of as an absolute, just as laws of the society are applicable to all citizens, regardless of rank or status. However, in particularistic and collectivistic cultures, social sensitivity and tact might override the importance of blunt truthfulness.[37] "White lies"—vague or ambiguous and untrue statements that are said to preserve harmony in a closely knit group—are widely forgiven in particularistic cultures. Here again, the notion of saving face by saying things that may not be absolutely true is of paramount importance.

Elaborate versus Succinct Communication

Another barrier to communication is the extent to which members of a given nation or culture prefer elaborate versus succinct ways of communicating. **Elaborate communication** uses a large quantity of words to convey a message, and it often includes exaggeration, metaphors, analogies, and proverbs to make a point. On the other hand, **succinct communication** uses the fewest words necessary to convey a message. The practice of *mubalaqha,* translated as "exaggeration," is common in the Middle East. Arabs are expected to make inflated statements to those who are not members of their in-group or culture, such as Westerners. If they do not, they are considered to be ineffective at managing the process of communication.[38] An example concerns the manner

> **PRACTICAL INSIGHT 9.5**
>
> **AD CITING KASHMIR STIRS FURY IN INDIA**
>
> An advertisement run last week by Cadbury India, the local unit of the multinational candy and soft drink maker Cadbury Schweppes, has stirred up a national political controversy and obliged the company to issue a public apology.
>
> The ad, promoting the company's Temptations brand of chocolates, appeared in copies of *The Times of India* distributed in and around Bombay on Aug. 15, the 55th anniversary of Indian independence. It included a map of India highlighting the state of Jammu and Kashmir—all of it, including the portion that has been controlled for years by Pakistan, which also claims the whole state.
>
> "I'm good," read the text of the ad. "I'm tempting. I'm too good to share. What am I? Cadbury's Temptations or Kashmir?"
>
> Politicians and activists of the Hindu nationalist Bharatiya Janata Party reacted with fury, saying the ad trivialized the conflict over Kashmir, the only predominantly Muslim state to remain part of India when Pakistan was formed. The Kashmir dispute has led to two of the three wars fought by the two countries since 1947, and they appeared on the brink of another war over it earlier this year. Political violence in the state has claimed tens of thousands of lives; India has accused Pakistan of backing extremist groups and infiltrating provocateurs into the state to foment trouble.
>
> After the B.J.P. staged protest rallies outside Cadbury India's offices in Bombay and newspaper editorials lambasted the company for insensitivity, Cadbury India issued a statement on Tuesday retracting the ad.
>
> **Source:** "Ad Citing Kashmir Stirs Fury in India," *New York Times*, August 23, 2003. Copyright © 2003 The New York Times Co. Reprinted with permission.

in which then U.S. Secretary of State James Baker told the Iraqi leader in 1991 that the invasion of Kuwait would lead to massive retaliation. Analysis by commentators suggested that the reason why such threats were not taken seriously was because Baker did not deliver his threats with sufficient exaggeration. Because of this, Iraqi Foreign Minister Tariq Aziz did not think the threats were credible.

Silence

As we discussed earlier, use of **silence** is regarded as effective strategy for communicating in some parts of the world. For example, Americans describe talking as pleasant and important for maintaining smooth communication, whereas Chinese perceive silence and quiet as a way of responding to communication.[39] Expatriate managers from the West working in countries where silence is a valued tool in the communication process must recognize its importance and respect its use.

In Practical Insight 9.6, some ways to avoid problems in cross-cultural communication are highlighted.

The Role of Information Technology in Communication across Borders and Cultures

The use of sophisticated information technology and management information systems—that is, computer-mediated communication systems—allows managers and employees of global corporations to communicate with each other easily and frequently. It has been suggested that the increased use of e-mail, facsimile, Internet and intranets, and other related advances in technology has resulted in a convergence of communication styles. The extensive use of the Internet in multinational and global corporations is making transmission of data, information, and knowledge easier. Mobile phones are not only digital but also high-speed digital with Internet

PRACTICAL INSIGHT 9.6

POTENTIAL HOT SPOTS IN CROSS-CULTURAL COMMUNICATION

This is not meant to be an exhaustive list, but when working with other people, or traveling abroad for work or pleasure, it may pay to ask some experts about the following communication styles of the area you plan to visit. A little research at the outset can stave off a host of misunderstandings:

1. *Opening and Closing Conversations:* Different cultures may have different customs around who addresses whom when and how, and who has the right, or even the duty, to speak first, and what is the proper way to conclude a conversation. Think about it: no matter where you are, some ways of commencing a conversation or concluding one will be considered as rude, even disrespectful. These are artificial customs, to a certain degree, and there is probably no universally right or wrong way to go about these things, short of behaviors that all cultures would likely consider to be vulgar or abusive. This topic includes modes of address, salutations, levels of deference to age or social position, acceptable ways to conclude gracefully and so on. Obviously, and to the dismay of many of us in the West, this will also cover gender differences.

2. *Taking Turns during Conversations:* In some cultures, it is more appropriate to take turns in an interactive way, and in others, it is more important to listen thoroughly and without comment, without immediate response, lest a response be taken as a challenge or a humiliation, particularly depending on the context of the conversation, the audience, and the levels of personal knowledge/relationship between the two people interacting. For example, a Western couple or pair of executives may feel perfectly comfortable interacting in a give and take way in a public market, but if that public market is in a part of the world where such a public display of give and take is considered to be in bad taste, then they may be giving offense without ever realizing it.

3. *Interrupting:* The same issues arise over the issue of interrupting. In some cultures, interruption, vocal, emotional expression, etc. are considered to be the default conversational style, particularly among those considered to be equals, or among men. Many people of Northern European or American extract might mistake this kind of conversation for argument and hostility, but that would not be the case.

4. *Use of Silence:* In some forms of communication, silence is to be expected before a response, as a sign of thoughtfulness and deference to the original speaker, yet at other times, silence may be experienced as a sign of hostility. In the West, twenty seconds of silence during a meeting is an extraordinarily long time, and people will feel uncomfortable with that. Someone invariably will break in to end the uncomfortable silence. But the same customs around silence are not universal.

5. *Appropriate Topics of Conversation:* In some places, it is considered vulgar to speak openly about money, for example, let alone about the kinds of intimate family issues that commonly form the basis of afternoon television "talk" shows in the West. Travelers or business people should learn the customs that surround the making of deals, the transaction of commerce, and the degree to which details are specified in advance and enumerated in writing across cultures (not all places are as prone to hire lawyers and create detailed contracts as we are in the West).

6. *Use of Humor:* In the West, we often try to build immediate rapport through humor, but of course, this is not universally seen to be appropriate in all contexts. The use of laughter can be experienced as a sign of disrespect by some, and so it is important to understand that this is another area where misunderstandings can be very likely to occur.

7. *Knowing How Much to Say:* In some places, less is definitely more, whereas in other places, it is more valued to wrap a rather small point up in a longer preamble, followed by an extended wrap-up. For Westerners, this can be maddening, as we tend to value speaking directly and to the point. Then again, there are clearly circumstances where Westerners say too much and lose their ability to communicate well, depending on the context. Of course, patterns around presumed areas of deference based on age and social standing can influence how much is appropriate to say, depending on the culture.

8. *Sequencing Elements during Conversation:* At what point during a conversation—or an extended conversation or negotiation—is it appropriate to touch upon more sensitive issues? Or how soon in a conversation is it appropriate simply to ask for directions? Since all cultures develop customs through which sensitive issues can be addressed in a way that connotes respect to all involved, and since those systems all can differ, it is important to understand the influence that sequence has on effectiveness. For us in the West, think about the process of asking, or being asked out on a date (a very Western process and one whose customs can be very fluid indeed). The right question, asked in the right way, but asked too soon or too late, according to custom, can connote very different things to the listener, and highly influence subsequent behavior. Sequencing and timing do matter.

Source: Copyright © 2003 A. J. Schuler. Dr. A. J. Schuler is a speaker, consultant and leadership coach. To find out more about his programs and services, visit www.AJSchuler.com or call (703) 370-6545.

PRACTICAL INSIGHT 9.7

THE WAY TO REACH AN ITALIAN? NOT E-MAIL

Italians are famous for their mobile-phone addiction: More than 80% of them own at least one. But an aversion to e-mail may be just as profound, much to the chagrin of Lucio Stanca, the former head of IBM's European operations. As Italy's new technology minister, Stanca must automate as many government procedures as possible. Yet he's having trouble just getting his colleagues to log on. His first report recommends the government adopt across-the-board Internet communication by the end of 2003. But it was sent to government offices only by snail mail because Stanca says that, from what he can tell, "no one opens their e-mail" in Italy.

Maybe Stanca could learn a few tricks from Telecom Italia chief executive Marco Tronchetti Provera, who was looking to gather his telecom managers for a March 6 meeting. Rather than bother with e-mail, Provera sent 2,000 short text messages to their cell phones. The result: record turnout. Perhaps Stanca should learn to make his reports shorter.

Source: Reprinted from Kate Carlisle, "National Aversions: The Way to Reach an Italian? Not E-mail," *BusinessWeek*, April 15, 2002, by special permission. Copyright © 2002 by The McGraw-Hill Companies, Inc.

---

access available. We are increasingly seeing the merging of various forms of communication technologies, such as e-mail, Internet, mobile phone, PCs, and personal organizers.

These changes, along with the widespread use of English in international communications, will lead to strong tendencies to develop similar communication patterns in dissimilar countries and cultures. However, English may not always be the dominant language of the Internet. Since the use of language and culture are intertwined, whether these technological developments will lead to a universal style of communication is not clear. About 4,000 to 5,000 different languages are spoken in over 140 countries around the world. While the largest group of people in the world, about 1.1 billion, speak Mandarin Chinese, English is the second most commonly used language.[40] Chinese and other East Asian languages use characters for entire words, rather than using an alphabet, so that developing a keyboard for use in computer-mediated communications is a difficult endeavor. This means that global corporations using English as the primary business language must make changes in their patterns of communication with their Chinese subsidiaries. An increase of more than 70 percent in non-English Internet sites and users has been estimated.[41]

Computer-mediated communication increases the amount of information that is available to users on a global scale. However, it does not guarantee that the information will be absorbed correctly or change the preexisting value systems of the receivers. Members of multinational work teams retain their culture-specific ways of communicating, problem solving, and decision making.[42] This is true for virtual teams of global corporations, composed of members of different cultures.[43] E-mail communication is not as personal as face-to-face communication, which is preferred in many parts of the world. Some factors that lead to divergence of communication patterns cannot be reduced simply by using the same language and the same type of technology. However, if Internet communication can reflect subtleties and nuances of language and business practices, it will foster more effective communication. International managers should be concerned with managing both convergence and divergence of communication patterns. Some of these are illustrated in Practical Insight 9.7.

Guidelines for Managing across Borders and Cultures

The role of communication in successfully coordinating activities of multinational and global corporations is increasing every day. Over 80 percent of a manager's day is spent communicating.[44] As globalization spreads to different parts of the world, and cultural diversity increases in multinational and global corporations, successful communication is critical. Managers should have appropriate communication abilities and skills to carry out their activities and operations—to negotiate and make decisions, to motivate employees, and to exercise leadership. As discussed in this chapter, there are significant problems in encoding and decoding messages that are sent across borders and cultures. A tendency to rely heavily on computer-mediated communication, such as the Internet or e-mail, might lead to the belief that people around the world are beginning to form common patterns of communication. However, this is not necessarily true. National and cultural differences in customs, beliefs, values, attitudes, and intentions regarding how one should communicate to co-workers, supervisors, and customers can make significant differences. These differences have implications for productivity in multinational and global companies.

The following guidelines will be helpful in effective communication across borders and cultures:

- **Learn the language of the country.** It is important to have fluency in the language of the country where one is posted. Even if fluency is lacking, some knowledge of the language is a significant plus in communicating effectively with colleagues, customers, workers, and government officials. Some companies offer language training programs to improve language skills. General Electric and ExxonMobil conduct language training for the families of expatriate managers.

- **Develop cultural sensitivity in communication.** Traveling around the globe and encountering different cultures is the best way to develop cultural sensitivity, but such travel is not always possible for young expatriates or managers of global corporations. Therefore, it is important that companies train expatriates and managers who will be dealing with those from different cultures. General Electric and ExxonMobil, beyond language training, also offer programs for expatriate managers and families to address diverse cultural issues, such as customs and cultural mores, relevant to communication and other functions. It is important to learn the language of the country in which one is going to be located, but this is not enough. Developing cultural sensitivity in communication requires understanding the bits and pieces of the customs, practices, and manners of the country. Communication patterns that sustain harmony and save face should be emphasized in dealing with collectivists from East Asia, as well as from other parts of the world.

- **Learn to properly encode and decode messages.** Communication, as we discussed earlier, involves clear encoding by senders and distortion-free decoding by the receiver. Managers need to choose the medium with enough richness to be effective in the cultural context. Even when the language of communication is equally understood by the parties concerned, several factors that induce noise and distortion are linked to differences in cultural backgrounds. It is necessary to be sensitive to the various barriers for effective communication as discussed earlier.

- **Develop appropriate feedback mechanisms.** Communication effectiveness is improved when individuals and global organizations develop and implement

- **Develop empathy.** Active listening involves trying to understand the other person's point of view and considering that it might be the correct one for that person—given his or her national and cultural background. It is important to develop empathy, which is putting oneself in the speaker's shoes. When this occurs, some of the listener's beliefs might be challenged; however, to be effective, keeping an open mind and listening sensitively are essential.

Summary

Multinational and global corporations cannot be successful in conducting their businesses worldwide without effective uses of communication. Such communication occurs among managers in dissimilar national and cultural contexts, and various types of media are used. Success or failure of communication is determined by whether the receiver understands the sender's message. A number of national and cultural factors influence the effectiveness of communication across national borders. Noise in communication due to the type of medium used, status and power differences, and differences in verbal and nonverbal expression can exercise powerful effects.

Other barriers to effective communication are related to selective attention to certain types of informational cues and also to the context of the communication. For example, high-context cultures emphasize nonverbal aspects of communication more than do low-context cultures. Therefore, e-mail may not be as acceptable in high-context cultures (like Japan) as it is in low-context cultures (like the United States or United Kingdom). Extensive use of computer-mediated communication may improve speed and accuracy of data, information, and knowledge transmission; however, there is no guarantee that people in different parts of the world will develop similar styles of communication. Perhaps the central message of this chapter is the importance of awareness of national and cultural differences in styles and modes of communication. Increased awareness of differences is likely to be translated into more effective forms of communication as multinational and global corporations expand their business operations in dissimilar nations and cultures.

Key Terms and Concepts

communication, *332*
computer-mediated communication, *337*
elaborate communication, *349*
etiquette, *347*
gestures, *339*
harmony in communication, *344*
high-contact cultures, *339*
high-context cultures, *340*
humor, *349*
kinesic behavior, *338*
low-contact cultures, *340*
low-context cultures, *340*
nonverbal communication, *334*
perception, *345*
proxemics, *339*
saving face, *343*
self-disclosure, *346*
silence, *350*
stereotyping, *345*
succinct communication, *349*
trust in communication, *343*
truthfulness, *349*
verbal communication, *334*

Discussion Questions

1. What is communication, and why is it important in managing multinational and global corporations?
2. Think of the communication model shown in Exhibit 9.1. How do your own experiences in communicating with people from other cultures illustrate some of the processes shown? What were the difficulties? What would you do to overcome these difficulties in the future?
3. What are the various forms of communication that are used in international corporations? Give examples of each type.

4. How do stereotypes and selective perception act as obstacles to effective communication? How important are these factors in communication across cultures?
5. Managers of many global corporations believe that the Internet and e-mail are making communication much easier. Is this necessarily true? Explain why or why not.

Minicase

Johannes van den Bosch Sends an Email

Joseph J. DiStefano

After having had several email exchanges with his Mexican counterpart over several weeks without getting the expected actions and results, Johannes van den Bosch was getting a tongue-lashing from his British MNC client, who was furious at the lack of progress. Van den Bosch, in the Rotterdam office of BigFiveFirm, and his colleague in the Mexico City office, Pablo Menendez, were both seasoned veterans, and van den Bosch couldn't understand the lack of responsiveness.

A week earlier, the client, Malcolm Smythe-Jones, had visited his office to express his mounting frustration. But this morning he had called with a stream of verbal abuse. His patience was exhausted.

Feeling angry himself, van den Bosch composed a strongly worded message to Menendez, and then decided to cool off. A half hour later, he edited it to "stick to the facts" while still communicating the appropriate level of urgency. As he clicked to send the message, he hoped that it would finally provoke some action to assuage his client with the reports he had been waiting for.

He reread the email, and as he saved it to the mounting record in Smythe-Jones's file, he thought, "I'm going to be happy when this project is over for another year!"

Message for Pablo Menendez

Subject: IAS 1998 Financial statements

Author: Johannes van den Bosch (Rotterdam)

Date: 10/72/99 1:51 P.M.

Dear Pablo,

This morning I had a conversation with Mr. Smythe-Jones (CFO) and Mr. Parker (Controller) re the finalization of certain 1998 financial statements. Mr. Smythe-Jones was not in a very good mood.

He told me that he was very unpleased by the fact that the 1998 IAS financial statements of the Mexican subsidiary still has not been finalized. At the moment he holds us responsible for this process. Although he recognizes that local management is responsible for such financial statements, he blames us for not being responsive on this matter and inform him about the process adequately. I believe he also recognizes that we have been instructed by Mr. Whyte (CEO) not to do any handholding, but that should not keep us from monitoring the process and inform him about the progress.

He asked me to provide him tomorrow with an update on the status of the IAS report and other reports pending.

Author's Note: The author prepared this mini-case as a basis for class discussion rather than to illustrate either effective or ineffective handling of a business situation. The mini-case reports events as they occurred. The email exchanges in both cases are reported verbatim, except for the names, which have been changed. Professor DiStefano acknowledges with thanks the cooperation of Johannes van den Bosch in providing this information and his generous permission to use the material for executive development.

Therefore I would like to get the following information from you today:

- What has to be done to finalize the Mexican subsidiary's IAS financials;
- Who has to do it (local management, B&FF Mexico, client headquarters; B&FF Rotterdam);
- A timetable when things have to be done in order to finalize within a couple of weeks or sooner;
- A brief overview why it takes so long to prepare and audit the IAS f/s; and
- Are there any other reports for 1998 pending (local gaap, tax), if so the above is also applicable for those reports.

As of today I would like to receive an update of the status every week. If any major problems arise during the finalization process I would like to be informed immediately. The next status update is due January 12, 2000.

Mr. Smythe-Jones also indicated that in the future all reports (US GAAP, local GAAP and IAS) should be normally finalized within 60 days after the balance sheet date. He will hold local auditors responsible for monitoring this process.

Best regards and best wishes for 2000.

Johannes

JOHANNES VAN DEN BOSCH RECEIVES A REPLY

A little more than an hour later, with his own patience again wearing thin, Johannes van den Bosch watched with relief as Pablo Menendez's name popped into his Inbox messages. His smile quickly turned to disbelief, and then horror, as he read the response from Mexico City. Not only was the client's need still unmet, but now he had another problem! Stung by the apparent anger from Menendez, and totally puzzled as to the cause, he reread the email to make sure he had not misunderstood the message.

——Original Message——

From:	Menendez, Pablo (Mexico City)
Sent:	Wednesday December 10, 23:11
To:	van den Bosch, Johannes (Rotterdam)
Subject:	RE: IAS 1998 financial statements
Importance:	High

Dear Johannes,

I am not surprised of the outcome of your meeting with Mr. Smythe-Jones (CFO). However, I cannot answer your request until I heard from local management. As it was agreed on the last meeting, we were precluded from doing any work without first getting approval from management at the headquarters and we were instructed by local management from not doing anything until they finalized what was required from us. It appears to me to be a Catch 22 game! I believe we (your Firm and ours) should not fall in the game of passing the ball to someone else before getting a clear understanding of what is going on. We have had several meetings with local management where the issue has been raised and were responded that other priorities were established by the headquarters (on my end I thought they tell you everything they have been instructed of locally, unfortunately it does not seem to be the case). In my opinion it looks very easy that you accept from management at the headquarters to hold us accountable from something we are not responsible of, and this does not mean I do not *understand the pressure you are receiving from your end. However, we are not the enemy. I am not sending copy of this message to our client because I believe that internal issues have to be primarily dealt of internally without involving our clients in the internal politics. The last is what myself truly believe.*

Could you tell me how can you accept a deadline from our Firm without first having involved local management? Don't you think they are the first to be involved local management? Don't you think they are the first to be involved on this? I may be wrong but if we are in an international Firm I think we should understand the other side and not just blame someone else of our client's problems.

I really do not want to be rude, but you do not let me any option.

Despite the differences we have had, it has been a pleasure working with you.

Best regards and seasons greeting.

Pablo Menendez

Worried that he had somehow offended Menendez, van den Bosch printed off a copy of the email which he had sent the day before, and asked the two partners on either side of his office for their reaction to the message. The audit and tax specialists, one Dutch and the other Belgian, had nearly identical replies. "It seems to me that you got the point across clearly, Johannes," they said. "You laid out the facts and proposed actions to solve the problem. Why do you ask?" they queried. When he showed them the letter, they too were puzzled. "Smythe-Jones will no doubt be the next person to send me a message!" he thought. As a frown reflected his increasingly grim mood, van den Bosch wondered what he should do now.

Source: Copyright © 2000 by IMD-International Institute for Management Development, Lausanne, Switzerland. Not to be used or reproduced without written permission directly from IMD.

DISCUSSION QUESTIONS

1. Why is Mr. Smyth-Jones upset with the situation? Is his upset reasonable? Should he hold the Rotterdam company responsible for the process?
2. Is Mr. van den Bosch correct in assuming that the e-mail from Mr. Menendez reflects anger? Is there anything in Mr. van den Bosch's e-mail that would have upset Mr. Menendez? If so, why?
3. Would you have done anything differently? Why or why not?
4. What should Mr. van den Bosch do to continue with his assignment and monitor the financial statements?

Notes

1. H. Mintzberg, *The Nature of Managerial Work* (New York: Harper & Row, 1973).
2. From an anonymous student at the University of Memphis, 2003.
3. R. Mead, *Cross-Cultural Management Communication* (New York: John Wiley & Sons, 1990).
4. L. Beamer and I. Varner, *Intercultural Communication in the Global Workplace,* 2nd ed. (Boston: McGraw-Hill/Irwin, 2001).
5. E. T. Hall, *The Silent Language* (New York: Doubleday, 1959).
6. Beamer and Varner, *Intercultural Communication.*
7. Ibid.
8. "The 21st Century Corporation," *BusinessWeek,* November 6, 2000.
9. M. McCance, "IM: Rapid, Risky," *Richmond (VA) Times-Dispatch,* July 19, 2001, p. A1; C. Hempel, "Instant-Message Gratification Is What People Want," *Ventura County (CA) Star,* April 9, 2001.
10. J. L. Graham, "The Influence of Culture on the Process of Business Negotiations: An Exploratory Study," *Journal of International Business Studies* 16 (1985), pp. 81–96; H. Morsbach,

"Aspects of Non-verbal Communication in Japan," in L. A. Samovar and R. E. Porter, eds., *Intercultural Communication: A Reader* (Belmont, CA: Wadsworth, 1982), pp. 300–316.

11. R. A. Barraclough, D. M. Christophel, and J. C. McCroskey, "Willingness to Communicate: A Cross-Cultural Investigation," *Communication Research Reports* (1988), pp. 187–192.

12. J. Wiemann, V. Chen, and H. Giles, *Beliefs about Talk and Silence in a Cultural Context,* paper presented to the Speech Communication Association, Chicago, Illinois, 1986.

13. O. Klineberg, "Emotional Expression in Chinese Literature," *Journal of Abnormal and Social Psychology* (1983), pp. 517–530.

14. D. Morris, P. Collett, P. Marsh, and M. O'Shaughnessy, *Gestures, Their Origins, and Distribution* (Briarcliff Manor, NY: Stein & Day, 1979).

15. E. T. Hall and M. R. Hall, *Understanding Cultural Differences* (Yarmouth, ME: Intercultural Press, 1990).

16. Ibid.

17. Ibid.

18. Ibid.; M. Rosch, "Communications: Focal Point of Culture," *Management International Review* 27, no. 4 (1987), p. 60.

19. Hall and Hall, *Understanding Cultural Differences.*

20. H. C. Triandis, *Culture and Social Behavior* (New York: McGraw-Hill, 1994), p. 186—section dealing with the role of status on intercultural communication.

21. S. Ting-Toomey, "A Face Negotiation Theory," in Y. Kim and W. Gudykunst, eds., *Theories of Intercultural Communication* (Newbury Park, CA: Sage, 1988).

22. Ibid.

23. Triandis, *Culture and Social Behavior,* chap. 7 on culture and communication.

24. E. Glenn, and P. Glenn, *Man and Mankind: Conflicts and Communication between Cultures* (Norwood, NJ: Ablex, 1981); J. Hooker, *Working across Cultures* (Stanford, CA: Stanford University Press, 2003).

25. I. Ratiu, "Thinking Internationally: A Comparison of How International Executives Learn," *International Studies of Management and Organization* 13 (1983), pp. 139–150.

26. M. Won-Doornink, "Self-Disclosure and Reciprocity in Conversation: A Cross-National Study," *Social Psychology Quarterly* 48 (1985), pp. 97–107.

27. D. Barnlund, *Public and Private Self in Japan and the United States* (Tokyo: Simul Press, 1975).

28. J. P. Dillard, S. R. Wilson, K. J. Tusing, and T. A. Kinney, "Politeness Judgments in Personal Relationships," *Journal of Language and Social Psychology* 16 (1997), pp. 297–325.

29. G. M. Guthrie, "Cultural Preparation for the Philippines," in R. B. Textor, ed., *Cultural Frontiers of the Peace Corps* (Cambridge, MA: MIT Press, 1966), pp. 15–34.

30. Z. Lin, "Ambiguity with a Purpose: The Shadow of Power in Communication," in P. C. Earley and M. Erez, eds., *New Perspectives on International Industrial/Organizational Psychology* (San Francisco: New Lexington Press, 1997), pp. 363–376; G. Gao, "'Don't Take My Word for It'—Understanding Chinese Speaking Practices," *International Journal of Intercultural Relations* 22 (1998), pp. 163–186; P. C. Earley and A. Randel, "Self and Other: Face and Work Group Dynamics," in C. Granrose and S. Oskamp, eds., *Claremont Symposium on Applied International Psychology* (Thousand Oaks, CA: Sage, 1997).

31. W. B. Gundykunst, "Individualistic and Collectivistic Perspectives on Communication: An Introduction," *International Journal of Intercultural Relations* 22 (1998), pp. 107–134.

32. M. Brein and K. H. David, "Intercultural Communications and the Adjustment of the Sojourner," *Psychological Bulletin* 76 (1971), pp. 215–230.

33. H. C. Triandis, "Culture, Training, Cognitive Complexity, and Interpersonal Attitudes," in R. W. Brislin, S. Bochner, and W. J. Lonner, eds., *Cross-Cultural Perspectives on Learning* (New York: Wiley, 1975), pp. 39–77.

34. C. Ward and A. Rana-Deuba, "Home and Host Culture Influences on Sojourner Adjustment," *International Journal of Intercultural Relations* 24 (2001), pp. 291–306.
35. N. Sugimoto, "Norms of Apology Depicted in U.S. American and Japanese Literature on Manners and Etiquette," *International Journal of Intercultural Relations* 21 (1998), pp. 175–193.
36. P. B. Smith and M. H. Bond, *Social Psychology across Cultures,* 2nd ed. (Boston: Allyn & Bacon, 1999).
37. Ibid.
38. A. Almaney and A. Ahwan, *Communicating with the Arabs* (Prospect Heights, IL: Waveland, 1982).
39. H. Giles, N. Coupland, and J. M. Weimann, "Talk Is Cheap . . . but My Word Is My Bond: Beliefs about Talk," in K. Bolton and H. Kwok, eds., *Sociolinguistics Today: Eastern and Western Perspectives* (London: Routledge, 1992).
40. W. Bright, ed.-in-chief, *International Encyclopedia of Linguistics* (New York: Oxford University Press, 1992).
41. Thomas Dwyer, "Web Globalization: Write Once, Deploy Worldwide," Aberdeen Group Insight Report 108 (www.aberdeen.com), reported in Lois Enos, "English-Only a Mistake for U.S. Sites," *E-Commerce Times,* May 17, 2001, www.EcommerceTimes.com.
42. P. C. Earley and C. B. Gibson, *Multinational Work Teams: A New Perspective* (Mahwah, NJ: Lawrence Erlbaum, 2002), pp. 40–43.
43. C. Simmers, *The Internet in the Classroom: Case Analysis across the Network: Across the Globe,* paper presented at the 10th Annual Mid-Atlantic Regional Organizational Behavior Teaching Conference, Philadelphia, March 9, 1996.
44. J. Greenberg, *Managing Behavior in Organizations* (Upper Saddle River, NJ: Prentice Hall, 1996).

CHAPTER TEN

Negotiation and Decision Making across Borders and Cultures

Chapter Learning Objectives

After completing this chapter, you should be able to:

- Understand the processes of negotiation and decision making and their significance for multinational and global corporations.
- Explain the environmental context of international business negotiations and the concept of multinational negotiating strength.
- Identify the various patterns of negotiation and conflict resolution in different national and cultural contexts.
- Understand the influence of national and cultural variations in decision making.
- Become aware of the errors in decision making.
- Discuss the importance of computer-mediated communication in negotiation and decision making.

Opening Case: Political Impact on Global Negotiation

Negotiators have a general understanding of their own local political environment. They are raised in a business milieu that clearly distinguishes who the key players are, and who has to be pitched about a proposal. They learn the roles that each level of government may bring to the table, and its impact on the negotiations.

When negotiators take their proposals abroad and negotiate with a foreign power, they may not fully realize the impact that different political systems will have on the manner in which the negotiation should be conducted. The scope of the impact by the governments of individual nations will vary in the degree of influence they may have on international negotiations.

A major U.S. defense contractor, Raytheon, found out for themselves several years ago just how differently this impact can affect their negotiations. Their first initial foray into international negotiations occurred in Europe. Raytheon was attempting to put together a consortium of European companies to produce a NATO weapons system. They had thoroughly researched all the possible contenders and compiled a list of those companies that they believed were best able to handle the contract they were trying to put together.

Raytheon then contacted those companies and started negotiations. Talks became suddenly stalled in their tracks when, much to Raytheon's dismay, the governments of several European nations abruptly advised Raytheon to cease negotiations with the firms within their respective countries. These European governments said it was not up to Raytheon to decide who they would conduct business with in their respective countries. They would decide which companies could be contacted, and Raytheon had no choice in the matter if they expected to fulfill the contract.

Raytheon realized that they had no choice in the matter. Accepting the political reality of the situation, they terminated talks with the companies that they had initially chosen. They then entered into talks with the consortium of companies chosen by the respective NATO members instead, and successfully completed the weapons system contract.

Several years later, the U.S. government convinced Raytheon to develop a similar weapons system for Japan. Having learned their lesson with the European consortium, they immediately initiated their talks with the Japanese government instead of going to individual companies like they did in the NATO situation. They sat back and waited for the Japanese government to tell them which companies to use in their weapons system project.

Nothing happened. The Japanese government remained curiously quiet. Some time elapsed before a senior executive from Raytheon had a conversation in private with the Japanese deputy minister of defense. The deputy minister advised the Raytheon executive that it was up to the U.S. company to make the decision about which companies to use, and not the Japanese government. It turned out that since two of Japan's main electronics firms were considered as possible contenders, the Japanese government did want to anger either of these companies by choosing one over the other on behalf the American firm. The reason was because both of these companies wielded some considerable political clout with the Japanese government.

It's a valuable lesson to remember that situations with individual nations are going to vary. What works in one country may very well not work in another country, so never make assumptions about what the political reaction will be.

Source: www.negotiations.com/case/political-impact.

Discussion Questions

1. Why did the Japanese government remain quiet in the process of negotiating with Raytheon?
2. What are some of the insights that we can glean from this case on political consequences of negotiations in the global context?

What Is Negotiation?

Negotiations between and among multinational and global corporations occur daily. As businesses expand globally, international negotiation has become a routine activity for many global organizations rather than an occasional event. Global managers must negotiate with parties in other countries to develop specific strategies for exporting, setting up joint ventures, and managing subsidiaries. The art of effective negotiation is difficult at best, and it can be challenging for even the most experienced global managers. Effective negotiation requires attention to important aspects of the process before, during, and after the negotiation session itself.

Negotiation is a basic form of interchange between two or more individuals, groups, or organizations—a process that is used in labor–management relations; business deals, such as sales agreements and mergers; and international relations. In simple terms, negotiation is a process in which an individual, a group, or an organization tries to change the beliefs, preferences, and behaviors of another individual, group, or organization. It can be defined as the process of verbal and nonverbal exchanges between two or more parties with the goal of reaching a mutually satisfactory agreement. However, mutually satisfactory agreements are not always possible in real-life situations, as we discuss later.

In everyday life, the concepts of bargaining and negotiation are used interchangeably, but they have different meanings. **Bargaining** is the process of arguing and haggling over prices and other details involved in transactions of goods and services, and it is seen in flea markets, bazaars, and fairs all over the world. Negotiation is a more formal process reflecting genuine concerns by the parties to reach an acceptable solution when interests conflict.[1]

Negotiations take place in order to reach peaceful solutions to conflicts between nations or to end a labor dispute. The process is not necessarily only for professionals, because we encounter the need for negotiating with people we work and live with daily. Individuals tend to negotiate about different things in many different situations, and knowledge about what and how to negotiate is essential for people who need to work with others to accomplish objectives. Sometimes people fail to negotiate because they do not have relevant information, time, and/or power to be effective.

Discussions between the United States, Canada, and Mexico to create the North American Free Trade Agreement (NAFTA), the ongoing diplomatic communications between the United States and Japan aimed at improving the free flow of goods and services between these countries, and the establishment of strategic alliances between Xerox and Fuji-Xerox are examples of **international negotiation.**

Situations in which negotiators may find themselves vary widely according to national contexts. Smart negotiators recognize the impact of situational cues on the bargaining process from their own as well as from their opponent's cultural backgrounds. In preparing for effective negotiations across borders, it is important to imagine how the proposal might look to the other negotiating parties. What are their distinct needs, compared to ours? What kind of outcome is at stake? What is their time frame—long term or short term? Do they prefer a sequential or a holistic approach? Some of the specific situational characteristics that influence the process of cross-border negotiation are:

- **Context of the negotiation.** Is it taking place at their office or yours or at a neutral location? When negotiations take place in comfortable locations, such as on a yacht or at a resort, the party that provides such surroundings generally tends to achieve desired outcomes. A division of Caterpillar Company in California succeeded in controlling negotiations with its international clients by having them on a luxurious yacht.[2]

- **Physical arrangements.** Paying attention to the seating arrangements of both parties is not trivial. In traditional American negotiations, the two parties face each other across a large table. Negotiators from east Asian countries, however, may view this process as more confrontational and open than their usual format. The Japanese like both parties to sit on the same side of the table, indicating that they are facing the problem rather than confronting each other. Holistic approaches to arranging the physical layout are particularly important in south and east Asian as well as Arabic countries.

- **Time limits.** The duration of negotiation is remarkably important. American negotiators are given a limited time to bring about a successful negotiation. They often communicate with their bosses through e-mail and faxes and respond to sequential processes emphasized in their headquarters. Negotiators from collectivistic cultures realize that Americans are particularly impatient and expect to spend a minimal amount of time negotiating. It is not unusual for Russian and Chinese negotiators to delay the final stage of negotiations until immediately before the Americans are ready to leave for home. Herb Cohen's book *You Can Negotiate Anything* provides a number of interesting examples of situations in which open-minded Americans lost negotiations with Russian counterparts because of the Americans' impatience.[3] And one Brazilian tour guide reported to the second author of this text that he succeeded

PRACTICAL INSIGHT 10.1

CULTURE SHOCK: IF YOU DON'T LEARN TO BRIDGE THE GAP, YOU MAY RISK ALIENATING POTENTIAL BUSINESS PARTNERS

Did you know that in Japanese, there are 19 different ways to say "no"? In a world increasingly dominated by international, multinational and transnational corporations, culture plays an important role in negotiation. The literature on this subject is large, fascinating and goes far beyond curious questions of international etiquette.

For example, the Japanese eschew direct confrontation, preferring an exchange of information. Russians love combat; their very word for "compromise" is borrowed from another language. Spanish negotiators are individualistic; Koreans are team players. Nigerians prefer the spoken word, Indians the written one. Asian languages are high in context, so you must pay attention to inflections, body language and what is *not* said. Latin American cultures are physically demonstrative. And we Americans alienate everyone with our impatience and obsession with getting things done . . . fast, fast, fast!

Sensitive negotiators allow for these sorts of differences. Take a tip from Stephen Covey, the author of *The Seven Habits of Highly Successful People* (Simon & Schuster): "Seek first to understand, then to be understood." For one thing, your opponent may not be speaking to you in his mother tongue. The subtleties of negotiating may be lost in translation. Make sure you are really connecting, and be especially clear, lest you talk past each other.

Moreover, those who negotiate outside their culture regularly should study the etiquette, ethics and attitudes of their opponents. It's just part of learning more about how the other side actually negotiates. If you know what to expect when you sit down to bargain, you will dramatically enhance your ability to get what you want. Let General George S. Patton lead you to the negotiating table: "I have studied the enemy all my life. I have read the memoirs of his generals and his leaders. I have even read his philosophers and listened to his music. I have studied in detail the account of every one of his battles. I know exactly how he will react under any given set of circumstances. So when the time comes, I'm going to whip the hell out of him."

Of course, you may not want to be quite so combative. In any case, all sorts of expertise is available on a country-by-country basis, from scholarly treatises to seasoned consultants, to learn about cultural idiosyncrasies. Consider adding a guide to your team, whether it's a professional, a friend who knows how "they" think, or simply a translator. Just be careful whom you choose. A line in one of Jimmy Carter's 1977 speeches in Poland was mistranslated: "I desire the Poles carnally."

Source: "Culture Shock," July 2003, www.entrepreneur.com. Reprinted with permission from *Entrepreneur* magazine.

---

in making good sales of Brazilian jewelry just before Americans departed for home. He found that Americans were not interested in negotiating just before departure.

- **Status differences.** Americans, in particular among Westerners, favor an egalitarian, informal approach to life, and negotiations tend to de-emphasize status differences. However, negotiators from the United Kingdom, Germany, and France are noted for using status as an informal mechanism for attempting to achieve gains in cross-border negotiations. Managers from most countries respect hierarchy and formality more than do Americans and feel more comfortable in situations explicitly recognizing their status. Chinese and Japanese negotiators present their business cards to Western managers with both hands and expect them to read the card immediately and recognize their status from the titles given. Americans tend to focus on the content and openness of the negotiation and less on the status of the members of the negotiation party.

The Negotiation Process

The process of negotiation consists of four fundamental elements:

1. Two or more parties involved in real or perceived conflict over important goals.
2. Shared interest in reaching an agreeable solution.

3. Background preparations leading to the process of negotiation.
4. A goal, but not a certainty, of reaching mutual agreement.[4]

Negotiation involves continuous communication, as discussed in Chapter 9. In the past, negotiations involved face-to-face meetings, but now negotiations can occur through postal mail, telephone, videoconferencing, e-mail, and the Internet.

The negotiation process entails five stages: (1) preparation, (2) relationship building, (3) information exchange, (4) persuasion, and (5) making concessions and reaching agreement, as illustrated in Exhibit 10.1. The importance and duration of each stage varies across cultures.[5] Cultural, national, and organizational influences are also seen in the exhibit. All of these influences are discussed later, but you must remember that they exert significant pressures on negotiators of all parties.

Preparation

In this stage, negotiators focus on gathering information, planning their strategies, and learning as much as possible about the other party or parties. The headquarters of multinational and global corporations are the appropriate settings for this step. Managers who were involved in previous negotiations of the same kind play the role of coaches, teaching the negotiation team about the other party's objectives, needs, preferences, and so on.

EXHIBIT 10.1 Stages of Negotiation in International Management

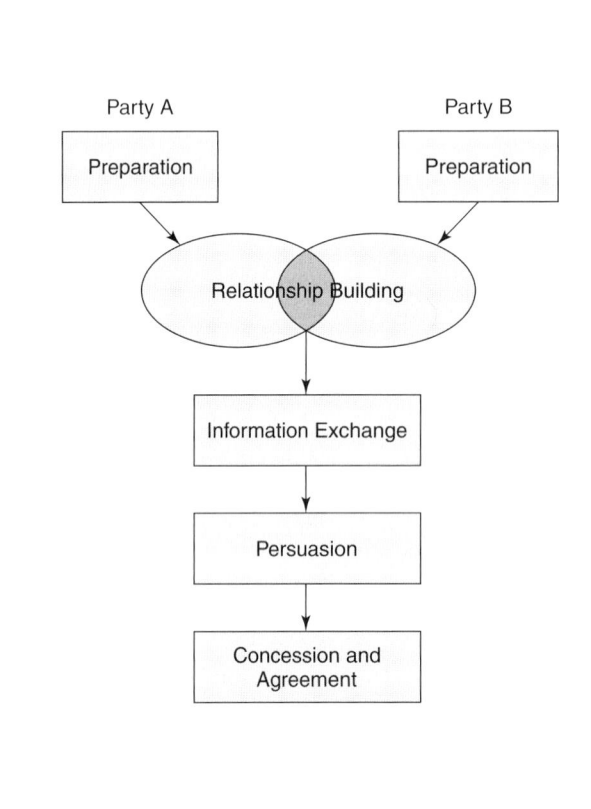

Cultural, National, and Organization Influences		Cultural, National, and Organization Influences
Cultural Variables	Party A → Preparation Party B → Preparation	Cultural Variables
Political and Legal Pluralism	↓	Political and Legal Pluralism
International Economic Situation	Relationship Building	International Economic Situation
Nature of Regulations and Control Processes	↓	Nature of Regulations and Control Processes
Political Risk and Instabilities	Information Exchange	Political Risk and Instabilities
Differences in Ideology	↓	Differences in Ideology
Organizational Stakeholders	Persuasion	Organizational Stakeholders
Administrative Heritage	↓	Administrative Heritage
Nature of Organizational Control Processes	Concession and Agreement	Nature of Organizational Control Processes
Patterns of Past Successes and Failures		Patterns of Past Successes and Failures

Relationship Building

In this stage, parties meet to discuss their mutual interests in the negotiation and get to know each other. This stage involves both formal and informal meetings at mutually agreeable and neutral locations. Exchange of business cards, many days of conversation, dinners, and other forms of entertainment often accompany this stage. The emphasis on building relationships and the need to know about the other group depend on national and cultural factors. Although U.S. negotiators do not like to spend much time in this stage, in much of the rest of the world, moving rapidly to the task of negotiating is not only inappropriate but may violate certain established protocols of behavior. French negotiators do not like to talk about business during dinner. They would rather enjoy fine wines and get to know their counterparts during evening hours. Similarly, Mexican negotiators often schedule sightseeing tours to important cultural sites and expect foreigners to pay some attention to their heritage and culture.

Information Exchange

During this stage, each party formally presents an initial position, and discussion of the issues involved follows. The other party has the opportunity to ask questions and clarify important points. American managers consider this to be the start of the real negotiating process and expect the other party to present relevant information in a succinct, logical, and comprehensive fashion. However, negotiators from other parts of the world may not follow this protocol and may even be skeptical of presenting a great deal of information up front.[6] In fact, in most countries, particularly those with a strong norm of collectivism, the emphasis on relationship building is regarded as the real beginning of the negotiation process.

Persuasion

During this stage, each party is concerned with changing the beliefs, preference structures, attitudes, and interests of the other parties. Attempts are made to work toward a mutually satisfactory agreement that can succeed in both the short term and long term. The role of cultural variables is particularly important in this stage. International studies of negotiation have revealed the use of certain tactics and strategies that are culture-specific.[7]

Differences in the use of threats, promises, recommendations, self-disclosure, appeals, and rewards are common. Exhibit 10.2 shows some of the differences in three countries, Japan, the United States, and Brazil, which are culturally disparate.

Making Concessions and Reaching Agreement

This final stage of negotiation is the stage in which parties make appropriate concessions and reach agreement. The agreements could be for the short term or the long term. Skilled negotiators generally decide on the number of final concessions they can make (the bottom line) during the preparation stage. Concessions and agreements may be reached without revealing total strategies that could be of value in future negotiations. Cultural differences play a significant role in the way concessions and agreements are made. U.S. negotiators negotiate sequentially (one issue at a time) and conclude the process with a legal contract, binding on all parties. Many east Asian negotiators do not like the idea of negotiating one issue at a time and find legal contracts to be less honorable than agreements based on mutual trust and respect.[8] Similarly, Russians attach less meaning to contracts and prefer to reach agreements based on a thorough discussion of the whole, rather than one issue at a time.

PRACTICAL INSIGHT 10.2

BUILDING TRUST WITH THE JAPANESE

Japanese believe, once the first contacts and introductions are completed, the next stage involves the development of trust through deeper knowledge of what the Westerners have to offer: how we handle ourselves as business people and managers, our efficiency, manufacturing methods, the standard of quality of our products and whether or not we are people they can do business with.

There are times when the seller wonders: "what else does it take?" For some the answer is:

- "It will take 'two years of eating and drinking' before you will get an order."
- "Attitude. Consider yourself not on business, but on a personal visit. There is no such thing as 'outside business hours.' You have to be friends to do business here. And you are always on the job, 24 hours a day."

The friendship dimension often involves extended social contacts. It is not just drinking at bars, but karaoke (where the visitor is expected to sing however poor his voice), as well as golf, fishing, going to the track, perhaps tennis. In some ways, the Japanese are better at this, and treat it as more a part of their professional life, than are most Caucasians.

Business competence aside, friendship and maintaining a harmonious and pleasant atmosphere are not the only important factors, from the viewpoint of Japanese managers. Most hope Westerners will show interest in Japan and that they will ask questions about the country and its culture, and will have done some advance study in this regard. Most Western managers successful in Japan believe in and practice this, and warn generally against companies sending managers to Japan who are ignorant of, or show no interest in, Japan or the Japanese.

The manner in which we handle tests of trustworthiness and our patience and endurance are noted carefully by the Japanese. How we handle objections, complaints, response to their discovery of mistakes our side has made and our honesty are all contributing factors to our evaluation.

When asked how they would:

1. Respond to a demand from the Japanese to meet a contract provision, even though he had already explained why his side could not meet the demand,
2. Handle a situation where the foreigner had inadvertently caused a loss of face to a Japanese,

Senior managers have stated:

1. "In this case, you have to play the sincerity game. Be sincere, explain why you cannot comply, and that there would be advantages for them. Treat their threat about losing the contract seriously, and be sure all your comments spring from sincerity."
2. "I would formally apologize, make a special visit to them, explain that it was a misunderstanding or an error, or whatever. Even if they did not believe me, it does not matter as long as I restore the relationship, and show them proper respect." "It's a different world, and things happen," another manager said. He was talking about inadvertent mistakes. "Take responsibility for whatever happens."

Consistently, the respondents state that from experience they have learnt that honesty is the only policy.

Some go further, arguing that they have found it best to be unstinting in their praise of the Japanese company and its expertise. This, if sincere, even if overdone, does no harm, these managers say. Indeed, others say that the strongest position to take with the Japanese is that of the student, wanting to learn, asking questions, and presenting any proposals with modesty and a little hesitation—for this is how the Japanese would themselves do it.

Keeping on top of the paperwork is clearly important for maintaining effective relationships with many Japanese customers. Also, much communication is indirect, so you are expected to pick up the nuances, the underlying meaning—the infamous when "yes" means "no."

In the early stage of trust building, it can be difficult for inexperienced managers to know whether or not the Japanese are really interested in their proposals. Commenting on this "Will they? Or won't they?" stage of waiting, experienced hands have observed:

- "If they don't call and you have to call them, something is probably wrong."
- "If they haven't said anything positive, such as 'we are interested,' then their attitude is probably negative."

- "Expect nothing, and then you will not be disappointed. Walk away, and get on with your life. If they come back to you, think of it as a surprise bonus"—words of wisdom particularly useful for smaller companies.

Many managers in the early stages of their dealings with the Japanese employ, and learn to effectively use, bilingual consultants and interpreters. Such professionals provide cultural and linguistic interpretation in situations where exactly what the Japanese are thinking or saying is unclear. Interpreters are important because "they style your language" into polished, sophisticated Japanese. This greatly enhances the Japanese perception of you.

One of the surprise twists of the early trust building, pre-agreement or pre-alliance stage is that the people with whom you have meetings can change in status. In the beginning, it may have been the urbane senior manager, but soon you are handed on to a younger, operations level Japanese. Probably someone at section manager level. As the age of the Japanese team gets younger, so their orientation becomes more factual, detailed, and bottom-line oriented. Their human relations skills are less polished. It is not until the negotiations are well advanced that senior managers re-appear. Indeed, when it is smaller Western firms, key Japanese people may not appear at all until negotiations have advanced substantially. When larger Western companies are involved, one experienced negotiator explained that he has learnt from experience that senior Japanese managers are very busy people, involved in many projects at the same time. They will not appear, and cannot justify appearing, until a project is close to agreement. So he advises Westerners to remain aware of the composition of the Japanese teams they face. When a senior manager or director appears, he says, you are very close to a deal. They wouldn't be there otherwise. In short, while it is the only sign you may get, it indicates that your trust building has been successful.

An Australian telecommunications company withdrew from a negotiation with a Japanese team before it was concluded. The manager's story was:

> I was working for AWA in the 1980's and we were looking at a major component for colour monitors from the Japanese. I was the project manager, and we had to source a fairly sizeable order. We made enquiries of 3 or 4 suppliers of the component, got samples, and trialed them. One Japanese company's product was particularly good, and their price was competitive. We had them make some modifications, send us further samples, and provide more detailed price data. At the eleventh hour however, our internal politics stepped in, and we had to go with another supplier. When I told the first supplier that we had decided to give the business to another company, they spat the dummy. They fumed—"What a terrible way to do business! You have no ethics! We'll never do business with you again."
>
> Their view was that they had the contract in their pocket because of the amount of work they had done. Privately I sympathized with them. And ever since then I have been very careful about how to ask questions of Japanese suppliers."

So what should the Western executive bear in mind when preparing to meet a Japanese business client, supplier or associate? Think of the process as reciprocal, universal, getting to know and trust each other. It need have no connection to business. You meet someone for the first time, and warm to each other immediately. So you meet again; in the process you will choose to exchange information on families, pastimes, interests. You will probably decide to do something together socially. Perhaps your families will meet. Perhaps you will go take in some form of recreational activity together: a movie, concert, etc. As the relationship warms further, you both think about what you can do together of a more serious nature—go into business, for instance. When you have got to that point, you will have established the requisite foundation of mutual trusting. Keeping a business relationship personal is often the not so hidden secret to successful human relationships across many other cultures as well.

Dr. Bob March is one of Australia's leading specialists on Japanese business and culture. He is the author of six books on Japan, including: *The Japanese Negotiator* (Kodansha International 1989, available in paperback). He has been a consultant on Japanese negotiation and business relationships for the past 20 years.

Source: www.negotiations.com/articles/building-trust.

EXHIBIT 10.2 Differences in Negotiator Strategies and Tactics in Three Countries

Source: J. L. Graham, "The Influences of Culture on the Process of Business Negotiations: An Exploratory Study," *Journal of International Business Studies* 16 (1985). Reproduced with permission of Palgrave Macmillan.

Individual Tactics as a Percentage of Total Tactics	Japanese N = 6	American N = 6	Brazilian N = 6
Promise	7	8	3
Threat	4	4	2
Recommendation	7	4	5
Warning	2	1	1
Reward	1	2	2
Punishment	1	3	3
Positive normative appeal	1	1	0
Negative normative appeal	3	1	1
Commitment	15	13	8
Self-disclosure	34	36	39
Question	20	20	22
Command	8	6	14

Occurrences in a 30-Minute Bargaining Session			
Number of times word *no* used	5.7	9.0	83.4
Silent periods of 10 seconds or more	5.5	3.5	0
Conversational overlaps (interruptions)	12.6	10.3	28.6
Gazing (minutes per random 10-min period)	1.3 min	3.3 min	5.2 min
Touching	0	0	4.7

Environmental Context of International Negotiations

As shown in Exhibit 10.3, cultural, national, and organizational variables significantly impact each stage of negotiation.

Cultural Variables

The cultural value of individualism influences the way American, Australian, and British managers approach the process. They are expected to make decisions by themselves, defend their points of view, and stand firm on issues that are important to them.

EXHIBIT 10.3 Comparison of Cultural Approaches to Negotiation

Source: Adapted from P. Casse and S. Deol, *Managing Intercultural Negotiations: Guidelines for Trainers and Negotiators* (Washington, DC: International Society for Intercultural Education, Training, and Research, 1985), pp. 148–152.

American Negotiator	Indian Negotiator	Arab Negotiator	Swedish Negotiator	Italian Negotiator
Accepts compromise when deadlock occurs	Relies on truth	Protects "face" of all parties	Gets straight to the point of the discussion	Dramatic
Has firm initial and final stands	Trusts instincts	Avoids confrontation	Avoids confrontation	Emotional
Sets up principals but lets subordinates do detail work	Seeks compromises	Uses a referent person to try to change others, e.g., "Do it for your father"	Time conscious	Able to read context well
Has a maximum of options	Is ready to alter position at any point	Seeks creative alternatives to satisfy all parties	Overly cautious	Suspicious
Respects other parties	Trusts opponent	Mediates through conferences	Informal	Intrigues
Is fully briefed	Respects other parties	Can keep secrets	Flexible	Uses flattery
Keeps position hidden as long as possible	Learns from opponent		Reacts slowly to new propositions	Concerned about creating a good impression
	Avoids use of secrets		Quiet and thoughtful	Indefinite

On the other hand, the value of collectivism influences the way Chinese and other east Asian managers approach negotiations. They emphasize decisions arrived at by consensus, defend group interests over individual interests, and often take a long-term view of the process.[9]

The definition of negotiation and what should occur during the process are also influenced by cultural differences, such as the amount of power distance (real or imagined) between the parties.[10] Selection of negotiators and the use of protocol and formality in the process also differ according to the cultural context of uncertainty avoidance and masculinity versus femininity.[11] Cultural values also have a significant effect on the choice of long- versus short-term goals and objectives.[12] In the United States, where "time is money" and "faster is better" is a general belief, there is an emphasis on achieving short-term goals, even at the expense of long-term goals. The Japanese, French, and others are more inclined to focus on long-term goals and objectives and may choose to ignore short-term objectives. This can cause surprise and confusion. The amount of time that may be spent in formal settings of negotiation also varies from country to country. Americans are seen as always being in a hurry and impatient. They spend less time on negotiating the details, unlike people in most other countries, and this leads to Americans accepting hurried agreements that they regret later.[13]

National Variables

Political Systems

The world consists of more than 200 countries, and each has its own distinct political system. International negotiators often get caught in the conflicting values they find between foreign policies of two or more countries. For example, because of the Russian invasion of Afghanistan, the Carter administration stopped the construction of a trans-Siberian pipeline in the former Soviet Union in the 1980s. Since American foreign policy was hostile toward Russia at the time, the U.S. government demanded that American companies (e.g., Dresser Industries) stop supplying equipment such as transformers and generators and related items to the construction. Current U.S. policy bans the sale of any technology, products, or services to organizations located in countries that support construction of nuclear weapons or warheads and countries that support terrorism.

In the past, political upheaval has often resulted in nationalization of foreign-owned companies. These issues are covered in Chapter 3, but they are mentioned again here because they can affect the negotiation process in numerous ways.

Legal Systems

Each country has its own legislation that influences negotiations in areas such as export and import quotas, antitrust regulations, labor–management relations, patent and trademark protection, product liability and marketing, maintenance of a minimum wage, and taxation. For example, a German company transferring technology to a Japanese collaborator must ensure that the transaction is legal in both Germany and Japan. Each country has laws that put limits on certain types of transactions. Certain sectors of the economy, such as the telecommunications and automobile industries, are often protected from wholly owned foreign investments. General Motors, Ford, Volkswagen, Toyota, and other automobile companies have set up manufacturing plants in India and China by establishing joint ventures with Indian and Chinese companies to meet legal restrictions. The joint venture agreement has an impact on how two parties might negotiate over important issues such as quality control, global marketing rights, the significance of and rights to technology, transfer to the joint venture, profit sharing, and royalty payments. Negotiators should be aware of the legal traps that might transform a good-faith agreement into a nightmare. Furthermore, it is essential that negotiators understand issues of political risk and be careful to avoid illegal activities, such as bribing or encouraging corruption.

International Economic Situation

Unlike purely domestic transactions, international business transactions occur with multiple currencies that fluctuate daily. Fluctuations in exchange rates, as reflected in the various currency crises around the world during the mid- to late 1990s, can affect negotiations in many ways. The currency crises in Mexico, Indonesia, and Russia caused significant problems for international firms that negotiated business transactions before the devaluation of currencies in these countries. A business deal that is not appropriately structured to compensate and protect against fluctuations in currency exchanges can lead either to disastrous consequences or to a windfall. Other international economic issues might concern regulation by the International Monetary Fund (IMF), the World Bank, and the United Nations.

Differences in Ideology

Negotiators from Western countries share a common ideology of capitalism and free enterprise, a strong belief in individual rights, protection of human rights, and the importance of making a profit. Negotiators from other countries, particularly from the socialistic or communist traditions (Russia, China, and Cuba), do not necessarily share this ideology. Group rights, as opposed to individual rights, are emphasized more in these countries, often leading to significant clashes during the negotiation process. Countries driven by strong values of idealism versus pragmatism are often unwilling to engage in win–win situations, making negotiation tricky and troublesome. Communication challenges in these types of cross-border negotiations exist because the parties strongly disagree on some of the fundamental issues of what is being negotiated and how long the outcomes of such negotiations are binding.[14]

These differences in ideology also reflect whether the parties follow distributive or integrative approaches to negotiation. Negotiators adopting a *distributive approach* view the negotiation process as a zero-sum game with fixed outcomes. The ideology of a distributive negotiation is such that the goals of one party stand in sharp contrast to those of the other party. In this approach, parties compete to maximize their outcomes, and if one party wins, the other loses. Negotiations between consumer groups and corporations, as well as labor–management negotiations, often reflect this approach.

On the other hand, negotiators using an *integrative approach* accommodate the other parties' interests and are willing to examine the range of possible outcomes that could result. The emphasis is on creating win–win scenarios in which both parties leave the negotiation with a sense of satisfaction. In integrative negotiations, each party is willing to spend time working toward satisfying the goals of the other party as much as possible, according to the circumstances.

The process of integrative negotiation is fundamentally different from that of distributive negotiation. The negotiators must be willing to explore the true mind-set of the other party to understand everyone's needs, which are often a product of the national cultural values and political and legal requirements. Negotiations between two successful multinational corporations that result in the setting up of a joint venture to produce a good or service that benefits both parties is an example of an integrative approach to negotiation.

Organizational Variables

Organizational Stakeholders

Stakeholders of multinational and global organizations are those persons and institutions with an interest or stake in the final outcome of negotiations. Examples include competitors, employees, labor unions, consumers, organized business groups (such as the Chamber of Commerce and other industry associations), and the company's shareholders and board of directors. All of these groups are capable of exerting pressure by lobbying for or against a proposed business arrangement, such as a joint venture or strategic alliance.

Competitors may launch a hard-nosed campaign to lobby against a proposed business agreement, especially if they feel that such agreements are detrimental to their own business. For example, agricultural companies in France and Spain did not favor the European Union entering into agricultural transactions with U.S. companies. Their fear was rooted in the fact that the U.S. agricultural sector was so industrialized that they could not effectively compete.

Employees and labor unions also affect the outcome of negotiations by getting involved. Collective bargaining agreements and labor contracts prevent companies, such as Caterpillar,[15] United Airlines, and American Airlines, from competing with firms that do not have such agreements.

Consumer groups that are likely to be affected, either positively or negatively, by the outcome of negotiations between two international firms may also become involved. U.S. consumers do not support business negotiations that might increase the price of popular Japanese products, such as consumer electronics and autos.

Organized business groups, such as the Chamber of Commerce and various industry groups, can also affect the process of international business negotiations. The positive attitude of a country's Chamber of Commerce, such as the U.S. Chamber of Commerce in Washington, D.C., or the U.K. Chamber of Commerce in London, can provide impetus for sustaining a negotiation, even when parties have difficulty reaching agreements. Visits of senior executives organized by the U.S. Chamber of Commerce were a major factor in setting up joint ventures and strategic alliances of American companies with their counterparts in China, India, Russia, and eastern Europe as these countries liberalized their markets.

Organizational Processes

Differences in decision-making processes and control mechanisms of global and multinational corporations play a crucial role in the way two or more corporations reach satisfactory agreements. Japanese multinationals are particularly noted for their group decision making, which affects the power of Japanese negotiators.[16] As discussed in Chapter 7, control mechanisms of Indian public bureaucracies are well known for their rigid and slow approach to negotiation, which leads to significant difficulties for Western multinationals. While there have been important changes in streamlining the bureaucratic processes to allow international companies to invest in India after 1991, problems continue.

Companies that have been repeatedly successful in negotiating internationally are those with administrative heritages that allow occasional failures. They succeed in situations that are complex or uncertain, require considerable advance preparation, and consume a great deal of time. It is essential that the organizational culture be

PRACTICAL INSIGHT 10.3

HOW TO AVOID BEING THE "UGLY AMERICAN" WHEN DOING BUSINESS ABROAD

You know the stereotype: They're bold, brash, and all business. They've got lots of money but little culture. They're immune to self-doubt and oblivious to cultural nuance.

They're the Ugly Americans.

The 1958 book and 1963 film adaptation gave the stereotype its name. How closely does the stereotype fit the reality of Americans doing business abroad today? How "ugly" are American businesspeople as they work with foreign partners in this our globalized world?

"Americans have a much greater willingness to adapt to other cultures than they did when that book was written," says Prabhu Guptara, director of the Executive Development Centre for UBS bank in Wolfsberg, Switzerland. "But Americans often still need to improve self-consciousness to understand that the qualities that make you win in the U.S. could as easily make you fail in Europe or Asia."

American execs need to be especially sensitive about three aspects of communications when they go abroad:

1. The rhythm of negotiations. Speed and directness are not necessarily qualities that foreigners appreciate, even though Americans like them.
2. The dynamics of personal relationships. Business in most of the developed world is people-based, not deal-based, so don't parachute in with the "lawyers and the dollars."
3. The depth of presentation. Slick speeches and PowerPoint slide shows may not get you far in cultures that value depth. You'd better have all the numbers and know what they mean.

Why these areas in particular? "Because Americans tend to value fast and agile dealmaking, and intense and skilled marketing, while not putting much value on personal relationships in business," explains Ann McDonagh Bengtsson, a France-based international consultant specializing in change management, especially where a number of different cultures are involved. "Whereas, most Europeans and many Asians want to develop a solid personal relationship before even considering a deal, and then expect very detailed and painstaking research to have gone into the preparation of any accord," Bengtsson says.

Says Japanese intercultural expert Shinobu Kitayama: "American culture emphasizes the core cultural idea of independence by valuing attending to oneself and discovering and expressing individual qualities while neither assuming nor valuing overt connectedness. These values are reflected in educational and legal systems, employment and caretaking practices, and individual cognition, emotion, and motivation."

In contrast, Bengtsson and Kitayama argue that Asian and European cultures tend to emphasize interdependence by valuing the self and individuality within a social context, connections among persons, and attending to and harmoniously coordinating with others. When Kitayama asked 65 middle-class American and 90 Japanese students attending the same Oregon university to list situations in which they felt that they were winning or losing, the American students focused more on ways in which they won individually, while the Japanese students won when the group with which they were associated enjoyed a success.

American execs abroad have to take these differences into account. So, when abroad:

Slow Down

The rhythm of negotiations and all business discussion is much slower outside the United States, as executives from the New York–based Bankers Trust had to learn when it merged with the Frankfurt-based Deutsche Bank two years ago.

Deutsche Bank was a very large, "universal" bank, as the Germans call such an entity. The bank was active in all sectors of banking, but the area where it needed the most reinforcement was investment banking. Hence the plan to merge with investment house Bankers Trust, a dedicated merchant bank with an American, "deals-based" culture.

The American executives quickly found that they could not fathom their German partners, reports international management professor Terry Garrison of the Henley Management College (Henley-on-Thames, England). "Accustomed to making split-second decisions, and managing on a project basis in which planning rarely extended beyond a given deal, the Bankers Trust 'hot-shots' found themselves working with 'universal' bankers who planned several years at a time, for whom a given 'deal' was something they felt they could take or leave, and who operated within a corporate governance framework that looked and felt completely alien to the Americans."

Garrison ran a seminar in which he helped the American execs get in tune with Continental banking culture. "It was a matter of teaching the Americans to slow down and think in different terms," Garrison says. "Those Germans who had spent a lifetime in a credit-management culture saw themselves as needing not just a crash course in merchant banking but a whole new vocabulary rooted in American capitalism."

Deutsche Bank executive Siegfried Guterman admits that "there were a lot of unmeasurable factors that were difficult to take into account before we accomplished the merger."

It is not that Asians and European cultures do not value efficiency. Rather, business for them is more conceptual and long-term. A given transaction is only interesting if it is part of the accomplishment of a much more stable, greater objective. "Attempts to hurry your foreign interlocutors along may just make them withdraw from the discussions altogether," Bengtsson points out.

Don't Arrive with "the Lawyers and the Dollars"
Personal and business relationships are more intertwined in Europe and in Asia that they are in the United States.

"Achieving trust with European and Asian partners is a key factor in success outside the U.S.," Guptara says. "Americans may not like each other, but if there is a 'deal' on the table, they do business. Most Asians and Europeans—even the British—want to get to know you first. They want to assure themselves that you are reliable, that you will not only go the distance for them this time, but that you will be there to do it again when they call upon you."

So, take the time to go for lunch with your prospective business partners abroad. Don't talk business right away—ask them about what things are like in their country. Find something that you have in common with them. Maybe you both like a certain sport? Perhaps you share an interest in Italian wine?

During this time, you can observe your interlocutor's reactions. What makes him laugh? Does he react with hostility to certain kinds of expressions? "When you get around to dessert, bring up the subject of the business at hand in a very casual way. Get some indications from his reaction about how to proceed. But let your interlocutor lead you through it all," says Guptara.

Negotiating experts agree that forcing a conclusion with a foreign partner can only cause problems. "Don't be afraid to drop the matter and to talk about the weather," says Garrison. "Don't be too serious, especially at the outset. Show your interlocutor that you are in no hurry to conclude, and he will assume that you are serious. Insist on a conclusion, and he will assume that you are desperate."

Establishing trust is a factor that an American businessperson abroad must take into account not only in negotiations, but also in working with Europeans or Asians on a day-to-day basis.

Disney had to endure an expensive lesson of this type when it opened EuroDisney outside Paris. The management expected the French employees to conform to American expectations in their work, and did little to build up trust. A long and agonizing conflict with French labor unions was the only result of this policy. Finally, Disney gave up and hired French managers. Labor difficulties were smoothed out when managers and workers began to trust each other.

Get the Details Right
Although the British may accept a slick PR demo while negotiating, most of the cultures on the Continent and many in Asia do not.

"There is a real academic side to business in Europe and in parts of Asia," Guptara says. "A business presentation to such interlocutors is like defending a Ph.D. thesis. They expect you to have real depth, all the numbers, and to be able to answer every question. Fail at this and they will never trust you. The word that Europeans apply to a businessman who can't answer key questions is *liar*."

It may seem useless pedantry on the part of your prospective business partners to insist on great detail, "but their view is that the details are the easy part," says Bengtsson. "And a thoroughness in knowledge of your subject means—especially to Europeans, rightly or wrongly—that the risks are being adequately managed."

One American manufacturer recently hit all the wrong buttons in discussions with a French acquisition. Arriving in Paris, the American company promptly invited the board of the French company to lunch. The French board was of the most traditional sort—all graduates of the *grandes écoles,* they perceived themselves to be fashionable, witty, and cultivated.

When the French businessmen arrived at the lunch, they were astonished to find their American colleagues wearing baseball hats and T-shirts with the name of the acquiring company on them. There was also a pile of such hats and shirts on the table, and they were bidden to put them on.

This suggestion did not go over well. But even worse was the period at lunch when the French—after what they thought was a decent delay—began asking strategic questions. It became obvious that the American executives knew little or nothing about the company they were acquiring apart from its balance sheet.

After that, the massive departure of the French businessmen from the company should not have taken the Americans by surprise.

Play by the Rules—Their Rules
When an American executive goes abroad, it's very easy for cultural assumptions to slip into her suitcase. "When negotiations are prolonged, or frustrating, these cultural assumptions tend to jump out of the suitcase, onto the negotiating table," Bengtsson points out. The point to remember at times like this is that you are in someone else's culture and, for the time being, you need to play by their rules.

Because of tighter budgets, companies are sending fewer executives abroad these days, so the executive who is sent to a foreign country has mission-critical work to do. Thus it's essential that the executive adapt to a different culture's rules: for communication, interaction, and negotiation. If he doesn't, if he acts the proverbial "Ugly American," his chances for success are small.

Source: Andrew Rosenbaum, "How to Avoid Being the Ugly American When Doing Business Abroad," December 2002. Reprinted by permission of *Harvard Management Communication Letter.* Copyright © 2002 by the Harvard Business School Publishing Corporation; all rights reserved.

designed to tolerate failures in negotiating in east and south Asian, Arabic, and Latin American countries. Long-term objectives in bringing about negotiations should be emphasized, as opposed to coming to a quick agreement, which is the usual practice in Western-style negotiations.

Consider negotiations between members of monochronic cultures and members of polychronic cultures.[17] *Monochronic cultures* tend to allocate time with a higher emphasis on tasks, while *polychronic cultures* tend to allocate time with a higher emphasis on relationships.[18] Monochronic cultures tend to have bureaucracies, which are governed by rules and policies and tend to be task-oriented, because the societies in which they exist are both. Polychronic cultures, on the other hand, are characterized by flatter organizational charts with fewer levels, which are sprawling and unstructured.[19] Hall suggests that polychronic organizations tend to be flatter because managers deal with many matters and people simultaneously.

Managers from Western MNCs complain about sluggish bureaucracies in their own countries, but their burden tends to be lighter compared to that of managers in polychronic cultures. Without well-established hierarchies for handling negotiations, each bureaucrat in a polychronic culture insists on signing off on pending negotiations. The sheer volume of procedures gets multiplied, as a result. A study of one joint venture in pharmaceuticals revealed that the U.S. government required 26 documents to be filed along with 9 administrative details, the Japanese government required 325 documents in 46 administrative procedures, and the South Korean government required 312 documents in 62 administrative procedures.[20] The interesting point to be noted is that the joint venture was undertaken in South Korea, and the paperwork took two years and nine months.

Monochronic bureaucracies tend to be massive, and the procedures are routinely implemented and are self-perpetuating. If an employee in a corporation in Memphis, Tennessee, wants to be transferred to another location, he or she will consult the company policy and file a request. An employee in a public bureaucracy in Colombia or India is more likely to ask a boss about the transfer or to call a senior colleague who may have influence in affecting a transfer. In polychronic bureaucracies, negotiations are routed through friends, family members, or other network connections. Monochronic organizations give equal treatment to employees of a given rank, and fairness is the organizing principle in these societies. Negotiating with representatives from polychronic bureaucracies will be slow, frustrating, and cumbersome. One may wish to conclude the negotiations out of sheer frustration. However, a satisfactory outcome may be reached if there is a guarantee that the boss will (1) be tolerant of occasional failures in dealing with these bureaucracies and (2) provide more time than would be the case in dealing with monochronic organizations.

Negotiating with the Chinese

In preparing for a business trip to mainland China, most Western managers are given a book of etiquette "how-tos," including such things as carrying a stack of business cards, having one's own interpreter, speaking softly and in short sentences, and wearing conservative clothing. These strategies are easy to implement and may win meager gains; however, according to Graham and Lam, these precautions will not sustain long-term negotiating relationships.[21] Four significant issues in Chinese culture, bound together for 5,000 years, influence Chinese business negotiations, according to these authors.

The first is *agrarianism*. In contrast to the United States and western Europe, where a majority of the population is urban, most Chinese people still live in rural agricultural areas engaged in rice or wheat cultivation. Group cooperation and harmony result from the communal, not individualistic, nature of peasant farming. Many of China's modern entrepreneurs are from agricultural areas, and thus agrarian values influence their negotiation approaches. Americans generally believe in openness and (what they believe to be) universally valid approaches to negotiation, whereas Chinese are more interested in outcomes that result in communal and harmonious relationships over the long term.

The second issue relates to *morality,* based on Confucian writings, which proposed that a society organized under a benevolent moral code would be stable, prosperous, and relatively immune from external aggression. Morality is also based on Taoism, which proposes that the key to life is compromise—a balance between the *yin* (dark, passive forces) and the *yang* (light, active forces). Chinese negotiators are more concerned with how the process occurs than with the outcomes, so negotiations involve long, drawn-out haggling to work through difficulties.

Pictographic language is the third issue, because Chinese is written in pictographs, that is, thousands of pictures rather than different combinations of 26 letters. As children learn through memorization of these pictures, their thinking becomes more holistic. Researchers have found that Chinese children are good at seeing a cohesive picture, whereas American children focus on details.[22]

Wariness of foreigners is the fourth and final issue. Because of the historical background of China, a violent history of wars with both external and internal aggressors, Chinese distrust rules. Most Chinese are confident only of those in their own in-groups. Exhibit 10.4 shows the resulting differences in negotiation processes.

EXHIBIT 10.4
Differences between American and Chinese Culture and Approaches to the Negotiation Process

Source: Adapted from J. L. Graham and N. M. Lam, "The Chinese Negotiation," *Harvard Business Review*, October 2003, p. 85.

Contrast of Basic Cultural Values	
American	**Chinese**
Task- and information-oriented	Relationship-oriented
Egalitarian	Hierarchical
Analytical	Holistic
Sequential, monochronic	Circular, polychronic
Seeks the complete truth	Seeks the harmonious way
Individualist	Collectivist
Confrontative, argumentative	Haggling, bargaining

Approach to the Negotiation Process	
Nontask Sounding	
Quick meetings	Long courting process
Informal	Formal
Make cold calls	Draw on intermediaries
Information Exchange	
Full authority	Limited authority
Direct	Indirect
Proposals first	Explanations first
Means of Persuasion	
Aggressive	Questioning
Impatient	Patient
Terms of Agreement	
A "good deal"	A long-term relationship

When a country believes so strongly in its own intellectual superiority, it does not give up its way of dealing with or negotiating with foreigners in accordance with modern practices. This is particularly true when the country perceives that its superiority is based on moral and spiritual values, as China does.[23]

According to Richard Lewis, who has taught communication and negotiation skills to Western managers in order for them to be effective in the Eastern cultures of Asia, traits that sustain the self-assessment of the Chinese are a sense of pride in their cultural history, a sense of duty, filial piety, kindness, courtesy, respect for hierarchy, loyalty, and humility. Given these self-ascribed qualities of the Chinese, Western managers might be inclined to think that Chinese managers are easy to negotiate with and, when faced with a dilemma, will do the right thing. However, Richard Lewis's observation is that the Chinese view of what is right does not necessarily match our (Western) view of what is right. Western managers emphasize truth before diplomacy, but the Chinese do just the opposite in many situations.* However, one thing is certain: Western managers must familiarize themselves with *guanxi,* which refers to a set of special relationships within the Confucian framework. These relationships exercise strong influences on the exchange of favors with individuals of different social statuses or rank. *Guanxi* guarantees that two people who believe in *guanxi* are linked in a relationship of mutual interdependence for a considerable period, if not for lifetime. Individuals who emphasize *guanxi* do so on the basis of intuition and do not necessarily engage in calculating or instrumental relationships.

The concept of face, which we discussed in Chapter 9, is also an important issue in dealing with the Chinese. Western managers dealing with the Chinese must learn to respect the significance of face as a living reality.

Using the Internet to Manage Negotiations

The use of the Internet in managing negotiations is also increasing.[24] Global organizations with sophisticated computer-mediated communication systems are evolving strategies of managing negotiations through the Internet. Decision support systems can provide support for the negotiation process by:

- Reducing the amount of time that is necessary for feedback from headquarters in order to carry out effective negotiations.
- Providing a large amount of data and information on alternative scenarios that may result from the negotiation process.
- Increasing the likelihood that important data and information are available when needed.

However, just because information can be sent by electronic media before, during, and after the course of a negotiation, it should not be assumed that negotiations can proceed without hurdles. Significant national and cultural blinders may prevent correct interpretation of information.[25] In other words, the message may not be accurately perceived because of selective filters and cultural biases, as discussed in Chapter 9.

Managing Negotiation and Conflict

Negotiations can become extremely complex in developing joint ventures, strategic alliances, and foreign direct investments (as discussed in Chapter 6) and in dealing with foreign governments. Conflicts can arise in any negotiation, but they are

---

* See endnote 23 for more discussion on the Chinese approach to negotiation.

especially frequent in international and cross-border negotiations. Since conflicts can be costly and lead to dysfunctional outcomes, they need to be properly managed. The process of managing conflict for multinational and global organizations becomes tricky because a great many factors must be considered. Differences in cultural, national, and organizational variables, as discussed above, create the potential for conflict to arise.[26]

As we have already discussed, much of the negotiation process involves both explicit and implicit conflict between the parties. **Conflict** can be understood as a state of disagreement or opposition between two parties, in which the accomplishment of one party's objectives neutralizes the other party's ability to achieve its desired outcomes. Conflicts present before, during, and after negotiation can cause significant disruptions, such as creating a showdown, a lose–lose situation. The presence of conflict may indicate that the parties will not engage in future negotiations and will not consider alternative scenarios.

The extent of globalization in the two organizations strongly influences the process of managing negotiation and conflict. Other factors that should be considered are the degree of interdependence in joint ventures and strategic alliances and the extent of economic deregulation that exists in the countries involved. We have already alluded to this in describing the stages of negotiation, as depicted in Exhibit 10.1. Knowledge of Internet technology, as well as the negotiation parties' effectiveness in using it, also plays a strong role. Companies that are relatively inefficient in using Internet and computer-mediated technologies to prepare global managers are at a considerable disadvantage. In the era of globalization, the use of Internet and related technologies should be incorporated to enhance the speed and effectiveness of the negotiation process. Such strategies are also needed to lower the degree of conflict that is otherwise inherent in negotiations across national borders and cultures. It is important to remember, however, that while modern technologies offer significant potential for improving the process of negotiation, some of the nonverbal cues and information that are necessary for sustaining the negotiation cannot be conveyed through Internet technologies. So, while there is a significant gain in one respect, there is also some loss of the richness that is always present in face-to-face meetings while negotiating with members of different cultures.

National and cultural factors, as presented in Exhibit 10.3, are often responsible for creating severe conflicts, leading to a breakdown in communication and negotiation. Negotiators from low-context cultures, as discussed in Chapter 9, tend to approach conflict directly through confrontation. A distinction is also made between the people involved and the conflict itself. On the other hand, negotiators from high-context cultures tend to approach conflict indirectly and subtly, through references to the history of previous conflicts between the parties. Rarely is a distinction made between the person engaged in the conflict and the conflict itself. The differences between members of low-context and high-context cultures in the handling of conflict are illustrated in Exhibit 10.5.

For example, Western businessmen report that while the Chinese put great emphasis on building relationships based on friendship and mutual respect, Americans are interested in getting to the point and are willing to reveal their objectives in the initial stages. The implicit communication styles used by Chinese and other east Asian negotiators also conflict with the explicit styles of communication used by Western negotiators.

Even with the emergence of China as a global economic power in the 1990s, most negotiations are still accomplished within the framework of budget allocations, mandated by the government for the project, as opposed to the potential profitability of the

EXHIBIT 10.5
Nature of Conflict between Members of Low- and High-Context Cultures

Source: W. Gudykunst, L. Steward, and S. Ting-Toomey, *Communication, Culture, and Organizational Processes* (New York: Sage, 1985).

Key Questions	Low-Context Conflict	High-Context Conflict
Why	Analytic, linear logic; instrumental-oriented; dichotomy between conflict and conflict parties	Synthetic, spiral logic; expressive-oriented; integration of conflict and conflict parties
When	Individualistic-oriented; low collective normative expectations; violations of individual expectations create conflict potentials	Group-oriented; high collective normative expectations; violations of collective expectations create conflict potentials
What	Revealment; direct, confrontational attitude; action- and solution-oriented	Concealment; indirect nonconfrontational attitude; "face-" and relationship-oriented
How	Explicit communication codes: line-logic style: rational-factual rhetoric; open, direct strategies	Implicit communication codes; point-logic style: intuitive-effective rhetoric; ambiguous, indirect strategies

project. In addition, the negotiation tends to be understood in the context of culturally ingrained values of politeness and emotional restraint.

The overlapping of work with family and other social obligations enters the context of negotiation in ways that Western negotiators do not understand. The concept of *saving face* in any negotiation is of critical importance in the east Asian cultures. Westerners often do not understand how powerful this concept is and how it affects the entire process of negotiation. If the negotiation leads to unsatisfactory outcomes for the east Asian parties, appropriate concessions must be made to allow them to save face. Future negotiations are likely to be problematic, if not impossible, if the outcomes do not result in saving face for the east Asian negotiators.

In managing effective international negotiations, it is useful to focus on:

- Dealing with people, especially building relationships with members of cultures for whom this is important.
- Allowing time for relationship building, thinking through various unexpected issues, and using interruptions to think through the issues in sufficient detail.
- Assessing possible barriers to communication, such as language and style differences, tendencies to stereotype, explicit versus implicit forms of communication, and the use of interpreters with resulting translation difficulties (see Chapter 9).
- Clarifying agreements, so that a signed, legally enforceable agreement is finalized. This can be an issue for some countries where a handshake is regarded as signifying a contract. Emphasis on too much formality might signal a lack of trust.
- Exercising power, bearing in mind mutual dependencies and differences in power between the parties. Too much difference in power might lead to negotiations that might not be honored in the long term.

Some of these issues are discussed in Practical Insight 10.4.

Ethics in International Negotiations

Accepting bribes, encouraging corrupt practices, and lying about one's true motives and capabilities in honoring the terms of a contract are all unethical. The U.S. Foreign Corrupt Practices Act of 1977, revised in 1998, is an example of a country-specific approach to maintaining *universalism*—ethical standards and values applicable worldwide. This legislation was designed to prevent American companies from accepting or giving bribes and engaging in other illegal actions that take place outside the United States and its territories with international companies, foreign governments, and others.

Another view of ethics is *relativism*—a belief that values, rules, and regulations are local and cannot be applied in cross-border and international negotiations. In fact, it is precisely because of this view of ethics held by traditional Asian, Latin American, and African cultures that the U.S. Foreign Corrupt Practices Act was developed. Modifying the terms of a contract after the deal is signed is not uncommon in these cultures, reflecting the notion that what matters is what works. These issues are discussed in detail in Chapter 14. Practical Insight 10.4 presents ethical considerations for doing business in third-world countries.

What Is Decision Making?

The nature of decisions that the parties make during the negotiation process determines the success of the outcomes. Decisions made before, during, and after negotiations should be carefully thought out for their implications and consequences. Effective decision making is crucial in today's highly competitive and global business environment. Managers are faced daily with a variety of decisions that have important cross-border implications for expanding their operations, as well as protecting their businesses. Correct choices can affect the success of global corporations, and the careers of individual managers are often linked to correct decisions, particularly in the West.

One of the first things to understand about decision making is that individualistic and collectivistic cultures promote different styles of information gathering. In individualistic cultures, people often consider their own information and that of experts in the area. In collectivistic cultures, people live in a sea of information embedded in the in-group context.[27] For example, they use an open office design to promote information flow between individuals. Decisions in collectivistic cultures are more often made on a group basis rather than on an individual basis.

The Decision-Making Process

Decision making is the conscious process of moving toward objectives after considering various alternatives.[28] It is concerned with making an appropriate choice among a multitude of possible scenarios. Effective decision making has been called one of the most important management tasks.[29]

Decision making is studied primarily by the descriptive approach and the prescriptive approach. The *descriptive approach* focuses on the various steps that are involved in the way managers carry out the task of decision making. When you describe the various steps that managers take in cross-border transactions, you are using the descriptive approach. It may involve consideration of such issues as the amount of information they need, the kind of approvals that are required, the chain of command they must respect, and the amount of time they have to make the decision. Decisions involved with implementing a joint venture agreement or launching a new product in the global marketplace can be described using this approach.

The *prescriptive approach* is concerned with understanding the rational processes that managers use to reach an optimal outcome. The importance of *rationality*—the use of reason and logic—in making a decision is the key to the prescriptive approach. The prescriptive approach highlights the importance of both subjective and objective factors that must be considered in the art and science of making a decision. When

PRACTICAL INSIGHT 10.4

A WHOLE WORLD OF ETHICAL DIFFERENCES

Doing business in the Third World often means demands for bribes. Here's how one man formulated his code of guiding principles.

You've just finished negotiating the deal, and it's time for a celebration, drinks and dinner all around, and you go to bed only to wake up the next morning to learn that the other side wants to start all over again. Or you try to buy something—a collection of antique vessels, say, for resale for decorative uses—and you're told that the artifacts are yours, but only for a price. You wonder, should I agree to pay a bribe just this once?

So it sometimes goes when it comes to the business of doing business abroad, which has been the case for my company, Rhodes Architectural Stone, ever since its launch (under another name) in 1998. Ours is the business of buying artifacts slated for demolition in areas of the world such as Africa, China, India, and Indonesia, and, in turn, selling them to discriminating clients in the U.S.

Ethical Yardstick

If there is one thing we've learned, it's that the ethical landscape is different in the Third World. In the U.S.—notwithstanding the recent spate of corporate scandals that have set a woefully new low for ethical business behavior—the fact remains that standards exist against which improprieties can be measured.

Not so in some other countries. The tenets that underlie our U.S. business language—that your word is your bond, that transparency is expected in joint ventures and contractual engagements, that each party walks away from the table getting as well as giving something—are not always understood.

This inherent conflict between First World and Third World business standards has meant that our journey as a design-driven firm has been extremely difficult at times. A core value of the company, which we call "value in the round"—meaning that value must be created for all parties in the deal—has involved familiarizing ourselves with an alien environment in order to establish business fundamentals. Needing to respect cultural differences must be carefully investigated and evaluated, while all the time taking care not to cross the line to engage in practices we abhor.

Black and White

In short, in the world of grays that characterizes business dealings in countries in which ethics are at best rudimentary by U.S. standards, and at worst nonexistent, we've taken the position that we must establish and adhere to a black-and-white policy.

Let me explain. Take the word "transparency," for example, which in the U.S. involves a baseline understanding of capitalism and allows each party to get something in a negotiation without necessarily having to cheat the other. With that common understanding, negotiators don't need to resort to taking money out of the game—bribing, to be precise—because all of the money is in the game. Nor is there a need to renegotiate a deal that has already been agreed upon because of a belief that the deal that was struck couldn't be good. Why would the parties have agreed to it in the first place?

In countries whose business laws are nascent, if they exist at all, and whose thinking has been shaped by philosophies vastly different from our own, our first challenge is to take what I call the "entry-level" business players, who disproportionately populate the developing countries in which we do business, and bring them up to speed in the business fundamentals of the U.S.

In the all-too-common instance of being asked that a deal be renegotiated, we see it as our duty to teach the fundamentals that underlie the business practices of the West, such as your word being your bond, and that, while it's all right to take as much time as you need to negotiate a deal, once you've agreed, you stand by it.

Shades of Gray

In the wake of a request to go back to the table after the celebratory dinner, for example, I begin by outlining what it's going to take to do business with us. We put it down in writing, even though I've learned that such documents are unenforceable. And if they ask again to renegotiate, we walk. In short, in a

---

you describe how managers arrive at the decision to undertake a joint venture, you are using the prescriptive approach. This approach takes into account the role of situational factors such as time and market pressures, as well as concessions that are needed for an optimal decision. Therefore, international managers must understand the role of culture and other variables, such as the national and organizational contexts, in the decision-making process.

The decision-making process is not just the province of managers. People make decisions on a daily basis when confronted with problems and opportunities. Some problems are routine, and managers can implement standard operating procedures or

world in which business fundamentals come in shades of gray, we've determined a black-and-white process as our blueprint for doing business.

Now, back to the bribes: Simply put, we don't pay them. In the case of our wanting to buy the collection of antique vessels, for example, we walked when told we would have to make such a payment. The good news in that case was that we were actually invited back a year later to make the purchase on our terms.

The matter of bribes, however, is more than just "'shall we" or "shall we not." It goes to the heart of the other issue underlying doing business in the Third World—the need for a way to respect cultural differences without crossing the line and engaging in practices that are, by Western standards, inappropriate or immoral.

Looked at this way, Rhodes Architectural Stone not only draws the line at paying bribes, but also at child labor and the mistreatment of women. The matter of child labor will serve to illustrate the dilemma. Imagine an American entrepreneur, traveling in the bitter cold in the remote countryside and dressed in a Gore-Tex parka, thinsulite socks, and the most comfortable and technologically advanced clothing money can buy. He arrives and states that we will not buy anything fabricated or procured with child labor. Now contrast that with the local reality, where the labor of the entire family is required to put bread on the table and a roof over one's head.

For the Children?

If my children were starving, I suppose I would do the same. In fact, our own forebears in the U.S. did employ children in factories well into the 20th century, and because of that, we don't have to do it any more. In this moral gray area, we've established another black-and-white policy: We cannot and will not do business with entities that engage in the practice of child labor, but we will not go to the next step and preach. In other words, we will not tell them they are wrong.

Surely, we bring a powerful lever when it comes to backing up this moral stance. Unlike foreign companies that go into native countries to sell products people can't afford, we are there to buy what they have to sell. We bring the twin carrots of hard currency and jobs.

That advantage notwithstanding, the decision to establish a moral black-and-white approach wasn't easy. It's one thing to come to that imperative in the matter of formulating business standards where none exist, for that involves the neutral task of teaching. It's quite another to tread into territory in which the actions are criminal or immoral by Western standards and, yet, understandable within the context of the foreign culture. The decision to do so, therefore, is actually a process, one of thought and reflection and, in the final analysis, leadership.

When to Walk

In coming to the imperatives that Rhodes Architectural Stone has determined for its business dealings overseas, I was fortunate to have the counsel of a member of our board, a former Whirlpool executive, with extensive business experience throughout the world.

This individual taught me that when dealing with the grays of the Third World's business landscape, it is necessary to establish a black-and-white, both for the way you will conduct business and also account for your moral imperatives. If the reality differs considerably when you are actually at the table, it is necessary to be strong enough to walk away.

In sum, you must ask yourself questions such as: Who am I? How do I feel about this or that action? Can I sleep at night if I engage in this or that behavior? In the milieu of grays that characterizes the world beyond our oceans, be strong enough to formulate your black-and-whites, which, in turn, will become your guiding principles.

Richard Rhodes, 39, CEO of Rhodes, Ragen & Smith, is a founding partner and nationally recognized entrepreneur, artist, and designer. He founded Rhodes Masonry, one of its principal affiliated companies, in 1984.

Source: Richard Rhodes, "A Whole World of Ethical Differences," *BusinessWeek,* March 27, 2003.

---

explicit rules. These are **programmed decisions.** On the other hand, some problems are new or complex, requiring consideration of many alternatives—they are **nonprogrammed decisions** and follow the following seven basic steps (see Exhibit 10.6):

1. *Defining the problem* is the first step in decision making, and it is probably the most important. A problem represents a state of affairs different from normal and desired functioning. If the problem is not well defined or if it is defined incorrectly, the solution will not solve the problem. For example, if the problem in an international negotiation is due to differences in political ideologies but the parties focus only on cultural preferences, the problem will worsen.

EXHIBIT 10.6
Steps in the Decision-Making Process

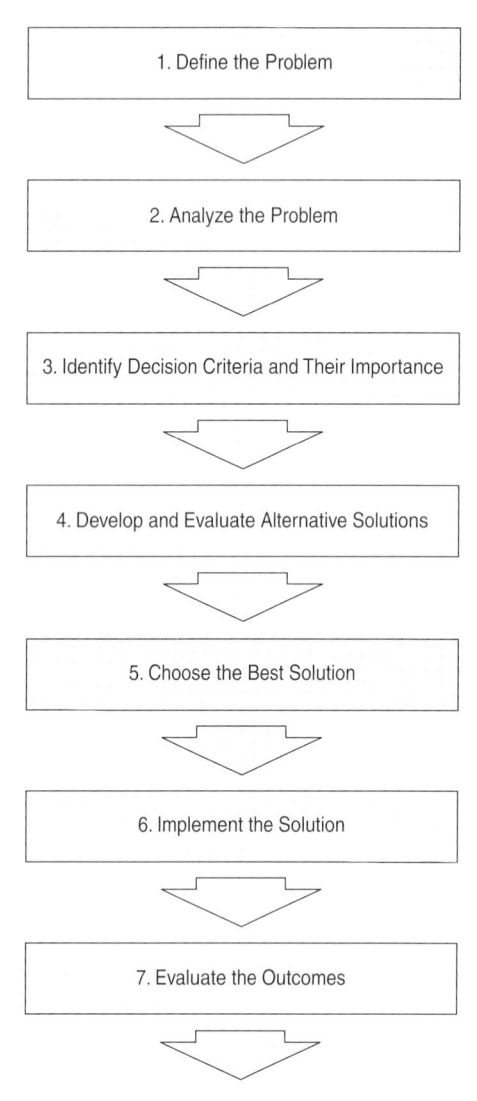

1. Define the Problem
2. Analyze the Problem
3. Identify Decision Criteria and Their Importance
4. Develop and Evaluate Alternative Solutions
5. Choose the Best Solution
6. Implement the Solution
7. Evaluate the Outcomes

2. *Analyzing the problem* focuses on finding the key factors responsible for the problem. These factors could be present in the task, the people, or the nature of the situation. In launching a new product, if the key factor is lack of global market demand but the manager identifies product quality as the key factor, he or she is analyzing the wrong factor to reach a decision.

3. *Identifying decision criteria and their importance* helps narrow the goals or objectives. For example, in selecting a new site for manufacturing, the manager may want to maximize the benefit of having a qualified workforce and minimize the importance of local taxes and tariffs. If the criteria for making decision are inappropriate, chances are high that the outcome will be poor.

4. *Developing and evaluating alternative solutions* enables the manager to consider different ways to solve the problem or take advantage of opportunities. The more alternatives considered, the more likely that an optimum solution will be found.

5. *Choosing the best solution* is not as easy as it may sound. A manager may come up with a set of solutions that look equally attractive, but the one that will maximize

PRACTICAL INSIGHT 10.5

CULTURE QUIZ

What Do You Do When . . . ?

1. The Chinese have stalled and stalled and stalled. Now, you have only one more day in Beijing before your flight home. Suddenly, during the final day of the negotiations, they appear to soften some of their demands—but of course, they expect you to give up some of yours as well. How could you have handled this better from the start?

2. You are introduced to Mr. Zhang Minwen at a banquet. You address him as Mr. Minwen, and become aware of his unfavorable reaction. You guess that you've said something wrong. But what?

3. You admire a beautiful Ming vase at your Chinese associate's home. Suddenly, before you leave, he thrusts a paper bag into your hands. You peek inside and see the vase. What do you do?

4. You've finally closed the deal, after exhausting both your patience and your company's travel budget. Now, two weeks later, the Chinese are asking for special considerations that change the terms of the agreement. How can they do this? Why are they doing it? And most important, what do you do?

5. On a business trip to Shanghai, you are invited to a banquet. Should you ask if your spouse may accompany you?

Culturally Sensitive Behavior Would Be . . .

1. This is a typical Chinese negotiating tactic. One way around this is to tell them you're leaving Friday—and actually leave the following Wednesday.

2. His name is Mr. Zhang. Chinese put their family name first.

3. You take it—because you admired it. You also reciprocate as soon as possible with an equally valuable gift.

4. The contract, for most Americans, represents the end of the negotiation. For the Chinese, however, it's just the beginning. Once a deal is made, the Chinese view their counterparts as trustworthy partners who can be relied upon for special favors . . . such as new terms in the contract.

5. Spouses (wives or husbands) aren't welcome at business social functions.

Source: Valerie Frazee, "In Keeping Up on Chinese Culture," *Personnel Journal* 75, no. 10 (October 1996). Reprinted with permission. Copyright Crain Communications, Inc.

---

the outcome is not always clear. Such dilemmas are routine in international transactions. When confronted with political risk in China, some companies pull out completely without recognizing the long-term benefits of continuing to work with the political system.

6. *Implementing the solution* involves putting the decision into practice. The manager must consider factors such as the amount of time needed, the nature of preferences of those implementing the plan, and the amount of resources needed to implement the decision correctly.

7. *Evaluating outcomes* is particularly important and often missed. In this step, managers consider whether the outcome actually solved the problem they defined in the first step. If it does not, they need to assess whether the problem was defined correctly, whether all possible viable alternatives were identified, and whether important criteria were considered when choosing the solution. International managers should pay special attention to this step because there are many conflicting factors that must be carefully considered in decision making in the global context.

Internal and External Factors

External factors identified in the section on negotiation earlier in this chapter are relevant here. The importance of political factors in some countries, such as Brazil, India, and Egypt, requires that managers focus on the political preferences of the key parties involved rather than on profitability alone. Economic factors, including volatility of exchange rates and the nature of foreign direct investment, are also factors for consideration. Decisions involving organizational factors include a consideration of whether the decision is made in the headquarters, at subsidiaries, or with an alliance partner.

Internal factors important in decision making relate to differences in thought and reasoning processes found in different parts of the world. In most Asian cultures, managers are unwilling to make rapid decisions. This is also true of managers in France and in Middle Eastern, Latin American, and Mediterranean countries. They focus on different aspects of the issues, like to negotiate for a long time, and have a tendency to engage in a great deal of relationship building. This process delays the speed at which decisions are made. There is also an emphasis on associative thinking, leading to associations among factors that are not necessarily logically linked in most Western countries.[30]

Some differences in reasoning are based on cultural preferences for inductive or deductive reasoning. Societies emphasizing **inductive reasoning** encourage managers to consider all of the specific facts and objective observations and slowly move toward generalizations and then a decision. Societies emphasizing **deductive reasoning** encourage managers to start with broad generalizations or categories and then evaluate the details to arrive at a decision. The difference between the two is illustrated in Exhibit 10.7.

Decisions arrived at through deductive reasoning appear poorly thought out and rapidly executed to people from inductive cultures. "Jumping to a conclusion" is the way many Japanese managers describe U.S. decision making.[31] The speed with which people think and the manner they use to approach the task affect decision making. The use of Internet and computer-mediated technology is making speed an even more important factor in cross-border negotiations and decision making. However, as we have discussed, national differences inherent in the process of decision making are not likely to disappear just because the countries are connected through the Internet.[32]

Sources of Errors in Decision Making across Borders and Cultures

Different Approaches to Heuristics and Biases

Given the number and complexity of decisions that global managers need to make, it is not suprising that managers tend to simplify things and use certain rules of thumb that they might have found useful in previous situations. The rules of thumb that

EXHIBIT 10.7
Deductive versus Inductive Styles of Decision Making

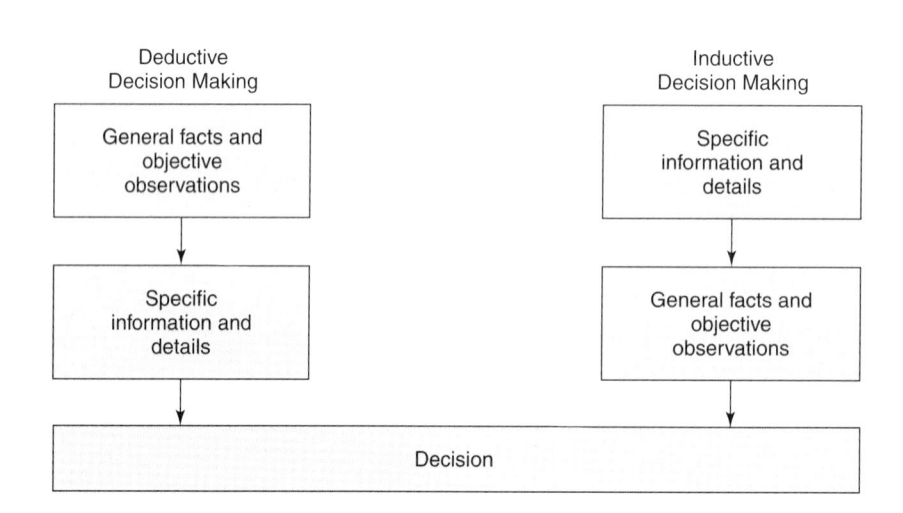

Deductive Decision Making: General facts and objective observations → Specific information and details → Decision

Inductive Decision Making: Specific information and details → General facts and objective observations → Decision

people use to simplify decision making are called *heuristics*. These heuristics differ considerably across cultural boundaries. Managers from abstractive cultures tend to use more scientific methods in coming to decisions, whereas managers from asssociative cultures are more inclined to emphasize practices that value the significance of cultural norms, such as the strong importance of *guanxi*. Heuristics may facilitate the decision-making process, but they also lead to biases in decision making. *Biases* are systematic errors that are rooted in the person and organization and in the society in which they function. Japanese managers use heuristics and are subject to biases that are different from Canadian managers or Russian managers. It is important to understand the nature of heurisitics and biases that are embedded in the cross-cultural and international decision-making context.

Escalation of Commitment

A major source of error in decision making is *escalation of commitment,* that is, the tendency of decision makers to invest additional resources (time, money, and effort) in efforts to improve decisions that were faulty to begin with. One is tempted to think of the example of the Iraq war that started due to incomplete intelligence from the Central Intelligence Agency in March 2003. In order to justify the continued existence of American troops in Iraq, which has cost the American economy dearly, increased expenditure of money was justified by the Pentagon. The escalation of commitment is also a major error that leads to sustaining justification of poor-performing loans in banking situations.*

Implications for Managers

Styles of negotiation, conflict resolution, and decision making may become similar as our knowledge and understanding of other nations and cultures increase. The importance of being explicit about how much each party knows about the other's background cannot be overstated.[33] Increased familiarity with country-specific factors, such as tax and tariff laws, labor relations, and political structure, on the part of expatriates is also leading toward satisfactory outcomes in cross-border business relationships.[34] Being aware of business protocols, such as dress, greeting,[35] and meeting, and taking more time to conduct negotiations are also helping the process. When managers make a conscious attempt to understand the nuances and subtleties of another culture, it becomes easier to develop appropriate approaches to negotiation, conflict resolution, and decision making. Prior knowledge of factors such as whether the other party is likely to take a distributive or an integrative approach to negotiation or is likely to use inductive or deductive reasoning are useful considerations. Effective uses of information technology enhance the quality of decisions that can be made for implementation in dissimilar countries and cultures, but that is not to say that greater use of information technology guarantees improved decision making. Managers are human beings and are subject to errors in judgment that will always be present. Attempts can be made by experienced managers to improve the quality of decision making by sharing their experiences. However, there should be room for tolerating the consequences of well-intentioned but poorly executed strategies of negotiation and decision making in the international context. Some of these considerations are illustrated in Practical Insight 10.6.

---

*More on this source of error can be found in the chapter on judgment and decision making in M. A. Stevenson, J. R. Busemeyer, and J. C. Nelson, *Handbook of Industrial and Organizational Psychology,* Vol. 1, 2nd ed. (Palo Alto, CA: Consulting Psychologists press, 1990).

PRACTICAL INSIGHT 10.6

A CULTURAL DILEMMA

Maria and her family hold closely to their Greek roots. Nine siblings and cousins, including Maria, are working in the family's importing business, and their connection to one another is strong.

While Olympia Imports is now in its second generation, leadership is still in the hands of the first-generation patriarch, Nick, who is 73. He and his brother, An, 65, who is Maria's father, founded the company more than 40 years ago.

Given the current international economic scene, the $12 million business is performing fairly well. However, Maria, 35, and a few of her cousins and siblings want to effect some change. Maria heads up sales and sees new product opportunities.

"Times are changing, but my uncle and my father refuse to recognize that as being so," she says. "They come from a culture where leadership is exclusively male. Uncle Nick has no intention of retiring. When he dies, it will be my father's turn to run the business, and when he dies, the next-oldest male will take over."

Maria has a college degree, and so do most of her cousins and siblings, but the values of the males among them are still very rooted in their traditional culture.

"Succession planning really isn't an option for this family," says Maria. "The rules are prescribed in advance. The younger generation, and especially the women, want to be heard. I'd like to know how we can have a voice in decision-making. What happens to consensus? What happens to team-building? And how can we create a forum or structure to encourage the generation of ideas?"

Response 1: Raise the Bar[*]

Maria needs to realize this is not a Greek tragedy—not yet, anyway.

In a culture where leadership is traditionally male and where birth order dictates organizational hierarchy in a family business Maria's situation is typical if no less frustrating.

As such, Maria's challenges are more "generational" than "gender-based"—pitting her skills, goals, and objectives against the cultural ideologies of her father's generation.

This situation is something she cannot change today or first thing tomorrow.

The best way Maria can constructively bring about change in the business is by accepting this reality and focusing on raising the company's success bar, not by dwelling on the dramatics of "having her voice heard."

Let's look at this from another perspective. Maria already directs sales—a critical role in any business and one that her mother or aunts likely never could have achieved.

In her father's mind, Maria may have already reached rare heights for a female, and she is perceived as a "modern woman and as living proof that an evolution is taking place."

To move forward, Maria must focus on effectively communicating her ideas and goals both for herself and for the business.

If Maria can succeed in delivering on an aggressive sales objective or in carving out a new sales or product initiative, then she will best position herself to have the professional respect and the "ears" that she will need for her ideas.

Response 2: Build Your Own Team[†]

If we accept Maria's statement that "succession planning really isn't an option," then we must look for other ways to meet the needs of the younger family members.

They must clearly separate issues of participation in and contribution to the company from the issue of who will be the leader. Given the traditional values of the younger males, can this generation present a reasonably congruent view of the future, especially across gender lines?

Can they agree on the direction in which to move the business, on the changes to make, on a timetable for such changes, and on the roles they will play? As these questions suggest, they must begin team-building among themselves.

Would it be possible to assemble the entire family, look 10 years into the future, and talk about the goals and dreams of each family member, for both the family and the business?

If the whole family cannot be brought together, perhaps the younger generation can gather on its own.

Maria, her siblings, and her cousins may find it easier to get their fathers to accept change if the ideas come from their fathers' peers. It might be useful to look outside the company for men their fathers know and respect, men who are not so wedded to tradition and who can act as champions for the younger generation and help begin the process of introducing change.

Maria must decide if her needs can be met at Olympia Imports under any circumstances. Going to another company may be her only means of making a contribution. And if things at the family firm improve, she could rejoin it with more experience.

[*]By Olga Staios, executive director of the Family Enterprise Institute in Cincinnati.

[†]By Paul L. Sessions, director of the Center for Family Business at the University of New Haven in West Haven, Connecticut.

Source: "A Cultural Dilemma," *Nation's Business,* March 1999. Reprinted with permission of U.S. Chamber of Commerce. Copyright 1999 U.S. Chamber of Commerce.

Summary

In this chapter, we described the basic processes of negotiation, conflict resolution, and decision making. Multinational and global corporations must be aware of the significance of these issues and how they affect their interest worldwide. Different environments result in different styles of negotiation, conflict resolution, and decision making.

Cross-border negotiations are vital for competition in the global marketplace. Negotiations between corporations occur each day. In order to effectively negotiate across cultures and borders, each step in the negotiation process must be performed with cultural context in mind. Success in negotiation depends on understanding the other party's needs and goals and the situation of the negotiation itself. Cultural, national, and organizational differences can affect success. For example, behaviors and concepts that we take for granted are not considered acceptable negotiating tactics in all cultures.

Much negotiation deals with conflict between two parties, and conflict can also result from breakdowns in communication. Some of these breakdowns are due to cultural and national factors, which can be overcome through understanding and education of the negotiators. Some conflict is also created because cultures promote different types of decision making. Understanding the process of decision making can alleviate some of the problems encountered in negotiating across cultures and borders.

Key Terms and Concepts

bargaining, *362*
conflict, *377*
decision making, *379*
deductive reasoning, *384*
inductive reasoning, *384*
international negotiation, *362*
negotiation, *361*
nonprogrammed decisions, *381*
programmed decisions, *381*

Discussion Questions

1. Define *negotiation*. Discuss the significance of negotiation involving cross-border and cross-cultural transactions. Give examples.
2. What are the stages of negotiation in international management? Give examples of each stage from your own experience in negotiations or from other sources.
3. Why are negotiations difficult to conduct in international transactions? List as many factors as you can think of from cultural, national, and organizational influences that affect the outcome of negotiations.
4. How do conflicts arise between low- and high-context cultures? How would you advise managers of low-context cultures to be more effective in handling conflicts with managers from high-context cultures?
5. Discuss the different types of decision making. How would inductive reasoning affect the way decisions are made? Give an example of how inductive reasoning might conflict with the process of deductive reasoning in negotiations.

Minicase

Conflict Resolution for Contrasting Cultures

An American sales manager of a large Japanese manufacturing firm in the United States sold a multimillion-dollar order to an American customer. The order was to be filled by headquarters in Tokyo. The customer requested some changes to the product's standard specifications and a specified deadline for delivery.

Because the firm had never made a sale to this American customer before, the sales manager was eager to provide good service and on-time delivery. To ensure a coordinated response, she organized a strategic planning session of the key division managers that would be involved in processing the order. She sent a copy of the meeting agenda to each participant. In attendance were the sales manager, four other Americans, three Japanese managers, the Japanese heads of finance and customer support, and the Japanese liaison to Tokyo headquarters. The three Japanese managers had been in the United States for less than two years.

The hour meeting included a brainstorming session to discuss strategies for dealing with the customer's requests, a discussion of possible timelines, and the next steps each manager would take. The American managers dominated, participating actively in the brainstorming session and discussion. They proposed a timeline and an action plan. In contrast, the Japanese managers said little, except to talk among themselves in Japanese. When the sales manager asked for their opinion about the Americans' proposed plan, two of the Japanese managers said they needed more time to think about it. The other one looked down, sucked air through his teeth, and said, "It may be difficult in Japan."

Concerned about the lack of participation from the Japanese but eager to process the customer's order, the sales manager sent all meeting participants an e-mail with the American managers' proposal and a request for feedback. She said frankly that she felt some of the managers hadn't participated much in the meeting, and she was clear about the need for timely action. She said that if she didn't hear from them within a week, she'd assume consensus and follow the recommended actions of the Americans.

A week passed without any input from the Japanese managers. Satisfied that she had consensus, she proceeded. She faxed the specifications and deadline to headquarters in Tokyo and requested that the order be given priority attention. After a week without any response, she sent another fax asking headquarters to confirm that it could fill the order. The reply came the next day: "Thank you for the proposal. We are currently considering your request."

Time passed, while the customer asked repeatedly about the order's status. The only response she could give was that there wasn't any information yet. Concerned, she sent another fax to Tokyo in which she outlined the specifications and timeline as requested by the customer. She reminded the headquarters liaison of the order's size and said the deal might fall through if she didn't receive confirmation immediately. In addition, she asked the liaison to see whether he could determine what was causing the delay. Three days later, he told her that there was some resistance to the proposal and that it would be difficult to meet the deadline.

When informed, the customer gave the sales manager a one-week extension but said that another supplier was being considered. Frantic, she again asked the Japanese liaison to intercede. Her bonus and division's profit margin rested on the success of this sale. As before, the reply from Tokyo was that it would be "difficult" to meet the customer's demands so quickly and that the sales manager should please ask the customer to be patient.

They lost the contract. Infuriated, the sales manager went to the subsidiary's Japanese president, explained what happened, and complained about the lack of commitment from headquarters and Japanese colleagues in the United States. The president said he shared her disappointment but that there were things she didn't understand about the subsidiary's relationship with headquarters. The liaison had informed the president that headquarters refused her order because it had committed most of its output for the next few months to a customer in Japan.

Enraged, the sales manager asked the president how she was supposed to attract customers when the Americans in the subsidiary were getting no support from the Japanese and were being treated like second-class citizens by headquarters. Why, she asked, wasn't she told that Tokyo was committed to other customers?

She said: "The Japanese are too slow in making decisions. By the time they get everyone on board in Japan, the U.S. customer has gone elsewhere. This whole mess started because the Japanese don't participate in meetings. We invite them and they just sit and talk to each other in Japanese. Are they hiding something? I never know what they're thinking, and it drives me crazy when they say things like 'It is difficult' or when they suck air through their teeth.

"It doesn't help that they never respond to my written messages. Don't these guys ever read their e-mail? I sent that e-mail out immediately after the meeting so they would have plenty of time to react. I wonder whether they are really committed to our sales mission or putting me off. They seem more concerned about how we interact than about actually solving the problem. There's clearly some sort of Japanese information network that I'm not part of. I feel as if I work in a vacuum, and it makes me look foolish to customers. The Japanese are too confident in the superiority of their product over the competition and too conservative to react swiftly to the needs of the market. I know that headquarters reacts more quickly to similar requests from their big customers in Japan, so it makes me and our customers feel as if we aren't an important market."

Said the U.S.-based Japanese: "The American salespeople are impatient. They treat everything as though it is an emergency and never plan ahead. They call meetings at the last minute and expect people to come ready to solve a problem about which they know nothing in advance. It seems the Americans don't want our feedback; they talk so fast and use too much slang.

"By the time we understood what they were talking about in the meeting, they were off on a different subject. So, we gave up trying to participate. The meeting leader said something about timelines, but we weren't sure what she wanted. So, we just agreed so as not to hold up the meeting. How can they expect us to be serious about participating in their brainstorming session? It is nothing more than guessing in public; it is irresponsible.

"The Americans also rely too much on written communication. They send us too many memos and too much e-mail. They seem content to sit in their offices creating a lot of paperwork without knowing how people will react. They are so cut-and-dried about business and do not care what others think. They talk a lot about making fast decisions, but they do not seem to be concerned if it is the right decision. That is not responsible, nor does it show consideration for the whole group.

"They have the same inconsiderate attitude toward headquarters. They send faxes demanding swift action, without knowing the obstacles headquarters has to overcome, such as requests from many customers around the world that have to be analyzed. The real problem is that there is no loyalty from our U.S. customers. They leave one supplier for another based solely on price and turnaround time. Why should we commit to them if they aren't ready to commit to us? Also, we are concerned that the salesforce has not worked hard enough to make customers understand our commitment to them."

Source: C. C. Clarke and G. D. Lipp, "Conflict Resolution for Contrasting Cultures," *Training & Development,* 1998. Copyright © 1998, T&D Magazine (formerly Training & Development), American Society for Training & Development. Reprinted with permission. All rights reserved.

DISCUSSION QUESTIONS

1. How are the managers of the Japanese manufacturing firm different from the American managers in the way they approach conflict resolution and decision making?
2. Why do the Japanese consider the Americans managers impatient?
3. What would you do to increase the amount of cooperation between the two parties?
4. Why did the Japanese not respond to the e-mails and written messages from the Americans?

Notes

1. R. J. Lewicki, J. A. Litterer, J. W. Minton, and D. M. Saunders, *Negotiation,* 2nd ed. (Burr Ridge, IL: Irwin, 1994).
2. N. J. Adler, *International Dimensions of Organizational Behavior,* 4th ed. (Cincinnati: South-Western, 2002).
3. H. Cohen, *You Can Negotiate Anything* (New York: Bantam Books, 1989); H. Cohen, *Negotiate This! By Caring, but Not THAT Much* (New York: Warner Books, 2003).
4. S. E. Weiss and W. Stripp, "Negotiating with Foreign Business Persons: An Introduction for Americans with Propositions on Six Cultures," New York University Graduate School of Business Administration, Working Paper 85–6 (1985); I. W. Zartman, ed., *The 50% Solution* (Garden City, NY: Anchor Books, 1976).
5. J. L. Graham, "A Theory of Interorganizational Negotiations," *Research in Marketing* 9 (1987), pp. 163–183.
6. Lewicki, Litterer, Minton, and Saunders, *Negotiation.*
7. J. L. Graham, "Brazilian, Japanese, and American Business Negotiations," *Journal of International Business Studies,* Spring/Summer 1983, pp. 47–61; J. L. Graham, "The Influence of Culture on the Process of Business Negotiations: An Exploratory Study," *Journal of International Business Studies* 16 (1985), pp. 81–96; J. L. Graham, D. K. Kim, C. Y. Lin, and M. Robinson, "Buyer–Seller Negotiations around the Pacific Rim: Differences in Fundamental

Exchange Processes," *Journal of Consumer Research* 15 (1988), pp. 48–54; J. L. Graham, A. T. Mintu, and W. Rodgers, "Explorations of Negotiation Behaviors in Ten Foreign Cultures Using a Model Developed in the United States," *Management Science* 40, no. 1 (1994), pp. 72–95.

8. G. Fisher, *International Negotiation: A Cross-Cultural Perspective* (Chicago: Intercultural Press, 1980).

9. R. J. Janosik, "Rethinking the Culture–Negotiation Link," *Negotiation Journal* 3 (1987), pp. 385–395; L. W. Pye, *Chinese Negotiating Style* (New York: Quorum Books, 1992); G. Hofstede, *Culture's Consequences: International Differences in Work-Related Values,* 2nd ed. (Thousand Oaks, CA: Sage, 2001).

10. D. A. Foster, *Bargaining across Borders: How to Negotiate Business Successfully Anywhere in the World* (New York; McGraw-Hill, 1992).

11. Weiss and Stripp, "Negotiating with Foreign Business Persons"; Foster, *Bargaining across Borders.*

12. Hofstede, *Culture's Consequences.*

13. J. L. Graham, "A Comparison of Japanese and American Business Negotiations," *International Journal of Research in Marketing* 1 (1984), pp. 50–68; J. L. Graham, "The Japanese Negotiation Style: Characteristics of a Distinct Approach," *Negotiation Journal* 9 (1993), pp. 123–140.

14. J. W. Salacuse, "Making Deals in Strange Places: A Beginner's Guide to International Business Negotiations," *Negotiation Journal* 4 (1988), pp. 5–13.

15. U. S. Rangan and C. A. Bartlett, "Caterpillar Tractor Company Case," in C. A. Bartlett and S. Ghoshal, *International Management, Text, Cases, and Readings in Cross-Border Management,* 3rd ed. (New York: McGraw-Hill/ Irwin, 2000), pp. 259–279; Harvard Business School Case 385-276, 1985.

16. J. L. Graham and Y. Sano, *Smart Bargaining* (New York: Harper Business, 1989).

17. J. Hooker, *Working across Cultures* (Stanford: Stanford University Press, 2003).

18. E. T. Hall, *The Silent Language* (Garden City, NY: Anchor Books/Doubleday, 1959).

19. E. T. Hall, *Beyond Culture* (Garden City, NY: Anchor Press/Doubleday, 1976).

20. B. L. DeMente, *Korean Etiquette and Ethics in Business* (Lincolnwood, IL: NTC Publishing Group, 1994).

21. J. L. Graham and N. M. Lam, "The Chinese Negotiation," *Harvard Business Review,* October 2003, pp. 82–91.

22. M. Bond, *The Psychology of the Chinese People* (Hong Kong: Oxford University Press, 1986).

23. Chapter 9 from Richard D. Lewis, *The Cultural Imperative: Global Trends in the 21st Century* (Yarmouth, ME: Intercultural Press, 2003).

24. T. J. Mullaney and R. Grover, "The Web Mogul," *BusinessWeek,* October 13, 2003, pp. 62–70.

25. R. S. Bhagat, B. L. Kedia, P. Harveston, and H. C. Triandis, "Cultural Variations in the Cross-Border Transfer of Organizational Knowledge: An Integrative Framework," *Academy of Management Review* 27, no. 2 (2002), pp. 204–221; R. S. Bhagat, B. L. Kedia, P. Harveston, and B. Srivastava, "Creation, Transformation, and Flow of Knowledge across the Individualism–Collectivism Divide: Implications for MNCs," in *European International Business Academy Proceedings* (Copenhagen: Copenhagen School of Business, 2004).

26. Hooker, *Working across Cultures;* Graham and Lam, "The Chinese Negotiation."

27. Hall, *Beyond Culture;* Bhagat, Kedia, Harveston, and Triandis, "Cultural Variations in the Cross-Border Transfer of Organizational Knowledge."

28. F. A. Shull, Jr., A. L. Delbecq, and L. L. Cummings, *Organizational Decision Making* (New York: McGraw-Hill, 1970).

29. H. J. Mintzberg, *Mintzberg on Management: Inside Our Strange World of Organizations* (New York: Free Press, 1998); P. Evans, V. Pucik, and J-L. Barsoux, *The Global Challenge* (New York: McGraw-Hill, 2002).

30. E. Glenn and P. Glenn, *Man and Mankind: Conflicts and Communication between Cultures* (Norwood, NJ: Ablex, 1981).

31. L. Copeland and L. Griggs, *Going International* (New York: Random House, 1985).
32. F. Cairncross, *The Death of Distance: How the Communications Revolution Is Changing Our Lives* (Boston: Harvard Business School Press, 2001).
33. S. E. Weiss, "Negotiating with 'Romans'—Part 1," *Sloan Management Review,* Winter 1994, pp. 51–61; S. E. Weiss, "Negotiating with 'Romans'—Part 2," *Sloan Management Review,* Spring 1994, pp. 85–99.
34. J. S. Black, H. B. Gregersen, M. E. Mendenhall, and L. K. Stroh, *Globalizing People through International Assignments* (Reading, MA: Addison-Wesley, 1999).
35. R. R. Gesteland, *Cross-Cultural Business Behavior: Marketing, Negotiating, and Managing across Cultures* (Copenhagen: Copenhagen Business School Press, 2001).

CHAPTER ELEVEN

Motivating and Leading across Borders and Cultures

Chapter Learning Objectives

After completing this chapter, you should be able to:

- Explain how people's conceptions of work and working differ in different national environments.
- Discuss the significance of models of work motivation from a U.S. perspective and the extent to which they might be applied in non-U.S. cultures.
- Understand how various cultural dimensions support different patterns of motivation and related work outcomes in different environments.
- Distinguish among the different patterns of motivation, job involvement, job satisfaction, and organizational commitment.
- Understand the significance of organizational rewards and various monetary and nonmonetary aspects of compensation in motivating different types of people in different parts of the world.
- Explain the significance of leadership in international management.
- Understand why some U.S. theories are applicable outside the United States and why some are not.
- Identify the factors that affect the quality of leadership in different countries and the significance of non-Western theories of leadership in the global context.
- Understand the role of effective global leadership.

Opening Case: My Way or the Highway at Hyundai and Kia

On the morning of Monday, Feb. 4, about 20 of the top executives at the Irvine (Calif.) headquarters of Kia Motors America left their warm offices to stand outside in near-freezing cold. They were awaiting the arrival of Byung Mo Ahn, the president of Kia. The group organized itself into a receiving line and stayed in formation for more than 15 minutes until Ahn arrived in a chauffeur-driven Kia Amanti sedan. Although some of the executives were shivering, it would have been bad form to return inside: Standing to greet top brass is customary at Hyundai Motors, Kia's Korean parent. After spending a full week in Irvine, Ahn performed another ritual that has become common at the company: sacking the American leadership team. On Feb. 8 he axed Len Hunt, president and CEO of Kia America, and Ian Beavis, marketing vice-president.

It marked the fourth shakeup in three years for Kia's American operation. The U.S. unit of Hyundai, meanwhile, has churned through four top executives in five years. Many of the departures have come at awkward times. Hunt and Beavis got the news at the airport as they were about to fly from

Irvine to an annual dealer meeting in San Francisco. According to several sources, Hunt's predecessor, Peter Butterfield, was dismissed during a dinner meeting with dealers at the Bellagio Hotel in Las Vegas—between the entree and dessert. The companies declined to comment on any of these executive departures.

The management shakeups at the American divisions of Hyundai and Kia—two once-separate manufacturers that are now essentially run as one company—come at a critical period. Both brands, which were originally marketed to American consumers as utilitarian econoboxes, are trying to move upscale and sell sedans that can compete with Cadillac and BMW. They are also banking on rapid growth in the U.S. Kia sold 305,000 cars in America in 2007, 13% shy of its target of 350,000. Given their aggressive growth plans, both Hyundai and Kia "need North American auto expertise," says James N. Hall, president of 2953 Analytics, an auto industry consultancy near Detroit.

The problem is that the companies keep booting out American talent. And many of the American executives who do stay find parent Hyundai's corporate culture to be suffocating. According to several current and former managers, Hyundai Chairman Chung Mong Koo, Kia's Ahn, and other top executives run the companies in a far more authoritarian style than do most American CEOs. The critics say his team micromanages details, rarely listens to advice from local managers, and displays little tolerance for disagreement. "It's a very feudal approach to management," says Bob Martin, a former sales executive who left Hyundai in 2005 to become a consultant at CarLab, a Santa Ana (Calif.) consulting firm. "There's a king, he rules, and everyone curries his favor. It's very militaristic."

While Chung's top-down management style might rub some Americans the wrong way, his long-term track record in the U.S. is impressive. Under his leadership, Hyundai has nearly doubled sales in the country since 2000, to 467,000 cars last year. Kia has posted almost identical growth. Chung, who was convicted of embezzlement in Korea last year but had his prison sentence suspended, has won praise for creating a highly disciplined company. When quality complaints started to plague Hyundai during the 1990s, he ordered engineers to attack the problem. By 2004, Hyundai had soared up the rankings in quality surveys. Unlike Detroit's Big Three, Hyundai and Kia have fewer management layers to hold up decisions. "I can see where Americans would feel uncomfortable," says Alice Amsden, a professor of political economy at MIT who has written books about Korea and other developing Asian economies. "American management is used to a different style. But Hyundai deserves a lot of credit."

Both Hyundai and Kia, speaking through representatives at their American units, said that all of the American managers who have left the companies in recent years were treated fairly. Even some of the executives who have departed praise the companies' management culture. "Being aggressive doesn't make them bad," says Robert Cosmai, who was CEO of Hyundai's American unit for two years before getting fired in January 2006.

Boldness is part of Hyundai's DNA. Like many of Korea's early corporate patriarchs, founder Chung Ju Yung had a simple strategy: Build factories first, worry about sales later. Starting with a small construction company in 1947, he moved into autos, shipbuilding, and other industries. Hyundai became one of the most successful Korean chaebols, family-controlled conglomerates with close ties to the government. But it was broken up into several pieces in the late 1990s in the wake of the Asian financial crisis. In 2007, global revenues of Hyundai and Kia grew 7%, to $63.5 billion.

Chung Ju Yung's heirs continue to run Hyundai, and his business philosophy still prevails. In America, the two companies often establish sales targets based on what their auto plants can produce—a persistent source of tension with local managers. Several past executives say that Hyundai and Kia have set unhealthily aggressive sales goals that are causing inventory to pile up. Hyundai has about 32,000 Sonata sedans parked in lots around its Montgomery (Ala.) plant with no orders from dealers. "The production-oriented style of pushing all the time won't work anymore," says Kim Ki Chan, professor of auto economics at Catholic University of Korea.

One consequence of this philosophy is that both Hyundai and Kia have been forced to sell more cars to rental fleets—a practice that tends to make brands lose cachet with buyers. But consumer psychology is something that Hyundai has never mastered, says consultant Hall. At bottom, it has always had the mindset of a manufacturer, not a marketer. Many of the products made by Chung Ju Yung's original conglomerate, such as locomotive engines and tanks, were sold to business. Hyundai's leadership team "lacks marketing savvy," says Yoo Young Kwon, a Seoul-based auto analyst at Prudential Investment & Securities. "What they need in the U.S. is to let American executives implement marketing strategy in a sustainable way."

But handing over the reins to American marketers is not something that seems to come naturally to Hyundai. After walking through the receiving line on that Monday morning in February, Kia CEO Ahn spent the day criticizing the company's advertising. The brand has marketed itself as sporty and fun as opposed to the more serious Hyundai. In one of the meetings, Ahn said he hated an ad depicting a Kia dealer doing an impression of the film *Flashdance,* dancing wildly as the jingle "He's a maniac, maniac, and he's selling like he's never sold before" plays. Ahn halted the spots and said Kia's message should lose the campy humor.

Four days later, Kia America CEO Hunt and marketing vice-president Beavis lost their jobs. The firings came as a surprise to the Kia dealers gathered in San Franciso's Moscone Center. Some say they're worried that the brand's marketing message will become diffuse. "It doesn't inspire a lot of confidence," says Ed Tonkin, a Portland (Ore.) Kia dealer who opened one of the brand's original U.S. stores. "The danger is that every time you get a new person, they will go with different marketing and advertising."

Since the meeting, Ahn has taken over Hunt's old office and expanded it. He has tried to mollify dealers with offers of increased corporate support. Kia and Hyundai are also making a greater effort to improve the morale of disgruntled American executives. Kia spokesman Alex Fedorak says many of them get training from a Korean culture coach.

Cross-cultural outreach is long overdue. Several Americans expressed resentment at the so-called coordinators, the Korean overseers whose job it is to keep an eye on American managers. Culled from the ranks of up-and-coming stars in Seoul, they sit alongside American managers, monitoring decision-making and results. Both Hyundai and Kia have about a dozen coordinators. They must agree to major decisions—and sometimes smaller ones, such as whether to award vacations to dealers who hit sales goals. Japanese automakers also have coordinators in their U.S. operations, but they play more of an advisory role while the American executives have free reign to make major decisions.

Mark Barnes, chief operating officer at Volkswagen Group of America, who worked as a sales executive at Hyundai America until 2006, says the coordinators applied pressure to achieve targets. "If you were subpar, they would ask what you're going to do to get your numbers up," Barnes says. During some conference calls, he adds, the coordinators would speak Korean to managers in Seoul, all but shutting out the Americans.

Kia spokesman Fedorak says the coordinators serve a valuable purpose: bringing the corporate vision from Seoul to America, then relaying the needs of the local market back to headquarters. Since few American employees speak Korean, the coordinators also act as translators. While acknowledging that Kia has a Confucian-influenced corporate culture in which "father knows best," he said this was not the main source of conflict with American executives. Instead, he attributed the tension to Korean managers' greater comfort with "stretch goals."

At the moment, the stretch goal that is stressing out American executives at Hyundai is the company's insistence on trying to move into the low end of the luxury business. For years, executives in the U.S. have been telling their counterparts in Seoul that the two brands are not strong enough to sell for much above the price range of $12,000 to $25,000. But their warnings have been ignored. Chung believes that going upscale is essential for Hyundai and Kia. The weak dollar has hurt profits, and concessions made to the Korean unions are eroding the company's cost advantage. So both Hyundai and Kia have launched a slate of vehicles priced near or above $30,000. In 2005, for example, Kia released the Amanti (Ahn's limo) with a mandate to sell 20,000 a year.

The company didn't come close to hitting that number, selling just 5,500 of the sedans, priced between $25,000 and $30,000, last year. Still, nobody expects Chung to heed the advice of some

American managers and pull back. "The top-down management style hasn't changed at Hyundai," says Lee Hang Koo, auto industry specialist at the Korea Institute for Industrial Economics & Trade. "This is bound to lead to cultural clashes with Americans. We've seen management churn in the past, and there's no reason to believe it will stop."

Source: D. Welch, D. Kiley, and M. Ihlwan, *BusinessWeek*, March 17, 2008, p. 48.

Discussion Questions

1. What motivators of individuals in Korea may not motivate people in the United States? How could a Korean manager encourage motivation in the United States?
2. Explain how Confucian philosophy may affect a manager's style of leadership.
3. On the basis of this case, discuss why it is important for managers to understand motivational differences across national borders and cultures.

What Is Motivation?

Managers talk about motivation constantly, and they work to improve the motivation of their subordinates in order to increase productivity and morale in the workplace. One theme runs through the previous chapters: Because people and societies differ in various ways, international managers must understand the significance of unusual circumstances and become culturally sensitive to differences in varied work environments. Managers of global corporations have firsthand knowledge, and some instinctively feel that cultural differences found in different parts of the world have important influences on how people feel when they work, what energizes them, and what makes them remain committed to their jobs and careers and companies. The motives for working differ widely, according to the important national and cultural values of each society.[1] However, before we can discuss the significance of cultural influences on motivation, we should define motivation.

Two thousand years ago, Confucius noted that all people are basically the same but they are motivated to do different things at different points in their lives. Recently, Honda Motor Company cofounder Takeo Fujisawa observed that while Japanese and American managers are 95 percent the same, they differ in the most important aspects. Philosophers from Germany, France, India, Greece, and other countries have all observed that differences in cultural upbringing makes a difference in how we think and how we behave in work organizations.

Motivation is the amount of effort that an employee is willing to put into work to accomplish an organizationally valued task. Motivation is a cognitive process; that is, it lies in the mind of the worker. It explains how workers get started on a task, how they maintain performance, why they keep working, and why they might quit working. Motivated workers have pleasant internal reactions while performing a task. They come to work earlier, put in longer hours, and do not mind "walking the extra mile" to get the job done. Another way of looking at motivation is to view it as the willingness to exert high levels of effort to accomplish organizational goals, to the extent that these efforts are rewarded.[2]

Managers cannot see motivation by observing employees, unless definite yardsticks measure the output of employees. An employee who produces 10 units an hour is probably twice as motivated as another employee who produces 5 units an hour, if other circumstances that affect productivity are identical in both situations. Motivation is not the only factor that affects productivity. Managers must take note of appropriate job descriptions that improve the employee's perceptions of the work role of the job, as well as job-relevant ability and other constraints on performance. New employees are unlikely to have a clear-cut perception of what is needed on the job in order to accomplish flawless performance. It takes some time for them to understand the job and to play an active role in removing various constraints that might hinder performance in one way or another. *Ability* is clearly the most important factor in performing a job. Ability reflects the cumulative influence of a multitude of work-related experiences that can be applied to a job to improve performance to a maximum level.[3]

Companies can also create work environments that facilitate productivity on the job. Global companies like Microsoft Corporation and Hewlett-Packard have created work environments in which one can report to work whenever one feels the impulse to contribute in a meaningful manner to a creative task. In the early 1980s, Apple Computers created work environments in which programmers and hardware engineers could arrive almost any time at the centers and design computers such as Apple I and Apple II. Such environments facilitate work performance and motivate workers to continue working for a long time without experiencing mental or physical fatigue.

Theories of Work Motivation

Why do we need theories of work motivation? People in all cultures, whether advanced industrialized countries or emergent economies or traditional cultures, have implicit theories to explain why people come to work, what they might want from work, and why they continue to work. However, the difficulty with these implicit theories is that they are not systematically developed and can be understood only as insightful "hunches," which, while helpful in some circumstances, are often at a loss to describe more than one situation.

Theories of motivation began to evolve in the United States and in some parts of Western Europe. You already know some of these theories, but a quick overview is helpful. We begin with the needs theories, outlined in Exhibit 11.1. These theories provide some important foundations for understanding patterns of motivation, not only in the United States, but in dissimilar cultures as well.

Recent research shows that individualistic cultures foster people to look at themselves in a highly context-free manner. In other words, people look at themselves primarily in terms of their interests, aspirations, and occupational accomplishments and do not necessarily link these processes with those of the groups they might have belonged to in the past or belong to now. This process is called *self-construal*. The motivation that employees experience in individualistic countries is strongly influenced by the degree to which they construe or conceptualize themselves in an independent manner. The tendency to engage in activities that are primarily geared toward developing the personal image of the individual worker or his or her occupational worthiness will be engaged in more than is the case in collectivistic cultures. Collectivistic cultures such as Japan, China, South Korea, India, and Brazil socialize individuals to construe or conceptualize the development of their personal selves in line with those of their peers.

A person does not seek to engage in activities in a highly independent fashion but takes the time to examine the relevance of engaging in those activities for the members of the group he or she belong to at present or might have belonged to in the past. *Self-actualization,* an important concept developed by Maslow that we are about to discuss next, is much less relevent in collectivistic cultures than it is in individualistic cultures like the United States, United Kingdom, Australia, Netherlands, and France. The point is that U.S. theories are the only theories we currently know of that provide some scientific foundations for the study of work motivation. The various concepts

EXHIBIT 11.1 Comparing Needs Theories of Motivation

Source: Adapted and expanded from S. L. McShane and M. A. Von Glinow, *Organizational Behavior*, 2nd ed. (New York: McGraw-Hill/Irwin, 2003), p. 135.

Rewards from the Job	Maslow's Needs Hierarchy Theory	Alderfer's ERG Theory	Herzberg's Motivator-Hygiene Theory	McClelland's Achievement Motivation Theory	
Opportunities for advancement Meaningful work Use of valued skills and abilities Opportunities for ongoing learning	Self-actualization	Growth	Motivators: Advancement Growth Achievement	Need for achievement	Generally referred to as higher-order needs and are fulfilled in professional, managerial, and creative positions
Acknowledgement of contributions Influence on work processes Respect and appreciation	Esteem			Need for power	
Supervisory support Co-worker support Social support from work	Affiliation	Relatedness	Hygiene factors: Working conditions Job security Salary	Need for affiliation	Generally referred to as middle-order needs and are fulfilled in administrative, technical, and clerical positions
Job security Fringe benefits Healthy working conditions	Security	Existence			
Basic pay	Physiological				Lower-order needs fulfilled in lower-level jobs

of the models are etic (see Chapter 4), but the degree of emphasis that is put on those concepts or factors differs considerably across borders and cultures.[4] Practical Insight 11.1 depicts one firm's global motivation practices.

Needs Theories

Maslow's Motivation Theory

Maslow suggested in the early 1950s that human beings are motivated by five basic needs and that these needs form a hierarchical structure.[5] According to this U.S.-based theory, the higher-order needs for self-esteem and self-actualization become activated and motivate behavior only after lower-order needs have been satisfied. For example, workers cannot feel motivated to perform on a job that requires complex learning skills if they are frightened about safety at work or do not get enough nutrition to sustain their bodily functions.

It is likely that two or three of the steps in Maslow's hierarchy are universal. However, the physical and economic environment in some countries might activate lower-level needs, thus making it difficult for the emergence of higher-order needs. In many countries, pressures of daily living preoccupy the minds of workers to such an extent that they are not able to move forward in the hierarchy of needs as proposed by

> **PRACTICAL INSIGHT 11.1**
>
> **EMPLOYEE MOTIVATION THE RITZ-CARLTON WAY**
> The upscale hotelier's staff meetings rely on techniques designed to engage staffers. Here's how you can incorporate them in your own shop.
>
> It didn't surprise me to find the Ritz-Carlton on *BusinessWeek*'s 2008 Customer Service Champs ranking (BusinessWeek.com, 2/21/08). When I was researching inspiring leaders, I spent time with Ritz-Carlton President Simon Cooper, who discussed how his company strives to engage its staff to increase employee satisfaction and improve customer service. I saw his strategies in practice when I attended staff meetings run by managers at the San Francisco Ritz-Carlton and described a few of them in a previous column (BusinessWeek.com, 2/13/07). Now, I've returned to my notes to expand on ways you can incorporate techniques from the upscale hotelier in your own company.
>
> **Share "Wow Stories"**
> Every day, employees of every department in every Ritz-Carlton hotel around the world gather for a 15-minute staff meeting where they share "wow stories." These are true stories of employee heroics that go above and beyond conventional customer service expectations. In one, a hotel chef in Bali found special eggs and milk for a guest with food allergies in a small grocery store in another country and had them flown to the hotel. In another, a hotel's laundry service failed to remove a stain on a guest's suit before the guest left. The hotel manager flew to the guest's house and personally delivered a reimbursement check for the cost of the suit.
>
> Telling stories in these pep talks accomplishes two goals. It reinforces a customer service skill the hotel is trying to encourage. Most important, it gives an employee "local fame." Employees want to be recognized in front of their peers. Giving them public recognition is a powerful motivator.
>
> **Demonstrate Passion**
> Moods are contagious. Managers who walk around with a smile on their face and demonstrate passion for their jobs have an uplifting effect on others. I attended a staff meeting for housekeepers at the San Francisco Ritz-Carlton one morning and discovered a group of employees whose happiness rivaled higher-paid employees in other professions. I quickly learned the enthusiasm started at the top. The supervisor was dressed impeccably in a three-button blue suit, white shirt, purple tie, and shined black shoes. His wardrobe communicated respect. "Good morning, everyone," he said enthusiastically. The housekeepers returned an energetic greeting. This manager was all smiles and showed respect for his team. He said they returned his commitment through their hard work.
>
> **Sell the Benefit**
> In every daily staff meeting, Ritz-Carlton managers reinforce one of 12 service values all employees are expected to embody on the job. On the day I attended a meeting in San Francisco, the theme was service value No.2: "I am always responsive

Maslow. We can see differences in environmental effects in countries such as Mexico, Nigeria, and central Asian republics, where global organizations have difficulty in finding highly trained workers.[6]

However, some of the general predictions of Maslow's theory do not apply across cultural and national borders. Some findings involving this theory of motivation, which has been useful in U.S. organizations, are conflicting. In countries where uncertainty avoidance is high, such as Greece and Japan, the need for security has been found to be more important for improving work motivation than the need for satisfying self-actualizing needs. The need for security in these countries dominates the thoughts of the workers and they rarely get beyond this stage of the hierarchy. On the other hand, in countries that are low in uncertainty avoidance, such as the United States, the United Kingdom, and New Zealand, individuals are more inclined to seek opportunities for satisfying their own self-actualizing needs because their needs for security are much lower and more easily met.

Contrasting with the U.S. pattern, satisfaction of interpersonal needs become more important in countries such as Denmark, Norway, and Sweden, which stress quality of life and social interrelatedness, qualities that are feminine in terms of cultural values.[7] In collectivistic countries such as Japan, Venezuela, Mexico, and Egypt, the need to satisfy group goals, which are often social in nature, is more important than it is in

to the expressed and unexpressed wishes and needs of our guests." The housekeepers were encouraged to discuss how this value applied to their daily tasks.

"What is an expressed wish?" the supervisor asked the group.

"If a guest asks for extra pillows," a woman said.

"That's exactly right," he said. "But it's the unexpressed wishes that create the Ritz-Carlton mystique," he continued, offering the example of a housekeeper who notices a champagne bottle sitting in melted ice and replaces the ice before being asked to do so. The question was then asked: "Why do we do it? Why do we go the extra mile?"

One housekeeper volunteered: "It offers a personal touch that shows we care."

"That's exactly right," another added. "It reflects our commitment to five-star service."

Employees need to understand how their daily actions have an impact on the customer. Use staff meetings to make the connection.

Ask for Feedback

Employees are encouraged to speak up during staff meetings. During a housekeeping meeting, the employees were debating the benefit of one cleaner over another. It seemed as though they preferred the old product over a new one. At first glance, it was a rather mundane discussion. But I noticed something about their supervisor. He was listening intently, as if the discussion were the most important thing in his life at the moment: nodding, maintaining eye contact, and asking questions. He showed genuine interest in the topic. If it is important to his staff, it is important to him. "Why do you think you have earned so much respect from your staff?" I later asked. "Because I listen to their concerns," the supervisor said. "And they know I will follow up."

Praise Effectively

Ritz-Carlton managers don't focus on what employees have done wrong but instead seek to help them improve on a given task. Supervisors use staff meetings to publicly praise employees. Criticism is done in private. One supervisor suggested sandwiching constructive criticism among the praise. "You did a great job this week cleaning the coffee pot," he would say, "but you're still struggling here. Let's work together on improving it." By offering the criticism in the middle of praise, he inspires his employees to exceed the expectations of the hotel's guests.

I chose to attend housekeeping meetings to make a key point: Motivation can and should take place everywhere within an organization. Simon Cooper cannot personally motivate each of his 35,000 employees worldwide, so it's up to his department managers to reinforce the brand and its values through daily interactions with their teams. Are your employees engaged? Are they inspired to follow your vision? Five-star service does not begin with them. It begins with you.

Source: Carmine Gallo, *BusinessWeek,* February 29, 2008.

---

individualistic countries such as the United States, the United Kingdom, and Australia.[8] In less developed countries, such as Nigeria and other eastern Africa nations, which depict high uncertainty avoidance, low individualism, high power distance, and relatively low emphasis on career success, community values dominate any individualistic tendencies, and condemnation of self-seeking individualism is common.[9] In fact, in some communities, self-seeking tendencies are considered to reflect mental abnormalities. While definitive conclusions are difficult to draw, one thing is certain: Maslow's theory cannot be applied universally to explain motivation patterns of workers or managers in countries that are different from the United States in cultural values.

ERG Theory

Alderfer developed the ERG (existence, relatedness, and growth) theory to provide a more simplified hierarchy of needs with the following three levels[10] (shown in Exhibit 11.1):

- **Growth needs**—similar to Maslow's needs for self-actualization and self-esteem.
- **Relatedness needs**—similar to Maslow's need for affiliation; these needs are fulfilled through meaningful and effective support from the work group.
- **Existence needs**—lower-order needs for security, safety, and survival.

Motivator–Hygiene/Intrinsic–Extrinsic Need Theory

The intrinsic–extrinsic dichotomy is a useful way to understand workforce motivation, regardless of the cultural context of the country involved. This thinking was developed by Herzberg (motivator–hygiene theory).[11] **Intrinsic factors** are concerned with opportunity for personal growth, development, and advancement, and they deal with the quality of work being performed. Intrinsic factors include complex learning and skill acquisition, as well as autonomy in decision making. Intrinsic factors tend to be more important in countries that are individualistic and low in uncertainty avoidance, such as the United States and the United Kingdom.

Extrinsic factors are concerned with the context of the workplace, such as level of pay, working conditions, and fringe benefits. Extrinsic factors are found to be more important in collectivistic and high uncertainty avoidance cultures, such as Zambia.[12] One's pay and fringe benefits can benefit the family and other important people in the in-group. Since the well-being of the in-group is of primary importance in collectivistic cultures, it makes sense for individuals in countries high in collectivism to be more concerned with extrinsic rewards from the workplace. Similarly, uncertainty avoidance can be dealt with more effectively if the worker gets appropriate extrinsic rewards from the workplace. Pay and medical benefits and other forms of financial compensation can lower the amount of uncertainty that a worker may face in life. Job dissatisfaction tends to increase when companies do *not* provide for these factors.[13] Adequate pay, medical insurance, and safety procedures in the workplace are examples of these extrinsic factors. The extrinsic and potentially demotivating factors largely correspond to the lower-order (physiological and safety) needs of Maslow.

Classifying needs to explain motivation and job satisfaction has been questioned in the U.S. context.[14] This process is more complicated in countries whose cultural values are different from those in the United States. For example, **organizational commitment** differs across cultures. Organizational commitment is the worker's involvement in identification with the work organization. Individuals in some cultures have been found to remain motivated on a particular job because of its value in sustaining commitments made in public, even though such commitments may be contrary to their self-interest.[15] For example, in India, if a manager has committed to work without pay on a government project for the benefit of the community, the manager will continue to work because of the public commitment. The job itself may be boring in terms of its intrinsic properties, but the manager will continue working on the project nevertheless.[16] Cultures that are more interested in quality of life, such as Sweden and Norway, and those that are more collectivistic, such as Egypt, Mexico, and India, focus on developing systems and work methods and restructuring employees into work groups to achieve increased work motivation and productivity.[17] Managers entering a new country to manage a venture should keenly observe local culture to determine which factors appear important in creating motivation and should not assume that their prior experience in the United States or other contexts is easily transferable.

Achievement Motivation Theory

The achievement motivation theory developed by McClelland during the 1960s has been highly influential in the United States.[18] Here, needs are learned through the variety of experiences that one undergoes in life. The research revealed that humans have three distinct patterns of needs: need for achievement, need for affiliation, and need for power.

The **need for achievement** reflects a desire to take on tasks and accomplish them satisfactorily. Individuals high in need for achievement enjoy challenges and thrive on stimulating environments. They prefer responsibility and the autonomy to pursue goals that they value, and they appreciate constructive feedback. Achievement motivation is high in the personality profiles of entrepreneurs and reflects the willingness to take risks. Employees with a high need for achievement tend to get more raises and promotions than those who are higher in their need for power or affiliation. Achievers are not always the best managers because they have difficulties working within hierarchies of organizations.

The **need for affiliation** reflects the desire of individuals to belong to a social group and to participate with others and create friendships. Individuals high in need for affiliation seek to enhance their sense of social esteem. They prefer harmony to individual achievements, seeking work environments that do not produce conflicts. These individuals do not like to get involved in difficult decisions that might result in unpleasant reactions from subordinates. They prefer to work in egalitarian organizations where the hierarchy is less restricting.

Individuals with a high **need for power** are comfortable in executive positions where they can make decisions in highly competitive situations. They place a high value on status and advancement. High power orientation may also reflect a strong tendency to lead and a willingness to accept responsibility for managing others, an attribute which reflects Hofstede's cultural dimension of masculinity. Unlike the need for achievement, the need for power is not necessarily associated with entrepreneurship, yet some with a high need for power have begun successful new ventures. This theory has generally found support in the U.S. context.

Countries that are inclined to foster a higher need for achievement in individuals, such as the United States, experience higher rates of economic growth. However, research has shown that emphasis on individual achievement can be considered an undesirable tendency and may even be perceived as antisocial in countries such as China, Indonesia, Malaysia, and perhaps in Africa and Latin America.[19] In paternalistic societies, such as India, achievement may not be valued if it is not part of the immediate family or close referent group, because of the close ties to group goals at the expense of personal goals. In hierarchical cultures, such as Mexico, the need for achievement is considered to be destructive, because conformity to the existing social order and one's duty to the community are valued more. Individuals with a high need for power are more valued for leadership positions, and managers with a high need for affiliation are regarded more favorably by their subordinates. This tendency has been observed in Mexico and especially among the Islamic cultures in Southeast Asia.[20] In Nordic countries, as well as in some Latin nations, motivation for both managers and subordinates reflects social esteem, human interaction, and friendship bonds more strongly than it does in other countries that are lower on the dimension of femininity, another dimension of Hofstede.[21]

Applicability of Needs Theories across Borders and Cultures

The applicability of these needs theories across cultures is somewhat limited by the fact that most researchers have focused on higher-order needs (need for achievement, need for self-actualization, and growth needs) and frequently ignore the lower-order needs.[22] The world's working population largely remains focused on trying to fulfill the lower-order needs of job security, safety, and good pay for maintaining their families, especially in developing and emerging nations (e.g., Mexico, India, China, and Brazil) as well as Romania, Bulgaria, and Poland. Kenyan and Malawi managers emphasize security needs and not higher-order needs.[23] Russian managers have been found to emphasize needs for security and social needs as opposed to higher-order needs.[24] In fact, research shows that the hierarchy of needs proposed by Maslow is generally valid with middle-class, white, Anglo-Saxon Americans and western Europeans but does not represent the hierarchy found in other parts of the world.[25] Economic factors, ecological conditions, and traditions and customs, along with dominant cultural values, significantly influence the hierarchy of needs.

In the collectivistic contexts of eastern Asia, achievement motivation is best understood on a group basis as a driving force, as opposed to individually based achievement motivation. In many environments, Japan in particular, individual achievement is neither valued highly nor rewarded. The individual desire to excel in the job at the expense of others may be strongly sanctioned.[26] Achievement motivation is more quickly aroused in individualistic countries than in more collectivistic countries.[27] Therefore, managers of international and global corporations should pay special attention to the selective influences of cultural context before implementing U.S.-based theories of motivation.

Process Theories

In contrast to the needs theories, which explain why people have different needs in their lives and careers, process theories are designed to explain how these needs deficiencies are translated into motivation that energizes performance. Three widely known process theories of motivation are expectancy theory, equity theory, and goal-setting theory. We briefly discuss them because they have been useful in explaining different patterns of motivation in different parts of the world. Managers of multinational corporations should be aware of the basic mechanisms illustrated in these theories.

Expectancy Theory

Expectancy theory proposes that individuals are driven by the expectations that their acts will produce certain anticipated results and rewards.[28] Expectancy theory helps us identify the significance of an individual's perception of the link between effort and performance, as well as of the manager's ability to identify and provide desired rewards. Expectancy theory has advanced our knowledge of motivational processes in the U.S. context, but application of this theory is subject to some cross-cultural variations. According to expectancy theory, motivation is the result of:[29]

- The expectancy that an effort will result in the desired level of performance.
- The likelihood that the performance will be linked with important intrinsic and extrinsic outcomes (first- and second-level outcomes).
- The value or attractiveness of the outcome or reward to the individual.

First-level outcomes are those that derive directly from performing the work itself, such as monetary rewards and job satisfaction. Second-level outcomes are those that are derived from the first-level outcomes, such as buying a car or house with the money earned, improvement of personal self-esteem, and improved quality of life.

Performance can be understood as a function of motivation, ability, role perception, and organizational factors that facilitate work, as follows:

$$\text{Work performance} = f(\text{Motivation} \times \text{Job ability} \times \text{Job perception} \times \text{Situational contraints})$$

In some countries, workers who are motivated and have appropriate cumulative experiences to do well on the job do not get to perform at a high level because they lack the kind of support they need from the workplace and often lack the technology that would assist them.

Motivation, in its turn, is a function of two kinds of beliefs and the importance or the attractiveness of the rewards. In other words, motivation is

$$\text{Motivation} = f(\text{Effort} \rightarrow \text{Performance}) \times (\text{Performance} \rightarrow \text{Rewards}) \times \text{Value of rewards}$$

This formulation, which has been tested in the United States and western Europe, has generally been found to accurately portray the degree of work motivation that employees experience when they believe (1) that there is a clear link between their effort and accomplishment of adequate performance on the job (i.e., expectancy) and (2) that performance leads to valuable rewards (i.e., instrumentality).[30]

Motivation is very much related to the features of one's work and nonwork life. Both of these contexts are greatly influenced by cultural variables, which affect emotional predispositions and behaviors of individuals and groups on the job. The frameworks presented in Chapter 4 are helpful and should be kept in mind as we try to understand the scope of applicability of these theories in non-U.S. contexts.

As shown in Exhibit 11.2, expectancy theory explains motivation as several steps. The first is the worker's expectation that he or she can successfully perform the job with the effort expected. The next step is the expectation of receiving the outcome promised if the performance is successful. First-level outcomes are important, but some are important only because they lead to others. For some workers, pay is valuable as a first-level outcome because of its purchasing value; for others, it has a secondary outcome, such as being a way to keep score with others ("I make more than ———"). Each outcome (at both the first level and the second level) has a *valence,* that is, a value to the worker. Values are different for each worker and for each outcome. For example, some workers value praise more than others. Extrinsic outcomes are physical outcomes such as money. Intrinsic outcomes are higher-level outcomes, such as self-esteem.

In countries that are individualistic, employees see their relationship with the organization from a more calculated and rational perspective, which implies that if the link between their performance and outcomes is unclear or lacking, they feel demotivated and begin to look for opportunities elsewhere. In collectivistic countries, the ties between the individual and the organization have a moral component.[31] Individuals

EXHIBIT 11.2 The Expectancy Model of Motivation

Source: From J. R. Hackman, E. E. Lawler, and L. W. Porter, eds., *Perspectives on Behavior in Organization* (New York: McGraw-Hill, 1977), p. 34. Copyright © 1994 The McGraw-Hill Companies, Inc. Reprinted with permission.

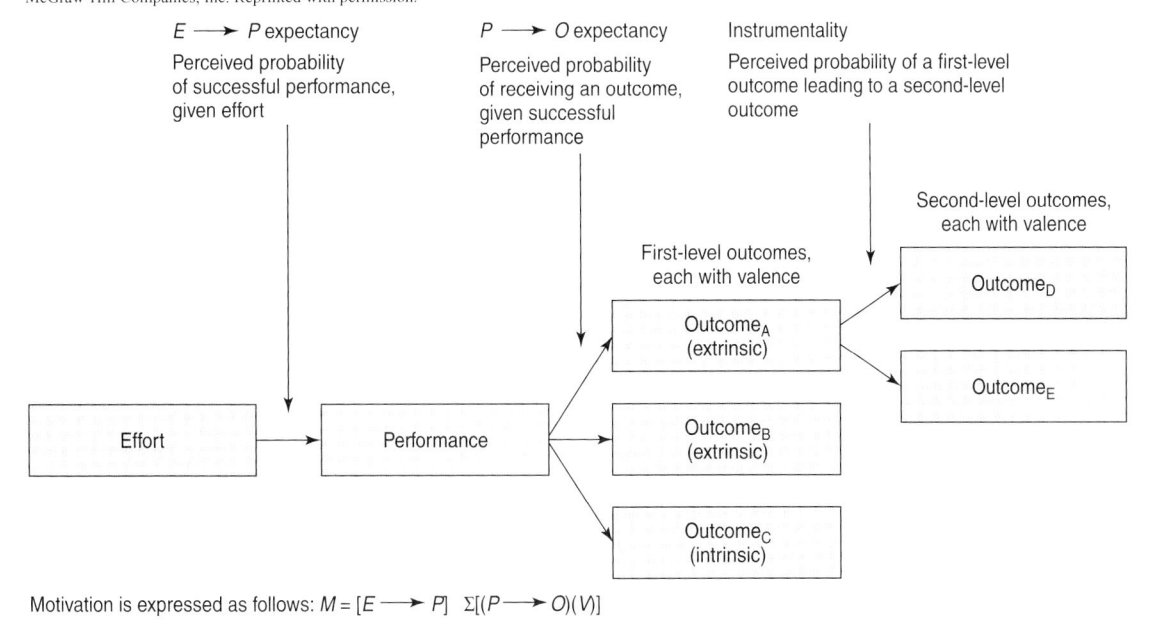

$E \longrightarrow P$ expectancy
Perceived probability of successful performance, given effort

$P \longrightarrow O$ expectancy
Perceived probability of receiving an outcome, given successful performance

Instrumentality
Perceived probability of a first-level outcome leading to a second-level outcome

Effort → Performance → First-level outcomes, each with valence:
- Outcome$_A$ (extrinsic)
- Outcome$_B$ (extrinsic)
- Outcome$_C$ (intrinsic)

Second-level outcomes, each with valence:
- Outcome$_D$
- Outcome$_E$

Outcome$_A$ leads to Outcome$_D$ and Outcome$_E$.

Motivation is expressed as follows: $M = [E \longrightarrow P] \; \Sigma[(P \longrightarrow O)(V)]$

using a moral component in their commitment are likely to be more tolerant, even if they do not see a strong link between their performance and outcomes. Personal ties with managers, owners, and co-workers are much more important in collectivistic contexts, where they act as guides for enhancing motivation. Therefore, application of expectancy theory in all contexts is not possible.

In many collectivistic countries, employees expect their firms to take care of their personal needs, whereas in the United States and other individualistic countries, employees have no such expectations. In Latin America, especially Brazil, where personal and work lives are highly integrated, major companies frequently assist their employees with personal financial problems such as financial difficulties that might arise from family illness.

Equity Theory

The basic premise of the equity theory of motivation, developed by Adams,[32] is that people try to balance their inputs and outcomes in relation to those of others. Inputs include an employee's level of education, work experience, personal characteristics, and loyalty to the company. Outcomes are derived in the context of working, such as pay, benefits, working conditions, co-worker relationships, and opportunities for growth. Each person has his or her own perception regarding the value of the inputs and outcomes. Motivation results when an employee compares inputs with the outcomes received. Each individual compares his or her outcomes with those of another person, called a "comparison other." When the ratio of the individual to the comparison other is about equal, little motivation is likely.

Motivation results when the two outcomes are unequal, resulting in a tension or discomfort that encourages the employee to equalize the ratio. This is seen in the following equation:

$$\frac{\text{Outcomes}_{self}}{\text{Inputs}_{self}} = \frac{\text{Outcomes}_{other}}{\text{Inputs}_{other}}$$

An important point to consider is that the norms regarding what is equitable differ from country to country. Among the more important norms that compete with the **norm of equity**, which is strongly emphasized in individualistic cultures of the West, are the norm of need and the norm of equality.[33] The **norm of need** emphasizes distribution of rewards according to the needs of employees. The **norm of equality** is concerned with distribution of equal rewards to everyone performing the same work, usually in a group context. When a person is severely deprived, the only norm that may make sense is the norm of need. In informal situations, the equality norm is more important in the distribution of rewards. For example, at a party it is assumed that resources such as food are shared equally, rather than according to the contributions each makes to the party. This equality norm is also more prevalent in work contexts characterized by strong loyalty to the in-group, which is emphasized in collectivistic cultures.

Goal-Setting Theory

Many companies set goals for employees to motivate them and clarify role perceptions.[34] However, goal setting involves much more than simply telling employees to do their best. It is a process of various steps to maximize effort toward achieving goals.[35] When applied properly, goal-setting techniques require adequate participation from both the employee and the supervisor in specifying and developing the goals while ensuring that the goals are challenging and achievable. It also requires feedback from both the employee and the supervisor regarding any problems that might arise in the process of achieving goals. This process should be separated from the pay process to maximize goal achievement and minimize less than optimal goal setting. Often, companies use management-by-objective (MBO) processes to formalize this theory application.[36] Use of MBO intensifies the effort of the employees to practice specific behaviors that should enable them to achieve their goals.[37]

Application of Process Theories across Borders and Cultures

Hulin and Triandis emphasized that in designing reward systems of global organizations, managers should take a close look at how cultural, subcultural, demographic, and personal factors influence motivational and job satisfaction outcomes.[38] For example, motivations of workers in collectivistic countries include:

- Adjustment of personal needs relative to the needs of the in-group.
- Preference for group goal setting and easier acceptance of assigned goals.
- Preference for group-based incentives and rewards.

In contrast, individualists are less sensitive to the needs of others with whom they work. Also, they prefer goals that are individually negotiated and do not easily tolerate group-based incentives.[39] Countries that are horizontal collectivistic (see Chapter 4) in orientation use group goals, whereas vertical collectivistic countries accept assigned goals without a lot of discussion.[40] To compete with the Japanese, many U.S. companies implemented quality circles and teamwork to improve motivation and performance of groups. However, these attempts have been mostly unsuccessful because of a lack of mutual commitment of members of work groups as well as commitment between work groups and the organization.[41]

Exchanges in individualistic cultures are based on *equity,* which means that individuals are rewarded on the basis of contributions measured by annual or semiannual performance appraisals. The more horizontal the culture is, the more likely that the principle of equality will guide the distribution of rewards. Collectivists apply the principle of equality when exchanging rewards with members of in-groups, but they pay more attention to equity when dealing with out-groups.[42] Equality is associated with harmony, solidarity, and good feelings for members of in-groups. On the other hand, equity leads to enhancement of individual-level productivity, competition with members of the work group, and continuous attention to individual career goals. All other research using concepts from process theories has shown that the psychological significance of rewards works differently in collectivistic and feminine societies than in individualistic and masculine societies.

One country stands apart from this, however. Japan, the world's second-largest economy, built its solid economic growth on collectivistic norms of cooperation, harmony, and lifetime commitment. The CEO of Nissan, the second-largest automotive manufacturer in Japan, earns about 10 times more than the lowest-paid worker. On the other hand, the CEO of Ford, the second-largest automotive manufacturer in the United States, earns over 540 times more than the lowest-paid worker.[43]

The Meaning of Working across Nations and Cultures

The concern that U.S.-based studies may not be applicable in all cultural contexts was addressed in the **Meaning of Working (MOW) study.**[44] This study examined what working means to people in Japan, Yugoslavia, Israel, the United States, Belgium, the Netherlands, Britain, and Germany. The researchers assessed the meaning using three key concepts:

1. **Work centrality.** The degree of general importance and value attributed to the working role in an individual's life.
2. **Societal norms about working.** The degree of normative beliefs and expectations regarding entitlement (specific rights) and obligations (duties) attached to working. The entitlement norm represents the underlying work rights of individuals and work-related responsibilities of organizations and society toward individuals. "This norm reflects notions that all members of society are entitled to meaningful and interesting work, proper training to obtain and continue in such work, and the right to participate in work/method decisions."[45] The obligation norm reflects the duties and responsibilities that individuals have in their work roles. "This norm includes the notions that everyone has a duty to contribute to society by working, a duty to save for their own future, and the duty to value one's work, whatever its nature."[46]
3. **Work goals.** Work-related outcomes preferred by individuals in the entire span of working life. The 11 goals studied included such things as interesting work, good pay, good job security, opportunity to learn, and a good match between the worker and the job.[47]

The clear implication of the MOW research study was that the higher the mean work centrality score, the more motivated and committed the workers are in that society. Of obvious importance to managers is that the score provides specific reasons for valuing work and the pattern of needs that working satisfies in different societies. Exhibit 11.3 shows that the mean centrality score was highest in Japan (7.78) and lowest in Britain (6.36).

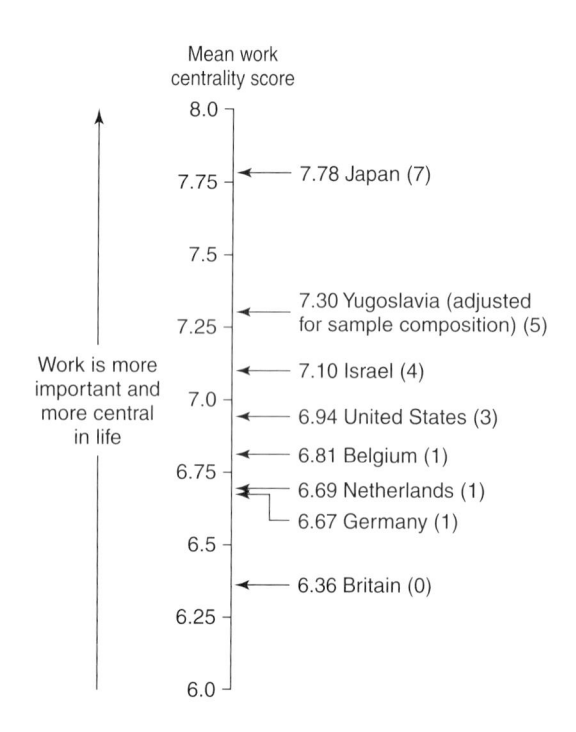

The relative importance of work goals is illustrated in Exhibit 11.4. In four countries, interesting work was ranked highest out of 11 possible work goals. The importance of pay was highest in Britain (ranked 2 of 11) and in Germany (ranked 1 of 11).

EXHIBIT 11.3
Work Centrality Scores

Source: Reprinted from *The Meaning of Work: An International Perspective*, MOW International Research Team. Copyright © 1987, with permission from Elsevier.

Mean work centrality score

- 7.78 Japan (7)
- 7.30 Yugoslavia (adjusted for sample composition) (5)
- 7.10 Israel (4)
- 6.94 United States (3)
- 6.81 Belgium (1)
- 6.69 Netherlands (1)
- 6.67 Germany (1)
- 6.36 Britain (0)

Work is more important and more central in life

EXHIBIT 11.4 The Importance of Work Goals

Source: Reprinted from *The Meaning of Work: An International Perspective,* MOW International Research Team. Copyright © 1987, with permission from Elsevier.

	Countries															
Work Goals	Belgium (N = 446)		Germany (N = 1248)		Israel (N = 772)		Japan (N = 2897)		Netherlands (N = 967)		United States (N = 988)		Yugoslavia (N = 512)*		Britain (N = 742)	
Interesting work	8.25	1	7.26	3	6.75	1	7.38	2	7.59	2	7.41	1	7.47	2	8.02	1
Good pay	7.13	2	7.73	1	6.60	3	6.56	5	6.27	5	6.82	2	6.73	3	7.80	2
Good interpersonal relations	6.34	5	6.43	4	6.67	2	6.39	6	7.19	3	6.08	7	7.52	1	6.33	4
Good job security	6.80	3	7.57	2	5.22	10	6.71	4	5.68	7	6.30	3	5.21	9	7.12	3
A good match between you and your job	5.77	8	6.09	5	5.61	6	7.83	1	6.17	6	6.19	4	6.49	5	5.63	6
A lot of autonomy	6.56	4	5.66	8	6.00	4	6.89	3	7.61	1	5.79	8	5.42	8	4.69	10
Opportunity to learn	5.80	7	4.97	9	5.83	5	6.26	7	5.38	9	6.16	5	6.61	4	5.55	8
A lot of variety	5.96	6	5.71	6	4.89	11	5.05	9	6.86	4	6.10	6	5.62	7	5.62	7
Convenient work hours	4.71	9	5.71	6	5.53	7	5.46	8	5.59	8	5.25	9	5.01	10	6.11	5
Good physical working conditions	4.19	11	4.39	11	5.28	9	4.18	10	5.03	10	4.84	11	5.94	6	4.87	9
Good opportunity for upgrading or promotion	4.49	10	4.48	10	5.29	8	3.33	11	3.31	11	5.08	10	4.00	11	4.27	11

Note: Mean ranks. The rank of each work goal within a given country. Rank 1 is the *most* important work goal for a country, while rank 11 is the *least* important work goal for a country.

*Combined target group data were used for Yugoslavia.

The importance of achieving a good match between the worker and the job was highest in Japan and lowest in Belgium. The MOW study also found that importance of work remained fairly constant in the United States from immediately after World War II until the early 1980s. In Britain, the centrality of work declined from after World War II to the early 1980s, attributed to the strong influence of unions.

While the results might be different today, due to increased pressures to achieve uniform management practices in multinational and global corporations, the MOW study highlights an important fact: Individuals differ in their emphasis on the meaning of working, and such differences are rooted in national and cultural differences.

When a manager of a subsidiary located in a culture which is dissimilar to his or her home-country culture disregards the importance of these cultural differences, the result is likely to be demotivating and frustrating for employees. In Thailand, for example, the introduction of an individual merit bonus plan for merit pay raises for individuals, which ran contrary to the societal norm of group-based cooperation and incentive in the workplace, failed to improve productivity and resulted in a decline of morale.[48] Managers must recognize the importance of needs, goals, values, and expectations of culturally dissimilar employees. People in every society are driven to achieve goals and fulfill needs according to their cultural preferences and values, but what those goals and needs are may not always be clear.

Applying Cultural Frameworks

Before we can attempt to understand the influences of cultural factors, ecological factors, and the level of economic development on the process of generating work motivation, we need to examine the World Values Survey.[49] This survey summarizes the attitudes of

EXHIBIT 11.5 Ranking of Top Four Work Characteristics in Nine Countries

Source: Adapted from R. Inglehart et al., *World Values Surveys and European Values Surveys, 1981-1984, 1990-1993, and 1993-1997* (Institute for Social Research, 2000). Reprinted with permission.

Work Values	United States	Germany	Turkey	Russia	Japan	Peru	Nigeria	India	China
Generous holidays	1	1	1	3		1	1	1	1
Job respected	2	2			1		4		
Good hours	3	3	4	4	4	3	2	4	
Use initiative	4			2	2		3	2	3
Responsibility		4	3	1					2
Interesting job			2			2		3	4
Achieve something					3	4			

people toward work and life in 50 countries inhabited by more than three-fourths of the world's population. As shown in Exhibit 11.5, the relative importance of work characteristics varies in nine countries located in different continents. This shows that in some societies work is central and absorbs much of a person's life. People in these societies are willing to work very hard and have a strong commitment to success at work.

Americans work the longest number of hours in a year, followed by the Japanese.[50] In fact, as globalization encompasses more aspects of American life, the distinction between doing work at home and doing it at the office has almost disappeared. Immigrants (legal residents born outside the United States) perceived Americans to be excessively concerned with performing activities in their work life that enhance their feelings of self-worth.[51] Work, for Americans, expands into the family arena, and when strong conflicts arise because of the simultaneous pursuit of work and personal life goals, work goals take precedence over family life. Taking this issue further, Florida analyzed the development of a new class of workers, which he called "the creative class," who are professionals somewhat akin to white-collar workers but their every waking hour is packed with work activities, most of which they truly enjoy.[52] These professionals process symbols and tend to be attracted to companies that allow creative expression at work, regardless of other concerns.

The Role of Cultural Variations in Work Motivation and Job Satisfaction

The amount of motivation or excitement that individuals experience is very much a product of the demands and joys of work and personal life. The context of work and personal life is highly influenced by ecological factors, societal culture, and the level of economic development of the country in which one works. Political frameworks, as discussed in Chapter 3, also provide important influences. For example, workers from East Germany who worked for over half a century under the Soviet communist system developed patterns of motivation very different from those of West German workers.[53]

To make meaningful and practical conclusions about the role of motivation in the international context, it is useful to apply Hofstede's research regarding individualism–collectivism, uncertainty avoidance, power distance, masculinity–femininity, and long-term versus short-term orientation.[54] Exhibit 11.6 shows the role of cultural variations in the meaning of work and work motivation.

Individualism–Collectivism

Countries that are high in individualism are likely to have more people who are motivated by opportunities for individual achievement and increased autonomy on

EXHIBIT 11.6 The Role of Cultural Variations in the Meaning of Work and Work Motivation

Source: Adapted and expanded from R. M. Steers and C. J. Sanchez-Runde, "Culture, Motivation, and Work Behavior," in M. J. Gannon and K. L. Newman, eds., *Blackwell Handbook of Cross-Cultural Management* (Oxford, UK: Blackwell Business, 2003), p. 194.

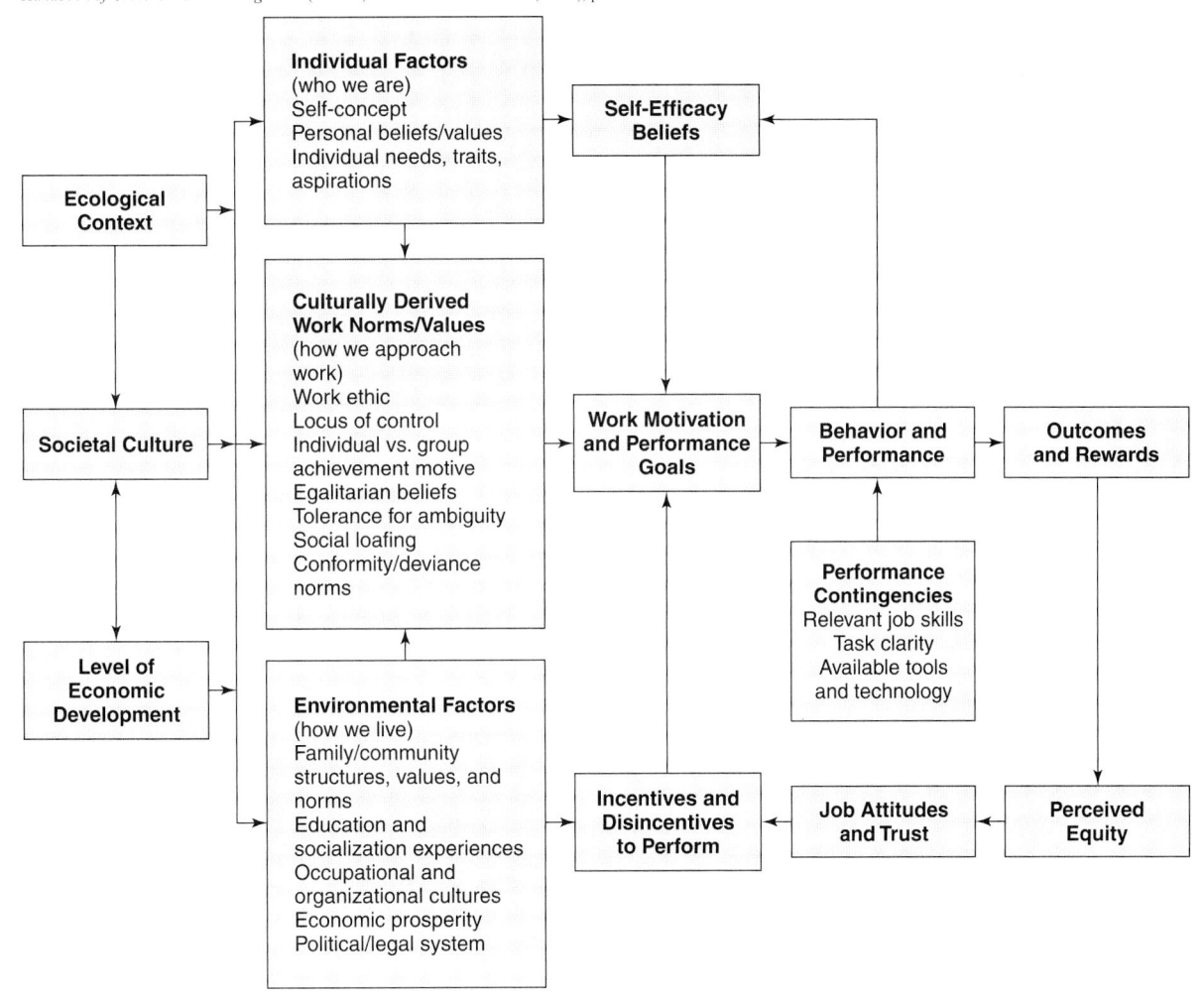

the job than do countries that are high in collectivism, which are likely to have more people who are motivated by work designed to sustain group goals and community-based activities and rewards. Performance by individualists who were working in groups was lower than the performance of individualists working alone.[55] In contrast, collectivists performed better while working in groups than they did when working alone.

Power Distance

The decision structures within the organization influence the relationship between power distance and process of work motivation. High power distance countries have many layers of management and a large proportion of supervisory personnel. Subordinates rely on formal rules and regulations in performing tasks and are not likely to be consulted by their supervisors in designing work and reward systems. In contrast, in low power distance countries, hierarchy is de-emphasized, and when it does exist, it is for convenience and only temporary. Subordinates expect flexibility in performing tasks and expect to be consulted in the design of work and reward systems. Intrinsic motivation is easily fostered in low power distance countries, and creative tendencies are strongly encouraged by supervisors who do not explicitly supervise the day-to-day performance of subordinates. Research by Peterson and his colleagues found that unclear expectations about how to perform the job, called **role ambiguity,** and excessive work, called **role overload,** are generally higher in cultures with high power distance.[56] These two characteristics, often called *work-related stressors,* can reduce work motivation, especially creativity and innovation. The ability to influence work conditions improved reactions to strains experienced at work.[57]

Uncertainty Avoidance

Individuals in high uncertainty avoidance countries generally have a high need for job security and are unwilling to take risks and make independent decisions. In these countries, subordinates expect managers to make decisions and then give explicit instructions, which reduces the potential for creativity and innovation. A preference for tasks with calculated risks and continuous problem solving characterizes low uncertainty avoidance countries. In fact, even the themes of traditional stories reflect higher levels of achievement motivation in low uncertainty avoidance countries in contrast to those in high uncertainty avoidance countries, which reflect strong security motivations.[58] The differences between the two preferences have clear implications for work motivation, job satisfaction, and organizational commitment.[59] In countries in which individuals are able to engage in appropriate problem-solving strategies in the workplace, they experienced lower levels of strain.[60] In general, when people are strongly motivated in both intrinsic and extrinsic senses, they are likely to do better in their careers and to progress toward further growth. Progress is usually more rapid in low uncertainty avoidance countries.

Masculinity–Femininity

High degrees of masculinity suggest that most people will be comfortable with traditional divisions of work and nonwork roles. *Work roles* consist of duties and responsibilities in the work organization, such as the role of nurse, mechanic, or manager. *Nonwork roles* are roles that individuals play outside the context of the work organization, such as the role of father, mother, husband, wife, sister, and friend. Work and nonwork roles tend to be distinct in masculine societies. In feminine cultures, the boundaries between work and nonwork roles are more flexible. Because of this, people feel motivated by having accommodating work schedules, such as flextime, part-time, and shift work, and they prefer jobs that nurture quality of work life. Competition, as a societal norm for sustaining motivation, is higher in masculine than feminine countries.[61] While the significance of this cultural dimension has not been widely examined, Hofstede maintains that it has important implications for understanding variations of the quality of work life around the globe. For example, Sweden and Norway are feminine countries in which the quality of work life and the sociotechnical method of improving work processes are emphasized. In contrast, in masculine countries, such as the United States and Germany, job design processes are geared toward sustaining performance rather than quality of work life.[62]

Long-Term versus Short-Term Orientation

Countries emphasizing short-term orientation foster short-term results, that is, the immediate or intermediate bottom line, as opposed to those emphasizing long-term orientation. Short-term virtues and norms about workplace values are emphasized,

PRACTICAL INSIGHT 11.2

TREAT EMPLOYEES RIGHT IN TOUGH TIMES
If employees really are your company's most important asset, mass layoffs and salary freezes are a poor way to show it.

Time after time, I have heard senior managers say: "People are my organization's most important asset," or "Employees are No. 1 in my organization." But I'm fed up being told that, and I don't want to hear it anymore.

Yes, praise for employees sounds good. But even when the economy is strong, there's an enormous gap between the rhetoric and the reality in many companies. Now that the economy is turning down, companies face a tough test in demonstrating how important their people are to them.

Often the first reaction of companies to hard times is to reduce labor costs. It's pretty much expected that they will lay off employees and freeze or reduce wages and benefits. This is probably the right move when human capital is not a key source of competitive advantage. But what about when it is—such as at knowledge-work companies where employees are expected to add significant value to products and services? In those kinds of businesses, it hardly seems wise to focus on cutting labor costs and decreasing a key asset. Rather, it makes much more sense to think of an economic downturn as a chance to gain or increase a competitive advantage that is based on human capital.

Down times in the economy create a buyer's market in talent, just as they create a buyer's market in real estate. Human capital-focused companies realize this and see downturns as a chance to raise the quality of their most important asset—their human capital. The most obvious way is by hiring individuals who, in good times, are not within their reach or are very difficult to recruit. Because they see people being laid off in their companies and are told salaries are frozen, they will listen to job offers that in good times they wouldn't.

But even in a downturn people won't necessarily take a low-ball offer, even if things are tough in their company. They may want to hang on because they have high seniority. Thus, unless a company is doing very well in the downturn, like Google (GOOG), it may have to offer them a higher salary to recruit them.

In the best of all scenarios, even in a downturn, a company can afford to hire new talent without reducing present staff; but if that's not the case, there is nothing wrong with making some performance-based reductions in existing staff while recruiting new talent. If this is executed well, it can simultaneously serve to reinforce a company's emphasis on performance while upgrading its talent.

But what if an organization needs to reduce its head count and it is not obvious that this can be done by eliminating sub-par performers? In this case, a company's objective should be to reduce its staff in a way that will not harm but may in fact enhance its employer brand.

For example, in the dot-com downturn, Cisco (CSCO) took a number of steps to ensure it would continue to be seen as a good employer even though it had to reduce its workforce. The company offered sabbaticals to some of its employees and offered to pay partial salaries to laid-off workers who went to work for charities and community ventures. It also helped subsidize the continuing education of former employees who wanted to advance their skills or change careers. Not surprisingly, when it came time for Cisco to start hiring again, it had no problem attracting a very talented pool of applicants because it was seen as a good place to work.

The Cisco approach isn't right for all companies, but every company needs to consider the impact that cost-reduction actions can have on its brand as an employer. If handled poorly, even small reductions can have a big long-term impact.

Witness Northwest Airlines (NWA). Its management recently sent a booklet to employees subject to a layoff, advising them how they could save money after being laid off. Among the things included in the *101 Ways to Save Money* booklet were buying jewelry at pawnshops, getting auto parts at junkyards, taking shorter showers, and finding valuable things in the trash by "dumpster diving"!

Employee outrage followed the distribution of this would-be helpful booklet. Management apologized for issuing it, but the damage had been done. Indeed, one of the positive outcomes of the proposed Delta/Northwest merger may be the disappearance of the Northwest employer brand.

So far, it doesn't appear that U.S. companies are responding to the current downturn as if people are their most important asset. More and more companies are reporting layoffs and salary freezes. But if your company wants to make people your most important asset, you can strengthen the company and prove that you mean what you say. The key question is, what kind of company will yours be? Will you take advantage of this opportunity to improve your talent level and strategic capabilities?

Source: Edward E. Lawler III, *BusinessWeek*, June 5, 2008.

---

resulting in employees valuing work outcomes that satisfy immediate needs.[63] Compensation schemes and reward systems should reflect these differences in orientation in order to enhance motivation, job satisfaction, and organizational commitment. The idea of encouraging good work habits is a constant across cultures, as shown in Practical Insight 11.2

Motivation in International and Global Corporations

International and global companies are culturally diverse organizations that require extensive coordination of practices from a variety of perspectives. Subsidiaries located in different parts of the world provide interesting insights as well as challenges in the way motivation in these companies should be understood and managed. Even within a country context, if the country is culturally diverse, such as the United States, or is in the process of becoming diverse, such as the United Kingdom, France, and Germany, management of conflicting values, norms, and attitudes becomes important. Therefore, the framework for managing a globally diverse workforce to enhance motivation is not significantly different from that of addressing issues on a domestic scale, but the range of issues is more complicated in some contexts. National characteristics and cultural characteristics interact in the design of effective incentive systems. For example, countries that are isolated geographically and have the cultural value of social needs tend to design rewards that enhance social interaction as an incentive for motivation.[64] Managers of global corporations need to pay attention to the combination of national and cultural characteristics before designing incentive systems and jobs. In some cultures, rewards may be given in the form of individual bonuses based on performance compensation systems, whereas in other cultures bonuses and performance incentive systems are not highly valued by workers. In the Netherlands and Sweden, for example, bonuses are not regarded as highly as is time off from work, enabling the worker to deal with nonwork obligations.

Sirota and Greenwood studied the work goals of 19,000 employees in a large multinational electrical equipment manufacturing company, operating in 46 countries.[65] In every country, the four most important goals were:

- Achievement, especially individual achievement.
- Quality of the immediate work environment.
- General features of the organization.
- Employment conditions, such as pay and work hours.

However, there were some major differences among the countries:

- English-speaking countries ranked higher on their emphasis for individual achievement and lower on their need for security.
- French-speaking countries gave greater emphasis to security and less to challenging work.
- Northern European countries put more emphasis on job accomplishment and less on getting ahead. There was also greater concern for people and less for the organization itself—it was important to separate personal lives from the influence of work lives.
- In Latin American and southern European countries, individual achievement as an organizational reward was less important than job security, and fringe benefits are important in both of these groups.
- Getting ahead was important in Germany, along with an emphasis on security and fringe benefits.
- Interestingly, Japan was low on individual achievement but ranked job-related challenges high. The need for job autonomy was lowest in Japan, but there was a strong emphasis on good working conditions and a friendly work environment.

What Is Leadership?

One of the most challenging tasks that international managers face is the need to work with and lead people of different national and cultural backgrounds. The process of leading others to accomplish tasks effectively is one of the most complex yet least understood areas of management. In the remainder of this chapter, we examine the concept and theories of leadership as they evolved in Western countries, particularly in the United States, and analyze their suitability in other nations and cultures.

Managers of multinational and global corporations need to understand the factors that enable the manager to be an effective leader not only in Western countries but also in non-Western countries. Examples of indigenous and non-Western theories of leadership need to be understood to enhance this process, and we discuss examples of these approaches as well.

Leadership has existed as a concept since the beginning of recorded history, but the word *leadership* seems to be relatively new. Descriptions of great leaders who have accomplished important goals for their followers and succeeded despite significant hardships exist in culturally diverse books and manuscripts, such as Homer's *Iliad,* the Indian *Gita,* the Bible and other religious texts, including the writings of Confucius. Powerful, influential leaders have moved masses and accomplished objectives that ordinary men and women might find impossible.

Despite 50 years of research on this topic, no generally accepted definition of leadership exists.[66] Generally, **leadership** is defined as the process of influencing and motivating people and providing a work environment that enables them to accomplish their group or organizational objectives. Effective leaders create appropriate conditions to help groups of people define their goals and find appropriate ways of achieving them.[67] Definitions given by researchers in the West tend to focus on the ability of individuals to influence their followers toward goal accomplishment.[68] Acceptance of this definition seems to be growing in different parts of the world; however, differences rooted in beliefs, attitudes, values, and norms present important challenges in understanding the importance of leadership in different nations and cultures.[69] Terms for leaders include boss, administrator, supervisor, director, manager, coach, head, chief, chair, master. In the United States, distinctions in titles, such as assistant vice president, managing director, division head, senior vice president, and president have a great deal of meaning. Not all countries make such fine distinctions between ranks as is found in U.S. corporations.

The difference between being a leader and assuming other organizational roles is the degree of influence that leaders have over their followers. Effective leaders tend to exercise both substantial and subtle influence over their followers to perform actions that go beyond simple compliance with their job descriptions.[70] Administrators and managers can get routine tasks accomplished without practicing acts of leadership, but tasks that force individuals to go beyond the normal requirements of their jobs demand the act of leadership. Effective leaders achieve effective group and organizational performance by emphasizing creativity and involvement of the followers over the long term. Their vision tends to have significant appeal for a large majority of their followers, and such vision has the potential to transform a collection of individuals into a group that can accomplish tasks with a sense of continued commitment and satisfaction.

No matter how leadership is defined around the world, only about 8 percent of executives in large firms think that their organizations employ a sufficient number of leaders.[71] Programs for enhancing leadership skills of managers and supervisors exist in both large and small corporations. Universities and many consulting organizations have programs to train leaders from both profit and non-profit organizations. Although individuals may say "Oh, I'm not a leader," when they are able to get tasks accomplished using their influence, they are exercising leadership.

Perspectives on Leadership

Research on the role of leadership in organizations has been conducted mostly in the United States, and it is often understood in terms of five phases, as shown in Exhibit 11.7. Each has its own distinct theoretical approach. We examine trait-based theories, behavioral theories, contingency theories, implicit theories, and transformational theories in this section.

Trait-Based Perspectives

Louis Gerstner Jr., who went to IBM as chairman and chief executive in 1993, with no previous experience in the computer industry, is credited for having turned this computer industry giant into the industry leader. Gerstner is recognized for his drive and his love of winning.[72] Among numerous examples of such leaders is Lee Iococca of Chrysler Corporation, who also turned a failing company into a success in the early1980s. Iacocca was credited for his vision and his sustained energy.

From these accounts, it appears that these individuals possess several leadership traits or competencies. The **trait-based perspective** of leadership developed from the belief that certain leadership competences or traits were natural to some and not to others. Leadership competencies include natural and learned abilities, values, personality traits such as drive, ability to forecast the future, and other characteristics that lead to the ability to create a credible vision and inspire others to follow.

For the first part of the twentieth century, management scholars used scientific methods to determine personality traits and physical characteristics that distinguished leaders from others. The "great men" theories of the early 1900s, however, failed to identify traits that are both necessary and sufficient for exhibiting

EXHIBIT 11.7
Perspectives on Leadership

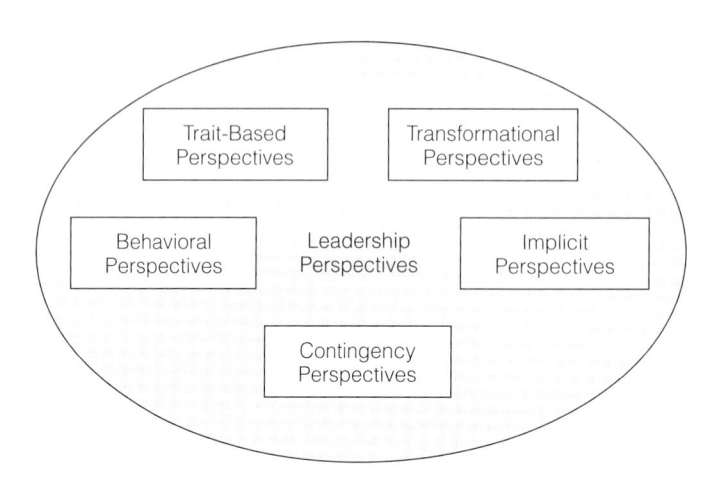

leadership. We do not know if certain traits are important in all situations of leadership. Recent research has shown that some individual traits are related to the emergence of leaders and their effectiveness.[73] These traits are described in Exhibit 11.8.

Leaders who are high in need for achievement are driven to succeed. Their inner motivation sustains their vision and encourages others to move forward with them. We can see this drive in IBM's Gerstner. Leadership motivation is concerned with a strong need for power, and this motivation is kept in check by a strong sense of personal and social responsibility.[74] Effective leaders tend to seek power, not necessarily for themselves, but for the benefit of their work group and organization. Integrity, as a leadership trait, refers to the leader's truthfulness and reliability in translating his or her vision into action.

Traits of self-confidence, intelligence, knowledge of the business, and emotional intelligence are all necessary in different combinations for leadership. The last of these traits, emotional intelligence, has only recently been studied and is regarded as crucial for effectiveness.[75] Leaders who are high on this trait are able to monitor their own and other's emotions, discriminate among them, and use the information to guide their thoughts and actions.

Behavioral Perspectives

The **behavioral perspective** of leadership focuses on behaviors that make leaders effective. Studies have identified two clusters of leadership behaviors with more than 1,800 items.[76] One cluster is called **consideration,** which reflects people-orientated behaviors, such as showing trust, respect, and a concern for others' well-being. Leaders rated high on consideration supported employees' interests and treated employees with respect. The other cluster is called **initiation of structure,** which focuses on behaviors that define and structure work roles. Leaders rated high on initiation of structure were concerned with assigning specific tasks, clarifying their duties and procedures, ensuring that they follow company rules, and encouraging them to reach their maximum performance potential. In general, the findings of these studies suggest that, with some exceptions, leaders high on both consideration and initiation of structure tend to achieve higher subordinate performance.

EXHIBIT 11.8
Leadership Traits

Source: Most elements of this list were derived from S. A. Kirkpatrick and E. A. Locke, "Leadership: Do Traits Matter?" *Academy of Management Executive* 5 (May 1991), pp. 48–60. Several of these ideas are also discussed in H. B. Gregersen, A. J. Morrison, and J. S. Black, "Developing Leaders for the Global Frontier," *Sloan Management* 40 (Fall 1998), pp. 21–32; R. J. House and R. N. Aditya, "The Social Scientific Study of Leadership: Quo Vadis?" *Journal of Management* 23 (1997), pp. 409–473.

Leadership Trait	Description
Drive	The leader's inner motivation to pursue goals
Leadership motivation	The leader's need for socialized power to accomplish team or organizational goals
Integrity	The leader's truthfulness and tendency to translate words into deeds
Self-confidence	The leader's belief in his or her own leadership skills and ability to achieve objectives
Intelligence	The leader's above-average cognitive ability to process enormous amounts of information
Knowledge of the business	The leader's understanding of the company's environment to make more intuitive decisions
Emotional intelligence	The leader's ability to monitor his or her own and others' emotions, discriminate among them, and use the information to guide his or her thoughts and actions

A number of cross-cultural studies have shown the importance of these two dimensions.[77] The findings show that considerate, or relationship-oriented, leaders are generally able to improve subordinates' satisfaction. The influence of initiation of structure, or task orientation, is more complex, and it is not clearly understood. Some researchers have suggested that a culture-specific interpretation of what task orientation means is important. The responses of subordinates to relationship-oriented leadership is consistently positive across cultures; however, the responses to task-oriented leadership depends on the nature of the culture in which the leader functions. Leaders must adapt their behavior to the situation and understand the needs of the followers in a clearer fashion in cross-cultural situations.

Contingency Perspectives

The **contingency perspective** framework was developed in the United States to account for leadership effectiveness that did not follow the predictions of behavioral theories. The contingency model, developed by Fiedler, presented the idea that the nature of the situation moderates the relationship between the leader's style and group effectiveness.[78] A leader's style is assessed by the Least Preferred Co-Workers (LPC) scale, and it reflects the leader's ability to work with the least preferred co-workers in his or her work group. The nature of the situation is determined by the leader's position power, quality of leader–member relations, and the amount of structure in the task itself. This theory predicts that a leader with stronger position power tends to improve group performance in highly structured task situations. On the other hand, leaders who are more relationship-oriented get the best out of groups in situations where the task is somewhat unstructured and where the nature of power that they have is less defined.

A number of cross-cultural studies have been conducted using this approach.[79] Filipino managers, who were more task-oriented, were better at creating high-performing groups, but Chinese managers, who were more relationship-oriented, were more effective in achieving goals. Research on this theory in Japan has not succeeded in finding support for this, and support in Mexico, where self-monitoring (being sensitive to one's behavior and the reactions of others) was used as another leader characteristic, is mixed.

The *path–goal theory* identified four leader behaviors and a number of situational and follower characteristics that influence the relationship between leader style and follower satisfaction and performance.[80] While there is good support for this theory in the United States, it has not been adequately tested in other countries. Cultural differences may be a key situational characteristic that, as we have seen, has many different dimensions.

Substitutes for leadership theory is another approach to highlighting the role of contingency.[81] The characteristics of subordinates, such as their degree of interest in the task, skill level, and professionalism, may substitute for leadership behavior, such as being directive or showing consideration. Contradictory results have been found, but the cross-cultural and international applicability of the substitutes for leadership theory has not been fully tested.

Implicit Perspectives

Implicit perspective theories, developed in the United States, focus on the way subordinates perceive a leader.[82] Followers develop prototypes or mental representations of leaders through their life experiences and interactions with others, according to this theory. Specific leader behaviors do not necessarily make a person a leader unless the followers perceive him or her as a leader.

The idea that different cultures have different prototypes for leader behavior has found support in international studies. Leaders who meet the expectations of their followers gain their trust and are effective in some cultures.[83] Results from this and other international studies suggest that some characteristics of leaders are universally accepted and preferred.

Transformational Perspectives

The **transformational leadership** theories focus on the process of a leader using his or her charisma to inspire followers to go beyond their immediate self-interests for the good of the work group and the organization.[84] **Charisma** is a special quality of interpersonal influence that some leaders possess and that enables their followers to develop respect and trust for the leader.

Examples of charismatic leaders are found in almost all nations and cultures. Churchill, Gandhi, and Mandela have had great influence on their followers that led to admiration, respect, trust, ongoing commitment, and loyalty for these leaders. Charismatic leaders are self-confident, have an ideal vision, and are deeply committed to their goals. They are seen as being unconventional and radical thinkers who can bring about important changes.

Some researchers argue that charismatic leaders are more effective than noncharismatic leaders regardless of national and cultural differences. This notion is supported across cultures.[85] Research on the effectiveness of this transformational perspective in countries like the Netherlands, Singapore, and the Dominican Republic has shown that, while the charismatic leader is perceived as being effective, the processes leaders use to influence subordinates toward accomplishing goals vary a great deal from country to country. However, in Japan this perspective of leadership does not have a great deal of validity.[86] Charismatic leadership has been found to have more effect on U.S. employees than on Mexican employees.[87]

This perspective has the best potential for being applicable in different countries and cultures, but more research needs to be done to fully understand how charisma and cultural differences act together to produce effective leaders.

Leadership across Cultures and Borders

The emergence of leadership, especially the way a leader influences followers, is often a product of cultural factors. Deeply ingrained values regarding the rights and duties of employees differ from country to country and present different worldviews. These values, reflected in laws, constitutions, and various social customs, provide prescriptions for leader behavior. Like other aspects of culture, discussed in Chapter 4, these are taken for granted by the members of a society, whether others see them as correct or not. If a leader violates core values, for example, by engaging in immoral or illegal activities or if the leader behaves in a more individualistic manner in a country that is more collectivistic, he or she can lose authority over subordinates and would be less effective. In some cases, the leader may immediately lose the positions of leadership.

The act of leadership is often a product of socially and culturally constructed legal, moral, ethical, and work obligations. For example, in Western countries, such as the United States and Norway, women are becoming organizational leaders, and the concept of equalizing pay between men and women has received considerable attention. Although some social barriers conflict with the cultural ideals of equality, most Westerners clearly anticipate that women have the potential for leadership.

In contrast, in high power distance countries, women do not have much opportunity to advance their careers or to become leaders in their organizations. A study of Arab executives and foreign expatriates in the United Arab Emirates reported that a consultative or participative style was preferred by both groups.[88] However, other studies have found that in Jordan and other Middle Eastern countries, an authoritative management style was preferred.[89] Autocratic styles of leadership have also been found in Indian managers.[90]

The political values of a country also influence the type of leader that will emerge and how leaders function. Political culture reflects idealized values about effective leadership and can exercise strong influences on how leaders should act in the workplace. Countries with democratic traditions have well-defined processes that encourage participative leadership, whereas countries with autocratic political philosophies, such as most Middle Eastern and Asian countries, tend to favor no participation by followers.

The culture of the organization affects the type of leaders that will emerge and how they function. One view proposes that the leaders' major contribution is the effective management of organizational culture.[91] Leaders create, maintain, and play a major role in changing organizational culture, but we should note that they are also influenced by the constraints and values of their company. For example, a leader who favors equal participation of men and women in senior management ranks might find difficulty in sustaining this in a company where the past tradition did not favor equal treatment of women. Similarly, a leader who has a preference for decentralized decision making may not find support for the change in an organization that has traditionally had centralized decision making.

Functions of Leadership across Borders and Cultures

As we discussed earlier, Western theories focus on traits, behaviors, interaction patterns, leader–member relationships, perception of followers, and influence as determinants of leadership. Research examining the role of societal culture is important, especially because it helps us draw implications for what international managers can do to provide effective leadership in different parts of the world.

Some functions of leadership are similar across borders and cultures; however, the definition of an effective leader varies greatly across cultures. The generally accepted images of leaders in different countries are important to understand. Industry leaders in Mexico, India, Italy, and France are highly regarded for their social status and access to political power. In Latin American countries such as Brazil and Chile, organizational leaders are expected to present a holistic view of themselves, be prominent in society, and have a strong appreciation for the arts. Decisiveness and knowledge of the industry are respected in leaders in Germany and Russia, where they receive a great deal of formal organizational prestige.[92]

Research on leadership clearly tells us that no style of leadership works well in all cultures and nations. A significant amount of research supports the idea that culture acts as a contingency factor in exercising leadership. This means that culture-based norms, beliefs, roles, and values about what is expected of leaders, the influence they have over their subordinates, and the amount of organizational status or prestige that they are given vary across nations.

Leadership in Guilt versus Shame Cultures

Most of us have a commonsense understanding of guilt versus shame. *Guilt* results from violating established social and moral principles and standards. Embezzling company resources and using company credit cards for personal benefits are acts that should result in feelings of guilt. On the other hand, *shame* results from acts that lead to public embarrassment. In other words, you can feel guilty about something you do, but shame does not occur unless the act becomes known to the relevant social group. One feels ashamed when one assumes that the female president of a company is a secretary and asks her during a boardroom meeting to make coffee for everyone. However, one may not feel guilty for this.

A relationship-based culture regulates interactions among co-workers with whom one already has established relationships through the mechanism of shame. Shame results when an individual is admonished or punished by superiors, as well as when one loses face or suffers humiliation in a work context. The fact that people can feel ashamed of their behavior is of supreme importance in sustaining moral leadership in many parts of east Asia, but it is particularly important in Japan.[93] For example, Shohei Nozawa, as president of Yamaichi Securities, stood before world TV cameras and profusely apologized, weeping, for announcing his firm's inability to pay stockholders. He showed shame, as appropriate in Japanese culture. This was the largest bankruptcy in post–World War II Japan. Many non-Japanese viewers, particularly Westerners, were shocked and disgusted by the display of tears.[94] Contrast this with the public display of confidence by Martha Stewart, CEO of Martha Stewart Living Omnimedia, Inc., who, despite being convicted of obstruction of justice, refused to show any shame.

Western scholars implicitly believe that leaders should feel guilty and show shame when they engage in inappropriate behaviors, such as wrongful treatment of subordinates, downsizing, sexual harassment, and presiding over corporate failures due to excessive greed. However, public displays of shame are rare in the United States and western European countries. For example, the former CEOs of Enron and WorldCom, Kenneth Lay and Bernie Ebbers, each refused to express any shame for having engaged in some of the largest bankruptcies in the history of global business. However, such mechanisms of social control in the form of shame are of critical importance in the behavior of public officials as well as businesspersons in many east Asian countries.

We do not advocate shame versus guilt as a mechanism for controlling wrongful and unethical impulses on the part of leaders. The point is that leaders managing across borders and cultures should carefully scrutinize the nature of the culture in which they are managing subsidiaries and work groups. One method that has been found particularly effective is to pay keen attention to a confidante and listen to the suggestions about how to be sensitive to using the appropriate mechanism.

The GLOBE Project on Leadership

The largest study on leadership effectiveness is the Global Leadership and Organizational Effectiveness (GLOBE) research program.[95] A global network of more than 170 management scholars and social scientists from 62 countries collaborated for the purpose of understanding cultural influences on leadership in organizations, using both quantitative and qualitative methods to collect data from over 18,000 managers representing a majority of the world's population.

The goal of the GLOBE project is to understand patterns of leadership that are universally accepted and those that are subject to the unique influences of the cultural context in which they operate. Findings show that specific leader behaviors—being trustworthy, encouraging, an effective communicator, a good bargainer, and a team builder, for example—are accepted almost everywhere. Negative behaviors that are universal include being uncooperative, egocentric, ruthless, and dictatorial. Behaviors that are dependent on the cultural context include group orientation, self-protectiveness,

EXHIBIT 11.9 Definitions of Various Aspects of the Concept of Culture and Sample Questionnaire Items from the GLOBE Project

Source: Reprinted from W. H. Mobley, M. J. Gessner, and V. Arnold, "Cultural Influences on Leadership and Organizations: Project Globe," *Advances in Global Leadership*, Vol. 1, pp. 171–234. Copyright © 1991, with permission from Elsevier.

Culture Construct Definitions	Specific Questionnaire Item
Power distance: The degree to which members of a collective expect power to be distributed equally.	Followers are (should be) expected to obey their leaders without question.
Uncertainty avoidance: The extent to which a society, organization, or group relies on social norms, rules, and procedures to alleviate unpredictability of future events.	Most people lead (should lead) highly structured lives with few unexpected events.
Humane orientation: The degree to which a collective encourages and rewards individuals for being fair, altruistic, generous, caring, and kind to others.	People are generally (should be generally) very tolerant of mistakes.
Collectivism I: The degree to which organizational and societal institutional practices encourage and reward collective distribution of resources and collective action.	Leaders encourage (should encourage) group loyalty even if individual goals suffer.
Collectivism II: The degree to which individuals express pride, loyalty, and cohesiveness in their organizations or families.	Employees feel (should feel) great loyalty toward this organization.
Assertiveness: The degree to which individuals are assertive, confrontational, and aggressive in their relationships with others.	People are (should be) generally dominant in their relationships with each other.
Gender egalitarianism: The degree to which a collective minimizes gender inequality.	Boys are encouraged (should be encouraged) more than girls to attain a higher education. (Scored inversely.)
Future orientation: The extent to which individuals engage in future-oriented behaviors such as delaying gratification, planning, and investing in the future.	More people live (should live) for the present rather than for the future. (Scored inversely.)
Performance orientation: The degree to which a collective encourages and rewards group members for performance improvement and excellence.	Students are encouraged (should be encouraged) to strive for continuously improved performance.

participative skills, humaneness, autonomy, and charisma. The major concepts investigated in the GLOBE research project are nine aspects of culture that were measured by administering questionnaires. These are reproduced in Exhibit 11.9.

Some of the findings of the GLOBE project show that being a participative leader is regarded as more important in Canada, Brazil, and Austria than in Egypt, Mexico, and Indonesia. In Brazil, a leader who is charismatic, group-oriented, participative, and humane but does not function autonomously is more effective. In the United States, the leaders should stand out through their individual achievements, inspire others through their optimism, stand up for their beliefs, have a clear focus for their efforts, seek continuous improvements, and strive for excellence.[96] The charismatic leader, according to the GLOBE project, is one who is a visionary, acts as an inspiration to subordinates, and is high on performance orientation. The participative leader is one who is willing to delegate responsibility to subordinates and is comfortable in sharing decision-making responsibilities. An autonomous leader is an individualist and does not score as high as a leader in countries where participation in decision making is highly regarded.

Some of the other findings from the GLOBE project are:

- Americans like two kinds of leaders, those who provide workers with empowerment, autonomy, and authority and those who are bold, forceful, confident, risk takers.
- Malaysians expect their leaders to be humble, modest, dignified, and group-oriented.
- Arabs treat their leaders as heroes and worship them as long as they remain in power.

- Iranians expect their leaders to exhibit power and strength.
- The French expect their leaders to appreciate the finer aspects of French culture and arts and to have a good knowledge of mathematics.
- The Dutch place high value on equality and are not so sure about the importance of leadership. Terms like *leader* and *manager* often carry a social stigma. Children don't like to tell their schoolmates that a parent is employed as a manager.

Other research that provides us with important insights about the relative level of preference for autocratic versus participative leaders is based on the work of Hofstede, discussed in Chapter 4. He noted that participative management approaches that are recommended by U.S. researchers to improve satisfaction and productivity of work groups may not work in high power distance and masculine countries.[97] Employees in high power distance countries, such as Mexico, the Philippines, and Malaysia, are likely to prefer an autocratic leader who also exhibits some degree of paternalism toward subordinates. Employees in low power distance countries are more likely to prefer a consultative, participative leadership style, and they expect their superiors not to deviate from this style.

As we discussed in implicit perspectives of leadership, to understand the significance of leadership in different countries, we must focus on the perceptions and attitudes that followers have about their leaders. *Subordinateship* (attitude toward leaders) is a strong factor in determining the types of leaders that are likely to be effective in each situation. This attitude is strongly conditioned by the beliefs, norms, and values of not only the society in which the leader functions but also the political, organizational, and industry cultures. In high power distance cultures, regardless of the educational level of the subordinate, the ideal boss is a benevolent autocrat, or a good father, and less powerful people take it for granted that they will be dependent on the more powerful. In practice, Hofstede notes that less powerful people are at one extreme or the other:[98] those who have strong emotional dependence on their leaders and those who do not have any emotional dependence on their leaders. Exhibit 11.10 shows the kind of subordinate behaviors found in countries characterized in terms of three levels of power distance.

EXHIBIT 11.10 Subordinateship for Three Levels of Power Distance

Source: Reprinted from Geert Hofstede, "Motivation, Leadership, and Organization: Do American Theories Apply Abroad?" *Organizational Dynamics*, Vol. 1, Copyright © 1980, with permission from Elsevier.

Low Power Distance	Medium Power Distance (United States)	High Power Distance
Subordinates have weak dependence needs.	Subordinates have medium dependence needs.	Subordinates have strong dependence needs.
Superiors have weak dependence needs toward their superiors.	Superiors have medium dependence needs toward their superiors.	Superiors have strong dependence needs toward their superiors.
Subordinates expect superiors to consult them and may rebel or strike if superiors are not seen as staying within their legitimate role.	Subordinates expect superiors to consult them but will accept autocratic behavior as well.	Subordinates expect superiors to act autocratically.
Ideal superior to most is a loyal democrat.	Ideal superior to most is a resourceful democrat.	Ideal superior to most is a benevolent autocrat or paternalist.
Laws and rules apply to all, and privileges for superiors are not considered acceptable.	Laws and rules apply to all, but a certain level of privilege for superiors is considered normal.	Everybody expects superiors to enjoy privileges; laws and rules differ for superiors and subordinates.
Status symbols are frowned upon and will easily come under attack from subordinates.	Status symbols for superiors contribute moderately to their authority and will be accepted by subordinates.	State symbols are very important and contribute strongly to the superior's authority with the subordinates.

Regarding expectations about managerial authority versus participation,[99] Americans and Germans prefer more participation than Italians and Japanese. Indonesians are comfortable with an autocratic style of decision making, but managers in Sweden, Denmark, and Great Britain believe that subordinates should participate in decision making and problem solving. Results of this study seem to conflict with the common knowledge about Japan's participative style of decision making. However, the research by Hampden-Turner and Trompenaars found that although Swedish managers are the most willing to delegate authority, Japanese managers rate second in terms of their willingness to delegate to their subordinates.[100]

In Exhibit 11.11, we provide a model of leadership effectiveness that incorporates the role of cultural differences. This model shows that factors external to the organization interact with those internal in origin and determine the content of the leadership process. The outcome of this interaction is reflected in the level of convergence and divergence between external factors and internal factors that are present in the work context. This level of convergence and divergence affects the way leaders interact with followers and work groups and exhibit acts of leadership. Follower behaviors are important in the process, as shown in Exhibit 11.11. Leader–follower interaction determines the first-level outcomes of group performance, satisfaction of the followers, feelings of well-being, and so on. These first-level outcomes lead to second-level outcomes such as organizational effectiveness, high morale, and creativity and innovation. The feedback arrow shows that second-level outcomes potentially change the nature of content factors specific to what the leaders and followers bring to the work. International and global managers can use this model to examine the role of both company culture and societal culture in determining the type of leadership that is likely to be valued.

EXHIBIT 11.11 An Integrative Model of Leadership Effectiveness across Nations and Cultures

Environmental Factors	Content Factors	Leader–Follower Interaction	First-Level Outcomes	Second-Level Outcomes
External in Origin: Political, Economic, Technological, Social, Cultural ↓ Level of Convergence and Divergence ↑ Internal in Origin: Organizational structure, culture, and climate, Availability of resources, Management systems	Specific to Leaders: Ability, Experience, Personality, Image, Position power, Style, Motives, Cultural awareness — Specific to Followers: Beliefs, Attitudes, Motives and motivation, Locus of control, Experience — Specific to Work Groups: Values, Norms, Work roles, Patterns of decision making, Substitutes for leadership	Acts of Leadership: Autocratic versus participative, Task versus people orientation, Transactional versus transformational — Follower Behavior: Desire for achievement versus affiliation, Value of rewards, Sensitivity and response to leadership	Amount of effort, Group performance (quality and quantity), Satisfaction of followers, Feeling of well-being, Absenteeism, Turnover	Accomplishment of individual group and organizational goals, Organizational effectiveness, High morale, Creativity and innovation

Arrows indicate possible causal influence

We emphasize that outcomes of leadership are embedded in a complex web of societal, cultural, and organizational factors. The types of leaders that emerge and the leaders' effectiveness are determined by the interaction of these factors.

Non-Western Styles of Leadership

Leadership in Japan

Descriptions of Japanese management have existed for a long time; however, a careful evaluation of leader behavior in this culture, which is highly group-oriented, is rare.[101] Misumi's performance-maintenance (PM) theory identifies leaders on the basis of two dimensions, performance and maintenance. The *performance dimension* comprises behaviors that lead a group toward goal accomplishment, including those that put pressure on followers and emphasize planning. Misumi defines pressure as supervisory behavior that puts strong emphasis on regulations and production, whereas planning concerns the scheduling and processing of work. The *maintenance dimension* is concerned with keeping harmony in the group and preserving the importance of the group in the organization. The effectiveness of PM leadership has been found in the Japanese context,[102] but its applicability in other countries depends on the specific leader behaviors that followers perceive to be effective in their unique cultural context. Recent research indicates that the performance- or task-oriented dimension is affected more strongly by cultural values of the subordinates than is the maintenance dimension.[103] Managers should be aware of this framework in understanding the nature of the leadership process in Japan.

Leadership in India

India is an emerging economic giant. The findings from the GLOBE research program confirm the complexity and diversity of Indian society and culture, resulting in the need for special types of leadership. Indian culture has functioned by referring to the past, but it is currently undergoing a rapid transition to a modern society. Values of individualism tend to characterize a large portion of Indians in urban areas. Although management in India was based on autocratic processes, formal authority, and charisma, a move toward emphasizing democratic processes in the workplace is under way. Family values tend to influence a significant number of leaders in their decisions, and **nurturant leadership** (taking a personal interest in the well-being of each subordinate) is still expected from managers, but changes, particularly in high-technology firms, are apparent.

Companies such as Texas Instruments and Microsoft are encountering these issues and are developing programs that integrate Indian values into the work context. Failure to include an Indian partner who understood the styles of Indian management and leadership led to problems between former energy giant Enron and the Indian government, and Enron decided not to build plants in India in 2001.[104]

Leadership in the Arab World

Leadership behavior in Arab countries is strongly influenced by the belief systems of the Islamic religion and past traditions, as well as by some Western values.[105] Along with these influences, the rigidity of a bureaucratic mentality introduced by the Ottoman Empire (from the thirteenth century until the end of World War I) and Europeans complicates matters even further. The patriarchal approach found in these cultures is called **sheikocracy**.[106] This style reflects an emphasis on hierarchical authority, personal connections, human relations, and conformity to rules and regulations based on the personality and power of those who made the rules. Efficiency and effectiveness are not as important. The combination of this leadership style with influences from Western management practices has produced a duality in managers in the Arab world, who aspire to become more sophisticated and modern in their leadership styles yet remain tied to traditional values. The Arab world is an important and growing part of the global marketplace, and international and global managers should be aware of this duality.

Leading in an Increasingly Interconnected World

The meaning of leadership will change in a world where companies are flexible and fluid, and the pace of change is rapid. Leading in e-business and virtual organizations is different from leading in traditional organizations. The differences between leadership in traditional organizations and e-businesses are the speed at which decisions must be made, the importance of flexibility, and the need to create an ongoing vision of the future. While data may be available to make rapid decisions, the knowledge that results from the data may be hard to obtain. Maintaining flexibility is easier said than done. Leaders must move with the flow of businesses and should be able to redirect their group or organization when they find that something that worked in the past does not work any longer.

Continuous focus on the vision is difficult. In a cyber world, people expect more from their leaders. The rules, policies, and regulations that are used in traditional companies reduce uncertainty for both leaders and followers, but this is not the case in a cyber world. Since formal guidelines have short life spans in digital organizations, it becomes the leader's responsibility to provide continuous direction as to where the company is headed. Getting employees to accept the vision may require more radical actions—actions that might not have been necessary in the past. Regardless of whether the digital company exists in an individualist or collectivistic culture, there is a convergence of what leaders of e-businesses are expected to be. Thus, cultural and national differences may not matter as much as differences rooted in the company culture.

Implications for the Practice of Global Leadership

Leadership entails continuous interaction with others, and we have discussed the role of various societal and cultural influences on this critical management function. Of the Fortune 500 firms surveyed, 85 percent think they do not have an adequate number of effective global leaders, and 65 percent believe that their existing leaders need to acquire additional skills and knowledge before they can meet or exceed needed capabilities in the global marketplace.[107]

Characteristics of **global leadership** are an inquiring mind, integrity, the ability to manage uncertainty and tensions, and emotional connections with people throughout the company's worldwide operation. Leaders should also possess an acute sense of their business to recognize worldwide market opportunities quickly and organizational savvy to manage the unique capabilities of their companies to capture new market opportunities.[108]

A global leader should have the skills and abilities to interact and manage people from diverse cultural backgrounds who work in the multinational or global corporation in different parts of the world. Some of these traits are:[109]

- A combination of the skills of a strategist with those of a builder of organizational architectures and the ability to coordinate the architecture seamlessly.[110]
- A strong cosmopolitan orientation encompassing the ability to operate flexibly and keep a sensitive eye toward distinctive demands of different cultures in which the corporation operates.
- Intercultural communication skills and cultural sensitivity. The role of effective communication cannot be overemphasized. It is critical for a leader to develop

PRACTICAL INSIGHT 11.3

REMOTE LEADERSHIP

More and more leaders are finding themselves in virtual boss/direct report relationships. Separated in space and often in time (zones), they struggle to communicate effectively, stay aligned, and achieve desired goals. It's all too easy for difficult-to-close gaps to open up when you are working virtually—in assessments, priorities, and expectations. Keeping this from happening is the central challenge of remote leadership.

Dictionaries list two quite distinct definitions for the word "remote," both of which can apply to the challenge of dealing with a virtual boss. One meaning is "operating effectively from a distance," for example using a remote control. This is of course the primary objective in a virtual boss-subordinate relationship: to have coordination and control work as well from a distance as it does up close.

The other, less benign, meaning of "remote" is "distant or unapproachable." Sometimes the black-hole boss is the problem. Try as you might, you really can't pin her down and get direction from her—in person or electronically.

More commonly, though, it's the direct report who doesn't make enough effort to make communication work across the distance. Particularly at risk for falling into this trap are those leaders who have a strong independent streak and a burning desire to prove themselves. They relish the opportunity to operate remotely and to chart their own course. So they don't put out the effort they should to get feedback and direction from their distant bosses.

This is, unfortunately, akin to sailing by dead reckoning when you are out of sight of land (in the days before GPS, naturally). You may navigate effectively and end up at the desired destination. But if you lack a reference point and get off course, it could take a long time to figure it out, and you may have a lot of distance to make up when you finally do.

What does it take to make remote leadership work? Here are some basic guidelines:

1. **Find a way to spend some face time with the new boss early on.** As soon as you know you are taking on a new role with a virtual boss, secure a significant block of face-to-face time. Regardless of how far away you are and how much you feel you need to do back home, force yourself to spend some time in the same room. It is difficult to make a personal connection and lay the foundation for a strong working relationship solely through electronic means.

2. **Discipline yourself to choose the right modes of electronic communication.** Email and instant messaging have revolutionized business communication, but they can never convey the sorts of contextual cues and emotional subtleties that are exchanged in conversation. Bias yourself toward electronic conversation and away from messaging in virtual relationships. Pick up the phone more than you would if you were located nearby. If you can't talk in real time, make more use of voice mail.

3. **Find windows of opportunity to check in with your boss.** You and your boss are both busy and it's all too easy for an "out of sight, out of mind" dynamic to creep in. So take the time to figure out your boss's routines and identify times when she is more likely to be available. One accomplished virtual manager I recently spoke with described how he arranged calls when his boss was in the car on the way to or from work.

4. **Discipline yourself to make the connection.** Think of yourself as having 100% responsibility for making the relationship work with your virtual boss. Force yourself to take the initiative to reach out regularly. Put reminders to do so into your calendar. Above all, keep in mind that the consequences of getting disconnected, and going off course as a result, will mostly be borne by you.

Have you experienced particular challenges in dealing with virtual bosses? Do you have suggestions for how to make remote leadership work?

Source: Michael Watkins, Harvard Business Online, September 18, 2007. Special permission from *BusinessWeek*.

---

appropriate skills to communicate face-to-face as well as through videoconferencing, e-mails, and other computer-mediated methods.
- The ability to acculturate rapidly without being judgmental and to be highly selective in perceiving culturally dissimilar cues and processes.
- Eagerness to continue learning not only about economic, institutional, political, and cultural influences relating to how organizations function but also about the significance of the meaning of working in different parts of the world.

Building on trust is important for strengthening leadership culture, as shown in Practical Insight 11.3, as is being able to understand cultural differences and their effect on business, as shown in Practical Insights 11.4 and 11.5.

PRACTICAL INSIGHT 11.4

A LEADER'S REAL JOB DESCRIPTION

Jack Welch has his "4E" framework for what makes for a great leader: positive energy, ability to energize others, edge to summon the courage to make tough decisions, and ability to execute. The Welch framework is just one of many in the leadership literature. Leadership gurus from Warren Bennis to Ram Charan have their own well-known and well-advanced formulas.

I humbly submit mine here. It may not be as catchy as some of the others, and I make no claims to originality. But it is informed by my experiences as an executive and as a consultant to dozens of global clients in assignments too numerous to mention. And it is the product of much reading, thinking, and agonizing over what it takes to be a great leader. Besides, as a consultant, I feel guilty when I don't present a framework to help people. A consultant, after all, is not unlike an optician who prescribes a new pair of glasses—or framework—to improve your eyesight.

My modest prescription: Every leader should be mindful that the opportunity to effect meaningful change is limited by time. In other words, leaders should always have a time frame in mind. Leaders work against the clock and the calendar. The TIME framework below describes the four essential actions every leader should master. Most important, this framework allows a leader to simultaneously deal with the myriad cognitive, spiritual, emotional, and power plays of the world.

Think. Little is more important to leadership than the opportunity for deep reflection. Often, leaders are so caught up doing triage at work, reacting to the daily grind of getting the job done, that they fail to set aside time for the proactive work. Thinking is the part of leadership that leads to innovating, discovering a purpose, creating a vision, and choosing a strategic position. It is the most essential part of the job, the part that focuses on the future.

Inspire. This is the most visible component of leadership. You've heard this before, but probably with an entirely different spin. Of course, the most effective leaders inspire. To use Welch's word, they energize. But they also sell the vision, act as an example, tell stories, confront reality, ask the right questions, demonstrate possibilities, reassure, and give hope for a bright future. The leader's job is to make people comfortable with what the company does so they can shape the task themselves in response to changing positions. Then, they can "do strategy with their fingertips," to borrow Andy Grove's phrase.

Too many people, however, confuse inspiration with feelings. No wonder, because many leadership writers just happen to be real or imaginary psychologists. But inspiration at its core is a spiritual concept, not rooted in psychology. Inspiration is the spirit in you. A spirit is not a sentiment. It helps us redefine what is possible.

Mobilize. The leader's third role is to mobilize people to perform a task. Every leader must be able to move a team to action, to build coalitions, define campaigns, set targets, and encourage networks. Unlike inspiring, which is typically directed at large numbers of people, mobilizing requires leaders to engage with and influence key players and their specific contributions. The skill to mobilize people is nearly equal to the skill to manage the politics and neutralize opponents. You have to clear the way for action to occur.

Empower. Leaders get most things done through others, so execution depends on managing authority correctly and delegating power generously. And part of this task involves allocating resources, scrutinizing and overseeing the deployment of those assets, and disempowering those who misuse them. People have to be equipped to perform their tasks. Assets have to be acquired and deployed. The overall organization has to be designed.

Thinking about what we do in all four dimensions is a passport to great leadership. But it's also important to say clearly that leadership is ineffective or flawed largely when someone is unbalanced on some or all of these dimensions. The best leaders must operate on all four levels.

Source: Nikos Mourkogiannis, *BusinessWeek*, December 26, 2007.

An interesting way leaders are developing their skills is by participating in multiplayer online computer games. The tools and techniques that they use are likely to change how leaders can be developed in global corporations in the twenty-first century. The *Harvard Business Review* reports that online interactions with members of dissimilar cultures are a significant way to develop leadership abilities.[111]

PRACTICAL INSIGHT 11.5

INDIA'S GOT A JOB FOR YOU

More companies on the subcontinent are looking for Western executives to provide international experience. There's no shortage of applicants. Like most senior executives, Carol Borghesi is no stranger to recruitment consultants. An acclaimed 26-year career in customer service, including a senior position at British Telecom Company (BT), has made her an attractive candidate for headhunters looking to fill senior positions across the globe. Yet it was only when India's mobile carrier Bharti Airtel came calling that Borghesi, 50, decided to leave a lucrative managing director role at BT to run Airtel's customer service business. "It's a deliberate choice to be in India at this time—it's a booming economy, and I wanted to be part of the action," says Borghesi, a Canadian native, who since October, 2006, has lived in a plush apartment in Gurgaon, just outside New Delhi, with her husband and 11-year-old daughter.

These days, she's not the only senior executive heading to the subcontinent. Borghesi is at the vanguard of a trend sweeping the country as fast-growing Indian companies eye Westerners for senior positions. "Everybody wants to be part of the India growth story now," says Deepak Gupta, managing director at Korn Ferry (KFY) in New Delhi. According to the executive search company, there are now around 1,000 foreigners holding senior positions in India, compared to 143 in 2005. By 2009, the number is expected to double.

It's not just the attraction of India's position, alongside China, as an engine of global economic growth. Hiring practices among fast-expanding India companies are becoming more global. Govind Iyer, partner at international search firm Egon Zehnder, notes that half of senior management searches are targeting non-Indians. Two years ago 70% of the searches, at companies' instigation, were for non-resident Indians, whom big companies saw as an easier option often willing to accept pay cuts to be part of the India growth story, and who were more attuned to cultural differences.

What changed? For one thing, Indian companies, many of which are making huge investments at home and abroad, are increasingly competing on a global scale and want the best person for the job. Meanwhile there are shortages of qualified managers in key areas such as infrastructure, aviation, retail, and life sciences. "India has good talent, but it's not deep enough for some of the new sectors," says Iyer.

The change of mindset shouldn't be underestimated. Just three years ago, even as entry-level and mid-level Western hires were in vogue, companies rarely conceded they lacked expertise in senior management. Not anymore. At Airtel, President & Chief Executive Officer Manoj Kohli says Borghesi is just what his firm requires. "Carol brings immense global experience," he says. "Her culturally diverse background adds richness to our leadership team."

India watchers also note a change in the types of executives that are relocating to India. Back in the 1990s, most senior level managers sent to India were charged with researching or establishing operations. Often, notes Rama Bijapurkar, a Mumbai business consultant, those who went were either brand managers, sent to test the water in a newly liberalized India, or older executives on the verge of retirement. "Now it's seriously different," she says. "They are getting senior people with a clear mandate to grow the business."

New recruits don't come cheap. Most expect Western-sized salaries and perks, often including stock options. Headhunters estimate that foreign salaries range from $300,000 to $600,000 including perks for senior positions. Contracts are typically for three to five years.

Yet with India booming the disparities appear to engender relatively little unease among locally hired colleagues. "Their compensation is justified for selective specialized functions," says K. V. Subramaniam, CEO of Reliance Life Sciences, a Mumbai-based biotech company. "They bring years of domain experience and are involved in developing competencies among Indian understudies." Reliance has 15 expatriates—several in senior positions—receiving compensation three times that of their Indian counterparts.

Of course India does hold special challenges. Bureaucracy, slow decision making, and cultural differences remain major headaches. Often, spouses of executives, especially those raising families, bear the brunt of the culture shock. Lamon Rutten, joint managing director of India's Multi Commodity Exchange, admits his family is still getting accustomed to living in India.

Rutten, his wife, and two children relocated in June, 2006, to Juhu, a suburb of Mumbai, from the calm of Geneva, after he gave up a post as chief of finance and risk management in the commodities branch at the United Nations Conference on Trade and Development. While he enjoys the job, Rutten laments the lack of green space and the time it takes to get things repaired. "With India opening up, it has to adapt," he says.

Business life can also throw up unusual problems. U.S. native Rudy Vercelli, 47, chief operating officer of Mumbai International Airport, is often mistaken for a tourist at the airport he is helping modernize. He also has to contend with the 80,000 squatters that occupy 60% of the airport's land. "We have 960 acres of airport land, but what we need is 4,000 acres. There is no room except on top," he says. Still, Vercelli, formerly a vice-president at Bechtel, has no regrets. "I will stay in India until they kick me out. My family looks upon every move as an adventure," he says.

Source: Nandina Lakshman, *BusinessWeek*, June 19, 2007.

Summary

Effectively motivating worldwide employees and leading global organizations are key success factors regarding the achievement of sustainable competitive advantages for the multinational enterprise. For example, people seek various rewards from work organizations, depending on their cultural values, norms, and attitudes. This chapter analyzed the nature of situations where U.S.-based theories of motivation are easily applicable and where they are not. Security is extremely important for some people, whereas others seek status and success over everything else. Some people look for satisfying and fulfilling work, while still others want agreeable relationships.

Human needs exhibit similarities around the globe, but cultural and environmental contexts determine the order of importance of these needs. Expectancy theory of motivation is applicable in many countries if managers specify the type of rewards that are likely to motivate a given group of workers based on their cultural background. This means that managers must know the type of motivational rewards that are important in the culture in which they operate.

As global companies expand into different countries, they face variations in patterns of motives. Even if the country culture suppresses achievement motives, the experience of working for a multinational subsidiary may create new expectations and therefore make people more achievement-oriented than they were before they started working.

Similar to motivation, leading global initiatives must be tailored to local cultures and contexts. The process of leading others is one of the most complex yet least understood areas of management. Managers must consider non-Western views of leadership as globalization spreads economic activities through the world. The perception of what a good leader is, in terms of both traits and behaviors, varies a great deal from society to society, and the act of leadership itself is a product of culture.

Although no generally accepted definition of leadership exists, it can be defined as the process of influencing others to achieve goals. Although trait leadership theories were popular in the United States in the early 1900s, no traits both necessary and sufficient for exhibiting leadership have been found. Behavioral theories of leadership have been found useful, but responses to task-oriented leadership vary across cultures. Contingency theory is applicable to cross-cultural leadership situations because a vast number of variables can affect the emergence and exercise of leadership. The notion of charismatic leadership is also supported across cultures, but influence processes differ across cultures.

Like other aspects of culture, leadership and leadership behaviors are taken for granted by society members, and they may not be transferable across cultures. For example, leadership in an individualistic culture may differ markedly from one in a collectivistic culture. Outcomes of leadership are embedded in a complex web of societal, cultural, and organizational factors that determine the emergence and effectiveness of leadership.

Key Terms and Concepts

- behavioral perspective, *415*
- charisma, *417*
- consideration, *415*
- contingency perspective, *416*
- extrinsic factor, *400*
- global leadership, *424*
- implicit perspective, *416*
- initiation of structure, *415*
- intrinsic factor, *400*
- leadership, *413*
- Meaning of Working (MOW) study, *405*
- motivation, *395*
- need for achievement, *400*
- need for affiliation, *401*
- need for power, *401*
- norm of equality, *404*
- norm of equity, *404*
- norm of need, *404*
- nurturant leadership, *423*
- organizational commitment, *400*
- role ambiguity, *410*
- role overload, *410*
- sheikocracy, *423*
- trait-based perspective, *414*
- transformational leadership, *417*

Discussion Questions

1. Explain the importance of understanding work motivation in managing multinational and global organizations.
2. Explain how global managers could design culturally appropriate reward systems.
3. What are the implications of Hofstede's cultural dimensions on work motivation?
4. What is the significance of self-construal in the process of developing work motivation?
5. What are some of the major differences between independent and interdependent modes of construal in the way they influence different types of performance in the work context?
6. Do you expect globalization to create workforces in different countries who experience similar types of work motivation and perform different facets of job performance in similar ways? In other words, does globalization happen to create uniform patterns of motivation and job performance in dissimilar nations and cultures?
7. Discuss the concept of leadership and its importance in achieving organizational goals.
8. How can we use the cultural dimensions of Hofstede to gain insights into leader–follower relationships around the world? Give specific examples, and explain.
9. How will the exercise of leadership in a digital organization differ from that in traditional organizations?
10. From Practical Insight 11.5, which describes the challenges of globalization in the Indian subcontinent, what are some of the specific qualities that Western managers would need in becoming effective leaders in this cultural setting?

Minicase

All Eyes on the Corner Office

After more than a decade at the head of Siemens, the icon of German industry, Chief Executive Heinrich von Pierer is something of an icon himself.

In 2003, his name was floated briefly as a candidate for the German presidency. After years of investor criticism that he moved too slowly to transform the $93 billion electronics conglomerate into a global competitor, von Pierer is getting the last laugh. While competitors such as Netherlands-based Philips Group suffered losses during the recent economic downturn, Siemens remained profitable. The share price has doubled over the past year, to almost $87 on the New York Stock Exchange. "He has done good work," allows shareholder advocate Daniela Bergdolt, a Munich lawyer who once told von Pierer at a stockholders' meeting that he should leave the company.

Now Bergdolt is worried about what will happen when von Pierer does just that. The 63-year-old executive's contract expires in September. He is widely expected to accept a two-year extension, but the question of who will succeed one of Germany's most important executives is fast becoming a hot topic in Germany—and elsewhere in Europe, where a new generation of CEOs is fast taking over. The race to succeed von Pierer, in fact, has already started in earnest. Von Pierer and Siemens supervisory board members are now closely watching a handful of candidates. Front-runners include former U.S. division chief Klaus Kleinfeld and Thomas Ganswindt, who runs the fixed-line telecom equipment business.

The oddsmakers currently favor 46-year-old Kleinfeld. Last November, he was promoted to the seven-member central committee of the management board in recognition for his work as CEO of Siemens' $20 billion U.S. operations from January, 2002, until December, a post seen as good training for the top slot. Like Siemens worldwide, the U.S. operations are a collection of fiefdoms that often need to be strong-armed into cooperating. But there are other credible candidates, including 47-year-old Johannes Feldmayer, another central committee member.

Whoever prevails, a new generation of managers is already moving into Siemens' top echelons. In just a year, the average age of top management has fallen from 58 to 53, J.P. Morgan Chase & Co. calculates. While rising forty-somethings won't foment revolution at consensus-driven Siemens, they are likely to speed the company's shift away from its conservative German roots. The new managers will focus more intensely on profit, move faster to unload underperforming units, and shift more production to cheaper locations abroad. "Obviously, von Pierer will be a tough act to follow," says

Henning Gebhardt, head of German equities at DWS, the fund management arm of Deutsche Bank. "But after 10 years, sometimes a change at the top is good." Von Pierer wrought mighty changes, even if his slow-but-steady pace didn't always satisfy investors. When he took over in 1992, Siemens relied heavily on government contracts, rarely disciplined managers who delivered poor results, and employed 61% of its workforce in high-wage Germany. Transparency? The company published no profit figures for its divisions, and often even employees didn't know if their units were making money.

Now Siemens gives detailed company and divisional results quarterly and has sacked numerous underperforming managers. Net return on sales has risen from 2.4% in 1993, the year after von Pierer took charge, to 4% in the latest quarter. Von Pierer responded to criticism that Siemens, which makes everything from locomotives to X-ray machines, had too many moving parts. He spun off dozens of units, including chipmaker Infineon Technologies and the electronic components unit known as Epcos. Now, 60% of employees work outside Germany and the domestic workforce has been cut by a third, to 167,000. Von Pierer, an engineer with a politician's touch, managed that without provoking extensive labor unrest—no small feat in a land where layoffs are deemed unpatriotic.

The new generation of managers, though, is likely to be more willing to bust heads. Consider the way Ganswindt turned around the company's $8.9 billion Information & Communication Networks division. He cut the workforce by nearly 40%, or 20,000 workers, to reduce costs by $4.4 billion. He shifted production to Brazil and China. From a loss of nearly $865 million in the fiscal year that ended Sept. 30, 2002, ICN returned to a profit of $64 million in the last quarter.

Despite the improvements, Siemens still gets heat for mediocre margins. Ganswindt and the other young managers are sensitive to the criticism. "You can't innovate if you don't have money to invest," he says.

Rising managers will also continue pushing the engineer-dominated company to focus more on customers' needs. They will maintain Siemens' steady drive to globalize—not only by investing in Asia and the Americas but also by importing non-German ways of doing business back to Munich.

There is no question, however, of Siemens transforming itself into something other than a German company. "A new CEO will mean change, but I don't expect a radical departure from the existing philosophy and strategy," says analyst Roland Pitz of HVB Group in Munich. The fear is that some company directors will try to keep things too German. The supervisory board could name a lower-profile candidate such as Kurt-Ludwig Gutberlet, head of BSH Bosch & Siemens Household Appliances, a profitable joint venture with Stuttgart-based Robert Bosch. "It could be someone who is not the strongest but has the strongest consensus among the gray heads," says a source who works closely with Siemens. Still, it's clear that at Siemens, gray heads are becoming ever more scarce.

Source: Jack Ewing, *BusinessWeek Online,* March 1, 2004, www.businessweek.com/magazine/content/04_09.

DISCUSSION QUESTIONS

1. What leadership skills have contributed to the success of the incumbent CEO, Heinrich von Pierer? Describe his leadership style.
2. Siemens faces challenges in the global marketplace. The company will likely require a different leadership style than von Pierer's to face these challenges. What style would you recommend to Siemens?
3. Why would the age of the leader be an important consideration in a global company? Would it be important in your consideration of the candidates for CEO of Siemens? Why?

Notes

1. C. L. Hulin and H. C. Triandis, "Meaning of Work in Different Organizational Environments," in P. C. Nystrome and W. H. Starbuck, eds., *Handbook of Organizational Design* (New York: Oxford University Press, 1981), pp. 336–357; H. C. Triandis, "Motivation to Work in Cross-Cultural Perspective," in J. M. Brett and F. Drasgow, eds., *The Psychology of Work: Theoretically Based Empirical Research* (Mahwah, NJ: Lawrence Erlbaum Associates, 2002), pp. 101–117.
2. S. P. Robins, *Organizational Behavior: Concepts, Controversies, and Applications,* 7th ed. (Upper Saddle River, NJ: Prentice Hall, 1996), p. 212.
3. M. D. Dunnette, "Aptitudes, Abilities, and Skills," in M. D. Dunnette, ed., *Handbook of Industrial and Organizational Psychology* (Chicago: Rand McNally College Publishing, 1976), pp. 473–520.

4. H. R. Markus and S. Kitayama, "Culture and the Self: Implications for Cognition, Emotion and Motivation," *Psychological Review* 98 (1991), pp. 224–253; R. S. Bhagat, J. R. VanScott, P. K. Steverson, and K. S. Moustafa, "Cultural Variations in Individual Job Performance: Implications for Industrial and Organizational Psychology in the 21st Century," in G. P. Hodgkinson and J. K. Ford, eds., *International Review of Industrial and Organizational Psychology,* Vol. 22. (New York: John Wiley and Sons, 2007).

5. A. Maslow, *Motivation and Personality* (New York: Harper & Row, 1954).

6. S. Suterwalla, "Immigration and Reality," *Newsweek,* January 28, 2001.

7. G. Hofstede, *Cultures' Consequences,* 2nd ed. (Thousand Oaks, CA: Sage, 2001).

8. Ibid.

9. G. K. Stephens, and C. R. Greer, "Doing Business in Mexico: Understanding Cultural Differences," *Organizational Dynamics,* Summer 1995, pp. 39–55.

10. C. P. Alderfer, R. E. Robert, and K. Ken, "The Effect of Variations in Relatedness Need Satisfaction on Relatedness Desires," *Administrative Science Quarterly* 19 (1974), pp. 507–553; C. P. Alderfer, *Existence, Relatedness, and Growth: Human Needs in Organizational Settings* (New York: Free Press, 1972).

11. F. Herzberg, "One More Time: How Do You Motivate Employees?" *Harvard Business Review* 87, no. 5 (1987), pp. 109–117.

12. P. D. Machungwa and N. Schmitt, "Work Motivation in a Developing Country," *Journal of Applied Psychology,* February 1983, pp. 31–42.

13. Herzberg, "One More Time."

14. E. Locke, "The Nature and Causes of Job Satisfaction," in Dunnette, *Handbook of Industrial and Organizational Psychology,* pp. 1297–1350.

15. J. B. P. Sinha, "Culture Embeddedness and the Developmental Role of Industrial Organizations in India," in H. C. Triandis, M. D. Dunnette, and L. M. Hough, eds., *Handbook of Industrial and Organizational Psychology,* Vol. 4., 2nd ed. (Palo Alto, CA: Consulting Psychologists Press, 1994), pp. 727–764.

16. R. House et al., "Cultural Influences on Leadership and Organizations: Project GLOBE," in W. H. Mobley, M. J. Gessner, and V. Arnold, eds., *Advances in Global Leadership,* Vol. 1 (Stamford, CT: JAI Press, 1999).

17. R. N. Kanungo, "Work Alienation: A Pancultural Perspective," *International Studies in Management and Organization* 13 (1983), pp. 119–138. See also O. Shenkar and S. Ronen, "Culture, Ideology, or Economy: A Comparative Exploration of Work Goal Importance among Managers in Chinese Societies," *Managing in a Global Economy III: Proceedings of the Third International Conference* (Amherst, MA: Eastern Academy of Management, 1989), pp. 162–167.

18. D. C. McClelland, "Toward a Theory of Motive Acquisition," *American Psychologist* 20, no. 5 (1965), pp. 321–333.

19. S. Ronen and O. Shenkar, "Clustering Countries on Attitudinal Dimensions: A Review and Synthesis," *Academy of Management Review* 10 (1985), pp. 435–454; G. Flynn, "HR in Mexico: What You Should Know," *Personnel Journal* 73, no. 8 (1994), pp. 34–44.

20. Flynn, "HR in Mexico."

21. P. T. Poulsen, "The Attuned Corporation: Experience from 18 Scandinavian Pioneering Corporations," *European Management Journal* 16, no. 3 (1988), pp. 229–235.

22. R. M. Steers and C. J. Sanchez-Runde, "Culture, Motivation, and Work Behavior," in M. J. Gannon and K. L. Newman, eds., *Blackwell Handbook of Cross-Cultural Management* (Oxford, UK: Blackwell Business, 2002), pp. 190–216.

23. P. Blunt and M. L. Jones, *Managing African Organizations* (Berlin: Walter de Gruyter, 1992).

24. D. S. Elenkov, "Russian Aerospace MNCs in Global Competition," *Columbia Journal of World Business* 30 (1995), pp. 66–78.

25. R. S. Bhagat and S. J. McQuaid, "Role of Subjective Culture in Organizations: A Review and Directions for Future Research," *Journal of Applied Psychology Monograph* 67, no. 5 (1982), pp. 653–685; R. S. Bhagat, B. L. Kedia, S. E. Crawford, and M. R. Kaplan, "Cross-Cultural

Issues in Organizational Psychology: Emergent Trends and Directions for Research in the 1990's," in C. L. Cooper and Ivan T. Robertson, eds., *International Review of Industrial and Organizational Psychology,* Vol. 5 (New York: John Wiley & Sons, 1990), pp. 59–99; Steers and Sanchez-Runde, "Culture, Motivation, and Work Behavior."

26. J. C. Abegglen and G. Stalk, *Kaisha: The Japanese Corporation* (New York: Basic Books, 1985); R. M. Steers, Y. Shin, and G. Ungson, *The Chaebol: Korea's New Industrial Might* (New York: Harper Business, Ballinger Division, 1989); Steers and Sanchez-Runde, "Culture, Motivation, and Work Behavior."

27. A. Sagie, D. Elizur, and H. Yamauchi, "The Structure and Strength of Achievement Motivation: A Cross-Cultural Comparison," *Journal of Organizational Behavior* 17 (1996), pp. 431–444.

28. V. H. Vroom, *Work and Motivation* (New York: John Wiley & Sons, 1964). See also V. H. Vroom and A. G. Jago, *The New Leadership: Managing Participation in Organizations* (Englewood Cliffs, NJ: Prentice Hall, 1988).

29. D. A. Nadler and E. E. Lawler, "Motivation: A Diagnostic Approach," in J. R. Hackman, E. E. Lawler, and L. W. Porter, eds., *Perspectives on Behavior in Organizations* (New York: McGraw-Hill, 1977), p. 34.

30. E. E. Lawler III, *Motivation in Work Organizations,* 1st classic ed. (San Francisco: Jossey-Bass, 1994); L. W. Porter, R. M. Steers, and G. A. Bigley, *Motivation and Work Behavior,* 4th ed. (New York: McGraw-Hill, 2002).

31. R. Nath and W. K. Narayanan, "A Comparative Study of Managerial Support, Trust, Openness, Decision-Making and Job Enrichment," *Academy of Management Proceedings* 40 (1980), pp. 48–52.

32. J. Adams, "Toward an Understanding of Inequity," *Journal of Abnormal and Social Psychology* 67 (1963), p. 97.

33. H. C. Triandis, *Culture and Social Behavior* (New York: McGraw-Hill, 1994), p. 100.

34. L. A. Wilk and W. K. Redmon, "The Effects of Feedback and Goal Setting on the Productivity and Satisfaction of University Admissions Staff," *Journal of Organizational Behavior Management* 18 (1998), pp. 45–68; A. A. Shikdar, and B. Das, "A Field Study of Worker Productivity Improvements," *Applied Ergonomics* 26 (1995), pp. 21–27.

35. E. A. Locke and G. P. Latham, *A Theory of Goal Setting and Task Performance* (Englewood Cliffs, NJ: Prentice Hall, 1990).

36. T. H. Poister and G. Streib, "MBO in Municipal Government: Variations on a Traditional Management Tool," *Public Administration Review* 55 (1995), pp. 48–56.

37. Locke and Latham, *A Theory of Goal Setting and Task Performance.*

38. C. L. Hulin and H. C. Triandis, "Meaning of Work in Different Organizational Environments."

39. H. C. Triandis, "Generic Individualism and Collectivism," in Gannon and Newman, *Blackwell Handbook of Cross-Cultural Management,* pp. 17–46.

40. M. Erez, "The Congruence of Goal-Setting Strategies with Socio-cultural Values and Its Effects on Performance," *Journal of Management* 12 (1989), pp. 83–90; M. Erez and P. C. Earley, *Culture, Self-Identity, and Work* (New York: Oxford University Press, 1993); Erez, "A Culture-Based Model of Work Motivation."

41. R. E. Cole, *Work, Mobility, and Participation: A Comparative Study of American and Japanese Industry* (Berkeley: University of California Press, 1980); E. E. Lawler III, "Total Quality Management and Employee Involvement: Are They Compatible?" *Academy of Management Executive* 8 (1994), pp. 68–76.

42. K. Leung, "Negotiation and Reward Allocations across Cultures," in P. C. Earley and M. Erez, eds., *New Perspectives on International Industrial and Organizational Psychology* (San Francisco: Lexington Press, 1997), pp. 640–675.

43. Triandis, "Generic Individualism and Collectivism."

44. MOW International Research Team, *The Meaning of Work: An International Perspective* (London: Academic Press, 1987).

45. Ibid., p. 94.

46. Ibid.
47. Ibid., pp. 118–119.
48. E. Rieger and D. Wong-Rieger, "A Configuration Model of National Influence Applied to Southeast Asian Organizations," *Proceedings of the Research Conference on Business in Southeast Asia,* University of Michigan, May 12–13, 1990.
49. R. Inglehart et al., *World Values Surveys and European Values Surveys, 1981–1984, 1990–1993, and 1993–1997* (Ann Arbor, MI: Institute for Social Research, 2000).
50. J. B. Schorr, *The Overworked American: The Unexpected Decline of Leisure* (New York: Basic Books, 1993).
51. R. S. Bhagat and K. S. Moustafa, "How Non-Americans View American Use of Time: A Cross-Cultural Perspective," in P. Boski, F. J. R. van de Vijver, and A. M. Chodynicka, eds., *New Directions in Cross-Cultural Psychology: Selected Papers from IAAP Congress in Warsaw, Poland* (Wydawnictwo: Polish Psychological Association, 2002), pp. 183–192.
52. R. Florida, *The Rise of the Creative Class* (New York: Basic Books, 2002).
53. "Togetherness: a Balance Sheet," *The Economist,* September 28, 2000, pp. 25–27.
54. G. Hofstede, *Cultures' Consequences,* 2nd ed. (Thousand Oaks, CA: Sage, 2001).
55. P. C. Earley, "East Meets West Meets Mideast: Further Explorations of Collectivistic and Individualistic Work Groups," *Academy of Management Journal* 36 (1993), pp. 319–348.
56. P. Peterson et al., "Role Conflict, Ambiguity, and Overload: A 21-Nation Study," *Academy of Management Journal* 38 (1995), pp. 429–452.
57. R. S. Bhagat, M. P. O'Driscoll, E. Babakus, and L. T. Frey, "Organizational Stress and Coping in Seven National Contexts: A Cross-Cultural Investigation," in G. P. Keita and J. J. Hurrell Jr., eds., *Job Stress in a Changing Workforce* (Washington, DC: American Psychological Association, 1994); Bhagat, Kedia, Crawford, and Kaplan, "Cross-Cultural Issues in Organizational Psychology."
58. Hofstede, *Cultures' Consequences.*
59. Peterson et al., "Role Conflict, Ambiguity, and Overload."
60. R. S. Bhagat, B. Krishnan, R. Renn, D. L. Harnish, and K. S. Moustafa, "Organizational Stress and Psychological Strain in Eight National Contexts: Do Cultural Variations Matter?" *Journal of International Business Studies* 35, no. 1 (2004).
61. Hofstede, *Cultures' Consequences.*
62. Ibid.
63. Ibid.
64. Y. P. Huo and R. M. Steers, "Cultural Influences on the Design of Incentive Systems: The Case of East Asia," *Asia Pacific Journal of Management* 10, no. 1 (1993), p. 81.
65. D. Sirota and M. J. Greenwood, "Understanding Your Overseas Workforce," *Harvard Business Review* 14 (January–February 1971), pp. 53–60.
66. P. W. Dorfman, "International and Cross-Cultural Leadership," in J. Punnett and O. Shenkar, eds., *Handbook for International Management Research* (Cambridge, MA: Blackwell, 1996), pp. 276–349.
67. D. Miller, M. F. R. Ket de Vries, and J. M. Toulouse, "Top Executive Locus of Control and Its Relationship to Strategy-Making, Structure, and Environment," *Academy of Management Journal* 25 (1982), pp. 237–253.
68. G. Yukl, *Leadership in Organizations,* 3rd ed. (Upper Saddle River, NJ: Prentice Hall, 1994).
69. R. J. House, N. S. Wright, and R. N. Aditya, "Cross-Cultural Research on Organizational Leadership: A Critical Analysis and a Proposed Theory," in Earley and Erez, eds., *New Perspectives on International Industrial/Organizational Psychology,* pp. 535–625.
70. D. Katz and R. Kahn, *The Social Psychology of Organizations,* 2nd ed. (New York: John Wiley & Sons, 1978).
71. M. Groves, "Cream Rises to the Top, but from a Small Crop," *Los Angeles Times,* June 8, 1998.
72. S. Lohr, "He Loves to Win. At I.B.M., He Did," *New York Times,* March 10, 2002, sec. 3, p. 1.

73. Dorfman, "International and Cross-Cultural Leadership."
74. R. J. House and R. N. Aditya, "The Social Scientific Study of Leadership: *Quo vadis?" Journal of Management* 23 (1997), pp. 409–473.
75. D. Goleman, "What Makes a Leader?" *Harvard Business Review* 76 (November–December 1998), pp. 92–102.
76. Yukl, *Leadership in Organizations.*
77. L. M. Ah Chong and D. C. Thomas, "Leadership Perceptions in Cross-Cultural Context: Pacific Islanders and Pakeha in New Zealand," *Leadership Quarterly* 8, no. 3 (1997), pp. 275–293.
78. F. E. Fiedler, *A Theory of Leadership Effectiveness* (New York: McGraw-Hill, 1967).
79. M. Bennett, "Testing Management Theories Cross-Culturally," *Journal of Applied Psychology* 62, no. 5 (1977), pp. 578–581; J. Misumi, *The Behavioral Science of Leadership: An Interdisciplinary Japanese Research Program* (Ann Arbor: University of Michigan Press, 1985); J. Misumi, and M. F. Peterson, "Supervision and Leadership," in B. M. Bass, P. J. D. Drenth, and P. Weissenberg, eds., *Advances in Organizational Psychology: An International Review* (Newbury Park, CA: Sage, 1987), pp. 220–231.
80. J. House, "A Path-Goal Theory of Leader Effectiveness," *Administrative Science Quarterly* 16 (1971), pp. 556–571; R. J. House, and T. R. Mitchell, "Path–Goal Theory of Leadership," *Contemporary Business* 3 (1974), pp. 81–98.
81. Dorfman, "International and Cross-Cultural Leadership."
82. R. G. Lord and K. J. Maher, *Leadership and Information Processing: Linking Perceptions and Performance* (Boston: Unwin-Everyman, 1991); R. G. Lord, R. J. Foti, and C. L. DeVader, "A Test of Leadership Categorization Theory: Internal Structure, Information Processing, and Leadership Perceptions," *Organizational Behavior and Human Performance* 34 (1984), pp. 343–378.
83. D. C. Thomas and E. C. Ravlin, "Responses of Employees to Cultural Adaptation by a Foreign Manager," *Journal of Applied Psychology* 80 (1995), pp. 133–146.
84. B. M. Bass, *Leadership and Performance beyond Expectation* (New York: Free Press, 1985); T. Burns, *Leadership* (New York: Harper & Row, 1978); J. A. Conger and R. Kanungo, "Toward a Behavioral Theory of Charismatic Leadership in Organizational Settings," *Academy of Management Review* 12 (1987), pp. 637–647; R. J. House, "A 1976 Theory of Charismatic Leadership," in J. G. Hunt and L. L. Larson, eds., *Leadership: The Cutting Edge* (Carbondale: Southern Illinois University Press, 1977), pp. 189–207.
85. Dorfman, "International and Cross-Cultural Leadership."
86. Bass, *Leadership and Performance beyond Expectations;* G. Howell, "Culture Tails: A Narrative Approach to Thinking, Cross-Cultural Psychology, and Psychotherapy," *American Psychologist* 46 (1994), pp. 187–197.
87. J. P. Howell and P. W. Dorfman, "A Comparative Study of Leadership and Its Substitutes in Mixed Cultural Work Settings," paper presented at the Western Academy of Management Meeting, Big Sky, Montana, April 1988.
88. A. J. Ali, A. A. Axim, and K. S. Krishnan, "Expatriates and Host Country Nationals: Managerial Values and Decision Styles," *Leadership & Organization Development Journal* 16, no. 6 (1995), pp. 27–34.
89. O. Dahhan, "Jordanian Top Managers: Characteristics, Activities, and Decision-Making Style," *Abhath Al-Yarmouk, Humanities and Social Sciences* 4, no. 1 (1988), pp. 37–55; M. K. Badawy, "Styles of Mid-Eastern Managers," *California Management Review* 22, no. 2 (1980), pp. 51–58.
90. R. Kaur, "Managerial Styles in the Public Sector, *Indian Journal of Industrial Relations* 28, no. 4 (1993), pp. 363–369.
91. E. H. Schein, *Organizational Culture and Leadership,* 2nd ed. (San Francisco: Jossey-Bass, 1992).
92. L. Copeland and L. Griggs, *Going International* (New York: Random House, 1985).
93. J. Hooker, *Working across Cultures* (Palo Alto: Stanford University Press, 2003).

94. Ibid.
95. R. J. House, P. J. Hanges, S. A. Ruiz-Quintanilla, P. W. Dorfman, M. Javidan, M. Dickson, V. Gupta, and GLOBE Country Co-Investigators, "Cultural Influences on Leadership and Organizations: Project GLOBE," in Mobley, Gessner, and Arnold, *Advances in Global Leadership,* pp. 171–234.
96. M. Hoppe and R. S. Bhagat, "Leadership in the United States of America: The Leader as Cultural Hero," in R. House, ed., *Anthology of Leadership around the World* (Thousand Oaks, CA: Sage, 2004).
97. Hofstede, *Cultures' Consequences.*
98. G. Hofstede, *Cultures and Organizations: Software of the Mind* (New York: McGraw-Hill, 1991).
99. A. Laurent, "The Cultural Diversity of Western Conceptions of Management," *International Studies of Management and Organization* 13, no. 1–2 (1983), pp. 75–96.
100. C. Hampden-Turner and A. Trompenaars, *The Seven Cultures of Capitalism* (New York: Doubleday, 1993).
101. Misumi, *The Behavioral Science of Leadership.*
102. Ibid.; M. F. Peterson, "PM Theory in Japan and China: What's in It for the United States?" *Organizational Dynamics* 16 (1988), pp. 22–38; Dorfman, "International and Cross-Cultural Leadership."
103. Ah Chong and Thomas, "Leadership Perceptions in Cross-Cultural Context"; M. F. Peterson, P. B. Smith, and M. H. J. Tayeb, "Development and Use of English Version of Japanese PM Leadership Measures in Electronics Plants," *Journal of Organizational Behavior* 14 (1993), pp. 251–267.
104. "Enron Switches Signals in India," *BusinessWeek,* January 8, 2001; "Enron Calls on Guarantees by India to Collect Debts," *Wall Street Journal,* February 9, 2001.
105. A. J. Ali, "Management Theory in a Transitional Society: The Arab's Experience," *International Studies of Management and Organization* 20 (1990), pp. 7–35.
106. A. Al-Kubaisy, "A Model in the Administrative Development of Arab Gulf Countries," *Arab Gulf* 17, no. 2 (1985), pp. 29–48.
107. S. P. Robbins and M. Coulter, *Management,* 7th ed. (Upper Saddle River, NJ: Prentice Hall, 2001).
108. H. B. Gregersen, A. J. Morrison, and J. S. Black, "Developing Leaders for the Global Frontier," *Sloan Management Review,* Fall 1998, pp. 21–32.
109. R. Rosen, P. Digh, M. Singer, and C. Phillips, *Global Literacies: Lessons on Business Leadership and National Cultures* (New York: Simon & Schuster, 2000); A. Morrison, "Global Leadership," in P. W. Beamish, A. J. Morrison, A. C. Inkpen, and P. M. Rosenzweig, *International Management: Text and Cases* (New York: McGraw-Hill/Irwin, 2003).
110. C. A. Bartlett and S. Ghoshal, "What Is a Global Manager?" *Harvard Business Review,* September–October 1992, pp. 124–132.
111. B. Reeves, T. W. Malone, and T. O'Driscoll, "Leadership's Online Labs," *Harvard Business Review,* May 2008.

CHAPTER TWELVE

International Human Resources Management

Chapter Learning Objectives

After completing this chapter, you should be able to:

- Understand the various approaches that multinational and global organizations undertake for managing and staffing subsidiaries in diverse parts of the world.
- Distinguish between various functions of international human resources management.
- Identify the various strategies for selecting staff for foreign assignments.
- Explain how training programs prepare managers for overseas assignments.
- Understand the various schemes for compensation and benefits used by multinational and global organizations.
- Identify the issues inherent in repatriation and explain why multinational and global companies need to address issues concerning managers returning from overseas assignments.
- Understand that labor relations practices differ in each country and explain how these differences affect multinational and global companies.

Opening Case: How to Avoid Culture Shock

The biggest hurdles to overcome when doing business internationally often have less to do with technology than with culture. "When we first went to Europe, we were shocked by the number of things that were different from the way we thought they were going to be," says Larry Schwartz, president of Hill Arts & Entertainment Systems Inc., a software VAR in Guilford, Conn. "The way they do business is just very different."

And each country has its own idiosyncrasies. For example, Schwartz had a difficult time cracking the German market because his company had first established a presence in England. "They saw us as English," he says, "which is even worse than being American."

When Schwartz finally did win German customers, he learned that the colors Americans find pleasing on a graphical user interface seemed ugly to the Germans.

"The Germans said, 'What are these?' They wanted garish colors, the brighter and bolder the better," he says. Schwartz realized why it's difficult for Americans to program for European customers. The English have one color preference, the Germans have another and the Italians look at color another way. "If you don't know the customs," Schwartz says, "you're just sunk."

Schwartz also made a gaffe during his first day of meetings in Munich by calling people by their first names, American style. "I was with one of my European people and I asked her why the Germans kept referring to each other by their last names, Herr This and Herr That, and she said that's what is expected in Germany." He adds that as an American, if you go in using first names at a meeting, from day one you've started alienating people.

Schwartz says the best thing to do is realize that business etiquette changes from country to country, and find local guides who can help you.

Don Howren, director of strategic alliances at Platinum Software Corp., Irvine, Calif., says his company has stepped on plenty of land mines while trying to expand into foreign markets. "We've done all the ugly American things you can come up with," he says. "But having good partnerships can help you dodge any issues that could hold you back."

Platinum tries to form partnerships with VARs and consultants in each new market. "There are a lot of things outside of the technical sphere that you have to deal with," Howren says. "Those are the greatest challenges for companies moving into those markets." For example, in the burgeoning Latin American market, Platinum is dealing constantly with a whole set of issues that are unique to those markets, such as hyperinflation and political situations.

American companies should also be aware that in some countries there is a cultural bias working against them before they even show up.

"I have found that the most difficult markets to break into are Germany and Japan," says Jennifer Meighan, an international business development consultant in San Francisco. "Both cultures are very tightly knit, very uniform and wary of American companies."

Some aspects of American business culture do have appeal in Europe, says Denise Sangster, president of Global Touch Inc., a channels consulting company in Berkeley, Calif.

"Europeans like nothing better than American-style service," Sangster says. "With some software companies in France, if you call during lunchtime with a question or a problem, they'll tell you to call back after lunch. So if you can provide them immediate support and service, they love you."

Also, European customers aren't accustomed to the "solution selling" approach that American software VARs espouse, but they appreciate it, Sangster says.

"If you can bring over that style of business, that approach of 'Let me help you solve your business problem,' which is not the normal way of doing things there, you'll have a tremendous opportunity," Sangster says. "You can win some very loyal and dedicated customers."

It can be tricky, though, to convince your European business partners, including VARs and distributors, to adopt your "solution sell" approach. "A lot of it has to do with your presentation," Sangster says. "There's a fine line between saying, 'Hey, look, we do things better, we're the best,' and saying, 'Let us show you a different way of looking at the same situation.'"

This kind of finesse is even more crucial in Asia, according to Bob Hoover, general manager of Asia/Pacific for Speedware Corp. in Toronto.

For example, forget about cold calling or making deals on the phone. Business is done in person, and introductions from mutual acquaintances or business contacts are often necessary, Hoover says. And it's important to build strong relationships before a deal is done, which means that compared to the West, business in Asia can seem to take forever.

"It took me 18 to 24 months to build ties there, work that would have taken about three months in the States," Hoover says.

The biggest mistake that U.S. companies make is to see Asia as a single entity. "Each country has a unique business culture," Hoover says. For example, in Japan and Korea, decisions are made by groups, so sales cycles are long—as much as three times longer than in the States. And Korean and Japanese companies tend to think strategically, with a long-term view.

In Taiwan, however, the business culture is built around small, family-owned companies. "Decisions are made very quickly. They tend to think tactically rather than strategically," Hoover says. "With Taiwanese customers you're always talking about new things, trying to keep them excited."

Hoover has a list of dos and don'ts that he gives to his sales reps when they move to Asia. Perhaps the biggest "don't" has to do with emotion. "You must never show emotion or lose your temper," Hoover says. "It's a sign of weakness. Customers will become very concerned about doing business with your company."

Americans should also avoid behaving in a way that is seen as stereotypically American: loud, fast-talking, slapping people on the back. Rather than trying to crack into Asian markets on your own, Hoover suggests hiring a well-connected consultant who can help you make connections. "This really can help you shorten the start-up period."

Source: Daniel Lyons, *VARBusiness,* June 15, 1995.

Discussion Questions

1. Discuss gaffes (mistakes) made when dealing with different cultures and their effects on management of companies.
2. How do you think the failure to understand cultural differences affects managing human resources?
3. What other insights can be gained from this case?

What Is International Human Resources Management?

International human resources management (IHRM) is concerned with the development of human resource capabilities to meet the diverse needs of various subsidiaries of multinational and global corporations. Management of human resources in multinational and global organizations differs greatly from that in domestic companies. Each multinational and global organization has a different approach for managing its employees. In most cases, how organizations find employees and pay, train, develop, and promote them varies in each subsidiary. These issues are complex, because they require a continuous link between corporate strategy and human resources management. National and cultural differences play important roles in the selection, compensation, training, development, placement, and promotion of employees.[1]

In this chapter, we discuss international human resources management. This field includes three major functions:

1. Management of human resources in global corporations, including issues of expatriation and repatriation.
2. Implementing corporate global strategy by adapting appropriate human resources management practices in different national, economic, and cultural environments.
3. Adopting labor relation practices in each subsidiary that match local requirements.

International human resources management is increasingly being recognized as a major determinant of success in the global environment. In the highly competitive global economy, where factors of production—capital, technology, raw material, and information—can be easily duplicated, the quality of human resources in the organization will be the sole source of competitive advantage.[2] Multinational and global corporations need to pay careful attention to this most critical resource, which, in its turn, can provide appropriate access to other resources needed for effective implementation of global strategy.

During the past decade, the number of multinational corporations engaged in business worldwide increased from 37,000 to more than 60,000. Foreign affiliates have increased from approximately 200,000 to more than 350,000. Foreign multinationals operating in the United States are employing more than 5 million Americans. About 80 percent of mid- to large-size U.S. multinationals have managers working in subsidiaries in other countries, and their numbers are increasing.[3] According to recent estimates by the National Foreign Trade Council, over 400,000 U.S. expatriates are working in different countries.

As multinational corporations from all countries are increasing, so too is the strategic pressure to select and staff overseas subsidiaries with the appropriate managers. The following sections discuss the critical issues associated with this strategic imperative.

Managing and Staffing Subsidiaries

Multinational and global organizations take different approaches to managing and staffing subsidiaries. These approaches are linked with the company's overall strategy, and they reflect its human resources policies and practices. The four major approaches are as follows:[4]

1. **Ethnocentric staffing approach.** The company uses the approach developed in the home country, and the values, attitudes, practices, and priorities of headquarters determine the human resources policies and practices. Managers from the home country are preferred for leadership and other major positions in the subsidiary. Foreign staffing decisions are made in the headquarters.
2. **Polycentric staffing approach.** The company considers the needs of the local subsidiary when formulating human resources policies and practices. Individuals from host countries are selected for managerial positions; however, promotion of a manager from foreign subsidiaries to headquarters is rare. Human resources decisions, policies, and practices are developed at the local level.
3. **Regiocentric staffing approach.** The company considers the needs of an entire region when developing human resources policies and practices. Managers from the host country are often selected for managerial positions in their own countries, and some may be promoted to regional positions. Subsidiaries in a given region, such as Latin America, may develop a common set of human resources management policies that are uniquely applicable in the particular regional context.
4. **Geocentric (global) staffing approach.** The company's priority is the optimal use of all resources, including human resources, and local or regional considerations are not considered important for the success of the corporate strategy. Managers are selected and promoted on a global basis without regard to their country of origin or cultural background. HRM policies are developed at headquarters, and these policies are generally consistent across all subsidiaries.

Companies with ethnocentric or geocentric approaches generally have human resources policies and practices that are consistent globally. Those taking a polycentric or regiocentric approach vary their policies and practices depending on the local or regional culture and practices.

While international corporate strategy determines the choice of one of the four approaches, the following important factors should be considered in the ultimate selection of an IHRM approach:[5]

- **National concerns.** Subsidiaries have to function within the legal framework of the host country. For example, some countries require that an employee who is laid off must be given compensation at a certain percentage of his or her basic pay. Some countries restrict the number of employees the subsidiary may bring from outside the country. In these countries, the head and a few senior managers of the subsidiary may be from the headquarters or another country, but the majority of the managers and employees must be local. Laws governing occupational safety also vary a great deal from country to country and have to be incorporated into the formulation of international human resources management practices. In addition, political volatility inherent in some countries requires that global corporations provide appropriate measures for the physical well-being and safety of not only their expatriate managers but the local workforce as well.

- **Economic concerns.** The cost of living, such as housing, food, and other expenses, varies widely from country to country. This often poses significant economic concerns that must be addressed by the corporation as it formulates its international human resources management policies and practices.
- **Technological concerns.** Another concern, which is growing in importance, is the availability of skilled employees, especially for global service corporations, such as Citicorp and McKinsey & Company. As the use of highly sophisticated manufacturing technology and the need to produce high-quality products on a global scale increase, IHRM managers need to ensure that skilled employees are selected and developed in all of the subsidiaries. When the basic product must be modified to appeal to local or regional markets, a polycentric or regiocentric approach makes more sense.
- **Organizational concerns.** The stage of the internationalization of the company and the product life cycle are important determinants of the IHRM approach. For example, when a company first ventures into international business, it often adopts an ethnocentric approach, but as subsidiaries are added and managed by locals, a polycentric approach makes more sense. Later, growth, increased productivity, and cost control may cause the firm to adopt a regiocentric or geocentric approach. As operations become strictly global in nature, a complete geocentric IHRM policy is the best approach.
- **Cultural concerns.** The differences between the corporate and societal cultures of the headquarters and subsidiaries also influence the IHRM approach. If the corporate cultures are different, as is often the case for many European multinationals, it becomes necessary to adopt a polycentric or regiocentric approach. If the societal cultures are different, a polycentric or regiocentric approach may be more appropriate. For example, the cultural need for extended bereavement leave in many cultures, such as east Asian and Polynesian cultures, makes most U.S. and European HRM policies pertaining to such leave difficult to enforce. In some countries, the societal culture encourages the adoption of an ethnocentric HRM approach, as is the case with most Japanese multinationals.[6] For example, most Japanese multinationals hire only Japanese as senior managers, which is acceptable and expected in their culture. Furthermore, if the number and degree of cultural differences among the subsidiaries are of paramount significance, the adoption of a geocentric HRM policy will be difficult, regardless of its usefulness in implementing the overall corporate strategy.

The choice of an approach to IHRM is difficult, at best. A multinational or global corporation whose overall corporate strategy is reflected in its HRM practices will be more competitive in launching new products and services. We should, however, note that of all corporate functions, IHRM tends to be more reflective of local norms, customs, traditions, values, and practices.[7] While U.S. researchers emphasize the need for consistency between corporate-level strategy and adoption of IHRM policies of subsidiaries, European managers are less inclined to emphasize consistency in practice. European HRM managers are likely to closely follow guidelines from top management, and this gives them less control and strategic autonomy in running the HRM operations of subsidiaries, as compared to their American counterparts.

Major IHRM Functions

International human resources managers have the responsibility for the five functional human resource areas: recruitment and selection, performance evaluation, compensation and benefits, training and development, and labor relations. Management of expatriate workers is an additional function of IHRM. Exhibit 12.1 summarizes the way that aspects of strategy influence IHRM.

Recruitment and Selection

Recruitment and selection are key processes through which a multinational or global corporation brings new employees into its network. *Recruitment* is the process of attracting a pool of qualified applicants for available positions. *Selection* is the process of choosing qualified applicants from the available candidates and ensuring that the skills, knowledge, and abilities of the selected employees match the requirements of the positions.

EXHIBIT 12.1 Strategic Approach, Organizational Concerns, and IHRM Approach

Source: D. A. Heenan and H. V. Perlmutter, *Multinational Organization Development.* Copyright © 1979. Used with permission of Pearson Education, Inc., Upper Saddle River, NJ 07458.

Aspects of the Enterprise	Ethnocentric	Polycentric	Regiocentric	Global
Primary strategic orientation/stage	International	Multidomestic	Regional	Transnational
Perpetuation (recruiting, staffing, development)	People of home country developed for key positions everywhere in the world	People of local nationality developed for key positions in their own country	Regional people developed for key positions anywhere in the region	Best people everywhere in the world developed for key positions everywhere in the world
Complexity of organization	Complex in home country, simple in subsidiaries	Varied and independent	Highly interdependent on a regional basis	"Global web"; complex, independent, worldwide alliances/network
Authority; decision making	High in headquarters	Relatively low in headquarters	High regional headquarters and/or high collaboration among subsidiaries	Collaboration of headquarters and subsidiaries around the world
Evaluation and control	Home standards applied to people and performance	Determined locally	Determined regionally	Globally integrated
Rewards	High in headquarters; low in subsidiaries	Wide variation; can be high or low rewards for subsidiary performance	Rewards for contribution to regional objectives	Rewards to international and local executives for reaching local and worldwide objectives based on global company goals
Communication; information flow	High volume of orders, commands, advice to subsidiaries	Little to and from headquarters; little among subsidiaries	Little to and from corporate headquarters, but may be high to and from regional headquarters and among countries	Horizontal; network relations
Geographic identification	Nationality of owner	Nationality of host country	Regional company	Truly global company, but identifying with national interests ("glocal")

Classifying Employees

Employees of multinational and global organizations are typically classified into three categories:

1. **Parent-country national (PCN).** The nationality of the employee is the same as that of the headquarters of the global organization. For example, a U.S. citizen working for a U.S. company, such as Microsoft, in Italy is a PCN.
2. **Host-country national (HCN).** The employee's nationality is the same as that of the subsidiary. For example, an Italian citizen working for a U.S. company, such as Microsoft, in Rome is an HCN.
3. **Third-country national (TCN).** The employee's nationality is neither that of the headquarters nor that of the local subsidiary. For example, an Italian citizen working for a U.S. company, such as Microsoft, in Brazil is a TCN.

The classification of employees is important because it determines the adoption of the IHRM approach. While such classification helps us understand the general approach that characterizes most IHRM policies of multinational and global corporations, it is important to note that the classification scheme does not cover all possibilities. In many countries, classifications are related to seniority, compensation, and stage of career.

In multinational and global corporations, the staffing policy strongly affects the type of employee the company prefers. Companies with an ethnocentric orientation usually staff important positions with PCNs. Those adopting a polycentric orientation usually select HCNs for subsidiaries while PCNs manage headquarters. Those with regiocentric orientations staff positions with PCNs or with HCNs and TCNs from the region—the needs of the company and the product strategy determine the staffing. Those adopting a geocentric approach are likely to favor the selection of the most suitable person for the job, regardless of type.

It is important to consider the prevalent practices of the headquarters, as well as the practices and legal requirements of the countries in which the subsidiaries are located, as discussed earlier. In many countries, such in Mexico, it is common practice to recruit family members to work in the same subsidiary[8]—a practice that is strongly discouraged in the United States, United Kingdom, and western Europe. In some eastern European countries, such as Hungary, the need to reduce unemployment means that multinationals must obtain permission from the ministry of labor before hiring an expatriate.[9]

A balance must be struck between internal corporate consistency and sensitivity to local needs and practices. Different cultures emphasize different attributes in the selection process. Some cultures emphasize the need for universal criteria—what the person can do for the organization is more important than who the person is. Other cultures emphasize ascriptive criteria—who the person is, and his or her family background and connections, is more important than what he or she can do for the organization. The selection process in achievement-oriented countries, such as the United States, United Kingdom, Australia, and western European countries, highlights skills, knowledge, and abilities. While family or social connections might help, the emphasis is on hiring those who are best able to perform the job. In an ascriptive culture, age, gender, family background, and social connections are important, and the emphasis is on selecting someone whose personal characteristics fit the job. For example, in Japan and parts of Latin America, advertisements in newspapers might explicitly state that the company is looking for a young male within a specific age range for a job, while such specifications may be external to the job requirements.

Such advertisements would be violations of the Fair Employment Practices Act in the United States. Many countries place few restrictions on recruitment, selection, or hiring, and an employer can ask any question or actively recruit candidates who fit certain personal characteristics.

Companies using a geocentric approach to IHRM have considerable difficulties in integrating the practices of various subsidiaries because the subsidiaries often vary from being heavily regulated by governments to having little regulation. One approach emphasizes the need for selecting applicants on the basis of not only ability and motivation but also the fit between the person and the organization, with selection modifications to suit cultural requirements.[10] This is important, for example, in some east Asian cultures such as Korea and Japan, where answering a question immediately is not seen as a positive attribute. The geocentric approach also highlights the development of a global system, based on achievement motivation, which may not be suitable in every country. Japanese managers feel that too much attention to qualifications and not enough on personal characteristics leads to selecting the wrong person for the company. The tendency in Japan is to recruit by emphasizing the fit with the entire company rather than with a specific job.

Performance Evaluation

Performance evaluation is the process of appraising employees' job performance. It is a systematic process, and in Western multinational organizations performance appraisals are usually done on a routine basis. Supervisors are required to discuss the results of appraisal with each employee.

Performance evaluation is often challenging, because it has two explicit purposes, which often conflict. The first is evaluative, while the second is developmental. Evaluative aspects of performance appraisal provide information for organizational decisions relating to compensation and advancement. Developmental aspects focus on feedback to help employees develop and improve their performance.

For international and global corporations, the complexity of performance evaluation increases because such organizations have the responsibility of developing systematic processes for the evaluation of employees from different countries who work in different locales. The need for developing consistent performance evaluations is often in conflict with the need to consider cultural factors. For example, in China, saving face is very important, and public criticism of an employee is counterproductive and may lead to turnover. This is also true in Mexico, where public criticism as a part of performance appraisal is avoided.[11] Developing a balanced performance review system for the Mexican situation requires an appreciation of Mexican culture, where tact and courtesy are key factors.

The organization's overall HRM strategy is the major determinant of the effectiveness of its performance evaluation system. A company with an ethnocentric approach designs appraisal systems that use the same techniques developed in headquarters, regardless of the need to incorporate some unique characteristics of each local subsidiary, such as national culture or legal issues. Some such companies translate their appraisal form into local languages. Multinational companies with polycentric or regiocentric approaches tend to be more sensitive to local conditions within each country or region. Those with a geocentric orientation use the same system of evaluating employees in various subsidiaries, but unlike ethnocentric organizations, the company develops universally applicable performance appraisal systems. Developing a global system of performance appraisal is time-consuming and requires a comprehensive consideration of many factors, as discussed earlier.

Compensation and Benefits

The compensation and benefit function of HRM is designed to develop uniform salary systems and other forms of remuneration, such as health insurance, pension funds, vacation, and sick pay. An international system of compensation is more difficult to develop, in that it must be concerned with the comparability across various subsidiaries located in various economic locales. The system must also be competitive, in order to attract and retain qualified employees. The salary structure of employees in different locations should reflect appropriate compensation schemes, taking into account local market conditions as well as consistency throughout the organization. Another concern is the overall cost of compensation to the multinational or global organization.[12]

Regardless of the approach to IHRM, compensation and benefit schemes reflect local market conditions. The availability of qualified local people to fill positions, the prevailing local wage rates, the use of expatriates, and various labor laws influence the level of compensation and benefits. If the supply of qualified applicants is limited, the wage rates typically rise. To lower such expenses, international HR managers may consider bringing in home-country or third-country nationals.

Typically, a global company attempts to develop a policy and apply it uniformly, offering salaries and benefits representing a specific market level. When the company emphasizes the quality of its products and employees, it often has a global policy to pay high wages everywhere to improve retention of quality employees. Another method is to pay high salaries in those countries where the company has its R&D operations but pay average wages elsewhere. Practical Insight 12.1 illustrates the linkage between various cultures and distinct compensation and benefit requirements as reported in 2008.

Training and Development

The training and development function involves planning for effective learning processes, organizational development, and career development. In the United States, there is a recognized field of HR called *human resource development (HRD)*. In global organizations, human resource development professionals are responsible for the training and development of employees located in subsidiaries around the world. They specialize in training employees for assignments abroad and in developing managers with a global mind-set, that is, managers who understand the complexities of managing in different countries.

The delivery of international training programs is either very centralized or decentralized.[13] A centralized approach originates at the headquarters, and corporate trainers travel to subsidiaries and adapt the program to local situations. This is an ethnocentric approach to training. In contrast, a geocentric approach allows the development of programs using inputs from both headquarters and subsidiary staff. Trainers are sent from headquarters or subsidiaries to any location where they are needed. In more polycentric approaches, the cultural backgrounds of the trainers and trainees tend to be similar. Subsidiary HR managers develop training materials and techniques for use in their own countries.

It is important to understand the learning process in order to implement effective training programs. Cultural differences in learning processes must be taken into account in developing training programs. An effective training program should focus on the specific needs of a subsidiary in a specific country and the cultural background of the trainees. In individualistic countries, the tendency is to emphasize learning mechanisms on an individual level; whereas in collectivistic countries, learning as a group is more effective. Similarly, where power distance is small, the relationship between the trainer and the trainee tends toward equality and challenging the trainer is acceptable. On the

EXHIBIT 12.2 Impact of Culture on Training and Development Practices

Source: Adapted from M. Marquardt and D. W. Engel, *Global Human Resource Development* (Prentice-Hall, 1993), pp. 25–32.

	United States/ Canada	East Asia	Middle East/ North Africa	Latin America
HRD roles	Trainer and trainee as equals; trainees can and do challenge trainer; trainer can be informed and casual.	Trainees have great respect for trainer, who should behave, dress, and relate in a highly professional, formal manner.	Trainer highly respected; trainees want respect and friendly relationship; formality is important.	Preference for a decisive, clear, charismatic leader as trainer; trainees like to be identified with and loyal to a successful leader.
Analysis and design	Trainer determines objectives with input from trainees and their managers; trainees openly state needs and want to achieve success through learning.	Trainer should know what trainees need, admitting needs might represent loss of face to trainees.	Difficult to identify needs because it is improper to speak of other's faults; design must include time for socializing, relationship building, and prayers.	Difficult to get trainees to expose weaknesses and faults; design should include time for socializing.
Development and delivery	Programs should be practical and relevant, using a variety of methodologies with lecturing time limited.	Materials should be orderly, well organized, and unambiguous; trainees most accustomed to lecture, note taking, and limited questioning.	Need adequate opportunity for trainer and trainees to interact; rely on verbal rather than written demonstrations of knowledge acquired; avoid paper exercises and role playing.	Educational system relies on lecture and has more theoretical emphasis; training should be delivered in local language.
Administration and environment	Hold training in comfortable, economical location; trainee selection based on perceived needs of organization and individual.	Quality of program may be judged on the basis of quality of location and training materials; ceremonies with dignitaries, certificates, plaques, and speeches taken as signs of value of program.	The learning process should be permeated with flourishes and ceremonies; program should not be scheduled during Ramadan, the month of fasting.	Value and importance judged by location, which dignitaries invited for the ceremonies, and academic affiliation of trainer; time is flexible: beginning or ending at a certain time not important.

other hand, in countries where power distance is large, a trainer receives great respect and challenging the trainer in any way is not acceptable. Exhibit 12.2 shows the impact of culture on training and development practices in four different parts of the world: The United States and Canada, east Asia, Middle East/north Africa, and Latin America. It also identifies the main differences among the regions, although the specifics of training practices may differ somewhat from country to country within each region.

Labor Relations

The labor relations function is designed to assist managers and workers determine their relationships within the workplace.[14] The concept and practice of labor relations vary greatly in different parts of the world. In the United States, labor relations practices generally are formal and confrontational and are governed by union contracts. In Japan, the relationship between management and unions is cooperative, and union leaders are determined by managers. In many countries, the government regulates labor relations. Therefore, a polycentric approach is generally more effective in managing this aspect of the HRM function. It has been suggested that even though labor relations are best addressed at the local or regional level, organizations should coordinate and develop labor relations policies uniformly across various subsidiaries.[15]

PRACTICAL INSIGHT 12.1

THE RIGHT PERKS
Global hiring means getting a handle on how different cultures view salaries, taxes, and benefits.

Brazilian supermodel Gisele Bundchen may be able to decide, as she did recently, that she would rather be paid in euros than once-mighty dollars. But for most mere mortals toiling away in cubicles around the globe, pay and benefits are a decidedly local affair. In Latin America, for instance, past financial crises mean employees aren't much interested in deferred compensation plans such as 401(k)s, which are common in the U.S. Why be rewarded in stocks and bonds that could collapse?

As expat packages decline and global growth requires attracting local talent, employers that ignore local quirks do so at their own risk. Peter D. Acker, a global rewards consultant for Hewitt Associates, reports that he sees companies extend their stock-option plans around the world, thinking everyone will love them. But local tax treatments for such options mean that's often not the case. Other companies, he says, have rolled out bonus plans in China that focus on individual performance, only to find that rewarding group achievements might have been a better cultural fit. Using data from benefits consulting firm Mercer, we compiled snapshots of pay and perks in 10 countries, including benefits ranging from company-owned ski chalets in France to bodyguards and bulletproof cars for top executives in Brazil:

India
- Cost-of-living rank (Bangalore): 134
- Salary, head of sales & marketing: $56,171
- Salary, data-entry operator: $1,913
- Projected average pay increase for 2008: 14.1%
- Days off: 31
- Local perk: CEOs might grumble about rising health-care costs for U.S. workers. But at least they don't have to pay for employees' aging parents, which is common for companies operating in India. Rosaline Chow Koo, Mercer's head of health and benefits consulting in Asia, says this is one reason health-care spending is rising swiftly: "It's growing so much faster than wages that it's become a hot issue."

Hong Kong
- Cost-of-living rank: 5
- Salary, head of sales & marketing: $149,905
- Salary, data-entry operator: $16,139
- Projected average pay increase for 2008: 3.8%
- Days off: 26
- Local perk: In recent years, Hong Kong workers have been asking for traditional Chinese medicine coverage as a supplement to regular health insurance. The plans, which cover everything from herbal therapies to fees for Chinese medicine practitioners, are offered by 55% of employers, says Mercer's Chow Koo.

Philippines
- Cost-of-living rank (Manila): 137
- Salary, head of sales & marketing: $95,286
- Salary, data-entry operator: $6,829
- Projected average pay increase for 2008: 7.4%
- Days off: 19
- Local perk: For years, many Filipinos received bags of rice as a benefit. Employers later converted the sacks to "rice allowances" paid in cash and now offer "flex" packages, where less tradition-minded workers can exchange the cash for perks such as free mobile phones.

China
- Cost-of-living rank (Shanghai): 26
- Salary, head of sales & marketing: $92,402
- Salary, data-entry operator: $4,034
- Projected average pay increase for 2008: 7.5%
- Days off: 23
- Local perk: Companies operating in China are required by the government to chip into a housing fund that's available to their Chinese employees, who also make contributions. When employees are ready to buy a home, they can draw from the funds to help. About 20% of multinationals currently chip in more to the housing fund than required, according to Mercer.

Japan
- Cost-of-living rank (Tokyo): 4
- Salary, head of sales & marketing: $148,899
- Salary, data-entry operator: $30,933
- Projected average pay increase for 2008: 2.5%
- Days off: 35
- Local perk: Japanese workers often receive "family allowances" *(kazoku teiate)* on top of their pay from employers, depending on the size of their family. Stemming from the country's tradition of lifetime employment, the stipends are most prevalent among native companies and range from about $100 to $300 a month. Some employers have

been recasting them as incentives for workers to have kids in order to combat Japan's declining birthrate.

Mexico

Cost-of-living rank (Mexico City): 104
Salary, head of sales & marketing: $163,591
Salary, data-entry operator: $11,017
Projected average pay increase for 2008: 4.8%
Days off: 23

Local perk: Some companies having difficulty luring qualified expats to polluted Mexico City offer "pollution-escape trips," or all-expenses-paid getaways to the Pacific or Gulf coasts. One local holiday quirk: Mother's Day is on a weekday, and employees get a day or a half-day off to take Mom out to lunch, prompting massive traffic snarls.

Brazil

Cost-of-living rank (Rio de Janeiro): 64
Salary, head of sales & marketing: $208,691
Salary, data-entry operator: $11,829
Projected average pay increase for 2008: 5.0%
Days off: 40

Local perk: It's more of an essential safety precaution than a perk, but to foil kidnappers, top executives in Brazil are chauffeured in bulletproof cars and followed by bodyguards. (This benefit also shows up in Mexico.) "It's kind of a strange way to think about it," says Hewitt's Acker. "But if your executive is kidnapped for a month, your business really suffers."

USA

Cost-of-living rank (New York): 15
Salary, head of sales & marketing: $229,300
Salary, data-entry operator: $35,400
Projected average pay increase for 2008: 3.7%
Days off: 25

Local perk: To get a handle on those fat pay packages, U.S. CEOs commonly receive financial-planning benefits—averaging about $20,000 a year, reports executive pay consultants Pearl Meyer & Partners. The money helps pay their cadre of accountants, estate lawyers, and financial planners. The benefit is much rarer elsewhere. And unique to the U.S.'s litigious society, Mercer says, are group or prepaid legal services, which some companies offer employees. As with group health insurance, employees pay premiums to get free or discounted access to attorneys for needs such as wills, adoptions, or real estate transactions.

Russia

Cost-of-living rank (Moscow): 1
Salary, head of sales & marketing: $117,135
Salary, data-entry operator: $10,325
Projected average pay increase for 2008: 10.2%
Days off: 39

Local perk: Company-sponsored mortgages are seen as an attractive perk in Russia, where consumers have traditionally had less access to credit and where the cost of living is high. Companies who offer this perk secure the loans, says Hewitt's Acker, and in some cases, help employees pay more favorable rates. Corporate help for loans occurs in other emerging markets, such as India and Brazil.

France

Cost-of-living rank (Paris): 13
Salary, head of sales & marketing: $188,771
Salary, data-entry operator: $28,857
Projected average pay increase for 2008: 3.0%
Days off: 40

Local perk: As if the high number of days off were not enough, some French employers offer the use of company-owned ski chalets and beach houses to employees for a nominal fee. Such perks are also occasionally seen in Germany, says Charles Nelson, who leads Mercer's health and benefits practice in Britain and Ireland.

Data: Data are provided by Mercer, except where noted. Cost-of-living rank is based on Mercer's 2007 survey of the comparative cost of cities for expatriates. Salaries represent midpoint annual base salaries, using exchange rates from local currencies to U.S. dollars on Jan. 14. Days off combine minimum vacation days required by law and public or nationally recognized holidays for employees working five days a week after 10 years' service. China and the U.S. do not mandate vacation days nationally, but 15 days is common in the U.S. for employees with 10 years of service and 12 days is average in China, though numbers vary from city to city. Mercer notes that in Mexico, many companies supplement required public holidays with an additional 4 to 6 days.

Source: Jena McGregor, "The Right Perks," *BusinessWeek,* January 28, 2008, p. 42.

Although some unions are termed "international," most unions are organized at the local, company, regional (within country), or national level. Furthermore, some unions are in the process of developing regional (groups of nations) offices in various countries. These offices focus on issues that arise as a result of multiple-country trading blocks, such as the European Union, MERCOSUR, or NAFTA. In Europe, more than 50 industrywide, cross-continent unions have emerged. Still, multinational and global companies have been slow to negotiate with them. An example of a worldwide union is the International Trade Union Confederation, which is the world's largest trade union. Formed in November 2006, it represents approximately 160 million workers worldwide and is represented in the majority of the countries in the world.

During the past 15 years, union membership has dropped significantly throughout the world. Still, in some countries and in some industries in those countries, powerful unions are a part of the business landscape. Exhibit 12.3 illustrates the change in specific trade unions in Europe from 1993 to 2003.

Selecting Expatriates

Most research indicates that technical competence is the primary decision criteria used by global firms in selecting employees for overseas assignments.[16] (A person living in a foreign land is known as an **expatriate**.) Companies continue to endorse this practice,

EXHIBIT 12.3
European Trade Union Membership Figures, 1993–2003

Source: *European Industrial Relations Observatory*, May 21, 2004.

Country	1993	1998	2003	Change, 1993–2003 (%)
Austria	1,616,000	1,480,000	1,407,000	−12.9
Belgium	2,865,000	3,013,000	3,061,000	+6.8
Bulgaria	2,192,000	778,000	515,000	−76.5
Cyprus	159,000	167,000	175,000	+10.1
Denmark	2,116,000	2,170,000	2,151,000	+1.7
Estonia	—	—	93,000	—
Finland	2,069,000	2,084,000	2,122,000	+2.6
France	1,256,000	1,425,000	889,000	−320%
Germany	11,680,000	9,798,000	8,894,000	−23.9
Greece	721,000	656,000	639,000	−11.4
Hungary	—	—	936,000	—
Ireland	432,000	463,000	515,000	+19.2
Italy	10,594,000	10,763,000	11,266,000	+6.3
Latvia	nd	252,000	180,000	−28.6
Luxembourg	97,000	112,000	139,000	+43.3
Malta	74,000	82,000	87,000	+17.6
Netherlands	1,810,000	1,936,000	1,941,000	+7.2
Norway	1,325,000	1,489,000	1,498,000	+13.1
Poland	6,500,000	3,200,000	1,900,000	−70.8
Portugal	1,150,000	—	1,165,000	+1.3
Romania	—	—	4,399,000	—
Slovakia	1,583,000	854,000	576,000	−63.6
Slovenia	nd	nd	360,000	—
Spain	—	—	2,108,000	—
Sweden	3,712,000	3,562,000	3,446,000	−7.2
United Kingdom	8,804,000	7,852,000	7,751,000	−12.0

and other criteria that can have substantial effects on expatriates' adjustment and performance are not given enough attention.[17] This overemphasis on technical and job-related competence has guided the selection process because it is easier to measure these factors. Host-country organizations also prefer technically competent expatriates. However, as we discussed in Chapter 4, cultural and national differences make expatriate adjustment difficult, and the ability to adapt to unfamiliar conditions is crucial.[18] Language skills and knowledge of the local area are straightforward criteria that could be incorporated, but what is not understood very well is that the factors that can ease adjustment to the new environment are generally less concrete.

Culture Shock

Culture shock—a state of anxiety and disorientation caused by exposure to a new culture—can be a significant barrier to the adjustment and performance of an expatriate. Differences in daily styles of interactions, including such things as whether to shake hands or not, when to present a gift, when and how to pay complements, cause difficulties in adjusting to the new environment. Coupled with this is the difference of familiar signs and ways of doing things, such as street signs, driving rules, and use of telephone and e-mail, that creates further problems for the expatriate.

The effects of culture shock on adjustment can be shown as a U-shaped curve, as shown in Exhibit 12.4. Individuals who visit a country for a short time, such as tourists and others on short-term missions, do not go through the various degrees of adjustment. However, people who go to work or live abroad for a long period of time go through the phases of adjustment shown in the exhibit. The first phase, the *honeymoon,* begins with the initial contact with another culture, and a sense of optimism and euphoria are common. Expatriates live in pleasant surroundings and are welcomed by colleagues and other host-country nationals, who may arrange special welcome events and make them feel comfortable.

In the second stage, *culture shock,* difficulties in language, inadequate schooling for the children, lack of adequate housing, crowded buses and subways, differences in shopping habits, and other problems can create stress, unhappiness, and a dislike for

EXHIBIT 12.4
Effects of Culture Shock on Adjustment

Source: From D. C. Thomas, *Essentials of International Management: A Cross-Cultural Perspective.* Copyright © 2002 by Sage Publications, Inc. Reprinted by permission of Sage Publications, Inc.

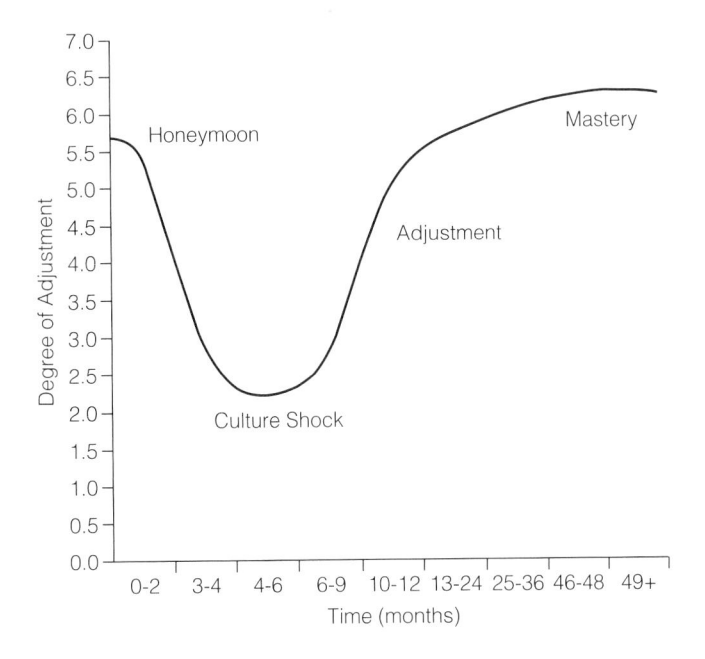

the country. During this period, expatriates often seek others from their home country with whom they can compare experiences about their difficulties. They may try to escape through drinking and socializing, as they experience a sense of powerlessness and alienation. Over time, these feeling may intensify in some expatriates and lead to depression and physical health problems. In addition, since the September 11, 2001, terrorist attacks on the World Trade Center and Pentagon, the incidences of terrorism are affecting placement of expatriates. Practical Insight 12.2 offers some tips for staying safe on foreign assignments. While there are no guarantees that the guidelines provided are foolproof, they will help.

In the third stage, *adjustment,* expatriates begin to develop new sets of skills that enable them to cope with their new environment. Anxiety and depression become less frequent, and expatriates begin to feel more positive about their new surroundings. Furthermore, the expatriate begins to become more productive at work and reverts back to being the confident manager who was selected for the overseas assignment.

In the fourth and last stage, *mastery,* expatriates know how to deal with the demands of their local environment and have learned enough about local customs and culture to feel "at home." Still, it is important for expatriates to continually realize that they will never know the entire culture as locals do and, thus, it is their responsibility to attain new knowledge and skills every day.

Managing Expatriates

Multinational and global organizations that make use of parent-country and third-country nationals must develop a process of handling the complexities of moving people outside their home countries. Employing expatriates may be linked with the global strategy, but it tends to be an expensive process most of the time. Careful managing of expatriate HRM is extremely important.

Cost of Failure

The cost of failure of the overseas assignments is much more than simply the cost of the executive's salary and transfer. Because of additional compensation, an expatriate stationed in an expensive city such as Tokyo, London, or Paris could cost a company up to $350,000 in the first year.[19] It is more cost-efficient to prevent a bad transfer than to have an expatriate return home because of difficulties in adjusting to foreign assignments.

Some managers fail because they are unhappy in their assignment. This is often due to the poor organizational support that promotes the feeling within the company that overseas assignments are not high-profile ones and do not lead to advancement.[20] It can also be due to the lack of family adjustment to the new culture.

Compensation Issues

Sending home-country nationals abroad is expensive. Doing so costs one to two times more than keeping managers at home, and estimates indicate that it costs 10 times more than hiring a host-country national.[21] Until there is a global salary system, companies are generally forced to resort to one of two types of compensation systems.

1. **Headquarters salary system.** This system is based on the headquarters pay scale plus differentials. The salary for the same job at headquarters determines the base salary of the home-country national. The differential can be a positive addition to an expatriate's salary, or it can be a negative allowance to account for the extra

PRACTICAL INSIGHT 12.2

STAYING SAFE ON FOREIGN ASSIGNMENTS

Overseas travel has become an increasingly important part of conducting business in the era of globalization. This article outlines some of the precautions which human-resource specialists can take to help to protect their company employees who travel abroad.

Business Travelers Make Easy Targets

Increasing crime directed at business travelers abroad makes it more important than ever that human-resource specialists have a strategy for protecting company employees who travel overseas for the firm.

While companies see foreign trade as an exciting opportunity in the era of globalization, so too do some of the world's criminals.

Says Alan Stokes, of insurer CIGNA International: "Business travelers make easy targets. They often travel in unfamiliar territory, wear formal clothes, carry expensive laptop computers in readily-identifiable bags, use mobile telephones and wear watches which can cost more than a year's salary in less-privileged countries. All these factors combine to make them highly visible.

"Improved travel has made so many destinations accessible that business travelers can almost forget they are on foreign territory. The security of corporate-credit-card bookings, executive-club lounges and international hotel chains can cocoon them into a false sense of security. But believing they can go anywhere in the world and behave exactly as they do at home can make business travelers an easy target for anything from mugging to armed-car theft and even kidnap.

"The challenge for human-resource professionals is not only to ensure the personal safety of the individual, but also to ensure that their organization is not exposed to the business implications of losing the services of a key employee, of disruption to customer relationships or the loss of a contract, by preparing corporate travelers in advance."

Assets to Be Protected

"Companies generally send key personnel to conduct business overseas, so they should be seen as an asset to be protected."

Mr Stokes offers the following advice to human-resource specialists:

1. *Prepare the ground.* Make use of free pre-travel advice from the travel agent or insurance company. Do some homework on the destination. Check well in advance about inoculation and visa requirements. Find out about any dress codes and ask which taxi company to use on arrival at the destination. Make sure there is a contact number for the embassy and know if there are any areas of town which should be avoided.

2. *Check the insurance.* Make sure your company insurance covers the basics such as medical expenses, repatriation, personal injury and sickness for the area the executive is traveling to. Insurance bought with a travel ticket may be geared towards the needs of the holidaymaker. Business travelers need different support, such as cover for business equipment. Encourage the executive to carry the helpline number listed in the insurance documents, so that help is always at hand.

3. *Do not stand out from the crowd.* Avoid business luggage tickets. If the executive has a laptop computer, make sure he or she carries it in an ordinary holdall or briefcase. To the average thief, computer bags scream: "I have $2,000 of equipment on my shoulder."

If possible, the executive should travel in casual clothes. Expensive business clothes mark him or her as someone likely to be carrying valuable possessions and part of a larger, wealthy organization. Thieves target airports in the knowledge that business travelers will be carrying cash and credit cards. Keep credit cards on one's person and in separate places.

Thieves know which hotels are used by comparatively wealthy business travelers. If the executive feels like taking fresh air or sightseeing, he or she should ask the hotel staff where is safe to walk alone and which areas to avoid. Leave valuables such as jewellery and passport in the hotel safe, or keep them with money in a concealed money belt.

Take care when showing a gold or platinum credit card. Something which is taken for granted at home can also be a status symbol which clearly marks a person out as a target.

If the executive is to be met at an airport, ask the driver to use a code by which he or she can be recognized. Name and company on a card advertises the executive as a target to follow.

Such simple precautions can help to prevent a dream trip to an exotic foreign location from becoming a nightmare.

Source: *Human Resource Management International Digest,* May–June 1999.

benefits that might be associated with the particular overseas placement. When an expatriate is provided free housing and transportation and an equivalent sum is subtracted from his basic pay, the amount deducted is a negative allowance. Under the headquarters salary system, host-country nationals are entitled to neither the base salary nor the differentials of home-country nationals. Their salaries are based on local salary standards. Third-country nationals pose a unique compensation challenge. The company may treat them either as home- or host-country nationals, so inequities arise. The headquarters salary system is the more ethnocentric of the two compensation systems.

2. **Citizenship salary system.** The citizenship salary system solves the problem of what to do about the third-country nationals. The manager's salary is based on the standard for the country of his or her citizenship or native residence. An appropriate differential is then added, based on comparative factors between the two countries. This system works well as long as expatriates with similar positions do not come from countries with different salary scales. It is difficult to avoid this problem, however, and inequities arising from either compensation program are noticed by the managers.

Benefits   In the United States, approximately 27 percent of compensation for home-country employees is benefits. Issues surrounding expatriate benefits are different from those affecting benefits of host-country employees. Expatriates need vacations to return home for extended visits. Multinational companies often pay airfare for home visits, emergency leave, illnesses, and a death in the expatriate's family. However, other questions must be dealt with on a country and case-by-case basis. For example, some benefits are taxable overseas but tax-deductible at home, and some countries provide government-sponsored social benefits, such as universal health care. The company must reach an agreement with either the government or the home-country manager about coverage for these necessities.

Allowances   Multinational and global companies often pay allowances for cost of living, relocation expenses, housing, cars, and club memberships in the host country. In addition, education allowances for children are often expected, either to allow the children to attend private school in the host country or to allow them to be educated in the home country. Hardship allowances are often required to attract qualified individuals to less desirable locations, such as the Middle East or other less developed areas.

Incentives   Only 20 percent of companies pay higher compensation to expatriates than to home-country managers. Instead, most offer a one-time lump-sum premium.[22]

Incentives are beginning to be phased out, because the manager sees the assignment as its own reward or as a step toward globalization.[23]

Taxes   Often multinational and global companies pay any extra tax burden. Taxes can be an extremely complex area in compensating expatriates. In some countries, expatriates' salary is taxable only when paid locally. In most countries, local authorities do not tax compensation based on a worldwide scheme. American companies prefer a tax equalization plan that allows the company to withhold the expatriate's U.S. tax liability and pay his or her local taxes. British companies, on the other hand, change their policy depending on the country in which the subsidiary is located. The tax equalization plan may create a situation in which the company pays taxes in multiple countries because taxes paid on behalf of an expatriate by the headquarters are also taxable locally. International compensation experts have suggested that companies with operations in many countries should adopt a policy of tax equalization. The company would gain in some countries and lose in others. However, if the scale of international operations is limited, it is best to leave the payment of local taxes to the expatriate and adjust other allowances in accordance with local standards.[24]

Managing Dual-Career Expatriates

A current critical strategic concern for multinational corporations is the consideration of attracting the right expatriates when their spouses also have careers, which are often not transferable overseas. The number of dual careers grew from 52 percent of all couples to 59 percent in the early 1990s, and the trend is on the rise. Over 50 percent of the expatriates being transferred abroad have spouses who worked before relocating.[25]

The dual-career expatriate couple has become a major concern of global companies, especially companies in which overseas experience can significantly advance one's career. In an interesting phenomenon, couples sustain their marriages by using the Internet and e-mail; this is becoming common as married men and women with careers take assignments in different parts of the world. Global companies must have sound policies to lessen the chances that a talented male or female manager will terminate employment because of the difficulties associated with separation from his or her spouse. Some of the suggestions for policies are:

- For transcontinental commuter marriages, providing for frequent visitation trips by the family or the expatriate to prevent the pain of separation from becoming too intense. One trip every two months is not unreasonable.
- Providing a generous allowance for long-distance telephone calls and other costs of communication. A phone conversation can ease the tension and loneliness of the expatriate and the family.
- Seeking employment opportunities for the spouse within the company or in the local area if the spouse is willing to quit his or her job in the home country to be with the married partner. The U.S. State Department has the practice of finding local jobs for spouses of employees sent abroad.
- Making connections with other global companies for employment of spouses. For example, the Hong Kong subsidiary of an international company, such as Proctor & Gamble, might be in a position to hire the spouse of an IBM expatriate manager working in Hong Kong.

Repatriation

Most overseas assignments last for five years. **Repatriation** is the term given to the return of the home-country manager. Managers return for a number of reasons:[26]

- The time of the overseas assignment is up.
- Children's education.
- Unhappy with the assignment.
- Family unhappiness.
- Failure—the expatriate does not meet stated objectives.

Readjustment problems occur when individuals arrive back after their overseas assignments. Tung found that the longer the assignment, the more problems with reabsorption.[27] Transition strategies are needed to retain these individuals and the experience they have acquired. One study showed:

- Three-fourths of expatriates felt they returned to a demotion,
- 60 percent felt they were unable to use their overseas experience because it was devalued by the organization.
- 60 percent believed that the company lacked any commitment to them on their return.[28]

The study also found that 25 percent of the expatriates left the organization within a year after their return.

Other readjustment problems are more personal, such as adjusting to lower pay and benefits after the overseas assignments. Some find difficulty in the housing market after they sold their house to go overseas. Children of expatriates may find that returning to public school is difficult after the smaller classes in private school. The change in the cultural lifestyle can affect those who transfer from cultural centers such as Paris or London or New York to less cosmopolitan areas in the home country.

Companies can prevent some of these problems by using transition strategies. One useful strategy is the use of repatriation agreements. These agreements define the company's responsibilities to the expatriate on his or her return, thereby providing the security often sought by managers on overseas assignments. Some companies have set up separate departments to deal with expatriates' special needs.[29] Another strategy used by some companies is the purchase of the manager's home until the foreign assignment is complete. This allows the expatriate to keep up with the generally increasing housing market while overseas. Some companies assign senior managers to be sponsors of expatriate managers.[30] These mentor programs maintain the individual's communication lines with headquarters, which is of crucial importance to expatriates on their return. Assigning expatriates to projects that are centered at the home office also enhances communication with headquarters. Practical Insight 12.3 illustrates the strategic importance of managing the expatriate's relocation to a new country.

International Human Resources Management and Competitive Advantage

In an era of globalization, when technology and capital flow freely across national and cultural boundaries, human resources take on new importance as critical strategic assets or factors of production that largely are not easily mobile. People resist permanent moves across cultures and boundaries, even if doing so means that they refuse better compensation and adequate living facilities. While political barriers to intercountry mobility have largely been removed, as in the case of integrated European Union countries, where free movement of labor is allowed, the actual size of the flow of talented people across national boundaries remains small. The main barriers are rooted in language differences, cultural preferences, and natural propensities to stay and work in the country of birth.

Intercountry competition in a global economy is likely to result in successes and failures of many large to medium-size organizations. One of the major ways failures can be averted and sustained competitive advantage maintained is by recruiting talented personnel from a global workforce who are able to manage technology and knowledge, motivate people in various worldwide subsidiaries, and exercise proper

PRACTICAL INSIGHT 12.3

CULTURE SHOCK IN AMERICA?

Imagine you're embarking on your first foreign assignment. You had an outstanding academic career and are now in great demand in your field. After only a few years on the job, you're an undisputed star at your company. You've become so stellar, in fact, that with your ability to speak the international language of business-English, you're the obvious choice to be sent abroad. It's a developmental assignment, shall we say: five, maybe 10, years overseas. Then you'll return home with a skill set bulging with international savvy and your own personal spotlight on the world stage of business.

With confidence, you accept that exotic assignment abroad. Destination: the United States of America. But you soon discover that the Land of Opportunity is really the Land of "What's Your Social Security Number?" Without that nine-digit track record of your material viability, it doesn't matter where you came from or where you're going. You find yourself struggling to open accounts; to get an apartment, a phone, and electricity; and to figure out the bus route while you're waiting for a car loan to come through. You have somehow dropped into the Dead Zone; you're stuck in Culture Shock Purgatory.

It's ironic that this would be the case in a country with one of the world's most-traveled populations. Still, being sent to the United States on foreign assignment is not just a stressful business—it's a lonely one. From New Delhi to Cape Town to Minas Gerais, the observation is the same: Americans are friendly but hard to make friends with. We gregarious Americans don't truly bring international assignees into our lives, because we don't bring them into our homes after work.

What about corporate support? With rare exception, Corporate America is still focused more on making Americans' adventures abroad successful than on providing the same levels of support to those coming here on corporate assignments. This perspective will eventually come at great cost to any U.S. corporation with international ambitions, says Willa Hallowell, a partner with Brooklyn, N.Y.–based Cornelius Grove and Associates, a consultancy emphasizing cross-cultural support. You have to regard this person coming in as a business investment, and you therefore must guard that investment in every possible way. "If you don't, the mess you will have to clean up will be an even greater expense," Hallowell says. The costs associated with the mess include loss of productivity, the diminishment of the employee's self-confidence, the potential destruction of the employee's home life, and the corrosion of the company's reputation abroad.

"If things aren't going well, the returning employee will spread the seeds of discontent," Hallowell says. "Then, the next round of employees brought here will be prepared for problems, or they might choose to come here to look for another job."

The good news is that companies are moving toward seeking support services for their expatriates from all nations. "More and more companies are bringing expats to us," says Franchette Richards, until recently manager of Arthur Andersen's International Employment Solutions group. "We're helping them deal with visas and other immigration issues—financial obstacles, cultural differences. It's important for companies to realize that they must be consistent in the support of their expats, whether the employees are coming here or going outbound. An expat is an expat is an expat."

And no matter where they come from, expats share a critical concern: how well their spouses adjust to their new life. "It is the main reason why employees go home early," says Cornelius Grove, partner at Grove & Associates and an expert on the physiological effects of the stress of culture shock.

Most damaging to a spouse's accommodation: Under U.S. immigration laws, most spouses are not allowed to find jobs while they are "in country," so they are without the automatic social network that the office provides the employee.

Source: M. Finney, *Across the Board,* May 2000, p. 28.

---

leadership and negotiating skills. Increasing the recruitment of women is one way to ensure continued success in the global workforce. Women are joining men as examples of successful global leaders and effective expatriates. (The Section 3 ending case highlights Christina Gold's international leadership at Western Union.) Still, despite such successes, many multinationals, particularly from collectivistic and developing economies, remain reluctant to employ women as senior-level managers in leadership roles. In addition, corporations avoid placement of women in cultures where they feel women are not accorded proper respect. While some of these assumptions might be true, research conducted in the human resource field shows that women are more effective than men as expatriate managers in parts of the world where relationship-oriented managers do much better.

Summary

International human resources management is the process of managing human resources globally. An organization's corporate strategy drives the approach it takes to IHRM. The approach can influence implementation of major functions such as recruitment and selection, performance evaluation, compensation and benefits, training and development, and labor relations.

Multinational companies adopting a purely ethnocentric approach attempt to impose their home-country methods on their subsidiaries. Polycentric and regiocentric approaches tend to follow local practices more consistently. The geocentric or global approach develops practices for uniform worldwide use.

Management of expatriates is one of the major concerns of IHRM. Because expatriates function in dissimilar economic, political, and cultural environments and also need to function effectively in foreign work and living situations, they need special attention. It is important to motivate them in their assignments and upgrade their compensation and benefits to make foreign assignments attractive.

Approaches to IHRM are both converging and diverging worldwide. Large global corporations, such as Microsoft, IBM, Sony, Toyota, and Unilever, prefer uniform practices, whereas smaller companies prefer IHRM practices tailored to the local needs. International managers have the important responsibility of managing human resources in various countries and should upgrade their knowledge continuously in order to effectively implement corporate strategies.

Key Terms and Concepts

culture shock, *449*
ethnocentric staffing approach, *439*
expatriate, *448*
geocentric (global) staffing approach, *439*
international human resources management (IHRM), *438*
performance evaluation, *443*
polycentric staffing approach, *439*
regiocentric staffing approach, *439*
repatriation, *453*

Discussion Questions

1. What is international human resources management? Why is it more difficult to manage human resources on a worldwide basis than on a national basis?
2. What are the various functions of international human resources management? How does the process of recruitment and selection differ in international corporations compared to domestic corporations?
3. How does the process of performance appraisal differ in organizations that adopt a geocentric approach compared to the ones that adopt an ethnocentric approach?
4. When should an international corporation use universal compensation policies and practices? When should it use policies and practices tailored to local needs?
5. Explain the concept of culture shock. What is the role of the spouse of an expatriate in adjusting to foreign countries?

Minicase

Cracks in a Particularly Thick Glass Ceiling

Women in South Korea are slowly changing a corporate culture.

South Koreans are a bit conflicted about career women. Gender wasn't much of an issue in the selection of a female astronaut to fly this month on the country's first space mission. But when women are seeking workaday corporate jobs, some South Korean men still resist change. Outer space is one thing, but a woman in the next cubicle is something else.

For years, most educated women in South Korea who wanted to work could follow but one career path, which began and ended with teaching. The situation started to change after the 1998 Asian financial crisis. Thousands of men lost their jobs or took salary cuts, and their wives had to pick up the slack by starting businesses in their homes or seeking part-time work. A couple of years later, the government banned gender discrimination in the workplace and required businesses with more than 500 employees to set up child-care facilities. It also created a Gender Equality Ministry.

These days the government hires thousands of women (42% of its new employees last year), many for senior positions in the judiciary, international trade administration, and foreign service. Startups and foreign companies also employ (and promote) increasing numbers of Korean women. But at the top 400 companies, many of which are family-run conglomerates, it's hard for women to reach the upper ranks. In all, about 8% of working women hold managerial positions. (In the U.S. nearly 51% do.) "We have a long way to go," says Cho Jin Woo, director of the Gender Equality Ministry.

South Koreans are grappling with traditional attitudes about women, a hierarchical business culture, and the need to open up the workplace to compete globally. A senior manager at SK Holdings, which controls the giant mobile phone carrier SK Telecom, says he avoids hiring women because he believes they lack tenacity. When deadlines are tight, he says, "you need people prepared to put in long hours at the office." Park Myung Soon, a 39-year-old woman who is in charge of business development at the carrier, says, "Many men are preoccupied with the notion that women are a different species." To get ahead, Park says she had to achieve 120% of what her male colleagues did—as well as play basketball and drink with them after work. "Luckily, I like sports, and I like to drink," she says.

When Choi Dong Hee joined SK's research arm in 2005, she was the only woman there and had no major assignment until she created one. After conducting a yearlong study, Choi, 30, proposed changing the company's policy to allow subscribers to use any wireless portal. Her managers ignored her. She persisted. Finally, they agreed to let her brief the division head, who agreed to let her make her case to the company chairman. Choi worked on the presentation for three weeks straight, sometimes alone in the office overnight (to her boss's horror). In the end, the company did adopt the open policy she advocated. Now her managers are quick to say that women's perspectives can help SK better serve its customers.

Sonia Kim, who is in charge of TV marketing at Samsung Electronics, says her male colleagues rarely argue with the boss, even if they think he's wrong. Kim, though, persuaded her manager to let her develop a promotional campaign rather than rely on an ad agency she thought had lost its creative edge. Kim also says some of the men used to overturn decisions made during the day while out drinking after hours. Since she and other women at Samsung complained, Kim says, the practice has mostly stopped.

Source: Moon Ihlwain, "Cracks in a Particularly Thick Glass Ceiling," *BusinessWeek,* April 21, 2008, p. 58.

DISCUSSION QUESTIONS

1. Should gender be a consideration when staffing local management positions?
2. Should gender be a consideration when selecting an expatriate for an overseas assignment?
3. Discuss what factors must be considered if a U.S. multinational corporation decides to staff a leadership position in South Korea with a woman.

Notes

1. P. J. Dowling, R. S. Schuler, and D. E. Welch, *International Dimensions of Human Resource Management,* 2nd ed. (Belmont, CA: Wadsworth, 1994).
2. J. L. Laabs, "HR Pioneers Explore the Road Less Traveled," *Personnel Journal,* February 1996, pp. 70–72, 74, 77–78.
3. J. S. Black and H. B. Gregersen, "The Right Way to Manage Expats," *Harvard Business Review,* March/April 1999, pp. 52–62.
4. B. S. Chakravarthy and H. V. Perlmuter, "Strategic Planning for a Global Business," *Columbia Journal of World Business* 20, no. 2 (1985), pp. 3–10; Dowling, Schuler, and Welch, *International Dimensions of Human Resource Management.*
5. C. D. Fisher, L. F. Schoenfeldt, and J. B. Shaw, *Human Resource Management,* 2nd ed. (Boston: Houghton Mifflin, 1993).
6. R. Tung, *The New Expatriates: Managing Human Resources Abroad* (Cambridge, MA: Ballinger, 1988).

7. P. M. Rosenweig and N. Nohria, "Influences on Human Resource Management Practices in Multinational Corporations," *Journal of International Business Studies* 25 (1994), pp. 229–251.
8. M. B. Teagarden, M. A. Von Glinow, M. C. Butler, and E. Drost, "The Best Practices Learning Curve: Human Resource Management in Mexico's Maquiladora Industry," in O. Shenkar, ed., *Global Perspectives of Human Resource Management* (Upper Saddle River, NJ: Prentice Hall, 1995).
9. D. C. Bangert and J. Poor, "Human Resource Management in Foreign Affiliates in Hungary," in Shenkar, *Global Perspectives of Human Resource Management*.
10. J. Artise, "Selection, Coaching, and Evaluation of Employees in International Subsidiaries," in Shenkar, *Global Perspectives of Human Resource Management*.
11. M. E. de Forest, "Thinking of a Plant in Mexico?" *Academy of Management Executive* 8 (1994), pp. 33–40.
12. Dowling, Schuler, and Welch, *International Dimensions of Human Resource Management*.
13. M. Marquardt and D. W. Engel, *Global Human Resource Development* (Upper Saddle River, NJ: Prentice Hall, 1993).
14. R. M. Hodgetts and F. Luthans, *International Management*, 2nd ed. (New York: McGraw-Hill, 1994).
15. Dowling, Schuler, and Welch, *International Dimensions of Human Resource Management*.
16. E. L. Miller, "The Job Satisfaction of Expatriate American Managers: A Function of Regional Location and Previous Work Experience," *Journal of International Business Studies* 6, no. 2 (1975), pp. 65–73; R. L. Tung, "Selection and Training of Personnel for Overseas Assignments," *Columbia Journal of World Business* 16 (1981), pp. 68–78.
17. A. Haselberger and L. K. Stroh, "Development and Selection of Multinational Expatriates," *Human Resource Development Quarterly* 3 (1992), pp. 287–293.
18. R. J. Stone, "Expatriate Selection and Failure," *Human Resource Planning* 29, no. 1 (1991), pp. 9–17; R. L. Tung, "American Expatriates Abroad: From Neophytes to Cosmopolitans," *Journal of World Business* 33, no. 2 (1998), pp. 125–144.
19. D. R. Briscoe, *International Human Resource Management*. (Upper Saddle River, NJ: Prentice Hall, 1995).
20. M. L. Kraimer, S. J. Wayne, and R. A. Jaworski, "Sources of Support and Expatriate Performance: The Mediating Role of Expatriate Adjustment," *Personnel Psychology* 54 (2001), pp. 71–99.
21. C. Reynolds, "Expatriate Compensations in Historical Perspective," *Journal of World Business* 32, no. 2 (1997), p. 127.
22. R. B. Peterson, N. K. Napier, and W. Shul-Shim, "Expatriate Management: A Comparison of MNCs across Four Parent Countries," *Thunderbird International Business Review,* March–April 2000, p. 155.
23. G. W. Latta, "Expatriate Incentives: Beyond Tradition," *HR Focus,* March 1998, p. 24.
24. D. Young, "Fair Compensation for Expatriates," *Harvard Business Review* 51, no. 4 (1973), p. 119.
25. J. S. Lubin, "Companies Use Cross-Cultural Training to Help Their Employees Adjust Abroad," *Wall Street Journal,* August 4, 1992, p. B1.
26. I. Torbiorn, *Living Abroad* (New York: John Wiley & Sons, 1982), p. 41; Kraimer, Wayne, and Jaworski, "Sources of Support and Expatriate Performance"; Y. Zeira and M. Banai, "Attitudes of Host-Country Organization toward MNCs' Staffing Policies: A Cross-Country and Cross-Industry Analysis," *Management International Review* 21, no. 2 (1981), p. 34.
27. R. L. Tung, "Career Issues in International Assignments," *Academy of Management Executive,* August 1988, p. 242.
28. J. E. Abueva, "Return of the Native Executive," *New York Times,* May 17, 2000, p. C1.
29. Tung, "Career Issues in International Assignments," p. 243.
30. Ibid.

Case III

Christina Gold Leading Change at Western Union

Alison Konrad and Jordan Mitchell

INTRODUCTION

In early 2003, Christina Gold, chief executive officer (CEO) of Western Union, had just begun implementing a new organization structure. Gold had joined Western Union in May 2002 with a key focus of unifying the company's U.S. operations with its international division. In guiding the company to act as one entity, Gold proposed a change from a U.S. centric product line focus to a regional structure with three main divisions: the Americas; Europe, Africa, the Middle East and South Asia; and Asia-Pacific.

Changing the structure sent out a clear message of Gold's desired change in mindset to a new type of global culture. Already, Gold was finding that leaders in the United States were reluctant to give up control of product lines. At the regional level, she had keen leaders who wanted to push out the responsibility within their own regions and move towards a decentralized plan. While Gold supported this notion in principle, she wanted to ensure that the right leaders could be placed in decentralized offices in order to execute on the six strategic pillars that she had laid out for the organization. As well, she wanted to match responsibility with authority by giving the regional heads profit and loss responsibility. With this responsibility at the regional level, she wondered how new products would develop under a regional structure. Gold was also aware of the need to consider recruiting, training and development of new leaders as the company was growing most rapidly in emerging markets, such as India, China, Eastern Europe and Africa.

One thing was certain—Gold had made it clear that no revenue decreases would be forgiven amidst the change. Many considerations had arisen: What pace of change should she take? How would she deal with the resistance to change? How could she ensure that the new structure would support Western Union's global expansion?

CHRISTINA GOLD

Born in 1947 in the Netherlands, Gold moved to Canada at age five. She attended Carleton University in Ottawa where she earned a degree in geography in 1969, and upon graduating, secured a job at a coupon-center clearinghouse. A year later in 1970, she joined Avon Canada as an entry-level inventory control clerk. Gold worked her way up through more than 20 positions before being promoted to president of the entire Canadian Avon division in 1989. Gold became well known for training sales representatives on selling techniques and time management. Dedicating time to joining representatives on sales calls, Gold explained her rationale, "I'd go out with the sales reps who were doing well and with the ones who were doing badly, and I'd pass what the successful ones were doing on to the others."[1]

In November 1993, Gold was selected from a number of candidates to run the entire North American Avon organization in New York. For several months, she and her husband maintained a commuting marriage between New York and Montreal before he was able to relocate to New York. Within

---

Jordan Mitchell prepared this case under the supervision of Professor Alison Konrad solely to provide material for class discussion. The authors do not intend to illustrate either effective or ineffective handling of a managerial situation. The authors may have disguised certain names and other identifying information to protect confidentiality. Ivey Management Services prohibits any form of reproduction, storage or transmittal without its written permission. This material is not covered under authorization from CanCopy or any reproduction rights organization. To order copies or request permission to reproduce materials, contact Ivey Publishing, Ivey Management Services, c/o Richard Ivey School of Business, The University of Western Ontario, London, Ontario, Canada, N6A 3K7; phone (519) 661-3208; fax (519) 661-3882; e-mail cases@ivey.uwo.ca. Copyright © 2005, Ivey Management Services. Version: (A) 2005-12-13. Reprinted with permission of Ivey Management Services on August 5, 2008.

[1] Claudia Deutsch, "Avon's Montreal recruit has Gold touch with reps," *New York Times*, April 5, 1994, p. B10.

six months at Avon, she was credited with rejuvenating the energy level among sales representatives, with one sales representative sending her flowers with a note saying, "Thanks for bringing springtime back to Avon."[2] In a show of appreciation to the sales force, Gold asked that all salaried Avon employees hand-write 100 thank-you notes to representatives. But Gold clarified an important aspect of communication, "Motivation isn't all prizes and things. It's listening."[3]

In 1996, Gold was promoted to lead the development of global direct-selling in an executive vice-president role, and in the same year was named one of the top 25 U.S. managers. During the same time, Gold was one of the three women insiders predicted to be promoted to the CEO post of Avon; however, all three of the internal candidates were passed over for Charles Perrin, former CEO of Duracell International Inc.[4] Gold left Avon in early 1998 after a 28-year career and established The Beaconsfield Group, a consultancy focused on global direct-selling and marketing/distribution strategies.[5] In September 1999, Gold was selected as the CEO of Excel Communications, a $1.3 billion Dallas-based firm, to lead the company's rollout of direct telecommunications selling. With the changing infrastructure in the telecommunications landscape within the next three years, Gold successfully launched a direct-selling strategy. In May 2002, Gold transitioned after Bell Canada Enterprises (BCE) sold the company. Gold became president of First Data Corporation's largest division—Western Union.

FIRST DATA CORPORATION IN BRIEF

First Data Corporation was established in 1992, when American Express spun off the division through an initial public offering.[6] Three years later in 1995, First Data merged with First Financial Management Corporation, which owned Western Union.

First Data's focus was facilitating the purchase of goods and services through almost any form of payment. In carrying out its business aim, First Data provided electronic commerce and payment services solutions to three million merchants, 1,400 card issuers and millions of individuals by the end of 2002. As First Data stated on its website, "You may not realize it, but First Data touches your life every day. Whether writing a check at the supermarket, buying dinner with your credit card or ordering a book online, we're connecting with you to make those transactions happen—safely and securely."[7] It had four central business segments: payment services, merchant services, card issuing services and emerging payments.

First Data had realized steady growth and had experienced a compound annual growth rate of 7.5 percent in revenues and 21.6 percent in net income from 1998 to 2002.[8] As of the end of 2002, First Data had revenues of $7.6 billion and net income of $1.2 billion.[9] First Data's strategy to grow hinged on expanding the reach of its core businesses, developing long-term contractual agreements with customers for steady and predictable revenue flows and responding to new e-commerce initiatives.

WESTERN UNION IN BRIEF

Western Union was founded in Rochester, New York, as The New York and Mississippi Valley Printing Telegraph Company in 1851. When the name changed to Western Union, the intent was to integrate acquired companies and unite the United States from east to west. Western Union had a number of firsts, such as the invention of the stock ticker in 1866, the electronic money transfer in 1871, the credit card in 1914, the singing telegram in 1933 and intercity facsimile service in 1935.[10]

---

[2] Ibid.

[3] Ibid.

[4] "Avon chooses outsider as heir apparent," *The Record,* December 12, 1997, p. B03.

[5] "New CEO at Excel Communications . . .," *PR Newswire,* September 15, 1999.

[6] First Data Fact Sheet, Company Documents.

[7] First Data Corporate Website, *www.firstdatacorp.com*, accessed December 23, 2004.

[8] First Data Annual Report, *www.sec.gov*, accessed December 31, 2002, p.17.

[9] Ibid.

[10] Western Union Fact Sheet, Company Documents.

Western Union posted sales of $3.2 billion in 2002, an 18 percent increase from the prior year.[11] Eighty percent of Western Union's revenues came from consumer-to-consumer (C2C) money transfers.[12] The number of consumer money transfers grew from 55.8 million in 2001 to 67.8 in 2002 with predictions that the number of these transfers would rise to more than 80 million in 2003. The remaining 20 percent of revenues was derived from consumer-to-business (C2B) transactions.

By early 2003, Western Union had approximately 4,500 employees of which 40 per cent were based in the United States. Most of the workforce was non-unionized except for 1,200 call center employees located in the Missouri, U.S., branch office. Western Union operated in 182,000 locations in 195 countries. More than 59,000 of the locations were located in North America (United States, Canada and Mexico), while the remaining 123,000 were made up of international agent locations. Agreements with international agents were typically made with banks and national post offices.

AGENT NETWORK

All of Western Union's international agents entered information into a common data processing system, where the payment was processed and made available to the receiving location. A consumer sending money paid a transfer fee on the amount sent to the receiver. Both the "sending" and "receiving" agents received a commission as did Western Union's corporate operation. Western Union also benefited from the differences in exchange rate spreads, which it recorded as additional revenue.

Robin Heller, Western Union's soon-to-be vice-president, operations, talked about how the company maintained consistency across its expansive agent network:

> We have to ensure the same brand promise whether someone is at a retail brick-and-mortar location, online or by telephone. We do that by asking for the same pieces of information in the same order and we make it very easy to execute. From that, we look at what we need to do to add to our training, the forms we use or the screens that agents use. We use the same system across the entire world.

Christina Gold shared her view of what it took to lead a geographically separated operation:

> You have to be sensitive to other cultures and other people, and that's true in New York City as well as in Bangkok. Each person's needs are different, and the leader has to be aware and flexible enough to work with each person effectively. One thing that does get in the way is language and communication issues. Using abbreviations and acronyms in Japan, for example, can make people feel ostracized. It's not inclusive. People feel left out or misunderstood. Another thing that can happen is that people do not understand what you are asking of them—they don't see it as a directive, but rather as a general comment. So to be effective in a global team requires more patience, more focus, you need to repeat things and get feedback to ensure people understand each other. Everything takes more thought and more patience. It's important not to jump to conclusions and to really listen.

WESTERN UNION'S CONSUMER

Western Union's major consumer segment was the migrant worker who earned money in one country and used money transfer services to send funds to family and loved ones in another country. This target consumer typically did not have a bank account. Hikmet Ersek, senior vice-president, EMEA (Europe/Middle East/Africa and South Asia), Western Union, stated, "We're dealing with a lot of immigrants who may experience problems in their host countries and where they work. The idea is that they will be served well and with a smile."

Heller spoke about the importance of customizing the Western Union experience to significantly different audiences:

> Our agents will try to localize the look and feel and the location of the office. They do the marketing at a local level. Take Africa for instance: in Africa there's a big festival culture so, we do skits or little plays at the festival to advertise our services.

---

[11] First Data Annual Report, *www.sec.gov*, December 31, 2002, p.33.
[12] *Ibid.*

EXHIBIT 1 Examples of Global Western Union Advertising

Source: Company files.

| Colombia, Ecuador and Peru | United States and Canada | Multilingual — European | Ukraine |

| Senegal | Congo | Mali |

See Exhibit 1 for an example of Western Union's advertising from around the world.

WESTERN UNION'S STRATEGY

By late 2002, Gold and her executive team had developed six core strategies for Western Union:

1. Develop a global brand
2. Enhance global network distribution
3. Expand adjacent markets such as WesternUnion.com and Prepaid services
4. Develop future business leaders within the organization
5. Increase productivity
6. Execute on service excellence

Gold talked about the driver of Western Union's growth and the challenges going forward:

> [The driver is] obviously the core business, which is the money transfer business. The consumer-to-consumer business is the growth engine. We're looking to grow our commercial business, our bill-payment business in the United States. And we're now extending that globally. We are starting to develop (our prepaid business) around the globe. Our challenge and our opportunity is to keep that growth in the double digits. I think part of it's really looking at building the right brand for Western Union. The fact we're growing so quickly and growing around the globe are key things as we develop our business and our brand in India and China.

REORGANIZATION

In order to align the company's organizational structure to the six core strategic focuses, Gold began a reorganizing program in early 2003. Prior to the reorganization effort, the structure mirrored Western Union's parent company, First Data, in that it had a U.S. business and an international business.

The executive team was made up of Christina Gold as president and six other senior executives. Four senior vice-presidents were in charge of the following product lines: Consumer Money Transfer, Mexican Money Transfer, Bill Payments and Corporate Services. One executive commented on the individuals responsible for the worldwide development of products: "The four executives run those products for the entire world, but they are very U.S.-centric."

The other two executive positions were Western Union's chief financial officer (CFO) and the senior vice-president of Western Union International. Annmarie Neal, senior vice-president, Talent, First Data, and co-acting senior vice-president of human resources for Western Union, was one of the first to draw out a rough version of the new structure on a white board. She talked about the goals in making a change to the structure:

> The main impetus is to allow Western Union to bring their services to market more effectively. The second major reason is to manage redundancy. We have a head of marketing for both the U.S. and international businesses. So one of the biggest thrusts is to have brand consistency across the globe. We also want to build the financial infrastructure and really place the financial decisioning in the right areas. With information technology, the aim is to have common platforms. For human resources, the idea is to have the ability to move talent around the globe. Whether that be from South East Asia or to the Americas. Western Union is very domestic in resources, but we see all the growth coming from other areas.

ALTERNATIVES CONSIDERED

In developing the new proposed structure, Gold and her executive team first established the core strategic focuses and looked at each region and considered structures that would be effective. Alternatives included making minor changes to the product line–focused structure, rolling out a structure organized by functional area such as sales, marketing, operations, finance and IT or considering a structure based on geography. The team chose to reorganize the company into a decentralized structure covering three main regions: the Americas; Europe, the Middle East and Africa; and Asia/Pacific. Annmarie Neal described the process for choosing a regional structure:

> We really wanted to reflect the global business and cut down on the idea of a domestic and international business. So, it became pretty obvious that we would choose a regional structure, but our organizational structure is constantly evolving. When we looked at a product organization structure, we realized pretty quickly that it wasn't going to work, simply because we had a number of products in the domestic business. But we really had only one business in the international market, which was money transfers. So we discarded that option pretty quickly. One of the big debates was the corporate role of marketing and what should be done at the regional level. We decided that strategy for loyalty and brand would reside at the corporate level whereas the execution of such strategies would be done in the regions.

Gold gave her view:

> Currently, we have a domestic business and an international division. It doesn't make sense for a global business the way it is now; whatever country you're in is "domestic." So, [the idea is to] have a regional structure. [My hope is that] we will have common goals and share a lot more ideas. There will be a lot more communication and sharing of resources. For example, the plan is to have a global marketing plan whereas currently we have separate marketing for domestic and each international area. It'll be much better from a customer perspective because the global services allows each region to spend their time focusing on specific customer needs.

CHALLENGES WITH REORGANIZING

In making the change, Gold had to first convince the First Data management team and then the First Data board of directors. The total cost of the restructuring was estimated at US$4 million and included provisions for relocation and recruitment in a few key positions. Gold's one central mandate for the organization was that revenues could not be negatively affected. In facilitating the change, Gold used her executive team, as well as the services of human resources, to define the key processes, design the structure of the new organization and define responsibility within the structure.

DEFINING RESPONSIBILITY

In defining responsibility, two main issues had arisen: Who would lead the development of new products? and Who would have profit and loss accountability in the organization?

Development of New Products

The company had been promoting three new business areas: commercial services, the website, WesternUnion.com and the prepaid card. Prepaid cards included a gamut of products ranging from prepaid wireless and telephone cards to prepaid debit cards.

Company executives needed to decide whether there should be a product leader or whether regional leaders could take on the responsibility. Some executives argued that sufficient time could not be devoted to developing them at a regional level. Ersek stated:

Something like the prepaid card is led by a product manager. I think that until it becomes big enough, it should stay under the product manager and then it is handed over to the regional heads. See, prepaid cards for me makes up about $200,000 in revenues, out of over $1.5 billion in revenues. My priority will be the larger numbers. But a product manager can put the marketing effort into this, build the product and then hand it off.

Profit and Loss (P&L) Responsibility

Another central challenge was deciding on whether profit and loss responsibility should rest with the regional heads or whether it should be based on corridors. Western Union defined corridors as, "country-to-country money-transfer pairs"[13] such as the U.S.-Mexico, UAE-India and Spain-Morocco. The company's worldwide operations had approximately 15,000 corridors[14] with approximately 500 of the top corridors making up 80 percent of money transfer activity. Changes in the corridors were heavily influenced by immigration patterns, country regulations and geo-economic conditions.[15]

While it was common that many corridors would be based within one region, such as the United States to Mexico under the Americas canopy, it was also common that corridors crossed international frontiers. Ersek explained:

> We have the unique challenge of sending and receiving. If I send money from Spain to Brazil, I need someone in Brazil. One of the big discussions is whether to have region or corridor heads. Some people feel that we needed to give the P&L responsibility to corridor heads. I am against this. Part of the reason, is that there have been big dynamic changes in corridor traffic.

Some managers felt that changes to corridor traffic were heavily linked to external factors outside of the control of Western Union making it too difficult to hold leaders responsible for top-line revenue results. Other executives believed that responsibility would be clearer if it mirrored the transaction flow between countries.

DECENTRALIZATION AT THE REGIONAL LEVEL

While decentralization was not a prerequisite in the new regional design, some executives felt that decentralization would enable the regions to get closer to the company's customers.

In the Europe, Middle East, Africa and South Asia division, the recently appointed Vice-President, Hikmet Ersek, wanted to decentralize the region by opening up a number of smaller offices in each

---

[13] First Data Annual Report, *www.sec.gov*, December 31, 2002, p.34.
[14] Ibid.
[15] Ibid.

country. Ersek believed the plan would put Western Union closer to its customers and agents allowing faster response times and enhanced service. Ersek stated, "I want to move from having five offices to having 35 or more different offices—like small agile teams. Obviously, there are some things that need to be central, like creating the brand and network development."

However, moving to the decentralized plan had its challenges. Ersek indicated:

> In order to decentralize, there are lots of questions from the legal and finance departments at the headquarters in Denver. Eventually, I want to put an office in Tashkent. However for many people Tashkent is an unknown quantity and they have some concerns. Finding the right people is a challenge. In a place like Tashkent, in Uzbekistan, we would have to find people who understood the code of conduct. We have to have people that we can trust. They need to accept and understand what it means to be part of a U.S. and a global company. Also, many of the local agents think that we are opening up branches. So, we have to assure them that we are opening up offices to support the agents.

Other executives felt that decentralization had its limits due to cost and human resource constraints. Neal balanced Ersek's view:

> I want to listen to all of the ideas around the globe. But, decentralizing regions could add to a significant increase in infrastructure cost. There's colonization in spirit and I think with some adaptation it could work. Where it gets tricky, is making a change without thinking through implications for the rest of the organization. We need to think about leveraging opportunities around the globe.

RECRUITING FOR NEW POSITIONS

Proposed changes in leadership included moving the head of Western Union International in Paris, France, to the company's headquarters in Colorado to assume the position of president of Western Union Americas, including all countries on both continents.

Formerly the senior Vice-President for Eastern Europe, Hikmet Ersek, had taken the role as the senior vice president responsible for Europe, the Middle East, Africa and South Asia. A role was still required to be filled for the Asia-Pacific division as the former president of the Asian division had left the company. Two new corporate roles were set to be created: senior vice-president of business development to be filled by Mike Yerington, a 30-year Western Union veteran, and senior vice-president, operations, to be filled by Robin Heller. Scott Schierman would continue as chief financial officer with greater day-to-day operational duties.

Overall, Western Union recruited approximately 500 individuals a year—some of the roles were to fill the four percent attrition rate, while others were to fill positions created by internal growth. One of the major challenges was recruiting individuals who possessed an understanding of operating in China and India. While growth was through adding agents in both countries, Western Union did not have to recruit staff in each location. However, the company needed to place people at the corporate level to manage the marketing, operations and information technological consistency. As Neal explained: "A lot of folks confuse being global with being from a different country. It doesn't mean that you're global if you have a different colored passport. We're looking for people that have a global mindset."

EXECUTIVE DEVELOPMENT PROGRAMS

As of early 2003, First Data was making changes to the company's development program. Previously, the program was called First Leaders, which contained 12 modules whereby participants could learn about aspects of leadership such as enhancing communication, risk-taking, conflict resolution and motivating employees. Jana Johnson, vice-president, executive development, First Data, commented on the old program:

> What you had was a director sitting in a room with administrative assistants and attendance was not mandatory. So, a lot of times people wouldn't come or people would attend a call on their cell phone and the types of issues that were coming up weren't necessarily helpful for everyone.

With the effectiveness of the old program dwindling, First Data executives planned a new leadership series, "First Executives," that was more in line with developing a pipeline of leaders for top management positions. Johnson explained the burning need at the First Data level, "At the First Data level, one of the critical things was succession planning and we identified 134 top critical positions. Specifically the goal was to have three high-confidence candidates per critical role by 2007."

The new program—First Executives—had 30 participants at an original cost of $7,500 per person in First Data of which 15 were Western Union executives. The plan was to add another 30 participants by the end of 2003. Each participant was given an executive coach that helped develop managerial and leadership abilities. In addition, they were all given mentors and given the opportunity to shadow a senior executive.

THE CULTURE CHANGE

The words "culture change" were frequently talked about within both First Data and Western Union. First Data had the reputation of being a conservative culture steeped in the financial industry. Some observers felt that the Western Union had a stronger identity due to its history and product focus. Ersek talked about the difference in the culture between Western Union and its parent:

> A company like First Data is driven by statistics, this has to be the case if you are listed on America's "Most Admired" list and if you are a major employer. With Western Union outside of America we still have the pioneering spirit that made Western Union famous in America. For Western Union International, the sky is the limit. We are still growing in double-digits.

Johnson talked about change in both organizations:

> It's a culture of change and we need leadership change. We're big and we know we're big. We know we need to change but we're just not sure what we need to change into. You can't control change, but you have to learn how to manage it and how to lead it. It's the messiness of change. And, it is messy.

Heller offered her view of changing Western Union:

> The biggest issue is probably the fear of the unknown and the fear of change. It's very important that we have the talent in place first and then we can look at the restructuring. You can always do any amount of restructuring or managing change that you need to do if you have the right people.

GOLD AS THE LEADER OF THE CHANGE

"She was masterful at reading the organization's readiness," commented Neal on Gold's leadership in initiating the organizational design change. Executives credited Gold with instilling a deep understanding of branding and marketing at Western Union while managing disparate personalities and cultures. Heller explained how Gold fostered leadership among Western Union executives and how she was leading the change:

> She doesn't bring rank into the situation. She always has time for us—she has a high level of accessibility and with her grinding schedule it's amazing. She's very much about inquiring and asking instead of telling. She gives feedback and ideas and listens openly to other ideas. Everyone has a voice. But don't take that the wrong way. She can make decisions. She can definitely make decisions! She takes it all in and then makes the call.

Ersek talked about his relationship with Gold:

> She gives autonomy, but she also keeps a hand on things. She is tough and has high standards and expects all her managers to adhere to these standards. This is something I admire very much about her, because she doesn't expect anything of anybody she cannot deliver herself. And, sometimes, I say, "Christina, that's not doable," and she says, "I'll help you do it." After she understood my region, her leadership has basically been, "What's your decision Hikmet?" And through that, she is sending signs to others that the responsibility is being pushed into the regions.

Neal observed Gold:

> Christina's a very tough executive. And by tough, I mean that she sets very high objectives. She is constantly stretching her executives. Christina is masterful in managing the globe and I don't mean just the employees. I'm talking about developing strong relationships with our agents and with government officials. I think a major thing about her leadership is how she empowers her revenue-generator executives. It's hard to keep track with some being several hours away and in a different time zones. But, she seems to manage this exceptionally well.

CONSIDERATIONS MOVING FORWARD

Gold was eager to lead Western Union through a major structural change from a company organized by product line to a geographically aligned organization. Gold wanted to ensure that the structure would support the company's strategic aims and give strength to Western Union's global expansion. She had a number of considerations: the pace of change, how to assuage resistance to the change and how to ensure that the new structure would help to follow the new strategic direction.

SECTION FOUR

Social Initiatives

CHAPTER THIRTEEN

Global Social Enterprise

Chapter Learning Objectives

After completing this chapter, you should be able to:

- Understand the development of global social enterprise initiatives.
- Integrate knowledge and innovation into developing global communities.
- Understand the importance of reciprocity in the collaborative efforts among multinational enterprises, local governments, and local communities that represent the poorest communities in the world.
- Develop a comprehensive framework for understanding the linkages among investment, local enterprise networks, and sustainable outcomes.

Opening Case: Beyond the Green Corporation

Imagine a world in which eco-friendly and socially responsible practices actually help a company's bottom line. It's closer than you think.

Under conventional notions of how to run a conglomerate like Unilever, CEO Patrick Cescau should wake up each morning with a laserlike focus: how to sell more soap and shampoo than Procter & Gamble Co. But ask Cescau about the $52 billion Dutch-British giant's biggest strategic challenges for the 21st century, and the conversation roams from water-deprived villages in Africa to the planet's warming climate. The world is Unilever's laboratory. In Brazil, the company operates a free community laundry in a Sao Paulo slum, provides financing to help tomato growers convert to eco-friendly "drip" irrigation, and recycles 17 tons of waste annually at a toothpaste factory. Unilever funds a floating hospital that offers free medical care in Bangladesh, a nation with just 20 doctors for every 10,000 people. In Ghana, it teaches palm oil producers to reuse plant waste while providing potable water to deprived communities. In India, Unilever staff help thousands of women in remote villages start micro-enterprises. And responding to green activists, the company discloses how much carbon dioxide and hazardous waste its factories spew out around the world.

As Cescau sees it, helping such nations wrestle with poverty, water scarcity, and the effects of climate change is vital to staying competitive in coming decades. Some 40% of the company's sales and most of its growth now take place in developing nations. Unilever food products account for roughly 10% of the world's crops of tea and 30% of all spinach. It is also one of the world's biggest buyers of fish. As environmental regulations grow tighter around the world, Unilever must invest in green technologies or its leadership in packaged foods, soaps, and other goods could be imperiled. "You can't ignore the impact your company has on the community and environment," Cescau says. CEOs used to frame thoughts like these in the context of moral responsibility, he adds. But now, "it's also about growth and innovation. In the future, it will be the only way to do business."

A remarkable number of CEOs have begun to commit themselves to the same kind of sustainability goals Cescau has pinpointed, even in profit-obsessed America. For years, the term "sustainability" has carried a lot of baggage. Put simply, it's about meeting humanity's needs without harming future generations. It was a favorite cause among economic development experts, human rights activists, and conservationists. But to many U.S. business leaders, sustainability just meant higher costs and smacked of earnest U.N. corporate-responsibility conferences and the utopian idealism of Western Europe. Now, sustainability is "right at the top of the agendas" of more U.S. CEOs, especially young ones, says McKinsey Global Institute Chairman Lenny Mendonca.

You can tell something is up just wading through the voluminous sustainability reports most big corporations post on their Web sites. These lay out efforts to cut toxic emissions, create eco-friendly products, help the poor, and cooperate with nonprofit groups. As recently as five years ago, such reports—if they appeared at all—were usually transparent efforts to polish the corporate image. Now there's a more sophisticated understanding that environmental and social practices can yield strategic advantages in an interconnected world of shifting customer loyalties and regulatory regimes.

Embracing sustainability can help avert costly setbacks from environmental disasters, political protests, and human rights or workplace abuses—the kinds of debacles suffered by Royal Dutch Shell PLC in Nigeria and Unocal in Burma. "Nobody has an idea when such events can hit a balance sheet, so companies must stay ahead of the curve," says Matthew J. Kiernan, CEO of Innovest Strategic Value Advisors. Innovest is an international research and advisory firm whose clients include large institutional investors. It supplied the data for this *BusinessWeek* Special Report and prepared a list of the world's 100 most sustainable corporations, to be presented at the Jan. 24–28 World Economic Forum in Davos, Switzerland.

The roster of advocates includes Jeffrey Immelt, CEO of GE, who is betting billions to position GE as a leading innovator in everything from wind power to hybrid engines. Wal-Mart, long assailed for its labor and global sourcing practices, has made a series of high-profile promises to slash energy use overall, from its stores to its vast trucking fleets, and purchase more electricity derived from renewable sources. GlaxoSmithKline discovered that, by investing to develop drugs for poor nations, it can work more effectively with those governments to make sure its patents are protected. Dow Chemical is increasing R&D in products such as roof tiles that deliver solar power to buildings and water treatment technologies for regions short of clean water. "There is 100% overlap between our business drivers and social and environmental interests," says Dow CEO Andrew N. Liveris.

Striking that balance is not easy. Many noble efforts fail because they are poorly executed or never made sense to begin with. "If there's no connection to a company's business, it doesn't have much leverage to make an impact," says business guru Michael Porter. Sustainability can be a hard proposition for investors, too. Decades of experience show that it's risky to pick stocks based mainly on a company's long-term environmental or social-responsibility targets.

Nevertheless, new sets of metrics, which Innovest and others designed to measure sustainability efforts, have helped convince CEOs and boards that they pay off. Few Wall Street analysts, for example, have tried to assess how much damage Wal-Mart's reputation for poor labor and environmental practices did to the stock price. But New York's Communications Consulting Worldwide (CCW), which studies issues such as reputation, puts it in stark dollars and cents. CCW calculates that if Wal-Mart had a reputation like that of rival TargetCorp, its stock would be worth 8.4% more, adding $16 billion in market capitalization.

Serious money is lining up behind the sustainability agenda. Assets of mutual funds that are designed to invest in companies meeting social responsibility criteria have swelled from $12 billion in 1995 to $178 billion in 2005, estimates trade association Social Investment Forum. Boston's State Street Global Advisors alone handles $77 billion in such funds. And institutions with $4 trillion in assets, including charitable trusts and government pension funds in Europe and states such as California, pledge to weigh sustainability factors in investment decisions.

Why the sudden urgency? The growing clout of watchdog groups making savvy use of the Internet is one factor. New environmental regulations also play a powerful role. Electronics manufacturers slow to wean their factories and products off toxic materials, for example, could be at a serious disadvantage as Europe adopts additional, stringent restrictions. American energy and utility companies that don't cut fossil fuel reliance could lose if Washington joins the rest of the industrialized world in ordering curbs on greenhouse gas emissions. Such developments help explain why ExxonMobil, long opposed to linking government policies with global warming theories, is now taking part in meetings to figure out what the U.S. should do to cut emissions.

Investors who think about these issues obviously have long time horizons. But they encounter knotty problems when trying to peer beyond the next quarter's results to a future years down the road. Corporations disclose the value of physical assets and investments in equipment and property. But U.S. regulators don't require them to quantify environmental, social, or labor practices. Accountants call such squishy factors "intangibles." These items aren't found on a corporate balance sheet, yet can be powerful indicators of future performance.

If a company is at the leading edge of understanding and preparing for megatrends taking shape in key markets, this could constitute a valuable intangible asset. By being the first fast-food chain to stop using unhealthy trans fats, Wendy's International Inc. may have a competitive edge now that New York City has banned the additives in restaurants. McDonald's Corp., which failed to do so, could have a future problem.

Rising investor demand for information on sustainability has spurred a flood of new research. Goldman Sachs, Deutsche Bank, UBS, Citigroup, Morgan Stanley, and other brokerages have formed dedicated teams assessing how companies are affected by everything from climate change and social pressures in emerging markets to governance records. "The difference in interest between three years ago and now is extraordinary," says former Goldman Sachs Asset Management CEO David Blood, who heads the Enhanced Analytics Initiative, a research effort on intangibles by 22 brokerages. He also leads Generation Investment Management, co-founded in 2004 with former Vice-President Al Gore, which uses sustainability as an investment criterion.

Perhaps the most ambitious effort is by Innovest, founded in 1995 by Kiernan, a former KPMG senior partner. Besides conventional financial performance metrics, Innovest studies 120 different factors, such as energy use, health and safety records, litigation, employee practices, regulatory history, and management systems for dealing with supplier problems. It uses these measures to assign grades ranging from AAA to CCC, much like a bond rating, to 2,200 listed companies. Companies on the Global 100 list on *BusinessWeek*'s Web site include Nokia and Ericsson, which excel at tailoring products for developing nations, and banks such as HSBC Holdings and ABN-Amro that study the environmental impact of projects they help finance.

Some of Innovest's conclusions are counterintuitive. Dell rates AAA, for example, where market darling Apple gets a middling BBB on the grounds of weaker oversight of offshore factories and lack of a "clear environmental business strategy." An Apple spokesman contests that it is a laggard, citing the company's leadership in energy-efficient products and in cutting toxic substances. Then there's Sony vs. Nintendo. Wall Street loves the latter for a host of reasons, not least that its Wii video game system, the first to let users simulate actions such as swinging a sword or tennis racket, was a Christmas blockbuster. Sony, meanwhile, has a famously dysfunctional home electronics arm, and was embarrassed by exploding laptop batteries and long delays in bringing out its PlayStation 3 game console. Nintendo's stock has more than tripled in three years; Sony's has languished.

Viewed through the lens of sustainability, however, Sony looks like the better bet. It is an industry leader in developing energy-efficient appliances. It also learned from a 2001 fiasco, when illegal cadmium was found in PlayStation cables bought from outside suppliers. That cost Sony $85 million. Now, Sony has a whole corporate infrastructure for controlling its vast supplier network, helping it avert or quickly fix problems. Nintendo, a smaller Kyoto-based company focused on games, shows less evidence of the global management systems needed to cope with sudden regulatory shifts or supplier problems, says Innovest. A Nintendo spokesman says it meets all environmental rules and is "always reviewing and considering" the merits of new global sustainability guidelines.

Here's another Rorschach test. Which is the best investment: ExxonMobil, BP, or PetroChina? Exxon, one of the best-performing energy biggies of the past five years, seems like the obvious stock pick. PetroChina Co. is riskier but also alluring. It's a prime supplier of fuel to booming China, has seen revenues and profits rocket, and has been a hot stock for two years. Analyst Shahreza Yusof of Aberdeen Asset Management PLC rates the company a buy. Because of its access to China's market and new reserves, he writes, one day it will be as big as today's major oil giants—"if not bigger."

By contrast, BP seems to disprove the sustainability thesis altogether. CEO John Browne has preached environmentalism for a decade, and BP consistently ranked atop most sustainability indexes. Yet in the past two years it has been hit with a refinery explosion that killed 15 in Texas, a fine for safety violations at a refinery in Ohio, a major oil pipeline leak in Alaska, and a U.S. Justice Dept. probe into suspected manipulation of oil prices. Browne has recently announced his retirement. BP's shares have slid 10% since late April. Exxon's are up around 12%.

Innovest still rates BP a solid AA, while labeling Exxon a riskier BB. And PetroChina? Innovest gives it a CCC. Here's why: BP wins points for plowing $8 billion into alternative energies to diversify away from oil and engages community and environmental groups. Exxon has done less to curb greenhouse gas emissions and promote renewables and has big projects in trouble spots like Chad. "I would still say Exxon is a bigger long-term risk," says Innovest's Kiernan. PetroChina is easier to justify. Begin with its safety record: A gas well explosion killed 243 people in 2003; another fatal explosion in 2005 spewed toxic benzene into a river, leaving millions temporarily without water. PetroChina has been slow to invest in alternative energy, Innovest says, and its parent company has big bets in the Sudan.

Many experts maintain sustainability factors are good proxies of management quality. "They show that companies tend to be more strategic, nimble, and better equipped to compete in the complex, high-velocity global environment," Kiernan explains. That also is the logic behind Goldman Sachs's intangibles research. In its thick annual assessments of global energy and mining companies, for example, it ranks companies on the basis of sustainability factors, financial returns, and access to new resource reserves. Top-ranking companies, such as British Gas, Shell, and Brazil's Petrobras, are leaders in all three categories. For the past two years, the stocks of elite companies on its list bested their industry peers by more than 5%—while laggards underperformed, Goldman says.

Still, BP's woeful performance highlights a serious caveat to the corporate responsibility crusade. Companies that talk the most about sustainability aren't always the best at executing. Ford Motor Company is another case in point. Former CEO William C. Ford Jr. has championed green causes for years. He famously spent $2 billion overhauling the sprawling River Rouge (Mich.) complex, putting on a 10-acre grass roof to capture rainwater. Ford also donated $25 million to Conservation International for an environmental center.

Still, the corporate responsibility field is littered with lofty intentions that don't pay off. As a result, many CEOs are unsure what to do exactly. In a recent McKinsey study of 1,144 top global executives, 79% predicted at least some responsibility for dealing with future social and political issues would fall on corporations. Three of four said such issues should be addressed by the CEO. But only 3% said they do a good job dealing with social pressures. "This is uncomfortable territory because most CEOs have not been trained to sense or react to the broader landscape," says McKinsey's Mendonca. "For the first time, they are expected to be statesmen as much as they are functional business leaders." Adding to the complexity, says Harvard's Porter, each company must custom-design initiatives that fit its own objectives.

Dow Chemical is looking at the big picture. It sees a market in the need for low-cost housing and is developing technologies such as eco-friendly Styrofoam used for walls. CEO Liveris also cites global water scarcity as a field in which Dow can "marry planetary issues with market opportunity." The U.N. figures 1.2 billion people lack access to clean water. Dow says financial solutions could help 300 million of them. That could translate into up to $3 billion in sales for Dow, which has a portfolio of cutting-edge systems for filtering minute contaminants from water. To reach the poor, Dow is working with foundations and the U.N. to raise funds for projects.

Philips Electronics also is building strategies around global megatrends. By 2050, the U.N. predicts, 85% of people will live in developing nations. But shortages of health care are acute. Among Philips' many projects are medical vans that reach remote villages, allowing urban doctors to diagnose and treat patients via satellite. Philips has also developed low-cost water-purification technology and a smokeless wood-burning stove that could reduce the 1.6 million deaths annually worldwide from pulmonary diseases linked to cooking smoke. "For us, sustainability is a business imperative," says Chief Procurement Officer Barbara Kux, who chairs a sustainability board that includes managers from all business units.

Such laudable efforts, even if successful, may not help managers make their numbers next quarter. But amid turbulent global challenges, they could help investors sort long-term survivors from the dinosaurs.

Source: P. Engardio, *BusinessWeek,* January 29, 2007, p. 50.

Discussion Questions

1. How can sustainability initiatives fit into a company's global enterprise posture?
2. Given a projected 85 percent of the world population living in developing nations by 2050, develop a list of potentially profitable initiatives that will help build these communities.

The Foundation of Global Social Enterprise

As the final chapter of this book discusses the integration of corporate social responsibility into the international management imperative, this penultimate chapter develops the notion of intersecting international strategy with **global social enterprise** initiatives. At the foundation of this concept is the combining of profits, both short and long term, with community development and social accomplishments. During the past few years, global social enterprise and social entrepreneurship have merged as critical initiatives in international management. Muhammad Yunus, the 2006 Nobel Peace Prize winner, suggests that social business is no longer a theoretical concept; rather, there is an exponential emergence of social businesses worldwide including his own Grameen Bank.[1] Previously, Prahalad and Hammond observed:

> Driven by private investment and widespread entrepreneurial activity, the economies of developing regions grow rigorously, creating jobs and wealth and bringing hundreds of millions of new consumers into the global marketplace every year. The resulting decrease in poverty produces a range of social benefits, helping to stabilize many developing regions and reduce civil and cross-border conflicts. Multinational companies expand rapidly in an era of intense innovation and competition.[2]

These authors present a business case and suggest that by serving the bottom of the pyramid—the poorest of the poor—multinational corporations will develop new and sustainable revenue streams, higher levels of efficiency in operations through tapping in to low-cost labor pools, and continued innovation and knowledge. For example, "the Swedish wireless company Ericsson has developed a small cellular telephone system called a MiniGSM, that local operators in the bottom of the pyramid markets can use to offer cell phone service to a small area at a radically lower cost than conventional equipment."[3] These benefits of market, cost, and knowledge directly reflect Ghoshal's earlier framework, reviewed in Section 1 of this text. Furthermore, these imperatives are critical for global firms not only to gain a competitive advantage but to sustain it as well as competitive pressures in many industries have exponentially grown during the past two decades. Practical Insight 13.1 depicts micro-financing initiatives, global enterprises that have indeed received the most attention thanks to Yunus's Grameen Bank. The lessons learned from these initiatives, especially the fusion of technology into the profit–community development marriage, can be translated to other industries. Also, as seen with Dell in the Practical Insight, these for-profit activities are migrating from rural areas into urban, poverty-stricken neighborhoods as well.

Global Development and Emerging-Nation Objectives

In 1990, Michael Porter suggested that emerging nations need to move beyond the simple factor-driven national advantages of inexpensive labor and access to natural resources.[4] During the past 18 years, through direct foreign investment, equity joint ventures, and strategic alliances, these countries have created advanced factors of competitive advantage including local technology capability, modern infrastructure, and a developed information base.

Historically, emerging-country initiatives have been directed at satisfying two specific objectives of economic reform. The first is the generation of hard currency, and the second is the attraction of developed-country partners into local ventures to learn technology and management know-how. As multinational enterprises and developing-country entities cooperate, it is critical that the partners have neither conflicting objectives nor conflicting strategic orientations; thus, there has been an emphasis on partnerships involving multinational enterprises and emerging-nation host governments to work to reduce the conflict associated with different goals.[5]

The issue of corporate social responsibility, and particularly the focus of poverty, is an integral piece of cooperative learning in emerging-country initiatives. The World Bank has advocated a new paradigm for poverty reduction, one visualized as a partnership among the state, business, and civil society, that is, nonprofit and nongovernmental organizations. Its arguments for business participation have elements of both self-interest and social capital. An example of self-interest is a private firm having the pick of the labor crop due to its favorable reputation created by its participation in a local micro-enterprise initiative. Social capital, for example, in the increase in generic organizational skills created in the individuals involved in the community project, may also be enhanced

Micro-Enterprise Collaboration and Global Development

Jones developed both theoretical and applied thinking in this area and emphasized that firm-level international strategy must address global development and poverty reduction. He explained the dual perspectives of this thinking. The first perspective focuses on country-level comparative advantage and suggests that Porter's Diamond, delineating country competitiveness, may be extended to include the critical knowledge flows that are derived from developing socially responsible micro-enterprise initiatives. The second perspective focuses on firm-level strategic advantages gained from collaborative social enterprise efforts in developing countries.[6] As exemplified in this chapter's opening case, firms understand the immediate and long-term profit implications of global social enterprise initiatives. Jones expands on the stakeholder approach that Freeman suggested helps to enlarge management's vision beyond shareholders to include the interests and claims of others in society who have an interest in the activities of the firm.[7] Subsequently, the multinational firm creates

PRACTICAL INSIGHT 13.1

TAKING TINY LOANS TO THE NEXT LEVEL

An idea, not a person, was the most powerful force in philanthropy in 2006. President Bill Clinton devoted a big chunk of his annual Clinton Global Initiative to exploring it. The mighty Bill & Melinda Gates Foundation endorsed it. The choice of the 2006 Nobel Peace Prize winner was a tribute to it. It was truly the year of microfinance.

The energy, money, and brainpower being devoted to the practice of lending to the world's poor is unprecedented. "Previously, if we screamed, people didn't listen. Now, if we whisper, the whole world will hear," says Muhammad Yunus, who shares the Nobel Peace Prize with his Bangladesh-based Grameen Bank. Yunus pioneered microfinance in the 1970s and continues to expand its boundaries. But some of the most exciting innovations reshaping the field spring from a new breed of philanthropists who hail, in large part, from the tech world.

Their approaches to tackling the immense problem of worldwide poverty range from the conventional, such as funding research, to the controversial, such as advocating a stronger focus on making profits from lending to the poor. As befits captains of the tech industry, their efforts center on bringing scale, efficiency, and transparency to a fragmented, often inefficient area.

At the heart of microfinance is microcredit, the practice of offering small, unsecured loans to poor people not served by banks. The loans, often just $50 to $150, are used to buy everything from buffaloes that produce milk to sell in markets to mobile phones that villagers can pay to use. Borrowers are usually women, in part because studies show that women are more likely to use their earnings to pay for family needs than men. Interest rates, which average a hefty 35%, are still far below rates charged by local moneylenders. Repayment rates are said to run from 95% to 98%, though some suspect that figure is overstated.

Proponents say the beauty of microfinance is how a small amount of money can have a ripple effect on so many lives. In capitalist terms, it's the power of leverage. In human terms, it's the story of Dorothy Njobvu Kanjautso, a 35-year-old mother of three in Malawi who was widowed eight years ago. Through Opportunity International, a nonprofit group that received the Gates Foundation's first-ever microfinance grant in late 2005, she has taken out six loans over the last three years to build a school with seven teachers and start a separate business selling frozen treats from a cart. She used her first $70 loan to buy mats and games for the children; subsequent loans let her add a primary school and expand enrollment.

Being able to employ other people in the community is one way Kanjautso's loans paid off. At home the loans have improved the nutrition and education of her children. Before their mother's business took off, Kelvin, 12, Natasha, 11, and Vanessa, 9, ate meat maybe once a month, and meals were not particularly nutritious. Now they eat meat once a week and have a more balanced diet. They go to a private school with a 30-to-1 teacher-student ratio, far better than the 70-to-1 ratio in government schools. Better education and nutrition greatly increase the odds of their being able to stay above the poverty line.

Almost as important as the Nobel in putting microfinance on the map is its embrace by the tech elite. Those include Microsoft's Gates and his $32 billion foundation, Michael and Susan Dell and their $1.2 billion foundation, and the $470 million Omidyar Network, created by eBay founder Pierre Omidyar and his wife Pam. The Omidyars split their money between a $270 million pool for not-for-profit ventures and a $200 million pool devoted to for-profit investments.

The technology and microfinance worlds converged at a pivotal November, 2004, meeting at the house of John Doerr, the preeminent Silicon Valley venture capitalist. Doerr, who has pumped close to $20 million into the sector, invited some of the leading digerati of the day, including Omidyar and Google Inc. founders Larry Page and Sergey Brin, to brainstorm with Yunus, Grameen Foundation President Alex Counts, and others. It was a "catalytic event," says Counts. "These are people who saw technology change the lives of the richest 1 billion people of the world in a relatively short period of time, and they played a significant role in it. Now, they want to do that with the poor."

The entrepreneurs come equipped with technological expertise, high-level problem-solving skills, and a finely honed sense of what it takes to get a business up to critical mass. They are invigorated, not put off, by complex problems. Says Omidyar: "This is just another large-scale systems challenge."

Like tech, microfinance makes a lot more financial sense when it achieves scale. Selling a little bit of software on thin margins isn't much of a business. But sell boatloads and you just might become Bill Gates. Similarly, lenders can't maximize impact if they operate with only a few hundred or thousand borrowers. So the new forces in microfinance want to bring more scale to the industry. There's a long way to go, but the effort is making progress. The Microcredit Summit Campaign, launched in 1997 to "reach 100 million of the world's poorest families . . . with credit for self-employment and other financial and business services by the year 2005," didn't reach that goal, but it should hit the mark by year-end. Its new goal is to reach a total of 175 million of the world's poorest families by 2015.

The most provocative argument about how microlenders can achieve scale comes from Omidyar. He maintains that there is no way philanthropy alone can deliver loans to the world's poor. "To scale [up], to get to 500 million people, I believe, is going to come from the for-profit side, because there isn't enough nonprofit capital to get there," he says. One tack: Omidyar Network's lead investment in the for-profit Unitus Equity Fund, an $8.5 million microfinance venture investor. The fund invests in microfinance institutions in Asia and Latin America with the aim of helping them grow and become more efficient.

Microfinance operations must streamline if they want to reach the maximum number of people. To facilitate that goal, this October the Gates Foundation gave $1.5 million to Unitus, the same Redmond (Wash.) organization that launched the equity fund. Unitus also works to help midsize microfinance institutions in India, Latin America, and other developing regions grow into more efficient operations that can pass savings along in lower interest rates for borrowers. Unitus used the Gates money to hire four consultants from the for-profit banking world to figure out ways to improve cost structures. Since some 70% of all microfinance institutions have fewer than 2,500 borrowers, "they're stuck small," says Unitus Chairman Mike Murray, a former Microsoft and Apple executive who has committed more than $10 million of his own money to the cause.

The Gates Foundation's efforts, which range from funding a trans-African network of commercial banks for the poor to a plan to bring credit unions to the poorest regions of the developing world, also support technologies that push beyond what is common in the West. In a region where banking services are often nonexistent, it has helped fund one of the more innovative approaches. A $2.2 million grant to Opportunity International in late 2005 included funds to help hand out biometric smart cards to clients of the group's microfinance institution in Malawi. The cards work much like ATM cards except they use fingerprint-reading technology. That's important because most clients don't have official identification documents since they don't drive and don't travel outside the country. When Malawi entrepreneur Kanjautso uses the ATM, she says she feels like one of the wealthy travelers that she associates with ATMs: "I look like a foreigner. I'm so proud of it." Now, Gates and others are trying to expand the use of mobile ATMS—armored machines on the back of Jeeps—to bring money to villages on a scheduled basis.

The Dells' foundation is also expanding the definition of microfinance, moving it from the rural areas where the practice got its start into India's most impoverished cities. It works with two institutions that focus on bringing financial services to urban slums in cities including Mumbai and Bangalore.

Toward that end, in May the Dell Foundation bought a 14% stake in Bangalore-based for-profit Ujjivan Financial Services. The year-old organization gives loans to the unemployed as well as to women who are employed, typically at local garment factories, who use the money to cover emergency family needs or to start a business. For the Dells, the Ujjivan investment is just a start; the foundation hopes to help launch 20 microfinance institutions to focus on the urban poor within five years.

Along with reaching new borrowers, microfinance will need to achieve a far greater level of standardization to attract more investment. Most lenders use homegrown programs to keep tabs on everything from loan repayments to their ability to lift the living standards of their borrowers. Omidyar has given a $1.4 million grant for the creation of software that helps microfinance institutions collect comparable data from borrowers. On Nov. 13, Seattle-based Grameen Technology Center launched a new software application called Mifos, a program designed to standardize the way repayment data, as well as information on how clients' lives improve as a result of getting loans, are collected. Grameen will give the software away in the hopes that it will become widely used. Omidyar is also focused on collecting better data on microfinance institutions. Over the past two years he has put $1.5 million into Microfinance Information eXchange, or mix Market, a nonprofit Web-based platform that collects financial data for more than 800 microfinance institutions. The idea: Standardize financial reporting and provide benchmarks so investors can make informed decisions about where to put their microfinance dollars.

In the wake of the Nobel and the buzz generated by having America's tech elite targeting microfinance, a site like mix Market may be ideally positioned. It's the kind of venture that can help move microfinance from being admired primarily as a good idea to a practice that becomes accepted as a good business. With microfinance, to use Yunus' words, "under the spotlight of the world," efforts like Omidyar's and his peers may enable it to rise to the challenge.

Source: Jay Greene and Jeffrey Gangemi, *BusinessWeek*, November 27, 2006, p. 76.

EXHIBIT 13.1
Collaboration Partners

Source: R. Jones, R. Kashlak, and A. Jones, "Knowledge Flows and Economic Development through Microenterprise Collaboration in Third-Sector Communities," *New England Journal of Entrepreneurship* 7, no. 1, p. 40.

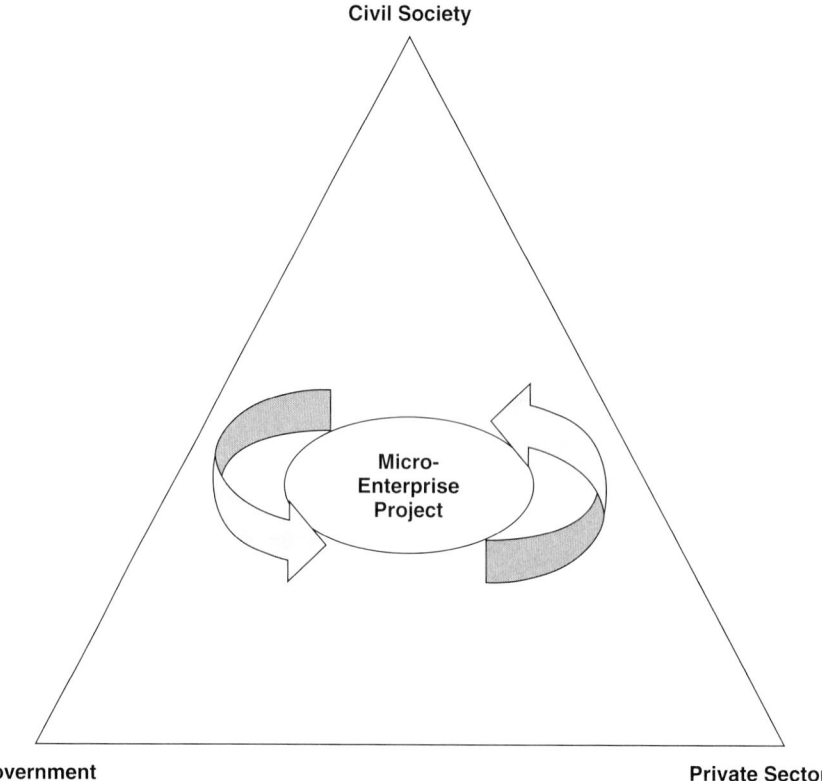

Civil Society

Micro-Enterprise Project

Government   Private Sector/MNE

more stakeholders from its international activities than would be found in a purely domestic operation. Waddock advocated that the treatment of stakeholders, including the communities and the environment, is to be considered part of the fundamental purpose of the firm.[8]

In 1999, Kofi Annan, former Secretary-General of the United Nations, suggested that his and similar organizations, which historically worked only with governments, must understand that peace and prosperity will not be achieved without partnerships involving governments, international organizations, the business community, and civil society. Increasingly, the global community concerned with economic development and promotion of democracies is focusing on developing programs to stimulate partnerships among three distinct sectors: the government sector, the civil society, and the private sector, including transnational corporations.[9] Exhibit 13.1 illustrates this proposed collaboration.

Thus, the new imperative of collaboration among these sectors follows Grosse and Behrman's suggestion that a better understanding of the many and diverse interactions between the various governments and multinational and local firms be more heavily incorporated into international business activities.[10] As suggested above, the lower-margin projected future revenue benefits from new market development activities in bottom-of-the-pyramid markets will be complemented by the efficiencies gained from the low-wage labor in these areas, whether rural or urban. Beyond these benefits to both the society and the multinational corporation lies the immense potential for new knowledge, new technology, and innovation, as discussed below.

Innovation and Knowledge from Global Enterprise Initiatives

As discussed previously in this text, collaborative initiatives are founded on core pillars of trust, reciprocity, and lack of opportunism. In the context of global enterprise, **reciprocity** of knowledge plays a key role, as shown in Exhibit 13.2. The modern organization is becoming increasingly informed in its strategies and practices by the concepts of learning and knowledge. An organization may be thought of as an idiosyncratic set of knowledge capabilities that are continuously enhanced and modified by unique learning routines. It is from the leveraging of this new and unique knowledge that sustainable competitive advantage may develop. Furthermore, as the prospect for success of host-country community-based projects and third-sector communities already involving the local governments and civil society organizations, including nongovernment organizations and development agencies, is evident, these benefits could be enhanced by combining the knowledge management resources of multinational enterprises. Subsequently, as discussed in Practical Insight 13.1, the multinational enterprise itself can develop a new set of knowledge and technological skills and advantages from these initiatives and then leverage those advantages in other major markets. At the center of this collaboration is reciprocity, which Kogut identified as fundamental to the achievement of long-term cooperation between partners.[11]

On the basis of Exhibits 13.1 and 13.2, Jones and colleagues suggested that at the foundation of this country-level approach to competitiveness are the various project- and sector-based approaches within the developing countries. It is at these levels that the third-sector communities may benefit through knowledge management and the subsequent transfer of specific technologies and skills when developing micro-enterprise projects. Specifically, both the knowledge management and organizational learning paradigms may be utilized to leverage the success of host-country community-based projects at two distinct levels: the micro level and the macro level.

At the micro level, *project-based knowledge management* suggests that partners succeed collectively as well as individually by learning from one another's historical competencies. Subsequently, the partners will learn from the new collective competency that has been and continues to be created in the collaboration. In addition to the learning dynamics of the individual project knowledge transfers among participants, separate learning may occur when sets of projects are reviewed, analyzed, and

EXHIBIT 13.2
Collaboration, Reciprocity, and Development

Source: Adapted from R. Jones, R. Kashlak, and A. Jones, "Knowledge Flows and Economic Development through Microenterprise Collaboration in Third-Sector Communities," *New England Journal of Entrepreneurship* 7, no. 1, p. 39.

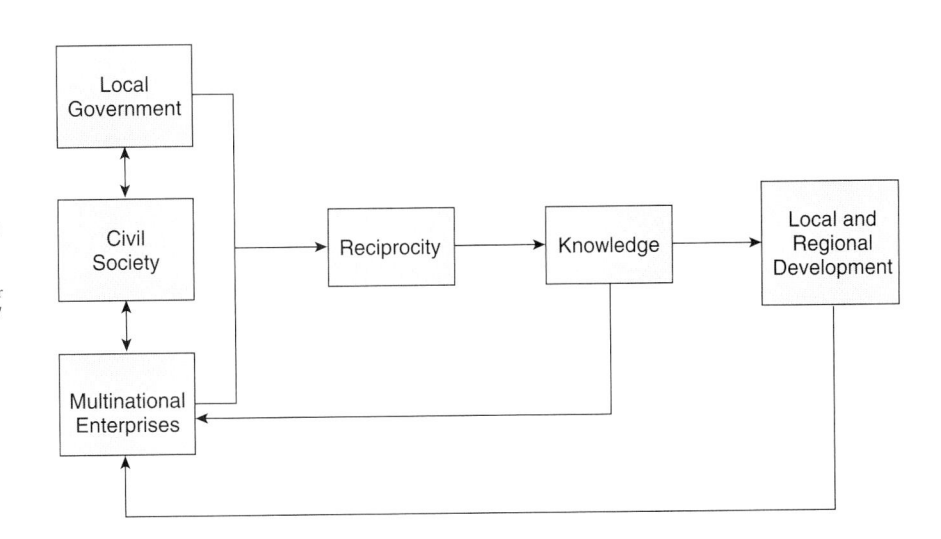

PRACTICAL INSIGHT 13.2

MINETTI OF ARGENTINA

Juan Minetti, SA, was founded in 1930 in the city of Córdoba. Today, Grupo Minetti has Argentinas second-largest production capacity of cement and concrete. The Minetti Foundation was created in 1987 to support micro-enterprise programs that facilitate the self-help development of individuals and their organizations, and to improve the standard of living of low-income populations. Since then, it has donated cement for community construction projects, provided training and other resources to unemployed workers and community organizations, and promoted corporate social responsibility (CSR) among other Argentine corporations.

The Minetti Foundation is considered a leader in CSR. It is a member of Argentina's prestigious Group of Foundations that includes Bunge and Born Foundation, YPF Foundation, Telefónica Foundation, Bank Boston Foundation, the Kellogg Foundation, and the ARCOR Foundation. As a result of its partnership with IAF, the Minetti Foundation now plays an even larger role than funding grants in the community. It is an example for Argentine corporations looking to improve their CSR programs. Between 1997 and 2001, the Minetti Foundation and the IAF contributed $285,000 each to create the "Building Bridges Fund," which provided grants to 28 micro-enterprises in the province of Córdoba. While the focus of this fund was primarily informal education, the guiding principle was that of building relationship capital for Grupo Minetti and for the grant recipients. More impressive, however, is that there were nearly 250 participating organizations that mobilized a total of $884,000 in cash and in-kind resources which was 150% more that the actual financing awarded through the Building Bridges grants. As a result of the track record established by "Building Bridges," in 2001 the Minetti Foundation leveraged $120,000 from Spain-based Telefónica Foundation to complement its $170,000 for a technical assistance fund for community organizations. In 2002, U.S.-based Hispanics in Philanthropy matched that $290,000 dollar for dollar. As part of its continuing leadership, the Minetti Foundation also held a workshop for several businesses in the province of Buenos Aires. The majority agreed on the benefits of adopting the Minetti Foundation's philosophy and methodology, i.e., shifting from simple donations to financing projects that strengthen local organizations. Already, five companies have joined forces to support a local educational project and plan to provide monitoring and other follow-up. While the Minetti Foundation was created to "do good" in the community, these are examples of the returns it has produced, especially from creating its first grant-making fund "Building Bridges."

Like Grupo Minetti, the Minetti Foundation takes calculated risks that yield high returns on a small investment. For example, "Building Bridges" provided a grant of 15,000 pesos

---

appropriately clustered, for example, at the sector level. Thus, at this macro level, *sector-based knowledge management* is evident. At the sector level of knowledge management, the partners respectively position themselves to succeed in community-based projects by learning from a single project or a cluster of projects in which they may or may not have participated.[12] Practical Insight 13.2 explores collaboration at a local level in Argentina.

Global Enterprise Networks and Sustainability

As initially identified in the chapter's opening case and as depicted in Figure 13.1, networks of different and distinct players are critical to the success of global enterprise initiatives. Wheeler and his team of researchers support Jones's suggestion that successful and sustainable global enterprises include for-profit businesses, not-for-profit organizations, and local communities. Furthermore, they developed a comprehensive model of **sustainability** of these initiatives. At the core of the model is the network of not only multinational and local corporations, government, and community but also investors and entrepreneurs. They suggest that with a strong investment anchor including human, social, financial, and ecological capital, an appropriately choreographed network will lead to not only sustainable profits but reinvestment in community and trade infrastructure that will enhance the community's quality of life and

to La Merced Housing and Service Cooperative in a semi-rural community both impoverished and isolated—physically, economically, socially and culturally. Both adults and children suffered high rates of illiteracy because the written word was virtually absent: no street signs, no sign indicating the name of the school, and worse, no books. With support from "Building Bridges," a group of concerned parents, educators and social workers initiated a program of educational support for at-risk students that evolved into an ongoing, youth-led project involving 80 children. Youth involved in "The Kid's Place" tutor their younger peers and develop other extra-curricular activities that help both groups stay in school—and succeed there. A follow-up grant was made to the organization that emerged from the project, Protagonism for Community Activities (PROCOM).

After three years, the progress has been significant. For instance, two 12-year-old librarians hunch over a notebook, writing slowly and carefully as they sign books in and out of a community children's library. The "Kid's" community center is covered with colorful posters listing the group's objectives and achievements, and each cubby and pencil holder is carefully labeled with a handwritten sign. Furthermore, visitors are given a copy of Little Workers, the youth's literary magazine filled with their own stories and poems. According to project coordinator Adriana Alanis, "More than just the money, it was the encouragement that we received in our visits from the Minetti Foundation, the training, and the opportunity to learn from other groups, such as how to start our library, step-by-step. The money is important, but the other is just as critical." One of the most dramatic project results is that the community has come together to make it sustainable. "There are many urgent needs in this community, even hunger, so we've begun producing food. If we secure outside help, we will be able to respond more quickly. If not, we will still succeed, just more slowly. But the commitment and protagonism are there. That's what's new." La Merced is often showcased as a model for community development—and has received unsolicited donations for its work. According to Ms. Alanis, "One woman who read the book called to say she wanted to help but wanted anonymity. So twice a week we go by and the manager of her apartment building hands us what we need to provide nutritional snacks to the children at 'The Kid's Place'." Others provide scholarships for the students. Support from "Building Bridges" has also given other grantee organizations the experience and track record that has allowed them to mobilize public and private resources, local and nationally.

Source: Audra Jones and Raymond Jones, in R. Jones, R. Kashlak, and A. Jones, "Knowledge Flows and Economic Development through Microenterprise Collaboration in Third-Sector Communities," *New England Journal of Entrepreneurship* 7, no. 1, pp. 39–49.

subsequently lead to self-reliance at both the individual and community levels.[13] This comprehensive framework, the sustainable **local enterprise network** model, is depicted in Exhibit 13.3.

EXHIBIT 13.3
The Sustainable Local Enterprise Network Model

Source: D. Wheeler, K. McKague, J. Thomson, R. Davies, J. Medalye, and M. Prada, "Creating Sustainable Local Enterprise Networks," *Sloan Management Review,* Fall 2005, p. 39.

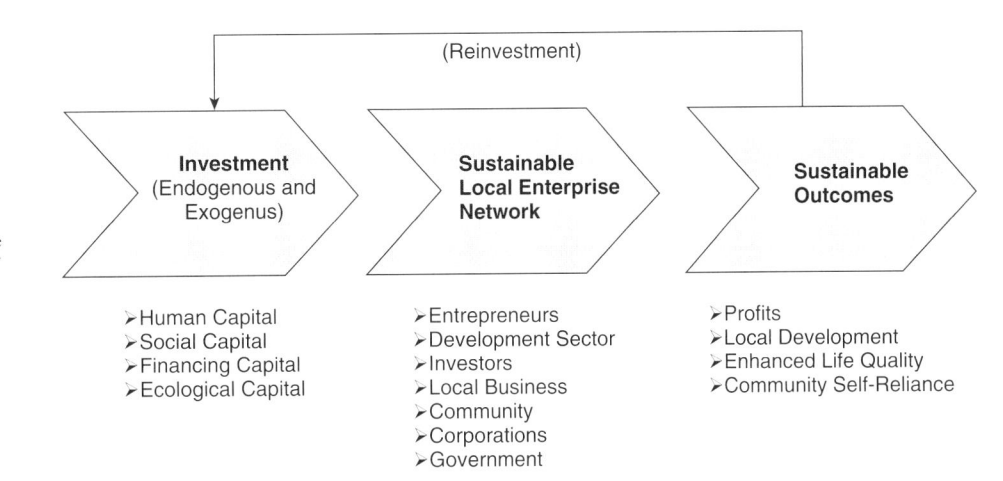

(Reinvestment)

Investment (Endogenous and Exogenus) → **Sustainable Local Enterprise Network** → **Sustainable Outcomes**

- Human Capital
- Social Capital
- Financing Capital
- Ecological Capital

- Entrepreneurs
- Development Sector
- Investors
- Local Business
- Community
- Corporations
- Government

- Profits
- Local Development
- Enhanced Life Quality
- Community Self-Reliance

Summary

This chapter introduced the evolving concept and strategy of global enterprise. Global social enterprise differs from corporate social responsibility (that is discussed in Chapter 14) as it incorporates the profit imperative for the multinational corporation. By collaborating with local businesses, governments, and development agencies, the firm can not only serve the world's poorest markets but also help to create a sustainable community and market for the future. A business case was presented to support the necessity of serving the poorest of the poor peoples of the world. By doing so, multinational corporations will develop long-term sustainable revenue streams, greater cost efficiency, and an important new source of innovation.

Knowledge as a sustainable competitive advantage was discussed. Similar to joint ventures and strategic alliances (discussed in Chapter 6), knowledge can be gained through collaboration with partners. In the case of global enterprise, collaborative efforts are most critical when partnering with local businesses and governments as well as nongovernment agencies. Furthermore, at the core of the collaborative relationships is reciprocity, whereby there is an equal sharing and benefit of the knowledge being developed at the "bottom of the pyramid" local level.

An integrative sustainable local enterprise network model was discussed to include all factors relevant to creating sustainable outcomes such as profits, local development, local trade opportunities, better quality of life, and eventual self-reliance of these communities. Key investment factors include financial, human, ecological, and social capital.

Key Terms and Concepts

global social enterprise, *474*
local enterprise networks, *481*
reciprocity, *479*
sustainability, *480*

Discussion Questions

1. In what ways must traditional firms from industrialized countries change their respective strategies, implementation techniques, and perspectives to compete in the bottom-of-the-pyramid market of billions of people worldwide?
2. In your opinion, how is global enterprise different from charity? Are both necessary parts of a multinational corporation's strategic portfolio?
3. Review the chapter figures illustrating the collaboration partners and the network model. What other factors, resources, or entities may be incorporated to ensure long-term sustainable outcomes?

Minicase

Rise of the Asian D-School: More Students Are Opting for Programs—and Jobs—at Home

Europe and the U.S. have long dominated design education, but Asian schools are quickly catching up. Having demonstrated their ability to teach engineering and technical skills, Chinese, Korean, Indian, and Taiwanese universities are now graduating thousands of design students every year. And a growing number offer programs in design strategy, innovative thinking, and sustainability.

Shih Chien University in Taipei, for example, is teaching "creativity management" classes. So is India's National Institute of Design. At Taiwan's National Cheng Kung University, a year-old graduate program called Institute of Creative Industry Design is fostering what one professor calls OCM thinking, for Own Culture and Manufacturing. Courses focus on topics such as creative industry planning and cognitive behavior research.

Global corporations chasing Asian consumer wallets are pouring money into research projects and workshops in design schools from Shanghai to Seoul. Oregon Scientific and LavAzza Coffee are teaming with graduate students at Hong Kong Polytechnic University to develop new business strategies. Levi Strauss, Estee Lauder, and Ford are tapping Shih Chien students for insights and designs. Autodesk, Inc. recently funded a faculty research chair at the National Institute of Design in India.

The influx of interest, funding, jobs, and internships means Asian design students are starting to see opportunity at home as well as abroad. In India, domestic companies such as Videocon, an industrial conglomerate, are setting up design departments for the first time. Meanwhile, Korean, Japanese, U.S., European, and other global companies keep flowing into India. "In terms of job opportunities, it's a very good time," says Ravi Poovaiah, a professor at Mumbai's Industrial Design Centre (IDC), part of the India Institute of Technology. The shift is seismic. "For years, we have sent our students to Europe and the U.S.," says Chiho In, a professor at Korea's Hongik University. "Now, we're also trying to build relationships in Asia." In fact, while the 11 Asian schools on *BusinessWeek*'s Global Design School list boast numerous partnerships in Europe and North America, many also link to nearby Asian institutions.

Sustainability is fast becoming a major issue in Asia, particularly in China. Beijing's Tsinghua University recently hosted a sustainable design workshop with Milan Polytechnic University. At Mumbai's IDC, it has been a driving force for years. "The Indian way of life is to not waste a thing," says IDC's Poovaiah. "It's part of how we look at products, too." That ethos is spurring IDC students to design fuel-efficient cars and bamboo products ranging from furniture to fixtures in its own Bamboo Lab.

Other schools take a broader view. Students at Hong Kong Polytechnic spent the summer of 2006 brainstorming ways design could assist rural ethnic minorities in China. One idea: Establish direct trade between farmers in the province of Yunnan and Hong Kong hotels that might purchase herbs for use in their toiletries. IDC students are designing mobile learning devices for migrant workers and carts for street-food vendors. "There are still so many things that need to be designed," says IDC's Poovaiah. "Asia is a gold mine of opportunity for designers."

Source: Elizabeth Woyke, *BusinessWeek*, October 15, 2007, p. 66.

DISCUSSION QUESTIONS

1. How can education be linked to the integrated model of sustainable local enterprise networks?
2. Are countries like China and India better positioned to design and develop future technologies and products that meet current and future needs of people at the bottom of the pyramid?
3. How are macro-level problems, such as the exponentially rising costs of fuel, catalysts to global enterprise initiatives?

Notes

1. M. Yunus, *Creating a World without Poverty* (New York: Public Affairs, 2007).
2. C. K. Prahalad and A. Hammond, "Serving the World's Poor Profitably," *Harvard Business Review,* September 2002, pp. 48–57.
3. Ibid., p. 54.
4. M. Porter, *The Competitive Advantage of Nations* (New York: Free Press, 1990).
5. R. Kashlak, "Establishing Financial Targets for Joint Ventures in Emerging Countries: A Conceptual Model," *Journal of International Management* 4, no. 3 (1998), pp. 241–258.
6. R. Jones, "Global Social Enterprise and Micro-Enterprise Collaboration," working paper, Loyola College, Maryland, Baltimore, 2004.
7. C. Freeman, "The Politics of Stakeholder Theory: Some Future Directions," *Business Ethics Quarterly* 4, pp. 409–421.
8. S. Waddock, "Strategy, Structure and Social Performance: Implications of the W-Form Enterprise," *Business and the Contemporary World* 8, no. 1, pp. 43–51.
9. R. Jones, R. Kashlak, and A. Jones, "Knowledge Flows and Economic Development through Microenterprise Collaboration in Third-Sector Communities," *New England Journal of Entrepreneurship* 7, no. 1, pp. 39–49.

10. R. Grosse and J. Behrman, "Theory in International Business," *Transnational Corporations,* February 1992, pp. 93–126.
11. B. Kogut, "The Stability of Joint Ventures: Reciprocity and Competitive Rivalry," *Journal of Industrial Economics,* December 1989, pp. 183–197.
12. Jones, Kashlak, and Jones, "Knowledge Flows and Economic Development."
13. D. Wheeler, K. McKague, J. Thomson, R. Davies, J. Medalye, and M. Prada, "Creating Sustainable Local Enterprise Networks," *Sloan Management Review,* Fall 2005, pp. 33–40.

CHAPTER FOURTEEN

Ethics and Social Responsibility for International Firms

Chapter Learning Objectives

After completing this chapter, you should be able to:

- Explain moral philosophies of relevance to business ethics.
- Define *business ethics* and describe the relationships among host-country laws, ethics, and cultural relativism.
- Discuss the process of formulating strategic corporate responsibility programs in the organization.
- Discuss the issues of bribery and corruption and their role in the international business arena.
- Discuss the ethics of child labor and sweatshops.
- Explain how a company can effectively inculcate ethics and business conduct in its managers and employees.

Opening Case: Scandals and Corruption— A Historical Perspective

The accounting scandals involving Enron, Arthur Andersen, WorldCom, Qwest Communications, Tyco and other once highly regarded companies have caused a crisis of confidence among many Americans. Some ask whether the problems are so severe as to represent an irreparable fault in the economic system.

From an historical perspective, the answer is that economies are capable of recovering and making progress, even after near devastation—not only from war, as in the case of Germany and Japan after World War II, but also from economic chicanery, which is scarcely new. After bubbles collapse and interfere with economic growth, the resulting loss of income stimulates efforts to maintain and increase income, both honestly and in corrupt ways.

Starting in 1600 with the establishment of the British East India Company, followed by its Dutch counterpart two years later, Europeans learned how to extract great wealth from the Far East. Warren Hastings, the first governor-general of India, and Robert Clive, a civil servant with the East India Company who became known as "the conqueror of India," were perhaps the earliest private malefactors of great wealth. Hastings accumulated £200,000 in India and transferred it to England in the 18th century; in the same period Clive transferred £280,000.

Edmund Burke, the 18th-century statesman, argued that Clive ought to be removed. At the same time Lord North, who served as Britain's prime minister from 1770 to 1782, contended that Hastings's

nominal salaries, clerks (known then as writers), cadets, assistant surgeons, ship captains and ship husbands, who handled charters, all found opportunities to acquire wealth.

Human nature has not changed. Andrew S. Fastow—who, while serving as Enron's chief financial officer, was also running partnerships, particularly LJM2 [private equity fund], set up by Enron to keep debt off the books—has been indicted on 78 counts of fraud, money laundering, conspiracy and obstruction of justice. The East India employees smuggled goods to Europe and dealt in opium with China. The role of ship commander was bought and sold, typically for £2,000 to £5,000, but sometimes for up to £10,000 and once for double that.

So egregious were their activities that British historians were not the only ones to single out Hastings and Clive. A German economic historian, Jacob van Klaveren, writing in the 1950's on the origins of corruption between the state and private business, asserted that corruption in business had begun with the East India Companies.

By the 19th century, business corruption was so much a fact of life that it became a prominent theme for European novelists. Among them were Honoré de Balzac in *The Human Comedy;* Charles Dickens, *Little Dorrit;* William Makepeace Thackeray, *The Newcomes;* Anthony Trollope, *The Way We Live Now;* Gustav Freytag, *Soll und Haben;* Alexandre Dumas, *Black Tulip;* and Emile Zola, *L'Argent.*

And like many European fashions, swindling found its place in America by the 19th century, where Mark Twain and Theodore Dreiser included it in the plots of their books, while Boston produced Charles Ponzi, a swindler so prominent that his name became synonymous with one type of chicanery. He borrowed money for 45 days at 50 percent interest and paid early investors with cash from later suckers whose money he kept.

The writers had abundant examples to inspire them, including Eugene Bontoux, founder and director of Union Générale, a French bank that collapsed in 1882, and in the United States, Daniel Drew, James Fisk Jr. and Jay Gould, who manipulated the stock of the Erie Railroad.

Financial scandals abounded on both sides of the Atlantic in the 20th century, as well. Among the perpetrators were the cabinet members involved in the Teapot Dome scandal during the administration of President Warren G. Harding; Ivar Kreuger, the Swedish Match King, who put together an empire of companies and became a private lender to governments before the empire collapsed, fraudulent accounting was exposed and he committed suicide in Paris in 1932; Robert L. Vesco, who looted Investors Overseas Services, the Swiss-based mutual fund empire founded by Bernard Cornfeld; Michele Sindona, the financier behind the Franklin National Bank in New York and Banca Ambrosia in Milan; and Nicholas Leeson, the rogue trader who brought down Barings Bank.

Two famous 18th-century swindlers—Sir John Blunt, chairman of the South Sea Trading Company, and John Law, a Scot, who persuaded the French government in 1716 to let him open a bank that could issue paper currency in Louisiana, which France owned—might be said to have a modern counterpart. Sir John's stock manipulation led to what became known as the South Sea bubble and produced the crash of the London stock exchange. Law's issuance of paper money, which was used to drive up shares that then plunged, became known as the Mississippi bubble.

Before the bubbles burst, each took vast earnings and invested in real estate. Sir John had six contracts to buy estates when the South Sea bubble burst in 1720; Law owned one-sixth of the Place Vendôme in Paris, plus a dozen estates in the French countryside, when the Banque Royale and the Compagnie d'Occident failed that same year.

Some figures in current scandals have also shown an eye for real estate. One of them is Kenneth L. Lay, the former chief executive of Enron. He acquired a multimillion-dollar penthouse in Houston, his home city, plus three large houses in Aspen, Colo., worth more than $5 million each, along with a building site valued at more than $1 million.

Investors have good reason to worry that next year may produce new disclosures of illegal insider trading, overstated profits and other dubious accounting practices. But the year could also bring new rules for corporate accounting, as the Securities and Exchange Commission, the new Public Accounting Oversight Board, federal and state governments, the courts and securities exchanges take up the issues raised by the scandals. It is still too early to say whether they will succeed in overhauling the rules and restoring investor confidence.

Source: Charles Kindleberger, "Corruption, Crime, Chicanery: Business through the Ages," *NewYorkTimes*, December 16, 2002. Copyright © 2002 The New York Times Co. Reprinted with permission.

Discussion Questions

1. As shown in this article, corruption and unethical behavior have been prevalent in history. Is it in human nature to be dishonest and corrupt? Can we legislate honesty and transparency in one's dealings with others?
2. Discuss the impacts of corrupt and unethical behavior on the well-being of society, which is affected by it.
3. Is giving a holiday gift to your mail carrier or local Police Athletic League any different from (a) bribing a customs officer to clear parcels through customs or (b) making payoffs to a politician to secure a business deal?

Business Ethics and Corporate Social Responsibility Defined

Most people would agree that a set of moral principles or values should govern the actions of executives, and most executives would agree that their decisions should be made in accordance with accepted principles of right or wrong. **Ethics** has been defined as "inquiry into the nature and grounds of morality where the term morality is taken to mean moral judgments, standards and rules of conduct."[1] It is a system of principles, a guide to human behavior that helps to distinguish between good and bad, or between right and wrong. Business ethics "is the moral thinking and analysis by corporate decision-makers and other members regarding the motives and consequences of their decisions and actions."[2]

International managers are confronted with a variety of decisions that create ethical dilemmas for the decision makers. The following situations illustrate some real-life ethical dilemmas faced by companies.

Situation 1 Should a company continue to market in a foreign country, where it is legal, a product that is banned in the home country because it is harmful? Companies in industrialized countries are continuing to sell products in foreign countries that are illegal at home but legal abroad. For instance, several pesticides such as Velsicol, Phosvel, and 2,4-D (which contains dioxin) are being sold directly or indirectly in other countries even though they have been banned in the United States. A strong link has been found between the chemicals in the pesticides and cancer. The manufacturers of these pesticides argue that the benefits of using the pesticides to increase crop yields in poor countries with severe food shortages far outweigh the health risk associated with their use. The profit motive is also involved in this issue. For example, American Vanguard Corporation, which was banned from selling the pesticide DBCP directly to American companies, continues to export it to other nations. American Vanguard claimed that it would have gone bankrupt had it not sold the DBCP in other countries.[3]

Situation 2 Cigarette smoking has been generally accepted as harmful to human health in most advanced countries. Scientific studies have proved that cigarette smoke causes cancer and that it is associated with the onset of heart disease. Laws in the United States require that product labeling on cigarette packets warn customers of the harmful side effects of smoking. Cigarette smoking has been banned in offices and restaurants in the state of New York. Almost all companies and government offices have a ban on smoking in the workplace. Still, smoking is big business in other countries, and especially in eastern Europe and Asia, where little has been done to make the public aware that smoking is harmful to health. Cigarette company giants like Philip Morris, RJR Nabisco, American Brands, and Rothmans International have targeted these world regions as the growth markets for cigarette sales to compensate for the mature home markets. The sales volume abroad of some companies like Philip Morris is larger than that at home. The ethical issue here is whether tobacco companies should target young men and women in other countries as potential long-term customers of a product when cigarette smoking is generally accepted to be addictive and harmful.

Situation 3   The search for enhanced efficiencies and lower costs has induced international companies to transfer labor-intensive operations to countries that offer cheap labor. Companies have also resorted to buying products made by contract manufacturers in foreign countries. International human rights groups have documented that in many cases the foreign contract manufacturers use child labor to make the goods. Chinese companies have used prison labor. The ethical question that arises in such cases is, Is it ethical for companies to sell products made by children or forced prison labor?

Situation 4   A foreign government official informs the vice president for marketing of a French aerospace company that the minister of defense will approve the purchase of aircraft from the aerospace company, worth several hundred million francs, if the selling price is hiked by 15 percent. He is also told to deposit the 15 percent increase in a numbered Swiss bank account. Failing to comply with this request, he is told, would cause the purchase order to be canceled and possibly given to a competing firm from another country. French law prohibits bribery in France but does not prohibit bribery of foreign officials abroad. If he refuses to give the bribe, the company would not get the order for the aircraft, and several hundred jobs at home would be lost. What should the vice president for marketing do?

The four situations presented above are illustrative of the innumerable ethical dilemmas faced by international managers almost daily. Unquestionably managers could use frameworks that could serve as benchmarks in identifying ethical problems and arriving at ethically sound solutions. To that end, we must define corporate social responsibility and subsequently draw on the field of philosophy to offer moral philosophies to better understand the basis of ethical dilemmas faced by managers.

Corporate social responsibility may be defined as the integration of business operations and values whereby the interests of all stakeholders, including customers, employees, investors, and the environment, are reflected in an organization's policies and actions. Consumers in many countries expect firms to meet high health and safety, worker, human rights, consumer protection, and environmental standards regardless of where their operations are located. Furthermore, investors and stakeholders are increasingly asking their suppliers to exhibit their respective corporate social responsibility programs.[4]

What are the drivers of corporate social responsibility? The following three specific motivations, as described by Maignan and Ralston, have emerged:[5]

1. From a utilitarian perspective, corporate social responsibility is an instrument useful to help achieve a firm's performance objectives defined in terms of profitability, return on investment, or sales volume.

2. The **positive duty approach** suggests that businesses may be self-motivated to have a positive impact regardless of social pressures calling for social initiatives. When this positive duty is prevalent, corporate social responsibility principles are a component of the firm's true identity, expressing values considered by organizational members as central, enduring, and distinctive values to the firm.[6]
3. From a **negative duty approach,** businesses are compelled to adopt social responsibility initiatives in order to conform to stakeholder norms defining appropriate behavior. When negative duty is prevalent, self-motivation is replaced by corporate social responsibility initiatives that are a reaction to what is expected from stakeholders.[7]

Moral Philosophies of Relevance to Business Ethics

A moral philosophy is "the set of principles or rules that people use to decide what is right or wrong."[8] Moral philosophies help explain why a person believes that a certain choice among alternatives is ethically right or wrong. Managers fall back on their personal principles, values, and belief systems to evaluate the "good" or "bad," and "right" or "wrong," aspects that are at the core of each alternative course of action available in decision making.

Managers and businesspersons are guided by moral philosophies when confronted with ethical and moral dilemmas as they formulate their strategies and action plans, but they do not all use the same moral philosophy. Some managers, for example, may view the producing of a product at the lowest cost to be of foremost importance and may therefore choose to locate the production plant in a country that offers the cheapest labor, even though the minimum health and safety standards that must be legally observed in production plants in that country would be considered below acceptable standards, and therefore illegal, in the home country. Other managers may believe that making profits at the expense of the health and safety of workers, although legal in the host country, is actually unethical and immoral and hence may decide to provide working conditions that are both healthy and safe for the workers, even at the expense of higher production costs and lower profits for the company. Some managers may believe that giving bribes to obtain business is unethical, whereas other managers may think that it is not wrong to obtain business by bribing politicians if doing so helps preserve jobs in the company.

Several moral philosophies appear in the literature on the subject. Studying each one is beyond the scope of this book. Therefore, we limit our discussion to those that are most relevant to the study of business ethics. The four moral philosophies that have evolved during the twentieth century and that serve as the principal foundations for the field of normative ethics are teleology, deontology, the theory of justice, and cultural relativism.[9]

Teleology

According to the moral philosophy called **teleology,** an action or behavior is acceptable or right if it is responsible for producing the desired outcomes, for example, a promotion at work, a bigger market share for a product or service, realization of self-interest, or utility. Teleological philosophies are often referred to as *consequentialism* by moral philosophers because of the emphasis placed by these philosophies on evaluating the morality of an action mainly by examining its consequences. The two key teleological precepts that serve as guides for managerial decision making are egoism and utilitarianism.

Egoism evaluates how right or acceptable a behavior is depending on its consequences on the person. The egoists profess that self-interest should be the primary determinant of a person's behavior. Self-interest may be different for different individuals. It may mean the acquisition of wealth, fame, or power; a good family life; leisure; or prestige. When faced with the prospect of having to choose among a set of alternatives, an egoist will probably choose one that maximizes her or his personal self-interest. A more calculating form of egoism does indeed consider the interests of others if in so doing the egoist's own self-interests are advanced. For example, a manager may promote community development projects not because of some deep-seated altruistic motive but because projects that benefit the community surrounding the company ultimately bring the manager personal prestige and elevate her standing within the company.

Utilitarianism, like egoism, holds that actions should be judged by their consequences; however, unlike egoists, utilitarians claim that behaviors that are moral produce the greatest good for the greatest number of people.[10] Utilitarians believe that a moral decision is one that creates the greatest total *utility*—that is, the greatest benefit for each and every person affected by a decision. A utilitarian would be inclined to make an analysis of the costs versus the benefits of each alternative course of action for those affected by the decision and to choose the one alternative that results in the greatest utility.

Selecting a decision that not only considers the interests but also maximizes the utility of all individuals and groups that are affected by the decision can be very difficult and perhaps impossible. A utilitarian can take a shortcut and reduce the complexity of utilitarian decision making by simply obeying the rules of behavior prescribed by a preferred ideological system. Some utilitarian philosophers, called *rule utilitarians,* have argued that general rules should be followed to decide which action is best.[11] They believe that certain principles or rules, when observed in ones's behavior, would result in the greatest utility. Decision making that is based on the foundation of rules or principles reduces the complexity of utilitarian decision making and erases the need to examine each particular situation. For example, some religious ideologies prescribe behavioral norms that, if followed, are supposed to improve the human condition. For instance, the Holy Koran preaches that craving excess profit is immoral. Guided by this principle, a Moslem utilitarian businessperson will make business decisions that do not, in his eyes, exploit workers, suppliers, or customers.

There are those who believe that bribery is bad for everyone. They theorize that bribery distorts the efficient allocation of resources by market forces and therefore everyone suffers because of the misallocation of resources. For example, a company whose product is far superior to those of its competitors may not get the business if a government official is bribed to buy from someone else. In this instance, the taxpayers are the losers, as their taxes have been misused to buy an inferior product. A rule utilitarian would refuse to bribe an official, even if that meant the loss of workers' jobs, but would firmly stick to the rule: "No bribes!"

Other utilitarian philosophers, called *act utilitarians,* profess that whether an individual action is right or wrong should be evaluated on the basis of its ability to create the greatest utility for the greatest number of people and that rules such as "bribery is bad" should serve only as guidelines in decision making. Act utilitarians would agree that bribery is wrong, not because bribery is inherently wrong but because the total utility decreases when bribery places self-interest ahead of societal interests. Act utilitarians would argue that offering a bribe to obtain business would be quite acceptable if the alternative is to lose hundreds of jobs in the factory, which in turn would adversely affect the welfare of the surrounding community.

Deontology: The Theory of Rights

Deontology (from the Greek word *deontos,* which means "binding, necessity") is "an ethical theory holding that acting from a sense of duty rather than concern for consequences is the basis for establishing our moral obligation."[12] Unlike utilitarians, deontologists argue that certain acts or behaviors must never be permitted, even though they might maximize utility. The German philosopher Immanuel Kant (1724–1804) was the main proponent of deontology. He believed that "some acts are right, and some acts are wrong, quite independent of their consequences. He professed that it is irrelevant in determining our moral obligation whether an action makes us happy, or whether it contributes to human pleasure. We do that which is right because it is the right thing to do. No other consideration is relevant to our moral deliberation."[13]

Deontology also refers to "moral philosophies that focus on the rights of individuals and on the intentions associated with a particular behavior, rather than on its consequences."[14] Deontologists believe that "human beings have certain fundamental rights that should be respected in all decisions."[15] The following are the fundamental rights, several of which have been incorporated into the U.S. Bill of Rights, that deontologists say should never be violated:

- **The right of free consent.** Every human being in an organization has the right to be treated only as he or she freely consents to be treated.
- **The right to free speech.** Every person has the right to truthfully criticize the behavior and actions of others so long as the criticism does not violate the rights of other persons.
- **The right to privacy.** Individuals have the right to keep from public scrutiny information about their private lives which they are not legally obliged to make public.
- **The right to freedom of conscience.** No one should be forced to carry out any order or to engage in any act that violates his or her moral or religious norms.
- **The right to due process.** Every human being has the right to a fair and impartial hearing when he or she believes that his or her rights are being violated.

Basing decisions on deontological principles is much easier than basing them on the utilitarian theory. One need only "do the right thing" and not interfere with the rights of others who might be affected by one's decisions. Consider a product that a manager cannot sell in her home country because of its cancer-causing properties. It is, however, not illegal to sell it in a poor, developing country. The manager still might choose not to sell it because her conscience tells her that to do otherwise would be wrong.

The Theory of Justice

There are three fundamental guidelines that the **theory of justice** provides to managers in their decision making: Be equitable, be fair, and be impartial. The behavioral prescriptions of the justice theory are captured in the following principles:

1. Do not treat individuals differently based on arbitrary characteristics. Those who are similar in relevant attributes should be treated similarly, and those who are different in the relevant attributes should be treated differently in proportion to the differences between them.
2. Attributes and positions of individuals that are the basis for differential treatment must be justifiably connected to the goals and tasks at hand.

3. Rules must be clearly stated and promulgated, administered fairly, and enforced consistently and fairly. Those who do not obey the rules because of ignorance or those who are forced to break them under duress should not be punished.
4. Do not hold individuals responsible for matters over which they have no control.[16]

Although not as difficult to apply as the utilitarian theory, justice theory demands that justifiable attributes be determined on which differential treatment of people may be based. Furthermore, this theory also requires the determination of facts to ensure the fair administration of rules as well as individuals' accountability.

Cultural Relativism

Cultural relativism asserts that "words such as 'right,' 'wrong,' 'justice,' and 'injustice,' derive their meaning and value from the attitudes of a given culture."[17] Thus, to the cultural relativist, ethical standards are culture-specific, and one should not be surprised to find that an act that is considered ethical in one culture might be looked on with disdain in another. For instance, the Koran forbids usury because it is considered unethical and immoral, and therefore Muslims must refrain from collecting interest on loans. Usury is therefore illegal in Saudi Arabia and in countries that have Islamic banking (discussed in Chapter 4). Christians and Jews do not share this belief. Relativists would argue that businesspersons in fundamentalist Islamic countries like Saudi Arabia and Iran ought to conform to the ethical and moral norms of those cultures when conducting business in those countries. Any other strategy might prove disastrous.

The Hindu religion considers the consumption of beef to be both unethical and immoral but not illegal. To succeed in India, companies in the food industry must respect this precept and not mix beef with nonbeef ingredients and attempt to pass off the products as nonbeef—even if they have foolproof ways to conceal the true identity of the ingredients. McDonald's in India does not sell any dishes that contain meat of any sort.

Exhibit 14.1 illustrates the effect of cultural relativism on the varying legal and ethical perceptions of six activities in the United States, China, and Saudi Arabia. For instance, where alcohol consumption, usury, and women drivers are legal, ethical, and commonplace in both China and the United States, these three activities are considered both illegal and unethical in Saudi Arabia. Thus path A in the exhibit links the similar perspectives of these three activities between the United States and China; path B, in contrast, links the diametrically opposing perspectives between the United States and Saudi Arabia.

As you can see, other activities are viewed differently in the three countries. For instance, child labor is ethically frowned on in the United States, which has many laws banning child labor. Thus there are ethically consistent home boycotts of U.S. companies that legally employ children overseas at low wages. In China and Saudi Arabia, child labor is more acceptable, from both the ethical and legal perspectives. Taking time to pray in the workplace setting is understood in Islamic cultures. However, even though many people in the United States believe that to pray is ethical, it still is illegal in the workplace under the U.S. Constitution. And under the current political regime in China, stopping work to pray is viewed as both unethical and illegal. Later in this chapter, we discuss the implications of bribery in different countries. Foreshadowing that discussion, Exhibit 14.1 illustrates that bribery, or facilitating payments, is also viewed differently between the United States and the other two countries depicted.

The motto of the cultural relativists might be summed up as, "When in Rome, do as the Romans do, ethically." Still, many firms that followed the laws of the host countries

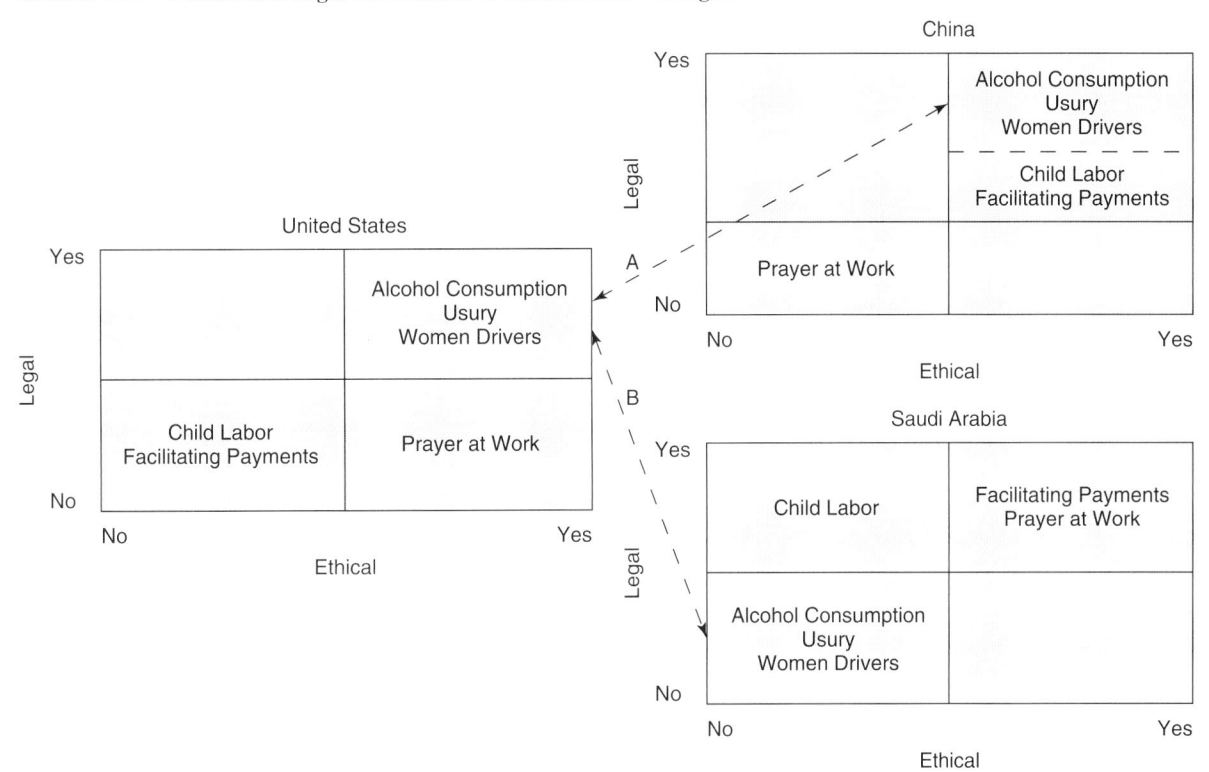

EXHIBIT 14.1 Ethical and Legal Distinctions in International Management

United States

	Ethical: No	Ethical: Yes
Legal: Yes		Alcohol Consumption, Usury, Women Drivers
Legal: No	Child Labor, Facilitating Payments	Prayer at Work

China

	Ethical: No	Ethical: Yes
Legal: Yes (upper)		Alcohol Consumption, Usury, Women Drivers
Legal: Yes (lower)		Child Labor, Facilitating Payments
Legal: No	Prayer at Work	

Saudi Arabia

	Ethical: No	Ethical: Yes
Legal: Yes	Child Labor	Facilitating Payments, Prayer at Work
Legal: No	Alcohol Consumption, Usury, Women Drivers	

in which they, or a licensee of theirs, did business have had problems at home. For instance, many U.S. firms have been accused of promoting sweatshops in Asia and have subsequently faced a backlash of protests in America. Nike is one example of a firm whose licensees in Asia do not break any host-country laws by employing children workers for long weekly hours at low wages. Still, protesters argue that Nike and other firms in these positions should be doing more for the host society, regardless of laws. Thus, in this age of globalization, home-country ethics now cause firms to rethink host-country practices.

Philosophers urge us to resort to ethical reasoning to ensure that managers make moral decisions. Nevertheless, as interpolated from Exhibit 14.1, different philosophies of ethical reasoning may lead to different behaviors in similar circumstances. Moreover, because of cultural differences, what is considered "right" and "good" in one culture may be actually taken as "wrong" and "bad" in another culture. Therefore, managers in two different cultures, adhering to the same ethical philosophy, may choose behavioral patterns that are at the opposite ends of a spectrum. For example, managers in India and the United States may interpret differently the following principle:

Principle: *Attributes and positions of individuals that are the basis for differential treatment must be justifiably connected to the goals and tasks at hand.*

Indian manager: "I must hire persons who belong to my caste because it is the right thing to do. The cohesiveness and morale of the group is the key for the success of my company."

American manager: "I must hire the best person for the job regardless of her class, race, religion, or national origin."

In this illustration, both managers are right in their judgment. In India, persons from the same caste are generally, if not always, given preference in hiring, whereas such a practice not only would be considered ethically unacceptable but is illegal in America. What this means is that moral philosophies provide the *criteria* for making ethical decisions; however, it is the manager who must reach into his or her system of *values and beliefs* and make the judgment call as to what makes an action ethical or unethical. But as Clarence C. Walton points out, the potential problem with this reality is that one rationale may be used as a foil against another, thus permitting the decision maker to employ whichever best suits his or her purposes at the time.[18]

The Basic Moral Norms

Multinationals may claim that because their foreign affiliates are citizens of each of the countries in which they operate, the pattern of behavior reflecting "good citizenship" may vary from country to country. Richard T. De George, a noted authority in the field of international business ethics, challenges this view:

> There is an important difference between customs, mores, and law on the one hand and ethics on the other. Customs, mores, and law do vary from country to country, and a business that wishes to succeed must consider these differences and on the whole respect them. Yet despite the claims of some simplistic critics, basic morality does not vary from country to country, even though certain practices may be ethical in one country and not in another because of differing circumstances. Getting this subtle difference straight is the crux of the matter.[19]

De George identified basic **moral norms,** which apply to any business operating anywhere. Application of these norms is essential for the effective functioning of a society or for business transactions to occur. "They are widely held, and everyone is expected to live by them and up to them; they are obvious, commonsensical, and available to all. If they were arcane or difficult or available only to an intellectual elite, they could not serve as basic norms governing all human interaction."[20] The following six moral norms are universally applicable.[21]

1. **No arbitrary killing of other members of the community to which one belongs.** A society must guarantee the safety of others who visit it or enter into alliances with it. Civil war that does not ensure safety of individuals would inhibit international trade and commerce. Criminal acts like kidnapping or killings of expatriate managers, as has happened in Russia and Colombia, would place a damper on international investments and trade.
2. **Telling the truth and not lying.** Interpersonal and interorganizational relationships are built on communications, that is, the transfer of knowledge and information between and among those involved in the transaction. Trust and faith between the communicators is built on the fundamental premise that the parties to the interaction are telling the truth. For a business firm this may mean truthfulness in advertising, in business negotiations, or in any interactions in which there is a transfer of information from the firm to its stakeholders, such as the employees, customers, stockholders, suppliers, governmental agencies, and the public at large.
3. **Respecting others' property.** All societies have the concept of property, although rules governing ownership, sale, and use of property may differ from society to society. Seizure of private property without reason or just compensation to the property owner for property seized should be deplored. Instances of expropriation without just compensation of property owned by foreign companies under the guise of nationalization have occurred mostly in developing countries of Africa, Asia,

and Latin America. Such actions caused a severe fall in foreign investments in these countries, with the resultant loss of valuable technology transfer from abroad, jobs, and international trade.

4. **Honoring contracts and exercising fairness in transactions.** A signed contract should be honored with the utmost integrity. The nuances of the contract language should not disguise hidden traps for either side in the agreement.
5. **Exercising fairness in business dealings.** Business dealings should be fair to all sides. The *Merriam-Webster's Dictionary* defines *fairness* as "marked by impartiality and honesty, free from self-interest, prejudice, or favoritism."
6. **Functioning in a fair market.** A fair market is one in which every person has an equal chance to succeed in a transaction. For example, equal access to relevant information must be available to all investors in the stock market. This means that some investors should not have privileged access to such information.

The noted ethicist Thomas Donaldson believes that both multinational and domestic corporations are bound to respect the following 10 rights:[22]

1. The right to freedom of physical movement.
2. The right to ownership of property.
3. The right to freedom from torture.
4. The right to a fair trial.
5. The right to nondiscriminatory treatment.
6. The right to physical security.
7. The right to freedom of speech and association.
8. The right to minimal education.
9. The right to political participation.
10. The right to subsistence.

All 10 rights should be the responsibility of peoples and governments in all societies regardless of their political ideology. Although the list may appear general and noncontroversial, it demands specific responsibilities and duties for corporations. The first four rights apply to societal obligations; the last six rights are directly aimed at the social responsibilities of companies worldwide. For example, the right to nondiscriminatory treatment requires that companies do not discriminate in their employment policies against women, certain racial groups, or religious groups. The right to physical security demands that companies provide safe working conditions to workers. The right to form workers' unions is reflected in the right to freedom of speech and association. Employing children in sweatshops means that they are in the factory and not in school. Nike, the athletic-shoe company, has the policy of not employing children. Nike provides schooling to children who are subsequently hired when the age of 16 years. The right to participate in the political process political party of one's choosing is inherent in the right to po right to a minimum wage is reflected in the tenth right

Incorporating Corporate Social Responsibility and Ethics into International Business Decisions

Of the moral philosophies discussed thus far, none can concern in the other philosophies. Utilitarianism, for produce the greatest good for the greatest number of peop

EXHIBIT 14.2
A Decision Tree Incorporating Ethics in International Business Decision Making

Source: Adapted from Gerald F. Cavanagh, Dennis J. Moberg, and Manuel Velasquez, "The Ethics of Organizational Politics," *Academy of Management Review* 6, no. 3 (1981), p. 368.

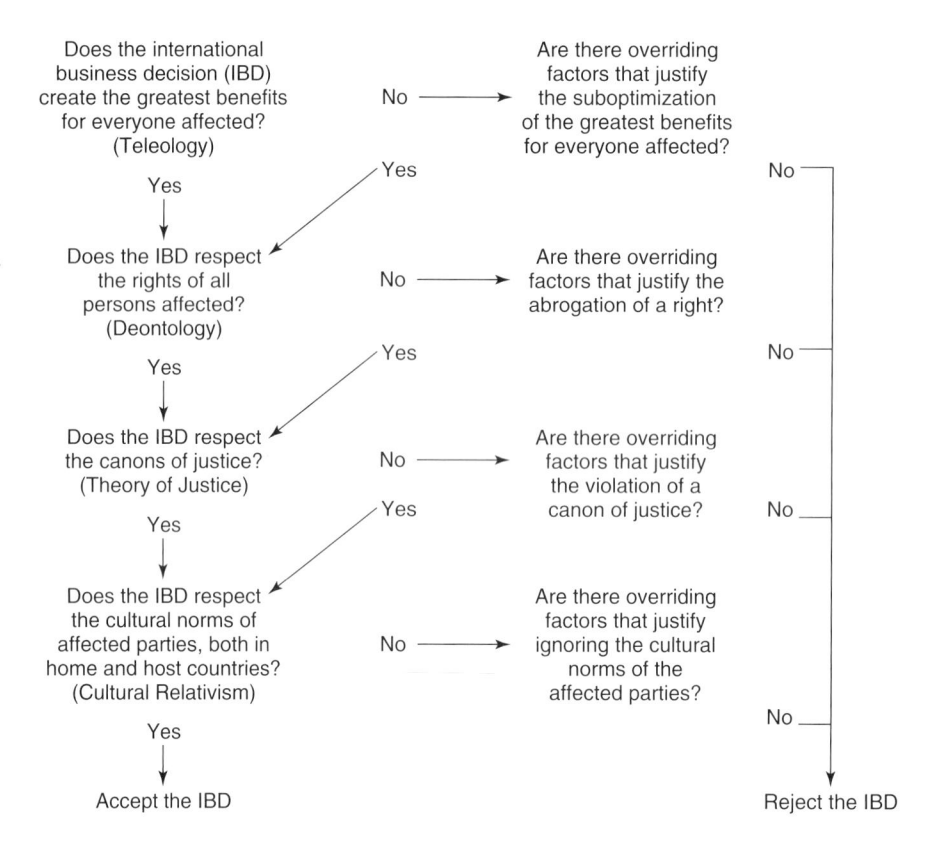

```
Does the international business decision (IBD)
create the greatest benefits for everyone affected?   ──No──▶   Are there overriding factors that justify
(Teleology)                                                     the suboptimization of the greatest benefits
         │                                                      for everyone affected?
        Yes ─────────────────────────────Yes──────────▶                    │
         ▼                                                                 No
Does the IBD respect the rights of all
persons affected?                                     ──No──▶   Are there overriding factors that justify the
(Deontology)                                                    abrogation of a right?
         │                                                                 │
        Yes ─────────────────────────────Yes──────────▶                    No
         ▼
Does the IBD respect the canons of justice?           ──No──▶   Are there overriding factors that justify
(Theory of Justice)                                             the violation of a canon of justice?
         │                                                                 │
        Yes ─────────────────────────────Yes──────────▶                    No
         ▼
Does the IBD respect the cultural norms of
affected parties, both in home and host countries?    ──No──▶   Are there overriding factors that justify
(Cultural Relativism)                                           ignoring the cultural norms of the
         │                                                      affected parties?
        Yes                                                                │
         ▼                                                                 No
   Accept the IBD                                                    Reject the IBD
```

brings forth this outcome may very well result in the abridgement of the rights of some people. By the same token, a decision that respects the rights of all persons affected may at the same time prove to be ineffective in optimizing the benefits for the people involved. And decisions that may appear to be equitable, fair, and impartial in one culture may have the opposite appearance in another culture. Approaches in business ethics based on such classical theories as teleology, deontology, justice, and cultural relativism have come under criticism for being too abstract and general to provide adequate guidance to managers.[23]

One way to resolve such problems resulting from a focus on one particular philosophy is to combine all four philosophical approaches into one unifying eclectic decision-making framework. With this is mind, we have incorporated all four moral philosophies in a decision tree, presented in Exhibit 14.2.

Integrating Corporate Social Responsibility with Business Operations

What the social responsibility of companies should be is a topic that is much discussed today, as it has been for the past 60 years or so. That companies should behave ethically is a concept that is accepted by corporate leaders. To behave ethically is to adhere to the norms of society that dictate what is acceptable behavior and what is not. Earlier in this chapter we referred to differences in ethical norms based on cultural parameters. Corporate ethical guidelines include principles for corporate behavior that address issues such as these: Give no bribes to secure business, uphold the primacy of worker safety on the shop floor, do not harm the environment, do not lie to the shareholders, and so on.

However, companies are now concerned with the concept of corporate social responsibility (CSR), which goes beyond that of corporate ethics. *Corporate social responsibility means a commitment to developing policies that integrate responsible practices into daily business operations. It refers to a concept whereby companies consider the interests of society by managing the business in a manner that accounts for the social and environmental impacts created by its operations.* Ideally, the CSR activities of a firm should be a non- zero-sum game between the firm and its external constituencies in which both the firm and one or more of the external constituents benefit.

Responsive CSR

Traditionally, firms have viewed corporate social responsibility in terms of the need to be a good "corporate citizen," often with the intention of deflecting criticism over its practices, a reactive response to negative publicity. This **responsive corporate social responsibility** views the community as an entity in tension or conflict with the company, rather than as a mutual partner with shared values. Responsive CSR would expect the company to deal with generic social issues that are unrelated to the firm's value chain or competitive environment solely to deflect criticism or for public relations purposes.

And where does corporate philanthropy fit into the concept of CSR? Companies donate money and sometimes time of employees to social causes such as the American Cancer Society, the local theater or museum, or the construction of a community center. If such donations of company time and money have a direct or indirect impact on enhancing the company's competitive posture while benefiting the recipients of the company's largess, they would qualify as the company's CSR. For instance, donations by pharmaceutical companies to the American Cancer Society could help promote fundamental research of benefit to the donor company as well as the general public. However, a similar donation by a retail garment chain would be responsive CSR, as it would not accrue any tangible benefits to the retail chain in the short or long term and therefore would probably help the donor company only in its image enhancement strategy and be of no benefit in improving the company's competitive positioning.

Strategic CSR

In contrast, **strategic corporate social responsibility** attempts to assess and implement the firm's CSR activities in a manner similar to its approach for other business choices: as an attempt to build or maintain competitive advantage and reach business goals. The strategic CSR view attempts to identify the intersection points between company and community to understand:

1. The social consequences of its value chain activities (inside-out).
2. The factors and forces in the external environment that have the potential to be of the greatest benefit to both the company's competitiveness and society (outside-in).

The ultimate aim of strategic CSR is to implement policies, processes, and procedures in strategically selected operations that would cause several different but interrelated outcomes:

1. Improve the value created for the company by the operation, and simultaneously create a beneficial qualitative and enduring impact on some element of society.
2. Directly influence competitive factors through deliberate social initiatives to produce a beneficial impact on society and improve the firm's competitive positioning in the industry.

498 Section Four *Social Initiatives*

EXHIBIT 14.3 The Value Chain and Inside-Out Impacts

Source: Michael Porter and Mark R. Kramer, "Strategy and Society: The Link between Competitive Advantage and Corporate Social Responsibility," *Harvard Business Review,* December 2006, p. 4.

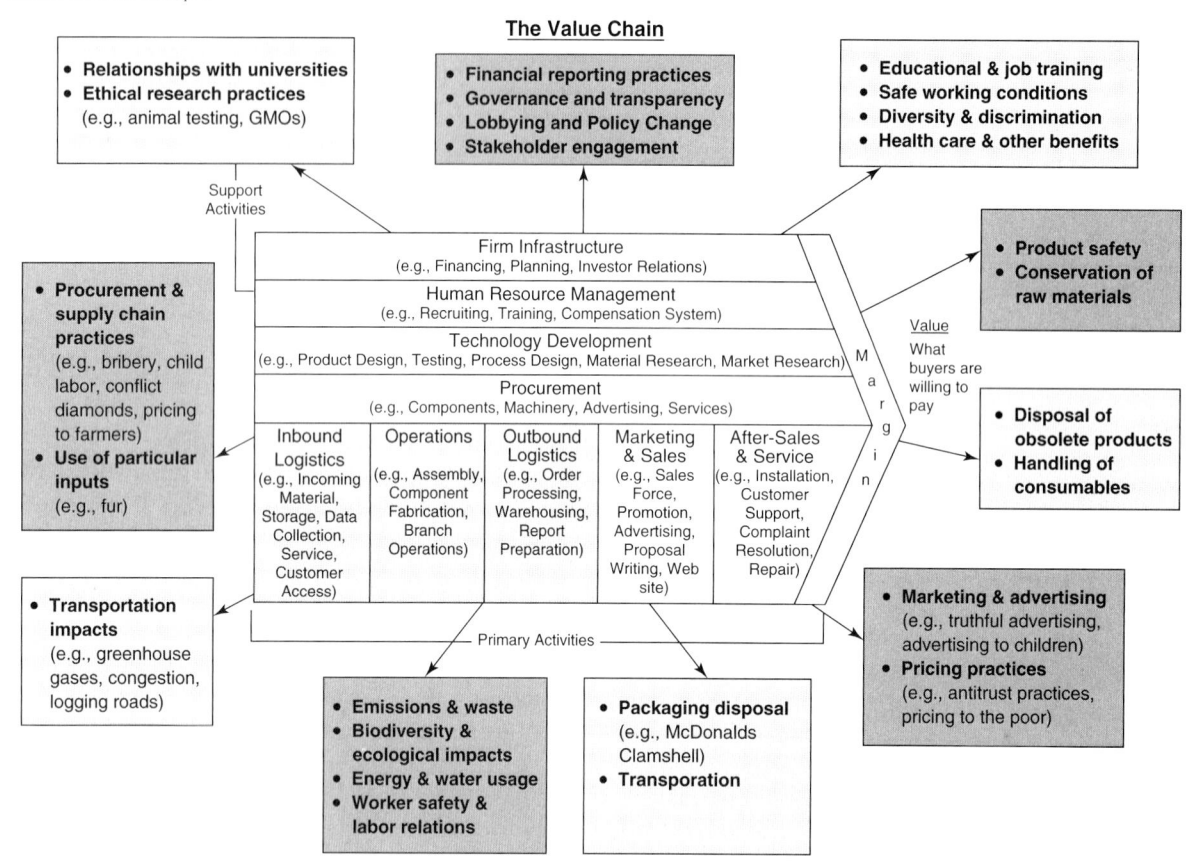

The Value Chain

- Relationships with universities
- Ethical research practices
  (e.g., animal testing, GMOs)

- Financial reporting practices
- Governance and transparency
- Lobbying and Policy Change
- Stakeholder engagement

- Educational & job training
- Safe working conditions
- Diversity & discrimination
- Health care & other benefits

Support Activities

Firm Infrastructure (e.g., Financing, Planning, Investor Relations)
Human Resource Management (e.g., Recruiting, Training, Compensation System)
Technology Development (e.g., Product Design, Testing, Process Design, Material Research, Market Research)
Procurement (e.g., Components, Machinery, Advertising, Services)

| Inbound Logistics (e.g., Incoming Material, Storage, Data Collection, Service, Customer Access) | Operations (e.g., Assembly, Component Fabrication, Branch Operations) | Outbound Logistics (e.g., Order Processing, Warehousing, Report Preparation) | Marketing & Sales (e.g., Sales Force, Promotion, Advertising, Proposal Writing, Web site) | After-Sales & Service (e.g., Installation, Customer Support, Complaint Resolution, Repair) |

Margin

Value — What buyers are willing to pay

- Product safety
- Conservation of raw materials

- Procurement & supply chain practices (e.g., bribery, child labor, conflict diamonds, pricing to farmers)
- Use of particular inputs (e.g., fur)

- Disposal of obsolete products
- Handling of consumables

- Transportation impacts (e.g., greenhouse gases, congestion, logging roads)

Primary Activities

- Emissions & waste
- Biodiversity & ecological impacts
- Energy & water usage
- Worker safety & labor relations

- Packaging disposal (e.g., McDonalds Clamshell)
- Transporation

- Marketing & advertising (e.g., truthful advertising, advertising to children)
- Pricing practices (e.g., antitrust practices, pricing to the poor)

Inside-Out Linkages and Strategic CSR

The company's impact on society comes about through its value chain activities, which can be either positive or negative. Porter and Kramer call these direct social impacts "inside-out linkages."[24] A company's value chain was discussed in Chapter 5. (See Exhibit 14.3.) It can be used to illustrate the many ways by which a company could integrate its value chain links with its strategic CSR responses. In the inside-out approach to strategic CSR, the value chain of a firm is altered to create a beneficial impact on society or to mitigate any of its negative impacts on society, while simultaneously enhancing the firm's competitive advantage.

Exhibit 14.3 illustrates the many ways in which the value chain links can have inside-out impacts.

The firm practicing strategic CSR identifies the social impacts of a value chain link and manages the relationship as part of the firm's overarching strategy. An example of such a strategic-proactive strategy is Toyota's development of the Prius. The Prius has allowed Toyota to sell a hybrid fuel-efficient product that benefits society through cleaner air and provides Toyota with a positive image as a forward-thinking, progressive auto manufacturer. Thus Prius has provided Toyota a "halo effect" that benefits not only sales of that model but sales of Toyota's other cars as well. Another Japanese manufacturer, Subaru, is seeking to gain competitive advantage by implementing a zero-waste manufacturing policy. This policy will benefit the environment by ensuring that landfills do not grow because of Subaru's manufacturing and hopefully will help the firm build competitive advantage by positioning it as a socially responsible actor. This positioning is in an industry in which competitors seek out ways to uniquely market themselves as "green."

Ice-cream manufacturer Mackie's of Scotland is also practicing inside-out strategic CSR. Mackie's has its own energy supply through wind turbines. Managing Director Mac says, "We are keen to find new ways to cut our energy consumption alongside our other environmental projects. The investment in wind turbines makes good sense for our business because our consumers have told us that it is important for them to know that our ice cream is made with 100% renewable energy. It also makes good financial sense, we are a rural business which needs significant power levels and will continue to need more as we grow."[25]

Timberland, the maker of outdoor boots and clothing, uses solar-panel-generated power as its primary source of electricity at its Ontario, California, distribution center. By lowering the emission of greenhouse gases, Timberland has minimized its environmental footprint. The Timberland solar panel will significantly reduce the amount of greenhouse gas emissions created by the Ontario distribution center, by an estimated 480,000 pounds of carbon emissions annually, therefore decreasing its dependency on electricity currently generated by fossil fuels and other sources. This makes good financial sense for the company and also has a beneficial impact on the environment.[26]

The Outside-In Linkages and Strategic CSR

In addition to understanding the social ramifications of the value chain, effective CSR requires an understanding of the social dimensions of the company's competitive context, consisting of its suppliers, buyers, the laws and regulations governing the industry, the degree of competition in the industry, factors that determine the demand for the industry's products, the transportation infrastructure, and so on. Porter and Kramer refer to this as the "outside-in" linkages that affect a company's ability to improve productivity and execute strategy.[27] Porter's diamond framework can be used to show how the company's competitive environment has an effect on its ability to compete. (See Exhibit 14.4.)

The outside-in approach to strategic CSR would result in a firm implementing strategies that somehow improve or alter one or more dimensions of its external environment, ultimately giving the firm a competitive advantage in the industry. It involves doing things differently from competitors in a way that lowers costs or better serves a set of customer needs.

An example of outside-in CSR is the strategic approach of the fast foods giant McDonald's. When it started operating in India, the company faced several challenges to its local value chain. It needed locally sourced items like tomatoes and potatoes. However, the locally sourced tomatoes were not up to the standards for firmness and taste, and the potatoes contained an inadequate amount of moisture. With the help of McDonald's, local suppliers of these items were taught how to grow them to meet the company's standards. McDonald's thus transferred critical knowledge in horticulture to the local farmers who were its key suppliers, thereby creating a multiplier impact of knowledge transfer and development of local entrepreneurs and jobs.

Nestlé is the world's largest direct buyer of coffee. It sources about 14 percent of our green coffee supply directly from farmers. This helps ensure that farmers get a better price for their produce. It also creates jobs at the buying centers, such as the Gagnoa buying center in Côte d'Ivoire. Nestlé's buying centers offer opportunities both to the farmers selling their coffee and to other locals. Thus, Nestlé helps local producers earn more for their produce and also creates jobs in the buying centers.

The Gujarat Cooperative Milk Marketing Federation (GCMMF), better known as Amul, is the largest cooperative movement in India, with 2.2 million milk producers

EXHIBIT 14.4 The Outside-In Approach to Strategic Corporate Responsibility

Source: Michael Porter, *The Competitive Advantage of Nations* (New York: Free Press, 1990)

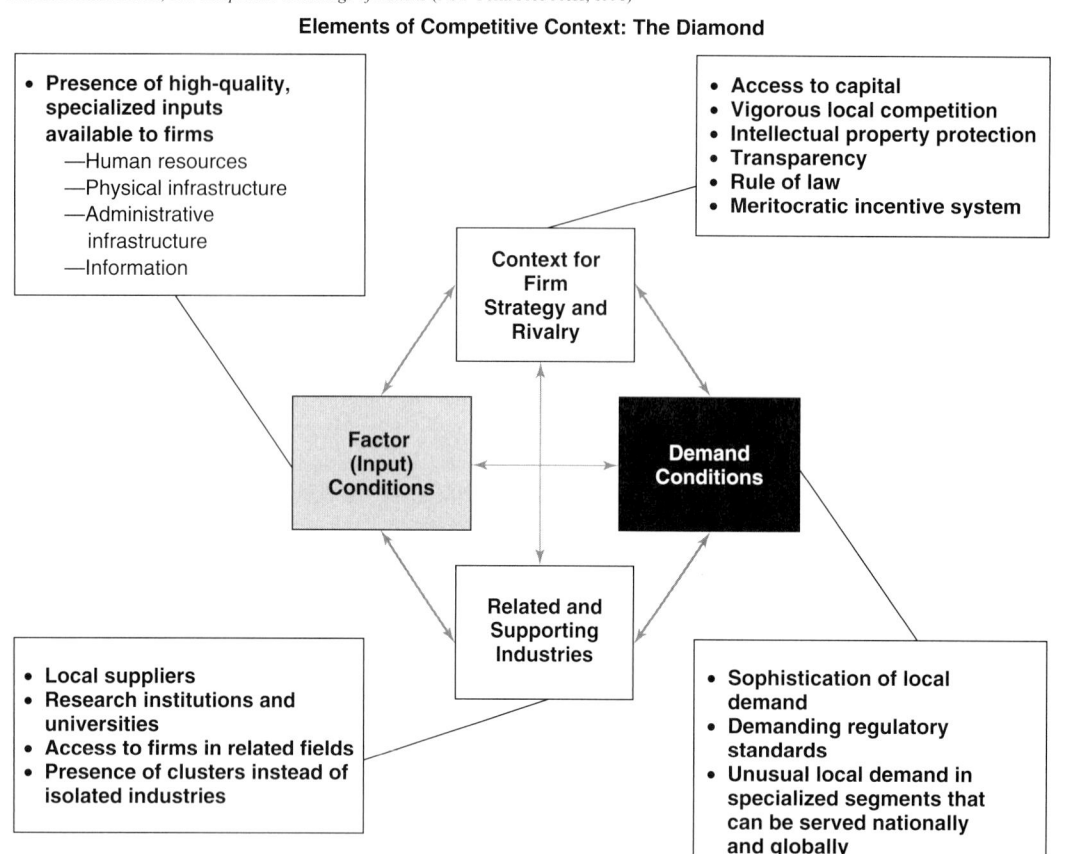

Elements of Competitive Context: The Diamond

- Presence of high-quality, specialized inputs available to firms
  — Human resources
  — Physical infrastructure
  — Administrative infrastructure
  — Information

- Access to capital
- Vigorous local competition
- Intellectual property protection
- Transparency
- Rule of law
- Meritocratic incentive system

Context for Firm Strategy and Rivalry

Factor (Input) Conditions

Demand Conditions

Related and Supporting Industries

- Local suppliers
- Research institutions and universities
- Access to firms in related fields
- Presence of clusters instead of isolated industries

- Sophistication of local demand
- Demanding regulatory standards
- Unusual local demand in specialized segments that can be served nationally and globally

---

organized in 10,552 cooperative societies in 2003–2004. The country's largest food company, Amul is the market leader in butter, whole milk, cheese, ice cream, dairy whitener, condensed milk, saturated fats, and long-life milk. Amul collects 447,000 liters of milk from 2.12 million farmers (many illiterate), converts the milk into branded, packaged products, and delivers goods worth $15 million to over 500,000 retail outlets across the country. The cooperative started in December 1946 with a group of farmers keen to free themselves from intermediaries and gain access to markets and thereby ensure maximum returns for their efforts. Amul's purchasing strategy is a classic example of a multiplier effect that has made millions of farmers more money than they would have made if the cooperative bought the milk supplies from wholesalers of milk.

Hewlett-Packard (HP) provides U.S. customers of inkjet print cartridges postage-paid recycling envelopes in their new inkjet print-cartridge boxes. With this expanded service, business customers and consumers can help protect the environment by mailing their empty HP inkjet cartridges to HP's state-of-the art recycling operations. The cartridges are then processed into recycled raw materials for use in new consumer products.

In each of these examples, the company has proactively impacted the demand or supply side of the diamond framework and, in doing so, has helped both itself and the social environment.

International Ethical Codes of Conduct for International Companies

The fact that cultural differences in various countries make it difficult to determine ethical conduct has not deterred countries and international organizations from promulgating codes of ethical conduct for international companies. Since 1948, we have seen a proliferation of intergovernmental treaties, conventions, agreements, accords, compacts, and declarations that have been intended to prescribe principles governing the activities of governments, groups, international companies, and individuals in areas such as consumer protection, environment protection, bribery, human rights and fundamental freedoms, and employment policies and practices.[28] Table 14.1 shows international treaties and conventions related to employment policies and practices.

The fact that several countries would agree on international codes of conduct signifies the need to recognize that, in spite of cultural differences in the world's community of nations, the nation-states find much "common ground." Codes of conduct are particularly relevant in a discussion of ethics in business, for they are seen as an alternative means to constitute an international *moral* authority by agreements among governments and to provide guidelines for multinational business activities.[29]

The Issues of Bribery and Corruption

Of all the issues of ethics confronting international managers, bribery and corruption have been the most troublesome and pervasive. *Bribery* may be defined as the payment voluntarily offered for the purpose of inducing a public official to do or omit to do something in violation of his or her lawful duty or to exercise his official discretion in favor of the payer's request for a contract, concession, or privilege on some basis other than merit. The greed of politicians and political parties has created systems of corruption and graft that one encounters to some degree in almost

TABLE 14.1 Employment Practices and Policies

Policy	Organization(s)
MNCs should not contravene the manpower policies of host nations.	ILO
MNCs should respect the right of employees to join trade unions and to bargain collectively.	ILO; OECD; UDHR
MNCs should develop nondiscriminatory employment policies and promote equal job opportunities.	ILO; OECD; UDHR
MNCs should provide equal pay for equal work.	ILO; UDHR
MNCs should give advance notice of changes in operations, especially plant closings, and mitigate the adverse effects of these changes.	ILO; OECD
MNCs should provide favorable work conditions, limited working hours, holidays with pay, and protection against unemployment.	UDHR
MNCs should promote job stability and job security, avoiding arbitrary dismissals and providing severance pay for those unemployed.	ILO; UDHR
MNCs should respect local host-country job standards and upgrade the local labor force through training.	ILO; OECD
MNCs should adopt adequate health and safety standards for employees and grant them the right to know about job-related health hazards.	ILO
MNCs should, minimally, pay basic living wages to employees.	ILO; UDHR
MNCs' operations should benefit lower income groups of the host nation.	ILO
MNCs should balance job opportunities, work conditions, job training, and living conditions among migrant workers and host-country nationals.	Helsinki

PRACTICAL INSIGHT 14.1

UNLAWFUL PAYMENTS TO FOREIGN OFFICIALS

Kazakhstan: United States vs. James H. Giffen

Hearings in the most far-reaching Foreign Corrupt Practices Act case in U.S. history, scheduled to begin in Manhattan on 14 May in *United States vs. James H. Giffen,* have been delayed until 3 June. This is the second delay for the court to hear pretrial motions submitted by attorneys for the defendant, who is charged with paying $78 million in bribes between 1995 and 2000 to former Kazakh Prime Minister Nurlan Balgimbaev and President Nursultan Nazarbaev, identified in court documents only as KO-1 and KO-2 until last month. Giffen, 63, the CEO of Mercator Corp., a small New York–based merchant bank, was indicted by a grand jury in April 2003.

Giffen is charged on 13 counts of violating the FCPA and 33 counts of money laundering. In March 2004, the government filed additional charges of tax evasion, charging that he omitted $2 million of income and reported only half of an $800,000 bonus paid to a staffer.

The four-year investigation unearthed a labyrinth of complex financial transactions to accounts in Switzerland and the British Virgin Islands allegedly made by U.S. oil companies Mobil (now ExxonMobil), Texaco (now ChevronTexaco), Phillips Petroleum (now ConocoPhillips) and Amoco (now BP) in connection with various fees for the purchase of oil and gas rights in the 1990s.

Part of the fees paid by U.S. oil companies were allegedly used by Giffen to purchase an array of luxury items, including millions of dollars in jewelry; fur coats for President Nazarbaev's wife, Sara, and a daughter, costing nearly $30,000; $45,000 for tuition at an exclusive Swiss high school; and tuition at George Washington University in the U.S. capital for Nazarbaev's daughter Aliya. Giffen also allegedly bought an $80,000 Donzi speedboat for Balgimbaev to present to Nazarbaev and two American snowmobiles for Nazarbaev and his wife.

The indictment revealed that Swiss authorities began investigating accounts "nominally owned by offshore companies but beneficially owned, directly or indirectly, by Balgimbaev and Nazarbaev . . . into which Mr. Giffen had made tens of millions of dollars in unlawful payments" in 1999.

Nazarbaev has criticized the case, coined "Kazakhgate," as an empty ploy by his political opponents but has seldom commented in detail on the allegations in the five years since they first surfaced.

Source: Marlena Telvick, EurasiaNet, May 31, 2004, http://forumkz.addr.com/2004en/en_forum_03_06_04.htm (a EurasiaNet Partner post from *Transitions Online*).

---

every country of the world. The phenomenon of bribery exists in rich industrialized countries as well as poor and underdeveloped countries, in democracies as well as dictatorships, in capitalist and socialist economies. Corruption scandals have affected the highest levels of government in Japan, South Korea, France, and several countries in Africa.

Business firms are required, and sometimes forced, to bribe government officials merely to perform what to an objective observer would look like ordinary business activities. The following example from Italy is illustrative of the nature and problem of bribery in many countries throughout the world:

> Virtually every major Italian political party and many of the country's most prestigious companies have been tarred by a bottomless, tangled-as-spaghetti scandal that swallowed trillions of taxpayer lire—billions of dollars.
>
> For decades, the (political) parties were routinely and generously financed by illegal kickbacks for public contracts and boosted by jobs-for-votes deals. In some regions of Sicily, there is no end to forest rangers on public payrolls, but hardly any trees.
>
> Payoffs, called *targenti,* were standard operating procedure at virtually every level in virtually every city.[30]

Many businesspeople believe that bribes are a necessary cost of doing business in certain countries. There is evidence to suggest that several American, as well as European and Asian, companies are involved in bribing foreign government officials to obtain business worth millions and sometimes billions of dollars. Practical Insight 14.1 provides one such example.

TABLE 14.2
Factors Responsible for Bribes

Home-Country Factors	Host-Country Factors
Competitors are giving bribes to obtain business.	Host government has control over business activity permits and licenses. Government officials are required to conduct normal business functions.
There is constant pressure for higher levels of performance by top management and shareholders.	Government officials are poorly paid and use bribes to supplement salary.
Bribery is an accepted practice in the host country. Cannot expect to get any business without conforming.	Bureaucratic delays can be costly for business (e.g., clear products through customs on time to meet delivery schedules).
Tax laws of the country encourage bribery (e.g., some bribes can be written off as a business expense in Germany but not in the U.S.).	Political pressure exists to make contributions to political parties or favorite political organizations or causes.

TABLE 14.3
Major Types of Bribe

Source: Subash C. Jain, "What Happened to the Marketing Man When His International Promotion Pay-Offs Became Bribes?" in Peter J. LaPlaca (ed.), *The New Role of the Marketing Professional*, American Marketing Association, 1977 Business Proceedings, Series No. 40. Reprinted with permission.

Facilitating payments: Disbursement of small amounts of cash or kind as tips or gifts to minor government officials to expedite clearance of shipments, documents or other routine transactions. Example: "In India not a single tile can move if the clerk's palm is not greased. Distribution of *bustarella* (an envelope containing a small amount of money) in Italy to make things move in an inefficient and chaotic social system."

Middlemen commissions: Appointment of intermediaries (agents and consultants) to facilitate sales in a nonroutine manner and payment to them of excessive allowances and commissions, which are not commensurate with the normal commercial services they perform. Often, the middlemen may request that part or all of their commission be deposited in a U.S. bank or a bank in a third country. Example: Northrup Corporation's payment of $30 million in fees to overseas agents and consultants, some of which was used for payoffs to government officials to secure favorable decisions on government procurement of aircraft and military hardware.

Political contributions: Contributions which can take the form of extortion since they are in violation of local law and custom. Also payments which, while not illegal, are specifically made with the intent of winning favors directly or indirectly. Example: Gulf Oil Corporation's payment of $3 million in 1971 to South Korea's Democratic Republican Party under intimidation and threat.

Cash disbursements: Cash payments made to important people through slush funds or in some other way, usually in a third country (i.e., deposit in a Swiss bank) for different reasons such as to obtain a tax break or sales contract or to get preferential treatment over a competitor. Example: Payment of $2.5 million, via Swiss bank accounts, to Honduran officials by United Brands Company for the reduction of the export tax on bananas.

Why Payoffs?

Why do companies feel obliged to pay huge sums of money to generate business abroad, and why do people in host countries accept such payments? The reasons that induce international companies to offer questionable payments abroad and the host-country factors that elicit bribes are presented in Table 14.2.

Types of Payoffs

Bribery takes different forms, and bribes are made in a variety of ways in different parts of the world. Table 14.3 depicts four categories of bribes used by international companies to obtain business in foreign countries, while Practical Insight 14.2 discusses bribes paid by Halliburton to Nigerian tax officials.

The Social Costs of Bribery and Corruption

Bribery, when used as the primary weapon to obtain business, has several dysfunctional consequences. First, a company that has the best product or service, or the best value at a given price, may not get the business. The business may go to the company

> **PRACTICAL INSIGHT 14.2**

HALLIBURTON DISCLOSES BRIBES IN NIGERIA

A subsidiary of Halliburton Co. paid a Nigerian tax official $2.4 million in bribes to get favorable tax treatment, the company disclosed in a federal filing. In a filing made Thursday with the Securities and Exchange Commission, the company said its KBR subsidiary "made improper payments of approximately $2.4 million to an entity owned by a Nigerian national who held himself out as a tax consultant when in fact he was an employee of a local tax authority."

The filing stated that the payments were found during a routine audit, and that several employees were fired as a result. Halliburton said it was cooperating with the SEC in its review, and added that none of the Houston company's senior officers were involved. A company spokeswoman told the *Houston Chronicle* for its Friday editions that the bribes were paid between 2001 and 2002.

Company officials are trying to determine how much it owes Nigeria in back taxes. It could be as much as $5 million, the filing said. Vice President Dick Cheney led the company until August 2000. Wednesday, the Bush administration denied there was any connection between Cheney's former role in running the company and a $76.7 million no-bid contract with the government to extinguish Iraqi oil well fires and help restart Iraq's oil industry. In Nigeria, the engineering, construction and oil-field services company is constructing a liquefied natural gas plant and developing an offshore oil and gas facility.

Source: "Halliburton SEC Filing Discloses Bribery," Associated Press, May 9, 2003. Reprinted with permission of The Associated Press.

that has given the biggest bribe to the government official who has the discretionary authority to decide which company may sell its products in the local market. In such a situation, the consumers are the real losers because their money does not fetch the best products or services that could have been available without the bribes. Second, if bribes are used to sell capital equipment like a factory or military hardware to the government, the taxpayer's money is being misallocated if government officials choose an inferior piece of equipment over one that may clearly be the better choice. Third, the incentive to compete on the basis of quality, price, and service is destroyed when these factors are rendered irrelevant by decisions influenced by factors such as bribery and corruption.

Thus, bribery can cause the misallocation of a country's resources because the intervention of bribes causes officials to direct resources away from where they can be best put to use based on a purely objective set of criteria like price, quality, and service. The economic costs of corruption can be quite significant. For instance, underreporting of income taxes in exchange for a bribe to the tax collector could reduce income tax revenues collected by the government by up to 50 percent. Also, the overinvoicing by government officials for public works projects or for imported capital goods could raise the prices of goods and services by as much as 100 percent. Ultimately, it is the country's consumers who bear the burden of these increased costs due to corruption.

Transparency International is an organization based in Berlin, Germany, that has served as a watchdog of corruption worldwide. It rates the extent of corruption in countries on a scale of 10 to 1, with 10 being the best—the least corrupt country—and 1 being the worst—the most corrupt country. Thus the higher the country score, the lower the level of corruption in the country. Results of the survey for the year 2007 are presented in Table 14.4.

Child Labor and Sweatshops

Child labor and its abuses in sweatshops are of great concern to most people of conscience. The following item, which appeared in the *Philadelphia Inquirer*, illustrates the cruelties of child labor in developing countries:

> Demanding an end to child labor, thousands of children and other protesters marched through Lahore yesterday to commemorate the killing this month of young activist Iqbal Masih.

TABLE 14.4 Global Corruption Perception Index

Source: Transparency International, www.transparency.org/policy_research/surveys_indices/cpi.

Country Rank	Country	2007 CPI Score*	Country Rank	Country	2007 CPI Score*	Country Rank	Country	2007 CPI Score*
1	Denmark	9.4	19	France	7.3	162	Central African Republic	2.0
1	Finland	9.4	20	USA	7.2	162	Papua New Guinea	2.0
1	New Zealand	9.4	21	Belgium	7.1	162	Turkmenistan	2.0
4	Singapore	9.3	22	Chile	7.0	162	Venezuela	2.0
4	Sweden	9.3	23	Barbados	6.9	168	Congo, Democratic Republic	1.9
6	Iceland	9.2	24	Saint Lucia	6.8	168	Equatorial Guinea	1.9
7	Netherlands	9.0	25	Spain	6.7	168	Guinea	1.9
7	Switzerland	9.0	25	Uruguay	6.7	168	Laos	1.9
9	Canada	8.7	150	Ecuador	2.1	172	Afghanistan	1.8
9	Norway	8.7	150	Kazakhstan	2.1	172	Chad	1.8
11	Australia	8.6	150	Kenya	2.1	172	Sudan	1.8
12	Luxembourg	8.4	150	Kyrgyzstan	2.1	175	Tonga	1.7
12	United Kingdom	8.4	150	Liberia	2.1	175	Uzbekistan	1.7
14	Hong Kong	8.3	150	Sierra Leone	2.1	177	Haiti	1.6
15	Austria	8.1	150	Tajikistan	2.1	178	Iraq	1.5
16	Germany	7.8	150	Zimbabwe	2.1	179	Myanmar	1.4
17	Ireland	7.5	162	Bangladesh	2.0	179	Somalia	1.4
17	Japan	7.5	162	Cambodia	2.0			

*10 = least corrupt.

About one-third of the 3,000 marchers were children, many of them workers in carpet-weaving factories and other industries that routinely employ child laborers for as low as one rupee, or about 3 cents a day. The march, which led to the governor's office in Punjab Province, was organized by the Bonded Labor Liberation Front, a private group trying to end the widespread practice of child labor in Pakistan.

The group two years ago rescued Iqbal, who was then 10 and had already spent six years working in carpet-weaving factories. Iqbal, who achieved international recognition for his activism, was gunned down April 17 in his village of Muridke, 22 miles northwest of Lahore. Eshan Ullah Khan, head of the Bonded Labor Liberation Front, alleges that people in the carpet industry who were angry at his campaign against child labor killed Iqbal.[31]

Few companies have taken steps to eliminate the abuses of child labor. Most argue that competition forces the company to use child labor. Others claim that the company itself does not employ child labor but its contractors do and that the company can do little to control the employment of workers whom it does not hire directly. In contrast, Levi Strauss & Company provides a fine example of how a company can indeed prohibit the use of child labor by manufacturing contractors linked with the company.

Levi Strauss has operations in many countries and diverse cultures. Robert D. Haas, chairman and CEO of the company, says: "We must take special care in selecting our contractors and those countries where our goods are produced in order to ensure that our products are made in a manner that is consistent with our values and reputation.

In early 1992, we developed a set of global sourcing guidelines that established standards our contractors must meet to ensure that their practices are compatible with our values. For instance, our guidelines ban the use of child labor and prison labor."[32] The company rules stipulate that working hours cannot exceed 60 hours a week, with at least one day off in seven, and wages must, at a minimum, comply with local law and prevailing local practice. The company accepts the fact that at times there are issues that are beyond the control of the local contractor, and therefore the company has a list of country-selection criteria. For instance, Levi Strauss refuses to source in countries where conditions such as human rights violations run counter to the values of the company and would adversely affect the company's global brand image.

Levi Strauss's phased withdrawal from China reflected its concern for human rights violations in that country. Another example of the application of this principle is the way the company handled the problem of two of its manufacturing contractors in Bangladesh and one in Turkey that employed underage workers. This was a clear violation of Levi Strauss's guidelines against the use of child labor. The company could have (1) instructed the contractors to fire the children, knowing that this action would have caused severe hardships on the children's families, many of whom depended on the earnings of the children as their only source of income, or (2) continued to employ the children, ignoring the company's position against the use of child labor. Neither of these options was acceptable to Levi Strauss, and therefore a third, win–win solution was found and implemented. The company worked out an arrangement with the contractors that called for the contractors to pay the children their salaries and benefits while they went to school on the factory site (the children did not work during this time), and Levi Strauss paid for books, tuition, and uniforms. The children would be offered full-time jobs in the plant when they reached working age. At times the contractors passed on to Levi Strauss, in the form of higher unit price, the costs of adhering to these company standards. In other cases the company has forgone cheaper sources of production due to unsatisfactory working conditions or concerns about the country of origin.[33] We end this section with these words of Robert D. Haas:

> There is a growing body of research evidence from respected groups that shows a positive correlation between citizenship and financial performance. These studies underscore that companies driven by values and a sense of purpose that extends beyond just making money outperform those that focus only on short-term profits. The former have higher sales, sustain higher profits, and have stocks that outperform the market. These findings mirror our experiences. Our values-driven approach has helped us:
>
> - identify contractors who really want to work for Levi Strauss;
> - gain customer and consumer loyalty because they feel good about having us as a business partner or about purchasing our products;
> - attract and retain the best employees;
> - improve the morale and trust of employees because the company's values closely mirror their own personal values;
> - initiate business in established and emerging markets because government and community leaders have a better sense of what we stand for and what to expect from us; and
> - maintain credibility during times of unplanned events or crisis.
>
> The conclusion is clear: There are important commercial benefits to be gained from managing your business in a responsible way that best serves the enterprise's long-term interests. The opposite is also clear: There are dangers of not doing so.[34]

So, what can companies do to ensure that employees do not engage in unethical behavior to obtain business abroad? Most companies have addressed this issue, in conjunction with a host of other ethical and moral dilemmas that employees face all over the world, in so-called company ethics programs. We consider this topic next.

What Companies Can Do to Integrate Ethics and Business Conduct

The issue of business ethics has attracted the attention of companies worldwide, and several companies have incorporated ethics training as part of the general orientation of all employees. The following are recommendations for integrating ethics into business conduct.

1. The Top Management Must Be Committed to the Company's Ethics Program Top management involvement is essential. At Chemical Bank, for example, some 250 vice presidents took part in a two-day seminar on corporate values that began with an appearance by the bank's chairman.

2. A Written Company Code That Clearly Communicates Management's Expectations Must Be Developed The code must be explicit in stating management's intent; for example, "The law is the floor. Ethical business conduct should normally exist at a level well above the minimum required law" (from "A Code of Worldwide Business Conduct," Caterpillar Tractor Company). Extensive interviews with managers at different levels of the organization, in various subsidiaries at home and abroad, may be conducted before and after the ethics code is drafted to ensure that the code is comprehensive in its coverage of the variety of ethical dilemmas that managers are most likely to encounter. For example, to develop the company's ethical guidelines, Levi Strauss formed a working group of 15 employees from a broad section of the company. The working group spent nine months developing the guidelines, during which time it researched the views of various key stakeholder groups—vendors, contractors, plant managers, merchandisers, sewing-machine operators, contract production staff, shareholders, and others.[35] The Code of Business Conduct of Rohm and Haas, specialty materials company, as it pertains to gifts and entertainment and the Foreign Corrupt Practices Act, is presented in Table 14.5.

3. Provide an Organizational Identity to the Ethics Program Most companies would agree that there should be strong organizational support for a company's ethics program. The best way to ensure that ethics is not downplayed is to establish a high-level ethics committee at the board of directors' level and an ethics committee at different organizational levels. For example, McDonnell Douglas has a Board of Directors Ethics Committee, an internal corporate committee led by a senior executive, and a committee at each division (component company) level reporting to the highest level. Further down the line, an ombudsman, who is a senior manager, is available to counsel employees who wish to have private and confidential advice.

In a similar vein, international companies could establish ethics committees at different organizational levels, starting with the top management levels of the parent company, and within the various divisions and subsidiaries of the company at home and abroad. The Boeing Company, a leading aircraft manufacturer, has "ethics advisers" in subsidiaries and a corporate office for employees to report infractions.[36]

4. A Formal Program Must Be in Place to Implement the Ethics Code Every employee must be made to go through a formal training program that teaches employees and indoctrinates them with the ethical code of the company. Case studies and role playing that highlights ethical dilemmas faced by international managers most frequently have proved to be very useful in encouraging participants to look at the operating

TABLE 14.5
Rohm and Haas Company: Political Payments and Gifts and Entertainment

Source: Rohm and Haas, "Code of Business Conduct," January 1994, pp. 1, 3.

The Company
Rohm and Haas Company is an ethical company which complies with applicable laws. This Code of Business Conduct applies to all directors, officers and employees of the Company, its subsidiaries and controlled affiliates.

Political Payments
(a) We encourage participation in the political process, and we recognize that participation is primarily a matter of individual involvement.
(b) Any payment of corporate funds to any political party, candidate, or campaign may be made only if permitted under applicable law and approved in advance by the General Counsel. U.S. laws generally prohibit payments of corporate funds to any U.S. political party, candidate, or campaign.

Gifts and Entertainment
(a) Gifts of cash or property may not be offered or made to any officer or employee of a customer or supplier or any government official or employee unless the gift is (1) nominal in value, (2) approved in advance by the appropriate regional director, business group executive, or corporate staff division manager, and (3) legal. In most countries it is illegal for corporations to make gifts to government officials or employees; any gift to a government official or employee must be approved in advance by the general counsel as well as the appropriate regional director, business group executive, or corporate staff division manager.
(b) Employees of the company should decline or turn over to the company gifts of more than nominal value or cash from persons or companies that do (or may expect to do) business with Rohm and Haas.
(c) Business entertainment (whether we do the entertaining or are entertained) must have a legitimate business purpose, may not be excessive, and must be legal. Business entertainment of government officials or employees is illegal or regulated in most countries; therefore, the propriety of such entertaining should be reviewed in advance with the general counsel or his delegates.

Translation
Translations of the code will be prepared in French, German, Italian, Portuguese, Spanish, and Japanese. Other translations will be prepared if necessary to ensure that recipients of the code are able to understand it fully. The general or resident manager in each country will be responsible for translations.

Dissemination
(a) A copy of the code in the appropriate language will be given to all employees of the company (including employees of domestic and foreign subsidiaries and controlled affiliates). New employees will be given a copy of the code at the time of their employment.
(b) The regional or staff division personnel directors are responsible for dissemination of the code.

Compliance
(a) All salaried employees of the company (its subsidiaries and controlled affiliates) will be asked to certify annually in writing their compliance with the code substantially as follows (with such exceptions as may be noted therein):

"I have reviewed and understand the Code of Business Conduct. I hereby confirm that (1) I have complied with the code during the preceding year, and (2) each recipient of the code who reports to me has certified in writing his or her compliance with the code."

(b) The regional and business directors will be responsible for obtaining certifications not later than February 1 with respect to the preceding year.

principles in the company code for guidance. For instance, Levi Strauss held training sessions for 100 in-country managers who would have to enforce the company's ethical global sourcing guidelines in the plants of the company's 700 contract manufacturers worldwide. The training included case studies and exercises in decision making. Following this training, the managers made presentations on the guidelines to the contractors, performed on-site audits, and worked with the contractors to make the necessary improvements.[37] Companies often require that employees sign a statement that they have read, have understood, and agree to comply with the company's ethics code.

5. The Line Managers, not Consultants, Train Employees in Ethics The line manager is the "role model" of ethical behavior for his or her subordinates. Each line manager must be cognizant of his or her own responsibilities in creating a culture of ethical norms that will be strictly adhered to. A line manager who deviates from the ethics code at crunch time will send the signal to subordinates that "the code is just a bunch

PRACTICAL INSIGHT 14.3

U.S. COMPANIES BACK OUT OF BURMA, CITING HUMAN-RIGHTS CONCERNS, GRAFT

A number of U.S. companies are backing out from their recent forays into Burma, partly because of pressure from human-rights groups and partly because doing business in the corrupt, junta-run country just isn't worth the trouble. Macy's said it would stop making clothing in Burma within 90 days because of a "lack of infrastructure" as well as corruption in the country.

The retailer, a unit of Federated Department Stores Inc., is the latest U.S. multinational to withdraw from the Southeast Asian nation, where the ruling military regime has been accused of widespread human-rights violations since it overturned a democratic election in 1990 that would have handed political power to civilians. Burma, which was renamed Myanmar by its military rulers in 1989, is "fast becoming the South Africa of the '90s," said Simon Billenness, an analyst at Franklin Research & Development Corp.

Only in the past few years has the long-isolated nation, with a population of about 43.5 million, even tried to woo foreign business. And it was beginning to have some success, albeit limited, mainly because of its low wages. However, in recent years, Liz Claiborne Inc. and Spiegel Inc.'s Eddie Bauer have pledged to stop importing apparel from Burma. Earlier this month, Starbucks Corp., the specialty-coffee company, asked that a new cold coffee drink it is creating not be bottled or distributed in Burma by PepsiCo Inc., which does business in Burma and is Starbuck's partner in the coffee-drink effort.

In withdrawing from Burma, the companies have acknowledged the human-rights concerns. "The consumer pressure is beginning to have an effect," says Thomas Lansner, a member of the Free Burma Action Group in New York. "Even if there's good business to be done in Burma, it has become an embarrassment for them to make money there." For its part, Macy's wasn't embarrassed—just disappointed because it was "impossible to make money there," a spokeswoman said. The company added that Burma's corruption "makes normal operations impossible."

Macy's had been contracting out private-label men's clothing in Burma for about 15 months. It thought the three factories it was using were private, but they turned out to be partly owned by the military government. Not all multinationals find Burma inhospitable. Unocal Corp., which has paid the Burmese government at least $10 million so far for rights to develop offshore gas fields, said it is "absolutely committed to this project." A spokesman added that Unocal thinks its involvement in Burma "will bring sustainable long-term benefits to (the) people of Myanmar."

Critics argue that such investment only nourishes the military junta. Burma's elected government-in-exile has called for economic sanctions against the country. But some investment advocates think private corporations actually may have more sway over such regimes than international bodies or other governments. "These companies can really press for change . . . because the country needs them and their investment," says Deborah Leipziger, director of international programs for the Council on Economic Priorities.

Source: G. Pascal Zachary, *Wall Street Journal,* Eastern Ed. Copyright © 1995 by Dow Jones & Co. Inc. Reproduced with permission of Dow Jones & Co. Inc. via Copyright Clearance Center.

---

of words that don't matter." The company's chief executive is the supreme line manager, and therefore ethical guidelines, of what is acceptable, what isn't, and why, are established by the messages sent by his or her own behaviors and actions over time.

6. Strict Enforcement of Codes Is Essential Employees who violate the company code ought to be punished. Chemical Bank has fired employees for violation of the company's code of ethics even when there are no violations of the law. Xerox Corporation has dismissed employees not only for taking bribes but also for minor manipulation of records and petty cheating on expense accounts.[38]

7. Actions Speak Louder than Words It is not what a company code or what a company's top management and line managers say but what they actually do in their decisions and actions on behalf of the company that counts. Companies like Federated Department Stores, Liz Claiborne, and Spiegel have pledged to stop their business activities in Burma because of human rights concerns in that country, whereas Unocal and others have decided to continue their involvement in Burma, giving as justification for their continued involvement the influence that they and other like-minded companies can have on changing the policies of the government of Burma. This is illustrated in Practical Insight 14.3.

Multinational companies play a dominant role in determining the well-being of people worldwide. Their behavior can have both beneficial and harmful consequences on the quality of life and living standards in various countries in which they conduct trade and commerce. This issue was covered in various chapters in this book. However, one should always be cognizant that decisions in companies are made by the people who manage them, so national or international companies can be no more ethical than the persons who run them. Companies that act with integrity are largely a function of individuals within firms who act with integrity. Executives in a firm's organizational hierarchy take their directions from their top management executives. As such, the board of directors and the chief executive officer are the crucial players in ensuring that the moral and ethical codes governing the behavior of the firm are communicated to all managers throughout the length and breadth of the global enterprise.

Summary

Business ethics and corporate social responsibility infuse the consideration of moral issues in corporate decision making and actions. Corporate social responsibility is specifically defined as the integration of business operations and values whereby the interests of all stakeholders—customers, employees, investors, and the environment—are reflected in the organization's policies and actions. It is motivated through a combination of utilitarian, positive duty, and negative duty approaches.

International managers may be confronted with a variety of ethical dilemmas, usually due to differences among different markets or nations in what constitutes legal or acceptable practice. Beyond the practical motivations for instituting corporate social responsibility initiatives, there are moral underpinnings as well. These include teleology, deontology (the theory of rights), the theory of justice, and cultural relativism. Regarding the latter theory, a host country's legal and ethical perspectives of an international firm's activities and products must be understood and related to the cultural relativism of the country.

Several prominent international accords address ethical behavior by international companies. One or more of these provide specific guidance with respect to employment practices and policies, consumer and environmental protection issues, political payments and involvement, and basic human rights and fundamental freedoms. Although the accords are not legally binding with force of law, they display the clear intent of the international community to foster ethical conduct.

Bribery and corruption are the most troublesome and pervasive ethical issues confronting international managers, and they are common to industrialized and developing countries alike. The line between proper and improper behavior is not always clearly drawn, and in many cases making a payoff may appear obligatory if the international company wishes to continue to do business. Laws and practices differ widely in different countries.

Increasingly, companies are coming to the realization that corporate social responsibility programs must be more than public relations ploys. Rather, the actions taken by companies must not only meet the demands of the external stakeholders but must also add value to the satisfaction levels of the consumers of their products or services and simultaneously improve their own competitiveness in the industry.

A growing number of international companies have adopted comprehensive ethics programs involving ethics training and, often, a published code of conduct for all company personnel. An effective integration of the company's ethics program and the business behavior of the company's people depends on top management and the entire organization demonstrating that they are serious about the program on an ongoing basis. Training, enforcement, and leadership by example are essential to success.

Key Terms and Concepts

corporate social responsibility, *488*
cultural relativism, *492*
deontology, *491*
egoism, *490*
ethics, *487*
moral norms, *494*
negative duty approach, *489*
positive duty approach, *489*
responsive corporate social responsibility, *497*
social costs of bribery, *503*
strategic corporate social responsibility, *497*
teleology, *489*
theory of justice, *491*
utilitarianism, *490*

Discussion Questions

1. Should "ethics" be a subject that must be taught in all business schools? Doesn't the axiom "Do the right thing" really say it all?
2. Think of an issue that poses an ethical dilemma, and apply Exhibit 14.2 to arrive at a decision on this issue.
3. In the text, we discussed five areas of interest to international companies that are covered by specific guidelines for ethical behavior from international accords. Find an article in the current business press that reports negatively on a company's behavior with respect to one of these five areas. What repercussions does the company face as a result of its actions? In your opinion, are they justified? Why do you suppose the company's decision makers acted as they did? Are "right" and "wrong" clearly defined in this situation? Discuss.
4. Give examples of how companies can implement strategic CSR with the inside-out approach.
5. Give examples of how companies can implement strategic CSR with the outside-in approach.
6. Different companies exhibit differing degrees of formality in their corporate ethical policies and programs, but all incorporate, to some extent, the seven recommendations contained in the chapter. Which of the seven is most critical to the success of a company's program, in your opinion? Why? Would your answer be the same for all firms in all industries? If not, what factors might determine the most essential recommendation for a given firm?

Minicase

Hondurans in Sweatshops See Opportunity

SAN PEDRO SULA, Honduras

Each morning, the workers spill off the buses and past the guards at the front gates of the industrial parks here, rushing to punch the clock before the 7:30 start of their workday. Outside, anxious onlookers are always waiting, hoping for a chance at least to fill out a job application that will allow them to become part of that throng.

With wages that start at less than 40 cents an hour, the apparel plants here offer little by American standards. But many of the people who work in them, having come from jobs that pay even less and offer no benefits or security, see employment here as the surest road to a better life. "In the countryside, a peon is a peon for all of his life," said Yensy Melendez, 29, a father of two and former farm worker who migrated seven years ago to this bustling city of 350,000 near Honduras's Caribbean coast and now has a factory job. "Here, it's not perfect, but at least you have a chance to improve your situation."

What residents of a rich country like the United States see as exploitation can seem a rare opportunity to residents of a poor country like Honduras, where the per capita income is $600 a year and unemployment is 40 percent. Such conflicts of standards and perceptions have become increasingly common as the global economy grows more intertwined, and have set off a heated debate about international norms of conduct and responsibility.

The recent controversy involving the television personality Kathie Lee Gifford and a line of clothing made here that bears her name provides a widely publicized case in point.

To critics in the United States, the apparel assembly plants here, known in Spanish as *maquiladoras,* are merely "monstrous sweatshops of the New World Order," to use the phrase of the National Labor Committee, the New York–based group that originally accused Mrs. Gifford of turning a blind eye to Hondurans working for "slave wages."

The National Labor Committee, a nonprofit group, is largely financed by foundations but also receives money from labor unions in the United States.

After the attacks on her, Mrs. Gifford has now endorsed efforts to monitor and improve conditions in apparel plants around the world. But the debate over what constitutes adequate wages, what minimum working conditions should be required and at what age it becomes permissible for minors to work continues here and in other developing countries that have eagerly welcomed assembly plants as a source of employment for their poor.

Whether workers think they are better off in the assembly plants than elsewhere is not the real issue, argues Charles Kernaghan, executive director of the National Labor Committee. Employers, he said, have a moral obligation to pay not merely what the market will bear, but a wage they know to be just.

LOW WAGE RATES DRAW CRITICISM

"The salaries being paid in a place like Honduras amount to less than 1 percent of the price of the garment in the United States," he said. "That's a crime." Companies could easily double their employees' wages, he added, and "it would be nothing."

But many of the people who work here and are most familiar with conditions in the plants argue that the situation in Honduras, at least, where about one-fifth of the clothing workers are unionized, is far more complicated than portrayed in the American debate over "sweatshops."

To make any kind of sweeping generalization is dangerous and misleading, many said during interviews here with more than 75 apparel workers and union leaders and visits to half a dozen plants, including the one that made clothes for the Gifford line.

Many here say critics from the north are more interested in protecting jobs in the United States than in improving the lot of Honduran workers.

Yes, workers and employers here say, some companies verbally abuse their workers on a regular basis, insist on compulsory overtime, impose unreachable production quotas or dismiss employees who become pregnant in order not to have to pay maternity benefits.

But other plants supply a subsidized lunch and free medical care to employees, are modern and air-conditioned, have agreed to union shops and generally respect workers' rights.

"You will find varying conditions and outlooks here," said Israel Salinas, president of the Federation of Independent Workers of Honduras, one of three rival labor groups seeking to organize the approximately 75,000 employees who work in the estimated 160 assembly plants in this country. "It all depends on whom you talk to and where you go."

A WORKER'S ESCAPE FROM RURAL POVERTY

The story told by one apparel worker, Eber Orellana Vasquez, is not unusual. He is one of some 450 employees at the King Star Garment assembly plant just south of here, a Taiwanese-owned company that produces beach shirts, shorts and other sportswear for the United States market.

At 26 he is a veteran of three years as an apparel worker and a strong supporter of the union that represents the employees in their dealings with the company.

"This has been an enormous advance for me," Mr. Orellana said, "and I give thanks to the maquila for it. My monthly income is seven times what I made in the countryside, and I've gained 30 pounds since I started working here."

Before he became an apparel worker here, Mr. Orellana explained, he worked for a decade on a dairy ranch, milking and herding cows and living in a rented shack. "My only possession there was a bicycle," he said, so small was his salary.

Now, thanks to his job as a quality control checker, he owns a house of his own, "made of brick with a zinc roof," he noted proudly, in contrast to the flimsy wood and thatch roof dwellings that are the norm in the countryside, and has access to electricity and water.

He has been able to bring his wife and a younger brother, now 17, from the ranch and find them jobs in the plant.

"Every time I go to visit the ranch, everyone wants to come back with me," Mr. Orellana said. "The work there is very hard, exhausting. You get up at 1 o'clock in the morning to start your chores, and the bosses are always mean. If you drink too much milk, they will fire you."

COMPANY ACCUSED OF RIGHTS ABUSES

The clothes for the Kathie Lee Gifford line were produced by the Global Fashion plant at the South Korean–run Galaxy Industrial Park just north of town, which has been singled out by human rights advocates here and abroad as being especially harsh and abusive to workers.

In recent testimony to Congress, a former employee at the factory, Wendy Diaz, 15, said she had been forced to work up to 74 hours a week by supervisors who regularly screamed at, hit and sexually harassed employees.

"We knew that factory wasn't the greatest," Mr. Kernaghan said in a telephone interview from New York. "We knew that conditions were pretty rough there, that people were being fired for trying to organize, that it was not a good place, not near to being among the better factories in Honduras."

Wal-Mart, which markets Mrs. Gifford's line of clothes, has no production contracts at the moment with Global Fashion. But it continues to have clothing made under contract at numerous other apparel plants in Honduras, and is being pressed by the National Labor Committee to consent to an independent monitoring program.

In an interview at the plant, Paul Kim, president of Global Fashion, acknowledged that his company required compulsory overtime of its employees, had a high employee turnover rate and might demand more effort of workers than some other companies here.

But he denied Miss Diaz's charge of systematic abuse, and described the regimen here as a form of tough love that works for the good of all concerned.

"Korea used to be a poor country, like Honduras," Mr. Kim said, speaking in Korean through a Spanish-language interpreter, "but we have had a lot of development because we worked very hard. The more you work, the more you earn. That's what Central America needs if it is going to become prosperous."

AN INDUSTRIAL BOOM BRINGS LABOR SHORTAGE

A decade ago, Honduras had virtually no assembly plants, and poor people had few options. Now, the factories have absorbed so many workers that they are creating labor shortages that have helped drive up wages for workers in other sectors, including agriculture, forestry, mining, fishing and even domestic work, traditionally the worst paid and most abusive.

"It used to be easy to get a nanny or a maid, but not now," said Jesus Canahuati, whose family owns an industrial park and several assembly plants here. "Everybody wants to work in the maquilas, because they represent an opportunity for a better life."

Within the apparel assembly industry itself, workers and employers agree, explosive growth has also encouraged the labor force to be on the move, always looking for the best offer. When workers do not like conditions where they are, both sides say, they often move to other jobs offering production incentives and increased benefits that in some cases double their base wage.

"If you don't pay more than the legal minimum, you don't get any employees," said Perry Keene, acting manager of Certified Apparel Services of Honduras, a plant here that makes infants' wear for department stores in the United States. "They will all go to other people, because it's a competitive labor market."

Another sharp difference of perspective surrounds the issue of teen-agers working in the assembly plants. The National Labor Committee and other critics in the United States contend that the practice, widespread here, is "destroying a whole generation of young women" and have called for American apparel concerns to stop doing business with all suppliers who hire children.

HONDURAN UNIONS DEFEND CHILD LABOR

But all three of the leading labor federations here, including unions that have worked closely with the National Labor Committee in denouncing abuses of workers, disagree with that position. Instead, acting in accordance with the demands of members whose own children are already working, they want the Honduran Government to enforce regulations that are already on the books. Under Honduran law, adolescents between the ages of 14 and 16 can be employed for up to six hours a day. To do so, they must first obtain the permission of their parents, which is usually readily granted, and of the Labor Ministry, also easily obtained in a country in which education for the majority of the population ends at sixth grade.

"This country is not the United States," said Evangelina Argueta, a labor organizer in Choloma, a suburb just north of here with a large concentration of industrial parks. "Very few Honduran mothers can afford the luxury of feeding children until they are 18 years old without putting them to work."

Nevertheless, responding to complaints from the United States and to the fears of blacklisting that have arisen as a result, the Honduran Maquiladora Association says its members have now stopped hiring any workers under 16. Union leaders and workers say factory owners have also been reviewing their personnel records and dismissing all employees who are minors.

But that does not mean the dismissed youngsters are returning to school. On the contrary, management and labor agree that most of the children have instead sought new jobs outside the assembly sector that are lower paying and more physically demanding or are buying fake documents in an effort to sneak their way back into the apparel plants.

CAMPAIGN BRINGS UNINTENDED RESULT

Mr. Kernaghan acknowledged that his group's effort to end child labor had produced unanticipated consequences. "Obviously this is not what we wanted to happen," he said.

He added that his group had discussed with Honduran factory owners an arrangement that would permit the 14- to 16-year-olds already employed to keep their jobs but shift future hiring toward adults.

"It's a tragic situation that needs to be resolved," he added. When asked how that should be done, he replied, "I may not be the right person to answer that kind of question, since I'm not an economist."

Many older workers who themselves began working at a young age assert that the American campaign may actually be hurting the very people it is intended to help.

Rene Javier Robertson, for example, left school at 13 to work as a fare collector on a bus "because with four kids besides me, my family needed me to work" and opportunities for teen-agers were limited.

"In 11 years on that job, I worked 14 hours a day, seven days a week, never got a day's vacation, didn't get paid when I was sick, and had to content myself with whatever wage the bus driver felt like paying me at the end of the day," said Mr. Robertson, who got a job on the assembly line three years ago and is now 27. "I was a slave, with no rights."

Teen-agers working at assembly plants "are a million times better off in here than out there on the street, because the maquila represents progress," Mr. Robertson added. "The work here isn't heavy, there are many benefits, and they have to respect your rights. I wish the maquila had existed when I started to work, because I could have avoided a lot of suffering."

Source: Larry Rohter, "Hondurans in Sweatshops See Opportunity," *New York Times,* July 18, 1996, p. A1. Copyright © 2003 The New York Times Company.

DISCUSSION QUESTIONS

1. Many employees in sweatshops, having come from jobs that pay even less and offer no benefits or security, see employment in a sweatshop as a means to a better life. What rights do human rights advocates from developed countries have to oppose the use of sweatshops by foreign firms?
2. Are organizations like the National Labor Committee acting in good faith on behalf of the workers in sweatshops? Or is their ulterior motive to save jobs of American workers that are exported to sweatshops abroad?
3. A decade ago, Honduras had virtually no assembly plants, and poor people had few options. Now, the factories have absorbed so many workers that they are creating labor shortages that have helped drive up wages of workers in other sectors, including agriculture, forestry, mining, fishing, and even domestic work, traditionally the worst paid and most abusive. Is this not an argument in favor of sweatshops?
4. Does free trade stimulate the growth of the number of sweatshops worldwide?
5. What would be the impacts on the global competitiveness of international companies if all nations do not adopt uniform policies that would eliminate sweatshops?

Notes

1. Paul W. Taylor, *Principles of Ethics: An Introduction to Ethics,* 2nd. ed. (Encino, CA: Dickenson, 1975), p. 1.
2. Sita C. Amba-Rao, "Multinational Corporate Social Responsibility, Ethics, Interactions, and Third World Governments: An Agenda for the 1990s," *Journal of Business Ethics* 12 (1993), p. 553.
3. Davis Weir and Mark Schapiro, *Circle of Poison* (San Francisco: Institute for Food and Development Policy, 1981), p. 22.
4. Kennedy Smith, "ISO Considers Corporate Social Responsibility Standards," *Journal for Quality and Participation* 25, no. 3 (2002), p. 42.

5. Isabelle Maignan and David A. Ralston, "Corporate Social Responsibility in Europe and the U.S.: Insights from Businesses' Self-Presentations," *Journal of International Business Studies* 33, no. 3 (2002), pp. 497–515.
6. R. Hooghiemstra, "Corporate Communication and Impression Management—New Perspectives: Why Companies Engage in Corporate Social Reporting," *Journal of Business Ethics* 27 (2000), pp. 55–68.
7. J. Handelman and S. Arnold, "The Role of Marketing Actions with a Social Dimension: Appeals to the Institutional Environment," *Journal of Marketing* 63 (1999), pp. 33–48.
8. O. C. Ferrell and John Fraedrich, *Business Ethics: Ethical Decision Making and Cases,* 2nd ed. (Boston: Houghton Mifflin, 1994), p. 60.
9. Tom L. Beauchamp and Norma E. Bowie, eds., *Ethical Theory and Business* (Englewood Cliffs, NJ: Prentice Hall, 1979).
10. J. S. Mill, *Utilitarianism* (Indianapolis:Bobbs-Merrill, 1957). First published 1863.
11. Richard Brandt, *Ethical Theory* (Englewood Cliffs, NJ: Prentice Hall, 1959), pp. 253–254.
12. Donald M. Borchert and David Stewart, *Exploring Ethics* (New York: Macmillan, 1986), p. 199.
13. Ibid.
14. Ferrell and Fraedrich, *Business Ethics,* p. 57.
15. Gerald F. Cavanagh, Dennis J. Moberg, and Manuel Velasquez, "The Ethics of Organizational Politics," *Academy of Management Review* 6, no. 3 (1981), p. 366.
16. Adapted from Cavanagh, Moberg, and Velasquez, "The Ethics of Organizational Politics," p. 366.
17. Thomas Donaldson, *The Ethics of International Business* (New York: Oxford University Press, 1989), p. 14.
18. Clarence C. Walton, *The Moral Manager* (Cambridge, MA: Ballinger, 1988), p. 110.
19. Richard T. De George, *Competing with Integrity in International Business* (New York, Oxford University Press, 1993), p. 11.
20. Ibid., p. 19.
21. Ibid., pp. 19–21.
22. Thomas Donaldson, "Can Multinationals Stage a Universal Morality Play?" *Business and Society Review,* 2001, pp. 51–55.
23. Thomas W. Dunfee, N. Vraig Smith, and William T. Ross Jr., "Social Contracts and Marketing Ethics," *Journal of Marketing,* July 1999, pp. 14–32.
24. Michael Porter and Mark R. Kramer, "Strategy and Society: The Link between Competitive Advantage and Corporate Social Responsibility," *Harvard Business Review,* December 2006, pp. 1–21.
25. www.mackies.co.uk/mackies/windturbine.html.
26. www.timberland.com/corp/index.jsp?eid=5022825705&page=pressrelease.
27. Porter and Kramer, "Strategy and Society."
28. Kathleen A. Getz, "International Codes of Conduct: An Analysis of Ethical Reasoning," *Journal of Business Ethics* 9, no. 7 (1990), pp. 567–578.
29. William C. Frederick, "The Moral Authority of Transnational Corporate Codes," *Journal of Business Ethics* 10 (1992), pp. 166–167.
30. William D. Montalbano, "A Challenge to Italy's Status Quo," *Philadelphia Inquirer,* March 21, 1993, pp. E1, E4.
31. "Thousands in Pakistan Call for End to Child Labor," *Philadelphia Inquirer,* April 26, 1995, p. A8.
32. Robert D. Haas, "Ethics in the Trenches," *Across the Board,* May 1994, pp. 12–13.
33. Ibid.
34. Ibid.
35. Ibid.
36. John Byrne, "Businesses Are Signing Up for Ethics 101," *BusinessWeek,* February 15, 1988, p. 5.
37. Haas, "Ethics in the Trenches."
38. Byrne, "Businesses Are Signing Up for Ethics 101," pp. 56–57.

CASE IV

The Tata Way: Evolving and Executing Sustainable Business Strategies

Oana Branzei and Anant G. Nadkarni

As corporate social responsibility is becoming increasingly important in attaining and sustaining competitive advantage, many companies have signed on to pro-environmental and pro-social initiatives. But can such initiatives promote doing good while strengthening a firm's competitive advantage? Starting with a Tata Workout in 2001, CEOs of the TATA companies have collectively evolved an integrated approach to embedding a sustainability mindset into their systems, people, and processes. In 2007, their efforts culminated in the launch of a Leadership Protocol that promotes both a systemic legacy and personality footprints for the next generation of TATA leaders. The authors discuss how this comprehensive approach for the execution of sustainability strategies can strengthen the connection between corporate social responsibility and global competitiveness.

Walmart has Sustainability 360. MacDonald's is greening its supply chains to promote fair-trade coffee and sustainable fisheries. Monsanto developed a trans fat-free soybean, helping make KFC's fried chicken a healthier choice and now works with farmers around the world to mitigate agriculture's overall impact on our environment. And Toyota's "Prius for the people" helps climate change mindful people make the right choice on their way to work.

Few corporate leaders would disagree that "today's companies ought to invest in corporate social responsibility as part of their business strategy to become more competitive" (Porter & Kramer, 2006). But connecting doing good and doing well poses new challenges in strategy formulation and execution. There are a handful of systematic guidelines that have helped disseminate best practices among future-minded corporations: the ISO 14000 Environmental Management Standard, the Global Reporting Initiative's Sustainability Reporting Guidelines, and more recently, the Social Accountability International's SA8000 code of conduct. As more companies sign on to these agreements, both the internal learning and external credibility stemming from sounder practices have become a source of competitive parity. But can a corporation blaze new competitive advantage at the junction of sustainability and business?

Take Tata's recently announced Nano, the world's most affordable car—for some perhaps another 4-wheel greenhouse threat, for many a revolutionary new way to reposition the auto industry. But both critics and advocates agree that the $2,500, two-cylinder car showcased at the New Delhi Auto Expo on January 10 offers an affordable transportation solution with a low carbon footprint. For Tata Motors, India's largest automobile company, the Nano is much more than a provocative new transportation choice for India's people. This little safe car stands as another bold embodiment of Tata's century of trust and cooperation with local communities. And the Nano is only one of the fruits of Tata companies' painstaking commitment to surfacing the best of business in the service of people, in India and globally.

Tata Consultancy Services Limited (TCS), a world leading provider of information technology consulting services, is winning global accolades from Business in the Community's (BitC) Corporate Responsibility Index (CRI), the leading UK benchmark of responsible business practice. In 2006, TCS achieved the gold band for its performance in the Community Index with a score of 94.7 percent. Known internationally for its business success, TCS has a warm spot in the heart of many Indians for the Computer Based Functional Literacy project. This program helped illiterate adults learn how

Oana Branzei is Assistant Professor of Strategy and David G. Burgoyne Faculty Fellow at the Richard Ivey School of Business. She is also a faculty member of the Cross-Enterprise Leadership Centre on Building Sustainable Value, the Research Network for Business Sustainability, the Corporate Sustainability Doctoral Academy, and the Sustainable Enterprise Academy. Anant G. Nadkarni is Vice President Corporate Sustainability for the TATA Group, Secretary of the Tata Council for Community Initiatives. He has worked with the United Nations Development Program and the Confederation of Indian Industry (CII) to advance the platform of sustainability.

to read in their own spoken language in a span of 30 to 45 hours spread over 10 to 12 weeks. The program is multimedia-driven, and targets 15 to 30 year olds—setting them on the path to acquiring other literacy skills, including writing and arithmetic ability without any interruption in their productive activities. Five years later, the project has spread to more than 1,000 centers in Andhra Pradesh, Tamil Nadu, Madhya Pradesh, Maharashtra, Uttar Pradesh and West Bengal, and it has helped more than 46,000 people learn how to read. It has also inspired TCS employees to closely marry their IT excellence with local initiatives in their global operations, and to embody and share the Tata values wherever they work.

There are many differences between Tata Motors and TCS—but also important commonalities. Both companies strive to share the human touch everyday and everywhere they go. The social and environmental value their respective operations create helps strengthen and promote the TATA brand as the group becomes a global presence. Their initiatives boil down century-old values of community stewardship in ways that leverage core operational impact to make a lasting impression on the communities in which they operate. This deep awareness of how business can benefit multiple stakeholders by mission and design constantly renews the Tata corporate identity in ways that continuously strengthen its brand and competitive advantage in markets at home and abroad.

THE TATA WAY

Why do so few corporations do business the Tata way? There is a catch. First, every single employee working for TATA companies, from the CEO to the most recent intern, shares in the deep values of their leaders, still a guidepost for every new project within the group. Second, Tata companies have evolved a collective commitment to evolving stronger connections between their values and first-in-class business practice—not by putting either one ahead of the other, but by finding mutually beneficial bridges between them.

> In a free enterprise, the community is not just another stakeholder in business, but is in fact the very purpose of its existence.—Jamsetji N. Tata (Founder, Tata Group, 1868)

> The Tata philosophy of management has always been and is today more than ever, that corporate enterprises must be managed not merely in the interests of their owners, but equally in those of their employees, of the customers of their products, of the local community and finally of the country as a whole.—J. R. D. Tata

Starting in the early 1990s, the group has invested in structures and processes that would gradually align its pro-social and pro-environmental values with excellence in business endeavors. These efforts culminated in 2003 with the introduction of The Tata Index for Sustainable Human Development, a pioneering effort aimed at directing, measuring and enhancing the community work that assists all TATA companies in their social responsibility efforts. The index had been developed by the TATA Council for Community Initiatives (TCCI), a council of Tata companies CEOs chaired by Mr. Kishor Chaukar, in partnership with TATA Quality Management Services (TQMS). Since June 2004, the Tata Index has been deployed annually to assure continuous improvement in the delivery of social responsibility initiatives at the company level. In 2005, reporting companies averaged almost half of its intended goal, i.e., 452.95 points on a 1000 point scale, with companies scoring as high as 712 (Tata Steel). In 2006/07, TCS scored 490. Tata Motors, now at 663, was one of the best performers on corporate sustainability within the group.

These scores were only the start. The purpose behind the Index was to seed new benchmarks and motivate continuous innovation in sustainability across each company's operations. TCCI offered a common platform where each company could share their challenges and achievements with the others and would learn how to nurture stronger internal leadership structures that promoted business excellence "the TATA way."

The Human Development Index was the very first initiative of its kind, both within TATA and across the world. The framework, originally initiated by TCCI in collaboration with the United Nations Development Program in India in 2001, has then been refined with training input from the Confederation of Indian Industry (CII), Price Waterhouse Cooper, the ICICI Bank, and the Ashoka group. Internationally, the index has both impressed and challenged the business community. It was showcased to the UN Secretary General Kofi Annan and 700 CEOs and global business leaders at the UN Business Leaders' Summit, as well as to governments and businesses in Switzerland,

FIGURE 1
The TATA Index

Source: TCCI, February 2008.

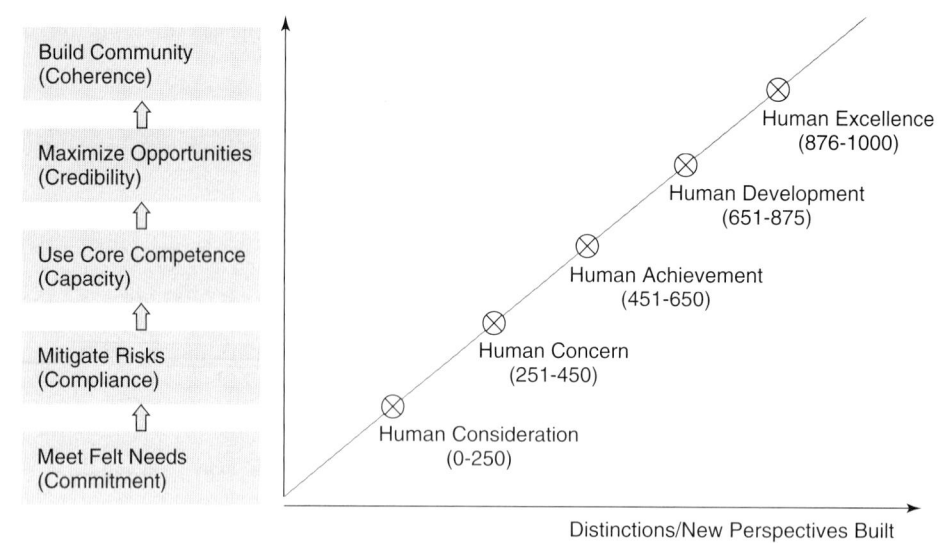

Build Community (Coherence)
⇧
Maximize Opportunities (Credibility)
⇧
Use Core Competence (Capacity)
⇧
Mitigate Risks (Compliance)
⇧
Meet Felt Needs (Commitment)

Human Excellence (876-1000)
Human Development (651-875)
Human Achievement (451-650)
Human Concern (251-450)
Human Consideration (0-250)

Distinctions/New Perspectives Built

Australia, Singapore, Bangkok, and Canada. Yet despite the appeal of assessing social impact, few companies in India and internationally have so far modeled TATA's approach.

The idea of explicitly tracking social impact originated with Tata Sons. Under the Chairmanship of Mr. Ratan N. Tata, the Group searched for a new way to harness collective synergies among the Tata companies. This led to the Business Excellence Model (TBEM), a detailed business process reform which began formalizing the set of core values that the Tatas had lived by for over a century. One of the offshoots of this effort was the adoption of a more systematic, unified TATA approach to CSR, rooted in Jamsetji Tata's social legacy, and the creation of the Tata Index for Sustainable Human Development, a trendsetting approach to mapping and measuring the social development endeavours of Tata Group companies.

The Index is now operational in most major Tata companies. Within each firm, a Corporate Head Social Responsibility (always a senior executive) manages a cross-functional CSR team of facilitators with specific responsibilities for community development, environmental management and volunteering. Mr. Nadkarni heads the operations of these teams and their leaders, i.e., the TCCI team, and functions as the Secretary of the Council—a group of 43 chief executive officers of Tata companies. TCCI operates across Tata companies as a network of more than 200 trained facilitations and over 11,500 volunteers.

The Index itself was a remarkable innovation. First, it broke down sustainability responses into three nested levels: systems (275/1000), people (175/1000) and program (550/1000), making it easy to measure, and easy to identify areas for improvement.

Second, the indexation exercise places great emphasis on process—not just outcomes. For example, Figure 2 shows how a company might apply the index to its own operations.

For each assessment, the Corporate Sustainability Facilitator representing a Tata company and the Community Head for the project would also identify specific opportunities for improvement. These might read: "The Company mentions of a regular convention of review. However, it is not clear as to how the review findings are incorporated into Company's strategy." Or "The Company trains its Facilitators / project leaders for leadership. However, it is not clear how the training imparted is actually benefiting them." Or "The Company declares 'underprivileged women' as its key community. However, there is no evidence on the process of identification of this community." Or "The Company states that the key community has benefited in terms of self-reliance. However, it is not clear as to how the key community has actually built self-reliance."

Each project leader is responsible for understanding the specific concerns of each community, defining the key beneficiaries, and placing a clear focus on how a company's core capabilities would contribute to a specific need. They would specify tangible measures both in terms of what will actually be done and in terms of the human achievement. The project leader will also determine the human excellence indicators and clearly identify which aspects have clear sustainability payoffs for the community engaged.

FIGURE 2 Example of Tata Company Self-Assessment Using the Tata Index

Source: TCCI, February 2008.

Assurance Item		Scores		
		Process	Outcomes	Total
Systems Level Response				
1	Leadership is by example	23	16	39
2	Deployment through networking and commitment	14	12	26
3	Strategy to build lasting businesses	12	8	20
4	Accountability towards value creation	13	12	25
	Total for Systems Response:	**62**	**48**	**110**
People Level Response:				
1	Put the best people!	10	8	18
2	Train and empower them!	9	7	16
3	Make them Leaders!	10	4	14
4	Most employees are like that!	8	4	12
	Total for People Response:	**37**	**23**	**60**
Program Level Response				
1	Managing risks	28	25	53
2	Opportunities to serve people	44	30	74
3	Build community and livelihoods	25	21	46
4	Encourage entrepreneurs and self-employment	34	23	57
	Total for Program Response:	**131**	**99**	**230**

Why do Tata companies care so much? Because that is the Tata way—and because their employees are trusted (and expected) to approach their tasks and their volunteering with society in mind. They do not do something because it pays. They do it because it matters—to their business model, to their own development as leaders, and to the legacy their company wants to leave behind. This selflessness may catch cynics by surprise, but it is part and parcel of forging a strong connection between sustainability and competitiveness. Much like, "Think not what society can do for your company, but what your company can do for society." There has been recent recognition by Harvard Business School professors Clayton Christensen and Michael Porter, among others, that such an orientation can trigger disruptive innovations. At Tata, the Index has made the disruption itself a way of doing business, to ensure that Tata's commitment to sustainable business will expand in the future and across its increasingly global base of operations.

> One hundred years from now, I expect the Tatas to be much bigger than it is now. More importantly, I hope the Group comes to be regarded as being the best in India—best in the manner in which we operate, best in the products we deliver and best in our value systems and ethics. Having said that, I hope that a hundred years from now we will spread our wings far beyond India.—Ratan Tata, 2005

The Group has been eager to leverage its learning by sharing the idea of indexation and the more practical how-to's of the Index with Tata suppliers, collaborators and competitors within India through the Confederation of Indian Industry (CII), and international organizations, such as the Global Reporting Initiative (the Group has been a founding member of GRI) and the Social Accountability Initiative. Although not every company may share the sustainability history or the ethos of Tata companies, the systematic approach of indexation can be easily adapted to work for different corporate identities, much as the GRI can be customized for specific activities and areas of improvement. If your firm has mustered the strategic commitment it takes to make the world a better place, the Index helps you execute by providing a guiding (albeit not forceful) approach to getting your systems, people and programs better every step of the way.

And then? You will soon need a parallel track to develop strong leaders that will continue to push your organization to the next level. Like every resource, sustainability processes can get stale and need periodic rejuvenation to bring your firm a competitive edge. Spearheaded by collaborations among Tata's strategic leaders on the Index, an even stronger linkage between sustainability and operational excellence was recently forged at TCCI's 6th workout since its founding, suggestively titled "Leadership for Corporate Sustainability." The deliverable was another world first: a Leadership Profile. This "*offers a set of suggestions to assist a Tata Company to develop its CSR practice with a greater*

FIGURE 3 The Tata Corporate Sustainability Leadership Profile: Process of Deployment

Source: TCCI, February 2008.

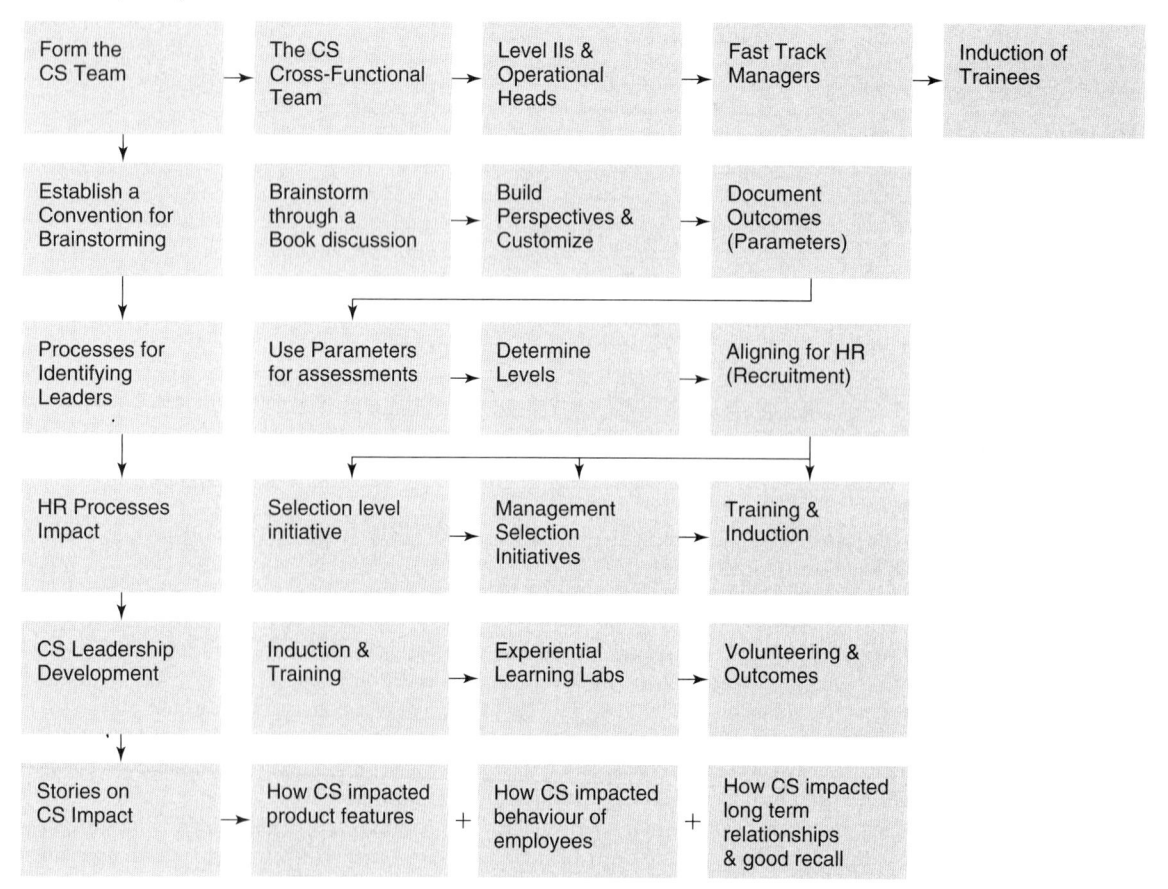

```
Form the            The CS              Level IIs &         Fast Track         Induction of
CS Team    ──▶    Cross-Functional ──▶ Operational   ──▶   Managers    ──▶    Trainees
                    Team                 Heads
  │
  ▼
Establish a         Brainstorm          Build               Document
Convention for ──▶  through a      ──▶  Perspectives & ──▶  Outcomes
Brainstorming       Book discussion     Customize           (Parameters)
  │                                                              │
  ▼                          ┌─────────────────────────────────┘
Processes for       Use Parameters      Determine           Aligning for HR
Identifying    ──▶  for assessments ──▶ Levels         ──▶  (Recruitment)
Leaders
  │                                                              │
  ▼                          ┌─────────────────────────────────┘
HR Processes        Selection level     Management           Training &
Impact         ──▶  initiative      ──▶ Selection      ──▶   Induction
                                        Initiatives
  │
  ▼
CS Leadership       Induction &         Experiential         Volunteering &
Development    ──▶  Training        ──▶ Learning Labs  ──▶   Outcomes
  │
  ▼
Stories on          How CS impacted     How CS impacted      How CS impacted
CS Impact      ──▶  product features +  behaviour of    +    long term
                                        employees            relationships
                                                             & good recall
```

focus on content and specific initiatives that have been collectively agreed upon at a group level. This version is specially designed to encourage CSR Facilitators and the TBEM Internal Assessors to work together in embedding CSR into the Internal Assessment process." (TATA Protocol—Corporate Social Responsibility, January 2007).

How do you develop Leaders for Corporate Sustainability? At Tata, this is a two-fold approach. On the one hand, the Index encourages a proactive application of the Tata Business Excellence model in ways that promote positive social and environmental contributions. Annual scoring ensures constant process improvement. The assessment triggers company-wide workouts that help strategic leaders work with their internal teams to jointly identify major risks, opportunities and innovations that can meet both sustainability and business excellence objectives. Using this collective understanding, the leaders then formulate a 3–5 year corporate sustainability strategy for their organization. This gives their company a more sustainable edge (competitively, socially and environmentally). It also gradually widens their own leadership bandwidth to make a larger difference in their community and competitive context by setting new standards of what businesses can achieve.

On the other hand, the Corporate Sustainability Leadership Profile guides their personality footprints to trigger a virtuous cycle of enhanced goodwill and reputation. First, the leaders assume responsibility for themselves and their leadership team, and work personally to tighten convergence between the trained corporate sustainability facilitators and their unit's business excellence goals. They lead for sustainability by example—through involvement in volunteering initiatives and through regular integration of sustainability issues in business meetings. Their performance on corporate sustainability is reviewed periodically (including their ability to promote and recognize such leadership among their subordinates). There is even a flowchart showing how any organizations can systematically implement leadership for sustainability.

At Tata, the Leadership Protocol translates the group mission statement into executable leadership for sustainability: "The Tata name is a unique asset representing leadership with trust. Leveraging this asset to enhance Group synergy and becoming globally competitive is the route to sustained growth and long-term success." (Group Mission Statement, 2007). Projects like the Nano or adult literacy in 40 hours do not happen by chance. But they can happen by design. Tata companies have unleashed a virtuous cycle of evolution and execution of sustainability strategies. The Index assesses and guides sustainability-enhancing processes; the Leadership Profile articulates the steps for strengthening leadership capabilities. By embedding a society-minded logic to value creation, Tata have given back many-fold to society. Their learning in turn has strengthened their corporate identity, and encouraged bold steps in rethinking transportation, information technology, or steel manufacturing.

Could your company follow their lead and make a difference? The Tata's approach is simple, but it is not easy. You can position your firm for a lasting competitive advantage by deliberately embedding sustainability assessments in both operations and leadership. Taking a comprehensive approach helps you identify and configure the various capabilities needed to create value sustainably—in systems, people and programs. And if your company is not changing fast enough, you can. Become the change you wish to see, and lead others by example:

- Take a holistic view of value creation.
- Demonstrate unusual creativity in solving tough problems for society.
- Practice strong ethical leadership with a deep sense of human purpose.
- Recalibrate the connection between your inner self and your footprints.

Source: *Ivey Business Journal,* March/April 2008. Reprinted with permission of Ivey Management Services on August 5, 2008.

Name Index

Abegglen, J. C., 432
Abueva, J. E., 458
Adams, J. Stacy, 404, 432
Aditya, R. N., 415, 433, 434
Adler, N. J., 389
Aeppel, T., 151
Agarwal, Sanjeev, 204, 237, 245, 247, 248
Ah Chong, L. M., 434, 435
Ahwan, A., 359
Ainuddin, R. Azimah, 317–328
Alanis, Adriana, 481
Alderfer, Clayton, 397, 399, 431
Al Emam, Rasha, 211
Alhabib, Maram, 211
Ali, A. J., 434, 435
Al-Kubaisy, A., 435
Almaney, A., 359
Al Sayegh, Abdullatif, 211
Altomonte, C., 105
Amba-Rao, Sita C., 515
Amin, Dimple, 188
Andersen, O., 204, 245
Anderson, Erin, 237, 247, 248
Annan, Kofi, 478
Appendino, Michele, 336
Aquino, Corazon, 73
Arino, A., 245
Armstrong, L., 252
Arnold, S., 515
Arnold, V., 420, 431, 435
Artise, J., 458
Aulakh, P., 247
Aupperle, K., 286
Axim, A. A., 434
Aziz, Tariq, 350
Aznar, Jose Maria, 337

Babakus, E., 433
Badawy, M. K., 434
Bafna, S. M., 183
Bailey, Jessica M., 107
Bailey, Michael, 54
Baker, James, 350
Baker, Stephen, 335–337
Bakhshian, Sara, 191
Balgimbaev, Nurlan, 502
Baliga, B., 287
Ball, Donald A., 23
Bamossy, G., 246
Banai, M., 458
Banerji, K., 245
Bangert, D. C., 458
Banks, John C., 246
Barkema, H., 205, 245

Barnevik, Percy, 265–266
Barnlund, Dean C., 346, 358
Barraclough, R. A., 358
Barshefsky, Charlene, 90
Bartlett, Christopher A., 189, 248, 268, 280, 286, 287, 288, 390, 435
Bass, B. M., 434
Baughn, Christopher C., 247
Beamer, K., 341
Beamer, L., 357
Beamish, Paul W., 315, 317–328, 435
Beauchamp, Tom L., 515
Behrman, J., 478, 484
Beinhocker, Eric, 179–181, 189
Bell, J., 205, 245
Bemish, Paul W., 246
Bengtsson, Ann McDonagh, 372, 373
Bennett, M., 434
Bennis, Warren, 426
Berg, D. M., 23, 105
Berlusconi, Silvio, 337
Berman, J. J., 146
Best, M. H., 315
Bhagat, R. S., 146, 297, 303, 307, 308, 315, 316, 390, 408, 431, 433, 435
Bhagwati, Jagdish, 43, 54, 248
Bhawuk, D. P. S., 147
Bigley, G. A., 432
Bijapurkar, Rama, 427
Billeness, Simon, 509
Bilsky, W., 147
bin Laden, Osama, 50
Birkinshaw, J., 287, 288, 304
Black, J. Stewart, 391, 415, 435, 457
Blokland, Paul, 182
Blunt, P., 431
Bochner, S., 114, 145, 359
Boddewyn, Jean J., 6, 23, 105
Boeri, Tito, 335
Bolton, K., 359
Bond, M. H., 141, 147, 359, 390
Borchert, Donald M., 515
Bordoloi, Sudnya, 223
Borghesi, Carol, 427
Boski, P., 433
Bowie, Norma E., 515
Bradach, J., 247
Bradbery, Raymond, 262
Brady, Aidan, 336–337
Brandt, Richard, 515
Brannen, Mary Yoko, 190, 192, 193, 194
Branzei, Oana, 516–521
Brett, Jeanne, 246, 430

Brewer, T., 105
Brewster, Chris, 118
Brien, M., 358
Bright, W., 359
Brin, Sergey, 476
Briscoe, D. R., 458
Brislin, R. W., 114, 145, 359
Brooks, Geraldine, 107
Brouthers, K., 105, 106, 246
Brown, Bernard E., 105
Buckley, Peter J., 23, 241, 248
Buckman, Bob, 306
Burns, T., 434
Burrows, Stephen J., 223
Bush, George W., 36, 56, 69, 73, 88
Butler, M. C., 458
Byas, Anand, 3
Byrne, John, 516

Cairncross, F., 391
Calori, R., 145
Capell, Kerry, 210–211
Carlisle, Kate, 335–337, 352
Carter, Adrienne, 223
Carter, Jimmy, 135, 363
Casse, P., 368
Casson, Mark, 23, 241, 248
Castro, Fidel, 66, 74
Cavanagh, Gerald F., 496, 515
Caves, Richard E., 13, 23
Cavusgil, S. T., 188
Cespedes, Frank V., 248
Chakravarthy, B., 287, 457
Chan, D-K., 147
Chan, Edwina H. S., 201
Chan, May, 190, 200
Chan, W., 287
Chandran, R., 105, 246
Chang, Sea-Jin, 24
Charan, Ram, 426
Chatterjee, S., 189
Chavez, Hugo, 55–57, 64, 73
Chen, V., 358
Chen Chong, 292
Cheney, Dick, 504
Cheng, J. L., 146
Chhabra, Vivek, 223
Child, J., 145
Chodynicka, A. M., 433
Choi, S. C., 130, 147
Choy, Linda, 189
Christophel, D. M., 358
Christopher, Warren, 127
Chu, Meng, 200

523

Clarke, C. C., 412
Clinton, Bill, 476
Clutterbuck, David, 287
Cohen, Herb, 362, 389
Cole, R. E., 432
Collett, P., 358
Conger, J. A., 434
Connolly, Norma, 195
Contractor, Farok, J., 234, 246, 247
Cooper, C. L., 432
Cooper, Simon, 398, 399
Copeland, L., 391, 434
Coplin, W., 106
Cosset, J., 106
Coulter, M., 435
Counts, Alex, 476
Coupland, N., 359
Covey, Stephen, 363
Crawford, S. E., 431
Cummings, L. L., 145, 390
Cushner, K., 146

Dahhan, O., 434
Daniels, John D., 23, 286
Das, B., 432
Das, T., 232, 246
Datta, D., 246
Davenport, T. H., 298, 315
David, K. H., 358
Davies, R., 481, 484
Dawson, C., 252
DeFillippi, R., 316
de Forest, M. E., 458
De George, Richard T., 494, 515
Delbecq, A. L., 390
Delene, Linda, 107
Delios, A., 106
Dell, Michael and Susan, 476, 477
Delphon de Vaux, Jean-Marc, 223
DeMente, B. L., 390
Deng Xiaoping, 140
Denning, S., 316
Deol, S., 368
De Soto, Hernando, 48, 54
Deutsch, Claudia, 459
DeVader, C. L., 434
de Witt, Melissa, 202–204
DiBenedetto, A., 105, 246
Dickson, M., 435
Digh, Patricia, 435
Dillard, J. P., 358
Dizard, J. W., 245
Domke-Damonte, D., 204, 245
Donaldson, Thomas, 515
Dorfman, P. W., 147, 433, 434, 435
Dowling, P. J., 457, 458
Doz, Yves I., 163, 189, 228, 246, 281–282, 287, 288
Drasgow, F., 430
Drenth, P. J. D., 434

Drost, E., 458
Drucker, Peter, 265, 286
Dunfee, Thomas W., 515
Dunlop, J. L., 146
Dunnette, M. D., 430, 431
Dunning, John J., 13, 23, 24, 239–242, 248
Dussuage, P., 245
Dwyer, Thomas, 359

Earley, P. C., 146, 358, 359, 409, 432, 433
Ebbers, Bernie, 419
Eccles, R., 247
Echikson, William, 53
Edmondson, Gail, 230–231
Einhorn, Bruce, 18, 197, 305
Ekeledo, I., 204–205, 245
Elenkov, D. S., 431
Elizur, D., 432
Eng, Dennis, 190, 200
Engardio, P., 474
Engdahl, R., 286
Engel, D. W., 445, 458
Englis, P., 303, 308, 316
Englund, George, 405
Erez, M., 146, 358, 432, 433
Erramilli, Krishna M., 204, 245, 247
Errunza, V., 106
Ewing, Jack, 98, 270, 430

Fahd, King, 127
Farrell, Diana, 179–181, 189
Fatehi, K., 106
Fealy, E., 106
Ferguson, G. J., 309
Ferguson, P. R., 309
Ferrell, O. C., 515
Fiedler, F. E., 416, 434
Finney, M., 455
Fisher, C. D., 457
Fisher, F., 287
Fisher, G., 390
Fishman, R., 107
Floisand, John, 262
Florida, Richard, 408, 433
Flynn, G., 431
Ford, D. L., Jr., 307
Fords, J. K., 431
Foster, D. A., 390
Foti, R. J., 434
Fowler, Geoffrey A., 201
Fox, Vincente, 36
Fraedrich, John, 515
Frankel, Jeffrey, 54
Frazee, Valerie, 383
Frederick, William C., 515
Freeman, C., 475, 483
French, D., 107
Frey, L. T., 433

Friedman, Thomas, 47, 86, 169
Fujisawa, Takeo, 395

Galbraith, J. R., 287
Gallo, Carmine, 399
Gamble, J., 106
Gangemi, Jeffrey, 477
Gannon, M. J., 409, 431, 432
Gao, G., 358
Garcia, Alain, 209
Garicano, L., 286
Garnier, G. P., 24
Garrette, B., 245
Garrison, Terry, 372
Garvin, D. A., 316
Gates, Bill, 292, 293, 476, 477
Gates, Melinda, 476, 477
Gatignon, Hubert, 237, 247, 248
Gelfand, M., 147
Gerstein, M. S., 287
Gerstner, Louis, Jr., 414, 415
Gessner, M. J., 420, 431, 435
Gesteland, R. R., 391
Getz, Kathleen A., 515
Ghoshal, Sumantra, 16–17, 24, 189, 248, 280, 286, 287, 288, 390, 435, 474
Ghosn, Carlos, 230–231
Gibson, C. B., 146, 359
Giffen, James H., 502
Giles, H., 358, 359
Gilpin, R., 54
Gitig, O., 107
Glenn, E., 358, 390
Glenn, P., 358, 390
Globerman, Stephen, 105, 106
Goldblatt, D., 54
Goldhar, J., 316
Goldsmith, Marshall, 346–347
Goleman, D., 434
Gomez-Mejia, L., 287
Govindarajan, V., 188, 189, 287, 315, 316
Graham, J. L., 246, 358, 368, 374–375, 389, 390
Granrose, C., 358
Greenberg, Cathy, 346
Greenberg, J., 359
Greene, Jay, 477
Greenwood, M. J., 412, 433
Greer, C. R., 431
Gregersen, Hal B., 391, 415, 435, 457
Griggs, L., 391, 434
Grosse, R., 478, 484
Grove, Andy, 426
Grove, Cornelius, 455
Grover, R., 390
Groves, M., 433
Gudykunst, W. B., 378
Guisinger, S. E., 23, 105
Gulati, Neeraj, 188

Gundykunst, W. B., 358
Gupta, A. K., 188, 189, 315, 316
Gupta, Deepak, 427
Gupta, U., 246
Gupta, V., 147, 435
Guptara, Prabhu, 372, 373
Gurr, Ted, 106
Guterman, Siegfried, 372
Guthrie, G. M., 114, 145, 358

Haaland, Jan I., 248
Haas, Robert D., 505, 506, 516
Hackman, J. R., 403, 432
Haleen, I., 107
Hall, Edward T., 131–132, 146, 147, 339, 358, 374, 390
Hall, G., 315
Hall, M. R., 339, 357, 358
Hall, R., 105
Hallowell, Willa, 455
Hamabe, Y., 106
Hamel, Gary, 24, 189, 236, 247, 248
Hamilton, R., 106, 274, 278, 287, 288
Hamm, Steve, 27
Hammond, A., 474, 483
Hampden-Turner, C., 422, 435
Hand, James, 112
Handleman, J., 515
Hanges, P. J., 147, 435
Harbison, M., 146
Harfenist, Jeffrey, 98
Harnish, D. L., 433
Harper, Stephen, 73
Harrigan, K., 245
Harris, M., 286
Hart, O., 286
Harveston, P., 316, 390
Harzing, A., 286
Haselberger, A., 458
Havrylyshyn, O., 106
Hayashi, Toshio, 178
Hayes, Samuel L., III, 134–135
Hedayati, Seyed Ali Asghar, 95
Hedlund, G., 286, 287
Heenan, D. A., 441
Held, D., 54
Hempel, C., 358
Hendrix, Anastasia, 331
Henisz, Witold, 105, 106
Hernandez, Greg, 196
Herskovits, M. J., 145
Herzberg, Frederick, 397, 400, 431
Hickson, D. J., 147
Hill, Charles W. L., 5, 23, 246, 247, 287, 315
Hill, Jonathan, 197
Hill, Richard E., 5, 23
Hitt, M., 287, 316
Hodgetts, R. M., 458
Hodgkinson, G. P., 431

Hofstede, Geert, 120–127, 131, 133, 137, 140, 146, 315, 390, 408, 421, 431, 433, 435
Holtshouse, D., 316
Hooghiemstra, R., 515
Hooker, J., 136–137, 147, 358, 390, 435
Hoppe, M., 435
Hoskisson, R., 287
Hough, L. M., 431
House, Robert J., 133, 147, 415, 416, 419, 431, 433, 434, 435
Hout, T., 189
Howard, John, 73
Howell, J. P., 434
Hu-Chan, Maya, 346
Hu Jintao, 104
Hulin, C. L., 430, 432
Hunt, J. G., 434
Huo, Y. P., 433
Hurrell, J. J., Jr., 433
Hurtha, Martin, 336
Hussein, Saddam, 74
Hwang, Peter, 247, 248
Hymer, S. H., 13, 23

Iacocca, Lee, 414
Ihlwan, M., 395
Imagawa, Toshihiro, 178
Imura, Hisako, 118
Inglehart, R., 408, 433
Ingrassia, Paul, 22
Inkpen, A. C., 246, 315, 435
Ip, Stephen, 196
Ireland, R., 287
Iwao, S., 147
Iyer, Govind, 427

Jabr, M. Hisham, 107
Jaeger, A., 287
Jago, A. G., 432
Jain, Subush C., 503
Janosik, R. J., 390
Javers, Eamon, 98
Javidan, M., 147, 435
Jawanda, Kanwal, 188
Jaworski, R. A., 458
Jennergren, P., 286
Jiang Zemin, 292
Jia Xinguang, 90
Johansson, J., 188
Johnson, J., 240, 248
Johnson, R., 315
Jonas, Adam, 231
Jones, C. A., 307
Jones, C. I., 105
Jones, M. L., 431
Jones, Raymond, 475, 478, 479, 481, 483, 484
Jons, Audra, 478, 479, 481, 483, 484
Josephberg, K., 107

Joshi, Mahesh, 154
Joyce, Romy, 286
Joyner, C., 106

Kagitcibasi, C., 130, 147
Kahn, R., 433
Kalemli-Ozcan, S., 107
Kamp, Mads, 270
Kanjautso, Dorothy Njobvu, 476, 477
Kant, Immanuel, 491
Kanungo, R. N., 431, 434
Kaplan, M. R., 431
Kashlak, Roger, 23, 105, 106, 154, 188, 189, 202–204, 246, 274, 278, 287, 288, 478, 479, 483, 484
Katz, D., 433
Kaufmann, D., 105
Kaur, R., 434
Keating, P., 286
Kedia, B. L., 297, 303, 308, 315, 316, 390, 431
Keita, G. P., 433
Ken, K., 431
Kerr, C., 146
Kerwin, Kathleen, 252, 291, 315
Ket de Vries, M. F. R., 433
Khan, Eshan Ullah, 505
Khidr, Qusai, 211
Khomeini, Ayatollah, 75
Kibaki, Mwai, 59
Kiley, D., 395
Kim, Chan W., 247, 248
Kim, D. K., 389
Kim, K., 286
Kim, U., 130, 147
Kim, Y., 358
Kindleberger, Charles, 248, 487
Kinney, T. A., 358
Kinsella, James, 112
Kirkpatrick, S. A., 415
Kitayama, Shinobu, 372, 431
Klineberg, O., 358
Kluckhohn, F., 117–120, 129, 146
Knickerbocker, F. T., 24
Knipp, Steven, 198
Kobrin, S., 67, 105, 106
Kogut, Bruce, 24, 205, 236, 240, 242, 245, 247, 248, 315, 479, 484
Kohli, Manoj, 427
Kolde, Endel J., 5, 23
Kolind, Lars, 270
Konigsberg, A. S., 245
Konrad, Alison, 459–467
Kotabe, M., 247
Koulecheff, Nadine, 337
Koza, M., 245
Kraay, A., 105
Kraimer, M. L., 458
Kramer, Mark R., 515

Kripalani, Manjeet, 182–183
Krishnan, B., 433
Krishnan, K. S., 434
Kukura, Sergei P., 75
Kumar, Sanjay, 188
Kundu, Sumit K., 234, 247
Kunii, Irene M., 18
Kwok, H., 359
Kwok, Lutricia S. M., 201

Laabs, J. L., 457
Lagace, Martha, 134–135
Lakshman, Nandini, 182–183, 223, 427
Lall, Sanjay, 248
Lam, N. M., 374–375, 390
La Monica, Paul R., 193
Landis, D., 146
Lansner, Thomas, 509
LaPlaca, Peter J., 503
La Porta, R., 107
Larson, L. L., 434
Latham, G. P., 432
Latta, G. W., 458
Laurent, Andre, 435
Lawler, Edward E., III, 287, 403, 411, 432
Lay, Kenneth, 419
Lee, John C. M., 201
Lee Kwan Yew, 72
Leggat, Rob, 90
Lei, D., 316
Leipziger, Deborah, 509
Le Marois, Jacques, 112
Leonard-Barton, D., 315
Lessard, D., 287
Leung, K., 432
Lewicki, R. J., 389
Lewin, A., 245
Lewis, Richard, 376, 390
Li, Sandy, 245
Lieberthal, Kenneth, 189
Li Kequiang, 104
Lin, C. Y., 389
Lin, Z., 358
Linn, J. J., 107
Lipp, G. D., 389
Litterer, J. A., 389
Liu, Donald, 190–201
Liu, Eva, 191
Locke, E. A., 415, 431, 432
Lohr, S., 314, 433
Lonner, W. J., 114, 145, 359
Lopez-de-Silanes, F., 107
Lorange, Peter, 246, 247, 287
Lord, R. G., 434
Lorenzi, Dena, 188
Loscher, Peter, 98
Losq, E., 106
Lu, C., 106

Lubatkin, M., 145, 189
Lubin, J. S., 458
Luqmani, Mushtaq, 107
Luthans, F., 458
Lyles, M., 227, 232, 246
Lyons, Daniel, 438
Lytle, A., 246

Machungwa, P. D., 431
Macridis, Roy C., 105
Madhok, Anoop, 246
Magee, Stephen, 240, 248
Maher, K. J., 434
Maignan, Isabelle, 488–489, 515
Makino, S., 246
Mallya, Vijay, 223
Malone, T. W., 435
Marcos, Ferdinand, 73
Markus, H. R., 431
Marquandt, M. J., 445, 458
Marr, Merissa, 201
Marsh, P., 358
Marton, K., 315
Masih, Iqbal, 504–505
Maslow, Abraham, 396–402, 431
Matoloni, Raymond J., Jr., 54
Matusik, S. F., 315
Mauborge, R., 287
McCance, M., 358
McCarthy, Michael J., 245
McClelland, David C., 397, 400, 431
McCroskey, J. C., 358
McCue, Andy, 342
McCulloch, Wendell H., Jr., 23
McGrew, A., 54
McKague, K., 481, 484
McManus, J., 240, 248
McMaster, John A., 336
McQuaid, S. J., 431
McShane, S. L., 397
Mead, R., 357
Medalye, J., 481, 484
Medvedev, Dmitry, 105
Mendenhall, M. E., 391
Meyer, J., 146
Mill, J. S., 515
Miller, D., 433
Miller, E. L., 458
Miller, Kent D., 24, 105, 106
Minetti, Juan, 480
Minton, J. W., 389
Mintu, A. T., 390
Mintzberg, H. J., 357, 390
Mirus, Rolf, 245
Misumi, J., 423, 434, 435
Mitchell, Jordan, 459–467
Mitchell, T. R., 434
Mitchell, W., 245
Mjoen, H., 247
Moberg, Dennis J., 496, 515

Mobley, W. H., 420, 431, 435
Mohammad, 93, 95, 134, 137
Mongkolporn, Usanee, 267
Montabaur, Daniela, 108–111
Montalbano, William D., 515
Moore, J., 286
Morita, Akio, 302
Morris, D., 358
Morrison, A., 162–164, 189, 246, 287
Morrison, A. J., 315, 415, 435
Morsbach, H., 358
Mourkogiannis, Nikos, 426
Moustafa, K. S., 408, 431, 433
Moutinho, Luiz, 107
Moy, Patsy, 200
Mugabe, Robert, 70
Mukherti, A., 287
Mulhern, Sarah, 336
Mullaney, T. J., 390
Muller, J., 252
Murray, Mike, 477
Murray, T., 315

Nadkarni, Anant G., 516–521
Nadler, D. A., 287, 432
Napier, N. K., 458
Napoleon, 92
Narayanan, W. K., 432
Nassar, Farid, 210
Natapermadi, Maman, 95
Nath, R., 432
Nathan, G., 316
Navaretti, Georgio Barba, 248
Nazarbaev, Nursultan, 502
Neider, Linda L., 316
Neuijen, B., 315
Newberry, W., 245
Newman, K. L., 409, 431, 432
Nohria, Nitin, 248, 286, 458
Nomani, A. Q., 146
Nonaka, I., 299, 301, 302, 315, 316
Noujaim, Matthew, 210
Nozawa, Shohei, 419
Nystrom, Paul C., 286, 430

Odinga, Raila, 59
O'Driscoll, M. P., 433
O'Driscoll, T., 435
Ohayv, D. D., 315
Omidyar, Pierre and Pam, 476, 477
Ono, Yomiko, 178
Orwall, Bruce, 192
Osborn, Richard N., 247
O'Shaughnessy, M., 358
Oskamp, S., 358
Ouchi, W., 287

Page, Larry, 476
Palau, Eduardo, 37
Palich, L., 287
Pan, Y., 205, 245

Paquet, G., 248
Park, Andrew, 18
Park, J., 286
Park, S., 246
Parkhe, Arvind, 232, 246, 247
Patton, George S., 363
Pearl, Daniel, 146
Penn, J. B., 36
Pennings, J., 205, 245
Perez, Antonio, 112
Perez, L., 107
Perlez, Jane, 22
Perlmutter, Howard J., 152, 188, 245, 441, 457
Perraton, J., 54
Peterson, M. F., 434, 435
Peterson, P., 410, 433
Peterson, R. B., 146, 458
Phatak, Arvind V., 23, 24, 54, 145, 176, 189, 286, 287
Phelan, S. E., 23, 105
Phillips, Carl, 435
Pinochet, Augusto, 64
Pitts, D., 286
Plamenatz, John, 105
Poister, T. H., 432
Pollack, J., 107
Poole, Henri, 112–113
Poor, J., 458
Porter, L. W., 403, 432
Porter, Michael E., 164, 189, 246, 475, 483, 515
Porter, R. E., 358
Poulsen, P. T., 431
Prada, M., 481, 484
Prahalad, C. K., 24, 163, 189, 236, 247, 248, 281–282, 288, 474, 483
Prescott, J., 286
Provera, Marco Tronchetti, 352
Prusak, L., 298, 315
Pugh, D. S., 146
Punett, Betty Jane, 23
Punnett, J., 433
Putin, Vladimir, 73, 105

Quaraeshi, Zahir A., 107

Racioppi, John, 262
Radebaugh, Lee H., 23
Rai, Saritha, 24
Ralston, David A., 488–489, 515
Ramaswami, Sridhar N., 204, 237, 247, 248
Rana-Deuba, A., 359
Randel, A., 358
Rangan, S., 287
Rangan, U. S., 390
Rao, C. P., 204, 245, 247
Ratiu, I., 358
Raviv, A., 286
Ravlin, E. C., 434

Redmon, W. K., 432
Redstone, Sumner M., 210
Reed, R., 316
Reeves, B., 435
Renn, R., 433
Resch, Inka, 335–337
Ressner, Jeffrey, 193, 198
Retsky, M., 107
Reynolds, C., 458
Richard, Alain, 337
Richards, Franchette, 455
Ricks, David A., 23, 146
Rieger, E., 433
Robbins, S. P., 435
Robert, R. E., 431
Roberts, Dexter, 90
Roberts, J., 204, 245
Robertson, Alistair, 346
Robertson, Ivan T., 432
Robins, S. P., 430
Robinson, M., 389
Robock, Stefan A., 106
Rodgers, W., 390
Roedy, Bill, 211
Rohter, Larry, 514
Ronen, S., 129–130, 146, 431
Root, Franklin R., 31, 245
Rosch, M., 358
Rosen, Robert, 435
Rosenbaum, Andrew, 373
Rosenberg, Tina, 54
Rosenzweig, P. M., 246, 315, 435, 458
Ross, William T., Jr., 515
Roth, K., 162–164, 189
Rowley, Ian, 230–231
Rudden, E., 189
Ruggles, R., 316
Rugman, Alan M., 23, 24, 248
Ruiz-Quintilla, S. A., 435
Ruki, Taufiqurrahman, 102
Russo, M., 246
Rutten, Lamon, 427

Saade, Edmond J., 55
Saaty, T., 188
Saban, C., 106
Sadrieh, Farid, 145, 146
Sagie, A., 432
Sagiv, L., 147
Salacuse, J. W., 390
Sambharya, R., 245
Samovar, L. A., 358
Sanchez-Runde, C. J., 409, 431, 432
Sanders, G., 315
Sano, Y., 390
Sanz, Antonio, 335
Saunders, D. M., 389
Schachter, O., 106
Schapiro, Mark, 515
Schein, E. H., 147, 434

Schmidt, Gidi, 262
Schmidt, Katherine A., 335–337
Schmitt, N., 431
Schoenfeldt, L. F., 457
Schorr, Juliet, 433
Schriesheim, Chester A., 316
Schuler, A. J., 351, 457, 458
Schuman, Michael, 193, 198
Schuman, Robert, 40
Schwartz, Adam, 95
Schwartz, Shalom, 130–131, 147
Schweiger, D., 162–163, 189
Sciolino, E., 146
Scoville, A., 107
Sessions, Paul L., 386
Sethi, D., 23, 105
Shamdasani, Ravina, 200
Shapiro, Daniel, 105, 106, 246
Shaw, J. B., 457
Shaw,, R. B., 287
Shay, A., 247
Sheehan, I., 304
Sheehan, T., 304
Shenkar, O., 129–130, 146, 431, 433, 458
Sherman, Hugh, 154
Shih, Stan, 305
Shikdar, A. A., 432
Shin, Y., 432
Shing, Jacky W. Y., 201
Shleifer, A., 107
Shull, F. A., Jr., 390
Shul-Shim, W., 458
Siddarthan, S., 248
Simmers, C., 359
Simon, J., 106
Singer, Marshall, 435
Singh, Bhavneet, 210
Singh, Harbir, 205, 236, 245, 247
Singh, Manmohan, 73
Singh, R. K., 315
Sinha, J. B. P., 147, 431
Sirota, D., 412, 433
Sivakumar, K., 205, 245
Skinner, David, 342
Smith, Geri, 55–57
Smith, Kennedy, 515
Smith, N. Vraig, 515
Smith, P. B., 359, 435
Snell, S., 287
Solmssen, Peter Y., 98
Somprasong Boonyachai, 267
Sood, James, 107
Sorenson, B., 107
Soru, Renato, 112
Spender, J. C., 316
Spero, Joan Edelman, 105
Srinivasan, Venu, 182
Sritama, Suchat, 197
Srivastava, B., 390
Staios, Olga, 386

Stalk, G., 432
Stanca, Lucio, 352
Starbuck, William H., 286, 430
Stark, Andrew, 515
Staw, B., 145
Steensma, H., 232, 246
Steers, R. M., 409, 431, 432, 433
Steiner, George A., 287
Stephens, G. K., 431
Stevens, Charles, 292, 293
Stevens, G. V., 105
Steverson, P. K., 431
Stewart, David, 515
Stewart, James B., 192
Stewart, L., 378
Stewart, Martha, 419
Stewart, T. A., 315
Stiglitz, Joseph E., 50, 54
Stokes, Alan, 451
Stone, R. J., 458
Stopford, John M., 248, 286
Streib, G., 432
Stripp, W., 389, 390
Strodtbeck, F. L., 117–120, 129, 146
Stroh, J. K., 391, 458
Subramaniam, K. V., 427
Sugimoto, N., 359
Suret, J., 106
Suterwalla, S., 431
Suzuki, Osamu, 182
Svensson, G., 189

Takeuchi, H., 299, 301, 304, 315, 316
Talal, Al Waleed bin, 211
Tallman, S., 247
Targetti, Lorenzo, 336
Tata, Ratan, 182–183
Tayeb, M. H. J., 435
Taylor, Paul W., 515
Taylor, R. R., 307
Taylor, V., 287
Tchuruk, Serge, 335
Teagarden, M. B., 458
Teece, David J., 247
Telvick, Marlena, 502
Teng, B., 232, 246
Terpstra, V., 245
Textor, R. B., 358
Thaksin Shinawatra, 267
Thomas, D. C., 434, 435, 449
Thomson, J., 481, 484

Thornton, Emily, 293, 315
Tierney, Christine, 291, 315
Ting-Toomey, S., 343, 358, 378
Torbiorn, I., 458
Toulouse, J. M., 433
Tretter, R., 286
Triandis, H. C., 111, 130, 132–133, 137, 145, 146, 147, 316, 348, 358, 359, 390, 430, 431, 432
Trompenaars, A., 422, 435
Trompenaars, Fons, 127–129, 146
Tse, D., 205, 245
Tsui, Sally P. M., 201
Tung, R. L., 453–454, 457, 458
Tusing, K. J., 358

Ungson, G., 432

Valery, Nicholas, 189
van de Vijver, F. J. R., 433
van Rooden, R., 106
VanScott, J. R., 431
Varner, I., 341, 357
Vayanos, D., 286
Veiga, J., 145
Velasquez, Manuel, 496, 515
Venables, Anthony, 248
Verbeke, Alain, 248
Vercelli, Rudy, 427
Vernon, R., 9, 23, 287
Very, P., 145
Victoriano, J., 107
Viner, Jacob, 32, 54
Vishny, R., 107
Vogel, Frank E., 134–135
von Blomberg, Peter, 98
Von Glinow, M. A., 397, 458
Vroom, V. H., 432
Vuchot, Didier, 335

Waddock, S., 478, 483
Wadia, Kris, 342
Wagh, Girish, 182
Walsh, Edward, 112, 113
Walter, I., 315
Walton, Clarence C., 494, 515
Ward, C., 359
Wayne, S. J., 458
Wee Liang Toon, 293
Wei, Shan-Jin, 54
Weinstein, David, 230
Weir, Davis, 515

Weiss, S. E., 227, 246, 389, 390, 391
Weissenberg, P., 434
Welch, D., 395
Welch, D. E., 457, 458
Welch, Jack, 426
Welford, Richard, 197
Wells, L., Jr., 286, 287
Wells, Louis T., 248
Wheeler, D., 481, 484
Whyte, W. F., 146
Wiemann, J., 358, 359
Wilk, L. A., 432
Williamson, Oliver E., 247
Wilson, S. R., 358
Wind, Y., 245
Won-Doornink, M., 358
Wong, Elyssa, 191
Wong-Rieger, D., 432
Woodcock, C., 246
Woodruff, David, 189
Wright, N. S., 433
Wright, Natanael, 337
Wrighton, Jo, 192
Wu, Helen, 199

Xi Jinping, 104, 105

Yamada, Kento, 178
Yamauchi, H., 432
Yan, A., 247
Yau, Charis, 195
Yoon, G., 130, 147
Yosha, O., 107
Young, D., 458
Young, Michael N., 190–201, 201
Yu, C., 245
Yukl, G., 433, 434
Yunus, Mohammad, 474, 475, 476, 477, 483

Zachary, G. Pascal, 509
Zander, Udo, 240, 242, 248, 315
Zanna, M. P., 147
Zeira, Y., 245, 458
Zellner, B., 106
Zhang Ying, 90
Zimman, Jon, 113
Zogby, James, 210
Zoido-Lobaton, P., 105
Zoltak, James, 192
Zou, S., 188

Subject Index

Ability, 396
Achievement cultures, 128
motivation theory, 400–401
her theories, 397
0
culture, 119
rvice's matrix
267
my, 131
s, 128
See also International
nd conventions
theory, 399
other theories, 397
rchy process, 155–156

Islamic law (Shari'ah)
in, 423–424
211–212
tures, 128
ols, rise of, 482–483
, 136
f South East Asian Nations
AN), 30
described, 37–38
Associative versus abstractive norms as barrier to communication, 344

Baby Shade Limited, 154
Bandwagon effect, 14
Banking and Islamic law, 93–95
Bargaining, 362
Barriers to effective communication, 341–350
associative versus abstractive norms, 344
content, 343
crossing the cultural chasm, 346–347
elaborate communication, 349–350
etiquette, 347–349
exaggeration, 349–350
harmony, 344
humor, 349
ideology versus pragmatism, 344
offshoring and, 342
potential hot spots, 351
practical insights, 342, 346–347, 350
saving face, 343–344
selective perception, 345
self-disclosure, 346–347
silence, 350
status differences, 342–343
stereotyping, 345–346
succinct communication, 349–350
symbols, 345
trust, 343
truthfulness, 349
Barter, 208–209
Basic human nature, culture and, 118–120
Basic registration, 88–89
Behavior control, 273
Behavioral perspective of leadership, 415–416
Being-oriented culture, 119
Berne Convention for the Protection of Industrial Property, 88
Bilateral treaty, 85
Black hole, 281
Bribery and corruption, 501–507
Asia-Pacific countries and, 102
in China, 98
defined, 501
factors responsible for, 503
FCPA and. *See* Foreign Corrupt Practices Act (FCPA)
Foreign Corrupt Practices Act and, 96–101
global corruption perception index, 505
in Kazakhstan, 502
as necessary cost of doing business, 502
in Nigeria, 504
OECD Antibribery Convention, 101, 102
practical insights, 1–2, 98
Rohm and Haas policy on, 508
Siemens and, 98
social costs of, 503–504
types of, 503
Buyback, 209–210

Cases
Americanization of Toyota, 249–252
Avoiding culture shock, 436–438
Beyond the green corporation, 470–474
CIENA's globalization, 184–188
Conflict resolution for contrasting cultures, 387–389
Cross culture in business and everyday life, 108–111
Email misunderstandings, 355–357
Global European consumer?, 53
Guide for multinationals, 284–286
High-tech transnationals, 25–27
Hondurans in sweatshops view opportunity, 511–514
Hong Kong Disneyland. *See* Hong Kong Disneyland case study
Islamic head scarves, 142–145
Leadership changes in China and Russia, 104–105
Love-hate relationship with Chavez, 55–57
Maytag's triad strategy, 150–152
My way or the highway at Hyundai and Kia, 392–395
Nora-Sakari. *See* Nora-Sakari: a proposed JV in Malaysia (revised) case study
Political impact on global negotiation, 360–361
Revival of I.B.M., 311–314
Rise of the Asian D-school, 482–483
Scandals and corruption, 485–487
Succession at Siemens, 429–430
Tata Cummins Limited, 202–204
Tata way: evolving and executing sustainable business strategy, 516–521
Tommy Hilfiger in India, 244
Trained manpower and low cost attract global giants, 2–3
Transferring knowledge at Ford, 289–291
U.S.-China misunderstandings, 330–331
Western Union. *See* Christina Gold leading change at Western Union
Women in South Korea, 456–457
World car, 22
Cash flows, counterattack strategy and, 174
Center for Economic Policy Research (CEPR), 48
Centrally planned economy, 62–64
Character of human beings, culture and, 118–120
Charisma, 417
Child labor, 504–507
China
commercial bribery in, 98
counterfeiting in, 90
cultural patterns of, 140–141
culture quiz on, 383
Dell Computers in, 18
encoding messages in words, 341
leadership changes in, 104–105
Microsoft in, 292–293
negotiating with, 374–376
guanxi, 376
-U.S. misunderstandings case study, 330–331

530 Subject Index

Christina Gold leading change at Western Union, 459–467
　advertising, 462
　agent network, 461
　alternatives considered, 463
　challenges with reorganizing, 464–466
　　decentralization at the regional level, 464–465
　　executive development programs, 465–466
　　recruiting for new positions, 465
　　responsibility, 464
　Christina Gold, 459–460
　considerations moving forward, 467
　consumers, 461
　culture change, 466
　First Data Corporation, 460
　introduction, 459
　reorganization, 463
　strategy, 462–463
　Western Union, 460–461
CIENA's globalization case study, 184–188
Citizenship salary system, 452
Civil law, 92–93
Civil society, 478
Civil strife, 73–75
Classifying employees, 442–443
Code law, 92–93
Codes of conduct of international companies. See Ethics, international codes of
Coercive potential, 74
Cold War era, 65–66
Collaborative strategy, 160
Collectivism, 120–121
　horizontal or vertical, 132
　individualism versus, 120–121, 408–409
　in-group, 133–134
　institutions and, 134
　knowledge management and, 302–303
　power distance versus, 122, 123
　in Trompenaar's framework, 128
Combination export manager (CEM), 206–207
Combination of knowledge, 302
Combination strategic control, 282
Commercial treaties, 85–90
Commoditization stage of knowledge life cycle, 304, 306
Common law, 92–93
Common Market. See European Union
Common market, 30, 31, 32. See also Economic integration
Common Market of the South, 38–39
Communication, 330–359
　appropriate language for, 332–334
　barriers to. See Barriers to effective communication
　cases, 330–331, 355–357

　computer-mediated, 337–338, 350, 352, 353
　cross-cultural process of, 332–334
　defined, 332
　effectiveness of, 332
　encoding messages in words, 341
　English and, 334, 335–336
　environmental context of, 340–341
　gestures, 339
　guidelines for managing, 353–354
　in high-contact cultures, 339–340
　in high-context cultures, 340–341
　information technology and, 350, 352
　jargon and, 333
　kinesic behavior and, 338–339
　in low-contact cultures, 340
　in low-context cultures, 340–341
　medium of, 334–340
　national and cultural influences on, 332–334
　noise, 332
　nonverbal, 334, 338–340
　practical insights, 335–336, 341, 351, 352
　proxemics and, 339–340
　summary, 354
　verbal, 334, 336
Company-specific risk, 69
Comparison of information, 299–300
Compensation, 450–453
　allowances and, 452
　benefits and, 444, 452
　citizenship salary system, 452
　headquarters salary system, 450, 452
　incentives and, 452
　as major function of IHRM, 444
　perks, 446–447
　practical insights, 446–447
　taxes and, 452–453
Competition, 150–201
　cases, 150–152, 184–188
　economic integration and, 33–34
　emerging markets and. See Emerging market environments
　ethnocentrism and, 152
　firm-level strategies, 171–179
　　core competency leveraging, 171–173
　　counterattack, 173–175
　　glocalization. See Glocalization
　foreign market. See Foreign market entry
　geocentrism and, 152–153
　managing a portfolio of country subsidiaries, 159–161
　modern international strategic orientation, 162–166
　　global orientation, 163
　　multidomestic orientation, 163–164
　　transnational orientation, 164

　value chain and. See Value chain
　overseas expansion. See Internationalization
　polycentrism and, 152
　practical insights, 154, 169, 178
　roots of international strategy, 152–153
　summary, 183–184
Competitive advantage
　international human resources management and, 454–455
　strategic objectives and sources of, 16–19
Competitive forces facilitating internationalization, 155
Competitive-strength matrix, 159–161
Competitiveness, country specific, 50–52
Complex integration strategies, 169–170
Computer-mediated communicating, 337–338, 350, 352, 353
Conflict
　defined, 377
　low- and high-context cultures and, 377, 378
　negotiation and, 376–378
　resolution of, for contrasting cultures case study, 387–389
Connecting information, 300
Consensus, 61
Consequences of information, 299–300
Consequentialism, 489–490
Conservation, 131
Consideration, 415–416
Context and culture, 131–132
Contingency perspective of leadership, 416
Contract manufacturing, 210
Contribution, 281
Controlling international strategies and operations, 271–286
　cases, 284–286
　comprehensive framework of control, 278–279
　designing effective, 279–282
　international environments and, 275–279
　　cultural distance, 276
　　economic factors, 277–278
　　political risk, 276–277
　　restrictions, 276–277
　managerial control process. See Managerial control process
　objectives of, 271
　practical insights, 281
　problems with, 274–275
　subsidiaries and. See Subsidiaries
　summary, 282–283
　types of systems, 272–274
　　behavior control, 273
　　input control, 272–273

Subject Index

knowledge of the transformation, 272
output control, 273–274
output measure availability and, 272
Convention on Combating Bribery of Foreign Public Officials in International Business Transactions, 101
Conventions, 85. *See also* International treaties and conventions
Convergence of cultures, 115–116
Conversation, 300
Copyrights, 88–90
Core competencies, 171–173
Core competency leveraging, 171–173
Core products, 171–172
Corporate social responsibility, 488–489. *See also* Ethics
defined, 488, 497
drivers of, 488–489
inside-out, 497–499
integrating with business operations, 496–500
negative duty approach to, 489
outside-in, 499–500
philanthropy, 497
positive duty approach to, 489
responsive, 497
strategic, 497–500
value chain activities, 497–499
Cost-reduction motives for establishing foreign operations, 11–13
Counterattack, 173–175
Counterfeiting, 88–90
Countertrade, 208–210
buyback, 209–210
counterpurchase, 209
defined, 208
downsides and risks of, 208
pure barter, 208–209
switch trading, 209
Country-level risk
internationalization and, 155
politics and, 58, 69, 76–77. *See also* Political risk
Country-specific economic integration, 30–31
Creation stage of knowledge life cycle, 303–304, 306
Cross-subsidization strategy, 14, 160–161
counterattack and, 174–175
Cultural complexity, 132
Cultural distance, 276
Cultural environment, 108–147
cases, 108–111, 142–145. *See also* Christina Gold leading change at Western Union
communication and. *See* Communication

controlling international operations and, 274–275
convergence of, 115–116
coping with culture shock, 118
defined, 111
dimensions of, 117–139
doing business in Islamic countries, 134–135
GLOBE studies. *See* Global Leadership and Organizational Behavior Effectiveness (GLOBE) project
Hall's framework, 131–132
Hofstede's framework. *See* Hofstede's framework for describing a culture
Hooker's framework, 136–137
Kluckhohn and Strodbeck's framework, 117–120
language barriers, 137
organizational cultures, 137, 139
religious differences, 137
Ronen and Shenkar's framework, 129–130
Schwartz's framework, 130–131
synthesis of, 133
Triandis's framework, 132
Trompenaar's framework, 127–129
divergence of, 116
errors in decision making and, 384–385
ethnocentrism and, 116
external, 115
geocentrism and, 116
glass ceiling for women in South Korea, 456–457
internal, 114–115
international management functions and, 114–117
knowledge management and, 306–308
language and. *See* Language and culture
leadership and. *See* Leadership, across cultures and borders
management styles and, 139–141
China, 140–141
Germany, 140
Islamic countries, 134–135
Japan, 139–140
Mexico, 141
needs theories and, 401–402
negotiation and, 368–369
objective, 111–113
organizations and, 114–117
parochialism and, 116
practical insights, 112–113, 118
process theories and, 405
sensitivity to, 116–117
subjective, 111–113
summary, 141

technology transfers and, 296–298
training and development practices and, 445
work motivation and job satisfaction, 407–411
Cultural relativism, 492–494
Cultural sensitivity, 116–117
Cultural syndrome
Hofstede's framework and, 120
Triandris's framework and, 132
Culture, 111. *See also* Cultural environment
Culture shock
in America, 455
avoiding, case study, 436–438
coping with, 118
defined, 449
negotiation and, 373
selecting expatriates and, 449–450
Customs union, 30, 31

Data, 299
Decision making, 380–381
deductive reasoning and, 384
defined, 379
descriptive approach to, 379
implications for managers, 385
inductive reasoning and, 384
internal and external factors, 383–384
nonprogrammed decisions, 381–383
prescriptive approach to, 379–383
process of, 379–389
programmed decisions, 380–381
sources of error in, 384–385
escalation of commitment, 385
Declaration, 85
Deductive reasoning, 384
Defensive (reactive) strategy, 160
Dell Computers in China, 18
Democracy, 62–64
Deontology, 491
Department of Justice, 96, 97
Dependent subsidiary, 281
Deprivation, relative, 73–75
Diffuse culture, 128
Diffusion stage of knowledge life cycle, 304, 306
Dimensions of value orientation, 117–120
Direct exporting, 207
Disneyland case study. *See* Hong Kong Disneyland case study
Dissemination risk, 234–235
Distributive approaches to negotiations, 370
Divergence of cultures, 116
Diversification, 79
Doing-oriented culture, 119
Dual-career expatriates, 453
Dynamic effects of economic integration, 33

Economic integration, 32–34
 country level, 30–31
 dynamic effects of, 33
 regional. *See* Regional economic agreements
 static effects of, 32–33
 supply-side effects of, 33–34
Economic union, 30–31
Economies of scale, 16–17, 33
Efficiency, global strategy and, 17
Egalitarianism, 131
Egoism, 490
Elaborate communications, 349–350
E-mail, 337–338
 in Italy, 352
 in Mexico, case study, 355–357
 misunderstandings case study, 355–357
 role of, 350, 352
Emerging market environments, 179–183
 design and, 183
 distribution and, 181
 middle-class market, 179–181
 packaging of, 181
 practical insights, 182–183
 pricing and, 181
 promotion and, 181, 183
Employment practices and policies, 501
End products, 172
Environmental protection
 EU laws concerning, 90–92
 host country laws, 96
Equity-based foreign ventures, 217–218
Equity international joint ventures (EIJVs), 219–228
 advantages of, 224–225
 conditions influencing, 221–222
  acquisition of knowledge and expertise, 222
  integrated network of subsidiaries, 221
  intellectual property, 221
  legislation, 221
  protecting a profitable market, 221
 cooperative strategies, 220
 defined, 219
 described, 219–221
 disadvantages of, 225–227
 importance of having the right partner, 227
 making them work. *See* Making international collaborative initiatives work
 motives for, 222–224
 negotiating, 227–228
 practical insight, 223
 typical, 220
Equity theory of motivation, 404

Escalation of commitment, 385
Ethics, 498–521
 bribery and corruption. *See* Bribery and corruption
 business conduct integrated with, 507–510
  actions not words, 509–510
  committed top management, 507
  formal program to implement, 507–508
  line managers to train employees, 508–509
  organizational identity, 507
  strict enforcement, 509
  written company code, 507, 508
 cases, 485–487, 511–514, 516–521
 child labor, 504–507
 corporate social responsibility and. *See* Corporate social responsibility
 defined, 487
 distinctions in international management, 493
 international codes of, 501
 moral norms and, 494–495
 moral philosophies and. *See* Moral philosophies
 negative duty approach, 489
 negotiations, 378–379
 positive duty approach, 489
 practical insights, 380–381, 502, 504, 509
 real-life dilemmas, 487–488
 relativism and, 379
 rights and, 495
 summary, 510
 sweatshops, 504–507
 universalism and, 378–379
 a whole world of ethical differences, 380–381
Ethnocentric staffing approach, 439
 compared to other approaches, 441
Ethnocentrism, 116
 international strategies based on, 152
Etiquette in communication, 347–349
Euro, 31
European Atomic Energy Community (EAEC), 40
European Coal and Steel Community (ECSC) Treaty, 40, 41
European Community (EC), 40–41. *See also* European Union (EU)
European Economic Community (EEC), 40–41
European Union (EU), 11, 27, 30, 31, 40
 achievements to date, 42
 from Common Market to economic union, 41
 described, 39–42
 environmental laws within, 90–92

 intellectual property and, 87
 Maastricht Treaty and, 42
 map of, 40
 origin of, 40
 Single European Act and, 41
 Treaty of Rome and, 40–41
Executive agreements, 85
Expatriates, 448–454
 culture shock and, 449–450
 defined, 448
 managing, 450–454
  compensation issue, 450–453
  cost of failure, 450
  dual-career, 453
  repatriation, 453–454
  safety issues, 451
Expectancy theory of motivation, 402–404
Expected return, internationalization of, 155
Explicit knowledge, 301
 knowledge creation and, 301–302
Export department, 207
Export sales subsidiary, 207
Exports (exporting), 206–207
 combination export manager, 206–207
 direct, 207
 glocalization of, 177
 indirect, 206–207
 manufacturer's export agent, 207
External-oriented cultures, 129
Externalization of knowledge, 302
Extrinsic factors, 400

Facilitating payments, 96
Facilitation, 74
Femininity as a cultural dimension, 122–125
 power distance versus, 125
 work motivation and, 410
Financial markets, globalization of, 46
Firm size, growth of, 33
First-to-file standard, 87
First-to-invent standard, 87
Ford case study, 288–291
Foreign Corrupt Practices Act (FCPA), 96–101
 affirmative defenses, 100
 antibribery provisions, 98–99
 background, 97
 basic provisions of, 97
 enforcement, 97, 98
 payment by intermediaries, 97
 permissible payments, 100
 sanctions against bribery, 100–101
 third-party payments, 99
 universalism and, 378–379
Foreign direct investment (FDI), 4
 as equity-based ventures, 217–218
 horizontal, 238
 modes of. *See* Modes of entry into foreign markets

theory of, 238–242
    alternative, 242
    choice of entry mode, 238–239
    fundamental questions, 239
    internalization of, 239, 240–241
    location advantage, 241–242
    market failures and, 240–242
    obtaining low-cost inputs, 238
    ownership advantages, 239
    serving local markets, 216
  vertical, 238
Foreign market entry, 156–159
  comparing and ranking targeted countries, 159
  decision making, 159
  identifying company objectives, 156
  key success factors, 157–159
  modes of. *See* Modes of entry into foreign markets
  opportunities and constraints, 72
  preliminary country screening, 157
Foreign product diversity, 254
Foreign sales as a percentage of total sales, 254
Foreign sales branches, 207
Foreign sales subsidiaries, 207
Foreign subsidiary roles, 280–281
Franchisee, 215–216
Franchising, 215–217
  agreements, 217
  defined, 215
Franchisor, 215–216
Free trade agreement, 34. *See also specific agreements*
Free trade area (FTA), 30, 31
Free Trade Area of the Americas (FTAA), 30
Freight costs, falling, 46–47
Friendship, commerce and navigation (FCN) treaties, 85–86
Future, society's view of the, 119, 127
Future-oriented culture, 119

Gender egalitarianism, 135–136
General Agreement on Tariffs and Trade (GATT), 27–29
  replacement of, 29
  Uruguay Round, 28, 29
  what was left undone, 28–29
Geocentric staffing approach, 439
  compared to other approaches, 441
Geocentrism, 116
  international strategies based on, 152–153
Geographic expansion, 252–253
Germany, culture and management styles in, 140
Gestures, 339
Global area structure, 260–263
  advantages of, 261–263

  drawbacks of, 263
  organization chart of, 261
Global companies, 8
  largest, 8–9, 10
Global European consumer case study, 53
Global labor force, 46
  backroom operations in India, 47
Global leadership, 424–427. *See also* Leadership
Global Leadership and Organizational Behavior Effectiveness (GLOBE) project, 419–423
  assertiveness, 136
  culture construct definitions, 420
  described, 419–420
  findings of, 420–421
  gender egalitarianism, 135–136
  human orientation, 136
  in-group collectivism, 133–134
  institutional collectivism, 134
  integrative model of effectiveness, 422
  performance orientation, 136
  power distance and, 421
  subordinateship and, 421
Global macroeconomic environment, 27
  cases, 25–27
  country specific, 50–52
  economic integration. *See* Economic integration
  GATT, 27–29
  globalization. *See* Globalization
  new global economy, 27–28
  practical insights, 36–37, 47
  regional agreements. *See* Regional economic agreements
  summary, 52
  trade blocs, 30–31
Global orientation, 163
Global political system, 62
Global product structure, 259–260
  benefits of, 260
  conditions favoring, 259–260
  drawbacks of, 260
  organization chart of, 259
Global social enterprise, 470–484
  beyond the green corporation, 470–474
  cases, 470–474, 482–483
  civil society and, 478
  defined, 474
  emerging-nation objectives, 475
  foundation of, 474–475
  innovation and knowledge from, 479–480
  local enterprise network, 480–481
  micro-enterprise collaboration and, 475–478
  Minetti of Argentina, 480–481
  practical insights, 476–477, 480–481
  reciprocity, 479–480

  summary, 482
  sustainability, 480–481
Global staffing approach, 439
  compared to other approaches, 441
Global strategy, 16–19
  achieving efficiency, 17
  innovation and learning, 18–19
  managing risks, 17–18
Globalization, 44–50
  case study, 184–188
  critics of, 44, 49–50
  defined, 44
  falling freight costs, 46–47
  of financial markets, 46
  global labor force, 46–47
  growth in international trade and commerce, 44–45
  innovations in information technology and transportation, 45
  porous borders between countries, 45–46
  supporters of, 44, 47–49
GLOBE studies. *See* Global Leadership and Organizational Behavior Effectiveness (GLOBE) project
Glocalization, 175–179
  defined, 176
  of exports, 177
  of foreign affiliates, 176–177
  of management, 176
  of production, 178–179
  of products, 177–178
Goal-setting theory, 404
Government. *See also* Political environment
  as facilitator of internationalization, 153
  policy uncertainties, 57–58
Green corporation, 470–474
Greenfield investment, 218
Gross domestic product (GDP), 8–9
  global, 44–45
Group-oriented society, 120
Growth strategies, 159–160
Guilt versus shame cultures, leadership in, 418–419

Halliburton's disclosure of bribes in Nigeria, 504
Hall's framework for describing a culture, 131–132
Harmony, 344
  as a cultural characteristic, 131
Harmony-with-nature orientation, 118
Headquarters salary system, 450, 452
Herzberg's motivator-hygiene theory, 400
  compared to other theories, 397
Heterarchy, 266–271
Hierarchical societies
  Kluckhohn and Strodtbeck's framework, 120
  Schwartz's framework, 131

High-contact cultures, 339–340
High-context cultures, 131
    communication in, 340–341
    conflict within, 377, 378
High-tech transnationals case study, 25–54
Hofstede's framework for describing a culture, 120–127
    collectivism, 120–122
    femininity, 122–125
    individualism, 120–122
    masculinity, 122–125
    power distance, 121–122, 123, 125
    scores for countries using, 126
    time orientation, 125, 127
    uncertainty avoidance, 122, 123
Home country risk, 76–77
Hondurans in sweatshops view opportunity case study, 511–514
Hong Kong Disneyland case study, 190–201
    company background, 190–191
    concluded deal, 196
    customer complaints, 200
    Disney in China, 193
    Disney in Paris, 192–193, 194
    Disney in Tokyo, 191–192, 193, 194
    external liaison with mainland travel agents, 201
    Hong Kong tourism industry and, 193–196
    human resources management, 198
    local cultural responsiveness, 198–199
    Lunar New Year holiday fiasco, 199–200
    marketing, 197–198
    negative publicity, 199–200
    new promotion, 200–201
    operations, 197–199
    product offerings, 197
    rocky start, 196–197
    setting the course for eventual success, 201
    working conditions, 200
Hooker's framework for cultural differences, 136–137
Horizontal foreign direct investment (HFDI), 238
Host-country attractiveness versus competitive-strength matrix, 159–161
Host-country environmental factors, 275–279
    comprehensive framework of international control, 278–279
    cultural distance, 276
    economic factors, 277–278
    political risk, 276–277
    restrictions, 276–277
Host-country national (HCN), 442–443
Host-country political risk, 71–75
    anticipated political decisions, 72
    assessing, 71–72, 76–77
    civil strife and, 73–75
    coercive potential and, 74
    control system and, 276–277
    decision-making processes and, 72
    facilitation and, 74
    government changes and, 73
    institutionalization and, 74
    key decision makers, 72
    party-leader changes and, 73
    past government policies, 72
    power of dominant groups and, 71
    regime legitimacy and, 74
    religious influences on, 73
    strength and bargaining power of legislative branch, 72
Host-country-specific laws, 95–96
Human orientation, 136
Human resources development (HRD), 445–446
Human resources management. See International human resources management (IHRM)
Human rights
    in Myanmar (Burma), 509
    theory of, 491
Humor in communication, 349
Hyundai case study, 392–395

I.B.M.'s revival case study, 311–314
Ideology versus pragmatism as barrier to communication, 344
Implementer, 281
Implicit perspectives of leadership, 416–417
In-group collectivism, 133–134
Independent subsidiary, 281
India
    backroom operations, 47, 169
    great Indian beer rush, 223
    humor backfiring in, 350
    job opportunities in, 427
    leadership in, 423
    mammoth middle-class market in, 179–183
    McDonald's in, 78, 158
    Tata Cummins Limited case study, 202–204
    Tata way, 516–521
    Tommy Hilfiger in, case study, 244
    trained manpower and low cost case study, 2–3
    world's cheapest car in, 182–183
Indirect exporting, 206–207
Individualism, 120
    collectivism versus, 120–121, 408–409
    horizontal or vertical, 132
    knowledge management and, 302–303
    power distance versus, 122, 123
    scores for countries in, 126
    in Trompenaar's framework, 128
Individualistic orientation, 120
Indonesian banking, 95
Inductive reasoning, 384
Information, 299
    transformation of, 299–300
Information technology, 45
    communications and, 350, 352
Initiation of structure, 415–416
Innovation
    global enterprise initiatives, 479–480
    as a global strategy, 18–19
Input control, 272–273, 274
Inside-out approach to strategic corporate social responsibility, 497–499
Institutional collectivism, 134
Institutionalization, 74
Insurance, 79–80
Integration strategies, 166–171
Integrative approach to negotiations, 370–371
Intellectual autonomy, 131
Intellectual capital, 299
Intellectual property and EIJVs, 221
Intellectual property rights, 86
Intellectual property theft, 84–90
    international custom and, 84–85
    international law creation and, 84
    Madrid Protocol, 88–89
    patents, 87–88
    practical insight, 90
    trademarks, copyrights, and manufacturing processes, 88–90
    treaties and conventions, 86–90
Interaction between international politics and economics, 62–67
    Cold War era and, 65–66
    demise of the Soviet Union and, 66
    international economic and political relations, 67
    nineteenth-century imperialism and, 65
    political concerns and economic policy, 66–67
Interdependence and multidirectional integration, 168
Internal-oriented cultures, 129
Internalization, 239, 240–241
    of knowledge, 302
International business, 5–6
International codes of conduct. See Ethics, international codes of
International collaboration imperative, 218–219
International companies, 7–9
    foreign market entry modes, 9
    global ranking of, 8
    largest, 8–9, 10
International competition. See Competition
International Court of Justice, 83

International custom, 84–85
International division, 256–258
	advantages of, 256–257
	disadvantages of, 257–258
	factors favoring the adoption of, 256
	as no longer an appropriate structure, 257–258
International economic situation, 370
International environment, 19–20
International events and political risks, 77
International human resources management (IHRM), 438–439
	cases, 436–438, 456–457
	competitive advantages and, 454–455
	defined, 439
	expatriates. See Expatriates
	major functions of, 441–448
		classifying employees, 442–443
		compensation and benefits, 444, 446–447
		labor relations, 445, 448
		performance evaluation, 443
		recruitment, 441
		selection, 441
		training and development, 444–445
	practical insights, 451
	subsidiaries. See Subsidiaries, managing and staffing
	summary, 456
International Labor Organization, 85
International law, 82–83
	intellectual property theft. See Intellectual property theft
	legal environment, 80–82
	nature of, 82–83
	sources of, 84
	treaties and conventions. See International treaties and conventions
	World Court, 83
	World Trade Organization, 83
International management, 2–24
	cases, 2–3, 22
	culture and, 114–117
		management styles and, 139–141
	defined, 6–7
	environment of international management, 19–20
	foreign direct investment and, 4
	global strategy. See Global strategy
	glocalization of, 176
	international business and, 5–6
	international companies and, 7–9
	model of, 21
	motives for foreign operations. See Motives for foreign operations
	practical insights, 18
	setting for, 3–5
	summary, 20–21

International matrix structure, 264–266
International Monetary Fund (IMF), 62
International negotiation, 362. See also Negotiation
International network theory, 242
International organizations and groups, political risk and, 76–77
International risk versus return portfolio, 161–162
International Searching Authority (ISA), 88
International strategic alliances, 228–232
	defined, 229
	making them work. See Making international collaborative initiatives work
	rationale for, 229
	between Renault and Nissan, 230–231
	risks of, 229–232
International treaties and conventions, 85–90. See also specific treaties and conventions
	definitions, 85
	friendship, commerce, and navigation, 85–86
	protection of international property rights, 86–90
Internationalization, 153–156
	analytical hierarchy process and, 155–156
	competitive forces and, 155
	country risk and, 155
	expected return and, 155
	facilitators of, 153–155
	government and political forces and, 153
	local products go global, 154
	locations for, 155–156
	market forces and, 154–155
	technological forces and, 153–154
Internet negotiations, 376
Intrinsic-extrinsic need theory, 400
Intrinsic factors, 400
Islamic law (Shari'ah), 93–95
	banking under, 93–95
	doing business under, 134–135
	women's head scarves, 142–145
Italy, e-mail in, 352

Japan
	building trust with, 366–367
	conflict resolution case study, 387–389
	culture and management styles, 139–140
	leadership in, 423
Jargon, 333
Joint ventures
	equity international. See Equity international joint ventures (EIJVs)

	making them work. See Making international collaborative initiatives work
	nature of, 218
	Nora-Sakari. See Nora-Sakari: A proposed JV in Malaysia (revised) case study
	as proactive hedges, 77–78
	strategic alliances. See Strategic alliances
	Tata Cummins Limited case study, 202–204

Kazakhstan, bribery in, 502
Kenya, political risk in, 59
Key success factors for foreign market entry, 157–159
Kia case study, 392–395
Kidnapping risk, 75
Kinesic behavior, 338–339
Kluckhohn and Strodtbeck's framework for describing a culture, 117–120
Knowledge, 298–310. See also Technology
	cases, 289–291, 311–314, 317–328
	creation of, 301–304, 307–308
	data, 298–299
	defined, 299
	explicit, 301
	global enterprise initiatives, 479–480
	information, 299
		transformation of, 299–300
	integration of strategic processes with, 306–308
	intellectual capital, 299
	learning organization, 309
	life cycle of. See Knowledge life cycle
	management of, 300–303, 306–308
	in organizations, 298–300
	strategic significance of, 298–300
	summary, 309–310
	tacit, 300–301
	of the transformation process, 272
	in transnational and global organizations, 308
Knowledge life cycle, 303–306
	commoditization stage, 304, 306
	creation stage, 303–304, 306
	diffusion stage, 304, 306
	fear of mistakes and, 304
	mobilization stage, 304, 306
	practical insights, 305
Knowledge-production system, 306
Koran, 93

Labor mobility, 33
Labor relations, 445–448
Language and culture, 114
	barriers created by, 137
	communication and, 332–334
	signs in English, 138

Lawmaking treaties, 85
Leadership, 413–435
　across cultures and borders, 417–423
　　functions of leadership, 418
　　GLOBE project, 419–423
　　in guilt versus shame cultures, 418–419
　in an increasingly connected world, 424
　cases, 429–430
　charisma and, 417
　consideration and, 415–416
　defined, 413
　global, 424–427
　India's got a job for you, 417
　initiation of structure and, 415–416
　non-Western, 423–424
　　Arab world, 423–424
　　India, 423
　　Japan, 423
　　nurturant, 423
　path-goal theory, 416
　perspectives of
　　behavioral, 415–416
　　contingency, 416
　　implicit, 416–417
　　transformational, 417
　perspectives on, 414–417
　　trait-based, 414–415
　practical insights, 425, 426, 427
　real job description, 426
　remote, 425
　summary, 428
Learning from foreign operations, 18–19
Learning organization, 309
Legal environment, 80–107
　cases, 104–105
　Convention for Combating Bribery, 101, 102
　equity international joint ventures, 221
　FCPA. See Foreign Corrupt Practices Act (FCPA)
　host-country, 95–96
　international law. See International law
　nation-states, 92–95
　　civil law, 92–93
　　classifications of, 92
　　common law, 92–93
　　complicating factors, 92
　　Islamic law, 93–95
　negotiators and, 369–370
　practical insights, 90, 95
　regional trade blocs, 90–92
　summary, 102–104
　treaties and conventions. See International treaties and conventions
　understanding laws in the international context, 80–82
　　concept of law, 81
　　functions of law, 82
　　requirements of an effective legal system, 81–82
Legitimacy, 61
Levi Strauss & Company, 505–506
Licensee, 210
Licensing, 211–215
　advantages of, 212
　agreements, 212–215
　　components of complex, 212–213
　　preparing, 215
　　steps before entering, 214
　defined, 211
　disadvantages of, 213–214
　reasons for use of, 210, 212
Licensor, 210
Lobbying, 78
Local enterprise network, 481
Location advantage, 241–242
Low-contact cultures, 340
Low-context cultures, 131–132
　communication in, 340–341
　conflict within, 377, 378

Maastricht Treaty on European Union, 42
Macro risks, 70–71
Macroeconomic environment
　global. See Global macroeconomic environment
　political. See Political environment
　uncertainty and, 57–58
Madrid Protocol, 88–89
Making international collaborative initiatives work, 232–234
　building trust in small steps, 232
　compatible partners, 232–233
　creating and maintaining equal power, 233–234
　management control, 234
　ownership control, 234
　patience, 234
Management, 6–7
Managerial control process, 271–275
　antecedent conditions, 272–273
　behavior control, 273
　input control, 272–273, 274
　knowledge of the transformation process, 272
　main elements in, 272
　output control, 273–274
　output measure availability, 272
　planning and, 272
　problems of, 274–275
　types of, 272–274
Manufacturer's export agent, 207
Market economy, 62–64
Market extension, 337
Market forces facilitating internationalization, 154–155
Market-seeking motives for establishing foreign operations, 9, 11

Masculinity as a cultural dimension, 122–125
　power distance versus, 125
　scores for countries in, 126
　work motivation and, 410
Maslow's need hierarchy theory, 397–399
　compared to other theories, 397
Mastery as a cultural characteristic, 131
　over nature, 118
Matrix structure, 264–266
Maytag's triad strategy case study, 150–152
McClelland's achievement motivation theory, 400–401
　compared to other theories, 397
McDonald's
　in India, 78, 158, 178
　in Japan, 178
Meaning of Working (MOW) study, 405–407
MERCOSUR (Mercado Común del Sur), 38–39
Mexico
　cultural patterns of, 141
　NAFTA and, 34–36
　Volkswagen, 49
Micro-enterprise collaboration, 475–478
Micro risks, 70–71
Microfinance, 475–478
Microsoft in China, 292–293
Minetti of Argentina, 480–481
Mixed-oriented culture, 119
Mobilization stage of knowledge life cycle, 304, 306
Modes of entry into foreign markets, 9, 202–248
　cases, 202–204, 244
　characteristics of, 235
　contract manufacturing, 210
　control and, 235
　countertrade, 208–210
　determinants of, 236–238
　dissemination risk and, 235
　environmental influences on, 204–206
　equity-based ventures, 217–218
　exporting, 206–207, 222–223
　　direct, 207
　franchising, 215–217
　international collaboration imperative, 218–219
　joint ventures. See Joint ventures
　licensing. See Licensing
　list of, 205
　practical insights, 210–211
　resource commitment and, 235
　risk and, 235
　summary, 243–244
　theory of multinational investment. See Foreign direct investment (FDI)
Moral norms, 494–495
Moral philosophies, 489–494

cultural relativism, 492–494
defined, 489
deontology, 491
egoism and, 490
teleology, 489–490
theory of justice, 491–492
theory of rights, 491
utilitarianism and, 490
Most-favored nation (MFN), 86
Motivation, 395–396. *See also* Work motivation
Motivator-hygiene theory, 400
 compared to other theories, 397
Motives for foreign operations, 9–16
 cost reduction, 11–13
 market seeking, 9, 11
 strategic. *See* Strategic motives for establishing foreign operations
MTV in the Arab world, 210–211
Multidimensional global structures, 263–271
 heterarchical structures and transnational mindsets, 266–271
 international matrix structure, 264–266
Multidirectional integration, 168
Multidomestic orientation, 163–164
Multilateral Investment Guarantee Agency of the World Bank (MIGA), 79
Multilateral treaty, 85
Multinational corporations (MNCs)
 emerging markets and. *See* Emerging market environments
 employment practices and policies, 501
 globalization and, 48–49, 50
 guide for, case study, 284–286
 international network theory and, 242

Nation-states, laws of, 92–95
National differences, 16–17
National treatment, 86
Nationalism, 69
Nature, cultural relationship to
 Kluckhohn and Strodtbeck's framework, 118
 Trompenaar's framework, 129
Need for achievement, 400–401
Need for affiliation, 401
Need for power, 401
Needs theories, 397–402
Negative duty approach, 489
Negotiation, 360–379
 bargaining and, 362
 cases, 387–389
 with the Chinese, 374–376, 383
 conflict and, 376–378
 context of, 362
 cultural variables, 368–369
  comparison of, 368
 culture shock and, 363
 defined, 361
 differences in strategies and tactics, 368

ethics and, 378–379
implications for managers, 385
international, 362
Internet use and, 376
national variables, 369–371
 distributive approach, 370
 ideological differences, 370–371
 integrative approach, 370–371
 international economic situation, 370
 legal systems, 369–370
 political systems, 369
organizational variables, 371, 374
 processes, 371, 374, 376
 stakeholders, 371
physical arrangements, 362
practical insights, 363, 366–367, 372–373, 383, 386
process of, 363–368
 building trust with the Japanese, 366–367
 illustrated, 364
 information exchange, 365
 making concessions and reaching agreements, 365
 persuasion, 365
 preparation, 364
 relationship building, 365
status differences, 363
summary, 387
time limits, 362–363
"ugly Americans," 372–373
Network structures, 269–270
Neutral cultures, 128
Nigeria, bribery in, 504
Nineteenth-century imperialism, 65
Nissan, 230–231
Nonprogrammed decisions, 381–383
Nontariff barriers, GATT and, 28
Nonverbal communication, 334, 338–340
Non-work roles, 410
Nora-Sakari: a proposed JV in Malaysia (revised) case study, 317–328
 decision, 325
 Finland: background information, 327–328
 Malaysia: background information, 326–327
 negotiation, 322–325
  arbitration, 325
  equity ownership, 324
  expatriates' salaries and perks, 324–325
  July 8 meeting, 323–325
  May 21 meeting, 322–323
  royalty payment, 324
 Nora Holdings SDN BHD, 319–321
  the company, 319–320
  the management, 320–321
 Nora's search for a JV partner, 318–319

 Sakari OY, 321–322
 technology transfer, 324
 telecom industry in Malaysia, 318
Norm of equality, 404
Norm of equity, 404
Norm of need, 404
North American Free Trade Agreement (NAFTA), 30, 141
 described, 34–36
Nurturant leadership, 423

Objective culture, 111–113
Offshoring, culture clashes and, 342
O-L-I framework for foreign direct investment, 239–242
 internalization, 240–241
 location advantages, 241–242
 ownership advantages, 239–240
Operational risk, 69
 scope of, 69–71
Organization for Economic Cooperation and Development (OECD)
 Convention on Combating Bribery and, 101, 102
 signatories to, 101
Organizational commitment, 400
Organizational context, 282
Organizational cultures, 137, 139
Organizing international operations, 249–287
 cases, 249–252, 284–286
 global hierarchical structures, 258–263
  areas structure, 260–263
  product structure, 259–260
 international division structure. *See* International division
 multidimensional structures, 263–271
  heterarchical structures and transitional mindsets, 266–271
  international matrix structure, 264–266
 practical insights, 262, 267, 270
 pre-international division phase, 255–256
 strategy-structure linkage, 252–255
 summary, 282–283
Output control, 273–274
Output measure availability, 272
Outside-in approach to strategic corporate social responsibility, 499–500
Outsourcing as simple integration strategy, 168–169
Overseas Private Insurance Corporation (OPIC), 70, 79
 described, 70
 hedges against political risk, 80
Ownership advantage, 239–240
Ownership risk, 69–71

Parent-country national (PCN), 442–443
Paris Convention for the Protection of Industrial Property, 88
Parochialism, 116
Particularistic cultures, 128
Past-oriented culture, 119
Patent Cooperation Treaty (PCT), 87–88
Patents, 87–88
Path-goal theory of leadership, 416
Perceived relative deprivation, 73–75
Perception, 345
Performance evaluation, 443
Performance-maintenance (PM) theory, 423
Performance orientation, 136
Performance risk, 230
Perks, 446–447
Person-embodied technologies, 294–295
Philanthropy, 497
Piracy of intellectual property, 88–90
Political environment, 55–107
    case, 104–105
    economics and. *See* Interaction between international politics and economics
    global negotiations case study, 360–361
    negotiations and, 369
    political system, 59–61
        consensus and, 61
        global, 62
        legitimacy and, 61
        players in, 59–61
        political process and, 62
    risk and. *See* Political risk
    summary, 102–104
    uncertainties and, 57–58
Political forces, 67–68
Political hazard, 68
Political ideology, 60–61
    negotiations and, 370–371
Political risk, 67–80
    case, 55–57
    in China, 68
    company-specific, 69
    country specific, 58, 69
    defined, 67–68
    environments of, 76–77
    global framework for assessing, 76–77
    home country, 76–77
    host-country. *See* Host-country political risk
    insurance for, 79–80
    international events and, 77
    international organizations and groups, 76–77
    in Kenya, 59
    kidnapping, 75
    macro, 70–71
    managing, 77–80
        proactive hedges, 77–78
        reactive hedges, 79–80
    micro, 70–71
    nature of, 68–69
    project-specific, 69
    risk forecasting, 58, 59=50
    scope of, 70–71
    summary, 102–104
    types of
        operational risk, 69
        ownership risk, 69–70
        transfer risk, 69
    uncertainties and, 57–58
Political union, 31
Polycentric staffing approach, 439
    compared to other approaches, 441
Polycentrism and international strategies, 152
Porous borders between countries, 45–56
Positive duty approach, 489
Poverty and globalization, 48–50
Power distance, 121–122
    individualism and collectivism versus, 122, 123
    knowledge management and, 303
    masculinity and femininity versus, 125
    scores for countries in, 126
    subordinateship and, 421
    work motivation and, 409–410
Present-oriented culture, 119
Privacy-oriented culture, 119
Proactive hedges, 77–78
Process-embodied technologies, 294
Process theories, 402–405
Procter & Gamble, 158
Product-embodied technologies, 294
Product expansion, 252–253
Product glocalization, 177–178
Product life cycle theory, 9
Production glocalization, 178–179
Productivity, 33
Programmed decisions, 380–381
Project-based knowledge management, 479
Project-specific risk, 69
Protocol, 85
Proxemics, 339–340
Public-oriented culture, 119
Pure barter, 208–209

Reactive hedges, 79–80
Reciprocity, 479–480
Recruitment of employees, 441
Regime legitimacy, 74
Regiocentric staffing approach, 439
    compared to other approaches, 441
Regional economic agreements, 34–42
    ASEAN, 37–38
    benefits of, 33–34
    European Union. *See* European Union (EU)
    global free trade and, 42–43
    laws of, 80–81, 90–92
    MERCOSUR, 39–40
    NAFTA, 34–36
    supply-side economics and, 33–34
Relational risk, 229–232
Relationship-oriented societies, 137
Relationships among people, culture and, 119–120
Religion
    cultural environment and, 137
    influence on government, 73
    Islamic. *See* Islamic law (Shari'ah)
Remote leadership, 425
Renault, 230–231
Repatriation, 453–454
Resource commitment, 235
Responsive corporate social responsibility, 497
Rights, 495
Risk
    dissemination, 235
    for global companies, 17–18
    performance, 230
    political. *See* Political risk
    relational, 229–232
    return portfolio versus, 161–162
    strategic alliances and, 229–232
    systemic, 235
Ritz-Carlton employee motivation, 398–399
Rogue Wave Software's global area structure, 262
Role ambiguity, 410
Role overload, 410
Roman law, 92–93
Ronen and Shenkar's framework for describing a culture, 129–130
Rule-oriented societies, 136–137
Rule utilitarians, 490
Russia, leadership changes in, 104–105

Safety issues on foreign assignment, 451
Saving face, 343–344, 378
Scale economies, 16–17, 33
Scandals and corruption case study, 485–487
Schengen Agreement, 42
Schuman Declaration, 40
Schwartz's framework for describing a culture, 130–131
Scope economies, 16–17
Sector-based knowledge management, 479–480
Securities and Exchange Commission (SEC), FCPA and, 96, 97
Selection of employees, 441
Selective perception, 345
Self-actualization, 396
Self-construal process, 396
Self-disclosure, 346–347
September 11, 69, 70, 135
Sequential cultures, 128–129

Shame versus guilt cultures, leadership in, 418–419
Sheikocracy, 423–424
"Shrinking world," 3–4
Siemens, 98
Silence, 350
Simple integration strategy, 168–169
Social costs of bribery, 503–504
Social responsibility
    cost reduction and, 13
    as proactive hedge, 78
Social uncertainties, 57–58
Socialization of knowledge, 302
Societal groups, 59–61
Societal norms about working, 406
Somalia, 70
South Korea case study, 456–457
Soviet Union, international economic system and demise of, 66, 68
Space orientation and culture, 119
Specific versus diffuse cultures, 128
Stand-alone strategies, 167–168
Static effects of economic integration, 32–33
Status
    communication and, 343
    negotiation and, 363
Stereotyping, 343–344
Strategic alliances
    in the automobile industry, case study, 230–231
    joint ventures. *See* Joint ventures
Strategic control, 281–282. *See also* Controlling international strategies and operations
Strategic corporate social responsibility, 497–500
Strategic leaders, 280
Strategic motives for establishing foreign operations, 13–16
    bandwagon effect, 14
    cross-subsidization, 14
    diversifying operations, 15–16
    exploiting brand names, 15
    first into a new market, 14
    following its customers, 13–14
    organizational knowledge, 15
    technology, 15
    third countries and, 15
    vertical integration, 14–15
Strategic objectives and sources of competitive advantage, 16–19
Strategic orientations of international firms and industries, 162–166
    global orientation, 163
    multidomestic orientation, 163–164
    transnational orientation, 164
    value chain and. *See* Value chain
Strategic significance of knowledge, 298–300
Strategy-structure linkage, 252–255

Subjective culture, 111–113. *See also* Cultural environment
Subjugation-of-nature orientation, 118
Subordinateship, 421
Subsidiaries
    control systems and, 279–282
        parent-subsidiary relationships, 280–282
        strategic, 281–282
        subsidiary roles and, 280–281
        substantive, 282
    dependent, 281
    global approach, 439, 441
    independent, 281
    integrated network of, 221
    managing a portfolio, 159–161
        host-country attractiveness versus competitive-strength matrix, 159–161
        international risk versus return, 161–162
    managing and staffing, 439–440
        ethnocentric approach, 439, 441
        geocentric approach, 439, 441
        polycentric approach, 439, 441
        regiocentric approach, 439, 441
        selection criteria, 439–440
    roles of foreign, 280–281
Subsidiary-parent interdependence, 281
Substantive control, 282
Substitutes for leadership theory, 416
Succession at Siemens case study, 436–438
Succinct communication, 349–350
Supply-side economics, economic integration and, 33–34
Surat Diamond Jewelry (SDJ), 154
Sustainability, 480–481
Sweatshops
    ethical issues, 504–507
    in Honduras, 511–514
Switch trading, 209
Symbols, 345
Synchronic cultures, 129
Systemic risk, 235

Tacit knowledge, 300–301
    knowledge creation and, 301–302
Taiwan's future, 305
Tariffs
    defined, 28
    GATT and, 28
Tata Cummins Limited case study, 202–204
Tata way: evolving and executing sustainable business strategies case study, 516–521
Taxes on expatriates, 452–453
Technological forces facilitating internationalization, 153–154
Technology, 289–298. *See also* Knowledge
    cases, 289–291, 311–314, 317–328

    defined, 294
    summary, 309–310
    understanding, 291–293
Technology transfer, 294–295
    cultural issues and, 296–298
        conceptual model of, 298
    defined, 294
    difficulties with, 296–297
        organizational and corporate cultures, 296–297
        societal cultures, 297
        strategic thinking, 296
        technological characteristics, 296
    factors influencing, 295
    Microsoft in China, 292–293
    of person-embodied technologies, 294–295
    of process-embodied technologies, 294
    of product-embodied technologies, 294
Teleology, 489–490
Terrorism, 70, 75. *See also* September 11
Theory of justice, 491–492
Theory of rights, 491
Thinking-oriented culture, 119
Third-country national (TCN), 442–443
Tightness versus looseness of culture, 132
Time orientation and culture
    Hofstede's framework, 125, 127
    Kluckhohn and Strodtbeck's framework, 119
    Trompenaar's framework, 128–129
Tommy Hilfiger in India case study, 244
Totalitarianism, 62–64
Toyota's Americanization case study, 249–252
Trade barriers, establishing foreign operations to bypass, 11
Trade blocs, 30–31. *See also* Regional economic agreements
    global free trade and, 42–43
    laws of, 80–81, 90–92
Trade creation, 32–33
Trade division, 32–33
Trademark Law Revision Act, 88
Trademarks, 88–90
Trait-based perspective of leadership, 414–415
Transfer risk, 69
    scope of, 70–71
Transferring knowledge at Ford case study, 289–291
Transformational leadership theories, 417
Transnational companies (TNCs)
    vis-à-vis national economies, 8–9, 10
Transnational orientation, 164
Transnational structure, 268–271
Transparency International, 502, 504
Transportation
    falling freight costs, 47
    innovations, 45

Treaties, 85. *See also* International treaties and conventions
　commercial, 85–90
Treaty of Rome, 27, 40–41
Triandis's framework for describing a culture, 132
Trompenaar's framework for describing a culture, 127–129
　individualism versus collectivism, 128
　neutral versus affective relationships, 128
　relationship to nature, 129
　relationship to time, 128–129
　specific versus diffuse relationships, 128
　universalism versus particularism, 128
Trust, 343
Truthfulness in communication, 349

Uncertainties and macroeconomic environment, 57–58
Uncertainty avoidance, 122, 123
　scores for countries in, 126
　work motivation and, 410
Unidirectional integration, 168
Union membership, 448
United Nations (UN), 62, 83
U.S. Chamber of Commerce, 371
United States-Japan Treaty of Friendship, Commerce, and Navigation (JFCN), 86
Universalistic cultures, 127–128
Utilitarianism, 490

Vacation policies, 96
Value chain, 164–171
　competitive advantage and, 165–166
　complex integration strategy, 169–170
　defined, 164
　dispersal of activities, 166–167, 169
　downstream activities, 165–166
　integration of activities, 166–171
　merging strategic orientation, 170–171
　primary activities, 165–166
　simple integration strategies, 168–169
　stand-alone strategies, 167–168
　support activities, 165–166
　typical, 165
　upstream activities, 165–166
Venezuela, case study, 55–57
Verbal communication, 334, 336
Vertical expansion, 252–253
Vertical foreign direct investment (VFDI), 239
Verticalness versus horizontalness of culture, 132
Vienna Convention on the Law of Treaties, 85
Volkswagen Mexico, 49

Wal-Mart, 158
Washington Consensus, 49
Western Union. *See* Christina Gold leading change at Western Union
Wholly owned equity-based ventures, 218
Women
　in South Korea case study, 456–457
　at Western Union. *See* Christina Gold leading change at Western Union
Work centrality, 406
Work goals, 406
Work motivation, 392–412
　ability and, 396
　cases, 392–395
　cultural variations, 408–411
　　individualism-collectivism, 408–409
　　long-term versus short-term orientation, 410–411
　　masculinity-femininity, 410
　　power distance, 409–410
　　ranking of, 408
　　uncertainty avoidance, 410
　defined, 395–396
　in international and global corporations, 412
　Meaning of Work study, 405–407
　practical insights, 398–399, 411
　at Ritz-Carlton, 398–399
　summary, 428
　theories of, 396–405
　　achievement motivation, 400–401
　　Alderfer's ERG, 399
　　applicability of, 401–402, 405
　　compared, 397
　　equity, 404
　　expectancy, 402–404
　　goal-setting, 404–405
　　intrinsic-extrinsic, 400
　　Maslow's motivation, 397–399
　　motivator-hygiene, 400
　　needs, 397–402
　　process, 402–405
　treating employees right in tough times, 411
Work-related stressors, 410
Work roles, 410
World Bank, 62
World car case study, 22
World Court, 83
World Intellectual Property Organization (WIPO), 86–88
World Trade Organization (WTO), 11
　dispute settlement procedure, 29
　global legal system and, 83
　global political system and, 62
　as replacement for GATT, 29